CONTEMPORARY MUSIC ALMANAC 1980/81

Ronald Zalkind

SCHIRMER BOOKS
A Division of Macmillan Publishing Co., Inc.
NEW YORK

COLLIER MACMILLAN PUBLISHERS
LONDON

Copyright © 1980 by Ronald Zalkind and Contemporary Communications Corporation, Inc.

All rights reserved. No part of this book may be reproduced or transmitted in any form or by any means, electronic or mechanical, including photocopying, recording, or by any information storage and retrieval system, without permission in writing from the Publisher.

A Contemporary Communications Corporation, Inc.–Zadoc Book

SCHIRMER BOOKS
A Division of Macmillan Publishing Co., Inc.
866 Third Avenue, New York, N.Y. 10022

Collier Macmillan Canada, Ltd.

ISSN: 0196-6200

Printed in the United States of America

Designed by Stanley S. Drate/Folio Graphics Co.

Printing number
1 2 3 4 5 6 7 8 9 10

CONTENTS

PREFACE   xi

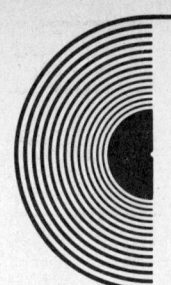

Rock Events 1979   1
Top Five Album Activity 1979   17
Top Five Singles Activity 1979   25
Calendar   33

LOOKING FORWARD, LOOKING BACK   59

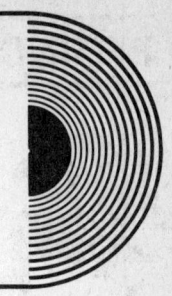

New Wave Music   61
Twenty-five Years of Rock 'n' Roll   81
Greatest Events in Rock 'n' Roll History   95
Best American Recording Studios 1979   102
Rock's Most Collectible Discs   112
Rock 'n' Roll Disc Jockeys   116
Motown Sound Revisited   123
Important Music Inventions   133
New Technology   144

WHO'S WHO   155

Artists   157
Music Business Professionals   351

BEHIND THE SCENES 371

Album Action 1979	372
Directory of Record Companies	415
Directory of Producers	418
Directory of Recording Studios	425
Directory of Personal Managers	430
Directory of Booking Agents	437
Top Twenty Songs 1979	439
Directory of Contemporary Music Publishers	442
Organizations for Performing and Recording Rights	447

GETTING STARTED 449

How To Get Your Song Published	451
Choosing the Right Attorney	458
Choosing the Right Publicist	460
How To Become a Record Producer	463
So You Want to Be a Record Executive	477
Getting Talent for Rock Concerts	485
How To Raise Money	491
How To Organize Your Business: Sole Proprietorship, Partnership, or Corporation	502
Trademarks in the Music Business	534
Colleges of Music	538
Music Business and Audio Engineering Schools	551

MUSIC BUSINESS CONTRACTS 565

Artist Recording Agreement	567
Exclusive Songwriter Agreement	578
Artist-Producer Exclusive Recording Agreement	584
Management Agreement	590
Production Agreement	595
Booking Agency Agreement	607
Co-publishing Agreement	610
Master Purchase Agreement	614

INSIDE THE ROCK BUSINESS 623

Pacesetting Radio Stations	625
Top 40	625
Rock Album Oriented	637
Concert Promoters	646
Concert Facilities	648
Rock Clubs	679
Rock Travel: 20 Major Cities	683
American Federation of Musicians (AFM) Locals	710
American Federation of Television & Radio Artists (AFTRA) Locals	719
Publicity Firms and Their Clients	720
Fan Clubs	728
Attorneys and Their Clients	730
Accounting Firms	745
Professional and Trade Organizations	746

PRINT AND FILM 749

Directory of Music Magazines	751
Contemporary Music Bibliography	770
Music Books 1979	781
ASCAP Deems Taylor Award Winners	793
Rock 'n' Roll Films	797
The 10 Best/10 Worst Rock Films	800
Rock 'n' Roll Film Directory	804

AWARDS 817

National Association Recording Merchandisers (NARM) Awards	819
Grammy Awards	827
Gold Record Awards — Albums	844
Gold Record Awards — Singles	876
Platinum Record Awards — Albums	892
Platinum Record Awards — Singles	897
Million Performance Songs	898
Academy Award Winners for Best Song, Best Musical Scoring	908
Tony Awards	913
Playboy Music Hall of Fame	918
Country Music Association Awards	919

PUZZLES AND QUIZZES 923

Word Choice Puzzles	925
Crossword Puzzles	928
Trivia Quizzes	934
Answers	939

Acknowledgments 945

READER QUESTIONNAIRE 947

PREFACE

The *Contemporary Music Almanac* is about rock music and the people who make it. The following sales percentages, broken down by repertoire (from a National Association of Recording Merchandisers survey), show rock to be far and away the most popular contemporary music:

Type of Recording	Percent of Business
Rock	41.7
Pop	13.1
Country	10.2
Disco	9.0
Soul	8.5
Middle of the Road	5.0
Jazz	3.8
Classical	3.4
Children's	2.6
Comedy	1.3
Other (includes spoken word, ethnic, language)	1.4
Budget/Economy	8.0

Each year we will publish a completely new edition of the *Contemporary Music Almanac*. In the present edition directories, calendars, articles, lists, and awards are intended to reflect the most successful parts of the music business. Out of a vast amount of information we have chosen to focus on what has drawn the most national attention during 1979. The size, scope, and focus of the book will no doubt change as readers, editors, and music business professionals give us their reaction to this first edition.

Rock music is heavily peopled with diverse mixtures of dynamic personalities. To give rock enthusiasts an affordable book that recalls significant events from the recent past and offers professionals a one-stop useful reference is a challenge we will continue to take seriously as we develop succeeding editions of this almanac. Enjoy this book, use it, and let us know what you think about it by filling out and sending us the questionnaire at the back of the book.

Rehearsal for UNICEF Concert, "A Gift of Song" UNICEF photo by Ruby Mera

ROCK EVENTS 1979

JANUARY 2

RCA Records announces plans to distribute 20th Century Fox Records, previously an independently distributed label. All 20th Century Fox field promotion and sales workers are let go. The move continues the trend away from independent distribution to branch distribution.

RSO Records announces plans to manufacture, promote, market and distribute Curtom Records. Curtom was formerly distributed by Warner Bros. Records. A desire to work with a smaller label is seen as the reason for Curtom's move.

JANUARY 3

Armed Forces, the third album by Elvis Costello, is released. The LP, along with Blondie's *Parallel Lines,* are the first albums by so-called new wave artists to achieve gold status.

JANUARY 4

Marshall Blonstein named president of Island Records. Working under the label's new distribution agreement with Warner Bros. Records, Blonstein pledges involvement in rock and "crossover" music in addition to reggae, which has long been a specialty of the label.

JANUARY 5

Charles Mingus, jazz composer, bassist and band leader, dies in Cuernavaca, Mexico at 56 from a muscular ailment known as Gehrig's Disease. Mingus, who played with jazz greats Louis Armstrong, Lionel Hampton, Dizzy Gillespie, Charlie Parker and others, was cremated.

JANUARY 9

A Gift of Song—The Music for UNICEF Concert is held at the United Nations General Assembly. Nine of the industry's top recording artists (ABBA, Bee Gees, Rod Stewart, Andy Gibb, John Denver, Kris Kristofferson, Earth, Wind & Fire, Olivia Newton-John, Donna Summer) perform songs and donate the copyrights to UNICEF; as much as $100-million is expected to be raised by the event.

JANUARY 10

Bob Siner named president of MCA Records, capping a year-long restructuring of the records division of MCA Inc. that included a new distribution system and the launching of the new Infinity Records label.

Bob Sherwood replaces Irwin Steinberg as president and chief operating officer of Phonogram Inc.; Steinberg continues as chairman of the Chicago-based company.

JANUARY 13

Donny Hathaway, the composer, arranger and singer, dies in New York City in a fall from a hotel window. Hathaway was best known for his collaborations with Roberta Flack ("Where Is the Love," "The Closer I Get to You"). He was 33.

The Volunteer Jam, hosted by the Charlie Daniels Band, is held in Nashville's Municipal Auditorium.

JANUARY 14

Warner Bros. Records announces the formation of RFC Records, a subsidiary disco label. The label is one of the many disco labels or disco departments formed by major labels to take advantage of the disco boom.

JANUARY 17

A&M Records announces a manufacturing and distribution pact with RCA Records. Prior to the move, A&M was the largest independently distributed label in the country. The announcement worries independent distributors, as the trend to branch distribution continues.

JANUARY 19

Dire Straits, the British folk-rock group, releases their self-titled debut record on Warner Bros. The album, which becomes platinum quickly, is the first critical and commercial success of the year for a new band.

JANUARY 21

The thirteenth annual MIDEM convention begins in Cannes, France; 5,500 people attend. Popular topics of discussion at the meeting are disco, piracy, and the acquisition of independent American record labels by majors.

JANUARY 27

Spirits Having Flown by the Bee Gees is released. The LP is the follow-up to the group's record-setting *Saturday Night Fever* album.

Rod Stewart's *Blondes Have More Fun* becomes number one. The success of the LP, spurred by the disco single "Da Ya Think I'm Sexy?," is a comeback for Stewart.

JANUARY 30

MCA Inc. buys ABC Records, following months of speculation concerning the sale of the label. Whether or not the label will retain its identity or become absorbed by MCA Records is not determined.

The Recording Industry Association of America releases their figures for 1978: 112 platinum and 254 gold records were awarded.

JANUARY 31

Paul McCartney & Wings sign to Columbia Records, ending a 16-year association between the former Beatle and Capitol Records. Although the terms of the deal are not disclosed, it is commonly believed that McCartney's royalty deal is potentially the most lucrative for any single artist ever.

FEBRUARY 1

Atco Records, Atlantic Records' sister label that specialized in rock during the 60s (when Atlantic specialized in R&B), is revived after five years of dormancy. The label will carry over a dozen acts.

FEBRUARY 2

We Are Family, the second album by Sister Sledge, is released; the LP is produced and written by Nile Rodgers and Bernard Edwards, who also produce, write and play for the group Chic. With Chic and Sister Sledge, Rodgers and Edwards are responsible for the popularity of disco in pop markets.

FEBRUARY 8

Capitol Industries-EMI, Inc., the London-based firm, buys United Artists Records for $3-million. Executives from both firms say that UA Records will retain its identity as a label. The purchase continues the string of mergers in the record industry.

FEBRUARY 9

Heroes of Rock 'n' Roll, a two-hour documentary, is aired on ABC Television. The show contains rare footage of several rock artists never before seen on television.

FEBRUARY 10

Cheap Trick at Budokan by Cheap Trick is released. Available only as an import for several weeks, the large sales of the LP at high import prices forced Epic to release the record domestically.

FEBRUARY 11

Elvis, a biography of the late singer, is shown on ABC Television. Pitted against *Gone with the Wind* and *One Flew Over the Cuckoo's Nest* on the other networks, *Elvis* won the largest share of the audience. The evening is reportedly the single most expensive evening of network programming in history.

FEBRUARY 15

Grammy Awards are presented. Billy Joel, the Bee Gees, Anne Murray, and Barry Manilow are multiple winners.

FEBRUARY 17

In its second week on the charts, *Spirits Having Flown* by the Bee Gees becomes the number one album.

FEBRUARY 20

David Geffen, the founder of Asylum Records and former manager of CSN&Y, Joni Mitchell, and the Eagles, is named to a newly-created consultancy position for Warner Communications Inc. music division. The appointment for Geffen comes after a three-year absence from a music industry job.

FEBRUARY 28

The Allman Brothers Band releases *Enlightened Rogues,* a reunion LP for the band that hasn't played together in over two years. The album also reunited the band with producer Tom Dowd.

MARCH 1

Paul McCartney & Wings resign with EMI for all countries worldwide except North America. The signing follows McCartney's February signing with Columbia for North America.

MARCH 2-4

The Havana Jam, sponsored by CBS Records and the Cuban government, is held in the 5,000-seat Karl Marx Auditorium in Havana. Weather Report, Stephen Stills, John McLaughlin, Billy Joel, and several Cuban artists appear.

The concerts are the first by American pop artists in Cuba in over twenty years.

MARCH 3

"I Will Survive" by Gloria Gaynor replaces Rod Stewart's "Da Ya Think I'm Sexy?" as the number one single. The move is representative of the strong showing of disco-oriented songs in the first half of the year. Of the top ten singles on the March 3 charts, nine are disco-oriented.

MARCH 4

Four weeks after its purchase of ABC Records, MCA Inc. announces the absorbing of the ABC roster into MCA Records. More than 300 ABC employees—all except a few high executives—are let go.

MARCH 10

Roxy Music, the British band that, according to some, was influential in the development of new wave, releases their first LP (*Manifesto*) in three years and begins U.S. tour.

MARCH 15

EMI Ltd. restructures its North American music operations, furthering the direction of consolidation and cutbacks in the industry. Under the new plan, EMI's three American concerns are grouped under the new banner, Capitol/EMI America/UA Records Group. Fifty UA workers are let go because of the move.

MARCH 16

L.A. (*Light Album*), with an extended disco song, is released by the Beach Boys. The group is one more in the long list of established rock acts (Rolling Stones, Doobie Brothers, Rod Stewart) to release a disco song.

MARCH 17

Rickie Lee Jones's self-titled debut LP is released. The album gains platinum status soon, as the singer-songwriter is hailed as one of the bright new stars of the year.

MARCH 20

President Carter hosts 300 recording industry executives at an afternoon reception in the White House. The reception highlights Carter's enthusiasm for all types of music and musicians. The same executives meet that night for the eleventh annual RIAA Cultural Awards ceremony in a Washington hotel. Beverly Sills, the opera singer, is the recipient of the year's cultural award.

MARCH 23

The twenty-first NARM (National Association of Record Merchandisers) convention is held at Hollywood, Florida. More than 2,200 (the largest crowd ever) attend meetings and presentations covering all aspects of the industry.

MARCH 24

The Second Annual Country Music Spectacular is held at the Silverdome in Pontiac, Michigan. Conway Twitty, Loretta Lynn, Johnny Paycheck, Earl Scruggs and others perform in what is called the world's largest indoor country music show. Close to 60,000 attend.

MARCH 28

Eric Clapton and Muddy Waters begin

U.S. tour in Tucson, Arizona. Waters, the Chicago blues guitarist, is one of Clapton's major influences.

APRIL 1

The International Brotherhood of Teamsters calls a strike against 73 major trucking companies, slowing delivery of records to retailers throughout the country. Record manufacturers quickly move product to airlines, UPS and non-union trucks. By April 11 the strike ends.

APRIL 4

Diana Ross begins a 28-city tour of arena-sized venues. The tour is the most extensive for the former Supreme since she went solo twelve years ago.

APRIL 5

The National Association of Independent Record Distributors (NAIRD) holds its eighth annual convention in Boston. As several independent distributors recently lost business to majors, survival of the independents is the focus of the convention.

APRIL 7

"Music Box Dancer," an instrumental song by Frank Mills, becomes the number one single—the first instrumental in several years to reach this status.

APRIL 9

Academy Awards are won by Paul Jabara ("Last Dance," best original song) and Giorgio Moroder (*Midnight Express*, best original score), representing a strong showing for disco material. Joe Renzetti's score for the *Buddy Holly Story* wins the best adaptation of a musical score award.

APRIL 10

NARM releases a study that categorizes record sales according to genre for the first time. In 1978 rock accounted for 41.7 percent of sales; pop 13.1 percent; country 10.2 percent; disco 9.0 percent; soul 8.5 percent, MOR 5 percent; jazz 3.8 percent; classical 3.4 percent; children's 2.6 percent; comedy 1.3 percent; and other 1.4 percent.

APRIL 18

CBS Inc. holds their annual meeting of shareholders in Nashville. Company officers predict a bright future. Bad sales and slow business at CBS's pressing plants brought CBS Inc.'s first quarter net income down 47 percent from 1978's first quarter showing.

APRIL 19

The Supreme Court rules eight to one that blanket licenses issued to broadcasters by ASCAP and BMI are not in violation of the nation's price-fixing laws. The decision ends a 9-year fight by CBS Inc., which alleged that blanket licenses were in violation of the anticompetitive provisions of the Sherman Act.

APRIL 21

"Heart of Glass," the disco single by Blondie, becomes the number 1 single, signifying the mass acceptance of a group that was originally labelled "punk."

Close to $500,000 is raised for leukemia research at the fourth annual T. J. Martell Foundation dinner at New York's Waldorf Astoria. The foundation is the only charity founded by and totally supported by the music industry.

APRIL 22

The Rolling Stones play two shows at the Oshawa Civic Auditorium near Toronto, ending a long legal battle between Stones' guitarist Keith Richard and the Canadian government. The shows were done in lieu of a sentence for Richard, who was found with heroin in Toronto two years ago.

APRIL 25

Bad Girls by Donna Summer is released and rises quickly to number one. The album is hailed by critics as the most successful rock-disco fusion yet.

APRIL 26

Several major and independent labels trim staffs, in response to soft first-quarter sales. Although most labels term their cutbacks as "streamlining" or "readjustments," definite cutbacks are reported at MCA, RCA, Fantasy, Polygram, and GRT Records.

MAY 6

The formation of MUSE (Musicians United for Safe Energy, Inc.) is announced by Jackson Browne, John Hall and Graham Nash. Headed by a 13-member board, MUSE announces plans for benefit concerts.

MAY 11

Lester Flatt, veteran bluegrass guitarist, singer and composer, dies in Nashville. With Earl Scruggs, Flatt composed "Foggy Mountain Breakdown" and the theme to the *Beverly Hillbillies* television show.

MAY 15

The Country Music Association presents Jimmy Carter their first Special Award for Carter's support of country music, in a ceremony at the White House.

MAY 20

The National Academy of Recording Arts and Sciences, meeting in Guadalajara, Mexico, expands the pop music categories for the Grammy Awards. Newly created categories are rock, disco and jazz fusion; rock had been part of the general pop music field.

MAY 21

Elton John begins a short tour of the USSR with a sold-out concert in Leningrad's 4,000-seat Oktyabrsky Concert Hall. The tour is one of the few by a Western pop star in recent Russian history. Tickets to the show are scalped at the equivalent of $150.

MAY 26

Three independent British labels sign distribution pacts with U.S. labels, highlighting American interest in British artists. Radar Records pacts with Polydor; Stiff with Epic and Columbia; Virgin with Atlantic.

JUNE 1

GRT Corp., the diversified tape manufacturer, lets go three vice presidents and several other employees because of loss of business incurred from manufacturer/distributor ties; in the recent past GRT's Janus Records folded, and the corporation lost the tape manufacturing account of ABC Records, which was bought by MCA Inc.

JUNE 4

Album sales in the U.K. are down five percent in the first quarter of 1979, compared to 1978; lack of superstar product and home taping are blamed. U.S. labels see the statistics as a mirror of their own sluggish sales.

JUNE 8-10

The Black Music Association, not yet a year old, holds its first conference in Philadelphia. Purpose of the meeting is to determine how the organization can improve the livelihood of its members throughout the industry. The conference is preceded on the 6th by a dinner and reception hosted by President Carter at the White House, and attended by 1,000 people from the government and recording industry.

JUNE 10

One of the many antinuclear concert/rally/demonstrations of the summer is held at the Hollywood Bowl. Peter, Paul & Mary, Graham Nash, Jackson Browne, Gil Scott-Heron and Lily Tomlin appear. This concert and other fundraising concerts demonstrate the strong economic power musicians hold in the antinuclear movement.

BMI awards Citations for Achievement for the most performed songs of 1978 to 136 writers and 105 publishers. The Bee Gees and Stigwood Music's "Night Fever" is the most performed BMI song of the year; Barry, Robin and Maurice Gibb receive eleven, seven, and six writing awards respectively.

JUNE 11

Chuck Berry, composer of rock classics such as "Johnny B. Goode," "Memphis" and "Sweet Little Sixteen," pleads guilty of income tax evasion in Los Angeles federal court. The charge stems from a 1973 debt of $110,000. On August 30, Berry begins serving his four-month sentence in a federal prison in Lompoc, California.

JUNE 12

The Kids Are Alright, the film and the album, are released by the Who. The film is viewed as an epic rock documentary.

JUNE 15

The dollar volume for the sale of records and prerecorded tapes in 1978 in the U.S. is tabulated at $4.1-billion, compared with $3.5-billion for 1977, making the record industry bigger than the film industry. Unit sales for the year, however, are up only four percent.

JUNE 22

Donna Summer captures the number one and number three singles positions with "Hot Stuff" and "Bad Girls," setting a record as the first solo entertainer to hold two of the top three positions simultaneously.

JUNE 25

WEA, distributor for Warner Bros., Atlantic, Elektra/Asylum, and other labels, raises its wholesale LP prices by 12 percent and ups their list price for singles; the move is seen as precedent-setting, and other major distributors soon follow. Retailers comment that buying will be more cautious, and the increase is passed on to consumers.

JUNE 28

The effects of slow business and low profits surface at CBS Records as 53 employees are laid off. Portrait Records, distributed by CBS, is restructured under the auspices of Epic/Portrait/Associated Labels. Workers on Portrait's formerly independent A&R and marketing staffs are incorporated into the CBS Records organization.

JUNE 29

Casablanca Records cuts 25 people from lower-level positions. As the label has done very well on the charts (with Donna Summer, Village People, Kiss and Mark Williams) during the year, the cutbacks are more of a reflection on the record industry economy in general; top-charted records in 1979 are not, as a rule, selling as much as top-charted records in 1978.

JULY 5

Capitol Records and CBS Records raise the list price of their singles, less than two weeks after WEA made the same move. Capitol also boosts their wholesale price on LPs.

JULY 10

Arthur Fiedler, conductor of the Boston Pops Symphony, dies of cardiac arrest at 84. Popular among classical and popular audiences, Fiedler's records sold over 50 million copies during his lifetime.

JULY 11

Bop Till You Drop, the first digital rock album, is released by Ry Cooder. Experimented with on classical recordings for some years, the digital process is catching on with pop artists. Several rock acts, including Fleetwood Mac, have recorded digital songs for future release.

JULY 12

Minnie Riperton, singer and composer, dies of cancer at 31. Riperton was very active as a fundraiser for cancer research and as a speaker.

Steve Dahl, staunch antidisco deejay on Chicago's WLUP-FM, hosts a "disco demolition" at Chicago's Comisky Park in between games of a doubleheader. As a gimmick Dahl burns disco records brought by fans for discount admission. Fans start their own fires and a mini-riot ensues, forcing the Chicago White Sox to forfeit the second game of the doubleheader. Soon after the incident, Dahl's parody, "Do You Think I'm Disco," becomes a popular single.

JULY 13

Cutbacks are quietly announced at MCA Records, RCA Records, Capricorn Records and Elektra/Asylum Records. As reasons for the cutbacks, officials cite an attempt to limit overhead costs in the sales slump.

JULY 16

Judgments totalling $3.2-million, the largest ever awarded in an antipiracy action, are imposed upon Magnitron Inc. by the district court of Oklahoma City. The decision, a major win in the fight against piracy, ends a five-year battle between CBS, A&M, MCA, Warner Bros., and Magnitron.

JULY 18

GRT Corp., hurt from loss of business and forced to cut a good part of its staff, files for financial relief under Chapter XI of the bankruptcy statutes, making the corporation the first large-scale, permanent casualty of the sales slump. GRT officials vow to continue operations.

JULY 19

London Records lays off employees. Following the lead of other labels, London officials term the cutbacks "restructuring."

JULY 27

Columbia Pictures Industries Inc. sells Arista Records to Ariola-Eurodisc, GmDH, a subsidiary of Bertelsmann AG of West Germany. Although the sale is rumoured to be the result of bad sales by Arista (the label had actually been doing relatively well), a statement said that the move gives Columbia "substantial flexibility in planning its future growth."

"Broadway Opry '79: A Little Country in the Big City, a 59-concert series featuring country music performers (Waylon Jennings, Conway Twitty, Ronny Millsap, Tanya Tucker and others) opens on Broadway. After half a dozen poor-selling concerts, the series closes, proving, according to some, that country music does not have a large audience in New York City. The organizers claim that insufficient planning was the only problem and vow to return next year.

AUGUST 3

Get The Knack, the debut LP by the Knack, jumps into the #1 position on the charts; the group's first single, "My Sharona," also reaches the top spot. The success of the Knack is a phenomenal overnight sensation. More specifically, the top 40 radio acceptance of the band is precedent-setting—proving that the back-to-the-basics, "power pop" rock exemplified by the Knack is gaining in popularity.

AUGUST 7

Reacting to the bad sales climate and retailers' discontent over new pricing structures, MCA Distributing unveils a new $5.98 pricing discount to apply to new, developing artists, and selected catalogue product. Soon after the move, other major distributors follow suit with similar discount structures.

AUGUST 10

CBS Records dismisses "slightly over 100" field and label people in middle and lower level positions.

AUGUST 13

The German music industry suffers its worst first half of the decade, as record and tape sales decline when compared with the same period in 1978. Home cassette taping and cheap import LPs are cited as part of the reason for the slump.

AUGUST 15

Bob Dylan's *Slow Train Coming* is released amid reports of Dylan's conversion to Christianity. The album contains several specific religious references (for which Dylan is berated by some critics), but the LP is also hailed as one of the artist's best—musically—in some years.

AUGUST 17

A&M Records becomes the latest label to implement cost-controlling measures as

34 staffers are cut. Horizon Records, A&M's jazz-oriented subsidiary label, is dissolved; Horizon artists are absorbed into the A&M roster.

AUGUST 25

Jazz bandleader/composer Stan Kenton dies in Los Angeles at age 67. Kenton led bands continuously from the 40s, seeing such players as Maynard Ferguson, Stan Getz and Lee Konitz pass through his ranks.

AUGUST 29

Polygram Inc. calls in its loans ($5 million) to Capricorn Records, a label Polygram had distributed, taking possession of Capricorn's master tapes, artist contracts, studio equipment, and apparently signalling the end of the Macon, Georgia-based label. The future of the label name and of the label's artists is to be decided by the courts.

AUGUST 31

Led Zeppelin's *In Through the Out Door,* debuts in the charts at the #1 position, the second time in the history of chart-making an album has entered the charts in the top position. Retailers are optimistic over the event and look forward to more "superstar" products.

CBS Records and Phonogram/Mercury introduce a $5.98 pricing structure following the lead of MCA. At the same time though, CBS and WEA raise their wholesale prices for new products by three percent, and CBS implements a 20 percent ceiling return policy, causing discontent among retailers.

Several thousand copies of *Lieder des Papstes* (Songs of the Pope) sung by Pope John Paul II in Polish and German, are imported to the U.S. Demand is so great that, soon afterward, Infinity Records buys the U.S. rights for the LP, making it available at domestic prices.

SEPTEMBER 5

IBM, the nation's leading computer company, and MCA join forces and form DiscoVision Associates, to manufacture videodiscs for the consumer and videodisc players for the industrial market. The move underscores the importance the industry places on the future of videodiscs; the partnership is IBM's closest contact with the manufacture of consumer product.

SEPTEMBER 9

President and Mrs. Carter host an informal gospel concert and picnic on the south lawn of the White House for the Gospel Music Association; 16 acts perform in a three-hour program. Carter's support of gospel music is in stride with his often-mentioned support of country music, jazz and black music.

SEPTEMBER 9-12

1200 radio programmers, managers, syndicators and advertisers attend the second annual National Association of Broadcasters programming conference in St. Louis. The effect of disco on radio and the sound of radio in the '80s are the principle topics of discussion.

SEPTEMBER 14

New LPs by Foreigner (*Head Games*) and Cheap Trick (*Dream Police*) are released to a retail market eager for big-name products. These releases, and other imminent releases, cause manufacturers and retailers to optimistically speculate about a strong fourth quarter of sales.

SEPTEMBER 15

ABBA, the Swedish group that has sold more records worldwide than anyone in the history of recorded music except Elvis Presley, starts their first North American tour.

SEPTEMBER 17

Capitol Records becomes the latest manufacturer to offer discount list prices with the introduction of a $5.98 series of anthology LPs.

SEPTEMBER 19

Singer/songwriter Elton John, after a successful tour of Russia and a popular disco record, begins his first U.S. tour in four years.

SEPTEMBER 19-23

Five benefit concerts are presented at Madison Square Garden by Musicians United for Safe Energy (MUSE). Bonnie Raitt, Jackson Browne, Graham Nash, Bruce Springsteen and others perform. $1.5 million is grossed; after expenses close to $1 million is available for the organizers to distribute to dozens of anti-nuke/pro-solar groups throughout the country. An LP and film are planned.

SEPTEMBER 24-29

The New York Music Task Force, a non-profit organization, Manhattan borough president Andrew Stein, and *Record World*, a trade magazine, present *New York City Music Week* in parks, plazas and nightclubs throughout the city. Endorsed by Mayor Edward Koch and governor Hugh Carey, the week-long series of events was organized to salute the industry in New York and to bring attention to the fact that New York City is once again becoming the center of the music industry.

SEPTEMBER 26

Elektra/Asylum releases *The Long Run* by the Eagles and starts the label's biggest new-release campaign ever. In its first week in the charts, the LP reaches the #2 position. New LPs by Blondie and Village People are also released, fueling industry-wide hopes of a sales upswing.

SEPTEMBER 27

Polygram Distribution becomes the latest major distributor to announce wide-ranging policy changes, including a ceiling of 18-22 percent on returns, and a minimum order size of $125 for LPs and tapes. The move, which follows similar changes by CBS and WEA, is explained as a means to deal equitably with large and small accounts and to combat increased operating costs.

OCTOBER 2

After a three-year court battle, a U.S. District Court judge rules that home copying of TV programs is not an infringement of the country's copyright laws. The decision, in favor of Sony Corporation against Walt Disney Productions and MCA, Inc., is seen as a victory for all manufacturers of home video equipment.

OCTOBER 9

The Country Music Association holds its annual awards ceremony at the Grand Ole Opry House in Nashville; Willie Nelson wins the entertainer of the year award; Kenny Rogers and Barbara Mandrell also win top awards.

OCTOBER 15

CBS Inc. and Warner Communications Inc., parent companies of CBS Records and the WEA Records family respectively, announce sales figures for the best third quarters in each company's history. At the same time, each of the corporation's music divisions report drops in income and profits. On a brighter note, Atlantic Records reports third quarter earnings of $45 million, the highest in the label's history. Atlantic is one of the few labels doing consistently well in the still-sluggish market.

OCTOBER 15

Multi-platinum sellers Fleetwood Mac releases the double-LP *Tusk,* the group's first record in over two-and-a-half years. Warner Bros. Records launches their most extensive marketing campaign ever. The group begins a world tour October 26.

OCTOBER 16

Phonogram/Mercury dismisses more than 20 employees and closes their Memphis office. Executives call the move "An adjustment to prevailing business conditions."

OCTOBER 17

RCA and A&M and Associated Labels become the latest manufacturer to announce a major change in returns policy, with a 22 percent ceiling on returns.

OCTOBER 19

Sony and Philips join forces in the development of a videodisc. As the Sony/Philips system will use laser beams to read signals (as opposed to a sapphire pick-up system used by RCA and others), there is much discussion about differences in equipment breaking up the market and slowing down the launching of the product in an industry badly needing new sales stimuli.

OCTOBER 21

KRTH-FM in Los Angeles takes out a full-page ad in the Los Angeles Times announcing their "Great Album Week;" in the week following the station plays new albums by top artists uninterrupted, ostensibly for listeners to tape on cassettes. The move fuels the growing controversy between radio and retailers over home taping. Manufacturers claim that home taping is taking a big dent out of record sales. At the same time New York station WPLJ takes out a similar ad in the Village Voice announcing their all-album program.

OCTOBER 30

Decca Ltd., the British company with several label and publishing interests, sells the majority of its concerns to the Dutch-German Polygram Group, adding to that corporation's diverse music operations. The sale is a bid to eliminate heavy losses in the Decca group, caused in part by losses in the record division.

Chief executives from most major record labels sign an open letter from the RIAA to radio broadcasters concerning the continuing home-taping controversy. The statement reads, in part: "The overt action to foster home-taping saps the lifeblood of the recording industry... this is an appeal from record executives to radio executives to stop fostering the home-taping of recordings." At the same time, the RKO radio chain (whose station KRTH had advertised its policy of playing new LPs uninterrupted for home-taping) issues a letter saying that the 11 stations in the chain will "no longer play albums in their entirety or work to promote the practice within the broadcast industry."

NOVEMBER 1

Several west coast retail chains—Wherehouse, Big Ben's, Tower Records and Music Plus—raise their LP prices by up to 16 percent. The retailers, many of whom hadn't raised their prices in three years, cite increases as manufacturer's prices and operating costs as reasons for the move.

A tape pirater is convicted of possessing stolen property with intent to sell in Jacksonville Florida, in a precedent-setting case. Traditionally pirates are charged in federal courts on copyright infringement. In this case the state contended that "since property is defined in the law as anything of value, including such intangibles as contract rights to royalties, the possession of the illegal tape with intent to sell represents the theft of rights and is, consequently possession of stolen property."

NOVEMBER 4-8

The fifth annual Musexpo Record and Music Industry Market is held in Miami. Over 2500 executives from 42 countries attend the conference, essentially a meeting place where licensing and sub-publishing deals transpire.

NOVEMBER 6

Thorn Electrical Industries buys EMI Ltd. for 169 million pounds—one of the biggest mergers in British history; the new company is called Thorn EMI. The deal is expected to bolster EMI's role as a complete leisure-time industry, with subsidiaries in over 30 countries.

NOVEMBER 7

Minor staff cuts are announced at Ariola-America, Elektra/Asylum and MCA record companies. As the cuts come in the middle of a slight upswing in sales, the smaller staffs are seen as a permanent reality, rather than a temporary reaction to sluggish sales.

NOVEMBER 15

MCA Records discontinues its Infinity label, the one-year-old company run by Ron Alexenburg. Most of the 100-plus employees at Infinity are cut, although the "best" are absorbed into the MCA structure, as selecte MCA employees are dismissed. Top Infinity artists are also absorbed by MCA. No figures are released but it is believed that Infinity lost in surplus of $10 million during its first year.

NOVEMBER 16

WEA unveils a new returns policy that rewards or penalizes retailers and wholesalers for limiting or exceeding a pre-determined returns quota. The policy sets an 18 percent break-even point for retailers and a 22 percent point for rackjobbers and one-stops. Returns below these levels are awarded with a rebate via label credit; customers sending back returns in excess of the number will face added charges. The new plan is lauded by retailers, many of whom had been disgruntled by new 18 percent-ceiling policies on returns recently put into effect by CBS, RCA and Polygram.

NOVEMBER 21

The Copyright Royalty Tribunal publishes the results from its first survey on home taping patterns. The survey finds that 70 percent of the tapers queried said that they would have bought the LP or tape had they not been able to tape it. Forty percent of the tapers said that they have increased their purchasing of prerecorded music since they began home-taping; another 40 percent said they had decreased their purchase of prerecorded music because of taping. The results are met with mixed reactions: sales are definitely being lost to home-taping, but the taping is also stimulating interest in music in general.

At the same time, independent radio consultant Kent Buckhart releases results from another survey, finding that 18 percent of radio listeners between the ages of 18 and 34 have taped entire albums off the air within the past three months. Pending further research, Burkhart does not advise any of the 120 Burkhart/Abrams SuperStars stations to alter any policies on full-album playing.

NOVEMBER 22

Warner Brothers Records lets go 55 employees (8 percent of the total staff). The layoffs termed "streamlining and consolidation," are the first for the label since the continuing industry-wide slump. According to a spokesman from the label, Warner Brothers was waiting to gauge the success of the new Fleetwood Mac LP *Tusk* before making any decisions on layoffs. The LP, with a $15.98 list price, drops from #4 to #6 in its sixth week on the charts this week, and is selling far below the rate of the group's last multi-platinum LP *Rumours*.

NOVEMBER 28

A&M Records dismisses 50 employees from field and home offices; the layoff reduces the company's staff by 14 percent. The news comes amidst unofficial estimates that 10 percent of the work force in the industry has been layed off in the last 18 months.

NOVEMBER 29

Ron Alexenburg, former head of Infinity Records, files suit against MCA Inc., the parent company that closed down Infinity recently. The suit seeks $2 million Alexenburg claims he is owed under his contract, as well as additional sums in damages.

DECEMBER 3

Eleven people die outside a Who concert in Cincinnati pushing (through three doors) to enter the coliseum for general-admission seats. The incident is the worst tragedy in the history of rock music. The future of "festival"-style, general admission seating is questioned in wake of the incident.

DECEMBER 4

No Nukes/The MUSE Concerts for a Non-Nuclear Future, a three record set featuring the Doobie Brothers, Jackson Browne, Crosby, Stills and Nash, James Taylor, Bruce Springsteen, Carly Simon, Bonnie Raitt, Graham Nash, Tom Petty, Ry Cooder and Chaka Khan, is released on Asylum Records.

DECEMBER 5

The economy is the reason given for the closing of four branch offices by MCA

Distributing in San Francisco, Houston, Charlotte and Hartford. At the same time, Nonesuch Records, the well-respected, budget classical label owned by Elektra/Asylum, is relieved of its director, Tracey Sterne, and put under the direction of Elektra/Asylum vice-president Keith Holzman. Elektra/Asylum vows the label will continue its activity.

DECEMBER 11

An independent study sponsored by the Recording Industry Association of America and the National Music Publishers Association finds that home taping costs the industry between 14 and 29 percent of its potential sales each year; 14 percent translates into a loss of album and singles totalling 201 million units. The report, coupled with a similar though not as pessimistic report released by the Copyright Royalty Tribunal, confirms labels' worst fears about home taping.

DECEMBER 22

More than one thousand feature film masters and six thousand-plus prerecorded bootleg home videocassettes are confiscated in raids in the U.K. and Holland in the biggest video piracy bust to date. The arrests of fifteen people in London and Rotterdam are coordinated by the Motion Picture Association of America, New Scotland Yard, and the Dutch police. Authorities note that as the home video industry grows, so too has bootlegging and piracy, causing alarm in video circles.

DECEMBER 26

Paul McCartney & Wings, Queen, the Who, Elvis Costello and Rockpile are some of the groups that perform at the Hammersmith Odeon in London to raise money for the people of Kampuchea (formerly Cambodia). The concerts are the outcome of talks between McCartney and U.N. Secretary-General Kurt Waldheim. Money raised from the concerts is directed to emergency relief work conducted by UNICEF and the International Committee of the Red Cross. The shows are filmed by EMI Ltd. for a spring airing.

DECEMBER 30

Composer and lyricist Richard Rodgers dies in New York City at age 77. Teaming with Lorenz Hart and Oscar Hammerstein II, Rodgers wrote Broadway musicals for more than 55 years. Among his most well-known scores are *Oklahoma*, *The Sound of Music*, *Pal Joey*, *Carousel*, *The King and I*, *Flower Drum Song*, and *South Pacific*.

JP

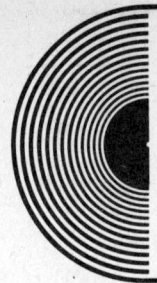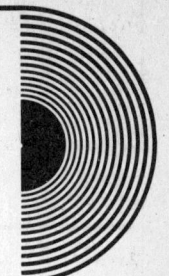

TOP FIVE ALBUM ACTIVITY 1979

JANUARY 6

Barbra Streisand's Greatest Hits, Vol. 2, Barbra Streisand (Columbia)
52nd Street, Billy Joel (Columbia)
A Wild and Crazy Guy, Steve Martin (Warner Bros.)
Grease—original soundtrack (RSO)
Double Vision, Foreigner (Atlantic)

JANUARY 13

52nd Street, Billy Joel (Columbia)
Barbra Streisand's Greatest Hits, Vol. 2, Barbra Streisand (Columbia)
A Wild and Crazy Guy, Steve Martin (Warner Bros.)
Grease—original soundtrack (RSO)
Greatest Hits, Barry Manilow (Arista)

JANUARY 20

52nd Street, Billy Joel (Columbia)
Barbra Streisand's Greatest Hits, Vol. 2, Barbra Streisand (Columbia)
Briefcase Full of Blues, Blues Brothers (Atlantic)
A Wild and Crazy Guy, Steve Martin (Warner Bros.)
Greatest Hits, Barry Manilow (Arista)

JANUARY 27

Barbra Streisand's Greatest Hits, Vol. 2, Barbra Streisand (Columbia)
Blondes Have More Fun, Rod Stewart (Warner Bros.)
Briefcase Full of Blues, Blues Brothers (Atlantic)
52nd Street, Billy Joel (Columbia)
A Wild and Crazy Guy, Steve Martin (Warner Bros.)

FEBRUARY 3

Blondes Have More Fun, Rod Stewart (Warner Bros.)
Briefcase Full of Blues, Blues Brothers (Atlantic)
52nd Street, Billy Joel (Columbia)
Barbra Streisand's Greatest Hits, Vol. 2, Barbra Streisand (Columbia)
The Best of Earth, Wind & Fire, Vol. 1, Earth, Wind & Fire (ARC/Columbia)

FEBRUARY 10

Blondes Have More Fun, Rod Stewart (Warner Bros.)
Briefcase Full of Blues, Blues Brothers (Atlantic)
Barbra Streisand's Greatest Hits, Vol. 2, Barbra Streisand (Columbia)
52nd Street, Billy Joel (Columbia)
The Best of Earth, Wind & Fire, Vol. 1, Earth, Wind & Fire (ARC/Columbia)

FEBRUARY 17

Blondes Have More Fun, Rod Stewart (Warner Bros.)

Briefcase Full of Blues, Blues Brothers (Atlantic)
Spirits Having Flown, Bee Gees (RSO)
52nd Street, Billy Joel (Columbia)
Barbra Streisand's Greatest Hits, Vol. 2, Barbra Streisand (Columbia)

FEBRUARY 24

Spirits Having Flown, Bee Gees (RSO)
Blondes Have More Fun, Rod Stewart (Warner Bros.)
Briefcase Full of Blues, Blues Brothers (Atlantic)
52nd Street, Billy Joel (Columbia)
Cruisin', Village People (Casablanca)

MARCH 3

Spirits Having Flown, Bee Gees (RSO)
Blondes Have More Fun, Rod Stewart (Warner Bros.)
Briefcase Full of Blues, Blues Brothers (Atlantic)
Cruisin', Village People (Casablanca)
52nd Street, Billy Joel (Columbia)

MARCH 10

Spirits Having Flown, Bee Gees (RSO)
Blondes Have More Fun, Rod Stewart (Warner Bros.)
Briefcase Full of Blues, Blues Brothers (Atlantic)
Minute by Minute, Doobie Brothers (Warner Bros.)
52nd Street, Billy Joel (Columbia)

MARCH 17

Spirits Having Flown, Bee Gees (RSO)
Blondes Have More Fun, Rod Stewart (Warner Bros.)
Briefcase Full of Blues, Blues Brothers (Atlantic)
Minute by Minute, Doobie Brothers (Warner Bros.)
Dire Straits, Dire Straits (Warner Bros.)

MARCH 24

Spirits Having Flown, Bee Gees (RSO)
Blondes Have More Fun, Rod Stewart (Warner Bros.)
Minute by Minute, Doobie Brothers (Warner Bros.)
Dire Straits, Dire Straits (Warner Bros.)
Cruisin', Village People (Casablanca)

MARCH 31

Spirits Having Flown, Bee Gees (RSO)
Minute by Minute, Doobie Brothers (Warner Bros.)
Blondes Have More Fun, Rod Stewart (Warner Bros.)
Dire Straits, Dire Straits (Warner Bros.)
Cruisin', Village People (Casablanca)

APRIL 7

Spirits Having Flown, Bee Gees (RSO)
Minute by Minute, Doobie Brothers (Warner Bros.)
Dire Straits, Dire Straits (Warner Bros.)
Blondes Have More Fun, Rod Stewart (Warner Bros.)
2 Hot!, Peaches & Herb (Polydor)

APRIL 14

Spirits Having Flown, Bee Gees (RSO)
Minute by Minute, Doobie Brothers (Warner Bros.)
Dire Straits, Dire Straits (Warner Bros.)
2 Hot!, Peaches & Herb (Polydor)
Blondes Have More Fun, Rod Stewart (Warner Bros.)

APRIL 21

Minute by Minute, Doobie Brothers (Warner Bros.)
Spirits Having Flown, Bee Gees (RSO)
2 Hot!, Peaches & Herb (Polydor)
Dire Straits, Dire Straits (Warner Bros.)
Breakfast in America, Supertramp (A&M)

APRIL 28

Spirits Having Flown, Bee Gees (RSO)
Minute by Minute, Doobie Brothers
  (Warner Bros.)
2 Hot!, Peaches & Herb (Polydor)
Breakfast in America, Supertramp
  (A&M)
Dire Straits, Dire Straits (Warner Bros.)

MAY 5

Spirits Having Flown, Bee Gees (RSO)
Minute by Minute, Doobie Brothers
  (Warner Bros.)
Breakfast in America, Supertramp
  (A&M)
2 Hot!, Peaches & Herb (Polydor)
Go West, Village People (Casablanca)

MAY 12

Breakfast in America, Supertramp
  (A&M)
Spirits Having Flown, Bee Gees (RSO)
Minute by Minute, Doobie Brothers
  (Warner Bros.)
2 Hot!, Peaches & Herb (Polydor)
Go West, Village People (Casablanca)

MAY 19

Breakfast in America, Supertramp
  (A&M)
2 Hot!, Peaches & Herb (Polydor)
Desolation Angels, Bad Company
  (Swan Song)
Minute by Minute, Doobie Brothers
  (Warner Bros.)
Spirits Having Flown, Bee Gees (RSO)

MAY 26

Breakfast in America, Supertramp
  (A&M)
2 Hot!, Peaches & Herb (Polydor)
Desolation Angels, Bad Company
  (Swan Song)
Bad Girls, Donna Summer (Casablanca)
Spirits Having Flown, Bee Gees (RSO)

JUNE 2

Breakfast in America, Supertramp
  (A&M)
Bad Girls, Donna Summer (Casablanca)
2 Hot!, Peaches & Herb (Polydor)
Desolation Angels, Bad Company
  (Swan Song)
We Are Family, Sister Sledge (Cotillion)

JUNE 9

Breakfast in America, Supertramp
  (A&M)
Bad Girls, Donna Summer (Casablanca)
2 Hot!, Peaches & Herb (Polydor)
Desolation Angels, Bad Company
  (Swan Song)
We Are Family, Sister Sledge (Cotillion)

JUNE 16

Bad Girls, Donna Summer (Casablanca)
Breakfast in America, Supertramp
  (A&M)
Rickie Lee Jones, Rickie Lee Jones
  (Warner Bros.)
Desolation Angels, Bad Company
  (Swan Song)
Cheap Trick at Budokan, Cheap Trick
  (Epic)

JUNE 23

Breakfast in America, Supertramp
  (A&M)
Bad Girls, Donna Summer (Casablanca)
Rickie Lee Jones, Rickie Lee Jones
  (Warner Bros.)
Desolation Angels, Bad Company
  (Swan Song)
Cheap Trick at Budokan, Cheap Trick
  (Epic)

TOP FIVE ALBUM ACTIVITY 1979

JUNE 30

Breakfast in America, Supertramp (A&M)
Bad Girls, Donna Summer (Casablanca)
Cheap Trick at Budokan, Cheap Trick (Epic)
Desolation Angels, Bad Company (Swan Song)
I Am, Earth, Wind & Fire (ARC/Columbia)

JULY 7

Breakfast in America, Supertramp (A&M)
Bad Girls, Donna Summer (Casablanca)
Cheap Trick at Budokan, Cheap Trick (Epic)
I Am, Earth, Wind & Fire (ARC/Columbia)
Desolation Angels, Bad Company (Swan Song)

JULY 14

Breakfast in America, Supertramp (A&M)
Bad Girls, Donna Summer (Casablanca)
Cheap Trick at Budokan, Cheap Trick (Epic)
I Am, Earth, Wind & Fire (ARC/Columbia)
Discovery, Electric Light Orchestra (Jet)

JULY 21

Bad Girls, Donna Summer (Casablanca)
Breakfast in America, Supertramp (A&M)
Cheap Trick at Budokan, Cheap Trick (Epic)
I Am, Earth, Wind & Fire (ARC/Columbia)
Discovery, Electric Light Orchestra (Jet)

JULY 28

Bad Girls, Donna Summer (Casablanca)
Breakfast in America, Supertramp (A&M)
Cheap Trick at Budokan, Cheap Trick (Epic)
I Am, Earth, Wind & Fire (ARC/Columbia)
Teddy, Teddy Pendergrass (Phila. Intl.)

AUGUST 4

Bad Girls, Donna Summer (Casablanca)
Breakfast in America, Supertramp (A&M)
Get the Knack, Knack (Capitol)
Cheap Trick at Budokan, Cheap Trick (Epic)
Teddy, Teddy Pendergrass (Phila. Intl.)

AUGUST 11

Get the Knack, Knack (Capitol)
Bad Girls, Donna Summer (Casablanca)
Breakfast in America, Supertramp (A&M)
Cheap Trick at Budokan, Cheap Trick (Epic)
Candy-O, Cars (Elektra)

AUGUST 18

Get the Knack, Knack (Capitol)
Bad Girls, Donna Summer (Casablanca)
Breakfast in America, Supertramp (A&M)
Candy-O, Cars (Elektra)
Cheap Trick at Budokan, Cheap Trick (Epic)

AUGUST 25

Get the Knack, Knack (Capitol)
Bad Girls, Donna Summer (Casablanca)
Breakfast in America, Supertramp (A&M)

TOP FIVE ALBUM ACTIVITY 1979

Candy-O, Cars (Elektra)
I Am, Earth, Wind & Fire
  (ARC/Columbia)

SEPTEMBER 1

Get the Knack, Knack (Capitol)
Breakfast in America, Supertramp
  (A&M)
Bad Girls, Donna Summer (Casablanca)
Candy-O, Cars (Elektra)
I Am, Earth, Wind & Fire
  (Columbia-ARC)

SEPTEMBER 8

In through the Out Door, Led Zeppelin
  (Swan Song)
Breakfast in America, Supertramp
  (A&M)
Get the Knack, Knack (Capitol)
Candy-O, Cars (Elektra)
Bad Girls, Donna Summer (Casablanca)

SEPTEMBER 15

In through the Out Door, Led Zeppelin
  (Swan Song)
Get the Knack, Knack (Capitol)
Breakfast in America, Supertramp
  (A&M)
Candy-O, Cars (Elektra)
Discovery, Electric Light Orchestra
  (Jet)

SEPTEMBER 22

In through the Out Door, Led Zeppelin
  (Swan Song)
Get the Knack, Knack (Capitol)
Midnight Magic, Commodores
  (Motown)
Breakfast in America, Supertramp
  (A&M)
Discovery, Electric Light Orchestra
  (Jet)

SEPTEMBER 29

In through the Out Door, Led Zeppelin
  (Swan Song)
Get the Knack, Knack (Capitol)
Midnight Magic, Commodores
  (Motown)
Breakfast in America, Supertramp
  (A&M)
Candy-O, Cars (Elektra)

OCTOBER 6

In through the Out Door, Led Zeppelin
  (Swan Song)
Midnight Magic, Commodores
  (Motown)
Get the Knack, Knack (Capitol)
Off the Wall, Michael Jackson (Epic)
Breakfast in America, Supertramp
  (A&M)

OCTOBER 13

In through the Out Door, Led Zeppelin
  (Swan Song)
The Long Run, Eagles (Asylum)
Get the Knack, Knack (Capitol)
Off the Wall, Michael Jackson (Epic)
Midnight Magic, Commodores
  (Motown)

OCTOBER 20

In through the Out Door, Led Zeppelin
  (Swan Song)
The Long Run, Eagles (Asylum)
Cornerstone, Styx (A&M)
Midnight Magic, Commodores
  (Motown)
Head Games, Foreigner (Atlantic)

OCTOBER 27

The Long Run, Eagles (Asylum)
In through the Out Door, Led Zeppelin
  (Swan Song)

TOP FIVE ALBUM ACTIVITY 1979

Cornerstone, Styx (A&M)
Midnight Magic, Commodores (Motown)
Head Games, Foreigner (Atlantic)

NOVEMBER 3

The Long Run, Eagles (Asylum)
In through the Out Door, Led Zeppelin (Swan Song)
Cornerstone, Styx (A&M)
Midnight Magic, Commodores (Motown)
Tusk, Fleetwood Mac (Warner Bros.)

NOVEMBER 10

The Long Run, Eagles (Asylum)
In through the Out Door, Led Zeppelin (Swan Song)
Cornerstone, Styx (A&M)
Midnight Magic, Commodores (Motown)
Tusk, Fleetwood Mac (Warner Bros.)

NOVEMBER 17

The Long Run, Eagles (Asylum)
In through the Out Door, Led Zeppelin (Swan Song)
Cornerstone, Styx (A&M)
Tusk, Fleetwood Mac (Warner Bros.)
Midnight Magic, Commodores (Motown)

NOVEMBER 24

The Long Run, Eagles (Asylum)
On the Radio—Greatest Hits—Volumes I & II, Donna Summer (Casablanca)
Cornerstone, Styx (A&M)
Tusk, Fleetwood Mac (Warner Bros.)
In through the Out Door, Led Zeppelin (Swan Song)

DECEMBER 1

The Long Run, Eagles (Asylum)
On the Radio—Greatest Hits Volumes I & II, Donna Summer (Casablanca)
Cornerstone, Styx (A&M)
Midnight Magic, Commodores (Motown)
In through the Out Door, Led Zeppelin (Swan Song)

DECEMBER 8

The Long Run, Eagles (Asylum)
On the Radio—Greatest Hits Volumes I & II, Donna Summer (Casablanca)
Cornerstone, Styx (A&M)
Midnight Magic, Commodores (Motown)
In through the Out Door, Led Zeppelin (Swan Song)

DECEMBER 15

The Long Run, Eagles (Asylum)
On the Radio—Greatest Hits Volumes I & II, Donna Summer (Casablanca)
Cornerstone, Styx (A&M)
Midnight Magic, Commodores (Motown)
Bee Gees Greatest, Bee Gees (RSO)

DECEMBER 22

On the Radio—Greatest Hits Volumes I & II, Donna Summer (Casablanca)
The Long Run, Eagles (Asylum)

Bee Gees Greatest, Bee Gees (RSO)
Cornerstone, Styx (A&M)
Midnight Magic, Commodores (Motown)

DECEMBER 29

The Long Run, Eagles (Asylum)
On the Radio—Greatest Hits Volumes I & II, Donna Summer (Casablanca)
Bee Gees Greatest, Bee Gees (RSO)
Cornerstone, Styx (A&M)
Kenny, Kenny Rogers (United Artists)

TOP FIVE SINGLES ACTIVITY 1979

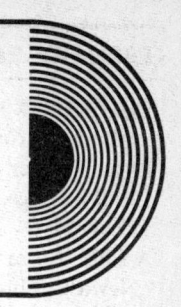

JANUARY 6

"Le Freak," Chic (Atlantic)
"Too Much Heaven," Bee Gees (RSO)
"My Life," Billy Joel (Columbia)
"You Don't Bring Me Flowers,"
　Barbra Streisand and Neil Diamond
　(Columbia)
"YMCA," Village People (Casablanca)

JANUARY 13

"Too Much Heaven," Bee Gees (RSO)
"Le Freak," Chic (Atlantic)
"My Life," Billy Joel (Columbia)
"YMCA," Village People (Casablanca)
"Hold the Line," Toto (Columbia)

JANUARY 20

"Le Freak," Chic (Atlantic)
"YMCA," Village People (Casablanca)
"Too Much Heaven," Bee Gees (RSO)
"My Life," Billy Joel (Columbia)
"Hold the Line," Toto (Columbia)

JANUARY 27

"Le Freak," Chic (Atlantic)
"YMCA," Village People (Casablanca)
"Too Much Heaven," Bee Gees (RSO)
"My Life," Billy Joel (Columbia)
"September," Earth, Wind & Fire
　(ARC/Columbia)

FEBRUARY 3

"Le Freak," Chic (Atlantic)
"Da Ya Think I'm Sexy?" Rod Stewart
　(Warner Bros.)
"YMCA," Village People (Casablanca)
"September," Earth, Wind & Fire
　(ARC/Columbia)
"Fire," Pointer Sisters (Planet)

FEBRUARY 10

"Da Ya Think I'm Sexy?" Rod Stewart
　(Warner Bros.)
"Le Freak," Chic (Atlantic)
"Fire," Pointer Sisters (Planet)
"September," Earth, Wind & Fire
　(ARC/Columbia)
"A Little More Love," Olivia
　Newton-John (MCA)

FEBRUARY 17

"Da Ya Think I'm Sexy?" Rod Stewart
　(Warner Bros.)
"Fire," Pointer Sisters (Planet)
"Le Freak," Chic (Atlantic)
"A Little More Love," Olivia
　Newton-John (MCA)
"I Will Survive," Gloria Gaynor
　(Polydor)

FEBRUARY 24

"Da Ya Think I'm Sexy?" Rod Stewart (Warner Bros.)
"Fire," Pointer Sisters (Planet)
"I Will Survive," Gloria Gaynor (Polydor)
"A Little More Love," Olivia Newton-John (MCA)
"YMCA," Village People (Casablanca)

MARCH 3

"Da Ya Think I'm Sexy?" Rod Stewart (Warner Bros.)
"I Will Survive," Gloria Gaynor (Polydor)
"YMCA," Village People (Casablanca)
"Fire," Pointer Sisters (Planet)
"Tragedy," Bee Gees (RSO)

MARCH 10

"I Will Survive," Gloria Gaynor (Polydor)
"Da Ya Think I'm Sexy?" Rod Stewart (Warner Bros.)
"YMCA," Village People (Casablanca)
"Tragedy," Bee Gees (RSO)
"Fire," Pointer Sisters

MARCH 17

"Tragedy," Bee Gees (RSO)
"Da Ya Think I'm Sexy?" Rod Stewart (Warner Bros.)
"I Will Survive," Gloria Gaynor (Polydor)
"YMCA," Village People (Casablanca)
"Fire," Pointer Sisters (Planet)

MARCH 24

"Da Ya Think I'm Sexy?" Rod Stewart (Warner Bros.)
"Tragedy," Bee Gees (RSO)
"I Will Survive," Gloria Gaynor (Polydor)
"YMCA," Village People (Casablanca)
"Heaven Knows," Donna Summer with Brooklyn Dreams (Casablanca)

MARCH 31

"Tragedy," Bee Gees (RSO)
"Da Ya Think I'm Sexy?" Rod Stewart (Warner Bros.)
"I Will Survive," Gloria Gaynor (Polydor)
"What a Fool Believes," Doobie Brothers (Warner Bros.)
"YMCA," Village People (Casablanca)

APRIL 7

"What a Fool Believes," Doobie Brothers (Warner Bros.)
"Tragedy," Bee Gees (RSO)
"I Will Survive," Gloria Gaynor (Polydor)
"Music Box Dancer," Frank Mills (Polydor)
"Knock on Wood," Amii Stewart (Ariola)

APRIL 14

"Music Box Dancer," Frank Mills (Polydor)
"Knock on Wood," Amii Stewart (Ariola)
"Tragedy," Bee Gees (RSO)
"What a Fool Believes," Doobie Brothers (Warner Bros.)
"I Will Survive," Gloria Gaynor (Polydor)

APRIL 21

"Knock on Wood," Amii Stewart (Ariola)
"Heart of Glass," Blondie (Chrysalis)

"Music Box Dancer," Frank Mills
   (Polydor)
"Tragedy," Bee Gees (RSO)
"I Want Your Love," Chic (Atlantic)

APRIL 28

"Heart of Glass," Blondie (Chrysalis)
"Reunited," Peaches & Herb (Polydor)
"Music Box Dancer," Frank Mills
   (Polydor)
"Knock on Wood," Amii Stewart
   (Ariola)
"I Want Your Love," Chic (Atlantic)

MAY 5

"Reunited," Peaches & Herb (Polydor)
"Heart of Glass," Blondie (Chrysalis)
"Music Box Dancer," Frank Mills
   (Polydor)
"In the Navy," Village People
   (Casablanca)
"Knock on Wood," Amii Stewart
   (Ariola)

MAY 12

"Reunited," Peaches & Herb (Polydor)
"In the Navy," Village People
   (Casablanca)
"Heart of Glass," Blondie (Chrysalis)
"Music Box Dancer," Frank Mills
   (Polydor)
"Knock on Wood," Amii Stewart
   (Ariola)

MAY 19

"Reunited," Peaches & Herb (Polydor)
"In the Navy," Village People
   (Casablanca)
"Heart of Glass," Blondie (Chrysalis)
"Hot Stuff," Donna Summer
   (Casablanca)
"Shake Your Body (Down to the
   Ground)," Jacksons (Epic)

MAY 26

"Reunited," Peaches & Herb (Polydor)
"Hot Stuff," Donna Summer
   (Casablanca)
"Heart of Glass," Blondie (Chrysalis)
"In the Navy," Village People
   (Casablanca)
"Shake Your Body (Down to the
   Ground)," Jacksons (Epic)

JUNE 2

"Hot Stuff," Donna Summer
   (Casablanca)
"Reunited," Peaches & Herb (Polydor)
"Shake Your Body (Down to the
   Ground)," Jacksons (Epic)
"In the Navy," Village People
   (Casablanca)
"Love You Inside Out," Bee Gees (RSO)

JUNE 9

"Hot Stuff," Donna Summer
   (Casablanca)
"Reunited," Peaches & Herb (Polydor)
"Shake Your Body (Down to the
   Ground)," Jacksons (Epic)
"Love You Inside Out," Bee Gees (RSO)
"We Are Family," Sister Sledge
   (Cotillion)

JUNE 16

"Hot Stuff," Donna Summer
   (Casablanca)
"Reunited," Peaches & Herb (Polydor)
"We Are Family," Sister Sledge
   (Cotillion)
"Love You Inside Out," Bee Gees (RSO)
"Just When I Needed You Most,"
   Randy Vanwarmer (Bearsville)

JUNE 23

"Hot Stuff," Donna Summer (Casablanca)

"Reunited," Peaches & Herb (Polydor)
"We Are Family," Sister Sledge
(Cotillion)
"You Take My Breath Away," Rex Smith
(Columbia)
"Just When I Needed You Most,"
Randy Vanwarmer (Bearsville)

JUNE 30

"Hot Stuff," Donna Summer
(Casablanca)
"Ring My Bell," Anita Ward
(Juana/TK)
"Bad Girls," Donna Summer
(Casablanca)
"You Take My Breath Away," Rex Smith
(Columbia)
"We Are Family," Sister Sledge
(Cotillion)

JULY 7

"Ring My Bell," Anita Ward
(Juana/TK)
"Hot Stuff," Donna Summer
(Casablanca)
"Bad Girls," Donna Summer
(Casablanca)
"You Take My Breath Away," Rex Smith
(Columbia)
"We Are Family," Sister Sledge
(Cotillion)

JULY 14

"Bad Girls," Donna Summer
(Casablanca)
"Ring My Bell," Anita Ward
(Juana/TK)
"Hot Stuff," Donna Summer
(Casablanca)
"I Want You to Want Me," Cheap Trick
(Epic)
"You Take My Breath Away," Rex Smith
(Columbia)

JULY 21

"Bad Girls," Donna Summer
(Casablanca)
"Ring My Bell," Anita Ward
(Juana/TK)
"Hot Stuff," Donna Summer
(Casablanca)
"I Want You to Want Me," Cheap Trick
(Epic)
"She Believes in Me," Kenny Rogers
(United Artists)

JULY 28

"Bad Girls," Donna Summer
(Casablanca)
"Ring My Bell," Anita Ward
(Juana/TK)
"Hot Stuff," Donna Summer
(Casablanca)
"She Believes in Me," Kenny Rogers
(United Artists)
"When You're in Love with a Beautiful
Woman," Dr. Hook (Capitol)

AUGUST 4

"Bad Girls," Donna Summer
(Casablanca)
"Ring My Bell," Anita Ward
(Juana/TK)
"Hot Stuff," Donna Summer
(Casablanca)
"When You're in Love with a Beautiful
Woman," Dr. Hook (Capitol)
"Gold," John Stewart (RSO)

AUGUST 11

"My Sharona," Knack (Capitol)
"Bad Girls," Donna Summer
(Casablanca)
"Good Times," Chic (Atlantic)
"When You're in Love with a Beautiful
Woman," Dr. Hook (Capitol)
"Gold," John Stewart (RSO)

AUGUST 18

"My Sharona," Knack (Capitol)
"Good Times," Chic (Atlantic)
"Bad Girls," Donna Summer (Casablanca)
"The Main Event/Fight," Barbra Streisand (Columbia)
"I Was Made for Lovin' You," Kiss (Casablanca)

AUGUST 25

"My Sharona," Knack (Capitol)
"Good Times," Chic (Atlantic)
"The Main Event/Fight," Barbra Streisand (Columbia)
"Bad Girls," Donna Summer (Casablanca)
"After the Love Has Gone," Earth, Wind & Fire (ARC/Columbia)

SEPTEMBER 1

"My Sharona," Knack (Capitol)
"Good Times," Chic (Atlantic)
"The Devil Went Down to Georgia," Charlie Daniels Band (Epic)
"After the Love Has Gone," Earth, Wind & Fire (Columbia-ARC)
"Lead Me On," Maxine Nightingale (Windsong)

SEPTEMBER 8

"My Sharona," Knack (Capitol)
"Sad Eyes," Robert John (EMI)
"The Devil Went Down to Georgia," Charlie Daniels Band (Epic)
"After the Love Has Gone," Earth, Wind & Fire (Columbia-ARC)
"Lead Me On," Maxine Nightingale (Windsong)

SEPTEMBER 15

"Sad Eyes," Robert John (EMI)
"My Sharona," Knack (Capitol)
"Don't Bring Me Down," Electric Light Orchestra (Jet)
"Lead Me On," Maxine Nightingale (Windsong)
"The Devil Went Down to Georgia," Charlie Daniels Band (Epic)

SEPTEMBER 22

"Sad Eyes," Robert John (EMI)
"My Sharona," Knack (Capitol)
"Don't Bring Me Down," Electric Light Orchestra (Jet)
"Lonesome Loser," Little River Band (Capitol)
"The Devil Went Down to Georgia," Charlie Daniels Band (Epic)

SEPTEMBER 29

"Sad Eyes," Robert John (EMI)
"My Sharona," Knack (Capitol)
"Don't Bring Me Down," Electric Light Orchestra (Jet)
"Lonesome Loser," Little River Band (Capitol)
"Sail On," Commodores (Motown)

OCTOBER 6

"Sad Eyes," Robert John (EMI)
"My Sharona," Knack (Capitol)
"Sail On," Commodores (Motown)
"Lonesome Loser," Little River Band (Capitol)
"I'll Never Love This Way Again," Dionne Warwick (Arista)

OCTOBER 13

"Sad Eyes," Robert John (EMI)
"Sail On," Commodores (Motown)
"Rise," Herb Alpert (A&M)
"Don't Stop 'til You Get Enough," Michael Jackson (Epic)
"My Sharona," Knack (Capitol)

OCTOBER 20

"Sail On," Commodores (Motown)
"Rise," Herb Alpert (A&M)
"Don't Stop 'til You Get Enough,"
  Michael Jackson (Epic)
"Sad Eyes," Robert John (EMI)
"Dim All the Lights," Donna Summer
  (Casablanca)

OCTOBER 27

"Rise," Herb Alpert (A&M)
"Don't Stop 'til You Get Enough,"
  Michael Jackson (Epic)
"Dim All the Lights," Donna Summer
  (Casablanca)
"Pop Muzik," M (Sire)
"Sad Eyes," Robert John (EMI-America)

NOVEMBER 3

"Don't Stop 'til You Get Enough,"
  Michael Jackson (Epic)
"Dim All the Lights," Donna Summer
  (Casablanca)
"Heartache Tonight," Eagles (Asylum)
"Pop Musik," M (Sire)
"You Decorated My Life," Kenny
  Rogers (United Artists)

NOVEMBER 10

"Heartache Tonight," Eagles (Asylum)
"Dim All the Lights," Donna Summer
  (Casablanca)
"Babe," Styx (A&M)
"Pop Muzik," M (Sire)
"You Decorated My Life," Kenny
  Rogers (United Artists)

NOVEMBER 17

"Babe," Styx (A&M)
"Heartache Tonight," Eagles (Asylum)
"No More Tears (Enough Is Enough),"
  Barbra Streisand/Donna Summer
  (Casablanca)
"Still," Commodores (Motown)
"Pop Muzik," M (Sire)

NOVEMBER 24

"No More Tears (Enough Is Enough),"
  Barbra Streisand/Donna Summer
  (Columbia/Casablanca)
"Babe," Styx (A&M)
"Still," Commodores (Motown)
"Heartache Tonight," Eagles (Asylum)
"Pop Muzik," M (Sire)

DECEMBER 1

"No More Tears (Enough Is Enough),"
  Barbra Streisand/Donna Summer
  (Columbia/Casablanca)
"Babe," Styx (A&M)
"Still," Commodores (Motown)
"Please Don't Go," KC & the Sunshine
  Band (TK)
"Heartache Tonight," Eagles (Asylum)

DECEMBER 8

"No More Tears (Enough Is Enough),"
  Barbra Streisand/Donna Summer
  (Columbia/Casablanca)
"Babe," Styx (A&M)
"Please Don't Go," KC & the Sunshine
  Band (TK)
"Escape (The Pina Colada Song),"
  Rupert Holmes (MCA)
"Still," Commodores (Motown)

DECEMBER 15

"Babe," Styx (A&M)
"No More Tears (Enough Is Enough),"
  Barbra Streisand/Donna Summer
  (Columbia/Casablanca)
"Please Don't Go," KC & the Sunshine
  Band (TK)

"Escape (The Pina Colada Song),"
  Rupert Holmes (MCA/Infinity)
"Ladies Night," Kool & the Gang
  (Delite)

DECEMBER 22

"Escape (The Pina Colada Song),"
  Rupert Holmes (MCA-Infinity)
"Babe," Styx (A&M)
"Please Don't Go," KC & the Sunshine
  Band (TK)
"No More Tears (Enough Is Enough),"
  Barbra Streisand/Donna Summer
  (Columbia/Casablanca)
"Ladies Night," Kool & the Gang (Delite)

DECEMBER 29

"Escape (The Pina Colada Song),"
  Rupert Holmes (MCA-Infinity)
"Please Don't Go," KC & the Sunshine
  Band (TK)
"Babe," Styx (A&M)
"Coward of the County," Kenny Rogers
  (United Artists)
"Do That to Me One More Time,"
  Captain & Tennille (Casablanca)

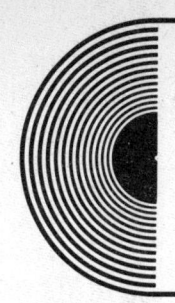

CALENDAR

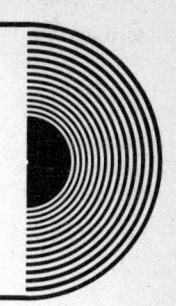

CAPRICORN

January 1	Country Joe McDonald, vocals, rhythm guitar, b. 1942 Hank Williams, d. 1953. (Born September 17.)
January 3	George Martin, producer of the early Beatles, America and Jeff Beck, b. 1926 Stephen Stills (Buffalo Springfield/CSN&Y, guitar and bass), b. 1945 John Paul Jones (Yardbirds/Led Zeppelin, bass and keyboards), b. 1946
January 6	Earl Scruggs, b. 1924
January 7	Eldee Young (Ramsey Lewis Trio, bass), b. 1936 Paul Revere (Paul Revere & the Raiders), b. 1942 Jan Wenner, *Rolling Stone* publisher, b. 1946 Kenny Loggins (Loggins & Messina, guitar and bass), b. 1948
January 8	Elvis Presley, b. 1935 Shirley Bassey, b. 1937 Anthony Gourdine (Little Anthony & the Imperials, lead vocals), b. 1941 Robby Kreiger (Doors, guitar), b. 1946 David Bowie, b. 1947 Terry Sylvester (Hollies, rhythm guitar), b. 1947
January 9	Joan Baez, b. 1941 Jimmy Page (Yardbirds/Led Zeppelin, lead quitar), b. 1945
January 10	Jerry Wexler, record producer, b. 1917 Jim Croce, b. 1942 Rod Stewart (Jeff Beck Group/Faces, lead vocals), b. 1945 Howlin' Wolf, d. 1976. (Born June 10.)
January 11	Denny Greene (Sha Na Na), b. 1949

January 12 Fred McDowell, b. 1904
"Long" (6'7") John Baldry, b. 1941
Cynthia Robinson (Sly & the Family Stone, trumpet), b. 1946

January 13 Fred White (Earth, Wind & Fire, drums), b. 1955

January 14 Alain Toussaint, producer, b. 1938

January 15 Gene Krupa, b. 1909
Captain Beefheart (Don Van Vliet), b. 1941
Ronnie Van Zant (Lynyrd Skynyrd, lead vocals), b. 1949
Melvyn Gale (Electric Light Orchestra, bass), b. 1952

January 16 William Francis (Dr. Hook & the Medicine Show, keyboard), b. 1942

January 17 Mick Taylor (John Mayall's Bluesbreakers/Rolling Stones, rhythm guitar), b. 1948

January 18 David Ruffin (Temptations, lead singer 1964-1968), b. 1941

January 19 Phil Everly, b. 1939
Janis Joplin, b. 1943
Rod Evans (Deep Purple, lead vocals), b. 1945
Dolly Parton, b. 1946
Robert Palmer, b. 1949
Dewey Bunnell (America), b. 1951

AQUARIUS

January 20 Eric Stewart (10 cc, lead guitar), b. 1945
George Grantham (Poco, drums), b. 1947
Paul Stanley (Kiss, rhythm guitar), b. 1952
Alan Freed, d. 1965. (Born December 15.)

January 21 Richie Havens, b. 1941

January 22 Sam Cooke, b. 1935
Addie "Mickey" Harris (Shirelles), b. 1940

January 23 Terry Kath (Chicago, guitar), d. 1978, accidentally shot himself. (Born January 31.)

January 24 Doug Kershaw, b. 1936
Neil Diamond, b. 1941
Ray Stevens, b. 1941

January 27 Bobby Bland, b. 1930
Kevin Coyne, b. 1944
Nick Mason (Pink Floyd, drums), b. 1945
Nedra Talley (Ronettes), b. 1947

January 28	Brian Keenan (Chambers Brothers, drums), b. 1944
January 29	Leadbelly (Huddie Ledbetter), b. 1889 David Byron (Uriah Heep, lead vocals), b. 1947
January 30	Marty Balin (Jefferson Airplane/Starship, Hot Tuna, vocals), b. 1943 Steve Marriott (Small Faces, Humble Pie, guitar and vocals), b. 1947
January 31	Roosevelt Sykes, b. 1906 Terry Kath (Chicago, guitar), b. 1946 Phil Collins (Genesis, drums and vocals), b. 1951 Phil Manzanera (Roxy Music), b. 1951 Johnny Rotten, b. 1956
February 1	Bob Shane (Kingston Trio), b. 1934 Don Everly, b. 1937 Ray "Dr. Hook" Sawyer (Dr. Hook & the Medicine Show, lead vocals), b. 1937
February 2	Stan Getz, b. 1927 Skip Battin (Byrds), b. 1934 Graham Nash (Hollies/CSN&Y, guitar), b. 1942 Alan McKay (Earth, Wind & Fire, guitar, percussion and sitar), b. 1948
February 3	Angelo D'Aleo (Belmonts, first tenor), b. 1940 Dave Davies (Kinks, rhythm guitar), b. 1947 Melanie (Schekeryk), b. 1947 Buddy Holly, (born Sept. 7), Ritchie Valens, (born May 13), Johnny Preston (born August 18) and The Big Bopper (born October 24) killed in plane crash in Ames, Iowa, 1959
February 4	John Steel (Animals, drums), b. 1941 Alice Cooper, b. 1948 Jerry Shirley (Humble Pie, drums), b. 1952
February 5	Alex Harvey, b. 1935 Cory Wells (Three Dog Night, lead vocals), b. 1942 Charles Winfield (Blood, Sweat & Tears, trumpet and fluegelhorn), b. 1943 Al Kooper (Blood, Sweat & Tears/Blues Project, lead vocals and keyboard), b. 1944 Bob Marley, b. 1945 Nigel Olsson, b. 1949
February 6	Natalie Cole, b. 1950
February 8	Lonnie Johnson, b. 1889 Adolfo De La Parra (Canned Heat, drums), b. 1946 Ted Turner (Wishbone Ash), b. 1950
February 9	Carole King, b. 1941
February 10	Roberta Flack, b. 1940

February 11	Gene Vincent, b. 1935 Tom Rush, b. 1941
February 12	Ray Manzarek (Doors, bass and keyboards), b. 1943 Stanley Knight (Black Oak Arkansas, guitar), b. 1949 Steve Hackett (Genesis, guitar), b. 1950
February 13	Peter Tork (Monkees, guitar), b. 1944 Ed Gagliardi (Foreigner, bass guitar), b. 1952
February 14	Eric Andersen, b. 1943 Tim Buckley, b. 1947
February 15	Brian Holland (Holland-Dozier-Holland), b. 1941 Mick Avory (Kinks, drums), b. 1944 Melissa Manchester, b. 1951
February 16	Sonny Bono (Sonny & Cher), b. 1935
February 17	Bobby Lewis, b. 1933 Eddie Holland (Holland-Dozier-Holland), b. 1941 Gene Pitney, b. 1941
February 18	Yoko Ono Lennon, b. 1933 Robin Bachman (Bachman-Turner Overdrive, drums), b. 1953

PISCES

February 19	William "Smokey" Robinson, b. 1940 Tony Iommi (Black Sabbath, guitar), b. 1948 Andy Powell (Wishbone Ash), b. 1950
February 20	Nancy Wilson, b. 1940 Buffy Sainte-Marie, b. 1941 Lewis Soloff (Blood, Sweat & Tears, trumpet and fluegelhorn), b. 1944 Randy California (Spirit, lead guitar), b. 1946 J. Geils (J. Geils Band, guitar), b. 1946
February 21	Nina Simone, b. 1933 Florence Ballard (Supremes), d. 1976. (Born June 30.)
February 23	Johnny Winter, b. 1944 Rusty Young (Poco, steel guitar), b. 1946 Steven Priest (Sweet, bass), b. 1950 Brad Whitford (Aerosmith, rhythm guitar), b. 1952
February 24	Paul Jones (Manfred Mann, lead vocals), b. 1944 Nicky Hopkins (John Mayall's Bluesbreakers/Quicksilver Messenger Service, keyboard), b. 1944

February 25	George Harrison, lead guitar, b. 1943 Stuart Wood (Bay City Rollers, guitar), b. 1957
February 26	Antoine "Fats" Domino, b. 1928 Johnny Cash, b. 1932 Paul Cotton (Poco, lead guitar), b. 1943 Bob "The Bear" Hite (Canned Heat, lead vocals), b. 1945
February 28	John Fahey, b. 1939 Brian Jones (Rolling Stones, rhythm guitar), b. 1942
March 1	Mike D'Abo (Manfred Mann), b. 1944 Roger Daltrey (Who, lead vocals), b. 1944
March 2	Willie Chambers (Chambers Brothers, guitar), b. 1938 George Benson, b. 1943 Lou Reed (Velvet Underground), b. 1944 Rory Gallagher, b. 1949
March 3	Junior Parker, b. 1927 Jance Garfat (Dr. Hook & the Medicine Show, bass), b. 1944
March 4	Mary Wilson (Supremes), b. 1944 Bobby Womack, b. 1944 Chris Squire (Yes, bass), b. 1948
March 5	Andy Gibb, b. 1958
March 6	Furry Lewis, b. 1893 Hugh Grundy (Zombies, drums), b. 1945 Kiki Dee, b. 1947 David Gilmour (Pink Floyd, lead guitar), b. 1947
March 7	Chris Taylor White (Zombies, bass), b. 1943 Peter Wolf (J. Geils Band, vocals), b. 1946
March 8	Randy Meisner (Poco/Eagles, bass), b. 1946 Rod "Pigpen" McKernan (Grateful Dead) found dead in his apartment, 1973, from liver damage. (Born September 8.)
March 9	Lloyd Price, b. 1933 Mickey Dolenz (Monkees, lead vocals, guitar and drums), b. 1945 Ray Royer (Procol Harum, lead guitar), b. 1945 Robin Trower (Procol Harum, lead guitar), b. 1945 Jimmie Fadden (Nitty Gritty Dirt Band), b. 1948
March 10	Dean Torrence (Jan & Dean), b. 1940 Tom Scholz (Boston, guitar), b. 1947
March 11	Mark Stein (Vanilla Fudge, keyboards), b. 1947
March 12	Paul Kantner (Jefferson Airplane/Starship, vocals and guitar), b.1942 James Taylor, b. 1948 Charlie Parker, d. 1955. (Born August 29.)
March 13	Neil Sedaka, b. 1939 Donald York (Sha Na Na), b. 1949

March 14	Quincy Jones, b. 1933 Loretta Lynn, b. 1940 Walter Parazaider (Chicago, woodwinds), b. 1945
March 15	Lightnin' Hopkins, b. 1912 Arif Mardin, record producer, b. 1932 Roy Clark, b. 1933 Phil Lesh (Grateful Dead, bass guitar), b. 1940 Mike Love (Beach Boys, lead vocals), b. 1941 Sly Stone, b. 1944 Howard Scott (War, lead guitar), b. 1946 Ry Cooder, b. 1947
March 16	Jerry Jeff Walker, b. 1942 Nancy Wilson (Heart), b. 1954
March 17	John Sebastian, b. 1944 Harold Brown (War, drums), b. 1946
March 18	Charley Pride, b. 1938 Wilson Pickett, b. 1941 Robert Harrison (Procol Harum, drums), b. 1947
March 19	Paul Atkinson (Zombies, guitar), b. 1946 Derek Longmuir (Bay City Rollers, drums), b. 1952 Gary Thain (Uriah Heep, bass), d. 1976
March 20	Carl Palmer (Emerson, Lake & Palmer, drums, percussion), b. 1947

ARIES

March 21	Son House, b. 1902 Rose Stone (Sly & the Family Stone, keyboard), b. 1945
March 22	Glen Campbell, b. 1936 Keith Relf (Yardbirds/Renaissance/Armageddon, vocals and harmonica), b. 1943 Jeremy Clyde (Chad & Jeremy), b. 1944
March 24	Lee Oskar (War, harmonica), b. 1946 Mike Kellie (Spooky Tooth, drummer), b. 1947
March 25	Johnny Burnette, b. 1934 Hoyt Axton, b. 1938 Aretha Franklin, b. 1943 Elton John, b. 1947
March 26	Rufus Thomas, b. 1917 Fred Parris (Five Satins, lead), b. 1936

Diana Ross, b. 1944
Richard Tandy (Electric Light Orchestra, guitar and keyboards), b. 1948
Steven Tyler (Aerosmith, lead vocals), b. 1948
Fran Sheehan (Boston, bass guitar), b. 1949

March 27 Leroy Carr, b. 1905
Wally Stocker (Babys, lead guitar), b. 1954

March 28 John Evans (Jethro Tull, keyboard), b. 1948
Charles Portz (Turtles, bass), b. 1945

March 30 Willie Nelson, b. 1933
Graeme Edge (Moody Blues, drums), b. 1944
Eric Clapton (John Mayall's Bluesbreakers/Yardbirds/Cream/ Blind Faith/Derek & the Dominoes, guitar and vocals), b. 1945
Jim Dandy (Black Oak Arkansas, lead vocals), b. 1948

March 31 G. Allan Nichol (Turtles, lead guitar), b. 1946
Mick Ralphs (Mott the Hoople/Bad Company, guitar), b. 1948
Tony Brock (Babys, drums), b. 1954

April 1 Rudolph Isley (Isley Brothers), b. 1939
Ronnie "Plonk" Lane (Faces, bass), b. 1948

April 2 Marvin Gaye, b. 1939
Leon Russell, b. 1941
Larry Coryell, b. 1943

April 3 Jeff Barry, songwriter, b. 1939
Jan Berry (Jan and Dean), b. 1941
Richard Manuel (Band, keyboard), b. 1944

April 4 Muddy Waters (McKinley Morganfield), b. 1915
Berry Oakley (Allman Brothers Band, bass guitar), b. 1948
Dave Hill (Slade), b. 1952

April 5 Tony Williams (Platters, lead), b. 1928
Allan Clarke (Hollies, lead vocals), b. 1942
"Anna" Ulvaeus (Abba, vocals), b. 1950

April 6 Michelle Phillips (Mamas & Papas), b. 1944

April 7 Billie Holiday, b. 1915
Freddie Hubbard, b. 1938
Mick Abrahams (Jethro Tull/Blodwyn Pig, lead guitar), b. 1943
Spencer Dryden (Jefferson Airplane/New Riders of the Purple Sage, drums), b. 1943
John Oates (Hall & Oates, guitar), b. 1949
Janis Ian, b. 1951

April 8 Steve Howe (Yes, lead guitar), b. 1947
Mel Schacher (& the Mysterians/Grand Funk Railroad, bass), b. 1951

April 9 Mance Lipscomb, b. 1895

CALENDAR

                Carl Perkins, b. 1932
                Terry Knight (& the Pack, lead vocals), b. 1943
                "Chico" Ryan (Sha Na Na), b. 1948
                Phil Ochs, suicide by hanging 1976. (Born December 19.)

April 10   Nathaniel Nelson (Flamingoes, lead), b. 1932

April 12   Tiny Tim, b. 1933
                Herbie Hancock, b. 1940
                John Kay (Steppenwolf, lead vocals and guitar), b. 1944
                David Cassidy, b. 1950

April 13   Lester Chambers (Chambers Brothers, percussion), b. 1940
                Jack Casady (Jefferson Airplane/Hot Tuna, bass guitar), b. 1944
                Al Green, b. 1946
                Roy Loney (Flaming Groovies), b. 1946
                Jim Pons (Turtles/Mothers of Invention, bass), b. 1946

April 14   Ritchie Blackmore (Deep Purple, lead guitar), b. 1945

April 15   Bessie Smith, b. 1894
                Dave Edmunds (Rockpile), b. 1944

April 16   Bobby Vinton, b. 1935
                Dusty Springfield, b. 1939

April 17   Don Kirshner, b. 1934
                Eddie Cochran, d. 1960. (Born October 3.)

April 18   Mike Vickers (Manfred Mann, guitar), b. 1942
                Lenny Baker (Sha Na Na), b. 1946

April 19   Alan Price (Animals, keyboard), b. 1942
                Mark Volman (Turtles/Mothers of Invention, vocals), b. 1947

April 20   Craig Frost (Grand Funk Railroad, keyboard), b. 1948

TAURUS

April 22   Charlie Mingus, b. 1922
                Peter Frampton (Humble Pie, guitar), b. 1950

April 23   Roy Orbison, b. 1936
                Peter Ham (Badfinger, lead guitar and keyboard), committed suicide 1975. (Born April 26.)

April 24   Barbra Streisand, b. 1942
                Doug Clifford (Creedence Clearwater Revival, drums), b. 1945
                Stu Cook (Creedence Clearwater Revival, bass), b. 1945
                Glen Cornick (Jethro Tull, bass), b. 1947

April 25	Ella Fitzgerald, b. 1918 Albert King, b. 1923 Bjorn Ulvaeus (Abba, guitar), b. 1945 Steve Ferrone (Average White Band, drums), b. 1950
April 26	Bobby Rydell, b. 1942 Gary Wright (Spooky Tooth, lead vocals), b. 1943 Pete Ham (Badfinger, lead guitar and keyboard), b. 1947
April 27	Paul "Ace" Frehley (Kiss, lead guitar and vocals), b. 1951
April 29	Duke Ellington, b. 1899 Carl Gardner (Coasters, lead), b. 1928 Albee Cracolici (Mystics, baritone), b. 1936 Frankie Lymon, drug overdose 1968. (Born September 30.)
April 30	Reverend Gary Davis, b. 1896 Johnny Horton, b. 1927 Bobby Vee, b. 1943
May 1	Little Walter (Marion Walter Jacobs), b. 1930 Judy Collins, b. 1939 Rita Coolidge, b. 1945
May 2	John Verity (Argent, guitar), b. 1944 Goldy McJohn (Steppenwolf, keyboard), b. 1945 Robert Henrit (Argent, drums), b. 1946 Lou Gramm (Foreigner, lead vocals), b. 1950
May 3	Pete Seeger, b. 1919 James Brown, b. 1928 Frankie Valli (Four Seasons), b. 1937
May 4	Maynard Ferguson, b. 1928 Ed Cassidy (Spirit, drums), b. 1931 Tammy Wynette, b. 1942
May 5	Bill Ward (Black Sabbath, drums), b. 1948
May 6	Peggy Lee, b. 1920 Bob Seger (Silver Bullet Band), b. 1945
May 7	Johnny Maestro (Crests/Brooklyn Bridge), b. 1939
May 8	Rick Nelson, b. 1940 "Sam" Samwell-Smith (Yardbirds/Renaissance, bass), b. 1943 Gary Glitter, b. 1944 Phillip Bailey (Earth, Wind & Fire, lead vocals and percussion), b. 1951
May 9	David Prater (Sam & Dave), b. 1937 Peter Birrell (Freddie & the Dreamers, bass), b. 1941 Richard Furay (Buffalo Springfield/Poco, rhythm guitar), b. 1944 Steve Katz (Blues Project/Blood Sweat & Tears/American Flyer, guitar and harmonica), b. 1945 Billy Joel, b. 1949

May 10 Danny Rapp (Danny & the Juniors), b. 1941
Donovan (Leitch), b. 1946
Graham Gouldman (10 cc, bass), b. 1946
Dave Mason (Traffic, guitar), b. 1946
Jay Ferguson (Spirit, lead vocals), b. 1947
Sid Vicious, b. 1957

May 11 Carla Bley, b. 1938
Eric Burdon (Animals/War, vocals), b. 1941
Les Chadwick (Gerry & the Pacemakers, bass), b. 1943
Lester Flatt, d. 1979. (Born June 28.)

May 12 Billy Swan, b. 1944
Ian McLagan (Faces, keyboard), b. 1946
Steve Winwood (Spencer Davis Group/Traffic/Blind Faith, guitar and keyboard), b. 1948
"Jocko" Marcellino (Sha Na Na), b. 1950

May 13 Ritchie Valens, b. 1941
Mary Wells, b. 1943
Magic Dick (J. Geils Band, mouth harp), b. 1945
Pete "Overend" Watts (Mott the Hoople, bass guitar), b. 1949
Peter Gabriel (Genesis, lead vocals), b. 1950
Stevie Wonder, b. 1950

May 14 Bobby Darin, b. 1936
Jack Bruce (John Mayall's Bluesbreakers/Manfred Mann/Cream, bass), b. 1943
Gene Cornish (Rascals, guitar), b. 1945

May 15 Eddy Arnold, b. 1918
Trini Lopez, b. 1937
Brian Eno, New Wave producer, b. 1948

May 16 "Red" Holt (Ramsey Lewis Trio), b. 1932
Jonathan Richman, b. 1951

May 17 Taj Mahal, b. 1940
Jesse Winchester, b. 1944
William Bruford (Yes/King Crimson, drums), b. 1950

May 18 Albert Hammond, b. 1942
Rick Wakeman (Yes, keyboard), b. 1949

May 19 Jerry Hyman (Blood, Sweat & Tears, trombone and recorder), b. 1947
Joey Ramone (Ramones), b. 1952

May 20 Joe Turner, b. 1911
Joe Cocker, b. 1944
Cher (Sonny & Cher), b. 1946
"Little" Jimmie Henderson (Black Oak Arkansas, lead guitar), b. 1954

GEMINI

May 21	Fats Waller, b. 1924 Ronald Isley (Isley Brothers, lead vocals), b. 1941 Hilton Valentine (Animals, lead guitar), b. 1943 Leo Sayer, b. 1948
May 22	Bernie Taupin, b. 1950
May 24	Bob Dylan, b. 1941 Derek Quinn (Freddie & the Dreamers, lead guitar), b. 1942 Patti LaBelle, b. 1944 Steve Upton (Wishbone Ash), b. 1946
May 25	Miles Davis, b. 1926 Jessi Colter, b. 1947
May 26	Levon Helms (Band, drums), b. 1943 Verden "Phally" Allen (Mott the Hoople, organ), b. 1944 Stevie Nicks (Fleetwood Mac, vocals), b. 1948
May 27	Ramsey Lewis, b. 1935
May 28	T. Bone Walker, b. 1910 Papa John Creach (Hot Tuna, acoustic fiddle and electric violin), b. 1917 Gladys Knight, b. 1944 John Fogerty (Creedence Clearwater Revival, lead guitar and vocals), b. 1945
May 29	Roy Crewsdon (Freddie & the Dreamers, rhythm guitar), b. 1941 Gary Brooker (Procol Harum, keyboard), b. 1949
May 30	Benny Goodman, b. 1909 Lenny Davidson (Dave Clark Five, drums), b. 1942
May 31	Peter Yarrow (Peter, Paul & Mary), b. 1938 Mick Ralphs (Mott the Hoople, lead guitar), b. 1944 John Bonham (Yardbirds/Renaissance/Led Zeppelin, drums), b. 1947
June 1	Ron Wood (Jeff Beck Group/Faces/Rolling Stones, rhythm guitar), b. 1947
June 2	Charles Miller (War, sax and lute), b. 1939 Charlie Watts (Rolling Stones, drums), b. 1941
June 3	Curtis Mayfield (Impressions), b. 1942 Michael Clark (Byrds/Flying Burrito Brothers, drums), b. 1944 Ian Hunter (Mott the Hoople, guitar and lead vocals), b. 1946 Suzie Quatro, b. 1950

CALENDAR

June 4   Roger Ball (Average White Band, sax), b. 1944
                 Gordon Waller (Peter & Gordon), b. 1945

June 5   Michael Monarch (Steppenwolf, guitar), b. 1946
                 Fred Stone (Sly & the Family Stone, guitar), b. 1946

June 6   Gary U.S. Bonds, b. 1939
                 Peter Albin (Big Brother & the Holding Company, bass), b. 1944
                 Edgar Froese (Tangerine Dream), b. 1944

June 7   Clarence White (Byrds), b. 1944
                 Bill Kreutzmann (Grateful Dead, drums), b. 1946

June 8   Chuck Negron (Three Dog Night, lead vocals), b. 1942
                 Boz Scaggs (Steve Miller Band), b. 1944
                 Mick Box (Uriah Heep, lead guitar), b. 1947
                 Julie Driscoll (Brian Auger & Trinity), b. 1947

June 9   Les Paul, b. 1923
                 Jackie Wilson, b. 1934
                 John Lord (Deep Purple, keyboard), b. 1941

June 10   Howlin' Wolf (Chester Burnet), b. 1910
                 Shirley Alston (Shirelles, lead), b. 1941
                 Matthew Fisher (Procol Harum, keyboard), p. 1946

June 11   James "Pookie" Hudson (Spaniels, lead), b. 1934

June 12   Roy Harper, b. 1941
                 Len Barry (Dovells), b. 1942
                 Brad Delp (Boston, lead vocals), b. 1951

June 13   Bobbie Freeman, b. 1940
                 Dennis La Corriere (Dr. Hook & the Medicine Show, guitar), b. 1949
                 Clyde McPhatter (Drifters), d. 1972 from a heartattack. (Born November 15.)

June 14   "Muff" Winwood (Spencer Davis Group, bass), b. 1943
                 Rodney Argent (Zombie/Argent, keyboard), b. 1945
                 Jim Lea (Slade), b. 1952

June 15   Waylon Jennings, b. 1937
                 Harry Nilsson, b. 1941
                 "Sam" Lutz (Brownsville Station, bass), b. 1949
                 Noddy Holder (Slade), b. 1950

June 16   Lamont Dozier (Holland-Dozier-Holland), b. 1941

June 18   Paul McCartney (Beatles/Wings), b. 1942

June 19   "Spanky" McFarlane (Spanky & Our Gang, lead vocals), b. 1942
                 Ann Wilson (Heart, lead vocals), b. 1950
                 Larry Dunn (Earth, Wind & Fire, keyboard), b. 1953

June 20   Chet Atkins, b. 1924
                 Billy Guy (Coasters), b. 1936

Brian Wilson (Beach Boys, keyboard and bass), b. 1942
Alan Longmuir (Bay City Rollers, bass guitar), b. 1953

CANCER

June 21 O. C. Smith, b. 1942
Ray Davies (Kinks, lead guitar), b. 1944
Joey Kramer (Aerosmith, drums), b. 1950

June 22 Kris Kristofferson, b. 1936
Peter Asher (Peter & Gordon), b. 1944
Howard Kaylan (Turtles/Mothers of Invention, lead vocals), b. 1947
Todd Rundgren, b. 1948

June 23 June Carter, b. 1929

June 24 Mick Fleetwood (John Mayall's Bluesbreakers/Fleetwood Mac, drums and percussion), b. 1942
Jeff Beck (Yardbirds/Jeff Beck Group, guitar), b. 1944
Chris Wood (Traffic, sax and flute), b. 1944
Colin Blunstone (Zombies, lead vocals and guitar), b. 1945

June 25 Carly Simon, b. 1945
Ian McDonald (King Crimson/Foreigner, rhythm guitar), b. 1946
Clint Warwick (Moody Blues, bass), b. 1949

June 26 "Big Bill" Broonzy, b. 1893
Larry Taylor (Canned Heat, bass), b. 1949

June 28 Lester Flatt, b. 1914
Dave Knights (Procol Harum, bass), b. 1945

June 29 Little Eva (Boyd), b. 1944
Ian Paice (Deep Purple, drums), b. 1948
Tim Buckley, d. 1975. (Born February 14.)

June 30 Lena Horne, b. 1917
Dave Van Ronk, b. 1936
Florence Ballard (Supremes), b. 1943
Andrew Scott (Sweet, lead guitar), b. 1949

July 1 Delaney Bramlett (Delaney & Bonnie), b. 1939
Deborah Harry (Blondie), b. 1950

July 3 "Mississippi" John Hurt, b. 1893
Mike Corby (Babys, rhythm guitar), b. 1955
Brian Jones (Rolling Stones, rhythm guitar), drowned in a swimming pool, 1969. (Born February 28.)

	Jim Morrison (Doors), died from a heart attack, 1971. (Born December 8.)
July 4	Louis Armstrong, b. 1900 Alan Wilson (Canned Heat, guitar), b. 1943 Jeremy Spencer (Fleetwood Mac/Albatross, lead guitar), b. 1948 John Waite (Babys, lead vocals and bass guitar), b. 1955 Donald McPherson (Main Ingredient), died of leukemia in 1971. (Born July 9.)
July 5	"Robbie" Robertson (Band, lead guitar), b. 1944
July 6	Bill Haley, b. 1927 Della Reese, b. 1932 Gene Chandler, b. 1937 R. K. Elswit (Dr. Hook & the Medicine Show, guitar), b. 1945
July 7	Ringo Starr, b. 1940 Jim Rodford (Argent, bass), b. 1945 Larry Rheinhardt (Iron Butterfly, guitar), b. 1948
July 8	Louis Jordan, b. 1908 Jaimoe Johanson (Allman Brothers Band, drums), b. 1944
July 9	Donald McPherson (Main Ingredient), b. 1941
July 10	Arlo Guthrie, b. 1947 Dave Smalley (Raspberries/Dynamite, bass), b. 1949
July 11	Blind Lemon Jefferson, b. 1897
July 12	Swamp Dogg, b. 1942 Christine McVie (Fleetwood Mac, keyboard), b. 1943 Minnie Ripperton, d. 1979. (Born November 8.)
July 13	Roger McGuinn (Byrds, guitar and lead vocals), b. 1942
July 14	Woody Guthrie, b. 1912
July 15	Linda Ronstadt, b. 1946
July 17	Spencer Davis, b. 1942 Mick Tucker (Sweet, drums), b. 1948 Terry "Geezer" Butler (Black Sabbath, bass), b. 1949 Phoebe Show, b. 1952 Billie Holiday, d. 1959. (Born April 7.)
July 18	Screamin' Jay Hawkins, b. 1929 Papa Dee Allen (War, percussion), b. 1931 Dion (DiMucci), b. 1939 Brian Auger (Trinity), b. 1939 Martha Reeves (Martha & the Vandellas), b. 1941 Wally Bryson (Raspberries, guitar), b. 1949
July 19	Alan Gorie (Average White Band, bass), b. 1946 Bernie Leadon (Flying Burrito Brothers/Eagles, guitar), b. 1947 Brian May (Queen, guitar), b. 1947

	Keith Goldchaux (Grateful Dead, piano), b. 1948 Clarence White (Byrds), d. 1973. (Born June 7.)
July 20	John Lodge (Moody Blues, bass), b. 1945 Carlos Santana, b. 1947
July 21	Cat Stevens, b. 1948

LEO

July 22	George Clinton (Parliament), b. 1940 Estelle Bennett (Ronettes), b. 1946 Don Henley (Eagles, drums), b. 1947
July 23	Cleveland Duncan (Penguins, lead), b. 1935 Dino Danelli (Rascals, drums), b. 1945 Andy Mackay (Roxy Music), b. 1946 David Essex, b. 1947 Blair Thornton (Bachman-Turner Overdrive, rhythm guitar), b. 1950
July 24	Steve Goodman, b. 1948
July 25	Jim McCarty (Yardbirds/Renaissance, drums), b. 1943 Verdine White (Earth, Wind & Fire, bass and percussion), b. 1951
July 26	Mick Jagger (Rolling Stones, lead vocals), b. 1943 Roger Taylor (Queen, drums), b. 1949
July 27	Nick Reynolds (Kingston Trio), b. 1933 Kim Fowley, b. 1942 David Weck (Brownsville Station, drums), b. 1949
July 28	George Cummings (Dr. Hook & the Medicine Show, steel guitar), b. 1938 Mike Bloomfield, b. 1943 Rick Wright (Pink Floyd, keyboard), b. 1945 Jonathan Edwards, b. 1946 Simon Kirke (Free/Bad Company, drums), b. 1949 Steven Took (T. Rex, vocals), b. 1949
July 29	Cass Elliot (Mamas & Papas), died choking on a sandwich in 1974. (Born September 19.)
July 30	Paul Anka, b. 1941 Jeffrey Hammond-Hammond (Jethro Tull, bass), b. 1946
July 31	Ahmet Ertegun, Atlantic Records chairman, b. 1923 Robert Welch (Fleetwood Mac, lead guitar), b. 1946 Hugh MacDowell (Electric Light Orchestra, cello), b. 1953 Jim Reeves, died in a plane crash, 1964. (Born August 20.)

CALENDAR

August 1 Ramblin' Jack Elliott, b. 1931

August 2 Doris Kenner (Shirelles), b. 1941
Garth Hudson (Band, keyboard), b. 1942

August 3 Beverly Lee (Shirelles), b. 1941
B. B. Dickerson (War, brass), b. 1949
John Graham (Electric Light Orchestra, guitar and percussion), b. 1951

August 4 Rick Derringer (McCoys), b. 1947

August 5 Rick Huxley (Dave Clark Five, bass), b. 1942
Jimmy Webb, songwriter, 1946

August 6 Isaac Hayes, b. 1938

August 8 Joe Tex, b. 1933
Jay David (Dr. Hook & the Medicine Show, drums), b. 1942
Jerry Garcia (Grateful Dead, guitar), b. 1942
Julian "Cannonball" Adderley, d. 1975. (Born September 15.)

August 9 Barbara Mason, b. 1947

August 10 Bobby Hatfield (Righteous Brothers), b. 1940
Ian Anderson (Jethro Tull, guitar and keyboards), b. 1947
Ronnie (Bennett) Spector (Ronettes), b. 1947

August 11 Michael Huggs (Manfred Mann, drums), b. 1942
Guy Villari (Regents, lead), b. 1942
Denis Payton (Dave Clark Five, tenor sax), b. 1943
Jeff Hanna (Nitty Gritty Dirt Band, lead vocals and guitar), b. 1947
Eric Carmen (Raspberries, lead vocals, guitar and bass), b. 1949
Erik Braunn (Iron Butterfly, lead guitar), b. 1950

August 12 Joe Jones, b. 1926

August 13 Tony Santini (Sha Na Na), b. 1948

August 14 Dash Crofts (Seals & Crofts), b. 1940
David Crosby (Byrds/Crosby, Stills & Nash, guitar), b. 1941
Larry Graham (Sly & the Family Stone/Graham Central Station, bass), b. 1946

August 15 Tom Aldrich (Black Oak Arkansas, drums), b. 1950

August 16 Elvis Presley, d. 1977. (Born January 8.)

August 17 Sib Hashian (Boston, drums), b. 1949

August 18 Johnny Preston, b. 1939
Sara Dash (LaBelle), b. 1945
Dennis Elliott (Foreigner, drums), b. 1950

August 19 Ginger Baker (Cream/Blind Faith, drums), b. 1940
Johnny Nash, b. 1940
John Deacon (Queen, bass), b. 1951

August 20	Jim Reeves, b. 1924 Jim Pankow (Chicago, trombone), b. 1947 Robert Plant (Yardbirds/Led Zeppelin, lead vocals and harmonica), b. 1947
August 21	Count Basie, b. 1904 Jackie DeShannon, b. 1944
August 22	John Lee Hooker, b. 1917 Fred Milano (Belmonts, second tenor), b. 1939 Joe Chambers (Chambers Brothers, guitar), b. 1942 Donna Godchaux (Grateful Dead, vocals), b. 1947 Ian Mitchell (Bay City Rollers, bass guitar), b. 1958

VIRGO

August 23	Keith Moon (Who, drums), b. 1946
August 24	David Freiberg (Jefferson Starship/Quicksilver Messenger Service, bass guitar), b. 1938 Kenny Rogers (New Christy Minstrels/First Edition), b. 1941 John Cipollina (Quicksilver Messenger Service, guitar), b. 1943 Jim Capaldi (Traffic, drums), b. 1944 "Mollie" Duncan (Average White Band, sax), b. 1945 Ken Hensley (Uriah Heep, keyboard), b. 1945
August 25	Gene Simmons (Kiss, bass), b. 1949
August 27	Phil Shulman (Gentle Giant), b. 1937 Tim Bogert (Vanilla Fudge/Cactus, guitar and bass), b. 1944 Cuba Gooding (Main Ingredient), b. 1944 Brian Epstein, Beatles manager, d. 1967. (Born September 19.)
August 28	Daniel Seraphine (Chicago, drums), b. 1948
August 29	Charlie Parker, b. 1920 Dinah Washington, b. 1924 Dick Halligan (Blood, Sweat & Tears, keyboard, flute and trombone), b. 1943
August 30	John Phillips (Mamas & Papas), b. 1945
August 31	Van Morrison, b. 1945
September 1	Barry Gibb (Bee Gees, guitar and vocals), b. 1946 Gregg Errico (Sly & the Family Stone, drums), b. 1946
September 2	Rosalind Ashford (Martha & the Vandellas), b. 1943 Mik Kaminski (Electric Light Orchestra, cello), b. 1951

CALENDAR

September 3
Memphis Slim (Peter Chatman), b. 1915
Freddie King (Billy Myles), b. 1934
Al Jardine (Beach Boys, rhythm guitar), b. 1942
George Biondo (Steppenwolf, bass), b. 1945
Don Brewer (The Pack/Grand Funk Railroad, drums), b. 1948
Woody Guthrie, died 1967, Huntington's disease. (Born July 14.)
Alan Wilson (Canned Heat), died 1970 from drug poisoning. (Born July 4.)

September 4
Gene Parsons (Byrds), b. 1945
Gary Duncan (Quicksilver Messenger Service, guitar), b. 1946
Greg Elmore (Quicksilver Messenger Service, drums), b. 1946

September 5
Joe "Speedo" Frazier (Impalas, lead), b. 1943
Buddy Miles, b. 1946
Loudon Wainwright, b. 1946
"Clem" Clempson (Humble Pie, guitar), b. 1949

September 6
Roger Waters (Pink Floyd, drums), b. 1947

September 7
Little Milton (Milton Campbell), b. 1934
Buddy Holly, b. 1936
Gloria Gaynor, b. 1949

September 8
Jimmie Rodgers, b. 1897
Patsy Cline, b. 1932
José Feliciano, b. 1945
Kelly Groucutt (Electric Light Orchestra, violin), b. 1945
Rod "Pigpen" McKernan (Grateful Dead, vocals, rhythm guitar), b. 1946
Freddie Mercury (Queen, lead vocals and keyboard), b. 1946

September 9
Jimmy Reed, b. 1925
Otis Redding, b. 1941
Luther Simmons (Main Ingredient), b. 1942
Doug Ingle (Iron Butterfly, lead vocals and keyboard), b. 1946
Billy Preston, b. 1946

September 10
Danny Hutton (Three Dog Night, lead vocals), b. 1942
John Entwistle (Who, bass), b. 1944
Barriemore Barlow (Jethro Tull, drums), b. 1949
Joe Perry (Aerosmith, lead guitar), b. 1950

September 11
Bernie Dwyer (Freddie & the Dreamers, drums), b. 1940

September 12
Gerry Beckley (America), b. 1952
Maria Muldaur, b. 1943
Donny Osmond, b. 1957

September 13
David Clayton-Thomas (Blood, Sweat & Tears, lead vocals), b. 1941
Peter Cetera (Chicago, bass), b. 1944

September 14
"Bowser" Bauman (Sha Na Na), b. 1947
Paul Kosoff (Free, guitar), b. 1950

September 15	Roy Acuff, b. 1903 Julian "Cannonball" Adderley, b. 1928 Lee Dorman (Iron Butterfly, bass), b. 1942
September 16	B. B. King, b. 1925 Bernie Calver (Hollies, bass), b. 1942 Kenny Jones (Faces, drums), b. 1949
September 17	Hank Williams, b. 1923 Phil Cracolici (Mystics, lead vocals), b. 1937 Lol Creme (10 cc, lead vocals & guitar), b. 1947
September 18	Frankie Avalon, b. 1940 Jimi Hendrix, died in 1970 from an accidental barbiturate overdose. (Born November 27.)
September 19	Billy Ward (The Dominoes), b. 1921 Brook Benton, b. 1931 Brian Epstein, Beatles manager, b. 1934 Bill Medley (Righteous Brothers), b. 1940 Cass Elliot (Mamas & Papas), b. 1943 David Bromberg, b. 1945 Gram Parsons (Byrds/Flying Burrito Brothers), d. 1973. (Born November 5.)
September 20	Jim Croce, killed in plane crash, 1973. (Born January 10.)
September 21	Donald Felder (Eagles, guitar), b. 1947
September 22	George Chambers (Chambers Brothers, bass), b. 1931

LIBRA

September 23	Ray Charles, b. 1930 Roy Buchanan, b. 1939 Bruce Springsteen, b. 1949 Robbie McIntosh (Average White Band, drums), died in 1974 from accidental drug poisoning
September 24	Gerry Marsden (Gerry & the Pacemakers, lead vocals and guitar), b. 1942
September 25	John Locke (Spirit, keyboard), b. 1943 Onnie McIntire (Average White Band, guitar), b. 1945
September 26	Bessie Smith, died in auto accident, 1937. (Born April 15.) Joseph Bauer (Youngbloods, drums), b. 1941 Bryan Ferry (Roxy Music), b. 1945 Olivia Newton-John, b. 1947

52 CALENDAR

September 27   Randy Bachman (Guess Who/Bachman-Turner Overdrive, lead guitar), b. 1943
Meat Loaf (Marvin Aday), b. 1947

September 28   Ben E. King, b. 1938
Nick St. Nicholas (Steppenwolf, bass), b. 1943

September 29   Freddie King, b. 1934
Jerry Lee Lewis, b. 1935
Mark Farner (The Pack/Grand Funk Railroad, lead vocals and guitar), b. 1948

September 30   Gus Dudgeon, record producer, b. 1942
Dewey Martin (Buffalo Springfield, drums), b. 1942
Frankie Lymon, b. 1942
Mike Harrison (Spooky Tooth, lead vocals), b. 1945
Marc Bolan (T. Rex, lead vocals & guitar), b. 1948

October 1   Jerry Martini (Sly & the Family Stone, sax), b. 1943
Scott McKenzie, b. 1944
"Cub" Koda (Brownsville Station, lead vocals and guitar), b. 1948

October 2   Don McLean, b. 1945
Michael Rutherford (Genesis, bass guitar), b. 1950

October 3   Eddie Cochran, b. 1938
Chubby Checker, b. 1941
Lindsey Buckingham (Fleetwood Mac, lead guitar), b. 1947
Janis Joplin, died in 1970 from heroin overdose. (Born January 19.)

October 4   Nona Hendryx (LaBelle), b. 1944
James Fielder (Blood, Sweat & Tears, bass), b. 1947

October 5   Carlo Mastrangelo (Belmonts, bass), b. 1938
Steve Miller, b. 1943
Brian Connolly (Sweet, lead vocals), b. 1948

October 7   Tony Silvester (Main Ingredient), b. 1941
Dino Valenti (Quicksilver Messenger Service, lead vocals), b. 1943
Kevin Godley (10 cc, drums), b. 1945

October 8   Michael Rosen (Average White Band, guitar), b. 1949

October 9   John Lennon, b. 1940
Jackson Browne (Nitty Gritty Dirt Band), b. 1950

October 10   Thelonius Monk, b. 1917
Alan Cartwright (Procol Harum, bass), b. 1945

October 11   Daryl Hall (Hall & Oates, electric organ), b. 1948
Andrew Woolfolk (Earth, Wind & Fire, sax and flute), b. 1950

October 12   Samuel Moore (Sam & Dave), b. 1935
Gene Vincent, died 1971 from bleeding ulcers. (Born February 11.)

October 13	Art Garfunkel (Simon & Garfunkel), b. 1942 Robert Lamm (Chicago, keyboard), b. 1944 (Olive) Marie Osmond, b. 1959
October 14	Cliff Richard, b. 1940 Justin Hayward (Moody Blues, lead vocals and guitar), b. 1946
October 16	Fred "C.F." Turner (Bachman-Turner Overdrive, bass), b. 1943 Bob "Ace" Weir (Grateful Dead, rhythm guitar), b. 1947
October 17	James Seals (Seals & Crofts), b. 1941 Gary Puckett (Gary Puckett & the Union Gap), b. 1942 James Tucker (Turtles, rhythm guitar), b. 1946
October 18	Chuck Berry, b. 1926 Ronnie Bright (Coasters, bass), b. 1938 Lauro Nyro, b. 1947
October 19	Larry Chance (Earls, lead), b. 1940 Peter Tosh, b. 1944 Keith Reid (Procol Harum lyricist), b. 1945 David Guard (Kingston Trio), b. 1934
October 20	Al Greenwood (Foreigner, keyboard, synthesizer), b. 1951 Ronnie Van Zant (Lynyrd Skynyrd, lead vocals), died in 1977 in a plane crash.
October 21	Dizzy Gillespie, b. 1917 Manfred Mann (Michael Leibowitz), keyboard, b. 1941 Elvin Bishop (Paul Butterfield Blues Band, lead guitar), b. 1942 Lee Loughnane (Chicago, trumpet), b. 1946 Tetsu Yamauchi (Free, Faces, bass), b. 1947 Eric Faulkner (Bay City Rollers, guitar), b. 1954
October 22	Edward Brigati (Rascals, percussion), b. 1946

SCORPIO

October 23	Eleanor Greenwich, songwriter, b. 1939 Fred Marsden (Gerry & the Pacemakers, drums), b. 1940 Greg Ridley (Spooky Tooth, Humble Pie, bass), b. 1947
October 24	Sonny Terry, b. 1911 "The Big Bopper" (J. P. Richardson), b. 1930 Helen Reddy, b. 1941 Bill Wyman (Rolling Stones, bass), b. 1941 Jerry Edmonton (Steppenwolf, drums), b. 1946 Dale Griffin (Mott the Hoople, drums), b. 1948

CALENDAR

October 25 — Jon Anderson (Yes, lead vocals), b. 1944

October 26 — Leslie West (Mountain), b. 1945

October 27 — Floyd Cramer, b. 1933

October 28 — Charlie Daniels, b. 1936
Rick Reynolds (Black Oak Arkansas, guitar), b. 1948

October 29 — Denny Laine (Moody Blues/Wings, vocals and guitar), b. 1944
Melba Moore, b. 1945
Peter Green (John Mayall's Bluesbreakers/Fleetwood Mac, lead guitar), b. 1946
Duane Allman, killed in a motorcycle accident in 1971. (Born November 20.)

October 30 — Eddie Holland (Holland-Dozier-Holland), b. 1939
Grace Slick (Jefferson Airplane/Starship, lead vocals), b. 1943
Timothy Schmidt (Poco/Eagles, bass), b. 1947

October 31 — Tom Paxton, b. 1937
Russ Ballard (Argent, guitar), b. 1947

November 1 — Rick Grech (Blind Faith/Traffic, bass), b. 1945

November 2 — Earl "Speedo" Carroll (Cadillacs/Coasters), b. 1937
Keith Emerson (Move/Emerson, Lake & Palmer, keyboard, Moog), b. 1944

November 3 — Nicholas Simper (Deep Purple, bass), b. 1946

November 5 — Ike Turner, b. 1931
Paul Simon (Simon & Garfunkel), b. 1941
Gram Parsons (Byrds/Flying Burrito Brothers, rhythm guitar, keyboard, and vocals), b. 1946
Peter Noone (Herman's Hermits, lead vocals), b. 1947
Johnny Horton, d. in 1960 in automobile accident. (Born April 30.)

November 6 — Glen Frey (Eagles, guitar), b. 1948

November 7 — Mary Travers (Peter, Paul & Mary), b. 1937
Dee Clark, b. 1938
Johnny Rivers, b. 1942
Joni Mitchell, b. 1943

November 8 — Bonnie Bramlett (Delaney & Bonnie), b. 1944
Donald Murray (Turtles, drums), b. 1945
Roy Wood (Move, lead guitar and vocals), b. 1946
Minnie Ripperton (Rotary Connection, lead vocals), b. 1948
Bonnie Raitt, b. 1949

November 9 — Tom Fogerty (Creedence Clearwater Revival, rhythm guitar), b. 1941

November 10 — Greg Lake (King Crimson/Emerson, Lake & Palmer, guitar, vocals), b. 1948
Donna Fargo, b. 1949

November 11	Lavern Baker, b. 1929 Jesse Colin Young (Youngbloods, lead vocals and bass), b. 1944 Chris Dreja (Yardbirds, rhythm guitar), b. 1945 Vincent Martell (Vanilla Fudge, guitar and bass), b. 1945 Barry Oakley (Allman Brothers Band, bass guitar), killed in a motorcycle accident in 1972. (Born April 4.)
November 12	Booker T. Jones (Booker T & the MGs), b. 1944 Neil Young (Buffalo Springfield/Crosby, Stills, Nash & Young), b. 1945
November 14	Keith Relf (Yardbirds/Renaissance, lead vocals and harmonica), electrocuted onstage in 1976. (Born March 22.) Freddie Garrity (Freddie & the Dreamers), b. 1940
November 15	Clyde McPhatter, b. 1931 "Frida" Anderson (Abba, vocals), b. 1945
November 17	Gordon Lightfoot, b. 1938 Eugene Clarke (Byrds, guitar), b. 1944 Junior Parker, d. 1971. (Born March 3.)
November 18	Hank Ballard, b. 1936
November 19	Fred Lipsius (Blood, Sweat & Tears, piano, sax), b. 1944
November 20	Dan McBride (Sha Na Na), b. 1945 Duane Allman (Allman Brothers Band, lead guitar), b. 1946 Joe Walsh (James Gang/Eagles, guitar), b. 1947
November 21	Dr. John (Mac Rebennac), b. 1940 Lonnie Jordan (War, keyboard), b. 1948

SAGITTARIUS

November 22	Steve Caldwell (Orlons, bass), b. 1942
November 24	Lee Michaels, b. 1945
November 25	Tina Turner, b. 1941 Bev Bevan (Electric Light Orchestra, drums), b. 1946
November 26	John McVie (John Mayall's Bluesbreakers/Fleetwood Mac, bass), b. 1945
November 27	Jimi Hendrix, b. 1942
November 28	Berry Gordy, producer of the "Motown" sound, b. 1929 Randy Newman, b. 1943

56 CALENDAR

November 29 John Mayall, b. 1933
Dennis Doherty (Mamas & Papas), b. 1941
Felix Cavaliere (Rascals, keyboard), b. 1944
Barry Goudreau (Boston, guitar), b. 1951

November 30 Dick Clark (American Bandstand), b. 1929
Paul Stookey (Peter, Paul & Mary), b. 1937

December 1 Billy Paul, 1934
Lou Rawls, b. 1936
John Densmore (Doors, drums and keyboards), b. 1945
Bette Midler, b. 1945

December 2 Tom McGuinness (Manfred Mann, bass), b. 1941

December 3 Ozzie Osbourne (Black Sabbath, vocals), b. 1948

December 4 Freddy Cannon, b. 1940
Chris Hillman (Byrds/Flying Burrito Brothers, vocals and bass guitar), b. 1942
Dennis Wilson (Beach Boys, drums), b. 1944
Tommy Bolin (Deep Purple, lead vocals), died in 1976 at age 25 from drug overdose

December 5 Little Richard (Pennimann), b. 1932
John Cale, b. 1940
Jim Messina (Buffalo Springfield/Poco/Loggins & Messina, bass), b. 1947

December 6 Dave Brubeck, b. 1920
Mike Smith (Dave Clark Five, lead vocals and keyboard), b. 1943
Leadbelly, died 1949. (Born January 29.)

December 7 Harry Chapin, b. 1942

December 8 Jerry Butler, b. 1939
Robert Elliott (Hollies, drums), b. 1942
Jim Morrison (Doors, lead vocals), b. 1943
Gregg Allman (Allman Brothers Band, guitar, organ and vocals), b. 1947

December 9 Rick Danko (Band, bass), b. 1943
Shirley Brickley (Orlons, lead), b. 1944
"Screamin' " Scott Simon (Sha Na Na), b. 1948
Donny Osmond, b. 1957

December 10 Chad Stuart (Chad & Jeremy), b. 1943
Johnny Rodriguez, b. 1952
Otis Redding, killed in plane crash, 1967. (Born September 9.)

December 11 Willie Mae "Big Mama" Thornton, b. 1926
David Gates (Bread, lead vocals and guitar), b. 1940
Sam Cooke, shot by a woman in a motel in 1964. (Born January 22.)

December 12	Charlie Rich, b. 1932 Dionne Warwick, b. 1940 Dickey Betts (Allman Brothers Band, guitar, vocals), b. 1943 Paul Rodgers (Free/Bad Company, lead vocals), b. 1949
December 14	Dinah Washington, died in 1963 from accidental overdose of sleeping pills. (Born August 29.)
December 15	John Hammond, talent scout, b. 1910 Alan Freed, disc jockey, b. 1922 Cindy Birdsong (Patti LaBelle & Bluebells/Supremes), b. 1939 Dave Clark (Dave Clark Five, drums), b. 1942 Fats Waller, d. 1943. (Born May 21.) Carmine Appice (Vanilla Fudge/Cactus, drums), b. 1946
December 16	Anthony Hicks (Hollies, lead guitar), b. 1945 Benny Andersson (Abba, piano), b. 1946
December 17	Tommy Steele, b. 1936 "Little" Booker, b. 1939 Paul Butterfield, b. 1942 Jim Bonfanti (Raspberries/Dynamite, drums), b. 1948
December 18	"Chas" Chandler (Animals, bass), b. 1938 Sam Andrew (Big Brother & the Holding Company, guitar), b. 1941 Keith Richard (Rolling Stones, lead guitar), b. 1943
December 19	Professor Longhair (Ron Byrd), b. 1918 Phil Ochs, b. 1940 Maurice White (Earth, Wind & Fire, lead vocals and percussion), b. 1941 Alvin Lee (Ten Years After, guitar and vocals), b. 1944
December 20	Bobby Colomby (Blood, Sweat & Tears, drums), b. 1944 Peter Criss (Kiss, drums), b. 1947 Bobby Darin, d. 1973. (Born May 14.)

CAPRICORN

December 21	Frank Zappa (Mothers of Invention), b. 1940 Carl Wilson (Beach Boys, guitar), b. 1946
December 22	Barry Jenkins (Animals, drums), b. 1944 Robin and Maurice Gibb (Bee Gees, lead vocal and guitar), b. 1949

December 23	Tim Hardin, b. 1940 Jorma Kaukonen (Jefferson Airplane/Hot Tuna, lead guitar), b. 1940 Ronald Bushy (Iron Butterfly, drums), b. 1945 Luther Grosvenor (Spooky Tooth, lead guitar), b. 1949 Johnny Contardo (Sha Na Na), b. 1951
December 24	Jan Akkerman (Focus, guitar and lute), b. 1946
December 25	Billy Horton (Silhouettes, lead), b. 1929 O'Kelly Isley (Isley Brothers), b. 1937 Henry Vestine (Canned Heat, lead guitar), b. 1944 Jimmy Buffet, b. 1946
December 26	Phil Spector, record producer, b. 1939
December 27	Leslie Maguire (Gerry & the Pacemakers, keyboard), b. 1941 Michael Pinder (Moody Blues, keyboard), b. 1941 Peter Quaife (Kinks, bass), b. 1943 Mick Jones (Spooky Tooth, Foreigner, lead guitar), b. 1944
December 28	Earl "Fatha" Hines, b. 1905
December 29	Ray Thomas (Moody Blues, sax and flute), b. 1941
December 30	Brownie McGhee, b. 1915 Bo Diddley, b. 1928 Del Shannon, b. 1939 Michael Nesmith (Monkees, bass), b. 1942 Davy Jones (Monkees, tambourine), b. 1946 Jeff Lynne (Electric Light Orchestra, guitar, Moog, and lead vocals), b. 1947
December 31	Odetta, b. 1930 John Denver, b. 1943 Burton Cummings (Guess Who, lead vocals and keyboard), b. 1947 Donna Summer, b. 1948 Tom Hamilton (Aerosmith, bass guitar), b. 1951

LOOKING FORWARD, LOOKING BACK

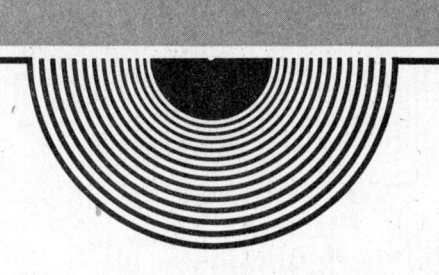

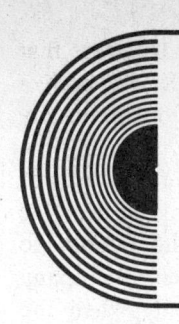

NEW WAVE MUSIC

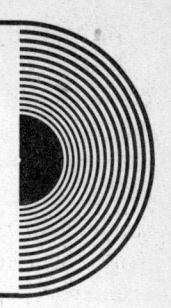

Until a variety of forces on two sides of the Atlantic teamed up to create, in 1977, a musical revolution that came to be known as "New Wave," the trend of rock music had been towards a shrinking number of megastar bands playing middle-of-the-rock for stadium-sized audiences who couldn't relate to their musical idols' ritzy lifestyles. The avenues open to novice (or novel) groups were nearly nonexistent, and the excitement and creativity level of the music was strikingly low. In the early Seventies, the groups who had led rock into the big leagues following the initial rush of 1964's British invasion had become, by and large, complacent, detached, and disinterested in any further challenge of the boundaries that limited the music. The pioneers had all settled down, and no real innovators seemed prepared to pick up the torch. With the Beatles dissolved into less creative individual parts, the Stones off living the chic life, the Who and Led Zeppelin working in a semi-retired mode, rarely touring, the new groups that emerged in the early Seventies were little more than substitutes for the giants of the Sixties. By 1975, the failure of new talent to replace old left rock 'n' roll in the sorry state of being more a business than a music. Something had to change. And it did.

What the new wave amounted to, in brief, was a violent short-circuiting of the normally slow process involved in bringing new groups and new music to the record buying public. In place of the long and arduous trek from garage band to album deal, the new wave created instant records, by groups that were new enough to be fresh, innovative, and unencumbered by the usual commercial considerations required to make it in the music business. By making the young groups appear to be an asset to the record companies, the new wave shifted the focus of the industry away from the older, stagnant performers and towards the radically different groups, sporting a new look, and playing music that recaptured all the missing excitement of the unsophisticated early days of rock. The new wave broke all the established rules of the rock world, created a whole flock of new ways of working, and brought to the fore an amazing assortment of people and ideas that brought rock 'n' roll out of its doldrums. In England, after some initial resistance and problems, the movement proved thoroughly successful, and was ultimately adopted and institutionalized by the very forces it sought to evade. In a sense, the idealism of the new wave was lost as its commercial aspects took hold, but the resulting changes brought about more than justify whatever sense of failure there might have been.

In America, where new wave never really took on the social implications that it had in England, its effects have been more gradual and subtle. As both a domestic and imported phenomenon, new wave took a long time to acquire any national success, although numerous bands on a local level were capturing the same sort of following and importance as the English groups. Here, instead of one cohesive movement acting positively, the tag "New Wave" took on negative meaning to record buyers and concert goers, and groups that either took the name themselves or were cubbyholed by others suffered from record company disinterest, radio blacklisting, and media stereotyping. It was only when the witch scare ended that new groups began being considered on their individual musical merits, and the music that had been dismissed as "Punk" or "New Wave" turned out to be both good and popular with a wide audience. It was primarily the sensationalist aspects of British new wave that turned the American public off—safety pins in cheeks, militaristic and sadistic clothing, bizarre haircuts, and violent posturings that slowed (and nearly stopped) the march of new wave progress in the States, yet those superficial accoutrements had less to do with the leaders of the British movement than their overzealous fans. Ultimately, it's hard to say whether or not such successful emergent groups as the Cars, Cheap Trick, Blondie, Elvis Costello and the Police are actually part of the new wave or simply the visible beneficiaries of its effects. It is safe to say, however, that all of them would have had much slower and tougher climbs to reach their current level of fame and fortune had the new wave not occurred when it did. In America, the primary value of new wave has been the introduction of a huge number of creative and talented bands that might otherwise never have reached a mass audience.

In addition to the major effects, new wave has spawned several intriguing side effects that have been most welcome. The return to prominence of singles, once the mainstay of rock 'n' roll, and bands that actually understand the differences between a 45 and a cut from an album. Also, the renewed interest in picture sleeves, custom labels, extended-play 7" records, and non-LP B-sides stems directly from new wave. Home-made records, cottage-industry record labels, colored vinyl, numerous fanzines, new rock related companies of all sorts, books, buttons, posters, T-shirts, a revitalization of bands' commitments to touring regularly and widely, and a whole slew of novel marketing ploys, from limited-edition give-away records at concerts and in albums to oddly-sized and shaped records are only some of the wonderful results of this startling revolution in music.

Tracing the new wave back to its beginnings requires some initial agreement as to what qualifies a band as new wave. Judging by recent criteria, the only valid consensus would seem to be based on attitude more than anything else. Any rock band that sets itself against blandness and boredom, stagnation and complacency and tends towards the weird, outrageous, unusual, or unpopular would have to qualify. An aggressive stance and a sense of humor are also common denominator traits to look for. Copycat groups that ape the music without understanding or ascribing to the attitude can't really be considered as new wave.

In a very real sense, the Beatles and the Stones had a lot in common with new wave when they started out in 1963. With their (then) far-out clothes and hair, wild music, and defiant pose, they seemed as threatening to the folks they pushed aside in the charts (The Singing Nun, Bobby Vinton, Four Seasons) as the punks did in 1977. However, once ensconced in the superstar club, they stopped being bad boys and joined the record industry as willing, albeit careful and clever, participants. In contrast, some of the new wave bands have kept struggling against the established order, and some have gone down fighting. The obvious temptation to relax and enjoy the luxuries and comforts of commercial popularity has gotten to many new wave bands, but some have remained resolute, and managed to keep their original beliefs and ethics, whatever the material cost. As a result, record companies have been forced to deal with the new bands on their own terms, even before their commercial potential has been determined.

The first really significant rock band to set the tone for much of what the new wave ultimately came to stand was the Velvet Underground. Formed in New York in 1966 by Lou Reed and John Cale, the band was firmly rooted in areas previously uncharted by rock music. Decidedly decadent, and with songs about hard drugs, odd sexuality, and various subculture mysteries, the interest and aid of Andy Warhol gave the group all the chicness it needed to take New York's artistic and trendy community by storm. By apparently living the lifestyle they sang about, the Velvets gave rock fans a heavy dose of reality—the seamy side of life—and they earned a devoted (and odd) following. By making music that gained its intensity from druggish hypnotic sounds in place of any attempts at technical virtuosity, the Velvets were the first major group since the fifties to suggest that talent, in the accepted sense of the word, wasn't always necessary in rock 'n' roll. Intensity of emotion (a basic factor in new wave music) could be more important than any classic chromatic logic. In short, the Velvets, to those who understood and/or appreciated them, were nothing less than a revelation in musical style.

Around the same time as Eastern parents were cringing at their off-springs' new-found fad, the Velvet Underground, the Midwest found that it had an equally crazed bunch in its midst. Iggy and the Stooges, Detroit's greatest contribution to the punk world, set out, in 1967, to stun, startle, and scare the world by playing harder, louder, sloppier, and more intensely than any one else in the vicinity. With one musical foot in heavy metal and the other in a Doors-type region, the Stooges added spice to their performances by Iggy's antics, which at times ranged from self-mutilation to reckless dives into audiences. Always pushing to be more outrageous, less concerned, and closer to the manic edge, Iggy set a standard of lunacy that few have ever been able to match on stage. Songs like "Now I Wanna Be Your Dog," "No Fun," and "Dirt" preached the Stooges' nihilism to a heavy beat and inspired, ten years later, numerous imitators.

Signed to Elektra Records in 1969, the Stooges were as non-mainstream a band as has ever been contracted to a major label. With total disregard for convention, taste, or melody, they banged out two albums of primal rock with a

Lou Reed

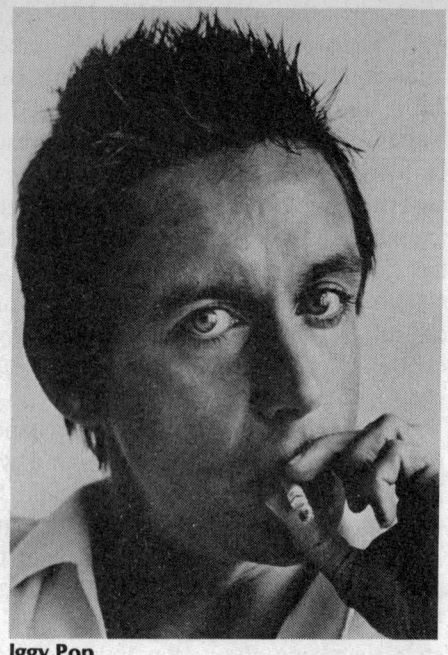

Iggy Pop

sound as raw as uncooked steak that remain classics of the genre to this day. Guaranteed by their total uncommerciality to become a cult band, they fulfilled their duty, and over the years Iggy has become almost the patron saint of punk.

Musically, the significance of the Stooges and the Velvets (and a few others—the Mothers of Invention, Fugs, Doors, MC5, Alice Cooper—to a lesser extent) was not in any similarity of sound, but in their shared outlook on the purpose and direction of rock music in general. Disavowing the conservatism of the mainstream chart groups, these upstart bands commited themselves fully to the idea of pushing rock beyond the accepted boundaries of the day. They were more daring, more violent, crazier, louder, faster, and always closer to that vague line between chaos and control. Without trying to sound poetic, many of the musicians lived fast and died young, giving themselves fully to their rock lifestyles. As these Sixties bands were a response to the failure of the successful English and American acts to keep up with the changes of the rock culture and audience on a street level, the Mid-Seventies new wavers were responding to complacent jet-setting tax exiles and mundane touring machines leaving their fans in the lurch. How excited can a young rock devotee be about an idol that tours once every three years, and then plays in a stadium to 75,000 people for some exorbitant ticket price? The immediacy of rock 'n' roll excitement is a very intimate affair, and the large majority of superstar acts have not made any effort to bring rock back to the people. And one major facet of new wave, at the start, was to bring bands and fans as close as possible—hence the English theatres without seats, low stages, and small halls.

PHIL MANZANERA   PAUL THOMPSON   DAVE SKINNER   BRYAN FERRY   GARY TIBBS   ANDY MACKAY
Roxy Music

    An important transitional stage between the early avant garde music and new wave was the glitter rock era. Originally (and primarily) an English fad, glitter bands brought theatrics—makeup, costumes, gimmicks—to a breed of loud, yet melodic, simpleminded pop music, and became huge stars with immense European followings. T. Rex, Sweet, Bowie, Slade, Sparks, Garry Glitter started the whole trend, and were later joined by more sophisticated outfits like Roxy Music, Cockney Rebel, Mott the Hoople, Roy Wood, and Be-Bop Deluxe who brought other styles into the genre. Short-lived, and more fun than serious, glitter took a while to catch on in America (although a few of the bands found quick success here), yet it had a lot of importance to the cult that developed around them. Appealing both to very young fans and to more sophisticated Anglophiles, glitter served to polarize the rock world with the sexual androgyny and bizarre fashions that the groups nurtured and inspired. Such was the perfect setting for the group that would more or less invent the idea of new wave, five years before it would catch on.

    Had the New York Dolls appeared in 1977 rather than 1972, they would have made the Sex Pistols seem like pale imitators, and would have been, no doubt, the leaders of the new wave movement without a challenge. As it happened, the Dolls had been and gone by the time the new wave began in earnest, and although always given due respect in articles and interviews, they never really benefitted from the popularization of their musical style. Maybe the new wave would have still occured without the Dolls, but the similarities between their best years and the early English explosion are undeniable.

The New York Dolls were five outrageous non-musicians who brought the notion of glamor and camp in rock a few (hundred) steps further than anyone had thought possible. They did everything imaginable to outrage and terrorize—from full drag queen makeup and clothes to unbelievable lyrics and statements. The suggestion of drugs and other forms of self-abuse were never far from the Dolls, and, in fact, their first drummer died a drug-related death while the group was in England at the end of 1972. Around the Dolls grew a New York scene, consisting of a small set of bands (from the Magic Tramps to Kiss), a couple of concert places (a dilapidated hotel, an arts center, and a bar in Queens), and an amazing amount of press coverage, both in America and England. Within a short span of time, the Dolls became very well known in rock circles, and soon became the first "New York Band" to be inked to a recording contract, despite general industry fears about their threatening image, lack of musical skill, and wild personal mythology.

The release of the first Dolls album in April 1973 proved a couple of major things; first and foremost that the weird side of rock could survive in the straight record industry; secondly that the press could more or less force the hand of record executives to support a group that hardly fits any commercial stereotypes. Both facts were to play a significant role in the explosion of similar new wave bands four years later. Unfortunately, for both the Dolls and the future, their two albums failed to impress any large segment of the American rock populace, and that certainly put a damper on the enthusiasm of their label and others considering an investment in the New York scene. After they were dropped by Mercury, the Dolls began to splinter and, with their demise, the first great New York prelude to new wave ended, with much ill will and little hope for years to come.

Amazingly enough, despite the bleakness of the commercial chances for underground bands, the end of the Dolls exactly coincided with the beginning of a wider, bigger, and more viable New York scene that was to succeed where the Dolls failed. A new club, originally dedicated to folk music, opened up on the Bowery, named itself CBGB's, and began booking the new bands—Television, Patti Smith, Blondie, the Ramones, Marbles, Fast, Planets, Tuff Darts—that had begun springing out of the woodwork. Some had been around the local circuit for several years, others were new arrivals in New York, and the rest were fresh from ethnic neighborhoods and bars in the outer regions of the city. The scene quickly grew, attracting audiences from all walks of life, and new bands kept springing up, almost daily. The final barrier, the record companies, finally overcame their fear of the dark, dingy clubs housing the new music (which by and large was original, well-played, and diverse), and began sending scouts down to look over the local talent to see which acts might be able to make it on the national, or even international scale. By the end of 1975, contracts had been signed between domestic record labels and Patti Smith, the Ramones, Blondie, and the Dictators, and the rush was on to observe and groom up-and-comers like Talking Heads, Mink DeVille, Richard Hell, Television, and a few others. New York had gone national, and it appeared to be a deep lode of saleable talent.

David Bowie

Patti Smith

The Motors

Ian Dury

Deborah Harry of Blondie

Rubinoos

David Johansen

Elvis Costello

Nick Lowe

The Boomtown Rats

The Clash

Over on the other side of the Atlantic, things were developing in a simultaneous-but-different way towards a similar end result. London had always supported a strong club circuit, filled with folk, blues, and rock acts that seemed content to earn a thin living by staying within the safe confines of the small bars and nightspots. Around 1972, a new breed of rock groups began infiltrating the club scene, playing more aggressive, sweatier rock 'n' roll, and attracting bigger, crazier, and more devoted crowds. Dubbed "Pub Rock" by the music press, groups like Ducks Deluxe, Brinsley Schwarz, Bees Make Honey, and Kilburn and the High Roads quickly became the most vital and exciting trend in England. Although the first slew of pub bands failed to sell huge quantities of records, they set the stage for successes to come in two ways. The bands which followed, led by Dr. Feelgood, did make the charts in a big way, and many of the original pub rockers later surfaced in significant new wave bands. Some of the names fans might recognize include Nick Lowe, Ian Dury, members of Graham Parker's band, the Motors, members of Elvis Costello's band, and quite a few of the obscure names appearing on labels like Stiff.

The release of Dr. Feelgood's debut LP, in January 1975, broke the field wide open, and legitimized the whole genre, which immediately began strengthening, expanding, and exploring the terrain. First to follow were the younger and hotter Eddie and the Hot Rods, whose fans began showing their appreciation by demolishing the concert halls where the Rods appeared. The polarization between youth and authority was beginning, and the seeds of rebellion were being firmly planted.

With the inspiration of the breakthroughs of Dr. F. and the Hot Rods, a tidal wave of new bands began flowing from the lower social strata of English society. Economically disenfranchised youths, faced with a choice of either menial labor jobs or welfare, began flocking to rock music as both a culture and as an occupation, whether a paying one or not. With varying degrees of political and social conscience, bands began taking on the role of generational spokesmen, expressing the frustrations and anger of British youth, who felt largely discarded by the social/economic machine. With the economy of England very weak, the time was perfect for some sort of grass-roots political movement, and, although not organized or ideological in the traditional sense, the new bands took up the banner.

English record companies, at the time even more stagnant and retrogressive than their American counterparts, paid little mind to the local bands at first. The Rods and Feelgoods had been signed by forward looking talent scouts (the same ones who had supported the pub bands a few years earlier) and few others could discern the good from the bad among the new crop. So nothing much happened at first. Then a few tentative steps—Graham Parker, with a band drawn from Ducks Deluxe and Brinsley Schwarz alumni, inked to Phonogram, and released his first LP in the summer of 1976. Compared to Springsteen, Van Morrison, and Bob Dylan, Parker set the style for the lone cowboy punk so perfectly captured a year later by Elvis Costello. One by one, labels began getting the message, and the future of new wave was looking better every day.

In 1976, two developments that would greatly affect the style and direction of new wave began in a couple of different cities. Most importantly, a number of independent, alternative record companies began surfacing to provide a viable home for many of the new artists. Secondly, several American new wave bands made their first trip to England, and set off a fire that sparked the entire insurgence of the movement there.

In San Francisco, Beserkley Records ("Home of the Hits"), which had been issuing neat, but mail-order only, singles for nearly two years, put their name on the musical map with a sampler collection album, *Beserkley Chartbusters*. Including tracks by Jonathan Richman and the Modern Lovers, Greg Kihn and Earth Quake, the album contained little that could be called new wave, but the insouciant and dedicated spirit of the label set the tone for many entrepeneurs to follow. The mere fact that a totally independent and unfinanced label could exist on a national scale and become well-known at that removed a lot of obstacles from other like-minded outfits.

At roughly the same time, two labels opened up shop in England, starting a British industry that has flourished in a way that no one could have imagined. Chiswick Records, run by the owner of a rare record shop, started with a roster of R&B/rock 'n' roll bands, but quickly expanded their scope to include a number of punk bands from near and far. Eventually, rockabilly and pop came in, and the label now has a fascinating catalog of weird and wonderful records.

Several months after Chiswick's inception, another new label, destined to become the definitive (and most successful) independent record company of the new wave set up shop. Stiff ("The World's Most Flexible Label"), formed by a trio of pub rock oddballs that included Jake Riviera and Dave Robinson, both former managers of local bands, issued their first release, on August 14, 1976. It was a single by Nick Lowe that was immediately recognized as an all-time classic 45. Stiff quickly established both the style and the standards for all the labels that followed them, and performed numerous crucial roles in leading the fight to legitimize and popularize new wave in England, and later, in America.

(In the interests of accuracy, there were a few other independents operating before 1976, most notably Skydog in France and Dynamo in Holland. But neither was as creatively significant or internationally successful as the class of '76.) The primary strength of the new labels was their disregard for the accepted rules of the record business. Despite a canny sense of the commercial, the new labels regularly tried things that majors would have dismissed as too expensive, too hard, or too chancy. Package tours, expensive record sleeves, customized labels, lunatic marketing campaigns, and clever publicity strategies, combined with a dedication to artists that could only be expected from a close relative became the staples of their style. Within a year, the independents in England had become commercially viable, nationally known, and highly respected for their selection of new artists. The majors began to find themselves aced out of numerous areas, from signings to advertising visibility, and many began to seriously consider getting aboard the bandwagon as fast as possible. Several deals between the new labels and the established ones served to familiarize both sides with the workings of the other, but the majors quickly realized that they had better shots at signing some of the new bands—they could offer more money, American distribution, international representation, etc. And the race was on.

In time, the majors began looking at the independents as sort of a testing ground for discovering new bands. Since many of the small labels could only commit themselves (for monetary reasons) to a short term deal, the majors found it easy to see what sort of response a band would get from an initial single release before considering offering them a longer term contract. The sudden rise of bands putting records out on their own also became a useful tool in the same manner.

The second major event of 1976 was the introduction of two US bands to the UK new wave populace. Patti Smith played London in May, and the Ramones followed in July. (As an interesting aside, the Ramones opened for the revived Flamin' Groovies, who had been, back in 1968, the first band to release their own record.) For the British, just on the verge of a whole rock revolution, these performances had earthshaking significance, instantly uniting all the diverse, unorganized elements that had been brewing a new music into a cohesive force of change. In the wake of the Ramones came a deluge of new bands, magazines (the most important of which, *Sniffin' Glue,* was named after a Ramones song), new places for the groups to play, and a huge subculture of fans for anything with the label "New Wave." The general feeling that anybody could form a punk band, get up on a stage, and be a rock star gave license to play, and prompted all sorts of new ideas and creative talents to be injected into the rock world. The music, after many years, once again belonged, truly, to the fans.

While the English musical scene was undergoing a tremendously exciting and consistently intriguing musical upheaval, with new (and different) bands and records emerging every day (or so it seemed), the image conveyed to America (thanks to sensationalist and irresponsible journalism on the part of many) was much less favorable. What Americans saw (and heard) of punk was the safety pins through the cheeks, militaristic and masochistic clothes, crazily dyed and cut hairstyles, mindless dancing, and the rumors of violence. There is no denying that many punk gigs ended up with people being hurt, but fan violence is certainly nothing new to rock concerts. The American view was based on the followers of the music, an approach that managed to dissuade many from giving the music a fair listening. Kind of like the objections to the Beatles' long hair in 1964, isn't it?

The group at the forefront of the new wave (whether or not they chose to accept the role) was the Sex Pistols. As the focal point for both media and fans, the Pistols blazed a niche in rock history by setting a stylistic example for bands to follow, by standing up to the record industry in an unprecedented lunatic fashion, by contributing to (if not setting) a revolution in fashion, and by making it cool for English bands to sing with English accents. In less than two years (they played their first gig in late 1976 and broke up at the end of 1978), they went through three record companies, two bassists, tons of money, and a great deal of public furor. With their unique sound—a blend of precise heavy metal with crazed chaos fronted by the amazing voice of Johnny Rotten—and their thorough disregard for any and all sacred tenets of the record business, they set a defiant style that perfectly captured the general feelings of rebellion and aggression that drove the new wave bands. By being commercially huge (everywhere but the US), they proved that one could successfully use the record giants without accepting their rules. And that was a significant change in the relationships between band and label.

It was obvious from the very beginning that the Pistols could not survive indefinitely. Their very nature was self-destructive, nihilistic, and generally untenable, but, during their tenure, they were so powerful and influential that they caused sweeping changes in the rock world of the Seventies that will undoubtedly last on into the Eighties. Even in America, where the general rock public found them more obnoxious than inspiring, and their album, *Never Mind the Bollocks,* with its cocky political sentiments, impenetrable vocal accent, and stunningly intense music, less exhilarating than, say, Boston, they struck a responsive note in many young rock 'n' roll neophytes who had never really felt, in any of the bands of the Seventies, the true power of the music. As the giants of the Sixties, the Beatles, Stones, Who, Hendrix, and the like, had captivated their audience, the Pistols were something for new rock fans to feel attached to and draw from, emotionally, as well as musically. And as the idols of the Sixties died one by one, it was fitting that the Pistols, as leaders of a movement, should fall by the wayside, leaving the banner in the hands of their followers.

Which is precisely what happened. In the wake of the Pistols' overnight stardom (all it took was a few dirty words on British television), the commercial viability of the English new wave became a truism to the record business, and within months of the first Pistols 45 ("Anarchy in the UK"), numerous bands (Jam, the Clash, Vibrators, Generation X) were signed to majors, while others (Adverts, Buzzcocks, Damned, Elvis Costello, Nick Lowe) were hooked up with independent labels. The race was on—new wave bands kept popping up, signing up, putting out records—compilation albums, samplers, spin-off bands—each day brought new surprises.

In America, the growth of new wave was much slower and more diffuse, really lacking the characteristics of a cohesive movement. Bands that were signed to major labels were chosen by individual merit and saleability, not because of their identification with any popular trend. Blondie, Talking Heads, Television, Dead Boys, Mink DeVille, and the Dictators joined Patti Smith and the Ramones in the record shops, but public response was only slightly different than any new band with a debut LP could expect. Mink DeVille, with a decidedly old wave sound, received a lot of airplay and sold quite well, but no momentum of a collective spirit existed, and each band pretty much had to fend for itself in the radio and retail arenas. Each band, in turn, toured England and Europe, establishing varying levels of stardom, but found their status unchanged when they returned. After all the enthusiasm abroad, many of the groups found American nonchalance hard to comprehend, and their future, stateside, hardly seemed assured.

Into this uneasy environment came the Sex Pistols, in January of 1978, who had finally decided to tour the intimidating giant. With all of the American new wave hopes riding on their shoulders, they planned and executed dates in a foolish choice of cities, refusing to cooperate with their record company on issues of press access and promotion, ultimately picking California for the scene of their dissolution. The tour was a disaster, with everybody involved disappointed and dispirited. The group's fans, unable to see them in the obscure choice of locations, were unhappy. The press, denied free tickets or transportation to the concerts were alienated. The record company, which spent a lot of money, was quickly losing interest in the group. So much for the new wave's championship shot. As far as America was concerned, all the movement had consisted of was one group, and they were out for the count.

Fortunately, the enthusiasm of the local American bands didn't falter as a result of the Pistols' demise, and British bands didn't give up on eventually conquering America. It just took a while longer than anyone had expected or hoped. It wasn't until the negative connotations of the alarmist labels "punk" and "new wave" were shunted aside that the music could be given a fair shot in the rock marketplace. As the British new wave bands began to find themselves selling more-than-respectable quantities of "product" overseas, US labels took some notice, and began considering the problems involved in bringing similar success here. While America failed to produce any truly great (or commercially significant) independent labels, bands were a different story. In 1978, the Cars broke through in a multi-platinized way, and in 1979, such luminaries as Blondie, Devo, Cheap Trick, and David Johansen became new stars in the American rock world. Also, the few British bands to find their gold pot at the American end of the rainbow—Joe Jackson, Elvis Costello, the Police—have proven the market does indeed exist for innovative, vaguely punky, musical groups. Future scores by new wave-ish bands seem inevitable, as each month brings announcements of new signings of promising local outfits, from Philadelphia to Los Angeles. Whether all of these bands actually qualify officially as new wave (who's to judge?), and it seems obvious that the diversity is too great to attach any single classification, there is no denying that they all owe, to some degree, their careers and their successes to the removal of barriers brought about by the new wave. As the Seventies draw to a close, the styles that launched the new wave—pop, punk, and avant-garde (now called "no wave")—have seemingly found a place in the commercial music arena of America. Bands that were both unknown and unacceptable a few years ago are now spawning imitators, as the record business, as has been its historical wont, rushes to replicate bands that sell with cheap clones that can follow the leader to platinum heaven. Fortunately, the rash of new signings over the last two years has allowed some fairly subversive bands into the rock mainstream, and they are gaining enough of a toehold to begin changing the rock industry's perceptions of what should and shouldn't be put on vinyl. If forward lookers like Devo and Elvis Costello continue to sell records, they will drastically influence the direction and development of rock 'n' roll over the next few years.

The most interesting trend of 1979 has been the recognition of a cult following in America for many of the top English new wave acts. Without being able to sell millions of records, and in some cases almost without American record releases, many of the good bands—the Clash, Boomtown Rats, Jam, Tom

Robinson, Damned, XTC, Squeeze, and others—have been able to do tours of clubs in such a bargain manner that they can make money doing a few dates to relatively small audiences. For some, the hipper cities like New York, Los Angeles and Cleveland can muster two or three thousand people to a headlining show at a medium-sized hall. This bodes well, suggesting more long-term hope for British bands who were originally judged too far-out to make it in America. Even if platinum goals are out of the question, the existence of a steady, committed, clientele for tours, import records, and relevant publications gives new bands a chance to try their wares here without bankrupting their record company or themselves.

For the future, another good sign is the recent tie-ups between credible new wave labels and majors as distributors or backers. Beserkley goes through Elektra; Stiff has ties with Columbia, Epic, and others; Virgin has a deal with Atlantic and also plans to release product through Jem/PVC, an independent label owned by a record importer; a new outfit called the Independent Recording Syndicate has recently been set up in conjunction with A&M; and Radar is now releasing records through Polydor. The situation seems to be improving steadily, and new breakthroughs keep adding hope and fuel to the dreams of a real change in the American record industry. After a very tenuous beginning, America is starting to accept the new wave, even if the label has been forgotten in the process.

The English new wave scene, circa 1979, is largely coasting on the successes of the past. Independent labels have become as firmly entrenched as those they originally sought to replace. The whole star trip that early new wavers attempted to downplay if not avoid has taken hold, with all remnants of a communal spirit gone. The stylistic continuity of the early bands has drifted into the same old used-to-be, with the struggle to be noticed as boring and mundane as the pre-new wave groups. Whatever non-conformism originally motivated the new wave has been replaced by old fashioned greed, and as many terrible bands are emerging as in the worst days of the early Seventies. It's an unfortunate commentary, but the major thing that has changed is the ability to assume that any new band coming along was going to be, at least, interesting. Similarly, the guarantee of certain record companies to be consistently entertaining are gone, and the resurgence of *caveat emptor* (coupled with the steadily spiraling prices of records) makes the fun of the whole thing a lot more problematic. There are still intriguing bands coming out of the post-new wave era in England, but they are fewer, further between, and less original than their predecessors.

As with any cultural movement, cubbyholes are bound to be misused, and the new wave label has certainly been hung on all sorts of bands that wouldn't think of themselves as part of any phenomenon or style. Unlike the days when the tag meant commercial death, it now amounts to a fairly innocuous mistake when misapplied. It's possible that a broader-than-necessary definition of new wave appeals to many in the record world, and the resulting confusion hardly matters.

Cheap Trick, a band that had served its apprenticeship playing Mideast clubs for several years before signing with Epic Records, has become a late Seventies superstar act with much of their early following coming from fans of new wave. Jonathan Richman, an early new wave hero because of recordings done in 1971, turned to a simplistic style of clever folk singing yet retained some of his new wave credibility. The Rubinoos, another Beserkley Records act, are a pure pop band, yet they had the support and dreams of new wave riding with them when a single, "I Think We're Alone Now," climbed in the charts a few years back. Tom Petty, another successful pop artist, was tagged "power pop" at the start, but when that term lost its popularity, he was associated with new wave, for whatever reasons. Nick Lowe, the Knack, the Records, the Motors, Shoes, Cars, and Blondie, for whatever personal backgrounds may tie in with new wave, all make music that is, plain and simply, pop music in the greater Sixties' tradition. They all share something—perhaps a common attitude regarding the purpose of playing rock 'n' roll, having as much to do with personal enjoyment and youthful fantasies of emulating past heroes as with financial rewards and the various benefits of stardom. Between them, they helped to revitalize the sound of American radio, the choice in American record shops, and the attitudes of record companies and rock fans everywhere. Compared to the crassness of assembly line disco and emotionless heavy metal retreads, the new pop bands have brought exuberance and fun back to the music which spawned it. Unlike the old-time superstars who are trading on their former greatness, these new bands are rising to the challenge of being fresh, creative, and experimental. They've also helped remove the feeling of alienation between audience and performer. By being more attentive to the people who buy their records, the new pop bands make an effort to be as close to their fans as possible in the hustle bustle world of rock stardom. In any case, they've got a better attitude than the megabands who show up two hours late to their own gigs, play a while with bored expressions, take the money and run. There's a sense of commitment to their audience that keeps the feeling of communication alive, whether through small magazines, fan clubs, personal appearances, or whatever. The people who make up these bands haven't forgotten why they love rock 'n' roll, and to a large degree, many of them are as big fans of rock as their fans are. And that's a good way to keep the feeling alive.

RECOMMENDED NEW WAVE RECORDINGS

(The following list is a personal selection of albums that can be loosely fit into the range of new wave. Records not released in the United States are marked with an asterisk to indicate import only. The order of the list is random.—IAR)

ALBUMS
CLASH—Clash Clash (CBS)*
ELVIS COSTELLO—This Year's Model, (Columbia)
SEX PISTOLS—The Great Rock 'n' Roll Swindle (Virgin)*
GENERATION X—Generation X (Chrysalis)

DAMNED—Damned Damned Damned (Stiff)*
DEVO—Q. Are We Not Men? A. We Are Devo (Warner Bros.)
TELEVISION—Marquee Moon (Elektra)
SHOES—Black Vinyl Shoes (PVC)
BOOMTOWN RATS—Boomtown Rats (Phonogram)
RAMONES—Rocket to Russia (Sire)
TOM ROBINSON BAND—Power in the Darkness (Harvest)
DICTATORS—Dictators Go Girl Crazy (Epic)
BLONDIE—Plastic Letters (Chrysalis)
PERE UBU—The Modern Dance (Blank)
XTC—White Noise (Virgin)*
VIBRATORS—Pure Mania (Epic)
NEW YORK DOLLS—New York Dolls (Mercury)
IGGY & THE STOOGES—Fun House (Elektra)
SKIDS—Scared to Dance (Virgin)*
MC5—Back in the USA (Atco)
JAM—In the City (Polydor)
VELVET UNDERGROUND—White Light/White Heat (Verve)
STRANGLERS—Rattus Norvegicus (A&M)
NICK LOWE—Pure Pop for Now People (Columbia)
EDDIE & THE HOT RODS—Life on the Line (Island)

NEW WAVE CHRONOLOGY

1966
The Velvet Underground is formed in New York by the collusion of John Cale and Lou Reed.

1967
MARCH: Release of the first Velvet Underground album by Verve Records.
OCTOBER: First public performance by Iggy and the Stooges.

1968
The Flamin' Groovies record and release their very own 10" album, *Sneakers*.

1969
MARCH: Detroit politico band, the MC5, have their first album, *Kick Out the Jams*, released amid controversy regarding lyrical content.
AUGUST: Debut album by the Stooges released.

1970
Lou Reed breaks away from the Velvet Underground to begin a solo career.
Stooges release *Fun House* album.
The second MC5 album, *Back in the USA*, produced by Jon Landau, released by the group's second record company, Atco.

1971
FEBRUARY: Alice Cooper release their third, yet crucially significant, album under the name *Love it to Death*.
NOVEMBER: As their national popularity grows, Alice & Band release *Killer* LP.

1972

New York Dolls begin playing clubs around New York in the Spring.

Boston's premier underground group, the Modern Lovers, flown to California to record demos for Warner Bros. with John Cale producing.

NOVEMBER: While in London playing a concert with the Faces, Dolls' drummer Billy Murcia dies a drug related death.

Miss Christine, of the GTO's, dies of a drug overdose.

1973

JANUARY: Another New York club band makes its debut under the name "Kiss."

APRIL: First New York Dolls album, produced by Todd Rundgren, released on an unsuspecting world.

JULY: Several years after breakup of the Stooges, Iggy Pop releases comeback album, *Raw Power*, with production assistance by new friend David Bowie. Series of dates are arranged—at New York's Max's Kansas City, Iggy slits open his chest with a broken glass during a performance.

AUGUST: First release (Flamin' Groovies EP—*Grease*) by new French independent record company, Skydog.

NOVEMBER: Patti Smith, accompanied by Lenny Kaye on guitar, makes her rock debut in New York.

DECEMBER: Tom Verlaine and Richard Hell form Television in New York. Interesting triple bill at New York's Academy of Music: Iggy Pop, Blue Oyster Cult, and Kiss.

1974

MARCH: First performances by Television, also the Ramones.

MAY: CBGB's opens in New York.

Dolls' second album, *Too Much Too Soon*, released.

Sparks' best album, *Kimono My House*, released, making them huge stars in England.

AUGUST: Blondie, consisting of Debbie Harry and three male musicians, forms in New York.

Privately issued 45, "Piss Factory", is first recording by Patti Smith.

SEPTEMBER: New York Dolls, as originally constituted, disband, various versions of the lineup carry on for several months.

DECEMBER: Traditional English pub R&Bers, Dr. Feelgood, signed to United Artists Records.

1975

JANUARY: Formation of Talking Heads in New York. Major pub rock package covers England: "Naughty Rhythms Tour."

FEBRUARY: Dr. Feelgood's debut disc, recorded in mono, appears in England. Stranglers begin gigging around London area.

APRIL: Johnny Thunders, Jerry Nolan, and Richard Hell form the Heartbreakers.

JUNE: Talking Heads begin gigging on New York underground circuit.

OCTOBER: Patti Smith's first album, *Horses*, released by Arista.

NOVEMBER: Debut concert by new London group, the Sex Pistols.

DECEMBER: Eddie and the Hot Rods signed to Island Records in England. First release on Chiswick label—Count Bishops EP.

1976

JANUARY: Graham Parker and the Rumour signed in England. Ramones signed to Sire in America.

FEBRUARY: Hot Rods release their first 45, complete with picture sleeve.
MARCH: Beserkley Records, based in San Francisco, releases their first album, *Beserkley Chartbusters.*
APRIL: London rock club, the Nashville, features a bill of Sex Pistols and 101ers, led by future Clashman Joe Strummer.
MAY: Release of first Ramones album.
Patti Smith tours England—support band in London is the Stranglers.
JULY: Ramones English debut as opening act for the Flamin' Groovies.
London punk band, the Damned, make first appearance.
Clash formed as a five piece band after breakup of 101ers.
Long time pub band, Kilburn and the High Roads, featuring Ian Dury, breaks up. Dury goes solo.
AUGUST: Clash begin playing in London clubs.
Stiff Records releases Nick Lowe 45 and begins revolution in British music business.
First European Punk Rock Festival held in France—bill includes Nick Lowe, Damned, Hot Rods.
SEPTEMBER: Punk Festival at London's 100 Club—lineup includes Sex Pistols, Clash, Damned, Buzzcocks, Siouxsie and the Banshees.
OCTOBER: Second Patti Smith album released. Sex Pistols sign recording contract with EMI.
NOVEMBER: "Anarchy in the UK," first 45 by the Pistols, released by EMI.
Damned release their first 45 on Stiff.
National tour begins in England—Pistols/Clash/Heartbreakers/Damned.
DECEMBER: Pistols outrage United Kingdom by using four-letter words on a TV talk show. England is plunged into controversy.
Stranglers sign recording contract in England.

1977

JANUARY: EMI unloads Sex Pistols in wake of fracas surrounding the group. Large cash settlement eases the band's disappointment.
FEBRUARY: Stiff releases first British punk LP—The Damned's Diamond in the Rough.
Sex Pistols fire their original bassist, Glen Matlock, and hire Sid Vicious to replace him.
MARCH: Sex Pistols sign second deal, this one a one-week affair with A&M. First 45 by the Clash, "White Riot," issued by CBS UK.
APRIL: Clash release a stunningly impressive first album.
Damned become first British punk band to play in America. First Jam single, "This is the Modern World," released in England.
MAY: Undaunted, Sex Pistols sign third contract (with Virgin) and release second single ("God Save the Queen.")
JUNE: Second Dictators' LP, *Manifest Destiny,* appears in US.
JULY: Ramones 45, "Sheena is a Punk Rocker," grazes US singles charts. Elvis Costello's first album, *My Aim is True,* issued by Stiff.
AUGUST: Avowed homosexual, Tom Robinson, signed to EMI in England.
SEPTEMBER: Ian Dury solo LP, *New Boots and Panties,* enters UK charts and remains there for over one year.
OCTOBER: With package tour on the road in England (Costello, Lowe, Dury), Stiff owners Robinson and Riviera go their separate ways, leaving Stiff Elvisless.
NOVEMBER: Pistols album released after much confusion and many delays.

1978

JANUARY: Sex Pistols' US tour opens in Atlanta. Sex Pistols break up in San Francisco.
FEBRUARY: Nick Lowe's first solo album, *Pure Pop For Now People* (a.k.a *Jesus of Cool*) released.
MARCH: Three UK new wave bands play in America—Stranglers, Jam, X-Ray Spex. Second Elvis Costello LP, *This Year's Model,* issued.
APRIL: Blondie's single, "Denis," goes to Number One in the English charts.
MAY: Tom Robinson Band release their debut LP.
AUGUST: Television disband.
OCTOBER: Sid Vicious arrested in New York for murder.
NOVEMBER: Talking Heads second album breaks the Top Thirty in US charts.
DECEMBER: Clash LP, *Give 'Em Enough Rope,* released in US and UK.

1979

FEBRUARY: Sid Vicious dies in New York. The new wave reaches its Altamont.

IAR

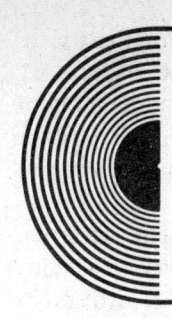

TWENTY-FIVE YEARS OF ROCK 'N' ROLL

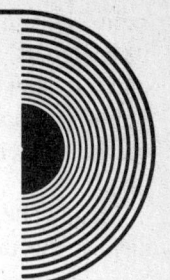

In the 1940s, a series of monumental changes in the music industry opened the door for the emergence of a new kind of music. As it took shape in the 50s, the music had the earmark of a fad—at most, a craze. Teenagers, an apparently unstable target group for the industry, embraced rock 'n' roll; the more conservative musical establishment condemned it as coarse and obscene. White church groups in the South attempted to suppress it as a black conspiracy. Congress held hearings to determine whether this new music was, indeed, a conspiracy. Best-selling writer and witch hunter Vance Packard testified that it was.

All the time that rock was being suppressed, no one thought it would last. Major labels signed few rock artists, taking the attitude that (in the words of British writer Charlie Gillett) "Rock 'n' roll singers, who seemed to be flash-in-the-pan novelties with only one style, promised to be redundant before a couple of years were up." So everyone thought, right through 1955.

But on August 18, 1979, eighteen of the top thirty LPs in the *Record World* national chart were albums of rock music. All other records—disco, jazz, comedy, soul/fusion—together accounted for little more than a third of the best-sellers. No soundtrack albums or country and western acts were to be found. And more often than not, it is a rock act which captures the weekly "Top Box Office" position in *Billboard*'s computation of live performance revenues. There is no escaping the conclusion that rock music is the best-selling form of music in the United States. A "flash-in-the-pan" has proven to be a consistent bullseye for more than a quarter of a century, and the gunpowder of rock is still dry. As soon as the music industry stopped withholding the nourishment it had denied rock 'n roll in its infancy, the music found a sustained audience reception and was able to thrive.

Beginnings

The American Society of Composers, Authors and Publishers (ASCAP) began losing its long-standing control of popular music in America as the country headed into World War II. ASCAP was Tin Pan Alley grown up; it held the rights to most of the elegant and superficial show tunes by established commercial songwriters. ASCAP-licensed songs were often performed live on radio, and in 1941 the Society began charging prohibitive rates for the use of its members' material on the air. ASCAP wanted everything to be classy, live, and on staff paper, and sneered at the phonograph record as a method of publishing songs. Radio, to which records were a lot more useful than sheet music, suddenly had to look to new writers for less exorbitantly-priced songs to play.

Meanwhile, the dance bands which played ASCAP's tunes went on strike against the record companies in an attempt to force radio to carry the bands live. The move backfired: singers left the bands and continued to record, radio played the singers' discs, listeners bought more and more of them, and by the war's end pop music was headed away from the band era and into the age of stars who were simply singers.

Throughout the 30s, a handful of big labels including Decca, Columbia, and RCA Victor had controlled the three popular record markets: the pop market, the country market, and the black music market. During the 40s, a wartime austerity program required that each record company cut production. The majors then concentrated on pop, leaving R&B and country and western to others. The "others" were independent labels which proceeded to develop their own regional talent—less polished artists who wrote and sang songs licensed by the new Broadcast Music Incorporated (BMI), an organization backed by radio, which was hated by the rival ASCAP. By the late 40s, the major record companies were supplying smoothly-produced pop "product" (Doris Day, Perry Como, Guy Mitchell) but had lost touch with idiosyncratic regional markets which demanded either "race" or "hillbilly" music.

As greater numbers of blacks moved from the South after the war, migrating to urban centers like Chicago, they brought blues music with them. The southern country blues of Robert Johnson and Charlie Patton were recreated and electrified up north through the music of Muddy Waters, Howlin' Wolf, Elmore James, John Lee Hooker, and Floyd Jones. These men built careers even as they circumvented the music establishment. They recorded for independent labels like Chess in Chicago; they could license their songs through BMI; they found radio audiences through the specialized "race" stations, whose sometimes powerful beams began spreading the blues to younger listeners, many of them white.

Postwar prosperity gave these listeners unprecedented spending power. The majors tried to woo them with nonconformist Caucasian singers such as Frank Sinatra, Frankie Laine, and the tearful Johnny Ray, but most of these were in the dance band tradition. By the early 50s, the urban kids had enough awareness of R&B to prefer performers who laid down more of a beat and sounded less like singers their parents listened to. They were drawn to dance songs (Ray Brown's ground-breaking "Good Rockin' Tonight" in 1948, Jackie Brenston's "Rocket 88" in 1951), slower blues (Ivory Joe Hunter's "I Almost Lost My Mind"), and the raw, aching-heart country songs of Hank Williams ("Your Cheating Heart," "I'm So Lonesome I Could Cry").

The stage was all set for a musical change. Major labels could try to have adult crooners cover some of these emotional songs, but most crooners couldn't rock. Too often, crooners could sing only of contrived situations in robot voices, mere mouthpieces of the A&R men at the majors. The real solution was to develop new artists, people who could express the alternate sound directly to a teen audience, with or without the help of the music establishment. Bill Haley from Detroit and producer Sam Phillips of Memphis were in the wings, preparing to create that expression.

School Days and Blue Suede Shoes

Apart from its artist roster, an independent label in the early 50s was often a one-man operation. Some would-be music moguls even handled their own distribution, selling the records they'd produced from the trunks of their cars. They found demand for their product. Often its very rawness provided just the edge of emotion the blues and country fans were seeking from music.

Sam Phillips ran a storefront studio in Memphis, a city in which blues and country converged. He recorded both types of music, sometimes by the same singer. He even had a sort of house band, headed by bassist Bill Black, which played a hybrid of the two styles. In 1953, Phillips recorded Herman "Junior" Parker singing an original tune, "Mystery Train," which combined the structure and beat of R&B with a jaunty country mood. That same year, former country-swing singer Bill Haley was recording for Essex Records, taking Dixieland-style songs, changing the beat, and ending up with performances like "Crazy Man Crazy." Haley, white and showbusinesslike, was more acceptable to mass-market programmers than the more parochial Parker, and his indie production made the Hot 100.

But Phillips went Haley one better when he introduced the younger, sexier Elvis Presley with such country-rhythm classics as "That's All Right," "Good Rockin' Tonight," and Parker's "Mystery Train." Presley had the emotion, the youth, and the rebellious charm that restless teenagers were looking for. A Mississippi rustic, he'd absorbed enough of the black singing style—an African transplant based on prayer-song, with exotic bending of pitch and unfaltering rhythmic awareness—to make many country fans around Memphis assume he was black when they heard his songs.

By 1955, Presley was on the national country chart with "Baby Let's Play House," and by 1956 Presley and producer Chet Atkins had broken the rock 'n' roll market wide open with "Heartbreak Hotel," recorded for RCA in an echoey Nashville stairwell. Though Atkins could no longer give Elvis the unique, regional sound Phillips strove for, it was appropriate that such a natural talent as Presley's should triumph commercially in a form fairly close to the original. Presley was a singer who'd started by simply singing songs he and Phillips liked, local songs. (By contrast, Bill Haley's anthem, "Rock around the Clock," had been composed by 63-year-old ASCAP member Max Freedman with the express purpose of cracking the youth market.) He was luckier than his equally well-intentioned black contemporaries, like Joe Turner and Lloyd Price, in having the muscle of RCA Victor and Colonel Tom Parker behind him, and millions of record buyers including white teens in his pocket. But he was reasonably authentic.

Crazed Georgian rock preacher Little Richard Penniman also fared better than Turner, as did the athletic, duck-walking Chuck Berry with his 1955 hit, "Maybellene." Such singers were already well plugged-in to show business and knew how to give the public the kind of shows and songs it wanted. Berry, who wrote slick, rocking accounts of cars and school days, was especially shrewd.

Huey Smith, Fats Domino, the Everly Brothers, Carl Perkins, Jerry Lee Lewis, Roy Orbison, and Chuck Willis all continued to record in a heartfelt rocking style well into 1957, but by the end of the year rock was largely in the hands of businessmen, behind-the-scenes writers, technicians, A&R men, and producers. Few rock experiments again took place to match Phillips' Sun sessions until the 60s were underway. The true rockers were displaced as if by conspiracy: the Army drafted Elvis, the Marines got the Everlys, and a plane disaster snuffed the life of BMI writer and hitmaker Buddy Holly, along with companions Ritchie Valens and the Big Bopper. A car crash killed Eddie Cochran and injured Gene Vincent. The songwriting establishment lobbied in Washington and hounded DJ Alan Freed to ruin under the guise of a Payola investigation. The law went after Berry, and Lewis was driven from his home base for marrying a young cousin. Bill Haley became dated, while the remarkably influential Bo Diddley was overlooked for years.

The Industry-at-Large Gets In on the Action

In the early days of rock 'n' roll, the major record and management companies were reluctant to put a real stake in what they feared (or hoped) was only a short-term craze. Columbia Records A&R chief Mitch Miller, for example, sided with the ASCAP stand that portrayed rock as a threat to established musical values, especially adult suburban buying patterns. It was also considered a possible threat to the still-viable singing careers in which the companies had long-term investments. Few executives had the far-sightedness to fortell that the youth culture wouldn't only sustain but renew itself each year as younger kids entered their teens. Consequently, signings by majors were rare prior to 1956. Bill Haley's contract with Decca (now MCA) was exceptional.

But as independent labels and regional radio flourished on rock, big-label executives started to relax their opposition. Still groping blindly for the key to the whole rock phenomenon, A&R men had their easy-listening artists cover the rock and R&B songs that showed hit potential. RCA's first "rock" hit was a Perry Como cover of Gene and Eunice's "KoKoMo." Mercury had the Crew Cuts and Georgia Gibbs copy original singles by the Chords and by LaVern Baker, while smaller mainstream labels such as Dot developed their own watered-down rockers like Pat Boone, who hit with a white-bucks version of Fats Domino's "Ain't That a Shame."

In theory the cover versions, which tended to smooth away the regional Negro accents of many originals, were supposed to be more acceptable to the mass market. (The same principle applied years later to the white blues revival which made stars of Johnny Winter and the early Fleetwood Mac.) And radio usually went along with the majors, which not by coincidence were the companies that could supply them most efficiently with broadcast records. With certain exceptions—such as the spirited Bill Haley versions of Joe Turner and Jackie Brenton songs—most of the covers had less fire than the originals. The changeover to rock music couldn't be complete until the majors started recording real rock 'n' rollers instead of using their on-hand imitators.

The progress of rock grew with the intercession of three mass-media powers. RCA signed Elvis Presley, buying his contract from Sam Phillips and setting him up in Nashville to record right away. WINS-New York hired Cleveland rock DJ Alan Freed. And the film industry boosted rock 'n' roll by turning out feature films like *Blackboard Jungle* and *Rock around the Clock,* both of which featured beat music on the soundtrack or rock 'n' rollers in the cast. Mirroring the moviemakers' policy of including veteran R&B singers in cameos, Alan Freed promoted riotous live shows which featured similar artists performing before a new teen audience. Barriers between pop and "race" music, between the tastes of young white and black listeners, started showing signs of weakening, and the anemic pop bloodstream got a welcome transfusion. Following RCA's success with Presley, Capitol signed Gene Vincent, Decca leased the recordings of Buddy Holly and the Crickets, and Liberty signed and developed Eddie Cochran, whose gunburst guitar style was an inspiration to later rockers including the Who and young Neil Diamond. Sun, which had lost Elvis, came back with Jerry Lee Lewis and Carl ("Blue Suede Shoes") Perkins. A growing number of southern and southwestern rockers watched their regional American style capture the teen population of the English-speaking world.

By 1958, the rockers with a combination of hit material and good management realized they had a greater potential for career longevity than their detractors would have had them believe. These singers and their labels also were aware that concessions to the powerful conservatives in the music business would have to be made for the sake of these longer careers. The transfusion slowed to a trickle: the outrageous quality of rock 'n' roll was starting to mellow and blend with the mainstream of Tin Pan Alley. Buddy Holly and the Everly Brothers spent much more time in New York, working on songs intended as hits as methodically as a group like Foreigner does today.

The growing popularity and influence of movies, TV and the teen stereotypes they fostered helped produce a rash of easygoing, boyish-looking pop stars including Rick Nelson, James Darren, and Tommy Sands, who struck paydirt with material developed for, not by, them. Such performers, who had styles that fell in between a teen and an adult orientation, became even more dominant as many of the first wave of rock singers died in accidents or were drafted. (Those that returned did so with slicker, more calculated styles.) Record and management companies tended to favor personalities such as Annette Funicello, who could manage lucrative multiple careers. Even Elvis Presley, as he got more deeply involved in making movies, started to sing fluffy material without displaying the conviction he'd brought to relatively lightweight early songs such as "We're Gonna Move" and "You're So Square."

The increasing attention paid to production values helped smooth-sounding urban harmony groups, usually of black or Italian background and singing with a mixture of gospel and Neapolitan coloring, take precedence over the blues and country-rock stylings of the early, fiery rockers. These groups included the Orioles, the Skyliners, the Drifters, the Elegants, and Dion and the Belmonts. Pop and pop-rock was now a national industry, and control was passing to executives and impresarios based in cities where the largest record companies, TV facilities, and film studios were located. Pop magnates like Alan Freed and Dick Clark had a finger in every record, dance hall, concert and radio/TV/movie pie within reach, and "conflict of interest" was a ground rule for success.

The Hit Factories and the Folk Revival: 1958 to 1964

The rock and pop of 1958 through 1963 had as its basis a triumph of sound over emotion. Pop was less concerned with the striving for a sense of freedom that had typified country-rock and R&B ("Mystery Train," "Blue Suede Shoes," Roy Orbison's "Down the Line") than with pandering to the stereotypical puppy-love longings which adults attributed to teens. Though such records were all the rage of the sub-debutante set, too much of the adolescent image held by grown men in the record industry was drawn from *The Many Loves of Dobie Gillis* and *Gidget Goes Hawaiian*. It was all too pat and mindless. Novelty records ruled the airwaves: "Witch Doctor," "Purple People Eater," "Battle of New Orleans," Chipmunks, and the Blob. Even the good records of the era were based on the premise of echo and "total sound." Jan and Dean sounded terrific singing "Baby Talk," but the words of the song were totally vacuous. Teen cliches like girl gossip at the ice cream fountain were departure points for the girl-group records of the Shangri-Las, the Angels, and the Chiffons, such as "Leader of the Pack" (produced by Shadow Morton) and "My Boyfriend's Back." After Morton, other producers took the concept of total sound a step further: Phil Spector and Brian Wilson both experimented with the infinite overdub and the "wall of sound."

Songwriting teams became a tool of mass production. Pomus-Schuman, Lieber-Stoller, Goffin-King, Sedaka-Greenfield, and, a little later, Holland-Dozier-Holland for Motown (though the Four Tops sang their early hits with a lot of feeling). Structure and cuteness inevitably took precedence over content. A few isolated rock musicians managed to break through with experimental guitar styles (Duane Eddy, Link Wray) and emotional, blues-inspired pop (Jackie DeShannon). Molasses-voiced prizefighter Lee Dorsey clicked with engaging New Orleans dance records like "Ride Your Pony" under the guidance of studio mentor Allen Toussaint. Two singers, Del Shannon and Roy Orbison, turned the concept of total sound into something like a melodic art in their respective singles, "Hats Off to Larry" and "Crying." Each of these artists had an influence on the course of 70s pop.

As girl groups continued to sing about lipstick, pillows, and popsicles, a substantial portion of the country's young record buyers were turning to the relatively unaffected story-songs of such groups as the Kingston Trio, Bud and Travis, the Chad Mitchell Trio, and the Journeymen. These duos and trios produced a blend of folk melody, calypso, and latin rhythm, and recycled Weavers harmonies that became the basis of the 60s folk rock of the Byrds and the Youngbloods, and later the West Coast styles of Crosby, Stills, Nash & Young, the Eagles, and Fleetwood Mac. Group albums such as the Kingston Trio's *Time to Think* helped open the way for mass acceptance of the message songs of Joan Baez and Bob Dylan, for the Trio's songs had subjects including integration, union rights, and disarmament. Accused at the time of crass commercialism by folk purists, the pop-folk groups reached huge audiences that their less-stagy predecessors—Leadbelly, Pete Seeger, Woody Guthrie and Bob Gibson—had been unable to. It is ironic that the Kingston Trio, which has realigned to tour for the past ten years, sounds so spare and ingenuous next to the slick style of its heirs—the Eagles, Poco, Firefall—that the group could almost be taken today as a genuine exponent of country-flavored folk song.

In early-60s America, the recording of intense, emotional music was left mainly to soul singers—Ray Charles, James Brown, Wilson Picket, and the cooler, more pop-oriented Sam Cooke. All of them brought gospel singing technique to existing R&B styles. Brown also developed a "flash" stage show with colorful costumes and a choreography sorely missing from the performances of most pop purveyors. Subsequent soul singers like Sam and Dave, Aretha Franklin, and Smokey Robinson tended to work the soul factories—Stax/Volt's Memphis studios, Atlantic Records in New York, and Motown Records in Detroit—where the improvisatory, gospel quality of their music became part of a producer's formula. Even so, the music of artists like Joe Tex, Otis Redding, Percy Sledge, and the Stax rhythm section, which recorded separately as Booker T. and the MGs, was a strong antidote to pop blandness and cuteness. Like other R&B music (Allen Toussaint, Bobby Womack) it became a powerful influence on white artists from the Rolling Stones and Rod Stewart to the Band and Little Feat.

Rock Comes of Age—The British Invasion

While American pop stars went right on sleepwalking, a bunch of English boys, many of them art students, were rediscovering the brasher side of rock 'n' roll. In Liverpool, then in Manchester, Birmingham, Newcastle and London, young guitarists and hopeful tunesmiths formed "beat groups." Beat groups played a variety of styles, including rockabilly and R&B, but evolved most directly from the British skiffle craze which had its roots in traditional jazz but turned out more like England's answer to the American folk fad. Kids played warhorse tunes to their own banjo and washboard accompaniment, gradually adding electric guitar and real drums. The folk and skiffle trends signalled a change from the image pop singer who rarely played guitar and was backed by a band that got little attention. Twenty years after the skiffle days, rock 'n' roll staging would still demand that a band provide its own accompaniment (much to the chagrin of formula-style producers).

In 1961 and 1962, beat groups toured as backing bands for featured pop singers like Frank Ifield and Tony Sheridan. They followed the models of Cliff Richard and the Shadows, or American Bobby Vee and the Crickets. But working-class audiences, whose temperament suited young bands better than melodramatic singers, clamored for the music of the beat groups alone.

At the same point in pop history, columnists were starting to celebrate young American stars—both singers and businessmen. The jet set seemed to embrace the likes of Joey Dee and Phil Spector, for to be a self-made young success in the pop industry was to be chic. Trendy people came to hear pop in the clubs, and much of club society was British: actors, designers, denizens of the ballet and the galleries, looking for a style of their own.

As outspoken beat groups like the Beatles, the Searchers and the Who began to get exposure, and the "mod" youth culture got more visible, the international entertainment industry changed. Rock music started to stand as a symbol of social change. Musicians were found sharp and amusing in interviews, designers and former models got in on image making, film and theatrical upstarts (the Stamp brothers, Richard Lester, David Hemmings) became involved with pop, and a new breed of business and recording managers (Brian Epstein, George Martin, Tony Hatch) took a large part of the pop domain away from the old-liners. Sheet music sales slid in the face of the exploding record industry. Groups were in, soloists were out. The strength of the beat groups came not just from their youth and irreverence, but from the music they played and the way it was recorded. The British rock records sounded simple and a bit rough, almost like demos. They were much more exciting than the records produced by American echo- and stringmeisters. They blended familiar influences into something fresh: the Hollies from Manchester, for example, combined the southern U.S. rock sound of Roy Orbison and Buddy Holly with the hypnotic rhythms and high-pitched singing of the Impressions. The Rolling Stones drew heavily from Otis Redding, Chuck Berry, Rufus Thomas and Solomon Burke, but added their London perspective in such songs as "Play with Fire." The Searchers favored Fats Domino, Jerry Lee Lewis and the Everly Brothers. The Beatles had original songs, deft management, cheeky working-class appeal, and a monstrous promotional campaign that included the rich and powerful backing of Capitol/EMI Records. All the groups were young, white, and marketable. Together, they brought rock back to life and took it beyond the teens.

Americans Plug In—Folk Rock and Progressive Rock

America was expected to answer Britain, and it answered with "folk rock." Folk rock developed partly from pop-folk, partly from the California rock of Sonny Bono, Jack Nitzsche, and ex-Journeyman John Phillips, and partly from the Chicago bar blues. Bob Dylan's topical and sometimes surreal lyrics had become favorites with the folkies by 1964, but his accompaniments were based largely on blues guitar patterns. His switch to electric backing on "Subterranean Homesick Blues," widely protested by his folk fans in the mid-60s, was a logical move musically and commercially. It followed the example of the urban bluesmen and was designed to make his voice heard louder in a rocking world.

The West Coast group the Byrds took the rhythms of Nitzsche/Bono songs as played by the Searchers ("Needles and Pins") and covered Dylan's most tuneful songs, sugar-coating them into danceable hits. Though the Byrds helped put the emphasis in pop on lyrics and popularized folk rock, they were less its originators than Dylan and the aforementioned writers were. With the help of seasoned West Coast session men like Leon Russell, Hal Blaine and Larry Knechtel, the Byrds rode the wave of pop adulation. In more recent lineup shuffles and incarnations—Crosby/Nash and McGuinn, Clark and Hillman—they've become solid musicians themselves, and have played live with a precision and power the early Byrds lacked.

The next step in rock after it had experimented with expressive lyrics was to experiment in other areas: sound, light, drugs. By late 1965, rock had become much more sophisticated at the creative end: the mass audience just hadn't caught up. The kids going to Dave Clark Five concerts in Newark or Trenton could never have anticipated what filmmaker Antonioni was soon to do with the Yardbirds in *Blow-up*. These showgoers had never even heard the names of the drugs that music business personalities were toying with after hours, or the names of the exotic eastern instruments that the Rolling Stones, the Beatles and the Yardbirds were preparing to use on records-in-progress. The music-hall tunes creeping into the work of the Kinks, Alan Price (late of the Animals), and Ian Whitcomb would take a little getting used to. Rock musicians were known to be amusing in interviews, but not known to be instructive. Up to this point, rock, however exciting to teenage girls, was simply entertainment to the masses.

All at once, rock 'n' roll started to take on artistic respectability. The music industry released a series of projects through which pop music grew up. Bands like the Rolling Stones, which had once appeared to be little more than retread R&B with a scruffy British image, were suddenly writing all their own songs and searching out metropolitan shops for new records and instruments to spark their own development. The Kinks, led by the droll and dandyish Ray Davies, added harpsichords and social comment to their repertoire. The Beatles and the Yardbirds introduced raga elements to their music and still scored hits. Rock began to push aside folk and jazz as the preferred musical form at colleges.

First at university stations, then on larger commercial outlets, rock invaded FM radio formats where album tracks like those of Bob Dylan and the Stones ("Ballad of a Thin Man," "Going Home") could be played at length. Rock music and its creators were given more and more space in print. And its spokesmen were regarded as leaders, unofficial behavior guides for young people disenchanted by the Vietnam war and the evident hyprocrisy of conventional models. If music was recorded in an atmosphere of drug experimentation, fans assumed it would sound better if they listened while stoned.

The center of innovation seemed to shift from London to San Francisco, whose Haight-Ashbury district symbolized creative and personal freedom. Record companies inked Frisco rockers as quickly as they'd snapped up British acts a few years earlier. Scotsman Donovan Leitch, who'd had several hits but no mass impact, became an enormous star after making an album, *Sunshine Super-*

man (back by a San Francisco band called The Jagged Edge) in which he laced his lyrics with coded drug allusions and the names of the trendiest West Coast personalities. East Coast girls took their pet ducks and fled to hip San Francisco, where they lived in communes and spent all their time in the glow of colored strobes, incense, and "cannon" hashish pipes, listening to Dylan, the Doors, Jefferson Airplane, Jimi Hendrix, Cream, and Big Brother and the Holding Company with Janis Joplin.

Periodicals such as *Crawdaddy!* in the east and *Rolling Stone* in the west arose with the express purpose of unraveling the rockers' trippy lyrics, as well as reporting the pearls of wisdom that dropped from the mouths of the acid-ravished celebrities. The Beatles, the Beach Boys, and Eric Burdon meditated and uttered pronouncements instead of wisecracks. Cult bands like the Grateful Dead and Pink Floyd were signed to major labels. It was as if everyone were in college, but no one had to go to class. "Psychedelia" had created the stereotypical drop-out rock audience, the national answer to the San Francisco image, and music business was good. Many people took rock 'n' roll seriously, though few besides Paul Simon and Art Garfunkel denied that it was still fun.

The Return to Rock Simplicity—1968

In 1968, rock 'n' rollers divided into two opposing factions. Progressive rock, loved in hippie and neoclassical circles, had gotten too protracted and complicated in form for those who liked their music punchy and simple. The back-to-rock-basics crowd, which was most vocal in England, didn't advocate one specific style, but demanded simply that the music be straightforward. The reissue of Eddie Cochran's crunchy-sounding teen anthems, along with a spate of brilliant new 45s by the Who ("Magic Bus"), Manfred Mann ("Fox on the Run"), and Creedence Clearwater Revival ("Susie Q") suited their demands well enough.

There was room in the revivalists' philosophy for non-nonsense blues, as well. Most of the blue-eyed blues outfits of 1968—John Mayall's Bluesbreakers, the original Fleetwood Mac, the Savoy Brown Blues Band—kept themselves manageable as quartets or quintets, to retain as raw a sound as possible. Mayall whittled a formerly large band down to a four-piece, and Savoy Brown and Fleetwood Mac used supplementary instrumentation like piano or sax only on select dates and recording sessions. In America, the Paul Butterfield Blues Band retained a larger lineup.

There was room for singer-songwriters who kept their sound in perspective: Bob Dylan and his LP *John Wesley Harding,* with its Nashville spareness and history-evoking atmosphere, for instance. And there was room for hard rock, Michigan-style, with the Seeds, the Bob Seger System, and later the MC 5 and Brownsville Station, who made hard rock out of oldies revivals.

The split viewpoint in no way reflected on the health of the rock scene, for the industry was firmly behind rock—any rock that sold. A greater percentage of LP releases consisted of rock albums, and smoothly-run concerts were beginning to give live rock 'n' roll a better reputation than it had enjoyed until then. Performers who would become stadium headliners in the 70s, like the Who, Rod Stewart, the Kinks, Traffic, Neil Young, and Eric Clapton, had the chance to work their shows out in clubs and mid-size halls where there was enough audience contact to make the gradual road to stardom seem real.

In 1969, the phase of gradually-accelerated careers gave way to a boom-or-bust phenomenon. The idea that rock wasn't just communal, but tribal, seized ritual hold of the fans. A number of rock performers were elevated to a position above even that held by legendary jazzmen. The rockers stood just above the kings, in the vicinity of the gods. Promoters and publicists bandied the catch-words "superstar" and "supergroup," and press and radio went along, blowing the musicians' significance so far out of proportion that the rock stars themselves couldn't meet the pressures or expectations of their supplicants, the public. Many stars tried to escape into drugs. Albino Texas blues-rocker Johnny Winter, who'd been signed by Columbia Records in a wash of hype for a sum more than ten times what RCA had paid for Elvis Presley, has said recently that "I wanted to die." He survived the trip and he scaled down his tour schedule to lead a more private life, but he still feels his brush with drugs and death was close.

Supergroups, Woodstock, and the Near Burn-out of Rock

The fatalities of Winter's contemporaries, Jimi Hendrix, Brian Jones, Jim Morrison, and Janis Joplin, were among the busts. The boom that these people witnessed the beginning of had to do with the supergroups and rock festivals. As the Beatles, the Hollies, the Byrds, Cream, Buffalo Springfield and other old bands split up, new ones rose from their ashes, did one-off tours and albums, and held the fans in thrall. Crosby, Stills and Nash, joined later by Neil Young, became inflated with more spurious divinity than all of the equally-excellent bands they'd come from put together. The same thing happened with Blind Faith (Cream plus Traffic) and nearly happened with Ginger Baker's Air Force. Rock musicians, at least those with the best business sense, were suddenly command-ing unprecedented six- and seven-figure sums for recording contracts. These were sometimes signed more on the strength of their legends than on any de-liverable goods, and nine years later similar signings would help throw the record and concert businesses into turmoil with layoffs and bankruptcies. Back in 1969 and 1970, the supergroups produced several fine albums, notably *Deja Vu* by Crosby, Stills and company, and *Blind Faith*. But in-group bickering and a string of personal disasters kept these two bands from delivering follow-up studio albums.

Fans stayed happy by trekking to a series of outdoor tribal gatherings held during the summer of 1969. Outstanding among these were the Atlantic City Pop Festival and the Woodstock Festival, which took place from August 15 through 17 in upstate New York. At Woodstock, there was a minimal amount of feuding and discomfort, as when the Who's Pete Townsend threw his guitar at Abbie Hoffman when the activist tried to make the rock platform into a political platform, but the festival-goers got to frolic in the nude and returned home generally pleased, elated with the Who's performance of selections from the "rock opera" *Tommy* as the sun rose on the last morning of the festival. Other acts of the decade which performed were Blood, Sweat & Tears and Sly & the Family Stone, whose funky, exuberant style is said to have anticipated disco.

Cotillion Records released ten longplaying sides of Woodstock music. Although not all the artists were represented, enough contractual problems were resolved to make the *Woodstock* albums a document befitting the musical and communal power of the late 60s. *Woodstock* included the Who's excellent set, quality performances from CSN&Y, plus the guitar pyrotechnics of the flashy and ill-fated Jimi Hendrix. Similar live records followed from other festivals: Monterey Pop, the Big Sur Festival, and in the 70s the Mar y Sol Festival and the *Over the Rainbow* LP.

The rock festival survived into the late 70s with such events as the California Jams (I and II) and the Texas Jam, all featuring Ted Nugent and Aerosmith, plus the Havana Jam that brought a cultural exchange between the U.S. and Cuba. Despite these notable successes, rock festivals lost some of their tribal good vibes after 1969. One big reason for this was the Altamont Speedway debacle, which almost wiped out the spirit of Woodstock the same year in California. The Rolling Stones, agreeing to play a free concert at a festival that also featured Jefferson Airplane, recruited local Hell's Angels as security guards. The mood at the disastrous festival was one of life or death, and by the end of the concert one person had been born and three others had died. Somehow the birth didn't compensate for the knifing that took place right in front of the Pennebaker brothers' camera, and the film that resulted, *Gimme Shelter*, was a chronicle of a great 60s bust, an epitaph to flower power and the Summer of Love.

Old Trends to New—The Seventies

It's convenient but somewhat arbitrary to identify periods of musical development according to their decade. Aspects and trends of the 60s remained with rock 'n' roll in the subsequent years. Even if the heyday of Bob Dylan, Brian Wilson and the Beatles' *Sergeant Pepper's Lonely Hearts Club Band* has passed, its legacy remains. Pop lyrics still express more than moon/June banality in the work of writers who care. Songs of some albums still contain connecting threads of mood and meaning, like the concept albums of the 60s (Fleetwood Mac's conceptual *Future Games* and *Bare Trees* are 70s albums; so is John Martyn's *Bless the Weather*.) It is still considered desirable for musicians to control their work environment instead of letting it control them. Only the most crass business considerations like those behind the disposable disco phenomenon debase the better musicians' work. For 70s rockers seem less willing than their predecessors to take what comes. The experienced among them are less at the mercy of any one producer or manager than some of the bygone rock 'n rollers were. Good production is now sought out rather than submitted to. Karl Richardson and Albhy Galuten did not force the Bee Gees to adopt a dance beat for *Saturday Night Fever,* for the Bee Gees are capable of making more than one kind of saleable pop record.

The actual innovations of 70s rock had as much to do with look as with sound. Deep Purple and Emerson, Lake & Palmer treated rock 'n roll as theatre, with their smoke bombs, tossed daggers, and aerial piano stunts. The even more fanciful staging pioneered by England's David Bowie was paralleled in America at a national level by Alice Cooper, and at a local one in the decadent, glittery turbulence surrounding the New York Dolls (the sort of turbulence forecast a few years earlier in the night-city imagery of Lou Reed's notorious Velvet Underground). By the mid-70s, Kiss, Queen, and Pink Floyd had established truly eye-popping stage set-ups, visuals that gave the fans something more than a beat to respond to.

Heavy music became a concert mainstay as bands acquired larger, more potentially deafening P.A. systems. There was some justification for cranking up to such volumes. At the core of rock is the throb of the bass drum and bass guitar, and in heavy music this beat pulses at the pace of a giant heart. Fans who attended Robin Trower's 1975 stadium shows, for which the biggest-ever heavy-metal P.A. was used, got a bigger kick in the chest from the relentlessly-pounding bass drum than anything they'd ever felt at a rock concert. Musically, the heavy rock style of Led Zeppelin, Nugent, Trower and others was adapted from the blues revival style of the late 60s, augmented with technoflash guitar effects in the spirit of Jimi Hendrix. That same blues revival, whose sounds got crossed with country music, also inspired the 70s southern rock of the Allman Brothers, Elvin Bishop, Lynyrd Skynyrd and the Amazing Rhythm Aces, and the British-American boogie style of Foghat.

In the west, the country rock of the Eagles, Linda Ronstadt, Jackson Browne and Firefall superceded the loose-jam format of San Francisco rock. The related but somewhat funkier Doobie Brothers grew greatly in popularity after a big promotional push from their record company and years of touring and practice. New Orleans R&B was blended with the soul of Memphis and resurfaced in the popular and influential music of the Band (and its splinter acts, Levon Helm and Rick Danko), as well as musicians' favorites Little Feat—now gone like so many others. In the east, Humble Pie veteran Peter Frampton sold millions of live albums, and Bruce Springsteen rode the crest of a Spectorian rock revival, using lyrics derived from a bygone era. Paul McCartney soared and dipped with Wings. Jeff Lynne, late of the Move, guided ELO to stardom. Eric Clapton and Dire Straits copied J. J. Cale and Bob Dylan, and outsold their models. Genesis, Yes, Stories, U. K. and Steve Hackett brought quasi-classical backgrounds and, usually, electronic expertise to commercial rock. Elvis Presley, once the "King," died in 1977; mad mod drummer Keith Moon followed a year later.

By 1977, rock had become so big, and evidently so corporate, that there was a musical backlash. Tired of squinting through binoculars at tiny Boston, tiny Foreigner, tiny Elton John, and miniature Rolling Stones perched on tiny stages in tremendous coliseums, a substantial number of fans went in search of rock played from the heart in smaller halls and clubs. There they found Rockpile, George Thorogood and the Destroyers, Roy Loney and the Phantom Movers, the Flamin' Groovies, Susan, and the Knack. They even rediscovered Carl Perkins and Jerry Lee Lewis. The very spareness and straightforwardness of this music was a throwback to the simpler days of rock 'n' roll, and an antidote to the emotionless electronic pulse of that commercially potent, assembly-line offspring of rock called disco.

The fate of these new rock 'n rollers is in question as pop enters the 80s. Rockpile and the Knack may become too big to keep playing the modest-sized venues that helped make them special. At the same time, they are unlikely to draw as many customers as the Bee Gees, John Travolta, Olivia Newton-John and Frankie Valli did with the film/LP combinations *Saturday Night Fever* and *Grease,* the sort of productions that are necessary for really good business in the pop world. But from any but the most rigid business point of view, rock 'n' roll—genuine rock 'n' roll—is showing more signs of health now than it has for the past six years. The music has proven its detractors wrong by twenty-five-years-plus in their pessimistic predications of the 50s. It could well be headed for a second twenty-five.

R H

GREATEST EVENTS IN ROCK 'N ROLL HISTORY

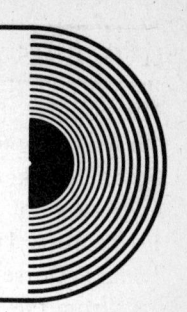

ALAN FREED ON THE AIR IN CLEVELAND

Alan Freed, the "Pied Piper of Rock 'n' Roll," made his mark in the history of rock when he first appeared on radio station WJW in Cleveland in 1951. This station was Freed's launching pad to national prominence, as well as a springboard for many black musicians into national acceptance. Freed began to play R&B records on his show, but in order to avoid the racial stigma then associated with the music he called his program "Moondog's Rock 'n' Roll Party," thereby inventing the term. The success of the music among his young white audience led Freed and a group of promoters to produce the first rock 'n roll stage shows. His first, in March 1962, was cancelled when 35,000 kids tried to pack into the 10,000-seat Cleveland Arena. In 1954, Freed moved his radio show and stage productions to New York, deejaying over WINS. His career soared through the 50s, with his production of three motion pictures (*Rock around the Clock, Rock, Rock, Rock,* and *Don't Knock the Rock*) as well as acceptance of composing credits from musicians in return for giving a song airplay ("Maybelline" with Chuck Berry). But his career was cut short during the payola scandals of 1960-62. There are those who claim to this day that Freed was the fall-guy for an entire industry.

BILL HALEY AND THE COMETS RECORD "ROCK AROUND THE CLOCK"

This overweight, middle-aged hillbilly rocker was the first idol of the rock era, predating the great Elvis himself. In 1955 his career and the direction of rock music was established with the recording of "Rock around the Clock," a recording which, by the early 70s, had sold more than 17 million copies. It was a career that began only four years earlier when Haley cut "Rockett 88" for Sam Phillips' Sun Records in 1951. The subsequent "Rock This Joint" sold what was then considered a walloping 75,000 copies. Haley's country and western feeling made rhythm and blues palatable for those early pop music tastes. His huge following overseas is often pointed to as an early stimulus for the English musical groundswell that came to a head in the 60s. It was this movement that eventually put Bill Haley out of the rock 'n' roll business.

ELVIS GOES ON TELEVISION

The popular story about Elvis going on Ed Sullivan and being filmed only from the waist up, following his release from the Army in 1960, was another one of Colonel Parker's publicity claims to fame. The appearance (three Sundays in a row) was not actually the first time Elvis had encountered the Eisenhower era TV censors. The camera cropping of Elvis's pelvis first occurred on Jimmy and Tommy Dorsey's "Stage Show" in January, 1956. For the Ed Sullivan shows, the "from the waist up" business was promoted to generate a bit of controversy and convince everyone that the rock 'n' roller still had a rebellious soul. Actually, his famed pelvic gyrations were learned from the frenzied swaying of the preacher in his First Assembly of God church choir. Sam Phillips, who had been producing Muddy Waters and other R&B artists, became convinced that a white singer doing black numbers would be an overnight sensation. Elvis proved him right, but Phillips will go down in history with the Indians selling Manhattan for twenty-four dollars when he sold Elvis's contract to RCA for a measly $35,000. In 1956, "Heartbreak Hotel," his first RCA recording, hit number one. In 1958 Elvis was inducted into the Army (a great piece of rock trivia: what was his enlistment number? answer: Private U.S. 53310761). His appearance on Ed Sullivan in 1960 marked the fact that "the King Was Back."

AMERICAN BANDSTAND HITS TV

This American classic television program that captivates the disco crowd today the way it enthralled the boppers in the 50s was the brainchild of two Philadelphia DJs, Bob Horn and Lee Stewart, in 1952. The show, originally called "Philadelphia Bandstand," was a series of interviews with pop artists, but, when it was discovered that the teenage audience would get to their feet and boogie, the dance show was born. The show pioneered the now common practice of lip-synching. It was when Dick Clark stepped on the scene that the show's success began to register. Clark, with his well-groomed Brylcreem image, was the perfect replacement for Horn, who was in trouble for drunken driving, had gotten himself nabbed in the payola scandals, and was subsequently dropped from the program. Within a year, Clark talked ABC into carrying the show nationwide as "American Bandstand." Clark, who singlehandedly created stars of the Frankie Avalon-Fabian-Chubby Checker breed, weathered his own payola investigations and came through them into the 60s unscathed.

TAMLA/ATLANTIC/STAX ARE BORN

These three, originally small, independent labels, the products of just a few individuals with a special love of black music and a keen eye for the marketplace, made rhythm and blues mass market. Up to this point R&B had been considered race music with limited sales. Tamla was Berry Gordy's first label, which began with a Smokey Robinson song in 1959. From 1961-62, Gordy, a songwriter who wrote between shifts on the Ford assembly line in Detroit, signed the Supremes, the Marvelettes, Martha & the Vandellas, the Temptations, and Marvin Gaye. Later, he would sign the Four Tops, Jr. Walker and the All Stars, the writing team of Holland, Dozier, Holland, and Stevie Wonder. Today his company, Motown, is the largest, solely-owned black company in America. Atlantic Records pioneered R&B. The company was first formed as early as 1947 when Ahmet Ertegun and Herb Abramson put together some money from the sale of Ahmet and his brother Nesuhi's collection of old jazz and blues records (15,000 of them). In 1953 Abramson split from the company and Jerry Wexler hopped aboard. This reorganized company recorded the Coasters, the Drifters, Clyde McPhatter and LaVern Baker in the 50s and the likes of Ray Charles, Aretha Franklin, and the Young Rascals in the 60s. It was with Atlantic that the famed writing team of Leiber and Stoller got their start, signing on as apprentices in 1956. Stax Records pioneered the Memphis Sound, founded by Jim Stewart, a bank teller and country fiddler and his sister, Estelle Axton. During the 60s, Jim and Estelle recorded Sam & Dave, Booker T and the MGs, Otis Redding, Isaac Hayes, and the Staple Singers. The stories of these three independents reveal the potential for success for the small label, which traditionally has been the source of new and creative music.

PHIL SPECTOR FORMS PHILLES RECORDS

Phil Spector, the "First Tycoon of Teen," is noted as the first great rock innovator in record production, as well as being the writer of such classics as "Spanish Harlem." His best-known work came in 1962 after he bought out his partners in Phil-Les Records, which he had formed with Lester Sill only one year earlier. He was the first to use overdubbing extensively. His "wall of sound" took record production to new levels of sophistication and complexity. He was the first to recruit session musicians (Leon Russell, Glen Campbell, for example). The Spector touch was indelibly placed on such artists as the Crystals, Ronettes, Righteous Brothers, as well as the Beatles. He was a millionaire before he was 21, and along with Brian Wilson is considered one of the bona fide rock 'n' roll eccentrics.

THE BEATLES COME TO AMERICA

What do you say when the most important group in rock 'n' roll history first visits a country smitten by Beatlemania? They were at an all-time high, with five records topping the Billboard Hot 100 chart ("Can't Buy Me Love," "Twist and Shout," "She Loves You," "I Want to Hold Your Hand," and "Please, Please Me.") With Brian Epstein at the helm, this group of English working-class kids from Liverpool led a musical explosion in mod England. This came to a head in February, 1964, when Epstein led the boys to the States. The event was perfectly staged by Epstein, who made sure they got appearances on the Ed Sullivan show for three weeks in a row. Their success filled a major void in the American teen pop scene and produced a flood of other English groups aping the Beatle image formula, the clothing, haircuts, etc.: Dave Clark Five, Jerry & the Pacemakers, the Searchers, Freddie and the Dreamers. The English invasion was in full gear.

DYLAN GOES ELECTRIC

It was at the Newport Folk Festival in July 1965 that the folksinging genius, Bob Dylan, turned his back on his devoted following and appeared on stage with an electric guitar and began playing rock 'n' roll, along with future members of the Band and the Paul Butterfield Blues Band. His followers split, and Dylan became a rock 'n' roll hero by default. As the story goes, Dylan was influenced to go electric by hearing the Animal's version of "House of the Rising Sun." During the years between 1961-64. Dylan was the penultimate folk singer of the Phil Ochs, Tom Paxton variety. There was the Peter, Paul & Mary hit of "Blowing in the Wind," as well as the activist anthemns like "A Hard Rain's Gonna Fall" and "The Times They Are a Changin'." John Hammond's discovery had proven to the music industry that there was a place for a folk singer on the record charts. Then the British revival of American rock 'n' roll caught Dylan's eye, and with the album *Bringing It All Back Home* he began his attempts to synthesize the two separate camps of rock and folk. Dylan would continue to change and search for years to come.

SGT. PEPPER'S LONELY HEARTS CLUB BAND

If one album can be sighted as an influential event in the history of rock 'n' roll, it would be *Sgt. Pepper's*. The prior release of *Rubber Soul* (December 1965) and *Revolver* (August 1966) revealed that the Beatles were exploring mysticism and music. These untrained musicians were writing songs more elaborate in structure. Meanwhile, George Martin was leading them through the paces of the early technical recording innovations. With the release of *Sgt. Pepper's* in 1967, popular music was revolutionized with cleverly overdubbed tapes made on a four-track machine.

MONTEREY

The Monterey Pop Festival was held on June 19, 1967, and besides being the first of the major rock concerts it was the first major presentation of the California music scene. It brought together the burgeoning acid-rock elements from the west with the folk-rock scene of the east. The Beach Boys were no longer the only spokesmen for this Pacific Ocean state. Produced by Lou Adler, Paul Simon and John Phillips, Monterey featured such artists as Jefferson Airplane, the Grateful Dead, Moby Grape, Janis Joplin, Big Brother & the Holding Company, Quicksilver Messenger Service, the Mamas & the Papas, as well as Jimi Hendrix and Otis Redding. Adler would go on to manage Carole King and start

Dunhill and eventually Ode Records. Monterey would always be pointed out as the first sign that a major rock concert could be pulled off. Woodstock would later smash all concert promotion restrictions. Monterey set the stage.

FM GOES ROCK

By 1967 more and more stations were sprinkling cuts from albums along with the standard Top 40 fare. As a result of a 1966 FCC ruling, which declared that FM and AM could no longer simulcast, FM radio was suddenly open territory for all comers—rock radio won out. Pioneered by three radio personalities, B. Mitchell Reed, Murray the K (Kaufman), and Tom Donahue, FM radio proved that it was a viable alternative to the playlist 2½-minute ditty programming of AM. Kaufman, after leaving AM radio because of the enforcement of playlists, first toured with the Beatles and then joined RKO's WOR-FM in New York, where he experimented with long versions of new music and mixing and molding three and four-cut sets. Meanwhile, on the west coast, B. Mitchell Reed, once a well-listened-to member of the WMCA Good Guy staff, set up shop on L.A.'s first album-oriented program on WFWB. In 1967 Reed met Tom Donahue and together they convinced Metromedia to open up progressive FM stations in L.A. (KMET) and San Francisco (KPPC).

WOODSTOCK/ALTAMOUNT

It is said that the flower generation only bloomed for the four months between Woodstock (July-August 1969) and Altamont (December 1969). If Woodstock showed that goodness and peace could come out of rock music's alliance with the anti-war, love generation, Altamont showed that there was an equally powerful brutal subculture at work. Woodstock was actually held in Walkill, N. Y., a small town over fifty miles away from the arts community of Woodstock. Half a million people crammed the fields of Max Yasgur's farm to prove that, despite the rain, mud and other inconveniences, they could have a good time. For at least those few days the social possibilities of the counter culture became real, while such acts as Crosby, Stills, Nash & Young, Jefferson Airplane, Grateful Dead, Jimi Hendrix, Canned Heat, Country Joe and the Fish, Joni Mitchell, Mountain, The Who, Janis Joplin, and Richie Havens played day and night. Altamont was to be a gift, a free concert from the Rolling Stones to America. But the concert was mis-managed and the Stones misguided and uninformed about the American Hell's Angels. Altamont resulted in many beatings and the stabbing to death of Meredith Hunter by the motorcycle gang who had been hired to "police" the affair.

DEATHS OF JIMI HENDRIX, JANIS JOPLIN, JIM MORRISON, BRIAN JONES, DUANE ALLMAN

In the two-year span between 1969 and 1971, five major members of the rock community died as a result of their excesses. Jimi Hendrix, Janis Joplin, Jim Morrison, Brian Jones and Duane Allman all epitomized the reckless fast pace of the rock musician pursuing his own image of fame and fortune and succumbing to drugs and booze. Meanwhile, Altamont was happening and the Beatles were breaking up. These were hard times for the rock generation. Brian Jones died of a supposed asthma attack on his A. A. Milne estate in England—he had been failing for a number of years, an acid burn-out who was allegedly being moved out that year (1969) from the Rolling Stones' headlines by Jagger and Richard. Jones had founded the group, and believed in the simple R&B style while the others toyed with psychedelia. Joplin died of a heroin overdose at the age of 27 in Los Angeles. Hendrix died in London, also at the age of 27, two weeks earlier on September 18. Jim Morrison died in July 1971 of a supposed heart attack. Duane Allman died on the verge of superstardom in a motorcycle accident on October 29, 1971. During those years rock 'n' roll suffered fatal losses from which it still hasn't recovered.

DISCO

A musical foster child of R&B, disco first made its mark in the gay clubs of 1974 when the Hues Corporation recorded their "Rock the Boat," followed by George McCrae's "Rock Your Baby," and Gloria Gaynor's "Never Can Say Goodbye." Meanwhile, in the Miami area, the same sound was being bred in the large numbers of clubs and cabarets, creating a Miami sound characterized by KC & the Sunshine Band on the TK label. The music was easy to dance to and sparked a new interest in stylized dancing that had lost ground to shapeless and loose boogeying during the 60s. The music industry, ever anxious to hop on and take advantage of a new trend, saw the disco boom as an opportunity to break records outside of radio stations. Dance programs returned to the television screens, and with the success of Robert Stigwood's 1977 *Saturday Night Fever*, disco became the sound of the late 70s. The Bee Gees soundtrack from the movie became the largest-selling record ever, selling 32 million units around the world. On March 18, 1977, the group did what only the Beatles had done before them—they captured four of the top 5 discs on the Hot 100 charts ("Love Is Thicker than Water," "Emotion," "Stayin' Alive," "Night Fever").

PUNK GOES BACK TO THE BASICS

With the glitter and glamour of disco all the rage, and the limousine-cocaine bug biting most of the rockers of the 60s, a new movement, or wave, was needed to shake up traditional rock 'n' roll. Punk rock and the broader based new wave sought a return to the roots and more straightforward rock. By 1976, the underground musicians of New York and London were making themselves heard. With instrumentation reminiscent of the 60s British explosion, with homage to such precursors as Lou Reed, the MC5, and David Bowie, the punks, led by the leaders of vulgarity and the safety-pin/razor set, the Sex Pistols, kicked the rock establishment on its ass. The Sex Pistols joined and then left two labels in 1977. Although they were banned on the concert circuit, and their "God Save the Queen" was banned on the radio, the record climbed the U. K. charts. In true "punk" style, Johnny Rotten, the group's leader, left the group, rejecting the publicity and hype—giving punk a death blow. But the lesson had been learned by the major labels. They picked up on the best of the new wave and produced stars like Blondie, Elvis Costello, Graham Parker, Talking Heads, Patti Smith, and Joe Jackson. With a bit of production and marketing, these underground characters made the charts, and while another subculture was being gobbled up by industry, a second limousine/cocaine rock establishment was born.

MP

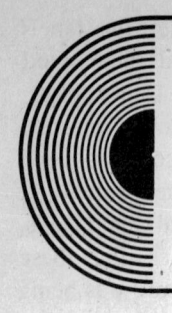

BEST AMERICAN RECORDING STUDIOS 1979

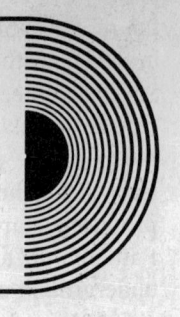

(in alphabetical order)

A&R STUDIOS, New York

As a result of the production success of co-owner Phil Ramone with such megatalents as Paul Simon and Billy Joel, A&R has gained the reputation of being one of the top examples of the New York City sound. The studio was originally established twenty years ago by Ramone and a partner simply to make demos in a small studio modified for 3-track recording. Skyscraper construction forced them out of their first facility, but luckily they were simultaneously offered a ready-made facility in the old CBS Records building. They are there to this day, although two additional studios have since been added in a building a couple blocks away. A&R is run today by Art Ward, former manager of the group called the Honeydreamers. Ward is president, and Don Frey, a former senior sound mixer at NBC, is acting as vice president of operations. Noted for its versatility, A&R does both advertising jingles and LP recording. However, it is the record work that has gained the studio its name. Most recently, it was responsible for Billy Joel's *52nd Street,* Quincy Jones's *The Wiz,* and the latest releases by Phoebe Snow, Kenny Loggins, and Steely Dan.

A&M RECORDING STUDIO, Los Angeles

Often called the studio that Herb Alpert built, A&M is noted (along with Atlantic Studios) as the leading major-label, in-house recording facility. It opened with eight tracks in 1968, inside the sound studio that Charlie Chaplin first built for movie sound, and is often credited with a "classic" sound. Technologically the studio has stayed a step ahead of its time, and is the home of one of the few existing 32-track digital 3M machines. Much of the credit for the studio's success, both musically and financially, is given to Alpert, who, as a businessman and musician, can straddle the individual requirements of these often two different worlds. It is the studio where the Village People, Dolly Parton, Barry Manilow, Gladys Knight, Chicago, Kris Kristofferson, and Rita Coolidge do much of their recording.

ATLANTIC STUDIOS, New York

It was from Atlantic Studios that Neshui and Ahmet Ertegun and Jerry Wexler launched their legendary R&B label in the 50s, beginning in 1959. Designed by producer Tom Dowd, the studio originally had one room and two mastering rooms, but was renovated in 1975 by adding a second studio, another remix room, and tape duplicating facilities. In 1970, the studio was sold (along with Atlantic Records) to Warner Communications, but all involved, excluding Wexler, remained as officers. A rather simple, straight-ahead studio, it is noted for its special and so-considered "unduplicated" sound. This is the home of the Tom Dowd sound, where many of the recordings that made Ray Charles and Aretha Franklin famous were made. More recently, Atlantic was responsible for Carly Simon's *Spy* LP, the work of Foreigner, Chaka Khan, Roxy Music, and others. It was also the home of one of the first MCI consoles, the first of the standardized boards, which, ten years ago, put an end to the dead-end trend of individually customized console equipment.

CARIBOU RANCH, Nederland, Colorado

Caribou Ranch was the brainchild of James Guerico, former bass player for Chad and Jeremy, and Frank Zappa, as well as producer for the Buckinghams, Blood, Sweat & Tears and Chicago. It was opened in 1972 with the concept that a studio was needed that would offer an opposite environment to the Los Angeles/New York urban style. The Caribou facility was originally a horse ranch in the 1930s, and sits on 3,000 acres at the foot of the Rocky Mountains. The buildings are rustic log cabins, built of cedar, pine and oak, and each contain grand pianos and antiques. The studio itself is a converted barn. Caribou is responsible for most of the recordings by Chicago, as well as work by Waylon Jennings, Tony Orlando, Elton John, and the recent Beach Boys *L.A. Light* LP.

CHEROKEE STUDIOS, Los Angeles

Founded by the Robb Brothers, who were formerly a recording and television act with Dick Clark in the late 1960s, Cherokee was originally founded in Chatsworth, California in 1971 as a 4-track studio. By 1974 it was 24-track, and moved later that year into the former MGM Records studio in Hollywood. Cherokee is noted for its exclusive clientele and tight security. It is said they only select the most elite acts, and that they cater almost exclusively to foreign artists. They have no staff engineers. Only people directly involved are admitted to the compound, which, according to reports, is rather plush and customarily offers wine and fruit in the lounges. It has one very large studio that can hold up to fifty strings easily; a mixdown studio; and another regular sized studio. Cherokee possibly has the largest selection of vintage microphones in the world. It is noted as the studio where most of Rod Stewart's recordings are made, as well as the studio for many LPs by Barbra Streisand, David Bowie, and most recently the Cars' *Candy-O*.

CRITERIA RECORDING STUDIO, Miami, Florida

Often erroneously called the studio that the Bee Gees built, Criteria Recording has been at its present location in Florida since 1954, when it was opened by owner Mack Emerman. Emerman was involved in mobile recording of local jazz musicians as a hobby by night, after working with his father's candy business by day. Today, Criteria is in the process of opening a Criteria West facility in Hollywood, California, as well as a new wing in the Miami facility which will be called Super Studio and will have all digital MCI equipment. Part of the success of Criteria has been this close affiliation with the Miami-based manufacturer, MCI, which revolutionized the recording business with its standardized consoles, but also has been noted as a studio that really knows how to treat an artist well. Visiting artists are often given beach mansions to live in, and free access to Emerman's yacht. Criteria's success is often pointed to as the cause of a recent boom in the south Florida recording business, an explosion that has led many to believe that along with Nashville, New York, and Los Angeles, Miami now stands as an industry center. Of course, the nine gold singles in the late 70s by the Bee Gees was a major stimulus for this success; all had been recorded at Criteria. This success brought the big acts down to Florida; producers followed the hits to Mack Emerman's door like lemmings following the sea. Criteria has most recently been responsible for: *Saturday Night Fever*, by the Bee Gees; the Allman Brothers Band's *Enlightened Rogues;* the Eagles' *Hotel California;* Andy Gibb's *Shadow Dancing;* and Crosby, Stills, and Nash's *CSN.*

ELECTRIC LADY, New York

Electric Lady Studios, on Eighth Street in New York's Greenwich Village, was originally built in September 1969 by guitar virtuoso Jimi Hendrix and Michael Jeffreys. Jimi made it for his personal use, but died within a year. Jeffreys had it for another year, but died in an airplane crash. The state then took over, and the studio was run by appointee managers until litigation problems were taken care of. As a result of bad management and no regular maintenance, the studio—considered the most sophisticated of its kind—decayed badly. Things changed for the better when Hal and Allen Selby bought it in October, 1977. When the studio was first opened, it became one of the first to use 24 tracks, and under Hendrix's direction it even toyed with early 2-track digital machines. Today, under Selby's direction, it is again in the forefront of professional audio technology, and is noted for its constant use as a "contained" studio, where it is turned over for periods of months to a single act or artist. Electric Lady is also noted as the home of Eddie Kramer, who designed the studio's original console, and who was the producer for Hendrix, Led Zeppelin, early Stones, Aerosmith, and Kiss. The late-60s murals are still on the wall, reflecting the studio's concern with its tradition, but all the rooms have since been done over in wood and brown tones, which changed the atmosphere which was often referred to as early-dungeon. It has been responsible for the latest work by Kiss, Stanley Clark, Peter Frampton, Foghat, Chuck Mangione, Joni Mitchell, and David Bowie.

FILMWAYS/HEIDER, San Francisco and Los Angeles, California

Quite simply the largest independent recording studio in the United States, with four studios in the San Francisco operation and ten studios in Hollywood, Heider studios was originally started by Wally Heider in 1964. Originally, Heider was a lawyer and musician who started his business by adding a little trailer behind his car—his first mobile recording unit. Today, the corporation, which has been bought out by Filmways Inc. (International Pictures, *Hollywood Squares*, etc.) has four mobile control rooms with 48 tracks in each one. The rooms in each city vary in size and style from a former aircraft hanger (which has held the entire Los Angeles Philharmonic with 150 musicians) to a room that just takes one or two musicians. While most of the credit for this success goes to Wally Heider, whose understanding of the business as well as the music has set a pattern for many other successful studio owners throughout the country, it was the early affiliation with such emerging talents as Crosby, Stills, Nash and Young that sent the small studio on the road to prosperity. The recordings of the Rolling Stones' *Get Your Ya Yas Out* and Cream's *Wheels on Fire* pushed Heider's studio even further ahead. Most recently, Filmways/Heider was responsible for the *Grease* soundtrack, Peter Frampton's *Where I Should Be* and *Comes Alive,* almost all of John Denver's recordings, as well as recent work by Kenny Loggins and Paul McCartney and Wings.

HIT FACTORY, New York

The recent interest in the New York sound is often attributed to the special success formula of the Hit Factory, which was originally opened by songwriter and producer Jerry Ragovoy in 1969. It was later taken over by former Record Plant New York stockholder Eddy Germano, who ushered in renovation as well as a third room. In terms of physical uniqueness, each studio is on a separate floor with a lounge and closed-circuit TV security. The carpets are changed every six months, and the colors change to fit the personalities of those working in the studio at the time. Artists who have recently recorded at the Hit Factory include: The Roaches, Talking Heads, the Village People, Meat Loaf, Hall and Oates, Patti Smith, Sara Dash, and Felix Cavaliere.

HOUSE OF MUSIC, Orange, New Jersey

The House of Music is often called the great New York studio that somehow ended up in New Jersey. It is owned by Charles Conrad and Stephen Golfas, and first took off when Conrad recorded Blind Faith on an 8-track machine in 1971. By 1975 it was a full 24-track facility, and a second room was added in 1978. Located on seven acres of land, the studio is actually an addition to the Conrad home. There's a barn, pool, pond, and river, and is noted as a warm, homey place, private but close to Manhattan. It is a favorite of many New York studio musicians like the components of Stuff, David Spinoza, as well as Patti Smith, Meat Loaf, and Kool and the Gang.

KENDUN STUDIOS, Los Angeles

Kendun Studios is the brainchild of Kent Duncan, who started in the business as a disc mastering engineer at the age of 25. In 1971 he built his first eight-track room, but his business didn't take off until Stevie Wonder heard about his mastering abilities and had him help master much of the *Innervisions* album. The success of Kendun illustrates how one landmark recording can build a small studio into a giant. Duncan shrewdly sent five hundred copies of his mastering "feat" all over Los Angeles, and the studio took off over night. So much so that this year Kendun will gross $4-million. The studio has over 230 gold and platinum records to its name. Known as a service-oriented company, and also known as the most expensive studio around, Kendun's reputation has been built on its staff producers, and on its ability to get an act in and out on time. It has been responsible for all of Steve Martin's LPs, Chuck Mangione's *Children of Sanchez*, as well as records by Bob Dylan, Heart, Frank Zappa, REO Speedwagon, and Chick Corea.

MEDIA SOUND, New York

The parent studio for several major New York recording facilities, Media Sound is a lasting offspring itself of the Woodstock festival of the summer of 1969. Originally owned and operated by Joel Rosenman, John Roberts, Harry Hirsch and Bob Walters, it was financed out of the capital raised by Rosenman and Roberts from Woodstock. For six months the foursome was hunting for the proper locale when they happened upon a Baptist church on 57th Street, a unique situation that has made it one of the more original of the New York brand of recording studio. The group started out with two 12-track studios and one eight-track room and went to 16-track and added a fourth room in the early 70s. They are presently in the early stages of planning a fifth room, with Rosenman and Roberts still in control and Hirsch (Soundmixers) and Walters (Power Station) having long since gone off on their own. The main room of "Media" has the old world charm of a small cathedral with buttresses, candelabra and the original woodwork, as well as a ceiling that is thirty-five feet high. Another room is octagonal shape, designed in cypress wood. "Media" is noted by many for its almost guild operation—all employees start at the bottom where they gain a full picture of what the studio business is about, meanwhile experiencing from the bottom the "service" nature of the studio game. Media Sound has been responsible for much of the work by Barry Manilow, the Ramones, Blondie, Barbra Streisand's *Songbird* LP, James Taylor's *Flag,* as well as recent work by Steve Khan, Aerosmith, Eileen Foley, and Desmond Child & Rouge.

MUSCLE SHOALS SOUND STUDIOS, Sheffield, Alabama

A major recording studio in Alabama? It seems strange, but it is true. As a result of producing by Jerry Wexler and a long string of hit records by Bob Dylan, the Rolling Stones, the Allman Brothers Band and numerous Atlantic R&B artists, Muscle Shoals' laid-back Alabama sound has contributed much to the recent history of music. To a large degree, it is a story of a particular rhythm section, the Muscle Shoals Rhythm Section, which also has placed its stamp on many landmark recordings. First started as Fame Studios and Publishing by Richard Hall in 1958 (who produced the Osmonds and Mac Davis), the studio brought together some of the best rhythm section players, all of whom became part owners in the facility. The rhythm section includes Jimmy Johnson on guitar, Barry Beckett on keyboards, Roger Hawkins on drums, and David Hood on bass. In 1970, the studio had a building which was part of a cemetery; caskets were actually stored there. Later they were in a venetian blind factory. Finally, in April 1978, they moved to their present location in a 31,000 square foot building on the Tennessee river. It has two studios with a third being planned and room for four or five, along with lounges, offices, and full recreation areas. Most recently, Muscle Shoals has been responsible for Bob Dylan's *Slow Train Coming,* Lynyrd Skynyrd's *First and Last, The Jukes,* by Southside Johnny and the Asbury Dukes, and recent records by Dr. Hook, the Amazing Rhythm Aces, Kate Taylor, and Joan Baez.

POWER STATION, New York

A major studio can be born overnight. This seems to be the case with the Power Station in New York, which only started in full operation in November, 1977. The facility was started by two individuals from Media Sound, Tony Bongiovi and Bob Walters. A two-room facility, the Power Station features control rooms that are identical, studios designed with no parallel surfaces, and a special "whispering dome" in Studio A. In terms of expansion, the Power Station is its own building and has an entire third floor where they presently park their cars. For the time being they seem to have *the* sound, producing all three disco hits by Chic, Blondie's newest release, *Eat to the Beat,* the Kinks' *Low Budget,* Ian Hunter's *You're Never Alone with a Schizophrenic,* Foghat's *Stone Blue,* as well as recent work by Bruce Springsteen and Carlene Carter.

RECORD PLANT, Los Angeles, San Francisco, New York

The Record Plant is a perfect example of how a name studio can proliferate and how the studio business becomes big industry. Started by Gary Kelgun and Tom Wilson in the 60s, Record Plant, under the management of Chris Stone, made its name with artists Jimi Hendrix and Frank Zappa. Wilson was a producer for Columbia, responsible for Bangladesh. In 1968 the New York facility was opened up, but one year later it was sold to Televisions Communications Co., which later sold it to Kinney, which became Warner Communications. Apparently the company, which originated in Sausalito, California, sold its New York facility, because it saw a market in Los Angeles but didn't have the money to make the move. The L.A. space was opened in December, 1969. There are now four rooms in Los Angeles, two in Sausalito, and five rooms in New York. New York is not affiliated with Los Angeles: New York is Record Plant Studios Ltd.; the L.A. and Sausalito facilities are the Sausalito Music Factory Inc., Doing Business as Record Plant. Record Plant suffered a setback several years ago as a result of the deaths of Gary Kelgun and Tom Wilson, both in 1977. Kelgun drowned in his swimming pool; Wilson died at the age of 41 of a heart attack only eight months later. Kelgun will be remembered as the man who brought the concept of the "living room" to the studio business. Jacuzzi's are a main feature in many Record Plant rooms. The L.A. facility is also the home of one of the few 32-track digital machines. With Chris Stone at the helm, the Record Plant has produced numerous hit records in recent years, including Fleetwood Mac's *Rumours,* McCartney's *London Town,* Donna Summer's *Love and More,* the Blues Brothers' *Briefcase Full of Blues,* as well as work by the Eagles, Moody Blues, and Robin Williams.

SIGMA SOUND STUDIOS, Philadelphia and New York

Sigma Sound Studios was built on the combination of owner Joe Tarsia, who was chief engineer with Cameo Parkway, having worked with everyone from Chubby Checker to Bobby Rydel, and the success team of Philadelphia International's Gamble and Huff, in 1971. New rooms opened at three separate studios in Philadelphia, keeping pace with the growing national acceptance of the "Sound of Philadelphia." A New York facility was opened in June, 1976. Recent hits have been produced at the Sigma facilities by the Village People, Ashford and Simpson, the O'Jays, Teddy Pendergrass, and McFadden & Whitehead. Most recently it made its mark with the work of DJ disco producer Tom Moulton, who is credited with the original editing of pop hits into long disco versions of the same music.

Sigma Sound Studios

SOUND 80, Minneapolis, Minnesota

Sound 80 is a perfect example of how studio equipment manufacturers help create studios of state-of-the-art excellence in their backyard. Sound 80 is often called the testing ground for equipment innovations by the nearby 3M Company. It was where the earliest 3M digital experiments were carried out, and is noted for producing top-notch engineerings like Tom Jung. Sound 80 actually began in the living room of owner Herb Pilhofer, who later moved to his basement with his 8-track machine. Sound 80 moved to its present location, which has two studios, in 1971. Today it has two other studios on the fortieth floor of a nearby office building. The technical excellence of Sound 80 has brought some of the biggest names of the music business to this arctic northern city. The Doobie Brothers, Cat Stevens, Bob Dylan, and others have recorded there.

SOUNDMIXERS, New York

Another New York studio that was born out of a splinter from Media Sound in New York. President and founder Harry Hirsch was a former partner in Media Sound who went off on his own when he figured New York needed yet another big studio complex. Opened in May, 1977, Soundmixers originally had only one room; today, it has four. All the studios are MCI 24-track and are completely automated, with complete sound services able to hand films, video, as well as records. Soundmixers is a favorite of Bob James, Kenny Loggins, Average White Band, Peter Brown, and Peter Tosh.

Soundmixers

UNIVERSAL RECORD, Chicago

One of the leading advertising studios in the country, Universal Record is noted as the leading studio in the midwest and is becoming, of late, more and more involved with making hit LPs. Founded by two audio engineers, Bill Putnam and Bernie Clapper, the two would later split, with Putnam going to Los Angeles to found United Western Studio, and with Clapper moving the studio to its present location. Universal made its move for the top in the late 60s, under the direction of Murray Allen, who opened four studios, two mixing theaters, and an editing room. Three of the studios are in the Prudential Plaza. Today, Universal has ten separate rooms including one studio that is 24 feet high and 54 X 54 feet, and can hold as many as 100 musicians. The punchy sound of Universal is sometimes credited as being the forerunner of the disco beat, a sound that was originally perfected for advertising jingle work. Most recently, artists like Tyrone Davis, Ramsey Lewis, Aerosmith, Shirley Bassey, Tower of Power, and the Blues Brothers have recorded at Universal in the "Windy City."

VILLAGE RECORDER, Los Angeles

Considered by some as the ultimate in elegant studio design as well as privacy, Village Recorder is the home of the new Studio D, built in 1978 for the exclusive use of Fleetwood Mac, which used it for the entire year to produce its recent *Tusk* LP. Village was started by George Hormel along with Dick La Palm and Edwin A. Mathews, who share the company presidency on a rotating basis, in 1968. From the beginning the studio was designed to hold four main rooms. There were two studios by the end of 1968 and three by the end of 1969. Studio D, which cost $1.5-million, was conceived and completed within ten weeks. Village was the first studio to use 16-track dolby. Besides keeping up with state-of-the-art equipment, Village has always been in the forefront of studio luxury design. They have several times demolished one room to make an entirely new one. They can project images on a backwall of a studio for a visually pleasant atmosphere. Surfaces are made to be changed. They are louvered so that they can be opened or closed to change acoustic response. Studio D is done in English wood and oak, with a wood called conzolo alvare, from South America, which is the densest wooden surface possible. The lounge has panels from an old English library. There's an isolation room that has an arched stained glass window that came out of a French cathedral. Besides the recent work by Fleetwood Mac, Village has been responsible for Frank Zappa's *Sheik Yer Bouti,* Steely Dan's *Aja* and *Royal Scam*, Neil Diamond's *Beautiful Noise*, the Band's *Last Waltz,* as well as Supertramp's *Breakfast in America.*

WOODLAND SOUND STUDIO, Nashville

There wouldn't be a Nashville sound without Woodland Sound Studio. Founded in 1967 by Glen Snoddy, who originally was chief engineer for Columbia's

Acuff-Rose Recording in Nashville, Woodland began as a four-track facility in an old Nashville theater. Today it is owned by the Crescent Company, which is a holding company in Nashville involved in everything from banking to bowling alleys. The studios are simple but noted for their attention to detail and quality. Woodland has been responsible for Kansas' *Point of No Return,* Neil Young's *Comes the Time,* as well as Charlie Daniels' *Million Mile Reflections.*

MP

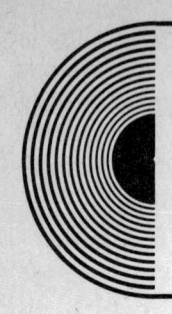

ROCK'S MOST COLLECTIBLE DISCS

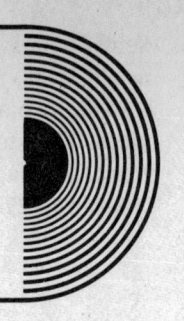

Early in 1954, delivery-truck driver Elvis Aaron Presley dropped by the Memphis Recording Studio at 706 Union Avenue in the seedy downtown area. For a four-dollar fee, the teenage Presley cut a Sun disc. Its title was "That's When Your Heartaches Begin" (later the flip side of "All Shook Up" on RCA). The single was backed by the old chestnut of "My Happiness." The record was then given to Presley's mother, Gladys, as a surprise gift.

Outside the Presley family, nobody has seen or heard this record, save those present at Sun that historic Saturday afternoon. Such a disc represents the ultimate in Presleymania, and would no doubt stand as the rock 'n' roll collector's dream, albeit not one that will likely take form in reality. Such one-of-a-kind items must be placed in the Priceless category. Other records, though, manufactured and released on a commercial basis, can be compared and now have had prices established.

The pricing rule of thumb is determined by the artist's collectability (the interest in his/her/their discs) and the number of copies available on a first-issue basis. With this last thought in mind, here are the fifteen most valuable rock records being sought today:

1. **"My Bonnie," by Tony Sheridan and the Beat Brothers.**
   Decca 31382 $800 Mint

This was really the Beatles when they were an unknown backup band for an English Elvis imitator. Former drummer Pete Best (now a Liverpool baker) is featured on this pre-Ringo session. The above price refers to the regular-release, black Decca single; the pink promo (DJ) copy is worth less than half, which is a big drop in value but not enough to cause the owner of a Decca DJ disc to trade it for a stack of Peter Frampton LPs. The intro to this disc features a slow beginning as opposed to the rapid intro of the MGM version (MGM 13213). The Decca single is a must for any Beatle collector who seeks their *complete* recording efforts.

2. **Yesterday and Today, by the Beatles**
   Capitol LP 2553(S) $500 Mint

Five hundred dollars for a million-selling album? The catch here is that this is the mint price paid for the infamous "Butcher Cover," a 1966 pop-art experiment by the Fab Four whose efforts appalled Capitol Records executives. Supposedly, less than 1,000 butchers hit the racks, and even they were yanked within hours. The next 8,000 albums were then pasted over with the common, staid trunk photo. A butcher picture beneath the white trunk photo can be detected by dark arcs along the right and left sides near the bottom of the front picture. Steaming is the only way to remove the top layer, and it's *very* difficult to do well.

3. **The Beatles and Frank Ifield (On Stage), by the Beatles and Frank Ifield**
   Vee Jay LP 1085(S) $500 Mint

Like every other company that could capitalize on pre-Capitol Beatle tapes, Vee Jay released this as their fourth—and least successful—Beatle album. A mono copy of this rarity is worth less than half of the stereo version. Still, don't expect to run across a pile of either at your local thrift store. Everyone knows the Beatles, to be sure. But Frank Ifield? He is remembered for his brief appearance in the spotlight in 1962 with a Top 5 single, "I'll Remember You," issued, naturally, on Vee Jay Records.

4. **"The Surfer Moon," by Bob and Sheri**
   Safari 101 $300 Mint

For a while, rumor had it that this was really the Beach Boys under an assumed name. After all, it *was* written and produced by Brian Wilson and *did* feature the Beach Boys' old L.A.-area address on the label. In reality, Bob was a Hawthorne High (Calif.) football buddy of Brian Wilson, and Sheri was Bob's girl friend at the time. The then-nameless Beach Boys played in the background on "The Surfer Moon"—a garage single—and the tune appeared in all its revised glory two years later on the Beach Boys' *Surfer Girl* album. The ultimate pre-popularity Brian Wilson/Beach Boys find.

5. **"Milkcow Blues Boogie," by Elvis Presley**
   Sun 215 $200 Mint

This was Elvis's third—and poorest-selling—Sun single, sure to escalate over his other four Suns because of its scarcity. "Milkcow Blues Boogie" begins with a slow, bluesy lead-in. Elvis then calls a halt to the proceedings. "Hold it, fellas," he exclaims. "That don't *move* me. Let's get real, real *gone* for a change!" Presley then switches to a white-hot rockabilly tempo which shows all the raw talent he would carry over to his more sophisticated and polished RCA product.

6. **"That's All Right," by Elvis Presley**
   Sun 209 $200 Mint

Elvis hid in a movie theater the day this single was first aired on Memphis radio. The timid Presley feared people would jeer his debut commercial effort, an upbeat Arthur Crudup blues song. But the song quickly became a local hit (Sun supposedly pressed about 7,000 copies). Try to find a clean copy today.

7. "Movie Magg," by Carl Perkins
   Flip 501 $200 Mint

Of Perkins' early work, the top prize is his obscure "Movie Magg," a 1955 rockabilly number cut for the small, independent Tennessee label called Flip. (Neither the song nor the label saw major commercial success.) Like Elvis, Carl Perkins found fame on Memphis's Sun label. Late in 1955, Carl attended a dance and heard a nearby man admonish another, "Don't step on my blue suede shoes!" That night, Perkins, jotted down those simplistic but now-immortal lines on a brown shopping bag. "Blue Suede Shoes" later became one of Sun's biggest chart hits. Carl's first Sun single was "Let the Jukebox Keep on Playing," fairly obscure and another must for the Perkins collector.

8. ("Do" The Screw," by the Crystals
   Philles 111 (DJ only) $200 Mint

Production genius Phil Spector wanted to bail out of his contract with partner Lester Sill (Philles = Phil + Les). Spector owed Sill another Crystals single, so Spector carried through. The result, however, was a purposely bad record of handclaps and a bass, punctuated by the Crystals and Spector's attorney saying "Do the screw!" The ultimate Spector/Philles 45.

9. "Zoot Suit," by the High Numbers
   Fontana 480 $200 Mint

The Who stand as one of the few surviving major forces of the mid-60s British invasion. Their first manager disliked the name Who and insisted the quartet call itself the High Numbers. His rationale was that there would be a strong identity with the group when it reached the "high numbers" of the British singles charts. But "Zoot Suit" failed, and the manager was fired. (He later returned to his former job as a doorknob manufacturer.) Peter Townshend then took on new management, and once again the group became the Who. Their next waxing was "I Can't Explain," and the London lads were on their way.

10. "Good Rockin' Tonight," by Elvis Presley
    Sun 210 $150 Mint

This was Presley's follow-up to the locally successful "That's All Right." The tune was originally done by bluesman Wyonie Harris in 1948 at the time Elvis was entering his adolescence. Roy Brown, best known for his Top 40 hit of "Let the Four Winds Blow" in 1957, penned "Good Rockin' Tonight." In the genre of black slang, the good rockin' had nothing at all to do with dancin'.

11. "That'll Be the Day," by Buddy Holly
    Decca EP 2575 $150 Mint

Avid Holly fans are aware of Buddy's early, country-flavored Decca discs. His three pre-Crickets sessions in Nashville yielded a pair of 1956 singles. A year later, the Crickets hit big with an electrified "That'll Be the Day." Decca then issued Holly's earlier, less sophisticated version in hopes of capturing some sales spinoff. While the original Decca album is also a rare item ($100-125), it's the Decca EP that takes the top prize here. Of course, the accompanying cardboard cover is a necessity, as it is with any EP or album.

12. "Stay Close to Me," by Lou Giordano
Brunswick 55115 $150 Mint

Recent efforts to track down Mr. Giordano have proven fruitless. So why should an obscure artist—and an equally obscure record—be on this list? The reason is that not only did Buddy Holly write "Stay Close to Me," but he produced and played lead guitar on it as well. "Stay Close to Me" has been bootlegged on a yellow DJ single, but the big money goes for the standard commercial release on the maroon Brunswick label.

13. "Ooby Dooby," by Roy Orbison
Je-Wel 101 $150 Mint

Roy Orbison made a chart breakthrough in 1956 with "Ooby Dooby" on Sun. (He then disappeared from the charts until 1960, when he returned with the two-million-seller of "Only the Lonely.") Roy's Sun Records hit had first been done on the tiny Je-Wel label. When Roy and his band, the Teen Kings, signed with Sun, the song was recut; therefore, the versions differ. Trivia note: the cowriter of "Ooby Dooby" was a college professor of English.

14. "Barbee," by Kenny and the Cadets
Randy 422 $150 Mint (colored wax)

A Hawthorne, California, group once came into contact with a Los Angeles couple who had recording connections. The man-and-wife team reasoned that their chances of scoring a hit single would be doubled with two songs from two "different" groups. "Barbee" was said to be by Kenny and the Cadets, while "Surfin' " (cut at the same time) was by the Pendletons, the group's real name. But when "Surfin' " was issued, the label read *Beach Boys,* much to the chagrin of the Pendletons. In the meantime, "Barbee" died a quiet death. A black vinyl version of "Barbee" would be worth about half the above price.

15. "Salt Lake City," by the Beach Boys
Capitol 2937 (DJ only) $150 Mint

"Salt Lake City" arrived years after the Beach Boys had shed their Kenny and the Cadets/Pendletons tags. By this time, they had established themselves as America's number-one band. This single was a white-label Capitol promotion item, pressed to hype the Beach Boys' new *Summer Days and Summer Nights* album. The disc was reasonably well-distributed in the Salt Lake City area, but even the most trashed copy rarely turns up there today.

RCH

ROCK 'N' ROLL DISC JOCKEYS

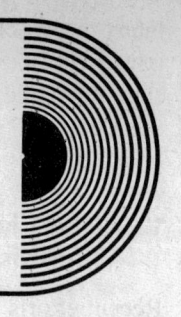

"Okay kats and kittens, get on your boppin' mittens. We're gonna freak and squeak 'til we crack our beak, lay down some crass sass on the mellow grass. Alroot! Alreet! Tweet! Tweet! Tweet!"

The days of the primitive rock & roll disc jockey are over. There was a time though, not so long ago, when tuning in your radio was akin to eavesdropping on outer space, so much raw individuated craziness lurked amidst the airwaves. The hysteria was caused by old DJs trying to find a broadcasting approach to equal the sounds of the frantic new music. Throughout the early and middle '50s, individual broadcast styles evolved from mello tones to black mello tones to black jive to teenage slang to speed rap. They'll all be illustrated lavishly in the pages ahead, but first, let's try and pinpoint the origins of the R&R jock (after all, he didn't just mutate out of Arthur Godfrey's ukelele).

Our story begins in 1946. In Nashville, a guy named Randy Wood is introduced to Gene Nobles, a local DJ. Wood has a problem. He recently bought a home appliances repair and sales shop in nearby Gallatin. Back in the storeroom he's come across some 2000 78s (*the* speed of the time) of "race" artists—that meant black in those days—and he doesn't know what to do with them.

Nobles, an ex-carny, recalls the popularity of the old Southern minstrel shows —every outfit used to carry one—and how popular their music always was with a white audience. Maybe his listeners would dig it—hell, they might even *buy* it—for, with some isolated exceptions, downhome blues, R&B—dirty stuff—just wasn't on the air.

Bibles & Baby Chickens

Luckily Nobles had his show over WLAC, a station with 50,000 watts that reached Montreal in the North, El Paso in the West and the Caribbean in the South. He and Wood bought a one minute spot to advertise the records at six for a dollar. Nothing happened so they bought 15 minutes. Still nothing. They were about ready to pack it in when on the third or fourth Monday they were hit by a *flood* of mail and in no time at all Gallatin's third class post office became a first class one.

From 1946 on, Albert Ammons's "Swanee River Boogie" introduced Nobles' delicious double entendre shows. (Years later the tune served as the theme for shows by John Richbourg and Bill "Hoss" Allen.)

The word spread. Up the Eastern seaboard to bored college kids ready for a new fad, and around to the potential black audience itself. Allen himself was a native of Gallatin, a town with more blacks than whites. His hipness to Southern black customs and speech—plus a deep, slow drawl—did not read as white to his listeners. "I used to say it was 'get down time.' That's what the pimps call the hour they put their girls out on the street. My opening would always be 'The Horseman's down for Royal Cream (a hairdressing) and Randy's Record Mart. The world's largest mail order record shop. In the business of sending out those phonograph records to *you*, my friends, by mail C.O.D. guaranteed safe delivery no matter where you be. Just pay Uncle Sam and he'll lay it on you, man!' " Hoss also pushed bibles and baby chickens, just as he does today on his gospel show on the same station.

Unlike Allen, John Richbourg ("John R way down in Dixie") was a soap opera announcer from New York who had to learn the lingo from scratch. He began "breaking" new records on his one to three o'clock in the morning show. Randy's Record Mart Show became so popular that a promo man from an independent label would bring in only an acetate and 100 bucks to insure its being played. If, after ten days, the major distribution centers in Charlotte and New Orleans hadn't placed any orders, the acetate would be scrapped and no records would have even been pressed!

Musically and culturally the Richbourg show's influence is inestimable. Shreveport's Bob Smith, now the famous Wolfman Jack, admits his style—"Dis is da WOOFMAN talkin' to ya baybeh! HowwooooOOO! Ca-ca-caRREEE!"—derived from Richbourg and Allen. While down in the Caribbean WLAC was the only U.S. station receivable. Without "Randy's," reggae music might have been another kind of animal.

But in spite of the fact that Nobles was voted best DJ by Ol' Miss, his Northern white audience was a minority—dominant, yes, and able to turn others on, but still a minority. It wasn't until 1951 that Alan Freed, then a classical music DJ in Cleveland, noticed white kids in a record store freaking out on greasy, raucous black R&B. Freed dug it, established "The Moondog Show" and the rest is—as they say—history.

Today an onslaught of freedom has caused the '50s to be bathed in a wash of nostalgia, a nostalgia which on one hand celebrates the very conventions and restrictions once thought so suffocating; and, on the other hand, falsifies and neutralizes the now-quaint rebellious/sexual drives that once challenged them. The film *American Hot Wax* portrays Freed, once "the poisoner of youthful minds," as merely a cultural relic, a harmless memory in a Frank Lovejoy bag suit and handkerchief square. (One thinks of Orson Welles or Lillian Hellman recently feted on TV; apparently any rebel this country would honor must first be defanged by time.)

Hit-pickin' Hunter

However, for a while there, Freed and other white DJs like him were really opening doors and literally "causing" riots. Over WAOK in Atlanta Zenas Sears was promoting Little Richard, Piano Red, Chuck Willis and staging Ray Charles concerts. On the West coast there was "Jumpin'" George Oxford of KSAN San Francisco/Oakland with his juicy, ham actor's voice. In between plugs for E-Z Credit furniture stores he sounded as if he was about to do a dirty-old man on the young chicks ("Ole jumpin' daddy, you make me want to *shout!*") whose squeals punctuated his spiels.

Los Angeles boasted "Huntin' with Hunter" with host Hunter Hancock, a near infallible hit picker. His KGFJ show was also known as "Harlematinee," an apt title since only black artists were played. Chuckling like some manic, square Babbit, Hunter's high-pitched voice cracked countless cornball jokes while he seemingly urged you to share his recently-discovered musical toy.

There were also the slurred-voiced maestros Poppa Stoppa and Jack the Cat, both fiercely loyal (over WJMR and WWEZ) to the great R&B artists of New Orleans, their hometown. But the man who originated and wrote the Poppa Stoppa show, Vernon Winslow, was black. When he was finally let on the air himself—as the maniacal Doctor Daddy-O—he was forced to broadcast out of Cosimo's Recording Studio because the hotel which housed the radio station wouldn't let him in. Some years later they relented, only to make him take the freight elevator entrance.

Soon the black DJs on the assorted indie stations became terrifically influential. Men like Bugs Scrugs from Memphis, Sugar Daddy Birmingham out of Winston-Salem, Jockey Jack Gibson in Atlanta and Shreveport's Professor Bop all played sounds as funky as their names.

"Cop Some Nod, Chill My Chat"

In Chicago, WOPA's Big Bill Hill made a hit out of Wilbert Harrison's "Kansas City" when the owner of the Fury Label—Bobby Robinson—sent over a fifth of Hill's favorite scotch. In between plays of Joe Turner and Little Willie John, the great Dr. Hepcat (nee Lavada Durst) blew minds all over central Texas with his spontaneous bop chatter. His Lord's Prayer recitation is still a classic: "I stash me down to cop a nod, if I am lame I'm not to blame, the stem is hard. If I am skull orchard bound don't clip my wings no matter how I sound. If I should cop a drear before the early bright—when Gabe makes his toot—I'll chill my chat, fall out like mad with everything alroot."

The "stem" refers to the street. If the jargon's confusing I'll try to "carve your knob" and help you to understand. For instance, Dr. Hepcat might say that if he had a pony to ride he could domino the nabbers, cop some presidents, gas his moss and maybe get togged with some beastly ground smashers. Then he'd be mellow to puff down the stroll where he'd motivate his piechopper to latch onto a fly delosis. In layman's parlance, that meant that: If he had a job he could avoid the police, make some money, get his hair conked, outfit himself with new shoes then be in the right frame of mind to ride down the street where he'd use his mouth to effect an introduction to a cute girl. Yet, even with all his mindboggling terms, the Doctor still had a fairly smooth, even rational delivery. Once you copped a dictionary of early '50s bop talk (which the good Doctor wrote and sold himself over KVET in Austin) everything was copasetic.

To get *really* down in the alley we must focus on Louisiana and a very esoteric DJ indeed. Like all great primitive artists his contributions lose something when transformed into cold print, but here goes. It's the mid-'50s. A gospel record has just ended.

"*Amen*...an' don't forget to write me a cahd or lettuh to Groover Boy KWKShreveport2. Well—we'll saynomorebayeh. Gonna get right on ahead wit' de music 'cause we know we got one right chere dat everyone want to heah. I got about fifty *re*-quests fo' dis an' don't has tahm to read 'em all but ANYHOW HERE'S DE REKKID BY JOE LIGGINS AN' HIS ORCHISTRA titled 'ooooOOOOOHHHWHHUUU! HOW I MISS YA'!"

Orgasmic Groover Boy

In the days when the KKK was distributing "literature" about how kids were being corrupted by "screaming moronic nigger music from the jungles of Africa," Groover Boy must've wiped 'em out—especially when he'd throw an orgasmic fit right in the middle of some farting sax solo. His approach to sponsors was no less idiosyncratic than his odd sense of humor.

"Dis is de KWK tahm on amerigofutenam(?)—feeuuuuuuuum! A man full— of *mud*—in Shreveport. Ya know—I like t'get serious jus' a minute chere baybeh. By de thousands peoples is turnin' to de rich, foamy mellocutions of Palmer's Skin Success Soap. Ya whips up ya soothin' foamy mellocution an' allows it to remain on an' luxurize three minutes. *Now*—here's whut dis gentle, foamy mellocutions do. ONE: it relieves de irritation of upset . . . *skin*, blackheads, rashes and pimples. TWO: it act as a deodorant, removin' de skin back-teh-rye-uh— chief cause of ah-ffensive puhspuhration odor, an' THREE: it hygienically cleanses luv-ly com-plex-ions an' *soothes* with its lano-*lin!* Tooooooo-day! Only twenny five cents at drug and toiletrie counters!"

After that he might have played "It Ain't The Meat But The Motion" by The Swallows or even Bull Moose Jackson's "Big Ten Inch." And it was these kinds of songs with their thinly disguised leer-ics that riled far tamer, more mainstream groups than the Klan. Once the hounds of decency were unleashed (in the form of civic groups, organized parents and the Catholic Church), both record producers and dee jays were told to quite literally "clean up their act."

White Smoke From a Chicken Leg

Not all the wild DJs capitulated overnight. Some of the white jocks had begun to pick up the jive patter and breathless delivery of their black confreres.

At a jazz and R&B concert in Detroit in the late '50s, my date and I were about the only whites in the place. All of the city's really "happening" black society was there, including the top-rated soul DJ Prophet Jones. The Prophet was dressed all in green (allegedly because it was the color of money). He entered, prancing gay, and flanked by two bodyguards. Black women shivered. He was heavy business. *Ebony* reported how he had foretold the coming of the atom bomb when he saw a puff of white smoke escaping from a chicken leg he had placed on his plate during a church social. He swept into his seat, the lights went down, the spot went up and the MC, Frantic Ernie, came out. And he was white!

Frantic Ernie was an exception; he had developed a credible R&B-based style that endeared him to both blacks and whites. The majority of "boss jocks" came on like second-rate hucksters, playing down the teen audience with every trick gimmick known. Some, however, were actually clever.

One of St. Louis' WIL's main men was Jack Carney who had a personality like a games director at a summer camp. He created the mythical Pookie Snackenberg and a fan club with buttons to go along with him. Among other accomplishments, he once conducted a contest whose winner was personally driven to school for a week by Carney in a rented limousine.

Surefire Gimmick

Another was the stay-awake marathon. New York's "Curly-Haired Boy In The Third Row," Peter Tripp, staged one in an empty recruiting office on Times Square. For five days and nights he stared back sleepless at the freaks who made faces at him through the plate glass. Finally his rap began to disintegrate. His face turned white, his lips went blue and he set his sportjacket on fire.

Alan Freed

Perhaps the best of the hip teen jocks was another Philadelphia resident, Joe Niagra of WIBG ("Wibbageland"). An early rhymer ("Hear the word from this rockin' bird!"), Niagra never let his speech patterns become predictable drone or babble. He had a knack for the odd pause or peculiar but just right emphasis that gave one the impression he was not only excited about a record's success but downright proud to serve his audience: "I predicted this would make it big and *you* proved me right!"

Besides being the sincerest of supersalesmen, Niagra may also have invented payola. Philly was the largest center for indies who, having less influence than the major labels, had to constantly grease the wheels. The story, as told to former Philly jock Oaky Miller by indie record producer Harry Finffer, is as follows: One day in the early fifties when Niagra was still only playing pop, he has lunch with Finffer. Harry asks Joe to play a new record and Joe agrees. Harry picks up the lunch tab—which is somewhere around three dollars—and they leave the restaurant. Outside, Joe, who makes then maybe $60.00 a week, sees a $100 dollar suit in a store window and flips over it. Next day at the station the suit arrives, addressed to Joe with a note from Finffer asking him to please play more of his records. Joe is like a kid at Xmas and plays the hell out of any product Finffer brings in. Payola is born.

Kovacs & Paar

"The indies tried to get the DJs boozed, fed and laid," claims Oaky Miller. He maintains, as do many others, that he accepted gifts but only played records if he thought they had merit (reminiscent of Melina Mercouri in *Never On Sunday* who'd only play for pay with men who turned her on). Miller, now a comic and actor, follows in the tradition of Steve Allen, Jack Paar, Ernie Kovacs, Garry Moore, Bob & Ray, Jonathan Winters and Soupy Sales (formerly Heinz), all of whom worked as mad-hatter DJs before scaling the heights of stardom. Miller's success story is pure Horatio Alger.

In '57 Miller was in Atlantic City, New Jersey looking for a summer job in between college semesters. One evening on the boardwalk he noticed a dance emporium. A DJ in the window was playing records, but there were only about six people in the place. Oaky, with no broadcasting experience at all, had a showman's confidence; he walked in, buttonholed the owner and asked the jock's salary. When he heard "25 bills a week," he was shook. He knew he could do better than the lame kid in the window and to prove it he asked the owner to walk with him down the crowded boardwalk. "If a hundred people don't stop me to say hello," he boasted, "forget I asked you for the job!"

Oaky had been a BMOC athlete at a big Philly high school. Atlantic City was where all the city's teens came for summer fun. When the owner saw his popularity he asked him to start work that very night. Oaky agreed, but for 50 dollars a night. He was in.

Oaky didn't know an A from a B side, but he learned fast. A couple of stations later he was at WEEZ outside of Philly in Chester, hosting a dance party on TV out of Scranton, hauling in $1000 a week on an average. And this isn't counting the record hops where the real money was.

How'd he score so big? Well, the major problem—that of establishing an on-air identity—was already taken care of. His delivery was typically good-natured jive: "The big bad O is back on the go. Hi everybody! This is Oaky Miller. I come on like a herd of turtles in the month of May and for the next solid three I've got goodies for thee, etc." Basically his appeal came from the way he involved his youthful audience; he might thank a high school's Number One tough for protecting him at a dance or complain how he was in love with Miss Canada but she was too far away. He started a fake feud with a woman who broadcast a cooking program on the station. He leaked out the police's phone number, telling the kids "That's where Elvis is staying!" and he urged them to cut school and attend his birthday party in a city park. To cool out the authorities he invented "Homework Corner"—a 20 minute show segment where students could exchange schoolwork questions and answers.

Recognizing the potential of another DJ—Jerry Blavat—Miller hired him under a one year contract, to host record hops. Blavat went on, over WCAM and WHAT, to perfect an incredibly sappy, near mindless crooning style—the forerunner of late '60s thorazine delivery. In his "hiptionary" ladies were "foxes" or "amazons" while guys were "studs" or "coyotes." Over a lush string backing he would breathe: "... The *coyote* needs someone ... and that someone ... that's the fox ... and the *fox* needs someone ... and that someone ... that's the coyote ... like the bee need the honey ... like the flower need the rain ... like the farmer need the crop ... like the ocean need the salt ... that's how the amazon needs the stud ... and teenage love ... wow ... it had no beginning ... had no end ... it will never end as long as there are teenagers ... there will be amazons and foxes falling in love with coyotes ... that's good, y'know?"

Blavat's style for introducing up-tempo numbers was more traditional though no less irritating: "... Unh! ... Unh! ... Unh! ... Up into the sky for thee! Yuh! Teenpopulationofthisherefabulousnation ... once again hello and a hi! and a huh! Big boss with the hot sauce. YourstrulyJerryBlavat. The geator with the heator. So—withoutfurtherado, let's try and appease huh?, your musical appetite huh? Let's try and appease you the yon teenage population. I along with you will rock the big tick tock ...."

"More Moves Than OJ"

Meanwhile, down in Pittsburgh on WAMO, Porky Chedwick billed himself the "Daddio of the raddio, a porkulatin' platter-pushin' poppa" who had "more jams than Smuckers." This "head snapper and dapper rapper" admitted he was "not Cary Grant" but could "do what he can't," declared he got his "PhD in insanity at the University of Spinner Sanctum" and confessed to always having a grape in his ear "to make my head ferment."

Accompanying the jive rappers, yet another style was quietly sliding out of the broadcast lab: weird sound effects. Traces of this go back to the early '50s when Al "Jazzbo" Collins did his "Purple Grotto" show on WNEW, New York.

The strange noises coupled with the jock's bizarro rap probably bagged more listeners than the good jazz he consistently played.

Squawks & Ginsburgers

Sometime later, Bob (*Hogan's Heroes*) Crane at WICC, Bridgeport, pioneered the super-production format with effects and way out voice tracks. Eventually moving to KNF in New York he was built a special console on which he could have staged the Battle of Little Big Horn.

Such new audience-nabbing devices weren't lost on the rock rappers. Arnie "Woo Woo" Ginsberg ("Woo woo to you you") backed up his youthful, eager to please voice on Boston's WMEX with pops, squawks, whistles, clangs, beeps and aroogahs. His "Night Train" show became an institution in the New England area for years. He was the first (and possibly only) jock to have a hamburger named after him. The name? The Ginsburger, natch.

In the early '60s Russ "Weird Beard" Knight's rhyming patter reverberated through countless echo-plexes, overlaid with flying saucer and rocket sounds right out of a sci-fi movie. KLIF's pick hits—the Knight Bullseyes—were introduced by an arrow in flight—"whhiirrr!"—that hit a target—"thock!" The show, "Beamed from a space capsule," was so damned *busy* the records began to sound just like one more electronic surprise—and this was still only a precursor of the McLuhanesque folly that was to follow.

The Boy on the Psychiatrist's Couch

As radio moved into the mid-'60s it followed Bill Drake's lead of super-sock-it-to-'em top 29 programming. Drake came up with his form of totally commercial radio (in Fresno and San Francisco). The thoroughly successful format carried over to the decade's end. Overlap sound, no dead airtime *ever,* stinger jingles of a second or less, constant harping on the station's call letters and punch! punch! punch!

While the new style set definite limits on the free-ranging "personality jock," some survived and prospered. One of these was B. Mitchel Reed, who arrived at WMCA, New York preceded by his rep as "the fastest tongue in the west," "The Boy On The Psychiatrist's Couch," "The Mad Monk In The Monastery" or simply "BMR." He would prepare for the verbal spill chute by downing some drinks, a joint and a few amphs. "After that, I felt loose and ready." Below is a rap, the like of which beat out both Cousin Brucie and Murray the K in popularity, and took him but 17 seconds to complete. Care to try *your* luck?

"Hey scooters, it's your leader BMR, WMCA jumpin' with my hat in my hand with the nuttiest show in the entire New York turf, read me back with the smashbacks or the Good Guy's survey or headed that way. This hour the name of the winner of the musical love letters contest—first portion to be presented from the lobby of the Nile Hilton Hotel. Hey, name, claim, style will go to Conneticus(?) second call city of Lalassitude(?) five thousand and like that there schmeer call right now."

(Reed, of course, successfully grew out of the hyperthyroid approach, and went on to pioneer a solid FM style, which he pursues today over Los Angeles' KMET.) For pure mid-'60s boss jock surrealism nobody topped the Real Don Steele. In 1966 the pyromaniacal Real fired this minibrushfire out over KHJ, Los Angeles, a city so used to glittery-eyed freaks it didn't even roll over. Sixteen seconds was all it took.

"Three o'clock in *Boss* Angeles! AndgehHEY! thitz me, The Real Don Steele, a billion dollar weekend there, and you're looking out of sidewalk call; I got nothing but those groovy golds—we're gonna fit Chuck out here on a fractious Friday, boy, got to get a set outside that (indecipherable word resembling blowing bubbles in water) jumbo city, take a trip. When you chase 'em, daylight."

Beautiful Drool

What more can you say? Only that after those strange mutants, some early FM rock jocks flirted briefly with an "Oh, wow man, like you know—*beautiful*" drool which often put you to sleep before the disc came on. New York's Rosko on WOR was the most famous exponent.

Some excitement was generated in L.A. in the late '60s by the Magnificent Montague whose popular exhortation to "Burn, baby, burn!" was belatedly exonerated from charges it helped ignite the Watts riots. In the '70s, sporadic outbursts of early broadcast mania have included such figures as the ubiquitus Dr. Demento and record producer Huey Meaux (whose infrequent Texas stories as The Crazy Cajun feature scratchy old records, prisoners' dedications and a flamboyant shouting style reminiscent of the best asbestos-larynxed oldtimers). Los Angeles' 'underground' KROQ FM recently had a weekly show by one Young Marquis; resembling a coked-out scion of the House of Usher, the Marquis mixed hard rock, heavy production and the styles of Zacherley and Don Steele. The results, if not always humorous, were at least "different."

Times, however, *have* changed. Nowadays fans of early rock radio probably spend their days holed up with the entire *Cruisin'* series. The medium's wild eccentrics seem to have disappeared from the airwaves about as completely as the fresh fowl, secret tonics and rebellious music they peddled. Perhaps a diligent few hold out hope that a generation of future Poppa Stoppas and Groover Boys is growing up somewhere out there right now and that one day, while nobody's listening, the real batwing madness will jump up and prowl the bands all over again.

RB

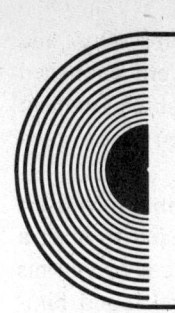

THE MOTOWN SOUND REVISITED
With Recommended "Vintage" Recordings

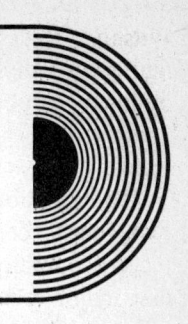

Motown. A somewhat over-used household word, employed these days to conjure up the image of a vast, slick vinyl and celluloid empire. Perched high atop the Hollywood ladder, this company is perceived today, especially among the young, as the storybook fulfillment of the black American dream. It seems rather elementary by today's standards; establish a music-making machine called "Hitsville" within the bowels of a mid-western inner city, churn out the hits, accrue a minor fortune and go west to cop the big enchilada.

Looking back over it all, Motown's ultimate significance lies not in the fact that they have won the game in a big way, but rather in how they played it and what they left behind in the wake of their climb. Throughout much of the 1960s, the word "Motown" represented a fusion between a city and a sound. The city was Detroit (affectionately known as Motortown), a rough, working class environment which has given rise to some of the best rock 'n' roll ever made, while the sound was young, basic, sensual and the very essence of the streets from which it rose. At the same time, the Motown sound certainly was "produced," it owed as much to the studio wizardry of such pioneers as Phil Spector and Leiber & Stoller as it did to the church music of the black man and the blues music of the city stoops. What emerged from all this was a magic brew, a body of music which cross-pollinated the concerns and emotions of old and young, transcending all social and racial barriers and forever changing the face of popular music.

Dubious legend has it that Berry Gordy Jr., Motown's celebrated founding father, launched his enterprise by borrowing several hundred dollars from his family's credit union. This strains all bounds of credibility when one considers the level of music business success already achieved by Gordy at the time Motown was formed. By 1960, when the first Tamla-Motown records began to appear, Gordy had authored or co-authored well over a dozen songs which had placed on the national bestseller lists. These included "Everyone Was There" by Bob Kayli (actually Gordy's brother Robert), "Bad Girls" by the Miracles, "Come To Me," "You've Got What It Takes" and "I Love The Way You Love" by Marv Johnson and, most importantly, a series of collaborations with writer-producer Billy Davis (masquerading as Tyran Carlo) for fellow-Detroiter Jackie

Wilson: "Reet Petite," "To Be Loved," "Lonely Teardrops," "That's Why" and numerous others. Additionally, many of Gordy's compositions were published by his own Jobete Music Company (an amalgam of his three daughters' names: Joanne, Betty and Terry), which effectively doubled his income on those copyrights.

More credible rumor has it that Gordy actually formed the company with his own funds (certainly more than several hundred dollars was needed to start a record company—even then), running into problems only when he achieved his first major independent hit—"Shop Around" by the Miracles—and found himself a victim of the classic dilemma; no money forthcoming from slow-paying distributors and a mountain of advertising and pressing bills to be paid. At this point, the humor mill persists, in stepped that allegedly non-existent secret society with an unsolicited and non-refusable offer of assistance, a cross which Gordy would have to bear for many years to come. In fact, some insist that it was this problem which ultimately prompted him to abandon Detroit for L.A.

So much for the "how;" as for the probably "why" underlying the formation of Motown (financial considerations aside), this would appear to rest with the music itself. One need only listen to Gordy's pre-Motown recordings in sequence to understand his rapid progress and frustrations. Some of his first efforts, "Got A Job" and "Money" (not the Barrett Strong composition) by the Miracles, and "What's Gwyne On" by Tony Spade, were parcelled out to such R&B labels as End and Backbeat. Nothing more than adequate, these records were merely a reflection of the doo-wop era in which they were produced. The Bob Kayli records were silly novelties and equally as undistinguished. But of utmost importance was the Jackie Wilson connection, which began in 1957 and propelled both Gordy and Wilson to stardom. Wilson had recorded as Little Mr. Midnite during the early 50s before replacing Clyde McPhatter as lead singer of Billy Ward's Dominoes. Now on his own, Wilson associated himself with Gordy and began turning a series of his compositions into major hits. What was wrong with these records was that Gordy's songs, and Wilson's delivery, were powerful and unrestrained R&B, while the arrangements and productions, at the hands of such bandleaders as Milton DeLugg and Dick Jacobs, were syrupy schlock. Gordy recognized that immediately, and, rather than buck the policies of major labels, resolved to set out on his own. His first attempt appears to have been "Bad Girl" by the Miracles, originally released as Motown #1. Although arguably yet another doo-wop, this record had an intangible special quality which stands up today alongside anything the Miracles have done since. Gordy was not able to meet the demand for this record and was forced almost immediately to lease it to Chess. Undaunted, Gordy established another label, Tamla, and began working with Marv Johnson, a former member of the Detroit-based Serenaders. Their first collaboration, "Come To Me," was released as Tamla 101. The vocal was a total steal of Jackie Wilson's style, but gone were the whitewashed backgrounds. Instead, this record featured bouncy R&B chants, a good, steady rock & roll track and a thumping tambourine. The year was 1959 and the Motown "sound" had been born. But, unfortunately, Berry Gordy still was not quite ready. Unable to handle demand for "Come To Me," which became a major national hit, he found himself obliged to turn Marv Johnson over to United Artists, eventually losing out on such goodies as "You've Got What It Takes," "I Love The Way You Love" and "Move Two Mountains." (Johnson later re-affiliated with Gordy's label, but was unable to recreate his early success.)

The late 50s proved an ideal training period for Berry Gordy, since these experiences helped him achieve a very delicate but important balance in his music. On one hand, the Jackie Wilson records were too "white" for his taste and pushed him more in the direction of R&B. On the other hand, his experiences with the record company establishment did instill in him, whether he was aware of it or not, a certain restraint which prevented his productions from becoming too ethnic for their time. While the days were yet to come when an operation such as Stax-Volt could make a total commitment to R&B and still achieve major commercial success, such certainly was not the case in 1960. It was this perfect balance, therefore, that yielded an absolutely unique pop sound which would soon take the music world by proverbial storm.

As the 60s unfolded, several small record labels sprang up in Detroit (Harvey, Anna, Tri-Phi, Miracle, etc.), most established by friends and associates of Gordy. These were methodically attracted into the Tamla-Motown family, providing Gordy with an unstoppable stable of artists, writers and producers (in fact, during later years, Motown swallowed virtually every other Detroit-based R&B label, including Ric-Tic, Myto, Golden World and others; the only company eluding their grasp seems to have been Westbound). Motown records were marketed in black areas, but soon broke out and reached the ears of white kids. Mid-west garage bands began incorporating Motown material into their repertoires, and British superstars-to-be were playing it in such places as the Marquee, the Flamingo and the Star Club. (After the "British Invasion," several of the bands issued recordings here of their interpretations of Motown hits: "Please Mr. Postman" and "Money" by the Beatles, "Do You Love Me" and "You've Got What It Takes" by the DC 5, and countless others.) In fact, many of the British bands have been quoted as saying that they would anxiously await the new Motown releases, hoping to learn and perform them before their competitors!

Late in 1963, as the spearhead of the British invasion was beginning to form, Motown was bombarding the charts, both Pop and R&B, with releases by the Marvelettes, Miracles, Contours, Martha & The Vandellas, "Little" Stevie Wonder, Marvin Gaye, Mary Wells and some minor entries by a group called the Supremes. How much more successful could they possibly get, the industry asked itself, since the British machine was preparing to mow down virtually every American R&B star? No one, including Berry Gordy himself, could possibly have provided an answer to that one, or could even have been remotely prepared for the monster that was about to be unleashed: the Temptations, Four Tops, Stevie Wonder (infinitely more devastating as an adult than with his "Little" prefix), the "polished" Supremes (10 number one records between 1964 and 1967, six of them consecutive!), Marvin Gaye & Tammi Terrell, Brenda Holloway, Junior Walker & The All Stars, the Holland-Dozier-Holland jukebox and, although somewhat later, the Jackson Five. With a roster of only a dozen and a half artists, Motown not only stood up to the British invasion but indeed helped fuel it. Even more astounding was the fact that this compact little operation was blowing the biggest of the majors off the charts, all the while remaining completely self-contained. Motown managed its own artists, sent them to its own finishing school, taught them choreography, poise and stage presence, assisted them with their money management, and provided the hits with unrelenting efficiency.

As the 1960s gave way to the 70s, the world began to change. Accordingly, so did the ways of the entertainment business; musical tastes altered dramatically, record buying patterns and marketing techniques became extremely complex and the creators of music sought increasing independence and control of their own affairs. And so, even though the hits continued to come, the Motown machine began to crumble as its various elements dispersed. Motown today is the very establishment with which Berry Gordy grappled nearly 20 years ago. They churn out the obligatory disco and funk records, but no longer is a Motown release a guaranteed hit. Their ultimate success appears to be in films and movie-related music, which is kind of sad. It seems that they have settled into a cushy, civil-service type of existence rather than to remain creatively at the forefront of contemporary popular music.

And what of the "sound"? Fortunately, that has never died, but rather has flourished and become a cornerstone of today's music. You hear it in the Stones, Meat Loaf and Springsteen, you hear it behind the stage antics of many new wave bands, you hear it transmutated into reggae and, on occasion, you hear it reproduced exactly in records such as Maxine Nightingale's "Right Back To Where We Started From" or Billy Ocean's "Love Really Hurts Without You." In short, you hear it everywhere.

No overview of Motown history, no matter how brief, could be complete without specific discussion of at least some of the records. When the editors of *Rocker* asked me to focus on about a dozen, I immediately sought some rational basis on which to select so few from so vast a number of possible choices. Would it be the 12 biggest hits, my 12 favorite records, or 12 records of a specific category or era? The answer turned out to be none of these, and yet a combination of them all. What follows is a list of "vintage" Motown records, along with some comments and recollections, based on the concept that these were the first to come immediately to mind, without any type of research. A record with that kind of power, I suppose, has done its job fully.

"MONEY"—Barrett Strong, Anna 1111 (Feb. 1960)

The label appears to have been the first viable Gordy venture, owned by Berry's sister Gwen and named after yet another sister, Anna (presently married to Marvin Gaye). The roster included Joe Tex, Paul Gayten, Johnny Bristol, Davin Ruffin (future lead of the Temps), Lamont Dozier and Barrett Strong, among numerous others. Anna's output was quite undistinguished with the singular exception of Barrett Strong's "Money"—an instant rock & roll classic so outrageous as to be completely out of place not only on its own label, but in its era. Produced by Roquel Davis and co-authored by Berry Gordy and Janie Bradford, the record defies classification; it is difficult to tell for what market it was intended, what with the Dick Clark bullshit being peddled to the white kids during this period and the largely slick, harmony oriented material making it in the R&B market. Its closest cousin would probably be Ray Charles' "What'd I Say," which had been a major hit during the previous summer, but Strong's "Money" came miles closer to the essence of rock 'n' roll than ol' Uncle Ray. In fact, Strong's wailing delivery came across with more than a hint of a "punk" attitude:

> "Yo' love gives me such a thrill,
> But yo' love don't pay my bills,
> Gimme money." © 1959, Jobete

Almost immediately upon its release, "Money" achieved a status claimed by only a few songs such as "Shout" (Isley Bros.), "Louie Louie" (Kingsmen, etc.) and "Gloria" (Them, Shadows Of Knight, etc.)—it became an obligatory staple item for every bar and garage band, an absolute standard. It also did not escape the notice of the fledgling British bands, most notably the Beatles, who ultimately recorded it.

"DEVIL WITH A BLUE DRESS"—Shorty Long, Soul 35001 (1964)

Frederick "Shorty" Long was a native of Birmingham, Alabama, and began singing in his local Baptist Church. After teaching himself R&B by listening to the records of Johnny Ace and Little Willie John, he became a resident singer on the chittlin' circuit and eventually hosted his own radio show in Alabama. Just how Shorty Long came to the attention of Berry Gordy is somewhat of a mystery, but the fact that Gordy decided on him to launch a subsidiary label called Soul is not. "Devil With A Blue Dress," Long's own composition, is about as close to hard core R&B as Gordy ever got, but with that undeniable Motown sound haunting it throughout. It was a slow, grindy, teasing ballad, and an absolutely wonderful record. Unfortunately, however, probably because it strayed too much from the established Motown formula, it never cracked the national top 100. It did become quite a sizable hit in Detroit, where it came to the attention of a teenage club band called Billy Lee & The Rivieras. They added it to their act, speeded it up just a little more each time they performed it, and, years later, turned it into their all-time biggest hit as Mitch Ryder & The Detroit Wheels. Long came to national attention in 1968 with a piece of garbage called "Here Comes The Judge," foisted on him by the record company to exploit the "Laugh-In" craze. He died just over one year later in a boating accident.

"LOVE IS LIKE A HEAT WAVE"—Martha & The Vandellas, Gordy 7022 (July 1963)
"DANCING IN THE STREET"—Martha & The Vandellas, Gordy 7033 (July 1964)

I've listed two records here, because they tie in my mind as the all-time great Martha records. Not that such goodies as "Quicksand," "Nowhere To Run,"

"Jimmy Mack," "Honey Chile" and "I'm Ready For Love" should be dismissed without consideration, but these two win. In any event, "Heat Wave" originally was titled just that, but was retitled as above to avoid confusion with the Irving Berlin standard (as if that could ever happen!). Who could ever forget first hearing that record, totally unlike anything that had ever come before it—that pounding beat, those sax riffs, Martha's uncompromising vocals and a track that rivaled anything that ever had to compete with the restrictions of an AM radio. And right up there with it was "Dancing In The Street," released exactly one summer later, one of the absolute celebrations of Motown and young music in general. I think Martha said it all, when she appeared on a Murray The K show in 1964 and modified the lyrics just slightly as she came to the end of the song:

> "Across the ocean blue,
> The Beatles too,
> They're dancin' in the street!"
> © 1964, Jobete

What's Martha doing today? Recording for Fantasy and seemingly unable to get to first base. The ultimate cruncher is that she's doing Richard Nader shows, singing the aforementioned classics as if they were ghosts of a prior life. Absurd!

"WHERE DID OUR LOVE GO"—The Supremes, Motown 1060 (June, 1964)

July, 1964. I'm working overtime at Broadcast Music, Inc. (BMI), and it's quite late at night. The air-conditioning has gone off hours ago, and it's hot as a bitch! Off in the distance, I hear the computers humming and the almost unintelligible drone of a radio cranking out WWRL, New York's hot R&B shouter. Suddenly, I perceive the sound of running footsteps coming closer and see the face of Gretta, a fellow night worker. Gretta is a good friend of such folks as Sam Cooke, Jerry Butler, Major Lance and Gene Chandler, and she knows that I'm a soul freak. Particularly, she knows that I'm crazed on Motown, and there's something on the radio that I've gotta hear *right now!* I follow her back to her department, and to her radio, and there it is:

> "Baby, baby,
> Where did our love go . . ."
> © 1964, Jobete

I don't know who's singing, but I do know this; if you've got any juices flowing in you at all, this one's gotta get you in the ol' gonads! And get me it did—that incessant beat, the discordant harmony of the "oohs" and that haunting come-hither little voice up front. Well, we all know what happened to Diana Ross & The Supremes. Or do we? As of last report, Mary Wilson still sings with the group, the only original member. Florence Ballard slid down into the welfare line and died a few years ago, virtually penniless, under rather mysterious circumstances. And Diana Ross? She now stands alongside such MOR megastars as Liza Minnelli and Bette Midler, cranking out movie music and pretending she's 12-year-old Dorothy. Really!

"UPTIGHT (EVERYTHING'S ALRIGHT)"—Stevie Wonder, Tamla 54124 (Nov. 1965)

This record blew me away the moment I first heard it, but not without conjuring up some pain. Flashback to the late summer of 1963. I am attending a performance of the Motown Revue in some area of Brooklyn (quite likely the Brevort Theatre) where 20-year-old white kids fear to tread! I have settled into the audience, crouched down as low as possible so that no one could see me (sure fooled 'em, didn't I?). I've really gotten into the Miracles, Marvelettes, Contours, etc., when they suddenly bring out this little blind kid. Two men guide him to the mike, and, just as suddenly, he's on his own. He breaks into a long version of "Fingertips," sporadically raising a harmonica to his lips and bouncing around. It's quite a long number, and somewhere in the middle, he bounces a little too hard and splits his lip on the mike. He starts bleeding profusely, spitting blood into the audience and severely drenching his shirt, but *he doesn't know it!* The audience thinks it's very funny and starts goofing on him, laughing, pointing and saying things he doesn't understand. Naturally he assumes they're goofing on his blindness, so he performs even harder, bleeding that much more. Here is this kid, literally pouring his guts out, and the fucking audience thinks it's at the circus! Well, that was my first impression of "Little" Stevie Wonder, and it hung in there for a long time. Until I heard "Uptight," that is, an absolutely magic Motown item (with horns yet, way before Stax!) that served almost instantly to blot out the past. How about *that,* Stevie, the music prevailed after all!

"PLEASE MR. POSTMAN"—The Marvelettes, Tamla 54046 (Aug. 1961)

Having been both into R&B and girl-groups, I was excited to say the least when the 2 genres seemed to cross at last with the release of this record in 1961. True, we did have the Chantels, but they were much closer to R&B than to girl-group. "Please Mr. Postman" was hardly a typical Motown record, trading off the traditional pop treatment for a heavy R&B track, yet, at the same time, addressing itself squarely to the teenager with lyrics such as:

"Deliver de letter
De sooner de better..."
© 1961, Jobete

Or, as in the follow-up, "Twistin' Postman":

"Look, look,
Here comes the postman,
Twistin' down the avenooh..."
© 1961, Jobete

The Marvelettes continued with an 8-year string of hits, and although their music became somewhat more sophisticated, it was still primarily for the younger kids. During the early 70s, the group retired into private life, selling their name to a promoter who assembled a new group to do oldies shows. The Marvelettes who tour today are younger than some of the kids for whom the original group sang back in 1961!

"I HEARD IT THROUGH THE GRAPEVINE"—Marvin Gaye, Tamla 54176 (Oct. 1968)

One of the classic pop songs of all time, co-written by Norman Whitfield and Barrett Strong, the first five notes are as instantly recognizable as the first four notes of Beethoven's Fifth. The song first became known late in 1967 via Gladys Knight & The Pips, for whom Motown had pulled out all the production stops to put across their newly signed act. It was a rousing version, with a robust gospel-style delivery from Gladys and a harmonic series of vocal semantics from the Pips. Marvin Gaye's version, by contrast, was simple, understated, beautiful and fine. Interestingly enough, however, Gaye's version reportedly was recorded *prior* to the Pips' release, having been held back because of Gaye's successful pairing with Tammi Terrell. When Tammi succumbed to brain damage during 1967, the record company continued to release their material "out of the can." This eventually ran out, and the company turned to Gaye to record more solo material. Severely depressed and unable to record, Gayle laid back and watched Tamla issue his earlier "Grapevine" track, which, to the amazement of all concerned, went on to become a multi-million seller and the most successful record in Motown history. The song became a standard, and returned once again to the Pop charts, several years later, via an unusual interpretation by Creedence Clearwater Revival.

"REACH OUT I'LL BE THERE"—The Four Tops, Motown 1098 (Aug. 1966)

Originally known as the Four Aims, this group had quite an unusual background and came up here with an equally unusual record. They first began recording in 1956, providing some R&B tracks for Chess. As the years went by, they drifted more towards pop, recording for labels including Red Top, Singular, Riverside and Columbia. When they finally wound up at Motown, they were signed as a *jazz act* and relegated to the subsidiary Workshop label. They were even dispatched on a tour with Billy Eckstein to promote their jazz image. That didn't work, of course, and a new plan was devised: switch them to the parent label, put them together with Holland-Dozier-Holland, and wait for the hits to come. And come they did, in rapid succession—"Baby I Need Your Loving," "I Can't Help Myself," "It's The Same Old Song," "Shake Me, Wake Me" and numerous others. But nothing before or after ever came close to touching "Reach Out," a record which almost defies description. Levi Stubbs' lead vocal delves into areas that transcend both pop and R&B; Phil Spector once attempted to define it as "black Dylan," a bizarre sound if there ever was one! The production was rich and full, and if I'd have to call it anything, I'd call it "black Spector." I'm sure the ol' wall-of-sound man himself would not disagree.

"YOU'VE REALLY GOT A HOLD ON ME"—The Miracles, Tamla 54073 (Nov. 1962)

It's hard to pick one Miracles record, especially when you consider that they've placed more than 3 dozen on the national charts since 1959. To complicate matters, Dylan once referred to Smokey Robinson as "America's most important living poet." Some compliment, considering the source. But, if I've got to go with one, this is it. I saw him perform it numerous times, mostly on Murray The K and similar type shows. But you ain't seen nuthin' unless you saw him do it at the Apollo, or at the Howard in Washington, DC. In those environments, Smokey simply sang his ass off and each and every lady in the audience was *convinced* it was for her. During Motown's entire history, Smokey has been there and he is one of the major cornerstones of both the sound and the company. He has substantially retired from performing these days to devote more time to his duties as Executive Vice President.

"BYE BYE BABY"—Mary Wells, Motown 1003 (Jan. 1961)

Although Mary became best known for her slick pop hits with material provided by the likes of H-D-H and Smokey, I've always liked this one the best. She wrote it herself, talked her way into Berry Gordy's office for an audition, and convinced him to release it as his third Motown entry. Off-key and rough-edged throughout, this record displays pure urban raunch and revels in it! White records such as "The One Who Really Loves You" and "You Beat Me To The Punch" are not to be sneezed at (I never really cared for "My Guy" although it was by far her biggest hit), it would have been interesting to hear what would have happened if the company had let her pursue her original direction. We'll never know, but as Berry Gordy printed blatantly on his record labels, "It's What's In The Grooves That Counts."

"DO YOU LOVE ME"—The Contours, Gordy 7005 (July 1962)

Motown's only "rap" record (they are common in other areas of R&B), "Do You Love Me" was actually a reincarnation of the Isley Brothers' "Shout." Their personal appearances featured the "little bit louder now, little bit softer now" techniques, and the audience response was similar. The group came to Gordy because of member Hubert Johnson, who was a distant cousin of Jackie Wilson. Jackie arranged the audition, and Gordy snapped them up for his namesake label and provided them with one of the most uptempo pieces of material ever to come out of Motown. The record very nearly reached the top of the national charts and created a real awareness among black kids of dancing ability. For some odd reason, the Dave Clark Five chose to cover the record and sent the song back into the American top 10 some two years after the original.

"SHOTGUN"—Jr. Walker & The All Stars, Soul 35008 (Jan. 1965)

Autrey DeWalt, Jr. was his real name, and he hailed from Blytheville, Arkansas. Seems he toured with several mid-western bands, eventually settling in Battle Creek, Michigan and forming his own band there. It was there that he also hooked up with Harvey Fuqua, former lead of the Moonglows, and proprietor of the Harvey label. Signed to this label, Walker came to Motown when Harvey was absorbed some years later. His first hit was "Shotgun," one of the best "dance" records of the 60s (and there were many) and one of the first "sax" records in some time. His real contribution, of course, was his unique style on the saxophone, which appeared in all his later hits (most notably "What Does It Take" in 1969) and which was copied to perfection in Carole King's recent hit of "Jazz Man."

"I WANT YOU BACK"—The Jackson Five, Motown 1157 (Oct. 1969)

Not since the Frankie Lymon era was anyone able to sell an 11-year-old kid, but leave it to Motown to pull it off! The J5 had originated in Gary, Indiana, where they had briefly recorded for the local Steeltown label and had become the town stars. The mayor of Gary brought them to the attention of Diana Ross, who, in turn, delivered them to Gordy. "I Want You Back" opened with some of the best guitar work ever heard around Motown, featured exquisite production and young Michael Jackson and went from nowhere straight to number one. They followed with three consecutive number one records, and two more that stopped just short. Motown obligingly created a writing entity called "The Corporation" to churn out "clever" lyrics for their find, and they undoubtedly reached their pinnacle with "The Love You Save":

"Isaac said he kissed you, beneath the apple tree,
When Benjie held your hand he felt electricity,
When Alexander called you, he said he rang your chime,
Christopher discovered you're way ahead of your time.
Stop, the love you save may be your own."   © 1970, Jobete

Kid Rock of the highest order, and big business. When I saw the J5 at Madison Square Garden, their reception was rivaled only by what the Beatles got at Shea, and in my mind, they just about tied. As fine as this stuff was, an unfortunate aftereffect was some of the "dreck" which followed in other quarters, including some of Michael Jackson's solo work. Chee-Chee & Peppy (remember them?) and the Osmonds (although "One Bad Apple" wasn't half bad; producer Mike Curb reports that he offered this one to the J5 first, but that they turned it down).

"CLOUD NINE"—The Temptations, Gordy 7081 (Oct. 1968)

The Temps had been one of the staples of the Motown sound, and, towards the late 60s, they were plagued with personal problems which would lead one to expect a change in the sound of the group. Nobody was ready, however, for the change they pulled off in 1968. Out of nowhere, with no warning, here comes The Temps with "Cloud Nine," a totally new sound quickly tagged by the trade as "psychedelic soul." Wah-wah pedals, echo, spacey production and lyrics full of drug references and social problems, they were all abundantly present in this record. The Temps stuck with this style for several years to come, ultimately refining it in the classic "Papa Was A Rollin' Stone."

RMN

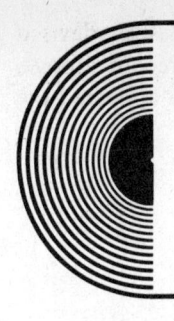

IMPORTANT MUSIC INVENTIONS

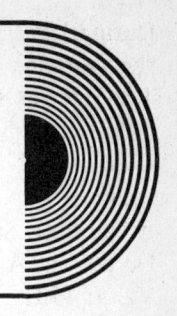

INVENTION: Phonograph record
INVENTORS: Thomas Edison, Charles Cros, Emile Berliner, Peter Goldmark
YEAR: 1877-1957

The matter of whether the phonograph and record were invented by French poet Charles Cros or Thomas Edison, the Wizard of Menlo Park, depends primarily on whether you're French or American. The former described a process for recording sound only a few months before Edison actually built his hand-cranked phonograph. Ten years later, Emile Berliner improved on it by creating the lateral-cut flat disc which led in 1948 to the invention of the long-playing microgroove record by Peter Goldmark, director of CBS Laboratories. Goldmark's record not only had a playing time of 23 minutes per side, obtained by using a super-thin recording groove and cutting record speed from 78 revolutions per minute to 33⅓, but used a new virtually unbreakable substance, vinyl.

Edison's original phonograph, patented in 1877, consisted of tin foil wrapped around a rotating cylinder. The vibration of his voice as he spoke into a recording horn caused a stylus to cut grooves into the tin foil. The first sound recording made was Edison reciting "Mary Had a Little Lamb."

During 1957, engineers for London and Columbia Records and Westrex devised rival systems for squeezing two channels of sound into a single record groove. The Westrex system won out, and the first commercial stereo disc appeared the following summer.

INVENTION: Stereo/multichannel recording
INVENTOR: A. D. Blumlein
YEAR: 1931

Stereo recording can trace its beginnings back to 1931 when A. D. Blumlein, chief engineer for Electric & Musical Industries Ltd. in England began experimenting with microphone placement and the simultaneous recording of two independent channels of sound. The first commercial use of stereo came with the recording of the soundtrack of Walt Disney's *Fantasia* some nine years later. Despite several attempts to put stereo on the air and on records in the 1940s and early 1950s, it wasn't until Westrex developed a technique for cutting left and right stereo channels in the same record groove in 1957 that stereo became a medium for popular music. The first stereo tape recorder appeared in 1949 when Magnecord created one by adding a second record head directly below the first. Multichannel recorders developed since have simply used the same technique, adding the required number of record heads and expanding tape width as required. Stereo radio broadcasts, involving one AM and one FM station, date from the late 1940s, but it wasn't until 1961 that the current multiplex system of broadcasting stereo from a single station was adopted. Developed by Zenith and General Electric, it leaned heavily on work done by FM's inventor, Major Edwin Armstrong, as early as 1935, and by Murray Crosby.

INVENTION: Dynamic loudspeaker
INVENTOR: Chester W. Rice, Edward W. Kellogg
YEAR: 1924

Radio was the craze of the 1920s, but until the development of the moving coil loudspeaker by two General Electric engineers, Edward Kellogg and Chester Rice, it was necessary to listen through hard bakelite headphones, and to phonograph records through an acoustic horn. The Kellogg-Rice design called for an electromagnet fixed to a paper cone which could move back and forth to set up sound vibrations. Over the past half-century, there have been refinements in manufacturing techniques, but the speaker in use in your home stereo system or at a rock concert is easily recognizeable as the one Kellogg and Rice developed. The Kellogg-Rice loudspeaker was first used in the Radiola 1, a $250 table radio introduced in 1925. With the coming of talking pictures in 1927, engineers like Robert Stephens and James B. Lansing experimented with a number of speaker designs for use in theaters, which led to the development of high fidelity loudspeakers for the home in the late 1940s.

IMPORTANT MUSIC INVENTIONS

Fellophone Super Two, two-tube radio C.1925 with loudspeaker

INVENTION: Power amplifier
INVENTORS: Thomas Edison, John Fleming, Lee De Forest
YEAR: 1883-1925

Just as Thomas Edison's incandescent electric light bulb led inevitably to the diode developed by John Fleming in the laboratories of the Marconi Company and the Fleming diode led to the development of the triode tube by Lee De Forest in 1907, the invention of these vacuum tubes led inevitably to the development of the three-stage amplifier circuit in the mid-1920s. Edison's contribution was a filament burning in a near-vacuum inside a glass envelope. Fleming and De Forest put the light bulb to work as a detector of and amplifier for audio signals, and De Forest showed how several tubes could be used in combination to produce signals loud enough to drive a loudspeaker. That basic design was adapted to radio design in the early 1920s by a number of manufacturers; to the phonograph by Brunswick-Balke-Collender in 1926; and to high fidelity use by Hermon Hosmer Scott in 1947. The basic design was used in movie houses with the coming of sound in 1927, later in public address amplifiers by David Bogen, and more recently in theatres and concert halls demanding very high levels of power with minimum distortion.

IMPORTANT MUSIC INVENTIONS

INVENTION: Microphone
INVENTORS: Alexander Graham Bell, Thomas Edison, Emile Berliner
YEAR: 1876-77

Alexander Graham Bell, an acoustician who became interested in telegraphy as a means of teaching deaf-mutes to talk, fashioned a crude microphone using the structure of the human ear as a model, complete with diaphragm. Berliner, a draper's assistant in Washington, DC, felt sure that he could improve on Bell's design by using the diaphragm to interact with a fixed plate, generating tiny electrical signals. At just about the same time, Edison created a microphone based on the same principle which used carbon granules, leading to a lengthy patent fight between the two which ultimately was resolved in Edison's favor. From Berliner's and Edison's basic designs stem such microphone designs as ribbon and condenser microphones as well as dynamics and piezo-electric types. Next to loudspeakers, microphones have undergone fewer changes in basic design since their introduction than just about any other electronic device.

First recording microphone.

INVENTION: Tape recorder
INVENTORS: Valdemar Poulsen, Fritz Pfleumer, George Eash
YEAR: 1898-1964

Danish telephone engineer Valdemar Poulsen was working on a system for making telephone lines more efficient when he came up with the idea of using an electromagnet to store sounds on a spool of piano wire. His telegraphone, patented in 1898, was the first wire recorder. In 1932, a German chemist named Fritz Pfleumer approached the giant I. G. Farbenindustrie with an idea for gluing particles onto a strip of plastic as a substitute recording medium. Two years later, Farben's BASF division had produced the first magnetic tape, and AEG a recorder to use it. Because Adolf Hitler considered the tape recorder so important, little was said about it until the end of World War II. In 1949, engineers for Magnecord found that by using two recording heads—one positioned above the other—it was possible to record stereophonically, a concept embodied in the first self-contained tape cartridge, developed by Cleveland inventor George Eash in 1954. Eash's cartridge, designed so that the inventor could listen to music in his car, led to the introduction of the 8-track cartridge by William Lear in 1965. A year earlier, engineers at Philips Gloebenlampenfabrik in Holland had miniaturized the twin-reel system developed by BASF and AEG and put it inside a cassette shell for use as a pocket dictating system.

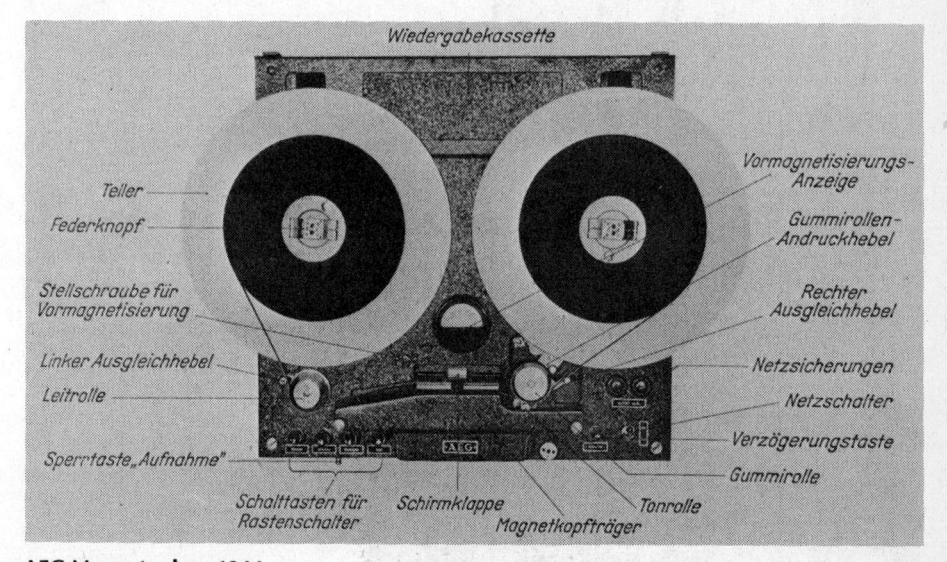

AEG Magnetophon 1944

IMPORTANT MUSIC INVENTIONS

INVENTION: Broadcasting
INVENTORS: Guglielmo Marconi, Lee De Forest, Edwin H. Armstrong, et al.
YEAR: 1895-1939

Electrical experimentation was all the rage in the 1890s when 20-year old Guglielmo Marconi began building his own Morse code sending and receiving equipment and set up experimental stations in his father's garden. Within four years, he was sending wireless messages from France to England, and by 1901 from England to America. However, it wasn't until the invention of the three-element audio tube by Lee De Forest in 1906 that voice transmission became practical, a step which led directly to the introduction of commercial radio broadcasting as we know it in 1920. While serving as a Signal Corps officer in France in 1918, Major Armstrong developed the superheterodyne receiver, a circuit designed to get maximum amplification from weak signals detected by the audion tube. Armstrong went on, in the 1930s, to develop frequency modulation broadcasting and to outline the techniques which resulted in commercial FM stereo broadcasting in 1961.

Marconi console radio, early 1930s.

IMPORTANT MUSIC INVENTIONS

INVENTION: Transistor
INVENTORS: John Bardeen, Walter Brattain, William Shockley
YEAR: 1947

Actually the result of work by a research team of Bell Telephone Laboratories physicists who were looking for a device which would be much smaller and much more energy-efficient than the electron tube, the transistor led inexorably to the integrated circuit (IC) and large-scale integrated circuit (LSI) which form the building blocks for most modern-day sound and recording equipment. Bardeen, Brattain and Shockley evolved a number of theories involving the practical use of semiconductor crystals and conducted thousands of experiments before discovering that under certain circumstances, germanium crystals could amplify a human voice as much as forty times. That discovery earned the three a Nobel Prize for physics in 1956. Engineers from Zenith substituted transistors for vacuum tubes in a portable radio in the late 1940s, and within 15 years the transistor had revolutionized not only radio but also tape recording and personal listening habits.

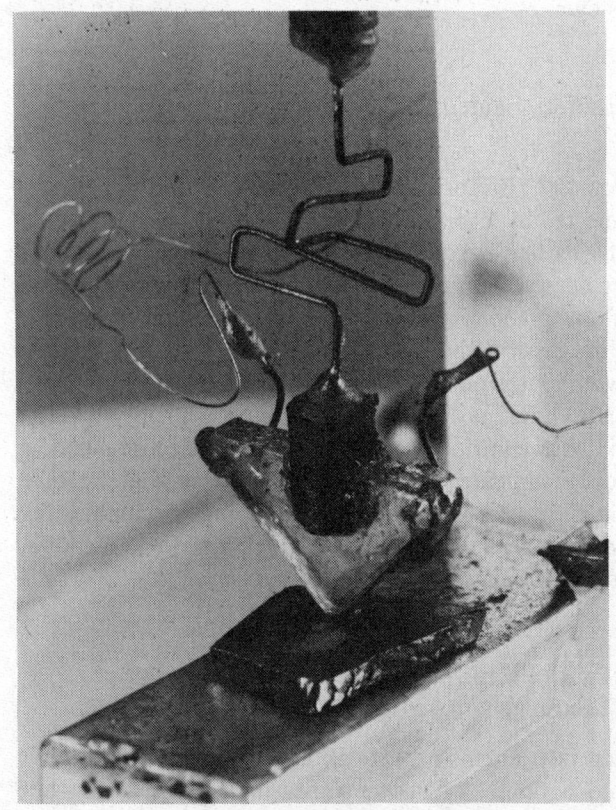

The original transistor developed by Shockley, Brattain and Bardeen.

INVENTION: Synthesizer
INVENTOR: Thaddeus Cahill, Leon Theremin, Robert Moog
YEAR: 1896-1964

Thaddeus Cahill's telharmonium weighed over 200 tons and took several railroad flatcars to move from one place to another, but it constituted the first true music synthesizing device. It led in 1920 to preliminary work on the theremin, a pole which generated musical sounds when hands were waved around it invented by Leon Theremin, the man also responsible in 1931 for the first electronic rhythm device. Laurens Hammond, the man who invented the electric organ in 1935, also developed the Novachord, an instrument which found steady work in recording studios during the 1950s, and a unit which led to the development in 1964 by Robert Moog of the Moog synthesizer. Moog, a technically-oriented musician who had been manufacturing and selling a do-it-yourself theremin kit, presented a paper before the Audio Engineering Society in which he outlined the possibility of combining significant features of the theremin, the Novachord, the Ondes Martenot, a 1929 device invented by Maurice Martenot, and the RCA Synthesizer Mark II in a single, reasonably compact, reasonably-priced device which could imitate virtually any musical instrument as well as create musical sounds of its own.

INVENTION: Piano
INVENTOR: Bartolomeo Cristofori, Laurens Hammond, et al. (electric piano)
YEAR: 1709-1965

Harpsichord maker Bartolomeo Cristofori one day built a keyboard instrument in which tiny hammers connected by levers to the keys struck the strings, instead of plucking them, as in the earlier harpsichords and virginals. The invention achieved little attention for nearly seventy years, until Mozart began performing on and composing for the piano. A hundred years later found the piano firmly ensconsed not only in classical music, but in the better parlors of rural American and the best bawdy houses of New Orleans and along the Mississippi River. During the late 1930s, Laurens Hammond, the man who invented the electronic organ, created the Novachord, a precursor of today's electric piano. A similar instrument, the Solovox, appeared at about the same time, and together, they found regular work in film studios and in the recording of commercials for radio and later for television. By the 1960s, the electric piano we know today had become an integral part of rock music.

INVENTION: Guitar
INVENTOR: Unknown; Les Paul (electric guitar)
YEAR: about 1300; 1927 (electric guitar)

The earliest plucked stringed instruments predate Biblical times. By the Middle Ages, they had evolved into a family of instruments which included the lute and cittera, which in turn metamorphosed into something like the classic guitar. Because it was portable, relatively easy to play and relatively simple to make, the guitar quickly became the people's musical instrument, used to accompany ballads and provide entertainment and dance accompaniment. It found its way early into American jazz. In 1927, a young jazz musician with an avid interest in the new field of electronics, Les Paul, experimented with the addition of a ceramic phono pickup mounted directly on his guitar and connected to a rudimentary amplifier. Result: the electric guitar as we know it. Later improvement consisted of better-quality amplifier circuits and more sophisticated pickups, but today's electric guitar is essentially the one developed by Paul.

INVENTION: Distortion devices (wah-wah pedal, fuzz-tone, reverb, etc.)
INVENTORS: Unknown
YEAR: 1924

These oscillating devices share a common ancestry with the electronic synthesizer and can trace their history back to the oscillators built by kitchen tinkerers in the early 1920s which resulted in the theremin and later the small synthesizer. Deliberately-introduced distortion didn't occur in recordings (or in live performances) until the mid-1960s, when the Rolling Stones introduced the fuzz-tone and the wah-wah pedal. Reverberation, which had been used to "correct" an otherwise dull, lifeless recording, had been around since the early 1950s, but it wasn't until the mid-sixties that it was used deliberately to create musical effects. An early reverb "unit," used by Columbia Records while the company maintained headquarters on Seventh Avenue in New York, was the building's stairwell. Later, more compact units consisted of a spring mounted in a box. Very sophisticated electronic reverb units appeared in the mid-1970s which permit adjusting very precise degrees of reverberation.

INVENTION: Laser
INVENTORS: Charles Townes, Arthur Schawlow, N. Basov, A. Prokhorov, T. H. Maiman
YEAR: 1957-1960

The theory of light amplification by stimulation of emission of radiation (laser) was the result of more than ten years' work by two physicists associated with Bell Telephone Laboratories. Charles Townes had been working on gas spectrascophy in the 1940s when he developed the maser, a device using a ruby for microwave relay of energy. Working with Arthur Schawlow, he stumbled on helium neon gas as a more satisfactory medium. However, the task of building the first working laser fell to two Russians, N. Basov and A. Prokhorov in 1958, a year after the Townes-Schawlow theoretical research. Almost yearly for the next 20 years, Townes, Schawlow and other Bell Labs scientists improved on the idea to the point in the early 1970s where lasers could be used as replacements for conventional stage lighting at rock concerts. The Electric Light Orchestra and Todd Rundgren are only two acts which use this very sophisticated narrow-beam lighting to create a number of very unusual effects.

144 NEW TECHNOLOGY

INVENTION: Psychedelic lighting
INVENTOR: Unknown
YEAR: 1923-1943

The effects of black, or ultraviolet, light were known in the time of the cave man, and attempts to create it naturally were part of the witchcraft of the Middle Ages. But it didn't exist in electric form until the invention of mercury lamps in the 1920s, when electricity was discharged through mercury in a tube to produce it. Used initially by stage magicians and for decoration, it quickly found industrial application in the photochemical and medical fields. Stroboscopic lights, another type of electrical discharge lamp, appeared in the early 1930s, when they were used in stop-motion photography and certain industrial applications. Their association with rock music began in France with the disco movement of the mid-1960s, when these and certain other industrial lamps were integrated into the total musical experience. Flashing incandescent lamps (great-grandchildren of Thomas Edison's incandescent bulb) and high-voltage tubing are among the other types of lighting commonly associated with rock.

INVENTION: Video disc
INVENTOR: John Logie Baird
YEAR: 1924

In 1924, 34-year old John Logie Baird was experimenting with the transmission of pictures by radio waves as well as sound, using a cardboard disc cut from a

"Magnavision" optical videodisc player by Magnavox.

hatbox and a projection lamp housed in an empty biscuit tin. An offshoot of his research was a wax-coated cardboard disc which revolved at high speed and contained about one minute's worth of a very blurry picture. The device was demonstrated the following year at Selfridge's Department Store. Nearly half a century later, in 1970, research teams for two European electronics gaints, Decca in England and the German-based Telefunken Company, came up with similar ideas for a disc which could record pictures in full color as well as sound on a long-playing disc. Since then, research teams made up of engineers from the world's leading electronics firms have been hard at work on videodisc systems which would be better and cheaper than Teldec's. The first to reach the market in the United States was one developed more or less jointly by MCA in the United States and Philips in Holland. Others include systems developed by Matsushita, RCA, JVC, and others.

RA

NEW TECHNOLOGY

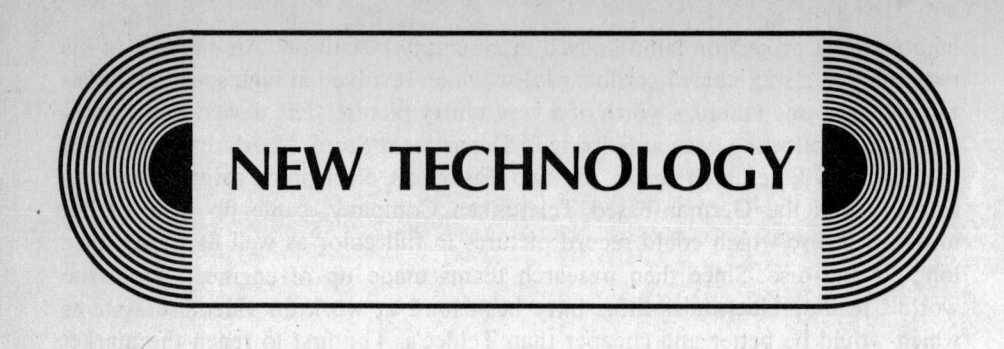

The unparalleled success of contemporary music in recent years has been due, in no small part, to the proliferation of ever better high fidelity stereo equipment which has brought the sounds of today's music into millions of homes throughout the United States and the world at large. Never content with current state-of-the-art hi-fi equipment, those manufacturers and engineers who are responsible for the development and advancement of electronic sound reproduction are forever seeking to achieve the ultimate in sonic realism.

A number of technological breakthroughs have resulted in new audio products in recent years, and still other advances promise to revolutionize the fields of recording and sound reproduction in the near future. Technological advances in audio may be divided into three categories: improvements in conventional analog sound reproducing techniques, developments in the field of digital sound storage and reproduction, and the integration of audio and video technologies. The past year has witnessed significant advances in each of these areas.

Advances in Home Recording Equipment

The stereo cassette tape deck has emerged as the most popular home recording instrument, with nearly 100 million cassette recorders of varying degrees of quality now in the hands of the American public. From its inception, however, the slow-speed cassette tape format has suffered from an inability to capture the true dynamic range (loudest louds and softest softs) of live music. While cassette tape and cassette tape hardware has improved in quality since Philips Company of the Netherlands introduced this recording format some fifteen years ago, residual tape hiss and the limited maximum recording levels which could be stored on the small tape package have continued to plague the industry.

Now, a new type of recording tape known as pure-metal particle tape, promises to improve cassette tape performance by a whole order of magnitude. Already introduced by at least three major tape firms, the new tape can handle much higher recording levels, particularly at high frequencies, where earlier tapes tended to introduce high orders of distortion. There are, however, obstacles to the wide acceptance of the new tape formulation. While music recorded on new metal tape can be played back on conventional cassette machines, such machines are incapable of *making* proper recordings using the new tape, or of erasing previous recordings on this tape. Accordingly, millions of tape decks

NEW TECHNOLOGY

are rendered obsolete as far as metal tape is concerned. Acting in their usual mercurial fashion, makers of high fidelity cassette tape decks have, in the past few months, managed to come up with new decks in a variety of price categories, that can handle the new tape. Both the tape and the new machines are generally costlier than previous conventional software and hardware, but that may well change as acceptance of the new recording medium becomes widespread. Figure 1 illustrates the increased recording capability of the new metal particle tape compared with older, conventional tapes.

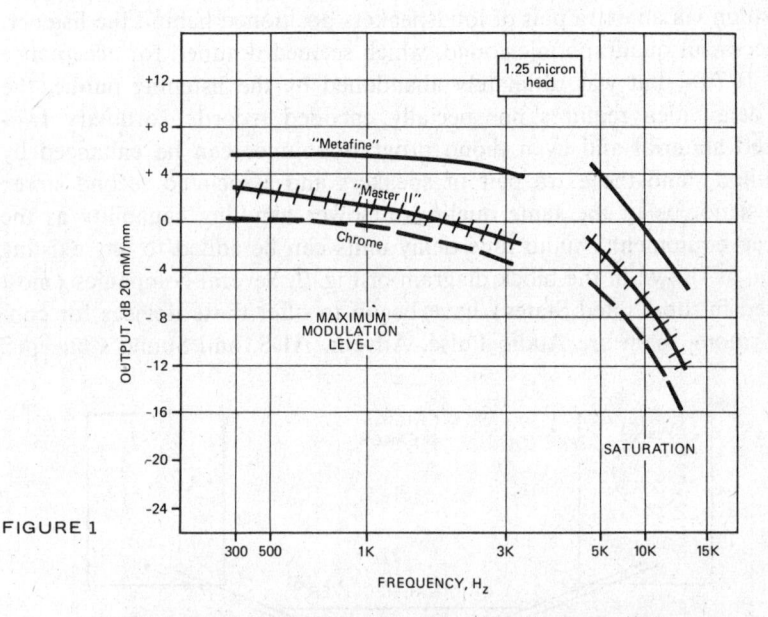

FIGURE 1

3M's "Scotch" Brand Metal Particle Tape, Called Metafine, provides higher maximum output levels (recording levels) particularly at high, trebel frequencies where conventional oxide tapes tend to saturate quite easily.

One of the newly introduced pure-metal cassette tapes which promises improved fidelity in home stereo cassette recorders.

Recreating the Concert Hall at Home

Even the very finest recorded stereo program sources, reproduced over the best stereo equipment in a home listening environment suffers from a degree of unrealism caused by the room acoustics in which the music is played. In a large concert hall, delayed reflected sounds reach our ears from the distant walls, ceiling and other remote surfaces of the listening space. Our ears tell us that we are in a large hall.

Now, electronic devices known as audio time delay units are able to recreate that same sonic illusion by delaying the music signals and reproducing them in echo-like fashion via an extra pair of loudspeakers positioned behind the listener. Unlike unsuccessful quadraphonic sound, which seemed destined for acceptance in the early 1970's, but was ultimately abandoned by the listening public, the audio time delay idea requires no specially encoded records (ordinary two-channel stereo material and even mono program sources can be enhanced by the new method) and the extra pair of speakers and associated second stereo amplifier need not be of the same quality or power handling capability as the primary stereo equipment. Audio time delay units can be added to any existing stereo system, as shown in the block diagram of Fig. 2. Several companies (most of them based in the United States) have begun to offer these devices for consumer use. Among them are Audio Pulse, Advent, ADS, and Sound Concepts.

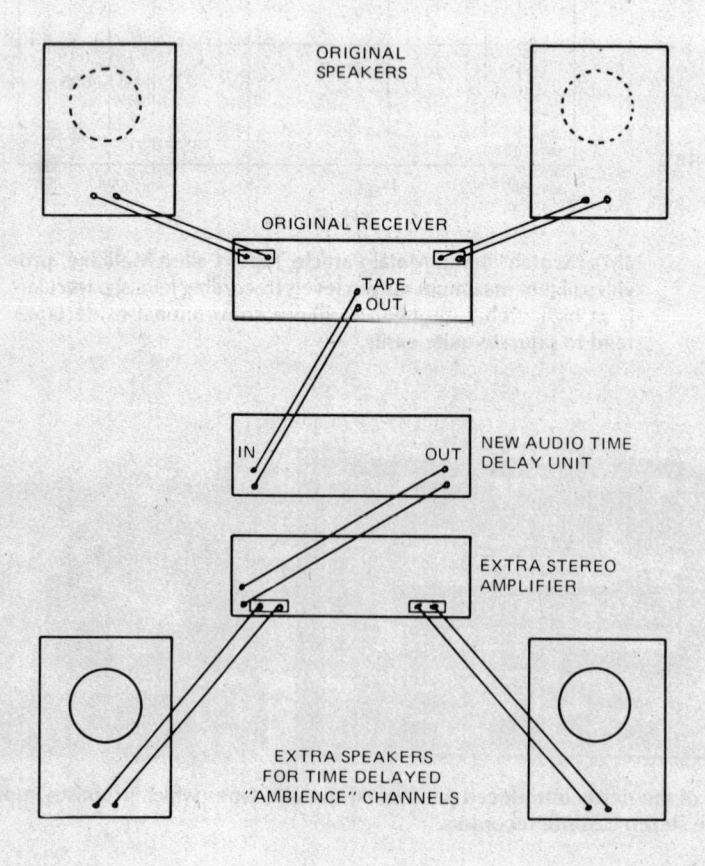

FIGURE 2

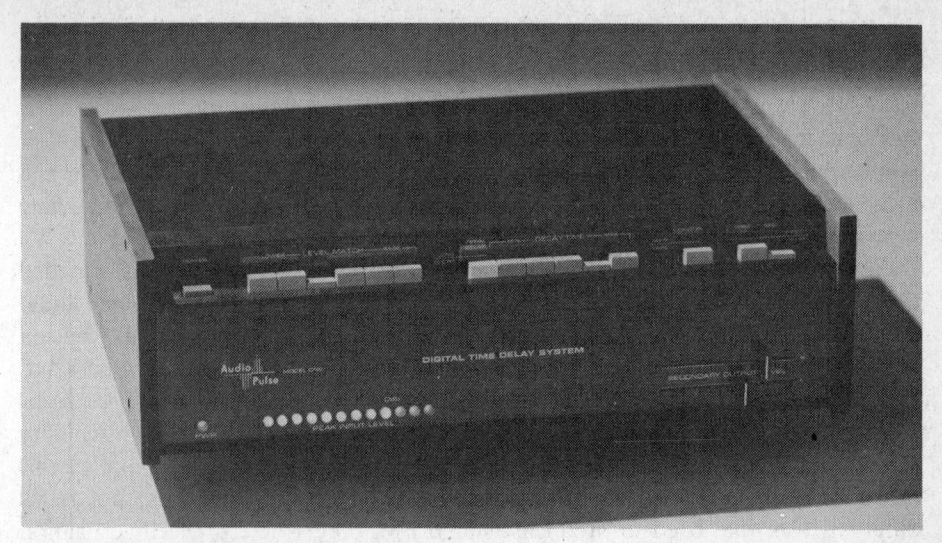

One of the first Audio Time Delay units developed to help recreate the ambience of a concert hall in a home listening room environment.

New Program Sources for Music

In the late 1950's, FM radio stations were suffering great economic hardships. Despite FM's greater fidelity and inherently noise-free reception, AM radio was king of the airwaves and those pioneering entrepreneurs who had gambled on the inherent superiority of FM radio were facing commercial disaster. The Federal Communications Commission, intent on saving FM radio, authorized a system of transmission which would permit FM stations to broadcast in two-channel stereo, which was, by the beginning of the 1960's, gaining favor in the recording industry. Whether the ultimate success of stereo was due to FM broadcasting or vice versa is difficult to say, but the fact is that today, FM radio is commercially healthier than AM. Small wonder, then, that now it is the AM broadcasters who are crying for assistance and again, the FCC intends to come to the rescue.

Currently, some six different techniques for broadcasting stereo over AM are being considered by the FCC. As the case in FM, new receivers will be needed when the FCC makes its decision, but these are not expected to be much costlier than existing radios. Advantages of Stereo AM radio, when it does come, will be particularly noted in car radios, where stereo FM radio has been anything but a total success. AM signals can be picked up at greater distances than FM and will be less susceptible to fading, distortion caused by changing antenna orientation (as when cars change direction of travel) and the other problems which have vexed drivers while trying to listen to stereo FM. Current predictions are that the Federal Communications Commission may make its decision by late 1979 or early 1980, after which there is likely to be a transition period from six to twelve months before broadcasting begins, to permit manufacturers to re-tool for stereo AM set production and distribution. To be sure, conversion of AM to stereo AM will not render that broadcast service any improvement in overall fidelity (generally, AM signals contain frequencies only up to about 5,000 Hertz, whereas FM broadcasts include all frequencies up to 15,000 Hz, sufficient for true high fidelity reproduction) but high fidelity reproduction offers less audible benefit in a moving vehicle than it does in a home music system and it is expected that the new broadcast format will enjoy almost immediate acceptance by the driving public.

In October of 1978, the Japanese Broadcasting Authority, NHK, launched dual-channel audio broadcasting on its TV network. The dual channel audio facility is currently being used both for bi-lingual audio service (push a button and you can listen to the dialogue of a film either in Japanese or in English) and for stereophonic transmission of music programs. Outpaced by Japanese technology, American industry is now urging the FCC to investigate the possibility of stereo-TV in the United States. The technology needed to accomplish this has been well known in this country for many years and is, in fact, not much different from that used to broadcast stereo FM. Nevertheless, the investigation process (several differing techniques are being proposed for stereo-TV) and the rule-making process are likely to take from three to four years, after which time we may see an approved stereo audio system for U.S. TV. By the time stereo TV arrives, it is probable that millions of homes will also be enjoying large-screen TV, so that the present objections to wide-spaced sound accompanying a small-screen picture may no longer be as valid as they are today.

Improving Conventional Phonograph Discs

Most mass produced records are produced from master tapes which, in turn, are edited from a series of individual recorded tape tracks. This technique of multi-track studio tape recording affords tremendous flexibility to both the recording artists and the recording engineers. But the successive "dubbings" on tape do tend to add noise or hiss to the resulting master tape from which the master disc is cut and, as noted earlier, tape also imposes limitations on dynamic range.

In recent years, many small recording companies have actually reverted to a system of record making that pre-dates the use of the tape recorder. The system is known as direct-to-disc recording and, as its name implies, the intermediate taping process is eliminated entirely. That means that the performers must create their music in real-time. There are no opportunities for correcting errors or poor performances. Any mistake in the performance means a complete re-do of the entire contents of one side of the finished disc. On the other hand, eliminating the tape process permits making records with much quieter background noise levels and, in many instances, much more realistic extremes of dynamic range. Usually, extra care is taken in the subsequent processing steps from master disc (lacquer), to the final vinyl disc product. Because of this methodology, however, only a limited number of pressings or copies can be obtained, so that each direct-to-disc offering is in effect a limited edition recording. These discs, now sold primarily through high-fidelity audio outlets and some record shops, carry a premium price which is generally more than double that of conventionally mass produced records. Although there are already more than one hundred album titles available in the direct-to-disc format, it is highly unlikely that the direct-to-disc format will ever supplant the easier-to-produce tape-mastered discs which have been responsible for the burgeoning contemporary music record industry in the past decade.

Noiseless Discs

While direct-to-disc records eliminate the noise contributed by the intermediate taping process, these and all discs have their own level of surface or background noise which, until recently, always masked attempts to inscribe truly soft passages of music on a record.

Now, a company called dbx, Inc. has launched a program to introduce discs to the listening public which are literally surface-noise free. Their system involves a coding and decoding scheme known as companding. During the recording process, all signals are linearly compressed. That is, soft sounds are made louder while loud sounds are made softer. In this way, the great dynamic range of live music (normally ranging from 80 to 90 dB between softest and loudest sounds) can be contained in a decibel span of only 40 to 45 dB, since compression is at a uniform rate of two-to-one. If one were to listen to such a disc using ordinary playback equipment, it would sound terrible. However, if a complementary expander device is inserted in the signal path during playback, the original dynamic range is fully restored. Even more important, since, in the encoding process, the soft sounds have been "pushed up" well above the surface noise level, during playback, those soft passages are restored to their correct relative levels while the surface noise level is pushed down even further (by the action of the playback expander), rendering them all but totally inaudible.

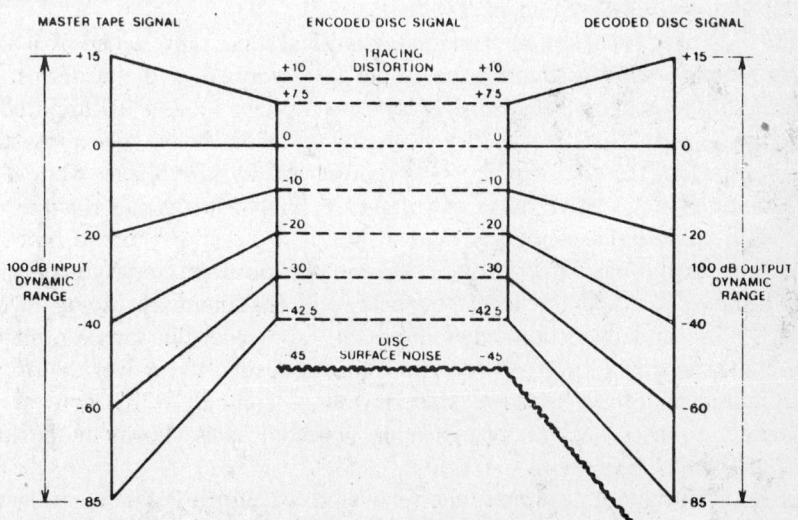

FIGURE 3

Diagram depicting the combination of signal compression during encoding and expansion during decoding that results in surface noise reduction and dynamic range retention on dbx encoded discs.

To encourage widespread acceptance of this new form of disc, dbx, Inc. has developed a low-cost decoder which will sell for little more than $100.00 and which can be connected to any stereo component system. By the end of 1979, dbx, Inc. claims that there will be more than 100 album titles. dbx, Inc. is currently licensing several smaller record firms for their system and, in addition to permitting them to issue dbx-encoded discs on their own, is making guaranteed purchases of discs which will be distributed by the company through their normal hardware outlets. The principle of companding employed by dbx in their encoded discs is illustrated in the diagram of Fig. 3.

The Digital Recording Revolution

All of the improvements in music reproduction which we have dealt with thus far lie in the analog domain. That is, music is represented by continuous signals (the wiggles in a record groove are a good example) which are *analogous* to the amplitudes of sounds we hear. Thanks to advances in computer technology, there is another way of representing any continuous event such as a pattern of music. It is based upon digital technology, in which any event or amplitude can be represented by a number or numerical code. In simple terms, if we had a numbering system consisting of only the numbers 0, 1, 2, 3 and 4, a signal that was instantaneously low in amplitude might be represented by a "0" while a loud instantaneous amplitude of sound might be represented by the number "4". In digital work, however, normal numbers are not used. Instead, a binary numbering system consisting of only "0's" and "1's" is used. If we needed only four numbers plus the number "0", all of these could be represented by various combinations of 0's and 1's, requiring only three "bits" of information. Thus, conventional zero would be represented by the digital notation "000", conventional "1" would be written 001, 2 would be 010, three would be 011 and 4 would be written as 100.

Referring to Fig. 4 we see how an analog musical tone, represented by a single cycle or alternation of a sound wave, could be described in digital terms. The tone's amplitude is sampled at nine points (A through I) and its amplitude at each of those points is described by a digital number. Now, to express these numbers in electronic circuitry, a "0" is represented by no voltage, while a "1" is represented by a positive pulse of voltage, as shown in the table at the right of the figure. These pulses, or absences of pulses are easily recorded onto tape and so long as the base-line zero-voltage and the positive going voltage pulse are well above the tape-hiss level and below the maximum recording level of the tape, noise and distortion inherent in the tape recording process play no part whatever in digital tape recording. All that is needed to recover the original analog equivalent of the tone we started with is a circuit which converts the pulses and no-pulses back to recognizable amplitudes, as shown in the lower portion of Fig. 3.

Clearly, in our simple example, the recovered waveform is far from identical to the original one (though the general form is correct). If, however, we sampled the waveform at hundreds or even thousands of points (instead of at eight points) we could come even closer to a perfectly faithful representation

NEW TECHNOLOGY

Sampling Point	Value	3-Bit Binary	Equivalent Pulse Code
A	2	010	⎍
B	3	011	⎍
C	4	100	⎍
D	3	011	⎍
E	2	010	⎍
F	1	001	⎍
G	0	000	—
H	1	001	⎍
I	2	010	⎍

Signal waveform to be translated to digital code.

Recovered waveform from digital code.

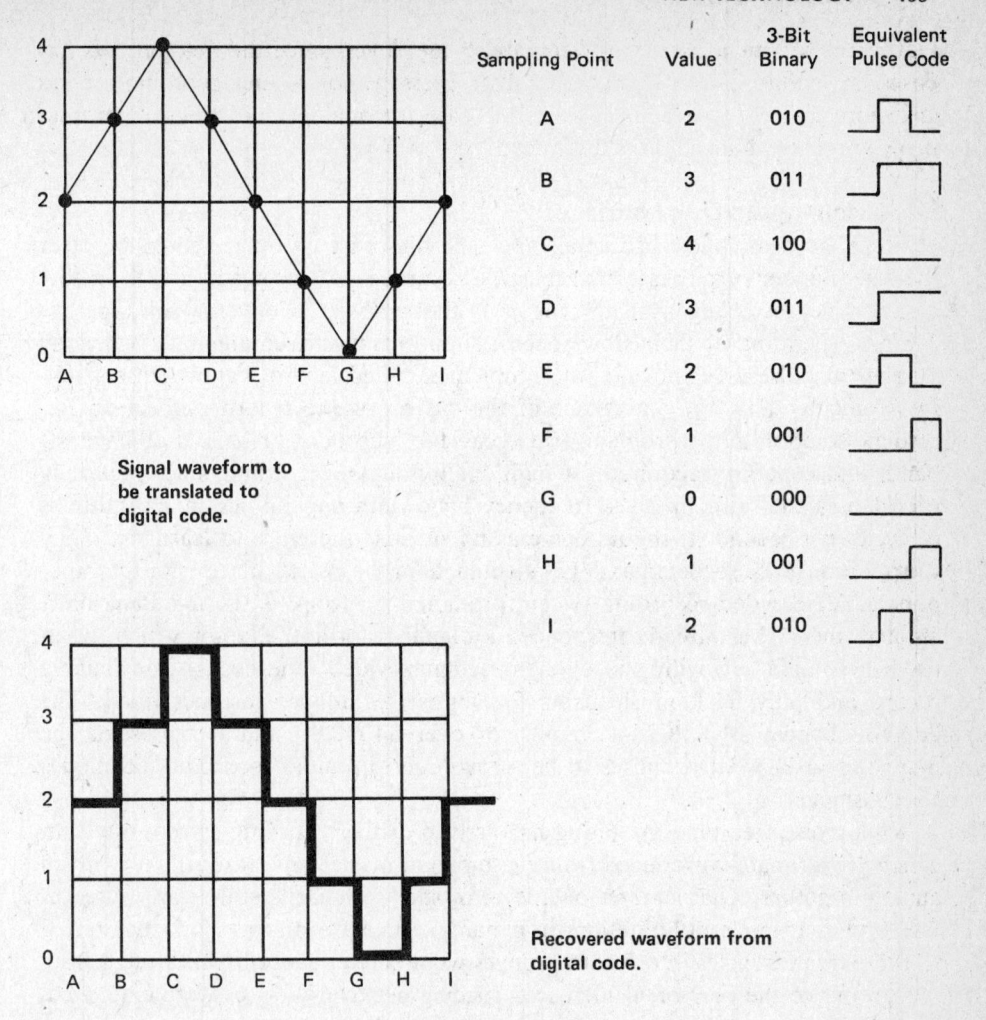

FIGURE 4

of the original signal. In newly developed modern digital tape recorders, that is just what is done. In a sixteen-bit digital system (as opposed to our three-bit system illustrated), as many as 32,000 distinct levels or amplitudes of a tone may be expressed in "zeroes" and "ones"—more than enough to faithfully describe the loudness levels of any musical pattern.

Tape recording systems which employ this digital principle are already in use in major recording studios around the country. Since such tape recording systems do not add noise or distortion to the finished master tape, digital recording on tape offers all the advantages of direct-to-disc recording along with all of the flexibility and editing possibilities of the older, analog master taping process now used by most recording companies.

Already, there are several commercially available discs which were mastered using digital tape. While these initial digitally-mastered discs now sell for about as much as the premium direct-to-disc records discussed earlier, it is expected that prices for such discs will eventually come down, since the new process imposes no limitations on numbers of discs pressed, nor is the recording session any more difficult to execute than is the case for analog multi-track recordings used for mass-produced discs until now.

The Video/Audio Disc Marriage

From the description of digital tape recording just given, it should be clear that the number of pulses which must be recorded per second in a high-quality digital tape recording system runs into the *millions*. Conventional tape recorders, operating at their slow speeds, simply cannot accommodate that great number of pulses. Technically, the problem is called lack of bandwidth capability. Coincidentally, the emergence of the video cassette recorder offers an immediate solution to the problem. Video cassette recorders, or VCR's *do* have the bandwidth capability required for high quality digital recording, since recording of video signals also involves frequency bandwidth capabilities in the millions of cycles per second. It should come as no surprise therefore to learn that Sony Corporation (whose Betamax VCR's compete in the marketplace with the other popular VHS video recording system promoted by RCA, JVC and Panasonic, among others) has already introduced a digital recording adaptor which, when used in conjunction with one of their Betamax video tape decks, can actually record and play back music using the digital techniques just described. The adaptor, known as a PCM-1, retails for over $4000.00, but it represents the first product in what promises to be a revolution in audio recording techniques for consumers.

While noise-free tape mastering has arrived at the recording studio, the *discs* which are ultimately produced from these digital master tapes are still very much analog in nature. That is, their own level of surface noise is still clearly discernible, and their inherent limitations in dynamic range are still present, since trying to cut extreme wiggles into record grooves would either cause breakthrough from one groove to the next or, if increased spacing between grooves were employed, recording time would be reduced.

An all-digital music disc is clearly in the future, however, and once again the technology for it derives from progress made in the video field. In mid-1979, Magnavox Company began test-marketing its video disc in Atlanta and Seattle. Immediate sell-outs of available inventory resulted. Magnavision, as the company calls its new video disc, involves what looks very much like a silver-coated phonograph record. However, this disc contains no visible grooves nor is there any form of needle or stylus needed to play it back. Instead, the disc contains microscopic pits or shadow areas imbedded beneath its protective surface. A complex system of a laser beam and reacting mirrors "reads" the pattern of shadows and translates them into the necessary video signal pattern needed to activate your TV set and produce full-color pictures on your home TV screen. Clearly, the wide bandwidth needed for picture reproduction that is built into the Magnavision video disc system would also lend itself to a fully digital *audio* recording.

While Magnavox has not yet indicated their intention to offer an audio version of their video disc (the audio track on the present Magnavision disc uses conventional analog signals), other high technology companies have. JVC (Japan Victor Company) for example, recently demonstrated their new video/audio digital disc system which, unlike the optical-laser approach of Magnavox, uses a different principle employing what they call a capacitive pickup. In this disc system, there are also no grooves, as such, but a flat pickup-needle rides along the surface of the disc and translates conductive patterns from beneath the surface of the disc into electrical signals that are either equivalent to a video signal (in the case of the picture version of the disc) or to a digital audio signal which can then be converted to conventional analog waveforms for reproduction over your stereo high fidelity system.

Still other systems have been proposed (both for video discs and digital audio discs) by companies such as RCA and Panasonic. Unfortunately, none of these systems is compatible with the other and there are fears that unless a standard system is agreed upon by these major manufacturers, marketing of the new video/audio disc format will prove difficult. The failure of quadraphonic sound to attract the buying public because of the multiplicity of systems and formats that were proposed for 4-channel sound is cited as an example of why the video/digital audio disc makers had better come to some agreement as to format and system very quickly.

To further complicate the matter, the giant Philips Company of the Netherlands has recently demonstrated yet another version of a digital audio disc. This version is designed strictly for *audio* and has no potential for video reproduction. The disc is much smaller in size than other audio/video discs proposed, and Philips argues that a true digital audio disc should be designed strictly with audio requirements in mind and should not be a spin-off from video technology and requirements.

While it is clear that the industry is in for some soul-searching and a period of internal struggle as all of these systems sort themselves out, there is no question but that the music industry (or at least the recording industry segment of it) is about to undergo a major upheaval. Industry pundits are predicting that the phonograph record, as we now know it, may be an obsolete relic in a decade or so.

LF

WHO'S WHO
ARTISTS

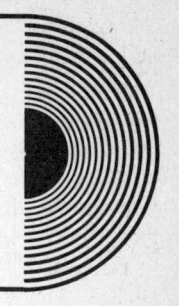

ABBA

The great Swedish vocal group led by producers/writers Benny Andersson and Bjorn Ulvaeus swept the AM airwaves in the U.S. and around the world with their bright, spirited harmonies and clever hooks. Their songs have the kind of innocence that rock 'n' roll has not enjoyed since its halcyon days, and their first hit, "Waterloo," won the Eurovision song contest in the original Swedish version before the group even thought of trying to dent the U.S. charts. Since then they have scored with "Fernando," "S.O.S.," "Dancing Queen" and others.

RECOMMENDED: *ABBA* (Atlantic).

AC/DC

Australians AC/DC play garage rock at excruciating volume with a self-parodying panache epitomized by guitarist Angus Young's schoolboy-gone-mad schtick and original songs like "Rock 'n' Roll Damnation" and "She's Got Balls." Formed by Angus and guitarist Malcolm Young in 1974, AC/DC moved from their home turf of Sydney pop center Melbourne, where they found drummer Phil Rudd, bassist Mark Evans (since replaced by Britisher Cliff Williams), and one-time crayfisherman and journeyman singer Bon Scott. Like Scott, the Youngs are native Scots who emigrated to Australia. AC/DC now command a fanatical heavy metal following in Australia, England and America based on the jagged-edge sound of their albums (produced by Harry Vanda and George Young, brother of the band members) and their tireless touring.

RECOMMENDED: *High Voltage, Let There Be Rock* (Atlantic).

ROY ACUFF

A native of Tennessee, Acuff was perhaps country music's first superstar, since he surfaced at a time when radio was taking the music out of the Deep South and spreading it around the nation. He was also the link between the strictly oral folk traditions of mountain music and the commercial sounds beginning to emanate from Nashville when he joined the Grand Ole Opry in 1938. A fiddler and singer, some of his biggest songs ("Tennessee Waltz," "Mule Skinner Blues," "Night Train to Memphis," "Great Speckle Bird," "Wreck on the Highway," "Wabash Cannonball") have become country music standards. He's also a demanding businessman who, along with Fred Rose, founded the first music publishing company south of the Mason-Dixon line today. Acuff-Rose has one of the largest catalogs in the industry.

RECOMMENDED: *Greatest Hits* (Columbia).

AEROSMITH

Photo by Ron Pownall

Formed by vocalist Steven Tyler, guitarist Joe Perry, and bassist Tom Hamilton in Sunapee, New Hampshire, where they gigged at the local inn, Boston based Aerosmith picked up drummer Joey Kramer, rhythm axman Brad Whitford (replacing original Ray Tabano), and a Columbia contact (1972) in that order, with their self-titled debut issued in 1973. Their roots are in 60s British Invasion rock (they covered the Yardbirds' "Train Kept a Rollin' "), but those roots are updated into a mega-amped 70s heavy metal attack that's yielded platinum sales. Aerosmith played neo-fascist rockers in the otherwise creampuff *Sgt. Pepper* film in 1978.

RECOMMENDED: *Aerosmith, Rocks, Live Bootleg* (Columbia).

JAN AKKERMAN

One of the greatest electric guitarists ever to come out of Holland, Akkerman was the leader of one of Holland's top groups, Brainbox, when he was tabbed to fill out the lineup on the fusion supergroup Focus, which he subsequently led to brilliant aesthetic and commerical heights until the group's mid-70s split. Akkerman started his solo projects while Focus was still extant and his album, *Profile*, included Pierre VanderLinden, Bert Ruiter, Ferry Maat, Jaap vanEyck and Frans Smit. Though several of these European musicians played on subsequent Akkerman solos, he also worked with such musicians as ex-Vanilla Fudge bassist Tim Bogert and drummer Carmine Appice.

RECOMMENDED: *Jan Akkerman* (Atlantic).

ALLMAN BROTHERS

This firebrand group of Southern rockers from Daytona Beach, Florida, was led by Duane Allman, one of the greatest American rock guitarists of the 70s, and his brother Gregg, who sang and played lead. After starting out in groups called the Hour Glass and the Allman Joys and playing a lot of sessions, the Allman Brothers were formed at the end of the 60s, a band that owed as much to British power blues bands like Cream as they did to their roots in southern R&B and jazz. Dickey Betts played second lead guitar, Berry Oakley, bass, and Jai Johanny Johanson and Butch Trucks, drums and percussion. When Duane Allman and Berry Oakley were killed in motorcycle accidents within a year of each other, the band added keyboardist Chuck Leavell and bassist Lamar Williams. The band broke up, then reformed in 1979 with the four original members plus Dan Toler and David Goldflies.

RECOMMENDED: *The Allman Brothers Band At Fillmore East, Eat A Peach, Brothers and Sisters* (Capricorn).

DUANE ALLMAN

Florida-bred Allman was one of the great American rock guitarists; a brilliant musician whose rhythmic sense and state of the art performances on single line leads, slide guitar and dobro, are unmatched in the field. Along with brother Gregg he formed local Florida groups Hour Glass and Allman Joys in the 60s while doing a number of sessions. Duane had been one of the top session guitarists in Muscle Shoals, Alabama, recording with such stars as Wilson Pickett and Aretha Franklin. After forming the landmark Southern rock band the Allman Brothers in the late 60s and recording the legendary *Layla* album with Derek and the Dominoes, Allman died in a tragic motorcycle accident.

RECOMMENDED: *Anthology Vol. 1, 2* (Capricorn).

GREGG ALLMAN

Keyboardist/vocalist Allman grew up listening to rock and R&B records in his home state of Florida, eventually forming several groups with his brother, guitarist Duane Allman. Their first two recording groups, Hour Glass and the Allman Joys, were heavily influenced by British rock bands, especially Cream, and when the two went on to form the Allman Brothers they combined those elements with a fine sense of their jazz and R&B roots. Allman's bluesy, gut-wrenching vocals spearheaded the band's tough sound, and when Duane Allman died Gregg was called on to lead the band. The tragedy struck deep, though, and Gregg floundered after his brother died. Eventually the Allman Brothers disbanded. Gregg recorded a solo album, *Laid Back,* then toured on his own before marrying Cher. After his much publicized breakup with Cher, Allman went on to reform the Allman Brothers for a fine comeback, *Enlightened Rogues.*

RECOMMENDED: *Laid Back* (Capricorn).

HERB ALPERT

Despite his years leading the Tijuana Brass, trumpeter Herb Alpert is most successful as the "A" in A&M Records (the "M" is former West Coast promo man Jerry Moss). The son of an immigrant Russian father and Hungarian mother, Alpert blew into his first horn at age eight and, after a year's army service (1956), tried his hand at songwriting and production with Lou Adler. The pair produced an early Jan and Dean single, "Baby Talk." Originally recording solo for RCA as Dore Alpert, Alpert decided he could best sell his own music, a jazz-laced pop set to amiable AM melodies on his own record label, and he was right. The first A&M single was the 1961 Tijuana Brass hit, "The Lonely Bull," an alternate version of "Twinkle Star" given an overhaul after Alpert and Moss saw a bullfight in Tijuana, Mexico —hence the Tijuana Brass. Besides recording his own material and co-running A&M, Alpert has also produced LPs by saxophonist Gato Barbieri and African singer Letta Moulu and collaborated on record with trumpet contemporary Hugh Masakela.

RECOMMENDED: *Herb Alpert and the Tijuana Brass—The Lonely Bull, Greatest Hits, Greatest Hits Vol. II; Herb Alpert and Hugh Masakela—Herb Alpert and Hugh Masakela; Rise* (A&M).

AMAZING RHYTHM ACES

The Memphis-based Amazing Rhythm Aces are a collection of enviably talented players equally at home in rock, R&B, and southern-fried country music. What is amazing about the Aces is that they haven't let their relative anonymity get them down. Since forming in 1972, lead singer Russell Smith, drummer Butch McDade, bassist Jeff Davis, guitarist Duncan Cameron (replacing Barry Burton in 1978), and keyboardists James Hooker and Billy Earhart have scored a respectable pop hit out of Jesse Winchester's "Third Rate Romance" and a 1976 Grammy for "The End Is Not in Sight" as Best Country Vocal Performance.

RECOMMENDED: *Stacked Deck, The Amazing Rhythm Aces* (formerly ABC, now Columbia).

AMBOY DUKES

One of the few 60s garage bands to make good without cleaning up their tattered act, Detroit's Amboy Dukes were led by guitarist Ted Nugent. Himself a Detroit native, Nugent originally formed the Amboy Dukes in 1965 in Chicago, later taking the name with him back to Detroit to reform the Dukes with new members and, after one unsuccessful album, chart a classic slab of acid-tinged raunch called "Journey to the Center of Your Mind." Dukes came and went, but Nugent stuck it out, going through a new set of players with almost every Amboy Dukes album until he just put pretence behind him and billed the group in the mid-70s as Ted Nugent and the Amboy Dukes. While the Amboy Dukes were a seminal part of the 60s Detroit scene with the MC5 and the then-Psychedelic Stooges, only Nugent has gone on to bigger things. Rusty Day sang for a time with Cactus, while keyboardist Andy Solomon and drummer Dave Palmer cut an LP of doo-wop spoofs (imagine a streetcorner take of "Purple Haze") for Atlantic in 1972.

RECOMMENDED: *Journey to the Center of Your Mind* (Mainstream); also various compilations of Mainstream recordings.

AMERICA

Dan Peek, Gerry Beckley, and Dewey Bunnell, all sons of U.S. servicemen stationed in England, formed America in 1969. They had an acoustically-based West Coast sound and first toured the U.S. as headliners in 1972 on the strength of "Horse with No Name" and the *America* LP. Later under the producing tutelage of Beatle-mentor George Martin, they found renewed commercial life with pop hits like "Sister Golden Hair." Now down to a duo (America lost Dan Peek in 1977), America now records gospel sides for the Texas-based Word label.

RECOMMENDED: *America, Homecoming* (Warner Bros.).

ERIC ANDERSEN

One of many Greenwich Village hopefuls in the 60s folk boom, Eric Andersen distinguished himself not only with his ability to write elegant ballads like the oft-covered "Violets of Dawn," "Thirsty Boots" (a classic example of dust bowl romanticism), and "Close the Door Lightly." Relying on his own songwriting muse rather than the old standards, Andersen came close to stardom several times. Beatle manager Brian Epstein planned to make Andersen a more handsome Dylan, a plan that was effectively scotched when Epstein died in 1967. Andersen has gone through several major record companies since, although he still gigs regularly on the club and intimate concert hall circuit. After nearly fifteen years as a performer, Andersen still sees his name in advertisements and on marquees spelt "Anderson."

RECOMMENDED: *Bout Changes 'n Things* (Vanguard); *Blue River* (Columbia); *The Best of Eric Andersen* (Arista).

ANGEL

Born in 1975 out of the ashes of forgotten Washington, DC groups like the Cherry People, Angel play music steeped in early 70s traditions like glitter-rock, heavy-metal, and Kiss-cum-Alice Cooper theatrics. In fact, it was Kiss who saw the group in a DC club only a month after their formation and suggested to Neil Bogart of Casablanca Records that he sign the band. He did, and four typical macho-rock recordings laced with pseudo-spiritualism have been the result. Gregg Giuffria (keyboards), Frank Domino (vocals), Barry Brandt (drums), Felix Robinson (bass, replacing Mickey Jones in 1977), and Punky Meadows (guitar and heavily made-up glam rock looks) have established a cult following, but their biggest claim to fame comes from Frank Zappa, who recorded a scathing but unreleased parody of Meadows called "Punky's Whips."

RECOMMENDED: *Angel, White Hot* (Casablanca).

ANIMALS

In 1964 it was Eric Burdon's blues-inflected howl, combined with the snarling instrumental attack of Alan Price (organ), Hilton Valentine (guitar), Chas Chandler (bass), and John Steele (drums) that gave the Animals the edge over all but three British Invasion groups (the Beatles, Stones, and Dave Clark Five). Originally the four-piece Alan Price Combo until former art school student Burdon joined in 1962, the Animals made their white-boy R&B reputation in their native Newcastle until producer Mickie Most dragged these generally unkempt lads (hence their name) to London to record, after two near-misses, the number 1 "House of the Rising Sun" (1964). Successive hits included John Lee Hooker's "Boom Boom," "Don't Let Me Be Misunderstood," and "Don't Bring Me Down." Price split for solo pastures in 1966, the rest a year later, leaving a blissed-out Burdon to court a new hippie audience with a new set of Animals (including guitarist Andy Summers, now with Police) until calling it quits in 1969. Burdon has since recorded with War (two early 70s LPs), Jimmy Witherspoon (*Guilty*), and made three indulgent but soul-charged solo LPs. The original Animals reunited twice; for a Christmas 1968 gig in Newcastle and for a 1976 reunion LP. Price is still a successful solo artist, while Chandler's into production and management (Hendrix for a time, then Slade).

RECOMMENDED: *The Animals; Before We Were So Rudely Interrupted* [reunion LP] (Jet/UA).

PAUL ANKA

One of the pop crooners who took over in the late 50s between Elvis and the Beatles when payola scandals were rampant, Anka scored his first hit, the multi-million selling "Diana," when he was just fifteen years old. In the next few years his wistful, crying style clicked with "Loneliest Boy In the World," "I Wish," and "I Can't Help Loving You." When the Beatles hit, guys like Anka were relegated to the Las Vegas circuit, where he did fine through the 60s and made a comeback in the 70s.

RECOMMENDED: *21 Golden Hits* (Roulette).

ROD ARGENT/ARGENT

Rod Argent formed Argent with his cousin, Jim Redford (bass), an ex-Unit 4+2 member Russ Ballard (guitar), and Bob Heniet (drums) in 1969 after the dissolution of his former group, the Zombies. The band's debut LP the following year took several stylistic cues from the Zombies as applied through Argent's prodigious abilities on organ and piano. But as a reaction to the increasing pomposity of British art-rock as practiced by Genesis, Yes, and ELP, Argent, both the band and the man, started turning the amps up and the virtuosity on. The group's best moments were the lyrical *Ring of Hands* (1971), and their big hit single, "Hold Your Head Up." The self-indulgence and creeping vapidity of subsequent LPs caused guitarist Russ Ballard, the pivotal musical force of the band, to go solo in 1974. Guitarists John Grimaldi and John Verity were brought in but Argent called it quits two years later. Rod Argent has since busied himself with sessions and a solo LP released in 1979. Redford is with the Kinks at this writing, Heniet holds drum clinics, and Ballard continues to write and record.

RECOMMENDED: *The Best of Argent— An Anthology* (Epic).

JOAN ARMATRADING

Born in the West Indies, Joan Armatrading is, in the words of Nina Simone, young, gifted and black; in that order. As a singer, she possesses the urgency of youth; as a songwriter, she is gifted with a lyrical perception that recalls the outspoken yet poetic muse of Van Morrison; and as a black, she has honestly and effectively crossed the color barrier to communicate universal pain and pleasure in song. One of six children, she moved from the island of St. Kitts, with her family, to Birmingham, England, at age seven, where she spent subsequent childhood years playing guitar, piano and trying her teenage hand at songwriting. By 1973, she had entered into a songwriting partnership with a fellow West Indian, Pam Nestor, to record *Whatever's for Us*. The next two years were spent finding her voice, literally and figuratively, as a solo artist, a two years well spent considering the ecstatic reviews that have greeted recent works *Back to the Night, Joan Armatrading, Show Some Emotion,* and *To the Limit*. The hit single continues to elude her, but hopefully not for long.

RECOMMENDED: *Joan Armatrading* (A&M).

ASHFORD & SIMPSON

For years, Nikolas Ashford and Valerie Simpson were two of the best-known unknowns behind the scenes in soul. Now, they are two of the best-known singers, songwriters, and producers in contemporary R&B. Both born and raised in New York's Harlem ghetto, Ashford and Simpson have sustained a personal as well as business relationship since they sold their first batch of co-written songs for seventy-five dollars when Valerie was 17 and Nikolas 21. Their first hit record as writers was Ray Charles' blowsy version of "Let's Go Get Stoned," after which they worked in Motown's songwriters' gallery, expanding into production on Marvin Gaye and Tammi Terrell hits "Ain't No Mountain High Enough," Diana Ross's "Reach Out and Touch (Somebody's Hand)," and as recently as 1979, Ross's LP *The Boss*. Simpson recorded two superb solo LPs for Motown before the pair signed for the first time as recording artists to Warner Bros. in 1973. Since then, they've curtailed outside projects in favor of their own records.

RECOMMENDED: *Is It Still Good to Ya, Stay Free* (Warner Bros.)

ASLEEP AT THE WHEEL

Originally an unlikely quintet of East Coast college students with an affinity for the southern sounds in life, Asleep at the Wheel have become a freewheeling fusion of cowboy schmaltz, wild western swing, jazz facility (check their version of Count Basie's "Jumpin' at the Woodside"), and rock drive. Personnel changes have been the rule rather than the exception, starting with their formation in the early months of 1970 by singer/guitarist Ray Benson (real name Ray Seifert, and rarely seen without a ten-gallon hat), Lucky Oceans (real name Reuben Gosfield), and drummer Leroy Preston. Female vocalist Chris O'Connell joined fresh out of high school, and with a rotating series of fiddlers, bassists and piano players AATW served apprenticeships in West Virginia and Berkeley, California, before settling in Texas. They recorded their debut LP for United Artists, then one for Epic, and have recorded all subsequent albums for Capitol. Though less raucous than Commander Cody's retired Lost Planet Airmen, AATW consistently deliver the goods live and on wax.

RECOMMENDED: *Asleep at the Wheel* (Epic); *Served Live* (Capitol).

CHET ATKINS

Born in 1924 in the Clinch Mountains town of Luttrell, Tennessee, Atkins was a formidable country guitarist by the time he left high school. He worked radio stations all over the south, settling with the Grand Ole Opry at WSM in Nashville in 1950. By then he was also a popular RCA artist, and working numerous sessions. When RCA opened a Nashville studio in 1957, Atkins was tapped to run it. He produced dozens of artists, and also became one of the jazz-influenced pickers crucial in shaping the contemporary Nashville Sound. Though he has been a top-ranking RCA exec for many years, he never stopped recording everything from stone country to classical to Spanish to Boston Pops. He has won nearly every award in the country music industry, and he remains one of the most influential instrumentalists the music has produced.

RECOMMENDED: *Down Home, Solo Flights, A Legendary Performer* (RCA).

ATLANTA RHYTHM SECTION

Sessionmen made good, the Atlanta Rhythm Section were just that: the house band at producer Buddy Buie's Studio One in Doraville, Georgia, until Buie recorded them with original material for their self-titled 1972 debut. Singer Rodney Justo split after the first LP, replaced by noted Dixie throat Ronnie Hammond, but the line-up is otherwise stable; J. R. Cobb (guitar), Dean Daughtry (keyboards), Barry Bailey (guitar), the rotund Paul Goddard (bass), and Robert Nix (drums). Their presession experience included numerous local Georgian bands: Roy Orbison, the D.C. popsters, the Candymen, and the Classics IV ("Spooky," "Stormy"), and that pop element shows in their studio-honed sound, a less hedonistic variation on the Neanderthal boogie usually associated with southern rock. The combination of chops and class made their 1977 LP, *A Rock and Roll Alternative*, their major commercial breakthrough.

RECOMMENDED: *Atlanta Rhythm Section* (Decca); *A Rock and Roll Alternative, Champagne Jam* (Polydor).

BRIAN AUGER

A former piano prodigy (he started at age 3), Auger is a well-respected player who has never capitalized on the jazz-rock phenomenon he helped bring into the world. His credentials are impeccable: 1964 *Melody Maker* Jazz Poll for Best New Artist and Keyboardist (this during the throes of Beatlemania), time in the legendary Steampacket with Rod Stewart and Long John Baldry, and two stunning LPs with model-turned-singer Julie Driscoll. But even incessant touring of U.S. clubs during the bulk of the 70s with his Oblivion Express didn't improve Auger's commercial fortunes. His most recent LP was a 1978 reunion album with Driscoll, now a highly-touted voice in London's avant garde circles and wife of British jazz pianist Keith Tippett.

RECOMMENDED: *Streetnoise* (Atco); *Oblivion Express, Encore* (Warner Bros.)

FRANKIE AVALON

Kingpin of the industry-contrived, cleancut "Philadelphia Sound" of the late 50s, Avalon was a national heartthrob whose biggest hit was "Venus." When the Beatles wiped out his ilk, Avalon turned to Hollywood and the Las Vegas nightclub circuit. He starred in all the *Beach Party* films as well as *The Alamo, Voyage to the Bottom of the Sea, Guns of the Timberland, Skiddoo, I'll Take Sweden,* and *Ski Party*.

RECOMMENDED: *Fifteen Greatest Hits* (Roulette).

AVERAGE WHITE BAND

Not only can white men sing the blues, but English white men can sing the blues and play them with conviction. That's the moral of the Average White Band story, a tale of both trial (the accidental death in 1974 of drummer Robbie McIntosh of heroin poisoning) and triumph. A collection of English and Scottish ex-sessionmen and pub band players, AWB, Alan Gorrie, Onnie McIntyre, Hamish Stuart, Roger Ball, Malcolm "Molly" Duncan, and Steve Ferrone (replacing McIntosh), got their first rave notices opening a 1971 London show for Eric Clapton. Their effortless blend of R&B grit, melodic pop sensibility, and instrumental facility ran counter to the prevailing hippie pretensions of the day, but by 1975 and their hit instrumental "Pick Up the Pieces," AWB had made R&B fashionable again for white rockers. Given their roots in Motown, jazz, and bluesy ballads, it was entirely appropriate that the group recorded one of the LPs with former Drifters vocalist Ben E. King (*Benny and Us*) in 1977.

RECOMMENDED: *Average White Band, Person to Person* (Atlantic).

HOYT AXTON

A singer-songwriter better known for his songwriting than his singing, Hoyt Axton has recorded steadily since the early 60s on a variety of labels, but his songs have all been hits for other people: "Greenback Dollar" for the Kingston Trio (1962), the bitter "The Pusher" for Steppenwolf (1968), "Joy to the World" for Three Dog Night (1970), and "No No Song" for solo Beatle Ringo Starr (1975). Songwriting was in his family; his mother, Mae, wrote "Heartbreak Hotel." Only recently has Axton himself scored recognition outside of critics' circles, notching an occasional hit (e.g., "When the Morning Comes") on the country charts.

RECOMMENDED: *Southbound* (A&M).

KEVIN AYERS

Kevin Ayers is one of those elusive figures in so-called progressive English rock who never seems to get the public recognition they deserve. Quitting school at age 16 (he spent his preteen years in Malaysia), he moved to Canterbury where he became a charter member of that neighborhood's post-psychedelic society, soon to spawn the legendary Wilde Flowers (for whom he sang and played guitar), Caravan, and Soft Machine (for whom he sang and played bass). He quit the Softs, an experimental outfit with an interest in multimedia and burgeoning jazz roots, in 1968, after one album and a U.S. tour with the Jimi Hendrix Experience. After recording his first solo LP, *Joy of a Toy*, he formed The Whole World in 1971, a group that included a 16-year old Mike Oldfield on guitar and bass. Since then, his solo output has been erratic if consistently fascinating. Of his ten albums, only five were released in the U.S., the last in 1977.

RECOMMENDED: *Banamour* (Sire U.S./Harvest U.K.); *June 1, 1974*—with John Cale, Brian Eno, Nico (Island).

BABYS

The Babys began as a teen-oriented quartet modeled on the Small Faces. They played British rock at once hard-edged and tuneful, with subtle overtones of American R&B. The band won notoriety in 1977 thanks to a huge promotion push from its business mentors. This "Buzz on the Babys" started when Chrysalis Records honchos viewed a videotape of the Babys' performance, signed the foursome on the strength of their pretty-boy image, and set a media blitz into motion. Then the band's manager circulated a story that the Babys had been kidnapped, and brought in the FBI to "find" them. The Babys had arrived. By the time of the spring 1977 date in New York, squealing girls were throwing cardboard boxes at singer John Waite and keyboard player Mike Corby in adoration. After scoring such AM hits as "Isn't It Time," the Babys replaced Corby with Jonathan Cain, while bassist Ricky Phillips stepped in to make the band a quintet and nudge it out of its teenybop phase. The Baby's flair for showmanship draws on a mixture of music-hall staging and rock tradition, and the band's live shows are among the most visually appealing in recent pop years.

RECOMMENDED: *The Babys, Head First* (Chrysalis).

BACHMAN-TURNER OVERDRIVE (BTO)

Bachman-Turner Overdrive had their heyday in the years 1973-75 when the four-piece heavy metal outfit scored hits like "Let It Ride," "Takin' Care of Business," and "You Ain't Seen Nothin' Yet," bash 'n thrash anthems which clicked with young America through sheer weight of rhythm and amplification. In fact, weight was one of the Canadian band's distinguishing features. Guitarist Randy Bachman (who left the Guess Who in 1970) and bassist C. F. Turner (who played with Bachman in a pre-BTO band called Brave Belt) both tipped the scales at well over 200 pounds, causing caustic critics to dub the band Bachman-Turner Overweight. But BTO, supplemented by two more Bachman brothers for a time, continued notching up hits until the eldest Bachman went solo a second time, recording *Survivor* for Polydor and later forming a BTO-soundalike called Ironhorse. BTO (they can't use Bachman's name due to legal complications) still plows on, playing their wheatfield wrath & wroll with both spunk and predictability.

RECOMMENDED: *Best of BTO (So Far)* (Mercury).

BAD COMPANY

Formed in 1973 from the ranks of two important British bands, Bad Company evaded the stigma of being a futile supergroup by playing stripped-down hard rock at a time when major groups were moving towards overproduced, undanceable music. Paul Rodgers had been the vocalist with Free, and Simon Kirke the drummer. Mick Ralphs had been the guitar star of Mott the Hoople, and Boz Burrell came from King Crimson, where he had sung in addition to playing bass. At first Bad Company seemed an unlikely combo, but their first LP proved that the chemistry for stardom was there, and a track from their debut, "Can't Get Enough of Your Love," became a huge hit single, providing the perfect antidote for the pomposity and pretension that had been glutting rock music. Unfortunately, Bad Company's simple, heavy-handed musical approach combined with macho lyrics grew boring after a couple of albums, and their popularity began to wane as new wave captured the market in energetic rock. It wasn't until 1979's *Desolation Angels* was released that the group rediscovered its audience and became a major concert draw in both America and England.

RECOMMENDED: *Bad Company, Straight Shooter, Desolation Angels* (Swan Song).

BADFINGER

A youthful quartet comprised of guitarist Joey Molland and bassist Tom Evans, from Liverpool, and guitarist/songwriter Peter Ham and drummer Mike Gibbins, from Swansea, the Iveys (as they were originally called) submitted tapes to the Beatles' Apple Corp. in 1968 and were immediately rewarded with a recording contract, a name change to Badfinger, a Paul McCartney song ("Come and Get It"), and a hit record in that order. Recordings made while they were still the Iveys were included on their first LP, released in 1970. Several Beatlesque hits followed, like "No Matter What" and "Baby Blue," but their biggest hit was, in fact, a Pete Ham song ("Without

You"), taken Top 20 by Harry Nilsson. But despite the appealing quality of their songs, schoolboy harmonies, and a jangly harmonic guitar sound, Badfinger suffered the tag of surrogate Beatles. They toured the States to no avail, and finally broke up in 1975, despondent after Peter Ham committed suicide (May 1, 1975). Molland played for a time in Natural Gas, but come 1979 he'd resurrected the band name with Evans and recorded an LP for Elektra.

RECOMMENDED: *No Dice* (Apple); *Badfinger* (Warner Bros.).

JOAN BAEZ

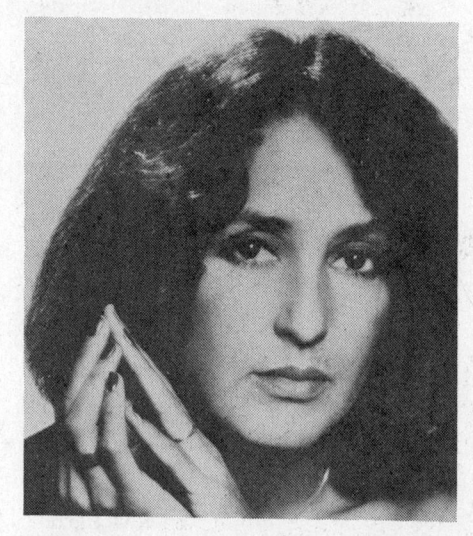

The "Queen of folk music," New York born Joan Baez emerged as a full blown star in her professional debut at the premier Newport Folk Festival in 1959. She had spent a lot of time listening to Odetta and Harry Belafonte and her crystalline voice was an instant crowd pleaser, garnering her a cover of *Time* magazine. When Bob Dylan came on the scene in the early 60s Baez helped introduce him by bringing him onstage during her concerts. Baez linked her folk music ideals to political causes early, singing at many benefits from the early 60s on, marrying radical student leader David Harris in 1968, and most recently campaigning for the Vietnamese refugees called the boat people.

RECOMMENDED: *Joan Baez, In Concert, Part One and Part Two* (Vanguard).

GINGER BAKER

The man most responsible for rock drum solos got his start with the blues-playing Graham Bond Organization before being deified as Cream's endless drummer. "Toad" was his trademark with Cream, and when he formed his own group, Air Force, he recorded it over again. Air Force included Bond, Denny Laine, Chris Wood, Stevie Winwood and Rick Grech, but Baker folded up his tent before he could do anything with such a stellar lineup and moved to Africa, only to resurface in the mid-70s with another lineup and a new record.

RECOMMENDED: *Ginger Baker's Air Force* (Atco).

LONG JOHN BALDRY

Long John Baldry is an English original in the sphere of blues and boogie. He uses unlikely combinations of singing styles, crossing the rumbling bass sounds of Righteous Brother Bill Medley with the drawing-room patter of Noel Coward. In the mid-50s, Baldry set out as a folk-blues artist on a tour with Jack Elliott. By the early 60s, Baldry had forsaken folk to concentrate on the urban blues that would help shape the British Invasion. In 1961 he was instrumental in putting together Alexis Korner's Blues Incorporated, a band which then included Mick Jagger and Charlie Watts. Baldry moved on to Cyril Davies' All Stars for two years before forming the Hootchie Cootchie Men with Mick Waller, Brian Auger, Julie Driscoll, and Baldry's discovery, Rod Stewart. The Hootchie

Cootchie Men gave way to Steampacket, followed in 1966 by Bluesology. For the latter, Baldry drafted pianist Reg Dwight, who later combined the names John Baldry and Elton Dean into his stage name, Elton John. After a spell as a crooner, Baldry returned to his blues roots to make the album *It Ain't Easy*, produced by Elton John and Rod Stewart in tribute to the man who launched their careers. Baldry has done time in a mental hospital, but in 1979 managed a shot at a comeback with the hard-rocking and soulful *Baldry's Out!*

RECOMMENDED: *Long John's Blues* (Ascot-UA).

BAND

As the Crackers and later Hawks, Robbie Robertson (guitar), Levon Helm (drums), Richard Manuel (piano), Garth Hudson (organ) and Rick Danko (bass) got their musical education playing bars and roadhouses across Canada and the U.S., backing up the great rockabilly guitarist Ronnie Hawkins. All Canadians except for Levon Helm (who is from Arkansas), the group didn't become the Band until after serving a brief period as Bob Dylan's backup group and recording the *Basement Tapes* with Dylan in a frame house in West Saugerties, New York. Robertson's songwriting and skillful guitar playing directed the Band through a range of material dealing with the myth of America for one of the most moving and graceful bodies of work a rock band has ever produced. The group's last act as a unit was to make a film, directed by Martin Scorcese, of their final concert at Winterland in 1977, called *The Last Waltz*.

RECOMMENDED: *Music from Big Pink, The Band, Rock of Ages* (Capitol).

BAR-KAYS

The original Bar-Kays were the house band at Stax Records in the mid-60s. They had one big hit ("Soul Finger" in 1967) and several smaller ones on their own, and they toured as Otis Redding's backup band. All but one of them were killed, however, in the plane crash that snuffed out Redding's burgeoning career in 1967. James Alexander, who took a different flight, picked up the pieces a year later, forming a new band to record both on its own and behind other Stax artists. When Stax Records folded in the mid-70s, the group moved to Mercury. Though their brand of funk has done reasonably well on the R&B charts, they have still barely dented the pop field.

RECOMMENDED: *Black Rock* (Volt); *Money Talks* (Stax).

SYD BARRETT

The early 60s were a time of pop rock and blues revivals among British rock musicians, so when a group surfaced playing strange, Eastern modalities and using weird, out of tune electronic effects and distortion, it really stood out. Pink Floyd was the first British psychedelic group, and in fact predated the American acid rock movement. The leader and visionary of the group was Syd Barrett, and by the end of the 60s Barrett had placed Pink Floyd at the top of the psychedelic trend in both countries. Barrett left the band before the notoriety translated into prosperity in the 70s, living as a recluse and venturing forth to record two solo albums.

RECOMMENDED: *The Madcap Laughs*.

BAY CITY ROLLERS

The Bay City Rollers, five well-meaning Scots from Edinburgh who originally called themselves the Saxons, created such pubescent excitement in England in 1975 that observers, particularly in America, couldn't help but yawn and decry Rollermania as a bad 70s imitation Beatlemania. In the end, they were right, because it didn't last. After setting teenage hearts afire up and down the length of England, vocalist Les McKeown, guitarist Stuart Wood, guitarist Eric Faulkner, and rhythm section brothers Alan and Derek Longmuir discovered, despite the Machiavellian efforts of manager Tam Paton, that their peers would not take them seriously and that terminally cute hits like "Saturday Night" and "Rock & Roll Love Letter" only filled the band coffers, not the rave reviews sack. Since Arista launched the Rollers in the States (1976) in a flurry of hype, the Rollers have gone through several disillusioned members (Ian Mitchell, Pat McGlynn) and commercially fizzled. McKeown is now out, and Alan Longmuir back in after an unsuccessful spell as a solo artist.

RECOMMENDED: *Greatest Hits* (Arista).

BEACH BOYS

The Wilson brothers, Brian, Carl and Dennis, formed this group with cousin Mike Love and Al Jardine in 1961. Originally Carl and the Passions, this vocal group started to call themselves the Beach Boys to connect the surfing craze that was going on with Brian Wilson's songs about being young in California. The first records were simple instrumentally but rich with varied vocal arrangements. By the time of *Pet Sounds*, Brian Wilson's adventurous musical ideas had led the group in a concept direction, including sound effects on many of the tracks, an approach which influenced the Beatles when they went in to record *Sgt. Pepper's Lonely Hearts Club Band*. As Wilson's compositions became more esoteric, unusual instrumentation and additional players were added to the group's line up for advanced recordings like *Smiley Smile* and *Surf's Up*.

RECOMMENDED: *Endless Summer* (Capitol); *Surf's Up, 16 Big Ones* (Warner Bros.).

BEATLES

It's probably the greatest rock & roll story ever told, but the Beatles story has been told so many times before and in such painstaking historical detail that it doesn't bear repeating here. What does bear repeating is the impact the Beatles, collectively and individually, had and continue to have on pop music, pop culture, and more importantly, the public's attitude toward rock 'n' roll and rock 'n' roll musicians. Much of the effect the Beatles had on screaming teenage fans in England, America, Japan, and the rest of the world is attributable to the managerial finesse of former record store manager Brian Epstein. But the Beatles could not have been the Beatles as we know them if John Lennon (b. October 9, 1940), Paul McCartney (b. June 18, 1942), George Harrison (b. February 25, 1943), and Ringo Starr (b. Richard Starkey, July 7, 1940) had not brought to their music the enthusiasm and aggressive inquisitiveness and experimentation that made them repeatedly break down timeworn pop traditions. Orchestras were nothing new to pop recordings, but the Beatles on *Sgt. Pepper* redefined their role in songs like "She's Leaving Home" and "A Day in the Life." George's use of the sitar, first on *Rubber Soul's* "Norwegian Wood" gave rock a new improvisatory tool. The Beatles individually haven't created the kind of excitement they did as a group; Ringo's had a few hits while making a respectable name in film cameos, George has recorded steadily if not with the frequency of Paul and his group Wings, and John has withdrawn into a reclusive existence and hasn't recorded since '75, but it is testimony to the lasting impact of the Beatles and everyone's fervent hope that maybe they'll reunite that the New York Post ran a page one headline "The Beatles Are Back" in its September 21, 1979 issue. It was a false alarm, a premature report of a possible reunion on behalf of the Vietnamese boat people, but you can bet it sold a lot of papers.

RECOMMENDED: (U.S. albums): *Rubber Soul, Revolver, Sergeant Pepper's Lonely Hearts Club Band, Hey Jude, Yesterday and Today, The Beatles, The White Album, Abbey Road, Let It Be* (all Capitol through *The Beatles*, then Apple, except *A Hard Day's Night* which is U.A.); there are untold numbers of Beatle albums, compilations, rip-off packages from the Beatlemania years, bootlegs, and information on most is in Nicholas Schaffner's *The Beatles Forever* and the discography by Castleman and Podrazik, *All Together Now*. Beatle books also number in the hundreds; Hunter Davies' *The Beatles* is the authorized biography and Wilfred Mellers' *Twilight of the Gods* the only book devoted to a serious analysis of their music.

BEAU BRUMMELS

Adding an element of West Coast cool and sophistication to the pop of the British Invasion, San Francisco's Beau Brummels were in 1964, the first American group to seriously challenge the likes of the Beatles with classic singles like "Laugh, Laugh" and "Cry Just a Little." Discovered by the late Frisco FM pioneer Tom Donahue, they were produced for his Autumn label by Sly Stone during their brief hit-making period. But as the music matured into a progressive-rock age, so did the Brummels, reduced by 1967 to single Sal Valentino, guitarist/writer Ron Elliott, and bassist Ron Meagher. Undaunted, they recorded the lush brooding *Triangle* and a year later one of the first country-rock fusion LPs, *Bradley's Barn*. Lack of commercial success finally forced them to break up; Elliott recorded solo, Valentino joined Stoneground, except for one reunion LP and tour in 1974.

RECOMMENDED: *Best of Beau Brummels* [compilation of Autumn recordings] (Warner Bros.).

BE-BOP DELUXE

Built around super-guitarist Bill Nelson, Be-Bop Deluxe burst out of Britain in mid-1974, playing a futuristic, Bowiesque music punctuated by Nelson's poetic images and superlative guitar technique. Fast and fluid, yet expressive and sensitive, Nelson's playing earned him a reputation as an axe hero. The group, however, had some early problems, and soon after the release of their first LP a new set of backup musicians was acquired for Nelson. After some adjusting, Be-Bop settled down as a quartet with bassist Charlie Tumahai, drummer Simon Fox, and keyboardist Andrew Clark, and remained as such until Nelson dissolved the band in late 1978. During their best period, Be-Bop was a fascinating band, both on record and in concert; for Nelson, apparently, that wasn't enough, and he formed a short-lived unit called Red Noise before retreating to the studio, away from the mainstream of rock competition.

RECOMMENDED: *Live! In the Air Age, Best and the Rest* (Harvest/Capitol).

JEFF BECK

One of the great rock guitarists, Jeff Beck has been one of the least consistent and public rock heroes of the past five years, surfacing only occasionally with a tour or an album. His recent change of direction from rock to jazz-fusion guitar playing has won him many new fans and lost him many old ones, but there is no question that Beck has mastered yet another style on a par with giants like Jan Hammer and Stanley Clarke. Beck's first important band was the Yardbirds, where he replaced an exiting Eric Clapton in late 1964. After swiftly earning a reputation as an incredible guitarist, he quit the band and formed a band of his own with Rod Stewart and Ron Wood. After two amazing albums with that once-in-a-lifetime outfit, Beck's volatile personality interfered, and new sidemen were recruited. Beck managed another pair of LPs before joining a new "supergroup" with ex-Vanilla Fudge players, Tim Bogert and Carmine Appice. One album later, Beck was ready to retire, and didn't resurface for two years, when the surprisingly instrumental jazz LP, *Blow by Blow,* brought him back to his former level of superstardom. For a few years, it looked as if Beck was back to stay, but he has not made a studio record since 1976, and nothing is presently on tap for this strange master.

RECOMMENDED: *Jeff Beck Group, Beck, Bogert & Appice* (Epic).

BEE GEES

The singing trio of Robin, Barry and Maurice Gibb come out of Australia in 1967 with a hit single, "New York Mining Disaster 1941," and a style closely patterned on the Beatles. As the band continued to write and record hit single after hit single, it became obvious that the Gibbs were not merely Beatles clones but one of the great male harmony groups. Their lush melodicism eventually led the Bee Gees to record with orchestral backups and their conceptual Masterpiece, *Odessa,* used orchestration to marvelous advantage. After a lapse in popularity during the mid-70s, the group came storming back to the forefront during the disco boom with their contribution to the soundtrack of *Saturday Night Fever.*

RECOMMENDED: *Bee Gees Gold Vol. 1, Saturday Night Fever, Spirits Having Flown* (RSO).

GEORGE BENSON

The singer-guitarist whose *Breezin'* is the biggest selling jazz record of all time, Benson began playing guitar at age eight and later worked as a vocalist in a number of R&B bands in his home town of Pittsburgh. He was offered his first recording contract when he was only ten years old and became known over the years as a good R&B-style instrumentalist, cutting his teeth with Jac McDuff before recording a series of albums for Columbia, Verve, CTI, and sessioning on dozens of other records. When he decided to try his hand at singing on *Breezin'*, Benson's career skyrocketed as "This Masquerade" became an enormous hit single and *Breezin'* won three Grammy Awards in 1976.

RECOMMENDED: *Breezin'* (Warner Bros.).

CHUCK BERRY

The St. Louis-born "father of rock 'n' roll" started out as a blues guitarist before arriving at a formula progression inspired by Guitar Slim which has become the standard model for thousands of rock 'n' roll songs. Berry's flashy style, big beat sound and patented "duck walk" stage maneuvers incited rock 'n' roll fans to riot across the country in the 50s and raised plenty of eyebrows along the way. His list of singles is amazing—"Sweet Little 16," "Memphis," "Johnny B. Goode," "Roll Over Beethoven," "Carol," and "Back in the U.S.A." After serving time in jail during the late 50s Berry returned in the early 60s and kept right on making hits, including "No Particular Place To Go." In the early 70s he had his biggest hit "My Ding A Ling." After several years hiatus Berry returned in 1979 with a strong album.

RECOMMENDED: *Golden Hits* (Mercury), *Golden Decade Vol 1-3*, *London Sessions* (Chess).

DICKEY BETTS

Jacksonville, Florida-born Dickey Betts was playing in a band called the Second Coming with bass guitarist Berry Oakley in 1968 when the guitarist met Duane and Gregg Allman. The Second Coming often jammed with another band called the 31st of February, which included drummer Butch Trucks and, on a temporary basis, the two Allmans. From this bandstand alliance sprang the Allman Brothers Band in 1969, with Betts playing second-line leads behind guitarist Duane until Allman died in a 1971 motorcycle crash. Betts stepped up front; he'd already written the Allmans' most popular instrumental, "In Memory of Elizabeth Reed," to co-lead the group with Gregg until the Allman Brothers dissolved in a public display of fraternal feuding centering on Gregg's court testimony against roadie Scooter Herring in a drug trial. Betts started his own band, Great Southern, for the space of two Arista albums, but participated in the Allmans' reunion that resulted in 1979's *Enlightened Rogues*.

RECOMMENDED: *Great Southern* (Arista).

BIG BOPPER

J. P. Richardson was a radio personality and a popular recording star in the late 50s. Based at radio station KTRM in Beaumont, Texas, for which he was also the program director, Bopper wrote and recorded a monster hit single called "Chantilly Lace" in 1958. He was on tour with Buddy Holly in 1959 when their privately chartered plane crashed outside of Fargo, North Dakota, killing Big Bopper, Buddy Holly and Ritchie Valens.

RECOMMENDED: *Chantilly Lace* (Pickwick).

BIG BROTHER & THE HOLDING COMPANY

One of San Francisco's early psychedelic bands, Big Brother found their key to the bigtime in the person of a gutsy little blues belter from Texas by the name of Janis Joplin. When she hooked up with them in 1967, they were good but not great; with her, they had everything they needed to make it big. The original band consisted of Sam Andrew and James Gurley on guitar, Peter Albin on bass, and David Getz on drums, and it was the pairing of Janis and Big Brother that made their appearance at the 1967 Monterey Pop Festival (among such competition as the Who, Jimi Hendrix, and the Jefferson Airplane) so great. Their second album together, recorded for the most part at their home base, Bill Graham's Fillmore West, and adorned with original R. Crumb cartoonery was a masterpiece of acid burnout playing and inspired vocal styling. The fuzzboxes and vibrato bars tended to hide the band's musical shortcomings, but the overall effect was an amazing earful. The alliance, although propitious, was ill-fated, and ended before another LP could be recorded. Janis went on to further success as a solo performer, although she organized a backup band, the Full Tilt Boogie Band, before her death in 1970. The guys she left behind, Big Brother, attempted to hold themselves together after Joplin's departure, but were never able to recapture the same level of fame and fortune.

RECOMMENDED: *Cheap Thrills* (Columbia).

BIG STAR

If Big Star had had a nickel for every rave review they got, this Memphis-based cult favorite would still be with us today. Led by former Box Top singer Alex Chilton (only 17 when the Box Tops scored with "The Letter"), Big Star included Chris Bell on guitar, Andy Hummel on bass, and Jody Stephenson on drums. Together, they recorded Anglophilic hymns á la Raspberries and Badfinger with a sensitivity and sophistication their forebearers rarely matched. They recorded two albums and played one of their few gigs, typically enough, at a 1973 rock critics' convention. Nary a negative word was heard when their first LP, *#1 Record*, was released, and while minimal sales and the departure of Bell threatened to send them spinning into oblivion, Big Star recorded a second critics' hit in 1974, *Radio City*. The band called it a day, however, when a third album languished in the vaults for lack of a record label. *Big Star Third* then became, as expected, a collector's item among cognescenti until its posthumous release in 1979 on the PVC label.

RECOMMENDED: *#1 Record, Radio City* (Argent); *Big Star Third* (PVC).

BLACK OAK ARKANSAS

Critics called Black Oak Arkansas, led by the flamboyant Jim "Dandy" Mangrum, a southern rock joke. But the joke was on the pundits, because in its eight-year recording span Black Oak peddled high-decibel raunch with great success, overcoming serious musical deficiencies with a dynamic presentation centered on the Beefheartian growl and comic-macho stage antics of Mangrum. Genuine rebels, Mangrum and the original BOA crew (Stanley Knight, Rick Reynolds, Harvey Jett, guitars; Pat Daugherty, bass; Wayne Evans, drums) grew up in the town of

Black Oak and thrived on trouble; they got their first P.A. system by stealing one from their high school. Originally known as the Knowbody Else (an LP on a Stax subsidiary), they emigrated to Los Angeles where former Iron Butterflies Lee Dorman and Mike Pinera produced their eponymous debut album. The band lived in their own self-sufficient community in the Arkansas wilds, but have since split up. Drummer Tommy Aldridge, who joined the group later, now slams the skins with guitarist Pat Travers.

RECOMMENDED: *Black Oak Arkansas* (Atco).

BLACK SABBATH

In the beginning, there was Earth. And Earth was vocalist Ozzy Osbourne, guitarist Tony Iommi, bass guitarist Geezer Butler, and drummer Bill Ward, all schoolmates from Birmingham, England. And Earth played the German club scene, including the famous Star Club in Hamburg. And in 1969, they became Black Sabbath, after the title of a song they'd written about the peace-and-love counterculture. They almost quit while they were ahead when Iommi joined Jethro Tull for all of two weeks. But Black Sabbath fortified the dark, fuzz-heavy bludgeon-rock sound they were soon to become famous for and recorded their first LP in 1970 for $1,200, in two days. Black Sabbath, a popular favorite despite critical negativity, went on to become a top record and concert attraction without altering their monotonic heavy-metal sound. Osbourne, whose singing has been likened to a poodle in pain, left the band in 1979 only to be replaced by singer Ronnie Dio (ex-Elf, Ritchie Blackmore's Rainbow). Butler took his leave later the same year.

RECOMMENDED: *Black Sabbath* (Warner Bros.).

RITCHIE BLACKMORE

After fighting for control of Deep Purple during the 60s and early 70s with vocalist Ian Gillan and Keyboardist Jon Lord, Blackmore set out on his own to search for his heavy metal vision. His band, Rainbow, opened its sets with the theme from *The Wizard of Oz*, "Somewhere over the Rainbow," then proceeded to blast its audience into oblivion with Blackmore's belching, acidic endlessly cascading lead guitar.

RECOMMENDED: *Ritchie Blackmore's Rainbow* (Polydor).

BLIND FAITH

Blind Faith was the first genuine supergroup, bringing together four great but disparate talents in Steve Winwood (Traffic), Eric Clapton (Yardbirds, Mayall, Cream), Ginger Baker (Cream), and the more obscure Rik Grech (Family). They made their debut in 1969 at a free concert in London's Hyde Park before 100,000, recorded one spotty album (featuring the obligatory "Toad"-like drum solo by Baker), toured U.S. coliseums, and broke up. Fortunately, they did give us a Clapton classic in "In the Presence of the Lord."

RECOMMENDED: *Blind Faith* (Atco).

BLONDIE

One of the best and most successful of the late 70s new wave bands to come out of the New York club scene, Blondie is fronted by lead singer Deborah Harry, who lives with guitarist and group leader Chris Stein. On stage, Stein and bassist Nigel Harrison, second guitarist Frank Infante, keyboardist Jimmy Destri and drummer Clem Burke all dress in severe early 60s styles while Harry struts in a sexy costume. The band's music is pure pop influenced heavily by 60s groups, and their clever amalgamation of hooks and catchy rhythms has yielded several hit singles under the expert direction of producer Mike Chapman, including the mock disco song "Heart of Glass."

RECOMMENDED: *Blondie* (Private Stock); *Parallel Lines, Eat To the Beat* (Chrysalis).

BLOOD, SWEAT & TEARS

Formed out of the ashes of the legendary New York rock band the Blues Project in the late 60s, Blood, Sweat & Tears was the big band vision of keyboardist/singer/songwriter Al Kooper and guitarist Steve Katz. The original band also included trumpeter Randy Brecker, saxophonist Fred Lipsius, trumpeter Jerry Weiss, trombonist Dick Halligan, bassist Jim Fielder, and drummer Bobby Colomby. The debut album was the most successful fusion of rock song structures, pop/R&B melodies and jazz horn charts of its time, maybe of all time, but Kooper's creativity led to internal problems and he left the group. Big-voiced singer David Clayton–Thomas was added for the second album, and the group came into its own commercially with a string of hit singles: "Spinning Wheel," "You've Made Me So Very Happy," "And When I Die," and "Lucretia Mac Evil."

RECOMMENDED: *Child Is Father to the Man, Blood, Sweat & Tears* (Columbia).

MIKE BLOOMFIELD

A guitar hero who relinquished his crown for the comforts of cultish obscurity, Michael Bloomfield was only 22 when he first recorded with the Paul Butterfield Blues Band and guested on Dylan's historic album, *Highway 61 Revisited*. The crisp, trebly sound of Bloomfield's Fender guitar striding up and down octaves became *the* standard for young white American blues guitarists. Bloomfield's reputation increased accordingly on the classic *Super Session* LP he recorded in 1968 with Al Kooper and Stephen Stills. But the flagging quality of albums he cut again with Kooper (*Live Adventures*), John Hammond, Jr. and Dr. John (*Triumvirate*), and his own group of hand-picked session friends (the solo 1969 *It's Not Killing Me*), and his own reclusiveness against the burgeoning popularity of Clapton and Hendrix caused his star to fall. His only group enterprise since the rise and fall of the Electric Flag in 1967-68 was a short-lived reformation of the Electric Flag and the superstar variation of same called KGB with which he lasted only one LP. Bloomfield, born in Chicago, lives in the country around San Francisco, gigs with pick-up groups on occasion, and records with increasing frequency for John Fahey's Takoma label.

RECOMMENDED: *Super Session, Live Adventures of Mike Bloomfield and Al Kooper* (Columbia).

BLUE CHEER

The kings of San Francisco heavy metal, Blue Cheer burst on the psychedelic scene in 1968 with an album, *Vincebus Eruptum,* that quickly became an anthem for tripsters from coast to coast. Acid chemist Owsley wrote the liner notes, but Fillmore impresario Bill Graham threw them out after one gig, calling Blue Cheer the worst band he ever heard. Guitarist Leigh Stevens played in an earsplitting fuzztone and feedback drone while bassist Dick Peterson and drummer Paul Whaley pounded out a furious doubletime that could well be considered a prototype for many new wave rhythm sections. Blue Cheer aced the Who on a cover version of Eddie Cochran's "Summertime Blues," which became the band's only hit single. After a quick fade, the band returned a few years later in a modified country rock format.

RECOMMENDED: *Vincebus Eruptum, Outsideinside* (Philips).

BLUE OYSTER CULT

If there is such a thing as intelligent heavy-metal, Blue Oyster Cult are its undisputed masters. Guitarist Allen Lanier, drummer Albert Bouchard, and lead guitarist Donald "Buck Dharma" Roeser were bored silly at Stony Brook College in 1970 when they formed one of two BOC forerunners, the legendary Soft White Underbelly, which played selected bar gigs, emulated the Music Machine ("Talk Talk"), and landed an Elektra contract which yielded only an unreleased single. A short afterlife as the Stalk Forrest Group (adding bassist and brother Joe Bouchard and singer and former roadie Eric Bloom) led to the name change to Blue Oyster Cult, courtesy of a poem by manager and producer Sandy Pearlman. Their self-titled debut album, a critics' choice to this day, defined the BOC style; bone-crushing chords, lead Dharma guitar of the kind even Jimmy Page professed to envy, and dark satanic lyrics with as much humor as menace. Consistent on album, BOC augment their live show with excruciating volume and a state-of-the-art laser show. To date, AM radio has only accepted Roeser's "Don't Fear the Reaper."

RECOMMENDED: *Blue Oyster Cult* (Columbia).

BLUES MAGOOS

The legendary cross between psychedelic blues and punk rock, the Blues Magoos (guitarist Mike Esposito, vocalist/organist Ralph Scala, Peppy Castro on vocals and rhythm guitar, bassist Ron Gilbert and drummer Geoff Daking) hailed from the Bronx and were New York's first acid rockers with the 1966 hit, "We Ain't Got Nothin' Yet." The band had suits designed that would light up during high spots in their stage show.

RECOMMENDED: *Psychedelic Lollipop, Electric Comic Book* (Mercury).

BLUES PROJECT

The Blues Project, New York City's first successful white electric blues band, proved the ability of the so-called 60s underground to sell records and concert tickets, even if the band, in its prime, only stayed together long enough to record one live and one studio album.

Original vocalist Tommy Flanders left just before release of *Live at the Cafe au Go Go,* Al Kooper took off after *Projections,* and bassist Andy Kulberg and drummer Roy Blumenfield recorded an album with their group Sea Train under the Blues Project name just to cover their legal obligations. But when they were hot, the Blues Project were hot, transcending their middle-class Jewish origins to make gutsy electric blues alongside comfortable melodic interludes like Steve Katz's "Steve's Song." Guitarist Danny Kalb got his reputation as a six-string flash during Project days. (The group name came from an Elektra blues compilation on which Kalb appeared, called *The Blues Project.*) Kalb tried a revival of the group with Blumenfield in 1971 and the entire band sans Flanders did a gig in New York in 1973, which was recorded for an album.

RECOMMENDED: *Live at the Cafe au Go Go, Projections* (Verve); *Reunion in Central Park* (MCA).

MARC BOLAN & T. REX

Marc Bolan (May 8, 1948-September 16, 1977) formed his first professional group, John's Children, in 1966, but it was not until the creation of an acoustic duo with Steve "Peregrine" Took in 1968 under the name of Tyrannosaurus Rex that his road to stardom really opened up. After four albums of quirky, fantasy-riddled folk music, Bolan went electric, shortened the band's name to a less cumbersome T. Rex, and began to add rock musicians to the lineup. From that point (1970) until 1973, T. Rex ruled the British single charts on a par with the likes of Bowie and Elton John. "Ride a White Swan," "Hot Love," "Bang a Gong," "Telegram Sam," "Metal Guru," and "Jeepster" were only some of his simple boogie classics. With the employment of Flo and Eddie as background singers, and the use of strings over basic guitar-based raunch, Bolan's childish lyrics made every record he put his name on an instant smash. As tastes changed, Bolan's popularity faded, although he continued, for a while, to make excellent records. The loss of his magic touch weighed heavily on Bolan, and he became fat and lazy. In 1976 he attempted a comeback, and released an album that showed some growth, a recognition that things had changed and that he was reconsidering his approach. Unfortunately, he was killed in a car crash, just as things were looking brighter.

RECOMMENDED: *T. Rex* (Reprise).

TOMMY BOLIN

A brilliant guitarist, Bolin played with a rock flash and jazz technique that enabled him to switch easily from stints with the James Gang (*Bang*) to Bill Cobham (*Spectrum*). On his own, Bolin leaned more in the straight-ahead rock direction although his 1975 solo album, *Teaser,* evidenced the lack of focus many group artists encounter when they set out on their own. *Teaser* offers moments of sheer virtuosity, like the slide guitar playing on "The Grind," and suggests that Bolin never got a chance to show his full potential as a solo artist before his tragic death in a Miami hotel room in 1976.

RECOMMENDED: *Teaser* (Nemporer).

BONZO DOG BAND

One of the most amazing organizations ever to exist under the aegis of rock 'n' roll, the Bonzo Dog (Doo Dah) Band existed in England from around 1965 to 1972, creating an unmatched level of humor and satirical music. With a variable lineup that included Viv Stanshall (later a solo artist), Neil Innes (who has worked with Monty Python and the Rutles), Roger Ruskin Spear (also a solo artist), and Legs Larry Smith (who toured for a while with Elton John), the Bonzos came out of the university world of dada theatrics and traditional jazz. More clever than musical at first, the Bonzos later established themselves as accomplished multi-instrumentalists, and their records show an astounding variety of styles and approaches. The Bonzos, always more a cult favorite than a commercial success, had one hit single, "I'm the Urban Spaceman," which was produced pseudonymously by Paul McCartney, whom they had met during the filming of the Beatles' *Magical Mystery Tour* show, in which the Bonzos have a featured role. Since the group's dissolution, the individual members have largely continued the farcical intent of their band, to varying degrees of success. There can be no doubt, though, that the Bonzos were a once-in-a-lifetime collection of talent and concept.

RECOMMENDED: *History of the Bonzos* (United Artists).

BOOMTOWN RATS

This Irish punk rock sextet came into prominence during 1977 in England with a debut album that was reminiscent of the early Rolling Stones for its power and alienated rage. Lead singer Bob Geldoff was a frothing punk intent on angering everybody in his path. The British press dutifully reports each of Geldoff's outrages with delighted remove. The Rats have since retreated from such a hard-edged musical stance, although the attempt to insult seems just as important in their program.

RECOMMENDED: *Boomtown Rats* (Mercury); *A Tonic for the Troops* (Columbia).

PAT BOONE

From his white shoes to his perfectly clean-cut hair Pat Boone was the epitome of the 50s crooner who could cash in on rock 'n' roll by offering safe, watered-down versions of top songs without the excitement of the originals. Invariably he would have hits while the originals languished. Boone also covered hymns right from the start, not exactly in a gospel vein, more in the line of devotional church music. After the British Invasion of the early 60s Boone attempted to cross over to country music with some success. Unlike other crooners of his generation, Boone did not attempt a major comeback in the 70s.

RECOMMENDED: *Pat's Great Hits* (Dot).

BOSTON

Epic Records initially promoted Boston with the catchphrase "Better music through science" on the strength of Tom Scholz's academic credentials and penchant for recording top quality heavy metal anthems on his own equipment in his own basement. But there is nothing scientific about Scholz's ability to write melodic songs ("More Than a Feeling," "Long Time") and then heighten their hooks with his own galvanizing guitar overdubs and Bradley Delp's octave-defying wail. Scholz, an MIT graduate with a master's degree in mechanical engineering, had labored in the Product Design wing of Polaroid's Boston headquarters by day, while he gigged with bar bands along the North Shore pickup circuit by night and tinkered with songs and home-made demos. (The demos that finally won Scholz and Boston their Epic contract are available on bootleg recordings and even in their rough form occasionally eclipse Boston's debut LP. Assembling Delp, guitarist Barry Goudreau, bassist Fran Sheehan, and drummer Sib Hashian, all Boston bar band alumni, Scholz created Boston. The multimillion-selling success of 1977's *Boston* and its single "More Than a Feeling" not only initiated a line of Boston clones eager to pick up a few crumbs of their phenomenal success but created an eagerness for Boston's second album, *Don't Look Back,* two years in the making. Another platinum album later, Boston stands as the high-water mark in rock's 70s fixation with studio sophistication and manufactured hits.

RECOMMENDED: *Boston* (Epic); *We Found It in the Trashcan, Honest* (bootleg of Boston demos).

DAVID BOWIE

The chameleonic David Bowie (b. David Jones, London, 1947) is not to be categorized lightly. After a short stint as a commercial artist in a London ad agency, Bowie (then Jones) started out in a semi-pro R&B band, playing saxophone. His blond boyish good looks made him perfect pop star material when he started recording formally as David Bowie (this after a period studying mime under Lindsay Kemp). He first realized his real singing and songwriting potential with *Man of Words, Man of Music* (1969) and its belated hit single "Space Oddity." The succeeding *The Man Who Sold The World* was a powerful if underrated rock 'n' roll statement made with his band that would soon become the Spiders From Mars. But it was the album *Ziggy Stardust and the Spiders from Mars* and its wild, if androgynously erotic, stage show that solidly established Bowie's reputation as a first-class entertainer and, given the album's mini-operatic theme of rock 'n' roll glory and death, a stylistic visionary. In fact, his vision usually outstripped that of his fans. Tired of the Ziggy personae, he announced his retirement on stage in London in July '73 and then gave his fans one more theatrical blast with the '74 *Diamond Dogs* tour. Not long after that, he retreated onto funkier turf with his white-man-got-soul routine on *Young Americans.* Another shift was detectable in the mechanical dance rhythms of *Station to Station,* but Bowie's interest in European avant-muzik only reached full flower in his work with Brian Eno on *Low, Heroes* (this with Robert Fripp), and *Lodger.* Bowie's film career, an excellent metaphor for his constant changing of masks, continues apace. *The Man Who Fell to Earth* was a marginally commercial success with critics giving Bowie the benefit of the doubt for his ability to look mysterious on screen. They haven't been so kind with his latest work *Just A Gigolo.*

RECOMMENDED: (U.S.) *Images* (London, a compilation of early and mid-60s recordings); *Space Oddity* (originally *Man of Words, Man of Music*), *Station to Station, Changes One* (RCA).

BOX TOPS

Memphis' answer to New York's Young Rascals, the Box Tops lit up Top 40 charts of the late 60s with a series of 45 RPM winners that artfully blended R&B grit with white uptown polish. Their debut single in 1967, "The Letter," sounds as fresh and exhilerating today as it did then, a welcome antidote to the psychedelic indulgences and sugary pop contrivances of the period. Singer Alex Chilton was only 17 at the time, but he carried in his voice a conviction that continued in later hits like "Cry Like a Baby" and "Sweet Cream Ladies." After the Box Tops (Chilton, Billy Cunningham, Gary Talley, Danny Smythe, John Evans) split, Chilton performed on the New York Greenwich Village folk circuit and then returned to Memphis to form Big Star, a highly underrated pop quartet that lasted through three LPs in various permutations. Chilton now records on his own and recently produced the voodoo rockabilly band the Cramps.

BRAND X

What the Average White Band are to R&B, Brand X are to jazz-rock; accomplished British session players who came together to make original music on their own. Bassist Percy Jones, guitarist John Goodsall, and drummer Phil Collins (of Genesis) all had hot reps of their own in and out of the studio when in 1973 they were called in by producer-keyboard player Robin Lumley to play back-up on an album by English singer Eddie Howell. Howell has since receded into obscurity, but the four jammed in the studio, liked the sound of it, and began recording. The name Brand X was chosen because they had no group name to put on the studio's recording log. Over the course of several personnel changes and (at this counting) five albums, Brand X has been accused of forsaking melodic sensitivity for chops, but on a good night (see live *Livestock*) they can't be beat. Members who have cruised in and out include percussionist Morris Pert (a Scot with concert music credentials), drummers Woody Dennard, Chuck Burgi and Michael Clark, keyboard ace Peter Robinson (replacing Lumley for a time), and guitarist Mike Miller (sitting in for Goodsall on one tour).

RECOMMENDED: *Unorthodox Behavior, Livestock* (Passport).

BRINSLEY SCHWARZ

Influential in the mid-70s pub-rock movement in Britain, Brinsley Schwarz (established 1970) made their first U.S. appearance at the Fillmore East in front of over 100 English pop journalists flown in especially for the gig. The band was disastrously bad that evening, and the reviews practically killed their chances of establishing a foothold here. But in retrospect, Brinsley Schwarz made good Workingman's Dead rock and, more important, gave us such talents as singer/songwriter/producer Nick Lowe, guitarist Brinsley Schwarz, keyboard player Bob Andrews, now with Graham Parker's Rumour, and Stiff recording artist Ian Gomm.

RECOMMENDED: *Brinsley Schwarz* (Capitol).

DAVID BROMBERG

This wacky, itinerant folklorist/singer/session musician made his living bumming around college campuses in the 60s playing "Bullfrog Blues" in a voice that resembled Andy Devine before coming to national attention as a session musician playing with Bob Dylan on *New Morning*. As a folkie/novelty item, Bromberg's engaging presence, ability to put together a series of hard-working, good-time bands and his multi-instrumental capabilities made him popular with a hard core of fans at the same time most critics were wondering how someone who sings this poorly ever got to make a record.

RECOMMENDED: *Out of the Blues* (Columbia).

JAMES BROWN

As a recent album proclaims, Brown is "The Original Disco Man," and a whole lot more. A Georgian, he reached the R&B charts in 1956 with his first release, "Please, Please, Please." For nearly ten years, he was a consistent soul hitmaker; his scorching 1963 *Live at the Apollo* LP is an awesome document of this period. But his music was so uncompromisingly "black," both rhythmically and in terms of Brown's shrieking vocals, that he never hit the pop Top Ten until "Papa's Got a Brand New Bag" in 1965. His flirtation with the white audience (through such classics as "I Got You," "Cold Sweat," and "I Got the Feelin'") continued for several years, and his frantic live performances became a legend. The man who once billed himself as "The Godfather of Soul" has gotten older, but he remains a hard-nosed and successful businessman and a sometimes social activist.

RECOMMENDED: *Live at the Apollo, Vols. 1-2* (King); *The Unbeatable 16 Hits, Soul Classics, Vols. 1-2* (Polydor).

JACKSON BROWNE

In 1967, Browne was known as a good, if somewhat quirky, songwriter who contributed to Nico's first album and played guitar for that strange songstress in her celebrated underground sessions at the Dom. When folk singer Tom Rush recorded Browne's writing alongside up-and-coming James Taylor and Joni Mitchell in 1968, the groundswell for Browne began. His first album was eagerly awaited and marked him as an important songwriter. With fiddler/guitarist David Lindley, bassist Doug Haywood, drummer Larry Zack, and keyboardist Jai Winding, Browne went on to record *Late for the Sky* and became the prophet of Southern Californian alienation and gloom. His best known song, "Take It Easy," was a big hit for the Eagles.

Photo by Lorrie Sullivan

RECOMMENDED: *Late for the Sky, The Pretender, Running on Empty* (Asylum).

BROWNSVILLE (BROWNSVILLE STATION)

Brownsville Station rose in 1969 from the ashes of Talisman and Koda Corporation, two Michigan rock 'n' roll bands whose leaders wanted to move on to something bigger. Brownsville played original teen anthems as well as oldies, did them loudly and never in the greasy Sha Na Na manner. The foursome, Cub Koda, Michael Lutz, Tony Driggins and T. J. Cronley, developed a unique in-person look: the tiny Koda hopped around the stage wearing round horn-rimmed glasses, gripping his harmonica in his mouth like an owl holding a mouse, while Cronley bashed the drums and Lutz circled Koda in a style Kiss later copied. Brownsville's hits include "Red Back Spider," "Smokin' in the Boys' Room," and "Kings of the Party." The band has never followed trends, brashly preferring just to be itself; Brownsville pounded out vintage rock before there was an oldies revival, played reggae before that was a fad, and blasted away like punks before anyone had heard of "the New Music." The band now consists of Lutz, Koda, Bruce Nazarian (bass) and Henry "H-Bomb" Weck (drums and explosives), a line-up which fully retains the power, cockiness and irreverance linked with the name of Brownsville for over ten years.

RECOMMENDED: *Yeah* (Big Tree); *Brownsville Station* (Private Stock).

LENNY BRUCE

Lenny Bruce was a culture hero because he was a comedian who made important early sick and black humor improvisations as well as trenchant social commentary. He used the stage as a platform to attack hypocrisy, racism, exploitation, corruption in politics, organized religion, and finally the U.S. justice system that hounded him with repeated arrests on obscenity and drug charges until his death from an overdose of morphine in 1966. By the time of his death, Bruce was virtually banned from working by nightclub owners across the country, but his effect on the loosening of public restrictions on the English language onstage and his fight for the right to uncensored performances opened the way for contemporary comedians from George Carlin to Richard Pryor. He influenced music figures as diverse as Phil Spector, Bob Dylan, Frank Zappa, Simon & Garfunkel, Grace Slick and John Lennon.

RECOMMENDED: *The Real Lenny Bruce* (Fantasy); *Lenny Bruce/Carnegie Hall* (United Artists); *The Law, the Language and Lenny Bruce* (Warner Bros.).

BILL BRUFORD

One of the best art rock drummers in the business, Bruford was the mainstay of the complex rhythmic switches Yes specialized in through that band's seventh album, at which point he joined King Crimson for the last few records of that group's brilliant run. Since then, Bruford has done the usual session chores with Genesis, Chris Squire, Roy Harper, Steve Howe, and Annette Peacock, before releasing his first solo album in 1978, *Feels Good to Me,* and joining the promising group, U.K. The U.K. association lasted long enough for Bruford and guitarist Allan Holdsworth to realize they should form their own band. The result is Bruford, and the band's 1979 debut added American R&B bassist Jeff Berlin and keyboardist Dave Stewart from the British avant garde band Hatfield and the North.

RECOMMENDED: *Feels Good to Me, One of a Kind* (Polydor).

TIM BUCKLEY

The American singer/songwriter community lost a unique, emotive voice when Tim Buckley died on June 29, 1975 of an overdose of heroin and morphine. Washington-born and New York-bred, Buckley moved to California at age 10 and was not long in joining local country bands and starting to write. His first album, 1966's *Tim Buckley,* was released when he was only 19, and already he was taking folk-rock into jazz-and-Brechttinged territory he would further expand with the classic *Goodbye and Hello*. But Buckley had barely begun to break through commercially when he left his prospective audience behind in a cloud of even jazzier dust on the dreamy, introspective LPs *Happy/Sad* and *Blue Afternoon*. Several ill-conceived and, worse, blatantly commercial albums later, Buckley was dead.

RECOMMENDED: *Tim Buckley, Goodbye and Hello, Happy/Sad* (Elektra).

BUFFALO SPRINGFIELD

An important collection of Southern Californian folk rockers, Buffalo Springfield pointed the stylistic direction for all American rock bands outside of heavy metal with their inspired cross-breed of folk, pop, country, rock, and R&B modes. The list of band members is a veritable Who's Who: Neil Young on lead guitar and vocals, Stephen Stills on second lead guitar and vocals, Richie Furay on rhythm guitar and vocals, Bruce Palmer and Jim Messina on bass, and Dewey Martin on drums. Young and Stills both wrote some of their best songs with this group, but the creative overload led to friction and unrest in the group until Young left. At their best moments, many experts believe this the best American rock band ever.

RECOMMENDED: *Buffalo Springfield, Buffalo Springfield—Greatest Hits, Retrospective* (Atco).

JIMMY BUFFETT

Known only at first by the underground dealers who dug him and the collection of Florida Keys weirdos he hung out with, Jimmy Buffett went on to become an unlikely star. An Auburn University dropout, he bounced around the Mississippi gulf coast for a while, playing the house at the Bayou Room in New Orleans, where a lot of his song ideas developed. Buffett went on to get a journalism degree at the University of Southern Mississippi before moving to Nashville to begin his recording career as a country rock singer/songwriter. After one unsuccessful album, he found himself with a new label and that Florida following. Writing songs about the sea, getting drunk and doing character cameos, Buffett clicked with the sultry hit "Margueritaville," and everything fell into place.

RECOMMENDED: *Changes in Latitudes, Changes in Attitudes, Son of a Son of a Sailor* (MCA).

SANDY BULL

This eclectic New York-based musician recorded a number of very interesting records for Vanguard in the 60s and 70s using a variety of instruments all played by himself in various musical styles from around the world. His early interest in Indian and other eastern styles and instrumentation is credited with influencing a lot of his peers in these directions, but he could also record such standards as "Tennessee Waltz."

RECOMMENDED: *Demolition Derby* (Vanguard).

PAUL BUTTERFIELD

Founder of the Butterfield Blues Band, the early 60s band that produced a powerful combination of white bluesmen and a black rhythm section, the Chicago-born harpist learned from playing with veteran blues harpists James Cotten and Junior Wells. His 1965 debut matched a front line of guitarists, Mike Bloomfield and Elvin Bishop, and organist Mark Naftalin against bassist Jerome Arnold and drummer Sam Lay. The performance was classic Chicago blues, but the second record, *East West* (with Billy Davenport replacing Lay), showed the band moving into a more free-form direction with exotic modalities and the kind of improvisational experimentation that was just starting to be explored. Butterfield went on to add horns to the outfit and his singing and harp playing continued to excel. In the mid-60s, Butterfield released several solo albums after disbanding the group.

RECOMMENDED: *The Paul Butterfield Band Live* (Elektra).

BYRDS

Roger McGuinn (b. James Joseph McGuinn, July 13, 1942, Chicago), Chris Hillman, Gene Clark (b. 1941, Tipton, Missouri), David Crosby (b. August 14, 1941, Los Angeles), and Michael Clark started out in 1964 as the Jet Set, then became the Beefeaters. But it was as the Byrds that they coined in sound if not word the term "folk-rock" and set off on a decade-long adventure: experimenting with old folk standards set to their trademark crackling Rickenbacker guitar sound, toying with Indian scales on *Fifth Dimension*, pre-dating country-rock by a good five years on *Sweetheart of the Rodeo*, and going through well over a dozen members before calling it quits in 1972. Through all this, Roger McGuinn (he changed his first name upon conversion to the Subud faith in 1968) was the center, gathering around him such talent as country enthusiast Gram Parsons, the late guitarist Clarence White, and songwriting bassist Skip Battin (who once had a teenybop hit as half of Skip and Flip). The five original Byrds made one vain reunion stab in '73, which only went to show how hard it is to recreate a past so glorious. McGuinn apparently owns the rights to the Byrds name, but the rest could probably care less. Crosby is one-third of Crosby, Stills, and Nash, Gene Clark makes sporadic solo appearances on record, and Chris Hillman surfaces every now and then with his own projects.

RECOMMENDED: *Mr. Tambourine Man, Sweetheart of the Rodeo* (Columbia).

J. J. CALE

Mark Knopfler admits to copping riffs for Dire Straits from him. Eric Clapton had adopted his languorous tone and recorded Cale songs like "After Midnight" and "Cocaine." Lynyrd Skynyrd used to open live sets with another Cale tune, "Call Me the Breeze." Yet J. J. Cale remains a relative unknown. The Tulsa-based singer/songwriter/guitarist was introduced by fellow Oklahoman Leon Russell, who signed him to record for his Shelter label. Cale has never gone in for big promotions. He just keeps turning out these marvelous white R&B records filled with songs driven by a relentless, slow-burn.

RECOMMENDED: *Really, Naturally, Okie, V* (Shelter).

JOHN CALE

Along with fellow Velvet Undergrounder Lou Reed, the Welsh-born and classically trained Cale is considered to be one of the new wave godfathers as well as one of rock's most convincing experimenters. Cale first met Reed in 1964 in New York, where the former had ditched classical studies to play electric viola with avant-garde composer LaMonte Young in his experimental group. Cale joined the Velvet Underground, contributing that experimental edge to Velvet pieces like "Sister Ray" and "European Son to Delmore Schwarz." Cale quit in 1968 to pursue a multi-career as producer (Modern Lovers, Stooges, Nico), arranger, composer, and performer, both solo and with fellow composer Terry Tiley on *Church of Antrax*. Cale produced a stunning debut album for Patti Smith. He tried his classical chops on his first solo LP *Academy of Peril*, but returned to song forms, however bizarrely rearranged, on successive albums.

RECOMMENDED: *Vintage Violence* (Columbia).

CAN

These experimental German rockers relied on the drone rhythms of Holgar Czukay's heavily damped bass guitar, and the electronically modified percussion of Jacki Liebezeit. On that wedge-like sound system, keyboardist Irmin Schmidt used his electronic music training under German composer Karl-Heinz Stockhausen to weave intricate patterns with guitarist Michael Karoli. Japanese lead singer Damo created an even weirder effect with his decidedly un-Teutonic vocals. Can has been recognized as Europe's most experimental rock band of the 70s, and has been called on to record soundtracks for several films.

RECOMMENDED: *Limited Edition* (United Artists).

CANNED HEAT

In the late 60s, Canned Heat were at the top. They played the Monterey Pop Festival with Hendrix, Joplin and the Who; they appeared at Woodstock; they had a hit single ("On the Road Again"); and they were a consistent album seller as well. Their unique blend of urban blues and progressive thinking made them a significant outfit, influencing many young guitarists and singers. As the 60s ended, their popularity (and the commercial viability of blues in general) began to wane, and the suicide death of co-founder Alan Wilson in 1970 ended the group, although various lineups have persevered. Canned Heat's original lineup was Bob Hite, vocals; Alan Wilson, guitar/vocals/harmonica; Henry Vestine, lead guitar; Larry Taylor, bass; and Frank Cook, drums (replaced early on by Adolfo de la Parra). These were total blues-R&B fanatics, with Hite owning an enormous personal collection of records. They drew from numerous blues styles and gradually developed a style all their own, which featured Hite's lusty singing and Wilson's whiny emotional plaint. Some of their early records are great, with all sorts of things thrown in, psychedelia, flute, jazzy improvisations, a potpourri of talent. Their demise was a loss for rock music fans everywhere.

RECOMMENDED: *Live at Topanga Corral* (Wand); *Future Blues* (Liberty).

CAPTAIN & TENILLE

Popping out of Southern California in 1975 with the treacly "Love Will Keep Us Together," the Captain & Tenille represented responsible young adult love to mid-America. They went for only the most insipid of pop schlock, presented a squeaky clean image, and proselytized for health foods in their spare time. They tried a sort of updated Sonny and Cher on TV one season (Toni played the bubbly wife, Darryl Dragon the dorky hubby), but even in a medium as bland as television, they came off as insubstantial.

RECOMMENDED: *Greatest Hits* (A&M).

CAPTAIN BEEFHEART

Don Van Vliet, alias the Spotlight Kid alias Captain Beefheart, was a childhood friend of Frank Zappa's in Los Angeles. His strange, other-worldly musical ideas, multi-stylistic interests and dada-like presentation made him one of the more interesting figures to come out of the west coast music scene of the 60s. He played with Zappa for a while before forming his own group, the Magic Band, and writing a series of songs as loved for their poetry as for their music. After the Magic Band dispersed in the 70s Beefheart worked briefly with Zappa again. Then, in 1978, Beefheart returned with one of his finest albums, *Shiny Beast/Bat Chain Puller.*

RECOMMENDED: *Mirror Man* (Buddah); *Shiny Beast/Bat Chain Puller* (Warner Brothers).

CARAVAN

One of the many fine bands to surface from the Canterbury section of England in the late 60s and early 70s, Caravan was a successor to the popular British group Wilde Flowers. Drummer Richard Coughlan and guitarist Pye Hastings (trained by Kevin Ayers) joined Wilde Flowers in 1965; keyboardist David Sinclair joined the band in 1967; and the following year the three formed Caravan when Wilde Flowers broke up. After recording three albums, Steve Miller replaced Sinclair on keyboards for one album, at which point Sinclair returned and bassist John Perry and electric violinist Geoff Richardson were added. The band's imaginative and eclectic sound has made Caravan one of the foremost British art-rock groups.

RECOMMENDED: *For Girls Who Grow Plump in the Night* (London).

ERIC CARMEN

As the leader of the Cleveland-based Raspberries ("Go All the Way," "Overnight Sensation," etc.), Carmen was a pioneer of power pop before that term was even coined. But after embarking on a solo career in 1975, he went soft, forgetting about the power and pouring on the pop. His music became self-consciously arty, saccharine and cloying, with only flashes of his previous zest. He still got the hit singles, but couldn't provide the thrills.

RECOMMENDED: *Eric Carmen* (Arista).

CARPENTERS

Richard and Karen Carpenter emerged from the upper-middle class suburbs of Los Angeles in 1969 with a cover of the Beatles' "Ticket to Ride." It was lush, syrupy, wholesome, lily white, and not a little mindless. It was also a huge success with adults and kids in their lower teens not yet ready for hard rock. Each record that followed was pretty much the same, only more so, until they started going "progressive" (and losing their audience) with *Passage* some eight years later. By that time they'd sold about thirty million records (eighteen gold) and won a lot of music business awards. By remaining absolutely true to their virginal, silver-spoon roots, the Carpenters also won a certain kind of perverse respect from critics, unusual for this kind of group.

RECOMMENDED: *The Singles, 1969-73* (A&M).

CARS

Ric Ocasek created the Cars in early 1977, fleshing out the image of experimental pop with song hooks that could lure even the most passive listener into its web of avant-garde notions, new wave intensity, and psychedelic gags. The band includes drummer David Robinson (ex-Modern Lovers), guitarist Elliot Easton, keys and sax man Greg Hawkes (ex-Martin Mull), and longtime musical partner bassist Ben Orr. Born Richard Otcasek in Baltimore (he admits to being

"The Ballad of Ira Hayes" and others. In 1968 he married June Carter and the two recorded several hits together including "Jackson" and "Guitar Pickin' Man." Cash went on to host his own television program for three years and continues to make hit records, the latest being his 1979 remake of "Ghost Riders In the Sky."

Photo by Elliot Gilbert

only 29 in press handouts), Ocasek went to Antioch College in Ohio, gigged around Cleveland in various bands, met Orr, and took off for Boston. He formed more bands there with various Cars in various combinations: Richard and the Rabbits, Cap'n Swing, before coming up with the Cars and, in 1978, a winner of a debut album. Hit singles like "My Best Friend's Girl," "Let's Go," and "Just What I Needed" (an FM hit in demo form back in Boston) epitomize the Cars' approach; pop cliches turned topsy-turvy with an intensity recalling Ocasek's love of the Velvet Underground, confidently rearranged into an electronic soundscape that takes Roxy Music several steps further. Outside the Cars, Ocasek's talents are also apparent on records and demos he has produced for new Boston bands and the New York primal electronic duo, Suicide.

RECOMMENDED: *The Cars, Candy-O* (Elektra).

JOHNNY CASH

The Arkansas born country singer and guitarist first recorded for Sun records in the 50s with the Tennessee Two, guitarist Luther Perkins and bassist Marshall Grant. During this period he recorded his classics "Folsom Prison Blues" and "I Walk the Line." Later, with Columbia records, Cash continued to make hits; "Don't Take Your Guns To Town," "Ring Of Fire," "In the Jailhouse House,"

RECOMMENDED: *Ring Of Fire, I Walk the Line, Folsom Prison* (Columbia).

CHAD AND JEREMY

Clean-cut though long-haired, Chad Stuart and Jeremy Clyde scored immediately in the post-Beatles English Invasion of 1964. They were melodic, their harmonies were smooth, and even their orchestrated pop-rock was inoffensive. They peaked when their sound became a little more folkish ("Summer Song" and "Yesterday's Gone"), but blew it by making the then-obligatory "meaningful" album. They were probably never meant to be anything more than pretty voices and pretty faces.

RECOMMENDED: *Best of Chad and Jeremy* (Capitol).

CHAMBERS BROTHERS

The first of the psychedelic black groups, the Chambers Brothers (George, Willie, Joe, Lester, and white drummer Brian Keenan) started out as a folk-gospel group in the early 60s, then hit the New York disco circuit. But their major claim to fame was "Time Has Come Today," a flower power anthem that went a little over ten minutes on record and up to thirty minutes in concert. At their peak, the stage show was full-out exuberance when it didn't become strained. Today, their old records are memorable more as artifacts than as innovative rock.

RECOMMENDED: *Time Has Come, Greatest Hits* (Columbia).

HARRY CHAPIN

Chapin is best known for his story songs ("Taxi," etc.), which tend to be slight, lugubrious ditties with catchy melodies that frequently pass for "meaningful" or "art." But they've won him a couple of gold records and Emmy and Oscar nominations. Born in Greenwich Village and now living happily on Long Island, he began playing with his brothers Tom and Steve. It's a musical family; his father was a drummer with the Tommy Dorsey and Woody Herman bands. Chapin went solo in 1971. He's also a social activist who cofounded the World Hunger Year project, and has worked in film (his *Legendary Champions* documentary was nominated for an Oscar in 1969). His *The Night That Made America Famous*, a multimedia Broadway show, was nominated for two Tonys in 1975, but did not do well at the box office.

RECOMMENDED: *Greatest Stories Live* (Elektra).

CHARLATANS

Those who were there swear that this was the first *real* San Francisco hippie band. They formed in 1965 and played what was then called good-time music and today would be called country-rock. The Charlatans dressed as Gold Rush dandies and seemed to be in the center of many "drug-related incidents." They were there when the Family Dog was staging its first events and the original Fillmore was starting up. When they were on, the Charlatans were truly inspired; unfortunately, their sole album barely reflects this (it wasn't released until 1969), and the group fell apart before they could benefit from the scene they helped create. Dan Hicks was the only one to see any success after that, and his was limited.

RECOMMENDED: *The Charlatans* (Philips).

RAY CHARLES

In 1955, Ray Charles fused the previously disparate forms of gospel and blues into an exhilarating song called "I Got a Woman" that laid the groundwork for modern soul music and much of the pop music that followed. Until then, the native Georgian (who went blind at a young age) had tried on a number of styles associated with other artists. After that, his unique skills as a singer, songwriter, pianist and arranger earned him the nickname The Genius. By 1959, he was a consistent entry in the pop charts; in 1962, his *Modern Sounds in Country and Western* (R&B arrangements of top country songs, another innovation) was the biggest album in the country. Despite a much-publicized heroin bust, his career has seldom flagged (though record sales have). In the last decade, he has devoted most of his efforts to pop music, but in the course of his career he has performed everything from Tin Pan Alley to deep blues, with every conceivable kind of group from rhythm combo to orchestra. This has only increased the demand for him as a live performer. In short, he has become a contemporary American institution.

RECOMMENDED: *The Ray Charles Story, Vols. 1-4* (Atlantic); *Greatest Hits* (ABC-Paramount).

CHEAP TRICK

Photo by Jim Houghton

This Illinois-based foursome first appeared on the national scene in early 1977 after spending several years establishing themselves as a major club attraction in the Midwest. Within two years, Cheap Trick had scored big with a chart-topping live album and single. Their following, built up by non-stop touring in the U.S., Canada, Europe and Japan, make them a huge concert draw everywhere. Their sound combines shattering hard rock energy with strong melodies and harmonies not usually found among such heavy duty outfits. Their live presentation is a frenetic visual hodgepodge built around the lunatic antics of pick-flicking guitarist Rick Nielsen and the debonair refinement of vocalist Robin Zander. Rounding out the group are drummer Bun E. Carlos and bassist Tom Petesson, whose collection of basses include eight, ten, and twelve-stringers. A group that records during brief breaks in their hectic tour schedule, Cheap Trick's success has spawned numerous imitators, but their particular blend of wit and wisdom will be hard to match.

RECOMMENDED: *Live At Budokan, Dream Police* (Epic).

CHUBBY CHECKER

An itinerant performer, Checker was in the right place at the right time when he recorded a version of the Hank Ballard tune "The Twist" in the early 60s, just in time to capitalize on that dance craze. Checker was the featured performer at the jet set mecca, New York's Peppermint Lounge, where the Twist was the dance of choice. When the Peppermint Lounge folded a few years later and the Twist fell from currency, Checker was quickly forgotten.

RECOMMENDED: *Do the Twist with Chubby Checker* (Roulette).

CHEECH AND CHONG

At a time when comedy was simply not very popular (early 70s), Tommy Chong (part Chinese) and Cheech Marin (Chicano) came out of Los Angeles pushing a sense of humor based entirely on drugs, which *were* popular. So, in little time, were Cheech and Chong, whose routines were unrelentingly sophomoric, excruciatingly obvious. But if you were too stoned to get up and change the record, they were probably what you wanted in the first place. Later, they were replaced by comics who expressed a more *complete* world view, but *Up in Smoke*, their 1978 feature film, was a surprise runaway hit, proving that there were still plenty of old dopers out there.

RECOMMENDED: *Cheech and Chong, Big Bambu* (Warner Bros.).

CHICAGO

Though named after their rough and tumble home town, these eight guys are slick all the way. First known as Chicago Transit Authority, they were one of the creators of the jazz-rock idiom. So what if it was a tepid jazz *and* a tepid rock; Chicago fused forty years of music together to create jazz for people who didn't like jazz and rock for people who didn't like rock. Their audience has always ranged from teenyboppers to veterans of the swing era, and those kind of demographics add up to many gold albums. In truth, they were nothing but a Midwestern show band with mushy liberal politics, and critics wouldn't treat them so harshly if they didn't sell so many records. But they've also been done in by their taste for overkill; purposely busy arrangements, ponderous packaging, and a logo that looks so much like the Coca Cola emblem that it's hard not to think they haven't conceived of themselves as a marketing project right from the beginning.

RECOMMENDED: *Chicago Transit Authority, Chicago II-III* (Columbia).

CITY BOY

The six-piece English band City Boy hail from Birmingham, home of the Move, ELO, Moody Blues, and it shows in their effortless blend of high vocal harmonies, involved pop composition, and arty instrumentalizing. Rarely as heavy-handed as the Moodies or as superficial as ELO, City Boy project an intelligent rock 'n' roll image that has proved more appealing to Americans than to the band's homeland. Chief writers and singers Lol Mason and Steve Broughton started out in local coffeehouses in the late 60s. City Boy began to take shape when they were joined in 1971 by pianist Max Thomas, in 1972 by bassist Chris Dunn, and in 1975 by lead guitarist Mike Slamer and dubbed themselves Back-in-the-Band. The weighty title went as drummer Roger Kent came in. Roy Ward subsequently took his place with the 1977 LP, *Young Men Gone West*.

RECOMMENDED: *City Boy* (Mercury).

ERIC CLAPTON

Clapton is revered as the first 60s guitar hero for his blues purish work with John Mayall, for pioneering the blues/rock power trio Cream, and then forming the first "supergroup," Blind Faith. Always shy and retiring, Clapton retreated when that group broke up, becoming a Delaney and Bonnie sideman and sinking deeper into despair. But then came his finest hour, *Layla*. Fronting a group he called

Derek and the Dominoes, augmented by the guitar of Duane Allman, it was rich, complex, jarring, desperate, passionate music. He descended into heroin for three years, bouncing back in 1974 with *461 Ocean Blvd*. This was a much quieter work that made explicit the spiritual side of Clapton that had been there all along and managed to capture the dignity and deep emotional undercurrent of Delta blues without aping the form. He hasn't really pushed himself since but has worked steadily. His magic hasn't strayed far from the country/blues/gospel synthesis of *461*, but he has yet to match that album's intensity.

RECOMMENDED: *History of Eric Clapton* (Atco); *At His Best, Clapton* (Polydor); *461 Ocean Blvd., Slowhand* (RSO).

DAVE CLARK FIVE

Dave was the drummer, from Tottenham; the front man was singer-keyboard player Mike Smith. From February 1964 to April 1966, the DC5 recorded fourteen straight Top 20 hits of ultracommercial British Invasion Studio sound. (They were always much more popular here than at home.) And for this they were roundly castigated by nearly everyone, teenybop crap, the critics said, mindless formulaic records. True enough, but there was something attractive in them anyhow. They put forth a glorious blare that in its very artlessness made for good AM radio. However formulaic they were, they did rock like crazy; all the emphasis was on drums and sax, and they hardly ever did a ballad.

RECOMMENDED: *Greatest Hits, More Greatest Hits* (Epic).

ALLAN CLARKE

The front man of the Hollies for thirteen years, Lancashire-bred singer Allan Clarke has sustained his position in pop with engaging riffy songwriting and a twangy, lead tenor voice. Clarke's impact goes beyond the commercial feat of filling three longplaying volumes of Hollies hits. He manages to mix classic rock elements: the rhythm of Lloyd Price, the urgency of Roy Orbison, the southern cockiness of early Elvis Presley, and the silkier vocal textures of Curtis Mayfield, into an overall sound that transcends its influences. From 1971 through 1973, Clarke fronted his own band, playing rhythm guitar and really rocking, but his three albums got little promotion. He developed a cult reputation for being ahead of his time by recording the songs of Gerry Rafferty, Mento Williams ("Draft Away"), and Buckingham/Nicks years before these writers became international chart forces. Needing to get back on his commercial feet, he rejoined the Hollies and nudged them back onto the U.S. charts with the 1974 hit, "The Air That I Breathe." Allan's original songs have been recorded or covered by the Searchers, Blue Mink, and Byron Lee and the Dragonaires.

RECOMMENDED: *My Real Name is 'arold* (Epic); *Headroom* (EMI).

STANLEY CLARKE

Born in Philadelphia, the virtuoso bassist Clarke started out playing in blues bands at age 16, went to the Philadelphia Music Academy, then did a series of sessions with jazz luminaries Horace Silver, Joe Henderson, Curtis Fuller, Art Blakey, Pharoh Sanders, Dexter Gordon, and Stan Getz. Clarke teamed up with pianist Chick Corea to form one of the most successful jazz/rock fusion bands, Return to Forever, and recorded his first solo album, *Children of Forever*, around the same time. After spending several years with Return to Forever and recording sporadically the group broke up and Clarke turned to a solo career. He has recorded several excellent albums in a variety of rock, jazz and disco styles while touring to a predominantly rock audience.

RECOMMENDED: *Children of Forever* (Polydor), *Stanley Clarke, School Days* (Nemporer).

CLASH

Along with the Sex Pistols, the Clash were at the front of the English new wave explosion in 1977, but unlike the Pistols, the Clash have managed to stay relatively intact and collectively productive. The four Londoners who make up the Clash: Joe Strummer (vocals/guitar), Mick Jones (guitar/vocals), Paul Simonon (bass), and Topper Headon (drums), play a fierce, politically conscious music that captures all the frustration and bitterness of English youth. Ruggedly independent and ethical about the business side of rock 'n' roll, the Clash have often crossed swords with their record company, have fired a pair of managers, and have had an extremely stormy career. Still, they are the most consistently exciting and stimulating music in Britain. Their two tours of America have brought them as many fanatic fans as they have in their own country.

RECOMMENDED: *Give 'Em Enough Rope, The Clash* (Epic).

JIMMY CLIFF

Born James Chambers in St. Catherine, Jamaica in 1948, Jimmy Cliff has been one of reggae's biggest stars outside of Bob Marley, principally because of his rough but realistic performance as the outlaw-reggae heroe in Perry Henzell's film, *The Harder They Come*. As early as 1962, Cliff was recording and scoring hits in Jamaica like "Hurricane Hattie" and "Miss Jamaica." He had moderate U.S. success introducing the reggae beat in the late 60s with "Wonderful World Beautiful People" and his "Many Rivers to Cross" has been covered extensively by everyone from Linda Ronstadt to the reformed Animals. Cliff has renounced Rastafarianism for the Moslem religion and continues to make albums that artfully combine his ethnic roots and commercial sensibilities.

RECOMMENDED: *The Harder They Come* (Mango); *In Concert* (Reprise).

CLIMAX BLUES BAND

The Climax Blues Band is stuck in the odd position of resolutely trying to carry on a tradition that often doesn't work on record. The tradition is that of white British blues. The playing of blues and blues-inspired music worked fine in clubs and halls around Stafford, the town in the English Midlands where the Climax Chicago Blues Band first boogied a decade ago in the manner of John Mayall's Bluesbreakers and the Savoy Brown Blues Band. It still worked when the five, Colin Cooper, Peter Haycock, Derek Holt, Arthur Wood and George Newsome, hooked up with producer Chris Thomas for a live-sounding studio album, *The Climax Chicago Blues Band*. For most of the ten years and ten records since, the group's output has been uneven, well-played but putting the audience to sleep. The band woke up in 1976 and broke through with *Gold Plated* and the single, "Couldn't Get It Right," but despite a display of studio savvy that manages to keep the band both full-sounding and blues-basic, Climax in the three years since has really been a sustained anticlimax.

RECOMMENDED: *Climax Chicago Blues Band* (Sire).

BILLY COBHAM

On his own, with Miles Davis or with John McLaughlin's Mahavishnu Orchestra, Billy Cobham is one of the most powerful and prolific jazz-rock drummers of the 70s. After sessioning with jazz stars George Benson, Horace Silver, Stanley Turrentine and Kenny Burrell while doing extensive background work on jingles and TV themes (Certs, Gillette, *Mission Impossible*), Cobham helped form Dreams, one of the first jazz/rock fusion bands. From there he played with Davis and McLaughlin before setting out on his own. His first album, Spectrum, which included guitarist Tommy Bolin and keyboardist Jan Hammer, was a big hit that even yielded a popular single. Cobham went on to record in a variety of group contexts, always with the accent on his big beat drumming.

RECOMMENDED: *Spectrum* (Atlantic).

EDDIE COCHRAN

Cochran came from Minnesota and became one of the most influential rockabilly guitarists. John Lennon and Paul McCartney of the Beatles got together over his "Twenty Flight Rock" and the Who did a version of "Summertime Blues" and "C'Mon Everybody." When his family moved to California in the mid-50s Cochran met lyricist Jerry Capeheart and the two formed a partnership, writing the above-mentioned songs and others. Cochran died in a car accident during a triumphant tour of Britain in 1960.

RECOMMENDED: *Eddie Cochran Legendary Master* (United Artists).

JOE COCKER

An English tribute to the influence of Ray Charles, Joe Cocker was and still is an important innovative white blues singer. Born in Sheffield, England, Cocker was a gas fitter who turned pro in 1964, recorded a flop version of the Beatles' "I'll Cry Instead," and returned to gas fitting while assembling the Grease Band. In 1968 Cocker recorded another Beatles song, "With a Little Help from My Friends," with indeed some superstar friends and scored his first hit. A Woodstock showing with the Grease Band strengthened his reputation and in 1970, when Leon Russell masterminded a traveling rock 'n roll circus called Mad Dogs and Englishmen fronted by Cocker, the singer became a household word courtesy of the concerts, resulting album and film. But constant drinking, rumors of drugs, and bad business management sent Cocker's star plummeting with only the periodic hit ("You Are So Beautiful") to revive his flagging fortunes.

RECOMMENDED: *Joe Cocker, Mad Dogs and Englishmen* (A&M).

LEONARD COHEN

Leonard Cohen (b. 1934, Montreal, Canada) was a poet first, songwriter second, and singer third. He had already published several volumes of poetry and two novels (*The Favorite Game* in 1963 and *Beautiful Losers* in 1966) before setting his poems to music and gaining pop recognition for sensitive covers of his songs like Judy Collins' "Suzanne." A reserved, almost academic figure whose periodic reclusiveness and concern for poetic form prevent him from ever becoming a star in commercial terms, Cohen records with increasing infrequency. After a period of inactivity, Cohen came back in 1978 with an album, *Death of a Ladies Man,* produced by Phil Spector, which was pounced on by critics as one of the great creative mismatches of the decade, a mismatch in which nobody won.

RECOMMENDED: *The Songs of Leonard Cohen* (Columbia).

NATALIE COLE

Photo by Tony Esparza

The daughter of Nat "King" Cole, Natalie was raised in a Hollywood showbiz household but didn't turn to singing herself until after her junior year of college at the University of Massachusetts. Four years later, in 1975, her first record ("Inseparable") was released, and she was an instant star. "This Will Be," from her debut album, won her two Grammies in 1976. Then, as now, she was produced by Chuck Jackson and Marvin Yancy. They're from the Chicago school of soul production, and Natalie sings a terrific soul tune. But as her career has progressed, it's become obvious that she longs for recognition as an all-around singer/entertainer. So she handles a lot of softer material as well and has been strongly influenced by white rock singers. All this has resulted in some checkered albums, but they go platinum or gold anyhow.

RECOMMENDED: *Inseparable* (Capitol).

JUDY COLLINS

This Seattle born folksinger started playing piano at age four and studied classical music through her teens until she became exposed to the late 50s folk music explosion. She learned to play guitar and started appearing in local Denver folk music hangouts. Her early 60s albums for Elektra earned her an ardent following on the folk music circuit. After moving to New York's Greenwich Village, Collins began recording songs by contemporary writers of the mid 60s, and her cover of Joni Mitchell's "Both Sides Now" brought Mitchell to public attention. Though she continued writing and recording through the 70s, her career waned until the daring pop album in 1979, *Hard Time For Lovers.*

RECOMMENDED: *The Judy Collins Concert, Wildflowers* (Elektra).

COMMANDER CODY

In the early 70s, George Frayne led Commander Cody and His Lost Planet Airmen, a group of Ann Arbor-via-Oakland "hillbilly hippies" who drove bar crowds wild after their rousing, tongue-in-cheek brand of country/western/swing/rockabilly/rock 'n' roll. The Commander played a rollicking boogie woogie piano and growled lead vocals on a few novelty songs. When the group, never a highly commercial proposition, broke up, he was the only one to try to make it solo. Odd, since not only did he have a good number of outside interests (he's an accomplished sculptor and painter), but he was perhaps the least musically ingenious member of the old group. His albums have tried unsuccessfully to capture a little of that old Airmen abandon and weirdness.

RECOMMENDED: *CC&HLPA—Lost in the Ozone, Live from Deep in the Heart of Texas* (Paramount).

RY COODER

His bottleneck guitar technique alone makes Cooder one of the most important practitioners of traditional American musical styles, but Cooder has also specialized in mandolin, accordion and slack key guitar styles. The Los Angeles native spent his salad days studying different blues guitarists before joining a group called the Rising Sons which also featured Taj Mahal. Since then, he has worked as a session musician and released an album a year of his own work since 1970. Each solo album covers a different aspect of American musical styles, and his most recent effort, *Bop Till You Drop*, besides being a great album, is rock's first digital recording.

RECOMMENDED: *Bop Till You Drop* (Warner Bros.).

SAM COOKE

The most popular of the late 50s-early 60s R&B singers, Cooke got his start singing lead with one of the famous gospel groups, the Soul Stirrers, before taking his smooth, mellow voice into pop music. His first hit, in 1957, was "You Send Me," followed by "Chain Gang," "Twisting the Night Away," "Shake," "Another Saturday Night" and "Ain't That Good News." Cooke died in a 1964 motel shootout with a woman but his influence on singers from Otis Redding to Rod Stewart outlived him.

RECOMMENDED: *Sam Cooke's Greatest Hits, Greatest Hits Vol. II* (RCA).

RITA COOLIDGE

Joe Cocker's Mad Dogs and Englishmen, the 1970 tour dedicated to the proposal that more is better, gave Coolidge her big break. She got a solo spot on that show, having previously sung only radio commercial ditties and backup with Delaney and Bonnie. After that, the Tennessee girl was on her way and in 1977 her slick, bland interpretations of rock and pop got results. Her *Anytime... Anywhere* LP yielded three hit singles, and while she has yet to match it, she's had hits ever since, but she still sounds first and foremost like a radio jingles singer. She tours with husband Kris Kristofferson, and also records duets with him.

RECOMMENDED: *Anytime . . . Anywhere* (A&M).

ALICE COOPER

Half Hollywood, half rock 'n' roll horror, Alice Cooper (b. Vincent Furnier in Detroit) was raised in Phoenix, Arizona, a preacher's son. Cooper formed a rock 'n' roll band with Neal Smith, Glen Buxton, Mike Bruce, and Dennis Dunaway that went under names like the Earwigs, Spiders, and Nazz (not to be confused with Todd Rundgren's band of the same name). A local hit in Phoenix wasn't enough to keep them there, so the band, renamed Alice Cooper with Furnier parading under the same name, moved to Los Angeles and developed a mondo-bizarro stage act that included killing chickens on stage while singing about "Refrigerator Heaven." The freak show shtick started turning the band a profit with *Love It to Death* and the Top 20 hit "I'm Eighteen." Cooper dismissed the band after 1973's *Billion Dollar Babies* LP and tour and 1974's *Muscle of Love*, and there started his descent into MOR-dom with sappy hits like "Only Women Bleed." His stage show is still heavy on the horror show gimmicks, but gimmicks they stay and his albums haven't rocked in years, despite a prestigious list of sessionmen like guitarists Dick Wagner and Steve Hunter who tore up Lou Reed's *Rock & Roll Animal* LP. Cooper's predeliction for alcohol forced him into semiretirement and hospital treatment in 1977/78, resulting in the *From Inside* album chronicling his stay.

RECOMMENDED: *Killer, School's Out, Billion Dollar Babies, Alice Cooper's Greatest Hits* (Warner Bros.).

CHICK COREA

A great musician who has stirred recent controversy following his conversion to Scientology, Corea was in the forefront of the early 70s jazz/rock fusion music. A native of Massachusetts who was classically trained, Corea began his professional playing in a Latin jazz bag with Mongo Santamaria, went on to play with Blue Mitchell and Stan Getz, then found his stride with the Miles Davis band that began exploring rock amplification techniques in a jazz harmonic frame. After leaving Davis, Corea formed the critically-acclaimed avant-garde jazz group Circle, a brain-twisting experience that apparently led him to the security of Scientology's quasi-religious program. It didn't affect his music, however, as the 1970 band Return to Forever proved with its adventurous blend of jazz and rock styles. Corea enjoyed success with this band until it broke up amid plenty of recrimination a few years ago. Since then, Corea has avoided solo albums and plays occasional acoustic piano duets with Herbie Hancock.

RECOMMENDED: *Return to Forever* (ECM).

LARRY CORYELL

Born in Texas and raised mostly around Seattle, Coryell was once considered the guitarist most likely to lead rock fans to jazz. He had a highly varied background, having played rock, jazz and country in Seattle. When he went to New York in the mid-60s, he worked first with a jazz/rock band called the Free Spirits and then took a seat in the band of vibist Gary Burton. His solos could crack around the room like a whip, but he also resorted to frenzied single-line outbursts that went nowhere and took a long time to do so. He has never sounded as good as a leader as he did as a sideman. Still, under the right circumstances, with the Jazz Composers Orchestra of America, for example, he can play tastefully and imaginatively.

RECOMMENDED: *At the Village Gate* (Vanguard).

ELVIS COSTELLO

Possibly the most unlikely looking rock star since Buddy Holly, Elvis Costello (b. Declan MacManus) came to prominence as the favored discovery of London's Stiff Records. With the help of manager Jake Riviera (b. Andrew Jakeman) and a trio of musicians known as the Attractions, Elvis has proven to be a talented performer of constant change and excitement. One of the 70s great songwriters, Costello's lyrics, about alienation, hate and frustration, are in the tradition of Bob Dylan and Pete Townsend, but his music draws on many varied forms, from reggae to R&B. An extremely private and intense individual, Costello rarely grants interviews and has built an air of mystery around himself and his comings and goings. Fortunately, his awesome abilities have made him a genuinely interesting musical figure, despite his occasionally overbearing image.

RECOMMENDED: *My Aim Is True, Armed Forces* (Columbia).

KEVIN COYNE

Little known even in his native England, singer/songwriter Kevin Coyne has subsisted mostly on critical acclaim for his perceptive, unflinching songs on the human condition and gruff, mannered, but affecting vocal style. An art college refugee, Coyne worked in various positions in psychiatric wards and mental institutions, from which he got the inspiration for many of his best songs, including a rare but superb English LP called *Case History*. His fortunes in the U.S. (Coyne records regularly for Virgin in the U.K.) have been low. With a band called Siren, he recorded two albums released by Elektra in 1970 and 1971 and was even touted for awhile as a possible replacement for Jim Morrison in the Doors. But his 1973 double album, *Marjory Razor Blade*, was reduced to one LP here, as was his last U.S. release, the live *In Living Black and White*. Coyne has also cowritten and appeared in several theatrical revues, as well as doing one-man shows.

RECOMMENDED: *Siren* (Dandelion/Elektra); *Marjory Razor Blade* (Virgin).

CRAZY HORSE

Originally known as the Rockets, Crazy Horse first attracted attention in 1969 when they backed Neil Young on his *Everybody Knows This Is Nowhere* LP and a subsequent tour. Their own debut LP showed that L.A. country-rock could be tough and driving as well as melodic and spirited. But Danny Whitten, the heart and soul of the group, died of a heroin overdose. The group disbanded for a couple years in the mid-70s, then came back with new member, Frank Sampedro. Though their work with Young, both live and on record, continues to dazzle, on their own they have simply lacked the spark that makes a great band.

RECOMMENDED: *Crazy Horse* (Reprise).

CREAM

The most successful white blues band to date, this supergroup trio (Eric Clapton, guitar; Jack Bruce, bass, vocals; and Ginger Baker, drums) plus producer/musician Felix Pappalardi existed for a little over two years only, yet changed the direction of rock music. Formed out of John Mayall's band and Graham Bond's "Organization," the threesome combined stunning instrumental virtuosity and improvisational skill with a diverse blend of musical influences that swung their sound between straight twelve-bar and sophisticated psychedelia. The rest of the rock world followed their lead. Definite trendsetters, Cream legitimized jamming, brought the bass guitar forward as a lead instrument, brought jazz and soloing to rock drumming, and served as inspiration for countless young guitarists. While they only recorded four official albums during their time together, several posthumous live collections served to downgrade the group's reputation, since their performances could be very spotty. In the studio, however, they were able to create some truly fascinating recordings, from the traditional drinking tune "Mother's Lament" to the outrageous acid song, "SWALBR." Since the group's breakup, in late 1968, none of the participants has been involved in musical ventures of this importance, although Clapton has certainly maintained his commercial viability.

RECOMMENDED: *Fresh Cream, Disraeli Gears, Wheels of Fire* (Atco, reissued by RSO).

CREEDENCE CLEARWATER REVIVAL

Their name wasn't catchy; they weren't much to look at; and their musical abilities were hardly of the first caliber. But John and Tom Fogerty, Stu Cook and Doug Clifford had a special sound that made them one of the hottest rock 'n' roll groups. Formed in California in the early 60s, they recorded a few singles as the Golliwogs before changing their name and fortunes. Their first LP, released in 1968, was a solid seller and went gold, but it was a single from their second release that made them superstars. "Proud Mary" was only the first of more than a dozen smashes over the next three years. With a style that combined R&B with Cajun and other southern forms, Creedence managed to please not only an AM hit singles following but an underground album audience as well. They played places like the Fillmore as easily as the stadiums that could hold their legions of fans. Their records showed a consistent desire to grow and develop, although the group never veered from its devotion to the simple formula of their sound, Creedence records had fewer studio tricks and less overdubbing than most groups'. And they never made a bad album. Since the group's demise, the result of John Fogerty's decision to go solo in 1972 (two years after his brother departed for the same reason), there have been some solo projects, and many reissued collections of the hits which still sound as good as when they first appeared.

RECOMMENDED: *Creedence Gold, More Creedence Gold* (Fantasy).

JIM CROCE

A midwestern singer/songwriter with folk leanings, Croce didn't achieve his greatest popularity until he died in a plane wreck in 1974. Although he wrote a couple of catchy songs ("Bad, Bad Leroy Brown," "You Don't Mess around with Jim"), he was overly derivative, sentimental and florid. A quiet and unassuming loner, he was often touted as a "poet of the everyday man."

RECOMMENDED: *Photographs and Memories—His Greatest Hits* (ABC).

STEVE CROPPER

This great Southern guitarist provided all those concise, bracing licks on Booker T and the MG's records, as well as on the efforts of nearly everyone else who ever used the Stax studios during the 60s soul explosion. He also had a hand in writing some of the standards of that era (Wilson Pickett's "In the Midnight Hour," Otis Redding's "Can't Turn You Loose," "Fa-Fa-Fa-Fa-Fa," and many more). But his own solo efforts were strangely cold and unimaginative. Most recently he's been playing behind the Blues Brothers, who at their best couldn't have shined his shoes.

RECOMMENDED: *With a Little Help from My Friends* (Volt).

DAVID CROSBY

An original Byrd, Crosby peaked during his tenure with Crosby, Stills, Nash & Young. He played guitar, sang leads and harmonies, wrote, and battled incessantly with his fellow band members, all of whom had egos as big as his own. His songs ran towards the pretentiously arty, and sounded like they'd been written by an est instructor. His guitar work was lackluster. When he released a solo album it was full of cosmic vacuities and aimless acoustic guitar noodling. His subsequent duet work with Graham Nash was a little brighter, and he's always right there when CSN&Y re-unite, but for the most part, he shows all the symptoms of boredom.

RECOMMENDED: with Nash—*Wind on the Water* (ABC).

CROSBY, STILLS, NASH & YOUNG

First it was just Crosby, Stills & Nash, three refugees from previously-popular groups; they were supposed to be the first American supergroup, back when terms like that were thrown around (1969), though their debut album sounds today more like "adult bubblegum" full of artificial sensitivity. Even their fabled harmonies grate. The addition of Neil Young for their first tour added some much-needed guts to the group, though on subsequent albums even he was muted. Live, they pioneered the idea of doing acoustic and electric sets; they were wildly erratic onstage, and their narcissism and forced brotherhood quickly became unbearable, but they were a very popular group. Of course the group dissolved quickly amidst great tension. When they reformed in the mid-70s (all but Young had fairly disastrous solo careers), they insisted it was for art, not profits, but they had nothing new to say, and they simply toured the huge halls playing old hits, took their money home at the end, and resumed doing pretty much nothing.

RECOMMENDED: *Crosby, Stills & Nash, Deja Vu* (Atlantic).

CRUSADERS

One of the hottest local Houston R&B jazz bands in the 50s, the Crusaders got their start playing with blues star Johnny Copeland. By the time keyboardist Joe Sample, bassist Wilton Felder, trombonist Wayne Henderson and drummer Stix Hooper moved to Los Angeles under the name Jazz Crusaders, they had established themselves as top musicians on their respective instruments and were sought after for session work. After streamlining the group's name to the Crusaders and heading in a hard funk direction, the band started to gain a national following. "Put It Where You Want It," an easy driving R&B instrumental, became their trademark hit. The introduction of session guitarist Larry Carlton to the Crusaders lineup provided another shot in the arm, and the band continued to make hit albums while branching out into the production field.

RECOMMENDED: *The Best of the Crusaders* (MCA).

BURTON CUMMINGS

Canadian born Cummings came to prominence in the mid 60s with the Canadian pop/rock band the Guess Who. This fiesty outfit from central Canada started out playing cover versions of other people's songs until they scored with the hit "These Eyes" in 1968. Cummings was the front man/lead singer for the band and co-writer with guitarist Randy Bachman. The band went on to become one of the biggest groups of the late 60s and early 70s with a string of hits that included "No Time," "Laughing," "Undun," "American Woman" and "Share the Land." Cummings kept the Guess Who together after Bachman left in the early 70s but by the mid-70s broke the band up to pursue a solo career.

RECOMMENDED: *Burton Cummings* (Portrait).

KING CURTIS

The best of the early rock saxophonists, Curtis appeared on virtually every rock 'n' roll hit record that required a saxophone break in the mid '50s. His honking, gutteral blues style created the tradition of rock 'n' roll saxophone soloing. Curtis appeared on the full range of Atlantic records vocal groups of the 50s and continued to record with all of that label's R&B stars of the 60s. Curtis went on to front his own group, making several excellent records, before being murdered in a Harlem street scuffle in the mid-70s.

RECOMMENDED: *Live At Fillmore West, King Curtis and Champion Jack Dupree* (Atlantic).

CHARLIE DANIELS BAND

A native of North Carolina, Daniels worked the southern bar circuit with various groups before settling down in the mid-60s as a Nashville sessions guitarist and fiddle player. He recorded behind Bob Dylan, Ringo Starr, Leonard Cohen, and numerous country stars. In 1971, he formed his own group, which plays a thundering (and frequently monotonous) brand of jazz-inflected southern boogie. Though he's never been much for hit singles (the 1973 novelty song "Uneasy Rider" being the primary exception), his constant touring has brought him a large and loyal audience.

RECOMMENDED: *Million Mile Reflections* (Epic).

BOBBY DARIN

The New York born singer was one of the better crooners of the kind that came out in the late 50s. He recorded for Atlantic records, which had the best lineup of rock and R&B performers at the time, and he was well directed, with good arrangements on many of his songs. His best moment was the party song "Splish Splash," which was about as good as this version of rock 'n' roll ever got. Darin also had a big hit in 1958 with "Queen of the Hop" before switching to the lounge circuit.

RECOMMENDED: *Bobby Darin's Greatest Hits* (Atlantic).

MILES DAVIS

One of America's greatest and most uncompromising jazzmen, trumpeter Miles Davis deserves inclusion in any rock book because of his wide-sweeping influence on the fusion of jazz and rock. Davis, having established a critical and commercial reputation with classic works like *Birth of the Cool, Kind of Blue,* and the orchestral *Sketches of Spain* started experimenting with rhythmic freedom in the mid-50s through 60s (*In a Silent Way*), culminating in a radical recording departure called *Bitches Brew* which featured players like Chick Corea, Lenny White (soon to drum for Return to

Forever), Wayne Shorter (Weather Report-to-be), guitarist John McLaughlin, and even rock bassist Harvey Brooks (once with Mike Bloomfield's Electric Flag). Davis followed up *Bitches Brew*, wildly acclaimed by rock critics and summarily dismissed by jazz purists, with similar works, heavy on the rhythmic accent and short on melodic content. Davis' output in the mid-to-late 70s has been sporadic.

RECOMMENDED: *In a Silent Way, Bitches Brew* (Columbia).

SPENCER DAVIS

This shrewd bandleader from the North of England was looking for recruits in the early 60s when he discovered a local group composed of keyboardist/vocalist Stevie Winwood, his brother Muff Winwood on bass and Peter York on drums. Davis hired them for the Spencer Davis group and soon Winwood's hard-edged R&B organ playing and bluesy, Ray Charles inspired singing were the key to the Spencer Davis sound. When Winwood left after the blockbuster singles "Keep On Running," "Somebody Help Me," "Gimme Some Lovin'" and "I'm a Man," Davis reformed the group with less success, eventually evolved into a more acoustic approach and disappeared in the early 70s.

RECOMMENDED: *Spencer Davis' Greatest Hits* (United Artists).

DEEP PURPLE

One of the first of the heavy metal bands, Deep Purple got its start in the mid-60s with a hit single called "Hush." Lead vocalist Ian Gillan, keyboardist Jon Lord, guitarist Ritchie Blackmore, bassist Roger Glover and drummer Ian Paice blasted out a high intensity drone that placed them in the forefront of 70s rock performance. Gillian became a huge star after his participation in *Jesus Christ Superstar,* Lord put together a number of special symphonic projects and Blackmore became known as one of the hottest lead guitarists on the circuit, but the resultant clash of egos created numerous problems for the band. Gillan finally left and was replaced by vocalist David Coverdale, but the band broke up soon after.

RECOMMENDED: *Shades of Deep Purple,* (Tetragramaton).

DELANEY AND BONNIE (BRAMLETT)

After sessioning in Los Angeles with Leon Russell at the helm, this southern husband-wife singing duo went to England where their down-home spirit and gospel roots appealed to the growing cartel of crack players looking for a medium. They put together a band for a British tour with Eric Clapton and Dave Mason on guitars, Carl Radle on bass, Jim Gordon on drums, Bobby Whitlock on keyboards, Jim Price on trumpet, and Bobby Keys on saxophone. Clapton, Gordon, Whitlock and Radle went on to form Derek and the Dominoes. Delaney and Bonnie made several other excellent records before their marriage split and they went separate ways.

RECOMMENDED: *On Tour, Motel Shot* (Atco).

SANDY DENNY

She never quite regained the touch she had with Fairport Convention, but Sandy Denny remained a compelling vocalist after she struck out on her own in 1970, first with a group called Fotheringay and then as a solo act. Her high, eerie voice remained strong, and while she failed to write a song as widely recognized as "Who Knows Where the Time Goes" (with Fairport Convention), she did have commercial success in England at least. In America, she was a cult artist just like Fairport had been. She died falling down a staircase in 1978.

RECOMMENDED: *Fotheringay* (A&M).

JOHN DENVER

This Texan who started out in the Chad Mitchell Trio writes cliched melodies, simplistic lyrics celebrating himself, his wife and the great outdoors, and sings in an Irish tenor that lacks depth. But he is still very popular and successful with a certain audience.

RECOMMENDED: *Poems, Prayers and Promises, Greatest Hits* (RCA).

RICK DERRINGER

Rick Derringer (b. Zehringer, 1947, Union City, Illinois) was only 18 when his group the McCoys (including brother Randy) was rescued from the Dayton, Ohio club circuit by producer Bert Berns, who gave them an R&B tune he'd written called "Hang on Sloopy." Stardom came too early for the McCoys, who grew up, tried to change with the psychedelic times, and failed commercially if not artistically on two subsequent Mercury albums. But after albino blues guitarist Johnny Winter again rescued the McCoys from the New York City bar scene and hired them as a back-up band, Derringer was back in the driver's seat, writing smash rock 'n' roll tunes like "Rock & Roll Hoochie Coo" and producing hits by Winter's brother, Edgar, like "Frankenstein" and "Free Ride." He formed his own band, Derringer, in 1976 after two solo LPs, and is frequently found on albums by pals like Alice Cooper and Todd Rundgren, who produced Derringer's latest.

RECOMMENDED: *All American Boy* (Blue Sky).

DEVO

The theory that motivates Devo is called "de-evolution," and it holds that five young men from Akron, Ohio should don futuristic industrial garb and attempt to stem the flow of backwards progress by playing ultra-precise and highly calculated rock music for the masses. The men behind the theory are two pairs of brothers, Jerry and Bob Casale (bass and guitar) and Mark and Bob Mothersbaugh (keyboards/guitars and guitar), plus drummer Alan Myers. Formed at Kent State University earlier this decade, the mysterious marauders managed to wangle a lucrative record contract in 1978 and have released two albums to date. Both feature the synthesizer-oriented rhythmic control that gives the group its instant recognition factor. The group's mascot, Booji (pronounced "boogie") Boy (in actuality Mark Mothersbaugh in a weird mask and costume) often appears on stage with Devo, and is also featured in several of their video shorts. Devo plays music for the 80s, with a definite nod towards the past. Their overhaul versions of "Satisfaction" and "Secret Agent Man" show the group's background, as well as their future.

RECOMMENDED: *Q. Are We Not Men? A. We Are Devo!* (Warner Bros.).

NEIL DIAMOND

A native New Yorker, he started out as a songwriter and then became a performer. He was a good one, too, as mid-60s singles "Solitary Man," "Cherry Cherry" and "Cracklin' Rosie" attest. But after going to UNI (now MCA) in 1967, he became increasingly grandiose, moving from his Brill Building roots to heavily orchestrated sensitivity and schlock rock in "She Walks on Water" and "I Am I Said." The more pompous his music, the more popular he became, both on record and live. In his five years at MCA he produced eight straight gold albums. In 1972, he switched to Columbia and retired from the stage for four years, which was a relief, as he had become a bad Elvis parody. Still, his popularity remains high, especially since he began performing again in 1977. The layoff had a salutory effect, too, as his music is now much less bloated. Even though he appeared with the rock elite at the Band's farewell concert, his heart is still primarily in Vegas.

RECOMMENDED: *Hot August Night, His 12 Greatest Hits* (MCA).

DICTATORS

A great idea that never achieved its potential or any commercial success, the Dictators were a bunch of Bronx, New York high school chums working under the tutelage of Sandy Pearlman, Murray Krugman, and Richard Meltzer, the behind-the-scenes creators of the Blue Oyster Cult. Despite loads of musical talent, strong songwriting, and a lot of contacts in the record industry, none of the Dictators' three LPs sold very well, and they eventually disbanded after a series of tumultuous personnel changes, in 1978. Ahead of their time, the Dictators' first album was a forerunner of new wave: tough, tight, youth-oriented, and snotty, yet only a few rock fans appreciated their special brand of humor and wit. Their second release was more heavy metal than new wave, and ironically made the Dictators seem uncool just as punk was coming in. A perfect case of zigging when they should have zagged, the Dictators left a recording legacy of pop metal that stands the test of time. Original lineup: Andy Shernoff (vocals, bass, keyboards), Top Ten Kempner (guitar), handsome Dick Manitoba (vocals), Ross the Boss Funicello (guitar), Stu Boy King (drums).

RECOMMENDED: *Dictators Go Girl Crazy* (Epic); *Manifest Destiny* (Asylum).

BO DIDDLEY

1955 was the year when rock 'n' roll made its big impact on America when Chess records released the first singles by Chuck Berry and Bo Diddley. The difference is that Diddley's record wasn't even so much of a song as a chant: pure rock 'n' roll, a jumping, infectious dance beat with African origins taken from a 40s popular tune called "Hambone." Even better, the song was called "Bo Diddley," making the point that the rhythm was the thing. Ever since then Diddley has made record after record and toured constantly playing that same beat over and over. Not only does it not tire with him, but hundreds of other groups have picked up on it and done their own versions.

RECOMMENDED: *Bo Diddley's 16 All Time Greatest Hits* (Chess).

AL DiMEOLA

A whiz-kid jazz guitarist, DiMeola broke into jazz-rock fusion as Bill Conners's replacement in the Return to Forever band, in which he remained until its demise. Berklee College of Music-trained, he had done stints with Larry Coryell and Barry Miles while still in school. His RTF experience brought him to the attention of Dee Anthony, the supermanager who engineered Peter Frampton and Joe Cocker's success. Anthony promoted DiMeola so well that his solo albums far outsell most good jazz records, and the guitarist has even made a cameo appearance in the pop film *Sgt. Pepper's Lonely Hearts Club Band*.

RECOMMENDED: *Elegant Gypsy* (Columbia).

DION AND THE BELMONTS

One of the most successful of the late 50s vocal groups, Dion and the Belmonts were Dion MiMucci, Angelo D'Aleo, Fred Milano and Carlo Mastrangelo. They were the original greasers and scored big with the hits "Teenager In Love," "Runaround Sue," "Lovers Who Wander" and "Lonely Teenager." Dion was the kind of show biz crooner that the music industry was trying to set up in this payola riddled era as an alternative to the more authentic forms of rock. The Beatles made this stuff obsolete, but Dion himself made a comeback in 1968 with the folk political lament "Abraham, Martin and John."

RECOMMENDED: *Greatest Hits* (Roulette).

DIRE STRAITS

The dark horse of 1979, Dire Straits, an English foursome peddling a bluesy, poetic blend of country-fried rock and American myth, was obscured by the dark clouds of British punk for most of 1978 despite a stunning debut album. Guitarist Mark Knopfler's ode to London's spiritual cousins of New Orleans' Basin Street swingers, "Sultans of Swing," made Dire Straits a multiplatinum act not just in America, but in most of the Western World and finally in England. The band: Knopfler (a former journalist and English teacher from Newcastle), younger brother Dave Knopfler (rhythm guitar), John Illsley (bass), and Pick Withers (drummer and one-time house player at Dave Edmunds' Rockfield Studio in Wales), first came to the public's attention in 1977 when the band sent a rough demo of Mark Knopfler tunes (including "Sultans") to BBC disc jockey Charlie Gillett, who promptly aired the tape and stirred record company interest. Knopfler is considered the band's greatest strength for his evocative tunes, six-string wizardry which recalls James Burton, Scotty Moore, Roy Buchanan and other Fender Strat Champs, and low vocal growl. Dylan recruited Knopfler and Withers to play on his new album *Slow Train Coming*.

RECOMMENDED: *Dire Straits, Communique* (Warner Bros.).

WILLIE DIXON

He wrote (or took credit for writing) any number of enduring Chicago blues standards, but produced them as well. He also played bass on a lot of Chess Records sessions. He was a sort of all-around troubleshooter and handyman for the label, the black liaison to black artists for the white men who ran the label. Yet for a supposed catalyst, his own albums, (he records rarely), have been remarkably stiff, and when he tours with the Chicago Blues All-Stars, he usually comes off as the weakest link in the group.

RECOMMENDED: *Blues Every Which Way with Memphis Slim* (Verve).

DR. FEELGOOD

A seminal forerunner of the British new wave, Dr. Feelgood burst on the London club/pub scene in late 1974, playing a stripped-down brand of R&B/rock 'n' roll that set them apart from the other bands in vogue at the time. Coming from a slummy suburb of London, Canvey Island, the foursome: Wilko Johnson (guitar), Lee Brilleaux (vocals, harmonica), John Sparks (bass), and Figure Martin (drums) blended super-tight arrangements and playing with spivey clothes that recalled the early Rolling Stones. Within the year, they were signed, and went on to become a huge success in Britain and Europe, where the tradition of America R&B and blues has never died. In their wake, younger and even more energetic bands arose, following the Feelgoods into the clubs where their career began. In early 1977, Wilko Johnson left the group to form a band called Solid Senders, and was replaced by John Mayo.

RECOMMENDED: *Sneakin' Suspicion* (Columbia).

DR. HOOK

This zany group fronted by comic-singer Dennis Locorriere and Ray Sawyer got its start in 1970 singing "Last Morning," a song from the film *Who Is Harry Kellerman and Why Is He Saying All Those Terrible Things about Me?* At the time, Dr. Hook played country rock with a seven-piece band including guitarists George Cummings and Rik Elswit, drummer Jay David, keyboardist Bill Francis, and bassist Jance Garfat. Their first few records were primarily covers of country humorist Shel Silverstein's songs, two of which, "Sylvia's Mother" and "The Cover of Rolling Stone," became substantial hits. Over the next few years, Dr. Hook's fortunes took a turn for the worse, for the band was forced to declare bankruptcy in 1974 yet decided to stay together and start from scratch. Bob "Willard" Henke replaced Cummings and John Wolters replaced Jay David as the band began to vary its musical style doing more pop, R&B and disco and concentrating on making hit singles.

RECOMMENDED: *A Little Bit More* (Capitol).

DOCTOR JOHN

New Orleans born Mac Rebenneck was a stalwart on the Louisiana session scene in the 50s, playing guitar and keyboards on countless records and learning from piano star Professor Longhair. In the 60s Rebenneck had an idea to produce a series of albums built around a mythical figure called Doctor John, and when he couldn't find a suitable front man for the idea decided to do it himself. He toured behind the painted face, gris-gris throwing witch doctor image for several years until a song called "In the Right Place," straight out of the Professor Longhair barrelhouse piano tradition, became a huge hit. In the late 70s Doctor John albums have been more straightforward pop affairs, even spilling over into disco.

RECOMMENDED: *In the Right Place* (Atco).

FATS DOMINO

Antoine "Fats" Domino was well known for his corpulent frame, easy grin and flat-top process as for his driving, New Orleans inspired piano playing and gruff, expressive voice. Domino became the strongest force in 50s rock probably because he was exciting enough to provide the audiences what they wanted while seeming innocuous enough to the political forces trying to stop rock 'n' roll's wilder side. It didn't matter, because Domino inspired his share of rock riots in theaters across the states and broke most of the attendance records at the time. The songs still sound good; "Fat Man," "Ain't That A Shame," "Blue Monday," "Blueberry Hill," "Let the Four Winds Blow." After disappearing for awhile Domino tried a comeback in the late 60s, covering the Beatles' "Lady Madonna," before once again returning to the revival shows.

RECOMMENDED: *The Legendary Master Fats Domino* (United Artists).

DONOVAN

In his first incarnation, he was the British answer to Bob Dylan, with "Catch the Wind" launching his career in 1965. That evolved into the druggy paranoia of *Sunshine Superman* (1966), and though he had not peaked commercially, his best years artistically were over. By 1968, he was singing children's songs; the soft innocence that had once served him so well had become muddled by drugs, the Maharishi, and who knows what else. He went on an antidrug crusade by which time his credibility with his audience was gone. He has persevered, resurfacing in a new guise (sometimes even as a full-out rocker) every so often, but he is a relic and he can't escape it.

RECOMMENDED: *Catch the Wind, Sunshine Superman* (Hickory).

DOOBIE BROTHERS

One of the most consistent hitmaking groups of the 70s, the Doobies began as a San José, California bar band in 1969 and had their first album out by 1971. It took a little longer to stake out a more distinct identity, but when they did, they sounded like a classic California rock band; washes of electric and acoustic guitars, vocal harmonies, smooth melodies. But not so much folk or country as to soften the overall impact. Personnel came and went over the decade as they evolved into a harder rock band, then took on R&B edges and finally a jazz-tinged direction. They are hard working live performers, and though their albums are usually instant gold, they are best heard on their long string of hit singles. Among the key alumni are Tom Johnston (who was replaced by Michael McDonald, the current pianist and a fine singer) and Jeff "Skunk" Baxter (who the Doobies had wooed away from Steely Dan).

RECOMMENDED: *What Were Once Vices Are Now Habits, Takin' It to the Streets, Minute by Minute* (Warner Bros.).

THE DOORS

Photo by Joel Brodsky

Jim Morrison's poetic talents are still debated more than eight years after his July 3, 1971 death of a heart attack. But no one disputes the effect the Doors, with Morrison playing psycho-sexual-conscience—had on its audience and on rock. Their music, an imagistic, psychedelic blend of blues roots, Robby Krieger's modal guitar runs and jazz-based impressions, John Densmore's jackhammer drumming, and Ray Manzarek's kaleidoscopic organ runs, was the perfect soundtrack for James Douglas Morrison's subliminal script, a fusion of rock 'n' roll aggression and dark, emotive poetry that somehow became lyrics to the Doors' songs. Morrison was a film student at UCLA when, in 1965, he met Manzarek. Reportedly, Morrison read him the lyrics to "Moonlight Drive" and Manzarek, a veteran of Chicago R&B bands, decided a group was in order. He enrolled Krieger and Densmore and they became the Doors, after William Blake's "The Doors of Perception." After the usual club rounds and one unsuccessful single ("Break on Through"), the Doors captured the imagination of the burgeoning underground in 1967 with *The Doors* and its signature single, "Light My Fire." Considered to be the Doors' finest hour, this album crystallized the group's sound and Morrison's erotic fury, particularly in the Oedipal drama "The End." *Strange Days*, released a year later, couldn't match its predecessor. The Doors tried hard to recapture their own fire but commerciality got the best of them on *Waiting for the Sun* and the flaccid *The Soft Parade*. Nevertheless both had their moments, which is more than can be said for *Absolutely Live,* an accurate reflection of the point the Doors had reached on stage and in the studio, by 1970. The group's underground reputation was back on the rise as a result of several police busts of Morrison, in 1967 in New Haven for obscene language and starting a riot and in 1969 at a Miami concert for indecent exposure. The 1970 album *Morrison Hotel* was a crude but hopeful document of the Doors' determination to get back into form, and by 1971, on *L.A. Woman,* they'd found new life. Morrison's bleak poetic vision found the perfect foil in the desperate blues played by the band on "The Wasp" and on the eerie "Riders of the Storm." But just as the Doors were riding their highest, Morrison decided to take a lengthy vacation with wife Pamela, a vacation that ended in his bathtub death from a heart attack. The rest of the Doors carried on for two more albums, in vain. Manzarek reportedly tried to groom the maniacal Iggy Pop for Morrison's place, but by 1974 he was recording solo and the others were pursuing their own projects. Jim Morrison and what he stood for in American rock has not been forgotten, least of all by the other three Doors. Over the last three years, Manzarek, Kreiger, and Densmore had been working on a compilation of Morrison's poetry recordings with snippets of Doors records and new music. The result, released in 1979, is *An American Prayer,* a clear look into the psychological impulses behind Jim Morrison the poet, lyricist, teen sex symbol, rock singer, and Lizard King.

RECOMMENDED: *The Doors, Absolutely Live, Morrison Hotel/Hard Rock Cafe, L.A. Woman* (Elektra).

NICK DRAKE

Nick Drake died at a tragically early age, 26, of a drug overdose, but he left a recorded legacy that leaves one wishing there was more. Born in 1948 in Burma, where his parents were stationed (his father was in the English foreign service), Drake came to England at age six and entered college in 1967, studying English literature. But music proved an irresistible sidetrack and, after being discovered performing by Ashley Hutchings (Fairport Convention, Steeleye Span), Drake started putting his songs on record. His three albums, *Five Leaves Left, Bryter Layer* (distilled into U.S. issue *Nick Drake*), and *Pink Moon,* are stunning in their instrumental subtlety, Drake's soft breathy singing, and his evocative but increasingly stark lyrical vision. At times, he eclipsed Van Morrison's considerable accomplishments on *Astral Weeks,* but after *Pink Moon* (an often harrowing album), Drake dropped out of music and sought psychiatric help. He started to record again just before his death on October 25, 1974.

RECOMMENDED: *Five Leaves Left, Bryter Layer* (U.S. Antilles).

DRIFTERS

The Drifters were put together in 1953 by Clyde McPhatter, who promptly led them to a big hit with "Money Honey," before leaving in 1954. They didn't do well without him and disbanded in '58 only to be reformed in '59 as a medium for the crack Leiber-Stoller songwriting team. With those writers the Drifters began their well known string of hits, "There Goes My Baby" and "Dance With Me." These featured lead singer Ben E. King. Doc Pomus and Mort Shuman wrote their next hits "Save the Last Dance For Me" and "This Magic Moment." After King left the group recruited lead singer Rudy Lewis for the hits "Up On the Roof," "On Broadway" and "Under the Boardwalk."

RECOMMENDED: *Drifters Greatest Hits, Drifters Golden Hits* (Atlantic).

DUCKS DELUXE

One of the first and best of the notorious British pub rock bands of the early 70s that paved the way for the punk rock and new wave groups that followed. Formed in early 1972 by guitarists Sean Tyla and Martin Belmont, bassist Nick Garvey, and drummer Tim Roper, the Ducks first recorded on Man's classic limited release record *Christmas At the Patti.* A year later they made their first album, then added organist Andy McMasters for a second album. Their two British releases were compiled into one U.S. record.

RECOMMENDED: *Don't Mind Rockin' Tonight* (RCA).

IAN DURY

A childhood victim of polio, an artist and university instructor, Ian Dury is as unlikely a new wave rocker as anybody imaginable. Fifteen years older than the other proponents of the genre, Dury has been at it since 1973, when he formed a pub rock band called Kilburn and the High Roads. Interesting but noncommercial, the Kilburns lasted three years and recorded one album before calling it quits. In 1977, Dury resurfaced as the leader of Ian Dury and the Blockheads, who were signed to Stiff just as the label was finding success with Elvis Costello. His first album became a huge seller in England; the result, probably, of new interest in the odd and the eccentric, two categories Dury fits perfectly. His European success attracted American attention, and the album was eventually released in the U.S., getting more attention from the press than from the record buying public. A second album, released in 1979, fared somewhat better, but Dury's Cockney accent and extreme English manner may be too obscure for most Americans' taste.

RECOMMENDED: *New Boots and Panties* (Stiff-Arista).

BOB DYLAN

Dylan (b. Robert Allen Zimmerman, May 24, 1941, Duluth, Minnesota) is as much mystique as music and the real fun begins when you try to separate the two. He first adopted the Dylan surname while at University of Minnesota, probably in homage to poet Dylan Thomas. He visited ailing Woody Guthrie in a New Jersey hospital when he first came to New York and made sure his singing/songwriting peers in the Village knew it. And he never made any secret of his desire to make it, making one of his first recorded appearances playing harmonica on a Harry Belafonte recording. Yet one more listen to "Like a Rolling Stone," an evening with *Blonde on Blonde,* a return to *Blood on the Tracks,* or another screening of D. A. Pennebaker's Dylan documentary *Don't Look Back* all reaffirm, as if his continued recorded product isn't enough, his preeminance as a rock 'n' roll voice, rivalled in its sharp tongue and eloquence only by the Beatles. The Dylan story is a matter of public record; his '65 appearance at Newport with electric backing, the '67 retirement after the alleged motorcycle accident, his C&W reincarnation in *Nashville Skyline,* the domestic strife chronicled on *Blood on the Tracks,* the '74 "comeback" tour with the Band, the riotous Rolling Thunder guerilla tour of '75. One place to start is Anthony Scaduto's biography *Bob Dylan,* and there are countless magazine articles and critical opinions. The fact that he can be interesting when he fails, e.g. his four-hour feature movie flop *Renaldo and Clara,* the indulgent *Self Portrait* album, is enough to keep us all coming back for more.

RECOMMENDED: *The Times They Are A'Changin'*, *Highway 61 Revisited*, *Blonde on Blonde*, *John Wesley Harding*, *Blood on the Tracks*, *Desire*, *Street Legal*, *Slow Train Coming* (Columbia); plus bootlegs, compilations, foreign pressings, early appearances on record, cover versions of Dylan tunes.

EAGLES

Photo by Lorrie Sullivan

The undisputed titans of L.A. country/rock, the Eagles hit it big with the release of their first album and single in 1971. But it was with 1974's *On the Border* that they exploded, and they've been instant platinum ever since. Their albums tend to be conceptual, and often quite pretentious. They've also taken a lot of flack for so fully embodying the laid back L.A. style, both in their music and in their lives. Much of the criticism is justified, but the release of *Hotel California* in 1977 showed a tougher, more self-aware Eagles; they won conciliatory praise from even some of their most severe critics. Though much of the songwriting in this group is transparently calculated, several of their singles ("Take It to the Limit," "Best of My Love," "Lyin' Eyes," "Life in the Fast Lane") are already standards. There have been personnel changes along the way, but the core of the group, Glenn Frey and Don Henley, has been there from the beginning.

RECOMMENDED: *One of These Nights*, *Greatest Hits, 1971-75*, *Hotel California* (Asylum).

EARTH, WIND & FIRE

This nine-piece R&B crossover group is the brainchild of Maurice White, who once drummed for Ramsey Lewis and in the Chess Records house band. Formed in 1972, EW&F grew steadily until 1975, when the personnel finally stabilized and *That's the Way of the World,* a film soundtrack, was released; it hasn't stopped selling, and the title song became their first gold single. By the end of the decade, they had four double platinum albums and another that was merely platinum, along with four gold singles and a Grammy. White is spiritually inclined, so that group's songs push brotherhood and cosmic awareness. As good as they can be, they also have an alarming tendency to sound like a black Chicago. Their no-expenses-spared stage show is one of the most spectacular around.

RECOMMENDED: *That's the Way of the World*, *Spirit* (Columbia).

EASYBEATS

The Easybeats should have been one of the world's biggest bands, but history has only given them one international smash, "Friday on My Mind," and a reputation not only as Australia's best pop group ever but as one of the most underrated pop groups anywhere. In Oz, the Easybeats, Harry Vanda, George Young, Steve Wright, Snowy Fleet and Dick Diamond, could do no wrong in 1965 and 1966, scoring eight consecutive Top Five records. When they emigrated to England to expand their winnings, they scored a preliminary round with "Friday," but lost to an unbeatable combination of management problems, wrangles with producers, and general bad pop star luck. But on what records were released in America, they left behind a legacy of talent, tongue-in-cheek humor, and songwriting ingenuity of which "Friday on My Mind" is the best known example. Vanda and Young continue to dominate Australian pop as songwriters and producers, particularly for the jock-rock band AC/DC which features Young brothers Angus and Malcolm on guitars. The dynamic duo have also recently surfaced on record as Flash and the Pan.

RECOMMENDED: *Friday on My Mind* (United Artists).

DUANE EDDY

One of the most celebrated rock guitarists in the early days, Eddy was built up mainly due to the fact that other guitarists admired his technique. But his music was always poorly packaged and often pretty bad, in spite of his tone. His record company kept putting the word "twang" in every one of his album titles, but Eddy ended up doing soundtrack music to films like *Gidget Goes Hawaiian*.

RECOMMENDED: *Have Twangy Guitar, Will Travel* (Pickwick).

DAVE EDMUNDS

A native of Wales, Edmunds' first taste of fame came with Love Sculpture in 1968. The group was short-lived, and he quickly retreated from the scene to become a producer. In 1970, he had a fluke international hit with "I Hear You Knocking," and followed that with a solo LP on which he played all the instruments. But it was as a producer that he earned his underground rep: Edmunds applied a folkie's sensibility to rock 'n' roll, and could recreate almost perfectly any genre of pop. He worked primarily with various British pub-rock bands during the mid-70s. But by the end of the decade, he was playing guitar and co-fronting (along with Nick Lowe) a very traditional-sounding band called Rockpile, which toured sometimes in support of a new Edmunds album and sometimes in support of Lowe's latest.

RECOMMENDED: *Rockpile* (MAM-London).

WALTER EGAN

A clever songwriter and an able singer-guitarist, Walter Egan became a pop fanatic while growing up in Forest Hills, New York through exposure to Elvis, Buddy Holly, the Kingston Trio and *American Bandstand*. In his teens, he fell victim to Beatlemania, got a Sears guitar, and joined his first band, the Malibooz. When Egan succumbed to psychedelia in the late 60s, the Malibooz became Sageworth, a group well known in New England but unknown elsewhere till it turned to a country-rock style. Egan found he could write in that idiom, and Gram Parsons and Emmylou Harris incorporated his material into their act. The connection with Harris led Egan to

California, backup work and a stint with Wheels. Singled out and signed as a soloist to Columbia, Egan soon met the stylistically-similar Fleetwood Mac, with whose members he has worked on all three of his solo albums. Egan's hook-filled musical explorations of the "teen wasteland" have won him chart hits with "Magnet and Steel" and "Tunnel of Love." In 1978 Egan formed The Professional Band and toured with Heart and Foreigner. Egan's most rocking, tradition-conscious material has come from his association with The Professional Band, notably the album *HiFi* (1979).

RECOMMENDED: *HiFi* (Columbia).

ELECTRIC FLAG

The Electric Flag, guitarist Mike Bloomfield's American music dream, survived for eighteen months. But in those eighteen months, the pioneer horn-rock band set a standard for assimilating punch-drunk blues, no-nonsense rock, and emotive R&B into a singular music that, at the time of the Flag's formation in 1967, was unlike anything heard before. Talent had a lot to do with it. Bloomfield, a prodigious blues guitarist who'd played on Paul Butterfield's first two albums, assembled around him drummer Buddy Miles, vocalist Nick "The Greek" Gravenites (later to write tunes for Janis Joplin), organist Barry Goldberg (like Bloomfield and Gravenites, a veteran of the Chicago blues scene), and a front line of horns that was the rival of any session crew, in sheer blowing power. But the weight of egos took its toll. After recording a soundtrack for the Roger Corman film *The Trip,* debuting at the Monterey Pop Festival, and releasing two albums the first of which is everything Blood, Sweat & Tears promised to be, the Electric Flag fell apart. Bloomfield tried again in 1974 with a core crew of Miles, Goldberg, Gravenites, and session bassist Roger Troy (replacing Harvey Brooks), but the magic was gone.

RECOMMENDED: *A Long Time Comin'* (Columbia).

ELECTRIC LIGHT ORCHESTRA

Jeff Lynne, Bev Bevan, and Roy Wood kept recording singles as the Move in the early 70s to finance their dream of forming an orchestral rock ensemble they would call the Electric Light Orchestra. A reality in 1971 with the release of *No Answer,* ELO was originally too close to that dream to make a commercial break. When Wood departed for rock 'n' rollier pastures with Wizzard, Lynne (who was a member of the Idle Race before joining the Move in 1970) and Bevan got down to the serious business of making records, and ELO is now one of the most popular bands on the planet. Both natives of the midland English industrial city of Birmingham, Lynne and Bevan run the ELO show with a group that now includes Kelly Groucutt (bass), Richard Tandy (keyboards), Mik Kaminski (violin) and Hugh McDowell and Melvyn Gale (cellos). The real ELO secret is Lynne's hit melodies, "Showdown," "Evil Woman," the revived Move hit "Do Ya," and a host of other top 10 entries.

RECOMMENDED: *ELO II* (United Artists); *A New World Record* (Jet).

EMERSON LAKE & PALMER

Emerson Lake & Palmer hit the art/rock scene in 1970 with a technically impeccable, conceptually fascinating display of classically-honed chops, lyrical pretension, and amplified bravado. And that was the band's bread-and-butter for the nine years they led British techno-rock. Keith Emerson was the showman, the same Keith Emerson who beat and raped his Hammond organ in performance with the Nice. Former King Crimsonite Greg Lake played bass and sang about such imperative cosmic subjects as the "Lucky Man" and the metallic monster they called *Tarkus* in a resonating tenor. Carl Palmer, a drummer at 16 with Chris Farlowe and later for Atomic Rooster, kept the beat with a very physical flair. Their ambitions too often got the better of them. In 1977 ELP hit the road after a lengthy absence with a full orchestra, a foolish economic proposition that backfired on them halfway through the trek when they sent the orchestra home. ELP's recorded output has been sporadic since 1974's egomaniacal three-record live set. There have been two *Works* issues, one consisting mostly of solo material, and recent word is that the group has dissolved for lack of interest; theirs, not the fans'.

RECOMMENDED: *Emerson Lake & Palmer* (Cotillion).

BRIAN ENO

This eccentric British electronic music experimentor was born in Woodbridge, Suffolk in 1948 and attended art school before working with avant garde composer LaMonte Young and joining the odd band Portsmouth Sinfonia. In 1971 he helped form Roxy Music, leaving that band to work on numerous solo projects. During that time he has worked with Robert Fripp, John Cale, Kevin Ayers, Nico, Robert Wyatt, Robert Calvert, Phil Manzanera and David Bowie.

RECOMMENDED: *Taking Tiger Mountain By Strategy* (Island).

EVERLY BROTHERS

Don and Phil Everly grew up in Kentucky listening to country and western and mountain music and developed a harmony singing style out of those influences that turned out to be influential on rock 'n' roll vocal groups. The duo's hits summed up the late 50s and pre-Beatles 60s very well; "Bye Bye Love," "Wake Up Little Susie," "Bird Dog," "Cathy's Clown."

RECOMMENDED: *The Very Best of the Everly Brothers* (Columbia).

FACES

The Faces, risen like an amplified phoenix from the ashes of the Small Faces after Steve Marriott's 1968 departure, may have been one of the 70s' biggest rock attractions, but they never fulfilled their early promise. Singer Rod Stewart and guitarist Ron Wood joined the Faces fresh from the frustrations of working in the Jeff Beck Group, and their first LP with the remaining Faces (they dropped Small in acknowledgement of Rod's comparatively greater height), *First Step,* was exactly that. But the drunken exuberance the Faces carried on to the stage too often carried over into the studio as well, resulting in a series of half-baked albums. As Rod Stewart continued to make a greater reputation with his solo activities, Ronnie Lane left, replaced by Mongolian bassist Tetsu Yamauchi (ex-Free). Ron Wood got friendly with the Stones and subbed on their 1974 tour, fueling rumors that he would join the band taking Mick Taylor's place. But Stewart was the one to sound the death knell, quitting in December 1975 to go full-time solo. Drummer Kenney Jones has since taken the late Keith Moon's drum stool in the Who, and pianist Ian McLagan is sessioneering about while working on occasion with the Stones.

RECOMMENDED: *A Nod's as Good as a Wink . . .* (Warner Bros.).

JOHN FAHEY

John Fahey collects turtles and has made a consistent if unextravagant living preserving American blues and developing a unique eclectic style on the acoustic guitar. Fahey is an intensely private figure, who records for his own Takoma label (he has recorded for Vanguard and Reprise in the past) and digs for the roots of American music (he wrote a biography of bluesman Charley Patton). As a guitarist, he blends blues figures, modal tunings, and other ethnic elements in a dazzling display of both technique and feeling.

RECOMMENDED: *Blind Joe Death* (Takoma); *John Fahey, Yellow Princess* (Vanguard).

FAIRPORT CONVENTION

Formed in 1967 as an American-sounding rock band, Fairport soon became *the* British folk-rock band. *Fairport Convention* and *Unhalfbricking* (both 1969) define the genre for all time. Using electric instruments and drawing their power from the dazzling guitar of Richard Thompson and the voice of Sandy Denny, Fairport did traditional British songs and contemporary American folkish songs and they all came out sounding positively medieval, stark, full of dread, more than a little spooky. They proved to be one of Dylan's finest interpreters. Though the group existed in one form or another for a decade, no one unit stayed together as long as two years; the earliest albums are the best.

RECOMMENDED: *Fairport Convention* (A&M).

ANDY FAIRWEATHER-LOW

Much like Scottish Frankie Miller, Andy Fairweather-Low is one of the great underrated English singers. As the vocalist for British 60s R&B band Amen Corner, Fairweather-Low racked up a series of Top Tenners out of such disparate material as the traditional blues "Gin House" the American Breed's punkish pop hit "Bend Me Shape Me," and Roy Wood's bulldozing rocker "Hello Susie." In 1970, when Amen Corner went the way of all pop groups, he went "progressive" with his own band Fairweather which made one unremarkable album and finally resurfaced three years later with a smart solo album *Spider Jiving* which he realized his potential not only as a soulful raver but as an effective songwriter.

RECOMMENDED: *Spider Jiving* (A&M).

ADAM FAITH

Rivalling Cliff Richard as Britain's top teen idol, Faith survived the competition by pursuing parallel careers in acting, producing, and management through the 60s and 70s. His biggest English hits, coming after an early stint in a late 50s skiffle group and a job in a film processing lab, were "What Do You Want?", "Poor Me," and "Lonely Pup," teen weepers in which he appealed to the young ladies for love and understanding. He got sixteen hits' worth in the years 1959-64. Most recently, he's returned to the British public eye and ear with a superb performance in the rock 'n' roll film *Stardust*, and his own recording activities, which include one 1974 American release, *I Survive*.

RECOMMENDED: *The Best of Adam Faith* (English EMI).

MARIANNE FAITHFUL

The daughter of a baroness, Marianne Faithful worked with Andrew Loog Oldham, the Rolling Stones manager, and parleyed her sultry good looks into a recording career when it was decided she could cover the Stones' "As Tears Go By." It was her only hit. She went on to a bit of acting, then became famous on the club circuit as Mick Jagger's girlfriend.

RECOMMENDED: *Marianne Faithful* (London).

FAMILY

Vocalist Roger Chapman, a gravel-throated madman who took out his frustrations on mike stands but could sing with subtlety and understanding when the song called for it, was a pivotal member of the band, along with guitarist Charlie Whitney with whom he formed Streetwalkers after Family finally broke up in 1973. Family was formed in Leicester, England in 1966, at first under the names Roaring Sixties and Farina. As Family (with bassist Rik Grech, Blind Faith-to-be), they recorded their long-playing debut with Traffic's Dave Mason as producer in 1968. Stylistically, they played an arresting combination of musics, folk, blues, rock, jazz, all channeled through an electric repertoire of original songs as interpreted by the manic Chapman, that yielded seven LPs and a handful of English hits. Always under-appreciated in the States, Family were best known here for the exploits of ex-members, particularly Grech in Blind Faith, and bassist John Wetton with King Crimson, Roxy Music, Uriah Heep, and U.K.

RECOMMENDED: *Music in a Doll's House* (Reprise); *Fearless* (United Artists).

RICHARD & MIMI FARINA

The story of these two folksingers is the tragic classic of lost love in the 60s folk scene. Mimi, Joan Baez's sister, met Richard, a firebrand revolutionary/novelist/songwriter, while the two were in Europe. Farina was writing *Been Down So Long It Looks Like Up To Me*. The two married and returned to the U.S., where Richard finished the novel and the two began playing together, recording several albums before Richard died in a motorcycle accident.

RECOMMENDED: *Celebrations for a Grey Day* (Vanguard).

JAY FERGUSON

Ferguson's spirited, funky keyboard playing and excellent blue-eyed soul singing were part of Spirit's great attack in the 60s. Ferguson also wrote two of that band's best songs, "Fresh Garbage" and "Uncle Jack." In the early 70s Ferguson formed Jo Jo Gunne, a hard rock funk band, and wrote one of that group's best songs, "Run, Run, Run." In the mid 70s following the breakup of Jo Jo Gunne, Ferguson embarked on a solo career, continuing his infectiously syncopated keyboard playing. Ferguson's friend Joe Walsh has guested guitar solos on his album.

RECOMMENDED: *All Alone In the End Zone* (Asylum).

BRYAN FERRY

Bryan Ferry, a miner's son from the coal-rich area of Newcastle, is best-known as the lead singer and flamboyant leader of England's Roxy Music, best of the post-Bowie experimental glam-rock bands. Under Ferry's direction, they became an early signpost to the British New Wave turning the techno-rock pretensions of a Yes and an ELP into inspiring pop. Ferry announced a period of "trial separation" for Roxy in 1976, after which he pursued a solo career already started in '73 with the oldies pastiche *These Foolish Things*. In England, Ferry has had the odd solo hit; no such luck in the States where the closest he came was Roxy's "Love is the Drug" in 1975. Roxy recently reunited for the *Manifesto* LP, but Ferry insists in interviews that his solo career will continue.

RECOMMENDED: *Another Time, Another Place, The Bride Stripped Bare* (Atlantic).

FLAMIN' GROOVIES

A band with a long and intricate history, the Groovies have been moving steadily backwards since beginning as San Francisco's first (and only) punk band way back in 1968. In their earliest incarnation, the Groovies played high energy, sloppy rock 'n' roll that was in sharp contrast with the hippie music that characterized their city. The first rock band to record and release a home-brew album, the Groovies were ultimately signed by a major label, released an LP, signed to another label, released another two LPs, emigrated to England, recorded a pair of singles produced by Dave Edmunds, underwent a number of changes in lineup, put out a live LP on a Dutch label, then signed to yet another label, where they have released three albums to date, each more 60s-oriented than its predecessor. Despite an immense talent for the creation of fragile pop classics, leader Cyril Jordan has had the band record numerous carbon-copy cover versions of songs by the Rolling Stones, Byrds, and Beatles. Perhaps in ten years they will have discovered the 70s. Meanwhile, founder guitarist Roy Loney has resurfaced recently after several years away from active rock performing with a new band, the Phantom Movers.

RECOMMENDED: *Flamingo* (Kama Sutra).

FLEETWOOD MAC

This most popular of adult rock bands dates back to 1967, when three John Mayall grads, guitarist Peter Green, bassist John McVie and drummer Mick Fleetwood, came together as yet another British blues band. Personnel changes have been frequent, as the group has tried on a variety of styles. By 1970, Green was gone and the sound was getting spacier. Christine McVie was added on keyboards, guitarist Jeremy Spencer left and was replaced by Bob Welch. The group became more melodic, with more emphasis on harmonies. When Californians Lindsey Buckingham and Stevie Nicks came on board after Welch left, the band flowered. *Fleetwood Mac* (1975) was a huge hit, with Buckingham's jagged guitar and Nicks' songwriting and stage presence providing a focus the band had previously lacked. Subsequent albums have also soared. Fleetwood Mac is now a "song" band, playing punchy numbers that talk about adult concerns, but they rock as hard (if not harder) as ever, perhaps because they retain that bluesy rhythm section. Few groups have ever attained across-the-board success and continued to grow musically.

RECOMMENDED: *Fleetwood Mac* (Epic); *Rumours, Tusk* (Warner Bros.).

FLO AND EDDIE

Pop satirists extraordinaire, Flo and Eddie, Mark Volman and Howard Kaylan, are the walking, talking, singing, wisecracking sound of rock's consciousness. Their send-ups of pop culture institutions like John Denver, George Harrison, and Mick Jagger (all in their pop star dildo routine) are as pointed as they are hilarious. But Volman and Kaylan (former members of the Inglewood, California chart band the Turtles from 1963 to 1970) are also brilliant tunesmiths, with an ear for catchy melodies and a love for ringing electric guitars and high teenage harmonies. One remarkable combination of all three was the 1968 satirical Turtles album, *Battle of the Bands*. But the pair have also plied their trade with Frank Zappa's Mothers (1970-72), as a recording solo act, and as a radio team on "Flo and Eddie by the Fireside," a mid-70s program that was syndicated to a large number of U.S. stations. And were that not enough, Volman and Kaylan also appear as background vocalists on several LPs, including three by T. Rex.

RECOMMENDED: *The Phlorescent Leech and Eddie* (Reprise).

FLYING BURRITO BROTHERS

After pioneering L.A. country-rock with the Byrds on *Sweetheart of the Rodeo*, Gram Parsons founded the Burritos in 1969 specifically to play country music, which he called "cosmic American music." Cofounder Chris Hillman (who came along with Parsons from the Byrds) was the only member to last out the group's entire four years. Initially, their druggy-mystical approach to country was unique and interesting, if not fully realized. But Parsons lost interest quickly, and once he did, the group drifted further from the original idea; musically, it might have been an improvement, but the sense of mission was gone. And the Burritos were never so much a band as the catalyst for a scene. Though they saw little commercial success, they were always critical favorites and the darlings of L.A. trendies, and they had an inestimable influence on all that has come out of Los Angeles since their demise.

RECOMMENDED: *Last of the Red Hot Burritos* (A&M).

FOCUS

This highly experimental Dutch jazz/rock/classical band was formed in 1969 by flutist This Van Leer, bassist Martin Dresden, and drummer Hans Cleuver. Guitarist Jan Akkerman left the legendary Dutch underground band Brainbox to make Focus a quartet. Bassist Bert Ruiter and drummer Pierre Van der Linden joined for later recordings, and while the group continued to try adventurous musical concepts they came up with a few commercial hooks ("Hocus Pocus" and "Harem Scarem") and eventually recorded with vocalist P. J. Proby.

RECOMMENDED: *In and Out of Focus* (Sire); *Hamburger Concerto* (Atco).

JOHN FOGERTY

As the guiding force behind Creedence Clearwater Revival, Fogerty was one of the true pop geniuses of the late 60s and early 70s. The songs he wrote were infectious, often witty, and wise beyond his years. When the group split, supposedly tired of his domination and of being rejected by critics as AM radio fodder, Fogerty appeared to be the one who could forge a successful solo career. What a huge puzzle and disappointment, then, that his albums have been sporadic and without spark. He's hardly written at all, and that wonderful gravelly voice has been mostly wasted.

RECOMMENDED: *Blue Ridge Rangers* (Fantasy).

FOGHAT

The backgrounds of the original members of this Anglo-American boogie-minded foursome, formed in 1972 in England, may actually be more interesting than their actual accomplishments as a group. Guitarist Lonesome Dave

Peverett, drummer Roger Earl, and original bassist Tone Stevens were all refugees from Savoy Brown. Peverett had actually played in a Swiss blues band (where he got the Lonesome tag), Earl once auditioned for Jimi Hendrix (and failed), and lead guitarist Rod Price was a member of an obscure English blues outfit called Black Cat Bones through whose obscure ranks passed the likes of Free/Bad Company drummer Simon Kirke. As Foghat, they have turned their backs on English indifference to their highly commercial brand of blues 'n' boogie and settled in the States, where they are headquartered in Long Island, New York. Stevens left, unable to keep up with Foghat's unrelenting touring schedule, and was temporarily replaced by Philadelphian Nick Jameson, who produced and engineered several Foghat LPs. Connecticut Yankee Craig McGregor stepped in permanently come 1977. Hit singles like "I Just Want to Make Love to You" (Willie Dixon's) and "Slow Ride" have consolidated Foghat's sales appeal with concert audiences, sending most of their nine albums to gold and beyond.

RECOMMENDED: *Fool for the City, Boogie Motel* (Bearsville).

FOREIGNER

In 1976 ex-Spooky Tooth guitarist Mick Jones and ex-King Crimson multi-instrumentalist Ian McDonald, both transplanted Englishmen living in New York, worked on a session fronted by Ian Lloyd of Stories that was to have been the groundwork for a new group. When that project failed, Jones and McDonald decided to form their own group and after hiring lead singer Lou Gramm, drummer Dennis Elliott and bassist Ed Gagliardi they dubbed the group Foreigner and proceeded to record a debut album that yielded three hit singles and eventually went triple platinum. The band continued to sell albums on the strength of their commercial blend of hard rock and melodic elements. Ex-Small Faces bassist Rick Wills replaced Galiardi for *Head Games,* which was produced by Queen/Cars producer Roy Thomas Baker.

RECOMMENDED: *Foreigner, Double Vision* (Atlantic).

FOUR SEASONS

Another of those great early 60s Italian vocal groups, the Four Seasons (Frankie Valli, Bob Gaudio, Tommy DeVito, Joe Long) brought pop music right up to the doorstep of the Beatles. The music was the kind of mindless pop that late 50s-early 60s vocal groups specialized in but there was something, arresting, even otherworldly, about Valli's incredible falsetto singing. The hits still sound good, too; "Rag Doll," "Ronnie," "Stay," "Let's Hang On," "Working My Way Back To You," "Walk Like A Man," "Dawn," "Sherry," "Alone," "Big Girls Don't Cry."

RECOMMENDED: *Four Seasons Gold Vault of Hits, Four Seasons Second Gold Vault of Hits* (Decca).

FOUR TOPS

Diehard Motown buffs often maintain that this group made the best records of 'em all for that label. Sometimes, as in "Reach Out, I'll Be There," it's hard to dispute. Certainly the Tops got the royal treatment, with most of their material written and produced by the crack team of Holland-Dozier-Holland. Levi Stubbs had the most urgent, frenetic voice of any of the Motown singers; his growling leads demanded that you listen to him. Sometimes he was even criticized for being overly frantic. But the Tops' string of hits speaks volumes for the group; quite simply, they made some of the most chilling records of the 60s, though they began slipping as soon as H-D-H left Motown in 1967. When Stubbs and company left Motown themselves, their work lost its bite entirely.

RECOMMENDED: *Reach Out, Still Waters Run Deep* (Motown); *Keeper of the Castle* (ABC-Dunhill).

PETER FRAMPTON

The Face of 1968 became the Conquering Hero of 1976 and 1977 with his 12-million selling *Frampton Comes Alive*. But a mere three-million selling follow-up and a film appearance in *Sgt. Pepper's Lonely Hearts Club Band* have done considerable if not irreparable damage to Peter Frampton's career in two short years. Frampton got an early start on stardom, joining a group called the Preachers at age 14 who enjoyed the patronage of Rolling Stone Bill Wyman. When the Preachers split, Frampton went with the part that became the Herd and he, in turn, became a teenybop fave on the basis of his looks and the Herd's British hits through the mid-60s. Eager for artistic credibility, he left in 1968 to form Humble Pie with Small Faces howler Steve Marriott, tiring of their increasing penchant for mindless boogie in 1971. As a solo artist, he made moderately successful albums and toured incessantly, building a concert audience that turned into a record-buying audience when he released *Frampton Comes Alive*, an accurate rendition of his live repertoire from *Winds of Change* on. But the phenomenal sales of *FCA* put a hex on Frampton, who went from cult hero to superstar in one unsuspecting shot. His every move was chronicled in that context, and when his next studio album, *I'm in You*, failed to match its predecessor's platinum pile, word went out that Frampton was a one-shot. The *Pepper* fiasco didn't help, and a June 1978 automobile accident in the Bahamas forced Frampton into recuperative seclusion for almost a year. *Where I Should Be* had respectable sales, but more than that, it represented a return to the good-natured rock 'n' roll style that made *FCA* such an agreeable, happy album in the first place.

RECOMMENDED: *Frampton Comes Alive, I'm in You* (A&M), and the soundtrack to the *Sgt. Pepper* film (RSO).

ARETHA FRANKLIN

Lady Soul was first signed by John Hammond and then kicked around Columbia for years while the label tried to figure out what to do with her. In 1967, Jerry Wexler signed her to Atlantic, took her down to Muscle Shoals, cut the epochal "I Never Loved a Man the Way That I Love You" and "Respect," and wrote a new chapter in the history of modern music. Never had a woman sung with such force, authority and fire. Given pretty much of a free rain, she proceeded to turn out soul classic after classic for the next few years before branching out into jazz, pop and even show tunes. She's without peer when she stays close to her church roots (her father is the famed Detroit preacher, Reverend C. L. Franklin), but in recent years seems to have lost some of her direction and drive. Still, nothing she does is without interest.

RECOMMENDED: *In Paris, This Girl's in Love with You, Spirit in the Dark, Young Gifted and Black* (Atlantic).

FREE

Free spawned some of the best musicians to grace British bands in the 70s while managing to turn out seven albums of their own, some of which are classic. Paul Rodgers and Simon Kirke, in from the start (1968) to the end (1973), went on to form Bad Company. Paul Kossoff was in the midst of a promising solo career as one of the world's premier lead guitarists when he died of drug problems in 1976. American keyboardist John "Rabbit" Bundrik is now a member of the Who, and Japanese bassist Tetsu Yamauchi was a member of the Faces after the departure of Ronnie Lane. Bassist Andy Fraser was in a number of bands after Free, most notably the Sharks, with Chris Spedding. Free themselves, despite the incessant turmoil they underwent, made a prime brand of straight-on rock 'n' roll, best exemplified by songs like "All Right Now" and "The Hunter."

RECOMMENDED: *Fire and Water, Free Live* (A&M).

ROBERT FRIPP

This eccentric British guitarist began recording in 1967 with a group called Giles, Giles and Fripp that made a strange rock opera record. A year later Fripp formed the trail-blazing British art rock band King Crimson and quickly became recognized as one of the finest and most inventive guitarists in rock. After recording a number of albums and touring virtually nonstop with Crimson through the mid-70s Fripp disbanded the group to concentrate on his solo project. On his own he had already recorded with Eno on the *No Pussyfooting* album and contributed largely to David Bowie's *Heroes*. In 1979 Fripp announced a five year, four record solo plan and kicked it off with a record called *Exposures* based around his new array of electronic gadgets which he calls Frippertronics.

RECOMMENDED: *Exposures* (Polydor).

THE FUGS

They may have been the craziest rock 'n' roll group ever. Their outrageous performances live in Greenwich Village legend to this day. Ed Sanders and Tuli Kupferberg were local poets who decided to set their poetry to music. They banded together with other poets and musicians; drummer Ken Weaver, fiddler/guitarist

Peter Stampfel, guitarist Steve Weber, bassist John Anderson and guitarist Vinny Leary, and recorded an album, *The Fugs First Album,* that is still one of the most arresting and individual statements ever made in rock. They weren't particularly interested in developing a recording career, so after a couple of more records they decided to call it quits.

RECOMMENDED: *The Fugs First Album, The Fugs* (ESP).

RICHIE FURAY

After leaving Poco in 1973 and then Souther, Hillman and Furay in 1976, guitarist/singer Furay retreated to his Colorado base to rethink his career as a musician and songwriter and put together the Richie Furay Band. Since then, he's released two albums of the kind of country/rock good-time music he's known for, playing with a backup band that now consists of guitarist Virgil Beckham, drummer John Mehler, bassist Billy Batstone, and keyboardist Gabriel Katona. Tim Schmit of the Eagles and David Cassidy made guest vocal appearances on Furay's latest album, *Dance a Little Light.*

RECOMMENDED: *I've Got a Reason* (Asylum).

PETER GABRIEL

Peter Gabriel was one of three students at the Charterhouse school in Surrey, England who formed a pop group in 1966 called the Garden Wall. The other two were Tony Banks and Anthony Phillips (and later Michael Rutherford), and together they would eventually become Genesis, for whom Gabriel would be the mesmeric frontman, slipping in and out of bizarre costumes to illustrate art-rock epics like "Watcher of the Skies" or commanding the band's all-white stage in a stark black outfit, a frontal lock of his hair removed and his face heavily made up in a pancake death mask. Then shortly after a U.S. trek to support the operatic *The Lamb Lies Down on Broadway,* Gabriel made the surprise announcement that he was leaving the group and just as surprisingly disappeared from public view until 1977, when he surfaced with his first and startlingly eclectic solo LP. His '78 effort, produced by Robert Fripp, is another fascinating document of Gabriel's creative idiosyncracies in song form.

RECOMMENDED: *Peter Gabriel* (Atlantic).

RORY GALLAGHER

One of the brightest rock stars ever to come out of Ireland, this rough and tumble guitarist first surfaced in the mid 60s with the group Taste, the Irish answer to such heavy metal monsters as Cream. Gallagher's studied blues technique did not keep him from playing full throttle, slicing great slide guitar leads into endless boogie rhythm patterns. As a solo Gallagher has recorded a number of albums in his rapid fire hard blues delivery for three different labels.

RECOMMENDED: *Rory Gallagher* (Atlantic); *Top Priority* (Chrysalis).

GALLAGHER AND LYLE

Determined to escape their native Scotland at almost any cost, Benny Gallagher and Graham Lyle headed for London ten years ago, signing on with newly-formed McGuiness-Flint. Though this band never really acknowledged the importance of Graham and Benny, the two were the principal songwriters and shaped the sound of the band on its first two LPs. At the same time as McGuiness-Flint was being launched, Apple Corps' Mary Hopkin waxed several Gallagher/Lyle tunes, including the hit single "Sparrow" and the highly-regarded album track, "International." On the strength of their track record as writers, Capitol signed Gallagher and Lyle as a light-rock recording partnership, and the duo cut an album on which they supplemented their singing with mandolin, accordion and harmonium which they played themselves. Their later (and for the most part their best) albums appeared on A&M from 1974 to 1977. Benny and Graham are still sought-after songwriters; their compositions and guest performances are on records by Bryan Ferry, Art Garfunkel, Ronnie Lane and Fairport Convention.

RECOMMENDED: *Seeds, Love on the Airwaves* (A&M).

JERRY GARCIA

Hippie in good standing for fifteen years, Jerry Garcia has been unfairly characterized as the original Mr. Good Vibes, the easy-going chieftain of Woodstock Nation because of his beatific bearded looks and his central role in the musical renaissance that started out as Haight-Ashbury and came to envelope the entire nation. But Garcia is also lead guitarist for the Grateful Dead and, as such, has defined a style of rock 'n' roll guitar playing that draws not just on rock and blues but country, jazz, and other musics. Garcia got his first guitar at 15, two years later joined the army, and nine months later returned to attend San Mateo Junior College with Robert Hunter, lyricist-to-be for the Dead. His fascination with bluegrass music led to the formation of temporary bands like the Wildwood Boys and Mother McCree's Uptown Jug Champions, various members of which eventually formed the Warlocks in 1965. They, in turn, became the Grateful Dead with Garcia dubbed Captain Trips. But in the Dead's decade and a half together, Garcia has not been afraid to experiment outside of the band.

He formed the New Riders of the Purple Sage with former Wildwood Boy David Nelson, tried bluegrass again with Old and In the Way, and occasionally tours with his own Jerry Garcia Band.

RECOMMENDED: *Garcia* (Warner Bros); *Reflections* (Round). Garcia also appears on New Riders' debut album, with Old and In the Way on Round, and collaborative albums with keyboardists Howard Wales and Merl Saunders.

ART GARFUNKEL

It was in the midst of recording Simon & Garfunkel's *Bridge over Troubled Water* that the latter made his film debut in *Catch-22*. The duo promptly broke up, leaving both men on their own. While Simon concentrated on his music, Garfunkel went on to appear in *Carnal Knowledge* and didn't get around to cutting a solo album until *Angel Clare* in 1973. Not surprisingly, given his role in the duo, it was smooth, lush, romantic mood music—gutless. He's not veered significantly from that since, but has secured a strong enough niche in the marketplace to indicate that a lot of people like cotton candy.

RECOMMENDED: *Angel Clare* (Columbia).

MARVIN GAYE

Another unbeatable Motown hitmaker, Gaye has been in a constant state of evolution, from "Hitchhike" to "I Heard It through the Grapevine" to *What's Goin' On*. But he's always been a tough one to pin down. Though much tension could be found in his early records, his own voice was always fluid, relaxed; he is a groove singer. Always a shy and extremely reluctant performer, he is still capable of putting on a terrific show. Along with Stevie Wonder, he was the first to win creative control over his records from Motown; the result was *What's Goin' On* (1971), a state-of-the-nation album that remains a landmark in black music. Since then, his releases have been sporadic and spotty, despite such classics as "Trouble Man" and "Let's Get It On," and he seems to be getting further and further away from both his audience and his muse.

RECOMMENDED: *Greatest Hits, Vols. 1-2, Super Hits, What's Goin' On* (Tamla).

J. GEILS BAND

The J. Geils Band were not just another bunch of white boys believing they could be as black as the blues they loved. The Geils Band (formed in 1969 in Boston as the J. Geils Blues Band) blew a lot of blood and guts into their blues, as evidenced by the feeling and fury that went into their first live album *Full House*. But Peter Wolf (vocals), Magic Dick (hot harp), J. Geils (savage six-string attack), Stephen Jo Bladd (drums), Seth Justman (assorted keys), Danny Klein (bass) also had a magic commercial touch that complemented the spirit of their sound. On one album they could send Smokey Robinson's "First I Look at the Purse" through the wringer and not much later score on the hit parade with a reggae-like "Give It To Me." The band ran into some flak with *Ladies Invited* and *Nightmares and Other Takes From the Vinyl Jungle* (both '74); critics bemoaning the lack of fire in their sound, and Wolf's highly publicized marriage to Faye Dunaway didn't do much for their street credibility. But the Geils guys have since bounded back on vinyl and there is no criticizing their stage show, as wild and wooly an evening as you're likely to see in a lifetime of Blues Brothers.

RECOMMENDED: *J. Geils Band, The Morning After, Full House* (Atlantic); *Sanctuary* (EMI America).

GENESIS

In their earliest incarnation, Genesis was a pop group, manipulated by Jonathan King into a corner they eventually found uncomfortable. Formed at the Charterhouse school in Surrey by singer Peter Gabriel, organist Tony Banks, and original guitarist Anthony Phillips as the Garden Wall, Genesis has since gone through musical and personnel changes that would have failed a lesser band. Drummers came and went until Phil Collins (ex-Flaming Youth) settled in 1970. Phillips left after *Trespass* in 1969, replaced by Steve Hackett who, in turn, left eight years later. Gabriel made a spectacular exit after the conceptual *The Lamb Lies Down on Broadway* tour of 1975 and as of this writing, Genesis is now down to three; Collins, Banks, and guitarist/bassist Michael Rutherford, a latecomer in the Garden Wall. And despite it all, Genesis continues to be a leading exponent of the classically rooted British art-rock of which Yes and ELP have been commercial proponents. Their cultish following, expanded in '72 with a debut U.S. performance in New York City, never really enabled them to crack the charts until *Trick of the Tail* and *Wind and Wuthering,* the two immediate post-Gabriel records, both of which were a long way from the dominantly acoustic sound of early records like *Trespass.*

RECOMMENDED: *From Genesis to Revelation* (London); *Genesis Live* (Charisma); *Trick of the Tail, Wind and Wuthering* (Atlantic).

GENTLE GIANT

As clever as they are sincere, Gentle Giant are one of the more likeable British art/rock outfits simply because they don't get too serious about the classicality of their sound. True, Kerry Minnear (keyboards, etc.) and Ray Shulman (bass, violin, etc.) are classically trained, but Shulman along with singing brother Derek and a third brother Phil played in several failed British pop and R&B bands before forming Gentle Giant in 1970. A parallel can be drawn between early Giant and King Crimson in the group's eclectic marriage of jazz and classical intentions to a rock beat, but Gentle Giant started forging its own sound with a few pop reverberations in its third album, 1972's *Three Friends.* Since then, they've expanded the sound with guitarist Gary Green and chrome-dome drummer John Weathers to considerable acclaim in the States with regular album releases and touring.

RECOMMENDED: *Little Giant* (Vertigo); *Giant for a Day* (Capitol).

LOWELL GEORGE

Lowell George made his show business debut at the age of six on the Ted Mack amateur hour in a harmonica duet with his brother, Hampton. By his teens George was absorbing jazz influences and playing guitar in his own band, Factory. The band worked briefly with Frank Zappa before disbanding, at which point George played session guitar with the Standells, the Seeds, and Zappa's Mothers of Invention. In 1971 George formed Little Feat; in Little Feat George's soulful singing and slide guitar made him the featured element, but his songwriting earned him a reputation outside the group. His most famous song, "Willin'," was recorded by a number of people, including Linda Ronstadt. As Little Feat progressed George started to work on a number of productions, producing records for Tret Fure, Howdy Moon, Valerie Carter and the Grateful Dead. In 1979 he left Little Feat for a solo career and died shortly after releasing his only solo album.

RECOMMENDED: *Thanks, I'll Eat It Here* (Warner Brothers).

ANDY GIBB

The youngest member of the star-studded Gibb family, Andy took a similar course on his own to the one that led his brothers to stardom as the Bee Gees. The Bee Gees returned to their British homeland when Andy was nine years old, after having been raised in Australia, and while his brothers were crooning Andy formed several bands on his own. When the time came for him to start his recording career in earnest, Andy decided to return to Australia until he had perfected his craft. Playing his own material as well as old Bee Gees numbers, Andy toured the country supporting groups like Sweet and the Bay City Rollers. Soon he began writing country-influenced songs, signed with Bee Gees manager Robert Stigwood, and went to the U.S. to record his first album with help from older brother Barry.

RECOMMENDED: *Flowing Rivers* (RSO).

NICK GILDER

Vocalist Nick Gilder, an Englishman who emigrated to Vancouver, Canada to seek his fortune, left the obscure Canadian rock band Sweeney Todd in 1977 for a solo career, taking with him the band's guitarist, James McCullogh. After their debut album failed, Gilder collaborated with mastermind pop producer Mike Chapman and struck paydirt with "Hot Child in the City," a stark, catchy tune which became a huge hit single during the summer of 1978. The band's rhythm section is comprised of bassist Eric Nelson, drummer Craig Krampf and keyboardist/guitarist Jamie Herndon.

RECOMMENDED: *City Nights* (Chrysalis).

GARY GLITTER

One of the prime movers of Britain's teenybopper-oriented glitter rock phase, Gary Glitter is best remembered for the innovative sound of his recordings. Basically drums and shouted choruses with deadly simple melodies and lyrics, his 1971-73 singles sound precisely like the worst aspects of disco music four years later. Interestingly enough, Glitter (born Paul Gadd) along with manager-producer Mike Leander became a huge star in England, despite the novelty sound of songs like "Rock and Roll Part 1" and "I Didn't Know I Love You (Till I Saw You Rock and Roll)." As the glam era ended, Glitter's career (actually his second time around, under the name Paul Raven, he recorded in the early 60s) faded somewhat, although he continues to release records of a more mainstream pop nature. His backing band became a recording group in their own right in 1975, and managed to have numerous hits by themselves.

RECOMMENDED: *Glitter* (Bell).

GONG

At one time a collection of playful psychedelic pixies led by former Soft Machine guitarist David Allen, Gong are testament to the old adage that the only constant is change. Under Allen's direction, the communal band specialized in a strange pastiche of musics; psychodaisical rock, free-spirited improv jazz, and electronic frivolity, framed by Allen's notion of an imaginary planet Gong and the mythology that went with it. Allen, an Australian beatnik who attended the Canterbury College of Art in the mid-60s and became part of the Canterbury school of 60s rock experimenters who later formed Soft Machine and Caravan, was left stranded in France in 1967 by visa problems and eventually formed Gong after various spells of writing poetry, composing songs, and jamming with French hippie musicians during the height of student unrest in Paris. He formed Gong in 1969 and continues to perform under the Gong banner with poet-wife, Gilli Smyth, although Gong drummer Pierre Moerlen also leads a Gong offshoot under the same name that peddles more conventional jazz-rock fusion music.

RECOMMENDED: *You, Shamal* (Virgin). (Virgin).

STEVE GOODMAN

It's a shame that Goodman is known almost exclusively for the hits he's written for others ("City of New Orleans" for Arlo Guthrie, "You Never Even Call Me By My Name" for David Alan Coe), because he is one of the most entertaining of the folk-based performers around today. Discovered in Chicago in 1971 by Kris Kristofferson, he has skillfully woven together various strains of American roots music (country, rural and urban blues, folk, early rock). He can often be precious and sentimental but he has a sense of humor that usually keeps him from going too far in that direction.

RECOMMENDED: *Somebody Else's Troubles* (Asylum); *The Essential Steve Goodman* (Buddah).

LESLEY GORE

In the early 60s the era of pajama parties and innocence as a teenage way of life was in its last gasp. Teenage girls teased their hair and waited for Johnny to ask them for that big date, while Johnny was usually too scared. The male versions of this myth were guys in white shoes like Pat Boone, but the last of the female versions was Lesley Gore, a suburban kid still in high school who sang about weekend heartbreak. "It's My Party and I'll Cry If I Want To" and "Judy's Turn To Cry" were her anthems and the songs hit home with their soap opera melodrama.

RECOMMENDED: *I'll Cry If I Want To* (Mercury).

GRAND FUNK RAILROAD

Hyped by Terry Knight, a former Detroit DJ, Flint, Michigan's Grand Funk Railroad [Guitarist Mark Farmer (b. September 29, 1948), bass guitarist Mel Schacher (b. April 8, 1951), and Don Brewer (b. September 3, 1948)] emitted some of the most abominable heavy-metal blather imaginable. Like Blue Cheer revisited, they covered the Animals' "Inside Looking Out" and Dave Mason's "Feelin' Alright" with the sensitivity of a bulldozer. Still, they sold lots of records, did two SRO shows at New York's 50,000-plus-seat Shea Stadium (1971), and were international teen heroes. Once they came out from under the manipulative spell of Knight ('72) and went into the studio with real producer (Todd Rundgren, Jimmy Ienner), Grand Funk, joined by baby-faced organist Craig Frost, started making hot rock 'n' roll records and placing them on the singles charts. They carried with them their punkish pasts (Farner and Brewer played in a Detroit band called the Pack once fronted by Knight), but a little instrumental technique didn't hurt when it came to pounding out "We're an American Band," Little Eva's "The Locomotion," or the soulful "Bad Time." And while the Zappa-produced *Good Singin', Good Playin'* was their least successful album, it was one red-hot swansong.

RECOMMENDED: *We're an American Band, Shinin' On* (Capitol); *Good Singin', Good Playin'* (MCA).

GRATEFUL DEAD

The Grateful Dead are proof that the 60s were not in vain. Often chastised as anachronistic idealists by 70s pragmatists, the Grateful Dead have survived near bankruptcy, the death of one member, a manager who robbed them, the shifting affections of critics, and the sobering experience of running a record company on the hippie ethic of art over commerce. And in spite of trials and tribulations that would have spelled curtains for a less committed band, the Dead have become rock's equivalent of a family, a family which includes the fanatic legion of Deadheads spread across America. The story of the Grateful Dead begins not with acid but with bluegrass and jug band music, the kind of sounds guitarist Jerry Garcia made while playing the San Francisco coffee-house circuit where he first met Bob Weir and Ron "Pigpen" McKernan (who died in May, 1973 of a stomach hemorrhage). Garcia went through a number of bluegrass bands with Dead lyricist-to-be Robert Hunter (who was participating in LSD tests at Stanford University), Weir, McKernan, and later drummer Bill Kreutzmann. Bassist Phil Lesh joined in 1965, just after they all formed an electric blues band called the Warlocks. Ken Kesey's notorious Acid Tests provided the freewheeling, LSD-fortified atmosphere for the Warlocks-turned-Grateful Dead to take their first bold creative steps and while the Dead's first LP was more or less inspired white-boy blues only partially capturing their live sound in the studio, the controversial *Anthem of the Sun* and the later *Live/Dead* showed them boldly improvising where no band had improvised before. Garcia's love of country music came back to the fore along with some stellar harmonies inspired by Crosby Stills and Nash on *Workingman's Dead* and *American Beauty*. Since then (1970), the Dead have further refined and defined their sound, tinkering with jazz, electronics, and exotic rhythms when they weren't pounding out class-A rock 'n' roll or funking up on a C&W riff. The Dead have only recently become a strong commercial proposition with the Arista label; touring and those legendary four-and-five hour shows were their economic mainstay for many years. Percussionist Mickey Hart has been in and out of the band, pianist Keith Godchaeux and his singing wife Donna have recently departed, and when the band isn't recording or touring, the individual players are busy with solo projects. For a detailed history of the Dead, consult Hank Harrison's *A Social History of the Grateful Dead* and the epic *Rolling Stone* interview with Jerry Garcia, published in book form as *Garcia—A Signpost to New Space*.

RECOMMENDED: *Live/Dead, Workingman's Dead, American Beauty, Europe '72, Skeletons From the Closet* (Warner Bros). Also numerous solo LPs by Garcia, Weir, and various offshoot bands as well as two MGM compilations of early live Dead material.

AL GREEN

Since "Back Up Train" in 1968, Green has gone against the grain in black music. As soul became funk and disco, he went backwards, returning to gospel. A heartthrob performer though his shows have been known to fall apart, he has a high, sensuous voice that he uses as another instrument in the overall sound developed by him and Memphis producer Willie Mitchell. After a 1974 attempt on his life by a spurned woman, he moved increasingly closer to the church; ultimately, he bought one and installed himself as the preacher. By *Full of Fire* (1977), his work was full of religious imagery, which he'd previously dealt in only sparingly. On the follow-up *The Belle Album,* he took over his own production and came up with a crackling, more disjointed sound that was equally intriguing. His fusion of the carnal and the spiritual, along with his own sexually ambiguous posture, makes him one of the more idiosyncratic characters around.

RECOMMENDED: *Al Green* (Bell); *Greatest Hits, Vols. 1-2* (Hi).

ELLIE GREENWICH

In the early 60s, when rock 'n' roll ceased to be a novelty and needed firm direction in order to refine its impact, independent producers and specialty writers began to become increasingly important. Often they worked together. The greatest of the producers, Phil Spector, used a number of writers for his different groups. By 1963 Spector had already established himself, and turned to a promising songwriting team, Jeff Barry and Ellie Greenwich. They supplied him with songs tailor made for his girl groups; "Then He Kissed Me" and "Da Doo Ron Ron" for the Crystals and "Be My Baby" for the Ronettes. After writing through the 70s Greenwich decided to try her hand at making her own album.

RECOMMENDED: *Let It Be Written, Let It Be Sung* (Verse).

GRIN

Based in the Baltimore-D.C. area, this effervescent trio was the original vehicle for Nils Lofgren, who was discovered by Neil Young. In many respects, they accomplished what Lofgren later tried to do as a solo, which was to play melodic rock with heart-of-gold lyrics. Lofgren wrote the material, sang lead, and played guitar and keyboards; bassist Bob Gordon and drummer Bob Berberich kept time.

RECOMMENDED: *Grin* (Spindizzy).

GROUNDHOGS

This power trio was primarily a vehicle for Tony McPhee, the only guitarist in the Hendrix mold to ever approach Jimi either technically or emotionally. They started as a blues band, and built a healthy following in their native England by the early 70s. But in America, they had little success.

RECOMMENDED: *Thank Christ for the Bomb* (United Artists).

ARLO GUTHRIE

The son of Woody Guthrie, America's best-loved folksinger, Arlo was born in Coney Island. He came of age musically in the mid-60s, so it wasn't surprising that the song that made him famous was "Alice's Restaurant Massacree" (1967), a long, sly talking blues that lampooned the draft and the Vietnam war. It was eventually made into a movie. Arlo had his musical ups and downs after that, but retained his high standing in what was left of the counterculture with his jabberwocky songs as well as the more serious topical material. He even had a hit single with "City of New Orleans," but his finest hour is the 1976 album, *Amigo*. Always the activist, he continues to ally himself with the environmental and anti-nuke movements, and a recent conversion to Catholicism has also become more evident in his music.

RECOMMENDED: *Alice's Restaurant, Amigo,* (Reprise); *Best of Arlo Guthrie, Pete Seeger & Arlo Guthrie Together in Concert* (Warner Bros.).

WOODY GUTHRIE

America's greatest folksinger/songwriter, Guthrie travelled through every state of the union in the 30s and 40s writing about the depression, labor unions, the hard times and the good times of America's working people. Of the over 1000 songs he wrote some of Guthrie's tunes became classics; "This Land Is Your Land," "Roll On, Columbia," "This Train Is Bound for Glory." After coming down with Huntington's Disease Guthrie was hospitalized for the last 15 years of his life, where many folksingers pilgrimaged to visit him. One of those was Bob Dylan, whose "Song To Woody" helped establish the young singer with the folk audience. Guthrie's son Arlo also became a folk singer, and eventually a movie was made about Woody's life, called *Bound For Glory,* starring David Carradine.

RECOMMENDED: *Woody Guthrie — A Legendary Performer* (RCA).

BUDDY GUY

When he arrived in Chicago from Louisiana in 1957, Guy played a more frenzied version of B. B. King-style guitar. His songs hauled out all the old blues cliches; he was like a walking encyclopedia, but that was part of his charm, because those cliches obviously lived in him. His early records had an incredibly nervous sound; music with knots in its stomach, and are all the more exciting for it. He made his name playing with harpist Junior Wells, with whom he still sometimes tours. Always a flamboyant showman, Guy was discovered by the hippies in the late 60s and came to rely increasingly on gimmicks to wow the whites. But that was at least somewhat consistent with his approach all along; even today, when he wants to, Guy can play shattering guitar.

RECOMMENDED: *Buddy Guy and Junior Wells Play the Blues* (Atco); with Junior Wells, *Blues Hit Big Town* (Delmark).

STEVE HACKETT

The London-born guitarist took his classical influences and space rock ideas to their logical conclusion as the lead guitarist with Genesis, one of Britain's top art groups, which he helped found. He left that band in the mid 70s to work on solo projects that were even more romantic and ethereal than his work with Genesis, but which were hooked around purely musical concepts without the Genesis theatrics. Hackett also guested with the American rock band Kansas, who played on one of his own albums.

RECOMMENDED: *Please Don't Touch* (Chrysalis).

SAMMY HAGAR

A former semipro fighter from Monterey, California, Hagar wanted to be a rock 'n' roller ever since he first heard Elvis Presley. He formed a series of copy bands and gigged around the San Bernardino area under the name of Skinny before joining up with Ronnie Montrose as lead singer and songwriter. After two records with Montrose, Hager set out on his own in 1976 and eventually took most of Montrose's band with him (bassist Bill Church, keyboardist Alan Fitzgerald and drummer Dennis Carmassi). His athletic stage antics and high energy band sound has made Hagar one of the top attractions on the U.S. concert circuit.

RECOMMENDED: *Nine on a Ten Scale* (Capitol).

BILL HALEY

Haley has often been credited with starting rock 'n' roll because his single "Rock Around the Clock" became the first chart topping rock 'n' roll hit and was used as the theme music for *Blackboard Jungle.* In fact Haley was pretty tame compared to some of the other rockers of his time, but in 1955 Bill Haley and the Comets really put the music on the map, playing with enough energy to inspire riots both in the U.S. and abroad, where Haley is worshipped to this day in places like England.

RECOMMENDED: *Golden Hits* (Decca).

JOHN HALL

Until he got Orleans off the ground in 1972, Hall's career was a checkered one that seemed to be headed nowhere; a few unmemorable bands, a couple good songs (cowritten with his wife Johanna), session work and sideman jobs, some so-so production gigs. It was nothing to be ashamed of; hell, Janis Joplin had recorded the Halls' "Half Moon" and John was working with other top artists, but Hall just didn't stand out in a crowd. With Orleans he got the major credit for some hit singles ("Let There Be Music," "Dance with Me," "Still the One") and his guitar work matured noticeably, taking on a harder and funkier edge. In 1977, he went solo. In addition to recording on his own, he provided sessions guitar for people like Little Feat and Jackson Browne and he produced Bonnie Raitt. There's something a little clinical, a little too studious, about his music, but maybe that's what happens when you let formal training get in your way. Hall is also deeply involved in the antinuclear movement and other political causes.

RECOMMENDED: *John Hall* (Asylum).

HALL AND OATES

Photo by Neal Preston

Daryl Hall and John Oates have spent the better part of the seven years they have been recording together (starting with *Whole Oats* in 1972) living down the "blue-eyed soul" compliments. The truth is that Hall and Oates can rock with the best of them, even if their hardest rocking LP, the Todd Rundgren-produced future-shock *War Babies,* was also their least successful. Hall (b. Pottstown, Pa.) and the diminutive Oates (b. New York City, moved to Philly with his family) first met in 1967 as students at Philadelphia's Temple University. Hall did session playing and songwriting at Sigma Sound Studios and played with Tim Moore in Gulliver; Oates studied journalism, after which they formed in 1970 a folkish duo with detectable R&B allegiances. Over the course of their recording career, Hall and Oates have refined their style, highlighting Hall's soaring tenor, the pair's exuberant harmonies, and the unique fusion of R&B emotion and rock 'n' roll energy, to very successful effect on "Sara Smile" and "Rich Girl."

RECOMMENDED: *Abandoned Luncheonette,* (Atlantic); *Bigger Than Both of Us, Along the Red Ledge,* (RCA); Hall has also appeared on Robert Fripp's *Exposure* and recorded a solo LP with Fripp, *Sacred Songs,* still unreleased at this writing.

JAN HAMMER

A Czechoslovakian-born keyboardist who was a child prodigy and underwent extensive classical piano training since age four, Hammer left his native land in 1966 to pursue musical studies at Boston's Berklee School of Music. After playing with a number of American jazz artists here, Hammer met John McLaughlin and helped form the Mahavishnu Orchestra, where his virtuoso synthesizer playing countered McLaughlin's lightning-fast guitar runs for the most lethal one-two punch fusion music has ever known. After leaving the Mahavishnu Orchestra, Hammer's synthesizer playing went more in the direction of reaching for the kind of gimmicky effects the instrument is capable of. He recorded an album about the creation of the universe, *The First Seven Days*, then after a brief stint with Jeff Beck (*Wired*), started to make his own rock 'n' roll albums and began singing.

RECOMMENDED: *The First Seven Days*, *Black Sheep* (Nemperor).

JOHN HAMMOND, JR.

John Hammond, Jr. became a well known folk and traditional blues guitarist after an appearance at the 1963 Newport Folk Festival. After working with a number of small blues and folk groups, one of which included the guitarist Jimi Hendrix, Hammond began an illustrious recording career and made a series of excellent blues rock records, playing with some of the best musicians of his generation, including Duane Allman.

RECOMMENDED: *Southern Fried* (Atlantic); *Triumverate* (Columbia).

HERBIE HANCOCK

Multi-keyboardist Hancock built a reputation as a west coast jazz pianist in the early 60s, accompanying local players like Hank Mobley and Lee Morgan, before his soundtrack music to *Blow Up* and its hit single, "Watermelon Man." After a series of critically acclaimed solo albums Hancock joined the Miles Davis band, staying on through that group's jazz fusion experiments before leaving to front his own band, Headhunters. Hancock's mid to late 70s albums pointed the way to disco funk, using electronic keyboards with great success, especially on the soundtrack to *Death Wish*. In '78 Hancock took time off to record a series of duet acoustic piano concerts with Chick Corea.

RECOMMENDED: *Maiden Voyage* (United Artists); *Thrust*, *V.S.O.P.* (Columbia).

TIM HARDIN

A 60s Village folkie with leanings toward jazz, Hardin wrote some of the genre's finest songs, "Reason to Believe," "If I Were a Carpenter," etc. But he could also get excessively soppy ("Misty Roses"). He had a soft, vulnerable voice that made him especially popular with women. But personal problems kept him from maintaining a career, and he barely made it past Woodstock.

RECOMMENDED: *Tim Hardin, Vols. 1-3* (Verve); *This Is Tim Hardin* (Atco).

STEVE HARLEY AND COCKNEY REBEL

Steve Harley, former journalist (born Steven Nice), created Cockney Rebel in 1973. He molded the group into an image of arty futurism, and within a few months, Cockney Rebel was signed to a huge record company, and had become the talk of London. Commercial stardom followed, and it wasn't until Harley attempted to make a name for himself in America that he ran into any obstacles. After five hit albums and a like number of singles in England and Europe, Harley's abrasive character and huge ego brought him down, and he has been casting about for the past few years attempting to regain his former stature, operating from an alternate base in Los Angeles. Despite various criticisms levelled at Rebel's music, the first three albums are wonderful collections of sophisticated pop poetry, all delivered in Harley's nasal vocals.

RECOMMENDED: *The Human Menagerie*, *Love's a Prima Donna* (all Capitol).

ROY HARPER

The ultimate stoned hippie-freak poet, Roy Harper is also one of England's most lyrically perceptive and melodically affecting singer-songwriters, highly touted by superstars like Paul McCartney, Ian Anderson of Jethro Tull (a long-time mate), and Jimmy Page of Led Zeppelin (who cowrote "Hats Off to Harper" for *Led Zeppelin III*). An early convert (age 13) to skiffle music, Harper joined the Royal Air Force as a teenager and secured his release by faking mental illness, resulting in a lengthy hospital stay chronicled in "Committed" from his first album. He worked the London folkie circuit through the 60s, but has since developed a style that draws on the angry frustration of the hardest rock and grafts it to an intelligent lyrical and musical presentation that has made him a well-respected figure in England but little more than a cult hero to his few American fans.

RECOMMENDED: *The Sophisticated Beggar* (Strike/Youngblood, U.K.); *Flat Baroque and Berserk* (Harvest); *Back to Reality* (Chrysalis U.S./Harvest U.K.).

EMMYLOU HARRIS

She was discovered by Gram Parsons playing bars in the Baltimore-D.C. area, and he wanted her to join the Flying Burrito Brothers. Instead, he left the group and brought her out to L.A. to sing backgrounds and duets with him on his solo albums. After he died, she had the contacts to get a good solo contract. Her debut album in 1975 was an immediate hit; her brand of L.A. country-rock is a lot closer to Nashville than any other music coming out of L.A., though she often does Beatles songs. She's also revived some obscure country classics, introducing them to a rock audience. At one point, she had Elvis Presley's band backing her. Harris approaches country music a little too much like a folkie (which she once was), and her albums have a way of being predictable in both material and arrangements, but that hasn't stopped her from appealing equally to rock fans and traditional country fans alike.

RECOMMENDED: *Pieces of the Sky,* (Reprise); *Quarter Moon in a Ten Cent Town* (Warner Bros.).

GEORGE HARRISON

Guitarist George started out the shy guy in the Beatles, but ended up the Eastern religion nut. His music suffered along the way. The religious pre-occupations began cropping up around the time the group went psychedelic. *All Things Must Pass* (1970), his first post-Beatles solo album, remains his most complete statement. Most often, he's self-righteous, vague and musically passive.

RECOMMENDED: *All Things Must Pass, Concert for Bangla Desh* (Apple); *Best of George Harrison* (Capitol).

ALEX HARVEY

Alex Harvey stands as living proof, along with Don Van Vliet (Captain Beefheart), that one does not have to hang it up at age 40. A boisterous but determined product of Glasgow, Scotland's legendary Gorbals slum area, Harvey (b. February 15, 1935) quit school at age 15 and held upwards of 40 jobs before turning to music. There were many years spent playing in skiffle groups, being proclaimed the "Tommy Steele of Scotland," and leading his own R&B revue (not to mention playing in the pit band for the London production of *Hair*). But Harvey didn't discover his own talent until he took a failing Scot rock band called Tear Gas renamed it the Sensational Alex Harvey Band, and formulated a stage show that portrayed him, pitted against the no-nonsense sound of SAHB, as a kind of friendly pirate, punkishly aggressive but genuinely sincere in his love for his audience which was usually as old as his own two kids. Harvey and band, guitarist Zal Cleminson (in mime makeup), keyboard player Hugh McKenna (later replaced by Tommy Eyre), drummer Ted McKenna, bassist Chris Glen, became a major U.K. touring and recording act, never really making a dent in the States, until tensions between Harvey and the boys led to a temporary and then permanent split in 1977. SAHB made one unspectacular album without Harvey and then went their own separate ways, Cleminson eventually to heavy-metal buccaneers Nazareth. Harvey, who once planned an album based on the Loch Ness monster, is currently staging a British comeback on his own.

RECOMMENDED: *Alex Harvey's Big Soul Band* (U.K. Polydor); *This is the Sensational Alex Harvey Band* (German Metronome); *The Impossible Dream, Tomorrow Belongs To Me* (Mercury).

RICHIE HAVENS

With his furious acoustic guitar strumming and his raspy, shouting voice, Havens was the darling of a lot of folkies, especially on the East Coast, as the 60s faded into the 70s. In fact, he was so revered that in front of his own audiences, he could get applause for forgetting the words to his songs. He has an eclectic repertoire.

RECOMMENDED: *Mixed Bag, Richard P. Havens, 1983* (Verve Forecast).

DALE HAWKINS

Hawkins was the king of the choogle, a southern guitarist from Louisiana who played with the down home swamp funk sound that characterized his greatest hit, the 1957 smash "Suzie Q," a tremendous inspiration on bayou rocker John Fogerty, who used it to get Creedence Clearwater Revival their first hit in the 70s. Hawkins recorded for Chess records, and brought some good young players through his band, most notably guitarist James Burton, who later became famous as Ricky Nelson's guitarist.

RECOMMENDED: *Best of Dale Hawkins* (Chess).

RONNIE HAWKINS

A southern singer/guitarist who wanted to play rock and roll in the 50s had few choices and Hawkins opted to try his luck in Memphis, Tennessee, where he floundered before deciding to move to Canada. There his gruff, nasty vocals, hard-edged rockabilly guitar playing and tough as nails approach went well with the hard drinking audiences he'd play to at local roadhouses, and Hawkins became a Canadian legend, attracting some of the best young players from that country to his band. One of his backing groups, which were known as the Hawks, featured the members of the Band in their salad days, and guitarist Robbie Robertson, who plays on Hawkins' classic version of "Who Do You Love," credits Hawkins with teaching him a lot.

RECOMMENDED: *Ronnie Hawkins' Greatest Hits* (Roulette).

HAWKWIND

Even if you can't stand Hawkwind's psycho-daisical version of the universe as one big cosmic playground for drug-happy hippies, you have to admire the British band's ability to survive in spite of all the cynicism. Formed in the late 60s by guitarist Dave Brock and saxman Nik Turner, Hawkwind was originally a musical commune consisting of musicians who could improvise endlessly on one riff. Surprisingly, they made it a career, becoming a people's bands by playing a lot of free gigs, getting busted for drugs often enough for the daily newspapers to take notice, and becoming England's closest stylistic if not musical counterpart to the Grateful Dead. Glitter-rock, singer/songwriter schlock, and the punk-rock attack of the late 70s did little to change Hawkwind's plan of action even though they suffered many personnel changes, the last of which included a recent name change to Hawklords. But Hawkwind did have a U.K. hit single in 1972 with "Silver Machine," recorded live at a benefit gig for alternative music guerillas the Greasy Truckers.

RECOMMENDED: *Hawkwind* (United Artists); *Warrior on the Edge of Time* (Atco).

ISAAC HAYES

With his partner David Porter he wrote and produced most of those sizzling Sam and Dave sides in the 60s. When he went solo with *Hot Buttered Soul* in 1969, he ushered in a new era of soul music, one that was marked by excess and left many longing for the good ol' days of Stax. Hayes sang lushy-orchestrated, extended (up to ten minutes) songs complete with virile, deep-voiced rap in the middle. He quickly descended into self-parody. His career floundered while people of less talent like Barry White took his bombast one step further. But for a while there, Hayes, a macho man wrapped in leather and chains, cut an imposing figure.

RECOMMENDED: *Hot Buttered Soul, Black Moses* (Enterprise).

HEART

Formed in Seattle in 1972, Heart was built around the Wilson sisters, guitarist Nancy and vocalist/flautist Ann. The rest of the band includes guitarist Roger Fisher, bassist Steven Fossen, keyboardist Howard Leese and drummer Michael Derosier. They began playing Led Zeppelin style material and their first album yielded the hit single "Barracuda"; as the band developed they expanded their sound into other areas and managed to continue their commercial success.

RECOMMENDED: *Dreamboat Annie, Little Queen* (Mushroom).

JIMI HENDRIX

One of the great rock guitarists, the Seattle-born Hendrix worked in R & B bands with Curtis Knight and the Isley Brothers before being discovered by Chas Chandler of the Animals, who took Hendrix back to England, encouraged him to put together a flashy act and financed the project. The Jimi Hendrix Experience was a trio with drummer Mitch Mitchell and bassist Noel Redding laying down a groove for Hendrix to solo over. Hendrix's first records were a marvel of playing and electronic technique and his performance at the Monterey Pop Festival in 1967, was immortalized in the film *Monterey Pop*. After breaking up the Experience, Hendrix put together another band with bassist Billy Cox and drummer Buddy Miles called Band of Gypsies. Hendrix was hard at work on a new project when he died in 1971.

RECOMMENDED: *Are You Experienced, Electric Ladyland* (Warner Brothers); *Band of Gypsies* (Capitol).

HERMAN'S HERMITS

These guys came out of Manchester, England in 1964 and were just too cute and too bubbly and too melodic and too lightweight not to make it big with twelve-year old girls and their parents. Does anyone remember when "I'm Henry VIII, I Am" was actually battling it out tooth and nail with "Satisfaction" for the top of the charts in 1965? Peter Noone (aka Herman) and the boys had other huge hits: "Mrs. Brown You've Got a Lovely Daughter," "I'm into Something Good," "Can't You Hear My Heartbeat," "Leaning on the Lamp Post," etc. But by 1968, they were gone; Noone in pursuit of an acting career that never panned out. Their records have recently become semi-popular with certain tune-conscious New Wavers with a twisted idea of what's camp, and a Noone-led group sporting the old name has begun playing again.

RECOMMENDED: *Best of Herman's Hermits,* Vols. 1-3 (MGM).

DAN HICKS

Dan Hicks once described the music of his band the Hot Licks as a "cross between the Andrew Sisters and the Jim Kweskin". Founded by Hicks, the original drummer with seminal San Francisco band the Charlatans, in 1968, the Frisco-based Hot Licks pursued a critically rewarding but financially unspectacular career playing Hicks originals that combined his love of traditional jazz, bluegrass, and old-time standards with his own tongue-in-cheek sense of humor. Hicks finally called it quits after the 1971 LP, prophetically titled *Last Train to Hicksville,* but surfaced again in 1978 with a soundtrack LP to a movie that was never released.

RECOMMENDED: *Where's the Money?, Strikin' It Rich* (Blue Thumb).

STEVE HILLAGE

Hillage is one of the most inventive and idiosyncratic British guitarists to come out of the late 60s. In answer to the acid rock scene in San Francisco several British groups from Canterbury made similar musical experiments and syntheses. One of the best of these groups, Gong, had Hillage on lead guitar. After making several excellent records with Gong, Hillage left that group to record his own albums. His first, *Fish Rising,* was based on a mythology of fishes; Hillage then put together a more conventional group for touring purposes.

RECOMMENDED: *Fish Rising* (Virgin).

CHRIS HILLMAN

An original Byrd and a co-founder of the Flying Burrito Brothers, Hillman as a solo act proved himself an exponent of L.A. country-rock cliches, and has accordingly become increasingly obscure. The beginning of the end for him was his participation in the manufactured "supergroup" Souther-Hillman-Furay.

RECOMMENDED: *Slippin' Away* (Asylum).

HOLLIES

The Hollies' tale is one of endurance, defying the usual short life of most rock bands and continually adapting to trends and fads without losing their own identity as one of pop's premier high-harmony bands. In 1963, the Hollies, from Manchester, England, scored with a fresh version of "Searchin'" and maintained an unbroken string of smashes (21) right through to 1970. Personnel changes were taken in stride [the classic Hollies line-up is still Allan Clarke (lead vocals), Graham Nash, Tony Hicks, Bobby Elliott, Bernie Calvert] as Nash left in 1968 to record what he thought was more substantial material with CSN, and Clarke took two solo sojourns. The Hollies' ability to mold pop trends to their own musical style still sounds remarkable on such hits as the post-British Invasion "Bus Stop" and "On a Carousel," the flower-power infected "Dear Eloise" and "King Midas in Reverse," and adult 70s excursions like "The Air That I Breathe" and "He Ain't Heavy, He's My Brother."

RECOMMENDED: *Bus Stop,* (Imperial); *He Ain't Heavy He's My Brother, Distant Light,* (Epic).

BUDDY HOLLY

One of the great stars of the late 50s, Holly used his Texas roots and a firm commitment to pop to create one of the earliest authentic rock sounds. His records, produced by himself and backing group the Crickets, and written by himself and manager Norman Petty, provided a tremendous influence both vocally and instrumentally on rock groups who followed him from the Beatles to the Grateful Dead. His hits still sound great; "Not Fade Away," "Peggy Sue," "Rave On," "That'll Be the Day," "Oh Boy," "Well All Right." Holly died in the 1959 plane crash that also took the lives of Richie Valens and the Big Bopper.

RECOMMENDED: *Buddy Holly's Greatest Hits* (MCA).

JOHN LEE HOOKER

A Mississippi bluesman who's been recording for years under a variety of names, Hooker made his mark in Detroit in the postwar era. A great guitar primitive, he's at his best working alone, or with a second guitar, when he can let his instincts guide him; dropping a bar or two here, adding there, declaiming lyrics that sound made-up on the spot even when they aren't; a stream-of-consciousness approach to blues. His voice is dark and brooding, his guitar work terse and choppy. When he works with a band, he has to iron out the eccentric timing and phrasing that makes him so unique in order for the band to follow him. In such cases, it usually sounds like the endless boogie as in his album with Canned Heat. He is one of the true blues masters.

RECOMMENDED: *It Serves You Right to Suffer, Never Get Out of These Blues Alive* (ABC-Impulse); *The Very Best of John Lee Hooker* (Buddah).

NICKY HOPKINS

Ray Davies of the Kinks wrote "Session Man" for his group in honor of this lyrical British pianist who played on the records of nearly every big English group of the late 60s and early 70s (and some American ones, too, especially after he moved to California). Hopkins also played with the Jeff Beck Group and Quicksilver, but didn't like performing live. His one solo album was proof positive that not all great session men can make the transition to front man.

RECOMMENDED: *The Tin Man Was a Dreamer* (Columbia).

SAM "LIGHTNIN'" HOPKINS

Often called the last of the old-time country bluesmen, Hopkins first played professionally in the 30s and is still going strong. Based in Houston, he plays guitar in a loose style and sings in a high voice that slides deftly around the words. There is genuine subtlety, a vision, even, in his best work; unfortunately, he has been over-recorded. The result is a slew of hurried and mediocre albums which dominate what should be a better rep than he has.

RECOMMENDED: *Early Recordings, Vols. 1-2, Texas Blues Man* (Arhoolie).

HORSLIPS

The Irish band Horslips first came together to perform on a commercial for lager beer. They play a unique commercial blend of Irish folk and arty rock 'n' roll. Horslips: Charles O'Conner (fiddle, etc.), Barry Devlin (bass), Jim Lockhart (keyboards, flute), Eamonn Carr (drums), Johnny Fean (guitar, replacing two other guitarists by time of first LP)—at first spiced their hard-rock with an assortment of traditional jigs and reels in authentic acoustic texture. But long-playing experiments like *The Tain* and *The Book of Invasions* found them expanding ancient Celtic legends into album concepts that combined the two musics into one playing style. That style, since *Book*, has given them a new popular base to work from in terms of both album sales and concert tours, although the band is a self-sufficient industry of its own in Dublin, where they release all their records on their own Oats label.

RECOMMENDED: *Dancehall Sweethearts* (RCA); *Book of Invasions* (DJM).

HOT CHOCOLATE

Though the members of this interracial quintet met and continue to live in London, most of them are from various islands in the Carribean. Their first release (in 1970) was a cover of John Lennon's "Give Peace a Chance," on the Beatles' Apple label. But it wasn't until they hooked up with British pop producer Mickie Most a couple years later that they really clicked, first in England and then in the States. Their quirky records, equal parts soul, pop and Carribean, generally have buoyant, optimistic brotherhood themes; the biggest hits include "Emma" (1975), "You Sexy Thing" (1975), and "Every 1's a Winner" (1978).

RECOMMENDED: *Hot Chocolate*, (Big Tree); *Every 1's a Winner* (Infinity).

HOT TUNA

Jefferson Airplane vocalist/guitarist Jorma Kaukonen and bassist Jack Casady originally formed this group to re-explore the folk and blues roots of the Airplane when the parent group became increasingly more rock-oriented. Sometimes acoustic and sometimes electric, Hot Tuna was reasonably popular completely independent of the Airplane. But they eventually ran into similar problems; lack of direction, volume over finesse, aimless jamming, apathy.

RECOMMENDED: *Hot Tuna, Burgers* (RCA).

H. P. LOVECRAFT

Chicago based folk rock band surfaced in the late 60s. The name is from the science fiction writer. The group was made up of guitarists George Edwards and Tony Cavallari, keyboardist Dave Michaels, drummer Mike Tegza and bassist Jeffrey Boyan. After a couple of albums the band was never heard from again.

RECOMMENDED: *H. P. Lovecraft* (Mercury).

HUMBLE PIE

Humble Pie's problem, in the end, was that their reach exceeded their grasp. Former Small Face Steve Marriott was as close as a one-time English mod could come to Ray Charles, but the Pie's descent into heavy-metal after Peter Frampton left for solo work is one of rock's greatest losses. Originally founded in 1968 by Marriott and Frampton (ex-of the Herd and a pop pin-up since age 15), Humble Pie got off to a quiet but impressive start with *Town and Country,* an acoustic album of winning songs bolstered with electric energy on *As Safe as Yesterday Is* (including Greg Ridley of Spooky Tooth on bass and Jerry Shirley on drums). Frampton was able to balance Marriott's occasional excesses more so than Colosseum guitarist Dave "Clem" Clempson, who joined in 1971. Humble Pie continued to tour the U.S., but their albums became more and more predictable by the time of their voluntary breakup in 1975. Marriott has since recorded solo, temporarily re-formed the Small Faces, and is currently trying to revive the Pie.

RECOMMENDED: *Performance-Rockin' the Fillmore, Smokin'* (A&M).

IAN HUNTER

The man behind the shades has been a major figure in rock 'n' roll since the first Mott the Hoople album way back in 1969. From Mott to a successful solo career, Ian Hunter has remained a talented and intriguing songwriter and vocalist. He has even written a popular book on the life of a rock star. Hunter first entered professional music when he auditioned for the job of singer with a band called Silence, which was about to change its name and record a debut album. Hunter's Dylan fixation and mysterious image fit perfectly, and Mott the Hoople was created. Mott finally connected after David Bowie and sidekick Mick Ronson tied up with the band, in "All the Young Dudes," a huge hit single and album. Two LPs later, the guitar job in the band opened up, and Mick Ronson served a brief spell before he and Hunter set off by themselves. A tour as Hunter-Ronson was a disappointment, but Ian began making albums with the help of Ronson. After a slow start, Hunter connected in 1979 with an LP called *You're Never Alone with a Schizophrenic* on Chrysalis Records.

RECOMMENDED: compilation on Columbia (1979).

JANIS IAN

When she was 15, Janis Ian became one of the most interesting offshoots of the mid-60s "protest music" folk-rock boom with a song about an interracial love affair, "Society's Child." Unable to follow it up successfully or effectively switch to other musical directions, Ian dropped out of music for several years, moved to California, and eventually wrote some songs with an eye to making a comeback. She returned in 1972 as part of the early 70s singer-songwriter trend with an album called *Stars* and has recorded sporadically and uneventfully since. Today she makes disco records.

RECOMMENDED: *Janis Ian, Night Rains* (Columbia).

IMPRESSIONS

They first appeared in Chicago in 1957 as the vehicle for Jerry Butler and Curtis Mayfield, but Butler left after one hit to pursue a solo career. The Impressions faltered until 1961, when Mayfield hit his stride as a singer and writer. "Gypsy Woman" was the perfect teen fantasy, and Mayfield gave his group a clean, light sound that contrasted sharply with the funkier soul records of the day. As staff producer for Okeh, he helped define the Chicago Sound (for Major Lance, Gene Chandler and others) that competed with Motown for much of the 60s. But he saved the best for his own group, which was moving on with songs that echoed the sentiments of Rev. Dr. Martin Luther King. His own wispy falsetto carried the melody; Sam Gooden and Fred Cash were indispensable with their church backup. In 1970, Mayfield left the group, and despite the efforts of his replacement Leroy Hutson, the Impressions could never match their former greatness.

RECOMMENDED: *Vintage Years* (Sire); *First Impressions* (Curtom); *People Get Ready* (ABC-Paramount).

INCREDIBLE STRING BAND

It probably wouldn't be fair to call the Scottish duo of Mike Heron and Robin Williamson folkies; their bizarre influences and musical interests went far too deep for that. They were different from the traditional British music bands that proliferated in the late 60s and resembled the more esoteric folkies of the Greenwich Village and San Francisco scene. Between them they covered a multitude of exotic instruments and combined their folklorists' sensibility with tales of magic and mystery from British history and Eastern mysticism before succumbing to an interest in scientology that eventually dried up their inspiration and led to the band's early 70s dissolution.

RECOMMENDED: *The Incredible String Band* (Elektra).

IRON BUTTERFLY

The beginning, and the beginning of the end of heavy metal, Iron Butterfly was an L.A. hard rock band. In 1968, at the height of mass psychedelia, they gave the world "In-a-Gadda-da-Vida," the heaviest song yet, which went on forever, made absolutely no sense, and impressed primarily acid victims. It became the biggest selling record in Atlantic Records' history up to that point, and paved the way for all manner of other similar atrocities. The group lumbered on a few more years without regaining the Midas touch, then splintered off into several other acts, none of which are around any more.

RECOMMENDED: *In-a-Gadda-da-Vida* (Atco).

IT'S A BEAUTIFUL DAY

A second-generation San Francisco band, It's a Beautiful Day was led by a classically trained violinist, David LaFlamme, who led the group through a series of personnel changes until calling it quits in 1972 after six albums. Remembered best for the self-consciously poetic but nevertheless entrancing "White Bird," the band never sustained the impact of that song on succeeding albums despite the stylistic thread of LaFlamme's violin contrasting with dreamy female vocals. LaFlamme has since resurfaced as a solo artist.

RECOMMENDED: *It's a Beautiful Day, At Carnegie Hall* (Columbia).

JOE JACKSON

A former student at the prestigious Royal Academy of Music, Joe Jackson arrived in 1979 with a single, "Is She Really Going Out with Him?" and an album of deceptively simple tunes that connected instantly with rock fans. A bit more acceptable than stylistic mentor Elvis Costello, Jackson presented the sanitized version of the new wave with only a little of the energy and bite. Coming out of a small band called Arms and Legs, Jackson recorded a demo tape of some of his songs and approached record companies. He got a song publishing deal, and then a record contract. Back in the studio, the album was recorded to sound just like the demos, sparse and simple, and that did the trick. American radio programmers found *Look Sharp!* to their taste, and Joe was on his way. A throat problem forced cancellation of much of his first U.S. tour, but a second album and new tour in the fall of 1979 should put his career back on the track.

RECOMMENDED: *Look Sharp!, I'm the Man* (A&M).

THE JACKSONS

Discovered by Diana Ross in their native Gary, Indiana, the Jackson Five were groomed for a year by Motown before the incendiary "I Want You Back" was unleashed in 1969. It was the first of four straight number 1 singles, with baby brother Michael taking the lead vocals. ("ABC" won a Grammy in 1971). It may have been teenybop music, but it was the wildest, most dynamic teenstuff ever heard. In 1976, the group (sans Jermaine) moved to Epic, became the Jacksons, and began experimenting. There was an increase in solo albums, the sound jumped from Motown to Philly and then all over the musical map. While they continue to put out solid records, with flashes of genius, nothing they've done can compare with the early Motown sides, which also turned out to be that company's last gasp with teen music.

RECOMMENDED: *Greatest Hits, Dancin' Machine, Moving Violation* (Motown).

MICK JAGGER

He writes songs and sings them for the Rolling Stones. Jagger was a middle-class student at the London School of Economics when he helped start the Stones. Like his peers, he had a bohemian, you might even call it "political," bent that found its outlet in black American music. In retrospect, it's obvious that

Jagger knew something about media manipulation and image making all along as the Stones grew and grew, evolving from scruffy social deviants to blues purists to soul men to rockers to psychedelic to politically aware outsiders to harder-edged rockers to the greatest rock band in the world to exiles on Main Street to jaded jet setters to untouchable narcissists to 60s survivors to scrappers holding their own against the challenge of the new wave. Along the way he acted in several movies, married a Nicaraguan aristocrat who later left him, and handled the Stones' business affairs in a way that made you think the guy might have attended the London School of Economics.

TOMMY JAMES & THE SHONDELLS

One of the few consistently excellent bands of the "bubblegum" era, the Shondells ran a string of hits from 1965 to 1970, although their first big single, "Hanky Panky," was actually recorded in 1960! Formed by a bunch of junior high school friends in Dayton, Ohio, Tommy James and the Shondells recorded a few local singles for small labels while going to school and playing the club circuit, but it wasn't until a deejay somewhere discovered one of those records and turned it into a regional, then national hit that they became full-time rock 'n' rollers. Once established as major stars, TJ and the Shondells went on to produce some of the more memorable 45s of the 60s; "I Think We're Alone Now," "Crimson and Clover," "Mirage," "Mony Mony," and "Gettin' Together." James's sexy voice and the band's organ-ized pop sound made every release a chart topper, until the changes in music and problems with drugs ended their reign, around 1970. Since the breakup of the group, Tommy James has returned as a solo performer (after a recuperative period away from music), while some of the group members formed a short-lived unit called Hog Heaven.

RECOMMENDED: *20 Greatest Hits* (Tee-Vee International Records).

JAN AND DEAN

Jan Berry (b. April 3, 1941, Los Angeles) and Dean Torrence (b. March 10, 1940, Los Angeles) sold nearly ten million records in their ten years as Jan and Dean, not counting their first record "Jenny Lee," credited to Jan and Arnie (Ginsberg) but also featuring Dean. Girls, surfing, and hot rods were usually the topic of Jan Berry's songs like "Surf City," "Little Old Lady From Pasadena," and the prophetic "Dead Man's Curve" (Jan was paralyzed for over a year from a 1965 automobile accident, suffering extensive brain damage from which he has never fully recovered). But these two good-looking California hunks with the high boyish harmonies also embodied everything that was Southern California, the teenage promised land, even to the point of playing the Abbott and Costello of pop in their roles as emcees of the *T.A.M.I. Show*. Jan's accident brought their collaboration to an end until 1973, when they staged an unsuccessful reunion show at a Surfer's Stomp. But in 1978, the pair tentatively tried again, making their official comeback performance at a Murray the K oldies show in New York and bringing the crowd to its feet as much for Jan's exhilirating defiance of his paralysis as for the exuberance of the songs they sang.

RECOMMENDED: Numerous 45 and album releases on the Arwin, Dove, Challenge, and Liberty labels. Best compilation is the *Jan and Dean Anthology Album* on United Artists.

AL JARREAU

One of the many figures in the jazz world to come to the popular forefront in the 70s after fusion and disco put a premium on expert performance in the studio, Jarreau is unusual in that he doesn't really fit those molds. He's an old fashioned scat singer, in the tradition of Lambert, Hendricks and Ross, born and bred in the heartland of Milwaukee. His mid-70s debut revealed Jarreau to be a consummate musician. He has gone on to expand his popularity to Europe, using a sparse but effective backup of piano, bass, drums and vibraphones.

RECOMMENDED: *Glow, We Got By* (Warner Brothers).

JAY AND THE AMERICANS

In the early 60s, Jay Black, Kenny Vance, Howie Kane, Sandy Deane and Marty Sanders were the last gasp of the vocal group explosion, a clean scrubbed package designed to translate easily from Asbury Park to Las Vegas. The theme song, "Only In America," gave you a good idea of where these guys were coming from, and other hits like "Come a Little Bit Closer," "Cara Mia," "Some Enchanted Evening," and "Let's Lock the Door (and Throw Away the Key)" kept them going for several years after being outdated.

RECOMMENDED: *Greatest Hits* (Cameo).

JEFFERSON AIRPLANE/STARSHIP

Psychedelic pied pipers of the San Francisco movement, the Airplane vocal attack featured the unabashed romanticism of Marty Balin and the steely bite of Grace Slick (who had replaced original female singer Signe Anderson early on). Paul Kantner and Jorma Kaukonen provided the guitar pyrotechnics; drummers came and went, while Jack Casady held down bass. Originally a folk-rock band, the Airplane grew increasingly louder, more complex, and, finally, more "political" by the end of the decade. Balin then left and the loss hurt immediately; there were solo albums and spinoff groups, but none came near the richness and power of the original Airplane. Neither, for that matter, did the Airplane itself, which put out a string of dispirited albums. Finally, in 1973, then-lovers Slick and Kantner formed the Starship; Balin was the only other Airplane member present, but he made a big difference. On record, the Starship is lighter and tighter, more melodic and less experimental, than the old Airplane. But the sound is right in tune with the 70s, and the hits started coming again. Always a turbulent group, their current status is questionable, as Balin has gotten fed up again and Slick is apparently leaving to fight her alcoholism.

RECOMMENDED: *Surrealistic Pillow, Crown of Creation, Bless Its Pointed Little Head, Volunteers* (RCA); *Dragonfly, Red Octopus, Spitfire,* (Grunt).

WAYLON JENNINGS

A West Texan who played in the last version of Buddy Holly's Crickets, Jennings spent years in Nashville trying, and failing, through little fault of his own, to forge a sound that would set him apart from other country singers. His music has always had more beat than Nashville could stomach, a result of his rocking heritage, but his records never showed it. Finally, in the early 70s, allied with Tompall Glaser and Willie Nelson, Jennings fought fiercely to become first an Outlaw, then the baddest Outlaw of 'em all. He took creative control of his own music and the results were impressive; he even used his own touring band (the Waylors) in the studio, a Nashville heresy. His songs all retain a cowboy-as-last-American-hero flavor, thanks in part to their themes and in part for his resonant voice and sense of arrangement; though he writes little, his material is amazingly consistent from song to song. He plays a rugged chicken-pickin' guitar, too. As his popularity has grown, Jennings has become increasingly self-conscious, sometimes even a self-parody, but for a few years there he was making some of the boldest and prettiest music in the country.

RECOMMENDED: *Best of Waylon Jennings, Vol. 1-2, Ramblin' Man* (RCA); with Willie Nelson—*Waylon and Willie* (RCA); with Willie Nelson, Jessi Colter, Tompall Glaser—*Wanted: The Outlaws* (RCA).

JETHRO TULL

Originally a progressive blues/jazz outfit in the late 60s, Jethro Tull changed character when founder/guitarist Mick Abrahams left soon after the first album's release. Under the subsequent leadership of flautist/vocalist Ian Anderson, Tull became a hybrid folk/heavy metal band, hugely successful through the release of records like *Aqualung, Thick as a Brick*, and *Songs from the Wood*. Over the years, personnel changes and musical shifts have brought the group varied levels of commercial success. With a recent taste for less rock and more traditional English music in their records, Tull would seem to be leaving their fans behind, however, their popularity as a major concert attraction has never seriously waned. The frenetic gyrations of ringmaster Anderson, combined with numerous theatric inventions, make a Jethro Tull concert into a true rock spectacle. The group's current lineup includes Martin Barre (guitar), John Evan (keyboards), Barriemore Barlow (drums), John Glascock (bass), and David Palmer (keyboards).

RECOMMENDED: *Aqualung, Living in the Past, Stormwatch* (Chrysalis).

BILLY JOEL

Trained on classical piano, born and bred in the music-rich Long Island environment, Joel spent his first years as a professional musician in the 60s playing with numerous Long Island bands, the most famous of which was the Hassles. After quitting that group to form a duo which never got off the ground, Joel concentrated on song-writing and played solo on the local lounge circuit before being discovered in the early 70s. Joel scored immediately with the hit single "Piano Man" and went on to become one of the most popular singer-songwriters of the 70s, with such hits as "Captain Jack," "Movin' Out," "Only the Good Die Young" and "Big Shot."

RECOMMENDED: *Streetlife Serenade, Turnstiles, The Stranger, 52nd Street* (Columbia).

DAVID JOHANSEN

Born in Staten Island, Johansen founded the New York Dolls in 1972 and led them by dressing up in drag and makeup and playing the most chaotic music imaginable. A vocalist of more spirit than talent, Johansen's nasal growl was a prime component of the Dolls' sound. They broke up in 1975 and Johansen resurfaced in a totally new band called The Staten Island Boys in which Johansen took his revamped New York soul music to the clubs of America and found a much more favorable response than he had ever received as a Doll. With two albums already released, he seems assured of a place in the rock world.

RECOMMENDED: *David Johansen* (Blue Sky).

ELTON JOHN

Born Reginald Dwight in Middlesex, England to music-minded parents, John was encouraged to play the piano and enrolled in the London Royal Academy of Music at age 11. At 14, he started out playing R&B in a band called Bluesology, then later joined Long John Baldry's blues band. While he was scouting around for his own recording contract, John came into contact with lyricist Bernie Taupin, and they began writing together. The two collaborated on all of John's biggest hits; "Crocodile Rock," "Bennie and the Jets," "Don't Let the Sun Go Down on Me," "Philadelphia Freedom," "Rocket Man," "Saturday Night's All Right for Fighting", and John went on to become an international media celebrity, fronting the covers of *Time* and *Newsweek* and starring in the film version of *Tommy*.

RECOMMENDED: *Elton John, Tumbleweed Connection, Madman across the Water, Goodbye Yellow Brick Road, Capt. Fantastic and the Brown Dirt Cowboy, Don't Shoot Me, I'm Only the Piano Player* (MCA).

ROBERT JOHNSON

Of Johnson, we know the following. He was born around 1910, and seems to be from the Clarkdale area of the Mississippi Delta. He played country dances; he rambled a lot, as far north as Canada, east to New York City, west to Texas. At first he was, according to Son House, a very ordinary country bluesman. He soon came to crystallize, to personify, the form; Son House said he must have sold his soul to the devil to play such perfect blues. Nearly all his songs are about doom: the flight from doom, embracing doom, facing doom down and maybe even whuppin' it; he recorded only 29 songs, in Houston, in 1936-37. His guitar playing was startling—piercing, tense, rhythmic; his voice was high and full of urgency. His lyrics, full of double entendres, are some of the most evocative in all of blues. He was killed in 1938, supposedly by a jealous lover. All else is mystery; there were not even any known pictures of Johnson until one was finally discovered in 1973. Johnson's undeniable influence lives on; in the blues of Muddy Waters, Johnny Shines and others, in the rock of the Rolling Stones, Eric Clapton, etc.

RECOMMENDED: *King of the Delta Blues Singers, Vols. 1-2* (Columbia).

BRIAN JONES

When the Rolling Stones formed in London in 1961, the only experienced musician in the band was Brian Jones. Jones had played in several blues bands when he met Mick Jagger and Keith Richards at a club called the Bricklayers Arms. After the Stones formed officially in 1963 Jones went on to provide an adventurous edge to the group's sound, playing lead and slide guitar as well as sitar, dulcimer, recorder and other instruments that were unusual for a blues band. When psychedelia became a force in the late 60s Jones helped the band put together its most adventurous album, Their Satanic Majesties Request. The Eastern musical influences and drug ambience were Jones' doing but when the album sold poorly Jones became depressed and eventually left the group in 1969. Jones died a month later, drowned in his own swimming pool.

RECOMMENDED: *Their Satanic Majesties Request* (London).

GRACE JONES

She rides onto the stage in a gleaming chrome motorcycle for one gig, then surrounds herself with male models in various states of undress for another. Grace Jones is the toast of the jet set, a disco queen who has been called the Dietrich of the New Decade. Her audience is made up of celebrities from Yves Saint Laurent, who designed an outfit on the spot when her clothes were torn from her body at a Paris show, to Bianca Jagger and Andy Warhol. The former model is not much of a singer, but that hasn't stopped her albums and disco hit, "I Need a Man," from doing well.

RECOMMENDED: *Portfolio* (Island).

JANIS JOPLIN

Janis Joplin (b. January 19, 1943, Port Arthur, Texas) created one of rock's few positive, assertive female images for females. She was determined to "take it to the limit" no matter what the consequence. In her case, the consequence was death of a drug overdose on October 4, 1970, shortly after recording the album *Pearl* which included her first Number One single, Kris Kristofferson's "Me and Bobby McGee." Janis' need to love and be loved was a constant theme in the songs she sang; from the down, dirty blues of Bessie Smith and Leadbelly she sang in Texas clubs to the electric blues she belted out with San Francisco's Big Brother and the Holding Company to songs recorded with her own bands after she left Big Brother in 1968. A year earlier, Janis had stepped into rock 'n' roll prominence with a white-hot set with Big Brother at the Monterey Pop Festival. While she left behind a comparitively brief recorded legacy (at least compared to Hendrix and Morrison), she also left behind a wild and wooly memory.

RECOMMENDED: *Cheap Thrills* (with Big Brother); *Pearl, Greatest Hits* (Columbia).

JOURNEY

Formed in the 70s around ex-Santana guitarist Neil Schon and keyboardist Gregg Rolie, this San Francisco hard rock outfit was completed by ex-Zappa drummer Aynsley Dunbar and bassist Ross Valory. Journey quickly became one of the west coast's best rock 'n' roll bands and gradually built a concert following in the rest of the country based on high energy sets that featured Schon's greased lightning guitar playing. After producer Roy Thomas Baker (Queen, Cars) began to work with them, Journey's albums started to sell as well. *Infinity*, which included the debut of vocalist Steve Perry, was the band's first platinum album. Dunbar left the band before their latest album, *Evolution*.

RECOMMENDED: *Journey* (Columbia).

KALEIDOSCOPE

Back when every other person on Sunset Strip was tripping on acid, back when eclectic was still a complimentary adjective, Kaleidoscope was the trippiest and most eclectic rock band in the country. They experimented with Indian and Eastern modes, with old jazz; they recorded country songs and Chicago blues. But everything they did rocked; it was an unusual and highly satisfying fusion. Of course they never enjoyed a shred of commercial success; in fact, hardly anybody outside of L.A. had even heard of them. All five members seemed to be ex-folkies who'd seen the rock 'n' roll light; all except the drummer played a variety of exotic instruments, and none except current Jackson Browne guitarist David Lindley seem to still be in the business (though one can't be sure, since some of them often switched names).

RECOMMENDED: *Side Trips, Kaleidoscope* (Epic).

DOUG KERSHAW

Kershaw's big break came in 1969, when he joined Bob Dylan as a guest on the first network *Johnny Cash Show*. Prior to that, he was known on the country circuit as an irrepressible Cajun fiddler, though he had been in Nashville so long that his Louisiana roots weren't all that conspicuous. After the TV show, he was known to the hippies, college students, and Bob Dylan fans in general. He played up to them shamelessly; his music became a catalog of flashy, empty gimmicks devoid of any of the deep feeling found in the best Cajun music *and* the best Nashville country. Still, his "Louisiana Man" (first recorded when he and his brother Rusty were a duo) remains a classic song.

RECOMMENDED: *The Cajun Way* (Warner Bros.); *Louisiana Man* (Hickory).

CHAKA KHAN

First she was the lead singer of Rufus, an integrated group that played a light brand of funk and turned out a handful of singles ("Show Me Something Good") that crossed over to the pop charts more readily than hard funk does. She's energetic, and her voice always conveys a cheerful, wholesome sexiness. When she left the group to go solo in 1977, she continued in that style, but with a more mature outlook and a fresh attack. Without her, the group was not successful.

RECOMMENDED: *Rufus, Rags to Rufus* (ABC); *Chaka* (Warner Bros.).

ALBERT KING

Born in Indianola, Mississippi, raised in several Arkansas towns, King was a key figure in the postwar St. Louis blues scene. His left-handed guitar playing owes something to B. B. King (no relation), but Albert has a tone of his own. His voice is a slight, wispy instrument in itself. King toiled long and hard in the urban blues jungle without ever quite reaching the status of a B. B. or a Muddy Waters, but in the late 60s, recording for a soul label, he came up with "Born under a Bad Sign," one of those songs that alludes directly to a current fad (astrology, in this case) and is therefore unstoppable. It won him bookings in the hippie halls but his concerts tended to drag on in long-winded displays of his (limited) guitar virtuosity.

RECOMMENDED: *Born under a Bad Sign, Live Wire/Blues Power* (Stax).

B. B. KING

A man who has made an enormous contribution to the blues, King started out playing country blues and gospel in Mississippi during the 40s before moving to Memphis where his live performance radio show earned him a big name in the blues world. His first records for Kent were instant hits; "Three O'Clock Blues," "Sweet Sixteen," "Don't Answer the Door" and a host of others. King worked nonstop through the 50s and 60s, making tremendous breakthroughs with young white audiences in the late 60s and netting his biggest hit "The Thrill Is Gone." King's greatest popularity came in the late 70s when he played everywhere from Las Vegas to the Soviet Union and made a series of big selling records with the Crusaders.

RECOMMENDED: *Midnight Believer, Lucille, Completely Well* (MCA).

BEN E. KING

The lead singer on a slew of 1959-60 Drifters hits; "There Goes My Baby," "Dance with Me," "This Magic Moment," "Save the Last Dance for Me," "True Love, True Love," King went solo in 1961 with the enduring "Spanish Harlem," one of Phil Spector's first productions. It was a Top 10 pop record, as was "Stand By Me" later the same year. For the rest of the 60s, he continued to score moderately high on the R&B charts, if not pop. Then he disappeared, until "Supernatural Thing" in 1975 became one of the first disco records to penetrate the pop Top 10. There followed a mildly-successful collaboration with the Average White Band in 1977, and King hasn't been heard from since.

RECOMMENDED: *Spanish Harlem, Greatest Hits* (Atco).

CAROLE KING

Along with her then-husband Gerry Goffin, she wrote who knows how many of those wonderful Brill Building hit singles in the early 60s. Later, she was a member of a soft rock group called the City. Her first solo album, in 1970, received rave reviews, but nobody was ready for what happened with the release of *Tapestry* the next year; it became the biggest selling album of all time (up until then). King's soothing soft rock voice, delicate piano, and love-won/love-lost lyrics put her at the top of the singer/songwriter pantheon, where she stayed a few years. Then she lost her edge; by the end of the decade, she was living in Colorado, releasing insubstantial albums, and keeping an even lower profile than before.

Photo by Jim McGuire

RECOMMENDED: *Tapestry, Greatest Hits* (Ode).

FREDDIE KING

One of the greatest guitarists to come out of Houston's Third Ward in the 50s, Freddie King used his hard-edged, T. Bone Walker-influenced blues playing to earn him the early hit single "Stumble." In turn, King went on to influence the blues guitar playing of Eric Clapton and Peter Green. King continued to play well into the 70s, recording with Leon Russell's Shelter label and scoring another hit with the blistering rocker "Going Down." King died in 1976 of hepatitis at the age of 42.

RECOMMENDED: *Texas Cannonball* (Shelter); *Larger Than Life* (RSO).

JONATHAN KING

This British singer/songwriter started out as an antihip singer in 1968 with his hit single "Everyone's Gone To the Moon" and went on to write a pop column, a novel, and host a television show. After doing some production work King started U.K. records in the early 70s and signed 10cc.

RECOMMENDED: *Jonathan King Or Then Again* (Pye).

KING CRIMSON

Guitarist Robert Fripp assembled King Crimson in 1969 to play his forward looking, heavy metal space rock with its technical demands and futurist themes. Ian McDonald played reeds, woodwinds, keyboards and vibes; Greg Lake played bass; Michael Giles, drums and Peter Sinfield wrote lyrics. It was a supergroup: McDonald and Giles went on to form their own band, with McDonald eventually starting Foreigner; and Greg Lake helped form Emerson, Lake & Palmer; Mel Collins, Keith Tippett and Peter Giles joined for the second album when McDonald and Lake left. Gordon Haskell and Andy McCullogh replaced the Giles brothers on bass and drums for the third album, then the rhythm section became Boz and Ian Wallace for *Islands*. Bassist John Wetton and drummer Bill Bruford provided Crimson's best rhythm section in the waning, mid-70s days of the group's existence.

RECOMMENDED: *In the Court of the Crimson King, Lizard, Lark's Tongue in Aspic*, (Atlantic).

KINGSMEN

They came out of the Pacific Northwest in the early 60s with one of the original punk rock sounds, heavily hooked around a tinny, repetitive organ. The group was formed in Portland, Oregon and made it big on the strength of a remake of a 1956 R & B song by Richard Berry called "Louie Louie." They did it crudely, with emphasis on the heavy staccatto beat and this is what made it such a big hit. The song's influence on the Kinks and the Who in England as well as a number of American groups was immediately obvious. The band scored another minor hit with "Little Latin Lupe Lu" before breaking up.

RECOMMENDED: *Kingsmen's Greatest Hits* (Wand).

KINGSTON TRIO

Dave Guard, Bob Shane and Nick Reynolds, known as the Kingston Trio, are credited with starting the folk craze of the late 50s and early 60s when their version of an old folk song, "Tom Dooley," became a big hit single. This California-based group sported a cleaner than clean cut image and always wore matching striped sports shirts while presenting a collegiate image that had a lot to do with the acceptance of folk music among the trendy college crowd. After woodshedding at a local San Francisco club called the Purple Onion the group hit it big and continued to enjoy popularity until 1968, when they broke up.

RECOMMENDED: *The Kingston Trio* (Capitol).

KINKS

The brothers Davies, Ray and Dave, have been musical partners in this long-lived band since 1963. In the course of over fifteen years, the Kinks have gone through numerous phases, some more musically rewarding than others, and contributed greatly to the growth and development of rock 'n' roll. In the beginning, the Kinks were a singles band, releasing a string of great songs ("You Really Got Me," "All Day and All of the Night," "Well Respected Man," "Tired of Waiting," and others) all penned by the perceptive and witty Raymond Douglas Davies. As time wore on, and Davies tired of short singles as his prime medium, the Kinks began to try larger and more grandiose projects: concept albums and soundtracks, all the while refining and improving their studio abilities and musical sophistication. After a somewhat dispiriting loss in popularity in the early 70s, the Kinks began fragmenting, and a series of changes in personnel shook the originally strong ties that bound the group. Eventually settling on a lineup that revolves around Ray and Dave as the foundation, with the other members relegated to support roles, the group has found a new audience, regained their commercial niche, and seems indestructible. Regardless of what the future may bring, the Kinks have already delivered many great albums.

RECOMMENDED: (recent LPs) *Sleepwalker* (Arista); *Every Body's in Show Business* (Warner Bros).

KISS

The biggest American band of the late 70s, Kiss was formed during the height of the early 70s glitter rock era and took their cues from Alice Cooper to put together a stage show that had a lot more spectacle than music. The idea was a huge success, as the band's Kabuki inspired outfits created a cartoon image that kids went nuts for and led to television, film projects and several top selling comic books. Bassist Gene Simmons is the fire breathing lizard man, guitarist Paul Stanley is the painted lover, guitarist Ace Frehley the man from space, and drummer Peter Criss the pussy cat. Their shows have featured some of the most imaginative staging in rock history.

RECOMMENDED: *Kiss, Double Platinum,* (Casablanca).

KLAATU

The only thing the Klaatu phenomenon proves is that, when it comes to the Beatles, there is one born every minute. When *Klaatu* was released in August 1976, little was known of the group and, judging by sales and critical response to its *Sgt. Pepper* overtones and psychedelic indulgences, few people cared to find out. The album had been purchased as a completed master from the Canadian Daffodil label and Klaatu manager Frank Davies without any background information. But when a rock columnist for the *Providence Journal* put forth the proposition that Klaatu was in fact the Beatles reunited, sales soared and everybody got into the act, searching out clues á la "Paul Is Dead." The sound of the album did recall late 60s Beatle works like *Pepper* and *The Beatles*, as well as juvenile Pink Floyd, and manager Davis did nothing to abate the hype. But, in fact, Klaatu was not the Beatles but a group of Canadian sessionmen too obscure to name here and after all was revealed, interest in Klaatu plummeted along with sales of later albums *Hope* and *Sir Army Suit.* Klaatu made charmingly oblique pop, richly colored and often graced with memorable song hooks (the Carpenters covered "Calling All Occupants of Interplanetary Craft"), but after the Beatle hoax, there was only one question left: Who cares?

RECOMMENDED: *Klaatu* (Capitol).

GLADYS KNIGHT & THE PIPS

Gladys and the Pips have been around for close to 25 years now; they first recorded "Every Beat of My Heart" when she was a shy Georgia teenager, and before that she'd won a Ted Mack Amateur Hour contest. The group has enjoyed a few uptempo hits, particularly when they were part of the Motown stable, but they have always had their best luck with ballads such as "Midnight Train to Georgia" and "Imagination." Then Gladys can give her smooth, silky voice full play; her timing and phrasing are impeccable, and the three male Pips "color" her words with their background singing. Gladys has also acted on TV and in the movies. In 1978, she recorded an LP without the Pips, and it remains to be seen whether she will work solo, continue with them, or do a little of both.

RECOMMENDED: *Second Anniversary, Still Together* (Buddah).

ALEXIS KORNER

Peter Townshend once said Alexis Korner should be carried around London for the rest of his life because of his role in bringing the Rolling Stones together. Add to that his part in the formation of Free and the general renaissance of English blues in the 60s and Alexis Korner deserves far greater than that. Born of Austrian and Greek/Turkish parents in Paris in 1928, Korner, after a period gigging with English traditional jazz bands, followed his own blues instincts by forming a band of his own, Blues Incorporated, and starting a club of his own, the Ealing Rhythm and Blues Club, in 1962. Soon he had gathered around him an all-star cast of would-be British rock stars that included not only various Stones but Jack Bruce, Lee Jackson (of the Nice), and John McLaughlin. Through the 60s and into the 70s, Korner continued to form bands and accept young singers and players as proteges (including a teenaged Robert Plant). He still records infrequently, his most recent release a rather disappointing superstar outing called *Get Off My Cloud* (Columbia). The *Bootleg Him* (Warner Bros.) compilation is far more representative of Korner's place in not just British but world rock history.

DANNY KORTCHMAR

One of the premier session guitarists in Los Angeles, Kortchmar is part of the crack studio band the Section, which has backed James Taylor, Jackson Browne, Carole King and Crosby, Stills & Nash. Kortchmar, a New York native, started playing when he was ten, and first recorded in a group called the King Bees. In the 60s he formed the Flying Machine with James Taylor, then The City with Carole King. He also was a member of Joe Mama and Attitudes. His solo album allows Kortchmar to stretch out and choose his own contexts to good effect.

RECOMMENDED: *Kootch* (Warner Bros.).

LEO KOTTKE

This Minnesota guitarist has enjoyed a small, but devout, following throughout the 70s. His image is that of the solo acoustic guitarist, though he has worked with bands and electric instruments. He's taken only a few shots at singing, since he himself says his voice sounds like "geese farts." Like John Fahey, he has woven many strands of American music, from blues, jazz and ragtime through pop and rock to country to folk, into a seamless and stately music that defies categorization, but does suggest the incredible breadth and depth of our native traditions.

RECOMMENDED: *My Feet Are Smiling, The Best* (Capitol).

KRAFTWERK

Kraftwerk's bleak industrial vision of music (Kraftwerk is German for "electric power plant") has not prevented them from reaping hits as unlikely as a 22-minute succession of mechanical rhythms, monotonic vocals, and electronic beeps arranged in hummable order and titled "Autobahn." Formed by two students from Dusseldorf, Germany, Ralf Hutter and Florian Schneider met at a classical music conservatory in 1968. Kraftwerk was the result of Hutter and Schneider' desire for a symphonic electronic sound, something the conservatory was not about to provide. They built their own studio in Dusseldorf, Kling Klang, and started making records at about the same time other German rock groups like Tangerine Dream, Can, Amon Duul II, and Faust were experimenting with electronics. The big difference was the Kraftwerk had hits in America—"Autobahn" and a series of *disco* hits based on a mathematical beat that actually transcends the cold impersonal melodic thread of their compositions. Kraftwerk rarely tour (one 1976 U.S. trek to capitalize on the AM-FM inroads made by "Autobahn") and still record at Kling Klang. David Bowie once called them his favorite group and despite the humanoid image projected by the press, Kraftwerk are treated with a cautious respect in discussions about electronic music and its pop possibilities. Hutter and Schneider have recorded as Kraftwerk both as a duo and as a four-piece with different personnel.

RECOMMENDED: *Autobahn,* (Mercury); *Radio-Activity,* (Capitol).

KRIS KRISTOFFERSON

A former Rhodes Scholar from Brownsville, Texas, Kristofferson as much as anybody increased the range of country music in the early 70s. He'd been kicking around town for some time as a janitor and songwriter of mainstream-sounding Nashville stuff, but his songs quickly became something entirely new. They were self-consciously poetic, used unusual metaphors and rhyme schemes and, perhaps worst of all in macho Nashville, presented the image of an emotionally vulnerable male. In the beginning, he had as big or as small a following among urban folkie types as among traditional country fans. But when Johnny Cash gave Kristofferson the seal of approval, the rest of Music City was quick to fall in line. Soon everybody was recording his songs "Me and Bobby McGee," "Help Me Make It through the Night," "Sunday Mornin' Comin' Down," etc. Next, Kristofferson began recording them himself. His first album was a landmark, so much so that nobody seemed to notice how many of the songs were *too* wordy, how similar were the melodies and arrangements, or how feeble a singer Kris was. Subsequent albums seemed to indicate that, with a few exceptions, he'd exhausted his songwriting talent on that first effort. He quickly moved into films, and before long was concentrating on his acting more than his music. He still tours, though, with wife Rita Coolidge, and still puts out albums regularly.

RECOMMENDED: *The Silver Tongued Devil and I, Me and Bobby McGee, Jesus Was a Capricorn* (Columbia).

JIM KWESKIN

New England bred Jim Kweskin formed one of the first of the jug band revival groups in 1963 in the folk music hotbed of Cambridge, Massachusetts. It was an all star group that included Geoff and Maria Muldaur, Richard Greene, Bill Keith, Mel Lyman and Fritz Richmond. The group helped popularize the good time jug band music to a young white audience and eventually broke up in 1968 after recording several albums. Kweskin went on to perform as a solo entertainer.

RECOMMENDED: *Jim Kweskin Jug Band* (Vanguard); *Jim Kweskin* (Warner Brothers).

LABELLE

Originally known as Patti LaBelle and the Blue Belles (of "I Sold My Heart to the Junkman" fame), this vocal trio is now best remembered for "Lady Marmalade," a New Orleans voodoo song that was a huge crossover hit in 1975. With their heads and feathers and spangles and space age finery, they were a special favorite among New York glitterati. But they soon broke up, with LaBelle and Nona Hendryx finding moderate (at best) success as solo acts.

RECOMMENDED: *Nightblrds, Chameleon* (Epic).

DENNY LAINE

The British singer/songwriter/guitarist got his start in the pop world when he formed the Moody Blues in the early 60s and led that band to its first hits, including "Go Now," before leaving in 1966 to form an experimental classical rock group with several string players from London's Royal Academy of Music. Laine went on to play with Ginger Baker's Air Force, where he sang his very fine song "Man of Constant Sorrow." More recently Laine has played with Paul McCartney & Wings.

RECOMMENDED: *Go Now* (London).

RONNIE LANE

One of the original members of the early 60s mod band the Small Faces, Ronnie Lane continued to be that group's bassist and second vocalist when Steve Marriott was replaced by vocalist Rod Stewart and guitarist Ron Wood. Even with Rod Stewart in the band Lane's vocal on "Maybe I'm Amazed" was always a high point of Faces concerts. After that band broke up in the late 70s Lane went on to make the interesting *Mahoney's Last Stand* with Ron Wood and the tremendous cooperative project with The Who's Peter Townshend, *Rough Mix*.

RECOMMENDED: *Rough Mix* (MCA).

NICOLETTE LARSON

The Kansas City bred Larson moved to L.A. in the mid 70s, hung around the singer/songwriter scene with Emmylou Harris and Linda Ronstadt, then sang backup harmonies for Neil Young on his albums *American Stars and Bars* and *Comes A Time* before recording on her own. She had guest-starred with Commander Cody and the Lost Planet Airmen on tour and got a lot of offers to record, but finally chose Warner Brothers, who rewarded her by turning "A Lotta Love" for her debut album into a late 70s hit.

RECOMMENDED: *Nicolette Larson* (Warner Brothers).

LEADBELLY

Called the "King of twelve string guitar," Huddie Ledbetter, aka Leadbelly, wrote and performed some of the best known blues songs of all time like "Midnight Special," "Good Night Irene," "Rock Island Line" and "Old Cottonfields at Home." Born in Louisiana, he worked the fields for years before setting out for a life as an itinerant musician. He collected many songs and experiences, landed in and out of jail, and was finally taken under the wing of Alan Lomax, who recorded him and arranged for several collegiate concert tours. He died in 1949.

RECOMMENDED: *Leadbelly* (Columbia).

LED ZEPPELIN

If Led Zeppelin are not the biggest rock group in the world right now (the Stones have a claim in, too), they are certainly the world's premier heavy-metal battalion. Robert Plant (b. August 20, 1948, Bromwich, England) is the classic macho screamer, John Bonham (b. May 31, 1949, Redditch, England) the thunder behind Plant's vocal lightning, John Paul Jones (b. John Baldwin, January 3, 1946, Kent, England) the anchoring bass and keyboard coloring, and Jimmy Page (b. January 9, 1944, Middlesex) the ultimate guitar hero and master of the six cosmic strings. Page deserves an entry all his own, documenting his extensive and lucrative session career which caused him in 1965 to turn down an offer to replace Eric Clapton in the Yardbirds (Jeff Beck was the lucky winner). But Page did join the band a year later, dueling on guitar with Beck until the latter left to pursue a solo career. Page was with the Yardbirds right down to their last 1968 gasp and when he went to form his own band after their demise he did so under the name New Yardbirds. He can thank the late Keith Moon for the name Led Zeppelin; Moon apparently made a crack about the band going down like a lead balloon and the name stuck. The Zeppelin repertoire, bolstered by a few Page originals and Yardbird bastardizations, consisted of blues standards and even the Beatles' "I Saw Her Standing There." Led Zeppelin got their Atlantic deal, as the story goes, on the strength of their reputations (manager Peter Grant apparently had no demo tape to play Atlantic exec Jerry Wexler). But their reputation as Led Zeppelin was made with their first two albums, brilliant if heavy-handed blues-rock offensives, the stop-time "Black Dog," that laid the base for later excursions, and their seven-minute standard "Stairway to Heaven." The holders of numerous record sales and concert attendance records, Led Zeppelin will be forever known as the archetypal blues-busting HM ensemble, although Page's interest in mysticism (and Aleister Crowley in particular) and Plant's considerable lyrical talents have resulted in classic Zep outings like the hypnotic "Kashmir" and "Stairway." But there's also "Whole Lotta Love," "Immigrant Song," and "Trampled Underfoot." With one foot in British blues, and another in the acoustic stream of groups like the Incredible String Band, plus singer/songwriters like Roy Harper, Led Zeppelin reigns supreme, even if their song remains the same.

RECOMMENDED: *Led Zeppelin, Led Zeppelin II, Led Zeppelin III, ZOFO* (the fourth album), *Houses of the Holy* (Atlantic); *Physical Graffiti, In Through the Out Door* (Swan Song).

ALVIN LEE

Alvin Lee became known as one of the hottest British electric guitarists in the mid-60s on the strength of his knowledgeable updates of jazz/R&B guitar stylists like Grant Green. With bassist Leo Lyons, keyboardist Chick Churchill and drummer Ric Lee he formed Ten Years After, which quickly became one of the most popular groups on the late 60s/early 70s concert circuit. Lee's greatest fame came after his high energy performance of "Goin' Home" at Woodstock became one of the centerpieces of the Woodstock film. Lee's first solo album with Mylon Lefevre was a high point for both performers in an easy country/rock mold while Lee's subsequent solo efforts have tried to rekindle the flash of his TYA days.

RECOMMENDED: *On the Road To Freedom* (Columbia); *Alvin Lee & Company* (London).

BRENDA LEE

A cute bobbysoxer from Atlanta, Georgia, Brenda Lee was a little girl with a big voice. She started to have hits when she was only eleven years old but her biggest hit came in 1960, when "I'm Sorry" hit the top spot on the hit parade. She continued to have hits in the early 60s; "I Want To Be Wanted," "You Can Depend On Me," "Emotions," "Fool Number One" and "Dum Dum," before retiring.

RECOMMENDED: *Ten Golden Years* (Decca).

THE LEFT BANKE

A deft New York-based pop quintet, the Left Banke appeared at the point in the mid-60s when experimentation in rock arrangements and instrumentation was spreading without yet being a really marketable idea. Leader Michael Brown, the son of a concert violinist, knew how to couple Baroque melodic styles with hit-parade lyrics. The results of his efforts, 45s like "Walk Away Renee," "Pretty Ballerina," and "Desiree," were given effective melancholy readings by the band's vulnerable-looking lead tenor, Steve Martin, also a songwriter. But after the third immaculate single, Martin quit. Tom Finn took over as frontman, then the Left Banke dwindled to trio size and was gone. Had the band survived through 1968, it might well have won a substantial album-buying following, but the rock market was still singles-oriented when the Left Banke rose and fell. In two years the group had such a profound effect on other musicians, though, that its influence is still evident on bands today: the Cars' "Let's Go" is largely a reworking of "Desiree."

RECOMMENDED: *The Left Banke* (Smash).

JOHN LENNON

Liverpool-born John Lennon went from being an Elvis Presley-inspired Teddy Boy to forming the Beatles after meeting Paul McCartney. During the Beatles' glorious 60s run Lennon provided controversial and experimental leadership, some of the best rhythm guitar playing in rock history and combined with Paul McCartney for the most celebrated songwriting duo of the decade. Lennon went on to make a number of great solo albums after the Beatles breakup, including one with the New York band Elephant's

Memory. Lennon and his wife Yoko Ono began staging some of their special events like the Bed In for Peace while the Beatles were still together and continued after that band's split. Lennon has been in semi-retirement for several years and is generally considered to be the major obstacle to the much talked about Beatles reunion.

RECOMMENDED: *Imagine, Mind Games* (Capitol).

GARY LEWIS

The son of Jerry Lewis, Gary had his father's goofy looks and a throwback pop attitude in the mid-60s, when he surfaced with a carefully assembled sound which yielded an impressive string of hits; "This Diamond Ring," "Everybody Loves A Clown," "She's just My Style," "Without A Word of Warning," "Time," "You Don't Have To Paint Me A Picture" and "Save Your Heart For Me." Partial architect of this foolproof sound was Leon Russell.

RECOMMENDED: *Golden Greats* (Imperial).

JERRY LEE LEWIS

"The Killer" came roaring out of Ferriday, Louisiana in 1957 with "Whole Lotta Shakin' Going' On" and "Great Balls of Fire" on Sun Records, and hasn't looked back since. His suggestive singing, pounding boogie piano and redneck ways defined the essence of rockabilly. But when he married his 13-year old second cousin in 1958, his career plummeted, though he never stopped working. It wasn't until 1968, when he began recording hard core country ("Another Place, Another Time") that radio programmers began playing his records again. Since then, he has been a fixture on the country charts and has occasionally even made new forays into rock 'n' roll. When he's not shucking, his live shows remain among the most exciting in contemporary music, but his wild personal life—frequent marriages, even more frequent pills-liquor-and-violence binges, often draws more attention than his music.

RECOMMENDED: *Original Golden Hits, Vols. 1-3, Sunday Down South* (with Johnny Cash) (Sun); *Best of Jerry Lee Lewis, Vols. 1-2* (Mercury).

GORDON LIGHTFOOT

This melancholy, Toronto-based folkie has hung in there about fifteen years now, writing songs that become standards ("Early Morning Rain"), having the occasional hit single, and touring semi-regularly. Commercially, he's outlasted nearly all his peers. He's worked every which way, solo, with accompanying orchestra, and though he's never been particularly innovative, he does have a flair for translating folk into pop.

RECOMMENDED: *Best of Gordon Lightfoot, Vols. 1-2* (United Artists); *Sundown* (Warner Bros.).

LINDISFARNE

One of England's most enduring folk-rock institutions, Lindisfarne are still far bigger at home than they are in America, although their good-time blend of folk intimacy and rock energy owes as much to the American C&W spirit as it does to British musical tradition. A Newcastle aggregation signed to England's Charisma label in 1968 reportedly because the record company prez liked Ray Jackson's harmonica playing, Lindisfarne (Jackson; Alan Hull, voice and songs; Ray Laidlaw, drums; Rod Clements, bass, fiddle; Simon Cowe, guitar), had a number one album in England with *Fog on the Tyne* and a Top Five single in "Meet Me on the Corner," both of which crystallized the Lindisfarne sound and enthusiasm. But intragroup differences caused a split down the middle in 1973; Clements, Laidlaw, and Cowe forming the very-Lindisfarne-like Jack the Lad. Lindisfarne itself survived the split for only two more albums. But at home in Newcastle, Lindisfarne would reunite for an annual stand of Christmas concerts that led to the band's reformation in 1977.

RECOMMENDED: *Fog on the Tyne, Dingley Dell* (Elektra); *Back and Fourth* (Atco).

LITTLE FEAT

Little Feat are one of the three classic American rock 'n' roll bands; the other two are the Allman Brothers and Springsteen's E-Streeters, and their near dozen albums are the proof. Blues, rockabilly, country-fried folk, and the odd shade of jazz are all detectable in the band's sonic mural, but the magic ingredient was the late Lowell George's songs; "Willin'," "Strawberry Flats," and "Dixie Chicken" are the American experience translated into rock 'n' roll terms everybody can understand. Not everybody, however, understood in the beginning. When Little Feat released their debut LP in 1969, their record label reportedly only pressed 10,000 copies, hardly a demonstration of faith. George (an ex-Standell and Mother of Invention), bassist Roy Estrada (also a former Mother), drummer Richie Hayward (ex-Fraternity of Man), and pianist Bill Payne next made the stunning *Sailin' Shoes* in '72, which also didn't reap the commercial reward critics expected. *Dixie Chicken* saw the arrival of more Feat in guitarist Paul Barrere, percussionist Sam Clayton, and bassist Ken Gradney and after breaking up when *Chicken* didn't fatten their purses, the Feats gave it another go on *Feats Don't Fail Me New*. While Little Feat never became the major attraction their fans and critics hoped they'd be, they enjoyed a strong cultish fame that was at its highest when George suddenly died on June 29, 1979 in Washington, D.C. in the middle of a tour to support his first solo LP *Thanks I'll Eat It Here*. The band's future without George is uncertain, although their last album with George *Down on the Farm* was recently released.

RECOMMENDED: *Sailin' Shoes, Dixie Chicken, Waiting For Columbus* (Warner Bros.).

LITTLE RICHARD

Legend has it that Little Richard Pennimann was washing dishes in a Memphis hash joint when he decided to bag it and become a rock 'n' roll singer. He was one of the wildest and one of the best of the 60s rockers, a real one man show who would wear a giant pompadour, make himself up heavily, scream uncontrollably during his songs, climb on top of his piano at the show's climax and proceed to strip, throwing his clothes to the audience. In addition, he wrote some of the greatest rock 'n' roll songs of all time; "Long Tall Sally," "Tutti-Frutti," "Rip It Up," "Keep a Knockin'," "Lucille," "Good Golly Miss Molly" and "Jenny Jenny." His influence was felt by such diverse stars as Mitch Ryder and Paul McCartney. After his wild rock days Richard became a preacher and renounced rock 'n' roll. He made a comeback in the 70s.

RECOMMENDED: *Little Richard's Biggest Hits* (Imperial).

NILS LOFGREN

As a solo act, Lofgren was a sort of link between punk and more mainstream rock. He had the punkish swagger down cold, but deep down you always knew he wasn't looking for trouble; he was instead a romantic, a big-hearted guy just looking for some girls and some fun. An unusually lyrical hard rock guitarist and an effectively wistful singer, he has never won the mass following his boosters always predicted for him. Perhaps that's why his later work sounds so much less convincing than earlier sides. Still, he's responsible for a few minor gems (especially "Moon Tears" and "Keith Don't Go"), and even when he's trying most desperately for a hit (as on "I Came to Dance"), it's hard to put him down.

RECOMMENDED: *Nils Lofgren, Cry Tough* (A&M).

LOGGINS & MESSINA

In 1970, Columbia Records A&R man Don Ellis put together a songwriter named Kenny Loggins, who'd written some material for the Nitty Gritty Dirt Band, and a producer named Jim Messina, who'd played bass in the Buffalo Springfield and Poco. Messina took such an active part in producing, playing and contributing songs, that the album was eventually called *Kenny Loggins with Jim Messina Sittin' In*. The two formed a duo and recorded several albums together before going their own ways in 1976.

RECOMMENDED: *Sittin' In, Full Sail* (Columbia).

JACKIE LOMAX

After making a name for himself in the early 60s around Liverpool and London, Lomax, along with his group the Undertakers, played in Hamburg's Star Club where Lomax met the Beatles, who liked his guitar playing and blues rock direction. Lomax became the first artist to be signed to the Beatles' Apple label, and his first solo album was produced by George Harrison. After the Apple dissolution, Lomax formed a group called Heavy Jelly, then went on to make two sensational solo albums for Warner Bros. In 1974 he formed yet another short-lived band called Badger before resuming his solo outings.

RECOMMENDED: *Livin' for Lovin'*, *Did You Ever Have That Feeling?* (Capitol).

LOVE

Love was and still is Arthur Lee by another name. Born and raised in Memphis and one of the few visible black 60s *rockers* along with Hendrix, Lee formed the group in Los Angeles in 1965. Love was at first a surrogate Byrds (guitarist/singer Bryan McLean was a former Byrds roadie); Lee's songs bolstered by crisp trebly guitars and a jumpy folk-rock beat. Their second and third albums, *Da Capo* and *Forever Changes*, however, showed Love and Lee moving into more exploratory directions, the latter using strings in a manner totally unlike most of the orchestral pretensions of post-*Sgt. Pepper* product. Love had always been plagued by merry-go-round personnel changes, many of these due to Lee's temperamental nature, but the next few Love albums usually had only Lee and his songs in common. Lee also recorded an LP in England with Hendrix that was never released (one track appeared on *False Start*), recorded an unreleased solo album with Paul Rothchild, and is still toting demos of new songs with a new Love around Los Angeles. But Love's impact is still felt in rock: the Move once covered "Stephanie Knows Who," the Rolling Stones lifted "She Comes in Colors" wholesale for "She's a Rainbow," and Led Zeppelin's Robert Plant cites *Forever Changes* as one of his favorite albums ever.

RECOMMENDED: *Love* (Elektra); *Reel to Real* (RSO).

LOVE SCULPTURE

In the mid-60s a number of the more adventurous British blues players started to get the idea to expand the limits of the music they had played. A number of power trios started which were designed to provide a lot of solo space for the lead guitarist over a rumbling, often boogie influenced rhythm section of bass and drums. One of the lesser known of these bands, Love Sculpture, never got more than a cult following in England, but the group is noteworthy because the featured guitarist was Dave Edmunds, who has gone on to great success in the 70s as a producer and solo artist as well as the leader of Rockpile.

RECOMMENDED: *Forms and Feelings* (Parrot).

LOVIN' SPOONFULL

Formed by John Sebastian, the autoharp and harmonica playing son of the greatest classical harmonica player of the 20th Century, guitarist Zal Yanovski, drummer Joe Butler and bassist Steve Boone, this good time group combined the folk/rock ambience of the mid-60s with a gift for melodic hooks that yielded up a succession of hit singles: "Do You Believe In Magic", "You Didn't Have To Be So Nice," "Day

Dream," "Did You Ever Have To Make Up Your Mind," "Summer In the City," "Nashville Cats," "Six O'Clock." The Spoonfull also did the soundtrack for Woody Allen's *What's Up Tiger Lily.* After the group broke up in the late 60s Sebastian went on to a solo career. His biggest moment came when he wrote the theme music for *Welcome Back Kotter.*

RECOMMENDED: *Do You Believe In Magic, Day Dream* (Kama Sutra).

NICK LOWE

The self-declared "Jesus of Cool," Nick Lowe has grown from a small-time (yet talented) club musician with an excellent but unviable band to an internationally recognized solo artist, producer, and songwriter. Along with manager Jake Riviera (who also runs Elvis Costello's career), Lowe has become famous and successful, playing bass with a band he co-runs with guitarist Dave Edmunds, and releasing records of immaculate pop under his own name. Born in England a little over thirty years ago, Lowe began his musical profession with a teenaged pop band called Kippington Lodge in 1965. After a series of moderately successful 45s, three of the group split off and formed a new band, named after guitarist Brinsley Schwarz (now with Graham Parker). When they broke up six albums later, in 1975, Lowe knocked around a bit before signing to Riviera's new independent label, Stiff Records, where his first solo single helped fuel the new wave's fires. He subsequently formed Rockpile with Edmunds, and has produced numerous albums for Elvis Costello, the Damned, Dr. Feelgood, Graham Parker, Clover, and others, in addition to releasing a pair of his own unique albums. A master rock craftsman, and a canny thinker as well.

RECOMMENDED: *Pure Pop for Now People* (Columbia).

LULU

Marie McDonald McLaughlin Lawrie, aka Lulu, was still a schoolgirl when she recorded her first hit, "Shout." The British singer relied on the strength of her cute good looks and squeaky innocent voice to carry her material, and soon became a star in England, scoring big with the cabaret audience and making films and television shows. In 1969 she placed first in the Eurovision song contest. The title song from her debut film, *To Sir With Love,* which also starred Sidney Poitier, was a number one single for six weeks in the U.S. In 1979 Lulu made a comeback album for Elton John's Rocket Records.

RECOMMENDED: *Don't Take Love For Granted* (Rocket).

FRANKIE LYMON

The history of rock 'n' roll is checkered with success stories involving young teenagers who ride one song to unheard-of popularity and become international stars overnight. Frankie Lymon was one such case, a kid from Detroit who felt the early spirit of rock 'n' roll in the 50s and wrote a song called "Why Do Fools Fall In Love" which rocketed his group, Frankie Lymon and the Teenagers, to the top. Lymon was only thirteen when it happened.

RECOMMENDED: *The Teenagers* (Gee).

LYNYRD SKYNYRD

They broke out of Florida in 1973, built a fervent following in the South, and then captured the Yanks as well. "Sweet Home Alabama," their 1974 single, became a calling card, along with the Duane Allman tribute, "Free Bird." Their three-guitar attack could be devastating, and Ronnie Van Zandt's whiskey-drenched vocals went for broke. As bruisingly aggressive as this band became, they still sounded clear as a mountain stream. They had a little of that country soul mixed in with their rockin' R&B. Always a big touring band. Skynyrd seemed certainly on the verge of superstardom in 1977 when a plane crash killed Van Zandt and other key members and staff. The survivors chose not to carry on—under the same name.

RECOMMENDED: *Lynyrd Skynyrd (Pronounced Leh-nerd Skin-nerd), One More from the Road, Street Survivors* (MCA).

TAJ MAHAL

It's no small coincidence that Taj Mahal (b. May 17, 1942, New York City) once played with rock ethnomusicologist Ry Cooder in a seminal 60s band called the Rising Sons. For like Cooder, Taj Mahal has dedicated his life to the preservation of black musical forms with an unabashed joy appropriate to the music itself. He got started early in life, studying black roots music as a member of the Pioneer Valley Folklore Society while a student at the University of Massachusetts. Once signed to Columbia as a solo artist. Taj dove straight into the blues, later taking on Cajun music, reggae, and even traditional jazz with his infamous tuba band on the live *The Real Thing* LP. Taj Mahal has never made a serious commercial dent in record sales, an ironic comment on the general American disinterest in its traditions, whatever the color, creed, or rhythm. But he continues to make records, excellent records, as he's also a facile multi-instrumentalist, so there's always hope.

RECORDINGS: *Taj Mahal, The Natch'l Blues, Evolution* (*the Most Recent*) (Warner Bros.).

MAHOGANY RUSH

At first castigated as a mindless Hendrix imitator who, according to publicity handouts, felt the soul of Jimi himself enter his body at an impressionable age, Frank Marino is actually an electric guitarist of considerable imagination who has developed an individual style based on Hendrix's innovative techniques. Born in Montreal, Marino began jamming with bassist Paul Harwood and drummer Jim Ayoub in 1970, at first for fun, and then for profit as they formed Mahogany Rush. In 1971 the band played in a huge pop festival at the Montreal Expo and their resounding reception led to a contract with the Canadian Kotai label. For a time, Marino himself reinforced the Hendrix myth during shows he would play guitar with his teeth and do rousing but note-for-note renditions of "Purple Haze" and Hendrix's adaptation of "The Star Spangled Banner." But those days are, for the most part, over and Marino has become one of Canada's most popular recording and touring rock attractions.

RECOMMENDED: *Maxoom* (Kotai-20th Century); *Mahogany Rush IV* (Columbia).

MAMAS & The PAPAS

In 1965 the Mamas & Papas first album yielded three hit singles, "California Dreamin'," "Monday Monday" and "I Call Your Name." John Phillips, Michelle Phillips, Cass Elliott and Denny Doherty sang a beautiful patchwork of harmonies that rocketed the group on to the American pop charts. After several more hits and a string of mid-60s albums the band split for solo projects, with Cass Elliott and John Phillips enjoying the greatest success until Elliott's death in London from choking on a sandwich.

RECOMMENDED: *Farewell to the First Golden Era* (Dunhill).

MAN

This band of Welsh rockers began performing in the early 70s with the only San Francisco psychedelic style rock available in England. Led by guitarists Mickey Jones and Deke Leonard, drummer Terry Williams, keyboardist Phil Ryan and bassist Will Youatt, the band built a fanatic British following and a modest but devoted audience in the states, particularly on the west coast. Bill Graham liked them so much when they played a warm-up set for another group in San Francisco that he invited them back to headline. He then introduced them to ex-Quicksilver Messenger Service guitarist John Cippolina, who jammed with the group and decided to join Man for a British tour which yielded the live album *Maximum Darkness*.

RECOMMENDED: *Revelation* (Pye); *Be Good to Yourself at Least Once a Day* (United Artists).

MELISSA MANCHESTER

The daughter of a bassoonist in the Metropolitan Opera orchestra, Manchester graduated from the High School of Performing Arts in New York and was writing songs professionally at the age of 15. She also sang in many commercial jingles and performed on the National Lampoon comedy album *Radio Dinner* before joining Bette Midler's backup group, the Harlettes. She was then signed for a recording career on her own and has enjoyed hits with "Midnight Blue," "Just You and I" and "Better Days."

RECOMMENDED: *Home To Myself* (Bell); *Melissa* (Arista).

BARRY MANILOW

Singer/songwriter Manilow worked in the CBS mail room, and through a contact, got a chance to do some arranging. Soon he was working as the musical director for the Emmy Award-winning WCBS-TV series *Callback!* Later, after working as a conductor/arranger for Ed Sullivan, Manilow met singer Bette Midler at New York's Continental Baths and became her arranger/conceptualist. Meanwhile, Manilow had been singing a lot of jingles on television, the most famous of which became the McDonald's theme song. As a solo artist, Manilow's late 70s recording career has been one hit single after another: "Mandy," "It's a Miracle," "I Write the Songs," "This One's for You," "Daybreak."

RECOMMENDED: *Barry Manilow Live* (Arista).

BARRY MANN

The first rock 'n roll records in the 50s were not often written by the performers who sang them. Rock 'n roll was a medium more for players and people who covered songs. But in the 60s the era of the rock 'n roll songwriter began. One of the best of these new specialists was Barry Mann, who wrote on his own and collaborated with Cynthia Weill. His first big record was the novelty song "Who Put the Bomp" from 1961. In '63 he put out his greatest work, "On Broadway," with Weill and Lieber and Stoller, an unusual combination of two songwriting teams. Then in '65 Mann's "Only In America" became a hit for Jay and the Americans. In the 70s Mann tried a solo career of his own.

RECOMMENDED: *Survivor* (RCA).

MANFRED MANN

Born in South Africa, Mann emigrated to England in the early 60s and became part of the "British Invasion" with a string of hit singles, the most notable of which are "Do Wah Diddy Diddy," "Pretty Flamingo," and "Mighty Quinn." "Quinn" was written by Bob Dylan, and when keyboardist Mann formed the jazz-rock Chapter III group in 1969 (which evolved into Manfred Mann's Earth Band in the 70s) he continued to record Dylan songs as a trademark. But Mann's biggest recent hit was a 1976 cover of Bruce Springsteen's "Blinded by the Light." The group's sound has settled into a melodic heavy metal style with Mann's hard-funk keyboard work giving way to synthesizer programs. Mann's early bands included Paul Jones, Klaus Voorman, and Mike D'Abo; currently it's guitarist Steve Waller, bassist Pat King and drummer John Lingwood. Mann wrote the soundtrack for the 1967 film *Up the Junction*.

RECOMMENDED: *Manfred Mann's Greatest Hits, Mighty Quinn* (EMI); *Manfred Mann's Earth Band* (Polydor).

PHIL MANZANERA

The British electric guitarist who became famous as the guts of the Roxy Music sound took the opportunity offered by that band's brief mid 70s hiatus to produce a solo album that featured him on 6 and 12 string guitars, tiple, acoustic guitar, synthesized guitar, bass, string synthesizer, organ and piano. He got help on the album from other Roxy members and an all star session cast. He displays the same spacy, romantic feeling in his solo performance as in Roxy. He recorded a second solo album with many of the same players in 1978.

RECOMMENDED: *Diamond Head* (Atlantic).

BOB MARLEY

To many non-Jamaicans, Bob Marley (b. February, 1945, St. Anns, Jamaica) *is* reggae, while to many Jamaicans Bob Marley represents a free spirit who speaks their mind through the language of Rastafarian doctrine and reggae's hypnotic beat. The son of a Jamaican mother and a British army captain, Marley was a welder when he formed his first group with Peter Tosh and Bunny Wailer nee Livingston, a harmony vocal outfit that would eventually become the Wailers. The Wailers were a substantial success in Jamaica, recording a wealth of singles under noted JA producers Coxsone Dodd and Lee Perry before being taken under the business arm of British reggae enthusiast Chris Blackwell, who signed the group to his Island label. Debuting the band in America on the album *Catch a Fire*, Blackwell was convinced reggae would be the next big thing in the States. And if reggae wasn't, Marley soon would be. He is an articulate Rastafarian spokesman and a charismatic performer who works magic with reggae rhythms and his own mystical presence. Marley is now usually accompanied by original rhythm section Wailers Carlton and Aston "Family Man" Barrett.

RECOMMENDED: *Rastaman Vibration, Babylon by Bus* (Island).

MARSHALL TUCKER BAND

Southern rockers from Spartanburg, South Carolina, the Marshall Tucker Band came to prominence in the early 70s after the Allman Brothers popularized a similar brand of blues-based instrumental jamming hooked with a dose of regional pride. Led by the Caldwell brothers, guitarist Toy and bassist Tommy, the group includes rhythm guitarist George McCorckle, singer Doug Gray, sax/flautist Jerry Eubanks, and drummer Paul Riddle. The Caldwell's interest in country music has led to the Marshall Tucker Band being the most country-derived of all the Southern rockers, with such popular songs as "Take the Highway" and "Can't You See."

RECOMMENDED: *The Marshall Tucker Band, Carolina* (Capricorn).

MARTHA AND THE VANDELLAS

The story of this group is Motown's biggest success story. Martha Reeves was a secretary at Motown's Detroit offices who got her shot at recording when another vocal team missed a session engagement and Martha said she could fill in with her friends Rosalind Ashford and Betty Kelly. The three did backup vocals for awhile before recording under their own name, at which point they exploded; "Come and Get These Memories," "Heat Wave," "Dancing In the Streets," "Nowhere To Run" and "Jimmy Mack." Martha Reeves went on to solo success in the 70s.

RECOMMENDED: *Greatest Hits* (Motown).

STEVE MARTIN

This weird comedian came into his own in the late 70s after years of knocking around the small club circuit and building a name through television appearances on *The Tonight Show*. Raised in California, Martin studied vaudevillians and slapstick comedians, then began writing for other comedians before going on his own. For several years he played opposite rock acts without much success. It was the television appearances that opened doors for him, particularly his several spots on *Saturday Night Live,* where he popularized a skit with Dan Akroyd about two Czechoslovakian brothers who were "wild and crazy guys."

RECOMMENDED: *Let's Get Small, Comedy Is Not Pretty* (Warner Brothers).

JOHN MARTYN

John Martyn fell under the spell of blues and traditional music in his late teens, when a folk revival was sweeping his native Scotland. A hoary Glasgow minstrel taught Martyn enough guitar fingering styles and open tunings to get him started playing in clubs. At 19, Martyn was moving ahead so quickly with his own songwriting that Island asked him to cut an album. On his next LP, *The Tumbler,* Martyn experimented with the jazz rhythms which have strongly colored his more recent work. Martyn's warm regard for traditions comes across in his husky baritone voice (as on "Spencer the Rover") without preventing him from sounding contemporary. He can play Jelly Roll Morton or Skip James blues on an improvisatory, Echoplexed, electrified guitar without losing their sense of the past. The casual, pub-like atmosphere of Celtic nonsense that Martyn creates in the most impersonal tour setting is phenomenal. Martyn's spare and tuneful original songs, such as "May You Never," "Man at the Station," and "Head and Heart," have enriched the songbags of many other singers and friends including Eric Clapton, Ian Matthews and Bridget St. John.

RECOMMENDED: *The Tumbler, Live* (Island).

DAVE MASON

Like so many British guitarists of the 60s, Dave Mason started playing blues songs based on American recordings. After playing with local bands like the Jaguars and Hellions, Mason got an insider's job as a roadie with the Spencer Davis group where he met vocalist/keyboardist Steve Winwood. Along with drummer Jim Capaldi and flautist Chris Wood, Mason and Winwood formed Traffic, one of the greatest British rock groups in history. Mason contributed a number of standards to that band, particularly "Feeling Alright," which became a hit for Joe Cocker, Grand Funk Railroad, and Three Dog Night. After playing with Delaney and Bonnie and Eric Clapton, Mason embarked on a solo career with a tremendous album called *Alone Together,* and continues to record on his own with great success.

RECOMMENDED: *Alone Together* (Blue Thumb).

IAN MATTHEWS

Country rock singer/guitarist Ian Matthews, who stepped into the limelight only after he'd worked solo for seven years and signed with a tiny label, was born in England in 1946 and christened Ian McDonal. At 20 he began his recording career with the London band, Pyramid. A year later he helped found Fairport Convention, singing male lead to offset Judy Dyble's soprano. Ian left Fairport, changed his name to Matthews to distinguish himself from the King Crimson/Foreigner Ian McDonald, and formed Matthews' Southern Comfort in 1969. This group had a more country style than Fairport, and helped popularize slide guitar and layered vocal harmonies in a country rock context. After scoring with the hit, "Woodstock," Matthews quit the band and cut two solo albums for Vertigo. He sang briefly in a new group, Plainsong, in 1971, and since then has worked solo. Matthews has consistently surrounded himself with varied, sympathetic musical stylists, and his pioneering work with country rock has been an inspiration to newer bands like the Eagles. He achieved belated solo success in 1978 with the hit 45, "Shake It," and the R&B-tinged LP *Stealing Home,* recorded under the supervision of the folk producer Sandy Roberton.

RECOMMENDED: *Tigers Will Survive* (Vertigo); *Stealing Home* (Mushroom).

JOHN MAYALL

Universally described as the father of the British Blues, John Mayall fronted groups since the late 50s, employing many important British rock-blues musicians; Eric Clapton, Mick Taylor, Jack Bruce, John McVie, Peter Green, Jon Mark, Aynsley Dunbar, Keef Hartley have all appeared on Mayall's lineup card at one time or another. Several strong changes of direction have taken Mayall away from his devotion to the blues, but he's always maintained a steady growth and progression, keeping his music interesting and fresh. The first recording group Mayall had was the Bluesbreakers, which lasted from 1963 until 1968. From there, Mayall tried an American sound that evolved into a love affair with the country. After several albums of American music played by English musicians, Mayall emigrated and began using American musicians like Larry Taylor, Sugarcane Harris, and Harvey Mandel. There are over two dozen albums with John Mayall's name, singing, guitar/organ/harmonica playing, and imprint. Some are better than others. Perhaps Mayall's prime contribution has been as a farm club for rising talent. For that, he has surely earned a place in rock history.

RECOMMENDED: *The Blues Alone, Turning Point, Diary of a Band* (London).

CURTIS MAYFIELD

A veteran of the Chicago R&B scene, Mayfield formed the Impressions in the late 50s with Jerry Butler, and when their first hit, "For Your Precious Love," became a huge hit, Butler left the group for a solo career and Mayfield joined him as a guitarist. Mayfield then reformed the Impressions in 1961 and led the group during its greatest years, writing their hits "Amen," "I'm So Proud," "Keep On Pushin'," "People Get Ready," and "We're A Winner." Mayfield left the Impressions in 1970 and formed his own record and publishing company, Curtom records, released a few solo albums, then scored the biggest hit of his career with the soundtrack to *Super Fly*.

RECOMMENDED: *Curtis Live, Super Fly* (Buddah).

MC5

As the anarchic spirit of Detroit rock (along with the Stooges and the unrecorded Up), the MC5 captured the revolutionary ethos of rock 'n' roll. The MC5 recorded their first album live in Detroit, complete with their "Kick out the jams, motherfuckers" anthem, played in Lincoln Park during the 1968 Democratic Convention riots in Chicago, and took out an ad in an underground journal deriding a record store who wouldn't stock the '5's first album because it had "motherfucker" on it. When the revolution fizzled (Sinclair went to the slammer on a dubious drug rap), the MC5 made *Back in the U.S.A.* a piledriving rock classic. *High Time* seconded the emotion, but neither sold and come 1972 the MC5 were no more. Wayne Kramer also went to jail on a drug bust (he's since been released), Rob Tyner tried writing and photography, Fred "Sonic" Smith lives with Patti Smith and gigs in Sonic's Rendevous Band, Michael Davis plays with Destroy All Monsters (he also served time), and Thompson played for a time with some ex-Stooges in the New Order. With the arrival of punk rock, the MC5 have enjoyed legend status even as they play punk venues with their respective bands.

RECOMMENDED: *Kick Out the Jams* (Elektra).

PAUL McCARTNEY

McCartney was the first of the Beatles to cut a solo album, *McCartney*, on which he played and sang virtually all instrumental and vocal parts, (maybe as if to say he didn't need the other three band members). After a second LP, *Ram*, made with session men and his wife, Linda, McCartney chose to return to a group format with Wings. Wings has released some fine records, like the rocking

"Junior's Farm" and the music hall-inspired "You Gave Me the Answer." But the only permanent Wing besides Paul and Linda is Denny Laine; all the rest have quit within three years. In the past three years, McCartney's music has been touch and go; quality records such as "With a Little Luck" and "Old Siam, Sir" have alternated with dismal experiments like the disco-styled "Goodnight Tonight." The triumphant 1976 Wings over the World tour proved that McCartney's spark didn't die with his exit from the legendary band, and the sell-out shows furnished a tangible link between the two groups.

RECOMMENDED: *Ram, Band on the Run, Venus & Mars, Wings at the Speed of Sound* (Capitol).

VAN McCOY

The man who became famous for the 1975 song "The Hustle," which ushered in disco as a mass-dance phenomenon, McCoy's career has kept him hustling. He started out singing with a local Washington, D.C. group called the Starlighters while majoring in psychology at Howard University. He started a record company in Philadelphia with his uncle, where he released his first recordings, including the modest hit "Mr. D.J." Then McCoy formed a production company which worked on Gladys Knight's "Giving Up," Barbara Lewis's "Baby I'm Yours," Ruby and the Romantics' "When You're Young and in Love," and on a number of songs for Peaches & Herb. All along he'd been writing, and his songs were often covered while Van occasionally recorded himself in between production projects. One of his own sessions yielded "The Hustle," and McCoy started solo performing on the strength of that song's popularity.

RECOMMENDED: *Disco Baby* (Avco).

COUNTRY JOE McDONALD AND THE FISH

Country Joe McDonald (b. January 1, 1942, El Monte, California) got an early radical start in life when his leftist parents named him after Joseph Stalin. When he was honorably discharged from the Navy, he combined his interests in country music and politics, and started performing his own songs in the coffeehouses of Berkeley. But he didn't hit on the magic combination until, after playing with a few jug bands, he formed Country Joe and the Fish in 1965. Frustratingly inconsistent in recorded output but refreshingly eclectic and often quite funny, Country Joe and the Fish included McDonald, guitarist Barry Melton, organist David Cohen, bassist Bruce Barthol, and drummer Chicken Hirsch in the best-known Fish configuration. They epitomized the free spirit of psychedelia, using it not only as rock 'n' roll entertainment but as a political tool. Perhaps because of this, their first album remains their best, *Electric Music For The Mind and Body,* but rampant personnel changes didn't help. Yet McDonald survived as a solo, maintained his political allegiances, sang the "Feel Like I'm Fixin' to Die" F-U-C-K cheer at Woodstock, toured army bases with an antiwar troupe, retreated to Europe disillusioned with America in the radically sterile 70s, and later returned to revive a solo career. It is appropriate that he sang at the Woodstock Reunion Concert in September of '79. For him, the spirit never died and his omnipresent voice in pop has been one of the things that kept it alive.

RECOMMENDED: *Electric Music For the Mind and Body, I-Feel-Like-I'm-Fixin'-to-Die, Incredible! Live! Country Joe!* (Vanguard).

KATE AND ANNA McGARRIGLE

This Canadian singer/songwriter duo provides one of the finest examples of late 70s folk style. Both became known for their songwriting before coming into their own as solo performers. Kate's "Work Song" became identified with Maria Muldaur's cover version, while Anna's "Heart Like A Wheel" provided one of Linda Ronstadt's best moments. On their own the McGarrigles combined their personal songwriting genius with a thoroughgoing knowledge of French folk material.

RECOMMENDED: *Dancer With Bruised Knees* (Warner Brothers).

ROGER (JIM) McGUINN

As jacket-and-tied banjo player for the Chad Mitchell Trio, Jim McGuinn was an unlikely candidate for future hip celebrity in early 60s folk–singing America. But by 1963 the lure of the 12-string guitar proved too strong for banjoist McGuinn, and he rambled to California to play sessions and clubs and write arrangements for Judy Collins. When the Beatles struck, McGuinn traded his ivied image for an electric Rickenbacker plus Dickensian cape and glasses. He sang the Collins songs himself, in a Bob Dylan-inspired nasal voice backed by the beat of the Byrds, and won AM radio cover. In various line-ups the Byrds made twelve consecutive albums; the one constant Byrd was Jim McGuinn, who changed his name to Roger following a spiritual revelation. McGuinn cut five post-Byrds LPs and a reunion album before hitting the road with Bob Dylan's Rolling Thunder Revue. In 1978 he reteamed with two original Byrds as McGuinn, Clark and Hillman. Roger has helped bring lyrical emphasis to amplified music, and his personalized, banjo-influenced guitar style brands him a rock original.

RECOMMENDED: *Peace on You, Cardiff Rose* (Columbia).

JOHN McLAUGHLIN

For the jazz-rock fusion, first thank Miles Davis. Then thank British guitarist John McLaughlin, who played on Davis' legendary *Bitches Brew* sessions and then went a step further with his own Mahavishnu Orchestra. Born in Yorkshire, England, McLaughlin started playing guitar in his teens after a preteen spell on violin and piano. His teenage interest in American blues and his own dazzling technical abilities on the guitar led to apprenticeships with Graham Bond and Brian Auger before taking a more exploratory jazz route on his own *Extrapolation* album (1969). This record led —through drummer Tony Williams' recommendation—to the call from Miles Davis to play on *Bitches Brew*. After recording an acoustic LP, *My Goal's Beyond,* which not only reflected his religious conversion to the teachings of

Sri Chimnoy but also included violinist Jerry Goodman and drummer Billy Cobham, McLaughlin formed an eclectic electric ensemble, the Mahavishnu Orchestra, with Goodman, Cobham, Czech keyboard player Jan Hammer, and bassist Rick Laird that broke the idea of a jazz-rock fusion wide open. The band's emotional impact and breathtaking technique are best on *The Inner Mounting Flame* and *Birds of Fire*. But McLaughlin's religious pre-occupations and mounting ego problems resulted in a split, after which McLaughlin indulged his religious excesses in a second Orchestra, complete with strings and horns. In 1976 he disbanded Mahavishnu for an acoustic group called Shakti and since then he has dabbled in both electric and acoustic guitar music that touches rock, jazz, and a wealth of ethnic bases without quite reaching the peaks of classic Mahavishnu. But it's still fascinating to watch him try.

RECOMMENDED: *Birds of Fire* (Columbia); with Carlos Santana—*Love Devotion Surrender* (Columbia).

DON McLEAN

A native of the beautiful Hudson River Valley area of New York, McLean grew up practicing the music he heard played by such folk groups as the Weavers. He became an itinerant folksinger at 15, travelling around upstate New York playing small clubs and cafes. In 1968 he got a grant from the New York State Council on the Arts to give free concerts in the Hudson River Valley to promote ecology. Folksinger Pete Seeger heard McLean and invited him to join the troupe of musicians who went up and down the Hudson playing music on Seeger's sloop Clearwater. The exposure through Seeger led to a wider following for McLean and a recording contract. His second album featured the song "American Pie," which became his trademark hit.

RECOMMENDED: *American Pie, Don McLean* (United Artists).

CLYDE McPHATTER

He was the original lead singer of the Drifters when they had a pre-Presley/Haley hit in 1953 with the driving "Money Honey." After it scored big, McPhatter went on to a solo career. McPhatter had been trained in the gospel group, the Dominoes, formed in 1950 by Billy Ward. As such McPhatter was one of the first singers to make the transition from gospel to rock 'n' roll, a much travelled route since. His biggest solo hit was the million selling 1958 smash "A Lover's Question."

RECOMMENDED: *Clyde McPhatter's Greatest Hits* (Atlantic).

MEATLOAF

Rock had become more of a stage spectacle than a player's music by the mid-70s when such big scale events as Kiss had taken over the concert scene. Meatloaf was designed to capitalize on that fact. The burly, gargantuan figure of Meatloaf careening across the stage to bellow out the nonstop lyrics to the epic songs written for him by group mastermind Jim Steinemann was calculated to appeal to the rock audience's love of overstatement. In order to translate this vision to vinyl an extraordinary producer was required and studio mastermind Todd Rundgren was tabbed for the job. With Rundgren at the controls and adding some of his own hot guitar licks, Meatloaf pulled off such FM fare as "Two Out of Three Ain't Bad" and "Paradise By the Dashboard Light."

RECOMMENDED: *Like A Bat Out Of Hell* (Epic).

MELANIE

Born Melanie Safka in Queens, New York, Melanie played folk clubs in Greenwich Village in the early 60s for spare change while studying acting at the American Academy in Manhattan. Her cute looks and wispy, even-natured singing enabled her to parley modest songwriting talents into mass success after appearing at Woodstock and writing a song, "Lay Down (Candles in the Rain)" about the experience. After the impact of her next hit, "Brand New Key," wore off, Melanie disappeared for several years and took up Scientology. Eventually she tried a comeback album, *Phonogenic*.

RECOMMENDED: *Melanie, Candles in the Rain* (Buddah).

LEE MICHAELS

He became famous for playing organ like a 747 taking off, but Michaels started out as a musician at age nine playing accordion in the pit band at a Mexican movie house in California. In the early to mid-60s, he played organ in obscure west coast bands like the Sentinels and Joel Scott Hill before forming his own band and eventually recording a good debut album called *Carnival of Life*. In the early 70s, Michaels hit on his super-heavy, slabs-of-sound organ delivery and achieved stardom in a duet with a drummer called Frosty who laid it on the skins as thickly as Michaels did on the organ. His career waned through the 70s despite several personnel changes.

RECOMMENDED: *Carnival of Life, Lee Michaels Live* (A&M).

BETTE MIDLER

In 1965, Bette Midler left her home in Honolulu with the money she made as an extra in the film *Hawaii* and moved to New York to become an actress. She tried go-go dancing in Union City, New Jersey bars and singing in Greenwich Village coffee houses before landing a part in the Broadway production of *Fiddler on the Roof*. From there she put together a stage show which became a huge hit at New York's Continental Baths, where she met pianist/arranger Barry Manilow, who put together a revue called The Divine Miss M. A recording contract ensued, then a Broadway Revue called *Clams On the Half Shell*, then television specials.

RECOMMENDED: *The Divine Miss M, Live At Last* (Atlantic).

BUDDY MILES

This powerful rock/R&B drummer surfaced in the late 60s with the Electric Flag after years on the R&B circuit backing up stars like Wilson Pickett and the Ink Spots. He quickly captured the imagination of the rock audience, who followed him through a solo career that began after leaving the Flag in 1968. With the Buddy Miles Express he toured the U.S. and recorded a number of popular albums. After working with guitarist Jimi Hendrix and bassist Billy Cox in Band of Gypsies, Miles again went out on his own, dropping his solo career only briefly to record with guitarist Carlos Santana.

RECOMMENDED: *Them Changes* (Mercury).

FRANKIE MILLER

This gutsy vocalist emulates Sam Cooke and Otis Redding and created turmoil in the British blues scene when he showed up in the early 70s. After stints singing lead in ex-Procol Harum guitarist Robin Trower's band and with pub rockers Brinsley Schwarz, Bees Make Honey and Ducks Deluxe, Miller formed his own band and recorded a series of critically-acclaimed solo albums; one, *Highlife*, produced in New Orleans by R&B master Allen Toussaint.

RECOMMENDED: *Once in a Blue Moon* (Chrysalis).

STEVE MILLER

Rock's leading pragmatist, Steve Miller (b. October 5, 1943, Milwaukee, Wisconsin) has always believed in his music but never forgotten the value of a dollar. The son of a pathologist, Miller led a number of bands in Wisconsin (one of which included Boz Scaggs), studied in Copenhagen, and jammed with fellow young white blues enthusiasts in Chicago (Barry Goldberg with whom he recorded a rare Epic album, Paul Butterfield, Mike Bloomfield) before moving to San Francisco to check out the Haight-Ashbury action. There he formed the Steve Miller Blues Band (later dropping the "Blues") and negotiated a landmark record contract that proved a model for other Frisco bands dickering with major labels. It's never been held that Miller was a great singer or a standout guitarist like Frisco brethren Jerry Garcia or John Cipollina, but Miller did have a good ear for what made exciting rock 'n' roll and driving blues and while *Children of the Future* was as psychedelic as he ever got, it still had plenty of that blues and rock, as have all of his successive LPs. Most recently, he's plugged into young America's commercial way of thinking, producing two hit albums, *Fly Like an Eagle* and *Book of Dreams*, that show not how Miller has changed with the times but how the times have caught up with him. After all, he wrote "Livin' in the U.S.A." ten years ago.

RECOMMENDED: *Children of the Future, Fly Like an Eagle, Book of Dreams* (Capitol).

JONI MITCHELL

When Joni Mitchell left her home in Alberta, Canada in 1965 with her new husband, Chuck Mitchell, to live in Detroit, she had already begun writing the folk songs that would soon make her a respected songstress. By the time her first album was released, Tom Rush and Judy Collins had already recorded her material, and Mitchell was an underground celebrity. After several tours in front of adoring audiences and the success of her song "Woodstock," written about the legendary upstate New York rock festival, Mitchell became a household word and has continued to support a large following despite an adventurous musical direction that has led her to record in a number of disparate styles. Most recently Mitchell collaborated on an album of jazz bassist/composer/arranger Charles Mingus' songs, the last project he worked on before his death.

RECOMMENDED: *Blue, Clouds* (Warner Bros.); *Miles of Aisles, Court and Spark, Mingus* (Asylum).

MOBY GRAPE

Unfortunately, San Francisco's Moby Grape is usually remembered only for the mondo-hype Columbia Records set in motion for the release of the Grape's first album in May, 1967. Five singles were released from the album simultaneously (all bombed), a massive party was thrown for them in Frisco, and all they had to show for it three albums later was the late Lillian Roxon describing them in her *Rock Encyclopedia* as "a psychedelic version of the Dave Clarke Five." Nothing, however, could have been further from the truth. True, the Grape; originally guitarists Jerry Miller, Peter Lewis, and former Jefferson Airplane drummer Skip Spence, bassist Bob Mosely, and drummer Don Stevenson, tried to overcompensate for the overpromotion on 1968's *Wow* with a lot of acidified art-rock gimmicks. But Moby Grape was, in its best moments, a fine rock 'n' roll band with the strongest six-string front line of any San Francisco group. Members gradually departed as public affection went to their Haight-Ashbury peers the Airplane and Dead; Spence by *Moby Grape '69* and Mosely by *Truly Fine Citizen*, but Moby Grape continues to exist in one form or another. Jerry Miller maintains a Grape-like group, gigs occasionally in the Frisco outbacks and even released a live album in '78 that included not only Miller and Lewis but the reclusive Spence.

RECOMMENDED: *Moby Grape* (Columbia); *20 Granite Creek* (Reprise); *Live Grape* (Escape).

MOLLY HATCHET

Jacksonville, Florida's Molly Hatchet, six bruisers named Dave Hluber, Duane Rolland, Steve Holland (all guitars), Danny Joe Brown (vocals), Banner Thomas (bass), Bruce Crump (drums), simply rock and roll hard with their songs about wine, whiskey and women on the road. They do sound a lot like Lynyrd Skynyrd, but that's not surprising since in their 1973-77 apprenticeship playing Florida bars Molly Hatchet could reputedly play at least twenty entries in the Skynyrd songbook note for note.

RECOMMENDED: *Molly Hatchet* (Epic).

EDDIE MONEY

San Francisco's Eddie Money follows the hitbound trail blazed by singers like Felix Cavaliere; Money's style mixes the rhythms of Detroit and Memphis with a blue-eyed rock 'n' roll savvy. His kind of are both ballsy and tuneful, the kind of juke box material that's hard to resist. Money's association with hard-rock guitar wizard Jimmy Lyon has a chemistry like that between Rod Stewart and Jeff Beck years ago. Some of this chemistry came across on the 1977 debut LP, *Eddie Money*, but the album was marred by melodramatic lyrics and by the absence of a tight band. On the sequel, *Life for the Taking*, Money sang more personally, backed by an improved band's fluid playing. He stretched melodies to the limits of his sandpaper voice, and with partner Lyon made a truly dramatic record that was highlighted by "Call on Me," "You Can't Keep a Good Man Down," and the title song. Though Money's flashy stage manner has earned him the reputation of an upstart white pop star, his songs have shown such attention to pop history that they have the earmark of musical maturity.

RECOMMENDED: *Life for the Taking* (Columbia).

THE MONKEES

Hollywood's answer to the Beatles, the Monkees were put together from a scripted formula for a television show about a cute rock group. From the thousands of applicants the four Monkees who were selected included only one musician, folk rocker Michael Nesmith. The other three were actors; Mickey Dolenz, Peter Tork and Davey Jones.

Dolenz had been the child star of *Circus Boy*, a weekly television series. Along with the songwriting team of Boyce and Hart and plenty of session musicians, the Monkees released a succession of bright, catchy pop singles; "Last Train To Clarksville," "Hey Hey We're the Monkees," "Pleasant Valley Sunday." They also made a feature film called *Head*.

RECOMMENDED: *The Monkees Greatest Hits* (Colgems).

MOODY BLUES

In 1965 the Moody Blues made an impression on the pop charts with the haunting ballad, "Go Now." The band was led by Denny Laine and Michael Pindar at that point, and after disappearing for two years the Moody Blues returned with *Days of Future Passed*, a beautiful album recorded with the London Symphony Orchestra. Laine was gone, so the new lineup was Pindar, Justin Hayward, John Lodge, Graeme Edge, and Ray Thomas. This new version of the band was lushly melodic and specialized in concept albums in which all the songs were related to a single theme and further enhanced through the use of orchestras or sound effects. "Tuesday Afternoon," "Nights in White Satin," "Ride My See-Saw" and "Questions" all became big hits.

RECOMMENDED: *Days of Future Passed, Seventh Sojurn, A Question of Balance* (London).

JIM MORRISON

The son of a Navy Admiral, Morrison was an aspiring writer/filmmaker when he met keyboardist Ray Manzarek at UCLA. Manzarek heard some of Morrison's lyrics and suggested they put together a band which, after the inclusion of guitarist Robbie Krieger and drummer John Densmore, became the Doors. Their 1967 debut album, *The Doors*, knocked the Beatles' *Sgt. Pepper* album from the top of the charts, and Morrison proceeded to become one of America's male sex symbols. Morrison was arrested for indecent exposure on stage in Miami, an event which triggered a downward slide which saw the Doors banned from public appearances in many places and finally forced Morrison into exile in Paris, where he died in 1971. A posthumous release of Morrison's poetry recited over Doors backing tracks was issued as a record in 1978.

Photo by Joel Broadsky

RECOMMENDED: *An American Prayer* (Elektra).

VAN MORRISON

Ireland's greatest musical resource, Morrison founded Them, one of the hottest blues bands of the early 60s. With his R&B vocals and harsh harmonica playing as the featured elements in Them he led that group to hits with "Mystic Eyes," "Here Comes the Night" and "Gloria." After leaving that group Morrison began a brilliant solo career in the mid 60s that has seen him recognized as one of rock's finest singers in the 70s. His solo albums have covered everything from hard edged R&B to lyrical, romantic Irish folk music.

RECOMMENDED: *Blowin' Your Mind* (Bang), *Astral Weeks, It's Too Late To Stop Now* (Warner Brothers).

MOTHERS OF INVENTION

The Soul Giants were a greasy little bar band playing dives around Southern California until Frank Zappa joined the band, or rather appropriated them for his own musical purposes, and renamed them the Mothers. MGM Records added "of Invention" for paranoia's sake, but it didn't stop Zappa and the ever-growing family of Mothers from making some of the most disconcerting music of the 60s and early 70s. The original Mothers, aside from Zappa, were singer Ray Collins, bass guitarist Roy Estrada, drummer Jimmy Carl Black (the self-styled "Indian of the group"), and a sax player, Dave Coronada, who split once he got wind of Zappa's plans for the band. Much has been made of the fact that the Mothers were Zappa's band and they did his bidding. Zappa has said so himself. But there is no denying that the Mothers were also good players and as zany a lot as Zappa could have possibly wished for in his mission to shock America right out of its brown shoes. Noted Mothers who have come and gone are saxist Ian Underwood, teen appeal merchant Motorhead Sherwood, percussionist Ruth Underwood, fuzak pianist George Duke, French violinist Jean-Luc Ponty, Flo and Eddie (Mark Volman and Howard Kaylan, ex-Turtles), synthesizist Don Preston, and guitarist Elliot Ingber, who played with Captain Beefheart under the unlikely name of Winged Eel Fingerling. History will probably point to *Freak Out, Absolutely Free,* and *We're Only In It For the Money* and the band's six-month 1966 stand at New York's Garrick Theater as the Mothers' finest moments. Zappa finally put the Mothers' name to quiet rest in 1976.

THE MOTORS

Like Graham Parker's band, the Rumour, the Motors rose from the ashes of pub rock bands. In 1977, Nick Garvey and Andy McMaster from Ducks Deluxe joined Bram Tchaikovsky and Ricky Slaughter to form a hard-rocking melodic pop group that walked a fine line between punk and chart rock. The Motors' first album showed strength in both departments and they found a home in the British charts easily. A tour of the States did little to bowl over the populace, yet a second album in 1978 showed even more songwriting prowess on the part of all concerned. A much poppier affair, the second LP gave rise to several hit English singles, but the group began showing inner problems, culminating in the departure of Bram Tchaikovsky for a profitable solo career in 1979. The current lineup includes Garvey and McMaster, but no new material has been forthcoming under the Motors log in over a year.

RECOMMENDED: *Approved by the Motors* (Virgin).

MOTT THE HOOPLE

Mott the Hoople was always everybody's band "most likely to". But all the goodwill in the world couldn't win them the rock 'n' roll reward they deserved. Mott, in an earlier 60s incarnation, was called Silence until Ian Hunter auditioneed for a job as singer and got it. As Mott (the name comes from a Willard Manus novel) they made four classic LPs, including the manic punkfest *Brain Capers* which anticipated the new wave by a good five years. By '72, Hunter, guitarist Mick Ralphs, organist Verden

Allen, bassist Peter "Overend" Watts, and drummer Dale "Buffin" Griffin were tired and frustrated, calling it quits with nothing to show for their efforts until Bowie encouraged them to reform, giving them their first hit in the process. That wasn't quite enough for Allen, who left shortly after *All The Young Dudes*, and Ralphs, who left after *Mott* and later founded Bad Company with Free men Paul Rodgers and Simon Kirke. Mott plowed on with Ariel Bender (aka Spooky Tooth's Luther Grosvenor) on guitar, but pressures mounted, Bender was out, Ronson stepped in, Hunter was hospitalized for exhaustion, and the end came, sort of, when Hunter pulled out in '74. Buffin, Watts, pianist Morgan Fisher, guitarist Ray Major, and vocalist Nigel Benjamin gave Mott an honest go, but it was never the same. Hunter with Ronson on guitar is now a successful solo act.

RECOMMENDED: *Mott The Hoople, Brain Capers,* (Atlantic); *All The Young Dudes* (Columbia).

MOUNTAIN

When bassist/engineer/producer Felix Pappalardi ended his successful association with Cream, he returned to his Long Island U.S. base to plot his next project. He formed Mountain in the image of Cream's power trio format in association with ex-Vagrants guitarist Leslie West and drummer Corky Laing, then went a step further by adding organist/keyboardist, Steve Knight. The result, *Mountain Climbing!,* was a watershed in heavy-metal conceptualization, slowing down the beat in order to lay on the sonic peanut butter. A wide range of new bands took their cues from that first Mountain album, which contained most of the songs ("Mississippi Queen," "Theme for an Imaginary Western," "Never in My Life," "Silver Paper") which would form the bulk of a live set that made Mountain one of the most popular concert attractions through the early 70s.

RECOMMENDED: *Mountain Climbing!, The Road Goes Ever On* (Windfall).

MOVE

It's an odd thing to say that the Birmingham, England band the Move never capitalized on their considerable talents and unbroken string of superb pop records, given the fact that in Britain the Move, guitarist/songwriter Roy Wood, singer Carl Wayne (left in '70), drummer Bev Bevan, bassist Trever Burton (later replaced by Rick Price), and rhythm guitarist Ace Kefford (gone by '68), also had an unbroken string of Top 20 hits. They also got an enviable pile of press clippings for such unorthodox concert antics as smashing up televisions and, in the case of "Flowers in the Rain," printing up a picture sleeve with a caricature of the Prime Minister in an uncompromising position (a lawsuit sent their royalties to charity). But the Move spent only three weeks touring in America in all of their seven years (1965-72), and in Britain they were never recognized properly for their long-playing achievements on *Shazam, Looking On,* and *Message From the Country*. Wood was certainly recognized as a pop genius, a songwriter of stunningly creative device, and when Jeff Lynne, from a rival Birmingham band the Idle Race, joined in 1970, he too was singled out as a musician and writer of no mean talent. In fact, Lynne specifically joined because he wanted to get in on Wood's plan to form a rock group with strings which would eventually become the Electric Light Orchestra. As for the Move's records, there are few that aren't rock & roll classics. From their first single "Night of Fear" (1967, an ingenious reworking of the riff from the *1812 Overture*), through *Shazam* (the 1969 album which showcased

Wood's songs in inventive, expanded arrangements), and finally to their one U.S. hit, Jeff Lynne's bruising rocker "Do Ya" (later revived by ELO), the Move demonstrated a grasp of rock 'n' roll possibilities and an eagerness to try them all.

RECOMMENDED: *Shazam* (A&M); *Looking On, Message From the Country* (Capitol).

MARIA MULDAUR

Famed for the sexy "Midnight on the Oasis," Muldaur nonetheless started out as a folksinger in the 60s playing the Greenwich Village coffee house circuit before marrying Geoff Muldaur and joining the Boston area band he played with, the Jim Kweskin Jug Band. After that band broke up, Geoff and Maria moved to Woodstock, New York and made two albums, *Pottery Pie* and *Sweet Potatoes*. In 1974 Maria went solo, and her first album soared behind the success of the single "Midnight at the Oasis." After moving to California and finding that the more overt R&B material clicked, Muldaur went more in that direction, then back to 30s big band arrangements, switching to a full orchestra for concert dates under the direction of venerable jazzman Benny Carter.

RECOMMENDED: *Maria Muldaur, Sweet Harmony* (Warner Bros.).

MICHAEL MURPHEY

One of the many aspiring musicians to migrate from Texas to California in the 60s, Murphey became a songwriter after majoring in creative writing at UCLA and hung out on the L.A. songwriter's circuit for several years before recording his first album, the highly regarded *Geronimo's Cadillac,* with producer Bob Johnstone. Hailed as one of the leaders in the country-rock field, Murphey went on to a successful recording career highlighted by sales of two million copies of his hit single, "Wildfire." Murphey has also written film scripts and did the music for a film on Native Americans called *The Divided Trail,* which was nominated for an Academy Award.

RECOMMENDED: *Michael Murphey, Blue Sky, Night Thunder* (Epic).

ANNE MURRAY

Canadian country/pop star singer Murray was born in Nova Scotia and became a singer on the Canadian television show "Sing Along Jubilee" while attending New Brunswick University in 1966. After recording for a small Canadian label before signing with Capitol records in Canada, Murray's first U.S. release, "Snowbird," became the first gold record a female Canadian recording artist ever received in the U.S. The song also did well on the country charts and earned her a spot on the Glen Campbell TV show. Since then she has pursued an active career in recording and television appearances, hosting nine specials for Canada's CBC and guesting on U.S. television shows from Johnny Carson to Dinah Shore, while producing hit after hit on pop and country charts.

RECOMMENDED: *New Kind of Feeling* (Capitol).

GRAHAM NASH

A product of Lancashire, England, Graham Nash began his career inauspiciously in a dawn-of-the-60s duo with Allan Clarke called the Guytones. Also known as the Two Teens, the Guytones became the Dominators of Rhythm, and, later, the Hollies. While with the Hollies, Nash wrote and sang the hits "On a Carousel," "Dear Eloise," and "King Midas in Reverse." In 1969 Nash joined David Crosby and Stephen Stills in California to form a supergroup which even today can sell out stadiums on the basis of only three studio albums in ten years. Nash became a gossip-column perennial because of his Laurel Canyon liason with Joni Mitchell and his alleged habit of dosing the drinks of unsuspecting guests with acid. On the creative front he wrote "Our House" and the politically-minded "Chicago," a song often performed by CSN as well as "solo" on an otherwise undistinguished Atlantic album. Nash's work with Crosby in a more directional duo format (1975-77) produced better musical results such as "Take the Money and Run," "Love Work Out," "Wind on the Water," and "Whistling Down the Wire." His lyrical style has had a strong influence on the music of other artists, including Little River Band, Keith, Mississippi, and even his own models, the Everly Brothers. Nash, who signed with Capitol last year, is a charming and energetic performer with a great flair for getting sedentary hippies to clap, dance and sing along with him.

RECOMMENDED: solo: *Songs for Beginners, Wild Tales* (Atlantic); *Crosby/Nash Live* (ABC-MCA).

NAZARETH

Guitarist/producer Manny Charlton, bassist Peter Agnew, drummer Darrell Sweet and cement mixer vocalist Dan McCafferty came roaring out of Scotland in 1968 as part of the proliferation of heavy metal bands spawned in the British Isles in the wake of Cream. No-nonsense hard rock and blues was the band's trademark, and McCafferty's Rod Stewart-influenced vocal delivery helped smooth over the rough edges in the group's first few years. On each album the group improved its sound until Charlton's production moves and multiguitar attack put them near the top of their field. Then, in 1979, a second guitarist (Zal Cleminson) from the Sensational Alex Harvey Band was added, and expanded their sound on the hard rocking extravaganza, *No Mean City*.

RECOMMENDED: *Expect No Mercy, No Mean City* (A&M).

RICK NELSON

The Adventures of Ozzie and Harriet made Ricky Nelson the first rock 'n' roll star whose career was launched by network television. Between 1957 and 1963, he had seventeen singles in the Top 10; "Poor Little Fool" (1958) and "Travelin' Man" (1961) went to No. 1. Though frequently criticized for helping turn raunchy rock 'n' roll into soft, suburbanized music (which is at least partially true), Nelson always fronted tough bands, and in retrospect, much of his work succeeds as well-crafted pop. He was aced out by the mid-60s British Invasion before bouncing back as first a country singer and then as an L.A. country-rocker; his Stone Canyon Band included several members who went on to become stalwarts of the current L.A. country-rock scene. Though "Garden Party" resurrected him briefly in 1972, he has been largely unable to exploit his connections well enough to rebuild a stable singing career.

RECOMMENDED: *Ricky Nelson, Legendary Masters Series #2* (United Artists).

WILLIE NELSON

After years at any number of odd jobs, including that of country musician, Willie Nelson left his native Texas for Nashville in 1961. His concise, cathartic songs were picked up by any number of country music stars, but Willie himself made little headway as a recording artist. By the early 70s, he'd packed his bags and left in frustration. Back in Texas, things started happening quickly. Willie forged an unlikely audience composed equally of hippies and rednecks, and thus came to be known as the father of the Outlaw, or progressive country, movement based in Austin. In 1973, he held the first of his annual Fourth of July festivals. But it wasn't until 1975, with "Blue Eyes Crying in the Rain" and *Red Headed Stranger* (country's first platinum album) that the rest of the country took to his flat, eccentric baritone the way Texans had for years. *Stardust,* a collection of pop standards, clinched it in 1978, and Nelson is now in the enviable position of being able to do whatever he wants, no matter how off-the-wall: his fans will buy anything with his name on it.

RECOMMENDED: *Best of Willie Nelson* (United Artists); *Stardust* (Columbia).

MICHAEL NESMITH

Michael Nesmith (b. December 30, 1942, Houston, Texas), easily the most talented of the Monkees in terms of songwriting, has long since lived down his reputation as the furry-capped guitarist in the made-for-TV rock combo created by Don Kirshner. Even before he joined the Monkees in 1965 he'd written a hit song in "Different Drum," sent Top 20 by Linda Ronstadt's Stone Poneys. By the time he'd quit the group, he'd already arranged an album's worth of his songs for an anonymous studio aggregation called the Wichita Train Whistle and shortly after turned toward country with his own First National Band. Disillusioned with record companies in general, Nesmith made his first stab at running his own with Countryside which fell afoul of distribution problems. He and his wife Kathryn now run a label called Pacific Arts which releases not only Nesmith products like the conceptual book-with-album *The Prison* or the more accessible but no less fascinating *Infinite Rider on the Big Dogma* but also issues items by jazz, country, pop, and assorted ethnic musicians. Nesmith's own music now runs an eclectic gamut, fusing country sympathies with a rock beat, learned but imaginative playing, and inviting lyrics.

RECOMMENDED: *The Wichita Train Whistle Sings* (Dot); *Tantamount to Treason Vol. 1* (RCA); *Infinite Rider on the Big Dogma* (Pacific Arts).

RANDY NEWMAN

Randy Newman's surprise hit of '77,

Photo by Bill King

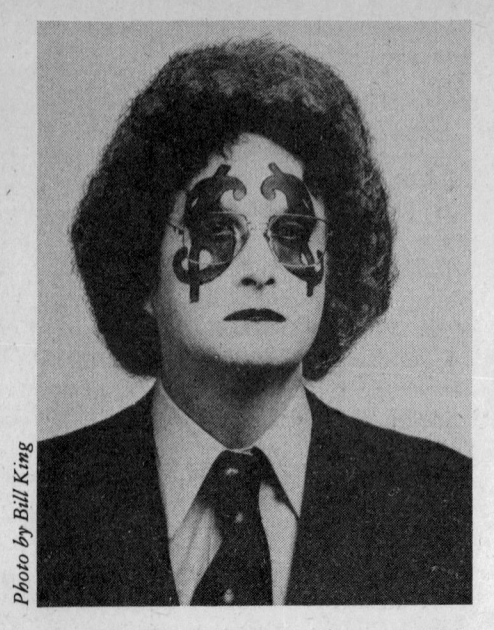

"Short People," and the controversy it sparked points up both the genius of the singer/songwriter/composer and the public's misunderstanding of it. Newman (b. November 28, 1943, Los Angeles) was not making fun of the world's population standing under five feet so much as he was pointing an accusing as well as amusing finger at those thoughtless folk who *do* make fun of short people. Similarly, his 1974 LP *Good Old Boys* took a fictional stand on behalf of America's redneck population, capturing in 10 simple but evocative songs the plight of the working man caught between his emotions and the pressures of making a living for himself and his family in an increasingly indifferent world. Newman does have a sharp satirical pen: on his *Born Again* album he takes a well-aimed poke at the Electric Light Orchestra in "The Story of a Rock & Roll Band," but when he sings about "Davy The Fat Boy" (from Newman's classic first LP), he does so with a sympathy one readily hears in his fragile melody and quavering, starkly human voice. Because of the deft combination of emotion, lyrical strength, and melodic impact, Newman's songs have always been popular with other singers. Alan Price covered a number of his songs on his first LP, Three Dog Night had a hit with "Mama Told Me Not to Come," and Newman's poignant "I Think It's Going to Rain Today" remains a perennial favorite since Judy Collins recorded it in 1966 for her *In My Life* album. Newman's own recording is usually at two and three-year intervals, and commercially he's never hit the big time with the exception of the freakish "Short People." But critical huzzahs always greet his albums and even forced Reprise to release a live promo-only LP in 1971. (Historically, one should note that Newman's uncle Alfred was a famous Hollywood film composer and that Randy has also worked in films: he did "Gone Dead Train" for *Performance;* he has also worked as an arranger and songwriter on sessions and did parts of the first Harper's Bizarre album.)

RECOMMENDED: *Sail Away, Good Old Boys, Little Criminals, Born Again* (Reprise).

NEW RIDERS OF THE PURPLE SAGE

The New Riders went for two years at the turn of the decade as the Grateful Dead's warmup band, a soft pedalling, pickin'-and-grinnin' troupe of country rock led by John "Marmeduke" Dawson on guitar and lead vocals, ex-Jefferson Airplane drummer Spencer Dryden, and the Dead's own Phil Lesh on bass and "Captain Trips" Garcia tinkering on pedal steel guitar. It was a great chance for Garcia to try his fairly sure hand at this country instrument, but it was the catchy tunefulness of songs like "Glendale Train" that made the New Riders the most popular unrecorded band in rock. After splitting from the Dead, the band employed steel guitarist Buddy Cage and bassist Stephen Love.

RECOMMENDED: *New Riders of the Purple Sage* (Columbia).

OLIVIA NEWTON-JOHN

This wholesome, rosy-cheeked pop singer came from Melbourne, Australia via Cambridge, England. Newton-John's heart-throb moralizations and clean-cut good looks made her the choice for crossover pop to country promotion, but she soon became one of the leading programmed singers on country music stations, much to the consternation of that genre's old timers. When the Country Music Association named her Top Female Vocalist of the Year in 1974, there was a near revolt from performers whose whole lives were spent recording country music, but her singles "Let Me Be There" and "I Honestly Love You" won her Grammy awards in both pop and country categories.

RECOMMENDED: *Let Me Be There* (MCA).

NEW YORK DOLLS

The New York Dolls, those glitter-rock gonzos of the early 70s, lived fast, played raunchy, and in the case of original drummer Bill Murcia who fell victim in 1973 to a potent mixture of pills and booze, died young. But despite their own self-destructive bent and the resistance of the record business, the Dolls emerged out of the New York underground rock scene to record two awesomely loud and arrogant rock 'n' roll documents (the first produced by Todd Rundgren) that predated the punk-rock movement by a good three years. The Dolls; singer David Johansen, guitarists Johnny Thunders (nee Genzale) and Sylvain Sylvain, bassist Arthur Kane, and drummer Jerry Nolan, played a brash, defiant mixture of R&B and streetcorner-wise rock 'n' roll, turned up to ten. They were visually highlighted by the Dolls' outrageous glitter-rock get-ups, which included high heels, feather boas, make-up, and other thrift-shop accoutrements appropriate to either gender. The band played its first gig at the end of '71 and its last in '75, when they were managed by Malcolm McLaren, who would later rise and fall as the guy holding the strings behind the Sex Pistols. By then, the glitter had turned red in a Chinese motif that did nothing to prolong the Dolls' life as a band. Drugs, poor record sales, and general rock 'n' roll excess had taken its toll. But the Dolls have lived on in a curious way. All of the ex-Dolls are now pursuing various solo careers and new wavers willingly light a fire at the Dolls altar.

RECOMMENDED: *New York Dolls, Too Much Too Soon* (Mercury).

NICE

Keith Emerson's flamboyant way with a Hammond organ and eccentric treatments of Bob Dylan's "She Belongs to Me" and Leonard Bernstein's "America" from *West Side Story* are the memories the Nice have left behind for most people, particularly those coming to the band through Emerson's later exploits with Emerson Lake and Palmer. But there was more, once the Nice: Emerson, bassist/vocalist Lee Jackson, drummer Brian Davison, and guitarist David O'List (who quit after the first LP), stepped out of their back-up gig for black British soulstress P. P. Arnold in 1967. For example, they turned Dave Brubeck's "Blue Rondo à la Turk" into a frantic rock 'n' roll dervish, they set fire to an American flag during a Royal Albert Hall performance of "America" in 1968 for which they were henceforth banned from the hall, and they capitalized on Emerson's classical training by playing and recording with orchestras as on 1970's *Five Bridges*. That, however, was also the same year they called it quits.

RECOMMENDED: *Nice* (Immediate): *Five Bridges Suite* (Mercury).

NICO

This tall, thin, very strange vocalist/writer/keyboardist first was a member of Andy Warhol's coterie who populated his avant garde films and art projects. In 1967 Warhol decided to form a rock band in his Max's Kansas City hangout and Nico became lead singer of the group, which was called Velvet Underground. Nico has since made a couple of very odd sounding solo albums and done some art projects.

RECOMMENDED: *Velvet Underground with Nico* (Verve).

NITTY GRITTY DIRT BAND

An eclectic country rock band, the Dirt Band started out in California playing all acoustic music and some jug band numbers. At the time Jackson Browne was one of the members of the band. The Dirt Band switched to electric instruments after that and in 1969 the group's lineup included Les Thompson on bass, mandolin and guitar, Jimmie Fadden on lead guitar, Jeff Hanna on drums and rhythm guitar, Jim Ibbotson on guitar and keyboards and John McEuen on banjo, mandolin, acoustic guitar and accordion. The group built their reputation during the 70s as one of the finest country-rock bands in the land, doing well with a cover of "Mr. Bojangles" and recording the landmark *Will the Circle Be Unbroken* album with top traditional country performers. McEuen now manages Steve Martin.

RECOMMENDED: *Uncle Charlie and his Dog Teddy, Will the Circle Be Unbroken* (United Artists).

TED NUGENT

The "Motor City Madman" is as well known for his gut-wrenching guitar playing and heavy metal sound with its earsplitting volume as for his fascination with firearms and hunting. He started out in the mid-60s as the guitarist who fronted the Amboy Dukes, who scored a hit single with "Journey To the Center of Your Mind." Nugent toured the midwest incessantly during the 70s before breaking through with a national following in the late 70s when his heavy metal style came into popularity.

RECOMMENDED: *State of Shock* (Epic).

LAURA NYRO

This reclusive New York poetess/singer/songwriter surfaced in the mid-60s with songs whose powerful emotional sentiment contrasted forcefully with her shy fragility and hauntingly understated singing and piano accompaniment. The song "Wedding Bell Blues" became a hit, as did the rousing "Save the Country," and Nyro was seen as one of the best of the contemporary songwriters. Her unwillingness to seek the spotlight led to a temporary retirement which ended in the early 70s with a live comeback album and the beautiful *Smile*.

RECOMMENDED: *Eli and the 13th Confessions, New York Tendaberry* (Columbia).

PHIL OCHS

Photo by Alice Ochs

Protest troubadour Phil Ochs (b. December 19, 1940, El Paso, Texas) became America's conscience in song during the 60s and paid dearly for his courage. A journalism student at Ohio State University, Ochs brought a reporter's eye for undisguised truth to his songs as well as an inate wit which made him a popular figure on the Greenwich Village club circuit. Yet Och's refusal to knuckle under to commercial requirements or censorship left him the victim of a broadcasting ban that kept him off American television and then restricted radio in the most crucial years of his career. His albums, however, withstand passing of the protest era, an ironic compliment after Och's steady decline in fortune into the 70s, culminating in a disastrous show at Carnegie Hall in which he appeared in a gold lamé Elvis suit, an electric band, and played Elvis and Buddy Holly medleys. In 1973, Ochs was the victim of a mysterious attack on a trip to Africa which damaged his vocal chords. Spotty showings on club stages and a snowballing drinking problem contributed to his depression and on April 8, 1976 he hung himself in the bathroom of his sister's home in Far Rockaway, New York. It was only two years after his last public appearance with Dylan at a benefit show for victims of Chile's military junta.

RECOMMENDED: *All The News That's Fit to Sing, I Ain't Marching Anymore,* (Elektra); a posthumous A&M compilation *Chords of Fame* with notes by Ed Sanders.

OHIO PLAYERS

This Cleveland-based funk R&B band surfaced in the late 60s as a heavily Sly & the Family Stone-influenced outfit known more for its sadomasochistic covers of titles like "Pain" than for its toe-tapping rhythms. As the 70s sound materialized, the band's musical concept jelled and hit singles like "Fire," "Sweet Sticky Thing," and "Love Rollercoaster" followed. Led by Clarence Satchell on alto, tenor, and baritone saxophones, flute and viatone, and Leroy Bonner on guitars, the group's big band sound utilized Ralph Middlebrooks and Marvin Pierce on trumpets, bassist Marshall Jones, drummer Jimmy Williams, keyboardist Billy Beck, guitarist Chet Willis, and percussionist Robert Jones.

RECOMMENDED: *Greatest Hits* (Chess).

THE O'JAYS

Eddie Levert, Walter Williams and Billy Powell had been singing together for almost ten years without ever getting a break when they clicked with the monster hit single "Back Stabbers" in 1972. They had come under the watchful hands of the Gamble-Huff production team and its Philly soul sound. The O'Jays followed with such hits as "Love Train," "Put Your Hands Together" and "Ship Ahoy", helped to usher in the disco craze, and became huge international stars. Today they are Yankee slugger Reggie Jackson's favorite group.

RECOMMENDED: *Family Reunion* (Philadelphia Intl.).

MIKE OLDFIELD

Mike Oldfield stunned those who heard his first album *Tubular Bells* released in 1973. A master of overdubbing, Oldfield played all the instruments himself on the record which made him a star overnight as well as a victim of "too much too soon" hype. Indeed, he got his start at 14 playing in a folk duo with his sister Sally called the Sallyangie and by 16 he was gigging and recording with English rock eccentric Kevin Ayers and his crew of experimenters in the Whole World. Upon that band's dissolution, Oldfield made a demo of his 50-minute composition *Tubular Bells* which was rejected by just about every record label in England as uncommercial, except for Virgin Records, an unconventional label that grew out of a chain of record shops. After *Bells* (copious amounts of which were used in the film *The Exorcist*), Oldfield struggled with a follow-up coming out with a Tubular encore called *Hergest Ridge* and a badly advised orchestral version of *TB* (the magic of *TB* was that it was an orchestral composition arranged for a *rock* orchestra). But he has since found his footing again, experimenting with new sounds and concepts without losing his touch for writing classical themes into his works.

RECOMMENDED: *Tubular Bells* (Virgin).

YOKO ONO

Japanese conceptual artist Yoko Ono (b. February 18, 1933) first met John Lennon at one of her art exhibitions in New York (Yoko was divorced with a child, Kyoko). Married March 20, 1969 they performed as a family of peace, staging bed-ins, periodically taking out "No More War" ads on billboards, and recording a fascinating series of albums as either John Lennon and the Plastic Ono Band or Yoko Ono and the Plastic Ono Band (*Live Peace 1969*, recorded at a Toronto rock festival, is a very hot rock 'n' roll record and Lennon's *Plastic Ono Band* "primal scream" album from 1970 is probably his best, an emotionally arresting experience). The couple took a sabbatical from each other in 1974, but reconciled in '75 and in that year Yoko gave birth to their long-desired son Sean.

RECOMMENDED: *Yoko Ono/Plastic Ono Band, Feeling the Space* (Apple).

ROY ORBISON

Known, simply, as The Voice, Orbison came out of Wink, Texas in 1956 to begin his career with Sun Records, whose sound was not exactly appropriate to his powerful, soaring ballad style. But between 1960 and 1964 at Monument, he ran up an impressive string of nine straight Top 10 records, including two ("Running Scared" and "Oh Pretty Woman") that went to No. 1. After that, big money and potential film deals lured him to MGM, and the hits quit coming. He has resurfaced and disappeared a number of times since. There have been great personal tragedies: the death of one wife in a motorcycle accident, two sons killed in a house fire, but at his peak Orbison was one of the most distinctive singers around, with total worldwide sales over 25 million and some 50 gold records to his credit.

RECOMMENDED: *Greatest Hits, More of Roy Orbison's Greatest Hits, The Very Best of Roy Orbison* (Monument).

ORLEANS

This white R&B band led by guitarist/songwriter John Hall was formed in upstate New York in 1972 and built a local reputation in bars between Ithaca and Woodstock, New York, playing tight, funky dance music. John Hall and Larry Hoppen developed a lead guitar harmony technique reminiscent of the Allman Brothers', while bassist Lance Hoppen and drummer Wells Kelly laid down the rock-solid foundation. Hall wrote most of the band's material with his lyricist/wife Joanna, who'd written "Half Moon" for Janis Joplin. "Please Be There" and "Let There Be Music" became the group's trademark hits.

RECOMMENDED: *Orleans* (ABC); *Let There Be Music* (Asylum).

OSMONDS

Singing families have always been a show business staple, and the Osmonds are the latest in a long line of sibling crooners. Donnie, Marie, Alan, Merrill, Jimmy, Jay and Wayne have graced America's television sets and jukeboxes through the 70s. From a strict Mormon upbringing, the Utah residents got their start as a barbershop vocal group on the Andy Williams show before getting their own network series, starting a long streak of hit singles with "One Bad Apple" in 1971, and eventually spawning a spinoff act, Donny and Marie Osmond, who got their own television show and hits.

RECOMMENDED: *Osmonds Live* (MGM).

OUTLAWS

Spawned in the late 60s in Tampa, Florida, it wasn't until the mid-70s that the Outlaws surfaced nationally, making them one of the last of the southern rock bands to make it. Their sound owed as much to the harmonies of Southern California folk-rock bands as to the blues-based jamming of most southern bands, which explains the early success of their harmony vocal-dominated hit, "There Goes Another Love Song." At that point, the band was composed of lead guitarists Hughie Thomasson and Billy Jones, rhythm guitarist Henry Paul, drummer Monte Yoho and bassist Frank O'Keefe. Harvey Dalton Arnold replaced O'Keefe for the third album, then Freddie Salem replaced Paul and a second drummer, David Dix, was added.

RECOMMENDED: *Outlaws* (Arista).

OZARK MOUNTAIN DAREDEVILS

Formed in the college town of Springfield, Missouri, the group is made up of vocalist/guitarist/keyboardist John Dillon, harpist/vocalist Steve Cash, vocalist/guitarist Randle Chowning, vocalist/bassist Michael "Supe" Granda, vocalist/drummer/guitarist/keyboardist Larry Lee, and pianist Buddy Brayfield. The band's impressive array of instrumental capabilities and vocal depth gives the Daredevils a unique sound composed of many elements of American music which enables them to play some experimental-sounding music yet score with hit singles like "Jackie Blues."

RECOMMENDED: *Ozark Mountain Daredevils, Men from Earth* (A&M).

PABLO CRUISE

This California funk band has melded its sinewy rhythms and glib commerciality into a fast-rising commodity on the U.S. pop market. The song "Zero to Sixty in Five" was used by ABC's *Wide World of Sports*. Vocalist/keyboardist Cory Lerios and vocalist/guitarist Dave Jenkins write most of the band's material, while Bruce Day adds harmony vocals in addition to playing bass and drummer Steve Price anchors the whole thing with supple rhythms. All except Day were formerly in the highly-touted band Stoneground.

RECOMMENDED: *Pablo Cruise, Worlds Away* (A&M).

JIMMY PAGE

Page got his reputation in the early 60s as a troubleshooting session guitarist on the London recording scene. He was the favorite of producer/entrepeneur Shel Talmy, who produced the early records of the Kinks and the Who. Page was always on hand in the studio to fill in a rhythm or lead track if Talmy didn't like the way the group's own guitarist played it, and controversy still rages to this day about Page's role on the solo of the Kinks' first hit "You Really Got Me." He joined the Yardbirds while Jeff Beck was still lead guitarist and learned from Beck before taking over for him after Beck left the group. Page had turned the Yardbirds into a Led Zeppelin prototype just as that band split, and after finding vocalist Robert Plant, put Led Zeppelin into operation. Today Zeppelin is one of the most popular rock music bands and their film *The Song Remains the Same* benefited from Page's sound production.

RECOMMENDED: *Live Yardbirds Featuring Jimmy Page* (Epic).

ROBERT PALMER

Blond, British, and sporting an impressive set of baby-blue eyes, singer Robert Palmer has been unjustifiably lumped in with the blue-eyed soul boys, if not for his looks, then for his affinity for R&B which has been in evidence since he first started gigging with British outfits. Born in Yorkshire, England and raised in Malta, Palmer exudes a confident air of cosmopolitanism that shows in the material he records: songs by the late Lowell George, Todd Rundgren, Toots and the Maytals, and on his most recent hit "Bad Case of Loving You", Moon Martin. Palmer expertly and with considerable imagination fuses soul, hard-core rock, reggae, and New Orleans gumbo funk in his albums.

RECOMMENDED: *Sneakin' Sally Thru the Alley, Some People Can Do What They Like* (Island).

FELIX PAPPALARDI

Felix Pappalardi (b. 1939, Bronx, New York City) first made his name as a producer for the Youngbloods, Joan Baez and most importantly, English blues-rock supergroup Cream. A former Greenwich Village folkie, he became a studio sensation until he fell under the spell of a bulky guitarist from Queens named Leslie West (formerly Weinstein), who was playing with the Vagrants, a group Pappalardi was supposed to produce. Instead, he produced a solo album for West, *Leslie West—*

Mountain, and formed a heavy-metal band with West called, obviously, Mountain. During its years as the four-man American Cream, Mountain, with Pappalardi on bass, had one major hit single in "Mississippi Queen" and toured endlessly, trading on West's guitar-hero schtick and the band's macho improv gymnastics which could prolong a five-minute item like "Nantucket Sleighride" to over 40 minutes (as it does on the live *Twin Peaks*). Pappalardi quit in '72, briefly rejoined in '74, and has since taken on a few select projects, like his '77 LP with the Japanese band Creation and his own first solo album, issued in '79.

RECOMMENDED: *Don't Worry Me* (A&M).

GRAHAM PARKER

Along with his band of pub-rock veterans, the Rumour, Graham Parker helped set the stage for England's new wave by bridging the gap between the older, more Americanized club bands and the energetic youngsters that came along in 1976 and 1977. Mixing a feel for vocal expression with a punky aggressive stance, Parker has not only produced exciting records, but also served as a focal point for many musicians of similar mind. A small fellow with a big voice, Parker had been a garage attendant before coming to the attention of a Phonogram A&R man in London. Armed with a batch of powerful songs (in the same direction as those of Mr. Costello, whose subsequent appearance certainly benefitted from Parker's groundbreaking efforts), and a band formed out of the remnants of several of the best; Ducks Deluxe, Brinsley Schwarz, and Bontemps Roulee, Parker attracted immediate critical attention in both England and America. Hampered by a lack of record company support in the U.S. and a general overshadowing by the greater talents of Elvis Costello, Parker's career never really took off commercially until 1979, when a new record label made his fifth album an American chart hit. In the meantime, the Rumour has recorded a pair of LPs without their star, and they both show a lot of talent in a thoroughly different direction than Parker's. The coexistence seems to be a comfortable arrangement, and the Parker/Rumour alliance shows no signs of weakening.

RECOMMENDED: *Howlin' Wind* (Mercury); *Squeezing Out Sparks* (Arista).

VAN DYKE PARKS

Van Dyke Parks (b. circa 1941, Mississippi) peddles ingenuity and pretension. In 1968, when he released his first album *Song Cycle,* Parks was the subject of debate, based on the eccentric orchestral rock arrangements and unconventional vocal treatments. Parks had moved to Hollywood with his family at age 13, worked as a child actor, studied composing, and reportedly wrote scores for Walt Disney movies. As a producer for the Mojo Men and Harpers Bizarre, he developed a reputation as a thinking man's popster, eventually collaborating with Beach Boy Brian Wilson on the ill-fated *Smile* LP. But *Song Cycle,* originally hyped tongue-in-cheek by Parks' record company as the most misunderstood and most commercially unsuccessful album of its time, ushered in along with *Sgt. Pepper* that dubious age of art-rock, while Parks himself has since indulged in such ethnic sounds as Caribbean steel band music (he produced the Esso Trinidad Steel Band) and calypso (he also produced Island superstar the Mighty Sparrow). He records infrequently; his last LP was released in 1975.

RECOMMENDED: *Song Cycle* (Warner Bros.).

PARLIAMENT-FUNKADELIC

One of the strangest groups in history, Parliament-Funkadelic has carved out a reputation based on a lead guitar concept of Jimi Hendrix, a funk bottom inspired by Sly & the Family Stone, and a hypnotic, disco-dance rhythm pattern all fused by the space age visions of group leader George Clinton. The huge musical organization includes keyboardist Bernie Worrell, drummer Tiki Fulwood, bassist Bootsy Collins, horn players like Fred Wesley, Maceo Parker, Michael and Randy Brecker, and a huge, chanting vocal chorus led by Clinton. The group's bizarre records are all based on long, hysterical concepts about extraterrestrial visitation which are illustrated in the stage shows by elaborate props including the "Mother Ship," a huge mock flying saucer that "lands" on stage in the middle of the set.

RECOMMENDED: *Mothership Connection* (Casablanca).

GRAM PARSONS

Gram Parsons (b. November 5, 1946, Winterhaven, Florida) has become a significant figure in American rock 'n' roll because of his enthusiasm for country music and efforts to marry it with rock. Those efforts bore early fruition on the Byrds' album *Sweetheart of the Rodeo* on which he was a major contributor (although rumor has it his playing was almost entirely mixed out of the final product after he split the Byrds on the eve of a South African tour in 1968). Even before that, Parsons, who was raised in Georgia and New Orleans, showed signs of interest in C&W before heading for New York in the mid-60s to play the usual protest tunes. At Harvard, he formed the International Submarine Band, which moved to L.A. and made one album, now a collector's item. With the Byrds, he first proposed a country/rock fusion, later articulating it on record with the Flying Burrito Brothers and then on his own as a solo act. He also "discovered" Emmylou Harris, who was his co-vocalist on both solo LPs, *G.P.* and the magnificent *Grievous Angel*. Unfortunately, Parsons died on September 19, 1973 in the desert outside L.A. under mysterious circumstances: no autopsy was performed because friend and road manager Phil Kaufman hijacked the body and cremated it according to Parson's wish at the Joshua Tree National Monument. Parsons never received the public and commercial recognition due him in his time, but his work has since come to be regarded as crucial in the development of American country/rock.

RECOMMENDED: *G.P., Grievous Angel* (Reprise).

LES PAUL

Paul was one of the important figures in the history of studio recording. In the late 40s the guitarist had a New Jersey radio show with singer Mary Ford based on show business pop music rather than jazz and Paul came up with the idea of using more than one guitar line at the same time by overdubbing in the recording process. From those crude origins Paul invented the technique of multitracking, making him one of the first musicians to become important for how he recorded what he played rather than the playing itself. In the 60s Paul took his discovery to its logical progression by building the world's first 16 track recording facility in his Englewood, New Jersey studio.

RECOMMENDED: *Still Waiting for the Sunrise* (Capitol).

TOM PAXTON

Tom Paxton arrived on the Greenwich Village folk scene in 1963 with a mixed bag of protest and patriotic songs. Among the topical songwriters, none had more credibility than Paxton: he had an Oklahoma background right out of Woody Guthrie's *Bound for Glory*, an honorable army discharge; yet he was seriously questioning American values in songs like "Daily News" and "What Did You Learn in School Today?" Paxton's early days in the Village were spent passing the hat but he made a breakthrough writing TV jingles, and in 1964 his first nationally-distributed album, *Ramblin' Boy*, set the tone for almost everything he'd do later. Carolyn Hester, the Kingston Trio, and Peter, Paul & Mary all covered his songs; the Chad Mitchell Trio even had a hit with "The Marvelous Toy." Later in the 60s, Paxton's base of popularity shifted to England, the country from which his melodic style was first drawn. He currently lives in New York, records occasionally for Vanguard.

RECOMMENDED: *Ramblin' Boy, The Compleat Tom Paxton* (Elektra).

PEARLS BEFORE SWINE

One of the weird, eclectic bands that surfaced out of the acid rock trends of the 60s, this Florida outfit featured Tom Rapp on guitar and vocals, Jim Bohannon on keyboards and percussion, Wayne Harley on banjo, autoharp, mandolin and vibraphone, and Lane Lederer on bass and guitar. Rapp went on to keep the name and record several solo albums in a more direct folk/rock style.

RECOMMENDED: *One Nation Underground* (ESP); *Stardancer* (Blue Thumb).

DAVID PEEL

David Peel is proof of the power of streetcorner singing. Peel first surfaced at Be-Ins in New York's Central Park in 1967 and after establishing a reputation as a rough, uncouth, but funny hippie howler, he landed an Elektra contract and recorded his first album with his group, the Lower East Side, right on the streets of New York, complete with hecklers and the highly unintelligent tune "Up against the Wall, Motherfucker," an underground hit since FM radio wouldn't touch it. Later, he entered the circle of Beatle John Lennon and recorded another album under his patronage. Peel still plays in New York in Greenwich Village bars and records albums on his own low-budget label.

RECOMMENDED: *Have a Marijuana* (Elektra).

PENTANGLE

British traditional music groups have flourished through the ages, but the interest during the late 60s for old and eclectic styles created a revival. Pentangle was formed by several accomplished musicians and folklorists in England who were interested in pursuing acoustic music: guitarists Bert Jansch and John Renbourn, drummer Terry Cox, bassist Danny Thompson and vocalist Jacqui McShee. The group not only met with popular support in their native land, but helped introduce traditional English music to a young American audience and spurred the solo careers of Jansch and Renbourn as well.

RECOMMENDED: *The Pentangle, Basket of Light* (Warner Brothers).

CARL PERKINS

In the mid 50s Sun records president Sam Phillips translated the country music and R&B mix called rockabilly into gold when he clicked with Elvis Presley. In an attempt to repeat that success Phillips signed a local Memphis guitar player named Carl Perkins who wrote one of the rock 'n' roll anthems, "Blue Suede Shoes." Perkins was unable to do as well as Presley with his hit, but the song was Sun's first million seller when Presley covered it. Perkins continued to record some hot sides before switching to playing country gigs with Johnny Cash. He made a comeback in the 70s.

RECOMMENDED: *Carl Perkins* (Sun).

PETER AND GORDON

This U.K. folksinging duo came to prominence in 1964 when almost every group with a British accent was making the U.S. charts. Peter Asher and Gordon Waller had a softer sound than most Merseybeat groups. Asher's sister Jane was Paul McCartney's girlfriend and McCartney wrote their first hit "World Without Love." After a few years without much luck the duo scored again with "Lady Godiva" in 1967. After the group broke up Asher went on to be A&R director for the Beatles' Apple records, then became an important producer of Los Angeles singer songwriters like Linda Rondstadt in the 70s.

RECOMMENDED: *Best of Peter and Gordon* (Capitol).

PETER, PAUL AND MARY

Peter Yarrow, Noel "Paul" Stookey and Mary Travers were all solo folkies when they met in 1960 on the Greenwich Village folk scene in New York and decided to form a trio dedicated to playing traditional folk music material. Mastermind manager Albert Grossman signed the three and used them to spearhead the early 60s folk boom that saw the group popularize such traditionals as "If I Had A Hammer" and record the first Bob Dylan song to ever become a hit, "Blowin' In the Wind." After ten years the band broke up in 1970.

RECOMMENDED: *Peter, Paul and Mary, Moving* (Warner Bros.).

SHAWN PHILLIPS

Shawn Phillips (b. February 3, 1943, Fort Worth, Texas) is not one to fall prey to pop fads or phenomena. While his peers jump on every bandwagon that passes by, Phillips continues to plow his own folk-oriented field, penning meditative musings on the world and its ways, arranging them with an exotic flair for rock orchestration, and singing them in a voice that runs from a soft whisper to an exhilarating very high C. His background is just as interesting; opening shows for Lenny Bruce at the Cafe Au Go Go in New York, touring as guitarist and sitarist for Donovan. As for the present, Phillips lives in a small Italian fishing village called Positano and tours solo with a dozen guitars and a synthesizer for support.

RECOMMENDED: *Spaced* (A&M); *Transcendence* (RCA).

WILSON PICKETT

Among 60s soul singers rooted deeply in gospel music, few voices stood out more than that of Pickett, who helped put the Memphis Sound on the map. After a

1962 hit ("I Found a Love") as lead singer of the Detroit-based Falcons and a couple minor hits on a small indie label in 1963, he signed with Atlantic. In 1965, backed by Booker T and the MG's and the Memphis Horns, he scored a No. 1 soul hit with "In the Midnight Hour," which quickly became a bar band staple. There were four more No. 1 soul hits, ending with "Don't Knock My Love" in 1971, and two of them ("Land of 1,000 Dances" in 1966 and "Funky Broadway" in 1977) were Top 10 pop hits. But he was unable to adapt his screaming style to the funk and disco of the 70s, and he spent most of the decade bouncing among a variety of labels with no significant hits to show for his efforts.

RECOMMENDED: *Best of Wilson Pickett, Vols. 1-2* (Atlantic).

PINK FLOYD

The first of the British psychedelic groups, Pink Floyd was formed in the mid 60s by guitarist Syd Barrett. The rest of the quartet was bassist Roger Waters, keyboardist Rick Wright and drummer Nick Mason. Barrett left after the first album and was replaced by guitarist Dave Gilmour. This is the lineup that went on to become Europe's biggest selling group and remains together to this day one of the world's most popular bands. The group's spacey, atmospheric rock was used as a soundtrack for the film *More* and led to the Floyd being asked to record the soundtrack for *La Valee*.

RECOMMENDED: *A Nice Pair, Atom Heart Mother, Dark Side of the Moon* (Capitol).

POCO

When the Buffalo Springfield, one of the greatest American bands of all time, broke up in the late 60s, the individual members went on to form the top country rock groups of the 70s. Perhaps the best of these offshoots was Poco, formed by ex-Springfield bassist Jim Messina and rhythm guitarist Richie Furay. Steel guitarist Rusty Young and drummer George Grantham filled out the group for their first album, then bassist Tim Schmit was added as Messina switched to second guitar. When Messina left to form Loggins and Messina in '71 Paul Cotten was added to the band and suddenly began to change the group's face with his prolific songwriting. After co-founder Furay left Cotton assumed direction.

RECOMMENDED: *Poco, A Good Feelin' To Know* (Epic).

POINTER SISTERS

Ruth, Anita, June and Bonnie Pointer are children of a preacher, the Reverend Elton Pointer, and spent their childhood singing with their two older brothers in the choir of the West Oakland Church of God. In 1969 they started out in San Francisco, backing up Elvin Bishop and Dave Mason before deciding to record on their own. The Sisters scored big with nostalgia-style songs like "Yes We Can Can" before switching to a more contemporary R&B direction. Then Richard Perry produced them on an album called *Energy*, and the Sisters had their biggest hit, a cover version of Bruce Springsteen's "Fire."

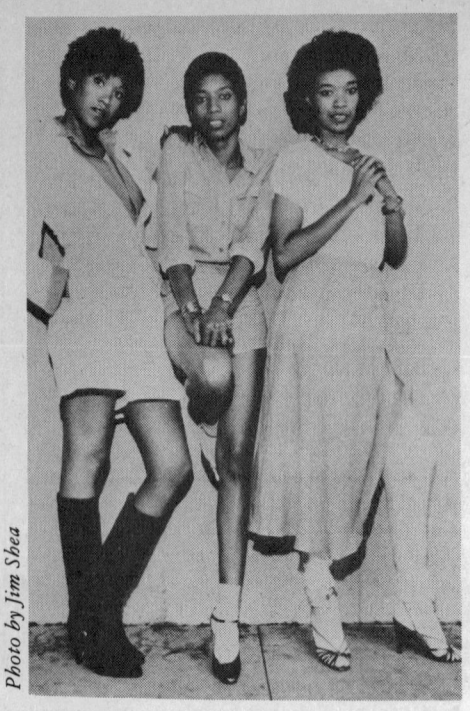

RECOMMENDED: *The Best of the Pointer Sisters* (ABC); *Energy* (Planet).

POLICE

One of the first English new wave bands to break through commercially in America, the Police are a trio composed of guitarist Andy Summers, bassist Gordon "Sting" Sumner, and American drummer Stewart Copeland. They came together in London during the height of the new wave movement, with the help of manager Miles Copeland, the drummer's brother. Andy Summers had been doing lucrative session work, while Stewart Copeland had been in the progressive group Curved Air. Sting's solid bass and anxious vocals blend well with Summers' skittish guitar and Copeland's reggae-tinged drumming. In early 1979, their first U.S. single, "Roxanne," made them overnight stars here, and the release of their debut album, *Outlandos d'Amour* (A&M) solidified their role as a major force in American rock 'n' roll.

RECOMMENDED: *Regatta de Blanc* (A&M).

JEAN-LUC PONTY

Conservatory trained master violinist Jean-Luc Ponty began his studies at the age of five. By fifteen he was a professional musician, playing classical and pop until deciding to concentrate on jazz. He came to the U.S. and immediately began playing with keyboardist George Duke and later collaborated with writer/arranger/guitarist/conceptualist Frank Zappa, recording both with Duke's small combo and Zappa's orchestra. Zappa worked with Ponty on some of Ponty's own records as well. In the mid-70s Ponty became fascinated with the possibilities of recording with electronic violin.

RECOMMENDED: *The Jean-Luc Ponty Experience* (Pacific Jazz); *Aurora* (Atlantic).

IGGY POP

One of America's truly perplexing rock figures, Iggy Pop (born James Osterberg in Ann Arbor, Michigan in 1947) has lived on the fringe of rock insanity since forming the Stooges in 1968. Through various lineups of that remarkable shambles of musical brilliance, a solo liaison with David Bowie, and finally a blossoming career as a major performer in the wake of the new wave, which the Stooges predated by almost a decade, Iggy first earned his notoriety through his abandoned concertizing: flinging himself headlong into audiences or onto tables, and smearing his body with anything handy, from peanut butter to the blood he regularly shed doing things like falling on broken glasses and throwing himself into amps and drumkits. The Stooges' music was loud, unruly, and chaotic, with lyrics covering a fairly revolting and nihilist set of subjects. As a solo artist, he has continued to espouse negativist philosophy, but the sophistication of his music has increased considerably. He has most recently followed the lead of Lou Reed and recorded in Germany, using electronics to further enhance his bleak images.

RECOMMENDED: *The Stooges* (Elektra); *Lust for Life*.

ELVIS PRESLEY

Elvis Aron Presley was born in 1935 to poor parents in Tupelo, Mississippi. When Elvis was thirteen the Presleys moved to Memphis, Tennessee. At first he made few friends there, expressing himself instead through church and amateur singing, and through the sort of flashy dress that years later would become integral to the concept of rock stardom. Appearing at country fairs from Memphis to Sweetwater, Texas, Presley became a regional star in 1954 and 1955 by blending country and western with rhythm and blues, and helping to create rock 'n' roll. But more than through his music, Presley brought rock into the musical mainstream through his marketability and appeal based on dark, menacing features, provocative plumed hairdo, suggestive stage motions, enthusiasm for work, and his expanding, rags-to-riches legend. Once he'd established himself as "The King of Rock 'n' Roll" with freewheeling, upbeat records like "Hound Dog" and "Don't Be Cruel," Presley and his advisers toned down his image and softened his repertoire to match a series of musical films and attract the most steadfast following possible. (With thirty-three movies and forty-five gold singles to his credit as of August 1977, the second figure rose after his death, Elvis proved the strategy correct.) But his place in rock 'n' roll hinged on his early brashness and emotional force, a fact he was aware of when he tried to recapture that fire with a late-60s return to the road and an emphasis on rhythmic singles like "Suspicious Minds" and "Any Day Now." By the time he was 42, he was considered a middle-of-the-road stylist, almost the sort of vocalist he had eclipsed twenty-one years earlier with "Heartbreak Hotel" and "Blue Suede

Shoe." It was largely his premature death which made people think of him again as a sexy, revolutionary pop singer, and prompted the release of enough exploitation films and stories to satisfy the most shameless necrophile. With the possible exception of the Beatles, no single phenomenon has had as much effect on the rock audience as Elvis Presley.

RECOMMENDED: *Elvis, For LP Fans Only, A Date with Elvis, Elvis' Golden Records Vols. 1-3, From Memphis to Vegas* . . . (RCA).

BILLY PRESTON

Preston, whose mother played "Sapphire" on the Amos & Andy radio show, was in show business from childhood. Born in Houston, Texas, he moved to California with his family and was playing keyboards with gospel star Mahalia Jackson at age 10 when a Hollywood producer tabbed him for the part of W. C. Handy as a child in *St. Louis Blues*. In 1962 he toured Europe with Little Richard, and met the Beatles in Hamburg. After a few years of rock 'n' roll work he returned to playing gospel with James Cleveland until he joined the Ray Charles group. When the Beatles formed Apple Records they signed Preston, and George Harrison produced two albums for Preston on that label. After touring with the Stones, playing the Concert for Bangla Desh and doing session work for dozens of big names, Preston toured successfully with his own band.

RECOMMENDED: *Original Billy Preston—Soul'd Out* (GNP Crescendo).

PRETTY THINGS

In 1964 the Pretty Things started out as one of the raunchiest British R&B bands, even a dirtier bunch than the Rolling Stones. In 1967 they enhanced their reputation by releasing the first rock opera, *S. F. Sorrow*. Then they stayed in the news in 1971 by releasing an album, *Parachute*, that was called album of the year by Rolling Stone Magazine. In 1973 the veterans were asked by Robert Plant to be the first group to sign with Led Zeppelin's Swan Song record label. Several successful tours followed, and lead singer Phil May has been recognized as one of the best rock vocalists. The rest of the band has featured keyboardist Gordon Edwards, lead guitarist Peter Tolson, keyboardist John Power, bassist Jack Green, and drummer Skip Alan.

RECOMMENDED: *The Vintage Years* (Sire); *Silk Torpedo* (Swan Song).

ALAN PRICE

An original Animal who first brought Burdon and the boys together as the Alan Price Combo, Alan Price (b. April 19, 1942, Fairfield, England) left the British Invasion bluesbusters early in the game (1965) to pursue solo activities. His first immediate success was to promote the songs of Randy Newman as his own British hit singles, "Simon Smith and his Amazing Dancing Bear" among others, and then to work on several English television specials. One collaborative LP with singer Georgie Fame later (1971), Price took film director Lindsay Anderson up on a proposition to play himself and write the score for the film *O! Lucky Man*, which initiated a whole new solo career for him. The "Jarrow Song," written about the British hunger marches of 1926, was a 1975 hit single for Price in Britain.

RECOMMENDED: *O! Lucky Man* (Warner Bros.); *Alan Price* (Jet).

LLOYD PRICE

Price was one of the handful of R&B singers who made the translation to rock 'n' roll in the 50s without much trouble.

His first hit was an R&B song "Lawdy Miss Clawdy," which made it in 1952, the pre-rock 'n' roll era. Elvis Presley became the first of many rockers to cover it later. After switching record companies in the late 50s Price came back with a string of hits; "Stagger Lee," "Personality" and "We're Gonna Get Married." After disappearing in the 60s, Price made a brief comeback in the 70s as the house performer at New York's Crawdaddy club.

RECOMMENDED: *Mr. Personality's Big 15* (ABC).

CHARLEY PRIDE

The first black singer to make it in modern country music, Pride is a product of the Delta cottonfields outside Sledge, Mississippi. He left there at 17 to take a shot at pro baseball, and played briefly with the L.A. Angels in 1961. During the off-season in 1963, he was discovered by country singer Red Sovine in Montana, where he worked in the zinc mines by day and sang at night. Sovine hooked him up with RCA's Chet Atkins, and his first record came out in 1965. Pride's career built slowly at first, largely because he and his business associates were leery about how the country audience would react to a black singer. But between 1969 and 1978, he had no less than nineteen No. 1 country records, an outstanding achievement for someone as low-key as Pride. In the process, he won nearly every award country music has to offer, and built one of the slickest stage shows in the business. Though he sometimes gets mired down in sentimentality, his creamy, sophisticated voice retains enough twang to satisfy the country purists. His albums (nearing 30, nearly half of them gold) represent the most consistent sellers in RCA's entire country catalog.

RECOMMENDED: *Best of Charley Pride, Vols. 1-3* (RCA).

JOHN PRINE

Photo by Gary Heery

An ex-mailman from Chicago, Prine's riveting social realism songs written with journalistic detail and deep love for the common man came to the attention of country singers like Kris Kristofferson, who urged him to record on his own. "Sam Stone," a song about a Vietnam veteran with a drug habit, made him one of the most respected songwriters of the early 70s. Though he's recorded since then in Nashville, his material has been covered by country, pop and rock performers and he's become one of the most successful folk singers in America.

RECOMMENDED: *The Best of John Prine* (Atlantic); *Bruised Orange* (Elektra).

PROCOL HARUM

A Bach-inspired organ tune might seem an unlikely basis for an international rock and soul hit, but the British Procol Harum with "A Whiter Shade of Pale" in 1967 made the idea a reality. With lyricist Keith Reid, the five musicians (Gary Brooker, Matthew Fisher, Robin Trower, B. J. Wilson and David Knights) went on to establish a level of imaginativeness and intensity that's rarely been matched in the twelve years of progressive rock which have followed. Personnel problems finally turned Procol Harum into a high-class pickup band, but not before the group had explored a wide range of melodies, dual-keyboard arrangements, haunting vocals and Gothic lyrics. Procol paved the way for mass acceptance of succeeding art-rock acts such as Genesis, Kansas, and Al Stewart. Procol broke up in 1977. Trower is a star bandleader; Brooker has gone solo; Wilson is a popular session drummer; organist Fisher is a respected record producer, as is Procol's Pete Solley, who's done keyboard work for Stewart. Both Reid and Knights went into artist management, and Reid hopes to find a singer-tunesmith to turn his recent verse into performable songs.

RECOMMENDED: *Procol Harum* (Deram-Regal Zonophone); *A Salty Dog, Live* (A&M).

PURE PRAIRIE LEAGUE

The name comes from a temperance union in old Dodge City, and the music is country/rock. Led by bassist Mike Reilly, drummer Billy Hinds and keyboardist Michael Conner, the band recently added guitarist Patrick Bolen and multi-instrumentalist Vince Gill in order to expand the stylistic and improvisational range. The band's pleasant blend of country rock and pop vocal influences enabled them to make a substantial hit single, "Amie."

RECOMMENDED: *Bustin' Out* (RCA).

SUZI QUATRO

Born into a musical family in Detroit at the beginning of 1950, Suzi Quatro entered professional music at age fourteen. In a series of bands with her sisters (one of who, Patti, was later in *Fanny*) and brother Mike, Suzi Q played a variety of instruments, eventually settling on the bass guitar when she signed up with famous English manager-producer Mickie Most in 1972. Most brought her to England, signed her to his record company (RAK), gave her a leather-clad sexy/tough image, and hired Mike Chapman and Nicky Chinn to write and produce her records. In the tradition of calculated chart successes, Suzi Quatro made the English charts sizzle with a clutch of amusing hits; "Can the Can," "48 Crash," and "Devil Gate Drive" and others. Despite efforts to make it in her native U.S., it wasn't until a guest appearance on the *Happy Days* TV show as Fonzie's friend Leather Tuscadero that Suzi's career began to take off. One guest shot turned into several, and soon a new recording contract, and then hit records, albeit in a somewhat different musical vein.

RECOMMENDED: *Suzi Quatro* (Bell).

QUEEN

Queen startled a sedentary rock world in 1973 by serving up a debut album of substance, quality, and originality. Mixing heavy metal guitar-based rock with ultrasophisticated multitrack recording wizardry under the tutelage of producer Roy Thomas Baker, Queen became one of the major rock influences of the mid-70s. The four Englishmen who make up Queen, Zanzibar-born vocalist Freddie

Mercury, astrophysicist guitar star Brian May, drummer Roger Meddows-Taylor, and bassist John Deacon, immediately became hugely successful, through singles, albums, and an extravagant stage presentation. Criticized by critics for pomposity and foolishness, Queen remains one of the most popular rock bands in the world, with regular chart-topping releases.

RECOMMENDED: *Queen, A Night at the Opera, Jazz,* (Elektra).

QUICKSILVER MESSENGER SERVICE

A San Francisco band, Quicksilver Messenger Service (the name came from their Virgo-heavy line-up) survived the end of the Acid Age, gigging long after their last album, a '75 reunion attempt, with a shifting set of musicians. But their best recorded work, *Quicksilver Messenger Service* (1968) and *Happy Trails* (1969), not only captured the spirit of the San Francisco sound in all of its mercurial glory but also the battle many Frisco musicians waged within themselves. For Quicksilver struck a rare balance between form: Cipollina's warbling vibrato guitar, the epic "The Fool," and feeling, the subtly spliced live "Who Do You Love" jam on *Happy Trails* and Dino Valenti's overbearing but often affecting growl on "What About Me." Formed in 1965, the classic Quicksilver was Cipollina, Duncan, drummer Greg Elmore, and bassist David Freiberg (now with Jefferson Starship). Dino Valenti was in and out until 1970, when he took over the reins and British pianist Nicky Hopkins appeared on three albums.

RECOMMENDED: *Quicksilver Messenger Service, Happy Trails, Solid Silver Anthology* (Capitol).

EDDIE RABBITT

His smooth, easy-listening voice and perky melodies have made Rabbitt one of the pre-eminent Nashville artists of the late 70s. Born in Brooklyn and raised in northern New Jersey, Rabbitt became a professional country musician in 1964; he moved to Nashville in 1967, and at first worked solely as a writer (Elvis Presley's 50th gold single was Eddie's song "Kentucky Rain"). It wasn't until 1974 that he launched his own career as a singer, and he didn't begin touring until 1977. But beginning in 1978, he racked up nine straight No. 1 country records, a few of which also made it onto the more lucrative pop charts, and the *big* crossover chart successes are almost certainly just around the corner.

RECOMMENDED: *Best of Eddie Rabbitt* (Elektra).

GERRY RAFFERTY

Scottish songwriter Gerry Rafferty made his first records in 1968 while working with the delirious Billy Connolly (Mr. Banana Boots) in the Humblebums. Three years later, Rafferty recorded his "solo" album, a musical poison-pen letter to the record industry. One of the sidemen for this LP was Joe Egan, with whom Gerry formed Stealers Wheel the next year. Rafferty's first worldwide hits came in 1972 and 1973 with the Stealers Wheel chestnuts "Stuck in the Middle with You" and "Star." Label and managerial problems coupled with Rafferty's unwillingness to tour led to the band's breakup after three albums. Rafferty retreated to the seclusion of his farm in Scotland, where contractual hassles kept him musically mute for three years. During that time he wrote the songs for *City to City,* an album so rich in material that it spawned four singles: three of them international smashes, and one, "Baker Street," the theme song to the summer of 1978. Rafferty's music combines the folk awareness of Fairport Convention with the AM adaptability of Paul McCartney, a man whose rural Scottish lifestyle closely resembles Rafferty's.

RECOMMENDED: *Can I Have My Money Back?* (Blue Thumb-Transatlantic); *City to City* (United Artists); *Gerry Rafferty* (Visa compilation of Rafferty-penned Humblebums songs).

BONNIE RAITT

The daughter of Broadway singing star John Raitt of *Carousel* and *Pajama Game,* Bonnie Raitt started her solo career in the early 70s as a brassy singer and interpreter of traditional blues guitar styles. Her first record included performances by Chicago bluesmen Junior Wells and A. C. Reed. As she went on, Raitt became known for selecting outstanding material from gifted but relatively unknown songwriters. Her instrumental accompaniment included John Hall of Orleans and members of Little Feat. More recently, Raitt has gone for a more slick delivery and the commerciality of Linda Ronstadt's producer Peter Asher.

RECOMMENDED: *Give It Up, Sweet Forgiveness* (Warner Bros.).

RAMONES

Dressed in sneakers and black leather jackets, the Ramones went through the mid-70s paving the way for hundreds of new bands. These groups would play loud and long in dark Manhattan bars like CBGBs and attract an audience of avant garde art and music fans who attached names like "new wave" and "minimalist rock" to them. But the Ramones remain essentially a pop group, making attempts at catchy hit singles like "Sheena Is A Punk Rocker" and "Rockaway Beach."

RECOMMENDED: *Ramones, Rocket to Russia* (Sire).

RASCALS

Lead singer Eddie Brigati, organist Felix Cavaliere, guitarist Gene Cornish and drummer Dino Danelli were the best band on Long Island's very hip summer dance circuit in the mid-60s. They were a burning outlet for blue–eyed soul that had their fans at clubs like the Barge wild with excitement. Their first album still sounds terrific 15 years later. The hits were legion: "Good Lovin'," "I Ain't Gonna Eat Out My Heart Anymore," "What Is the Reason," "I've Been Lonely Too Long," "Groovin'." After changing their name to the Rascals they mellowed out a bit and got into more jazz influenced, stretched out arrangements without losing the blues base. The band members went their separate ways in the early 70s.

RECOMMENDED: *Young Rascals, Collections, Greatest Hits,* (Atlantic).

RASPBERRIES

The band that earned Cleveland the nickname of "America's Liverpool," the Raspberries, led by Eric Carmen, hit the national charts in May 1972 with the single, "Go All the Way." With a sophisticated sound that had more to do with the Beatles and Beach Boys than anything of the 'Berries own decade, they successfully crossed the AM-FM bridge, appealing both to young kids and older listeners. In the space of a three-year, four-album recording career, the group mustered five hit singles, and earned a following that was stunned when the group disbanded in 1975 after undergoing a major personnel change before the recording of their final LP. The original drummer, Jim Bonfanti, was replaced by Michael McBride, and bassist Dave Smalley was replaced by Scott McCarl. After the split, Eric Carment went on to a smash solo LP and then quick oblivion from which no return has been made.

RECOMMENDED: *Raspberries, Fresh, Raspberries' Best* (Capitol).

OTIS REDDING

One of our best soul singers, Redding was born in Dawson, Georgia, and moved to Macon to start his recording career. Throughout the 60s and early 70s Redding's hits dominated the pop charts: "Pain In My Heart," "Respect," "I've Been Loving You Too Long," "I Can't Turn You Loose," "Satisfaction," "Don't Mess With Cupid," 'Fa-Fa-Fa-Fa-Fa," "Shake" and "Dock of the Bay." Redding's appearance at the Monterey Pop Festival in 1967 clinched his reputation as one of the most galvanizing live performers. He was certainly on the brink of superstardom when his light plane crashed later in the year, killing Redding.

RECOMMENDED: *Tell the Truth, The Dock of the Bay, History of Otis Redding* (Atlantic).

HELEN REDDY

Born in Melbourne, Australia, the daughter of show business parents, Reddy had a forgettable career in her homeland before winning a talent contest that sent her to the U.S. After knocking around in the States, she met Jeff Wald, who became her manager and husband. Wald tried her out on a number of songs until her cover of a song from *Jesus Christ Superstar,* "I Don't Know How to Love Him," became a huge hit. When she released "I Am Woman," Reddy's career was secure. She expanded to a film career, appearing in the Walt Disney movie *Pete's Dragon.*

RECOMMENDED: *I Don't Know How to Love Him, No Way to Treat a Lady* (Capitol).

LOU REED

About Lou Reed (b. Long Island, New York), Lester Bangs, in *Creem,* probably said it best when he wrote that the founding member of the Velvet Underground and increasingly unpredictable solo artist "gave dignity and poetry and rock 'n' roll to smack, speed, homosexuality, sadomasochism, murder, misogyny, stumblebum passivity, and suicide, and then proceeded to belie all his achievements and return to the mire by turning the whole thing into a bad joke." The worst joke of all was *Metal Machine Music,* a two-record set of beeps, hums, and other electronic nonsense that exhausted his audience's patience in 1975. But for all his infuriating behavior and audience baiting, Lou Reed, since the earliest days of the Velvet Underground, has made moving, emotional, thought-provoking rock 'n' roll and his failures are just as interesting as his successes. The Velvet Underground LPs are already recognized as classics in the canon of 60s urban rock, but Reed's solo outings are just as fascinating. *Transformer,* produced by Reed afficionado David Bowie in 1972, yielded Lou his solitary hit "Walk on the Wild Side," a soft shuffle which took a lyrically uninhibited but ultimately sensitive look at the social misfits populating Andy Warhol's circle of fast-living friends with *Berlin* the conceptual extension of that in darker colors. *Rock & Roll Animal,* recorded live in New York, produced electrifying takes of Reed stage standards "Sweet Jane" and "Rock and Roll." More recently, Reed unleashed his rapier wit in a set of monologues-and-music on the live *Take No Prisoners* and kicked ass on *Street Hassle.* Reed has gone through his phases, appearing on stage as a junkie (simulating shooting up) and a blond Frankensteinish android, but there is no contesting the fact that his discography is among the most fascinating in rock.

RECOMMENDED: *Lou Reed, Transformer, Berlin, Rock 'n' Roll Animal, Sally Can't Dance,* (RCA); *Street Hassle, Take No Prisoners* (Arista).

TERRY REID

Terry Reid came real close to a good thing when he was asked by Jimmy Page to be the singer in his New Yardbirds, which became Led Zeppelin, But Reid took a pass and instead suggested a young Birmingham blues wailer named Robert Plant. Reid continued slugging it out in cultish obscurity. His hoarse throaty, often pained vocal style is not the stuff of top 40 hits, but Reid, who came to London in 1964 and made the club band rounds until his discovery by producer Mickie Most, is still an effective singer whose emotive singing defies both description and classification. With Most he made two powerful and critically-acclaimed albums, *Bang Bang You're Terry Reid* (1968) and *Terry Reid* (1969), with only his scratchy guitar, Pete Solley's keyboards, and Keith Webb's drums. After voluntarily retiring to the States for a period, he briefly reappeared with the semi-acoustic *River,* again disappeared from public view, and again recorded, this time a more commercial effort called *Seeds of Memory.*

RECOMMENDED: *Bang Bang You're Terry Reid, Terry Reid* (Epic); *Seeds of Memory* (ABC).

RENAISSANCE

Few people who knew this band in its prehistory as ex-Yardbirds lead singer Keith Relf's follow-up project would recognize what became of it in the 70s. Led by the sky-high soprano of lead singer Annie Haslam and fleshed out instrumentally by bassist Jon Camp, guitarist Michael Dunford, drummer Terence Sullivan and keyboardist John Tout, Renaissance is a full-fledged classical/rock outfit, borrowing liberally and unabashedly from Debussy, Prokofiev and Rachmaninoff, with songs based on the *Scheherazade* legend and Alexander Solzhenitsyn's *A Day in the Life of Ivan Denisovitch.*

RECOMMENDED: *Prologue,* (Capitol-Sovereign); *Scheherazade and Other Stories, Live at Carnegie Hall* (Sire).

REO SPEEDWAGON

Granite-hard rock with a subtle melodic twist, that's REO Speedwagon. From

Champaign, Illinois where guitarist Gary Richrath (b. Peoria, Illinois) started the band while at the University of Illinois, REO Speedwagon (currently Richrath, singer/guitarist Kevin Cronin, bassist Bruce Hall, drummer Alan Gratzer, keyboard player Neal Doughty) has steadily built a national following on the strength of their concert performances, songs like "Ridin' the Storm Out," and a recent series of more commercially mature LPs on the order of *You Can Tune a Piano But You Can't Tune a Fish* and *Nine Lives*. The band now lives and works in Los Angeles.

RECOMMENDED: *Ridin' the Storm Out, REO Speedwagon Live, You Can Tune a Piano But You Can't Tune a Fish* (Epic).

PAUL REVERE AND THE RAIDERS

Paul Revere (his real name) and his colonially-garbed pop group have been dismissed as a teenypop phenomenon (they appeared daily on Dick Clark's mid-60s TV dance party *Where The Action Is*) with a few good singles ("Just Like Me," "Hungry," "Good Thing," "Kicks"). They were more than that. Revere, singer and dreamboat Mark Lindsay (he of the colonial ponytail), and the other Raiders who came and left (Phil Volk, Drake Levin, country singer-to-be Freddy Weller, among others) made some of the 60s punkiest hit singles. One of their first records was a raunchy pre-Kingsmen take of "Louie Louie." "Just Like Me" and "Steppin' Out" both had Lindsay growling over bulldozing riffs and wildly careening guitar solos, and "Him or Me, What's It Gonna Be" had an invigorating Byrds-like guitar sound that stood up well when the Flamin' Groovies covered it eight years later. Revere, the real mastermind behind the band, continues to lead a group of Raiders playing clubs and state fairs for fun and profit while Lindsay, after a few solo hits, had an A&R gig at United Artists Records at last report.

RECOMMENDED: *Paul Revere and the Raiders Greatest Hits* (Columbia).

CHARLIE RICH

Raised on a cotton plantation near Colt, Arkansas, Rich's first love was jazz, but his first records were for Sun, the Memphis rockabilly label. His rich, resonant voice and gospel-based piano were akin to Ray Charles. He hit in 1960 with "Lonely Weekends" and again in 1965 with "Mohair Sam," but those two records represented his only successes for about twenty years. Most of that time he simply bounced from label to label, a victim of bad producers and heavy drinking. Finally, in 1968, he settled in at Epic with producer Billy Sherrill providing him a mainstream country sound. By 1972, he had cracked the country Top 20, and in 1973, "Behind Closed Doors" was the No. 1 country record and a pop hit as well. In 1974, "The Most Beautiful Girl" topped both charts, and went platinum. When Rich went to Las Vegas his records became syrupy and lost all their vitality. A change of labels, to United Artists in 1978, gave him a commercial shot in the arm, but the music itself was no improvement.

RECOMMENDED: *Lonely Weekends* (Sun); *Best of Charlie Rich* (Epic).

CLIFF RICHARD

An amazingly durable singer, Cliff Richard (born Harry Webb in India) dominated the English record charts with his backing group, the Shadows, from 1959 until the Beatles came along. But Richard's durability brought him back to the top with regularity even after the Beatles had established themselves. The star of numerous films (among them, one great rock movie from 1959 called *Expresso*

Bongo), television shows, and stage productions, Richard has become a national institution in Britain, and shows no sign of weakening despite the fact that he's nearly forty and has been performing professionally for over twenty years. Never as big in America as at home, Cliff launched a successful assault on these shores in 1976 with a hit single, "Devil Woman," on Elton John's Rocket Records. Each time the contemporary rock world is prepared to write him off, Richard comes back with another hit record.

RECOMMENDED: *I'm Nearly Famous* (Rocket).

JONATHAN RICHMAN

Jonathan Richman (b. Natick, Massachusetts) has been alternately praised and reviled by critics and fans who see him as the rock 'n' roll innocent, writing such improbable songs as "Pablo Picasso" ("was not called an asshole") and "Here Come the Martian Martians" and singing them in a pained untrained tenor like a guitar-toting babe in the urban woods. Richman is remembered in Boston as the young kid who used to follow the Velvet Underground and worship the ground Lou Reed walked on. But with his group Modern Lovers Mark I, he made his own mark in the early 70s although ultimately their first Warner Brothers contract and John Cale-produced sessions went for naught. Under the aegis of independent record entrepreneur Matthew King Kaufman, Richman got back on record with a classic road song called "Roadrunner," formed a new acoustic-oriented Modern Lovers, and reverted into a child-like songwriting phase ("I'm a little mosquito/buzz, buzz, buzz") that confused his followers, some to the point of desertion. But with admirable pluck, Jonathan now carries on solo, still trying to find his place in the modern world.

RECOMMENDED: *The Modern Lovers, Back in Your Life* (Beserkeley).

RIGHTEOUS BROTHERS

Bill Medley and Bobby Hatfield called themselves the Righteous Brothers and the two became a powerful songwriting duo of the 60s. Under the direction of master producer Phil Spector, the Brothers put together an awesome series of swelling, romantic soul and R&B hits, the greatest of which, "You Lost That Lovin' Feelin'," was an amazing example of Spector's powerful "wall of sound". The Brothers went on to several other hits, most notably "Ebb Tide," "Unchained Melody" and "Soul and Inspiration." Medley left for a solo career in the late 60s. The Righteous Brothers made a movie called *A Swingin' Summer* in 1965.

RECOMMENDED: *Some Blue Eyed Soul, Greatest Hits* (Moonglow).

JOHNNY RIVERS

New York-born, Louisiana-bred Rivers worked as a songwriter in Nashville until 1963, when he moved to Los Angeles and got his big break opening the Whiskey au Go Go discotheque hangout for the stars. His white R&B singing and boogie guitar accompaniment led to a recording contract and a string of hit singles that included "Memphis," "Maybelline," "Mountain of Love," "Secret Agent Man," "Seventh Son," and "I Washed My Hands in the Muddy Water." He formed his own publishing company, Rivers Music, and his own record company, Soul City. His first discovery was a black lounge act called the Versatiles that Rivers suggested change its name to the Fifth Dimension. In addition to the Fifth Dimension, Rivers helped Jim Webb and Glen Campbell get their starts. In 1972 Rivers recorded the theme song for George McGovern's presidential candidacy, "Come Home America."

RECOMMENDED: *And I Know You Wanna Dance, Rewind, Blue Suede Shoes* (United Artists).

SMOKEY ROBINSON

At age 13, Smokey Robinson formed a band with three Detroit neighbors and called it the Miracles. When they later signed with Motown Records, they put that company on the map with its first million-selling single, "Shop Around." Over the years the Miracles were one of Motown's premier groups, with hits like "Get Ready," "My Girl," "My Guy," "Second That Emotion," and "Ain't That Peculiar." When Motown moved its offices to Los Angeles, Robinson quit the Miracles and recorded a series of acclaimed solo albums. At the same time, Robinson has pursued an acting career in television and also produced a movie called *Big Time*.

RECOMMENDED: *Pure Smokey, Deep in My Soul* (Motown).

TOM ROBINSON BAND

In the context of the British new wave, the short-lived TRB had a significant impact, both on the music and on the political nature of the movement. A self-avowed homosexual and political activist, Robinson had been a member of a small-time band called Care Society, which released one album in 1976 under the tutelage of Ray Davies of the Kinks. After a bitter split with Davies, Robinson "came out of the closet" and formed a quartet to militate for change. In the frenzy of activity in England in 1977, the Tom Robinson Band managed to get a recording contract with EMI Records, the label that had been the first to dismiss the Sex Pistols because of their controversiality. The release of a wonderful (and nonpolitical) single, "2-4-6-8 Motorway," put TRB on the pop charts. When their debut album was released in mid-1978, however, it was full of intense preaching and rhetoric with songs like "Up against the Wall," "Ain't Gonna Take It," "Glad to Be Gay," and "Long Hot Summer." America was intrigued, and the group's first tour here was quite well received. But there was no way to turn radical proselytizing into big business ten years after the Woodstock Nation and TRB seemed destined for cult status. Unfortunately, personnel problems erupted before the recording of the second album, and by mid-1979 the Tom Robinson Group was no more.

RECOMMENDED: *Power in the Darkness* (Harvest).

KENNY ROGERS

He left his native Houston at the age of 19 to hook up with such folkish L.A. groups as the Bobby Doyle Trio and the New Christy Minstrels. In 1967, he co-founded the First Edition, an innocuous rock band which moved toward country as it picked up hits ("Just Dropped In to See What Condition My Condition Was In," "Ruby, Don't Take Your Love to Town," "Ruben James," "Something's

Burning") and a national TV series. When the group broke up, Rogers went solo as a country artist peaking in 1977 with "Lucille," which won him a Grammy and numerous Country Music Association awards. Each new release since has been an instant hit, and Rogers has come to represent the modern country singer: soft, suave, soothing, bland. He also cuts occasional duets with Dotty West that are a little more country than his solo sides.

RECOMMENDED: *Kenny Rogers and the First Edition, Greatest Hits* (Reprise); *The Gambler* (United Artists).

ROLLING STONES

The Rolling Stones were introduced on the live *Get Your Ya-Ya's Out* as "the greatest rock 'n' roll band in the world." But they've earned their arrogance in their seventeen years as blues-smitten middle-class punks turned superstars. Led by the charismatic singer Michael Philip Jagger (b. July 26, 1943, Dartford, Kent, England) and a real rock 'n' roll outlaw in guitarist Keith Richards (b. December 18, 1943, Dartford, Kent), the Rolling Stones, Jagger, Richards, the late Brian Jones (b. Lewis Brian Hopkin-Jones, February 28, 1942, Cheltenham), bassist Bill Wyman (b. October 24, 1936), drummer Charlie Watts (b. June 2, 1941), and later guitarists Mick Taylor (ex-John Mayall) and Ron Wood (ex-Jeff Beck, Faces) have come to symbolize the riches and jet-set popularity that can come from rock 'n' roll as well as setting an example for expressive, lyrically incisive, R&B-inflected rock 'n' roll raunch. Their historical tale has been told from a number of angles: Anthony Scaduto wrote a scathing bio of Jagger subtitled *Everybody's Lucifer;* Robert Greenfield went on the Stones' '73 U.S. tour and came back with *S.T.P.: A Journey Through America;* Tony Sanchez concentrated on the sleaze for his *Up and Down With the Rolling Stones;* and British writer Roy Carr gives a detailed account of their musical career in *The Stones: An Illustrated Record.* Nor have the Stones ever come up short on headlines. The embryonic Stones (which included guitarist Dick Taylor of the Pretty Things) worked out their unique (in Britain's early 60s) fusion of blues, R&B, and teen rock 'n' roll enthusiasm in relative obscurity with the paternal help of Alexis Korner, first at his Ealing Club and later the Crawdaddy in Richmond. But it was Andrew Loog Oldham, upstart hustler, who capitalized on Jagger's pouting sensuality and the Stones' generally dirty looks, promoting them in the papers as Parental Enemy #1. The notorious drug busts of 1967 and 1968, Brian Jones' drowning in his swimming pool on July 3, 1969, the Altamont fiasco (a member of the audience stabbed to death by Hell's Angels at a free Stones festival in California, 1969), Jagger's marriage to Nicaraguan beauty Bianca Perez Morena de Macias, Mick Taylor's '74 break with the group, Keith Richards' run-in with Canadian authorities over drug charges in 1978, Jagger's divorce proceedings with Bianca and Margaret Trudeau's rumored fling with the Stones in '78— they all followed in succession. But the Stones' story cannot be told without the music, an unexcelled collection of successes, near-misses, and even interesting failures in which the Rolling Stones and particularly the Jagger-Richards songwriting team defied, pushed back, and refined to their own advantage the limits of rock, strutting confidently back to their roots on the bulldozing *Some Girls* in 1978. There are, for example, the powerful R&B sides they cut at Chicago's Chess studios in 1965, the superb *Aftermath,* a fascinating *Between the Buttons,* the Pepperlike psychedelia of *Their Satanic Majesties Request,* the improved-with-age *Exile on Main Street,* and "Jumpin' Jack Flash," everything the Stones have meant to rock 'n' roll in three electrifying minutes. With Ron Wood in the second guitar seat, trading riffs and guitar-hero grimaces with Richards, the Stones are back to grinding out first-class rock 'n' roll after some spotty albums in the mid-70s. The punks have issued a challenge to the Stones to rock or get lost, just as the Stones themselves did in 1962. That the Stones have taken them up on the challenge and made their most exciting music in years as a result augers well for the future: rock 'n' roll's as well as the Rolling Stones'.

RECOMMENDED: *December's Children, Aftermath, Between the Buttons, Let It Bleed,* (London); *Sticky Fingers, Exile on Main Street, Goat's Head Soup, It's Only Rock 'n' Roll, Black and Blues, Through The Past Darkly, Some Girls* (Rolling Stones).

RONETTES

A tough girl group, the Ronettes were three black singers who wore beehive hairdos and heavily made up faces and sang a brassy, challenging style that was cut by Phil Spector to fit his "wall of sound" production approach. Spector had already clicked with the girls group the Crystals and used the Ronettes as the flip side followup. Their mid-60s hits were "Be My Baby," "Walking in the Rain," "Baby I Love You" and "Do I Love You," among others.

RECOMMENDED: *Ronettes* (Philles).

LINDA RONSTADT

Photo by Jim Shea

In her work with the Stone Poneys and her solo records through 1973, Linda showed great feeling for such folk and country-derived songs as "2:10 Train," "Orion," "Long, Long Time," "The Only Mama That'll Walk the Line," and "Everybody Loves a Winner." But as manager Peter Asher maneuvered her further into the mainstream of American pop consciousness, Ronstadt lost her gruff persuasiveness and sensitive way with love songs. For the past few years she's seemed incapable of anything more than re-recording hits of the 50s and soundalike Jackson Browne and Warren Zevon songs in a sterile, calculated manner.

RECOMMENDED: *The Stone Poneys, Heart Like a Wheel* (Capitol); *Prisoner in Disguise, Simple Dreams* (Asylum).

ROXY MUSIC

One of the strangest of a bizarre collection of rock groups to surface out of the mannered glitter rock explosion of the early 70s, Roxy Music was led by the odd visions of singer/songwriter/conceptualist leader Bryan Ferry. Ferry's approach to writing took much from the metaphysical poets, and his arrangement of the band's musical direction took similarly unusual twists. At first his co-conspirator was synthesizer wizard Brian Eno, who left when the musical direction Ferry was taking did not appeal to him. Eddie Jobson became the keyboardist and string player, while the rest of the group consisted of guitarist Phil Manzanera, bassist John Gustafson, saxophonist Andrew Mackay and drummer Paul Thompson, After a brief respite to pursue solo projects, Roxy Music reunited in 1979.

RECOMMENDED: *Roxy Music* (Warner Brothers); *Siren* (Atco).

RUFUS

One of the most successful pre-disco funk and R&B bands of the mid-70s, Rufus was born in Chicago where keyboardist Kevin Murphy put the band together in 1973. The idea was to back up sultry vocalist Chaka Khan, a big voiced veteran of the Chicago supper club circuit who had performed with The Babysitters. The hit single "Tell Me Something Good," with its honking overlay of spongy funk textures, rocketed the band to stardom. The other members were David "Hawk" Wolinski on keyboards, guitarist Tony Maiden, bassist Bobby Watson, and drummer Richard Calhoun. Khan left the band in 1978 and Rufus has continued to record.

RECOMMENDED: *Rufus, Rufusized* (MCA).

RUNAWAYS

Under the guidance and direction of Los Angeles based Kim Fowley, five young girls from the better sections of Southern California were molded into the Runaways in 1976. The plan was simple enough: meld sex with rock 'n' roll and give teenage boys something else to dream about besides guitars and amplifiers. Unfortunately, the posturing and lack of talent by the unlikely nubettes, Cherie Currie, Lita Ford, Sandy West, Jackie Fox and Joan Jett, made the band more of a joke than a successful marketing ploy. Their first two albums were loud and abrasive, but too calculated to be entertaining. Then the inner tensions always present in unnaturally conceived groups began to affect the Runaways, and vocalist Currie was the first to leave, with much acrimony on all sides. Her one-album solo career went nowhere. Bassist Jackie Fox was replaced by Vickie Blue, and the four-piece group recorded a third album. Their recent existence has been sporadic, despite the release of a Japanese live LP from their 1977 tour.

TODD RUNDGREN

Upper Darby High School authorities would not acknowledge Todd Rundgren Day in 1977 because Rundgren, they said, was not a model student and hailing him as a hero would set a bad example for students. Rundgren, born and raised in the Philadelphia suburb of Upper Darby, Pa., is the closest thing rock 'n' roll has to a Renaissance man. As a teen, he came under the spell of that city's R&B scene, played in the obligatory British Invasion copy band, and established himself as a six-string guitarist with a blues band called Woody's Truck Stop. But he made his mark as the songwriting and conceptual mastermind behind Nazz, who made an impressive 1968 debut. He has spent prodigious spells as a producer and engineer for Ian and Sylvia, the Band, Grand Funk, Fanny, the New York Dolls, and later Patti Smith, the Tubes,

Tom Robinson, and Rick Derringer. He also has the ability to record "an ear-catching bouquet of pop melodies," as he describes them in the liner notes to has overdubber's delight *Something/Anything*, melodies which include "Hello It's Me" (dating back to Nazz days) and "I Saw The Light." Consider also his touring and recording work with Utopia (currently Roger Powell, Kasim Sulton, and John Wilcox) and finally his new interest in video and video discs. Not bad for a guy still not 30.

RECOMMENDED: *Runt,* (Ampex/Bearsville); *Something/Anything, Utopia, Back to the Bars* (Bearsville).

RUSH

Toronto-born and bred, Rush, guitarist Alex Lifeson, bass guitarist and singer Geddy Lee, and drummer Neil Peart (replacing John Rutsey in 1974), have taken criticism for: (a) Lee's screeching vocals, akin to Robert Plant on helium; (b) the conceptual 15-minute sci-fi fantasies (lyrics by Ayn Rand enthusiast Peart) they perform on record and stage; (c) their general heavy-metal-via Yes/Genesis sound. But after several years of taking abuse from Toronto bar owners, Rush has conquered much of America with a vengeance. A solid touring attraction, especially in the Midwest (they first broke in Cleveland via WMMS), Rush is consistently ignored by FM radio as well for the above reasons. Rush records consistently go gold and platinum here and back home in Canada where they have won a host of Junos (Canada's Grammy).

RECOMMENDED: *Rush, All the World's a Stage, Hemispheres* (Mercury).

TOM RUSH

Part of the Boston area early 60s folk scene, Rush gradually built up a local reputation after learning to play the guitar while he was at Harvard University. Born in Portsmouth, New Hampshire, Rush was suited to a folk background and combined a lot of different styles of traditional American and British music into his delivery before recording several records for Prestige, then Vanguard, at which point he was hailed by Paul Nelson of *Little Sandy Review* as "that artist none of us thought possible." Later Rush became known for popularizing rising songwriters like Joni Mitchell and Jackson Browne. Rush continued recording for Columbia in the 70s, making his classic *Ladies Love Outlaws* for that label.

RECOMMENDED: *Blues/Songs/Ballads* (Prestige); *Circle Game* (Elektra); *Ladies Love Outlaws* (Columbia).

LEON RUSSELL

In 1959 he backed Ronnie Hawkins and turned down a gig with Jerry Lee Lewis, choosing to become an L.A. session musician instead. He played on Phil Spector productions of the Crystals and Ronettes, on the Righteous Brothers' "You've Lost That Lovin' Feeling," on Gary Lewis's hits (which he cowrote), on the Byrds' "Mr. Tambourine Man," and on Ike and Tina Turner's "River Deep, Mountain High." On his own he recorded two albums under the name Asylum Choir with Marc Benno, then contributed to Delaney and Bonnie's first LP which led him to Joe Cocker. Russell wrote "Delta Lady" for Cocker, became his musical director, and spearheaded the Mad Dogs and Englishmen tour which was made into a feature film. Russell's solo career has flourished since, while many of his songs have been covered by other artists.

RECOMMENDED: *Leon Russell, Carney* (Shelter).

MITCH RYDER

Lillian Roxon described Mitch Ryder (real name Willard Levise, b. Detroit) as "one of those white singers who is still doing every trick in the 50s rhythm & blues book," all of which just goes to show "there [is] still a market for sweaty, bare-chested, hard-rock, bump-and-grind sexuality." Well, there is and Ryder, both in sound and spirit, continues to make the mighty noise he did in the 60s when belting out "Jenny Take a Ride," "Devil With the Blue Dress," and "Sock It to Me" in front of the furiously pumping Detroit Wheels. (In a previous incarnation they were Billy Lee, Ryder again, and the Rivieras, playing clubs in the metropolitan Detroit area.) As the hits started to come less frequently, Ryder's producer Bob Crewe sent him cabaret's way to no avail. But successive ventures like *The Detroit Memphis Experiment* produced by Steve Cropper and featuring the famed Memphis studio rhythm section and Ryder's early 70s band Detroit (one devastatingly hard rockin' album on Paramount) showed he'd never lost the touch. After a period of semi-retirement in which he wrote material with wife Kimberly, painted, and wrote an as-yet unpublished novel, Mitch Ryder is back in action with a new band and album (*How I Spent My Vacation,* on the independent Seeds and Stems label).

DOUG SAHM

Tex-Mex man Doug Sahm (b. November 6, 1941) has enjoyed only spotty commercial success and most of it with his original Sir Douglas Quintet on "She's About a Mover" and "Mendocino" (1965 and '69 respectively). But his contribution to the American rock 'n' roll canon and his steady representation of Texas in rock history makes him an important figure. He is certainly recognized by his peers: Bob Dylan played on the '73 LP *Doug Sahm and Band,* which was produced by heavyweights Jerry Wexler and Arif Mardin, and ex-Creedence Clearwater Revivalists Stu Cook and Doug Clifford were the rhythm section on 74's *Groover's Paradise.* Sahm also produced one of the great Tex-Mex records (picking up a lot from his original producer Huey Meaux) by a quartet of teens called Louie and the Lovers entitled *Rise.* It was classic Tex-Mex: an exhilarating hybrid of Texas R&B, garage-band rock rhythms, and stylistic Mexican spices. You can hear it all over Sahm's records and in his live performances. He's recently resurfaced on the club circuit after a period of relative inactivity.

RECOMMENDED: *The Best of the Sir Douglas Quintet* (Tribe); *Doug Sahm and Band* (Atlantic); *Groover's Paradise* (Warner Bros.).

SAM AND DAVE

These soul men exploded in the 60s with their double dynamite singing approach and one of the most kinetic stage acts of the time. Sam Moore and Dave Porter were the spearheads of the Stax-Volt sound, scoring with the singles "Hold On, I'm Coming," "You've Got Me Humming," "Soul Man," "Soothe Me," "When Something Is Wrong With My Baby," "Wrap It Up," "I Thank You," and "Can't You Find Another Way (Of Doing It)." Their "Soul Man" became a big hit again in 1978 in a version done by the Blues Brothers.

RECOMMENDED: *Hold On I'm Coming, Soul Men* (Atlantic).

SANTANA

Billed as the Santana Blues Band, this high-powered Latin rock outfit led by the searing lead guitar work of Carlos Santana played before half a million people at Woodstock without even a record contract. Ten years, eleven albums, and twelve different lineups later, Santana remains one of the hottest groups around. Over the years they've had success with singles like "Evil Ways," "No One to Depend On," and "Black Magic Woman," switched from high-powered rock to avant garde jazz and steaming salsa styles with ease, and featured some great players. Carlos Santana has stepped out of his leader's role in this band to record with John McLaughlin and Buddy Miles.

RECOMMENDED: *Santana, Abraxas* (Columbia).

SAVOY BROWN

Alexis Korner and John Mayall may have been the godfather and father respectively of white electric British blues, but Savoy Brown, under the leadership of guitarist Kim Simmonds, took the message to America. Relatively popular at home, Savoy Brown nevertheless made the U.S. concert circuit their second home, touring the States extensively with what seemed like a different set of personnel everytime. And, with the exception of Simmonds, Savoy Brown was something of a way station for British bluesbusters who rarely stayed with the band for more than three or four albums at a time. Simmonds organized the band in 1966, but the Savoy Brown line-up considered the best was Simmonds, singer Chris Youlden (with the battered top hat and omnipresent stogie), guitarist Lonesome Dave Peverett, bass guitarist Tone Stevens, and drummer Roger Earl. The last three broke away in 1971 to form Foghat, a British blues/rock outfit that moved to the States some years later, acknowledging the American teenage thirst for ballsy boogie. Simmonds kept the Savoys going with players from Chicken Shack, Keef Hartley's band, and former members of Noel Redding's Fat Mattress, to name a few, Simmonds also moved to America in '78, settling near Cleveland, Ohio, after recording one more Savoy Brown album as a trio. The band's future, at this date, is uncertain. Their past, however, made for some very exciting blues'd-out rock 'n' roll.

RECOMMENDED: *Shake Down* (U.K. Decca); *Street Corner Talking, Hellbound Train* (London/Parrot).

LEO SAYER

A working class kid from Shoreham-by-Sea, England, Leo Sayer moved to London as a teenager and earned his living playing Bob Dylan songs in the streets before joining several bands. He collaborated with David Courtney on some songs, and when Roger Daltrey of the Who was looking for material for his debut solo album he recorded an album of nothing but Sayer/Courtney tunes. Daltrey encouraged Sayer to stay at Daltrey's house and use his home studio to work on material for Sayer's own album. Sayer became a huge star in England and a moderate hit in the U.S., where his penchant for wearing a clown suit onstage gave him a recognizable image for the teen audience.

RECOMMENDED: *Endless Flight* (Warner Bros.).

BOZ SCAGGS

William Royce (Boz) Scaggs (b. June, 1944, Ohio) first played with Steve Miller in Texas at age 15 in Miller's Markmen. With Miller, he also went to the University of Wisconsin where the two played the usual fraternity-rock mixture of R&B and boozy rock 'n' roll. Scaggs also toured Europe on a musician's budget as a folksinger, recording one album *Boz* that was released only in Europe. He also gigged in Texas and Europe with a band that would become the Mother Earth rhythm section. None of this sounds terribly impressive, but as a rock 'n' roll education goes, Scaggs made the most of it because he would later play in the Steve Miller Band on the groundbreaking *Children of the Future* and *Sailor* albums and then formulate his own musical future, based on a slick but substantial R&B premise first established on the Muscle Shoal-style *Boz Scaggs* album and finally realized on the superb, not to mention best-selling, *Silk Degrees*.

RECOMMENDED: *Boz Scaggs* (Atlantic, a classic LP for Duane Allman's guitar solo on "Loan Me a Dime" alone); *Moments, Silk Degrees* (Columbia).

TOM SCOTT

Rock became more of a special interest medium in the 70s when its simple basic form adapted so well to any musical shape. One of the more vital aspects of the evolution of 70s rock was fusion, a combination of jazz harmonic complexity with rock rhythms. Many jazz players and rock players have appeared on the same sessions in the 70s, and no player represents that conjunction better than Tom Scott. Scott, a jazz saxophonist, has played in countless L.A. sessions, notably with Steely Dan and Joni Mitchell (on her live *Miles of Aisles*). Scott leads the L.A. Express, a band featuring Max Bennett on bass, John Guerin on drums, Robben Ford on guitar, and Larry Nash on piano.

RECOMMENDED: *Great Scott* (A&M); *Tom Cat* (Ode).

SEATRAIN

Formed after the breakup of the Blues Project in the late 60s by ex-Project flautist/bassist Andy Kulberg and drummer Roy Blumenfeld, the band also included ex-Jim Kweskin fiddler Richard Greene, guitarist John Gregory and vocalist Jim Roberts. After a mediocre debut the band switched personnel dramatically, filling in with drummer Larry Atamanuik, guitarist Peter Rowan and keyboardist Lloyd Baskin. The band's eclectic sound won them some admirers, but after several albums the group split up.

RECOMMENDED: *Seatrain, Marblehead Messenger* (Capitol).

JOHN SEBASTIAN

The son of a world famous harmonica virtuoso, John Sebastian was born in 1944 in New York City. An early pioneer in the Greenwich Village folk scene, he formed his first serious band, the Mugwumps (with two future members of the Mamas and the Papas) in 1962. Three years later, he formed the Lovin' Spoonful with guitarist Zal Yanovsky, bassist Steven Boone, and drummer Joe Butler. Sebastian himself played guitar, autoharp, harmonica, and sang such classics as "Do You Believe in Magic?", "Summer in the City," "Rain on the Roof," and "You Didn't Have to Be So Nice." A prolific songwriter, Sebastian wrote a pair of film scores (*What's Up Tiger Lily* and *You're a Big Boy Now*) with the Spoonful, and continued such projects after the group broke up in 1967, writing a Broadway show score and recording as a solo artist. Sebastian appeared at Woodstock and at the Isle of Wight Festivals, and wrote and recorded several hit records in the decade since the Spoonful, but his biggest success came when he was asked to write the theme song for a new TV show in 1976. The show, *Welcome Back Kotter*, became a hit, and so did the theme song, released as a single. Sebastian's goodtime music attracts new fans every time he makes a new album or plays a big concert. A real American folk musician.

RECOMMENDED: *John B. Sebastian, The Four of Us* (Reprise).

THE SECTION

Drummer Russ Kunkel, guitarist Danny Kortchmar, keyboardist Craig Doerge and bassist Leland Sklar are four of the finest instrumentalists on the Los Angeles session scene. Together and separately they've played with countless major artists from Bob Dylan to Barbra Streisand. In addition, the band has been closely involved in the musical careers of James Taylor, Carole King, Jackson Browne and Crosby, Stills and Nash. The band came together in the early 70s when they were backing James Taylor on his first national tour. They jammed during sound checks and after listening to recordings of the results decided to record on their own.

RECOMMENDED: *The Section* (Warner Brothers); *Fork It Over* (Capitol).

NEIL SEDAKA

Brooklyn-born Sedaka started writing songs with his lifelong musical partner, Howard Greenfield, at age 13. Five years later, Connie Francis's cover of Sedaka's "Stupid Cupid" became his first hit. Starting in 1959, Sedaka began his own recording career, scoring big hits with "Calendar Girl" and "Happy Birthday Sweet 16." After falling into obscurity during the 60s, Sedaka's brand of saccharine pop came back into fashion in the 70s and he was able to graduate from the oldies circuit to a second round of recording his own songs. Sedaka became a major force in 70s songwriting, penning "Love Will Keep Us Together" for Captain & Tennille, the song responsible for their initial fame.

RECOMMENDED: *Sedaka's Back* (Rocket).

SEEDS

The Seeds, led by pug-faced, mop-topped Sky Saxon, knew one song and got five albums out of it. Managed by the flamboyant "Lord" Tim Hudson, the Seeds: Saxon, drummer Rick Andridge, guitarist Jan Savage, keyboard player Daryl Hooper, had their biggest hit in 1967 with the seminal disaffected-teen anthem, "Pushin' Too Hard". A driving Bo Diddley-like sound, Saxon's punkish whine, and Hudson's ability to jump aboard every bandwagon enabled the Seeds to go from being a big underground band in Los Angeles to being a nationally-known band. During their four years, the Seeds went psychedelic, became the Sky Saxon Blues Band (liner notes by Muddy Waters), and faded into obscurity when their audience grew up. Saxon has recently resurfaced on record as Sky Sunlight.

RECOMMENDED: *The Seeds* (GNP Crescendo).

PETE SEEGER

More than any other professional folk singer, Seeger encouraged his audiences to follow his example and learn to accompany themselves on guitar and banjo (thus helping to spark the American folk revival). He's made three instructional record albums; some of those he's influenced, like Roger McGuinn, have since become stars. As a member of two seminal folk groups, the Weavers and the Almanac Singers, Seeger championed social causes and became notorious for his outspoken lyrics and comments in support of unions and socialized political programs. So strongly was he supported within the folk community that when the ABC-TV *Hootenanny* show blacklisted him in the 60s for alleged communist sympathies, top-line acts like the Kingston Trio and Joan Baez turned down offers for paid appearances on the program. Seeger's activism has tended to obscure his considerable writing talent: he wrote the melodies of "Where Have All the Flowers Gone" and "Bells of Rhymney," as well as providing words and 12-string guitar arrangements for other songs which later did well for the Byrds and Judy Collins. Seeger has recently crusaded for conservation in New York State, and took part in the anti-nuclear power rallies late in 1979.

RECOMMENDED: *American Favorite Ballads, Vol. IV & V, Quest, The World of Pete Seeger* (Columbia); *Circles & Seasons* (Warner Bros.).

BOB SEGER

After years of being the biggest rock attraction in Detroit but virtually unheard of everywhere else, Bob Seger made the late 70s hit single, "Night Moves." The talented singer/songwriter/guitarist started out in the mid-60s and had a top 10 hit in 1968, "Ramblin' Gamblin' Man." In the 70s he formed the Silver Bullet band: lead guitarist Drew Abbot, saxophonist Alto Reed, keyboardist Robyn Robbins, bassist Chris Campbell, and drummer Charlie Martin, and eventually quit playing guitar in live shows to enhance his stage presence.

RECOMMENDED: *Live Bullet, Night Moves, Stranger in Town*, (Capitol).

SEX PISTOLS

The leaders and innovators of the whole British punk/new wave explosion, the Pistols led a brief but tumultuous and influential life between 1976 and 1978, gaining the sort of notoriety usually accorded only the top names of rock. In that short time span, they were signed to three and fired from two major English record labels, collecting over $200,000 in severance money along the way. Their first 45, "Anarchy in the U.K.," served as the focal point and rallying cry for hundreds of followers and bands that sprung up in the Pistols' wake. After establishing their popularity as a top live act in England and Europe (despite attempts by various governments to prevent their appearing), the Pistols tried to crack the American market but failed miserably, ending the tour in chaos and dissolution. Bassist Sid Vicious, who perched in New York after the split, was arrested for the murder of his girlfriend, and later died from a drug overdose. Singer/leader Johnny Rotten reverted to his given name, Lydon, and formed a group called Public Image Ltd., while guitarist Steve Jones and drummer Paul Cook have pursued various musical ventures together, some under the name "Sex Pistols."

RECOMMENDED: *Never Mind the Bollocks* (Warner Bros.); *The Great Rock 'n' Roll Swindle* (Virgin import).

THE SHADOWS

One of the most successful, longstanding, and important British rock groups, the Shadows are not well known in America despite worldwide sales in the many millions. An instrumental guitar band, in the same vein as their imitators the Ventures and the Spotnicks, the Shadows began as a quartet, backing teen idol Cliff Richard in 1958. The original members, Hank B. Marvin, Bruce Welch, Terry Smart, and Ian Samwell, became overnight stars as the Drifters, and changed their name to the Shadows a year later, while Smart was replaced by Tony Meehan. Over the next five years, while remaining Richard's backing group on tours and records, the Shadows, despite numerous personnel shifts, recorded and released twenty hit singles. Some of the standouts are "Apache," "The Rumble," "Shadoogie," "Guitar Tango." All bore the distinctively clear twang of the Shadow's two guitar attack, and many became worldwide hits in countries the group would eventually tour: Poland, South Africa, Israel, Greece. In the late 60s, the Shadows broke up and reformed a few years later as Marvin, Welch and Farrar. In 1975, the name Shadows was revived, and they have continued where they left off. Many alumnae of the group have gone on to various important roles in British music, as performers and producers.

RECOMMENDED: *Shadoogie* (EMI-Pathe Marconi).

SHANGRI-LAS

The mid-60s saw a proliferation of girl vocal groups and the Shangri-Las were among the best. Their bad girl image and nasty, big beat sound were the stuff of pop legend, but their producer, Shadow Morton, took it one step further by identifying them with the motorcycle gang films of the time in their biggest single, "Leader of the Pack." Their other singles were "Give Him a Great Big Kiss," "Remember Walkin' In the Sand" and "I Can Never Go Home Anymore."

RECOMMENDED: *Golden Hits of the Shangri-Las* (Red Bird).

CARLY SIMON

The daughter of publishing magnate Richard Simon (of Simon & Schuster), Carly got her start in the music business as part of a singing duo with her sister Lucy when the two were at Sarah Lawrence College. Carly's solo career began in the early 70s after a successful songwriting collaboration with Jacob Brakman. Her sultry, big-voiced delivery and sensuality made her a popular, if infrequent, concert attraction, and in 1972 she married singer-songwriter James Taylor. A song from *No Secrets*, her Richard Perry-produced album of that same year, "You're So Vain," became a huge hit on the strength of a guest appearance by Mick Jagger and a surprise ending to the chorus. More recently, Simon has retired from the road, but her performances of songs like "Anticipation" and "Nobody Does It Better" continue to be used in commercials and television trailers.

RECOMMENDED: *Anticipation, No Secrets*, (Elektra).

PAUL SIMON

This diminutive singer/songwriter got his start in the late 50s singing with his pal Art Garfunkel. They recorded under the name of Tom and Jerry in an Everly Brothers fashion. Then, after the success of the New York folk scene and protest folk music in the early 60s, Simon and Garfunkel took the cue and scored a huge hit with the alienation anthem "Sounds of Silence." After several years of phenomenal success the duo split up. Since then Simon has been far more successful than his counterpart with an impressive string of hits from "Me and Julio Down by the Schoolyard" to "Fifty Ways To Leave Your Lover."

RECOMMENDED: *Paul Simon, There Goes Rhymin' Simon, Still Crazy After All These Years.*

SIMON & GARFUNKEL

New Yorkers Paul Simon and Art Garfunkel sang together as Tom and Jerry beginning with their high school days. In the mid-60s, Simon's songwriting talent broke wide open, and the folk-style duo signed with Columbia, a label on which ex-folkies Bob Dylan and the Byrds were racking up folk-rock hits. Columbia dubbed electric guitars and drums over the duo's record "Sounds of Silence," and Art and Paul quickly joined the label's hitmakers. They followed up their smash with an overnight image change that included Byrds capes and Dylanesque poses. Beneath the posturings, the music remained strong. Simon was soon scoring films *(The Graduate),* while Garfunkel turned to acting *(Catch-22, Carnal Knowledge).* Except for an occasional single or concert reunion, the two worked separately after 1971, with Garfunkel turning to a more crooning style. Simon's songs, many of them folk-rock evergreens ("Richard Cory," "I Am a Rock"), have been recorded by Wings, the Hollies, the Seekers, Del Shannon, the Cyrkle and many others.

RECOMMENDED: *Sounds of Silence, Parsley, Sage, Rosemary & Thyme, Bookends, Bridge over Troubled Water* (Columbia).

SLADE

The English town of Wolverhampton was the home, in 1971, of four lads with short haircuts and funny clothes, who made a string of British chart singles that continued non-stop for over two years. In the midst of the glitter-rock craze, Slade were the country bumpkins, playing hook-laden stomping music with misspelled titles and often vulgar lyrics at the highest conceivable volume. Despite all their shortcomings, they combined all the elements necessary for wonderful singalong singles, and England's teenyboppers made them national heroes. In America, they never quite caught on, but managed to attract a large cult following among future Kiss fans. Five years after their stint in the spotlight, Slade are still at it, a little more polished and subtle, but committed to good-time rock 'n' roll music. Their old records still sound great.

RECOMMENDED: *Slade Alive, Slayed?* (Polydor).

GRACE SLICK

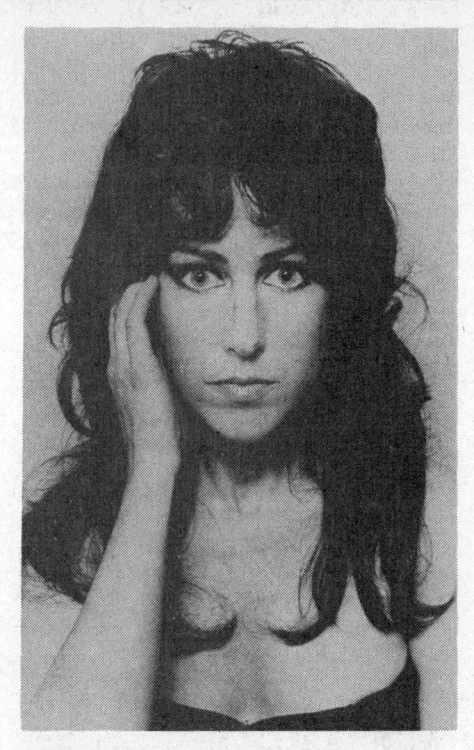

Charles Perry described Grace Slick as a voice that "had an element of icy fury; when she reached for a high note, it was as if she were zeroing in on something in order to throttle it." And in the twelve years that Grace Slick (b. Grace Wing, October 30, 1943, Chicago) sang with San Francisco's Jefferson Airplane, and before that with her husband and drummer Jerry Slick in the Great Society, she consistently sang at full throttle, bringing to life her classic Summer of Love songs "Somebody to Love" and "White Rabbit" while penetrating chilling psychic depths in her liberal interpretation of James Joyce's *Ulysses* "rejoyce." A dark mysterious beauty who put her husband through school through fashion modeling, Grace Slick joined the Airplane in 1966 after original vocalist Signe Toly Anderson retired to have a baby. Slick, of course, brought with her a remarkable voice and two hit songs. But she also brought with her a biting wit and a mysterious sensuality which was complemented by Marty Balin's shadowy romanticism. With the Airplane's Paul Kantner, she not only bore a child, China, but recorded several albums with musicians that eventually became the Jefferson Starship and one solo LP. As the Starship flourished on a string of highly commercial hits, Grace underwent personal changes, marrying the band's lighting director Skip Johnson, falling afoul of the law because of alcoholic overindulgences, and finally quitting the Starship after a stormy session with the band during a '78 European tour. Kantner has said in interviews, however, that the band will always keep a place open for her.

RECOMMENDED: all Jefferson Airplane and Jefferson Starship albums through *Gold* (1979) (Grunt).

SLY AND THE FAMILY STONE

One of the most influential figures in the history of popular music, Sylvester Stewart or Sly Stone took his Texas-to-California musical roots and his jive from experience as a disc jockey and fused rock instrumentation and sound with R&B rhythms and style for the group called Sly and the Family Stone that changed the face of rock, jazz and R&B, and practically invented disco. The hits tell the story: "Dance To the Music," "Life," "Everyday People," "Sing a Simple Song," "Stand," "I Want To Take You Higher," "Everybody Is A Star" and "Family Affair." After running into some problems in the mid-70s Stone came back strong in 1979 with the album *Back On the Right Track*.

RECOMMENDED: *Whole New Thing, Stand, There's A Riot Goin' On* (Epic); *Back On the Right Track* (Warner Brothers).

PATTI SMITH

At the end of 1973, poetess and rock critic Patti Smith made her performing debut at a club in New York City, reciting her work to the guitar accompaniment of fellow writer Lenny Kaye. In the five years that followed, Patti Smith formed a group, signed a recording contract, and went on to make a set of albums that established her as a major rock star. Born in Chicago in 1946, raised in New Jersey, her exodus to New York in 1967 opened the way to involvement in the underground world of poetry, art, and music. She has published several volumes of poetry, and has been involved in numerous avant garde projects. As a recording artist, Smith has assembled a strong band of talented musicians: quite a change from the rudimentary nature of the early lineup. Guitarist Lenny Kaye is still with the band, having forsaken a writing career to become a rock star. The others are Ivan Kral (guitar), Jay Dee Daugherty (drums), and Richard Sohl (keyboards). With four albums done, Patti seems to be getting better, stronger, and more popular each time out.

RECOMMENDED: *Horses, Wave* (Arista).

PHOEBE SNOW

The Jersey bred Snow was one of several talented women singer/songwriters to emerge in the early-to-mid 70s. Snow's vocal control and musical sophistication singled her out immediately and earned her a devoted following: a song from her first album, "Poetry Man," became an instant FM radio classic. She went on to write more about domestic bliss, then moved to California and mellowed out further while maintaining her staunch followers. In 1979 she made a duet television appearance with Linda Ronstadt on Saturday Night Live.

RECOMMENDED: *Phoebe Snow, Second Childhood* (Columbia).

SOFT MACHINE

The British band Soft Machine either because of or in spite of a never-ending series of personnel changes, did much to further the fusion cause on a remarkable series of albums that expanded the improvisational rock vocabulary. Before 1968 Soft Machine was testing the progressive rock waters as the Wilde Flowers, a seminal late 60s band from Canterbury which eventually evolved into Caravan and delivered bassist/singer Kevin Ayers, drummer Robert Wyatt, organist Mike Ratledge, and guitarist/Aussie beatnik David Allen to Soft Machine. They played happenings in the south of France, led England's psychedelic underground, and toured the U.S. with Hendrix in '67, recording a one-off single with Kim Fowley that went nowhere. The next ten years saw the mercurial Machine gain and lose personnel at an alarming rate while developing an experimental sound that borrowed eccentric rhythms and horn arrangements from jazz, balls from rock, and inspiration from everywhere. Probably the quintessential Soft Machine album is *Third,* a two-record four-song opus released in 1970. The last original member, Ratledge, left the band in 1978.

RECOMMENDED: *The Soft Machine* (Probe); *Third,* (Columbia).

SONNY & CHER

This husband and wife songwriting team seemed led by Sonny Bono when they first hit it big in 1965 with a modified protest song called "I Got You Babe" that made it on the strength of brilliant New Orleans style production. But as the duo's string of hits continued it became obvious that Cher was the main attraction, and by the time the duo got their own television variety program, *The Sonny and Cher Comedy Hour,* Sonny had been relegated to a no talent buffoon status in the combo. After her split with Sonny, Cher eventually went on to solo stardom.

RECOMMENDED: *Best of Sonny and Cher* (Atco).

JOHN DAVID SOUTHER

Born in Detroit and raised in Amarillo, Texas, Souther worked in a number of bands including Longbranch Pennywhistle, a duo with the Eagles' Glen Frey, before signing a recording contract. After a debut album and a tour, Souther joined Souther, Hillman and Furay, a short-lived group which recorded two albums. When that band broke up, Souther went back into the studio with producer Peter Asher and made a second solo album, *Black Rose,* which featured an all-star backup cast including Lowell George, Joe Walsh and Linda Ronstadt. Ronstadt has recorded a number of Souther songs on her own albums.

RECOMMENDED: *Black Rose* (Asylum).

SOUTHSIDE JOHNNY AND THE ASBURY JUKES

This blue eyed soul and R&B band from New Jersey plays a steaming version of the kind of hard blues rock heard in the 60s from the Memphis area. The band's Jersey reputation was exceeded only by Bruce Springsteen and the E Street band, which in fact took many of its cues from Southside Johnny's knife edged funk. The Jukes have slowly become one of the top live attractions of the late 70s. Southside Johnny sings lead and plays harmonica and the rest of the band is bassist Al Berger, drummer Kenny Pentifallo, keyboardist Kevin Kavanaugh, guitarist Willie Rush, saxophonists Eddie Manion and Carlo Novi, trumpeters Ricky Gazda and Tony Palligrosi and trombonist Richie Rosenberg.

RECOMMENDED: *This Time It's For Real* (Epic).

SPARKS

The irrepressible Mael brothers, mustachioed Ron on various keys and eccentric songs, pretty boy Russell on warbly high-pitched vocals, have operated as Sparks since 1971. Before that, they fronted the same band under the name of Halfnelson. What they put on vinyl was memorable, at least for the mobs of English teens who took Sparks to their hearts and made them a top singles act in Britain while Americans lumped them in with the glitter-rock bunch of the mid-70s. Noted L.A. producer Earle Mankey was an original Spark, but the Maels

(L.A. natives themselves) have made no secret of the fact that they are Sparks, a truth upheld by the long list that have gone through the Mael-led ranks. The Sparks sound, at least on hits like "This Town Ain't Big Enough For the Both of Us," was characterized by Russell's grating squeal offset by Ron's roller-rink keyboards set to a hyper-beat. Most recently, the Maels have fallen under the rock-disco fusion spell, recording underrated album co-produced with Euro-disco Giorgio Moroder.

RECOMMENDED: *A Woofer in Tweeter's Clothing* (Bearsville); *Number One in Heaven* (Elektra).

PHIL SPECTOR

The greatest producer of the 60s, and one of the greatest of all time, Spector revolutionized recording technique by recording layers and layers of instruments until it all blended together in what was called his wall of sound. He created some of the greatest hits of the 60s: Ike and Tina Turner's "River Deep, Mountain High;" The Crystals' "Then He Kissed Me," "Da Doo Ron Ron," "He's a Rebel," "Uptown" and "He's Sure the Boy I Love;" the Ronettes' "Be My Baby," "(Best Part Of) Breaking Up," "Walking In the Rain" and "Baby I Love You;" and the Righteous Brothers' "You've Lost That Lovin' Feelin'."

RECOMMENDED: *Phil Spector's Greatest Hits* (Warner Brothers).

THE SPINNERS

Four of the original members of this group that started out in high school in 1955 are still in the Spinners: baritone-lead singer Henry Fambrough, tenor-lead singer Billy Henderson, bass-lead singer Pervis Jackson, and tenor-lead singer Bobby Smith. The fifth member, another tenor named Phillipe Wynne, joined in 1971. They did moderately well as part of the Motown organization; their big hits were "Truly Yours" and "It's a Shame." Their greatest triumphs, however, occurred after singing with Atlantic Records, when their Thom Bell-produced string of hits began in the mid-70s: "Could It Be I'm Falling in Love," "One of a Kind Love Affair," "Mighty Love," and "Then Came You."

RECOMMENDED: *Spinners* (Atlantic).

SPIRIT

Spirit's first four albums are their best. The L.A.-based group's effortlessly eclectic blend of acid-enlightened rock, white boy blues, jazz cool, and learned but fluid playing has never been duplicated. Originally formed in 1965 as the Red Roosters, the classic Spirit was guitar wunderkind Randy California, pianist John Locke, bass guitarist Mark Andes, singer Jay Ferguson, and chrome-dome drummer Ed Cassidy (a colorful dude with a fascinating past as timekeeper for Cannonball Adderly, Thelonious Monk, and the seminal Taj Mahal/Ry Cooder band, the Rising Sons). Ferguson was to eventually form Jo Jo Gunne, then go solo; Andes eventually joined Firefall; Locke split for pastures unknown; and Cassidy and California, rumored stepfather and son, tried keeping the group going after a lapse in which Andes and Cassidy recorded with the Staehley Brothers as Spirit. California's Hendrix fascination became increasingly apparent on later Spirit albums (there was one passable reunion album in 1976), but look for them now on solo records. Spirit, finally California, Cassidy, and bassist Fuzzy Knight, broke up in 1979.

RECOMMENDED: *Spirit* (Ode); *The Twelve Dreams of Dr. Sardonicus* (Epic).

SPOOKY TOOTH

Spooky Tooth came from late 60s progressive rock, the product of English bands the V.I.P.'s and Art with the addition of American singer Gary Wright, to achieve modest success despite several bright recorded moments. The classic Tooth line-up is Wright on keys and vocals, Mike Harrison again on keys and vocals (their dueling vocals on the epic blues "Evil Woman" was a highpoint), guitarist Luther Grosvenor (later to show up in Mott The Hoople as Ariel Bender), bassist Greg Ridley (Humble Pie-to-be), and drummer Mike Kellie (various group escapades, now a new waver with the Only Ones). Together, their strangest album was *Ceremony*, a collaboration with French electronic musicman Pierre Henry. The band was no more by 1970, but in 1973 Wright gave it another go with Kellie, guitarist Mick Jones (now Foreigner), bassist Chris Stewart, and, later on, the late great English singer Mike Patto. A year and a half later, Spooky Tooth was once again a memory.

RECOMMENDED: *Spooky Tooth* (Bell), *You Broke My Heart So I Busted Your Jaw* (A&M).

DUSTY SPRINGFIELD

A member of the British folk-rock trio the Springfields ("Silver Threads and Golden Needles"), Dusty went solo in 1964. One of the gutsiest female singers, she had three Top 10 singles in the mid-60s ("Wishin' and Hopin'," "You Don't Have to Say You Love Me," "Son of a Preacher Man"), a fair number of lesser hits, and topped the decade off with her *Dusty in Memphis* album. Since then she has been a cult artist with only sporadic releases, but her depth and range justify the good reputation she maintains through thick and thin.

RECOMMENDED: *You Don't Have to Say You Love Me, Golden Hits* (Philips).

BRUCE SPRINGSTEEN

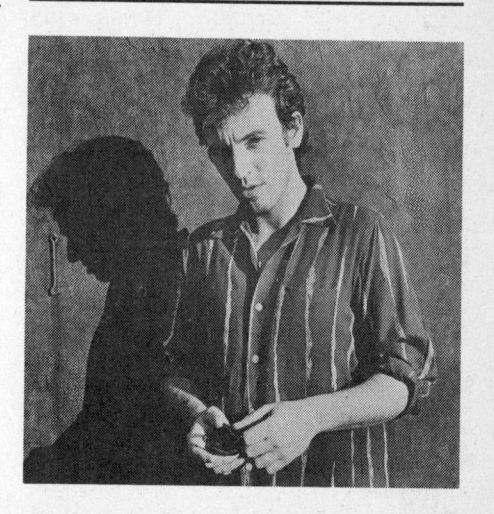

Jon Landau saw the future of rock 'n roll one night in a Massachusetts club and its name was Bruce Springsteen. With that, the hype on Jersey jiver Bruce Springsteen (b. September 23, 1949, Freehold, New Jersey) simply snowballed with help from his rabid fans of "De Boss" who swore his tales of teen angst and three-hour concerts were terrific. His albums, starting with the frenetic *Greetings From Asbury Park, N.J.* which earned him a "new Dylan" accolade simply because it was more vital and exciting than most "new Dylan", have spiritedly documented his growth not only as a songwriter and lyricist but as a streetwise romantic with the ability to put into song pain, emotion, and exuberant joy. Young Springsteen commuted to New York to play guitar at the Cafe Wha in the mid-60s, gigged in failed Jersey bar bands like Steel Mill and the wild Dr. Zoom and the Sonic Boom, and despite a short spell trying to study at college, tried music again under the managerial wing of Mike Appel in 1972. Appel badgered his way into see John Hammond, taunting him by saying that since he discovered Dylan and is supposed to have good ears, did he think he could discover this? Hammond took him up by signing Springsteen to Columbia and while Bruce never commercially paid off the bet until 75's *Born to Run*, there has never been any doubt in anyone's mind that if Bruce Springsteen isn't the future of rock 'n roll, he's one of the few brave enough to stare it straight in the eye. His E-Street Band consists of saxman Clarence Clemons (once one of James Brown's Famous Flames), drummer Max Weinberg, bassist Garry Tallent, pianist Bittan, organist Danny Federici, and longtime Springsteen man-about-Jersey Miami Steve Van Zandt on guitar. Springsteen and Appel severed their relationship after a long legal battle and Jon Landau, now both manages and produces him.

RECOMMENDED: *Greeting From Asbury Park, N.J., The Wild, The Innocent and the E-Street Shuffle, Born to Run, Darkness on the Edge of Town* (Columbia).

RINGO STARR

The ex-Beatle drummer kicked off his solo career with an unexpected record of country music songs backed up with the best of Nashville's session players. He went on to make another solo album of old time pop songs backed by lush orchestrations. Then Starr got his big solo commercial break when producer Richard Perry took him on for a super production, *Ringo*, that featured performances by the other Beatles, members of the band and L.A.'s top studio musicians. The record yielded three huge hit singles: "Photograph," "You're Sixteen" and "Oh My My!" Starr went on to make several more solo albums and star in several films, including a Dracula remake that also featured Harry Nilsson.

RECOMMENDED: *Ringo* (Apple).

STATUS QUO

One of the longest surviving British bands, Status Quo's career stretches from their first incarnation, "The Spectres," in 1965, through their term as a flower power singles outfit ("Pictures of Matchstick Men" and "Ice in the Sun") in 1968 to the "Number One Boogie Band in England" title, which they proclaimed themselves in 1972. Through nearly fifteen years of constant touring, the group has managed to retain both its lineup and its sense of fun. Led by guitarist Frank Rossi, the remainder of Status Quo is Rick Parfitt, Alan Lancaster, and John Coghlan. In the 70s, Quo has been popular in England, with legions of fans bopping to their simplistic Chuck Berry-like twelve bar boogies. Some of their records are enjoyable, and their concerts have a certain magic despite the basic format, which can be repetitive and boring.

RECOMMENDED: *On the Level, Live*.

STEELEYE SPAN

Folk-rock took many forms, but the music of Steeleye Span was among the most literal. Six British players and singers built a repertoire of 300-year old tradition songs which they set to a thumping rock beat, embellished by ringing vocal harmonies, an electric violin, a concertina, and a girl singer who took her shoes off and danced a jig around the audience. For variety, the group played covers of American pop tunes like the Four Seasons' "Rag Doll," made pornographic 45s under an assumed new-wave name, The Port Dukes, edited and published three songbooks, and resurrected a Mummers' play for a 1974 tour. A grueling road schedule and the domestic responsibilities of the band members shut Steeleye down in 1978. The spirit of the band lives on in frontwoman Maddy Prior's imported Chrysalis solo album, *Changing Winds*.

RECOMMENDED: *Below the Salt, Parcel of Rogues* (Chrysalis).

STEELY DAN

The name comes from an exotic dildo. Dan's 1972 debut *Can't Buy A Thrill*, listed six musicians as Steely Dan: bassist/vocalist Walter Becker, keyboardist/vocalist Donald Fagen, guitarists Jeff "Skunk" Baxter and Denny Dias, drummer Jim Hodder and vocalist David Palmer. Even then additional instrumentation was used and later the band became known as a revolving unit of session players under the direction of songwriters Becker and Fagen. "Do It Again" and "Reelin' In the Years" became enormous hits from the first album and Steely Dan has enjoyed tremendous, if quirky, pop currency ever since: "Rikki Don't Lose That Number," "Black Friday," "The Royal Scam" and "Peg." Of the original session players only guitarist Denny Dias has appeared on all Steely Dan albums up to the most recent, *Aja,* while such greats as Larry Carlton, Steve Khan, Lee Ritenour, Hugh McCracken and Rick Derringer have recorded with the group.

RECOMMENDED: *Can't Buy A Thrill, Aja* (ABC).

STEPPENWOLF

While most American bands were out taking a trip on the psychedelic bandwagon in 1968, Steppenwolf, led by singer John Kay (b. April 12, 1944, East Germany), bullied their way into the Top 40 with the biker's national anthem "Born to Be Wild" (written by original guitarist Dennis "Mars Bonfire" Edmonton) and monopolized underground playlists with their angry electric adaption of Hoyt Axton's anti-dope diatribe "The Pusher." Once a Canadian blues band called Sparrow, Kay's Steppenwolf went heavy macho with a hint of political conviction in original songs like the "Monster." The band was consistently on the charts into the early 70s, something which killed their underground reputation, but hit a few skids with a series of personnel changes that led to dissolution of the group in '72. They gave it a reunion go in '74 for three albums and decided their time was up. There are a dozen Steppenwolf albums, not including compilations and three John Kay solo LPs.

RECOMMENDED: *Steppenwolf, Steppenwolf the Second* (including "Magic Carpet Ride"), and *Monster* (Dunhill).

CAT STEVENS

Born of a Cypriot father and a Swedish mother, Stevens (b. Demetri Georgiou) decided to become a folk singer after hearing "He's Got the Whole World in His Hands," and clicked in the early 60s with a song called "I Love My Dog," which was followed by another hit, "Matthew and Son." His halting, jerky voice made him instantly recognizable, and when he returned after a long bout with tuberculosis to his songwriting career the singer-songwriter trend was in full swing. His comeback album, *Mona Bone Jakon*, put him on the map once again. A string of hits including "Peace Train" and "Wild World" kept him a strong box office attraction through the 70s.

RECOMMENDED: *Tea for the Tillerman, Teaser and the Firecat, Catch Bull at Four* (A&M).

AL STEWART

Singer/songwriter Al Stewart dropped out of public school in the south of England (where he'd moved with his family at age three) to make his fortune as a musician. He didn't really make that fortune until his Top 40 hit "Year of the Cat" enabled the album of the same name to become his first platinum. But Stewart, who cut his teeth on the English folk circuit in the mid-60s with co-patriots Ralph McTell, Roy Harper, and Bert Jansch, had been writing and recording songs of unrequited love and fatalistic reflections on history since 1967 when his first album *Bedsitter Images* was released in England. Stewart has very little good to say of his first four albums, only *Love Chronicles* was released in the U.S., but they all have their moments, usually when Stewart's whispery tenor meshed with the sound of his session musicians. Those musicians often included Jimmy Page (on *Love Chronicles*), Rick Wakeman, and Quiver guitarist Tim Renwick. But on his fifth album, Stewart examined the past, present, and future of European history and established a U.S. following that supported him through *Modern Times* and enabled him to score big with *Year of the Cat*. Stewart now lives in Los Angeles, ostracized by his English peers and the usually snobbish British press for selling out to U.S. commercial interests.

RECOMMENDED: *Love Chronicles* (U.K. CBS); *Year of the Cat* (Janus).

JOHN STEWART

Though he began his career as a rock 'n' roller at the close of the 50s, John Stewart first made musical headway as a songwriter for the Kingston Trio. He joined the Trio in 1961, and his tasteful lead guitar and banjo work helped bring the group hits such as "Rev. Mr. Black," "One More Town," and "Greenback Dollars." After the Kingston Trio disbanded in 1967, John was joined by his second wife, singer Buffy Ford, for an album and TV appearances (1968). Stewart wrote hits for the Lovin' Spoonful and the Monkees, and made solo LPs throughout the 70s. He toured the West, but never broke the ice nationally until, in 1979, RSO Records and two members of Fleetwood Mac got behind him and launched the hit singles "Gold" and "Midnight Wind." Stewart on stage is intense and witty, and carries an effective show with his tall figure, churning guitar rhythms, and graphic folk-rock vignettes of workaday America.

RECOMMENDED: *Bombs Away Dream Babies* (RSO).

ROD STEWART

Rasping Rod Stewart, the singer who best personifies jet-set, megabucks rock 'n' roll, was discovered by John Baldry in 1964 in the humblest of surroundings: an English railway station where the spindly Scot had gone to play his harmonica. Baldry made him a member of his blues band, the Hootchie Cootchie Men, and later, with Julie Driscoll, they both sang in Steampacket. Stewarts' specialties were the soul and R&B numbers of Sam Cooke and Jimmy Reed. But the guitar shuffles and boogie piano rhythms of Baldry's outfits became so integral to Stewart's style that he used them as recently as in "Blondes (Have More Fun)." In 1968, guitarist Jeff Beck hired Stewart as his singer. The Beck Group made two albums, *Truth* and *Beck-Ola*, which set standards for heavy music that still go unchallenged. Stewart's sandpaper voice was a foil to Beck's nervous lead guitar, and many who heard the Beck Group live and watched Rod's masterful stage movements remain Stewart fans today. Stewart spent the first half of the 70s working with hand-picked British Isles musicians on a series of five Phonogram albums that tended toward a relaxed, folky production style and spawned singles gems such as "Maggie May," "Angel," and "True Blue." He also sang on five Faces albums, and the taste he showed for Motown hits ("I Wish It Would Rain") has carried over to his late-70s Warner albums. When Faces disbanded, Stewart moved to America where he now sings with renewed power and fronts a seven-piece group that plays with a rare blend of rock energy and lyrical flair that only the best of Stewart's many bands have managed.

RECOMMENDED: *Every Picture Tells a Story, Never a Dull Moment* (Mercury); *Foot Loose and Fancy Free, Blondes Have More Fun* (Warner Bros.).

STEPHEN STILLS

This lanky guitarist/singer/songwriter got his reputation with the Buffalo Springfield and Crosby, Stills and Nash before developing his own solo career. The knack for hit songwriting first demonstrated on the Springfield classic "For What It's Worth," continued on Stills' first solo outing, with "Love The One You're With." The record included a stellar session lineup including guitarists Jimi Hendrix and Eric Clapton. Stills went on to assemble his finest solo outing with a band to go with it, Manassas. That band included guitarist Chris Hillman, bassist Fuzzy Samuels, steel guitarist Al Perkins, keyboardist Paul Harris, drummer Dallas Taylor, and percussionist Joe Lala. More recently Stills joined a Crosby, Stills and Nash reunion for the M.U.S.E. anti-nuclear power demonstrations.

RECOMMENDED: *Manassas* (Atlantic).

STRAWBS

From humble beginnings as a folk band, The Strawberry Hill Boys, Dave Cousins and Co., built a majestic rock group with grandiose production and visions of poetry. During a career that began in 1967, the various incarnations of the group (there have been many changes) have recorded over a dozen albums, some of which stand as superlative examples of the combination of English traditional and contemporary styles. Some of the alumnae of Strawbs are the late Sandy Denny, Rick Wakeman, Richard Hudson and John Ford, who went on to become a successful duo, Dave Lambert (now recording solo), and John Hawken (a keyboardist whose list of credentials include Renaissance and the early 60s Nashville Teens). The constant factor throughout it all has been Dave

Cousins, guitarist, vocalist, songwriter. His intriguing vocals and fey stage manner have given the group its consistent brand, although some of his more self-indulgent excursions have been the cause of the band's intermittent popularity. Despite several moments of major stardom, the Strawbs have been on the slide in the past few years.

RECOMMENDED: *Bursting at the Seams, Hero and Heroine* (A&M).

BARBRA STREISAND

In 1962 Streisand, a Brooklyn girl trying to make the Broadway big time, won a best supporting actress award for her comedic performance in *I Can Get It For You Wholesale*. Her recording contract and the lead role in *Funny Girl* were immediate results. Since then she has starred in a series of motion pictures including *Hello Dolly*, *The Way We Were* and *A Star Is Born*, and a number of Emmy award winning television specials, and has numerous Oscars and Grammys for acting and vocal performances.

RECOMMENDED: *Lazy Afternoon, Stoney End* (Columbia).

STYX

Formed as a garage band in the 60s called TW4 by organist Dennis DeYoung and twin brothers John (drums) and Chuck (bass) Panazzo, this was only one of many British-influenced bands spawned in the Chicago area at that time. After luring guitarist James Young from another group, the lineup was completed and the band, then calling themselves Styx, signed a contract in 1970. They recorded four albums which received moderate support and toured incessantly before getting an odd break. Seemingly out of nowhere, a melodic single from their second album, "Lady," became a hit even though it didn't have much to do with the band's live sound. By this time their nonstop touring had provided a hard-core audience, and when guitarist Tommy Shaw was added to the lineup for *Crystal Ball*, the group's sound became more dynamic.

RECOMMENDED: *Styx I* (Wooden Nickel); *Cornerstone, The Grand Illusion* (A&M).

DONNA SUMMER

Disco's premier chanteuse logged a lot of hanging-out time fronting rock bands and working in musicals, including the German production of *Hair,* before hooking up with mastermind disco producer Giorgio Moroder in 1975. Moroder made Summer the focus of his disco project, a session band called the Munich Machine in need of a plug-in singer, and "Love to Love You Baby," with its endless ecstatic groans and simulated lovemaking, started off a sizzling association for this crew. Summer's talent is more than the plug-in role requires, so she has become one of the few disco artists to grow within the genre, garnering accolades for her performance of "Last Dance" in *Thank God It's Friday* and climaxing with her powerful 1979 single, "Hot Stuff."

RECOMMENDED: *Love to Love You Baby, Bad Girls* (Casablanca).

SUPERTRAMP

Supertramp were late bloomers. For their first five years, leaders Rick Davies (guitars, keys) and Roger Hodgson (keyboards) struggled to keep the band together with the generous but short-lived patronage of an eccentric millionaire known simply as Sam. England, whence they came, wasn't interested in their art-rock sound. With the recruitment of saxophonist John Anthony Helliwell, bassist Dougie Thompson, and American drummer Bob C. Benberg (brother-in-law of Thin Lizzy guitarist Scott Gorham), Supertramp refined their sound, tuned their talent for penning insistent melodies within the frame of an expanded instrumental arrangement, tightened their schoolboy harmonies, and scored with the Ken Scott-produced *Crime of the Century* in 1974. With that album, they made impressive inroads in the American marketplace and have since relocated in Los Angeles. The move and a lengthy U.S. concert trek paid off in 1979 with the multi-platinum *Breakfast in America.*

RECOMMENDED: *Supertramp, Breakfast in America* (A&M).

SUPREMES

Diane Ross, Mary Wilson and Florence Ballard were Motown's top female vocal group during the 60s. With the crack session band providing excellent backup and the Motown songwriting team of Holland-Dozier-Holland working overtime, the Supremes strung together an impressive array of hits: "When the Lovelight Starts Shining Through His Eyes," "Where Did Our Love Go," "Baby Love," "Come See About Me," "Stop!

In the Name of Love," "Back In My Arms Again," "Nothing But Heartaches," "I Hear A Symphony," "My World Is Empty Without You," "Love Is Like An Itching In My Heart," "You Can't Hurry Love," "You Keep Me Hangin' On," "Love Is Here and Now You're Gone" and "This Happening." After leaving the Supremes Diana Ross went on to become a solo star.

RECOMMENDED: *Diana Ross and the Supremes Greatest Hits* (Motown).

SWEET

Starting out as a gimmick-ridden teenybopper singles band in England, the Sweet have shifted musical direction a number of times during their ten-year career but have always remained capable of excellent musicianship and studio mastery. Sweet was introduced to America through a number one single, "Little Willie," in early 1973, and followed that with a string of further hits: "Blockbuster," "Ballroom Blitz," "Fox on the Run," and "Action" in quick succession. During that period, they split with Mike Chapman and Nicky Chinn, the songwriting, producing and management team that made them stars, and began operating as an independent unit. Their momentum carried them for a while, but soon ran out of steam. Then, in 1978, a new single in a totally different vein, "Love Is Like Oxygen," put them back on top.

RECOMMENDED: *The Sweet* (Bell); *Cut above the Rest* (Capitol).

LORD SUTCH

This wildman vocalist goes all the way back in the British blues scene and is tight with some of the biggest names in English rock 'n roll. His first album, *Lord Sutch and Heavy Friends,* was produced by Jimmy Page and featured performances by Page, Noel Redding, Jeff Beck, John Bonham, and Nicky Hopkins. His second record *Hands of Jack the Ripper,* brought in Keith Moon, Matthew Fisher, Ritchie Blackmore and Victor Brox. Sutch hasn't been heard from since 1972.

RECOMMENDED: *Lord Sutch and Heavy Friends, Hands of Jack the Ripper* (Cotillion).

TALKING HEADS

Originally a trio (David Byrne, vocals and guitar; Christina Weymouth, bass; Chris Frantz, drums) playing the underground club circuit in New York, the Heads added guitarist/keyboardist Jerry Harrison (formerly of the Modern lovers) just before recording their first album. At first thought of as too new wave/weird for any sort of national following, the Heads had the most successful LP of all the punkish bands and following that, a year later, a bona fide hit single, "Take Me to the River." With three albums under their belts, the Heads are firmly entrenched in world rock consciousness, playing a progressive but clean music that deals lyrically with, as their second album put it, "Buildings and Food".

RECOMMENDED: *Talking Heads '77, More Songs about Buildings and Food* (Sire).

JAMES TAYLOR

After knocking around during the mid-60s writing songs and forming the short lived group Flying Machine with guitarist Danny Kortchmar, James Taylor became one of the first artists to be signed by the Beatles for their Apple label. After that celebrated debut Taylor signed with Warner Brothers and quickly became the figurehead of the early 70s singer/songwriter craze. Taylor blossomed into a marvelous singer and his backing group went on to record on their own as the

Section. Taylor married singer Carly Simon and the two have recently contributed their efforts to the anti-nuke M.U.S.E. concerts.

RECOMMENDED: *Sweet Baby James, Mudslide Slim and the Blue Horizon* (Columbia).

MICK TAYLOR

One of the great slide guitarists in rock, the British born Taylor got his start as a whiz kid in the John Mayall Blues Band. Taylor's playing on Mayall's landmark *Bare Wires* album earned him a reputation on the circuit which eventually led him to be selected to replace Brian Jones in the Rolling Stones. Taylor's lightning slide runs added a new element to the Stones' hard edged blues sound and Taylor helped create some of the Stones' hottest live moments. His high point in the studio with the Stones came on their classic *Exile On Main Street*, on which Taylor's slide guitar is the most frequently heard instrument. After a brief, unrecorded stint in a band with Jack Bruce and Carla Bley, Mick Taylor finally released his long awaited first solo album in 1979.

RECOMMENDED: *Mick Taylor* (Atlantic).

THE TEMPTATIONS

One of the hottest R&B vocal groups of all time, the Temptations started out with Motown records in 1960 and started to put together a series of hits in that label's style: "The Way You Do The Things You Do," "Beauty Is Only Skin Deep," "My Girl," "Ain't Too Proud To Beg," "I'm Losing You," "I Wish It Would Rain." The original band consisted of lead vocalist David Ruffin, Eddie Kendricks, Mel Franklin, Otis Williams, Paul Williams, but Ruffin was gone by 1968 and Dennis Edwards added. With Kendricks on lead they had hits like "Cloud Nine" in a harder edged, psychedelic mold.

RECOMMENDED: *Temptations Greatest Hits* (Motown).

10cc

In a letter to England's *Melody Maker*, a reader once wrote that "10cc are so bloody smart they have no feelings at all." English studio hounds 10cc always demonstrated on record such an overbearing ability to make Class-A pop 'n' roll records that one couldn't help feeling that they were all surface and no soul. Yet the magic they made as the original foursome, Eric Stewart (b. January, 1945), Graham Gouldman (b. May, 1946), Lol Creme (b. September, 1947), and Kevin Godley (b. October, 1945), provides a model of post-*Pepper* pop rendered with 70s sophistication. In the pre-*Pepper* days, all four worked hard apprenticeships, Stewart and Gouldman as members of the English beat invasion band the Mindbenders and Gouldman as a penman for the Yardbirds, Hollies, and Herman's Hermits, Creme and Godley in a variety of unremarkable band ventures. Their paths crossed as Hotlegs, a studio concoction that was really only supposed to test equipment and instrument sounds in a Manchester studio Stewart and

Gouldman had invested in called Strawberry. Hotlegs, ironically, had a 1970 hit with a nonsensical single called "Neanderthal Man" which gave the four the impetus to experiment further as 10cc, a name reportedly based on the fact that the normal male ejaculation is 9cc. They made enjoyable hits ("Donna," "I'm Not in Love") and albums (the incomparable *Sheet Music* in 1974). A rift developed between the pop faction (Stewart and Gouldman) and the art-school crew (Creme and Godley) and by 1976 the latter had split to record what became a three-LP extravaganza called *Consequences*. Under the banner of 10cc, Stewart and Gouldman continued to record, using a lot of overdubs, and created an expanded 10cc for touring and later recording purposes. Stewart suffered major injuries in a '79 car crash, but has since recovered. He and Gouldman also pursue outside projects (10cc recorded a Dr. Pepper commercial in '78), while Creme and Godley record and produce on their own, and promote the Gizmo, a guitar synthesizer featured prominently on *Consequences*.

RECOMMENDED: *10cc* (U.K.); *Bloody Tourists* (Polydor).

TEN YEARS AFTER

Ten Years After may as well have been just billed as Alvin Lee for all the recognition organist Chick Churchill, bassist Leo Lyons, and drummer Ric Churchill got in the band's eight-year tenure. Lee got all the credit as a guitar hero, on such blues-rock epics as "Love Like a Man," "Hear Me Calling," and "I'm Goin' Home." The latter practically made Lee's and TYA's fortune as performed at Woodstock and preserved on celluloid in the movie. But prior to that, TYA, formed in Nottingham, England (Lee's home) in 1967, had developed a reputation on that country's white blues circuit as a top attraction, fusing jazz improvisation with jock-rock aggression on a frenetic workout like Woody Herman's "Woodchopper's Ball." Woodstock and the American tour grind, however, reduced TYA to a popular riff factory dominated by Lee until they finally hung it up in 1975. Lee went on to record solo (he also did an LP with Dixie gospel-rock enthusiast Mylon LeFevre) and has since returned with a trio he calls Ten Years Later.

RECOMMENDED: *Ten Years After* (Deram); *Rock and Roll Music to the World* (Columbia).

THIN LIZZY

A hard-rocking Irish outfit that has suffered many ups and downs in a decade-spanning career, Thin Lizzy was formed by bassist/vocalist Phil Lynott in Dublin along with drummer Brian Downey and a series of guitarists that has included Eric Bell, Brian Robertson, Scott Gorham, Garry Moore, Midge Ure, and a few others. Lynott, a published poet, has been Thin Lizzy's mainstay, writing much of the band's material and presenting a unified image for the slick power that has gained the world-wide following that Lizzy enjoys. While England was growing fonder and fonder of Thin Lizzy throughout the first half of the 70s, it wasn't until the release of "The Boys Are Back in Town" from the *Jailbreak* LP (their sixth) that America tuned in in a big way. Since then (summer 1976), the fortunes of Thin Lizzy have been mottled, their major strength coming from live appearances charged with theatrics and high energy metallic rock. While their records have remained fairly uniform in their quality, sales have never matched their one big hit.

RECOMMENDED: *Jailbreak, Bad Reputation* (Mercury).

RICHARD AND LINDA THOMPSON

In 1967 guitarist Richard Thompson helped to form the British traditional music group Fairport Convention. His sinewy, economic playing echoed that of the Band's Robbie Robertson, one of his favorite players. Along with his wife, vocalist Linda Thompson, Richard left Fairport in the 70s to record several solo albums.

RECOMMENDED: *Richard and Linda Thompson* (Island).

THREE DOG NIGHT

Led by Danny Hutton, an Irish-born pop singer, the band formed as a vocal trio with Cory Yells and Chuck Negron at the end of the 60s. Adding bassist Joe Schermie, guitarist Mike Allsup and keyboardist Jim Greenspoon, the group woodshedded in the Los Angeles area before getting a long-term headlining deal at the Whiskey au Go Go which led to a recording contract. The group's first album shrewdly covered songs by some of the best pop writers of the day: Randy Newman, Robbie Robertson, Harry Nilsson, Stevie Winwood, Lennon/McCartney, and Nilsson's "One" became the first in a long string of catchy commercial hits characterized by the band's strong harmony vocals.

RECOMMENDED: *Joy to the World—Greatest Hits* (ABC).

THUNDERCLAP NEWMAN

Pete Townshend of the Who was involved in assembling this short-lived band built around three unlikely musicians: Andy "Thunderclap" Newman, pianist and sometime milkman; John "Speedy" Keen, drummer, vocalist, and composer of the Who's "Armenia City in the Sky;" and Jimmy McCulloch, fifteen-year old guitarist who would go on to join Paul McCartney's Wings five years later. Their solo album, a brilliant collection of songs that included the hit single, "Something in the Air," was produced by Townshend, who also played bass on the record. Despite their success, the internal pressures of the band brought it to an early end in 1970, eighteen months after it began. Both Keen and Newman launched solo careers with albums, but neither has made much headway. McCulloch, on the other hand, has become a guitar-for-hire, serving with a number of bands, including Blue, Stone the Crows, Small Faces, John Mayall, and Wings. Most recently, he has formed a band of his own and has started to step out as a vocalist and songwriter.

RECOMMENDED: *Hollywood Dream* (Track/Atlantic, reissued by MCA).

TOOTS AND THE MAYTALS

Frederick "Toots" Hibbert is singing testament to the influence American soul has had on Jamaican reggae. Hibbert sings with the enthusiasm and emotion of Otis Redding, roaring in jubilation even when he takes on the topic of his stay in jail on drug charges in "54-46." With Maytals Raleigh Gordon and Jerry Matthias, Toots has become a major musical attraction in Jamaica, rolling up hit after hit since the early 60s under the tutelage of the island's best producers, Coxsone Dodd, Byron Lee, Leslie Kong. Born in Maypen where he sang in Baptist choirs as a child, Toots moved to Kingston where he met Matthias and Gordon. Together, they have won the Jamaica National Song Festival a remarkable three times. Toots and the Maytals recorded a 1968 single with Kong entitled "Do the Reggay," a dance record with more of a Rock Steady beat but which was certainly prophetic in its use of the word.

RECOMMENDED: *Funky Kingston* (Island-Mango).

PETER TOSH

An original Wailer, Peter Tosh (b. October 19, 1944) has gradually modified his vision on recent solo albums to include such commercial trappings as disco ("Buk-In-Hamm Palace" on *Mystic Man*) and the support of Rolling Stones Mick Jagger and Keith Richards. But he's used them to his own advantage, saying in a '76 *Melody Maker* interview that "reggae is only what you hear and think is reggae." Tosh was not only responsible for one of the Wailers' most powerful songs "Get Up, Stand Up" (he left the group in '74). He also took the Jamaican belief that smoking herb is a right, not a crime, to the JA airwaves in 1975 with his hit "Legalize It." That record was banned, as was the previous "Mark of the Beast," a musical reply to the Jamaican police who beat him up wtihout provocation earlier that year. Jagger and Richards signed Tosh to Rolling Stones Records (their first label singing aside from the Stones themselves) in 1978, put him in front of stadium audiences to open for them on their summer '78 tour, and have promoted Tosh as the man to bring reggae into the American musical mainstream, something even Bob Marley has yet to accomplish.

RECOMMENDED: *Legalize It* (Columbia); *Bush Doctor* (Rolling Stones).

TOTO

Probably the most successful session group to go out on their own in recent years, Toto is made up of keyboardist David Paich, drummer Jeff Porcaro, bassist David Hungate, keyboardist Steve Porcaro, guitarist Steve Lukather and vocalist Bobby Kimball. Paich, Jeff Porcaro, Steve Porcaro and Steve Lukather all toured with Boz Scaggs and Paich co-wrote and arranged Scaggs' Silk Degrees album, so it's not surprising that the group sounds a lot like Scaggs on recent efforts. "Hold the Line" became a hit single for the band in 1978.

RECOMMENDED: *Toto* (Columbia).

ALLEN TOUSSAINT

More than any contemporary artist, Allen Toussaint embodies the spirit and soulfulness of the music of New Orleans. Born into a musical family, Toussaint began his career under the stage name "Toussan," recording an instrumental piano album which included the original version of his famous song, "Java." Toussaint cut his teeth as a producer with Minit Records, for whom he supervised Ernie K-Doe, Aaron Neville and Irma Thomas. In the late 50s and early 60s he was also an independent producer and writer for Lee Dorsey, the Meters, Clarence "Frogman" Henry and Chris Kenner. Writing under his mother's name, Naomi Neville, Toussaint penned and/or produced "Pain in My Heart," Mother in Law," and "I Like It Like That," songs which got a second lease on life with the mid-60s British Invasion. During the past decade, Toussaint not only toured and cut four solo albums but furnished material and arrangements for LaBelle, Dr. John, Wings, the Band, Little Feat, Claudia Lennear, and the Pointer Sisters. It was Toussaint's warm bayou voice and honeysuckle piano that first gave shape to "Southern Nights," a song with which Glen Campbell later struck gold. Unlike others behind the scenes in music, Toussaint doesn't advertise himself, he's shy and aloof, yet for twenty-five years he's been a moving force in hit records and AM radio.

RECOMMENDED: *Toussan* (RCA); *Southern Nights* (Reprise).

TOWER OF POWER

Originally known as the Motowns, this Oakland-based funk-soul band started out in 1967, recorded a first album for San Francisco Records in 1969, and went on to become one of the most popular bands in their genre. The group's appeal has always been in live performance; they got their first record contract based on an amateur night performance at the Fillmore West. The huge group was fronted by lead singer Lenny Williams until he left for a solo career in 1976 and was replaced by Edward McGee. The band's horn section: Lenny Pickett on sax, Steve Kupka on sax, Emilio Catillo on sax, Greg Adams on trumpet, and Mic Gillette on trumpet, has a reputation of its own, and is often called on for outside session work with Rod Stewart, Elton John, Van Morrison, Commander Cody, Santana and others.

RECOMMENDED: *East Bay Grease* (San Francisco); *Tower of Power* (Warner Bros.).

TRAFFIC

In their original formation, Traffic: Steve Winwood (b. May 12, 1948, Birmingham), Chris Wood (b. June 24, 1944, Birmingham), Jim Capaldi (b. August 24, 1944, Evesham, Worcestershire), Dave Mason (b. May 10, 1946, Worcestershire), epitomized the flower-happy optimism of English psychedelia, cast in the form of Winwood's inviting melodies and the band's fluid jazz-tinged playing. And despite personnel changes and break-ups, Traffic survived in one form or another for over seven years. The band was Winwood's idea. He was, in, 1967 fresh out of the R&B-mad Spencer Davis Group and the short-lived Powerhouse with Eric Clapton. And for all their experimental ambition, they weren't long in scoring hits, at least in Britain with the invigorating "Paper Sun" and Mason's whimsical "Hole in My Shoe." Mason first quit in '67, returned to lend a hand on the second album (which included his standard "Feelin' Alright"), quit again, and returned a third time before the entire band dissolved upon release of the 1968 farewell album *Last Exit.* Traffic reformed minus Mason in '70 for the ostensible reason of recording a Winwood solo record which became Traffic's *John Barleycorn Must Die.* An expanded line-up made two live albums, the highly successful *The Low Spark of High-Heeled Boys,* and an imitative *Shoot Out at the Fantasy Factory.* But it was a four-piece band, including black bassist Rosco Gee, that made the introspective *When The Eagle Flies,* the highly underrated album after which Traffic finally gave it up in 1974. It would be another four years before Winwood would reappear, this time as a solo artist on his own *Steve Winwood.* Capaldi and Mason continue to record solo.

RECOMMENDED: *Mr. Fantasy* (United Artists); *The Low Spark of High-Heeled Boys* (Island).

THE TRAMMPS

In their original incarnation, as the Volcanoes, this group hit in 1965 with "Storm Warning." Natives of Philadelphia, they evolved along with the Gamble-Huff sound. By the early 70s, under their current name, they were presiding over the birth of disco with such seminal classics as "Penguin in the Big Apple/ Zing Went the Strings of My Heart (Medley)" and "Sixty Minute Man." But it took the inclusion of their blistering, 11-minute "Disco Inferno" on the *Saturday Night Fever* soundtrack in 1977 to break them onto the pop charts. Unlike most disco groups, the Trammps have always delivered live; their stage show, with comedian as opening act, is reminiscent of the R&B revues of two and three decades ago, and the three vocalists, Earl Young (the driving force behind the whole 11-piece group), Jimmy Ellis and Robert Upchurch, likewise evoke the black vocal groups of the same era. All of this makes the Trammps perhaps the best evidence yet to support the argument that disco is primarily the latest wave in the evolution of black popular music.

RECOMMENDED: *Best of the Trammps* (Atlantic).

TROGGS

This group came out of England in 1966 with a great riff hit single, "Wild Thing," and a raunchy, almost disgusting attitude that made them one of the prototypical punk rock groups. Reg Presley's growling, grunting chant-like vocals were the distinctive elements in the band's sound and led them to other hits like "I Can't Control Myself" as well as the uncharacteristic ballad "Love Is All Around." The band disappeared in 1968, then returned with a comeback album in 1975.

RECOMMENDED: *The Troggs* (Pye).

ROBIN TROWER

Nurtured by the music of B. B. King, Muddy Waters, Ray Charles and Jimi Hendrix, Robin Trower achieved more with his agonized, wailing guitar playing in Procol Harum than many soloists can ever hope to. Trower's space in Procol was limited by the band's two keyboard players; when Robin quit early in 1972 to form a more spontaneous British power trio, he made sure his guitar was the only voice featured alongside Jim Dewar's gritty singing. Trower's biggest impact came with the 1974 LP *Bridge of Sighs*, which showcased original songs with droning metallic chords, frenzied guitar solos, wall-shaking drum rolls, and devotional lyrics that drew on blues and spiritual influences. Trower gradually modified his band line-up until he had a funky, four-piece R&B outfit which included former Sly Stone sidemen Bill Lordan (drums) and Rustee Allen (bass).

Shifting his musical emphasis from guitar virtuosity to structured songwriting, Trower created his two most straightforward albums, *In City Dreams* and *Caravan to Midnight*. Live, Trower's music is a pulsating blend of tradition and progressive innovation.

RECOMMENDED: *Bridge of Sighs, Caravan to Midnight* (Chrysalis).

TUBES

Seven-pieces strong shot through and through with a rapier wit manifest in one of the most extravagantly entertaining stage shows since Alice Cooper's plucked chicken days, the Bay Area-based Tubes have drawn rock fans into their macabre world of white punks on dope, bondage, and game shows gone gonzo, all held together by strong musical presentation that borders dangerously on art/rock with Michael Cotten's bank of synthesizers but comes back to earth with leader/guitarist Bill Spooner's dry punkish wit and singer/theatrical front man Fee Waybill's smarmy stage charm. Aside from transferring their stage show to record and indulging in a variety of video art projects, the Tubes are also featured in the porn classic *The Resurrection of Eve* doing their "Mondo Bondage" routine. As of this writing, the Tubes are, aside from Spooner, Waybill, and Cotten, guitarist Roger Steen, drummer Prairie Prince, bass guitarist Rick Anderson, keyboardist Vince Welnick, and dancer/sex interest Re Styles.

RECOMMENDED: *The Tubes; Now; What Do You Want From Life* (A&M).

IKE AND TINA TURNER

One of the many R&B groups to translate their skills into the rock 'n' roll era, this husband and wife team was the perfect combination. Ike led the band, a large touring organization with a crack rhythm section, Ike on guitar and a girl backing chorus, while Tina fronted the group as lead singer with her high intensity, gospel wail. The group had several R&B hits before turning to rock 'n' roll. Perhaps their greatest moment on record came when Phil Spector produced them for "River Deep, Mountain High." The Turners came to wider public attention playing on a Rolling Stones tour of the U.S., while Tina was given the part of the Acid Queen in Ken Russell's production of *Tommy*.

Photo by Harry Langdon

RECOMMENDED: *River Deep, Mountain High* (Philles).

TURTLES

"Nobody understood the Turtles," lamented critic Ken Barnes in his liner notes to the Sire Turtles anthology *Happy Together Again* and despite the fact that the L.A.-based band had a remarkable seventeen chart records in their five years together ('65-'69). The Turtles, led by Mark Volman and Howard Kaylan, were pegged as a folk-pop Top 40 band after their first three singles "It Ain't Me Babe" (Dylan's own), "Let Me Be," and "You Baby" became AM radio mainstays for the better parts of 1965 and '66. The band's inviting blend of crisp electric guitars, a steady but not oppressive rock beat, and the twangy folk harmonies of Volman and Kaylan can be traced back to the band's origins as 1) a surfer group 2) a bar band imitating British Invasion acts and 3) an acoustic folk group. The Turtles later parodied their own origins on a highly-overlooked '68 album called *Battle of the Bands* and, in fact, many of their albums and non-hit singles have been forgotten when they actually showed the band, Volman, Kaylan, drummer John Barbata (later with Jefferson Airplane), bass guitarist Jim Pons (replacing Chuck Portz), and guitarists Al Nichols and Jim Tucker, to be expanding the pop song form with both humor and style. The band finally broke up in '69, Volman and Kaylan becoming the Phlorescent Leech and Eddie, a recording, touring, and radio show act.

RECOMMENDED: *Happy Together Again* (Sire). *Turtle Soup* (White Whale).

BONNIE TYLER

With a raspy voice that made her sound like the female Rod Stewart, this Welsh-born singer had a No. 3 hit in 1978 called "It's a Heartache." The song was an international hit and zipped high on the country charts. Tyler has done nothing of note since, and she is beginning to look like one of those one-hit wonders.

RECOMMENDED: *It's a Heartache* (RCA).

UFO

UFO have defied key personnel changes and changing of the times to become a steady recording and touring heavy-metal attraction. And they are good at what they do; hammering out riffs with a finesse absent from most headbanging outfits. Vocalist Phil Mogg, bassist Pete Way, drummer Andy Parker (replacing a drummer who Mogg once said "smelled like a fish"), and guitarist Mick Bolton weren't even out of their teens when they banded together as UFO in 1970. They did less than spectacular business in their native England at first, but scored big in Japan and Germany with their first LP and a hamfisted 45 version of Eddie Cochran's "C'mon Everybody." Unfortunately, Bolton packed his bags in the middle of a '73 German tour, during which UFO borrowed German guitarist Michael Schenker from their support band Scorpions. With Schenker's whiplash guitar and a commendable songbook setting them apart from the rest of the heavy-metal assassins, UFO built a U.S. and U.K. following through steady recording and touring. Schenker mysteriously disappeared for a time in '77 and just as mysteriously reappeared. In '79 Schenker bowed out completely to record with Scorpions and his original sub Paul Chapman (guitarist with U.K. band Lone Star) took his place. UFO's next LP was produced by Beatle mentor George Martin.

RECOMMENDED: *UFO 1* (Rare Earth); *Strangers in the Night* (Chrysalis).

UNITED STATES OF AMERICA

The United States of America were making electronic rock before Emerson Lake & Palmer discovered the synthesizer, and in their brief time together made it better than most do today. Joseph Byrd was the ring (modulator) leader, writing most of the material, singing, and emitting a variety of beaps, bips, and bops from his electronic armory. Dorothy Moskowitz sang, Gordon Marron played violin, Rand Forbes laid the beat on bass, and Craig Woodson operated electric drums. No guitars. The sonic result, married to remarkably beautiful tone poems like "Love Song to a Dead Che" and "Cloud Song," as well as hard-nosed rockers on the order of "Hard Coming Love" and "The Garden of Earthly Delights" and the vaudevillian "I Wouldn't Leave My Wooden Wife for You, Sugar" brilliant. The band, based in New York, had only one album, and it's out of print. But it's worth the effort to beg, borrow, or steal it. The future they were making music for still isn't here yet.

RECOMMENDED: *The United States of America* (Columbia).

URIAH HEEP

If heavy metal were to be described in two words, those words would probably be Uriah Heep. The quintessential example of jock/rock thud married to artrock overreach, Uriah Heep has been universally reviled by critics for sins Heep consider to be virtues. But while Heep at their height were capable of turning out piledriving singles like "Easy Livin'," they have since fallen on harder times as they've been left behind in the dust of new wave upstarts and younger heavy-metallurigists like Van Halen and Judas Priest. Launched from London in 1970 by guitarist Mick Box, screecher David Byron, and keyboard player Ken Hensley, Uriah Heep went through a number of bass players (including Gary Thain who was electrocuted on stage in 1974, "invited" to leave in '75, and found dead in his flat in '76 of a drug overdose) and drummers (Lee Kerslake is the band's longest-standing entry there). Byron was unceremoniously sacked in '76, replaced for a time by John Lawton, English singer for German band Lucifer's Friend.

RECOMMENDED: *Uriah Heep, Uriah Heep Live* (Mercury); *Return to Fantasy* (all Warner Bros.).

UTOPIA

Utopia, aside from being a vision of life as we would like to know it, is Todd Rundgren's vision of a band as *he* would like to know it. Formed originally as a touring ensemble by Rundgren for a '73 trek to support his *A Wizard, A True Star* LP, Utopia hit rocky ground right from the start. On that tour, the band, which included Hunt and Tony Sales in the rhythm section and a synthesizer player named Jean-Yves Labat under the moniker of M. Frog, all wore black hair with a white streak down the middle and played spatial rock. Rundgren reformed and refined the band later, eventually trimming it down to the current four-piece line-up; Rundgren, keyboard and synthesizer maestro Roger Powell, drummer John "Willie" Wilcox, and bassist and singer Kasim Sulton. Their sound now is far more commercial but not less compromising.

RECOMMENDED: *Utopia, Adventures in Utopia* (Bearsville).

RICHIE VALENS

Richard Valenzuela was one of the more unusual rock stars of the 50s, not a country or R&B trained musician but trained in Latin music. His father was a guitar player in Latin bands and when the kid changed his name to Valens he wrote songs like "Come On, Let's Go" and "La Bamba," which became the hit that made Trini Lopez's career. He died in the same plane crash that killed Buddy Holly and the Big Bopper.

RECOMMENDED: *Richie Valens* (Del Fi).

VAN DER GRAAF GENERATOR

One of the great but misunderstood English rock ensembles, Van Der Graaf Generator asked for their own cult obscurity, defying every commercial dictum in their stormy eleven-year history. They broke up four times in that period but there is no question that when they were together, they could make dark, eerie, foreboding musical magic. Singer/songwriter and Van Der Graaf guiding light Peter Hammill is responsible for much of that. One of five students who originally formed the band at Manchester University in 1967, he writes songs in free verse, fleshed out in the context of Van Der Graaf by David Jackson's saxophone, Hugh Banton's cathedral-like keyboards, and Guy Evans' funereal drums (they are the most stable members of Van Der Graaf). Hammill records frequently as a solo and, with Van Der Graaf apparently a dead issue (the latest incarnation split in '77), still carries on the spirit of that band.

RECOMMENDED: *Aerosol Grey Machine* (Fontana); *The Least We Can Do Is Wave to Each Other* (Probe).

VAN HALEN

Van Halen play tight, tough, aggressive rock 'n' roll. Singer David Lee Roth guitarist Edward Van Halen and drumming brother Alex (both born in Holland to a musical family), and bassist Michael Anthony all started out in Southern California bar bands, finally coming together because the members of their respective bands couldn't keep up with their energy. Defying the usual demo tape bow-down-to-record company rules a new group usually follows, Van Halen (at one time called Mammoth) supported themselves by playing clubs, beer bars, backing up wet T-shirt contests, and hiring themselves out to backyard suburban teen parties until they'd built up enough of a following to promote their own concerts around their Pasadena home base. Then Gene Simmons of Kiss got them into a recording studio to make demos. But it was a live show at L.A.'s Starwood that convinced Warner Brothers execs, who finally signed the band in 1977, after three years of non-stop gigging.

RECOMMENDED: *Van Halen* (Warner Bros.).

GINO VANELLI

Montreal-born Vanelli started out playing drums along with his favorite jazz records at home, then switched to rock 'n' roll after hearing the Beatles. By age 12 he'd joined a band called the Cobras, then formed a group with his brother Joe called the Jacksonville Five, an R&B group that played James Brown, King Curtis, and Bar-Kays songs. Then after a few years, Vanelli returned to the business with a handful of songs he'd written and sold himself as a pop crooner. Vanelli soon became the heartthrob of Canada while maintaining respectable sales in the U.S.

RECOMMENDED: *A Pauper in Paradise* (A&M).

VANILLA FUDGE

One of the first and most characteristic heavy metal groups, the Vanilla Fudge built up their local Long Island reputation in 1967 with slowed-up arrangements of popular songs like the Supremes' "You Keep Me Hanging On," the Beatles' "Ticket To Ride" and "Eleanor Rigby" and Sonny and Cher's "Bang Bang." The band was made up of organist Mark Stein, guitarist Vincent Martell, drummer Carmine Appice and bassist Tim Bogert. After the novelty wore off Bogert and Appice went on to record with Cactus and Jeff Beck.

RECOMMENDED: *Vanilla Fudge* (Atco).

VELVET UNDERGROUND

When Andy Warhol wanted to expand his art projects into multi-media events using rock in the mid-60s, he picked up on the musicians in the Velvet Underground, gave them their name and introduced them to Nico, one of his superstars who fronted the band. The Velvet Underground was originally to be part of Warhol's Exploding Plastic Inevitable, a multi-media show. The musicians were guitarist Lou Reed, who did much of the writing, John Cale on electric viola, piano and bass, Sterling Morrison on rhythm guitar and bass and Maureen Tucker on drums. Eventually Nico, Cale, and Tucker left and multi-instrumentalist Doug Yule and drummer Moe Tucker were added. Reed and Cale went on to successful solo careers.

RECOMMENDED: *The Velvet Underground and Nico, White Light/White Heat* (Verve).

VILLAGE PEOPLE

DAVID HODO

VICTOR WILLIS

ALEX BRILEY

FELIPE ROSE

RANDY JONES    GLENN M. HUGHES

The emblematic disco group, Village People outraged a lot of people and amused the rest, but nobody could ignore the anthemic catchiness of "Macho Man" and "YMCA," the band's two blockbuster late 70s international hits. The Village People concept: six cliched male images singing unison harmonies over a nonstop disco vamp, was created by a French producer named Jacques Morali, who auditioned actors for all the parts except for the lead singer, which required a professional front man. Victor Willis, who is costumed as a policeman or sailor, was picked to front for "serviceman" Alexy Briley, "rocker" Glen Hughes, "Indian" Felipe Rose, "cowboy" Randy Jones and "hardhat" David Hodo.

RECOMMENDED: *Macho Man, Go West* (Casablanca).

GENE VINCENT

After Elvis Presley went from Sun records and scored big with the major company RCA, Capitol records organized a competition to find a new Elvis Presley. Gene Vincent, a young sailor from Virginia, was the winner, and Capitol set about turning him into a teen star. With a backing group called the Blue Caps and a leather jacketed motorcycle image, Vincent recorded a song "Be Bop A Lula," that achieved the desired effect. Vincent's popularity outside of the U.S. was even greater, especially in England where he became the idol of the rockers.

RECOMMENDED: *Gene Vincent's Greatest Hits* (Capitol).

WAILERS

The Wailers were originally Bob Marley, Peter Tosh, and Bunny Livingstone (nee Wailer), later fortified by the rhythmic brother team of Carlton Barrett (drums) and Aston "Family Man" Barrett (bass). With Tosh and Livingstone both departing to make magic on their own as roots rockers, the Wailers have become Marley's touring and recording band. The Barrett brothers are always there, marking reggae rhythm time with the perfection and soul that has also made them two of Jamaica's most in-demand sessioneers.

RECOMMENDED: see Marley, Bob.

LOUDON WAINWRIGHT III

This zany, singer/songwriter surfaced in 1970 and was immediately tabbed "the new Dylan," an epithet that has proven to be wrong. His father wrote for *Life* magazine and he studied acting in school, so Wainwright's talents were more for whimsical observation and engaging live performances than the dead serious attitudinizing of so many singer-songwriters. His sense of humor has remained throughout his records, even when he's singing about bad times he went through with his ex-wife. The song subjects range from dead skunks (a subject that produced his only hit) to ice hockey.

RECOMMENDED: *Loudon Wainwright III* (Atlantic); *T Shirt* (Arista).

TOM WAITS

Hunched over in a ratty suit, a butt of a Camel cigarette clutched precariously between two nicotine-stained fingers, goatee drooping from his long sad face,

Tom Waits (b. December 7, 1949, Pomona, California) may look like one of L.A.'s walking wounded, a member of the beatnik-turned-wino community, but he writes sensitive, witty, and emotionally affecting song portraits of people who live in the shadow of the urban underbelly: the strippers, the bums, the lonely lovers, and sings them in a deep beer-soaked growl, all of which has made him the object of a growing cult of fans affected as much by his songs as his appearance. Waits has, in fact, lived a life similar to those who are the subjects of his songs, working in greasy diners and pizza palaces. But upon his discovery by ex-Zappa manager Herb Cohen while Waits was playing a hoot night at L.A.'s Troubadour, Tom Waits took his songs and his rap, a sarcastic fusion of Jack Kerouac and Lord Buckley, to a bigger audience, one that grows with each new album. He lives out of a seedy L.A. motel even today, not far from his favorite haunts.

RECOMMENDED: *Closing Time, Nighthawks at the Diner* (Asylum).

RICK WAKEMAN

One of rock music's premier keyboard players, Wakeman has had three different careers in the rock world, and has been adept and successful at all of them. Starting as a session musician for people like David Bowie, Cat Stevens, and Magna Carta, Wakeman first joined a permanent band, the Strawbs, in 1970. It was with the Strawbs that Wakeman first became known as an organist, but after a short stint he left to fill the keyboard vacancy left in Yes by the departure of Tony Kaye. With Yes, Wakeman became a superstar, rivalled only by Keith Emerson on keyboard. Through four LPs *(Fragile, Yessongs, Close to the Edge* and *Tales from Topographic Oceans),* Wakeman's fun-loving, beer-drinking personality clashed with the group's macrobiotic bent, and Wakeman ultimately split to pursue solo recording projects which he had begun while in Yes. As a solo composer-creator, Wakeman has made a series of conceptual LPs, employing both rock musicians and symphony orchestras, and · has staged some spectacular concerts with actors, props, and stage effects. In 1977, Wakeman rejoined Yes, taking his place back from Patric Moraz in time for the recording of *Going for the One.*

RECOMMENDED: *Six wives of Henry VIII* (A&M)

JERRY JEFF WALKER

Jerry Jeff Walker is of Yankee stock (b. March 16, 1942, upstate New York), but his name is linked with the outlaw family of country/rock, singer/songwriters who claim Texas as their musical and spiritual home. Leaving home at 16 to seek his fortune, Walker wasn't long in hitting Texas after a stopover in New Orleans. But he was soon back in New York, first recording with a folk-rock group called Circus Maximus, and then setting out as a solo act. During this period, his most significant song out of four albums is "Mr. Bojangles," his sensitive acoustic portrayal of a destitute tap dancer which eventually became a chart record for the Nitty Gritty Dirt Band. Disgruntled with New York's music industry merry-go-round, Walker simply got off it, settling in Austin, Texas where he has lived ever since. He recorded one album *(Viva Terlingua)* in 1973 in Luckenbach, Texas where his one and only neighbor for two weeks of recording was Luckenbach's one and only citizen, mayor Hondo Crouch. It is Walker's gruff, deeply felt vocal manner and his stories-in-song that bring his material to life.

RECOMMENDED: *Driftin' Way of Life* (Vanguard); *Mr. Bojangles* (Atlantic); *Walker's Collectibles* (MCA).

JOE WALSH

Photo by Henry Diltz

This whiz-kid Ohio guitarist joined the James Gang in 1969 and proceeded to make that band one of the hottest American bands of the early 70s. Singing, songwriting, and handling guitar chores proved too much for Walsh, who quit after making four albums with that power group and went on to play a softer, lyrical music on his solo albums, where he mixed keyboard playing in with his guitar work. By the time he joined the Eagles in the mid-70s, Walsh was ready to rock out again while continuing to work on solo albums in his spare time.

RECOMMENDED: *The Smoker You Drink, The Player You Get* (ABC).

DIONNE WARWICK

There wasn't a whole lot happening on American pop radio between 1962 and 1964, but one of the best things that you could find there was Dionne Warwick, a bright-eyed, high-cheekboned singer who cracked both Top 40 and R&B lists with her heartfelt renditions of "Don't Make Me Over" and "Anyone Who Had a Heart." Both were written in the triple time signature usually alien to AM radio, and recorded using an echoey wall of strings and chorus to heighten emotion. They as well as Warwick's subsequent hits tended to center on the plight of a proud girl, usually wounded in love but trying to assert independence ("Walk on By"), and were composed, oddly enough, by two men. Hal David and Burt Bacharach. By 1965, Warwick was so popular that she was said to have first shot at recording any suitable David/Bacharach song, and was cast in a nude scene in the film *Slaves*. Since the lapse of her arrangement with the two writers, she has continued to record; but except for a mawkish collaboration with producer Barry Manilow ("I'll Never Love This Way Again"), her records haven't had the mass appeal of her earlier work for Scepter Records.

RECOMMENDED: *Decade of Gold, Windows of the World* (Scepter).

WAR

In 1969 a band called the Night Shift was playing around Los Angeles: drummer Harold Brown, saxophonist Charles Miller, guitarist Howard Scott, bassist B. B. Dickerson, keyboardist Lonnie Jordan, percussionist Pap Dee Allen. Then Eric Burdon discovered them, hired them as a backup band, changed the name to War, and brought in a friend who played harmonica named Lee Oskar. After two albums with Burdon, War went on their own and began to have hit singles. "Ballero," "The Cisco Kid," "Slippin' into Darkness," and "All Day Music" all sold well, while the band's tight, funky arrangements and exciting solo capability made them a popular concert attraction.

RECOMMENDED: *War, The World Is a Ghetto, Live* (United Artists).

MUDDY WATERS

Photo by D. Shigley

Muddy Waters (b. April 4, 1915, Rolling Fork, Mississippi as McKinley Morganfield) recorded a blues in 1954 called "Rollin' Stone." That one song not only inspired Bob Dylan to write "Like a Rolling Stone," but from it the Rolling Stones got their name as did *Rolling Stone* magazine. But Muddy Waters' imprint on rock 'n' roll, not to mention his contributions to American blues, goes far deeper. On his earliest recordings for the Library of Congress in '41 and '42, he sang and played guitar with power and anguish and intensity, from which rock 'n' roll would draw much of its rhythm, riffs, and spirit. The list of classic Muddy Waters tunes recorded in Chicago during the 50s and 60s and the number of white blues and rock musicians who have paid him public homage would fill books. While his long-time label Chess tried to capitalize on the 60s blues revival with a series of LPs that found Waters pandering to the psychedelic sound, it wasn't until 1977 that Muddy had his favors returned in kind, this time by albino guitarist Johnny Winter and young black harpist James Cotton who formed with Waters a blues triumvirate for a superb album *Hard Again* and tour highlighting many of his old standards with the same gruff, uncompromising edge but for a new, younger, and blues-hungry audience. At 62, Waters is still going strong.

RECOMMENDED: *McKinley Morganfield A.K.A. Muddy Waters* (a superb compilation on Chess); *Fathers and Sons* (with Mike Bloomfield and friends) (Chess).

WEATHER REPORT

One of the first and best jazz rock fusion groups, Weather Report was formed around keyboardist Joe Zawinul and saxophonist Wayne Shorter, players from Miles Davis's early 70s organization. Zawinul's advanced synthesizer conceptualizations have defined Weather Report's sound, while Shorter's playing is used sparingly, more for mood and coloration in the arrangements than as a solo voice. In a few years the band has repeatedly changed its music through the inexorable shifts of its powerful rhythm sections, which have matched a succession of remarkable bassists and drummers to Zawinul's incisive keyboard rhythms. The original band included drummer Alphonze Mouzon, bassist Miroslav Vitous and percussionist Airto Moreiro. Since then drummers Eric Gravatt, Ndugu, Ishmael Wilburn, Chester Thompson, Tony Williams and Peter Erskine have anchored the band, while Alphonso Johnson and Jaco Pastorius have played bass.

RECOMMENDED: *Weather Report, I Sing the Body Electric, Mr. Gone* (Columbia).

JIMMY WEBB

Jimmy Webb's star has been in eclipse for several years now, ever since he stopped churning out hits for Richard Harris (the mini-operatic "MacArthur's Park"), Glen Campbell ("Wichita Lineman," "By the Time I Get to Phoenix"), and the Fifth Dimension ("Up Up and Away"). And Webb (b. August 15, 1942, Elk City, Oklahoma) was only 22 when he walked away with eight Grammy Awards for his songwriting. But he has made a number of good, if not outstanding, solo albums that show he can still write affecting, melodic tunes although whether he can interpret them as well as the people he used to write for is another question. Webb's last major hit was a tune he penned for Art Garfunkel, "All I Know," released in '73.

RECOMMENDED: *Jim Webb Sings Jim Webb* (Warner Bros.); *Land's End* (Asylum).

BOB WELCH

Son of a Hollywood producer, songwriting guitarist Robert Welch came to rock through a fascination with jazz. Players responsible for inspiring Welch's light but supple style include Wes Montgomery, Herb Ellis, Kenny Burrell, and Grant Green. From 1965 through 1969 Welch played in the slick, Portland-based Seven Souls, his first West Coast R&B band. The Seven Souls backed James Brown and Aretha Franklin in Las Vegas, but stayed in Hawaii, whereupon Welch flew east to Paris to form Head West. After recording one album, Bob left the group, staying on in Paris as a record producer. A Fleetwood Mac audition announcement brought him to England in 1971, and he became the first American ever to join the blues/rock champions. Welch brought a new guitar sound with octave-playing, flatted and diminished chords to Fleetwood Mac and made five albums with the band. At the end of 1974 he left to form the power trio Paris with Glenn Cornick and Thom Mooney. Paris released two dismal albums. Welch's greatest success began three years ago as a pseudo-hip, cigar-smoking pop star who flaunts a contrived image of decadence and sensuality. His hits include "Sentimental Lady" and "Precious Love."

RECOMMENDED: *French Kiss* (Capitol).

WET WILLIE

This gutsy white R&B band was spawned in Mobile, Alabama in the late 60s and signed with the Allman Brothers' label, Capricorn Records, in 1970. Lead singer Jimmy Hall's sweating gospel delivery worked well on the covers of standard blues the band specialized in: Otis Redding's "Shout Bamalama," Little Richard's "Keep A-Knockin'," and Big Boy Crudup's "That's All Right." The rest of the band is Jack Hall on bass, John Anthony on keyboards, Lewis Ross on drums, and guitarist Rick Hirsch. When they finally charted a single in the Top 10 in 1974, "Keep on Smiling," Wet Willie graduated from the warm-up circuit.

RECOMMENDED: *Dixie Rock* (Capricorn).

WHO

One of the most widely respected and venerable rock institutions, the Who have not only survived the 60s, but the 70s as well, remaining the most consistently interesting and creative supergroup. Led by guitarist and rock songwriter Pete Townshend, the Who have undergone only one change in lineup; the replacement of the late Keith Moon by Kenny Jones in 1979. The other two components of the Who are bassist John Entwistle and vocalist Roger Daltrey. The Who made 1979 their big comeback year, after several years of general inactivity. With the release of two movies made by the Who, and a return to the concert stage in several countries (despite vows never to tour again), the Who spent 1979 reaching to old fans as well as those newcomers who are too young to recall hits like "Can't Explain," "My Generation," "I Can See for Miles," and "Pinball Wizard" firsthand. Formed in London in late 1963, the Who have released thirteen albums in the U.S., six of which have achieved platinum sales. In addition, the group have individually produced nearly a dozen solo LPs. Always a record-breaking concert attraction when they tour, the Who have remained on top of the rock heap for more than fifteen years now, and show no signs of weakening.

RECOMMENDED: *Tommy, Live at Leeds, Who's Next, Who Are You, Quadrophenia* (MCA).

HANK WILLIAMS

This singer/songwriter/guitarist from Montgomery, Alabama, was the single/most important figure in postwar country music and one of America's greatest songwriters. In the late 40s and early 50s Williams dominated the country charts and created more interest in country music than ever. His songs were universally loved by jazz, R&B, folk and rock performers: "Your Cheatin' Heart," "Move It On Over," "I'm So Lonesome I Could Cry," "Honky Tonk Blues," "Cold Cold Heart," "Honky Tonkin'," "Jambalaya," "Hey Good Lookin'," I Can't Help It If I'm Still In Love With You." Williams died in 1953.

RECOMMENDED: *24 Of Hank Williams' Greatest Hits* (MGM).

SONNY BOY WILLIAMSON

There were two Sonny Boy Williamsons, both of whom were important blues figures. The first, John Lee Williamson, was a harmonica whiz from Jackson, Tennessee who went to Chicago in 1932 and recorded for Bluebird Records but died at 22 when he was stabbed in the head. Rice Miller, also a harmonica player, named himself after the original. The second Sonny Boy recorded for Ace Records in the 50s and his biggest hit was called "Nights By Myself." In the 60s he found himself playing in England with a band of young white bluesmen called the Yardbirds.

RECOMMENDED: *Sonny Boy Williamson and the Yardbirds* (Mercury).

JACKIE WILSON

This gospel influenced soul singer from Detroit got his start in professional music replacing Clyde McPhatter in the gospel group the Dominoes, where he stayed until going solo in 1957. He developed a style that could appeal to more tastes when he would record ballads like "Danny Boy" with maudlin, dramatic overtones, but which enabled him to freak out on jump tunes like "Higher and Higher." In person Wilson was a sweating, ecstatic performer right out of the gospel mold and he continued to put his message across until being hospitalized in the mid-70s. He remains in a coma.

RECOMMENDED: *Higher and Higher* (Brunswick).

JESSE WINCHESTER

For a long time, Shreveport, Louisiana-born Jesse Winchester was more a cause celebre than a pop star. A year after graduating from Williams College in Massachusetts with a B.A. in German and extracurricular credits in rock 'n' roll, Winchester took his stand on the draft in 1967 and moved to Montreal, Canada where he gigged for a period with a group called Les Astronauts before deciding to live by his own songs. The Band's Robbie Robertson was so smitten by Winchester's lyrically rich, musically understated songs that he produced Winchester's first album, released in 1970. Critics gave him thumbs up, but his inability to tour kept him from reaping the same rewards as those artists like Joan Baez, Jimmy Buffett, and Jonathan Edwards who were covering his songs. On March 11, 1977, Jesse Winchester returned home to Memphis, Tennessee where he was a member of a very distinguished family (his grandfather gave the oration at W. C. Handy's funeral; a great-great-great grandfather hung out with Davy Crockett).

RECOMMENDED: *Jesse Winchester* (Ampex); *Let The Rough Side Drag, A Touch on the Rainy Side* (Bearsville).

WINGS

Wings is not Paul McCartney. Paul McCartney is the leader and musical focus. With the exception of McCartney and wife Linda, the only steady recording and touring member of Wings has been ex-Moody Blue Denny Laine, who plays a dependably supportive role on guitar and vocals. Other players have come and gone, drummers Denny Seiwell and Joe English (who went on to play with Sea Level), guitarists Henry McCullough (ex-Joe Cocker's Grease Band) and Jimmy McCullough (not related, first gigging with Thunderclap Newman at 16, he was found dead in his flat October 4, 1979). The latest additions to the Wings flock are guitarist Lawrence Juber and drummer Steve Holly. The hits, too, keep on coming for McCartney & Wings, gold and platinum for *Band on the Run* and *Wings at the Speed of Sound*. Wings tours sporadically: to date, their only American trek was a three-month roll through the States in 1976, documented on the live *Wings Over America*.

RECOMMENDED: *Band on the Run* (Apple/Capitol); *Back to the Egg* (Columbia).

JOHNNY WINTER

Texas blues star Johnny Winter took a handicap, his albino bodymark, and turned it into his calling card. Winter served his blues apprenticeship in Chicago clubs like the Rush Up and the Fickle Pickle. Returning to Texas, he added bassist Tommy Shannon and drummer "Uncle" John Turner and played local rock clubs. The trio moved north to immortalize Steve Paul's Scene with its blistering blues performances. With this same line-up, Winter recorded *Johnny Winter* and *Second Winter*, the album that broke him. When the Winter Band hit the national concert and radio circuit at the close of the 60s, the trio had a mystique that almost equalled that of Jimi Hendrix, Eric Clapton or the Rolling Stones. Winter's subsequent bands have often been farm teams for future groups; Rick Derringer, Bobby Caldwell and the Brecker brothers are all Winter alumni. Winter once drew critical scorn for being the wealthy son of a Mississippi mayor, but he turned a corner and proved his bluesworthiness three years ago when he toured, produced and recorded with the Muddy Waters Band. A memorable stage image, complete with beaked nose, jutting chin and leather cap, plus a flawless sense of timing, growling voice, and stinging electric guitar work, combine to keep Johnny Winter a perennial concert favorite.

RECOMMENDED: *Johnny Winter, Still Alive and Well, Nothin' but the Blues* (Columbia).

STEVE WINWOOD

Winwood burst on the British pop scene at the age of 16 as the lead vocalist and organist with the Spencer Davis group and gut-wrenching vocal performances on "I'm A Man" and "Gimme Some Lovin'". He went on to form Traffic with Dave Mason, Chris Wood and Jim Capaldi and led that band to the top of the British charts. After several years as Traffic's leader Winwood broke the band up and went into a brief retirement before making a single, excellent solo album in 1977, *Winwood*.

RECOMMENDED: *Winwood* (Island).

WISHBONE ASH

Wishbone Ash originally peddled driving blues/rock with the Gatling gun-like sound of dueling guitars, at first those of Andy Powell and Ted Turner and then (upon Turner's '74 departure) Powell and Laurie Wisefield. Drummer Steve Upton and drummer Martin Turner provided the rhythmic thunder and in their second album in 1971, *Pilgrimage,* Wishbone Ash was walking away with all the "Brightest Hope" and "Best New Group" accolades in the normally finicky English music press. Wishbone Ash, seven albums later, no longer get much press but they maintain a devoted following of fans.

RECOMMENDED: *Pilgrimage* (MCA); *Locked In, New England* (Atlantic).

BOBBY WOMACK

With his four brothers, Womack sang in storefront gospel sessions in the early 50s around their hometown of Cleveland. The Womack brothers came to the attention of Sam Cooke, who signed them to his label, SAR. Their first record, in 1962, was the R&B hit "Looking for a Love," which later became a remake hit for the J. Geils Band. After changing their name to the Valentinos, Womack & Co. scored with the Womack-penned "It's All Over Now," which was knocked off the charts by the Rolling Stones' cover version of the song. After working with Wilson Pickett and cowriting his hits "I'm in Love," "I'm a Midnight Mover," and "Ninety-Nine and a Half," Womack began a solo career that saw him use a smoother, crooning style.

RECOMMENDED: *Fly Me to the Moon* (United Artists); *The Roads of Life* (Arista).

STEVIE WONDER

Steveland Morris, blind from birth, sang and played harmonica so well as a child in Detroit that when he was ten years old his friend's big brother, Ronnie White of the Miracles, brought him to Motown Records. Berry Gordy signed the kid on the spot, changed his name to Little Stevie Wonder, and had a hit single and album with his first shot. Over the years, Stevie blossomed into one of the greatest composers, vocalists and keyboardists of our time, a truly universal musician whose songs appeal to the entire range of public taste from commercial to esoteric. In more recent albums, Wonder has incorporated creative use of the synthesizer into his compositions. Every one of Wonder's albums has been gold, several have made platinum, and his album *Songs in the Key of Life* won five different Grammy awards in 1977.

RECOMMENDED: *Stevie Wonder Live, Talking Book, Innervisions, Songs in the Key of Life* (Motown).

RON WOOD

Guitarist Ron Wood (b. June 1, 1947, Middlesex, England), with jet-black rooster coiffure and wide beery grin, may well be rock's Best Supporting Player. Beginning as guitarist in a London R&B band called the Thunderbirds (later just the Birds), Woody has played for Jeff Beck (playing bass in the first Jeff Beck Group with Rod Stewart at the mike), sat in with cultish English popsters the Creation, joined the Small-less Faces with Stewart in 1969, playing guitar on Stewart's solo LPs through *Smiler*, subbed for the just-departed Mick Taylor on the Rolling Stones' 1975 tour, and finally joined the Stones permanently in '76. Woody's solo career has progressed at a casual pace with two solo albums while with Faces and a '79 issue (*Gimme Some Neck*) followed up by an all-star tour, co-leading with Richards a cheery bar band called the New Barbarians (Wood, Richards, Stanley Clarke, Bobby Keyes, ex-Face Ian McLagan, and Meter Zig Modeliste). *Creem* named Wood 1975's Most Valuable Player for his consecutive tours with the Stones, then the Faces in the same year.

RECOMMENDED: *I've Got My Own Album to Do, Now Look* (Warner Bros.).

ROY WOOD

Roy Wood (b. November 8, 1946, Birmingham, England) set so many high standards for himself as guitarist, songwriter, and captain of high English pop band the Move that some critics and fans find his later solo and group work rather disappointing in comparison. Wood's love of classic rock 'n' roll (e.g. 50s rockabilly, Phil Spector) and his insistence on recording his solo records one overdub at a time are attempts to experiment with rock and return to roots in the hope of reaching the balance he struck so often with the Move. An art college drop-out, Wood first recorded with a local group called Mike Sheridan and the Night Riders, co-founding the Move shortly thereafter. He had long held the dream of creating a 50s rockabilly, Phil Spector) as does Movers Jeff Lynne and Bev Bevan being the Electric Light Orchestra. A combination falling-out with Lynne and disaffection with the direction of ELO led to his departure in 1972 after only one album. With the expanded Wizzard he simply rocked and rolled, concentrating on pop songs and forms on one-man outings like *Boulders* and the much-maligned *Mustard*. The hits haven't come with the frequency they used to with the Move, Wizzard, or as a solo, but Wood remains in form, recently producing an album for girlfriend Annie Haslam of Renaissance and records for British doo-wop rockers Darts.

RECOMMENDED: *Super Active Wizzo* (U.K. Warner Bros.); a worthwhile compilation is *The Roy Wood Story* (U.K. Harvest).

LINK WRAY

Legendary guitar hero Link Wray grew up in North Carolina and learned blues guitar from locals before switching to rock 'n' roll orchestra; the result with left him unable to sing so he worked on instrumentals. His first hit, "Rumble," became a classic rock guitar instrumental which influenced people like the Who's

Peter Townshend, then "Rawhide" followed with an even gutsier sound. Wray invented fuzztone technique with these numbers. Over a decade later Wray returned with a home-made comeback album which was every bit as good as his earlier stuff, and subsequently recorded several albums with Robert Gordon before releasing his 1979 album *Bullshot*.

RECOMMENDED: *Link Wray* (Polydor); *Bullshot* (Visa).

GARY WRIGHT

A former child actor who studied psychology in New York and Berlin Universities, Gary Wright (b. 1943, Creskill, New Jersey) made his living as a musician, most notably as the driving musical and vocal force behind British blues-heavy rock band Spooky Tooth and as singer-songwriter-synthesizist on his own *The Dream Weaver* LP with its hit single of the same name. Wright did take a solo sabbatical from Spooky Tooth in 1970, recording two albums of which *Extraction* was the more impressive hard-rock bruiser and gigging under the name of Wright's Wonderwheel (with Foreigner's Mick Jones as guitarist). He gave the Tooth one more go with Jones and original members Mike Harrison and Mike Kellie, but by 1974 Wright was developing his own electronic keyboard-oriented sound, the sound that would make "The Dream Weaver," with its atmospheric synthesized strains and Wright's own high-pitched tenor, a Number One entry on U.S. charts in '76. Wright's successive LPs have followed in a similar vein, though without the same spectacular success.

RECOMMENDED: *Extraction* (A&M); *The Dream Weaver* (Warner Bros.).

YARDBIRDS

With a lineup that included three of the great masters of the electric guitar, Eric Clapton, Jeff Beck, and Jimmy Page, the Yardbirds were one of the most important groups of the early-to-mid 60s. Formed in London in 1963, their five-year career had a profound influence on countless other bands and fledgling musicians, setting the stage for groups like Cream and the Jimi Hendrix Experience, which adopted many of the Yardbirds' innovative use of lead guitar, electronic and studio effects, feedback, progressive songwriting, and live jamming. The Yardbirds recording career was not especially wonderful, with the group facing a myriad of troubles from contracts to personal problems and a general series of bad breaks. They did, however, manage a brace of great singles that dented the charts; "For Your Love," "Heart Full of Soul," "I'm a Man," "Shapes of Things," and "Over Under Sideways Down," as well as four uneven studio albums and a live disaster that was taken off the market by legal order of Jimmy Page, by the time of release a member of Led Zeppelin. Playing everything from 12-bar blues to psychedelia and gregorian chants, the Yardbirds remained steadfastly ahead of their time, and the breakup of the group was under less than pleasant circumstances. The original members of the group have fared differently. Keith Relf, the vocalist, was electrocuted in 1976; bassist Paul Samwell-Smith has become a successful record producer; drummer Jim McCarty has formed several groups; and rhythm guitarist Chris Dreja has turned professional photographer.

RECOMMENDED: *Great Hits, Favorites* (Epic).

YES

Through a record industry friend, Jon Anderson found out that Sly and the Family Stone had neglected to show up for a gig at a London showcase club and this friend wondered if his band Yes could fill in at the last moment. A full house of press types were stunned by Yes' magnificent playing and fresh imaginative approach to songs by the Beatles ("Every Little Thing") and the Byrds ("I See You") as well as their own originals. Yes built a reputation in English, then America, finally international rock circles as a breath of fresh art-rock air which they maintain to this day. The original Yes, singer Anderson, bassist Chris Squire, guitarist Peter Banks, organist Tony Kaye, drummer Bill Bruford, lasted only two albums. Banks, Kaye, and Bruford, left over the course of three albums, but the enlistment of keyboard ace Rick Wakeman was a major factor in the Yes sound when *Fragile* was released in 1972, spawning a major hit single in "Roundabout." Wakeman left for the period of one album, the bloated *Relayer* on which Swiss multi-keyboard ace Patrick Moraz took his place, but Wakeman reconciled with the band (the conceptual *Tales of Topographic Oceans* was an original sore point) and Yes is back to punchy four-and-five-minute attacks of Steve Howe's eccentric guitar, Squire's thunderous bass bottom, Alan White's polyrhythmic beat-keeping, Anderson's angelic tenor, and Wakeman's masterful manipulation of the 88's.

RECOMMENDED: *Yes, Yesterdays* (Atlantic).

JESSE COLIN YOUNG

A product of the early 60s urban folk movement, Young was the leader of the Youngbloods, whose 1969 hit "Get Together" was the anthem of the peace-love-and-flowers brigade. That band deteriorated slowly over the next couple years, with Young finally going solo in 1972. Since then he's released an album per year, most of which have sold decently (though he's never broken the Top 20). A resident of Marin County, California, the singer-guitarist concerns himself mainly with wistful love ballads and songs about the wonders of rural life. As such, he can be quite vacuous at one moment and quite poignant at the next, but he continues to connect with his audience of 60s psychedelic rockers who've grown up and gone mellow.

RECOMMENDED: *Light Shine* (Warner Bros.); *American Dreams* (Elektra).

NEIL YOUNG

A mercurial personality, Neil Young (b. November 12, 1945, Toronto) stalled the release of his '78 album *Comes A Time* several times because of defects he found in the pressings. His first live album *Time Fades Away* (1973) was not an in-concert reprise of his best-known songs but a record full of unfamiliar new material which left fans who had been sold on the musical charm of *After the Goldrush* and *Harvest* confused and, if sales are any indication, disappointed. Young, the buckskinned lead guitarist with Buffalo Springfield and occasional member of CSN(&Y), has never capitalized on his ability to write melodies for young moderns. Rather, he's gone out of his way to make demands on his audience. His first solo album was a startlingly eclectic affair, featuring string arrangements and a lengthy acoustic blues "Last Train to Tulsa," although both had roots in his work with the Springfield on *Buffalo Springfield Again,* specifically the mini-opera "Broken Arrow." Young's recorded and touring work with Crazy Horse, the late Danny Whitten on guitar (eulogized in "Tonight's the Night") and later replaced by Frank Sampedro, bassist Billy Talbot, and drummer Ralph Molina, has been singularly powerful, often eclipsing the amplified arrogance claimed by New Wave upstarts. The electric side of *Rust Never Sleeps* contains some of the most exciting Young/Crazy Horse playing on record, finally the rightful successor to the furious guitar interplay of "Cowgirl in the Sand" and "Down by the River" on *Everybody Knows This is Nowhere*. Young also fancies himself a filmmaker, although his two commercially-released efforts *Journey Through the Past* and *Rust Never Sleeps* (your basic in-concert footage) seem more the work of a dilettante. Yet while he plays the brooding uncompromising outlaw, very much the loner of his song of the same name, Neil Young consistently writes insightful, affecting songs about the human condition and renders them on stage and record with a fury and emotion his contemporaries usually can't approach.

RECOMMENDED: *After the Goldrush, Harvest, Zuma, Decade* (Reprise).

FRANK ZAPPA

Photo by Lynn Goldsmith, Inc.

Francis Vincent Zappa, Jr. (b. December 21, 1940, Baltimore, Maryland) first wrote what he once called a "rancid" film score for a Grade-B movie called *The World's Greatest Sinner* in 1962. Armed with an imposing proboscis, a pair of dark, penetrating eyes, a deadly wit, an ear for good players (witness the names of Zappa alumni), and a musical imagination that draws on rock, jazz, doo-wop, and modern music, Frank Zappa has taken on the recording Establishment and despite the many lawsuits and run-ins his continued appearance indicates he's winning. Zappa, who moved to California with his parents in 1950, played in a variety of greasy R&B and lounge lizard dance bands, owned a studio in Cucamonga, wrote a TV rock opera *I Was a Teenage Malt Shop*, and appeared on the Steve Allen Show (1963) playing a concerto on bicycle before discovering another greasy R&B band called the Soul Giants in 1964 and appropriating them for his own musical purposes under the name of the Mothers (M-G-M Records later added "of Invention" for their own paranoid marketing purposes). Zappa's work with the Mothers in that initial 1965-1967 is usually regarded as a high water mark for both Zappa and the group. *Freak Out, Absolutely Free,* and *We're Only In It For The Money* (with its *Sgt. Pepper* parody cover) are among the most revolutionary rock albums of the period for their maddening yet carefully prepared mixture of satire, outrageous playing, and rock & roll intensity. He made public his love for 50s R&B with *Ruben and the Jets* (1968), a recreation so authentic some people took it for the real thing. During the Mothers' six-month residency at the Garrick Theatre in New York City in '66 and '67, they shocked/entertained audiences with a wild revue called *Absolutely Free* (whence the LP of the same name). But feeling a deepening frustration with the American public who *didn't* buy Mothers albums and kept the band on the brink of starvation (the band at one time numbered almost a dozen pieces), Zappa disbanded the

Mothers in the fall of '69, only to form another set featuring the high harmonies and obscene banter of ex-Turtles Howard Kaylan and Mark Volman ("The Phlorescent Leech and Eddie"). From that point, Mothers came and went until with the '76 LP *Zoot Allures* Zappa did away with the name all together. But there has always been more to Zappa than the Mothers. His interest in modern music was manifest as early as 1957 when he communicated with composer Edgard Varese. Ten years later, he released an album of unfinished ballet music called *Lumpy Gravy*. He gave the world a surrealistic view of rock & roll life on the road with the movie *200 Motels* and accompanying score. He unflinchingly foisted on the world Wild Man Fischer, Alice Cooper, and singing groupies the GTO's. He's launched a number of record labels (Bizarre, Straight, and now Zappa) and fought his undue share of lawsuits (Beatles management held up the release of *We're Only In It* . . . because of the *Pepper*-like cover; M-G-M and Capitol fought over *Lumpy Gravy* for 13 months; Zappa and Warner Brothers are haggling over money, possession of tapes, and unapproved releases as of this writing). Yet he refuses to give up and a whole new and remarkably young audience is giving Zappa their ears since his freak '73 hit album *Apostrophe* and single "Don't Eat The Yellow Snow." As he told *People* in a '79 interview, "I'm an American guy with a pioneer instinct. But a stinker." (Note: This "stinker" is also a family man with four children by second wife Gail.)

RECOMMENDED: with and without the Mothers—*Freak Out, Absolutely Free* (United Artists); *Apostrophe* (solo) (Discreet) *Sheik Yerbouti* (Zappa).

ZOMBIES

Formed in 1963 during the height of the rock 'n' roll boom in London, the Zombies consisted of lead singer/guitarist Colin Blunstone, keyboardist/writer Rod Argent, lead guitarist Paul Atkinson, bassist Chris White and drummer Hugh Grundy. Argent had a knack for writing excellent pop hooks which led immediately to the hit singles "Tell Her No" and "She's Not There." After recording two albums the band split up in 1967, Argent went on to form the group Argent and Blunstone also went on to solo success.

RECOMMENDED: *Time of the Zombies* (Epic).

ZZ TOP

Texas based hard rock power trio ZZ surfaced in the early 70s and carved out a reputation as the hottest band in the southwest. The sound was jackhammer crude, with Billy Gibbons' punchy lead guitar carrying the weight while bassist Dusty Hill and drummer Frank Beard pounded out a hard edged boogie grind. The sources were Cream and Jimi Hendrix, and the results were enough to keep the band's fans dancing. "La Grange," a tough boogie song about a Texas whorehouse, became a hit single. "That little ol' band from Texas" toured the globe in '76 with a stage shaped like the Lone Star state and a touring menagerie that boasted a train to carry it around as large as a circus train. The switch to a new label in '79 prompted the band to vow it will expand its Texas funk to new territory.

RECOMMENDED: *Tres Hombres, Fandango* (London).

MUSIC BUSINESS PROFESSIONALS

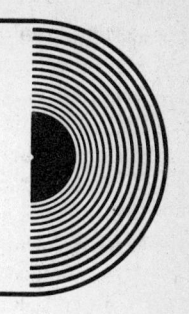

Richie Aaron, rock photographer.
Lee Abrams, radio programming consultant who developed the "superstars" FM format.
Ken Adamany, personal manager of Cheap Trick.
Stanley Adams, president of the American Society of Composers, Authors & Publishers (ASCAP) and an award-winning lyricist ("What a Difference a Day Makes").
Lou Adler, president of Ode Records; producer of Carole King, Mamas & the Papas, Cheech & Chong; director of **Up in Smoke.**
Michael Adler, president of Scorpio Music Distribution, a cutout firm.
Paul Adler, director of membership for ASCAP.
Brian Ahern, producer of Emmylou Harris.
Paul Ahern, personal manager of Boston.
Larry Aiken, Evansville, Indiana-based concert promoter; owns Aiken Management.
Steve Alaimo, vice president of TK Records.
David Alan, owner of the Boarding House club in San Francisco.
George Albert, publisher of **Cashbox** magazine.
Ron and Howard Albert, producers of Firefall and Crosby, Stills & Nash.
Dick Allen, Los Angeles-based agent of the William Morris Agency.

Barney Ales, president of Rocket Records; formerly president of Motown Records.
Vince Aletti, vice president of A&R at RFC Records, Warner Bros.' disco label.
Ron Alexenburg, former president of Infinity Records.
Buddy Allen, personal manager of the Trammps and Spinners.
Henry Allen, president of Cotillion Records.
Herb Alpert, vice chairman of A&M Records.
Billy Altman, New York editor of **Cream** magazine and author of books on country and rock music.
Stig Anderson, personal manager of ABBA.
Arma Andon, vice president of artist development at Columbia Records.
Dee Anthony, personal manager of Peter Frampton, Peter Allen, Gary Wright, and Al DiMeola.
John Antoon, co-publisher of the **Album Network** tip sheet.
Harry Apostoleris, owner of Alpha Distributors, a New York City-based independent distributorship.
Don Arden, president of Jet Records and personal manager of Black Sabbath and Electric Light Orchestra (ELO).
Pat Armstrong, personal manager of Molly Hatchet.

MUSIC BUSINESS PROFESSIONALS

Larkin Arnold, senior vice president of Arista Records.

Benjamin Ashburn, personal manager of the Commodores.

Richard Asher, deputy president and chief operating officer of CBS Records Group.

Peter Asher, producer of Linda Ronstadt and James Taylor; personal manager of Linda Ronstadt.

Bill Aucoin, personal manager of Kiss.

Bob Austin, publisher of **Record World** magazine.

Irving Azoff, personal manager of the Eagles, Jimmy Buffett, and Steely Dan.

Gary Bailey, New York-based agent of the William Morris Agency.

Roy Thomas Baker, producer of Foreigner, Journey, Queen, and the Cars.

Russell Barnard, editor of **Country Music** magazine.

Chuck Barnet, Beverly Hills-based agent of Athena Artists.

Steve Barri, producer of Cher and Yvonne Elliman.

Frank Barsalona, president of Premier Talent.

John Baruck, personal manager of REO Speedwagon.

John Bauer, Seattle-based concert promoter; president of John Bauer Concert Co.

Sandy Beach, program director of WKBW-AM, Buffalo NY.

Bobbin Beam, music director of WLPX-FM, Milwaukee WI.

Barry Beckett, co-owner of Muscle Shoals Sound Records; producer of Bob Dylan, Southside Johnny, and Phoebe Snow.

Jules Belkin, Cleveland-based concert promoter; co-owner of Belkin Productions.

Mike Belkin, co-owner of Belkin Productions; runs a personal management, independent record promotion, and label business.

Barry Bell, agent affiliated with Premier Talent.

Thom Bell, managing partner of Mighty Three Music; producer of Elton John, Spinners, Stylistics, O'Jays, Johnny Mathis; composer of "Rubber Band Man," "You Make Me Feel Brand New," many other hit songs.

Henri Belolo, president of Can't Stop Music and Stop Light Music, publishers of disco songs.

Victor Benedetto, president of C.A.M. Productions, a New York City-based production/publishing/management company.

Al Bennett, president of Cream Records.

Don Benson, program director of WQXI-AM, Atlanta GA.

Tony Berardini, program director of WBCN-FM, Boston MA.

John Berg, vice president of packaging, art and design for CBS Records.

Barry Bergman, owner of the Record Bar retail chain.

Al Berman, president of the Harry Fox Agency.

Ilene Berns, president of Bang Records.

Sid Bernstein, personal manager of Laura Nyro; brought the Beatles to Carnegie Hall, Shea Stadium in the 60s; managed the Rascals.

Ken Berry, president of Virgin Records.

Richard Bibby, general manager of Pickwick Records.

Irv Biegel, cofounder of Millenium Records; presently vice president of east coat operations at Casablanca Records.

Freddie Bienstock, managing partner of Hudson Bay Music Publishing Company.

Troy Blakely, agent affiliated with DMA.

Steve Blanck, Los Angeles-based agent of the William Morris Agency.

Bert Block, personal manager of Kris Kristofferson and Rita Coolidge.

Richard Block, east coast vice president of Album Graphics Inc. (AGI), a printing/packaging/artwork firm.

Susan Blond, vice president of Epic Records publicity.

MUSIC BUSINESS PROFESSIONALS

Marshall Blonstein, president of Island Records.
Howard Bloom, president of the Howard Bloom Organization, a New York-based publicity firm.
Mel Bly, president of Warner Bros. Music; executive vice president of Pacific Records.
Joyce Bogart, co-personal manager of Donna Summer.
Neil Bogart, president of Casablanca Records & Filmworks.
Armen Boladian, president of Westbound Records.
Tony Bongiovi, producer/engineer and co-owner of the Power Station recording studio in New York.
Bruce Botnick, producer of Eddie Money and the Doors.
John Boylan, producer of Boston and the Charlie Daniels Band.
Jack Boyle, Miami-based concert promoter; president of Cellar Door Concerts.
Al Brady, program director of WABC-AM, New York NY.
Jerry Bradley, vice president in charge of RCA Records' Nashville operations.
Danny Bramson, president of Backstreet Records.
David Braun, Beverly Hills-based attorney and personal manager.
Jerry Brenner, independent record promoter.
Zane Breslau, Chicago-based concert promoter; president of Twogether Productions.
Henry Brief, former executive director of the Recording Industry Association of America.
David Briggs, producer of Neil Young.
Bernie Brillstein, personal manager of John Belushi and Dan Aykroyd.
Dick Broder, personal manager of Marilyn McCoo & Billy Davis and Tony Orlando.
Jim Brown, program director of WOKY-AM, Milwaukee WI.
Denny Bruce, director of A&R for Tacoma Records, distributed by Chrysalis.
Buddy Buie, co-personal manager and co-producer of the Atlanta Rhythm Section.
Jesse Bullett, program director of WLUP-FM, Chicago IL.
Corky Burger, Buffalo-based concert promoter; vice president of Harvey & Corky Productions.
Samuel Burger, senior vice president of manufacturing operations for CBS Records.
Nat Burgess, New York-based agent of the William Morris Agency.
Kent Burkhart, partner in the Abrams/Burkhart radio consulting firm.
George Butler, vice president of A&R for CBS Records' jazz/progressive division.
Joleen Burton, financial executive and stockholder in A&M Records.
Charles Callelo, producer of Rex Smith.
Marvin Cane, chief operating officer of Famous Music.
Nick Caris, agent affiliated with DMA.
James Carmichael, producer of the Commodores.
Denny Carpenter, program director of KSTP-AM, Minneapolis MN.
Bud Carr, personal manager of Kansas.
Patrick Carr, freelance writer and radio producer.
George Carroll, Beverly Hills-based agent with Athena Artists.
John Carter, producer of Bob Welch and Sammy Hagar.
Dwight Case, program director for RKO General, Los Angeles CA.
Terry Cashman, president of Lifesong Records.
Ray Caviano, president of RFC Records, Warner Bros.' disco label.
Robert Cavallo, co-owner of Cavallo/Ruffalo Management.
Stan Cayre, chairman of Salsoul Records and vice president of Caytronics.
A. J. Cervantes, president of Butterfly Records.

MUSIC BUSINESS PROFESSIONALS

Mike Chapman, co-producer of Blondie, Exile, the Knack, and Suzi Quatro.

Todd Chase, program director of JB105, Providence RI.

Armand Chianti, program director of WZOK, Seattle WA.

Sal Chiantia, president of MCA Music.

Harold Childs, senior executive vice president of promotion at A&M Records.

Nicky Chinn, co-producer of Blondie, Exile and Suzi Quatro.

Robert Christgau, pop music editor of the **Village Voice** in New York.

Bobby Christian, program director of 96KX, Pittsburgh PA.

Phil Citron, New York agent of the William Morris Agency.

Bernie Clapper, owner of Universal Recording Studios in Los Angeles.

Dick Clark, host of **American Bandstand.**

Mike Clark, Dallas-based concert promoter; president of Friends Productions.

George Clinton, producer of Parliament-Funkadelic.

Bob Coburn, program director of WMET-FM, Chicago IL.

Frank Cody, program director of KBPI-FM, Denver CO.

Ronnie Cohan, agent affiliated with ICM.

Joe Cohen, executive vice president of the National Association of Recording Merchandisers (NARM).

John Cohen, owner of Disc Records retail chain.

Oscar Cohen, president of Associated Booking Corp. (ABC).

Michael Cohl, Toronto-based concert promoter; president of Concert Productions International Ltd.

Marvin Cohn, vice president of business affairs at CBS Records.

Paul Colby, owner of the Other End club in New York.

Bobby Cole, program director of KMEL-FM, San Francisco CA.

William Collins, producer of Bootsy's Rubber Band.

Charles Conrad, co-owner of House of Music recording studio in Orange, NJ.

Lionel Conway, president of Island Music and UFO Music Inc.

Alex Cooley, Atlanta-based concert promoter; owner of the Capri club.

Harry Coombs, executive vice president of Philadelphia International Records.

Jay Cooper, Beverly Hills-based attorney.

Mark Cooper, music director of KMEL-FM, San Francisco CA.

Mort Cooperman, owner of the Lone Star club in New York.

Cecil Corbett, Camden, SC-based concert promoter; president of Beach Club Productions.

Denny Cordell, president of Shelter Records.

Don Cornelius, host and producer of **Soul Train.**

Stan Cornyn, executive vice president of Warner Bros. Records.

Tom Cossie, co-owner of Ocean Records; executive producer of Chic.

Al Coury, president of RSO Records.

Larry Cox, producer of Jefferson Starship.

Jack Craigo, premier marketing executive, formerly with CBS Records.

Ed Cramer, president of Broadcast Music Inc. (BMI).

Luigi Creatore, co-president of H&L Records.

Bob Crewe, producer of the Four Seasons and Mitch Ryder.

Frankie Crocker, radio personality and program director for WBLS-FM (New York) and KUTE-FM (Los Angeles).

Dave Crockett, owner of Karma, an Indianapolis-based retail chain.

Jim Crockett, publisher of **Contemporary Keyboard, Guitar Player,** and **Frets** magazines.

Steve Cropper, producer of Poco and the Cate Brothers, wrote songs with Otis Redding; member of Booker T and the MGs.

Cameron Crowe, contributing editor of **Rolling Stone** magazine.

Peter Crowley, booking manager of

Max's Kansas City in New York.

Mike Curb, president of Warner-Curb records and Lieutenant Governor of the State of California.

Bill Curbishley, personal manager of the Who.

Chris Curtis, program director of WZUU-AM, Milwaukee WI.

Bud Daily and Don Daily, owners of Big State independent distributorship in Texas.

Damion, program director of KLOS-FM, Los Angeles CA.

Tom Daniels, program director of WLPX-FM, Milwaukee WI.

Ron Dante, co-producer of Barry Manilow.

Jack Darden, program director of KLIF-AM, Dallas TX.

Paul David, owner of the Stark/Camelot retail chain.

Cliff Davies, producer of Ted Nugent.

Allen Davis, president of CBS Records International.

Clive Davis, president of Arista Records.

Dan Davis, vice president of creative services at Capitol Records.

Walter Dean, executive vice president of CBS Records.

Ron DeBlasio, personal manager of Sister Sledge.

Rick Dees, top morning disc jockey in Los Angeles; created the "Disco Duck" hit single (RSO).

Ron Delsener, New York-based concert promoter; president of Ron Delsener Entertainments Ltd.

Alex Demmers, program director of WIOQ-FM, Philadelphia PA.

Don Dempsey, vice president and general manager of Epic/Portrait/CBS Associated Labels.

Joel Denver, program director of KSLQ-AM, St. Louis MO.

Murray Deutch, president of Buttermilk Sky Music Publishing.

Don DeVito, producer of Bob Dylan.

Denny Diante, producer of Maxine Nightingale.

Pat DiCesare, Pittsburgh-based concert

Clive Davis

promoter; president of DiCesare-Engler Productions.

Dieter Dierks, producer of Scorpions.

Judith Dlugacz, president of Olivia Records, a feminist label.

Donald K. Donald, Montreal-based concert promoter; president of Donald K. Donald Presents.

Tom Dowd, producer of Eric Clapton and Rod Stewart; designer of Atlantic Recording Studios.

Jack Douglas, producer of Aerosmith and Cheap Trick.

Ray Dowell, personal manager of Rush.

Tom Draper, vice president-director of Black music marketing at Warner Bros. Records.

Sidney Drashin, Jacksonville-based concert promoter; president of Jet Set Entertainments.

Paul Drew, personal manager of Pink Lady; former head of RKO radio programming.

Henry Droz, president of WEA Corp., the distributing arm of Warner Bros./Elektra-Asylum-Nonesuch/Atlantic Records.

Gus Dudgeon, producer of Elton John and Night.

Alan Dulberger, owner of the 1812 Overture retail chain and a Milwaukee-based concert promoter; president of Landmark Productions.

Kent Duncan, owner of Kendun Recording Studios in Los Angeles.

Dave van Dyke, program director of KAZY-FM, Denver CO.

Edward Dwyer, west coast vice president of Album Graphics Inc. (AGI), a printing/packaging/artwork firm.

John Eastman, New York-based attorney.

Lee Eastman, New York-based attorney.

Dave Edmunds, producer of Brinsley Schwartz, Foghat, and Del Shannon.

Bob Edson, senior vice president of RSO Records.

Bernard Edwards, coproducer of Chic and Sister Sledge.

Kevin Eggers, president of Tomato Records.

David Einstein, program director of WHFS-FM, Bethesda MD.

Herbert Eisenman, president of 20th Century Music Corp.

Susan Elliott, pop music editor of **High Fidelity** magazine.

Don Ellis, vice president, creative, of Motown Records.

Terry Ellis, president of Chrysalis Records.

Bill Elson, agent affiliated with ATI.

Mack Emerman, owner of Criteria Recording Studios in Miami.

Ken Emerson, staff writer with the **Boston Phoenix** and a contributor to many magazines.

Richard Engler, Pittsburgh-based concert promoter; vice president of DiCesare-Engler Productions.

Brian Eno, producer of David Bowie, Talking Heads, and himself.

John Entwistle, producer of the Who.

Michael Epstein, owner of My Father's Place club in Roslyn, NY.

Dennis Erokan, publisher-editor of BAM, The California Music Magazine.

Ahmet Ertegun, co-founder and chairman of Atlantic Records.

Nesuhi Ertegun, co-founder of Atlantic Records and president of WEA International.

David Eskin, New York-based record exporter.

Bob Esty, producer of Cher and Barbra Streisand.

Dick Etlinger, vice president of business affairs for Casablanca Records & Filmworks.

Bob Ezrin, producer of Alice Cooper, Guess Who, and Peter Gabriel.

Christine M. Farnon, national executive director of the National Association of Recording Arts & Sciences (NARAS).

John Farrar, producer of Olivia Newton-John.

Bob Fead, division vice president of RCA Records U.S.A.

Leonard Feist, president of the National Music Publishers Association (NMPA).

Barry Fey, Denver-based concert promoter; president of Feyline Presents Inc.

Barry Fiedel, co-publisher of the **Album Network** tip sheet.

Oscar Fields, vice president of Black music marketing at Warner Bros. Records.

Shelly Finkel, New York-based concert promoter; president of Cross-Country Concerts.

Tom Finnegan, owner of Great Gildersleeves club in New York.

Greg Fishbach, Los Angeles-based attorney.

Paul Fishkin, co-founder of Modern Records; formerly head of Bearsville Records.

Larry Fitzgerald, co-personal manager of Toto and the Brothers Johnson.

Mike Flicker, producer of Heart and St. Paradise.

Max Floyd, program director of KY102-FM, Kansas City MO.
Lou Fogelman, president of Music Plus retail chain in Los Angeles.
Jim Foglesong, chief executive of MCA Records' Nashville operations.
Jackie Forsting, music director of WROQ-FM, Charlotte NC.
Wayne Forte, New York-based agent of the William Morris Agency.
Fred Foster, president of Monument Records.
David Foster, producer of Alice Cooper and Hall & Oates.
Kim Fowley, producer of Helen Reddy and the Runaways.
Barry Fox, Chicago-based concert promoter; affiliated with Twogether Productions; personal manager of Trillion and the Boyzz.
Dick Fox, New York-based agent of the William Morris Agency.
Don Fox, New Orleans-based concert promoter; president of Beaver Productions.
Robert Fox, Detroit-based concert promoter; president of Brass Ring Productions.
Fred Frank, co-president of Roadshow Records.
Jeff Franklin, president of American Talent International (ATI) booking agency.
David Fricke, associate editor of **Circus** magazine and frequent contributor to other music publications.
Gil Friesen, president of A&M Records.
John Frisoli, president of Polygram Distribution.
Chris Fritz, Kansas City-based concert promoter; president of Chris Fritz & Co.
Ken Fritz, personal manager of George Benson.
Victor Fuentealba, president of the American Federation of Musicians (AFM).
Dave Fulton, editor-in-chief of **Cashbox** magazine.

Lewis Futterman, producer of Ted Nugent.
Jane G, agent affiliated with Premier Talent.
Bill Gallagher, president of Audio Fidelity Records.
John Gallagher, program director of WAAF-AM, Worcester MA.
Al Gallico, president of Al Gallico Music Corp.
Albhy Galuten, co-producer of the Bee Gees.
Kenneth Gamble, chairman of Philadelphia International Records, songwriter and producer; president-treasurer of the Black Music Association.
Glenda Garcia, executive director of the Black Music Association.
Eric Gardner, personal manager of Todd Rundgren.
Les Garland, program director of KFRC-AM, San Francisco CA.
Lew Garlick, chairman of Ivy Hill, a major supplier of packaging materials to the record industry.
Jon Garrett, hair stylist used by David Bowie, Fleetwood and others.
Curt Gary, music director of WEBN-FM, Cincinnati OH.
Bill Gavin, publisher of **The Gavin Report.**
David Geffen, founder of Asylum Records; currently a senior executive at Warner Communications Inc.
Arnie Geller, co-personal manager of the Atlanta Rhythm Section.
Bob Gelms, music director of WXRT-FM, Chicago IL.
John Gerhon, program director of WLS-AM, Chicago IL.
Eddy Germano, owner of the Hit Factory recording studio in New York.
Fred Gershon, president of the Robert Stigwood Organization.
Vernon Gibbs, rhythm and blues A&R director at Arista Records.
George Gillespie, owner of Soul Shack retail chain in Washington DC.

MUSIC BUSINESS PROFESSIONALS

Greg Gillespie, music director of KAZY-FM, Denver CO.

Charlie Gillett, author of **Sound of the City: The Rise of Rock and Roll** and other rock books.

Herman Gimble, chairman of Audiofidelity Records.

Clay Gish, program director of KRBE-AM, Houston TX.

Murray Gitlin, senior vice president and treasurer of Warner Bros. Records.

Dave Glew, senior vice president and general manager of Atlantic Records.

Jeff Glixman, producer of Paul Stanley (Kiss).

Steve Gold, co-owner of L.A. International Records; co-personal manager of War.

Danny Goldberg, co-founder of Modern Records.

Herb Goldfarb, former general manager of London Records; presently employed by Record Shack.

Irv Goldfarb, music director of WGRQ-FM, Buffalo NY.

Elliot Goldman, executive vice president of Arista Records.

Lynn Goldsmith, rock photographer.

Jerry Goldstein, co-owner of L.A. International Records; co-personal manager of War.

Stephen Galfas, co-owner of House of Music recording studio in Orange NJ.

Shep Gordon, personal manager of Alice Cooper, Teddy Pendergrass, Franki Valli and Blondie.

Berry Gordy, chairman of Motown Records.

Stan Gortikov, president of the Recording Industry Association of America.

Richard Gotterher, producer of Blondie and Richard Gordon.

Bill Graham, San Francisco-based concert promoter and personal manager of Van Morrison, Santana, and Eddie Money; president of Bill Graham Presents; opened the Fillmores East and West to rock music.

Arnie Granat, Chicago-based concert promoter; co-owner of JAM Productions.

Mickey Granberg, executive director of the National Association of Recording Merchandisers.

Peter Grant, founder of Swan Song Records.

Norman Granz, president of Pablo Records.

Florence Greenberg, former president of Scepter Records, a major R&B label of the late 50s and 60s.

Charles Greene, co-owner of Emerald City Records.

Jerry Greenberg, president of Atlantic Records.

Lewis Grey, Los Angeles-based concert promoter; president of Lewis Grey Productions.

Dick Griffey, president of Solar Records.

Meg Griffin, music director of WPIX-FM, New York NY.

Ed Grossi, co-owner of JEM Records, a rock importer.

Albert Grossman, president of Bearsville Records; former manager of Janis Joplin and Bob Dylan.

Alan Grubman, New York-based attorney.

Lee Guber, chairman of Casablanca Records & Filmworks.

James William Guercio, creator of Chicago; owner of Caribou Records and the Caribou Ranch/recording studio.

Gary Guthrie, program director of FM100, Memphis TN.

Fred Haayen, president of Polydor Records.

Ted Habeck, program director of KSHE-FM, St. Louis MO.

Tommy Hadges, program director of WCOZ-FM, Boston MA.

Ron Haffkine, producer-manager of Dr. Hook and the Medicine Show.

Claude Hall, publisher of **International Radio Report.**

Drake Hall, music director of WLRS-FM, Louisville, KY.

MUSIC BUSINESS PROFESSIONALS

Morton Hall, New York-based concert promoter.
Bill Ham, personal manager of Z.Z. Top, Point Blank, Jay Boy Adams.
Bob Hamilton, program director of KRTH-AM, Los Angeles CA.
Jim Halsey, president of the Jim Halsey Company.
Tac Hammer, program director of KQRS-FM, Minneapolis MN.
John Hammond, legendary talent scout of Bob Dylan, Bruce Springsteen, and Aretha Franklin.
David Handleman, chairman of Handleman Co., a Michigan-based rack jobber.
Chet Hansen, Beverly Hills-based agent of Athena Artists.
Larry Harris, former vice president and general manager of Portrait Records.
Rick Harris, program director of WLAC-AM, Nashville TN.
Mark Hartley, co-personal manager of Toto and the Brothers Johnson.
Roger Hawkins, co-owner of Muscle Shoals Sound Records.
Jack Hecht, president of Queens Litho, a New York-based design/print/packaging company.
Wally Heider, founder of Filmways-Heider recording studios in Los Angeles and San Francisco.
Ira Heilicher, former president of the Heilicher Bros. rack jobbing concern.
Tom Heiman, owner of Peaches retail chain.
Fred Heller, personal manager of Blood, Sweat & Tears and the Brecker Brothers.
Larry Heller, top executive at ASI, a market research firm whose clients are record companies.
David Hemmings, personal manager of Pat Travers.
Robert Hilburn, rock critic of the **Los Angeles Times.**
Warren Hildebrand, owner of All South, a New Orleans-based independent distributorship.
Harry Hirsch, owner of Soundmixers Recording Studio in New York.
Walter Hofer, attorney and chairman of the Copyright Service Bureau.
Brad Hoffman, music director of WZOK-FM, Seattle WA.
Elliot Hoffman, New York-based attorney.
Steve Holden, author of **Triple Platinum** and record critic for **Rolling Stone** magazine.
Cecil Holmes, senior vice president of Casablanca Records & Filmworks; president of Chocolate City Records.
David Hood, co-owner of Muscle Shoals Sound Records.
George Hormel, co-owner of Village Recorders in Los Angeles.
Leon Huff, vice chairman of Philadelphia International Records; composer, producer and keyboardist.
Dick Hungate, music director of WMMR, Philadelphia PA.
Paul Hutchinson, vice presidents and controller of Chrysalis Records.
Pete Hyman, president New York Records and Tapes, a cutout firm.
Jimmy Ienner, president of Millenium Records; producer of the Raspberries and Grand Funk Railroad.
Mel Ilberman, division vice president of business affairs at RCA Records.
Tim Illius, Los Angeles-based agent of the William Morris Agency.
Arthur Indursky, New York-based attorney.
Jimmy Iovine, recording engineer and producer of Patti Smith and Tom Petty.
Keith Isley, program director of ZETA4-FM, Miami FL.
Chuck Jackson, co-producer of Natalie Cole.
David Jackson, vice president of business affairs at MCA Records.
Mack Jagger, co-producer of the Rolling Stones.
Jay Jacobs, New York-based agent of the William Morris Agency.

Bob James, president of Tappan Zee Records.
Dick James, president of Dick James Music and DJM Records.
Nick Jameson, producer of Foghat.
Elizabeth Joel, personal manager of Billy Joel and Phoebe Snow.
Glyn Johns, producer of the Who and Small Faces.
Gloria Johnson, music director of KGON-FM, Portland OR.
Jimmy Johnson, co-owner of Muscle Shoals Sound Records.
Bob Johnston, producer of early Bob Dylan albums, Judy Collins, and Leonard Cohen.
Quincy Jones, president of Quincy Jones Productions and Quest Records.
William Joseph, general manager of Presswell, an independent pressing/plating/printing facility in New Jersey.
Susan Josephs, personal manager of England Dan and John Ford Coley.
Marvin Josephson, chairman of Marvin Josephson Associates, parent firm of ICM.
Timmy Judge, program director of WSHE-FM, Miami FL.
Ralph Kaffel, president of Fantasy/Prestige/Milestone/Stax Records.
Leonard Kalikow, publisher of **New on the Charts.**
Bruce Kaplan, president of Flying Fish Records.
John Kaplan, executive vice president of Handleman Co.
Bruce Kapp, Chicago-based concert promoter; president of Celebration Productions.
Art Kass, president of Buddha Records
Gary Katz, producer of Steely Dan.
Peter Kauff, co-syndicator of the "King Biscuit Flour Hour" and the "Robert Klein Radio Hour."
Matthew Kaufman, "reining looney" (i.e., president) of Beserkley Records.
Monte Kay, president of Little David Records.
Rick Kay, Detroit-based concert promoter; vice president of Brass Ring Productions.
Chuck Kaye, president of Almo-Irving/Ronder Music.
Tom Keenan, owner of Everybody's Records retail chain in Portland.
Bob Kelly, Memphis-based concert promoter; president of Mid-South Concerts.
Don Kelly, program director of WXLO-FM, New York NY.
Orrin Keepnews, vice president of jazz A&R at Fantasy Records.
David Kershenbaum, producer of Joe Jackson.
Kid Leo, music director of WMMS-FM, Cleveland OH.
John Killion, publisher of **Country Music** magazine.
Ken Kinnear, personal manager of Heart.
Charles Kipps, president of Charles Kipps Music Publishing.
Don Kirshner, discoverer of Bobby Darin, Carole King and Neil Sedaka; president of Kirshner Records; host of **Rock Concert.**

Don Kirshner

MUSIC BUSINESS PROFESSIONALS

Philip Kives, chairman of K-tel International.
Allen Klein, president of ABKCO Industries and former personal manager of the Beatles and Rolling Stones.
Gary Klein, producer of Barbra Streisand, Dolly Parton and Cheryl Ladd.
Michael Klenfner, head of Front Line Management's New York office.
Dick Kline, executive vice president of Polydor Inc.
Dick Klotzman, Baltimore-based concert promoter; president of International Tour Consultants.
Jim Koplik, Connecticut-based concert promoter; president of Cross Country Productions.
Charles Koppelman, president of the Entertainment Company.
Harvey Korman, co-owner and general manager of PIKS, an independent distributorship based in the midwest.
John Kosh, record jacket designer and illustrator.
Chris Kovarik, program director of KZEL-FM, Eugene OR.
Barry Kramer, publisher of **Creem** magazine.
Eddie Kramer, producer of Kiss, Ace Frehley, Foghat, and Jimi Hendrix.
Jack Kratish, vice president of financial affairs at TK Records.
David Krebs, co-personal manager of Aerosmith, Ted Nugent, Rex Smith, AC/DC, Mother's Finest, and other artists.
Marc Kreiner, co-owner of Ocean Records, executive producer of Chic.
Danny Kresky, Pittsburgh-based concert promoter; president of Danny Kresky Enterprises.
Gary Krisel, vice president and general manager of Disneyland Records.
Eric Kronfeld, personal manager of Lou Reed.
Barry Krost, personal manager of Cat Stevens.
Murray Krugman, co-personal manager and co-producer of Blue Oyster Cult.
Hilly Krystal, owner of CBGB's club in New York.
Phil Kurnit, executive vice president of Lifesong Records.
Cedric Kushner, New York-based concert promoter; president of Cedric Kushner Productions.
Gregg Lake, producer of Emerson Lake & Palmer.
Dennis Lambert, co-producer of Santana, Tavares, Glen Campbell, RockRose; co-owner of Haven Records.
Joe Lambusta, Lakeland-based concert promoter; secretary-treasurer of Beach Club Productions.
Brian Lane, personal manager of Yes and the Fabulous Poodles.
Jon Landau, personal manager and producer of Bruce Springsteen; formerly producer of Jackson Browne and staff writer at **Rolling Stone** magazine.
Dave Lange, program director of WDVE-FM, Pittsburgh PA.
Robert John Lange, producer of AC/DC, Graham Parker and the Outlaws.
Dick La Palm, co-owner of Village Recorders in Los Angeles.
Carmen LaRosa, general manager of DJM Records.
Larry Larson, personal manager of Kenny Loggins.
Phil Lashinsky, Charleston-based concert promoter; president of Entertainment Amusement Co.
Jay Lasker, president of Ariola Records.
Evan Lasky, president of Budget Records retail chain in Denver.
Len Latimer, publisher of **Songwriter** magazine.
Bob Laurence, program director of KDWB-AM, Minneapolis MN.
Don Law, Boston-based concert promoter; president of Don Law Co.
Hal Lazarref, agent affiliated with ICM.
Steve Leber, co-personal manager of Aerosmith, Ted Nugent, Rex Smith,

MUSIC BUSINESS PROFESSIONALS

AC/DC, Mother's Finest, and other artists.

Steve Leeds, New York-based independent record promoter.

Ed Leffler, personal manager of Sweet and Sammy Hagar.

Jerry Leiber, co-producer of the Coasters and Drifters; legendary songwriter.

Helen Leicht, music director of WIOQ-FM, Philadelphia PA.

Paul Lemieux, music director of WAAF-FM, Worcester MA.

Dave Leone, president of Diversified Management Agency (DMA).

Cy Leslie, founder of Pickwick International.

Aaron Levy, vice president of finance at Arista Records.

Leeds Levy, vice president in charge of song acquisitions at MCA Music.

Lou Levy, founder of Leeds Music.

Morris Levy, president of Roulette Records.

Randy Levy, Minneapolis-based concert promoter; president of Schon Productions.

Fred Lewis, personal manager of the Cars.

David Libert, president of the David Libert Agency.

Sal Licata, senior vice president of Chrysalis Records.

David Lieberman, chairman of Lieberman Enterprises, a major U.S. rack jobber.

Steve Litman, St. Louis-based concert promoter; president of Contemporary Productions.

Alan Livingston, president of 20th Century Fox Records.

Michael Lloyd, producer of Shaun Cassidy, Leif Garrett and Donnie & Marie Osmond.

Hank LoConti, owner of the Agora club in Cleveland.

John Long, program director of WHBQ-AM, Memphis TN.

Miles Lourie, personal manager of Barry Manilow.

Jerry Love, co-producer of the Spinners, Dionne Warwick and Ronny Dyson.

Nick Lowe, producer of Elvis Costello and himself.

Bill Lowery, president of the Lowery Group, a publishing/production organization.

Dave Lucas, Indianapolis-based concert promoter; president of Sunshine Promotions.

Bruce Lundvall, president of CBS Records United States (CRU).

Mike Lushka, vice president and general manager of Motown Records.

Moe Lytle, president of Gusto Records.

Marty Machat, personal manager of Electric Light Orchestra.

Jim Macnamara, owner of Gaspar's club in New York.

Carl Maduri, partner in Mike Belkin's personal management, independent record promotion and label business.

Larry Magid, Philadelphia-based concert promoter; president of Electric Factory Concerts.

Mike Maitland, former president of Warner Bros. Records and MCA Records.

Toby Mamis, president of Famous Toby Mamis publicity firm in Los Angeles.

Leonard Marcus, editor of **High Fidelity** magazine.

Arif Mardin, producer of Bette Midler, the Bee Gees (first dance LPs), and the Rascals.

Frank Marino, producer of Mahogany Rush.

Gil Markle, owner of Long View Farms recording studio in central Massachusetts.

Paul Marks, managing director of ASCAP.

Sam Marmaduke, president of Western Merchandisers, a Texas-based rack jobber and independent distributorship.

Denton Marr, program director of WEBN-FM, Cincinnati OH.

David Marsden, Boston based agent of Athena Artists.

MUSIC BUSINESS PROFESSIONALS

Dave Marsh, contributing editor of **Rolling Stone** magazine.
Paul Marshall, New York-based attorney.
Chuck Martin, program director of KHJ-AM, Los Angeles.
George Martin, producer of the Beatles and America.
Steve Massarsky, personal manager of the Allman Brothers Band.
Tony Martell, vice president and general manager of the CBS Associated Labels; organized the T.J. Martell Foundation in memory of his son, who died of leukemia.
Arthur Martinez, division vice president of international operations at RCA Records.
Harry Maslin, producer of Melissa Manchester.
Jerry Masucci, president of Fania Records.
Edwin A. Mathews, co-owner of Village Recorders in Los Angeles.
Mike Mayer, New York-based attorney.
Curtis Mayfield, president of Curtom Records; composer of "Superfly" motion picture soundtracks; recording artist.
Peyton Mays, music director of KZEL-FM, Eugene OR.
Jim Mazza, president and chief operating officer of EMI-America Records.
Paul McCartney, producer of Wings.
Jackie McCauley, program director of KSAN-FM, San Francisco CA.
Glenn McDermott, manager of Le Mudd Club.
Randy McElrath, Milwaukee-based concert promoter; president of Stardate Productions.
Bill McEuen, personal manager of Steve Martin.
Mark McEuen, program director of W4-FM, Detroit MI.
Terry McEwen, executive vice president of London Records.
Earl McGrath, president of Rolling Stones Records.
Michael McKay, music director of DC101-FM, Washington, DC.
Malcolm McLaren, producer of the Sex Pistols.
Ina Meibach, New York-based attorney.
George B. Meier, publisher of **Walrus** magazine.
Debbie Meister, Beverly Hills-based agent of Athena Artists.
Harvey Meltzer, supervisor of CBS Records' royalty computations.
Bhaskar Menon, chairman and chief executive officer of Capitol Records.
Billy Meshel, vice president and general manager of Arista Music Publishing Group.
Louis Messina, Houston-based concert promoter; president of Pace Concerts.
Bob Meyrowitz, co-syndicator of the "King Biscuit Flour Hour" and the "Robert Klein Radio Hour."
Wally Meyrowitz, agent affiliated with ATI.
Lorne Michaels, producer of **Saturday Night Live.**
Jerry Mickelson, Chicago-based concert promoter; partner in JAM Productions.
Ed Micone, agent affiliated with ICM.
Chris Miller, program director of KZAP-FM, Sacramento CA.
Doris Miller, music director of KZEW-FM, Dallas TX.
David Mintz, personal manager of the Average White Band.
Bob Mitchell, program director of WTIX-AM, New Orleans LA.
Fred Moch, Los Angeles-based agent of the William Morris Agency.
Fred Moelis, executive vice president of Don Kirshner Entertainment Corp.
Ivan Mogull, president of Ivan Mogull Music.
Noel Monk, personal manager of Van Halen.
Stan Monteiro, vice president of west coast promotion at Epic Records.
Jacques Morali, creator and producer of the Village People.
Jay Morgenstern, former vice president

MUSIC BUSINESS PROFESSIONALS

in charge of Infinity Records' music publishing operation.

Giorgio Moroder, producer of Donna Sumer; composer of the motion picture soundtrack for **Midnight Express.**

Doug Morris, president of ATCO Records.

Art Moskowitz, Los Angeles-based agent of the William Morris Agency.

Ira Moss, president of the Moss Music Group Inc.

Jerry Moss, chairman of A&M Records.

Mickie Most, producer of Herman's Hermits, Jeff Beck, Donovan and Hot Chocolate.

Tommy Mottola, personal manager of Hall & Oates.

Barry Mraz, producer of Styx and Fotomaker.

Susan Munao, co-personal manager of Donna Summer.

Scott Muni, program director of WNEW-FM, New York NY.

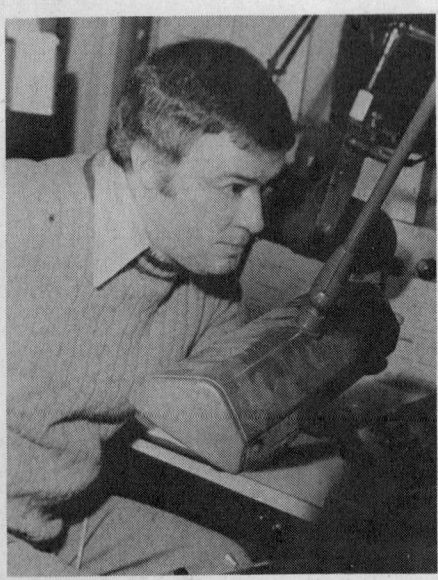

Scott Muni

Brian Murphy, Los Angeles based concert promoter; partner in Avalon Attractions.

Robert Muzzy, music director of Y100, Miami FL.

Jerry Nathan, Buffalo-based concert promoter; president of Festival East Concerts.

Nancy Nathan, Buffalo-based concert promoter; talent buyer for Festival East Concerts.

James Nederlander, Los Angeles-based concert promoter; president of James Nederlander Associates.

Harry Nelson, program director of WRKO-AM, Buffalo NY.

Dale Niedermaier, owner of the Parkwest club in Chicago.

Jack Nitzche, producer of Neil Young, Graham Parker and B.B. King; composer of the motion picture soundtrack to **One Flew over the Cuckoo's Nest.**

Richard Norton, karate instructor of James Taylor, Linda Ronstadt and ABBA.

Ted Nussbaum, New York-based attorney.

Harold Okinow, president of Lieberman Enterprises.

Milton Okun, producer of John Denver.

Andrew Loog Oldham, producer of the Werewolves and early Rolling Stones LPs.

Denise Oliver, program director of KSJO-FM, San Jose CA.

Keith Olson, producer of Foreigner and Fleetwood Mac.

Jack Orbin, San Antonio-based concert promoter; president of Stone City Attractions.

Harold Orenstein, New York-based attorney.

Mo Ostin, chairman of Warner Bros. Records.

Tony Outeda, personal manager of Foghat

Joe Owens, general manager of Mushroom Records.

Tom Owens, program director of KZEW-FM, Dallas TX.

Jimmy Page, producer of Led Zeppelin.

David Paich, producer of Cheryl Lynn and Toto.

William Paley, chairman of CBS Inc.
Robert Palmer, rock and jazz critic for the **New York Times, Penthouse, Rolling Stone,** and other publications.
Peter Parcher, New York-based litigator.
Sid Parnes, editor-in-chief of **Record World** magazine.
Alan Parsons, producer of Al Stewart and the Alan Parsons Project.
David Passick, co-personal manager of Renaissance and the Grateful Dead.
Martin A. Paulson, trustee of the Music Performance Trust Fund (MPTF).
Bruce Payne, personal manager of Ritchie Blackmore.
Sandy Pearlman, co-producer and co-personal manager of Blue Oyster Cult.
Monique I. Peer, president of Peer-Southern music publishing company.
Alan Pepper, co-owner of the Bottom Line club in New York.
Hugo Peretti, copresident of H&L Records.
Gary Perkins, Los Angeles-based concert promoter; partner in Avalon Attractions.
Freddie Perren, producer of Gloria Gaynor, Yvonne Elliman, Tavares and Peaches & Herb.
Al Perry, independent record promoter in Boston.
Quentin Perry, Atlanta-based concert promoter; president of Taurus Productions.
Richard Perry, producer of the Pointer Sisters, Carly Simon, Leo Sayer and many others; president of Planet Records.
Chris Peters, president of Peters International, a record importer.
Lennie Petze, vice president of A&R at Epic Records.
Beau Phillips, program director of KISW-FM, Seattle WA.
Sam Phillips, producer of early Sun recordings of Elvis Presley, Johnny Cash and Jerry Lee Lewis; more recently has produced John Prine.
Herb Pilhofer, owner of Sound 80 Recording Studio in Minneapolis.
Rich Piombino, music director of WKLS-FM, Atlanta GA.
Bob Pittman, program director of WNBC-AM, New York NY.
Jon Podell, agent affiliated with B.M.F.
Jeff Pollack, program director of WMMR-EM, Philadelphia PA.
Vini Poncia, producer of Peter Criss (Kiss).
Steve Popovich, president of Cleveland International Records.
Eddie Portnoy, owner of the Record Shack wholesale-retail chain in New York.
Neil Portnoy, senior vice president of 20th Century Fox Records.
Mel Posner, vice chairman of Elektra/Asylum Records.
Brian Potter, co-producer of Santana, Tavares, Glen Campbell and Rock Rose; co-owner of Haven Records.
Bud Prager, personal manager of Foreigner.
Spencer Proffer, personal manager of the Marshall Tucker Band and Billy Thorpe.
Thomas Pryor, editor of **Daily Variety** magazine.
Jimmy Pullis, owner of Trax and JP's clubs in New York.
Bill Putnam, owner of United Western Studios in Los Angeles.
Norbert Putnam, producer of Jimmy Buffett and Toby Beau.
Ray Quinn, program director of WFIL-AM, Philadelphia PA.
Ron Rainy, west coast head of Magna Artists booking agency.
Phil Ramone, producer of Billy Joel and Phoebe Snow; co-owner of A&R Recording Studios in New York.
Ron Ravitz, president of Controlled Sheet Music Service, an independent rack jobber of sheet music and folios.

Hal Ray, Los Angeles based agent of the William Morris Agency.

John Reid, chairman of Rocket Records.

Barry Reiss, senior vice president of business affairs at Infinity Records.

Jack Reinstein, vice president of finance at Elektra Records.

Bob Reno, president of Midland International Records and Midsong Music.

Malvina Reynolds, president of Cassandra Records, a feminist label.

Terry Rhodes, agent affiliated with ICM.

Paul Riann, program director of KLOL-FM, Houston TX.

Tandy Rice, personal manager of Billy Carter.

Keith Richard, co-producer of the Rolling Stones.

Jack Richardson, producer of Staez.

Karl Richardson, producer of Andy Gibb and the Bee Gees.

Julie Rifkind, president of Spring Records.

Ron Riley, program director of WCAO-AM, Baltimore MD.

Jim Rissmiller, Los Angeles-based concert promoter; president of Wolf & Rissmiller Concerts.

Steve Rivers, program director of WIFI-AM, Philadelphia PA.

Jake Riviera, personal manager of Elvis Costello, Dave Edmunds and Nick Lowe.

Ira A. Robbins, publisher of **Trouser Press** magazine.

John Roberts, co-owner of Media Sound Studios.

Elliot Roberts, personal manager of Joni Mitchell and Neil Young.

David Robinson, president of Stiff Records.

Jim Robinson, program director of KQFM-FM, Portland OR.

Irwin Robinson, president of Chappell Music.

Lisa Robinson, editor of **Hit Parader** magazine.

Michelle Robinson, music director of WSHE-FM, Miami FL.

John Rockwell, rock music writer for the **New York Times.**

Nile Rodgers, co-producer of Chic and Sister Sledge.

Brian Rohan, San Francisco-based attorney.

John Rook, program director of KFI-AM, Los Angeles CA.

Wesley Rose, president of Hickory Records and Acuff-Rose Publications.

Carl Rosenbaum, Chicago-based concert promoter; president of Celebration-Flipside Concerts.

Ed Rosenblatt, senior vice president of sales and promotion for Warner Bros. Records.

Joel Rosenman, co-owner of Media Sound Studios.

Michael Roshkind, vice chairman and chief operating officer of Motown Records.

Sheldon Roskin, partner in Solters & Roskin publicity firm.

Jack Rosner, vice president of administrations at Screen Gems-EMI.

Carol Ross, president of the Press Office publicity firm.

Steve Ross, chairman of Warner Communications Inc. (WCI).

Tom Ross, agent affiliated with ICM.

Gerald Rothberg, publisher-editor of **Circus** magazine.

Paul Rothchild, producer of the Doors, Paul Butterfield and other folk-oriented artists.

Eileen Rothschild, vice president of publishing at RSO Records.

Steve Rubell, co-owner of Studio 54 discotheque in New York.

Ed Rubin, east coast head of Magna Artists booking agency.

Peter Rudge, president of SIR Productions.

Kal Rudman, publisher of the **Friday Morning Quarterback** tip sheet.

Joseph Ruffalo, co-personal manager of Earth, Wind & Fire and Deniese Williams.

Tony Ruffino, Long Island-based concert

MUSIC BUSINESS PROFESSIONALS

promoters; president of Tony Ruffino & Larry Vaughn Productions.
Todd Rundgren, producer of Meat Loaf and Patti Smith.
Steve Runner, music director of WLVQ-FM, Columbus OH.
Frank Russo, Providence-based concert promoter; president of Gemini Concerts.
Sol Saffian, agent affiliated with Norby Walters.
Ed Salamon, program director of WHN-FM, New York NY.
Lee Salomon, New York-based agent of the William Morris Agency.
Milt Salstone, chairman of M.S. Distributing, an independent distributorship.
Johnny Sandlin, producer of the Allman Brothers Band and Rockets.
John Santangelo, Jr., publisher of **Hit Parader** magazine.
Steve Schankman, St. Louis-based concert promoter; partner in Contemporary Productions Inc.
Louie Shelton, producer of Seals & Crofts and Art Garfunkel.
John Scher, co-personal manager of Renaissance and the Grateful Dead; Passaic-based concert promoter; president of Monarch Entertainment Bureau.
Henry Schissler, manager of rock discotheques (e.g., Hurrah's, Trudy Heller's, Heat).
Marvin Schlacter, president of Prelude Records.
Tom Scholz, producer of Boston.
Ekke Schnabel, senior vice president of business affairs at Polydor Records.
Bill Schnee, producer of Pablo Cruise.
Richard Schory, president of Ovation Records.
Aaron Schroeder, president of Aaron Schroeder Intl. music publishing company.
Peter Schukat, New York-based attorney.
Dave Schulps, editor of **Trouser Press** magazine.

Albert Schultz, president of Albert Schultz Inc., a record exporting firm.
Sheldon Schultz, agent affiliated with ICM.
Irwin Schuster, vice president creative of Chappell Music.
Bert, James and Stu Schwartz, co-owners of Schwartz Brothers independent distributorship in Washington, DC.
Marty Scott, partner in JEM Records, a rock importer.
Ben and Tony Scotti, co-owners of Scotti Bros. Records; personal managers of Leif Garrett.
John Sebastian, program director of KUPD-AM, Phoenix AZ.
Harold Seider, president of United Artists Music.
Selby Brothers, owners of Electric Lady Studio in New York.
Scott Shannon, program director of WPGC-AM, Washington, DC.
Jason Shapiro, chairman of National Record Mart, a Pittsburgh-based retail chain.
Jerry Shapiro, president of Brookville Marketing, a TV direct mail firm.
Mickey Shapiro, Los Angeles based attorney.
Greg Shaw, president of Bomp Records.
Peter Sheils, Los Angeles based agent of the William Morris Agency.
Earl Shelton, vice president and general manager of Mighty Three Music.
Bob Sherwood, president of Mercury Records.
Dave Sholin, program director of RKO General, San Francisco CA.
Paul Shore, president of Shorewood Packaging, a jacket printing firm.
Carol Sidlow, Los Angeles-based agent of the William Morris Agency.
David Siebert, general manager of Siebert's, a wholesale division of the Handleman Co.
Mike Sigman, senior vice president and managing editor of **Record World** magazine.
Martin Silfen, New York-based attorney.

MUSIC BUSINESS PROFESSIONALS

Lester Sill, president of Screen Gems-EMI Music Inc.

Len Silver, president of Amherst Records; owner of Record Theatre retail chain in Buffalo.

Sam Silverman, president of United Records and Tapes, a Miami-based independent distributorship.

Syd Silverman, publisher of **Variety** and **Daily Variety** magazines.

Ed Silvers, chairman of Warner Bros. Music and president of Pacific Records.

Lou Simon, senior vice president of marketing at Mercury Records.

Joe Simone, president of Progress Distributing, an independent distributorship.

Stanley Sirote, president of Countrywide Distributing, a firm specializing in cutouts.

Barbara Skydell, executive agent affiliated with Premier Talent.

Scott Slade, program director of WAYS-AM, Charlotte NC.

Steve Slatin, music director of KISW-FM, Seattle WA.

Joe Slattery, president of the American Federation of Television & Radio Artists (AFTRA).

Bob Slavin, music director of WCOZ-FM, Boston MA.

C. Charles Smith, president of Pickwick International.

Joe Smith, chairman of Elektra/Asylum Records.

Paul Smith, senior vice president of marketing at CBS Records.

Rick Smith, vice president and general manager of CBS Music Publishing.

Stanley Snadowsky, New York-based attorney and co-owner of the Bottom Line club.

Glen Snoddy, owner of Woodland Sound Studio in Nashville.

Jack Snyder, program director of KMET-FM, Los Angeles CA.

Coen Solleveld, worldwide president of Polygram Corp.

Russ Solomon, owner of Tower Records retail chain in Los Angeles.

Seymour Solomon, president and classical A&R representative of Vanguard Records.

Larry Solters, partner in Solters & Roskin publicity firm.

David Sonenberg, personal manager of Meat Loaf.

Martin Spector, owner of Spec's Records retail chain in Florida.

Phil Spector, producer of the Beatles, Crystals and Ronettes; co-owner of Philles Records.

Tim Spencer, program director of KTXQ-FM, Dallas TX.

George Souvall, president of Alta Distribution Co.

Howard Stark, executive vice president of Ariola Records.

Steven Starr, owner of Starrs Nightclub in Philadelphia.

Seymour Stein, managing director of Sire Records.

David J. Steinberg, Philadelphia-based attorney.

Irwin Steinberg, chairman and chief executive officer of Phonogram/Mercury Records.

Michael Stewart, president of Interworld Music Group.

Robert Stigwood, chairman of the Robert Stigwood Organization; personal manager of the Bee Gees, Andy Gibb and Eric Clapton.

Rand Stoll, agent affiliated with Headliners.

Mike Stoller, co-producer of the Coasters and Drifters; legendary songwriter.

Arnold Stone, vice president of administration at MCA Records.

Brian Stone, co-owner of Emerald City Records.

Henry Stone, president of TK Records.

Phil Strider, music director of KBPI-FM, Denver CO.

Burt Sugarman, producer of **Midnight Special.**

Joe Sullivan, personal manager of Wet Willie and Charlie Daniels.

MUSIC BUSINESS PROFESSIONALS

Robert Summer, president of RCA Records.
Jesse Summers, music director of KPRI-FM, San Diego CA.
John Swenson, rock music writer and author of books on rock 'n' roll.
Warren B. Syer, publisher of **High Fidelity** magazine.
Bill Szmczyk, producer of the Eagles.
Michael Tannen, New York-based attorney.
Bill Tanner, program director of Y100-AM, Miami FL.
Nat Tarnapol, president of Brunswick Records.
Joe Tarsia, owner of Sigma Sound Recording Studios.
Creed Taylor, chairman of CTI Records and a jazz producer.
LeBaron Taylor, vice president of Black music marketing at CBS Records.
Al Teller, president of Windsong Records.
Ted Templeman, producer of Van Halen and the Doobie Brothers; vice president of Warner Bros. Records.
Jeff Tennenbaum, co-owner of JEM Records, a rock importer.
Tom Teuber, program director of WLVQ-FM, Columbus OH.
Doug Thaler, agent affiliated with ATI.
Peter Thall, New York-based attorney.
Marty Thau, president of Red Star Records.
Al Thomas, president of Virgin Records.
Dave Thompson, program director of KDWB-AM, Minneapolis MN.
Ross Todd, Cincinnati-based concert promoter; president of Ross Todd Presents.
D.H. Toller-Bond, president of London Records.
Allan Toussaint, producer of Joe Cocker.
Bob Travis, program director of WGCL-AM, Cleveland OH.
Rosalie Trombley, music director of CKLW-AM, Detroit MI.
Jim Tyrrell, president of T-Electric Records.
Larry Uttal, former president of Bell Records and Private Stock Records.
Elmer Valentine, owner of the Roxy and Whiskey clubs in Los Angeles.
Larry Vallon, Evansville-based concert promoter; president of Larry Vallen Presents.
Johannan Vigoda, personal manager of Stevie Wonder.
Gabe Vigorito, president of De-Lite Records.
Sheldon Vogel, executive vice president of Atlantic Records.
Jerry Wagner, president of CTI Records.
Jeff Wald, personal manager of Helen Reddy and Chicago.
Phil Walden, president of Capricorn Records.
Gary Waldron, program director of KCPX-AM, Salt Lake City UT.
Jo Walker, executive director of the Country Music Association.
Bob Walters, co-owner of the Power Station recording studio in New York.
Norby Walters, president of Norby Walters booking agency.
Art Ward, president of A&R Recording Studios in New York.
Lenny Waronker, producer of Randy Newman, George Harrison, and Ry Cooder; senior vice president of A&R at Warner Bros. Records.
Paul Wasserman, partner in Mahoney/Wasserman publicity firm.
Jon Waxman, New York-based attorney.
Dan Weiner, agent affiliated with Monterrey Peninsula Artists.
Harvey Weinstein, Buffalo-based concert promoter; president of Harvey & Corky Productions.
Judy Weinstein, president of For the Record, a New York-based disco pool.
Jerry Weintraub, personal manager of Neil Diamond, John Denver, Harry Chapin, John Davidson, the Carpenters and other artists.
Stu Weintraub, New York-based agent of the William Morris Agency.
Norman Weiser, president of SESAC Inc.

Nat Weiss, president of Nemperor Records.
Paulette Weiss, pop music editor of **Stereo Review** magazine.
Sam Weiss, owner of Win Records one-stop in New York.
Steve Weiss, New York-based attorney.
Lawrence Welk, legendary bandleader and president of the Welk Music Group.
Manny Wells, president of Surplus Records & Tapes, a cutout firm.
Stu Welz, Los Angeles-based agent of the William Morris Agency.
Jann Wenner, publisher of **Rolling Stone** magazine.
Tom Werman, producer of Cheap Trick, Ted Nugent and Molly Hatchet.
Steve West, program director of KJR-AM, Seattle WA.
Tommy West, vice president of Lifesong Records.
Logan Westbrooks, president of Source Records.
Jerry Wexler, producer of Aretha Franklin, Bob Dylan and Dire Straits; senior vice president of Warner Bros. Records.

Jerry Wexler

Dennis White, vice president of marketing at Capitol Records.
Jim White, program director of KILT-AM, Houston TX.
Maurice White, producer of Earth, Wind & Fire and Pockets.
Dick Whiteford, agent affiliated with ABC.
Norman Whitfield, president of Whitfield Records.
George Williams, music director of Southern Broadcasting, Winston-Salem, NC.
Bob Wilson, publisher of **Radio & Records** magazine.
Marty Winkler, president of Belwyn-Mills publishing company.
Jerry Winston, president of Malverne Distributors, a New York-based independent distributorship.
Muff Winwood, producer of Dire Straits.
Joe Wissert, producer of Boz Scaggs.
Sanford I. Wolff, executive secretary of AFTRA.
Richard Woodward, music director of WRKO-AM, Boston MA.
Chris Wright, co-owner of Chrysalis Records.
Marvin Yancy, co-producer of Natalie Cole.
Jules Yarnell, head of the anti-piracy division of the Recording Industry Association of America.
Walter Yetnikoff, president of the CBS Records Group.
Bill Young, program director of KILT-AM, Houston TX.
Saul Zaentz, president of Fantasy/Prestige/Milestone/Stax Records.
Michael Zager, co-producer of the Spinners, Dionne Warwick and Ronny Dyson.
Ronald Zalkind, author of **Getting Ahead in the Music Business** and founder of the Zadoc Institute for Practical Learning in New York.
Theodora Zavin, senior vice president of BMI.
Lee Zhito, publisher of Billboard magazine.
Don Zimmermann, president of Capitol Records.
Bob Zievens, Beverly Hills-based agent of Athena Artists.
Irv Zuckerman, St-Louis based concert promoter; partner in Contemporary Productions Inc.

BEHIND THE SCENES

ALBUM ACTION 1979

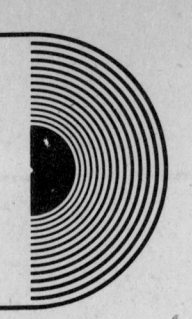

Album Artist (Label)	Producer	Engineer

JANUARY

Album Artist (Label)	Producer	Engineer
You Don't Bring Me Flowers Neil Diamond (Columbia)	Bob Gaudio	Rich Ruggieri, Ron Hitchcock
Back to Earth Cat Stevens (A&M)	Cat Stevens, Paul Samwell-Smith	Billy Sherrill
Briefcase Full of Blues Blues Brothers (Atlantic)	Bob Tischler	Warren Dewey
Touchdown Bob James (Columbia)	Bob James	Joe Jorgenson
If You Want Blood AC/DC (Atlantic)	Vanda, George Young	
T-Connection T-Connection (Dash)	Cory Wade	Gary Vandy
Angie Angela Bofill (Arista)	Dave Grusin, Larry Rosen	Larry Rosen, Jim Bayer
Love Beach Emerson, Lake & Palmer (Atlantic)	Keith Emerson, Greg Lake, Carl Palmer	Karl Pitterson, Jack Nuber
From the Inside Alice Cooper (Warner Bros.)	David Foster	H. Gatica, K. Olsen, D. DeVore, Tom Knox, H. Steele
Sanctuary J. Geils Band (EMI)	Joe Wissert	Dave Thoenes

Mixing/Mastering	Studio	Personal Manager or Contact	Booking Agent
/Doug Sax, Mastering Lab	Cherokee, Sunset Sound, J&M, Indigo Ranch	Management III	William Morris
/Bob Sawell, Master Control	Jack Clement	Barry Krost	—
Record Plant	Universal Amphitheater	Bernie Brillstein	—
Sound Mixers//Vladimir Miller, Idris Muhammad	CBS, Sound Mixers, A&R	Tappan Zee Records	—
Albert Studios	recorded live	Leber-Krebs	—
Cory Wade, T-Connection/ Ted Jensen	Studio Center Sound	Don Taylor	—
Jim Bayer, Larry Rosen/ Ted Jensen	Electric Lady, A&R	Grusin/Rosen Prod.	—
	Compass Point	Stewart Young	Premier Talent
K. Olsen, D. DeVore, A. Humberto	Davlen Sound, Hollywood Sound, Cherokee, Kendun, Studio 55	Alive Ent.	Entertainment Projects
Record Plant/Joe Bressco	Longview Farms, Record Plant	T&A Research & Development	Premier Talent

ALBUM ACTION 1979

Album Artist (Label)	Producer	Engineer
An American Prayer Jim Morrison (Elektra)	Doors, John Haeny	John Haeny
Bush Doctor Peter Tosh (Rolling Stones)	Peter Tosh, Robert Shakespeare	Geoffrey Tung, Errol Thompson
Greatest Hits Barry Manilow (Arista)	Barry Manilow, Ron Dante	Michael Delugg
Shakedown Street Grateful Dead (Arista)	Lowell George	Bob Matthews
Fly Away Voyage (Marlin)	Roger Tokarz	Steve Taylor
Light of Life Bar-Kays (Mercury)	Allen Jones	Wm. Brown III, R. Jackson, Allan Jones
Don't Cry Out Loud Melissa Manchester (Arista)	Harry Maslin	Milt Chase, Gary Starr, Gary S. Karvina
Jazz Queen (Elektra)	Roy Thomas Baker, Queen	Geoff Workman
C'est Chic Chic (Atlantic)	Bernard Edwards, Nile Rogers	Bob Clearmountain
Back to the Bars Todd Rundgren (Bearsville)	Todd Rundgren	Todd Rundgren
Bonnie Pointer Bonnie Pointer (Motown)	Jeff Bowen, Berry Gordy	Russ Terrana, Bob Robitaille, Art Stewart, Guy Casta, Glen Jordan, Gerry Napiur, Mike Stone
Misplaced Ideals Sad Cafe (A&M)	John Punter	
Instant Replay Dan Hartman (Blue Sky)	Dan Hartman	Darryl Rogers
Get Down Gene Chandler (20th Century Fox)	Carl Davis	Bill Bradley
Totally Hot Olivia Newton-John (MCA)	John Farrar	David J. Holman

ALBUM ACTION 1979   375

Mixing/Mastering	Studio	Personal Manager or Contact	Booking Agent
Cherokee	Hollywood Sound	—	—
Karl Pitterson/ Dennis King	Joe Gibbs Studio, Dynamic Sound	Herb Miller	—
		Miles Lourie	William Morris
Club La Front	Club La Front	Richard Loren	Bill Graham (west), Monarch (east)
Steve Taylor	Trident Studio	TK Records	
/Larry Nix	Ardent	Don Dortch	Don Dortch
Phil Schier	A&M, Village Recorders, Music Grinders	—	ICM
/George Marino at Sterling Sound	Mountain, Super Bear	John Reid	Howard Rose
/Dennis King at Atlantic Sound	Power Station	Marty Itzler	Steve Ellis
	recorded live	Eric Gardner	ATI
Russ Terrana/Jack Andrews	Motown, Gold Star, Record Plant, Marvin Gaye, Wally Heides	Motown Records	—
	Sawmill, Strawberry St. North, Indigo	Kennedy Street Mgt.	—
/Jose Rodriguez at Sterling Sound	Schoolhouse	Steve Paul	Premier Talent
/Walter Tragett	Universal	Carl Davis	—
David J. Holman/Allen Zentz	Hollywood Sound, Group III, Cherokee	Lee Kramer	ICM

ALBUM ACTION 1979

Album Artist (Label)	Producer	Engineer
Willie and Family Live Willie Nelson (Columbia)	Willie Nelson	Tom Walsh
Destiny Jacksons (Epic)	Jacksons	Pete Granet, Don Murray
Edwin Starr Edwin Starr (20th Century Fox)	Edwin Starr	Ric Pekkerman, Bob D'Orleans
Legend Poco (ABC)	Richard Sanford Orshoff	David Henson
Backless Eric Clapton (RSO)	Glyn Johns	Glyn Johns
TNT Tanya Tucker (MCA)	Jerry Goldstein	Ed Barton
Feel the Need Leif Garrett (Scotti Bros.)	Michael Lloyd	Humberto Gatica, Michael Lloyd
Playin' to Win Outlaws (Arista)	Robert John Lange	Rodney Mils
Patrice Patrice Rushen (Elektra)	Charles Mims, Jr., Reggie Andrews, Patrice Rushen	Pete Chaiken
Dire Straits Dire Straits (Warner Bros.)	Muff Winwood	Rhett Davies
Pleasure and Pain Dr. Hook (Capitol)	Ron Haffkine	Steve Melton, Gregg Harmon
Energy Pointer Sisters (Planet)	Richard Perry	Dennis Kirk
Q: "Are We Not Men?" A: "We Are Devo! ! !" Devo (Warner Bros.)	Brian Eno	Conrad Planck
Aerosmith Live Bootleg Aerosmith (Columbia)	Jack Douglas, Aerosmith	Jay Messina, Lee DeCarlo, Jack Douglas

Mixing/Mastering	Studio	Personal Manager or Contact	Booking Agent
Bradley Hartman	Showco Mobile	Media Consulting	Media Consulting
Weslake Audio/Masterlab	Cherokee, Total Experience, Heiders/ Filmways, Record Plant, Dawn Breakers	Weisner-Deamann/ Joe Jackson	Regency
Hollywood Sound/ Total Experience	Hollywood Sound, Total Experience		
/Joe Chiccareli	Crystal, Village	Hartmann & Goodman	Premier Talent
		Robert Stigwood Org.	—
Ed Barton/Wally Traugatt	Kendun	Far Out	—
		Stan Moress	ICM
Studio One/Sterling Sound	Studio One	Charles Brusco	ATI
Conway/Bernie Grundman	Conway, Group IV, Record Plant	Tentmakers	Regency
	Basing St.	Ed Bicknell	ATI
	Muscle Shoals	Bob Heller	William Morris
Bill Schnee/Doug Sax	Studio 55	Management III	—
Conny's Studio	Conny's, Different Fur	Lookout Mgr.	William Morris
/George Marino at Sterling Sound		Leber-Krebs	ICM

ALBUM ACTION 1979

Album Artist (Label)	Producer	Engineer
Against the Grain Phoebe Snow (Columbia)	Phil Ramone, Barry Beckett	Jim Boyer
Goin' Coconuts Donny & Marie Osmond (Polydor)	Michael Lloyd, Mike Curb	Humberto Gatica, Michael Lloyd
Hearts of Stone Southside Johnny & the Ashbury Jukes (Epic)	Steve Van Zandt	Jack Malken
Money Talks Bar-Kays (Stax)	Allen Jones, Phil Kaffel	William C. Brown III
Christmas Portrait Carpenters (A&M)	Richard Carpenter	Ray Gerhardt, Roger Young, Dave Iveland
To the Limit Joan Armatrading (A&M)	Glyn Johns	Doug Sax
Photo Finish Rory Gallagher (Chrysalis)	Rory Gallagher	Alan O'Duffy
Mother Factor Mother's Finest (Epic)	Tom Werman	Don Cody, Rodney Mills
Motor Booty Affair Parliament (Casablanca)	George Clinton	Jim Vitti, Pete Bishop, Mike Iacofeui, Greg Riley

FEBRUARY

Mirror Stars Fabulous Poodles (Park Lane)	Muff Winwood, John Entwhistle, Howard Kilgour	Cyrano Kilgour, Howard Kilgour
Every 1's a Winner Hot Chocolate (Infinity)	Mickie Most	
Shot of Love Lakeside (Solar)	Dick Griffey, Leon Sylvers, Lakeside	Don Blake
Head First Babys (Chrysalis)	Ron Nevison	Ron Nevison
You Fooled Me Greg & Hanks (RCA)	Zane Grey, LeRon Hanks	Mitt Calise, Steve Hirsch, Jim Cone, Larry Forkner

ALBUM ACTION 1979 379

Mixing/Mastering	Studio	Personal Manager or Contact	Booking Agent
Barry Beckett at Muscle Shoals	A&R	Home Run	Home Run
/Bob MacLeod at Artisan Sound	Kolob, Michael Lloyd	Osmond Entertainment Center	ICM
Bob Ludwig at Masterdish	Secret Sound	Steve Van Zandt	Premier Talent
/John Golden	Stax	Don Dortch	Don Dortch Intl.
/Bernie Grundman		Management III	William Morris
/Mastering Lab	Olympic	Mike Stone	Artists Heller Agency
	Dierks	Donald Gallagher	ICM
Studio I/Frank DeLuna at A&M	Studio I	Leber-Krebs	Rogers Agency
United Sound/Allen Zentz	United Sound, Super Disc	Leber-Krebs	William Morris

	Basing Street, Ramport	Park Lane Mgt.	Premier Talent
	RAK	Ian Wright	—
Steve Hodge	Studio Masters	Solar Records	—
Mike Reese	Hidden Valley Ranch Castle, Record Plant	Renaissance Mgt.	ATI
David Ruffo, Galen Senogles, Rick Hart	A&R Wally Heides, Sound Arts, Capitol	Don Sorkin	—

ALBUM ACTION 1979

Album Artist (Label)	Producer	Engineer
Trillion Trillion (Epic)	Gary Lyons	Gino Giorgiao
Blondes Have More Fun Rod Stewart (Warner Bros.)	Tom Dowd	Andy Johns
Minute by Minute Doobie Brothers (Warner Bros.)	Ted Templeman	Donn Landee
Equinoxe Jean Michel Jarre (Polydor)	Jean Michel Jarre	
Crosswinds Peabo Bryson (Capitol)	Peabo Bryson, Johnny Pate	Dave Ireland, Richard Cottrell
Let the Music Play Arpeggio (Polydor)	Simon Sousson	Bryce Robbley, Brian Levi, Joe Cannizzaro
Strangers in the Night UFO (Chrysalis)	Ron Nevison	Ron Nevison, Mike Clink
Somewhere in My Lifetime Phyllis Hyman (Arista)	Larry Alexander, Skip Scarborough	Don Cody, Michael DeLugg, Rick Rowe
Head East Live Head East (A&M)	Jeffrey Lesser	Lee DeCarlo
Exotic Mysteries Lonnie Liston Smith (Columbia)	Lonnie Liston Smith, Bert DeCoteaux	Dave Wittman
Instant Funk Instant Funk (Salsoul)	Bunny Sigler	Dick Devlin, Jim Gallagher, Jay Mark
John Denver John Denver (RCA)	Milt Okun	Ed Barta
Life for the Taking Eddie Money (Columbia)	Bruce Botnick	Rik Pekkonen
Bustin' Loose Chuck Brown & the Soul Searchers (Source)	James Purdie	Carl Paruolo
Nicolette Nicolette Larson (Warner Bros.)	Ted Templeman	Donn Landee

Mixing/Mastering	Studio	Personal Manager or Contact	Booking Agent
Chicago Recording Co./ George Marino	Caribou	Twogether Mgt.	ICM
Andy Johns, Tom Dowd		Bill Gaff	ATI
Sunset Sound	Warner Bros.	Bruce Cohn	Monterey Peninsula
Jean Pierre Janiaud	Jean Michel Jarre's private studio	Francis Dreyfus	—
Johnny Pate, Peabo Bryson, Dave Ireland/ Bernie Grundman	A&M	David Franklin	William Morris
Bob Stone, Mick Gugguski/Allen Zentz	Star Track	De-Air Mktg. Intl.	—
	Record Plant	Wilf Wright	ATI
/Jack Skinner	CBS, United Western Media Sound, Secret Sound	Command Performance Inc.	Willam Morris
Lee DeCarlo	Record Plant	Larry Boyd or Artistic Vision	Premier Talent
Dave Wittman	Electric Lady	Joe Fontana	Regency
Bob Bland/Jose Rodriguez	Alpha Intl., Sigma Sound, Philadelphia Music Works	Salsoul Records	—
	Filmways/Heider	Management III	William Morris
Andy Johns/Wally Traugott		Bill Graham	Premier Talent
Carl Paruolo, Present/Frankford Wayne	Sigma Sound	Dancer Prod.	Norby Walters
	Warner Bros.	White Rabbit Mgt.	—

Album Artist (Label)	Producer	Engineer
Move It On Over George Thorogood & the Destroyers (Rounder)	George Thorogood, John Nagy, Ken Irwin	John Nagy
Armed Forces Elvis Costello (Columbia)	Nick Lowe	
The Gambler Kenny Rogers (UA)	Larry Butler	Billy Sherrill
Love Tracks Gloria Gaynor (Polydor)	Dino Fekaris	Lewis Peters, Jack Rouben
Here My Dear Marvin Gaye (Tamla)	Marvin Gaye	Art Stewart, Fred Ross, Tony Houston, Bill Ravencroft

MARCH

Carmel Joe Sample (ABC)	Joe Sample, Stix Hooper Wilton Felder	Rik Pekkonen
Spirits Having Flown Bee Gees (RSO)	Bee Gees, Karl Richardson, Albhy Galuten	Karl Richardson
Bustin' Out of L Seven Rick James (Motown)	Rick James, Art Stewart	Carmine Rubino
Numbers Rufus (ABC)	Rufus, Roy Halee	Roy Halee
Awakening Michael Marada Walden (Atlantic)	Nardo Michael Walden, Patrick Adams	Bob Clearmountain, Michael Frondelli, Jimmy Shifflett, Alan Sides
Cheap Trick at Budokan Cheap Trick (Epic)	Tom Werman	Tamoo Suzuki
Super Mann Herbie Mann (Atlantic)	Patrick Adams	Bert Szerlip, Scott Litt, Ralph Moss
A Tonic for the Troops Boomtown Rats (Columbia)	Robert John L'ange	Stuff Brown, Tim Friese-Greene
The Man Who Built America Horslips (DJM)	Steve Katz	Dec O'Doherty

ALBUM ACTION 1979   383

Mixing/Mastering	Studio	Personal Manager or Contact	Booking Agent
Mixing Lab/Masterdisk	Dimension Sound	Rounder Records	Rosebud Music Agency
		Jake Riviera	—
/Bob Sowell at Master Control	Jack Clement	Kragen & Co.	ICM
/Artisian Sound	Mom and Pops Co. Store	American Worldwide Sounds & Music	Norby Walters
Art Stewart/Jack Andrews at Motown	Marvin Gaye Studio	Curtis Shaw	—
Rik Pekkonen	Hollywood Sound	Grief-Garris	William Morris
/George Marino	Criteria	Robert Stigwood Org.	William Morris
Art Stewart, Rick James/ Jo Hansch	Sigma Sound	Alive Ent.	—
Roy Halee, Rufus/ Allen Zentz	Dawnbreaker	Fitzgerald-Hartley	Regency
/Dennis King	Power Station, Electric Lady, Crystal Sound, Oceanway	Greg DiGiovine	Starloft
Jay Messina/Gary Ladinsky	recorded live	Ken Adamany	ATI
	Power Station, Sound Palace		
	Relight, Dieter Dierk's	Fatchna O'Kelly	ATI
Advision	Advision	Michael Deeny	William Morris

ALBUM ACTION 1979

Album Artist (Label)	Producer	Engineer
McGuinn, Clarke & Hillman McGuinn, Clarke & Hillman (Capitol)	Ron Albert, Howard Albert	Don Gehman
Outlandos d'Amour Polices (A&M)	Police	Nigel Gray, Chris Gray
New Kind of Feeling Anne Murray (Capitol)	Jim Ed Norman	Ken Friesen
We Are Family Sister Sledge (Cotillion)	Nile Rodgers, Bernard Edwards	Bob Clearmountain, Don Berman, Bert Szerlip
George Harrison George Harrison (Warner Bros.)	George Harrison, Russ Titelman	Lee Herschberg, Phil McDonald, Keemar Shankar
Feets Don't Fail Me Now Herbie Hancock (Columbia)	Herbie Hancock, David Rubinson & Friends	Bryan Bell
Take Me Home Cher (Casablanca)	Bob Esty	Michael DeLugg, Larry Emerine
Outline Gino Soccio (Warner Bros.)	Gino Soccio	Lindsay Kidd
Cut Loose Hamilton Bohannon (Mercury)	Hamilton Bohannon	Tad, Milan Bogdan, Joe Neal
Rock Billy Boogie Robert Gordon (RCA)	Richard Gottehrer	Rob Freeman
Tiger in the Rain Michael Franks (Warner Bros.)	John Simon	Glenn Berger
Hard Times for Lovers Judy Collins (Elektra)	Gary Klein	Armin Steiner, John Mills
Knock on Wood Amii Stewart (Ariola)	Barry Leng	Alan Winstanley, John Mackwith, Greg Walsh, Phil Harding, Steve Hohoyd, John Eden

Mixing/Mastering	Studio	Personal Manager or Contact	Booking Agent
Criteria	Criteria	Al Hersh	Magna Artists
	Surrey Sound	Miles Copeland	Paragon
	Eastern Sound	Balmur	APA
Power Station/Dennis King	Power Station	Ron DeBlasto	Steve Ellis
Phil McDonald/Lee Herschenberg	F.P.S.H.O.T.	Dennis O'Brien	—
	Bear West	Adam's Dad Mgt.	William Morris
Larry Emerine/Allen Zentz	Studio 55, A&M	Katz-Gallin	—
Mix Machine/Jack Skinner	Montreal	Unison Records	—
Joe Neal at Mastersound/ Glen Meadows	Mastersound, Studio One	Levi Bohannon	Paragon
Greg Calbi	Plaza Sound	Richard Gottehrer	Premier Talent
Glenn Berger	A&R	Fred Heller	William Morris
John Mills/Bernie Grundman	Round Labs, Capitol Records	Entertainment Co. or Rock Mountain Prod.	—
/Ian Cooper	T.W., Utopia, Marquee, Red Bus	Ariola Records	—

Album Artist (Label)	Producer	Engineer
More Songs about Buildings and Food Talking Heads (Sire)	Brian Eno, Talking Heads	Rhett Davies

APRIL

Album Artist (Label)	Producer	Engineer
Livin' Inside Your Love George Benson (Warner Bros.)	Tommy LiPuma	Al Schmitt
Enlightened Rogues Allman Brothers Band (Capricorn)	Tom Dowd	Steve Gursky
If You Knew Suzi Suzi Quatro (RSO)	Mike Chapman	Peter Coleman
Light the Light Seawind (Horizon)	Tommy LiPuma	Al Schmitt, Armin Steiner
Look Sharp! Joe Jackson (A&M)	Dave Kershenbaum	"Hot" Rod Hewison
It's Alright with Me Patti LaBelle (Epic)	Skip Scarborough	Don Cody
Oneness Devadip Carlos Santana (Columbia)	Devadip Carlos Santana, Glen Kolotkin Glen Kolotkin	
Sheik Yerbouti Frank Zappa (Mercury)	Frank Zappa	Peter Henderson, Davey Moire, Claus Wiedemann, Kerry McNab
Desolation Angels Bad Company (Swan Song)	Bad Company	Tony Patrick
Danger Money U.K. (Polydor)	John Welton, Eddie Jobson	John Punter
Manifesto Roxy Music (Atco)	Roxy Music	Rhett Davis, Phil Brown, Randy Mason, Jimmy Douglas

Mixing/Mastering	Studio	Personal Manager or Contact	Booking Agent
/Joe Gastwirt at Masterdisk	Compass Point	Gary Kurfirst	Talking Heads Tours Inc.
Capitol/Mike Reese at Mastering Lab	Columbia, Capitol, Atlantic	Ken Fritz	William Morris
Criteria/Criteria	Criteria	Steve Massarsky	Paragon
Decca, MCA-Whitney/ Gordon Vicary	EMI Electrola, MCA-Whitney	Chinnichap	—
Mike Reese at Capitol	Sound Labs	Ken Fritz	William Morris
	Eden	Albion Mgt.	—
/Stewart Romain at CBS	Total Experience, Alpha International	Great Eastern Mgt.	Regency
/Phil Brown at Automatt	Automatt	Bill Graham	Premier Talent
Joe Chicarelli, Frank Zappa	Village Recorders, Basing Street Remote, Remote Truck, Manor Remote, RCA Remote, The 'Ole Four Track	Glotzer Mgt.	—
Marquee	Ridge Farm	Swan Song Mgt.	—
/George Marino at Sterling Sound	A.I.R.	E.G. Records	Premier Talent
Atlantic	Ridge Farm, Basing Street	E.G. Mgt.	Premier Talent

ALBUM ACTION 1979

Album Artist (Label)	Producer	Engineer
Remote Control The Tubes (A&M)	Todd Rundgren	Todd Rundgren
The Promise of Love Delegation (Shadybrook)	Ken Gold	David Baker, Phil Harding, Ashley Howe
Breakfast in America Supertramp (A&M)	Supertramp, Peter Henderson	Peter Heinderson
"L.A. (Light Album)" Beach Boys (Caribou)	Bruce Johnston, Curt Beecher	Chuck Britz, Bill Fletcher, Joel Moss, Curt Beecher, Earl Mankey, Tom Murphey, Chuck Leary, Greg Venable, Jeff Guercio, John Hanlon
Feel No Fret Average White Band (Atlantic)	Average White Band, Gene Paul	Gene Paul
Fate for Breakfast Art Garfunkel (Columbia)	Louie Shelton	Joseph Bogan, Michael Stavrou, Elliot Scheiner, Ed Rakowitz, Bob Bullock, Jon Smith, Ed Sprig
Rockets Rockets (RSO)	Johnny Sandlin	Kur Kinzel
Night Rider! Tim Weisberg	Tim Weisberg, Lynn Blessing	Tom Flye
Rickie Lee Jones Rickie Lee Jones (Warner Bros.)	Lenny Waronker Russ Titelman	Lee Herschberg, Lloyd Clifft, Tom Knox, Roger "Joey" Nichols
Dr. Heckle and Mr. Jive England Dan & John Ford Coley (Tree)	Kyle Lehning	Kyle Lehning
Strikes Blackfoot (Atco)	Al Nalli, Henry Weck	Henry Weck
Disco Nights GQ (Arista)	Jimmy Simpson, Beau Ray Fleming	Randy Bean, Andy Abrams, Jimmy Simpson, Robin Martinez

Mixing/Mastering	Studio	Personal Manager or Contact	Booking Agent
	Ausex Corp., Music Room	Artists Intl. Mgt.	Monterey Peninsula Artists
	Lansdowne, Marquee, Roundhouse	Shadybrook	—
Crystal Sound	Village Recorders	Dave Margereson	Premier Talent
/Brian Gardner at Allen Zentz	Brother, Caribou, Sounds Good, Criteria, United Western, Kaye Smith, Super Sound, Brittania, Sound Arts/Dan Wyman, Westlake	Brother Records	Concerts West
Atlantic/George Piros	Compass Point	David Mintz	Premier Talent
	Sound Factory, A.I.R., A&R, Kendun Recorders, Dawnbreaker, Hit Factory	Arthur Garfunkel Ent.	—
/George Marino at Sterling Sound	Capricorn	Gary Lazar Mgt.	ATI
Tom Flye/Masterfonics	Record Plant	Red Sky Mgt.	Howard Rose
Warner Bros./ Warner Bros.	Warner Bros.	Nick Mathe	—
Elliot Scheiner, Bill Schnee/Mike Reese	Darlen Studios	Susan Josephs	ICM
	Subterranean, Sound Suite, Bee Jay	Al Nalli	DMA
	Sound Palace, Sigma Sound	Tony Lopez	Norby Walters

Album Artist (Label)	Producer	Engineer
Children of the Sun Billy Thorpe (Capricorn)	Spencer Proffer	Larry Brown
The Joy of Living Tony Williams (Columbia)	Tony Williams	Jan Hammer, Don Puluse, Fred Catero, Tom Suzuki, Stanley Tonkel, Jack Malker
Parallel Lines Blondie (Chrysalis)	Mike Chapman	Peter Coleman
Desmond Child & Rouge Desmond Child & Rouge (Capitol)	Richard Landis	
Madam Butterfly Tavares (Capitol)	Bobby Martin	
Village People Village People (Casablanca)	Jacques Morali	Gerald Block
Macho Man Village People (Casablanca)	Jacques Morali	Gerald Block
Smooth Talk Evelyn "Champagne" King (RCA)	T. Life	Joaquin J. Lopes, Boris Midney

MAY

Hot Number Foxy (Dash)	Foxy, Jerry Masters	Jerry Masters, Godfrey Diamond
Squeezing Out Sparks Graham Parker (Arista)	Jack Nitzsche	Mark Howlett
Tycoon Tycoon (Arista)	Robert John Lange	Tim Friese-Green
I Love You So Natalie Cole (Capitol)	Marvin Yancy, Charles Jackson	Butch Lynch, Serge Reyes, Mark Davis, Clay McMurray, Gordon Shyrock, Frank Kejmar, Reginald Dozier, Jerry Brown, Zolie Osage, Al Schmitt
Let Me Be Your Woman Linda Clifford (RSO)	Gil Askey	Roger Anfinsen, Fred Breitberg

ALBUM ACTION 1979   391

Mixing/Mastering	Studio	Personal Manager or Contact	Booking Agent
/Bernie Grundman	Pasha Music House	Robert Raymond	—
/George Marino	Red Gate, CBS, Automatt, Secret Sound	Monte Kay Mt.	—
Forum/MCA-Whitney	Record Plant	Chrysalis Records	Paragon
		Starflight Mgt.	Premier Talent
	Total Experience	Brian Panella	Regency
	Sigma Sound	Can't Stop Prod.	ATI
	Sigma Sound	Can't Stop Prod.	ATI
Joaquin J. Lopes/Jack Adelman	RCA, Alpha Intl.	Sight & Sound Mgt.	William Morris
/George Marino at Sterling Sound	Criteria, Media Sound	Don Kelley Org.	—
Cherokee/Mark Hawlett, Jeff Sanders	Lansdowne	A.R.S.E.	Premier Talent
/Sterling Sound	Wessex	S.C.S.	Monterey Peninsula Artists
/Capitol	Sound Factory, United Western, ABC, MCA-Whitney, Hollywood Sound, Love 'n Comfort	New Direction	William Morris
Custom, CBS, Custom Sigma Sound		Curtom Records	Norby Walters

ALBUM ACTION 1979

Album Artist (Label)	Producer	Engineer
Music Box Evelyn "Champagne" King (RCA)	T. Life	Rick Rowe, Darroll Gustamachio, Gene Leone
Inspiration Maze Featuring Frankie Beverly (Capitol)	Frankie Beverly	John Nowland, Bill Evans, David Farrell, Gene Thompson
Thanks I'll Eat It Here Lowell George (Warner Bros.)	Lowell George	George Massenberg, Don Landee, Ray Thompson
Everybody Up Ohio Players (Arista)	Ohio Players	Steve Kusiciel, Gary Platt, Jim Krause
Real Life Ain't This Way Jay Ferguson (Asylum)	Bill Szmcyck	Ed Marshall, David Crowther, Terry Nelson
Go West Village People (Casablanca)	Jacques Morali	Mike Hutchinson
Van Halen II Van Halen (Warner Bros)	Ted Templeman	Corey Bailey, Jim Fitzpatrick
The Message Is Love Barry White (Unlimited Gold)	Barry White	Frank Kejmar
Rock On Raydio (Arista)	Ray Parkers, Jr.	Ray Parkers, Jr.
Brazilia John Klemmer (MCA)	John Klemmer, Stephan Goldman	Rick Ruggeri, Billy Taylor
Land of Passion Hubert Laws (Columbia)	Hubert Laws	Chris Brunt, Buddy Brundo
Watcha Gonna Do with My Love? Stephanie Mills (20th Century Fox)	Reggie Lucas, James Mtume	Jay Mark, Carmine Rubino
Paradise Grover Washington, Jr. (Elektra)	Grover Washington, Jr.	Fred Galletti
You're Never Alone with a Schizophrenic Ian Hunter (Chrysalis)	Ian Hunter, Mick Ronson	Bob Clearmountain, Scott Litt, Don Berman
Forever Orleans (Chrysalis)	Orleans	Roy Cicala, Sam Ginsberg

ALBUM ACTION 1979

Mixing/Mastering	Studio	Personal Manager or Contact	Booking Agent
	Secret Sound, Alpha International	Sight & Sound Mgt.	William Morris
/Wally Traugott at Capitol	Studio in the Country	Leon Fisher	ABC
		Cavallo-Ruffalo Mgt.	—
/Sterling Sound	Fifth Floor, Ohio Players, Paragon	Spectrum Talent Intl.	—
/Ted Jensen	Santa Barbara, Bayshore	Marty Pichinson	Variety Artists
	Sigma Sound	Can't Stop Prod.	ATI
Westlake Audio	Sunset Sound	Van Halen Prod.	Premier Talent
		Soul Unlimited	ICM
/Bernie Grundman	Raydio	Cavallo-Ruffalo	Brighton Agency
/Mike Reese	A&M, Sunset Sound, Cherokee	Gary Borman	William Morris
/Vladimir Meller	CBS	Spirit Prod.	—
/Ted Jensen	Sigma Sound	Joey or Audrey Mills	ICM
/Rudy Van Gelder	Alpha International	Great Eastern Mgt.	William Morris
/George Marino	Power Station	Cleveland Ent.	—
	Record Plant, Bearsville	Sight & Sound	ICM

Album Artist (Label)	Producer	Engineer
Runnin' Like the Wind Marshall Tucker Band (Warner Bros.)	Stewart Levine	Kurt Kinzel
Minnie Minnie Riperton (Capitol)	Henry Lewy, Dick Rudolph, Minnie Riperton	Steve Katz, Henry Lewy, Dick Rudolph
Tales of the Unexpected Frank Marino & Mahogany Rush (Columbia)	Frank Marino	Billy Szawlowski, Louis Gauthier
The Music Band War (MCA)	Jerry Goldstein, Lonnie Jordan, Howard Scott	Chris Huston
Evolution Journey (Columbia)	Roy Thomas Baker	Geoff Workman
Alive on Arrival Steve Forbert (Nemperor)	Steve Burgh	Glenn Berger, Charles Clifton
Brother to Brother Gino Vannelli (A&M)	Gino Vannelli, Joe Vannelli, Ross Vannelli	Norm Kinney

JUNE

Album Artist (Label)	Producer	Engineer
Blue Kentucky Girl Emmylou Harris (Warner Bros.)	Brian Ahern	Brian Ahern, Donivan Cowart, Bradley Hartman, Stuart Taylor
Night of the Living Dregs Dixie Dregs (Capricorn)	Ken Scott	
Grey Ghost Henry Paul Band (Atlantic)	Ron Albert, Howard Albert	Don Gehman
New Chautaugua Pat Methany (ECM)	Manfred Eicher	Jan Erik Kongshang
Bad Girls Donna Summer (Casablanca)	Giogio Moroder, Pete Bellotte	Juergen Koppers, Steven Smith
Bob Dylan at Budokan Bob Dylan (Columbia)	Don DeVito	Tom Szuki, Teppei Kasai, Tetsuro Tomita, G. H. Sukegawa

ALBUM ACTION 1979

Mixing/Mastering	Studio	Personal Manager or Contact	Booking Agent
/Bernie Grundman	Bayshore	Joe MacDonald	—
/Bernie Grundman	A&M	Ken Fritz	William Morris
/Sterling Sound	Tempo	Leber-Krebs	Premier Talent
/Capitol		Far Out Prod.	William Morris
Cherokee/George Marino at Sterling Sound	His Master's Wheels, Cherokee	Nightmare Prod.	Premier Talent
A&R/Sterling Sound	A&R	Coconut Ent.	Premier Talent
Norm Kinney/A&M	Davlen Sound	Bill Johnston	David Bendett Agency
Enactron II	Enactron	Ed Tickner	Monterey Peninsula Artists
/Stan Ricker	Chateau Records, Mountain Records, Avis Montreaux	Lloyd Segal	Variety Artists
Criteria	Criteria	Sound Seventy Mgt.	—
	Talent	Ted Kurland	—
Rusk/Brian Gardner	Music Grinders, Rusk	Joyce Bogart-Susan Munao	William Morris
	Nippon Budokan	Management III	—

ALBUM ACTION 1979

Album Artist (Label)	Producer	Engineer
Flag James Taylor (Columbia)	Peter Asher	Val Garay
Exposure Robert Fripp (Polydor)	Robert Fripp	Ed Sprigg, Steve Short, Jim Bonneford
Hot Property Heatwave (Epic)	Phil Ramone	Andy Jackson, Per Hansen, Richard Goldblatt
Million Mile Reflections Charlie Daniels Band (Epic)	John Boylan	Paul Grupp
Great Balls of Fire Dolly Parton (RCA)	Dean Parks, Gregg Perry	Eric Prestidge
I Am Earth, Wind & Fire (Columbia)	Maurice White	George Massenberg, Tom Perry
One for the Road Willie Nelson, Leon Russell (Columbia)	Willie Nelson, Leon Russell	Roger Lin
The Boss Diana Ross (Motown)	Nick Ashford, Valerie Simpson	Mike Hutchinson, James Simpson
Lodger David Bowie (RCA)	David Bowie, Tony Visconti	Tony Visconti, David Richards
Do You Wanna Go Party KC & the Sunshine Band (TK)	H. W. Casey, R. Finch	Milam Bodgam, R. Finch
Let Me Be Good to You Lou Rawls (Phila. Intl.)	Kenneth Gamble, Leon Huff	Joe Tarsia, Don Murray, Art Stoppe, Peter Humphreys, Dirk Devlin, Jim Gallagher
Winner Takes All Isley Brothers (T-Neck)	Isley Brothers	John Holbrook
Night Owl Gerry Rafferty (UA)	Gerry Rafferty, Hugh Murphy	Barry Hammond
State of Shock Ted Nugent (Epic)	Cliff Davies, Lou Futterman	Tim Geelan

Mixing/Mastering	Studio	Personal Manager or Contact	Booking Agent
	Sound Factory, Media Sound, Atlantic	Peter Asher	ICM
	Hit Factory, Relight	E.G. Mgt.	—
/Ted Jensen	Utopia, Sound Track, Music Center	Bud Carr	Regency
Westlake Audio	Woodland Sound	Sound Seventy	Paragon
Spectrum/Bernie Grundman at A&M	Sound Labs, A&M, Salty Dog	Katz-Gallin	ICM
/Mike Reese at Mastering Lab	Hollywood Sound, Davlen	Cavallo-Ruffalo	Brighton
/Bernie Grundman at A&M	Paradise	Nelson: Media Consulting; Russell: Diane Sullivan	Nelson: Media Consulting; Russell: Magna
/Stewart Romain at Columbia	Sigma Sound	Multi-Media Mgt.	William Morris
Tony Visconti, Rod O'Brien at Record Plant/Gregg Calbi at Sterling Sound	Mountain	Pat Gibbons	ICM
Sound Stage	Sunshine Sound	Katz-Gallin	ICM
/Frankford Wayne	Sigma Sound, Sound Lab, Davlen Sound	B.N.B. Assoc.	William Morris
/Stan Kalina at CBS	Bearsville	Kelly O. Isley	Soul & Style
	Chipping Norton	United Artists London	—
	Quadrail Studios, CBS	Leber-Krebs	DMA

ALBUM ACTION 1979

Album Artist (Label)	Producer	Engineer
Monolith Kansas (Kirshner)	Kansas	Davy Moire, Brad Aaron
Straight to the Point Atlantic Starr (A&M)	Bobby Eli	Carl Paruolo, Jim Gallagher, Dirk Devlin, Kenny Present
Dionne Dionne Warwick (Arista)	Barry Manilow	Michael Delugg
Classics Kenny Rogers and Dottie West (UA)	Larry Butler	Billy Sherrill
Belle Du Jour St. Tropez (Butterfly)	William Michael Lewis, Laurin Rinder	Galen Senogles

JULY

Album Artist (Label)	Producer	Engineer
Black Rose Thin Lizzy (Warner Bros.)	Tony Visconti, Thin Lizzy	Kit Woolven
Jean-Luc Ponty Live Jean-Luc Ponty (Atlantic)	Jean-Luc Ponty	Ed E. Thacher
Wave Patti Smith Group (Arista)	Todd Rundgren	Todd Rundgren, George Carnell, Tom Edwards
Bombs Away Dream Babies John Stewart (RSO)	John Stewart	David Gertz, Wayne Neuendorf, Karla Frederick, Barbara Isaac, Lenise Bent, Jim Hilton, Don Gooch
McFadden & Whitehead McFadden & Whitehead (Phila. Intl.)	Gene McFadden, John Whitehead, Jerry Cohen	Dirk Devlin
Candy Con Funk Shun (Mercury)	Skip Scarborough, Con Funk Shun	Don Cody, Leslie Ann Jones
Warmer Randy Vanwarmer (Bearsville)	John Holbrook, Dell Newman	Brent Maher, Richard Dodd, John Holbrook, George Carnell, Scott Litt, Jess Hendrikson
Back to the Egg Wings (Columbia)	Paul McCartney, Chris Thomas	Phil McDonald

Mixing/Mastering	Studio	Personal Manager or Contact	Booking Agent
Capricorn	Axis, Apogee	Budd Carr	ICM
/Bernie Grundman at A&M	Sigma Sound	Earl Cole	Regency
	United Western	Paul Cantor	—
/Bob Sowell at Master Control	Jack Clement	Krogan & Co.	ICM
/A&M	Trident, Sound City, Producer's Workshop	Butterfly Records	Norby Walters

Mixing/Mastering	Studio	Personal Manager or Contact	Booking Agent
	Pathe Marconi, EMI, Good Earth	Chris Morrison	Howard Rose
Chateau/Stan Ricker at JKVC Cutting Center	recorded live	Michael Davenport	Magna
	Bearsville	Ina Meibach	Premier Talent
Jim Hilton, Eddie Ashworth at Larrabee Sound/ Kendun	Filmways/Heider, Village Recorders, Larrabee Sound	Management III	Regency
/Frankford Wayne	Sigma Sound	Phila. Intl. Records	—
Fred Catero, Don Cody/ Kendun	Automatt, Pre Production, Melody Sound	Don Dortch Int.	—
/Bob Ludwig at Masterdisk	Creative Sound Workshop, Scorpio, Bearsville, Power Station	Ian Kimmet	—
/Stan Kalina at CBS	Spirit of Ranchan, Lympne Castle, Replica, EMI	MPL Communications	—

ALBUM ACTION 1979

Album Artist (Label)	Producer	Engineer
Candy-O Cars (Elektra)	Roy Thomas Baker	Geoff Workman
Voulez-Vous ABBA (Atlantic)	Benny Andersson, Bjorn Ulvaeus	Michael B. Tretow
An Evening of Magic Chuck Mangione (A&M)	Chuck Mangione	Michael Guzauski, Larry Swist
Under Dog Atlanta Rhythm Section (Polydor)	Buddy Buie	Rodney Mills
Mirrors Blue Oyster Cult (Columbia)	Tom Werman	Gary Ladinsky
Communique Dire Straits (Warner Bros.)	Barry Beckett, Jerry Wexler	Jack Nuber
Duty Now for the Future Devo (Warner Bros.)	Ken Scott	Ken Scott
The Roches Roches (Warner Bros.)	Robert Fripp	Ed Sprigg
The Kids Are Alright The Who (MCA)	The Who, John Entwistle	Cy Langston
Teddy Teddy Pendergrass (Phila. Intl.)	Sherman Marshall, Kenneth Gamble, Leon Huff, Thom Bell, Gene McFadden, John Whitehead	Joe Tarsia, Dirk Devlin, Jeffrey Stewart, Jim Gallagher
Street Life Crusaders (MCA)	Wilton Felder, Stiv Hooper, Joe Sample	Rik Pekkonen
Dynasty Kiss (Casablanca)	Vini Poncia	Jon Mathias, Jim Galante

AUGUST

Live Killers Queen (Elektra)	Queen	John Estchelle
Devotion L.T.D. (A&M)	Bobby Martin	Bob Hughes

ALBUM ACTION 1979 401

Mixing/Mastering	Studio	Personal Manager or Contact	Booking Agent
George Marino at Sterling Sound	Cherokee	Fred Lewis	Monterey Peninsula Artists
Polar	Polar	Stig Anderson	ICM
/Chris Bellman at Allen Zentz	Filmways/Heider	Tom Iannaccone	Magna
/Bob Ludwig, Rodney Mills	Studio One	Buie-Geller Mgt.	Paragon
Gary Ladinsky at Record Plant	Kendun, CBS, Record Plant	Sandy Pearlman	ATI
Muscle Shoals/Warner Bros.	Compass Point	Ed Bicknell	ATI
/Bernie Grundman at A&M	Chateau	Lookout Mgt.	William Morris
	Hit Factory	Michael Tannen	Athena
/Mastering Lab	Rampart	Trinifold	Premier Talent
/Frankford Wayne	Sigma Sound	Alive Ent.	William Morris
A&M	Hollywood Sound	Grief-Garris	Monterey Peninsula Artists
/George Marino at Sterling Sound	Electric Lady, Record Plant	Aucoin Mgt.	ATI
Mountain/George Marino at Sterling Sound	recorded live	John Reid	Howard Rose
Total Experience/Bernie Grundman at A&M	Hollywood Sound	Tentmakers	Regency

Album Artist (Label)	Producer	Engineer
Spy Carly Simon (Elektra)	Arif Mardin	Lew Hahn
Where There's Smoke Smokey Robinson (Tamla)	Smokey Robinson	Michael Lizzio, Cal Harris, Roger Dollarhide
Mingus Joni Mitchell (Asylum)	Henry Lewy	Henry Lewy, Steve Katz, Jerry Soloman
Nils Nils Lofgren (A&M)	Bob Ezrin	Brian Christian, Ringo Hyrcyna, David Gertz, Jim Frank, Geoff Hendrikson, Damien Korner
Another Taste Taste of Honey (Capitol)	Larry Mizell, Fonce Mizell	Serge Reyes, Butch Lynch
Do It All Michael Henderson (Buddah)	Michael Henderson	Jim Gallagher, Jim Vitti, Mike Iacopella, Pete Bishop
Destination Sun Sun (Capitol)	Beau Ray Fleming, Byron Byrd	Phil Mehaffey, Charles Farris, Byron M. Byrd
Go for What You Know Pat Travers Band (Polydor)	Pat Travers, Tom Allom	Tom Allom
The Thom Bell Sessions Elton John (MCA)	Thom Bell	Don Murray
Images Ronnie Milsap (RCA)	Ronnie Milsap, Tom Collins	Ben Harris, Travis Turk
Get the Knack Knack (Capitol)	Mike Chapman	
Strange Man, Changed Man Bram Tchaikovsky (Radar)	Peter Ker, Nick Garvey, Bram Tchaikovsky	
Secrets Robert Palmer (Island)	Robert Palmer	Karl Pitterson

SEPTEMBER

When Love Comes Calling Deniece Williams (ARC)	J. P. Williams	Humberto Gatica, Ron Malo

ALBUM ACTION 1979   403

Mixing/Mastering	Studio	Personal Manager or Contact	Booking Agent
Atlantic/George Piros at Atlantic	Atlantic	Arlyne Rothberg	William Morris
Michael Lizzio, Smokey Robinson	Motown	Multi-Media Mgt.	William Morris
/Bernie Grundman at A&M	A&M, Electric Lady	Lookout Mgt.	ATI
/Bob Ludwig at Masterdisk	Power Station, Sound Stage, Filmways/ Heider, Utopia	Art Linson	—
/Mike Reese at Mastering Lab	Sound Factory, Golden Sound	B.N.B. Assoc.	William Morris
	Sigma Sound, United Sound	Media Consulting	—
	Cyberteknics	Beau Ray Fleming	Starloft
Bayshore	recorded live	New Age Mgt.	ATI
/Ian Cooper at Utophia	Kay Smith, Sigma Sound	John Reid	Howard Rose
/Masterfonics	Ground Star	Don Reeves	William Morris
	Whitney	Scott Anderson	William Morris
	Pebble Beach, Basing Street	Ozone Mgt.	ATI
/Greg Calbi at Sterling Sound	Compass Point	David Harper	Premier Talent
—	Sunset Sounds, Kendun Recorders, Devonshire Sound	Cavallo-Ruffalo	Brighton Agency

Album Artist (Label)	Producer	Engineer
Fickle Heart Sniff 'N The Tears (Atlantic)	Luigi Salvoni	—

OCTOBER

Album Artist (Label)	Producer	Engineer
Reality . . . What a Concept Robin Williams (Casablanca)	Brooks Arthur, Neil Bogart	Deni King, Bob Merritt
Invitation Norman Connors (Arista)	Norman Connors	Richard Hennan, Jackson Schwartz
Euphoria Gato Barbieri (A&M)	Jay Chattaway	Bob Clearmountain, Neil Dorfsman, Doug Epstein
Kid Blue Louise Goffin (A&M)	Danny Kortchmar	Dennis Kirk
Stay Free Ashford & Simpson (Warner Bros.)	Nick Ashford, Valerie Simpson	Mike Hutchinson, Jim Dougherty
Fear of Music Talking Heads (Sire)	Talking Heads, Brian Eno	Rod O'Brien, Joe Barbaria, Neil Teeman
Feel It Noel Pointer (UA)	Larry Rosen	Barney Perkins, Bruce Harves, Lionel Job, James Nichols
Highway To Hell AC/DC (Atlantic)	Robert John Lange	Mark Dearney, Tony Platt
"13" Chicago (Columbia)	Phil Ramone, Chicago	Jim Boyer
Born Again Randy Newman (Warner Bros)	Russ Titleman, Lenny Waronker	Tom Knox
Off The Wall Michael Jackson (Epic)	Quincy Jones	Bruce Swedien
Future Now Pleasure (Fantasy)	Pleasure, Marlon McClain, Phil Kaffel	Phil Kaffel, Wally Buck

ALBUM ACTION 1979 405

Mixing/Mastering	Studio	Personal Manager or Contact	Booking Agent
Steve Lipson	Regents Park Recorders	Robert Raymond	Monterey Peninsula Artists
Bob Merritt, Brooks Arthur	recorded live	Rollins & Joffe	ICM
/John Golden, Kendun Recorders	Kendun Recorders	Bill Krasilovsky	
Power Station/ Vladimir Meller, CBS	Power Station Media Sound	Herb Alpert	APA
—	Sound Factory	Lewis Kaplan	Howard Rose
/Steward Romain, Columbia	Sigma Sound	George Schiffen	William Morris
Sterling Sound/ Sterling Sound	Record Plant Remote, Hit Factory, Atlantic Studios, RPM Sound Studios	Gary Kurfirst	Talking Heads Tours
/Dominick Romeo, Frankford/Wayne	Electric Lady, Sound Ideas, Westlake, CBS, Soundmixers	Fred Kewley	Magna Artists
Basing Street Studio	Roundhouse Studios	Leber-Krebs	ATI
Ted Jensen, A&R	Le Studio, A&M	Jeff Wald Assoc.	William Morris
Lee Herschberg/ Lee Herschberg	Warner Bros.	Renaissance Mgt.	Athena
/Bernie Grundman at A&M	Allen Zentz Studio, Westlake Audio, Cherokee Studios	Weisner-Demann/ Joe Jackson	Regency
/Joe Gastwirt, David Turner at Kendun Recorders	Fantasy Studios	Double T. Promotions	William Morris

Album Artist (Label)	Producer	Engineer
Down To Earth Rainbow (Polydor)	Roger Glover	Gary Edwards
Fight Dirty Charlie (Arista)	Terry Thomas, Julian Colbeck	Stephen Short, John Branc, Colin Greer, Steven Taylor
Back On The Streets Tower of Power (Columbia)	Tower of Power, McKinley Jackson, Emilio Castillo, Rich Evans	Alan Chinowsky, Jim Gaines, Paul Serrano, Michael Stone
Joe's Garage, Act I Frank Zappa (Phonogram)	Frank Zappa	Joe Chicarelli, Claus Wiedmann, David Gray
Flirtin' With Disaster Molly Hatchett (Epic)	Tom Werman	Gary Ladinsky
Priority Pointer Sisters (Planet)	Richard Perry	Dennis Kirk
Unleashed In The East (Live In Japan) Judas Priest (Columbia)	Tom Allom, Judas Priest	Yoshihiro Suzuki, Neil Kernon
Volcano Jimmy Buffet (MCA)	Norbet Putnam	Gene Eichelberger, Geoffrey Emerick
Head Games Foreigner (Atlantic)	Roy Thomas Baker, Mick Jones, Ian McDonald	Geoff Workman
Kenny Kenny Rogers (United Artists)	Larry Butler	Billy Sherrill, Harold Lee

NOVEMBER

Brenda Russell Brenda Russell (Horizon)	Andre Fischer	John Rhys
Satisfied Rita Coolidge (A&M)	D. Anderle B. T. Jones	Ron Hitchcock, Peggy McCreary, David Andrele

Mixing/Mastering	Studio	Personal Manager or Contact	Booking Agent
Greg Colby	Chateau Pelle de Cornfeld	Thomas Talent	ATI
	Trident Studios	Dave Thomas	Monterey Peninsula Artists
	Record Plant, P.S. Studio, Universal, United Western	Tower Mgmt.	William Morris
Mick Glossop, Steve Nye/Stan Ricker at JVC Cutting Center	Village Recorders, Kendun Recorders	Glotzer Mgmt.	
/George Marino at Sterling Sound	Record Plant, Bee Jay Studios	Pat Armstrong	ATI
Bill Schnee at Studio 55/Mike Reese & Doug Sax at Mastering Lab	Studio 55	Management III	Monterey Peninsula Artists
Sterling Studio	recorded Live	Arnakata Mgmt.	ATI
/Glenn Meadows at Masterphonics	Air Studios, Quadrafonic Studios Sunset Sound	Front Line Mgmt.	Howard Rose
/George Marino at Sterling Sound	Atlantic Studios, Cherokee Studios	E.S.P.	Monterey Peninsula Artists
Larry Butler/ Glen Meadows, Masterfonics	Jack Clement Studios, American Studios	Kragen & Co.	ICM
Al Schmitt Capitol Studios/Mike Reese at Mastering Lab	Kendun Recorders, Conway Studios	Brenda Dash	
/Mike Reese at Mastering Lab	Sunset Sound	Bert Block	Magna Artists

ALBUM ACTION 1979

Album Artist (Label)	Producer	Engineer
Miss The Mississippi Crystal Gayle (Columbia)	Allen Reynolds	Garth Fundis
Sound Track of Quadrophenia The Who (Polydor)	John Entwistle	Cy Langston
Comedy Is Not Pretty Steve Martin (Warner Bros.)	Willam McEuen	
Dream Police Cheap Trick (Epic)	Tom Werman	Gary Ladinsky
8:30 Weather Report (Arc)	Joe Zawinul, J. Pastorius	Kim King, Warren Dewey, John Haeny
Don't Let Go Isaac Hayes (Polydor)	Isaac Hayes	Mark Harman, Joe Neil
Cornerstone Styx (A&M)	Styx	Gary Loizzo, Rob Kingsland
Victim of Love Elton John (MCA)	Pete Bellotte	Peter Luedman, Roman Olearczrek
Uncle Jam Wants You Funkadelic (Warner Bros.)	George Clinton (Dr. Funkenstein)	Jim Vitti Steve Bishop
Boogie Motel Foghat (Bearsville)	Foghat, Tony Outeda	Don Berman
One Voice Barry Manilow (Arista)	Barry Manilow, Ron Dante	Michael DeLugg
X-Static Daryl Hall & John Oates (RCA)	David Foster	Ed Sprigg
I Have A Right Gloria Gaynor (Polydor)	Dave Kershenbaum	Lewis Peters
Oasis Jimmy Messina (Columbia)	Jimmy Messina	Don Murray
The Long Run Eagles (Asylum)	Bill Szymczyk	Bill Szymczyk, Ed "Radar" Marshal
Live And Sleazy Village People (Casablanca)	Jacques Morali	Michael Hutchinson, Steve Mitchell, Joe Barbaria

ALBUM ACTION 1979   409

Mixing/Mastering	Studio	Personal Manager or Contact	Booking Agent
/Masterfonics	Jack's Tracks	Bill Gatzimos	William Morris
CTS Wembley, Ramport Studios	Ramport Studios	Trinifold	Premier
/Geoff Sykes at Kendun Recorders	The Boarding House	William W. McEuen	APA
Record Plant/ George Marino at Sterling Sound	Record Plant	Ken Adanany	ATI
Devonshire Sound	recorded Live	Cavallo-Ruffalo	Brighton Agency
/Masterfonics Glen Meadows	North Star Studio, Master Sound	Thalen Hurewitz	APA
	Pumpkin Studios	Derek Sutton	ICM
/Brian Gardner at Allen Zentz	Musicland, Rusk Sound	John Reid	Howard Rose
/Brian Gardner at Allen Zentz	United Studio	Leber-Krebs	David Libert Agcy.
/Bob Ludwig, Masterdisk	Boggie Motel	Tony Outeda	ATI
	United Western, Allan Zentz	Miles Lourie	William Morris
Humberto Gatica, Sunset Sound	Hit Factory	Champion Ent.	ATI
Mom & Pops Co. Store/ Brian Gardner, Allen Zentz	Mom & Pops Co. Store	Basement Music (Albion Mgt.)	William Morris
/Chris Belman at Allen Zentz	Santa Barbara Sound	Fitzgerald-Hartley	ICM
Bill Szymczyk, Bayshore/ Ted Jensen, Sterling Sound	Bayshore	Front Line Mgmt.	Howard Rose
Michael Hutchinson, Sigma Sound/Bruce Fergesen, Hit Factory	Sigma Sound, A&M, Hit Factory	Can't Stop Prod.	ATI

Album Artist (Label)	Producer	Engineer
Rise Herb Alpert (A&M)	Herb Alpert, Randy Badazz	Don Hahn, Mark Smith
Stormwatch Jethro Tull (Chrysalis)	Ian Anderson, Robin Black	Robin Black
Marathon Santana (Columbia)	Keith Olsen, David DeVore, Santana	Keith Olsen, David DeVore
Restless Nights Karla Bonoff (Columbia)	Kenny Edwards	Greg Ladanyi, Jim Nipar
Keep The Fire Kenny Loggins (Columbia)	Tom Dowd	Steve Gersky
Night In The Ruts Aerosmith (Columbia)	Gary Lyons, Aerosmith	Gary Lyons
Freedom At Point Zero Jefferson Starship (Grunt)		
Tusk Fleetwood Mac (Warner Brothers)	Fleetwood Mac, Richard Dashut, Ken Caillat	Richard Dashut, Ken Caillat, Herman Rojas

DECEMBER

Joe's Garage—Act I Frank Zappa (Mercury)	Frank Zappa	Joe Chicarelli
Journey through the Secret Life of Plants Stevie Wonder (Motown)	Stevie Wonder	Gary Olazabal, John Fishback, Jay Mark
Hydra Toto (Columbia)	Toto, Tom Knox	Tom Knox, Dana Latham
Survival Bob Marley & the Wailers (Island)	Bob Marley, Alex Sadkin	Alex Sadkin
Melissa Manchester Melissa Manchester (Arista)	Steve Buckingham	Ed Seay

Mixing/Mastering	Studio	Personal Manager or Contact	Booking Agent
/Bernie Grundman, A&M	A&M	A&M Records	
	Maison Rouge	Friday Mgmt.	Premier
Sound City/Joe Gaswirt, Artisan Sound	Automatt	Bill Graham	Premier
Bernie Grundman, A&M	Sound Factory	Norm Epstein Mgmt.	William Morris
	Filmways/Heider, Santa Barbara Sound	Larry Larson Assoc.	ICM
Mediasound/ George Marino, Sterling Sound	Mediasound, Record Plant	Leber-Krebs	ICM
Record Plant/ Mike Reese, The Mastering Lab	Record Plant	Bill Thompson	—
Rich Feldman, Soundstream/	Village Recorders	Seedy Mgmt.	ICM

Mixing/Mastering	Studio	Personal Manager or Contact	Booking Agent
Mick Glossop, Steve Nye /JVC Cutting Center, Star Ricker, Jack Hunt	Village, Kendun	Glotzer Mgt.	—
/Stan Ricker, JVC Cutting Center	I.A.M., Crystal, Lyon, Motown, Sigma Sound, Studio in the Country	Black Bull	—
—	Sunset Sound	Fitzgerald-Hartley	Monterey Peninsula
/Sterling Sound	Tuff Gong	Don Taylor	ABC
/Glen Meadows, Masterfonics	Web IV	Michael Lippman	ICM

ALBUM ACTION 1979

Album Artist (Label)	Producer	Engineer
Freedom at Point Zero Jefferson Starship (Grunt)	Ron Nevison	Ron Nevison, Michael Clink
On the Radio—Greatest Hits, Vols. I & II Donna Summer (Casablanca)	Giorgio Moroder, Pete Bellotte	Giorgio Moroder, Harold Faltermeyer
Willie Nelson Sings Kristofferson Willie Nelson (Columbia)	Willie Nelson	Bradley Hartman, Harold Lee
Twice the Fire Peaches & Herb (Polydor)	Freddie Perren	Rick Clifford Steve Bouliot
Are You Ready Atlanta Rhythm Section (Polydor)	Buddy Buie	Rodney Mills
Damn the Torpedos Tom Petty & the Heartbreakers (Backstreet-MCA)	Tom Petty, Jimmy Iovine	Shelly Yakus
One on One Bob James & Earl Klugh (Tappan Zee)	Bob James	Joe Jorgensen
Harder . . . Faster April Wine (Capitol)	Myles Godwin, Nick Blagona	Nick Blagona
Wet Barbra Streisand (Columbia)	Gary Klein	John Arrias, Juergen Roppers
Fire It Up Rick James (Motown)	Rick James	Tom Flye
Reggatta de Blanc Police (A&M)	Nigel Gray, Police	Nigel Gray, Angela Bofill, Larry Rosen
Classic Crystal Crystal Gayle (UA)	Allen Reynolds	Garth Fundis
Night in the Ruts Aerosmith (Columbia)	Gary Lyons, Aerosmith	Gary Lyons

Mixing/Mastering	Studio	Personal Manager or Contact	Booking Agent
/Mike Reese, Mastering Lab	Record Plant	Bill Thompson	ICM
/Brian Gardner, Allen Zentz	Westlake	Joyce Bogart, Susan Munao	William Morris
Bradley Hartman, Enactron	Shangri La, Jack Clement	—	Mark Rothbaum
/Jeff Sanders, Kendun	Mom & Pops Co. Store	Prime Time Prod.	Norby Walters
/Rodney Mills, Bob Ludwig	recorded live	Buie-Geller Mgt.	Empire Talent
Cherokee, Record Plant /Sterling Sound	Sound City, Cherokee	Tony Dimitriades	Premier Talent
Joe Jorgensen /Stan Kalina, CBS	Media Sound, Sound Palace, Sound Mixers	James-Tappan Zee Records; Klugh-Bert Block	Klugh-Magna
/George Marino, Sterling Sound	Le Studio	Terry Flood	ICM
/Mike Reese, Mastering Lab	Sound Labs, Capitol, Crimson, Village, Rusk Sound	Jon Peters	ICM
/Jim Sintetos, Kendun	Record Plant	Strout & Whitehouse	Mecca
/Ted Jensen, Sterling Sound	Surrey Sound, A&R, Electric Lady	Miles Copeland	F.B.I.
/Masterfonics	Jack Clement	Bill Gatzimos	William Morris
Media Sound/George Marino, Sterling Sound	Media Sound, Record Plant	Leber-Krebs	ICM

DIRECTORY OF RECORD COMPANIES*

A&M Records, 1416 North LaBrea, Los Angeles, CA 90028. 213-469-3411. **New York office:** 595 Madison Avenue, New York, NY 10022. 212-826-0477.
ABC Records—see MCA Records listing.
American Record Co. (ARC), 9885 Charleville Boulevard, Beverly Hills, CA 90212. 213-277-8137.
Ariola Records, 8671 Wilshire Boulevard, Los Angeles, CA 90211. 213-659-6530.
Arista Records, 6 West 57 Street, New York, NY 10019. 212-489-7400. **Los Angeles office:** 1888 Century Park East, Suite 1510, Los Angeles, CA 90067. 213-553-1777.
Asylum Records, 962 North LaCienega, Los Angeles, CA 90069. 213-655-8280. **New York office:** 665 Fifth Avenue, New York, NY 10022. 212-355-7610.
Atco Records, 75 Rockefeller Plaza, New York, NY 10019. 212-489-0955. **Los Angeles office:** 9229 Sunset Boulevard, Los Angeles, CA 90069. 213-273-3763.
Atlantic Records, 75 Rockefeller Plaza, New York, NY 10019. 212-484-6000. **Los Angeles office:** 9229 Sunset Boulevard, Los Angeles, CA 90069. 213-278-9230. **Atlanta office:** 250 Villanova Drive, Atlanta, GA 30336. 404-344-4033.
Bearsville Records, 75 East 55 Street, New York, NY 10022. 212-751-7030.
Blue Sky Records, 745 Fifth Avenue, Suite 1803, New York, NY 10022. 212-751-3400.
Buddah Records, 810 Seventh Avenue, New York, NY 10019. 212-582-6900.
Butterfly Records, 9000 Sunset Boulevard, Suite 617, Los Angeles, CA 90069. 213-273-9600.
CBS Records—see Columbia, Epic, Portrait listings.
Capitol Records, 1750 North Vine Street, Hollywood, CA 90028. 213-462-6252. **New York office:** 1370 Avenue of the Americas, New York, NY 10019. 212-757-7470. **Nashville office:** 38 Music Square East, Nashville, TN 37203. 615-244-1842.
Capricorn Records, 535 Cotton Avenue, Macon, GA 31208. 912-745-8511. **Los Angeles office:** 4405 Riverside Drive, Burbank, CA 91505. 213-849-1371.
Caribou Records, Caribou Ranch, Nederland, CO 80456. 303-258-3215.
Casablanca Records, 8255 Sunset Boulevard, Los Angeles, CA 90046. 213-650-8300. **New York office:** 137 West 55 Street, New York, NY 10019. 212-397-0660.
Chrysalis Records, 9255 Sunset Boulevard, Los Angeles, CA 90069. 213-550-0171. **New York office:** 115 East 57 Street, New York, NY 10022. 212-935-8750.

*Based on **Album Action Chart 1979**

DIRECTORY OF RECORD COMPANIES

Columbia Records, 51 West 52 Street, New York, NY 10019. 212-975-4321. **Los Angeles office:** 1801 Century Park West, Los Angeles, CA 90067. 213-556-4700. **Nashville office:** 49 Music Square West, Nashville, TN 37203. 615–259–4321.

Cotillion Records, c/o Atlantic Records, 75 Rockefeller Plaza, New York, NY 10019. 212-484-6000.

Dash Records, c/o TK Records, 495 SE Tenth Court, Hialeah, FL 33010. 305-888-1685.

DJM Records, 119 West 57 Street, New York, NY 10019. 212-581-3420. **Los Angeles office:** 6255 Sunset Boulevard, Los Angeles, CA 90028. 213-466-9771.

ECM Records, 509 Madison Avenue, Suite 512, New York, NY 10022. 212-888-1122.

Elektra Records, 962 North LaCienega, Los Angeles, CA 90069. 213-655-8280. **New York office:** 665 Fifth Avenue, New York, NY 10022. 212-355-7610. **Nashville office:** 1201 16 Avenue South, Nashville, TN 27203. 615-320-7525.

EMI-America Records, 6464 Sunset Boulevard, Penthouse Suite, Los Angeles, CA 90028. 213-464-2488. **New York office:** 1370 Avenue of the Americas, New York, NY 10019. 212-757-7470.

Epic Records, 51 West 52 Street, New York, NY 10019. 212-975-4321. **Los Angeles office:** 1801 Century Park West, Los Angeles, CA 90067. 213-556-4700. **Nashville office:** 49 Music Square West, Nashville, TN 37203. 615-329-4321.

Fantasy Records, 10th & Parker St., Berkeley, CA 94710. 415-549-2500. **New York office:** 1775 Broadway, Suite 617, New York, NY 10019. 212-757-2134.

Horizon Records, 1416 North LaBrea, Los Angeles, CA 90028. 213-469-2411. **New York office:** 595 Madison Avenue, New York, NY 10022. 212-826-0477.

Infinity Records, 10 East 53 Street, New York, NY 10022. 212-888-9700.

Island Records, 444 Madison Avenue, New York, NY 10022. 212-355-6500.

Kirshner Records, 1370 Avenue of the Americas, New York, NY 10019. 212-489-0440.

Marlin Records, c/o TK Productions, 495 SE 10 Court, Hialeah, FL 33010. 305-888-1685.

MCA Records, 100 Universal City Plaza, Universal City, CA 91608. 213-985-4321. **New York office:** 445 Park Avenue, New York, NY 10022. 212-759-7500. **Nashville office:** 27 Music Square East, Nashville, TN 37203. 615-244-8944.

Mercury-Phonogram Records, One IBM Plaza, Chicago, IL 60611. 312-645-6300. **New York office:** 810 Seventh Avenue, New York, NY 10019. 212-399-7485. **Los Angeles office:** 6255 Sunset Boulevard, Los Angeles, CA 90028. 213-466-9771. **Nashville office:** 10 Music Circle South, Nashville, TN 37203. 615-244-3776. **Memphis office:** 2000 Madison Avenue, Memphis, TN 38104. 901-726-6000.

Motown Records, 6255 Sunset Boulevard, Los Angeles, CA 90028. 213-468-3500.

Nemperor Records, 888 Seventh Avenue, New York, NY 10019. 212-541-6210.

Philadelphia International Records, 309 South Broad Street, Philadelphia, PA 19107. 215-985-0900.

Planet Records, 9120 Sunset Boulevard, Los Angeles, CA 90069. 213-275-4710.

Polydor Records, 810 Seventh Avenue, New York, NY 10019. 212-399-7100. **Los Angeles office:** 6255 Sunset Boulevard, Los Angeles, CA 90028. 213-466-9574.

RCA Records, 1133 Avenue of the Americas, New York, NY 10036. 212–598–5900. **Los Angeles office:** 6363 Sunset Boulevard, Los Angeles, CA 90028. 213-468-4000. **Nashville office:** 30 Music Square West,

DIRECTORY OF RECORD COMPANIES 417

Nashville, TN 37203. 615-244-9880.
RSO Records, 8335 Sunset Boulevard, Los Angeles, CA 90069. 213-650-1234. **New York office:** 1775 Broadway, New York, NY 10019. 212-975-0700.
Rolling Stones Records, c/o Atlantic Records, 75 Rockefeller Plaza, New York, NY 10019. 212-484-6000.
Rounder Records, 186 Willow Avenue, Somerville, MA 02144. 617-354-0700.
Salsoul Records, 240 Madison Avenue, New York, NY 10016. 212-889-7340.
Scotti Bros. Records, 9229 Sunset Boulevard, Suite 901, Los Angeles, CA 90069. 213-550-6262.
Shadybrook Records, 8913 Sunset Boulevard, Los Angeles, CA 90069. 213-652-4782.
Sire Records, 165 West 74 Street, New York, NY 10023. 212-595-5000.
Solar Records, 6255 Sunset Boulevard, Suite 923, Hollywood, CA 90028. 213-467-6527.
Source Records, 1902 Fifth Avenue, Second Floor, Los Angeles, CA 90018. 213-731-0693.
Stax/Fantasy Records, Tenth and Parker, Berkeley, CA 94710. 415-549-2500.
Memphis office: Mid Memphis Tower, 1407 Union, Suite 600, Memphis, TN 38104. 901-726-6360.

Swan Song Records, c/o Atlantic Records, 75 Rockefeller Plaza, New York, NY 10019. 212-484-6000.
Tamla Records, 6255 Sunset Boulevard, Los Angeles, CA 90028. 213-468-3500.
T-Neck Records, 1650 Broadway, New York, NY 10019. 212-582-5430.
TK Records, 495 SE Tenth Court, Hialeah, FL 33010. 305-888-1685. **New York office:** 65 East 55 Street, New York, NY 10022. 212-752-0160.
20th Century Fox Records, 8544 Sunset Boulevard, Los Angeles, CA 90069. 213-657-8310.
United Artists Records, 6920 Sunset Boulevard, Los Angeles, CA 90028. 213-461-9141. **New York office:** 1370 Avenue of the Americas, New York, NY 10019. 212-757-7470. **Nashville office:** 50 Music Square West, Nashville, TN 37203. 615-329-9356.
Unlimited Gold Records, 12403 Ventura Court, Studio City, CA 91604. 213-877-0535.
Warner Bros. Records, 3300 Warner Boulevard, Burbank, CA 91505. 213-846-9090. **New York office:** 3 East 54 Street, New York, NY 10022. 212-832-0600.
Nashville office: 1706 Grand Avenue, Nashville, TN 37212. 615-256-4282.

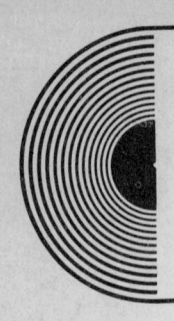

DIRECTORY OF PRODUCERS*

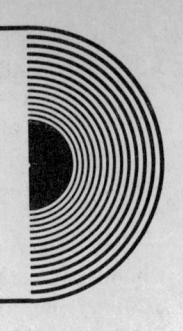

Aerosmith, c/o Contemporary Communications Corp., 65 West 55 Street, New York, NY 10019. 212-765-2600.

Herb Alpert, c/o A&M Records, 1416 N. LaBrea Ave., Los Angeles, CA 90028. 213-469-2411.

Ron and Howard Albert, c/o Fat Albert Productions, 1755 NE 149 Street, Miami, FL 33161. 305-947-5611; 305-893-7183.

Larry Alexander, c/o Command Performance Inc., 850 Seventh Avenue, New York, NY 10019. 212-586-1100.

Tom Allom, c/o David Hemmings, New Age Management, 712 Fifth Avenue, New York, NY 10022. 212-765-3850.

D. Anderle, c/o A & M Records, 1416 N. LaBrea, Los Angeles, CA 90028. 213-469-2411.

Ian Anderson, c/o Terry Ellis, Chrysalis Records, 9255 Sunset Blvd., Los Angeles, CA 90069. 213-550-0171.

Reggie Andrews, c/o Tentmakers, 6367 West Sixth Street, Los Angeles, CA 90048. 213-937-6650.

Brooks Arthur, c/o Palm Tree Productions, 8544 Sunset Boulevard, Los Angeles, CA 90069. 213-657-8210.

Nick Ashford, c/o George Schaffer, 1155 North LaCienega, Suite 6, Los Angeles, CA 90069. 213-659-5705.

Gil Askey, c/o Curtom Records, 5915 North Lincoln, Chicago, IL 60659. 312-769-4676.

Average White Band, c/o David Mintz, 123 East 54 Street, New York, NY 10022. 212-752-3080.

Bad Company, c/o Swan Song Management, 444 Madison Avenue, New York, NY 10022. 212-752-1330. 212-838-3320.

Randy Badazz, c/o Cooper Epstein & Hurewitz, 9465 Wilshire Blvd., Suite 800, Beverly Hills, CA 90212. 213-278-1111.

Roy Thomas Baker, c/o Rocket Records, 211 South Beverly Drive, Suite 205, Beverly Hills, CA 90212. 213-550-0144.

Barry Beckett, 1000 Alabama Avenue, Sheffield, AL 35660. 205-381-2060.

Bee Gees, c/o RSO Records, 8335 Sunset Boulevard, Los Angeles, CA 90069. 213-278-1680.

Curt Beecher, c/o Brothers Records, 10880 Wilshire Boulevard, Suite 306, Los Angeles, CA 90024. 213-475-0361.

Pete Bellotte, Revelation Music, 8 Munchen 81, Arabellahaus 5/139, Germany. 9232-3000.

Frankie Beverly, c/o Leon Fisher, 1764 Sycamore, Los Angeles, CA 213-851-2589.

Nick Blagona, c/o Le Studio, Morin Heights, PR 1, Quebec JOR 1H0 Canada. 514-226-2419.

Neil Bogart, Casablanca Records, 8255

*Based on **Album Action Chart 1979**

DIRECTORY OF PRODUCERS

Sunset Boulevard, Los Angeles, CA 90048. 213-650-8300.
Robin Black, c/o Chrysalis Records, 12 Statford Pl., London N1, AF, England. 01-408-2355.
Hamilton Bohannon, c/o Levi Bohannon, 289 North Oraton Parkway, East Orange, NJ. 201-643-6981; 201-672-2787.
Bruce Botnick, c/o Columbia Records, 1801 Century Park West, Los Angeles, CA 90067. 213-556-4722.
Jeffrey Bowen, c/o Motown Records, 6255 Sunset Boulevard, Los Angeles, CA 90028. 213-468-3500.
Buddy Buie Productions, 3297 Northcrest Road, Suite 203, Doraville, GA 30340. 404-491-0950.
David Bowie, c/o Pat Gibbons-Stan Diamond, 10850 Wilshire Boulevard, Los Angeles, CA 90024. 213-449-5142.
Steve Buckingham, Studio One Complex, 3864 Oakliff Industrial Court, Doraville, GA 30340. 404-449-5147.
Charles Callelo, P. O. Box 467, Kearny, NJ 07032. 201-997-4450.
Emilio Castillo, c/o Tower Mgmt., 606 Wilshire Blvd., Santa Monica, CA 90401. 213-451-8458.
Richard Carpenter, c/o Management III, 9744 Wilshire Boulevard, Beverly Hills, CA. 213-550-7100.
Mike Chapman, c/o Chinnichap Inc., 8919 Sunset Boulevard, Los Angeles, CA 90069. 213-657-8585.
George Clinton, c/o Leber-Krebs, 65 W. 55 Street, New York, NY 10019. 212-765-2600.
Jay Chattaway, c/o Tappan Zee Rec's., 888 Seventh Avenue, New York, NY 10019. 212-765-0580.
Julian Colbeck, c/o Dave Thomas, Trident Studios, 17 St. Ann's Court, London W1 England. 01-734-9901.
Chicago, c/o Jeff Wald Assocs., 9356 Santa Monica Blvd., Beverly Hills, CA 90210. 213-273-2192.
Mike Curb, c/o Warner-Curb Records, 3300 Warner Boulevard, Burbank, CA 91505. 213-846-9090.

Ron Dante, 311 Productions, 311 W. 57 Street, NY, NY 10019. 212-765-8200.
Carl Davis, 20 East Huron Street, Chicago, IL 60611. 312-943-0305.
Bert DeCoteaux, c/o CBS Records, 51 West 52 Street, New York, NY 10019. 212-975-4321.
David DeVore, c/o Cohen & Steinhart, 6430 Sunset Blvd., Suite 1500, Los Angeles, CA 90028. 213-463-1151.
Doors, c/o Tom Dowd, Atlantic Studios, 1841 Broadway, New York, NY 10023. 212-484-8490.
Jack Douglas, c/o Waterfront Productions, 314 East 69 Street, New York, NY 10022. 212-861-5638.
Tom Dowd, c/o Atlantic Studios, 1841 Broadway, New York, NY 10023. 212-484-8490.
Kenny Edwards, c/o Norm Epstein Mgmt., 644 N. Doheny Dr., Los Angeles, CA 90069. 213-271-5181.
Bernard Edwards, c/o Martin Itzler, Esq., 110 East 59 Street, 37th Floor, New York, NY 10022. 212-752-8855.
Keith Emerson, c/o Manticore Management, 170 East 61 Street, New York, NY 10021. 212-421-3470.
Brian Eno, c/o E. G. Records, 246 East 62 Street, New York, NY 10021. 212-355-5200.
John Entwhistle, c/o Trinifold, 112 Wardour St., London W1V 3LD, England. 01-439-8411.
Bob Erzin, c/o My Own Productions Co. Ltd., 125 Dupont Street, Toronto, Ontario, Canada. 416-961-0164.
Bob Esty, c/o Casablanca Records, 8255 Sunset Boulevard, Los Angeles, CA 90046. 213-650-8300.
Richard Evans, c/o David Franklin, Omni Int'l., Suite 1290, So. Atlanta, GA 30303. 404-688-2233.
John Farrar, c/o Dan Cleary, BNB Management, 9454 Wilshire Boulevard, Los Angeles, CA 90212. 213-273-7020.
Wilton Felder, c/o Grief-Garris Management, 8467 Beverly Boulevard, Los Angeles, CA 90048. 213-653-4780.
Andre Fischer, Sweet Street Prodn's.,

DIRECTORY OF PRODUCERS

P. O. Box 3875, Los Angeles, CA 90028. 213-980-4232.

Beau Ray Fleming, c/o Royal Gentlemen, P. O. Box 428, Mid City Station, Dayton, OH 45402. **N. Y. office:** 160 East 26 Street, Apt. 1G, New York, NY 10010. 212-889-1599.

David Foster, c/o Ned Shankman, 315 Pier Street, Santa Monica, CA 90405. 213-396-3185.

Foxy, c/o TK Records, 495 SE Tenth Court, Hialeah, FL 33010. 305-888-1685.

Robert Fripp, c/o E. G. Records, 246 East 62 Street, New York, NY 10021. 212-355-5200.

Foghat, c/o Tony Outeda, P. O. Box 398, Port Jefferson, NY 11777. 516-751-5300.

Lewis Futterman, Box 1085, Ansonia Station, New York, NY 10023. 212-873-2403.

Rory Gallagher, c/o Donald Gallagher, 45 A Finsborough Road, London SW 10, England 01-439-6325.

Albhy Galuten, c/o Criteria Recording Studios, 1755 NE 149 Street, Miami, FL 33161. 305-947-5611.

Kenneth Gamble, Gamble & Huff Productions, 309 Broad Street, Philadelphia, PA 19107. 215-985-0900.

Lowell George, c/o Cavallo-Ruffalo Management, 9885 Charleville Boulevard, Beverly Hills, CA 90212. 213-277-8137.

John Glemmer, c/o Gary Borman, 244 Ladera Drive, Beverly Hills, CA 90210. 213-275-8035.

Glimmer Twins (i.e., Mick Jagger and Keith Richard), Rolling Stone Records, 75 Rockefeller Plaza, New York, NY 10019. 212-484-6000.

Roger Glover, c/o Thames Talent, 1345 Avenue of the Americas, New York, NY 10019. 212-541-6740.

Ken Gold, c/o Screen Gems-EMI, Saint Margrets House, 19-23 Wells Street, London W1 England. 01-580-2090.

Steve Goldman, c/o Gary Borman Management, 244 LaDera Drive, Beverly Hills, CA 90210. 213-275-8035.

Jerry Goldstein, c/o Far Out Productions, 7417 Sunset Boulevard, Los Angeles, CA 90046. 213-874-1300.

Myles Goodwin, c/o Terry Flood, 354 Youville Street, Montreal, Quebec 1Z5 Canada. 514-284-1001.

Berry Gordy, c/o Motown Records, 6255 Sunset Boulevard, Los Angeles, CA 90028. 213-468-3500.

Richard Gottehrer, 44 West 77 Street, New York, NY 10024. 212-799-0228.

Nigel Gray, c/o Miles Copeland, 41 B. Blenheim Crescent, London W11 England. 01-727-0734. **N.Y. office:** 250 West 57 Street, Suite 603, New York, NY 10019. 212-245-5587.

Zane Grey, c/o Don Sorkin, 9368 Sierra Mar Drive, Los Angeles, CA 90069. 213-278-4700.

Dick Griffey, 6255 Sunset Boulevard, Suite 923, Hollywood, CA 90028. 213-467-6527.

John Haeny, c/o John Frankenheimer, Loeb & Loeb, 10100 Santa Monica Boulevard, Suite 2200, Los Angeles, CA 90067. 213-552-7783.

Ron Haffkine, P. O. Box 4115, Madison, TN 37115. 615-868-4090. **N.Y. office:** c/o Grapefruit Productions, 16 Douglass Street, Brooklyn, NY 11231. 212-834-1105.

Roy Halee, 1051 Villa View Drive, Pacific Palisades, CA 90272. 213-459-4983.

Herbie Hancock, c/o Adam's Dad Management, 827 Folsom Street, San Francisco, CA 94107. 415-777-2930.

Len Ron Hanks, c/o Don Sorkin, 9368 Sierra Mar Drive, Los Angeles, CA 90069. 213-278-4700.

Isaac Hayes, c/o Thalen Hurewitz, Cooper, Epstein & Hurewitz, 9465 Wilshire Blvd., Suite 800, Beverly Hills, CA 90212. 213-278-1111.

George Harrison, c/o Denis O'Brien-Dennis Morgan, Dark Horse Records, 3300 Warner Boulevard, Burbank, CA 91505. 213-846-9090.

Michael Henderson, c/o Media Consulting, 54 Main Street, Danbury, CT 06810. 203-792-8880.

DIRECTORY OF PRODUCERS

Peter Henderson, c/o Air Studios, 12 Stratford Place, London W1N 94F England. 01-408-2355.
Stix Hopper, c/o Grief-Garris Management, 8467 Beverly Boulevard, Los Angeles, CA 90048. 213-653-4780.
Leon Huff, c/o Gamble & Huff Productions, 309 South Broad Street, Philadelphia, PA 19107. 215-985-0900.
Ian Hunter, c/o Cleveland Entertainment Co., 538 Madison Avenue, New York, NY 10022. 212-935-8630.
Jimmy Iovine, c/o Record Plant, 321 West 44 Street, New York, NY 10036. 212–581–6505.
Charles Jackson, Jay's Entertainments, 1777 North Vine Street, Suite 303, Los Angeles, CA 90028. 213-462-1640.
Jacksons, c/o Weisner-Demann, 9200 Sunset Boulevard, Los Angeles, CA 90069. 213-550-8200.
McKinley Jackson, 606 Wilshire Blvd., Suite 412, Santa Monica, CA 90401. 213-451-8458.
Bob James, c/o Tappan Zee Records, 100 West 57 Street, New York, NY 10019. 212–765–0580.
Rick James, c/o Strout & Whitehouse, 280 South Beverly Drive, Suite 402, Beverly Hills, CA 90212. 213–858–8816.
Jean Michel Jarre, c/o Francis Dreyfus, Disques Motors, 26 Avenue Kleber, 75016 Paris, France, 723-4437.
Eddie Jobson, c/o E. G. Management Ltd., 63A Kings Road, London SW3 England. 01-730-2162.
Glyn Johns, c/o Interglobal Record Corp., 1501 Broadway, New York, NY 10036. 212-840-2200.
Bruce Johnston, c/o Brothers Records, 10880 Wilshire Boulevard, Suite 306, Los Angeles, CA 90024. 213-475-0361.
Allen Jones, c/o Don Dortch International, 3171 Director's Row, Suite 411, Memphis, TN 38131. 901-396-3780.
B. T. Jones, Media Consulting, 54 Main Street, Danbury, CT. 203-792-8880. **Los Angeles office:** 31721 Broad Beach Rd., Malibu, CA 90265. 213-457-2837.

Quincy Jones, c/o Fitzgerald-Hartley, 17175 Ventura Blvd., Encino, CA 91316. 213-995-8255.
Phil Kaffel, c/o Fantasy Records, Tenth and Parker, Berkeley, CA 94710. 415-549-2500.
Kansas, c/o Budd Carr, 9200 Sunset Boulevard, Suite 1207, Los Angeles, CA 90069. 213-858-7087.
David Kershenbaum, 1416 North LaBrea, Los Angeles, CA 90028. 213-469-2411.
Howard Kilgour, c/o CBS Records U.K., 17-19 Soho Square, London W1V 6HE England. 01-734-8181.
Gary Klein, 6430 Sunset Boulevard, Suite 803, Los Angeles, CA 90028. 213-466-6127. **New York office:** The Entertainment Company, 40 West 57 Street, New York, NY 10019. 212-586-3600.
John Klemmer, c/o Gary Borman, 244 Ladera Drive, Beverly Hills, CA 90210. 213-275-8035.
Tom Knox, c/o Fitzgerald-Hartley, 7250 Beverly Boulevard, Los Angeles, CA 90036. 213–934–8002.
Glen Kolotkin, c/o Beserkley Records, 1199 Spruce Street, Berkeley, CA 94707. 415-527-7664.
Danny Kortchmar, c/o Michael Rosenfeld, 270 North Canon Drive, Beverly Hills, CA 90210. 213-858-7788.
Greg Lake, c/o Manticore Management, 170 East 61 Street, New York, NY 10021. 212-421-4057.
Lakeside, c/o Solar Records, 6255 Sunset Boulevard, Suite 923, Los Angeles, CA 90028. 213-467-6527.
Robert John Lange, c/o Paul Schindler, 65 East 55 Street, New York, NY 10022. 212-688-6470.
Barry Leng, c/o Hansa Records, 12 Bruton Street, London W1X 7AH. England. 01-493-9766.
Kyle Lehning, 107 Crossroads Drive, Hendersonville, TN 37075. 615-824-0440. **Los Angeles office:** c/o Atco Records, 9229 Sunset Boulevard, Los Angeles, CA 90069. 213-273-3763.

DIRECTORY OF PRODUCERS

Jerry Lesser, 9617 Charleville Boulevard, Beverly Hills, CA 90212. 213-271-0887.

Henry Lewy, 6005 Paseo Canyon, Malibu, CA 90265. 213-457-2035.

T. Life, c/o Sight & Sound Management, 119 West 57 Street, New York, NY 10019. 212-541-5581.

Tommy LiPuma, c/o Horizon Records, 1416 North LaBrea, Los Angeles, CA 90069. 213-469-2411.

Michael Lloyd, c/o Warner-Curb Records, 3300 Warner Boulevard, Burbank, CA 91505. 213-846-9090.

Reggie Lucas, c/o Famous Music, One Gulf & Western Plaza, New York, NY 10023. 212-333-4131.

Gary Lyons, c/o Abe Hock, 211 West 56 Street, New York, NY 10019. 212-265-1501.

Barry Manilow, c/o Miles Lourie, 314 West 71 Street, New York, NY 10023. 212-595-4330.

Arif Mardin, c/o Atlantic Records, 75 Rockefeller Plaza, New York, NY 10019. 212-484-6000.

Bob Marley, c/o Don Taylor, 211 West 56 Street, New York, NY 10019. 212-582-2886.

Bobby Martin, c/o Tentmakers, 6367 West Sixth Street, Los Angeles, CA 90048. 213-937-6650.

Harry Maslin, c/o Arista Records, 1880 Century Park East, Suite 1510, Los Angeles, CA 90067. 213-553-1777.

Jerry Masters, c/o Criteria Recording Studios, 1755 NE 149 Street, Miami, FL 33161. 305-947-5611.

William E. McEuen, 10010 Tolucka Lake Drive, Tolucka Lake, CA 91602. 213-654-0938.

Jimmy Messina, c/o Fitzgerald-Hartley, 7250 Beverly Blvd., Los Angeles, CA 90036. 213-934-8002.

Charles Mims, Jr., c/o Tentmakers, 6367 West Sixth Street, Los Angeles, CA 90048. 213-937-6650.

Fonce Mizell, c/o Sky High Productions, 8515 Hollywood Boulevard, Los Angeles, CA 90069. 213-654-3760.

Larry Mizell, c/o Sky High Productions, 8515 Hollywood Boulevard, Los Angeles, CA 90069. 213-654-3760.

Jacques Morali, c/o Can't Stop Productions, 65 East 55 Street, New York, NY 10022. 212-751-6177.

Mickie Most, 42-48 Charlbert Street, London NW8 England. 01-586-2012.

James Mtume, c/o Famous Music, One Gulf & Western Plaza, New York, NY 10023. 212-333-4131.

Al Nalli, 312 South Ashley, Ann Arbor, MI 48104. 313-796-5454.

Willie Nelson, c/o Mark Rothbaum, 225 Main Street, Danbury, CT 06810. 203–792–2400.

Ron Nevison, c/o Michael Lippman, 333 North Foothill Road, Beverly Hills, CA 90210. 213–858–0585.

Jack Nitzsche, c/o North Spur Productions, 8235 Santa Monica Boulevard, Suite 201, Los Angeles, CA 90046. 213-645-8424.

Jim Ed Norman, 6255 Sunset Boulevard, Hollywood, CA 90028. 213-462-4020.

Milton T. Okun, c/o Windsong Records, 9744 Wilshire Boulevard, Beverly Hills, CA. 213-550-7100.

Keith Olsen, Cohen & Steinhart, 6430 Sunset Blvd., Suite 1500, Los Angeles, CA 90028. 213-463-1151.

Tony Outeda, P. O. Box 398, Port Jefferson, NY 11777. 516-751-5300.

Richard Sanford Orshoff, c/o John Frankenheimer, Loeb & Loeb, 10100 Santa Monica Boulevard, Suite 2200, Los Angeles, CA 90067. 213-552-7783.

Carl Palmer, c/o Manticore Management, 170 East 61 Street, New York, NY 10021. 212-421-3470.

Robert Palmer, c/o Island Records, 444 Madison Avenue, New York, NY 10022. 212-355-6550.

Ray Parker, Jr., c/o Cavallo-Ruffalo Management, 9885 Charleville Boulevard, Beverly Hills, CA 90212. 213-277-8137.

J. Pastorius, c/o Cavallo-Ruffalo, 9885 Charleville Blvd., Beverly Hills, CA 90212. 213-277-8137.

Gene Paul, c/o Atlantic Records, 75 Rockefeller Plaza, New York, NY 10019. 212-489-0955.

DIRECTORY OF PRODUCERS

Gregg Perry, 833 Stirrup Drive, Nashville, TN 37221.

Richard Perry, c/o Planet Records, 9120 Sunset Boulevard, Los Angeles, CA 90069. 213-275-4710.

Tom Petty, c/o Tony Dimitriades, Lookout Mgt., 9120 Sunset Boulevard, Hollywood, CA 90069. 213-278-0881.

Police, c/o Miles Copeland, 41-B Blenheim Crescent, London W11 England. 01-727-0734.

Spencer Proffer, c/o Pasha Music House, 5615 Melrose Avenue, Los Angeles, CA 90038. 213-466-3507.

John Punter, c/o Kennedy Street Management, Brazennose House East, 7th Floor, Brazennose Street, Manchester, England. 061-833-0382.

James Purdie, c/o Dancer Productions, 1638 R Street, Washington, DC 20009. 202-234-8860.

Queen, c/o John Reid Entertainments Ltd., 211 South Beverly Drive, Suite 200 Los Angeles, CA 90212, 213-275-5221.

Gerry Rafferty, c/o Continental U.A. London, 37-41 Mortimer Street, Mortimer House, London W1 England. Att: Rick Van Hingl.

Phil Ramone, 36 East 61 Street, Third Floor, New York, NY 10021. 212-759-6948.

Allen Reynolds, c/o Rivertown Prod'ns., P. O. Box 12647, Nashville, TN 37212. 615-385-2555.

Karl Richardson, c/o Criteria Recording Studios, 1775 NE 149 Street, Miami, FL 33161. 305-947-5611.

Smokey Robinson, c/o Motown Records 6255 Sunset Boulevard, Los Angeles, CA 90028. 213-468-3485.

Nile Rodgers, c/o Martin Itzler, Esq., 110 East 59 Street, New York, NY 10022. 212-752-8855.

Mick Ronson, c/o Bob Casper, 1780 Broadway, New York, NY 10019. 212-765-5038.

Larry Rosen, 330 W. 58 Street, #17E, New York, NY 10019. 212-245-7033.

Roxy Music, c/o E. G. Records, 246 East 62 Street, New York, NY 10021. 212-355-5200.

David Rubinson & Friends, 827 Folsom Street, San Francisco, CA 94107. 415-777-2930.

Dick Rudolph, c/o Ken Fritz Management, 444 South San Vicente, Los Angeles, CA 90048. 213-651-5350.

Rufus, c/o Fitzgerald-Hartley, 17175 Ventura Boulevard, Encino, CA 91316. 213-995-8255.

Todd Rundgren, c/o Eric Gardner, 184 Eighth Avenue, Brooklyn, NY 11215. 212-499-6384.

Patrice Rushen, c/o Tentmakers, 6367 West Sixth Street, Los Angeles, CA 90048. 213-937-6650.

Leon Russell, c/o Diane Sullivan, 4720 West Magnolia, Burbank, CA 91505. 213-980-5648.

Alex Sadkin, c/o Compass Point Studio, P. O. Box N4599, Nassau, Bahamas. 809-327-8282.

Luigi Salvoni, c/o E.S.P., 1790 Broadway, New York, NY 10019. 212-765-8450.

Joe Sample, c/o Grief-Garris Management, 8467 Beverly Boulevard, Los Angeles, CA 90048. 213-653-4780.

Johnny Sandlin, c/o Gary Lazar Management, 24548 Pierce, Southfield, MI 48075. 313-559-6760.

Devadip Carlos Santana, c/o Bill Graham Productions, 201 Eleventh Street, San Francisco, CA 94103. 415-864-0815.

Skip Scarborough, c/o Relmarc Productions, 11620 Wilshire Boulevard, Suite 580, Los Angeles, CA 90025. 213-464-0101.

Ken Scott, Chateau Recorders, 5500 Cahuenga Boulevard, North Hollywood, CA 91602. 213-464-5247.

Robert Shakespeare, c/o Rolling Stones Records, 75 Rockefeller Plaza, New York, NY 10019. 212-484-6000.

Louie Shelton, c/o Day 5 Productions, 216 Chatsworth Drive, San Fernando, CA 91340. 213-365-9371.

Bunny Sigler, c/o Salsoul Records, 240 Madison Avenue, New York, NY 10016. 212-889-7340.

DIRECTORY OF PRODUCERS

John Simon, c/o Mitchell Pines. 212-644-4020.

Jimmy Simpson, 301 East 21 Street, New York, NY 10010. 212-677-4915.

Valerie Simpson, c/o George Schiffer, 1155 North LaCienega, Suite 6, Los Angeles, CA 90069. 213-659-5705.

Lonnie Liston Smith, c/o Joe Fontana, 161 West 54 Street, New York, NY 10019. 212-247-3043.

Gino Soccio, c/o Unison Records, 1310 Rue LaRiviere, Montreal, Quebec, Canada. 514-527-4588.

Edwin Starr, c/o Kyle Management, 8960 Cynthia Street, Los Angeles, CA 90069. 213-271-9381.

Art Stewart, c/o Motown Records, 6255 Sunset Boulevard, Los Angeles, CA 90028. 213-468-3500.

Supertramp, c/o Mismanagement, 3805 West Magnolia Boulevard, Burbank, CA 91505. 213-849-7871.

Styx, c/o Derek Sutton, Stardust Ents., 4600 Franklin Avenue, Los Angeles, CA 90027. 213-660-2553.

Leon Sylvers, c/o Al Ross, 1900 Avenue of the Stars, Los Angeles, CA 90067. 213-277-5253.

Bill Szymczyck, c/o Pandora Productions, 2665 South Bayshore Drive, Suite 100, Miami, FL 33133. 305-856-5942.

Talking Heads, c/o Gary Kurfirst, Overland Productions, 405 Park Avenue, New York, NY 10022. 212-838-2330.

Ted Templeman, c/o Warner Bros. Records, 3300 Warner Boulevard, Burbank, CA 91505. 213-846-9090.

Terry Thomas, c/o Trident Studios, 17 St. Ann's Court, London WL England. 01-734-9901.

Russ Titelman, c/o Warner-Reprise Records, 3300 Warner Boulevard, Burbank, CA 91505. 213-846-9090.

Roger Tokarz, c/o TK Productions, 495 SE Tenth Court, Hialeah, FL 33010. 305-888-1685.

Peter Tosh, c/o Rolling Stones Records, 75 Rockefeller Plaza, New York, NY 10019. 212-484-6000.

Tower of Power, 606 Wilshire Blvd., Suite 412, Santa Monica, CA 90401. 213-451-8458.

Pat Travers, c/o New Age Management, 712 Fifth Avenue, New York, NY 10022. 212-765-3850.

Steve Van Zandt, 205 Second Avenue, Asbury Park, NJ. 201-988-3931.

Tony Visconti, c/o Chris Morrison, 52 Dean Street, London Wl England. 01-734-9734.

Narda Michael Walden, c/o Greg DiGiovine, P. O. Box 690, San Francisco, CA 94001. 415-626-0655.

Lenny Waronker, c/o Warner Bros. Records, 3300 Warner Boulevard, Burbank, CA 91505. 213-846-9090.

Grover Washington, Jr., c/o Great Eastern Management, 1913 Walnut Street, Philadelphia, PA 19103. 215-567-0990.

Henry Weck, c/o Al Nalli, 312 South Ashley, Ann Arbor, MI 48104. 313-769-5454.

Tom Werman, c/o Epic Records, 1801 Century Park West, Century City, CA 90067. 213-556-4700.

John Wetton, c/o E. G. Management Ltd., 63-A Kings Road, London SW 3 England. 01-730-2162. **New York office:** 246 East 62 Street, New York, NY 10021. 212-355-5200.

Barry White, c/o Soul Unlimited, 14724 Ventura Boulevard, Suite 1204, Sherman Oaks, CA 91403. 213-872-1314.

J. P. Williams, c/o Cavallo-Rufallo Management, 9885 Charleville Boulevard, Beverly Hills, CA 90212. 213-277-8137.

Tony Williams, c/o Monte Kay Management, 9200 Sunset Boulevard, Los Angeles, CA 90069. 213-278-7975.

Muff Winwood, c/o CBS Records U.K., 17-19 Soho Square, London, England. 01-734-8181.

Joe Wissert, c/o Columbia Records, 1801 Century Park West, Century City, CA 90067. 213-556-4700.

Marvin Yancy, c/o Jay's Entertainments, 1777 North Vine Street, Suite 303,

Los Angeles, CA 90028. 213-462-1640.
Stevie Wonder, c/o Black Bull, 6255 Sunset Boulevard, Hollywood, CA 90028. 213-468-3500.
Joe Zawinul, Cavallo-Ruffalo, 9885 Charleville Blvd., Beverly Hills, CA 90212. 213-277-8137.
Frank Zappa, c/o Glotzer Management, 824 North Robertson Boulevard, Hollywood, CA 90069. 213-278-8715.

DIRECTORY OF RECORDING STUDIOS[*]

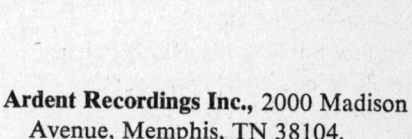

A&M Recording Studio, 1416 North LaBrea, Hollywood, CA 90028. 213-469-2411.
A&R Recording Inc., 322 West 48 Street, New York, NY 10036. 212-582-1070.
A I R Studios, 214 Oxford Street, London W1, England. 01-637-2758.
Abbey Road Studios, 3 Abbey Road, St. John's Wood, London NW8 9AY England. 01-286-1161.
ABC Recording Studio, 8255 Beverly Boulevard, Los Angeles, CA 90048. 213-658-5990.
Advision Ltd., 23 Gosfield Street, London W1 England. 01-580-5707.
Alpha International, 2001 West Moyamensing Avenue, Philadelphia, PA 19145. 215-271-7333.
American Sound Studio, 827 Thomas Street, Memphis, TN 38107. 901-525-0540.
Apogee Recording Studios, 125 Simpson Street NW, Atlanta, GA 30313. 404-522-8460.

Ardent Recordings Inc., 2000 Madison Avenue, Memphis, TN 38104. 901-725-0855.
Atlantic Studios, 1841 Broadway, New York, NY 10023. 212-484-8490.
The Automatt, 827 Folsom Street, San Francisco, CA 94107. 415-777-4111.
Axis Sound Studios, 1314 Ellsworth Industrial Drive, Atlanta, GA 30318. 404-355-8680.
Basin G Street Studios, 8-10 Basing Street, London W11 1ET England. 01-229-1229.
Bayshore Recording Studios, 2665 South Bayshore Drive, Coconut Grove, FL 33133. 305-856-5942.
Bearsville Sound Studio, Box 135, Speare Road, Bearsville, NY 12409. 914-679-7303.
Bear West Studios, 915 Howard Street, San Francisco, CA 94103. 415-543-2125.
Bee Jay Recording Studios, 5000 Eggleston Avenue, Orlando, FL 32810. 305-293-1781.

[*]Based on **Album Action Chart 1979**

DIRECTORY OF RECORDING STUDIOS

Brother Studio, 1454 Fifth Street, Santa Monica, CA 90401. 213-451-5433.

Britannia Row Recording Studios, 35 Britannia Row, Islington, London N1 8QH England. 01-359-5275.

The Burbank Studios, 4000 Warner Boulevard, Burbank, CA 91522. 213-843-6000.

Capitol Records, 1750 North Vine Street, Hollywood, CA 90028. 213-462-6252.

Capricorn Studio, 548 Broadway, Macon, GA 31201. 912-745-8511.

Caribou Ranch Recording Studio, Nederland, CO 80466. 303-258-3215.

Castle Recording Studio, 93 Castle Hill Road, Lancaster, England. 0942-58-777.

Chateau Recorders, 5500 Cahuenga, North Hollywood, CA 91601. 213-769-3700.

Cherokee Studios, 751 North Fairfax, Hollywood, CA 90046. 213-653-3412.

Chipping Norton Recording Studios, 28-30 New Street, Chipping Norton, Oxon, England. 0608-3636.

Jack Clement Recording Studio, 3102 Belmont Boulevard, Nashville, TN 37212. 615-383-1982.

CBS Recording Studios, 49 East 52 Street, New York, NY 10022. 212-975-5901. **Nashville studios:** 34 Music Square East, Nashville, TN 37203. 615-259-4321. **London studios:** 31-37 Whitfield Street, London W1P 5RE England. 01-636-3434. **Tokyo studios:** 4-14-14 Akasaka, Minatoku, Tokyo 107 Japan. 01-584-8111.

Conny's Studio, Koln, West Germany.

Conway Recording, 655 North St. Andrews Place, Hollywood, CA 90004. 213-463-2175.

Crimson Sound, 1454 Fifth Street, Santa Monica, CA 90401. 213–393–9444.

Criteria Recording Studios, 1755 NE 149 Street, Miami, FL 33181. 305-947-5611.

Crystal-Sound Recording, 1014 North Vine Street, Hollywood, CA 90038. 213-466-6453.

Custom Recorders, P. O. Box 8045, Universal City, CA 91608. 213-877-2557.

Davlen Studios, 4162 Lankershim Boulevard, Universal City, CA 91602. 213-980-8700.

Dawnbreaker Recording Studio, 216 Chatsworth Drive, San Fernando, CA 91340. 213-361-1283; 213-875-0277.

Devonshire Sound Studios, 10729 Magnolia Boulevard, North Hollywood, CA 91601. 213-985-1945.

Dierks Studios, Hauptstr 33, D5024 Pulheim, College 3, West Germany, 2238-2004.

Different Fur, 3470 19 Street, San Francisco, CA 415-864-1967.

Dimension Sound Studios, 368 Centre Street, Jamaica Plain, MA 02130. 617-522-3100.

Dynamic Sounds Recording Studio, 15 Bell Road, Kingston 11, Jamaica. 923-9168.

Eastern Sound Co., 48 Yorkville Avenue, Toronto, Canada M4W 1L4. 416-920-2211.

Eden Studios Ltd., 20-24 Beaumont Road, Chiswick, London W4 England. 01-995-5432.

Electric Lady Studios, 52 West 8 Street, New York, NY 10011. 212-477-7500.

Enactron Remote Recording Studio, 9500 Lania Lane, Beverly Hills, CA 90210. 213-271-9829.

Fantasy Studios, Tenth & Parker Streets, Berkeley, CA 94710. 415-549-2500.

Fifth Floor Studios, 517 West Third Street, Cincinnati, OH 45202. 513-651-1871.

Filmways/Heider Recording Studio, 245 Hyde Street, San Francisco, CA 94102. 415-771-5780. **Los Angeles studio:** 1604 North Cahuenga, Hollywood, CA 90028. 213-466-5474.

Gold Star Recording Studios, 6252

Santa Monica Boulevard, Hollywood, CA 90038. 213-469-1173.
Golden Sound Studios, 7000 Santa Monica Boulevard, Los Angeles, CA 90028. 213-462-6688.
Group IV Recording, 1541 North Wilcox Avenue, Hollywood, CA 90028. 213-466-6444.
Hit Factory, 353 West 48 Street, New York, NY 10036. 212-581-9590.
Hollywood Sound Recorders, 6367 Selma Avenue, Hollywood, CA 90028. 213-467-1411.
Indigo Ranch Studio (Malibu), P. O. Box 24-A-14, Los Angeles, CA 90024. 213-456-9277.
Kaye-Smith Studios, 2212 Fourth Avenue, Seattle, WA 98121. 206-624-8651.
Kendun Recorders, 619 South Glenwood Place, Burbank, CA 91506. 213-843-8096.
Lansdowne Studios, Lansdowne House, Lansdowne Road, London 11 England. 01-727-0041.
Larrabee Sound, 8811 Santa Monica Boulevard, Los Angeles, CA 90069. 213-657-6750.
Le Studio, Morin Heights, PR 1, Quebec JOR 1HO, Canada. 514–226–2419.
Long View Farm, Stoddard Road, North Brookfield, MA 01535. 617-867-7662.
Maison Rouge, 2 Wansdown Place, Fulham Broadway, London SW6 1DN, England. 01-381-2001.
The Manor Studios, Manor House, Shipton-on-Cherwell, Oxford, England.
Marquee Studios, 10 Richmond Mews, Dean Street, London W1 England. 01-437-6731.
Master Sound Studios, 1227 Spring Street NW, Atlanta, GA 30309. 404-873-6425.
MCA Whitney Recording Studios, 1516 Glenoaks Boulevard, Glendale, CA 91201. 213-245-6801.
Media Sound Studios, 311 West 57 Street, New York, NY 10019. 212-765-4700.

Meoldy Recording Service, 2093 Faulkner Road NE, Atlanta, GA 30324. 404-321-3886.
Mom & Pops Co. Store, 4028 Colfax Avenue, Studio City, CA 91604. 213-769-7282.
Motown Recording Studios, 6255 Sunset Boulevard, Los Angeles, CA 90028. 213-468-3500.
Mountain Meadow Recording, 570 Twenty-sixth Street, No. 1, Ogden, UT 84401. 801-394-3217.
Mountain Recording Studio, 8 Rue du Theatre, CH-1820 Montreux 2, Switzerland. 021-62-56-56.
Muscle Shoals Sound Studios, 1000 Alabama Avenue, Sheffield, AL 35660. 205-381-2060.
The Music Centre, Engineers Way, Wembley, Middlesex HA9 ODR England. 01-903-4611.
Music Grinder Studios, 7460 Melrose Avenue, Los Angeles, CA 90046. 213-655-2996.
Musicland Studios GmbH, Arabellastr. 5/139, D8000 Munich 81, Germany. 089-92-32-2700/3000.
North Star Prod'ns, 56624 Joshua Drive, Yucca Valley, CA 92284. 714-365-7145.
P. S. Recording Studios, 323 East 23 Street, Chicago, IL 60616. 312-225-2110.
Paradise Studio, 1700 Broadway, New York, NY 10019. 212-541-7920.
Paragon Recording Studios, 9 East Huron Street, Chicago, IL 60611. 312-664-2412.
The Pasha Music House, 5615 Melrose Avenue, Hollywood, CA 90038. 213-466-3507.
Pathe Marconi-EMI, 62 Rue de Sevres, F-92100 Boulogne, France. 331-603-17-11.
Pebble Beach Sound Recorders, 12-A South Farm Road, Worthing, Sussex, England. 0903-201-767.
Philadelphia Music Works, P. O. Box 947, Bryn Mawr, PA 19010. 215-525-9873.

DIRECTORY OF RECORDING STUDIOS

Plaza Sound Studios, 55 West 50 Street, New York, NY 10020. 212-757-6111.

Power Station, 441 West 53 Street, New York, NY 10019. 212-246-2900.

Producer's Workshop, 6035 Hollywood Boulevard, Hollywood, CA 90028. 213-466-7766.

Quadradical Cinema Corp. Sound Studio, 14203 NE 18 Avenue, North Miami, FL 33181. 305-940-7971.

Quadrafonic Sound Studio, 1802 Grand Avenue, Nashville, TN 37212. 615-327-4568.

RPM Sound Studios, Inc., 12 East 12 Street, New York, NY 10003. 212-242-2100.

Ramport Studios, 115-117 Thessaly Road, London SW8 England. 01-720-5066

RCA Studios, 110 West 44 Street, New York, NY 10036. 212-598-5900.

RCA Custom Recording Services, 13-17 New Burlington Place, London W1 England. 01-734-2998.

Record Plant, 321 West 44 Street, New York, NY 10036. 212-581-6505. **San Francisco studio:** 2200 Bridgeway, Sausalito, CA 94965. 415-332-6100. **Los Angeles studio:** 8456 West Third Street, Los Angeles, CA 90048. 213-653-0240.

Red Gate Studio, 5000 Eggleston Avenue, Orlando, FL.

Regents Park Recording, 27-A Queens Terrace, London NW8 6DY England. 01-586-5633.

Relight Studios, Goirlesedijk 12A, Hilvarenbeek, Holland. 04255-2589.

Roundhouse Recording Studios, 100 Chalk Farm Road, London NW1 8EH England. 01-485-0131.

RPM Sound Studios, 12 East 12 Street, New York, NY 10003. 212-242-2100.

Rusk Sound Studios, 1556 North LaBrea, Hollywood, CA 90028. 213-462-6477.

Salty Dog Recording, 14511 Delano, Van Nuys, CA 91411. 213-994-9973.

Santa Barbara Sound Recording, 33 West Haley Street, Santa Barbara, CA 93101. 805-966-6630.

Sawmill Studio, Goland, Fowey, Cornwall PL23 1LP England. 072-683-3337.

Secret Sound Studio, 147 West 24 Street, New York, NY 10011. 212-691-7674.

Sigma Sound Studios, 212 North 12 Street, Philadelphia, PA 19107. 215-561-3660. **New York studios:** 1697 Broadway, New York, NY 10019. 212-582-5055.

Sound Arts, 2825 Hyans Street, Los Angeles, CA 90026. 213-487-5148.

Sound City Inc., 15456 Cabrito Road, Van Nuys, CA 91406. 213-873-2842.

Sound Factory, 6357 Selma Avenue, Hollywood, CA 90028. 213-467-2500.

Sound Labs Inc., 1800 North Argyle, Los Angeles, CA 90028. 213-466-3463.

Soundmixers, 1619 Broadway, New York, NY 10019. 212-245-3100.

Sound Palace, 37 West 54 Street, New York, NY 10019. 212-541-4870.

Sound Stage Studios, 10 Music Circle, Nashville, TN 37203. 615-256-2676.

Sound Suite Recorders, P. O. Box 66, Manhattan Beach, CA 90266. 213-649-3554.

Sound Track Studio, Store Kongensgade 66, DK-1264 Copenhagen, Denmark. 01-15-50-00.

Star Track Recording Studio, 8615 Santa Monica Boulevard, West Hollywood, CA 90069. 213-855-1171.

Stax Studios, 10 Street and Parker, Berkeley, CA 94710. 415-549-2500.

Strawberry Recording Studios, 3 Waterloo Road, Stockport, Cheshire, England. 061-480-9711.

Studio Center Sound Recordings, 14875 NE 20 Avenue, North Miami, FL 33181. 305-861-0756.

Studio in the Country, P. O. Box 490, Bogalusa, LA 70427. 504-735-8224.

Studio Masters, 8312 Beverly Boulevard, Los Angeles, CA. 213-653-1988.

Studio One, 3864 Oakcliff Industrial Court, Doraville, GA 30340. 404-447-9492.

DIRECTORY OF RECORDING STUDIOS

Studio One, Inc., Box 69, Tazewell, VA 24651. 703-988-4150.
Studio Tempo Inc., 0707 Charlevoix Street, Quebec, Canada H3K 2Y1. 514-937-9571.
Sunset Sound, 6650 Sunset Boulevard, Hollywood, CA 90028. 213-469-1186.
Superdisc Inc., 14611 East Nine Mile Road, East Detroit, MI 48021. 313-779-1380.
Super Sound, 600 East Franklin, Suite E, Monterey, CA 93940. 408-649-4100.
Total Experience Recording Studio, 6226 Yucca Street, Los Angeles, CA 90028. 213-462-6585.
Trident Recording Studios, 17 St. Annes Court, Wardour Street, London W1V 3AW England. 01-734-9901.
TW Music, 211 Fulham Palace Road, London W6 England. 01-385-4630.
United Sound Systems, 5840 Second Boulevard, Detroit, MI 48202. 313-871-2570.
United Western Studios, 6000 Sunset Boulevard, Hollywood, CA 90028. 213-469-3983.
Universal Recording, 46 East Walton, Chicago, IL 60611. 312-642-6465.
Utopia Recording Studios, Spencer Court, 7 Chaclot Road, London NW1 8LH England. 01-586-3434.
Village Recorders, 1616 Butler Avenue, West Los Angeles, CA 90025. 213-478-8227.
Warner Bros. Recording Studios, 11114 Cumpston Avenue, North Hollywood, CA 91601. 213-980-5605.
Wessex Studios, 106 Highbury, New Park, London N5 2DW England. 01-359-0051.
Westlake Audio, 6311 Wilshire Boulevard, Los Angeles, CA 90048. 213-655-0303.
Westlake Studios, 8447 Beverly Blvd., Los Angeles, CA 90048 and 6311 Wilshire Blvd., Los Angeles, CA 90048. 213-654-2155.
Whitney Studios, 1516 Glenoaks, Glendale, CA 91201. 213-245-6801.
Woodland Sound Studios, 1011 Woodland Street, Nashville, TN 37206. 615-227-5027.
Allen Zentz Recording, 1020 Sycamore Avenue, Hollywood, CA 90038. 213-851-8300.

DIRECTORY OF PERSONAL MANAGERS*

Ken Adamany, 520 University Place, Madison, WI 53703. 608-251-2644.

Adam's Dad Management, 827 Folsom Street, San Francisco, CA 94107. 415-777-2930.

Alive Entertainments, 8600 Melrose Avenue, Los Angeles, CA 90069. 213-659-7001.

Albion Management, c/o John Telfer, 147 Oxford Street, London, England. 01-734-9072.

Herb Alpert, c/o A&M Records, 1461 N. LaBrea Avenue, Los Angeles, CA 90028. 213-469-2411.

American World Wide Sounds & Music, 405 Park Avenue, New York, NY 10022. 212-355-3270.

Stig Anderson, c/o Mildred Fields, Transaction Music, 225 East 57 Street, New York, NY 10022. 212-838-2590.

A.R.S.E., 157 West 57 Street, New York, NY 10019. 212-489-1731.

Pat Armstrong, P. O. Box 5067, 1019 Walnut Street, Macon, GA 31208. 912-742-1291.

Arnakata, 35 Homer Street, London, England. 01-723-8424.
New York office: 211 W. 56 Street, Suite 15L, NY, NY 10019. 212-765-4601.

Artistic Vision Ltd., 680 Craig Road, St. Louis, MO 63141. 314-567-9650.

Artists International Management, 258 South Beverly Drive, Beverly Hills, CA 90212. 213-275-9999.

Peter Asher Management Inc., 644 North Doheny Drive, Los Angeles, CA 90069. 213-273-9433.

Aucoin Management, 645 Madison Avenue, New York, NY 10022. 212-826-8800.

Balmur Ltd., 825 Eglinton Avenue West, Suite 406, Toronto, Ont. Canada M5N 1E7. 416-485-4653.

Beggar's Banquet Management, North 8 Hogarth Road, London SW5 England. 01-370-6175.

Sid Bernstein Productions, 4 East 75 Street, New York, NY 10021. 212-744-9000.

Ed Bicknell, c/o Mems, 31 Kings Road, London SW1, England. 01-730-9461.

Black Bull, c/o Chris Jones, 6255 Sunset Boulevard, Los Angeles, CA 90028. 213–468–3500.

Bernard Brillstein, Brillstein Company, 9200 Sunset Boulevard, Suite 425, Hollywood, CA 90069. 213-275-6135.

B.N.B. Associates, 9454 Wilshire Boulevard, Beverly Hills, CA 90212. 213-273-7020.

Bert Block, Block-Kewley Mgmt., 11 Bailey Avenue, Ridgefield, CT 06877. 203-438-3728.

Buddy Lee Attractions, 806 Sixteenth Avenue South, Nashville, TN 37203. 615-244-4336.

Rick Bloom's Office, 6338 Jackie Avenue, Woodland Hills, CA 91367. 213-883-7160.

Joyce Bogart-Susan Munao, c/o

---

*Based on **Album Action Chart 1979**

DIRECTORY OF PERSONAL MANAGERS 431

Casablanca Records, 8255 Sunset Boulevard, Los Angeles, CA 90069. 213-650-8300.

Levi Bohannon, 289 North Oraton Parkway, East Orange, NJ 07107. 201-643-6981; 201-672-2787.

Armen Boladian, c/o Westbound Records, 19631 West 8 Mile Road, Detroit, MI 48219. 313-255-7640.

Gary Borman Management, 244 Ladera Drive, Beverly Hills, CA 90210. 213-275-8035.

Larry Boyd, 791 Tenth Street, Carlyle, IL 62231. 618-594-4442.

Ariane Brener, c/o Eric Kronfeld, 1501 Broadway, New York, NY 10019. 212-840-2200.

Brothers Records, 10880 Wilshire Boulevard, Suite 306, Los Angeles, CA 90024.

Charles Brusco, 180 Allen Road NE, Atlanta, GA 30328. 404-252-9140.

Buie-Geller Organization, 3297 North Crest Road, Suite 203, Doraville, GA 30340. 404-491-0950.

Can't Stop Productions, 65 East 55 Street, New York, NY 10022. 212-751-6177.

Paul Cantor Enterprises Inc., 144 South Beverly Drive, Beverly Hills, CA 90212. 213-274-9222.

Career Management, Inc., 641 Lexington Avenue, New York, NY 10018. 212-289-6914.

Budd Carr, 9200 Sunset Boulevard, Suite 1207, Los Angeles, CA 90069.

Cavallo-Ruffalo Management, 9885 Charleville Boulevard, Beverly Hills, CA 90212. 213-277-8137.

Chinnichap Inc., 8919 Sunset Boulevard, Los Angeles, CA 90069. 213-657-8585.

Cleveland Entertainment Co., P. O. Box 783, Willoughby, OH 44094. 216-951-0993. **New York office:** 538 Madison Avenue, New York, NY 10022. 212-935-8630.

Coconut Entertainment Co., 157 West 57 Street, New York, NY 10019. 212-582-5285.

Bruce Cohn, 15000 Sonoma Highway, Glen Ellen, CA 95442. 707-996-4050; 415-957-1567.

Earl Cole, 6477 Atlantic Avenue, Suite 5148, Long Beach, CA 90805. 213-422-1368.

Command Performance, 850 Seventh Avenue, New York, NY 10019. 212-586-1100. Att: Larry Alexander.

Miles Copeland, 41 B Blenheim Crescent, London W11 England. 01-727-0734.

Crosseyed Bear Productions, 131 Congress Street, Buffalo, NY 14213. 716-883-1272. Att: Michael Davenport.

Dancer Productions, 1638 R Street, Washington, DC 20009. 202-234-8860.

Brenda Dash, c/o Sweet Street Prodn's, P. O. Box 3875, Los Angeles, CA 90028. 213-980-4232.

Carl Davis, c/o Chi-Sound Records, 20 East Huron Street, Chicago, IL 60611. 312-943-0305.

De-Air Marketing International, 9701 Wilshire Boulevard, Suite 800, Beverly Hills, CA 90212. 213-272-5919.

Ron DeBlasio, 1888 Century Park East, Los Angeles, CA 90069. 213-553-6006.

Michael Deeny, 12 Southwell Gardens, Lonodn SW 7 England. 01-373-5465.

Greg DiGiovine, P. O. Box 690, San Francisco, CA 94001. 415-626-0655.

Tonly Dimitriades, c/o Lookout Management, 9120 Sunset Boulevard, Hollywood, CA 90069. 213–278–0881.

Don Dortch International, 2605 Nonconnah Boulevard, Suite 150, Memphis, TN 38112. 901-345-6555.

Double T. Promotions, 712 SW Salmon, Suite B, Portland, OR 97205. 503-221-0288.

Francis Dreyfus, c/o Disques Motors, 26 Avenue Kleber, 75016 Paris, France. 723-4437.

Ed Elerbee, 200 West 72 Street, New York, NY 10023. 212-362-0702.

E. G. Management Ltd., 63 A Kings Road, London SW 3 England. 01-730-2162. **New York office:** 246

East 62 Street, New York, NY 10021. 212-355-5200.
Norman Epstein, 644 N. Doheny Drive, Los Angeles, CA 90069. 213-271-5181.
The Entertainment Company, 40 West 57 Street, New York, NY 10019. 212-586-3600. **Los Angeles office:** 6430 Sunset Boulevard, Los Angeles, CA 90028. 213-466-6127.
E.S.P., Inc., 1790 Broadway, New York, NY 10019. 212-765-8450.
Far Out Management Ltd., 7417 Sunset Boulevard, Los Angeles, CA 90046. 213-874-1300.
Leon Fisher, 1764 Sycamore, Los Angeles, CA 213-851-2589.
Fitzgerald-Hartley, 17175 Ventura Boulevard, Encino, CA 91316. 213-995-8255.
Mick Fleetwood, Limited Management, 1420 North Beachwood Drive, Hollywood, CA 90028.
Beau Ray Fleming, 160 East 26 Street, Apt. 16, New York, NY 10010. 212-679-5903.
Terry Flood, 354 Youville Street, Montreal, Quebec 1Z5 Canada. 514-284-1001.
Joe Fontana, 161 West 54 Street, New York, NY 10019. 212-247-3043.
David Franklin, c/o Omni International, Suite 1290 South, Atlanta, GA 30303. 404-688-2233.
Ken Fritz, 444 South San Vicente, Los Angeles, CA 90048. 213-651-5350.
Front Line Management, 8380 Melrose, Suite 307, Los Angeles, CA 90069. 213-658-6600.
Gaff Management, c/o Billy Gaff, 90 Wardour Street, London W1 England. 01-836-3941. **Los Angeles office:** 1245 North Doheny Drive, Los Angeles, CA 90069. 213-550-8798.
Donald Gallagher, 45 A Finsborough Road, London SW10 England. 01-439-6325.
Eric Gardner, 184 Eighth Avenue, Brooklyn, NY 11215. 212-499-6384.
Arthur Garfunkel Entertainments, c/o Sanford Greenberg & Richard Paysner,
600 New Hampshire Avenue NW, Suite 950, Washington, D.C. 202-333-8080. **New York office:** 460 Park Avenue, Suite 800, New York, NY 10022. 212-688-1531.
Bill Gatzimos, 50 Music Square W., Nashville, TN 37203. 615-327-2651.
Pat Gibbons, c/o Stan Diamond, 10850 Wilshire Boulevard, Los Angeles, CA 90024. 213-879-3444.
Glotzer Management, 824 North Robertson Boulevard, Hollywood, CA 90069. 213-278-8715.
Richard Gottehrer, 44 West 77 Street, New York, NY 10024. 212-799-0228.
Bill Graham Productions, 201 Eleventh Street, San Francisco, CA 94103. 415-864-0815.
Great Eastern Management, 1913 Walnut Street, Philadelphia, PA 19103. 215-567-0990.
Grief-Garris Management, 8467 Beverly Boulevard, Los Angeles, CA 90048. 213-653-4780.
David Harper, c/o Island Records, 444 Madison Avenue, New York, NY 10022. 212-355-6550.
Hartmann & Goodman, 1500 Crossroads of the World, Hollywood, CA 90028. 213-461-3461.
Bob Heller, Grapefruit Productions, 16 Douglass Street, Brooklyn, NY 11231. 212-834-1105.
Fred Heller Entertainments, 1756 Broadway, Suite 10H, New York, NY 10019. 212-265-1501.
Al Hersh, 2480 Neuz Way, Topanga Canyon, CA 90290. 213-455-1755.
Home Run Productions, 14 East 60 Street, New York, NY 10022.
Thalen Hurewitz, Cooper, Epstein & Hurewitz, 9465 Wilshire Blvd, Suite 800, Beverly Hills, CA 90212. 213-278-1111.
Ben Hurwitz, c/o Little David Records, 9229 Sunset Boulevard, Hollywood, CA 90069. 213-278-7975.
Hit & Run Music Ltd., 10 Maddox Street, London W1 R9PN England. 01-629-2846.

DIRECTORY OF PERSONAL MANAGERS

Tom Iannaccone, Gates Music, One Marine Midland Place, Rochester, NY 14604. 716-232-2490.

Kelly O. Isley, 1650 Broadway, New York, NY 10019. 212-582-5430.

Martin Itzler, Esq., 110 East 59 Street, New York, NY 10022. 212-752-8855.

Joe Jackson, 6255 Sunset Boulevard, Suite 1023, Los Angeles, CA 90028. 213-466-7315.

Bill Johnston, 9052 Elevado, Los Angeles, CA 90069. 213-271-8504; 213-275-9842.

Susan Josephs, c/o Twin Trumpet Productions, 6430 Sunset Boulevard, Suite 1531, Los Angeles, CA 90028. 213-462-6803.

Lewis Kaplan, 444 South San Vicente Blvd., Los Angeles, CA 90048. 213-653-1345.

Katz-Gallin Entertainments, 9255 Sunset Boulevard, Suite 1115, Los Angeles, CA 90069. 213-273-4210.

Don Kelly Organization, 1474 North Kins Road, Los Angeles, CA 90069. 213-656-4787.

Kennedy Street Management, Ltd., 7 Floor Brazennose House E, Brazennose Street, Manchester M25 AS England. 061-833-0382.

Fred Kewley Mgmt., 11 Bailey Avenue, Ridgefield, CT 06877. 203-438-3728.

Kragen & Co., 1112 North Sherbourne, Los Angeles, CA. 213-659-7914.

Lee Kramer, L. K. Productions, 9229 Sunset Boulevard, Suite 306, Los Angeles, CA 90069. 213-550-1168.

Gary Kurfirst, Overland Productions, 405 Park Avenue, New York, NY 10022. 212-838-2330.

Ted Kurland Associates, 46 Ashford Street, Boston, MA. 617-254-0007.

Brian Lane, Sun Arts, 9 Hillgate Street, London W8 England. 01-727-2791.

Larry Larson, 8732 Sunset Blvd., Los Angeles, CA 90069. 213-652-8700.

Gary Lazar Management, 24548 Pierce, Southfield, MI 48075. 313-559-6760.

Leber-Krebs, Inc., 65 West 55 Street, New York, NY 10019. 212-765-2600.

Fred Lewis Organization, 141 Bedford Road, Carlisle, MA 01741. 617-369-6182.

Art Linson, c/o Mike Rosenfeld, 270 North Canon, Beverly Hills, CA 90212. 213-858-7788.

Michael Lippman, 333 North Foothill Road, Beverly Hills, CA 90210. 213-858-0585.

Little Macho Music, 270 Madison Avenue, Suite 1410, New York, NY 10016. 212-532-2230.

Lookout Management, 9120 Sunset Boulevard, Los Angeles, CA 90069. 213-278-0881.

Tony Lopez, Tony Productions, 1860 Grand Concourse, Bronx, NY 10457. 212-299-2500.

Richard Loren, Box 3356, San Rafael, CA 94902. 415-457-2377.

Miles Lourie, 314 West 71 Street, New York, NY 10023. 212-595-4330.

Joe MacDonald, 300 East Henry Street, Spartanburg, SC 39302. 803-573-5033.

The Manhattan Transfer, 1474 North Kings Road, Los Angeles, CA 90069. 213-656-4870.

Dave Margereson, Mismanagement, 3805 West Magnolia Boulevard, Burbank, CA 91505. 213-849-7871.

Steve Massarsky, 515 Madison Avenue, Suite 1228, New York, NY 10022. 212-355-2671.

Management III Ltd., 9744 Wilshire Boulevard, Beverly Hills, CA. 213-550-7100. New York office: 1345 Avenue of the Americas, New York, NY 10019. 212-752-1563.

Nick Mathe, c/o Nexus, 6404 Hollywood Boulevard, Suite 209, Los Angeles, CA 90028. 213-466-4211.

William E. McEuen, 10010 Tolucka Lake Dr., Tolucka Lake, CA 91602. 213-654-0938.

Jonnie Mae Matthews, 17397 Santa Barbara, Detroit, MI 48221. 313-863-8522.

Media Consulting, 54 Main Street, Danbury, CT 06810. 213-792-8880.

Ina Meibach, Weiss & Meibach, 888 Seventh Avenue, New York, NY 10019. 212-765-4936.

Herb Miller, Music Fair, 2 Little Premier Plaza, Kingston 10, West Indies. 92-663-85.

Joey or Audrey Mills, 273 Primrose Avenue, Mount Vernon, NY 10552. 914-667-3399.

David Mintz, 123 East 54 Street, Suite 2B, New York, NY 10022. 212-752-3080.

Monte Kay Management, 9200 Sunset Boulevard, Los Angeles, CA 90069. 213-278-7975.

Stan Moress, c/o Scotti Brothers Entertainment, 9229 Sunset Boulevard, Los Angeles, CA 90069. 213-550-6262.

Chris Morrison, Morrison & O'Donnell, 52 Dean Street, London N1 England. 01-734-9734.

MPL Communications, c/o Eastman & Eastman, 39 West 54 Street, New York, NY 10019. 212-581-1330.

Multi-Media Management, 6255 Sunset Boulevard, Los Angeles, CA 90028. 213-468-3500.

Al Nalli Productions Inc., 312 South Ashley Street, Ann Arbor, MI 48104. 313-769-5454.

New Age Management, 712 Fifth Avenue, New York, NY 10022. 212-765-3850. Att: David Hemmings.

New Direction, c/o Kevin Hunter, 9255 Sunset Boulevard, Los Angeles, CA 90069. 213-550-7205.

Nightmare Productions, 1735 Pacific Avenue, San Francisco, CA 94109. 415-885-2561.

Denis O'Brien, c/o Dennis Morgan, Dark Horse Records, 3300 Warner Boulevard, Burbank, CA 91505. 213-846-9090.

Fachina O'Kelly, 44 Seymour Place, London W1 England. 01-753-8464.

Osmond Entertainment Center, 1420 East 800 North, Orem, UT 94059. 801-224-4444.

Tony Outeda, P. O. Box 398, Port Jefferson, NY 11777, 516-751-5300.

Ozone Management, 498/500 Harrow Road, London W9 England. 011-441-960-0955.

Brian Panella, 14020 Old Harbor Lane, Suite 207, Marina Del Ray, CA 90291. 213-827-1220.

Park Lane Management, 9 Hillgate Street, London W8 England. 01-727-2791.

Steve Paul, c/o Blue Sky Records, 745 Fifth Avenue, Suite 1803, New York, NY 10022. 212-751-3400.

Sandy Pearlman, P. O. Box 263, Setauket, NY 11733. 516-751-7420.

Jon Peters, 4000 Warner Boulevard, Burbank, CA 91522. 213–843–6000.

Marty Pichinson Management, 518 North LaCienega, Los Angeles, CA 90048. 213-659-7491.

Barry Platnick, 250 West 57 Street, New York, NY 10019. 212-757-4315.

Prime Time Productions, 8221 Georgia Avenue, Silver Springs, MD 20910. 301–565–3372. **L.A. office:** 3752 Tracy, Los Angeles, CA 90027. 213–665–6613.

Robert Raymond, 10845 Lindbrook, Suite 3, Los Angeles, CA 90024. 213-478-0041.

Ray Charles Enterprises, 2107 West Washington Boulevard, Los Angeles, CA 90017. 213-737-8000.

Red Sky Management, 8380 Melrose Avenue, Los Angeles, CA 90069. 213-658-6600.

Don Reeves, Ronnie Milsap Entertainments, 41 Music Square East, Nashville, TN 37203. 615-256-7575.

John Reid Entertainments Inc., 211 South Beverly Drive, Suite 200, Beverly Hills, CA 90212. 213-275-5221.

Renaissance Management, 433 North Camden Drive, Beverly Hills, CA 90210. 213-273-4162.

Jake Riviera, A.R.S.E., 157 West 57 Street, New York, NY 10019. 212-480-1731.

Major Reynolds, c/o Sound Suite, 14750 Puritan Avenue, Detroit, MI 48227. 313-273-3000.

DIRECTORY OF PERSONAL MANAGERS

Rollins & Joffe, 100 Universal Plaza, Universal City, CA 91608. 213-985-4321.
Arlyne Rothberg, 145 Central Park West, New York, NY 10023. 212-873-8288.
Peter Rudge, S.I.R. Productions, 112 Central Park South, New York, NY 10019. 212-489-0950.
George Schiffer, 1155 North LaCienega, Penthouse 6, Los Angeles, CA 90069. 213-885-0293.
S.C.S. Management, Park Townes South, 330 West 58 Street, Suite 7J, New York, NY 10019. 212-265-2520.
Scotti Brothers, 9229 Sunset Boulevard, Hollywood, CA 90069. 213-550-6262.
Peter Scarborough, c/o S.E.A. Ltd., 20 Great Portland Street, London W1 England. 01-441-580-4287.
Lloyd Segal, 9454 Wilshire Boulevard, Suite 500, Beverly Hills, CA 90212. 213-274-5857.
Shadybrook, 9039 Sunset Boulevard, Los Angeles, CA 90069. 213-275-5002.
Shankman & DeBlasio, 185 Pier Avenue, Main Street at Pier, Santa Monica, CA 90405. 213-396-3185.
Curtis Shaw, 6255 Sunset Boulevard, Los Angeles, CA 90028. 213-464-8424.
Sight & Sound Management, 119 West 57 Street, New York, NY 10019. 212-541-5581.
Ed Silvers, c/o Warner Bros. Music, 9200 Sunset Boulevard, Hollywood, CA 90069. 213-273-3323.
Solar Records, 6255 Sunset Boulevard, Suite 923, Hollywood, CA 90028. 213-467-6527.
Jon Somonds, 3932 Cumberland Avenue, Los Angeles, CA 90027. 213-666-3620.
Don Sorkin, 9368 Sierra Mar Drive, Los Angeles, CA 90069. 213-278-4700.
Sound Seventy Productions, 210 Twenty-fifth Avenue North, Nashville, TN 37203. 615-327-1711.
Soul Unlimited, 14724 Ventura Boulevard, Suite 1204, Sherman Oaks, CA 91403. 213-872-1314.
Julian Spear, The Basement, 216 Randolph Avenue, London W9 England. 011-441-624-7591.
Spectrum Talent International, 1680 Vine Street, Suite 817, Los Angeles, CA 91128. 213-462-3085.
Spirit Productions, 66 West 94 Street, New York, NY 10024. 212-724-8527.
Starflight Management, 2 West 45 Street, New York, NY 10036. 212-575-5036.
Robert Stigwood Organisation, 8335 Sunset Boulevard, Los Angeles, CA 90069. **New York office:** 1775 Broadway, New York, NY 10019. 212-975-0700.
Mike Stone, 9 Bryanston Mansions, York Street, London W1 England. 01-262-2840.
Strout & Whitehouse, 280 South Beverly Drive, Suite 402, Beverly Hills, CA 90212. 213-858-8816.
Diane Sullivan, 4720 West Magnolia, Burbank, CA 91505. 213-980-5648; 213-980-5644.
Derek Sutton, Stardust Ents., 4600 Franklin Ave., Los Angeles, CA 90027. 213-660-2553.
Swan Song, Inc., 444 Madison Avenue, New York, NY 10022. 212-752-1330.
T&A Research & Development, 405 Park Avenue, New York, NY 10022. 212-355-4920.
Michael Tannen, Esq., 36 East 61 Street, New York, NY 10021. 212-752-2276.
The Tanners Arms, Newbridge Street, Newcastle-upon-Tyne, England NE1 2NS. 011-44-632-24062.
Don Taylor, 211 West 56 Street, New York, NY 10019. 212-582-2886.
Tentmakers, 6367 West Sixth Street, Los Angeles, CA 90048. 213-937-6650.
Thames Talent Ltd., 1345 Avenue of the Americas, New York, NY 10019. 212-541-6740.
Bill Thomson, c/o Grunt Records, P. O. Box 99387, San Francisco, CA 94109. 415-668-2326.
Edward Tickner Management, 12230 Hesby Street, North Los Angeles, CA 91607. 213-877-6338.

Trinifold, c/o Left Field Services, 250 West 57 Street, New York, NY 10019. 212-541-9212.

Tower Management, 606 Wilshire Blvd., Suite 412, Santa Monica, CA 90410. 213-451-8458.

Twogether Management, 1559 Hunter, Wheeling, IL 60090. 314-870-1880.

Upstart Management, 6671 Sunset Boulevard, Los Angeles, CA 90028. 213-652-7011.

Van Halen Productions, P. O. Box 2128, Los Angeles, CA 91602. 213-462-1403. Att: Noel Monk.

Steve Van Zandt, 205 Second Avenue, Asbury Park, NJ. 201-988-3931.

Jeff Wald Associates, 9356 Santa Monica Boulevard, Beverly Hills, CA 90210. 213-273-2192.

Weisner-Demann, 9200 Sunset Boulevard, Suite 16, Los Angeles, CA 90069. 213-550-8200.

White Rabbit Management, 12230 Hesby Street, North Los Angeles, CA 91607. 213-877-6338.

Ian Wright, c/o MAM, 2425 New Pond Street, London W1 England. 01-629-9255.

Wilf Wright, 1140 North Alpa Lana, Los Angeles, CA 90069. 213-659-3612.

Stewart Young, c/o Manticore Records, 170 East 61 Street, New York, NY 10021. 212-421-4057.

DIRECTORY OF BOOKING AGENTS*

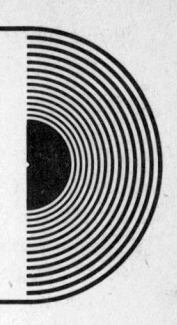

Associated Booking Corp. (ABC), 1995 Broadway, New York, NY 10023. 212-874-2400. **Los Angeles office:** 9595 Wilshire Boulevard, Suite 309, Los Angeles, CA 90212. 213-273-5600.

Artists Heller Agency, 7430 Sunset Boulevard, Suite 1516, Hollywood, CA 90028. 213-462-1100.

Athena Artists, 9100 Wilshire Boulevard, Beverly Hills, CA 90212. 213-273-9170. **New England office:** Box 715, Plymouth, MA 02360. 617-746-8701.

American Talent International (ATI), 888 Seventh Avenue, New York, NY 10019. 212-977-2300. **Los Angeles office:** 118 South Beverly Drive, Los Angeles, CA 90212. 213-278-9311.

Agency for the Performing Arts (APA), 120 West 57 Street, New York, NY 10019. 212-582-1500. **Los Angeles office:** 9000 Sunset Boulevard, Suite 315, Los Angeles, CA 90069. 213-273-0744.

David Bendett Agency Inc., 2431 Briarcrest Road, Beverly Hills, CA 90210. 213-278-5657.

Brighton Agency, 9884 Santa Monica Boulevard, Beverly Hills, CA 90212. 213-277-9182.

Concerts West, 700 112 Avenue NE, Bellvue, WA 98004. 206-455-9160.

The David Libert Agency, 1108 N. Sherbourne Dr., Los Angeles, CA 90069. 213-659-6776.

Diversified Management Agency (DMA), 17650 West 12 Mile Road, Southfield, MI 48075. 313-559-2600.

Don Dortch International, 2605 Nonconnah, Suite 150, Memphis, TN 38112. 901-345-6555.

Steve Ellis, 37 West 57 Street, Room 303, New York, NY 10019. 212-935-3600.

Empire Agency, P. O. Box 6518, Macon, GA 31208. 912-742-4521.

Empire Talent, 1237 South Jackson Spring, Macon, GA 31211. 912–742–4521.

F.B.I. (Frontier Booking Inc.), c/o ICM, 250 57 Street, New York, NY 10019. 212–245–5587. **L.A. office:** 8899 Beverly Boulevard, Los Angeles, CA 90045. 213–550–4000.

Bill Graham Productions, 201 Eleventh Street, San Francisco, CA 94103. 415-864-0815.

Home Run Productions, 14 East 60 Street, New York, NY 10022. 212-751-8920.

ICM, 40 West 57 Street, New York, NY 10019. 212-556-5600. **Los Angeles office:** 8899 Beverly Boulevard, Los Angeles, CA 90045. 213-550-4000.

Love Artists, 1901 Avenue of the Stars, Los Angeles, CA 90067. 213-553-5117.

Magna Artists Corp., 595 Madison Avenue, New York, NY 10022. 212-752-0363. **Los Angeles office:**

*Based on **Album Action Chart 1979**

DIRECTORY OF BOOKING AGENTS

9200 Sunset Boulevard, Los Angeles, CA 90069. 213-273-3177.

Mecca Artists, 1650 Broadway, New York, NY 10019. 212-489-1400.

Media Consulting, 54 Main Street, Danbury, CT 06810. 203-792-8800. Att: Mark Rothman.

Monarch Entertainment, 412 Pleasant Valley Way, West Orange, NJ 07052. 201-736-9828.

Monterey Peninsula Artists, P. O. Box 7308, Carmel, CA 93921. 408-624-4889.

Paragon Agency, 560 Arlington Place, Macon, GA 31208. 912-742-8931. **New York office:** 250 West 57 Street, New York, NY 10019. 212-541-9524.

Premier Talent Associates, Inc., 3 East 54 Street, New York, NY 10022. 212-758-4900.

Regency Artists, 9200 Sunset Boulevard, Suite 823, Los Angeles, CA 90069. 213-273-7103.

Renaissance Booking, 39 West 55 Street, New York, NY 10019. 212-586-6246.

Rodgers Agency, P. O. Box 76640, Atlanta, GA 30318. 404-992-1050.

Howard Rose Agency, 2029 Century Park East, Los Angeles, CA 90067. 213-277-3620.

Rosebud Music Agency, P. O. Box 1897, San Francisco, CA 94101. 415-566-7009.

Mark Rothbaum Associates, 225 Main Street, Danbury, CT 06810. 203-792-2400.

Soul and Style, 1650 Broadway, New York, NY 10019. 212-582-5430.

Starloft Agency, 250 West 57 Street, New York, NY 10019. 212-541-7900.

Sutton Artists, 505 Park Avenue, New York, NY 10022. 212-832-8302.

Talking Heads Tours Inc., c/o Overland Productions, 405 Park Avenue, Eighth Floor, New York, NY 10022. 212-838-2330.

Troy Entertainment, 600 Old Country Road, Garden City, NY 11530. 516-741-2101.

Variety Artists, 9229 Sunset Boulevard, Suite 610, Los Angeles, CA 90069. 213-273-6376. **Minneapolis office:** 4120 Excelsior, Minneapolis, MN 54416. 612-925-3440.

Norby Walters Associates, 1290 Avenue of the Americas, New York, NY 10019. 212-245-3939.

William Morris Agency, 1350 Avenue of the Americas, New York, NY 10019. 212-586-5100. **Los Angeles office:** 151 El Camino Drive, Los Angeles, CA 90212. 213-274-7451.

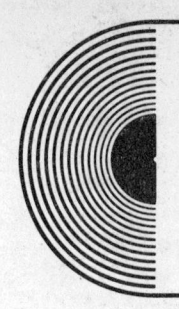

TOP 20 SONGS 1979

title • writer • publisher

"**A Little More Love**" J. Farrar (John Farrar/Irving).

"**After the Love Has Gone**" D. Foster, J. Graylon, B. Champlin (Ninth/Garden-Rake/Irving/Foster Frees/Jobette).

"**Ain't Love a Bitch**" R. Stewart, G. Grainger (Riva).

"**Ain't No Stoppin' Us Now**" J. Whitehead, G. McFadden, J. Cohen (Mighty Three).

"**Bad Girls**" D. Summer, Sudano, Hokenson, Esposito (Starrin/Earborne/Sweet Summer).

"**Big Shot**" B. Joel (Impulsive/April).

"**Blow Away**" G. Harrison (Ganga).

"**Boogie Wonderland**" J. Lind, A. Willis (Charleville/Irving/Deertrack/Ninth).

"**Broken Hearted Me**," Norman (Chappell/Sailmaker—ASCAP).

"**Chuckie's in Love**" R.L. Jones (Easy Money).

"**Cool Change**," Boylan and group (Screen Gems-EMI—BMI).

"**Crazy Love**" R. Young (Pirooting).

"**Cruisin'**," S. Robinson (Bertram—ASCAP).

"**Da Ya Think I'm Sexy**" R. Stewart, C. Appice (Riva/Warner Bros./Nite-Stalk).

"**Dance the Night Away**" E. Van Halen, A. Van Halen, M. Anthony, D. L. Roth (Van Halen).

"**Dancin' Shoes**" C. Storie (Canal).

"**Days Gone Down**" G. Rafferty (Gerry Rafferty).

"**Deeper Than the Night**" T. Snow, J. Vastano (Braintree/Snow).

"**Disco Nights (Disco Freak)**" E. Raheim, LeBlanc (G.Q./Arista).

"**Do It or Die**" Buie, Cobb, Hammond (Low Sal).

"**Does Your Mother Know**" B. Andersson, B. Ulvaeus (Countless).

"**Don't Bring Me Down**" J. Lynne (Jet).

"**Don't Cry Out Loud**" P. Allen, C.B. Sager (Irving/Woolnough/Jemava/Begonia-Unichappell).

"**Do That to Me One More Time**," D. Dragon (Moonlight & Magnolias—BMI).

"**Escape (The Pina Colada Song)**," R. Holmes-Boyer (Screen Gems-EMI—BMI).

"**Every 1's a Winner**" E. Brown (Finchley).

"**Every Time I Think of You**" R. Kennedy, J. Conrad (X-Ray/Jacon).

"**Fire**" B. Springsteen (Bruce Springsteen).

"**Gold**" J. Stewart (Bugle/Stigwood/Unichappell).

"**Goodbye Stranger**" R. Davies, R. Hodgson (Almo/Delicate).

"**Goodnight Tonight**" P. McCartney (MPL Communications).

"Good Times" B. Edwards, N. Rodgers (Chic).
"Got to Be Real" C. Lynn, D. Paich, D. Foster (Butterfly-Gong/Hudmar/Cotaba).
"Head Games," M. Jones, L. Gramm (Somerset Songs/Evansongs—ASCAP).
"Heart of Glass" D. Harry, L. Stein (Rare Blues/Monster Island).
"Heart of the Night" P. Cotton (Tarantula).
"Heaven Knows" D. Summer, G. Moroder, P. Bellotte (Rick's).
"He's the Greatest Dancer" D. Paich (Chic).
"Hold the Line" D. Paich (Hudmar).
"Honesty" B. Joel (Impulsive/April).
"Hot Stuff" P. Bellotte, H. Faltermeier, K. Forsey (Rick's Revelation/Editions Intro).
"I Don't Know if It's Right" T. Life, J.H. Fitch (Six Continents/Mills & Mills).
"I Just Fall in Love Again" Dorff, Sklerov, Lloyd, Herbstritt (Peso/Hobby Horse/Cotton Pickin' Songs).
"I Wanna Be with You," Isley Brothers (Bovina).
"I Want You to Want Me" R. Nielson (Screen Gems-EMI/Adult).
"I Want Your Love" B. Edwards, N. Rodgers (Chic/Cotillion).
"I Was Made for Dancing" M. Lloyd (Michael's/Scott Tone).
"I Was Made for Lovin' You" P. Stanley, V. Poncia, D. Child (Kiss/Mad Vincent).
"I Will Survive" D. Fekaris, F. Perren (Perren Vibes).
"In the Navy" J. Morali, H. Belodo, V. Willis (Can't Stop).
"Is She Really Going Out with Him" J. Jackson (Albion).
"Jane," D. Freiberg, J. McPherson, C. Chaquico, P. Kantner (Pods/Lunatunes/Little Dragon—BMI).
"Just When I Needed You Most" R. Vanwarmer (4th Floor).

"Knock on Wood" E. Floyd, S. Cropper (East Memphis).
"Lady" G. Goble (Screen Gems-EMI).
"Ladies Night," E. Deodata (Delightful/Gang—BMI).
"Lead Me On" A. Willis, D. Lasley (Almo).
"Le Freak" N. Rodgers, B. Edwards (Chic).
"Let's Go" R. Ocasek (Lido).
"Livin' It Up (Friday Night)" L. Bell (Mighty Three).
"Lonesome Loser" D. Briggs (Screen Gems-EMI).
"Lotta Love" N. Young (Silver Fiddle).
"Love Ballad" Scarborough (Unichappell).
"Love Don't Live Here Anymore" N. Whitfield (Maytwelfth/Warner-Tamerlane).
"Love Is the Answer" T. Rundgren (Earmark/Fiction).
"Love Takes Time" M. Mason, L. Hopper (Orleansongs).
"Love You Inside Out" B. Gibb, M. Gibb, R. Gibb (Stigwood/Unichappell).
"MacArthur Park" J. Webb (Canopy).
"Makin' It" F. Perren, D. Fekaris (Perren Vibes).
"Mama Can't Buy You Love" L. Bell, C. James (Mighty Three).
"Minute by Minute" M. McDonald, L. Agrams (Snug/Loresta).
"Music Box Dancer" F. Mills (Unichappell).
"My Life" B. Joel (Impulsive/April).
"My Sharona" D. Fieger, B. Averre (Eighties/Small Hill).
"New York Groove" R. Ballard (Island).
"No Tell Lover" L. Loughnane, D. Seraphine, P. Cetera (Com/Street Sense/Polish Prince).
"Ooh Baby Baby" W. Robinson, W. Moore (Jobete).
"Our Love (Don't Throw It Away)" B. Gibb, B. Weaver (Stigwood/Unichappell).

"Precious Love" B. Welch (Glenwood/ Cigar).
"Promises" R. Feldman, R. Linn (Narwhal).
"Reunited" D. Fekaris, F. Perren (Perren Vibes).
"Ring My Bell" F. Knight (Two-Knight).
"Rock 'n' Roll Fantasy" P. Rodgers (Badco).
"Rock with You," Jones (Almo/ Rondor—ASCAP).
"Sad Eyes" R. John (Careers).
"Send One Your Love," S. Wonder (Jobete/Black Bull—ASCAP).
"September" M. White, A. McKay, A. Willis (Songfire).
"Shadows in the Moonlight" R. Burke, C. Black (Chappell/Trichappell).
"Shake It" T. Boylan (Steamed Clam).
"Shake Your Body (Down to the Ground)" R. Jackson, M. Jackson (Peacock).
"Shake Your Groove Thing" F. Perren (Perren Vibes).
"Sharing the Night Together" E. Struzick, A. Aldridge (Music Mill/ Al Cartee).
"She Believes in Me" A. Gibb (Angel Wing).
"Shine a Little Love" J. Lynn (Jet).
"Somewhere in the Night" W. Jennings, R. Kerr (Irving).
"Soul Man" D. Porter, I. Hayes (Walden/Birdees).
"Strange Way" R. Roberts (Stephen Stills).
"Stumblin' In" M. Chapman, N. Chinn (Chinnichap).
"Sultans of Swing" M. Knopfleur (Almo).
"Sweet Life" Davis, Collins (Tanta/ Chappell/Web IV).
"Take the Long Way Home," P. Henderson and group (Almo/Delicate—ASCAP).

"Take Me Home" M. Allen, B. Esty (Rick's).
"The Devil's Went Down to Georgia" C. Daniels, F. Edwards, J. Marshall, C. Hayward, D. Gregario (Hat Band).
"The Gambler" D. Schlitz (Writers Night).
"The Logical Song" R. Davies, R. Hodgson (Almo/Delicate).
"The Main Event/Fight" P. Jabara, B. Roberts, B. Esty (Primus Artists/ Diana/Rick's).
"Time Passages" A. Stewart, P. White (DJM/Frabjous).
"Too Much Heaven" B. Gibb, M. Gibb (Music for Unicef).
"Tragedy" Bee Gees, K. Richardson, A. Galuten (Stigwood).
"We Are Family" N. Rodgers, B. Edwards (Chic).
"We Don't Talk Anymore," B. Welch (ATV—BMI).
"We've Got Tonight" B. Seger (Gear).
"What a Fool Believes" M. McDonald, K. Loggins (Snug/Milk Money).
"What You Won't Do for Love" B. Caldwell, Kettner (Sherlyn/ Lindseyanne).
"When You're in Love with a Beautiful Woman" E. Stevens (DebDave).
"Y.M.C.A." J. Morali, H. Belodo, V. Willis (Green Light).
"You Can't Change That" Ray Parker, Jr. (Raydiola).
"You Don't Bring Me Flowers" N. Diamond, A. Bergman, B. Bergman (Stonebridge/Threesome).
"You're Only Lonely," J. D. Souther (Ice Age—ASCAP).
"You Take My Breath Away" S. Lawrence, B. Hart (Laughing Willow).

DIRECTORY OF CONTEMPORARY MUSIC PUBLISHERS

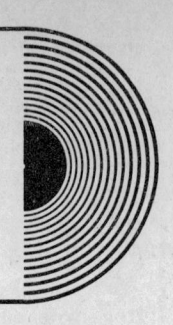

Adult Music, c/o Ken Adamany, 520 University Avenue, Madison, WI 53703.

Albion Music, c/o John Telfer, 147 Oxford Street, London W1 England. 01-734-9072.

Almo/Irving/Rondor Music Corp., 1352 North LaBrea, Hollywood, CA 90028. 213-469-2411.

Angel Wing Music, c/o James E. Cason, 2804 Azalea Place, Nashville, TN 37204.

April/Blackwood Music, 1350 Avenue of the Americas, New York, NY 10019. 212-975-4886. **Los Angeles office:** 1930 Century Park West, Los Angeles, CA 90067. 213-556-4790. **Nashville office:** 31 Music Square West, Nashville, TN 37203. 615-329-2374.

Arista Music Publishing Group, 6 West 57 Street, New York, NY 10019. 212-489-7400. **Los Angeles office:** 1888 Century Park East, Suite 1510, Los Angeles, CA 90067. 213-553-1777.

Badco Music Inc., c/o Swan Song Management, 444 Madison Avenue, New York, NY 10022. 212-752-1330.

Begonia-Unichappell Music, c/o Chappell Music, 810 Seventh Avenue, New York, NY 10019. 212-399-7100.

Bertram Music, c/o William Robinson, 6255 Sunset Boulevard, Hollywood, CA 90028.

Birdees Music Corp., c/o Cream Music, 8025 Melrose Avenue, Los Angeles, CA 90046. 213-655-0944.

Black Bull, c/o J. Vigoda, 1780 Broadway, Room 1001, New York, NY 10019. 212-586-7120.

Bovina Music, c/o Kelly Isley, 1650 Broadway, New York, NY 10019. 212-582-5432.

Braintree Music, c/o Segel & Goldman, 9200 Sunset Boulevard, Hollywood, CA 90069. 213-466-6428.

Bugle Music, c/o Chappell Music, 810 Seventh Avenue, New York, NY 10019. 212-399-7100.

Butterfly-Gong Music, c/o Eric Kronfield, 1501 Broadway, New York, NY 10036. 212-840-2200.

Canal Publishing Inc., 6325 Guilford, Indianapolis, IN 40220. 317-255-3116.

Canopy Music, c/o Bruce Grakal, 9777 Wilshire Boulevard, Suite 1018, Beverly Hills, CA 90212. 213-278-0066.

Can't Stop Music, 65 East 55 Street, Suite 302, New York, NY 10022. 212-751-6177.

Career Music, 6 West 57 Street, New York, NY 10019. 212-489-7400. **Los Angeles office:** 1888 Century Park East, Suite 1510, Los Angeles, CA 90067. 213-553-1777.

Al Cartee Music Inc., 1108 Avalon Avenue, Muscle Shoals, AL 35660. 205-381-5100.

Chappell Music, 810 Seventh Avenue, New York, NY 10019. 212-399-7100. **Los Angeles office:** 6255 Sunset Boulevard, Los Angeles, CA 90028.

DIRECTORY OF MUSIC PUBLISHERS 443

213-269-5141. **Nashville office:** 10 Music Square South, Nashville, TN 37203. 615-288-3382.

Chic, c/o Cotillion Music, 75 Rockefeller Plaza, New York, NY 10019. 212-484-6000.

Chinnichap Music, 8919 Sunset Boulevard, Los Angeles, CA 90069. 213-657-8585.

Cigar Music, c/o Glenwood Music, P. O. Box 218, World Way Postal Center, Los Angeles, CA 90080. 213-462-6251.

Com Music, c/o Green & Reynolds, 1900 Avenue of the Stars, Suite 1424, Los Angeles, CA 90067. 213-553-5434.

Cotaba Music, c/o David Foster, P. O. Box 2907, Van Nuys, CA 91404. 213-273-4660.

Cotillion Music Inc., 75 Rockefeller Plaza, New York, NY 10019. 212-484-6000. **Los Angeles office:** c/o Warner-Tamerlane Music, 9200 Sunset Boulevard, Suite 222, Los Angeles, CA 90069. 213-273-3323.

Cotton Pickin' Songs, 6255 Sunset Boulevard, Suite 1019, Los Angeles, CA 90028. 213-467-2181.

Countless Songs Ltd. c/o Ivan Mogull Music Corp., 4 East 49 Street, New York, NY 10017. 212-355-5636.

DebDave Music Inc., P. O. Box 2154, Donelson, TN 37214. 615-320-7227.

Deertrack Music, c/o Mitchell, Silberberg & Knupp, 1800 Century Park East, Los Angeles, CA 90067. 213-553-5000.

Delicate Music, c/o Rondor Music Inc., 1416 North LaBrea, Hollywood, CA 90028. 213-464-7581.

Diana Music Co., c/o Hect & Co., 1501 Broadway, New York, NY 10036. 212-391-4900.

Earborne Music, c/o Rick's Music, 8255 Sunset Boulevard, Los Angeles, CA 90046. 213-650-8300.

Earmark Music, c/o 4th Floor Music, 75 East 55 Street, New York, NY 10022. 212-751-9560.

East/Memphis Music Corp., c/o Cream Music Publishing Group, 8025 Melrose Avenue, Los Angeles, CA 90046. 213-655-0944.

Easy Money Music, c/o Rickie Lee Jones, 6404 Hollywood Boulevard, Suite 209, Los Angeles, CA 90028. 213-466-4211.

Edition Intro, 8000 Munchen, 81 Arabellhause 5/139 West Germany. 89-923-22700.

Eighties Music, c/o Upstate Management, 6671 Sunset Boulevard, Beverly Hills, CA 90028. 213-652-7011.

The Entertainment Company Music Group, 40 West 57 Street, New York, NY 10019. 212-265-2600. **Los Angeles office:** 6430 Sunset Boulevard, Los Angeles, CA 90028. 213-466-6127.

Evansongs, c/o Prager-Phantom Records, 1790 Broadway, Penthouse, New York, NY 10019. 212-765-8450.

Famous Music, 1 Gulf & Western Plaza, New York, NY 10023. 212-333-3433. **Los Angeles office:** 6430 Sunset Boulevard, Los Angeles, CA 90028. 213-461-3091. **Nashville office:** 2 Music Circle South, Nashville, TN 37203. 615-242-3531.

John Farrar Music, c/o Irving Music, 1352 North LaBrea, Hollywood, CA 90028. 213-469-2411.

Fiction Music, c/o 4th Floor Music, 75 East 55 Street, New York, NY 10022. 212-751-9560.

Finchley Music, c/o Arrow, Silverman & Parcher, 1370 Avenue of the Americas, New York, NY 10019. 212-586-1451.

Foster Frees Music, c/o Ned Shankman, 1888 Century Park East, Los Angeles, CA 90067. 213-553-6006.

4th Floor Music, 75 East 55 Street, Suite 505, New York, NY 10022. 212-751-9560.

Frabjous Music, c/o Kinetic Productions, 2059 Laurel Canyon Boulevard, Los Angeles, CA 90046. 213-654-6744.

Ganga Music, c/o Hardee, Barovick, Konecky & Braun, 9655 Wilshire

Boulevard, Suite 300, Beverly Hills, CA 90212. 213-278-2752.

Gear Music, c/o Punch Andrews, 567 Purdy, Birmingham, MI 48009. 313-642-0910.

Glenwood Music Corp., c/o Screen Gems-EMI, 1370 Avenue of the Americas, New York, NY 10019. 212-489-6740. **Los Angeles office:** P. O. Box 218, World Way Postal Center, Los Angeles, CA 90080. 213-462-6251.

G.Q. Music, c/o Tony Lopez, 1860 Grand Concourse, Bronx, NY 10457. 212-299-2500.

Green Light Music, 65 East 55 Street, New York, NY 10022. 212-751-6177.

Harrick Music, Inc., P. O. Box 1780, Miami, FL 33011. 305-888-1685.

Hat Band Music, 210 Twenty-fifth Avenue, Nashville, TN 37203. 615-327-1711.

Hobby Horse Music, 6255 Sunset Boulevard, Suite 1019, Los Angeles, CA 90028. 213-467-2181.

Hudmar Music, 24157 Lupin Hill Road, Hidden Hills, CA. 213-462-6011.

Impulsive Music, c/o Home Run Productions, 14 East 60 Street, New York, NY 10022. 212-753-9450.

Interworld Music Group, 25 West 56 Street, New York, NY 10019. 212-582-8810. **Los Angeles office:** 6255 Sunset Boulevard, Los Angeles, CA 90028. 213-467-5108.

Island Music Ltd. 7720 Sunset Boulevard, Los Angeles, CA 90046. 213-851-1466.

Jacon Music, c/o Jack Conrad, 2958 North Beachwood Drive, Los Angeles, CA 90068.

Dick James Music, 119 West 57 Street, New York, NY 10019. 212-581-3420. **Los Angeles office:** 6430 Sunset Boulevard, Los Angeles, CA 90028. 213-461-2881.

Jemava Music, c/o Beldock, Levine & Hoffman, 565 Fifth Avenue, Suite 600, New York, NY 10019. 212-758-2122.

Jet Music, 2049 Century Park East, Los Angeles, CA 900267. 213-553-6801. **London office:** 102-104 Glouchester, London W1H 3PH England. 01-486-6040.

Jobete Music, 6255 Sunset Boulevard, Los Angeles, CA 90028. 213-468-3500. **New York office:** 157 West 57 Street, New York, NY 10019. 212-581-7420.

Don Kirshner Music, 1370 Avenue of the Americas, New York, NY 10019. 212-489-0440. **Los Angeles office:** 9000 Sunset Boulevard, Hollywood, CA 90069. 213-278-4160.

Kiss Songs, c/o Aucoin Management, 645 Madison Avenue, New York, NY 10022. 212-826-8800.

Laughing Willow Music, c/o Arnold Liebman, 159 West 53 Street, New York, NY 10019. 212-765-3620.

Lido Music, P. O. Box 107, Carlisle, MA 01741. 617-369-6182.

Lindseyanne Co. Inc., 495 SE 10 Court, Hialeah, FL 33010. 305-888-1685.

Loresta Music, c/o Jeff Graubat, Chocolate Building, 900 North Point, Fourth Floor, San Francisco, CA 94100. 408-255-0345.

The Lowery Group, P. O. Box 9687, Atlanta, GA 30319. 404-233-6703.

Low-Sal Music Inc., 1224 Fernwood Circle, Atlanta, GA 30319. 404-233-6703.

Lunatunes, c/o Mietus Copyright, 527 Madison Avenue, Suite 317, New York, NY 10022. 212–371–7950.

MCA Music, 445 Park Avenue, New York, NY 10022. 212-759-7500. **Los Angeles office:** 100 Universal City Plaza, Universal City, CA 91608. 213-769-3565. **Nashville office:** 6 Music Circle North, Nashville, TN 37203. 615-327-4622.

Mad Vincent Music, c/o Satin, Tennenbaum, Eichler & Zimmerman, 9454 Wilshire Boulevard, Beverly Hills, CA 90212. 213-586-6015.

Maytwelfth Music, c/o Warner Bros. Music, 9200 Sunset Boulevard, Hollywood, CA 90069. 213-273-3323.

DIRECTORY OF MUSIC PUBLISHERS 445

Michael's Music, c/o Michael Lloyd, 405 North Camden Drive, Beverly Hills, CA 90212. 213-846-9090.

Midsong Music International Ltd., 1650 Broadway, New York, NY 10019. 212-541-5100.

Mighty Three Music, 309 South Broad Street, Philadelphia, PA 19107. 215-546-3510. **Seattle office:** 117 South Main, Suite 200, Seattle, WA 98104. 206-682-5278.

Milk Money Music, c/o Segel & Goldman, 9200 Sunset Boulevard, Los Angeles, CA 90069. 213-278-9200.

Mills & Mills, c/o Sight and Sound Management, 119 West 57 Street, New York, NY 10019. 212-541-5581.

Monster Island Music Publishing, c/o Peter C. Leeds, 485 Madison Avenue, New York, NY 10022. 212-688-9800.

MPL Communications, c/o Eastman & Eastman, 39 West 54 Street, New York, NY 10019. 212-581-1330.

Music for Unicef, c/o RSO Music, 1775 Broadway, New York, NY 10019. 212-975-0700. **Los Angeles office:** 8335 Sunset Boulevard, Hollywood, CA 90069. 213-650-1234.

Music Mill, P. O. Box 2413, Muscle Shoals, AL 35660. 205-381-5100.

Narwhal Music, 12839 League Street, Los Angeles, CA 91605. 213-765-2996.

Ninth Music, c/o Gelfan, Breslauer & MacNow, 431 South Palm Canyon Drive, Palm Springs, CA 92262. 714-325-5095.

Nite-Stalk Music, c/o Bill Gaff, 1245 North Doheny Drive, Los Angeles, CA 90069. 213-550-8798.

Orleansongs, c/o Infinity Music, 485 Madison Avenue, New York, NY 10022. 212-888-9700.

Peacock Music, c/o Richard Arons, 6255 Sunset Boulevard, Los Angeles, CA 90028. 213-466-7315.

Peer-Southern Organization, 1740 Broadway, New York, NY 10019. 212-265-3910. **Los Angeles office:** 6922 Hollywood Boulevard, Los Angeles, CA 90028. 213-469-1667.

Nashville office: 7 Music Circle North, Nashville, TN 37203. 615-244-6200.

Perren Vibes, c/o The Mom & Pops Co. Store, 4028 Colfax, Studio City, CA 91604. 213-877-2797.

Peso Music, 6255 Sunset Boulevard, Suite 1019, Los Angeles, CA 90028. 213-467-2181.

Pirooting Music, c/o Segel & Goldman, 9200 Sunset Boulevard, Los Angeles, CA 90069. 213-278-9200.

Polish Prince Music, c/o Greene & Reynolds, 1900 Avenue of the Stars, Los Angeles, CA 90067. 213-553-5434.

Primus Artists, 4000 Warner Boulevard, Burbank, CA 91522. 213-843-6000.

Rare Blue Music, 9255 Sunset Boulevard, Los Angeles, CA 90069. 213-550-0171.

Raydiola Music, c/o Cavallo-Ruffalo Management, 9885 Charleville Boulevard, Beverly Hills, CA 90212. 213-277-8137.

Revelation Music, 8000 Munchen 81, Arabellhause 5/139 Germany. 89-923-22700.

Rick's Music, 8255 Sunset Boulevard, Los Angeles, CA 90046. 213-650-8300.

Riva Music, c/o Gaff Management, 1245 North Doheny Drive, Los Angeles, CA 90069. 213-550-8798.

A. Schroeder International Ltd., 25 West 56 Street, New York, NY 10019. 212-582-8810.

Screen Gems-EMI Music Inc., 1370 Avenue of the Americas, New York, NY 10019. 212-489-6740. **Los Angeles office:** 6255 Sunset Boulevard, Los Angeles, CA 90028. 213-469-8371. **Nashville office:** 1207 Sixteenth Avenue South, Nashville, TN 37212. 615-320-7700.

Sherlyn Publishing Co., 495 SE 10 Court, Hialeah, FL 33010. 305-888-1685. **New York office:** 65 East 55 Street, New York, NY 10022. 212-752-0160.

Silver Fiddle Music, c/o Segel & Goldman, 9200 Sunset Boulevard,

Suite 525, Los Angeles, CA 90069. 213-278-9200.

Six Continents Music, c/o Interworld Music, 6255 Sunset Boulevard, Suite 709, Los Angeles, CA 90028. 213-467-5108.

Small Hill Music, c/o Upstate Management, 6671 Sunset Boulevard, Los Angeles, CA 90028. 213-652-7011.

Snow Music, c/o Greene & Reynolds, 1900 Avenue of the Stars, Los Angeles, CA 90067. 213-553-5434.

Snug Music, c/o Bruce Cohen Music, P. O. Box 878, Sohoma, CA 95476. 707-938-4060.

Songfire Music, c/o Cavallo-Ruffalo Management, 9885 Charleville Boulevard, Beverly Hills, CA 90212. 213-277-8137.

Special Rider Music, P. O. Box 860, Cooper Station, New York, NY 10003. 212-473-5900.

Bruce Springsteen Music, c/o Michael Tannen, 36 East 61 Street, New York, NY 10021. 212-752-2276.

Starrin Music, c/o Rick's Music, 8255 Sunset Boulevard, Los Angeles, CA 90046. 213-650-8300.

Steamed Clam Music, c/o Terrance Boylan, 80 Irving Place, New York, NY 10003.

Robert Stigwood Music, c/o Chappell Music, 810 Seventh Avenue, New York, NY 10019. 212-399-7100.

Stephen Stills Music, 5032 Lankersham Boulevard, North Hollywood, CA 91601. 213-766-7142.

Stonebridge Music, c/o Bicycle Music Co., 8756 Holloway Drive, Los Angeles, CA 90067. 213-659-6361.

Street Sense Music, c/o Greene & Reynolds, 1900 Avenue of the Stars, Los Angeles, CA 90067. 213-553-5434.

Sweet Summer Night Music, c/o Rick's Music, 8255 Sunset Boulevard, Los Angeles, CA 90046. 213-650-8300.

Tanta Music, c/o Susan Collins, 201 West 89 Street, New York, NY 10024.

Tarantula Music, c/o Segel & Goldman, 9200 Sunset Boulevard, Suite 1000, Los Angeles, CA 90069. 213-278-9200.

Threesome Music, 1801 Avenue of the Stars, Suite 911, Los Angeles, CA 90067.

Tri-Chappell—see Chappell Music

Scott Tone Music, c/o Herb Wasserman, 80 Van Cortland Park, Bronx, NY 10463. 212-796-2002.

Two-Knight Music, c/o Fred Knight, P. O. Box 874, Bessemer, AL 35020. 205-424-3756.

Unichappell—see Chappell Music.

United Artists Music, 6920 Sunset Boulevard, Hollywood, CA 90069. 213-461-9141. **New York office:** 727 Seventh Avenue, New York, NY 10019. 212-575-3000. **Nashville office:** 1013 Sixteenth Avenue Sought, Nashville, TN 37212. 615-255-1161.

Walden Music, c/o Atlantic Records Music Publishing, 75 Rockefeller Plaza, New York, NY 10019. 212-484-6000.

Warner Bros. Music, 9200 Sunset Boulevard, Los Angeles, CA 90069. 213-273-3323. **New York office:** 75 Rockefeller Plaza, New York, NY 10019. 212-484-8000. **Nashville office:** 16 Avenue South, Nashville, TN 615-255-5693.

Warner-Tamerlane Publishing Group— see Warner Bros. Music.

Web IV Music Inc., 2107 Faulkner Road NE, Atlanta, GA 30324. 404-325-9810.

Woolnough Music, 1550 Neptune, Leucadia, CA 92024. 213-752-6688.

Writers Night Music, c/o Paul Craft, P. O. Box 22635, Madison, TN 37202. 615-383-8318.

X-Ray Music, c/o Maynard L. Kennedy, 2711 Bowmont Drive, Beverly Hills, CA 90210. 213-275-3269.

ORGANIZATIONS FOR PERFORMING AND RECORDING RIGHTS

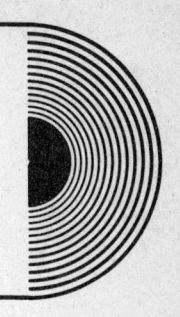

PERFORMING RIGHTS

ASCAP (American Society of Composers, Authors & Publishers), One Lincoln Plaza, New York, NY 10023. 212-595-3050.

BMI (Broadcast Music Inc.), 320 West 57 Street, New York, NY 10019. 212-586-2000.

SESAC Inc., 10 Columbus Circle, New York, NY 10019. 212-586-3450.

RECORDING RIGHTS

AMRA (American Mechanical Rights Association), 250 West 57 Street, New York, NY 10019. 212-246-4077.

Copyright Service Bureau Ltd., 221 West 57 Street, New York, NY 10019. 212-582-5030.

Harry Fox Agency Inc., 110 East 59 Street, New York, NY 10022. 212-751-1930.

SESAC Inc., 10 Columbia Circle, New York, NY 10019. 212-586-3450.

GETTING STARTED

HOW TO GET YOUR SONG PUBLISHED

1

It isn't easy to get a new song published today, but then it never was. It isn't impossible either. Thousands of new works are being published every year by thousands of publishers. ASCAP alone has more than 5,000 publisher members —large, medium, and small—spread across the country. While the biggest publishing firms are clustered in such music centers as New York, Nashville, and Los Angeles, there are others in smaller cities and you can find them by checking the classified pages of your local phone book. An incomplete but quite useful listing of most of the energetic publishing firms appears each September in *Billboard*'s annual Buyer's Guide. *Cash Box* and *Record World* also publish such lists.

2

Finding the address of a publisher may be less difficult than determining which one might be best for your song. There might be a first-class publishing firm in the Texas city in which you live, but, if your song is a rock work and that company specializes in gospel, it might not be the best for you. There are major publishing houses that are strong and active in many types of music, but also quite a few firms that are really successful only in two or three kinds of songs. If you'll read the music trade weeklies—and that's a must if you don't want to waste time and effort—you can figure out which firms do what best.

3

Before going on to how to present your song after you've made your choices—and you must realistically assume that the first one may not immediately sign up your "baby"—let's be clear about what a music publisher does. Some songwriters still think that a publisher's main job is to print up sheet music of your work. That hasn't been true for at least a quarter of a century, and today sheet music is rarely printed until after there's been a successful record to generate demand for it. The main job of a music publisher is to get your song to the right record company or to the manager of the right recording artist. That can lead to an album cut or even a hit single, and substantial income from record sales and from licensing the performing rights.

4

If the songwriter isn't also the performer, the record income may well be less than that generated by the performing rights. That's because the old U.S. Copyright Act of 1909 limited the fee that a record company had to pay to the owner of a copyrighted song to a ridiculous 2 cents single sold. The same applied to album cuts. Congress has since passed and President Ford signed into law in October 1976 the new Copyright Law of 1976 (effective January 1, 1978) which raised that to 2¾ cents or ½ of 1 cent per minute of playing time or fraction thereof, whichever amount is larger. As for performing rights income, in 1978 ASCAP alone collected for its members from almost 40,000 U.S. licensees and many foreign "users"—via sister licensing societies abroad—$119,000,000. Add to that the estimated* total of roughly $80,000,000 ASCAP's two smaller competitors, BMI and SESAC, collected and you'll see that performing rights income is significant. By the way, writers and publishers—at least all those in ASCAP—split equally the income from performing rights, and the general usage is that the same split applies to record sales. While many music licensing organizations in other countries collect for both disk sales and performances, in the U.S. ASCAP and BMI collect only for licensing performances and the copyright owner makes other arrangements for record and sheet music income.

5

Returning to what a publisher is supposed to do, the energetic and responsible music publisher won't stop after the first record of your song. For one thing, that record can be a flop. Even if it is a hit, the publisher should try for more records by other artists—now and later. Long after a song's initial success, a new artist with new style and interpretation can come along and make a new hit single. Some of the cases that come to mind immediately are the Barbra Streisand version of "Happy Days Are Here Again," the Esther Phillips disco smash of "What A Diff'rence A Day Made," and the Captain and Tennille edition of "Shop Around." It is up to the publisher to work the catalogue, and the writer isn't being pushy if he or she checks every year or so on what's being done with his/her earlier songs. A good song can have a long and profitable life, if it gets the right attention.

6

Now how do you present your song to that publisher whom you have so carefully chosen? First, you make a clear audible tape on a decent tape machine—not a

*Precise figures not available.

$19 model. It doesn't have to be a $2,000 machine either, but one good enough so that the listener will get an exact picture of both the music and the lyric. A single guitar or piano will do or you could offer it with a small group, but you don't need an elaborately and expensively produced demo. You should cut it in a place with reasonable acoustics, but that doesn't necessarily mean a studio. What you want is a tape that will give the potential buyer a precise idea of what you're selling, and, if your voice is as terrible as mine, you'd probably want a friend or relative who sings better to do it for you. Again, you don't need a great voice—just one that isn't rotten. If and when the publisher accepts the song, the publisher may very well make a better/costlier/more professional demo tape to send or play for the record company or artist.

7

Many publishing firms suggest that you put no more than three or four songs on one tape, with 12 or 15 inches of silent leader up front and between each song. Almost all publishers prefer reel-to-reel tape, but some listen to cassettes too. All want you to provide the typed-up lyrics for each song on a separate sheet of paper—three songs, three pages. If you write music, you can also send along "lead sheets," but not all of the people working at publishing firms today read music. They listen well.

8

How do you get them to listen?
You find out the name or names of the professional manager or assistant professional managers at that publisher by reading the music trade weeklies or by phoning, and you write that person a letter asking for an appointment. Some won't answer and some will answer negatively—the first time. At a 1976 National Academy of Recording Arts and Sciences (NARAS) Institute symposium that I chaired, the professional manager of one of America's most successful publishers said that he rarely brushed off anyone who had the brains and initiative to find his name and address. You write asking for a chance to play your tape, or to play your songs live. The letter should say that you'll be phoning in six or eight days for an appointment. Call when you say you'll call, and, if your call isn't productive, write or phone again two weeks later and then a month after that. Persist, firmly, but politely.

9

Just because the head office of the publisher is in Hollywood and you're in Philadelphia doesn't mean that you have to pitch your songs to someone in the California office. The firm may well have an office with a qualified professional manager or two in New York, a much less expensive trip. Wherever you go, don't get indignant if you don't get to play your tape for the president of the company. That's silly. Generally some middle-level person—who may be twenty-six or fifty-six—will listen, and these folks are usually honest and rarely rude. Some publishers may answer your letters or calls by suggesting that you drop off the tape, explaining that they're too busy to see you now, but will listen later. Some of them will actually listen later, but some won't and you'll just get your tape back in the stamped, self-addressed, sturdy envelope or mailer they expect you to leave with the tape.

10

Dropping off the tape isn't nearly as good an idea, so you should try—politely—to persuade the man or woman to see you and let you play it. When you arrive for the appointment, it is not necessary to recount the story of your life or give a long and passionate pitch on why this song is a sure hit. You can certainly express confidence in your work, but the drill is to get to playing the tape within three or four minutes after you arrive. Your songs—not you—are what may charm the publisher. Yes, you can bring two tapes with three or four songs in each, but keep in mind that it is probably best to have all the songs on any one tape of the same general kind—all blues or all rock or all country or all ballads or all soul. Mixing them up might just possibly confuse a publisher who doesn't know anything about you and is trying to get a definite first impression of a stranger.

11

It often makes a publisher uneasy to meet a new writer who confidently announces that "I can write anything," and there are two good reasons for this. First, very few people can write all kinds of songs. Second, almost nobody can write everything well.

12

Even if this publisher doesn't accept any of this first batch of songs, you can ask for an appointment in six or eight weeks to bring in some others. In the intervening weeks, repeat this process and offer the first batch elsewhere—to the second and third firms on your list. Success on the first try is extremely rare, so don't be discouraged or angry. Raging around to your friends that "all these publishers are jerks" is both dumb and unprofessional, and a professional songwriter is what you want to be. What's more, not too many of the professional people at music publishing firms are jerks. Most are quite capable, a few brilliant. None of them is perfect, and they'll all admit that their firms—at one time or another—misjudged and turned down a fine song or writer.

13

The great majority are honest. There's a very, very small chance that anyone might try to rip off your song. What happens much more often is that some amateur songwriter believes—usually erroneously—that a work later published was stolen from his, and a number of lawsuits follow. That's why so many publishers return unopened all envelopes containing unsolicited songs/tapes sent in by strangers. Writing ahead and phoning ahead gives them some clue that you're sensible, responsible, and at least semiprofessional.

14

The discussion of rip-offs inevitably leads to the question of when to copyright. Several fine publishers have told me that they don't bother to copyright a song until a definite recording commitment has been secured. They handle many songs and don't want too many unnecessary ten-dollar copyright fees. Obviously copyrighting is the safest thing to do, but there are a number of songwriters who don't copyright before sending a song to a publisher. If you do elect to copyright, you can get half a dozen copies of the required Form PA—with instructions— free by simply sending a postcard to the U.S. Copyright Office at the Library of Congress in Washington, D.C.

15

Do connections help? They might—certainly in terms of getting that first listening meeting. If your friend has a relative who works at Publisher A or has had songs published by B, the introduction could be useful. On the other hand, think twice if A or B isn't doing a solid job in the area of music for which you're writing. Even though getting a song published isn't easy—for while there are so many more publishing firms now, there are also so many more aspiring songwriters—merely getting it published doesn't assure success. You've got to find a publisher who believes in the song, has as much practical savvy as energy and enthusiasm, and knows the realities and personalities of the current music world. The right publisher—and these come in all sizes—will work hard for the song because the publisher gets half of the income it generates. You're partners.

16

Take your partner seriously, for the publisher may know things and people you don't. There's at least one matter you'll have to decide for yourself, and that's the choice of which performing rights organization you want to license your music. A publisher may have two separate firms, one in ASCAP and the other with BMI or SESAC. The publisher may recommend that you affiliate with one or the other, but you need not assent immediately. Ask why this one or that one is recommended, think about it, and then talk to some friends in the business. Then you—on your own—should write or phone at least two of the three to discuss what it considers are its strengths and advantages, how it pays royalties to writers, whether writers have any say in electing its board or serve on it, who its prominent members are, whether an "advance" might be possible and under what circumstances etc. Think it over—quickly but carefully. The odds are very good that the publisher with two separate firms will go along with your choice.

17

Sometimes differences arise between the community of songwriters and the world of music publishers, and there's another organization that you might want to consider. The American Guild of Authors and Composers is an energetic songwriter group. It is not the most popular organization with all publishers, and quite a few reject the form contract it recommends. A lot don't. Whether you'd want to join is something only you can decide—after you take the trouble to get the facts, check with AGAC and its members and its critics. Another thing that you'll certainly want to do is read over your publisher's contract carefully—perhaps discuss it with a couple of people who know more than you (or I) do before signing. There's nothing discourteous in such behavior, if done in an adult and nonbelligerent manner. After all, nobody who's mature signs any contract or other legal/business document without studying and understanding exactly what it provides. That is simply common sense, no matter how eager you are to get published.

18

It would be a serious mistake if you viewed music publishers as adversaries, and equally unrealistic to see them as all-powerful father figures. Publishers and writers are partners with a common goal: maximum income from promoting the song. Reviewing the contract before you sign should not be a sign of distrust but rather a sound and routine business practice. Both parties have obligations to each other, and those of the writer don't stop with delivery of the tape or lead sheet. If the publisher offers comments or suggestions, the professional songwriter considers his partner's ideas seriously. Maybe that third line of lyrics could be clearer, or more romantic. The publisher can also expect the writer to cooperate in joint efforts to publicize and promote their song, and to deal with him with the same candor, honesty, and responsible behavior that the writer expects. Cooperation doesn't mean that the writer automatically lets the publisher revise his or her work, but it does mean that any criticism be evaluated as a possible step toward a better and more profitable song. If either the writer or publisher sees the joint effort as a battle between art and business, it's probably going to be a bummer.

19

What will almost surely be a bummer is any deal with a publisher who wants you to pay money to have your song published, or for lead sheets or demo records. In very, very few cases will the writer benefit. Unless you're willing to accept such "publication" as a sop to your ego, stay away from "vanity" outfits. Some—as any Better Business Bureau will tell you—are "song shark" rip-off operations that live on the dreams of sadly untalented amateurs. Publishers pay writers, not the other way around. ASCAP's policy—and perhaps that of the other two licensing operations—is not to accept such "vanity" publication as valid compliance with requirements for joining.

20

There are obviously many other questions that this brief introductory note has not treated. One is whether it is advantageous to affiliate with a publishing firm that's part of a conglomerate which also owns a record company, a movie studio, or radio or television stations. If you asked that of nine songwriters, you could easily get twelve different answers. Some people believe that dealing with a publisher with a conglomerate can get your song a better chance for album cuts, and other people don't. As for the single, there isn't much evidence that the connection helps very often. A number of the most effective and successful publishing houses are now part of a bigger entertainment combines, while other top firms are not. I'm certainly not an authority on this issue, but it's my hunch that you should concentrate on getting your song to a good and vigorous publisher interested in your kind of song—and don't try to be too cunning in calculating corporate affiliations.

21

The appetite of the public and the pressure on the publishers for good, new songs is greater than it has ever been, for the music explosion of the past quarter century is still sounding loud and clear around the world. Since they hear so many poor songs, almost all publishers are very eager to find and work the relatively few good ones. Maybe your first songs won't be quite good enough, but perhaps your twenty-first will be terrific. It could be your sixty-first too. The publishers are rooting for you, because they can't do well if America's writers don't create those good songs. I'm rooting for both of you, because I—and hundreds of millions around the world—just happen to love the unique and delightful thing that is a good song. As a young ASCAP writer said to me last year, "Thank God for the 3-minute art form."

WW

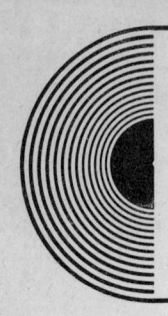

CHOOSING THE RIGHT ATTORNEY

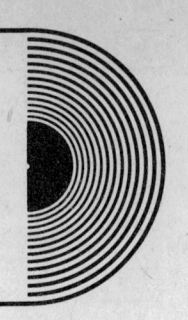

"Lawyers are a pain in the ass. They try to justify their bills by finding a zillion things wrong with a record contract." *

The above-cited quote is contained in a guide written for recording artists. Unfortunately, it is representative of how many artists view attorneys. I believe that the quality of these relationships would be greatly improved if artists applied the same amount of scrutiny to choosing an attorney as they do to the selection of a fellow band member or a manager.

Since most young artists simply do not know any attorneys on a personal basis, they often wind up choosing the lawyers who handled their family's house-closing or their friend's divorce. Although an artist may be well served by such an individual, it is really in his or her best interest to be represented by an attorney who has chosen the music field as a primary area of specialization.

Record contracts contain a number of clauses which can have a crucial effect on a performer's career. If an artist is not represented by someone who understands the nuances of these agreements, their success (not to mention their potential earnings) can be seriously compromised.

Another thing that an experienced music-business attorney can provide is clout. Clout with record executives to finalize a record deal. Clout with merchandise or endorsement people to deliver lucrative contracts. Clout with international record companies and music publishers in order to get the best possible deals for their clients. All of these things are really the function of a manager, but in reality many of them are ultimately accomplished by the attorney involved.

The best way to find the right lawyer for your needs is to solicit recommendations from your friends who are already in the music business. If you are a songwriter, ask other songwriters. If you are a producer, ask other producers. This will increase the likelihood that you will be dealing with an attorney who really understands the more subtle problems that can occur in your specific field.

Once you have identified a few attorneys who seem like good candidates, set up a meeting with them. (There should be no charge for this conference.) Don't be afraid to ask the attorneys some questions about their background, knowledge of the music business, or negotiating style.

---

*Earl Carter, *Guide for Future Recording Artists* (Los Angeles: Beaver Creek Publishers, 1967), p. 57.

Most young artists view legal fees as the biggest deterrent to hiring a good lawyer. This is something of a misnomer, since many attorneys are willing to accept clients who initially cannot afford to pay a regular retainer fee. In cases like this, the attorney will often agree to defer payment of fees until the artist is in a position to pay. Before entering into an arrangement of this type, be sure that the attorney agrees to give you the same priority in terms of time as any paying client would be entitled to receive. You should also ask for regular monthly bills, even though there is an understanding that they will not be paid immediately.

Another type of arrangement between attorney and artist is a "contingency" deal. This means that the lawyer will receive a small percentage of the artist's income from certain sources, if and when it is received. I don't think that this type of arrangement is as attractive to either party as the deferred payment situation which was previously described.

One mistake that many new artists make is to assume that their interests are adequately represented by the lawyer who was hired by their manager. Artists should not only be represented by their own counsel when negotiating a management contract, but they should continue to have their personal attorney review any contracts that the management company wishes to enter into on the artist's behalf.

The relationship between the artist and his or her attorney must be built on deep trust and respect. If this doesn't exist, it's time to find a new lawyer.

RED

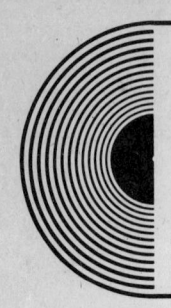

CHOOSING THE RIGHT PUBLICIST

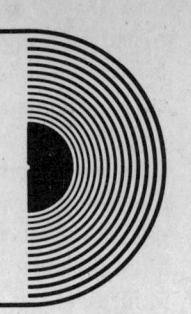

A music publicist's job is to set up, manipulate, and use the media to create, build, sell, and prolong the artist-client's career. This involves setting up press, radio, and TV interviews for the artist; organizing public appearances; spreading any news the artist wants the public to hear via press releases or phone calls; supervising all photo sessions; and devising a systematic plan for presenting the desired image of the artist to the public. Some publicists also become involved in designing album covers, posters, tour programs, as well as at least overseeing (if not running) the artist's official fan club.

In choosing which publicist to hire, the following questions should be considered:

1) What are my immediate needs from the media?
2) Which type of publicist can best fulfill these needs?
3) How much can I afford for PR? Who will pay for it?
4) Am I looking simply for media coverage, or do I also want image guidance and creative input?
5) Do I need a full-time publicist, or just one for the months I'm actively working?

Though all major record companies have in-house press departments, most moderately to highly successful artists choose to employ outside publicists to work with the record company for several reasons:

- Record company publicists are responsible for every act on the label, whether they personally like a particular act or not; outside publicists almost always work only for acts they personally want to work for and believe in.
- Record companies are only concerned with selling an act's current product; outside press reps are involved in every aspect of the artist's career, including touring and keeping interest high between records and tours.
- Record company "flacks" (slang for publicists) have many acts to work on at one time, and as a result they have limited time and energy for each artist; outside flacks work fewer artists at a time, and are able to give more time and attention to each client.

- Record label employees' jobs are for the label, and are not dependent upon the success of their work for any one artist; independents are hired by the act, and can be fired by the act if they don't deliver results to the client's satisfaction.
- Many decisions on game plans are largely determined by the label's corporate policy and budget limitations; personal publicists base their decisions on what they believe will best serve the client without much concern to the cost or traditional policies.
- Label press agents use their star clients in trade-off deals to get press on the unknown acts; independents almost never put any client in the position of being used to the advantage of another client.

The nonrecord company affiliated press agents fit into four categories:

Employees of Large PR Firms. There are several large PR companies centralized in the music industry. Most of these firms divide the workload among the staff based upon individual employee's personal taste and experience, and the particular needs of the client. The advantage in using a large PR firm is that it has clout with the media due to collective years of building important contacts, and offices in more than one area of the country so that artists can be sure they are covered wherever they go. The disadvantage is that these large companies don't get personally close to or familiar with the artist, and are thereby hampered in understanding the artist's image or the cause of the artist's popularity. Furthermore, these firms are quite expensive, with fees beginning at $800–1,000 per month and reaching as high as $2,500–3,000 per month.

Management Company In-house Publicists. These press reps are paid by the artist's personal manager to handle PR for all the company's clients and projects. The department usually consists of one publicist and one secretary-assistant. These flacks work closely with the label and the manager as a liaison between the artist and the media. The advantage in using these publicists is that their jobs depend on how much favorable publicity they get for the company's talent. The disadvantage is that they are easily tempted by the security and better money a record company offers, or the freedom of working free-lance. As a result, these flacks usually stay on the job for a short time before they leave the artist and the company to work with another publicist who has to start from scratch.

Free-lance, Independent, Self-employed Publicists. These publicists usually begin either at record companies or other PR firms, or as in-house publicists. Once they establish a reputation, however, they go out on their own. They can be hired for the months they are needed by artists and paid fees instead of salaries, either by the record company or the management company. Their fees range from $800–1,500 a month. They work either out of their homes, or they have their own small offices. The advantage in using a free-lance publicist is that they only accept clients they really believe in, and they only take on a few clients at a time. The disadvantage is that while their fees may be lower than those of a major PR firm, the independents charge back every expense from cabfares to long-distance telephone bills to the employer.

Personal, Private Publicists. These publicists work for one client at a time—usually twelve months a year for many years. They are more than just press agents. They are also secretaries, confidants, assistants, and advisors. They are hired by and paid by the artist, and are paid either a fee or salary, plus all expenses connected with their work. The advantage in using these publicists is that they are totally devoted to the artist and "on call" twenty-four hours a day, seven days a week, 52 weeks a year. The disadvantage is that they are often resented by other publicists (especially record company publicists) and the media as an obstacle to getting through to the artist.

There isn't an industry in the world that doesn't concern itself to some extent with public relations, and in the music business PR has become a major factor in building a performer's career.

LK

HOW DO YOU BECOME A RECORD PRODUCER

The biggest misconception most people have about record producers is that they are merely creative technicians—that their job consists entirely of recording, mixing, and editing tape until a finished master is achieved. That, in reality, is the *majority* of what any producer does for a living, but equally as important is the *minority* interest a producer has in his profession.

All successful producers have the following in common:

- They have the ability to pick hit songs and hit artists.
- They have a "feel" for the marketplace.
- They know how to present a potential new artist or song to a record company.
- They are generally familiar with standard operating procedures within the record business and specifically with production budgets and artist-producer deals.
- They know how to deal effectively with studio and record company personnel.

No professional producer, not even a staff producer on salary to a major record company, lives in a creative vacuum. Far from being a monothematic, exclusively musical personage, the successful producer of the '80s can best be characterized as a figment of his own multitrack recording environment. Here, for example, is how a producer's "tracks," if we can call them that, might look under spectrographic analysis:

Track A is the successful producer's ability to hear new, unrecorded music that has commercial possibilities. All producers, in addition to knowing how to conduct studio sessions, must have a marked aptitude for being talent scouts.

Track B, the ability to feel sympathetic pulsations from the marketplace, suggests that the successful producer must not only be business oriented but also sales oriented, since the producer must "sell" his concept of a new artist or sound to the record company. The successful record producer, therefore, must also be a gifted salesman.

Track C, the ability to present a potential new artist or song to a record company, means that the producer must be articulate, courteous, patient, and able to get along with other people in a variety of social circumstances. Henry Kissinger may play this gambit better, but all successful record producers must be clever, political strategists.

PRODUCER

Track A:
Talent scout

Track B:
Businessman and salesman

Track C:
Political strategist

Track D:
Quasi-lawyer and accountant

Track E:
Director of studio sessions

Track F:
Good team player

FIGURE 1.
Producers handle more today than just recording music.

Track D, which implies that a producer be well-versed in what are considered customary practices in the record industry, shifts the onus from being an isolated denizen of the recording studio to that of being an almost limited partner of the producer's lawyer, accountant, or perhaps business manager. By way of illustration, many of my friends tell me that I'm a better music business lawyer than their own high-priced attorneys. My profession, however, is record producer; what I've had to learn about contracts I've learned out of necessity and self-interest.

Tracks E and *F,* which encompass the producer's ability to record the artist in the studio and to deal effectively with studio and record company personnel, are the more technical end of the producer's multitrack talent spectrum. Recording technique, like dance, acting, or guitar technique, can readily—in fact speedily—be learned. But what also needs to be learned, if you want to be a successful record producer, are the elements covered in tracks A, B, C, and D.

This is why I suggested that the place to begin studying record production is not in the chapter devoted to getting a good sound, but here. Let it sink in that a successful record producer is more than a music man, more even than a talent scout: he's also part businessman, salesman, politician, counsellor, director of operations, attorney, and accountant. I haven't even covered some of the other functions undertaken or carefully monitored by the most successful producers, such as record promotion, public relations, manufacturing of records and tapes, and foreign licensing of product. What happens in the studio, although it occupies the majority of a producer's time, is but the tip of the iceberg. Today, record production is an all-encompassing creative as well as business vocation.

These preliminary "state-of-the-production business" remarks lead to some unavoidable conclusions. Nobody jumps into a career as a record producer without having tried something else first. Many producers, like myself, were originally artists; others were originally audio engineers, songwriters, personal managers, or A&R personnel. Regardless of the road you take, one of the keys to getting ahead in the production business is to get a job with an established, reputable company as early as possible. It can be a record or publishing company, a booking agency, a management office, or even a retail record store. But it's vitally important to be visible in some way to the industry, to see who's coming and going, and to learn the best and most inexpensive way possible—on the job.

The next conclusion may be the toughest pill of all to swallow. Although the majority of a producer's time is spent in the studio, it's what the producer does wearing his *minority*-interest hat (tracks A, B, C, and D) that has the greatest impact initially on being able to sign new artists and get production deals. Having an exclusive contract to produce a new artist, for example, means much more to a record company than whether the producer who has secured this contract from the artist is qualified to produce. Business comes before technique; one can always begin on the fringe of production and work up to the ultimate goal of creative control. If you become expert at tracks A, B, C, and D, you may never need to learn how to turn the tape recorder on. You may hire somebody to handle that mundane "chore," or you may get out of record production altogether and start your own record or personal management company.

Last but not least, the magic bullet for opening most doors in the music business is something highly impersonal. It's called either a hit song, a hit artist demo, or, less frequently, a hit master tape. The bottom line in this business isn't whether you went to Harvard, whether you wear clean or dirty underwear, or whether you're straight, gay, or somewhere in between. The bottom line, especially for record producers, is, "How good is this demo you brought to us?"

I don't wish to belabor this putting-the-cart-before-the-horse point any further. Let me summarize simply where I'd like each reader's focus to be at this particular juncture:

1. The term "record producer" is something of a misnomer in that it does not adequately describe the gamut of business as well as creative imperatives demanded by the job.

2. The best way to study record production generally is to plug yourself into a highly visible job within the music industry. Production technique can be studied specifically either by taking a course in record production or simply hanging out at recording studios (my production technique was developed using the latter method). Presently, however, there is no college-level program anywhere in the world that even remotely approximates what you will learn in time from working in the music business.

3. Leverage counts much more than knowledge of recording practices. Novice producers are encouraged to learn as much as they can about the utilization of recording equipment, but their primary emphasis should be on scouting talent and hopefully signing talent to exclusive production contracts. A legally enforceable contract, coupled with a crudely produced demo tape

of a potential hit song or artist, is worth many times what it will cost to produce a 24-track master tape recording of a bad song. As we say in the industry, "Who you know is more important than what you know."

4. *Less is best.* There is absolutely no need for beginning producers (especially those who haven't mastered Tracks A, B, C, and D) to think about producing expensive master tapes. A demo tape will do fine. If a postage stamp can do the job of a long-distance telephone call, use the postage stamp. Saving money, in short, makes a lot of sense, no matter how elevated your financial position may one day become.

Having established these general priorities, we're ready to define the different types of producers, their pecking order within the industry, and their cast of supporting players.

TYPES OF PRODUCERS

Producers are either staff producers, executive producers, or independent producers. *A staff producer* is a salaried employee of a record company. He takes direction from the record company's A&R (Artist and Repertoire) department, which periodically will assign him to listen to or work with new or established artists signed to the label. In addition to his regular salary, the parameters of which are presently $300 to $600 a week, most staff producers receive incentive production royalties of two percent of the retail list price of the records they produce, less standard packaging deductions. This is quite an improvement over the one percent staff-producer royalty that was customary a decade ago, and like day to night compared to what was customary two decades ago when staff producers only received a rather modest salary.

Executive producers are the heads of A&R, or executives functioning in primarily administrative capacities, at major record companies such as CBS, Warner Brothers, and Polydor Records. Unlike staff and independent producers, their purview is limited to what normally can be accomplished in an office. In the production business, this means that the executive producer directs the flow of "traffic"—i.e., demonstration tapes, talent scouting assignments, and actual production workloads—to the producers and A&R employees that he supervises. Executive producers are also in charge of approving production budgets, mediating disputes between artists, producers, and studio personnel, and developing the overall roster configuration for the label (e.g., how many rock, R&B [rhythm and blues], country, jazz, and classical artists the label should have). These jobs pay well—between the parameters of $50,000 to $100,000 a year, plus bonuses—but they are primarily paper-pushing jobs. The executive producer in the record business has, as his corollary, the executive producer of a motion picture or television series.

Independent producers are people who function pretty much on their own. They work for no one specific company, although they may have an agreement to make a certain number of records over a period of time for a given label. But for the most part, they're free to move from record company to record company, taking on the projects that are most interesting to them and most relevant to their particular style of production. Independent producers make their living through a combination of advances against royalties and independent production royalties. The parameters of independent production advances and royalties depend entirely on how "strong" the producer is, how much the record company desires his services, or the opposite side of that coin—how "hungry" the producer is to get his foot in the door at a particular label. Advances range from zero to $50,000 per album and higher; royalties, as a rule, are in the range of two percent to four percent of the retail list price of an album, with the present industry norm being three percent. If you're superstrong, you may be able to get as much as five percent.

The logic of which job is more desirable—staff producer, executive producer, or independent producer—can be expressed in a matter-of-fact way, using simple arithmetic:

Executive producers, as previously stated, make between $50,000 and $100,000 a year, plus bonuses. They receive excellent employee benefits, such as health and life insurance, pension plans, and stock options. Practically all of their business expenses are paid for by their employer, including meals, transportation, hotel accommodations, stationery, etc. Most of their paycheck —after deducting for federal, state, and local taxes (and if there's anything left after buying groceries)—can be put right into the executive producer's investment portfolio.

Staff producers earn a base salary of between $15,600 and $31,200 a year, plus bonuses. As company employees, they are also entitled to employee benefits and reimbursement of their business-related, out-of-pocket expenses. Assuming that the retail list price of an album is $7.98, which is the current industry standard (soon it will be $8.98), and assuming that the staff producer is involved annually in three different recording sessions (this is a typical workload for an established in-house staffer), the producer, whose current royalty is two percent of the retail list price of albums and singles less packaging deductions (which bring the royalty base price down to $6.98 approximately, rather than $7.98), will receive additional compensation as follows:

- $.14 (rounded off) for each album sold through normal United States distribution channels;
- $10,500 if, as an example, each of three albums sold 25,000 units;
- $126,000 if, as another example, album A sold 100,000 units, album B sold 300,000 units, and album C "went gold," or sold 500,000 units;
- $420,000 if, as still another example, each album reached the "platinum" album plateau of 1,000,000 units sold. Note that in each of these cases the staff producer's salary may technically be considered either a complete or partial advance against production royalties, when and if they are earned.

Independent record producers receive advances in lieu of a salary. They usually pay their own way for everything; in addition, the advances they receive are recoupable from the production royalties they will eventually receive. Assuming, however, that an independent record producer is getting a royalty of three percent of the retail list price of an album ($7.98) less packaging deductions ($7.98 becomes $6.98 approximately), and assuming that the independent record producer, like the staff producer above, is involved in three different recording sessions during a one-year period, his earnings will be:

- $.21 (rounded off) for each album sold through normal United States distribution channels;
- $15,750 if, as in the case of the staff producer above, each of the three albums sold 25,000 units; $189,000 if, as with the previous staff producer example, album A sold 100,000 units, album B sold 300,000 units, and album C sold 500,000 units, making it a gold record;
- $630,000 (plus three platinum album awards from the Recording Industry Association of America) if, as with the previous staff producer example, each album sold 1,000,000 units.

It's quite rare, incidentally, that any producer will be able to score a "hat trick" this way, with three different projects in a year each becoming platinum records, What *is* happening with greater frequency is that a single hit album sells in the multiplatinum range, anywhere from two to five million units. If you're in record production for the money, and you're able to produce artists who consistently sell in the multiplatinum range, you'll probably want to be an independent producer rather than a staff producer.

There are other, somewhat more realistic, parts of the production equation to consider, however. Very few of the many thousands of albums commercially released each year become multiplatinum, platinum, or gold records. Eight out of nine records released by established record companies, in fact, don't achieve break-even. In such cases the independent record producer's advance against royalties would be the only payment he receives for his professional services.

Many of you will certainly feel tempted by the "large figures" I've used. I hope they can be attained by everyone who tries, but realistically it's not going to happen overnight. The more reasonable way to begin a production career is with some financial security behind you—in other words, a salary. Start out being a record company gofer; work into the A&R department in the capacity of an assistant, if you can; ask the A&R executive producer to "give you a shot" as a demo producer; become a staff producer, and let the record company worry about getting business and making money. Only when you've established yourself as a proven-successful hit record producer, in my opinion, should you consider starting your own independent record production company.

CUSTOM LABELS

There is one other form of production entity associated with the record business, which goes by the generic term *custom label*. Custom label owners comprise the cream of U.S. and international record producers. In essence, a custom label, which is distributed by a major label, enables the producer-owner to function somewhat independently in the areas of deciding which artists to sign; how much to pay those artists; what material to record; when to release product; and how to promote product to radio stations, record stores, and to the public in general.

Because of their track records and the quality of the product they consistently tend to deliver, custom label owners are able to negotiate all-inclusive royalties (from which the custom label owner pays the artists and the producer, if the producer isn't the custom label owner) in the range of 12 percent to 20 percent of the retail list price of a $7.98 album. Some custom label owners go one step further: They become fifty-fifty partners with the major label that distributes their product. This means that after all expenses have been paid, including manufacturing, advertising, promotion, and artist royalties, the distributing-label owner and the custom-label owner split the net profits in half.

Crossing over to custom-label ownership should be weighed very carefully by each independent or staff record producer so tempted. Owning a custom label means that you're running your own minirecord company, and that you're going to have to compete with every other record company—large and small—for artists, airplay, and counter space. You'll only be able to spend a fraction of the time you might otherwise spend, if you remained a staff or independent producer, in the studio. You'll make more money as a custom label owner for each record you sell, but you will no longer be able to work with established artists signed to other labels.

The expense of running a custom label, which could include executive salaries for a national promotion director, operations chief, and A&R head;

Point-of-entry job within a record, publishing, or management company, booking agency, or retail record store.

Assistant in the A&R department of a record or publishing company (preferably making demo tapes.)

Staff recording producer with a major label.

Independent record producer.

Custom label owner (optional).

FIGURE 2.
Step progression of jobs taken by most successful record producers.

production costs; rent, telephone, postage, insurance, salaries, and employee benefits for secretaries and a receptionist; is staggering. You may be receiving a seven-figure advance against royalties from your distributor—you may even have one or two outstanding years back to back—but if you can't be "in the money" for a very long period of time, you'll be in the unenviable position of having to pay everybody else for their services, while you take home the remnants (if any) of the feast.

In 1973, after having had a number of years of success with different artists, including the Four Tops and The Grassroots, my partner, Brian Potter, and I decided to get a little more deeply involved with what we did and how we did it. We made a custom label deal with Capitol Records for a company called Haven Records, which Capitol distributed in the United States, and EMI, Capitol's parent company, distributed outside the United States.

Over the years, we delivered products to Capitol of the Righteous Brothers, Evie Sands, The Grassroots, and a number of new artists. Most of the talent that we had signed to us, in fact, was new, which, if I can speak frankly, is one of the problems we had with being a custom label. Artists feel more comfortable recording for companies whose image precedes them. Even if you're offering something extraordinary to the artist (in the case of Haven Records, it was the opportunity to work with Brian Potter and me not only as producers but as songwriters), the new custom label owner has a tremendous number of obstacles to overcome. When you start a new record company today, even one that's affiliated with a major international distributor, it's somewhat of a competitive liability.

Custom-label ownership is a difficult undertaking. My partner and I are no longer involved in Haven Records to the extent we were during the '70s because we found it to be too time-consuming and because we found trying to compete with major record companies too difficult. As producers, we felt that we had closed ourselves off too much from involvement with other record companies and other artists, many of whom were seeking us out to produce their records. These are some of the reasons I recommended thinking about custom label ownership as a possible, but not necessarily mandatory, final record production goal. Remaining independent, so as to play the entire field and stick primarily to the creative business of producing hit records, may be a more sensible career path for most producers to take.

THE RECORDING ENGINEER

The man who literally sits next to the producer in the studio control room is the *recording engineer*. This is the technical expert in charge of operating and maintaining the production equipment. The essence of his job is to help the producer achieve the sound the producer desires hearing. The majority of producers that I know are not engineers in their own right. It takes many years of hard work and a lot of practical experience to become a good engineer. It's a separate career unto itself. For some extroverted engineers, it is an avenue for becoming a producer, but the most direct route for becoming a producer is to do just that: become a producer.

There are fewer staff engineers today than there used to be, as recording studios are finding that most artists and/or producers prefer using independent engineers with whom they've established a working rapport. Large studio complexes, however, such as United Western in Los Angeles, do maintain a resident engineering staff. They earn anywhere from $200 a week, in the capacity of trainee-second-engineer, to $600 or $700 a week, when they become full-fledged mixers. I'm sure there are also bonuses built into what staff engineers do, based on the number of hours they actually spend on a particular production.

Independent engineers are hired for a particular project and paid an hourly fee of between $30 and $50 an hour. Assuming that the engineer spends the industry average of 300 to 500 hours making an individual album, and that, like the successful producer, the successful recording engineer keeps busy with at least three different projects each year, annual income of between $27,000 and $75,000 is possible. In addition, some producers, as I do, involve their engineers in a share of the bottom-line profit of a hit album (some record companies and artists do this, too). This is usually not a contractual obligation, but a gratuitous way of showing the engineer how valued his services are in making hit records.

As a rule, independent recording engineers bill record companies on a weekly basis. They are treated as independent contractors by the record company, although they do sometimes get preferential treatment: For example, a recording engineer who works with a number of artists signed to a label may be able to negotiate for up-front money in advance of his involvement in a scheduled recording project.

Most engineers are involved in all phases of recording. However, with the rise in popularity of disco product, there have been engineers and quasi-producers who have begun to specialize in mixing. A mixing specialist may be able to bill clients at higher hourly rates, but the job openings in this area at present are extremely limited. The best way to go, in my opinion, would be to learn how to be a full-service engineer, able to assist the producer from the inception to the completion of a studio project.

ARRANGERS

Producers rely on engineers for technical support; they rely on arrangers and possibly songwriters for musical support if the artists they're producing aren't a self-contained group. The arranger's job is to orchestrate a song along the lines suggested by the producer. Although I do some of my own arrangements, I've enjoyed working with a number of enormously talented free-lance arrangers, including Jimmie Haskell, Michael Omartian, Gene Page, and Tom Sellers. These men have been lured, from time to time, into the ranks of producers, but for the most part they return to their craft of orchestrator/arranger/conductor.

A really good arranger deserves the freedom to contribute his own spark to the music, rather than be limited by a producer who might insist, for example, on three trumpets, two saxophones, and a kazoo. Arrangers can charge anywhere from $200 per arrangement to $1,000 per arrangement, depending on how difficult and time-consuming the arrangement will be. Each local of the American Federation of Musicians (AFM) publishes a directory not only of arrangers but also of copyists, who are the people that write out the orchestral parts so that the musicians can actually read them. These directories, though, should only be consulted as a last recourse: The best way to secure a talented arranger is through word-of-mouth recommendations.

Understanding song structure and being able to contribute to the shaping process of a song is an important role for a producer. If the producer isn't working with singer-songwriter artists, and he himself isn't a songwriter, he must be able to obtain good songs from professional songwriters, most of whom are affiliated with major music publishers such as Chappell, Warner Brothers, and Screen Gems Music.

Any song that has received its first commercial recording can be "covered" by a different artist on a different recording, so long as recording royalties are paid by the cover artist's record company to the composer, lyricist, and publisher of the song. Most producers, even those like my partner and I who write a lot of original songs, keep a file of potential hit songs on tap for recording situations that might arise. It's also advisable for a producer to become professionally associated with several outstanding songwriters (in our case, we usually contact writers like Barry Mann, Cynthia Weil, Alan O'Day, etc.) so that they can either submit songs for an upcoming project, or consider collaborating with the artist-songwriter featured on the recording.

A&R EXECUTIVE

The last V.I.P. player in the record business, the A&R executive, is analogous to the editor of a publishing house or the adjudicator of a trial. His job is to say "Yea" or "Nay" to the producer, the artist, the manager, or whomever else solicits the participation of his company. Approaches may differ from one A&R department to another and one A&R executive to another—some do it nicely, some not so nicely—but the decision to either pass on a tape, request a live audition, or sight-unseen sign an unknown or establish artist is always determined by someone wearing an A&R hat.

Basically there are four ways to approach the A&R department of a record company:

1. *By submitting a demonstration tape.* At the most, the demo should have three or four songs on it, preferably with leader tape in between the songs so that the A&R executive can fast-forward his tape recorder from the beginning of one song to the next. It's also advisable to package demos with lyric sheets and the name, address, and telephone number of the producer and/or contact person for the artist.

2. *By submitting a finished master tape.* Masters have a tendency to physically stand out from demos. They look more expensive (hopefully they sound

more expensive!), and they usually *are* very expensive (anywhere from $2,000 to $30,000 or more) to produce, depending on the number of sides. There is absolutely no need, in my opinion, to go to the trouble and expense of producing a finished master unless you've tried repeatedly and unsuccessfully to interest record companies in demo tapes, and you still think you're right and the whole world is wrong. Masters somehow draw A&R people's attention more immediately. But it is a highly risk-oriented proposition to produce a master tape "on spec," and one that most successful producers have never had to take.

3. *By inviting someone from the A&R department to a live performance or rehearsal of the group.* It's amazing how much money is actually spent by major record companies sending A&R talent scouts not just around the block, but to all corners of the world to listen to artists who reportedly "have what it takes." This is the least expensive way to get evaluated, although it's somewhat anxiety-provoking if you're worried about the group sounding stale, flat, or nervous.

4. *Through referrals.* This gambit sometimes works for producers who have made a good impression on at least one previous employer who's well connected in the industry. The music business is very much a "family" business. Everybody knows everybody else, and it's very hard to keep a secret about talented newcomers with good production instincts. It's not even necessary, for people fitting this description, to have a demo or to be working with a group. A word-of-mouth recommendation may do the trick.

A possible fifth approach, the "do-nothing" approach, is unfortunately not applicable to producers. Unknown artists, if they're playing clubs that are highly visible to the industry, sometimes get "discovered" without really trying. Producers, on the other hand, have no choice but to be aggressive go-getters, ready to have the door slammed in their face a hundred times without giving up. Among the ingredients needed to succeed in our business, one of the most essential, albeit noncreative ingredients, is *persistence*.

THE PLAN

Here, ideally, is how the record production game should be played. First, the producer should make a commitment—then keep it— to focus his energies and pocketbook on becoming a producer, period. Some readers may consider this a "given" (i.e., a taken-for-granted assumption), but I'd rather not take that chance. The reason some people don't get ahead is not because they lack ability, but because they haven't learned how to channel their ability in a singular direction. If you want to be a producer, you shouldn't be trying to be a manager, agent, or concert promoter at the same time. Songwriting, arranging, and audio engineering courses can be justified perhaps as production-related activities, but anything else, until your production star has risen in the heavens, should be verboten.

Second, and this is a practical extension of step one: Establish contact with the music business in some capacity, and find out whether you can make a living being a record producer. This implies that you will realistically assess your ability to compete with other potential or established producers; determine the extent to which you like the business, and vice versa; and estimate the popularity quotient of the type of music you're into and its impact on your potential earnings. For instance, if you wanted to be a classical record producer, you can't realistically expect to sell three million units of the Beethoven Tenth Piano Sonata or Handel's *Water Music* (unless there are three million Mark Spitzes). Lower your financial expectations for classical music, jazz, spoken voice, foreign language, or children's recordings. Also, certain esoteric kinds of rock, country, and even pop music traditionally appeal to a more limited audience than mainstream rock, pop, R&B, and now disco music. This preproduction learning and familiarization stage is essential for drawing a heads-up, eyes-wide-open bead on a focused, income-generating production career.

Third, if you're not one of the lucky individuals invited to become a staff producer through word-of-mouth referral, find an artist, preferably a self-contained group, to record. The group should be at a parallel level to your production abilities. In other words, until you know how to direct a studio session properly, and until you or your friend-turned-recording-engineer have gained the upper hand over your equipment, you should not attempt to record professional ensembles. It would be better to learn from groups who, like you, have many things to learn and many mistakes (forgivable, under these circumstances) to get out of their systems. Once the mantle of quasi-professional has been attained, however (bearing in mind that you're not a real professional until you get *paid* to be a producer), the places to hang out in order to secure a potentially commercial group are recording studios; clubs; instrument repair shops; local offices of the AFM; college and high school social gatherings; music business schools and conservatories; and amateur-night showcases.

Fourth, on a personal or "gut" level, make sure there is a positive, emotional response engendered between the artists and the producer. You must be able to get along with each other as human beings, as business associates, as career planners, as dreamers, but especially—assuming that the producer and the artists are both newcomers—as struggling, almost desperate contestants in the hit record sweepstakes. There will be ninety-nine parts adversity for every one "lucky break" you occasionally receive. If the feeling between the producer and his artists isn't as strong as the feeling between a husband and wife who love each other, it's a very dangerous, divorce-laden situation.

Fifth, which is the most elusive step for most beginning producers, you should try signing the artists to an exclusive record production contract. This is the producer's insurance that he will at least be able to participate to some extent in the event that a major label offers the group a recording contract.

Sixth, which is the first real "money" decision, you have to decide which way to record or showcase the group, and how much money you're prepared to spend. The options available to the producer are as follows:

a) He can invite A&R personnel from various companies to hear the group perform live, either in rehearsal or in front of an audience;

b) He can record the group on a very cheap home tape recorder. This approach, by the way, is not to be sneered at: No A&R person expects a demo tape, no matter how many production values are built into it, to do anything other than *suggest* what a finished master tape might sound like. So long as the integrity of the song and the artist come through, the sound quality of a demo, whether it's bad, good, or excellent, is of secondary importance.

c) He can record the group in a more sophisticated home recording studio. Such a studio today, including building materials and equipment, will cost between $10,000 and $15,000. What you get for the money is the ability to produce very high quality demos and hands-on engineering experience. You won't have as much control over the final sound as you'd get working in a 16- or 24-track professional studio, but if you're planning to spend a lot of time in the studio you might actually save money (or be able to earn money, if you rent the studio out for demo purposes) by producing records at home.

d) He can record the group in a professional studio environment. The preferred way to do this is without having to spend what most 24-track studios are charging today: between $150 and $225 an hour. Over the years, I have listened to many tapes that were submitted to me by managers or artists where they had been given studio time at either reduced cost or gratis. There are no preestablished deal parameters in this regard. On the bottom line, you're dealing with human beings (i.e., studio owners) who have feelings and who understand that artists and producers have to somehow get started. The key is to find a studio that will allow you to record when sessions are over, or on a day when there are no bookings. Some studio owners will do it merely to help out; others will be approachable on the basis that either they get reimbursed later on by the artist's record company, that they receive a limited participation in the artist or producer's royalty income, or both. Getting the cooperation of a studio owner in this respect is as much a test of the producer's ability to sell himself and his product as anything else he'll encounter.

Many factors should be weighed before deciding which of these options, along with the related master tape option, should be taken. Chief among these factors, in my opinion, is what can be learned from the collective experience of thousands of aspiring producers who preceded us to the A&R lion's den. The quality of the artist and the artist's song come first. It's not how technically good an unsolicited tape sounds; it's whether the song and/or the artist embodied on that tape sounds unique. I, for one, don't recommend taking financial risks. My strategy, if I were a beginning producer, would be to spend as little of my own money as possible; concentrate on developing relevant, concise material for my artist, and a live presentation with a certain "punch"; and attempt to set up a live showcase for record company personnel. This plan, from a producer no less, does not even mention the absolute need for a demo tape.

Seventh, the penultimate step, the producer has to advertise his existence to major record companies, custom labels, studio owners, personal managers—anyone and everyone that the producer knows is involved with the manufacturing and distribution of phonograph records and tapes. The standard record producer calling card, of course, is the demonstration tape. Other approaches can be taken using master tape recordings, word-of-mouth referrals, or invitations to attend a showcase performance. In sending demos out to record companies, make sure you get the name and telephone number of a contact person in A&R so that, among other things, you know who to speak to about getting your tapes back.

Eighth, which is the most important step of all, the producer must get a response. This brings us back to the original sixty-four-dollar question: How do you actually make your tape more important than the hundreds of other tapes, stacked one on top of the other, in the corner of the A&R department's storage closet? What do you have to do to break down the barriers of ongoing record company business, regional staff meetings and conventions held outside the office, and the incessant politicking for new jobs that has precedence over all other considerations in a record company? Those of us who are survivors of the door-slammed-shut syndrome know the answer: dedication, persistence, faith, and ambition (a little luck never hurt anyone, either). However you do it, you must be able to get an answer. You must be able to be heard, to be seen, and to be at least tacitly regarded as an intelligent, creative young Turk.

Above all, I've tried in this general introduction to the record production business to portray the contestants, rules, and materials necessary to play the production game in realistic, commonsense terms. It may seem odd that some people can become successful producers without formal production training or even knowledge of recording technique. At the other end of the spectrum, the situation where an aspiring producer spends lots of money doing what is usually nonessential (such as producing an expensive master tape) rather than what costs practically nothing (such as coming up with great production ideas by listening to the radio) contains an inherent element of pathos.

Of one thing we can be confidently certain: Before you succeed, you will fail. Failing, for me, was my greatest motivation. It kept me pushing, kept me wanting it, until I learned how to stop making bad records. Mine isn't an overnight success story; practically no producer's story is. We *worked* to get where we are. That process, for better or for worse, is still the way most people get from A to Z in the production business: from just dreaming about becoming a producer to having a home, swimming pool, and tennis court built on the financial rewards of gold or platinum-selling records.

DL

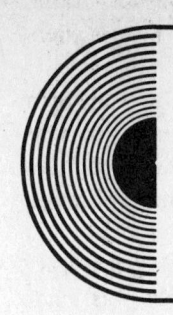

SO YOU WANT TO BE A RECORD EXECUTIVE

I remember the first time I tried to explain to my parents exactly what it was I did for a living. Even now, years later, I laugh when I think of the expressions on their faces.

My father, nose crinkled, eyes squinting, looking at me almost like he was inspecting some strange insect under a microscope. My mother nodding her head as if to say, "Yes, I see, uh huh, I understand," but behind her eyes I could hear her thinking, "Oh my God, my son is a raving lunatic." I had been around too much of something, I'm sure they concluded, after I left for the evening.

I actually did tell them the truth about my job—well, half of it anyway. I told them that I spent most of my waking hours listening to music. I started work at 10:00 in the morning, usually worked until 8:00 PM or so. I often had two-to three-hour business lunches at stylish restaurants. Five out of seven nights, I went to see a concert, or went to a party. A late dinner would usually follow. I spent a good portion of my time talking to, or talking about, rock and roll stars. I lived in a fabulous apartment, and traveled about the country like most people travel about their neighborhood. All this, and I was earning an equivalent salary of almost twice my father's, one year out of college, 24 years old.

You see, I am in the music business, and I was what's called a record executive.

I was on a "fast track," and I wasn't alone. On the track with me were plenty of other record company executive types, all pursuing their careers with the same zeal and enthusiasm as I pursued mine. By 26, I had climbed to the position of Director of Marketing Services for ABC Records, a company in serious financial trouble whose executive team was trying to turn from red ink to black. My corporate rocket was climbing straight up, with no sure end in sight. It was a pretty heady experience.

Then, in February 1979, ABC Records was sold to MCA, Inc. All 250 or so ABC employees were fired, including me. I looked around, but there simply were no executive jobs available in an industry that was having one of its worst years ever.

That was almost a year ago. Now, at 27, I'm a partner in an independent marketing and personal management firm. Our company is doing quite well;

I'm still on the fast track, although now I work for myself, with my partners, harder than ever.

Oh, what about the half of my job I didn't tell my parents? I didn't tell them about the bone-crushing corporate pressures, the back-stabbing politics, the late-night phone calls from artist's managers, the fear of not succeeding soon, because if I didn't make it big by 32 or so there was a good chance I never would. Brutal? Granted. But lots of fun.

So, you too want to be a record executive. You like the idea of a fast-track way of life, of big gambles and career risks. My mother probably was right. I *am* a lunatic. And so are you.

Well, then, let's get down to the basics. First of all, you're not alone. A lot of other lunatics are running around out there, and they too want a shot at the few available jobs. Second of all, your success will be determined by a combination of a lot of luck and some amount of preparation. There is nothing I can do about your luck, though perhaps I can help you a bit with your preparation.

Climbing the Ladder. Before discussing the how-tos of marketing records, it is important that you understand three ground rules for your success within the record company itself.

All industries have their own tone or personality, and the individual companies within the industry come to reflect that tone. This is easily understood. A company's primary goal is to do business. To offend or reject the mores of its industry may give the company an "outcast" image. Few companies want this.

The record industry is no different from others; its companies are no different, either. Even though the record business is show business and its people pride themselves on being iconoclasts, hip, elitest, in-the-know; even though many executives act like stars themselves; and even though many in the business see themselves as rugged individualists apart from the crowd; there are still accepted ways of doing business and particular traits which are rewarded.

The following are general rules, and are not meant for everyone. There are, to be sure, many music people who are quite successful who have never followed any rules but their own. In fact, these rules are more for the company-inclined than the entrepreneurial-minded. If your future lies in the company structure, you would do best to fit into the parameters of rewardable behavior.

Study the business and learn it fast. The record business is wonderful because it rewards the young. Many industries won't even consider people for the plum jobs until middle to late 40s. In a record company, you had better be on your executive way by late 20s/early 30s, or watch out. This means that your business skills must be honed early on in your career. Remember: The golden rule of business is to make money. Record companies are not concerned about walking on the frontier of art, for the most part, nor are they concerned with making social, cultural, political, or any other kinds of statements with the music they market. If an artist makes an important contribution to art and society, fine, but he or she had better sell some records or it's "see you later."

As an aside, and to be fair, most major labels do, in fact, have some artists on the company roster who make no money, perhaps even cost money: certain classical and experimental music artists are good examples. These artists are valuable, however, in that they provide an important image base for the company. And their expenses represent only a very small portion of the overall marketing budgets.

The record business is full of traditional ways of doing business that make no sense. Don't be afraid to ask questions of people whose abilities you trust. Many people feel that asking questions shows signs of weakness. Nothing could be further from the truth.

Be ambitious and aggressive, but don't be impatient. The record business prides itself on being a business which will give a chance to anyone who wants it badly enough. You can afford to speak plainly about your future goals and not feel threatened, but remember that there is no substitute for experience. For years, the attitude regarding the growth of the business was that the sky was the limit. At the middle management levels, no one felt they would stay in the same company position for more than a year, or two at most. And sure enough, the industry did expand, and people were promoted like clockwork. Expansion has now slowed, and companies are no longer promoting like they once did. However, the problems that now face the industry and which must be solved will require solid management skills. If you have the tools, you will eventually be rewarded.

Make as few enemies as possible. Because the record business is a "people business," your reputation is a valuable commodity because when all is said and done, there are are not many career people in the record business. It doesn't take long to learn the names of the most important players. And after a few years in the business, you will know most of the people who have any real impact. In any event, you simply cannot afford to be unfamiliar with the important people in the industry. If you make too many enemies (on the other hand, don't be obsessed with wanting everyone to like you), your chances of being tapped for a good job are reduced dramatically. The record business is show business, and egos are fragile.

Nuts and Bolts. Now that you have the proper attitude to begin your executive climb through the corporate catacombs, you need to have an understanding of how record companies are structured.

There are six basic marketing departments within a record company: (1) promotion; (2) sales and distribution; (3) advertising and merchandising; (4) publicity; (5) artist development; and (6) artists and repertoire, or A&R. Each department is usually helmed by a vice president who in turn either reports to the president or to a vice president of marketing. The A&R department almost always reports directly to the president. Within each department, there are typically a variety of titled positions and, of course, each company has its own guidelines as to who gets what title. Sometimes it gets pretty confusing trying to figure out who is responsible for what particular job.

Each department represents one large piece of the marketing puzzle. The more sophisticated companies have learned to effectively integrate each function into the overall marketing process.

Promotion. In the record business, promotion is defined as the efforts made to get a record played at a radio station. As such, promotion is generally considered to be the most pivotal marketing department within the company.

Without equal, the best way to sell music is to have someone hear it, and there are only two ways to expose music to a mass audience: radio and television. There are approximately 5,000 singles and 2,500 albums released in the United States each year. Most contemporary radio stations today limit their weekly playlist to about thirty current hit records. Some stations play only twenty, some stations play as many as forty-five. At thirty records per week and only at most four to five slots open each week per station for new records to be added to the playlist, the odds *against* a record being added are very good. Take radio exposure away from a record, and the chance of it becoming a hit are so small it's frightening. The job of the promotion department is to convince radio to play a record.

Sales and distribution. The job of sales and distribution is to sell and then distribute the records to record stores.

Selling a record requires the sales staff to go to their accounts and then "solicit" the record—to sell it to the buyer. This process occurs two to four weeks prior to the record's release date: the date it's shipped to accounts for sale to the consumer.

There are three types of record selling accounts: direct retail, racks, and one-stops. Direct retail accounts are regular record stores. They are either "mom and pop" shops or chain stores. They buy records directly from the label (i.e., the manufacturer). "Racked" accounts are most generally separate departments within larger stores, as for example Sears, J.C. Penney, and K-Mart. The stores purchase records from rack jobber companies that, in turn, stock the stores with hit records, sometimes providing sales personnel. "Racked" accounts represent a full fifty percent of all records and tapes sold.

One-stops are accounts which purchase records from record companies and then resell the records to retail record stores or juke-box operators, who for one reason or another are not in a position to purchase records directly from the label. A common example is a "mom and pop" store that, due to its small size, doesn't qualify for credit with the labels' credit department and so must go to a one-stop to purchase their records.

There are two ways to distribute records: independent distribution or branch distribution. Independent distributors, or "indies" as they're called, are separate independently owned companies which contract with labels to physically distribute records to accounts. Branch distribution is a structure in which local sales offices are owned and operated by the label. The sales staff is employed by the label and all records are warehoused at the label's facilities.

Branch distribution appears to offer greater control in bringing records to the marketplace, but a large yearly sales volume is necessary if the label is to be able to afford the cost of operating the system with its tremendous overhead.

Somewhere toward the end of 1978/beginning of 1979, the industry began to see a proliferation of distribution deals. That is, small record companies, once distributed by independents, now sought the protective umbrellas of the major labels' massive distribution arms. For a negotiated percentage of sales, the major labels would manufacture and market these smaller companies' records. The trend perhaps signaled the beginning of the end of independent distribution as it is now known.

Toward the middle of 1979, the industry saw itself shrink to an essentially six-company industry consisting of CBS, Warner/Elektra-Asylum/Atlantic, RCA, MCA, Polydor/Phonogram, and Capitol/EMI. Six major labels financed, manufactured, and marketed approximately ninety percent of the industry's business.

Advertising and merchandising. The purpose of advertising and merchandising is to support and further develop through the media and at point of purchase the image of the artist and record.

From an advertising point of view, there is general acceptance within the industry that the most effective ad campaign supports, rather than leads, airplay. Once airplay develops, radio, print, and perhaps television buys are then made to remind consumers of the records they have already been hearing on a favorite radio station.

Of course, once an artist has attained a certain level of success, some amount of advertising is normally done before airplay to simply inform the consumer that a new record is available.

Except for some nationally bought ads, most ad dollars are spent at the local level through radio, newspapers, and local television (as opposed to network buys). The buys are made through the branch or distributor. The purpose of this decentralized budgeting process is threefold: (1) strong local relationships often promote cost discounts when buys are made; (2) accounts are able to be "tagged"—that is, their name is mentioned in the ad itself (For example, "[recording artist] is now available at all ——— record stores." For this mention, the branch or distributor is able to sell more records than perhaps otherwise would have been normal to that particular account); (3) timing is a critical factor in advertising records. The difference between a hit record and a failure can literally be the ability for a company to react within a few short days. Being able to spend ad dollars on a local level means that a salesperson is able to confirm an order with an account on the spot, without waiting for approval from headquarters.

Many industries often speak of "co-op" ad dollars—the account pays for half the ad, and the manufacturer pays for half. Record companies also co-op ads with accounts, but the labels pay for 100 percent of the buy.

Merchandising relates to a label's point of purchase efforts in addition to any promotional gimmicks made to create interest in an artist's record.

Point of purchase has perhaps the single strongest impact on the consumer. Being in a record store and seeing a fabulous display or hearing the record played in the store can immediately trigger an album sale. For this reason, labels spend huge sums of money for point-of-purchase materials: posters, mobiles, die-cut graphics, neon signs, stand-ups, and so on. A strong album cover graphic is also of terrific importance. In fact, some record stores, realizing how important in-store play can be in selling a record, have gone so far as to charge labels for the privilege of playing their records in the store.

Publicity. A strong publicity or public relations campaign is an integral part of any well-developed campaign effort. The publicity function concerns itself with press and media.

A good publicist looks for an angle when pitching a story. Why is this artist different? What makes this album deserving of attention? Is it the proper time for an album review, interview, or feature story? Don't shy away from a bad review. Studies indicate that most readers have a short retention span for facts. Readers remember they read *something* about a particular artist, but they just don't remember *what* it was they read.

The press is a good place to build an image for an artist. The use of photos helps to reinforce a particular personality the artist wants to project, while a good campaign will attempt to get the artist's name into print before the album is released in order to develop expectation and interest in the new music.

Visibility is very important to the public's interpretation of someone's importance. The more the public sees and hears about an artist, the more important they perceive the artist to be.

Artist development. The responsibilities of the artist development department are perhaps the most difficult of any single department to define. As the name suggests, anything that affects an artist's career growth should have input from artist development.

On a day-to-day level, artist development is most concerned with guiding the artist's touring and other personal appearance (television) obligations. Concert appearances by an artist are one of the proven ways to sell records. If an artist has a good live show, you can count on selling records to people who went to the show. Concertgoers will tell friends how good an artist is, thus selling even more albums.

A record company only makes its money from selling records; it makes nothing from an artist's live appearance revenues. But live appearances do sell records, so it's in a label's best interest to see to it that an artist tours.

Unfortunately, the cost of touring is very high. It is not unusual for a group to spend $2,000 to $3,000 per day on the road. Because many artists do not earn enough from the concert revenues to offset the cost of touring, most labels must loan money to the band in the form of "tour support." Tour support is almost always recoupable against royalties. That is, as the artist sells records and begins to accrue royalties due, recoupable funds are applied to the royalty account of the artist. If no records are sold, recoupable monies are not returned to the label, but once records are sold, all recoupables are repaid to the label before royalties are paid to the artist.

In addition to coordinating the label's involvement with a tour prior to commencement, artist development is also responsible for monitoring the success of the tour once under way. Are tickets selling as expected? If not, is more advertising warranted? What is the profile of the artist's audience? Black, white? Male, female? Age? Is the show itself as good as it should be? If not, what changes are necessary?

A&R. A&R has traditionally been the talent-finding arm of the record company. A&R often helps artists find the proper producers for their records, sometimes recommends material to artists, acts as the label's liaison when the record is being made, and sees to it that all publishing and artist clearances, as well as other legal areas are properly administered.

Long considered the sexiest job to hold in a record company, the role of the A&R person has changed much in recent years, and continues to evolve still. Most artists today are fairly sophisticated in their approach to their music, and no longer require—or simply won't accept—the direct creative input from A&R. Most artists now bring to their project an independent producer who works not for the label but for himself, and with the growing trend of artists being brought to the label by attorneys and signed through the president's office, the real influence of A&R has been reduced considerably.

Still, A&R is important because new artists are the lifeblood of the record company and there must be someone in the company capable of evaluating the musical viability of an artist's music as it relates to commercial considerations. Does this artist fit well into the roster? Are musical changes necessary to make the album commercial? How much can the project be expected to cost? Is the artist capable of producing the album by himself?

Putting It All Together. The record business is changing very quickly, and in the short space of nine months we have seen the industry change much. When a business grows at the fast and furious pace that ours has and then slows almost overnight, the impact is devastating. Major companies have collapsed. Mergers have become commonplace. Executive realignments have taken place at just about all labels. As of this writing (August 1979), no one knows what Christmas will bring. If it's bad, like last year, I shudder to think what January 1980 will be like.

What was once a business of bold entrepreneurs is fast becoming dominated by large, well-financed corporations. Records is still a hustler's business, but now one must hustle at the corporate level, which is something new and very different to many people indeed.

The dismal truth is that most campaigns to establish artists or break a record are still flown from the seat of someone's pants. All too often, marketing campaigns are awkwardly assembled strategies developed from good intentions but not enough thought. To be sure, every label can point to a particular campaign for which it is proud. Perhaps it was even brilliant. The record sold fabulously; the artist is now a star. For my money, Capitol Records' campaign for The Knack is the best campaign in the last five years. CBS can point to Eddie Money; Warner Bros. has Rickie Lee Jones. Every label has at least one. Unfortunately, though, they are few and far between.

So after all this, you *still* want to be a record executive? Well, good for you, because the business will inevitably turn around and we'll start selling records once again. The people in the business care about what they do and have a good time with their jobs. But still, to find a job at a label is not easy. It requires determination and imagination, but it can be done.

If promotion or sales interests you, in which case you would most likely start as a local promotion or sales rep in a particular market, you should find out if there is a label's branch office in your city (also check the independent distributors, but remember that indies are even less stable now than labels). The distributing arms of the six major labels—CBS, WEA, Polygram, RCA, MCA, and Capitol—have about twenty branches in various cities throughout the country. Telephone, send letters, show up in person. Do whatever it takes to meet the branch manager or with whomever else you are told to speak.

If advertising/merchandising is your pleasure, a branch may also be able to provide an entry-level local position from which you can move to headquarters. Think about an ad agency. Most major cities have some nice-sized agencies. Gain some experience at an agency, then move to a label.

Many publicists come from journalism backgrounds and artist development sorts often come from talent agencies or concert promoters. Either way, persistent interest often opens a door.

A&R is a whole different ballgame. I've never met an A&R person who felt the way they got their job was typical. Labels often look to the promotion staff to fill A&R positions. The theory is that in promotion you are constantly trying to get records played at radio stations, and after a while you have a good feel for what will get played and what won't. Since airplay sells records, it makes sense to have someone look for new music and know if radio will play it.

And as for some advice after you've been hired—good luck!

ED

GETTING TALENT FOR ROCK CONCERTS

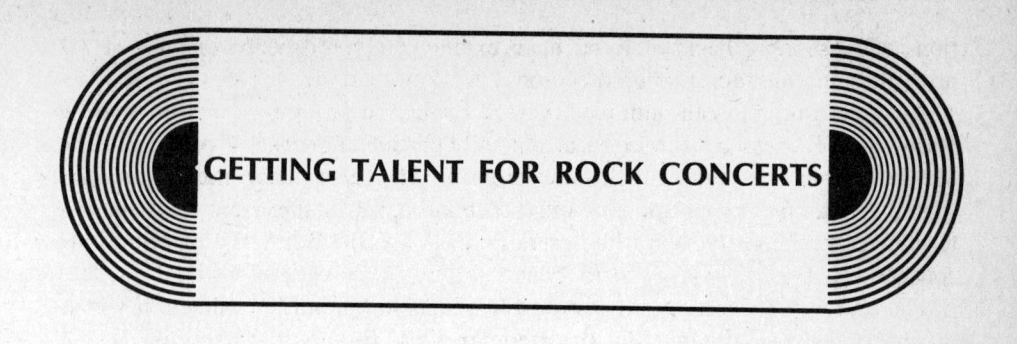

Deliverability: that's the key to becoming a successful concert promoter. Deliverability to you, by the agency, of an attraction. Having the attraction play for you, as opposed to the already established concert promoter. Those who have made any attempt at this realize how near-to-impossible it is for the novice to break the bonds that exist between the present buyers and sellers of talent.

However, there is a way to get your foot in the door that does not involve miracles. It means dealing with the realities of the concert promotion business: being patient, dedicated, and willing to sacrifice financially for several, perhaps many, years. If you really want it, and you're talented and lucky, it can be done.

I think the most important thing for the reader to realize is what a task it's going to be to get talent—how frustrating it's going to be. Inevitably, one starts to feel paranoid that the industry is not responding to "my" interest, "my" enthusiasm, or to "me" as a person. Everybody—every novice promoter, and I was no exception—has to pay his dues this way. We start by trying to shake an apple off a tree. If we persevere, eventually the agency is going to recognize our legitimate interest in promoting concerts.

I would recommend that before you call to discuss a specific engagement, try to have an initial meeting with an agent (not the president of the agency) in his office. Office appointments are better than meeting backstage or at a party, unless you're at a small party with someone who is well connected with the agent and who can make a personal introduction for you.

Receptionists and secretaries, who command the telephones and therefore control communications between the agent and the outside world, can be extremely important to your overall chances of getting an appointment. These are the people, often inundated with requests, who will first present your case to their boss. Try to become a face or a person to the secretary, as opposed to being merely another voice over the telephone, or another aspiring concert promoter on paper. If you're able to, go to the agency's office and hand-deliver your information. A secretary who's on your side and has the ear of a line agent can make a big difference.

Don't talk to personal managers or artists at the outset of your promotion career. Later on, your relationships with managers and artists may be strong enough for you to deal with them directly. But initially, you must deal with the artist's agent exclusively. If you try to cut out the agency at first, your negotiations will probably backfire to such an extent that you'll be frozen out of the promotion business for a long, long time.

An agent doesn't need another potential buyer calling up for Crosby, Stills, & Nash, The Eagles, or Linda Ronstadt. That's not the agent's problem. The agent's problem is finding work for the new attractions that the agency has signed. As a start-up promoter, your potential value to the agency will be determined by whether you are interested in and have the capability of promoting concerts for the agency's new attractions.

The best way to learn about new developments in the music business, if you're a total outsider, is by reading the trade papers: *Billboard, Cashbox, Record World, Radio & Records, Variety,* and *Amusement Business.* Pay particular attention to captioned photographs announcing the recent signing by record companies of unknown artists. Once an artist has been signed to a major record company, it is usually a matter of days or weeks before that artist is also signed to a major booking agency. By contacting the record company, or reading the trades for additional information on which agency the artist signed with, you may be able to get a head start on other promoters seeking to gain admittance at that particular agency.

Explain to the agent in your initial appointment that you're a new promoter, that you don't expect to be laden with gifts of superstars at the outset of the relationship, and that you're willing to serve a function for the agency by promoting its new attractions if the agency, in turn, can be influential in developing your career as a concert promoter. In the initial meeting you should discuss the kinds of attractions the agency has, the agency's conditions for dealing with the promoter, and what kind of service the agency expects from the promoter. It is very important for the promoter to make the agent feel comfortable with him as a business person. Personal references, trial balance sheets for projected concerts involving the agency's attractions, and a copy of the promoter's rental agreement with the facility can be very reassuring signs to the agent of the promoter's professionalism.

I would also, in the initial meeting, try to impress the agent with the fact that not only are you enthusiastic and willing to play a developmental role (a key concept) in the careers of their new acts, but that you are financially prepared to handle the burdens of being in business. Don't make an offer, get an acceptance, and then tell the agent that you're going to try to raise the money to produce the show. Have your finances at least partially nailed down before you go there.

Make sure you know what you're talking about. The easiest way for somebody to dismiss you mentally, from a business standpoint, is to consider you a flake—someone who has no idea what he's talking about, or who doesn't know the realities of the business. When the agent asks, "Is there a PC involved?" you should know that PC means percentage. When the agent talks about the GP, you should know that GP is the gross potential of the concert. When the agent asks for ticket prices, you should know how to scale the house, and how many seats there are in the facility. When the agent asks about taxes, you should know what types and percentages these taxes will be.

You must sound like a professional. If you write, which I don't recommend, you must write like a professional. The least you can do is impress the potential seller, the agent, with your comfort within the industry, your knowledge of it, and your fluency with its terminology.

The right person to talk to in this initial meeting is any agent you can get to see. It doesn't have to be the president of the agency. In fact, it's absurd even to think that you'll be able to see the president. Get in to see an agent. Break the ice. Try to get through. Get somebody there to respond to you.

After the initial meeting has been concluded, it's not necessary to have any written correspondence between the promoter and the agent to memorialize the meeting. This is a telephone industry. Try to develop telephone relationships rather than written ones. This is a very valuable thing for a new promoter: to be able to call an agency and have that call taken, instead of waiting for three days for a call to come back to you. Aside from contracts, it's all done on the phone. Deals are confirmed or turned down verbally in the concert promotion business, long before they've gone to contract.

After the initial meeting, the next step will be a discussion, either in person or on the telephone, concerning a specific concert proposal. While it is essential to have certain data and financial information available on the GP, less applicable taxes, the seating capacity of the facility, and the cost for you to promote the concert, less talent, and other variables, you're still not "in" with the agency. You will have to do a second selling job of yourself, your facility, and your services before the agency will award you its talent.

Good halls, in my experience, make very persuasive arguments for aspiring concert promoters. If you think you have the best hall in town for the artist you're attempting to promote, let the agent know it. Be able to describe the hall physically. Give the agent some idea who's played there before, and how successful those attractions were in that facility. Let the agent know who's playing near you, so that the agency doesn't think there's somebody coming in who's going to share your business. Try to explain, if you're already promoting concerts, that you're not playing anybody with a similar audience during that period of time, and that, to the best of your knowledge, none of your local competitors have booked similar attractions.

If the facility is really hot, and anything presented there is a sellout, bring along some newspaper clips or magazine stories about the hall. In short, stress the merits of the hall to the agent: who's played there, how the hall has been used in the past, and the success of the hall with the local audience.

You're not going to impress an agent by saying, "You know that opening act you have that's playing 500-seaters? Well, I believe in it so much that I'm going to put it in a 3,000-seater." Unless the agency wants to destroy you—and good agencies don't—they're going to think that's absurd. Smart agencies never want their acts to do badly. They especially don't want an attraction to develop the reputation of playing to empty auditoriums—of being a "loser" or a "dead act." If it's a new act and you're offering to headline them, the agency will want the act to headline in a small place where the business will at least be hearty. Good exposure, with the possibility of a turnaway crowd, is much more desirable to an experienced agent than the lure of quick money.

As I've already explained, the price of the act is not negotiable, even for start-up attractions. Either you take it or you leave it. The real key—and I can't emphasize it strongly enough—is how you, as opposed to somebody else, are going to get the attraction. What can you do to influence the agency's decision, so that eventually you will be able to promote their major attractions?

You're not going to get it by beating the price. Even when I competed with Ron Delsener, who is presently the major New York City concert promoter, there weren't more than three shows out of the hundreds and hundreds we did a year that Ron Delsener would take from me, or I would take from him, because one of us was willing to pay more. It never was that. It was, instead: Who deserves the act? Who should be playing the act? Who put his dues in with that act? Who worked with that agency? Who's willing to do more for that agency? Who's willing to commit himself more to that act?

If price were the only problem involved in getting talent, then the entire concert promotion industry would be the loser. We'd all have to be crazy to overpay attractions and fight against each other, at least in terms of financial return. Successful promoters get talent because of their abilities, and because of what they did for the agency in the act's early stages. You just hope, although there's no guarantee, that the agency will remember. You also hope that the attraction will remember, too.

This is why promoters can be such backstabbers against their competitors. After the show, which the promoter doesn't own, after the money, which the promoter will spend, he has nothing except his relationships with artists, agents, and managers. These relationships are the promoter's only tangible asset. If they change, he's out of business. If someone else comes in and creates a similar relationship, his business can be halved. The cutthroat nature of this business stems from the promoter's vital concern for protecting that next telephone call to the agency.

Sometimes it is the facility that decides which start-up promoter an agent will work with. Large facilities that draw sellout audiences translate into acceptable GPs for the attraction and the agency. If the promoter can somehow obtain control of an important facility (in the trade we call this an exclusivity), he must be taken seriously by the agent. Even so, if you're able to command a facility, you're not home free. You must be willing to serve the agency. You must be willing to promote whatever acts the agency wants promoted for at least a trial period. If you don't treat the agent with respect, he will either wait for another arena to be built in your city, or look to the surrounding suburbs.

How do you insure that your relationship with the agency will continue, and that eventually you will receive bigger attractions? By doing everything the way the agency wants you to do it. It may sound like pandering, but it's reality. If you have an engagement and you're required to send the agency a fifty percent deposit by certified check by March 15, make sure it gets there and is certified on time.

Don't surprise the attraction. Know the artist's concert rider backwards and forwards, and don't make any changes in it. If the rider states that the attracion is to receive four bottles of this wine and three cases of this beer, don't assume that you can replace "this beer" with "that beer." Don't assume that you can replace meat with cheese. Give the artist exactly what he wants.

Be there during the engagement. Make your presence known. You are the person the attraction is working for, and they want to see you working. They want to see your personal involvement.

You're usually not going to be the person who selects, or packages, the opening act talent that complements the headliner. You're usually going to have a package of two or more artists thrust upon you by the agency. More than likely, in order for you to have a headline attraction, the agency will tell you that you must expose another one of its new acts. Occasionally, when the agency doesn't have another suitable act available, they may let you go to another agency. It's more likely, however, that the headliner's agency will make the call for you: they want the supporting act's agency to feel that "Your agency owes my agency one act."

Expect to lose money over a certain number of start-up concerts when you start promoting. Chances of losing money are much greater with your early shows than with your later ones, when you've learned which advertising media work best and how many production personnel you actually need. But you never stop losing money as a promoter. There's always some favor you have to do that will hurt you in the pocketbook.

When you've figured out what your costs will be after the agent quotes you a price for the attraction, you may realize that the price is at a level where it's impossible for you to make a profit. Be forthright about it with the agent; tell him, "It's impossible for me to make a profit this way." If the agent answers, "We'd like you to do this for us, and in return we will start to give you acts that can make you some money," you have to determine if: (1) you're talking to an agent who has the authority to keep his word; and (2) it's a prudent business gamble.

Concert promotion is a business in which you're very often asked to lose money, or to do something that will more than likely lose money, on a handshake, on a verbal promise, on a nonlegal basis, on the provision that "We'll [the agency] make it up to you." You can't ask for anything in writing—you won't get it. You're constantly negotiating deliverability, not price. You're negotiating with an agent to become their promoter: to become a service arm of that agency. That's the magic.

You always seem to be dealing, in actuality, with future concerts. You're negotiating for the right to do a future concert with a bigger attraction than the one you're talking about. Each concert you do is going to have some bearing on the ones you get next, or the ones that you don't get next.

Even though it's a futures business, make sure, at the end of the year, that you've made more money than you've lost. There's a point where developing a relationship with a developing attraction should stop, and that's the end of the year, the bottom line. Evaluate your position carefully. You are not in business just to develop acts for agents and managers. You are in the concert promotion business to make money for yourself.

HS

HOW TO RAISE MONEY

If you need money to start a professional recording studio, record store, or music business magazine; if your group needs financing to make master tapes, purchase better instruments, or hire a top arranger; if your personal management company wishes to expand its purview into publishing, concerts, and films; if, in order to promote rock concerts, you require advertising, facility rent, and overhead subsidies; if your classical chamber ensemble needs money to finance an international concert tour, showcase in New York City, or commission a new work—for these and other reasons you may be required some day actively to seek investors.

Fund raising is a skill, like anything else. Some people can learn to become expert fund raisers; other people are born with the ability to raise money; still others will never focus on how fairly simple the fund-raising process actually is. I earnestly hope that none of my readers qualify for membership in the third category.

The ordering of chapters in this section should correspond to the orderly progression of steps one takes in assessing, developing, and communicating fund-raising proposals to others. Here, however, are some throw-out recommendations on raising money to get started:

1. *Never be afraid to ask.* This is the biggest hang-up for most beginners. God will not punish you if you ask for money. You will lose neither friends nor face if you ask for money properly. What you will most certainly lose, if you don't learn to open your mouth, are the chances for raising money. It's the easiest thing in the world to ask for funding—all you have to do is try.

2. *Have something specific to sell.* Potential investors need fast, accurate answers concerning the purposes, objectives, manpower and equipment needs, income, and expense projections for your venture. Until your business plan is well thought out, you are not ready to make telephone calls or write letters.

3. *The main thing to sell is experience.* This is the most important thing you have to offer an investor. You know what it's like out there. You've lived the experience. Now you've put two and two together, and you have a specific proposal. It will work for the following reasons (at this point you should begin listing what those reasons are). If, indeed, you are speaking with the Voice of Experience, you will be heard.

4. *Form letters are taboo.* Every potential investor should get a customized

fund-raising cover letter. Xerox copies of the company's prospectus are fine, but Xeroxed cover letters are a turnoff.

5. *Do not mix business with pleasure at first.* Paying back a loan is much more important over the long haul than becoming instant pals with your investor. Getting a check isn't the end—it's the beginning of the fund-raising relationship you want to establish with that angel. Until you are making as much money as the investor, your relationship should be that of servant to master.

CHOOSE BUSINESS-RELATED FUND-RAISING TARGETS ONLY

In order for there to be even a remote chance of raising money, there must be a mutuality of interests (I prefer calling it the common ground) between the seeker of funds and the provider of funds.

It's not likely, in other words, that a member of the New York Philharmonic's board of directors will want to invest $10,000 in a new rock group, or that a singer who's made millions in rock and roll will suddenly want to start a new career by performing the role of Carmen with the Metropolitan Opera (does this person, we might ask, even know how to read music?).

Investors generally like to get involved in things they feel comfortable with, rather than with polar opposites. It doesn't have to be exactly the same business, but investment seekers would be well advised not to waste time selling the equivalent of meat to a vegetarian, or peddling matching three-piece outfits to members of a nudist colony.

Here are some guidelines to use in deciding where to go for investment capital, depending on the specific nature of your involvement in the music business:

Contemporary pop artists who need better equipment, instruments, costumes, and so on. If you sign a recording contract, the record company might advance money to the group for this purpose (it would be justified internally as an artist development expense); if you do not yet have a recording contract, the money would most likely be obtained from either a personal manager or silent-partner investor.

Record producers who need financing for a master tape. If you have stature in the industry as a person with good ears, you may be able to swing a deal with a major label; otherwise you will have to seek out private investors—preferably one person, although the cost of the tape may require you to form a syndicate of investors.

Promoters who need backing in order to produce a concert. If the act is affiliated with a major record company, the company will pay either most or all of the advertising costs; the rest of the money will have to be raised from private investors.

Classical artists who need money for a showcase concert. This is not a good return-on-investment opportunity (i.e., you will be lucky if you sell fifty tickets; you will be luckier still if those fifty people actually show up). Enter competitions where the prize is a free showcase concert, or contact private foundations interested in music with original programming ideas.

Personal managers interested in expanding into other areas. If just one of your artists is signed to a major label and the product is selling, the record company may finance the entire expansion plan; if this is not the case, you will have to seek funds from private investors.

Persons interested in starting a club. It may be possible, in time, to finance expansion of a very successful club through commercial bank loans, but beginning club owners will almost certainly have to use a combination of their own money plus private investment capital.

Full-service music publishers. If you have impressive professional credentials, you may be able to raise money from foreign publishers who will want exclusive licenses to use your songs in their countries. Otherwise, you should use your own money—this is not an expensive business to get into.

Persons interested in starting a recording studio. If you are a respected producer, you may be able to raise the money from private investors; if not, there is an outside chance in some U.S. cities of getting a commercial bank to lend you the money.

Persons interested in starting an agency. This business does not require a lot of investment capital (i.e., you don't need an office at first, or a secretary, or fancy furniture—what you do need is at least one marketable artist and the ability to talk endlessly on the telephone). Money to finance expansion of an existing agency will usually come from private investors and/or other agents interested in merging with your firm.

Persons interested in starting a retail record store. If you have more than a pittance to invest and your business plan is carefully worked out, you may be able to get a loan from a commercial bank.

Persons interested in starting a classical music ensemble. If you have a considerable amount of artistic stature and a smattering of social graces, you may be able to assemble a group of Ensemble Friends (private individuals, local companies, foundations, arts councils) to help pay the bills. In order to enlist the Ensemble Friends, however, you will have to perform many concerts for little or no pay for at least several years.

Banks (correctly so) don't like to take chances. They will not lend money unless there is adequate collateral, such as cash, purchased equipment, or the money-seeker's home, to secure the loan. Private investors, on the other hand, sometimes relish highly speculative gambles. They may have a real affinity with another gambling type (i.e., the fund raiser), especially if their own money was made in a high-risk field. They may actually gain from losing 100 percent of their investment in a new business if they're in a very high tax bracket. They may also be interested in making new business contacts with people they might otherwise never meet except via the music business entrepreneur's venture.

There is one other very important reason for recommending private investors over any other potential source of capital. Private investors don't decide through committee meetings. Their actions are not restricted by charter guidelines or bylaws. They say either yes or no, but they decide for themselves and they usually decide quickly. Even if the answer is no, it's better to find that out and move on to another investment prospect than to agonize for months over whether the deal you want is going to go through.

NARROW YOUR FOCUS TO INVESTORS LOOKING TO INVEST

There is a tendency for beginning fund raisers to put the cart before the horse—i.e., to allocate most of their time to planning new ventures in minute detail before ascertaining if anyone is even remotely interested in the venture. My advice is to find out first if there are any potential common ground investors in the market at present. Only after you've made contact with a few likely investors should you go ahead (assuming they're interested) and develop an extensive plan.

There is no official directory of U.S. or international investors with which to begin narrowing down likely investment candidates. Much can be learned, however, by reading the music business trades. Investment bankers, lawyers, and accountants may also be able to provide good leads on who might presently be in the market to invest in your business. Tips may just as easily (less expensively, too, as a rule) be gotten from receptionists, secretaries, friends, and denizens of the music business jungle.

I am, admittedly, a professional fund raiser. That means that whoever I am with, no matter what the circumstances, I am never far from thinking about money. I am always ready to pounce on people who know other people that have a lot of money. Invariably, I ask these questions:

"How well do you know the person?"
"What's the person really like?"
"What's the person doing right now with his time?"
"Do you know if the person has ever invested money before, or if the person has ever made a charitable donation?"
"My project—do you think it might interest your person?"
"How would you advise me to contact the person?"

After that, my procedure is as standard as turning on an ignition switch. Either the person I pounced on (if he still likes me) offers to put in a good word first, or the very next day, while it's still fresh in my mind, I get in touch with the potential investor. I introduce myself as a friend of the person I pounced on. (Note: I will always first get permission from the person acting as a go-between to use his name.) Then I give a brief history of myself, describe my most recent accomplishments, and give a thumbnail sketch of my new business plans.

Depending on whether it's a for-profit or not-for-profit business, I conclude the selling part of the exploratory phone call with one of the following questions:

"Would you be interested in learning more about the venture?"
"Would you like to make an investment?"
"Would you consider making a tax-deductible contribution?"

Seconds later, I know where I stand. Most potential investors aren't interested —that's par for the course. But if a person is interested, it means I'm going to need documentation. It means I'm actually going to have to sit down and formulate a business plan. The point is, there should be a reason for planning a business. If no one out there is interested in your idea for a venture, there is not enough reason, in my opinion, to pursue it actively.

MATCH YOUR PROSPECTUS TO THE PERSONALITY OF YOUR INVESTOR

Unless the modus operandi is direct mail solicitation—a tactic used effectively by established nonprofit institutions such as The Metropolitan Museum of Art and the Los Angeles Philharmonic—every fund-raising crusade should be custom tailored to the individual potential investor. Some investors will expect a one-hundred-page prospectus. Other investors won't even look at your prospectus; they'll tell you they decided to invest at 2:00 in the morning because they like you and they admire what you're doing (at times such as these, the least you should remember to say is "Thanks"). Either way, it's important to get as much advance knowledge as you can about the idiosyncracies of a potential angel.

There are five basic components to a fund-raising proposal: (1) the cover letter, which summarizes the purposes, objectives, and financial prospects of the contemplated venture; (2) the prospectus, which includes historical background and the actual business plan; (3) public relations endorsements, such as press releases, photographs, chart listings, newspaper stories, sample product, or concert programs; (4) either an audited financial statement or an accountant's income statement and balance sheet for the most recent period of your present company's existence (if you have a company); and (5) a verbal sales pitch that covers the entire scope of your contemplated venture in no more than ten minutes. (Note: Very often when I meet with a potential investor for the first time I ask for five uninterrupted minutes in which to make my case; if I'm talking particularly well that day about my business, almost invariably I walk away with money.)

What one can realistically hope to accomplish by submitting thorough, typewritten, neatly bound *support documentation* is, frankly, not a great deal. If the written materials lend a feeling of seriousness and professionalism to your venture, that is the most that can be expected. But it is wrong to place any major significance on the influence of written business plans on the potential investor. The reason people give money is not because something looks good on paper; people give money because they want to—i.e., they are interested in a specific area, and they need someone with expert qualifications (you) to help translate their vision into working reality.

Let us agree, for the moment, that the fundamental secret to successful fund raising is being in the right place at the right time, and that the value of written materials to the potential investor may actually be negative. This would account for why so many apparently brainless, nonplanning people (albeit with experience) receive funding, while other people, busily perfecting cover letters and sometimes paying outrageous sums to professional fund raisers (not including myself) for this purpose, end up with nothing.

However, the written *business plan* is an absolutely indispensable survival prescription for the fund-raising seeker. A carefully conceived plan should tell whether there is substance or froth to your idea of starting a business. The plan should help bring you within the orbit of potential investors who don't need to be sold on the merits of the plan, but who may desperately need someone to take the idea and run with it. The principal beneficiary of business planning, in other words, is not the fund-raising target; it's you.

Here are some tips to use when the time comes to write down a business plan:

1. *Look at your business expenses on a monthly basis.* Will you be making more telephone calls, for example, in March than in January? Are you going to need part-time employees in May and June, or are you going to cut back full-time labor in November? Will you be needing an office for the entire year, or for only nine months? Go down your entire list of expense items in this way; it may substantially reduce your total estimated expenditures for the year.

2. *Look for the cheapest acceptable way to do things.* Most new businesses don't need fancy offices, fancy office furniture, and deluxe office equipment. If you can get by without a postage meter, do it. If you don't really need a paper copier, don't buy one. If you can work out of your home initially, save the money. Keep your expenses down to the bare bone, and maximize net profit.

3. *Don't forget to compute taxes.* Every employer with employees has to deal minimally with payroll taxes. There may also be duties, levies, freight charges, and other business-related taxes to deal with that are often overlooked by beginning music business entrepreneurs. Find out which taxes are applicable to your business, and factor them into the total expense equation.

4. *Add 15 percent to each of your expense estimates.* At the end of the year, it's better to show your investor that the business saved money (i.e., your expenses were less than budgeted) rather than that it was forced to reduce net profits. The most expedient way to plan for the unexpected is to formulate an exact estimate of something, then add 15 percent to that figure.

5. *Project income on three different levels.* There should be a minimum, middle-level, and maximum projected income listing for whatever business you're planning to develop. If, for instance, it's a recording studio, the schedule should reflect billings for partial, normal, and twenty-four-hour use; if it's a concert, the schedule should reflect ticket income based on 50, 75, and 100 percent of tickets sold; if it's an artist investment deal, the schedule should reflect income based on what the artist's debut LP (along with accompanying career development plans) will yield if 10,000 units, 100,000 units, and 500,000 units are sold. Again, these financial projects may not be very significant to the investor. But I think it's an excellent idea for beginning entrepreneurs to work up minimum income projections, subtract income from expense, and periodically ask themselves, "Am I crazy to be doing this?"

MAKE A FIRM OFFER:
TAKE IT OR LEAVE IT

The culmination of the fund-raising campaign—also the last page of the written prospectus—is the making of an offer, otherwise known as "the deal." It is the fund raiser's job to propose the deal. Deals should be based on how much money, time, and professional services a potential investor can be expected to contribute to the new venture. The deal maker should also ascertain whether the potential investor is passionately, enthusiastically, or only mildly interested in the project area.

As I said earlier, some investors would rather seem to lose money for tax purposes than make money. The magic phrase to use when speaking to the former group is the *tax shelter*. Other investors may want to make as much money, and also get as much equity in your business, as you let them. Giving up ownership is personally very distasteful to me. I would rather see beginning entrepreneurs use the following guidelines in formulating their first deals:

1. A corporation will be set up. The fund raiser will not be held personally liable for any debts incurred by the corporation, including the repayment of any loans to the investor in the event that the business goes broke.

2. Stock will be issued in the corporation. The fund raiser will maintain a controlling interest (at least fifty-one percent) in the corporation's stock.

3. Four-fifths of the investor's financial contribution to the corporation will be treated as a loan. The fund raiser will not have to begin paying back the loan, plus interest (the lowest interest rate allowed by the state), until two calendar years from the start of business have elapsed.

4. The remaining one-fifth of the investor's financial contribution will be treated as equity in the corporation. Depending on the size of the investment, the investor may be entitled to as little as five percent or as much as forty-nine percent of the business. For a forty-nine percent interest, however, the investor should be contributing at least a six-figure sum to the corporation.

5. The fund raiser will be the chief operating officer of the corporation, as well as the signer of all company checks.

6. The investor will be invited to join the board of directors of the corporation.

7. The investor will have the right to audit the corporation's financial records during normal working hours so long as the investor is a director of the corporation.

The deal should be for slightly more money than you actually need. Some investors like to haggle—initially over price, later over contract points—but most will accept your offer at face value. Having gotten this far, this is hardly the time for you to start acting squeamish. The last card you throw on the table must be a very positive ace: you've done your homework; you have a great idea, and the experience to back it up; you've made the investor a decent offer—now, Mr. Investor, what do you say?

GIVE YOURSELF A SALARY

When money is near at hand, a fund raiser should be in telephone contact with his attorney or business adviser. If the deal goes through, the lawyer will draft a letter of agreement and incorporation papers, as well as attend to any revisions of the letter of agreement following conversation with the investor's lawyer.

Attorneys, accountants, and business advisers should also be used as sounding boards and sources of expert knowledge by the fund raiser. When it comes time to offer a specific tax shelter plan, if you're not sure which way to slant the deal, or if there are legal or tax questions relating to the establishment of the contemplated venture, you will have a need to consult with these professional-services people. You will also, one day, be obliged to pay their fees.

There is nothing troublesome about the legitimacy of having to pay fees for services rendered. What constantly amazes me is how infrequently beginning fund raisers apply the principle to themselves.

Fund raising is an extremely time-consuming job. Many hours will be spent formulating a written business plan. Many, many more hours will be spent on the telephone with potential investors, or in the offices or homes of (let us hope) sure-shot contributors. By itself, the onerous chore of fund raising entitles one to financial remuneration, though perhaps not at the premium rate of $150 an hour, which some lawyers charge. It is advisable, however, to keep track of how many hours you work on a given fund-raising project: beginning fund raisers might value their time at $10 an hour; more advanced fund raisers, who have learned how to compress more work into less time, may figure $25 an hour; and so on.

Even more shocking than the aforementioned is the tendency of most beginning fund raisers to forget to budget themselves a salary as compensation for heading up the proposed venture. No matter if the business is a colossal success or failure, the same principle applies to the fund raiser as it does to the accountant or attorney—i.e., time is money. If you, the fund raiser, are obligating yourself to run a business, you should be paid for your time. (Such payment, incidentally, should be adjusted to include your work in the capacity of professional fund raiser.) You should not have to rely on net income (if there is any) as your sole source of earnings.

I think, however, that too many beginning fund raisers, after budgeting total proposed venture expenses, less salary, lose heart. They are afraid of appearing too greedy, or of having the investor's interest turn sour. These fears, in my experience, are simply not justified if a beginning music business entrepreneur includes a reasonable, subsistence-level salary for himself in the written business plan.

What must be avoided is any appearance that the fund-raiser's control of the expense tiller is less than rock steady. If you start a potential investor out with a $50,000 capitalization figure, only to come back a week later with an adjusted figure of $62,500, the difference being your salary, you will probably have lost an investor. It is perfectly all right to expect to be paid for your work, but is is poor planning to call attention to this fact after you have already stated your case.

STAY AWAY FROM BRAND-NAME
INSTITUTIONS UNTIL YOU'RE VERY BIG

Reference was made earlier to establishing whether a common ground exists between a person or organization seeking funds, and an organization or private investor able to contribute funds. The common ground mentality works at virtually every level of the fund-raising business. Money will be granted not only on the basis of a solid business plan, but on the basis of race, sexual orientation, religion, age, salesmanship, character, work experience, and personal reputation.

Another very real factor in deciding who gets money is how the contributor of funds slept the night before meeting the seeker of funds—as well as, in today's world, with whom it was that the contributor of funds was sleeping. There are also other factors at work.

Brand-name institutions, such as Bob Dylan, ABC, or the Ford Foundation, are hung up on the glamour of their names. They are unlikely sources of money for beginning music business entrepreneurs. Practically all brand-name institutional money goes to similarly respectable brand-name institutions or brand-name causes, such as the world peace movement, CARE, and Lincoln Center for the Performing Arts.

Private foundations, despite their impressive listing in the Columbia University Press edition of *The Foundation Directory* (every serious classical music fund raiser has a copy), are notoriously bad supporters of unattached, newly formed music organizations. Most private foundations—if they give any money at all to music—support one pet project started years earlier by the organization's founder. Either that, or the foundation supports established, brand-name symphonies and operas, usually the best in town. In panoramic perspective, most private foundations are not interested in funding any music organization that has not already established roots, trunk, foliage, and a women's auxiliary. (Note: This is not to denigrate the need for continued financial assistance of worthy, established cultural institutions. I am merely advising that for organizations getting started, it's going to be difficult to raise money from conservative private foundations.)

If you are a veteran of the armed forces, or if you have been subjected to racial, economic, religious, or sexual discrimination, you may have an effective hook (pardon my crudity) for receiving government funding at the federal, state, and local levels. Then again, you may not. Successful fund raising requires an incredible amount of brute work, for which there is no substitute. If there is an apparent common ground linkage between your venture and an existing program of the federal government, it is certainly worth exploring. But all too often, there are enormous lines asking for U.S. government aid. I frankly cannot recommend government aid as the most likely place—even for veterans—to receive seed money for music business ventures.

Successful fund raising is predicated not just on perceiving the common ground, but on having and applying good common sense. If you're starting up small, think small. Talk to people who can relate to you on more than a business level. Don't bother brand-name institutions until you can show an impressive track record. Above all, put yourself in the other person's shoes: See if the deal, the sales pitch, the purpose of the business, and you yourself appear legitimate. Until you can pass this test, you're not ready to seek funding from major sources.

YOU ARE THE ONE
(WHO DOES ALL THE WORK)

There are some other suggestions I'd like to make about fund raising before moving on. In the nonprofit area, it is much better to get ten small grants of $100 each than one large grant of $1,000. New investors are impressed by how many people preceded them to the slaughter, or altar, or however else they refer to the act of writing a check.

Again, for nonprofit seekers of capital, it is advisable to organize an active as well as an honorary board of directors. The honorary board will be a listing of the most prestigious national and local politicians, composers, performers, and arts patrons you can find. Their purpose is to lend legitimacy and prestige to the organization's letterhead. The active board of directors (so-called) includes friends, business associates, the fund raiser's attorney, and perhaps members of the ensemble. Unfortunately, it has been my experience that active boards specialize in being inactive. The only person who can be expected to do all the work at the inception of business is the person who initiated the venture: the fund raiser.

Even in the commercial area, inaction is the rule of thumb. Months may go by before the investor's lawyer and the fund raiser's lawyer have a chance to go over the papers. Unless it is a multimillion dollar deal, the arrangement is not considered important. These are the moments in a young person's life when it is imperative to keep the faith. Don't rely on people to do anything for a long, long time—certainly not until the venture's performance can be evaluated on a budget sheet.

Nobody makes it in a new business without having tremendous personal ambition. Nothing else can sustain the venture during the inevitable lean years. If you do not have ambition—if you're not burning with desire to make a lot of money or get to the top of your profession—you are not cut out to be a private entrepreneur.

But ambition needs to be harnessed. It must be fueled with enough money to support the fund raiser at a bare subsistence level (at least) during the early years. Untempered ambition is folly. Before setting up your own business, please see to it that you are able to survive in the wilderness not for months, but for years.

OPPORTUNITIES STILL EXIST FOR IDEA PEOPLE

Recently I had lunch with the operations director of a major U.S. record company with offices in Los Angeles. I was told that the company was expanding rapidly, and that within the next two years at least 500 new employees would be added to the company's Los Angeles labor force.

"Are each of these new employees already accounted for?" I asked, fearing the worst.

The answer was, "Yes, they are." As happens so often in this business, most of the 500 new Los Angeles employees will come from the ranks of the record company's existing labor force. The others will be transfer employees from established record companies, as well as experienced retailers, promoters, producers, and other industry employees who have captured the attention of the company's management hierarchy.

That's how big companies take on personnel. It's ninety-five percent hiring from within, first from within the company, then from within the industry. The other five percent will probably be sons, daughters, nieces, or nephews of the top cadre of managers, along with one or two unattached college reps. Still, there will always be career opportunities for outsiders in the music business—maybe not with major U.S. record companies, but with worthwhile alternatives.

The spark that will most often ignite a rewarding career in the music business in the future will be a great idea married to a common ground investor. More and more, this will be a business governed by cerebral intelligence as well as gut instinct.

The music still has to be in the grooves, but beyond that, so many potential investors have become aware of the staggering profits to be made in the music business that it is today an incredibly bullish market for idea persons. If you are an artist with an idea, a manager with an idea, a record retailer with an idea, a concert promoter or publisher with an idea—if it's really a great deal and it's presented properly, you have a better chance than ever before of getting into the music business as an independent entrepreneur.

The risks are greater than they used to be, but so are the rewards. Idea people are usually the principal officers in the company they help put together. If it is a workable idea and it succeeds, you're in, you've made it, plus you are your own boss. Congratulations!

Big companies are getting bigger. Medium-sized companies can no longer compete with big companies, and are either being acquired or going broke. I have no doubt that the music business will change. It has to, simply because there are so many capable young people who will grow frustrated at the closed-door policy of major companies. Whatever new direction the music business takes, it is a dynamic opportunity for men and women with intelligence, probity, luck, and a hand on the pulse of tomorrow. But take it from me: There's nothing like having your own business. If you can possibly do it that way, I urge you to try.

RZ

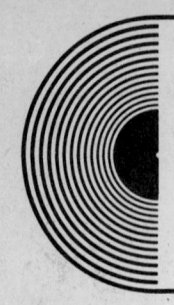

HOW TO ORGANIZE YOUR BUSINESS: SOLE PROPRIETORSHIP, PARTNERSHIP, OR CORPORATION

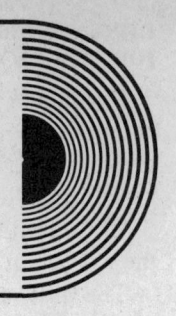

CHOOSING THE FORM OF BUSINESS OPERATION—AN OVERVIEW

One of the first decisions that confronts an entrepreneur, whether his business involvement is in the arts or in any other form of money-making endeavor, is the organizational form in which he is going to operate his business. This chapter is intended to present the entrepreneur with the background necessary to make an informed choice from the types of business organizations available, and the legal and tax consequences associated with the use of each.

All too often, unfortunately, an entrepreneur makes the very significant decision of how to conduct his business without considering the ramifications of his choice or other alternatives. Most people first beginning their own business, for example, find themselves operating their enterprise as a sole proprietorship—but by default, not by forethought. In fact, a proprietorship, as the mere alter ego of the entrepreneur, represents the *absence* of a legal organization, and may not be as suitable as other available means of conducting the same business.

Selecting the appropriate form of organization for one's business typically calls for an analysis of several considerations, each of which can affect the ultimate choice. Among the factors to be taken into account are the degree of exposure to personal liability resulting from the operation of the business, the extent to which capital is or will be required in the conduct of the business, the general financial condition and relative tax brackets of the owners or investors, and the potential for growth and the realization of income from the business. Since circumstances change, the choice of business organization should also be reviewed every few years.

In this country, most business organizations may be classified into one of the following three forms, listed below in order of increasing complexity:

Sole Proprietorship. As the most basic form of business enterprise, the sole proprietorship is the ownership by a single individual of a business conducted in noncorporate form. In this case, the individual and his business are legally one and the same.

Partnership. A partnership, which may be a general partnership or a limited partnership, is an association of two or more persons to carry on a business for profit as co-owners. At law, a partnership is treated as an aggregation of individuals for some purposes, but as an independent entity for others.

Corporation. A business corporation is an entity which is organized under state statute by an incorporator, owned by its shareholders, and managed by its directors and officers, but recognized as separate from any of these for nearly all legal purposes.

This chapter will explore the comparative advantages and disadvantages, both tax and nontax, associated with each of these three recognized legal structures. These structures are sufficiently flexible to accommodate virtually all nontax business objectives. Thus, an informed decision as to whether to operate one's business as a sole proprietorship or as a partnership, on the one hand, or through a corporation, on the other, will often be dictated by the very different treatment of each type of entity for federal income tax purposes.

Tax reasons are also the motivation behind the use of the fourth type of entity that will be discussed in this chapter. This entity, known alternatively as the "Subchapter S corporation" (by reason of the location of its relevant provisions in the Internal Revenue Code) or as an "electing small business corporation" (due to the affirmative election of this status that must be made with the I.R.S.), is a creation of the tax law and combines features of both the partnership and the corporation. The chapter concludes with a brief mention of the tax-exempt organization, which in both its organization and method of operation, is qualitatively different from other types of entities.

Other types of business organizations exist, but either are used for specialized purposes, or are uncommon and tend to resemble either a partnership or a corporation in their method of operation. Examples of the former, usually special-purpose business organizations formed to derive specific tax advantages available under the Internal Revenue Code, are cooperatives, regulated investment companies, Domestic International Sales Corporations, and certain corporations doing business in U.S. possessions. An example of the latter type of entity, going by a name not recognizable as a partnership or corporation, is the business (or Massachusetts) trust, which offers advantages and protection similar to that of the corporation and is taxed as a corporation.

SOLE PROPRIETORSHIP

It has been estimated that approximately 70 percent of all businesses being operated in the United States today are conducted as sole proprietorships. This form of organization—or more accurately, *lack* of formal organization—is popular because it is the most simple to begin and operate.

A sole proprietorship is a one-man enterprise. As the only owner of the business, the proprietor is answerable only to himself. He keeps all of the net profits of the business for himself, and, for tax purposes, all of the net income of the enterprise is taxable directly to him. The debts and obligations of the business are likewise the personal and direct responsibility of the proprietor, whose personal assets are subject to any judgments awarded against the business.

This last point—the unlimited liability of the owner of the business—is the most important legal aspect to bear in mind in connection with the use of the sole proprietorship. Unlike the legal liabilities of a corporation, the debts and obligations of which may only be satisfied from the assets of the corporation (and not from the assets of the corporation's stockholders), the legal liabilities of a sole proprietorship may be satisfied from the personal, nonbusiness assets of the sole proprietor. In practical terms, this means that if the business encounters legal difficulties or becomes overextended in its debts, the sole proprietor may lose not only his business, but everything else he owns as well.

There are means of avoiding this problem in a way that allows the owner of the business to still retain management and operational control. One such technique is to incorporate the business, a procedure discussed subsequently in this chapter. Short of incorporation, insurance is available for certain clearly defined risks to which the business may be subject (such as tort claims or workmen's compensation, for example).

Also, it is possible to place personal assets not needed in the business beyond the reach of creditors by transferring these assets into someone else's name, such as a wife's or an adult child's. These assets could then be leased back by the business without subjecting them to the fortunes of the business, if the terms of the lease are realistic. This technique calls for a measure of foresight and prudence, however, because the transferred property becomes subject to the creditors of the party to whom the property is transferred if that person becomes entangled in difficulties of his own. Furthermore, the courts will disregard the transfer and will allow creditors of the transferor to attach the transferred property if the transfer was made with the sole intention of defrauding creditors, or if the transfer was made gratuitously or for a nominal amount at a time when the transferor was insolvent.

Another fact of life for the sole proprietor is that lenders are seldom encouraged to loan funds to the business based on the limited personal assets of the owner. The owner, of course, cannot afford the lender any ownership in the business, since by definition the proprietorship is synonymous with the owner. Therefore, under most circumstances, the only source of outside financing for the business is by way of loans to the owner from his family or friends, and capital to meet unusual needs of the business may be unavailable unless a partnership or a corporation is formed.

A further drawback to the use of the sole proprietorship—but one of less significance than unlimited liability and the proprietor's usual inability to raise capital—is the lack of continuity to the business in the event of the owner's death, disability, or withdrawal from the business. A sole proprietorship may have the use of a valuable license or franchise in the business, but this right would terminate at the death of the owner. Also, since the business dies with the owner, estate planning is out of the question for the business itself (as opposed to planning for the devolution of any transferable assets used in the business).

For income tax purposes, the most important concept for a sole proprietor to remember is his complete individual identity with the operations of the business. This point is often little understood by beginning business people. The sole proprietorship itself does not pay income taxes; rather, its gains and losses are reported on Schedule C attached to the Form 1040 filed by the sole proprietor individually, who then combines the net income (or loss) of the proprietorship with his other items of income or loss for the taxable year. The sole proprietor must use the same tax reporting year for his business and non-business income, and is himself responsible for the payment of any taxes resulting from the operations of the business. However, the proprietor may report his business income on an accrual basis, even if he reports his nonbusiness income on a cash basis.

Because the business and the owner are considered one and the same, the owner cannot hire himself as an employee of the business, nor can the business deduct any amounts the owner withdraws from the business as his "wage." For example, if the net income of the business was $12,500 during a calendar year, and the owner withdrew $10,000 of this amount for his own purposes, the owner would be liable for income taxes on the full $12,500. Likewise, if the owner withdrew $15,000 from the business in this period, he would still pay tax on only the $12,500 generated by the business, and the additional $2,500 would be deemed for tax purposes nontaxable return of capital. As a self-employed individual, the sole proprietor will also be liable for self-employment tax, and in some states for unincorporated business tax.

Another corollary to the complete identity of the owner and the business for tax purposes is the inability of the business to provide for the owner any fringe benefits on a basis deductible to the business. A corporation employing its sole owner/employee, for example, may establish a plan to reimburse him on a tax-free basis for any medical expenses incurred by him and his dependents and deduct any costs involved in maintaining such a plan. A sole proprietor, on the other hand, must obtain any such coverage himself and pay for it on an after-tax, rather than a pretax, basis. Similarly, any other payments which the owner makes, whether personal and nondeductible (such as for medical expense coverage) or business related and deductible (such as travel or entertainment expenses incurred to benefit the business) are paid directly by the owner, and if deductible, are deducted by the owner himself and not by the business.

This merger of identity of the business and its owner in the view of the tax law must not be taken to suggest that the books and records of the business may be integrated with the personal records of the proprietor of the business. To the contrary, it is imperative that a separate bank account be opened for transactions of the business, that separate stationery be used for correspondence, receipts, and other paperwork of the business, and that separate ledgers be established to record the results of operations of the business. The owner will find that accurately maintaining business records and keeping them divorced from his personal records will not only simplify any I.R.S. audit, but will also render less complex the transformation of the proprietorship into a partnership or a corporation, if either of those paths is followed at some future time.

What other technicalities must a sole proprietor observe? Fortunately there are few, since a sole proprietorship is the least regulated of all the forms of legal organization. However, one common requirement imposed upon a sole proprietor is to file a statement known as a "doing business" certificate with the office of the county clerk. This is a local business license, entitling the owner to do business in that locality. Another common requirement is for the owner to file a "fictitious name" statement, if he is transacting business under a name other than his own. This document is filed at the same time or as part of the "doing business" certificate, and it affords protection against others who may wish to use the same (or a virtually identical) name to conduct their business.

Information as to any other local law requirements that must be satisfied is obtainable from the county clerk's office when these documents are filed. In general, a businessperson in the arts, whether involved directly in an artistic capacity (for example, as a composer or arranger) or indirectly in a service function (perhaps as a booking agent or personal manager), would not be subject to the myriad permit and licensing requirements to which most businesses are subject, or to conform to such local business nuisances as zoning laws, building codes, or health requirements. Even the state sales tax requirements can, in most cases, be avoided, since these generally apply only to the sale of tangible personal property; without checking, though, it is not safe to assume that sales taxes are completely inapplicable to the business, since in some states they extend to the sale of services, as well.

In summary, the advantages of utilizing the sole proprietorship to conduct business are that the organizational formalities are minimal, the proprietor has complete freedom of operation, and that all profits remain the property of the owner. Losses from the business are deductible from any other income of the owner for income tax purposes, in the same manner that income from the business is lumped together with all other income realized by the owner for the taxable period. If the business does generate income, these earnings need not be shared with anyone, and they may be retained in the business for its expansion or other needs.

The disadvantages are also clear. In case the business fails, the owner bears full responsibility for its debts and obligations, and his personal assets are subject to the claims of creditors. Additional funds for the needs of the business may be unavailable from recognized lending sources. Finally, a one-man operation—particularly if successful—may grow beyond the ability of the owner to administer or control and necessitate bringing in a partner. This, then, leads us to the comparative advantages and disadvantages of using the partnership format.

PARTNERSHIP

As in the case of a sole proprietorship, the formation of a partnership entails little or no organizational formality. Usually, only the doing business certificate and fictitious name statement would have to be filed. No formal partnership agreement is required or any writing at all for that matter, because a partnership is automatically created when two or more individuals, orally or otherwise, combine as co-owners of a business for profit. Thus, the term "partnership" covers a broad range of relationships, including those going by the name of "syndicate," "group," "pool," and "joint venture."

Partnerships offer possibilities usually unavailable to the sole proprietor. Additional capital becomes available through a combination of assets of the partners, so that borrowing becomes easier or even unnecessary. Personal abilities may be complemented by the introduction of additional skills into the business, and more ideas and energy can be generated than in a one-man business, where the owner is pressured to do everything himself.

Partnerships have distinct disadvantages, as well, for the independent entrepreneur. The proprietor who formerly ran a one-man show will find that he now has to share decision-making and forgo some of his independence. Partners may clash on crucial aspects of operating the business, and harmonizing the differing viewpoints into a working relationship may require both time and diplomacy. Most important, an individual partner has unlimited personal liability for all of the debts and obligations of the partnership incurred by him and by *every other partner* acting on partnership business. Thus, for example, if Partner A borrows a sum from the bank, and holds himself out to the bank as representing the partnership at the time he incurs the debt, every other partner in that partnership is legally responsible for the repayment of the debt, regardless of whether they signed any documents obligating themselves to that effect or even whether they had personal knowledge of the debt.

Of course, there are several means available of circumventing this most undesirable aspect of carrying the full financial burdens of the business. Where the business only requires an infusion of capital, one method which may be appropriate is to create a limited partnership, which traditionally is the meeting ground between the "idea" man and the "money" man.

Unlike a "general" partnership, comprised completely of "general" partners who are each completely responsible for all of the debts of the partnership's business (regardless of by whom incurred), a "limited" partnership is formed by one or more such "general" partners and by one or more "limited" partners, the latter having their personal liability limited to the amount they are obligated to contribute to the partnership. A limited partner typically invests money or other kinds of property (in fact, anything except services) in exchange for the right to share in whatever income is generated by the operations of the partnership.

To obtain and retain the legally sheltered status of a limited partner, however, the incoming investor must strictly refrain from participating in the management of the business; if he fails to observe this limitation, his status is converted to that of a general partner and he thereby becomes liable for all of the debts and liabilities of the partnership. Also, far greater formality is necessary in the formation of a limited partnership. Since the limited partnership is a statutory creation, the requirements of state law governing the formation of limited partnerships must be strictly observed. These invariably require the filing with local authorities of a certificate of limited partnership and publication in a locally circulated newspaper of the substance of the agreement of limited partnership (including the names and addresses of the investors and the agreed upon contribution of each). A limited partnership not formed in accordance with the dictates of state law is a general partnership vis-a-vis creditors of the partnership, and its partners are all general partners, regardless of whether they were under the mistaken impression that they were limited partners.

Aside from creation of a limited partnership, there are other methods short of incorporation of limiting the liabilities of the partners in a partnership, though none are completely foolproof. Insurance can be obtained for certain well-defined risks, or as explained previously in connection with sole proprietorships, personal assets of a partner can be placed into someone else's name. Indemnity agreements between the partners, limiting individual obligations to the partnership, may be executed (assuming the individual partners have adequate net worth to support such agreements), but these are only effective between the partners and do not bind creditors of the partnership. Also, the liability of a partnership may be limited by contract to the assets of a partnership, if a creditor finds such terms acceptable; most creditors, however, would deem such a proposal a sign of financial weakness on the part of the partnership.

Like the sole proprietorship, the partnership lacks the feature of continuity of life. In general, the death or withdrawal of a general partner in a general partnership or a limited partnership will cause a dissolution of the partnership under state law, unless, as discussed below, provision to the contrary is made in the partnership agreement.

Another feature which the partnership shares in common with the sole proprietorship is the inability of a partner to freely transfer his interest in the business. Absent provision to the contrary in the partnership agreement, a general partner in a general partnership or a limited partnership may not sell or assign his partnership interest without the consent of all of his partners. This prevents the partners from having some undesirable new partner forced upon them against their will, and is advantageous where all of the partners are making an active contribution to the success of the business. It becomes a distinct problem, though, where a partner insists on selling out or is compelled to withdraw his investment in the partnership.

A limited partner is not under the same constraints as a general partner in his ability to transfer his interest in a partnership freely. Unless the limited partnership agreement provides otherwise, a limited partner need not obtain the consent of the other partners to transfer his interest. As a practical matter, though, most partnership agreements will require the prior approval of the general partners to any transfer of a limited partnership interest—particularly if the limited partner has not paid in full for his interest at the time of transfer. Regardless of whether prior approval is or is not required, since a limited partner may not participate in the management of the business, the purchaser of a limited partnership interest acquires no more than the right to share in those profits of the partnership which would have been due his predecessor.

The astute reader will have gathered by now that the relationship between partners in a partnership is sufficiently complex to call for the understanding of the partners to be reduced to writing. As noted, a general partnership can be created and exist under state law without any written agreement, but to allow the relationship of the parties to remain on an oral basis is extremely unwise and virtually certain to lead to misunderstandings.

What specific provisions should a written partnership agreement contain? At a minimum, the agreement should unambiguously cover the following points:

- *Purposes.* The agreement should set forth at the very outset the nature of the partnership's business; the purposes of the enterprise should be sufficiently clear to all the partners to allow these goals to be succinctly stated in no more than a sentence or two.
- *Contributions.* This provision should spell out precisely what the amount or value of each partner's contribution is and whether it will take the form of cash, property, or services. Also, if any partner's contribution is not being made at the outset of the partnership's existence, the agreement should specify when the deferred payment will be made. There is no legal requirement that the contributions of the partners be equal in amount or be made simultaneously.
- *Sharing Arrangements.* The agreement must specify concisely how the partners are to share in the profits and losses to be realized by the partnership. Generally, the sharing ratios will be related to the capital contributions of the partners, and if some business end is to be served by allocating profits and losses in a different manner, this must be spelled out in the agreement. For example, if Partner A and Partner B contribute equal amounts of money to the partnership, but Partner A works full-time in the business and Partner B only works part-time, the partners may wish to allocate a greater share of the profits of the business to Partner A than to Partner B. Nevertheless, since it might be unfair in this case to charge a greater share of the partnership's losses to Partner A, the agreement may provide that any losses are to be shared equally by the partners.

The sharing provision should also clarify how gain or loss on the sale of contributed property is to be allocated between the partners. If a partner contributes property to the partnership instead of cash, and there is a difference between his cost or tax basis for the property and its present fair market value, his partners may be charged with unexpected tax liabilities. Assume, for example, that Partner A contributes $100 to the partnership and Partner B contributes a copyright which he purchased for $50 but is presently worth $100. If the partnership agreement provides for the equal sharing of gains between the partners, and the partnership sells the contributed copyright, Partner A will be charged with half of the gain on the sale, or $25, unless the agreement provides otherwise.

For income tax purposes, the sharing provision is probably the most significant one contained in the entire partnership agreement since it governs the tax consequences to each partner. As will be explained, a partnership itself is not a taxable entity; rather the partners are taxed on their allocable shares of the partnership's items of gain, loss, deduction, or credit. In general, the partners have complete flexibility as to the allocation of such items, and the I.R.S. will abide by the division spelled out in the partnership agreement unless the formula, in the phraseology of the Internal Revenue Code, "lacks substantial economic effect," or, in other words, is motivated by a tax avoidance purpose.
- *Payments.* To prevent otherwise inevitable disagreement between the partners, the agreement must provide procedures for the withdrawal of funds and the payment of profits. The partners have complete flexibility with respect to the amount and timing of partnership payouts, but, as explained subsequently, since partners are taxed on their respective shares of partnership income,

whether withdrawn or not, the partners should assure themselves in this provision of having sufficient cash in hand to pay their tax liabilities when due. This provision may also cover the issue of whether the partners are to be paid salaries for services rendered to the partnership or some amount of interest on their contributions of capital to the partnership, and, if so, whether such payments are to be made from profits of the partnership or made regardless of profits.

- *Continuity.* It is always advisable to provide in the partnership agreement that the partnership will continue to exist despite the death, disability, or withdrawal from the partnership of a general partner, since in the absence of such a provision any of those events will necessitate a forced liquidation of the business—almost always, at financial loss to the remaining partners. In the event only one partner remains in the partnership after such an occurrence, though, this provision will not prevent the automatic termination of the partnership, since a partnership must have at least two partners at all times. Thus, after the necessary winding-up of the partnership's business takes place, the remaining partner finds himself a sole proprietor.

To avoid this and deter premature withdrawal by a partner from the business, either before a specified amount of time elapses or before the partnership has attained certain business goals, the partnership agreement can provide penalties for such withdrawal. One common means of doing so is to provide that the withdrawing partner's interest will be purchased by the remaining partners at a substantial discount from its value.

Specific provisions should also be made, whether in the partnership agreement or in a separate document, for either an option or an absolute obligation upon the partnership or the surviving partners to purchase the partnership interest of a deceased partner. The purchase price in this case would be predetermined by a price or a formula contained in the agreement. Methods commonly used to fix the purchase price include the use of independent appraisers, book value, or the capitalization of earnings approach. In addition, if it appears that the partnership or the partners may lack the wherewithal to make the purchase, the use of life insurance can provide an effective solution. The insurance may be carried by the partnership to fund a redemption of the deceased partner's interest, or the insurance may be carried by the individual partners on each other's lives to fund a cross-purchase of the interest, but, in either case, the premiums paid on the insurance policies are a nondeductible expense. If the partnership relies heavily on the personal services of its partners, and does not use assets in its business that are susceptible of ready valuation—thus rendering it difficult or unfair to arrive at an immediately determinable purchase price for a deceased partner's interest—the agreement can provide that the estate or heirs will be paid for the interest out of a specified share of the partnership's earnings over a given period of time.

- *Miscellaneous Provisions.* Other useful provisions which the partners will generally wish to put into writing will concern the term of the partnership's existence (if it is to be of limited duration); the issue of how the partnership's organizational costs and the out-of-pocket business expenses of the partners are to be reimbursed by the partnership; and what limitations, if any, are to be placed on the financial and legal powers of each partner. Bear in mind, however, that any such limitations spelled out within the partnership agreement will not absolve any partner of partnership obligations incurred by his other partners.

Except in the case of an extremely simple arrangement, it is highly advisable to have the partnership agreement drawn by an attorney who is knowledgeable in tax and business matters. Such an attorney, by probing the prospective partners as to their intentions and desires, will assist them in clarifying their ideas and, in all likelihood, raise additional points that the parties had never considered. Then again, the organization and operation of the partnership can engender unanticipated tax problems, which an experienced practitioner will point out and attempt to resolve, to the extent he can do so, in the partnership agreement. Of course, the attorney will charge for his time, but this cost should be viewed as preventive medicine and absorbed by the parties as an indispensable expense of getting the business underway. In most cases, too, the lawyer's fee can be substantially reduced by thrashing out all essential details before visiting his office or by arriving at his office with a draft partnership agreement incorporating the provisions discussed above, thereby conserving the lawyer's time.

Prospective partners must be acquainted with the basics of those tax provisions governing the taxation of partnerships and partners. Reduced to its fundamentals, the law provides that a partnership (like a sole proprietorship) is not an entity subject to tax. While the partnership files an annual information return on Form 1065 with the I.R.S., it pays no income tax. Rather, the partnership serves as a conduit for tax purposes, so that the partners are taxed directly on their respective shares of taxable income realized by the partnership, *regardless of whether it is actually distributed to them,* and the partnership's income retains its character in the hands of the partners. The allocation of income provided by the partnership agreement will in most cases control the amount and type of income on which each partner is taxed, and therefore all or some portion of a partner's share of the partnership's income may be taxed at the favorable tax rates reserved for long-term capital gain and for personal service income.

Losses from partnership operations are also subject to the conduit principle and are thus passed on to the partners in the proportions provided in the partnership agreement. A partner's deductible loss, however, may never exceed the basis of his partnership interest. This basis is comprised initially of the cash and the basis of any property which the partner contributes to the partnership, as well as the partner's share of partnership liabilities (except, in some cases, liabilities with respect to which the partner has no personal liability). However, the partner's basis continually fluctuates; it is increased by his share of earnings of the partnership and subsequent contributions made by the partner to the partnership and is decreased by the partner's share of the losses of the partnership as well as by any withdrawals made by him from the partnership. If a partner's loss exceeds the basis of his partnership interest, the excess is not deductible by the partner and is carried forward indefinitely until he invests additional capital or has partnership earnings sufficient to raise his basis by an amount which can absorb the disallowed portion of the loss.

The partner's share of income or loss from the operations of the partnership is reported on Schedule E of the Form 1040 filed by the partner individually, and as in the case of the sole proprietor, these amounts are combined with the partner's other reportable items for the year. Another similarity to the sole proprietorship is the ability of the partnership to report on either the cash or accrual basis; the basis elected need not coincide with the method used by the individual partners to report their other business or nonbusiness income on their individual income tax returns. Also, like a sole proprietor, a partner cannot be an employee of his business. Thus, a partner pays self-employment tax for social security coverage (and, in some states, unincorporated business tax), and he pays out of his pocket for any "fringe" benefits, such as medical coverage.

A partner reports his share of partnership income or loss for the partnership tax period that ends within the partner's taxable year. However, in most cases, the partnership's taxable period will be the calendar year, since a partnership cannot freely elect a taxable year that is different from the one used by its "principal" partners (i.e., any partner who has an interest of 5 percent or more in the capital or profits of the partnership). A partnership must secure prior approval from the I.R.S. to report on the basis of a taxable year other than the calendar year if its partners report on the basis of a calendar year.

The income tax consequences associated with the organization, operation, and termination of a partnership can be extremely complex, and an extensive discussion of this subject is beyond the scope of this handbook. The basic pitfall to be aware of upon the initial formation of the partnership, however, is the crucial distinction to be drawn between a contribution of property and a contribution of services. A contribution of unencumbered property to a partnership is not a taxable transaction, even if the property has appreciated in the hands of the partner or if it has appreciated by reason of the formation of the partnership. On the other hand, a partner who receives a share in the capital of the partnership in exchange for services rendered (or to be rendered) is deemed to have realized ordinary income at that time in an amount equal to the value of that capital interest. If, however, the partner rendering services receives in exchange therefor a share in future profits of the partnership, he incurs no tax liability at that time unless the profits' interest is capable of being valued then.

The withdrawal of assets from a partnership, like the contribution of assets, does not generally represent a taxable event. A partner realizes no gain on a withdrawal or current distribution of money except if the amount of money received by the partner exceeds the basis of his partnership interest. Similarly, if a partnership is liquidated and the partnership's assets are distributed to the partners, each partner, as a general rule, will receive his proportional share of the assets distributed on a tax-free basis at that time and will subsequently realize gain or loss to the extent that the proceeds of sale of these assets is more or less than the basis for his partnership interest. If instead, the partnership is liquidated by a sale of its assets and a distribution of the proceeds of sale to the partners, the sale of the partnership's assets will result in gain or loss includable in each partner's share and the actual distribution of funds produces no additional tax, except to the extent that the proceeds exceed the basis of the partner's partnership interest.

The tax aspects of partnership taxation described above only control if the partnership, in its operations, resembles a partnership more than a corporation. Regardless of what name the partnership goes under, or how it is classified for state law purposes, the I.R.S. will attempt to tax the partnership as if it were a corporation, if the partnership has *more* corporate characteristics than noncorporate characteristics. Those corporate characteristics relevant to this distinction are spelled out in the Treasury Regulations as limited liability, continuity of life, centralization of management, and free transferability of interests. However, the Regulations provide, in essence, that an organization formed and operated under the provisions of the Uniform Partnership Act or the Uniform Limited Partnership Act (in effect in virtually all jurisdictions in this country) will generally not be taxed as a corporation, since it will lack the characteristics of limited liability, continuity of life, and centralization of management.

To summarize, the arguments in favor of doing business through a partnership, especially in contrast to the sole proprietorship, consist of the additional capital, energy, ideas, and viewpoints which the partners make available to each other and to the business. Then, too, the partners have nearly complete flexibility for tax purposes in deciding how profits and losses of the business are to be shared, and business losses are deductible by a partner from his personal income. Also, there is little organizational formality involved, and the partners themselves can decide how detailed or extensive their working agreement is to be.

On the other hand, a partnership curtails the independence of a businessperson, since he is answerable for his activities through the partnership to his other partners. In addition, a partner is personally liable for all debts incurred by the business—whether these obligations result from his own doing or from the actions of his partners. Any profits generated by the business must be divided between the partners, regardless of their contribution or lack of contribution to the activity generating those profits. Lastly, in the absence of agreement to the contrary, the partnership is automatically dissolved by the death or withdrawal from the business of any general partner in the partnership.

CORPORATION

Unlike a sole proprietorship or a partnership, both of which are legally indistinguishable from their owners, a corporation is recognized by the law as a distinct legal entity, which is separate from its owners. The corporation offers business and tax advantages which are unavailable to sole proprietors or to partners, but before incorporating a business, the entrepreneur must also be aware of the very real disadvantages that the corporate form entails.

The major nontax advantage often cited for the use of a corporation, as opposed to transacting business through a sole proprietorship or a partnership, is the limited liability afforded the stockholder of a corporation. A corporate stockholder, in theory, bears no personal responsibility for the debts and obligations of the corporation. His loss, it is said, is limited to his investment in the corporation's stock because a corporation is only liable to its creditors in an amount equal to the value of its assets. The stockholder of a small, newly formed corporation without substantial capital, however, will find illusory the concept that his own liability has become limited to the assets of his business merely because he has incorporated his business. Any bank or other creditor supplying financing to a small corporation will require the stockholders or officers of the corporation to give their personal guarantee of repayment. The responsible persons of the corporation can also find themselves personally liable for claims made against their corporations in other instances, as well—if they act with gross negligence, for example, or if they fail to pay over certain Federal and state taxes collected by the corporation.

Another presumed nontax advantage is the continuity of life of a corporation. The corporation continues to exist, regardless of the death or withdrawal of a stockholder, and under most state laws, it has a perpetual existence. However, practical problems arise, particularly in the case of a small, closely held corporation, upon the discontinuance of participation in the corporation's activities by a principal of the business, because no ready market exists for the corporation's stock. Thus, the heirs of a decedent stockholder may be left with an estate consisting of unmarketable stock, while finding themselves responsible for the payment of estate taxes due on the value of the stock.

Unlike a sole proprietorship or a partnership, the ownership interests in a corporation, represented by shares of stock, are freely transferable. Thus, the business does not terminate whenever a change of ownership occurs. As opposed to this flexibility, though, the stockholder in a corporation must consider the dilution of control which a sale of shares to outsiders may represent. A stockholder in a small corporation has every cause to be concerned by the potential loss of control that may take place when another stockholder dies or sells his stock, or when new stock is issued by the corporation.

To a large extent, the problems raised by the illiquidity of shares held by a decedent and by the potential sale of shares in a small corporation to possibly unfriendly outsiders can be resolved by restrictive or buy-sell agreements. However, there is no means of circumventing one distinct disadvantage of using the corporate entity—the increased formalities (such as corporate meetings and minutes, formal stock issuance, and other recordkeeping) and attendant legal and accounting costs, and a loss of flexibility on draws and expenses. Where corporate formalities and requirements are not observed, the corporation may not be treated as such for tax purposes, thereby destroying the anticipated tax advantages to be discussed, and the "corporate veil" could be pierced for nontax purposes, too.

The paperwork begins with the very birth of the corporation. The proprietorship or partnership comes into being when the owner or owners simply decide to transact business in that form; by contrast, the corporation may only be created by filing a "certificate" or "articles" of incorporation with the appropriate state authorities (generally the office of the secretary of state). The federal government does not charter the run-of-the-mill variety of commercial corporation, of the type under discussion here.

While requirements differ from state by state, the charter or incorporation document usually must contain the following information:

- *Corporate name.* The proposed name of the corporation may be rejected by the authorities if it is misleadingly similar to another corporate name in use or reserved for use in the state, unless written consent of the nameholder is obtained. The proposed name may also be rejected if it is off-color or otherwise offensive, or if it contains a specified word that is reserved in that state for special-purpose organizations (schools, banks, churches, etc.).
- *Purposes and powers.* In most states, the business purposes of the corporation must be explicitly spelled out, and the corporation may not engage in activities or exert powers not set forth in its charter unless the charter is amended. In some states, though, the charter may provide that the corporation will engage in any lawful business, and the full panoply of corporate powers provided by statutes may be simply incorporated by reference in the charter.
- *Location of principal office.* This provision permits the state to send required notifications, tax forms, and legal process to the corporation in timely fashion. Even if the principal office of the corporation is located outside of the state in which the corporation is chartered, the corporation is required to maintain an office for this purpose (usually, the mail drop of an agent) in the state of incorporation.
- *Stock issuance authorization.* The charter must specify the type and maximum amount of stock which the corporation may issue; unauthorized shares of stock are legally void. Typically, stock is classified as either "common" or "preferred". Common stockholders generally control the corporation by means of their ability to vote their shares at stockholder meetings; preferred stockholders usually have no vote but may be guaranteed a specified dollar dividend on their shares and have prior claim over common stockholders to corporate assets in the event of liquidation. All stock is issued either bearing an arbitrary value per share ("par value"), in which case it may not be legally sold for less than this value, or issued without an assigned value ("no par value"), in which case it may be sold for whatever value the board of directors considers appropriate.
- *Miscellaneous provisions.* Additional information sometimes called for, depending upon the state issuing the charter, may include the names of future stockholders of the corporation and the number of shares to which each subscribes, the minimum and maximum number of directors on the board of the corporation, whether or not the stockholders will be entitled to purchase a pro rata portion of any stock issued in the future ("preemptive rights"), and the anticipated tax reporting year of the corporation. In all jurisdictions, the names and addresses of the incorporators, or signatories to the charter, are required.

The requirements of state law must be strictly adhered to for the corporation to be legally organized; it does not begin its existence before the charter is approved or "filed" by the proper state official. Because these requirements are so detailed, and vary considerably from state to state, an attorney should be retained to draft and file the corporate charter.

Of course, an attorney's services are not *legally* required to organize the corporation, and the entrepreneur can himself prepare and file the charter if he has the energy and diligence to study the state's business corporation laws. However, the guidance of a skilled attorney, in addition to assuring the expeditious processing of the corporate charter, can be valuable in many other ways to the entrepreneur who has decided to incorporate his business. For one thing, the attorney should be able to advise the entrepreneur whether the laws of some other state render it more desirable to incorporate in that jurisdiction because the other state has relatively lower state taxes and organizational fees, fewer restrictions on corporate powers, and less stringent capital requirements. One location which informed entrepreneurs find attractive as a state in which to incorporate is the state of Delaware which has flexible and modern corporate laws concerning meetings of stockholder and directors, the issuance of stock, indemnification of officers and directors, corporate mergers, and so forth, as well as favorable tax laws and a judiciary with a generally probusiness perspective.

Then again, the attorney can advise the entrepreneur as to any other procedures that must be followed to lawfully organize the corporation under state law, in addition to filing the charter. Some states, for example, require that the proposed name of the corporation be reserved *prior* to the filing of the charter. Others require that a statement naming the elected officers be filed, or that formal permission to issue stock be obtained.

The attorney will also point out other steps that should be taken immediately after the charter has been filed, although these procedures may not be clearly spelled out in the law or, for that matter, even mentioned at all. For example, the incorporator should act promptly to elect an initial board of directors and adopt corporate bylaws. The initial board of directors should take action to approve the actions of the incorporator, elect officers, issue shares, open the corporation's bank account, determine the stated capital of the corporation, adopt a fiscal year, etc. A new federal identification number must be obtained for the corporation, and state tax and labor requirements met. If the corporation will be transacting business on an ongoing basis in states other than the one where it was incorporated, it must qualify to do business in those other states. These actions all have independent significance, and if not performed properly, can at the very least impede the effective operation of the corporation.

Most important, a knowledgeable attorney can apprise his client of the tax advantages to be gained through use of the corporate entity, which are substantially greater than those afforded the sole proprietor or the partner. A corporation is an entity separate from the entrepreneur but which can be owned solely by him, and can be paid (and taxed) upon income it is paid for the services or other work product of the entrepreneur, such as his musical compositions, entertainment skills, personal management services, etc. In return, as an employee of the corporation, the entrepreneur is paid a salary from the corporation, which the corporation claims as a deduction from its income for tax purposes, and which reduces the amount subject to tax in its hands. The tax payable on its earnings is not high (relatively speaking) since corporate tax rates are lower than individual rates on equivalent amounts of income. Moreover, the amount paid out as salary may be less than the income realized by the corporation during its taxable year, thus enabling the entrepreneur to spread income over a number of years. In the aggregate, the amount of tax payable by the corporation and by the entrepreneur may be substantially less than the amount which would have been paid by the entrepreneur had all of the income been attributable directly to him in the first instance.

Compare, for example, the amount of tax payable by an entrepreneur-artist with taxable income during the year of $100,000, with the amount of tax payable by a corporation realizing the same amount of income but which pays its employee-artist a salary of $25,000. In the first instance, assuming that the entrepreneur's income all qualifies as personal service income subject to the maximum tax rate, his federal income tax liability at 1979 rates, filing singly, would be $42,642, were he to realize directly the $100,000 taxable income. On the other hand, the total federal tax liability of both the corporation and the employee in the second instance would be $22,702—a savings of $19,940. This savings would be unattainable if the entrepreneur conducted his business through a proprietorship or partnership, since, as noted, those forms of enterprise act as conduits for tax purposes rather than as distinct taxable entities capable of themselves earning income or of being taxed on it.

Inherent in the fact that the corporation is a separate entity for tax purposes is the concept of the "double taxation" of corporate earnings. This aspect of the tax law is best demonstrated by the distribution of corporate earnings to the stockholders in the form of dividends: These earnings are fully taxed to the corporation at the time they are earned, without reduction for any amounts to be distributed to the stockholders as dividends, and are taxed a second time, when received by the stockholders, as dividends. In an extreme situation, if the corporation is taxed at the highest federal corporate tax rate (46% in 1979) on income which is distributed as a dividend to an individual shareholder who is himself taxed at the highest federal tax rate (70% in 1979), the total effective rate of federal income tax on the corporation's income is 83.80% and if state and local taxes were included, this percentage would be even higher.

One means of avoiding double taxation is for the corporation to elect "Subchapter S" status, discussed later on in this chapter, which has its own set of tax disadvantages to accompany this singular advantage. Another alternative is for a stockholder to forgo current dividend distributions from the corporation and instead to incur the stockholder level tax in the form of capital gains when he sells his shares or at the time the corporation liquidates in the future. However, to deter unreasonable accumulations of income in hopes of avoiding the double taxation, the tax law provides two penalty taxes—the accumulated earnings tax and the personal holding company tax—both of which are intended to compel the current payment of corporate income as dividends.

The accumulated earnings tax is a surtax, in the nature of a penalty, which is imposed on the earnings of corporations which retain income in excess of amounts reasonably required to meet their business needs. However, since a corporation may accumulate a minimum amount of $150,000 from its past and present earnings before this tax may be imposed, this tax poses little realistic threat to most fledgling corporations.

The personal holding company provisions, which impose another penalty tax, may present more of a problem, especially to corporations formed by entrepreneurs in the arts. An ordinary, non-Subchapter S corporation is a "personal holding company" if at least 60 percent of its ordinary gross income, as adjusted, consists of "personal holding company income" and at any time during the last half of its taxable year, more than 50 percent in value of its outstanding stock is owned, directly or indirectly, by or for not more than five individuals. The term "personal holding company income" means, for the most part, passive income such as dividends, interest, royalties, and rents. The term "personal holding company income" *also* includes amounts received by a corporation from contracts for personal services if the individual who is to perform the services is designated by name or by description in the contract, and at some time during the taxable year, the designated individual owned, directly or indirectly, 25 percent or more in value of the outstanding stock of the corporation.

Thus, for example, if an artist's wholly owned corporation was to make his services available under an agreement that called for him by name to perform those services, the income so derived by the corporation would constitute "personal holding company" income. If this "tainted" income in conjunction with income from passive sources (which, as noted, includes royalties), comprised 60 percent of the corporation's total income, the corporation could be liable for the penalty tax. However, since the designation in the personal service contract must be explicit in order for the income from the contract to be counted toward the 60 percent test, if the contract did not *name* the person who was to perform the services and the party contracting with the corporation was not given the right to designate the 25 percent stockholder to perform the services, then the income derived from the contract would not be "tainted", even in the case of a one-man corporation.

Since the personal holding company tax only applies to *undistributed* income of a regular corporation, it is clearly in the best interests of the stockholders to monitor the income and outflow of their corporation during its taxable year to insure either that the corporation is not a personal holding company or that it has little or no undistributed personal holding company income. If the corporation's "bottom line" can be brought down to or near zero by means of legitimate corporate business expenses, the penalty tax should have no impact and the problem of double taxation will be minimized.

Among the measures suggested by tax planners to avoid income tax at the corporate level are the following:

- *"Thin stock."* This technique calls for the creation of a high proportion of corporate debt in relation to corporate equity. The advantages of doing so are twofold: The investor is repaid the debt as a tax-free return of capital, and prior to repayment of the debt, the interest paid on it is deductible to the corporation. On the other hand, creditors and potential investors may refrain from dealing with a corporation that is burdened by a great deal of debt. Also, if the corporation's ratio of debt to equity is excessive (generally speaking, more than four to one), the I.R.S. may treat the "debt" as additional equity investment in the corporation. This would result in a disallowance of the corporation's interest deduction and the treatment of these "interest" payments to the recipient as dividends, as well as any repayment of the debt itself being deemed proceeds from the redemption of stock.

• *Leasing arrangements.* Since bona fide rental payments constitute a legitimate business expense to a corporation, stockholders may lease property used in the corporation's business to it in an attempt to reduce its taxable income. For the lease arrangement to be upheld for tax purposes, though, the rentals must approximate what would have been paid an outside lessor dealing at armslength with the corporation. Excessive rentals will be disallowed by the I.R.S. as a business expense deduction to the corporation and treated as dividend income to the recipient stockholder.

• *Salaries and fringe benefits.* The usual and preferred method of reducing or eliminating the double tax is to pay salaries and bonuses, and confer fringe benefits, on the stockholder-employees in an amount sufficient to offset the corporation's income. These expenses are deductible to the corporation, provided that the stockholder receiving this compensation has actually rendered services to the corporation and the amount of the compensation is "reasonable," a concept discussed subsequently. If the corporation's compensation deduction is unquestioned or unchanged by the I.R.S., the one tax incurred on this income is that paid by the recipient stockholder, who would report this income as qualifying for the 50 percent maximum federal tax on personal service income. On the other hand, compensation payments which the I.R.S. finds to exceed a reasonable amount are treated as dividend distributions, and may not be deducted by the payor corporation or reported as personal service income qualifying for the maximum tax rate by the stockholder-payee.

Practically speaking, compensation payments include not only the hard dollar amounts written on an employee's paycheck, but also the value of the nontaxable fringe benefits and employee benefit programs that an employee is provided by his employer-corporation. As noted, in a proprietorship or a partnership, the proprietor or the partners must pay for their own welfare programs themselves, and they obtain no business deduction for payments made to purchase their own benefits. By contrast, a corporation can provide substantial benefits to its employees, including its stockholder-employees, which are nontaxable to the employees but which are deductible by the corporation, so long as the value of these benefits, considered together with the amount of actual compensation paid to the employees, constitutes reasonable payment for services rendered.

These benefits include the following:

• *Tax-qualified retirement plans.* The most advantageous fringe benefit available through a corporation—in fact, one reason why many informed entrepreneurs choose to incorporate their business—is the ability to adopt a corporate pension or profit-sharing plan. A pension plan provides some type of retirement payment for participating employees, either based upon a predetermined retirement benefit or a fixed annual contribution to the plan; a profit-sharing plan, on the other hand, does not contain a predetermined formula for calculating an employee's retirement benefit or the employer's annual contribution, but instead provides for contributions in a varying amount, which are based upon the profits of the employer and made in the discretion of the board of directors of the corporation. Tax-qualified retirement plans are available through the installation of any such plan in a regular corporation (as opposed, for example, to a Subchapter S corporation) where the larger contributions are permitted and result in larger retirement benefits.

Provided that the plan has received formal approval from the I.R.S. and is operated in conformity with the law, contributions to the plan are immediately deductible to the employer-corporation—an especially beneficial feature in high-income years—though the participating employees are not taxed on these contributions (or any earnings on these contributions) until they are actually distributed or otherwise made available to them. Generally, the distribution would not take place until the death, disability, or retirement of the employee, and at that time, the distribution could qualify for favorable income or estate tax treatment.

- *Group term life insurance.* Premiums paid by a corporation on a plan of group term life insurance are deductible by the corporation and, to the extent coverage per employee does not exceed $50,000, such premiums are not treated as additional compensation to its employees. Premiums on coverage over $50,000 are taxed to the employee but the employee may nevertheless receive a substantial benefit through such coverage, since the actuarial tables of insurance coverage costs used by the I.R.S. in determining the includable income to the employee show costs significantly below those actually paid by the corporation. In addition, insurance proceeds received by beneficiaries of the employee are exempt from federal income tax.

- *Medical expense reimbursement.* The corporation may extend to its employees a medical expense reimbursement plan and/or a health or accident plan, under which the corporation pays the costs of medical care of the employee, either directly or through reimbursement to the employee, and/or the costs of the employee's Blue Cross-Blue Shield or similar health insurance and major medical insurance premiums, as well as premiums for accident or disability insurance. Corporate payments under these plans are excluded from the income of the employee and are deductible to the corporation, and, at present, these plans may cover only those key employees whom the corporation wishes to cover. After 1980, uninsured medical reimbursement plans will have to meet stringent new coverage standards if key employees are to continue to obtain the exclusion, but these standards will not apply to plans under which benefits are provided by a licensed insurance company.

- *Death benefit.* The corporation may pay a death benefit to the survivors of a deceased employee, and the corporation's payments, up to the total amount of $5,000, will be free of income tax to the employee's survivors while deductible to the corporation. The death benefit need not be paid under a plan or even under any contractual obligation of the employer. However, the income tax exclusion is only available if the deceased employee did not have immediately prior to his death a nonforfeitable right to receive the amounts while living, such as under a wage-continuation plan or an annuity. But where the right to receive the death benefit is forfeitable, either upon leaving employment or upon the failure to satisfy certain conditions, the death benefit qualifies for the $5,000 exclusion.

- *Deferred compensation.* A stockholder-employee may enter into a deferred compensation arrangement with the corporation based upon the promise of the corporation to pay a specified amount of income to the employee at a given time in the future. This precludes the employee from being charged with current taxable income, even if the deferred amount is nonforfeitable to the employee. When the deferred payment falls due, the employee may be in a lower tax bracket and therefore pay substantially less tax than were he to receive the payment currently. Also, these payments qualify as personal service income of the employee, whenever received, for purposes of the 50 per cent federal maximum tax rate.

There are two major disadvantages to nontax qualified arrangements of deferred compensation such as this. From the standpoint of the employer, the drawback is that its deduction of these payments is deferred until the year the employee includes them in his income. From the standpoint of the employee, the problem is that he may only preserve the current nontaxable status of these payments if they are not placed in escrow or otherwise funded by the employer. If the employer purchases an insurance policy to pay for these deferred amounts, the employee may have no interest in the insurance policy, either. Thus, the employee must rely on the ability of the corporation to pay these amounts when due and is unable to protect his right to payment in any real way.

As noted, the corporation may only deduct salaries and the cost of other benefits to the extent they are "reasonable" in amount; any portion found to be "unreasonable" would be subject to tax on the part of the corporation and a second time on the part of the recipient as unearned income. In determining reasonableness, the I.R.S. looks to the amount of salary paid counterparts of the employee in comparable business, as well as such other factors as the employee's duties, the complexity of the business, the value or uniqueness of the employee's services, and the percentage of the corporation's gross and net income paid out in salaries.

An entrepreneur in the arts, rendering his creative abilities or his personal services through a corporate entity, probably has little to fear from a claim of unreasonable compensation. Since all or most of the earnings of the corporation paid to or for the benefit of the entrepreneur is directly attributable to the talents or services of the entrepreneur, the compensation paid to him through his corporation is related to the services that he actually rendered and the value of those services in the marketplace. In an analogous situation, the courts have held that salary paid to a professional by his corporation is reasonable compensation to the extent that the payments do not exceed amounts received by the corporation for his services.

The I.R.S. has a stronger case for disallowing a deduction of compensation if the payment represents a return on capital invested in the business, rather than for services rendered to the business. For example, an incorporated entrepreneur might be tempted to place a portfolio of stocks into his corporation's name after having learned from his tax advisor that regular corporations are entitled to deduct from their income 85 per cent of dividends they receive from domestic corporations. If the corporation was to pay a portion of these dividends to the entrepreneur and attempt to deduct them as payments of compensation, however, the I.R.S. would most likely claim that these amounts represent a nondeductible distribution of corporate earnings, rather than deductible compensation for services rendered.

Another argument which the I.R.S. is apt to raise, especially in the case of a one-man incorporated talent or service business, is that the corporation's income is not taxable to it but is properly taxable to the person who earned it for the corporation. This contention, if upheld, can spell tax disaster for the entrepreneur, since the result is to invalidate the corporation's deduction of compensation and all the related corporate benefits that are compensation-related (primarily, pension or profit-sharing plan contributions).

The decided cases in this area suggest that this problem can be avoided through careful planning and documentation of the transactions involved. For example, in a well-known case involving the estate of Nat "King" Cole, Cole transferred to a related corporation his rights to receive royalties from the use of master recordings which he had previously made and he also agreed to record new masters for this corporation as its employee. Cole having since died, the Government sought to tax Cole's estate on income earned by the corporation from the contract rights to the royalties on the old masters and from the new masters recorded by Cole for the corporation. The U.S. Tax Court held, however, that the corporation had earned this income, since it had acquired the property generating this income under an arms-length agreement from the payor of the royalty income and under an employment agreement with Cole.

In so holding, the court relied upon an earlier case involving Fontaine Fox, the creator of several cartoon series, and his 98 per cent owned corporation, named Reynard. Under an employment agreement, Fox transferred to Reynard the copyrights to his previously published cartoons and his rights with third parties to royalties for the exploitation of his cartoon characters, and he agreed to render to Reynard his exclusive services as a cartoonist. Reynard then entered into syndication agreements for Fox's cartoons, and it paid Fox a salary for producing his creations for Reynard. The government attempted to attribute to Fox the income reported by Reynard from the royalty agreements and the syndication contracts. The Board of Tax Appeals disagreed and held that the corporation was taxable on the income it had derived from the disposition of property created by its stockholder-employee.

These cases, however, should be contrasted with another decision involving the entertainer Victor Borge. Borge was the sole stockholder of Danica, a corporation engaged in the business of raising poultry. Since Danica was experiencing losses of approximately $50,000 a year, Borge was counseled to channel his entertainment services through the corporation. Borge and Danica thereupon entered into a contract under which Borge agreed to perform entertainment and promotional services for Danica for a five-year period for compensation from Danica of $50,000 per year. Danica offset its poultry-derived losses against its entertainment-derived income (which far exceeded the $50,000 it had agreed to pay Borge for such profits). The I.R.S. proceeded to allocate a part of the corporation's income to Borge, and both the Tax Court and the Court of Appeals for the Second Circuit upheld the allocation, notwithstanding the fact that the corporation was a legally formed entity and the employment relationship between Borge and Danica was unquestionably genuine.

In its opinion, the appellate court reasoned:

> Danica did nothing to aid Borge in his entertainment business. Those who contracted with Danica for Borge's entertainment services required Borge personally to guarantee the contracts. Danica's entertainment earnings were attributable solely to the services of Borge and Danica's only profits were from the entertainment business. . . .
>
> Here . . . Borge was in the business of entertaining. He was not devoting his time and energies to the corporation; he was carrying on his career as an entertainer, and merely channeling a part of his entertainment through the corporation.

Thus, the Borge case, as well as others to the same effect, indicate that where an entrepreneur is conducting his own trade or business and channels a portion of his earnings from that trade or business to a controlled corporation, these earnings may be reallocated from the corporation to the entrepreneur, who will be taxed on this income as its true earner.

Prudence requires preparedness to ward off an I.R.S. attack of this type. In the first place, the entrepreneur's trade or business activities should be conducted entirely through the corporation, to the maximum extent feasible. Second, any preexisting agreements between the entrepreneur and outside parties for the services of the entrepreneur should be terminated; new contracts should then be entered into between the corporation and these outside parties and an employment agreement signed between the corporation and the entrepreneur. Third, the corporation at all times must act as a bona fide business entity. Thus, for example, all of its business expenses (such as office supplies, rental for office space, etc.) should be incurred on its own behalf, and all retainers, billings, and communications regarding the entrepreneur's services should likewise be in the name of the corporation. Finally, the corporation should withhold income tax on wages paid to its corporate employees, including the entrepreneur, and in all other respects conform to the tax laws respecting employers.

Having weighed the risks and rewards of operating in corporate form, and having concluded that the general arithmetic of incorporation seems favorable and its business advantages appear desirable, how does the entrepreneur convert his proprietorship or partnership into a corporation without incurring unexpected tax liabilities? An individual may incorporate his sole proprietorship on a completely tax-free basis by transferring the assets of the business to the corporation solely in exchange for its stock and securities, if immediately after the transfer he is in control of the corporation through ownership of at least 80 per cent of its voting stock and at least 80 per cent of the total number of shares of all other classes of stock of the corporation. If the sole proprietor and another person both transfer assets to a corporation, neither pay any tax if the exchange is solely in exchange for stock or securities of the newly formed corporation and in the aggregate they meet the 80 per cent ownership test immediately after the transfer. Likewise, a partnership may be incorporated on a tax-free basis if the partners contribute assets of the partnership to the corporation solely in exchange for stock or securities, and immediately after the exchange the partners meet the 80 per cent test of stock ownership. In no event do the transferors realize any loss from the exchange if the 80 per cent ownership test is met, and for this reason the transferors may wish to avoid meeting this test if depreciated (rather than appreciated) assets are transferred in an incorporation exchange.

Where more than one person transfers assets in an incorporation exchange, the stock or securities received by the transferor need not be substantially in proportion to the value of the assets contributed to the corporation. However, while any such disproportion will not render the exchange with the corporation taxable, the excess may represent a gift or taxable compensation.

The corporation takes as its tax basis in the transferred assets for purposes of depreciation or resale the same basis that the assets had in the hands of the transferor, even though their value may be more (or less) than their tax basis at the time of the exchange. The corporation's tax basis may be affected, though, if any gain is recognized to the transferor upon the exchange, which will be the case if the transferor receives any money or other property from the corporation in addition to receiving its stock or securities. If any of the transferred assets are subject to liabilities, the corporation may take the property subject to or assume these liabilities without the transferors realizing gain from the assumption or otherwise placing in jeopardy the tax-free nature of the exchange, except where certain types of liabilities exceed the tax basis of the transferred assets or if a tax avoidance motive is found to have been present for the corporation's assumption of the debt.

The withdrawal of capital from a corporation is a far more complex subject for tax purposes than are the relatively simple and clear-cut rules governing incorporation. In fact, the provisions of the Internal Revenue Code concerning capital withdrawals, whether in the form of stock redemptions or corporate liquidations, are among the most notoriously difficult and treacherous in the entire tax law. The barest rudiments are discussed here, but at no time should a transaction of redemption or liquidation be undertaken by an entrepreneur without first obtaining the advice of a competent tax professional.

In this area, the critical distinction to be initially drawn is between a redemption treated as a sale or exchange of stock and a redemption treated as a dividend; the former is subject to capital gain rates and the latter subject to ordinary income rates. A stockholder is deemed to have made a sale or exchange of his stock and therefore may report his redemption proceeds at capital gains rates if the redemption meets any of the following three tests:

- The distribution will not be treated as a dividend if it is "substantially disproportionate" with respect to the stockholder, which requires the stockholder to have his stockholdings reduced by more than 20 per cent in the redemption and own less than 50 per cent of the voting stock of the corporation after the redemption.
- The distribution will not be treated as a dividend if it is "in complete redemption of all stock of the corporation" owned by the stockholder, which requires a complete termination of the stockholder's stock interests, direct or indirect, in the corporation.
- The distribution will not be treated as a dividend if it "is not substantially equivalent to a dividend," which requires some showing of a diminution of corporate control on the part of the stockholder as a result of the redemption, though such diminution may be less than the degree necessary to satisfy the "substantially disproportionate" test.

If the stockholders make an actual sale or exchange of their stock to an outside purchaser, as opposed to "selling" stock to the issuing corporation in a redemption, the stockholders realize capital gain or loss and no taxable event takes place at the corporate level. If the corporation distributes its assets to its stockholders by way of a partial or complete liquidation, the stockholders also realize capital gain or loss upon the distribution, unless certain specific exceptions apply, and the corporation, as a general rule, realizes no gain or loss upon the liquidation. However, if the corporation sells its assets preliminary to a liquidation, it realizes gain or loss upon the sale and the stockholders also realize gain or loss upon the distribution in liquidation; in this case, however, the tax at the corporate level may be eliminated if the sale of assets by the corporation was pursuant to a plan of complete liquidation adopted within 12 months prior to the liquidation.

If the sale or distribution of corporate assets takes place before the corporation realizes a substantial part of the taxable income to be derived from certain types of property, the corporation may be said to be "collapsible", with the result that gain realized from the proceeds of sale or distributions in liquidation is treated as ordinary income. To be collapsible, however, the corporation must have been "formed" or "availed of" with a view to the premature sale or exchange of its stock or liquidation. Even if such a "view" is present, several defenses are available, among them that a substantial part of the taxable income from certain assets has been realized prior to the sale or liquidation; that the untaxed appreciation in those assets constitutes less than a specified percentage of the net worth of the corporation; and that the specified assets have been held by the corporation for over three years.

The collapsible corporation provisions only concern the treatment of gain; an investor's loss in a corporation's stock is treated as a capital loss and is subject to the limitations on deductibility applicable to capital losses. As an exception to this general rule of capital loss, however, Section 1244 of the Internal Revenue Code permits an individual to treat a loss from his investment in the common stock of certain "small business corporations" as an *ordinary* loss rather than as a capital loss. A "Section 1244 loss" includes a stockholder's loss incurred on a sale or exchange of his stock, in partial or complete liquidations of the corporation, in redemptions of the stock, or even if the stock becomes worthless. The maximum deductible amount is at present $50,000 ($100,000 in the case of a married couple filing jointly), and the stock must have been issued to the individual claiming the loss for money or property, but not for services or other stock. In addition, the corporation issuing the stock must have met certain standards having to do with its size and capitalization at the time the stock was issued and at the time the loss was sustained.

To summarize, the corporation from its birth to its death is the most complex of business organizations. Treated as an entity separate and apart from its owners, it insulates its owners from unlimited liability, allows them flexibility in transferring their ownership interests in the business without terminating it, and affords them significant tax advantages unavailable through the use of a sole proprietorship or a partnership.

There are prominent disadvantages, too. A corporation entails greater expense of organization and upkeep and more formalities than a proprietorship or partnership and may not in a practical sense provide a stockholder with limited liability. For tax purposes, the major drawback to the use of a corporation is the phenomenon of "double taxation," i.e., that corporate earnings are taxed initially to the corporation, and if distributed as a dividend, are then taxed a second time to the stockholder. Also, since the corporation is treated as an independent entity for all tax purposes, neither its gains nor its losses flow through to the stockholders; an entrepreneur who anticipates initial start-up losses in his business should therefore consider a proprietorship, partnership, or, as discussed below, a Subchapter S corporation.

SUBCHAPTER S CORPORATION

A Subchapter S corporation is a tax hybrid. For all nontax purposes, the Subchapter S corporation is a true corporation that operates in the same manner as any other validly formed corporation and that provides its stockholders with the same advantages and drawbacks of a regular corporation. But for tax purposes, this type of entity is treated generally as if it were a partnership—meaning that its net earnings are not taxed at the corporate level but instead flow through to the stockholders, who include their pro rata share of the corporation's income on their individual returns, regardless of whether this income is in fact distributed. Also, like a partnership (but unlike a regular corporation), any operating losses sustained by the entity flow through to its investor-stockholders, who may deduct such losses on their individual returns and thereby offset ordinary income by a like amount.

These two paramount advantages of the Subchapter S corporation—the avoidance of double taxation on corporate earnings and the availability of corporate losses to the stockholders individually—are only available to corporations which qualify to elect Subchapter S status *and* validly make the election. The eligibility provisions for making the election, which were liberalized by the Tax Reform Act of 1976 and the Revenue Act of 1978, are technical, but involve essentially the following five requirements:

- *Number of stockholders.* The corporation may have up to 15 stockholders; a husband and wife are treated as one stockholder for this purpose regardless of the legal ownership of the stock.
- *Type of stockholders.* The corporation may not have stockholders other than individuals (none of whom may be nonresident alien individuals) or certain types of trusts and estates.
- *Outstanding stock.* The corporation may have only one class of stock outstanding, thus, the issuance of any preferred stock or nonvoting common stock will disqualify the corporation from Subchapter S status.
- *Situs of incorporation.* The corporation must be a domestic corporation, i.e., incorporated and validly existing within one of the fifty states.
- *No subsidiaries.* The corporation may not be a member of an "affiliated group," or parent-subsidiary chain of corporations.

Because the technical term used in the tax law to refer to Subchapter C corporations is "electing small business corporation," the mistaken impression has been created that restrictions exist as to the size of a corporation eligible for the election. The law contains no such restrictions, however; a corporation as large in size as General Motors could elect to be taxed under Subchapter S if it met the five requirements outlined above.

Each stockholder of the corporation must consent in writing to the Subchapter S election, which is made on Form 2558, and which must be timely filed. For newly organized corporations, the election form must be filed within the first month of the corporation's taxable year; this first month is deemed to commence when the corporation has stockholders or acquires assets or begins doing business, whichever is the first to occur. For corporations already in existence, the election may be made for a corporate year at any time during the corporation's preceding year or during the first seventy five days of the year for which the election is desired.

A Subchapter S election terminates upon the occurrence of any of the following events:

- *Ineligibility.* If the corporation fails at any time to satisfy any of the eligibility requirements (for example, by issuing shares of a second class of stock or admitting a nonresident alien individual as a stockholder), the election terminates retroactive to the beginning of the taxable year of such ineligibility.
- *Affirmative refusal.* If a new stockholder files with the I.R.S. an affirmative refusal to consent to the election, Subchapter S status is terminated retroactive to the beginning of the taxable year of such refusal.
- *"Tainted" income.* If the corporation derives more than 80 per cent of its gross receipts from sources outside the United States or derives more than 20 per cent of its gross receipts from such passive income sources as royalties, rents, dividends, interest, annuities and sales, or exchanges of stocks or securities, the election is terminated retroactive to the beginning of the taxable year in which this mix of income is derived. As a limited exception to the passive income rule,

the law provides that the election will not terminate if the 20 per cent limitation is exceeded in the first taxable year in which the corporation commenced the active conduct of its trade or business or the next succeeding taxable year *and* the amount of such passive income for the taxable year is less than $3,000.

- *Stockholder revocation.* The Subchapter S election can also be terminated by its deliberate revocation, consented to in writing by all of the stockholders. Termination by revocation is effective only for the next succeeding taxable year unless it occurs within the first taxable month of the corporation. No new election of Subchapter S status can be elected for five years following the revocation (or termination) of the election, unless the I.R.S. consents to the election.

Once an election has been validly made, how is a Subchapter S corporation and its stockholders taxed? For most federal income tax purposes, an electing corporation is not a separate taxable entity, since it is not taxed on its ordinary income or, in general, on its capital gain income. Instead, the corporation files an information return on Form 1120-S, rather than the regular corporate return, and those persons who own stock in the corporation on the last day of its taxable year are taxed on its undistributed income for that year. Since this flow-through is limited to the corporation's undistributed earnings, all salaries, bonuses, and fringe benefits paid to or for the benefit of the corporation's employees (including stockholder-employees), to the extent reasonable and otherwise deductible by the corporation, reduce the earnings deemed distributed by the corporation at the end of its years. Also, income distributed during the year is taxed to those who receive it under the general dividend rules and such distributions further reduce the year-end "deemed distributions."

Net operating losses of Subchapter S corporations are passed through to those stockholders who hold stock in the corporation at any time during the year of the loss. The pass-through of loss to any stockholder is proportionate to the number of days on which he holds stock during the taxable year. For example, if a stockholder owned one-half of the outstanding stock for 60 days during the loss year, his share of the corporation's loss would be one-half of 60/365's of the loss. All Subchapter S derived income and loss derived by the stockholder is reported on Schedule E of his return filed for his year in which or within which ends the corporation's year.

A Subchapter S stockholder may only deduct his share of loss to the extent of the sum of the basis of his stock in the corporation and his basis in any indebtedness that the corporation owes to him. The basis of the stockholder in his stock is a fluctuating figure, which is increased by the share of undistributed Subchapter S income upon which he is taxed and which is decreased by his share of operating losses. If a stockholder has insufficient basis in his stock and corporate debt to permit him to fully utilize his share of corporate losses, he is generally not permitted to carry over excess losses to future years and these losses are permanently lost.

The taxation of distributions of earnings by a Subchapter S corporation is very complex, and special rules govern the determination of whether a distribution consists of previously taxed income or of current income, or whether it constitutes an ordinary dividend taxed as such to the stockholder. As a general rule, amounts taxed to the stockholders as year-end "deemed distributions", having been taxed once to the stockholder, are not taxed a second time and may be distributed tax-free to the stockholder within the first two and one-half months of the year following the year in which such amounts were earned by the corporation. However, this previously taxed amount is *not* distributable on a tax-free basis if the entitled stockholder transfers or disposes of all of his stock or if the Subchapter S election terminates for any reason, or to the extent that current earnings are not first distributed if the previously taxed income is distributed after the two and one-half month grace period.

Since undistributed earnings are taxable only to those persons who are stockholders on the last day of the corporation's taxable year, a transfer of shares to a low-bracket taxpayer before the close of the tax year will effectively reduce the tax payable by the stockholders on the corporate earnings. This shifting of interest is unavailable, however, to transfer corporate losses because, as noted, such losses flow through pro rata to every person who was a stockholder during the year of the loss.

In addition to the possibility of "income splitting" in a profitable year, a Subchapter S election may provide a substantial deferral of time for the stockholder to pay any tax due in connection with the year-end "deemed distribution." This comes about by reason of the corporation's ability to report on the basis of a fiscal year while the stockholder, if an individual, will generally report on the basis of a calendar year. For example, if the Subchapter S corporation's taxable year began February 1, 1978 and ended January 31, 1979, the undistributed earnings of the corporation would be taxable to those persons who are its stockholders on January 31, 1979 and includable in their incomes for their taxable years ending December 31, 1979, assuming they are calendar-year taxpayers. Thus, no tax would be paid on what are essentially 1978 earnings until the stockholders' returns, due April 15, 1980, are filed.

Another advantage that is often pointed out to electing Subchapter S status is that this type of corporation is not subject to the accumulated earnings tax or personal holding company provisions applicable to regular corporations. Logically, there is no reason why either penalty tax should apply—the distribution of corporate earnings which the accumulated earnings tax is intended to accomplish is effectuated by the "deemed distribution" provisions, and the prohibition on deriving more than 20 per cent of corporate receipts in the form of passive income precludes imposition of the personal holding company surtax.

A Subchapter S election is by no means an unmixed blessing. There are substantial drawbacks which may render such a corporation an unattractive or unfeasible choice of entity through which to conduct business. Some of the more prominent disadvantages are the following:

• The strict limitations on the amount of passive income that a Subchapter S corporation is allowed to derive may preclude such an election on the part of an entrepreneur in the arts who anticipates substantial income from royalty or license income.

• A Subchapter S stockholder is unable to carry forward and deduct in future years any flow-through losses in excess of his investment in the corporation (including debt); by contrast, a partner may carry forward and deduct his share of the partnership's losses in excess of his partnership basis at any time in the future that his basis is increased sufficiently by his investment of additional capital in the partnership or by his share of the partnership's earnings.

- Corporate income taxed to the stockholder at year-end as a "deemed distribution" generally loses the character it had when received by the corporation, and is taxed to the stockholder as a dividend, at rates as high as 70 per cent on the federal level, rather than as earned or personal service income qualifying for the 50 per cent maximum federal tax rate on personal service income. Thus, the election may be inappropriate for a high-bracket taxpayer whose employer-corporation could pay him all or most of its income as deductible compensation.

- Regular corporations are permitted to deduct substantially greater amounts as contributions to tax-qualified retirement plans than are Subchapter S corporations. Also, more liberal rules with respect to vesting, or nonforfeitability of employer contributions, and coordination with Social Security benefits are provided with respect to tax-qualified retirement plans adopted by regular corporations.

- Since previously taxed income of the Subchapter S corporation must usually be distributed within two and one-half months of the close of the taxable year to insure the tax-free nature of the distribution, an election may be inappropriate if the corporation will have inadequate cash flow or will be unable to borrow funds to distribute this income or otherwise must retain the income in the business.

- A Subchapter S corporation may not carry back or carry forward net operating losses from nonelection years to election years, with the result that tax refunds or savings attributable to these losses from years when the entity was taxed as a regular corporation will be lost.

- In many states, a Subchapter S election is not recognized for state franchise tax purposes, and the entity is taxed as any other corporation.

In short, the provisions governing the taxation of Subchapter S corporations are complex and the law's many restrictions may render the benefits of Subchapter S unavailable or unuseful for many entrepreneurs who wish to do business in corporate form. On the other hand, if the entrepreneur anticipates start-up losses in his business, he may elect Subchapter S status for the period in which the business will generate a loss. He then has the option of revoking the election when the business turns profitable, if he is a high-bracket taxpayer at that time, or wishes to attain the tax advantages available only to regular corporations.

TAX-EXEMPT ORGANIZATION

A word must be added at this point about the tax-exempt organization, which in its method of organization and operation differs greatly from the commercial business entity. To acquire tax-exempt status, the organization must be validly formed under state law to engage in a non-profit purpose which the tax law expressly declares to be tax-exempt and then obtain recognition of its tax-exempt status from the I.R.S.

In general, contributions to only certain types of tax-exempt organizations entitle the donor to a tax deduction of the amount or the value of any property contributed to the organization. These special organizations, listed in Section 501(c)(3) of the Internal Revenue Code, include those organized exclusively for, and operated for, charitable, educational, or literary purposes. No part of the net earnings of such organizations may inure to the benefit of private interests, nor may such entities attempt to influence legislation (unless an election is made to come under newly enacted provisions allowing certain lobbying expenditures) or participate to any extent in a political campaign for or against any candidate for public office.

The I.R.S. has ruled on numerous occasions that an entity formed to promote the arts may qualify as an educational, literary, or charitable tax-exempt organization, depending on its activities, so long as the activity furthers the public interest (as opposed to the private interest of the organization's founders or principals). For example, each of the following was found to qualify for recognition by the I.R.S. of its tax-exempt status:

- an organization which produced plays and made classic works of theatre available in cities and colleges by means of a touring repertory company;
- an organization formed to operate and maintain a school to teach the art of dance (with an emphasis on contemporary dance);
- an organization created to develop and promote an appreciation of jazz music as an American art form through the presentation of public jazz festivals and concerts;
- an organization formed to promote a public appreciation of group harmony singing and to educate its members and the general public in this type of music;
- an organization encouraging and promoting the advancement of young musical artists by conducting weekly workshops, sponsoring public concerts by such artists, and securing paid engagements for them to improve their professional standing;
- an organization created to sponsor a public art exhibit at which works of unknown but promising artists are selected by qualified judges for viewing and are gratuitously displayed;
- an organization formed to promote the art of filmmaking by conducting annual festivals to provide unknown independent filmmakers with the opportunity to display films and by sponsoring symposiums on filmmaking;
- an organization providing awards and grants, including scholarships and fellowship grants, to needy individuals to enable them to continue their work in the creative arts, as well as their education and studies, without any monetary benefit to the donor organization.

It is instructive to contrast the purposes of the foregoing organizations with those of entities that the I.R.S. ruled did *not* merit tax exemption. In one ruling, a group of artists formed and operated a cooperative art gallery for the purpose of exhibiting and selling their works. The I.R.S. held that the cooperative was a taxable entity, since the artists were being directly benefited by the exhibition and sale of their work. Since this benefit was substantial, rather than incidental to the avowed educational purpose of the organization, it failed to qualify for tax-exempt status.

In another instance, a nonprofit organization was formed by a group of art patrons to promote community understanding of modern art trends by selecting for exhibit, exhibiting, and selling art works of local artists. The artists had no control over the selection of which of their works were displayed. The organization retained a 10 per cent sales commission on any of its sales, which was less than customary commercial charges and not sufficient to cover the cost of operating the gallery. Nevertheless, the I.R.S. ruled that the organization was not tax-exempt because the major activity of the organization was to serve the private interests of the artists whose works were displayed for sale. The fact that 90 per cent of the sales proceeds was turned over to the individual artists signified that the direct benefit to the artists was substantial, rather than incidental to the organization's other purposes and activities.

The organization, therefore, must not only be formed for exempt purposes but actively operate in such a fashion as to further these purposes. The entity need not necessarily be a corporation—it may be an association or a trust—but it must be validly formed under state law under a written organizational document and procedural rules or bylaws. The formation of such an organization may entail the prior approval under state law of some department, especially if educational or charitable functions are present or proposed, and the continued supervision of some state watchdog agency, such as the attorney general's office. Usually, the services of a well-versed tax attorney are indispensable to forming the organization in a manner that complies with all state procedural and substantive requirements *and* satisfies I.R.S. requirements for tax-exempt status, which are imposed over and above the legal requirements of the state in which the entity is formed.

The application to the I.R.S. is filed on Form 1023. The instructions to the form are complex, and the form itself contains numerous traps for the unwary, designed to weed out the deserving from the undeserving organization. In most instances, the form is completed and submitted to the I.R.S. on behalf of the organization by the tax attorney who formed it under state law. It is inadvisable for a layman, however well educated he may be, to file the form, since the I.R.S. agent who will review the organization's application will sometimes suggest changes in wording or ask technical or seemingly insignificant questions, the answers to which have a direct bearing on whether the exemption will be denied or granted. If the response to these questions is unsatisfactory to the agent, either because the applicant misunderstood the question or the agent misunderstood the answer, the organization could be found to be taxable on the federal level, notwithstanding its nonprofit status on the state level. A lengthy appeal procedure and court review of the denial of exempt status is possible, but this anguish can be avoided by retaining a qualified attorney to handle the matter from the outset and avoiding the temptation to cut corners.

To retain exempt status once granted, the organization must thereafter comply with the involved filing requirements and other rules for organizations with tax-exempt status. Every such organization must file an annual information return with the I.R.S. on Form 990 or 990-PF, and the failure to do so in the absence of an express exemption from this requirement will cost the entity $10 a day (up to a maximum of $5,000) for every day the return is late, unless a showing of reasonable cause for the nonfiling or late filing is made.

Also, even though an organization is recognized as tax-exempt, it may still be liable for income tax on its "unrelated business income," which is income from a trade or business, regularly carried on by the organization, that is not substantially related to the charitable, educational, or other purpose constituting the basis for the exemption. The purpose of this provision is to deter a tax-exempt organization from using its insulation from federal tax liability to compete unfairly with regular commercial businesses. Thus, for example, if an exempt institution was to enter the travel business and derive revenues from performing the functions of a travel agent for its members, these revenues would be subject to tax in the same manner as if tax-exempt status was lacking. An exempt organization that has $1,000 or more gross income from an unrelated business must file Form 990-T, and if it has employees, regardless of whether Form 990-T is due, it is usually responsible for withholding, depositing, paying, and reporting federal income tax, social security taxes, and federal unemployment tax on taxable wages it pays to its employees, notwithstanding its own exempt status from federal income tax.

Additional filing requirements, excise taxes, and prohibitions are imposed upon "private foundations," as defined in the tax law. Despite the use of the term "foundation," any tax-exempt entity, regardless of how formed or categorized for state law purposes, or by whatever name it goes, may fall within the classification of a private foundation. The determination of whether an exempt organization is a private foundation or an organization other than a private foundation (the latter often called a public charity) usually hinges on the degree of public or governmental support derived by the organization. If the organization derives its receipts primarily from a handful of contributions or from investment income, rather than from broad public support, it may well be a private foundation and subject to myriad additional operational requirements. On the other hand, if the organization either has broad public or governmental support or actively functions in a supporting relationship to such an organization, it is probably a public charity and exempt from this overlay of requirements. However, even if an organization meets the tests of public charity status, it will be presumed to be a private foundation, with some exceptions, unless it gives timely notice—usually within fifteen months from the end of the month in which it was organized—to the I.R.S. that it is not a private foundation.

An extensive discussion of private foundations is beyond the scope of this handbook, but the principals of any tax-exempt organization must be aware of the requirements involved, and sensitive to the problems that the I.R.S. can raise in this respect. Further information on this subject is provided in two helpful (and free) pamphlets published by the I.R.S., Publication 557 ("How to Apply for and Retain Exempt Status for Your Organization") and Publication 578 ("Tax Information for Private Foundations and Foundation Managers").

IBS

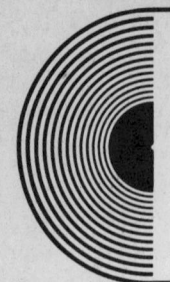

TRADEMARKS IN THE MUSIC BUSINESS

- Your band is breaking up—who has the right to continue using the name of the band?
- You are creating a new record label and have selected a name—how do you discover whether someone else already has preempted that name?
- Someone is selling T-shirts and posters with your name and picture on them, without your permission—can you stop them?
- You have written a song and want to call it "White Christmas"—do you need Irving Berlin's permission to do so?

These are just a few of the many questions involving trademarks which typically confront artists, managers, producers, record companies, and music publishers. An awareness of some of the basic concepts of trademark law is useful to everyone in the music business.

What Is a Trademark, and What Does It Do? A "trademark" is a word or logo used to identify goods from a particular source. Trademarks include *brand names* identifying goods ("Asylum" for phonograph records; "Sony" for tape recorders) and *service marks* identifying services ("Kiss" for recording and entertainment services provided by a rock band). The owner of a trademark for a particular product or service can sue to stop someone else from using the same term on the same goods or services, and the owner's rights also extend to different terms that are confusingly similar as well as to different goods or services if they are sufficiently closely related to create a likelihood of confusion of origin or sponsorship. The trademark owner also can license someone else to use the mark on any goods or services, although the owner must control the quality of the licensee's goods and services. In short, the law protects purchasers from being misled about the source of the goods or services, and it assures the owner of a trademark that he can profit from the commercial magnetism his trademark has developed.

Trademark Rights Are Obtained by Use. Trademark rights can be acquired in the United States (unlike most other countries) only by actually affixing the mark to the goods or to point-of-purchase displays for them, or by displaying the mark in the sale or advertising of the services. The first person to use a trademark generally has the exclusive right to it in the geographic area in which he has used it on a commercial scale. Therefore, in order to avoid infringing someone else's existing rights, it is a good idea to obtain a trademark search report before adopting a new trademark. Such a report normally can be ordered only by an attorney from a professional search service, and an experienced trademark attorney will know how to interpret the report and can advise whether or not it presents any significant problems, and, if so, how to deal with them.

Trademark Registration. Registration of a trademark is not mandatory, and unregistered rights will still be protected in a trademark user's local trading area. But if a trademark has been used in interstate commerce, the trademark owner normally should apply to register the mark in the U.S. Patent and Trademark Office (the application fee is currently only $35). The organization of a corporation, or the filing of a certificate of doing business under an assumed name, is *not* a substitute for obtaining a federal registration. When issued, a federal registration has significant advantages since, among other things, it is constructive notice of the registrant's exclusive ownership rights applicable nationwide to everyone who subsequently starts using that trademark, and it gives federal courts jurisdiction to hear infringement claims. Trademark rights continue indefinitely as long as the owner properly uses the mark, although federal registrations must be renewed every 20 years and a declaration of use must be filed during the sixth year after registration.

The Practical Significance of Trademarks. As indicated above, the law assures the owner of a trademark of the *exclusive* right to use the mark. This right can have tremendous economic value:

- *Recording Artists:* A popular group may sell millions of copies of a new album simply on the strength of its name alone. But the significance of trademark rights for a recording artist can extend far beyond the sale of records. In recent years, it has become commonplace to use recording artist and group names and logos on T-shirts, posters, books, musical equipment, bubblegum cards, and even pinball machines. Trademark law (combined with the related legal doctrines of unfair competition, the rights of privacy and publicity, and copyright) guarantee that a band or artist can share in the income from the merchandising of such goods. Indeed, groups such as "Cheap Trick" have been taking legal action to stop the sale of unauthorized merchandise bearing their trademarks right outside the concert halls in which they were performing.

A trademark search can be vital before money is poured into a new group name, and in addition to getting a normal search report, telephone calls to check the members of the AFM and AFTRA are a good idea. If such steps are not taken, an unknown preexisting regional group may come out of the woodwork and seek an injunction after another group has innocently adopted the same name, gotten a recording contract, and made a hit record which is moving up in the charts. This has happened a number of times in recent years, and the defendants have faced the choices of changing their names and losing the momentum they had finally achieved, or of making a substantial settlement payment to get the regional group to change its name.

It is important at the beginning, when everyone is cooperative, for the group members and the merger to clarify who owns the group name and who can use it if there is a change in group members or if there is a complete breakup. Once the group has made it, the significance of these arrangements—or of the failure to have made any arrangements—can be enormous. There have been long, expensive, and disruptive litigations involving a number of famous group names, such as "Grand Funk Railroad."

- *Record Labels:* As with group names, new record labels should be carefully checked before they are launched. In addition to the checks applicable to group names, the annual lists published by the music business trade magazines should be reviewed. Customers sometimes are attracted by a record's trademark if it has attained a certain reputation, such as the reputation of "London ffrr" for quality classical records. More often, they are more interested in the recording artist and the particular performance recorded. A label can be important in creating an image within the industry, however, and a forced change of name after labels, stationery, advertising, and all the rest have been printed should be avoided.

- *Show and Film Titles:* The titles of individual literary works (unlike titles used for a series of works such as a television series) generally are viewed as being descriptive and are not protectible until they have received a fair degree of public recognition, which is judged by such factors as the length of time the title has been in use, the extent of its promotion, and the volume of relevant sales or admissions. In some instances, prerelease publicity for a production has been so great that courts have enjoined as unfair competition the use of a similar title seeking to cash in on it (for example, "The Story of O" stopped "The Journey of O"). The Motion Picture Association of America, Inc. has a unique Title Registration Bureau giving its members and associate members a private way of reserving and objecting to film titles, which could enable a producer to avoid an instance such as when two films entitled "Harlow" were independently released at the same time. There is no analogous clearing house for other media titles. The point is that, once significant public recognition has been established for such a title, its goodwill can be exploited in a variety of ways, such as through commercial tie-ins, merchandising, sequels, and records. "The Pink Panther" is only one such example, and the opportunities for making big money seem to be increasing due to the multifaceted approaches to promoting musical productions like "Saturday Night Fever."

- *Song Titles:* Song titles generally are hard to protect (except for the most famous songs). As a practical matter, composers should steer clear of confusingly similar titles in order to avoid lost performance credits with ASCAP or BMI due to logging mistakes. Once a title becomes well known, however, it too can be protected and exploited by the music publisher, which usually has a contract obligation to pay a substantial portion of the net proceeds over to the composer. "Young at Heart" is an example of a song title that was purchased for use as a movie title for thousands of dollars. Another twist is that advertisers frequently seek to use popular songs for their commercials, often with special lyrics, for example "Up, Up, and Away (with TWA)." Music publishers may obtain significant compensation for permitting a song to be used in this way.

Conclusion. While trademarks provide financial opportunities for the owner, enforcing trademark rights and defending infringement claims can be difficult and costly. Therefore, careful, advance planning is necessary to avoid problems and to maximize income and promotion impact.

WMB

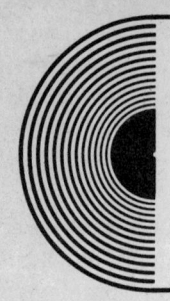

COLLEGES OF MUSIC

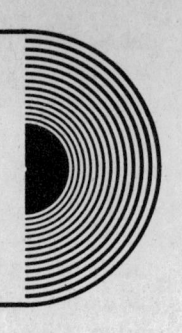

ALABAMA

Alabama State University, Montgomery, AL 36101. 205-832-6072.
Birmingham-Southern College, Birmingham, AL 35204. 205-328-5250.
Judson College, Marion, AL 36756. 205-683-6161.
Samford University, Birmingham, AL 35209. 205-870-2851.
University of Alabama, University, AL 35486. 205-348-7110.
University of Montevallo, Montevallo, AL 35115. 205-665-2521.
University of South Alabama, Mobile, AL 36688. 205-460-6138.

ALASKA

University of Alaska, Fairbanks, AK 99701. 907-479-7211.

ARIZONA

Arizona State University, Tempe, AZ 85281. 602-965-3371.
Northern Arizona University, Flagstaff, AZ 86001. 602-523-3731.
University of Arizona, Tucson, AZ 85721. 602-626-2997.

ARKANSAS

Arkansas State University, State University, AR 72467. 501-972-2094.
Arkansas Tech University, Russellville, AR 72801. 501-968-0369.
Henderson State University, Arkadelphia, AR 71923. 501-246-5511.
Hendrix College, Conway, AR 72032. 501-329-6811.
Quachita Baptist University, Arkadelphia, AR 71923. 501-246-4531.
Southern Arkansas University, Magnolia, AR 71753. 501-234-5120.
University of Arkansas, Fayetteville, AR 72701. 501-575-4701.
University of Arkansas at Little Rock, Little Rock, AR 72204. 501-569-3294.
University of Central Arkansas, Conway, AR 72032. 501-329-2410.

CALIFORNIA

Biola College, La Mirada, CA 90639. 213-944-0351.
California Institute of the Arts, Valencia, CA 91355. 805-255-1050.
California State University, Chico, CA 95929. 916-895-5152.
California State University, Dominguez Hills, CA 90747. 213-532-4300.
California State University, Fresno, CA 93740. 209-487-2654.
California State University, Fullerton, CA 92634. 714-870-3511.
California State University, Hayward, CA 94542. 415-881-3135.
California State University, Long Beach, CA 90840. 213-498-4781.

COLLEGES OF MUSIC

California State University, Los Angeles, CA 90032. 213-224-3448.
California State University, Northridge, CA 91330. 213-885-3184.
California State University, Sacramento, CA 95819. 916-454-6514.
College of Notre Dame, Belmont, CA 94002. 415-593-1601.
Holy Names College, Oakland, CA 94619. 415-436-1052.
Immaculate Heart College, Los Angeles, CA 90027. 213-462-1301.
Mount St. Mary's College, Los Angeles, CA 90049. 213-272-8791.
Pacific Union Colege, Angwin, CA 94508. 707-965-6201.
Pepperdine University at Malibu, Malibu, CA 90265. 213-456-4335.
San Diego State University, San Diego, CA 92182. 714-286-6031.
San Francisco Conservatory, San Francisco, CA 94122. 415-564-8086.
San Francisco State University, San Francisco, CA 94132. 415-469-1431.
San Jose State University, San Jose, CA 95192. 408-277-2905.
Sonoma State College, Sonoma, CA 94928. 707-664-2324.
University of Redlands, Redlands, CA 92373. 714-793-2121.
University of Santa Clara, Santa Clara, CA 95053. 408-984-4428.
University of Southern California, Los Angeles, CA 90007. 213-741-5389.
University of the Pacific, Stockton, CA 95211. 209-946-2415.

COLORADO

Colorado College, Colorado Springs, CO 80903. 303-473-2233.
Colorado State University, Fort Collins, CO 80523. 303-491-5533.
Metropolitan State College, Denver, CA 80204. 303-629-3180.
University of Colorado, Boulder, CO 80309. 303-492-6352.
University of Denver, Denver, CO 80208. 303-753-2196.
University of Northern Colorado, Greeley, CO. 303-351-2678.
University of Southern Colorado, Pueblo, CO 81001. 303-549-2552.
Western State College of Colorado, Gunnison, CO 81230. 303-943-3093.

CONNECTICUT

Hartt College of Music, West Hartford, CT 06117. 203-243-4468.
Neighborhood Music School, New Haven, CT 06511. 203-624-5189.
University of Bridgeport, Bridgeport, CT 06602. 203-576-4404.
University of Connecticut, Storrs, CT 06268. 203-486-3728.
Yale University, New Haven, CT 06520. 203-436-8740.

DELAWARE

University of Delaware, Newark, DE 19711. 302-738-2850.

DISTRICT OF COLUMBIA

American University, Washington, DC 20016. 202-686-2162.
Catholic University, Washington, DC 20064. 202-635-5414.
Howard University, Washington, DC 20059. 202-636-7082.

FLORIDA

Florida Atlantic University, Boca Raton, FL 33431. 305-395-5100.
Florida State University, Tallahassee, FL 32306. 904-644-5084.
Jacksonville University, Jacksonville, FL 32211. 904-744-3950.
Rollins College, Winter Park, FL 32789. 305-646-2233.
Stetson University, Deland, FL 32720. 904-734-4121.
University of Florida, Gainesville, FL 32601. 904-392-0223.

University of Miami, Coral Gables, FL 33124. 305-284-2433.
University of Tampa, Tampa, FL 33606. 813-253-8861.
University of West Florida, Pensacola, FL 32504. 904-476-9500.

GEORGIA

Augusta College, Augusta, GA 30904. 404-828-3211.
Berry College, Mount Berry, GA 30149. 404-232-5374.
Columbus College, Columbus, GA 31970. 404-568-2049.
Georgia College, Milledgeville, GA 31061. 912-453-4226.
Georgia Southern College, Statesboro, GA 30458. 912-681-5396.
Georgia State University, Atlanta, GA 30303. 404-658-2349.
Mercer University, Macon, GA 31207. 912-745-6811.
Shorter College, Rome, GA 30161. 404-291-2121.
Spelman College, Atlanta, GA 30314. 404-681-3643.
Truett McConnell College, Cleveland, GA 30528. 404-865-4626.
University of Georgia, Athens, GA 30602. 404-542-3737.
Wesleyan College, Macon, GA 31201. 912-477-1110.
West Georgia College, Carrollton, GA 30118. 404-834-1224.

HAWAII

University of Hawaii, Honolulu HI 96822. 808-948-7756.

IDAHO

Boise State University, Boise, ID 83725. 208-385-1771.
Idaho State University, Pocatello, ID 83209. 208-236-3636.
Ricks College, Rexburg, ID 83440. 208-356-2275.
University of Idaho, Moscow, ID 83843. 208-885-6231.

ILLINOIS

American Conservatory, Chicago, IL 60603. 312-263-4161.
Augustana College, Rock Island, IL 61201. 309-794-7343.
Bradley University, Peoria, IL 61625. 309-676-7611.
Chicago Conservatory College, Chicago, IL 60605. 312-427-0500.
Chicago Music College of Roosevelt University, Chicago, IL 60605. 312-341-3782.
De Paul University, Chicago, IL 60614. 312-321-7760.
Eastern Illinois University, Charleston, IL 61920. 217-581-3010.
Illinois Central College, East Peoria, IL 61635. 309-694-5113.
Illinois State University, Normal, IL 61761. 309-436-7631.
Illinois Wesleyan University, Bloomington, IL 61701. 309-556-3061.
MacMurray College, Jacksonville, IL 62650. 217-245-6151.
Millikin University, Decatur, IL 62526. 217-424-6302.
Music Center of the North Shore, Winnetka, IL 60093. 312-446-3822.
North Park College, Chicago, IL 60625. 312-583-2700.
Northwestern University, Evanston, IL 60201. 312-492-7575.
Quincy College, Quincy, IL 62301. 217-222-8020.
Rosary College, River Forest, IL 60305. 312-366-2490.
Sherwood Music School, Chicago, IL 60605. 312-427-6267.
Southern Illinois University, Carbondale, IL 62901. 618-453-2263.
Southern Illinois University, Edwardsville, IL 62026. 618-692-3900.

COLLEGES OF MUSIC

Springfield College in Illinois, Springfield, IL 62702. 217-525-1420.
University of Illinois, Urbana, IL 61801. 217-333-2620.
Vandercook College of Music, Chicago, IL 60616. 312-225-6288.
Western Illinois University, Macomb, IL 61455. 309-298-1544.
Wheaton College, Wheaton, IL 60187. 312-682-5098.
William Rainey Harper College, Palatine, IL 60067. 312-397-3000.

INDIANA

Anderson College, Anderson, IN 46011. 317-644-0951.
Ball State University, Muncie, IN 47306. 317-285-4435.
De Pauw University, Greencastle, IN 46135. 317-653-9721.
Indiana Central University, Indianapolis, IN 46227. 317-788-3225.
Indiana State University, Terre Haute, IN 47809. 812-232-6311.
Indiana University, Bloomington, IN 47401. 812-337-1582.
Jordan College of Music (Butler University), Indianapolis, IN 46208. 317-923-3451.
Manchester College, North Manchester, IN 46962. 219-982-2141.
Saint Mary-of-the-Woods College, Saint Mary-of-the-Woods, IN 47876. 812-535-4141.
Saint Mary's College, Notre Dame, IN 46556. 219-284-4095.
Taylor University, Upland, IN 46989. 317-998-2751.
University of Evansville, Evansville, IN 47702. 812-479-2741.
University of Notre Dame, Notre Dame, IN 46556. 219-283-6211.
Valparaiso University, Valparaiso, IN 46383. 219-464-5454.

IOWA

Clarke College, Dubuque, IA 52001. 319-588-6412.
Coe College, Cedar Rapids, IA 52402. 319-398-1550.
Cornell College, Mount Vernon, IA 52314. 319-895-8811.
Drake University, Des Moines, IA 50311. 515-271-3132.
Iowa State University, Ames, IA 50010. 515-294-5364.
Luther College, Decorah, IA 52101. 319-387-1208.
Morningside College, Sioux City, IA 51106. 712-277-5210.
Simpson College, Indianola, IA 50125. 515-961-6251.
University of Iowa, Iowa City, IA 52242. 319-353-3445.
University of Northern Iowa, Cedar Falls, IA 50613. 319-273-2024.
Wartburg College, Waverly, IA 50677. 319-352-1200.

KANSAS

Benedictine College, Atchison, KS 66002. 913-367-6110.
Bethany College, Lindsborg, KS 67456. 913-227-3312.
Emporia Kansas State College, Emporia, KS 66801. 316-343-1200.
Fort Hays State College, Hays, KS 67601. 913-628-4226.
Friends University, Wichita, KS 67213. 316-261-5800.
Kansas State University, Manhattan, KS 66506. 913-532-5740.
Marymount College, Salina, KS 67401. 913-825-2101.
Pittsburg State University, Pittsburg, KS 66762. 316-231-7000.
Saint Mary College, Leavenworth, KS 66048. 913-682-5151.
Saint Mary of the Plains College, Dodge City, KS 67801. 316-255-4171.

Southwestern College, Winfield, KS
67156. 316–221–4150.
Tabor College, Hillsboro, KS 67063.
316–947–3121.
University of Kansas, Lawrence, KS
66045. 913–864–3421.
Washburn University, Topeka, KS
66621. 913–295–6511.
Wichita State University, Wichita, KS
67208. 316–689–3502.

KENTUCKY

Asbury College, Wilmore, KY 40390.
606–858–3511.
Cumberland College, Williamsburg, KY
40769. 606–549–2030.
Eastern Kentucky University, Richmond,
KY 40475. 606–622–3266.
Kentucky State College, Frankfort, KY
40601. 502–564–6496.
Morehead State University, Morehead,
KY 40351. 606–783–3102.
Murray State University, Murray, KY
42071. 502–762–4288.
Southern Baptist Theological Seminary,
Louisville, KY 40206. 502–897–4115.
University of Kentucky, Lexington, KY
40560. 606–258–4936.
University of Louisville, Louisville, KY
40222. 502–588–6907.
Western Kentucky University, Bowling
Green, KY. 502–745–3751.

LOUISIANA

Centenary College of Louisiana, Shreveport, LA 71104. 318–869–5235.
Louisiana College, Pineville, LA 71360.
318–487–7336.
Louisiana State University, Baton
Rouge, LA 70803. 504–388–3261.
Louisiana Tech University, Ruston, LA
71270. 318–257–4233.
Loyola University, New Orleans, LA
71008. 504–865–3037.
McNeese State University, Lake Charles,
LA 70609. 318–477–2520.
New Orleans Baptist Theological Seminary, New Orleans, LA 70126.
504–282–4455.
Northeast Louisiana University, Monroe,
LA 71201. 318–342–2120.
Northwestern State University of
Louisiana, Natchitoches, LA 71457.
318–357–4436.
Southeastern Louisiana University, Hammond, LA 70402. 504–549–2184.
Southern University, Baton Rouge, LA
70813. 504–771–2011.
Tulane University, New Orleans, LA
70118. 504–865–4526.
University of Southwestern Louisiana,
Lafayette, LA 70501. 318–233–3850.
Xavier University of Louisiana, New
Orleans, LA 70125. 504–486–7411.

MAINE

University of Maine, Orono, ME 04473.
207–581–7534.

MARYLAND

Essex Community College, Baltimore
County, MD 21237. 301–682–6000.
Montgomery College, Rockville, MD
20850. 301–762–7400.
Peabody Conservatory, Baltimore, MD
21202. 301–837–0600.
Towson State University, Baltimore, MD
21204. 301–321–2143.
University of Maryland, College Park,
MD 20742. 301–454–2501.
Western Maryland College, Westminster,
MD 21157. 301–848–7000.

MASSACHUSETTS

Anna Maria College, Paxton, MA
01612. 617–757–4586.
Berklee School of Music, Boston, MA
02215. 617–266–1400.
Boston Conservatory, Boston, MA
02215. 617–536–6340.

Gordon College, Wenham, MA 01984. 617-927-2300.
New England Conservatory, Boston, MA 02115. 617-262-1120.
University of Lowell, Lowell, MA 01854. 617-454-8011.
University of Massachusetts, Amherst, MA 01003. 413-545-2227.

MICHIGAN

Albion College, Albion, MI 49224. 517-629-5511.
Alma College, Alma, MI 48801. 517-463-2141.
Andrews University, Berrien Springs, MI 49104. 616-471-3136.
Central Michigan University, Mount Pleasant, MI 48859. 517-774-3281.
Eastern Michigan University, Ypsilanti, MI 48197. 313-487-0244.
Grand Rapids Junior College, Grand Rapids, MI 49503. 616-456-4865.
Hope College, Holland, MI 49423. 616-392-5111.
Interlochen Center for the Arts, Interlochen, MI 49643. 616-276-9221.
Michigan State University, East Lansing, MI 48824. 517-355-4583.
Northern Michigan University, Marquette, MI 49855. 906-227-2656.
University of Michigan, An Arbor, MI 48109. 313-764-0584.
Wayne State University, Detroit, MI 48202. 313-577-1795.
Western Michigan University, Kalamazoo, MI 49008. 616-383-0910.

MINNESOTA

College of Saint Teresa, Winona, MN 55987. 507-454-2930.
Concordia College, Moorhead, MN 56560. 218-299-4414.
Gustavus Adolphus College, Saint Peter, MN 56082. 507-931-4300.
Hamline University, Saint Paul, MN 55101. 612-641-2231.
Macalester College, Saint Paul, MN 55105. 612-647-6382.
Mankato State University, Mankato, MN 56001. 507-389-2119.
Moorhead State University, Moorhead, MN 56560. 218-236-2101.
Saint Cloud State University, Saint Cloud, MN 56301. 612-255-3223.
Saint Olaf College, Northfield, MN 55057. 507-663-3180.
University of Minnesota, Duluth, MN 55812. 218-726-8207.
University of Minnesota, Minneapolis, MN 55455. 612-373-5400.
Winona State University, Winona, MN 55987. 507-457-2109.

MISSISSIPPI

Belhaven College, Jackson, MS 39202. 601-948-3818.
Delta State University, Cleveland, MS 38733. 601-843-3701.
Jackson State University, Jackson, MS 39217. 601-968-2141.
Mississippi College, Clinton, MS 39056. 601-924-5131.
Mississippi University for Women, Columbus, MS 39701. 601-328-5502.
University of Mississippi, University, MS 38677. 601-232-7268.
University of Southern Mississippi, Hattiesburg, MS 39401. 601-266-7276.
William Carey College, Hattiesburg, MS 39401. 601-582-5051.

MISSOURI

Central Methodist College, Fayette, MO 65248. 816-248-3391.
Central Missouri State University, Warrensburg, MO 64093. 816-429-4530.
Cottey College, Nevada, MO 64772. 417-667-8181.
Evangel College, Springfield, MO 65802. 417-865-2811.
Fontbonne College, Saint Louis, MO 63105. 314-862-3456.

Lincoln University, Jefferson City, MO 65101. 314-751-2325.
Northeast Missouri State University, Kirksville, MO 63501. 816-655-5121.
Northwest Missouri State University, Maryville, MO 64468. 816-582-7141.
Park College, Kansas City, MO 64152. 816-741-2000.
Saint Louis Conservatory of Music, Saint Louis, MO 63130. 314-863-3033.
School of the Ozarks, Point Lookout, MO 65726. 417-334-6411.
Southeast Missouri State University, Cape Girardeau, MO 63701. 314-651-2141.
Southwest Baptist College, Bolivar, MO 65613. 417-326-5281.
Southwest Missouri State University, Springfield, MO 65802. 417-836-5648.
Stephens College, Columbia, MO 65201. 314-442-2211.
University of Missouri, Columbia, MO 65202. 314-882-3650.
University of Missouri, Kansas City, MO 64111. 816-276-2731.
Washington University, Saint Louis, MO 63130. 314-889-5581.
Webster College, Saint Louis, MO 63119. 314-968-0500.
William Jewell College, Liberty, MO 64068. 816-781-3806.
William Woods College, Fulton, MO 65251. 314-642-2251.

MONTANA

University of Montana, Missoula, MT 59812. 406-243-6880.

NEBRASKA

Hastings College, Hastings, NE 68901. 402-463-2402.
Kearney State College, Kearney, NE 68847. 308-236-4446.
Nebraksa Wesleyan University, Lincoln, NE 68504. 402-466-2371.
Union College, Lincoln, NE 68506. 402-488-2331.

University of Nebraska, Lincoln, NE 68508. 402-472-2503.

NEW HAMPSHIRE

University of New Hampshire, Durham, NH 03824. 603-862-2405.

NEW JERSEY

Douglass College of Rutgers University, New Brunswick, NJ 08903. 201-932-9302.
Glassboro State College, Glassboro, NJ 08028. 609-445-6042.
Jersey City State College, Jersey City, NJ 07305. 201-547-3151.
Kean College of New Jersey, Union, NJ 07083. 201-527-2108.
Montclair State College, Upper Montclair, NJ 07043. 201-893-5103.
Trenton State College, Trenton, NJ 08625. 609-771-2551.
Westminster Choir College, Princeton, NJ 08540. 609-924-7414.
William Paterson College of New Jersey, Wayne, NJ 07470. 201-595-2314.

NEW MEXICO

Eastern New Mexico University, Portales, NM 88130. 505-562-2731.
New Mexico State University, Las Cruces, NM 88003. 505-646-2421.
University of New Mexico, Albuquerque, NM 87131. 505-277-2126.

NEW YORK

Eastman School of Music, Rochester, NY 14604. 716-275-3001.
David Hochstein Memorial Music School, Rochester, NY 14614. 716-454-4596.
Houghton College, Houghton, NY 14744. 716-567-2211.
Ithaca College, Ithaca, NY 14850. 608-274-3170.

COLLEGES OF MUSIC

The Juilliard School, New York, NY 10023. 212-799-5000.
Manhattan School of Music, New York, NY 10027. 212-749-2802.
Manhattanville College, Purchase, NY 10577. 914-946-9600.
Mannes College of Music, New York, NY 10021. 212-737-0700.
Nassau Community College, Garden City, NY 11530. 516-222-7000.
New York University, New York, NY 10003. 212-598-3493.
Nyack College, Nyack, NY 10960. 914-358-1710.
Roberts Wesleyan College, Rochester, NY 14624. 716-594-9471.
State University College, Fredonia, NY 14063. 716-673-3151.
State University College, New Paltz, NY 914-257-2404.
State University College, Potsdam, NY 13676. 315-268-2969.
State University College, Purchase, NY 10577. 914-253-5000.
State University of New York at Buffalo, Buffalo, NY 14214. 716-831-4116.
Syracuse University, Syracuse, NY 13210. 315-423-2191.
Westchester Conservatory of Music, White Plains, NY 10605. 914-761-3715.

Mars Hill College, Mars Hill, NC 28754. 704-689-1209.
Meredith College, Raleigh, NC 27602. 919-833-6461.
Pembroke State University, Pembroke, NC 28372. 919-521-4214.
Pfeiffer College, Misenheimer, NC 28109. 704-463-7343.
Queens College, Charlotte, NC 28274. 704-332-7121.
Saint Andrews Presbyterian College, Laurinburg, NC 28352. 919-276-3652.
Salem College, Winston-Salem, NC 27108. 919-723-7961.
University of North Carolina, Greensboro, NC 27412. 919-379-5560.
Wingate College, Wingate, NC 28174. 704-233-4061.
Winston-Salem State University, Winston-Salem, NC 27102. 919-761-2046.

NORTH DAKOTA

Minot State College, Minot, ND 58701. 701-857-3185.
North Dakota State University, Fargo, ND 58102. 701-237-7933.
University of North Dakota, Grand Forks, ND 58202. 701-777-2644.

NORTH CAROLINA

Appalachian State University, Boone, NC 28607. 704-262-3020.
Atlantic Christian College, Wilson, NC 27893. 919-237-3161.
Brevard College, Brevard, NC 28712. 704-883-8292.
Catawba College, Salisbury, NC 28144. 704-637-4111.
East Carolina University, Greenville, NC 27834. 919-757-6851.
Gardner-Webb College, Boiling Springs, NC 28017. 704-434-2361.
Greensboro College, Greensboro, NC 27402. 919-272-7102.

OHIO

Ashland College, Ashland, OH 44805. 419-289-4085.
Baldwin-Wallace College, Berea, OH 44017. 216-826-2361.
Bluffton College, Bluffton, OH 45817. 419-358-8015.
Bowling Green State University, Bowling Green, OH 43403. 419-372-2181.
Capital University, Columbus, OH 43209. 614-236-6411.
Case Western Reserve University, Cleveland, OH 44106. 216-268-2400.
Central State University, Wilberforce, OH 45384. 513-376-7114.

Cleveland Institute of Music, Cleveland, OH 44106. 216-791-5165.
Cleveland State University, Cleveland, OH 44115. 216-687-2031.
College of Wooster, Wooster, OH 44691. 216-264-1234.
Denison University, Granville, OH 43023. 614-587-0810.
Findlay College, Findlay, OH 45840. 419-422-8313.
Heidelberg College, Tiffin, OH 44883. 419-448-2505.
Hiram College, Hiram, OH 44234. 216-569-3211.
Kent State University, Kent, OH 44242. 216-672-2172.
Malone College, Canton, OH 44709. 216-454-3011.
Miami University, Oxford, OH 45056. 513-529-3014.
Mount Union College, Alliance, OH 44601. 216-823-3206.
Muskingum College, New Concord, OH 43762. 614-826-8315.
Oberlin Conservatory, Oberlin, OH 44074. 216-775-8200.
Ohio Northern University, Ada, OH 45810. 419-634-9921.
Ohio State University, Columbus, OH 43210. 614-422-6508.
Ohio University, Athens, OH 45701. 614-594-5587.
Ohio Wesleyan University, Delaware, OH 43105. 614-369-4431.
Otterbein College, Westerville, OH 43081. 614-890-3000.
University of Akron, Akron, OH 44325. 216-375-7591.
University of Cincinnati, Cincinnati, OH 45221. 513-475-3737.
University of Dayton, Dayton, OH 45469. 513-229-3936.
University of Toledo, Toledo, OH 43606. 419-537-2448.
Wittenberg University, Springfield, OH 45501. 513-327-7212.
Wright State University, Dayton, OH 45431. 513-873-2346.
Youngstown State University, Youngstown, OH 44503. 216-746-1851.

OKLAHOMA

Cameron University, Lawton, OK 73505. 405-248-2200.
Oklahoma Baptist University, Shawnee, OK 74801. 405-275-2850.
Oklahoma City University, Oklahoma City, OK 73106. 405-521-5316.
Oklahoma State University, Stillwater, OK 74074. 405-624-6133.
Phillips University, Enid, OK 73701. 405-237-4433.
Southeastern Oklahoma State University, Durant, OK 74701. 405-924-0121.
Southwestern Oklahoma State University, Weatherford, OK 73096. 405-722-6611.
University of Oklahoma, Norman, OK 73019. 405-325-2081.
University of Science and Arts of Oklahoma, Chickasha, OK 73018. 405-224-3140.
University of Tulsa, Tulsa, OK 74104. 918-939-6351.

OREGON

Lewis and Clark College, Portland, OR 97219. 503-244-6161.
Linfield College, McMinnville, OR 97128. 503-472-4121.
Marylhurst Education Center, Marylhurst, OR 97036. 503-636-8141.
Oregon College of Education, Monmouth, OR 97361. 503-838-1220.
Pacific University, Forest Grove, OR 97116. 503-357-6151.
Southern Oregon State College, Ashland, OR 97520. 503-482-6101.
University of Oregon, Eugene, OR 97403. 503-686-3761.
Willamette University, Salem, OR 97301. 503-370-6325.

PENNSYLVANIA

Allegheny College, Meadville, PA 16335. 814-724-3356.

Bucknell University, Lewisburg, PA 17837. 717-524-1216.
Carnegie-Mellon University, Pittsburgh, PA 15213. 413-578-2372.
College Misericordia, Dallas, PA 18612. 717-675-2181.
Curtis Institute of Music, Philadelphia, PA 19103. 215-893-5252.
Duquesne University, Pittsburgh, PA 15219. 412-434-6080.
Edinboro State College, Edinboro, PA 16444. 814-732-2555.
Elizabethtown College, Elizabethtown, PA 17022. 717-367-1151.
Immaculata College, Immaculata, PA 19345. 215-647-4400.
Indiana University of Pennsylvania, Indiana, PA 15701. 412-357-2390.
Lebanon Valley College, Annville, PA 17003. 717-867-4411.
Mansfield State College, Mansfield, PA 16933. 717-662-4080.
Marywood College, Scranton, PA 18509. 717-343-6521.
Millersville State College, Millersville, PA 17551. 717-872-5411.
Philadelphia College of Bible, Philadelphia, PA 19103. 215-561-8661.
Philadelphia College of the Performing Arts, Philadelphia, PA 19102. 215-545-6200.
Seton Hill College, Greensburg, PA 15601. 412-834-2200.
Slippery Rock State College, Slippery Rock, PA 16057. 412-794-7276.
Susquehanna University, Selinsgrove, PA 17870. 717-374-0101.
Temple University, Philadelphia, PA 19122. 215-787-8301.
West Chester State College, West Chester, PA 19380. 215-436-2628.
Westminster College, New Wilmington, PA 16142. 412-946-8761.

RHODE ISLAND

Barrington College, Barrington, RI 02806. 401-246-1200.
Rhode Island College, Providence, RI 02908. 401-456-8244.
University of Rhode Island, Kingston, RI 02881. 401-792-2431.

SOUTH CAROLINA

Anderson College, Anderson, SC 29621. 803-226-6181.
Baptist College at Charleston, Charleston, SC 10087. 803-797-4784.
Coker College, Hartsville, SC 29550. 803-332-1381.
Columbia College, Columbia, SC 29203. 803-786-3761.
Converse College, Spartanburg, SC 29301. 803-585-6421.
Furman University, Greenville, SC 29613. 803-294-2086.
Limestone College, Gaffney, SC 29340. 803-489-7151.
University of South Carolina, Columbia, SC 29208. 803-777-4280.
Winthrop College, Rock Hill, SC 29733. 803-323-2255.

SOUTH DAKOTA

Augustana College, Sioux Falls, SD 57102. 605-336-5451.
Northern State College, Aberdeen, SD 57401. 605-622-2497.
South Dakota State University, Brookings, SD 57006. 605-688-5187.
University of South Dakota, Vermillion, SD 57069. 605-677-5274.
Yankton College, Yankton, SD 57078. 605-665-3661.

TENNESSEE

Austin Peay State University, Clarksville, TN 37040. 615-648-7818.
Belmont College, Nashville, TN 37203. 615-383-7001.
Blair School of Music, Nashville, TN 37212. 615-327-8010.

Cadek Conservatory, Chattanooga, TN 37402. 615-755-4624.
Carson-Newman College, Jefferson City, TN 37760. 615-475-9061.
East Tennessee State University, Johnson City, TN 37601. 615-929-4270.
Fisk University, Nashville, TN 37203. 615-329-8529.
George Peabody College for Teachers, Nashville, TN 37203. 615-327-8061.
Maryville College, Maryville, TN 37801. 615-982-6950.
Memphis State University, Memphis, TN 38152. 901-454-2541.
Middle Tennessee State University, Murfreesboro, TN 37132. 615-898-2469.
Southern Missionary College, Collegedale, TN 37315. 615-396-4267.
Southwestern at Memphis, Memphis, TN 38112. 901-278-2030.
Tennessee State University, Nashville, TN 37203. 615-320-3544.
Tennessee Technological University, Cookeville, TN 38501. 615-528-3161.
Trevecca Nazarene College, Nashville, TN 37210. 615-244-6000.
Union University, Jackson, TN 38301. 901-668-1818.
University of Tennessee at Chattanooga, Chattanooga, TN 37403. 615-755-4601.
University of Tennessee at Martin, Martin, TN 38237. 901-587-7400.
University of Tennessee, Knoxville, TN 37916. 615-974-3241.

TEXAS

Abilene Christian University, Abilene, TX 79601. 915-677-1911.
Amarillo College, Amarillo, TX 79178. 806-376-5111.
Baylor University, Waco, TX 76703. 817-755-1161.
Corpus Christi State University, Corpus Christi, TX 78412. 512-991-6810.
Del Mar College, Corpus Christi, TX 78404. 512-881-6211.
East Texas State University, Commerce, TX 75428. 214-886-3303.
Hardin-Simmons University, Abilene, TX 79601. 915-677-7281.
Incarnate Word College, San Antonio, TX 78209. 512-828-1261.
Lamar University, Beaumont, TX 77710. 713-838-8927.
Midwestern State University, Wichita Falls, TX 76308. 817-692-6611.
North Texas State University, Denton, TX 76203. 817-788-2530.
Odessa College, Odessa, TX 79760. 915-357-5381.
Our Lady of the Lake University, San Antonio, TX 78285. 512-434-6711.
Sam Houston State University, Huntsville, TX 77341. 713-295-6211.
Southern Methodist University, Dallas, TX 75275. 214-692-2587.
Southwest Texas State University, San Marcos, TX 78666. 512-245-2375.
Southwestern Baptist Theological Seminar, Fort Worth, TX 38112. 901-278-2030.
Southwestern University, Georgetown, TX 78626. 512-863-6511.
Stephen F. Austin State University, Nacogdoches, TX 75961. 713-569-4602.
Texarkana College, Texarkana, TX 75501. 214-838-4541.
Texas A. and I. University, Kingsville, TX 78363. 512-595-2803.
Texas Tech University, Lubbock, TX 79409. 806-742-2270.
Texas Wesleyan College, Fort Worth, TX 76105. 817-534-0251.
Texas Woman's University, Denton, TX 76204. 817-387-1412.
University of Houston, Houston, TX 77004. 713-749-1118.
University of Texas, Austin, TX 78712. 512-471-1528.
University of Texas at Arlington, Arlington, TX 76019. 817-273-3471.
University of Texas at El Paso, El Paso, TX 79968. 915-747-5606.

West Texas State University, Canyon, TX 79016. 806-656-2016.

UTAH

Brigham Young University, Provo, UT 84602. 801-374-1211.
University of Utah, Salt Lake City, UT 84112. 801-581-6765.
Weber State College, Ogden, UT 84403. 801-626-6427.

VERMONT

University of Vermont, Burlington, VT 05401. 802-656-3040.

VIRGINIA

Hampton Institute, Hampton, VA 23668. 804-727-5402.
Hollins College, Hollins, VA 24020. 703-362-6512.
Madison College, Harrisonburg, VA 22807. 703-433-6211.
Mary Washington College, Fredericksburg, VA 22401. 703-373-7250.
Norfolk State College, Norfolk, VA 23504. 804-623-8544.
Old Dominion University, Norfolk, VA 23508. 804-489-6219.
Radford College, Radford, VA 24141. 703-731-5177.
Shenandoah Conservatory, Winchester, VA 22601. 703-667-8714.
University of Richmond, Richmond, VA 23173. 804-285-6334.
Virginia Commonwealth University, Richmond, VA 23284. 804-257-1166.
Virginia State College, Petersburg, VA 23803. 804-520-5311.

WASHINGTON

Central Washington State College, Ellensburg, WA 98926. 509-963-1216.
Eastern Washington University, Cheney, WA 99004. 509-359-2241.
Pacific Lutheran University, Tacoma, WA 98447. 206-531-6900.
Seattle Pacific University, Seattle, WA 98119. 206-281-2205.
University of Puget Sound, Tacoma, WA 98416. 206-756-3253.
University of Washington, Seattle, WA 98195. 206-543-1200.
Walla Walla College, College Place, WA 99324. 509-527-2561.
Washington State University, Pullman, WA 99164. 509-335-8524.
Whitman College, Walla Walla, WA 99362. 509-529-5100.
Whitworth College, Spokane, WA 99251. 509-466-1000.

WEST VIRGINIA

Salem College, Salem WV 26426. 304-782-5381.
West Liberty State College, West Liberty, WV 26074. 304-336-8006.
West Virginia University, Morgantown, WV 26506. 304-293-4091.
West Virginia Wesleyan College, Buckhannon, WV 26201. 304-473-8051.

WISCONSIN

Alverno College, Milwaukee, WI 53215. 414-671-5400.
Lawrence University, Appleton, WI 54911. 414-739-3681.
University of Wisconsin—Eau Claire, WI 54701. 715-836-4954.
University of Wisconsin—Green Bay, WI 54302. 414-465-2458.
University of Wisconsin—Madison, WI 53706. 608-263-1900.
University of Wisconsin—Milwaukee, WI 53201. 414-963-4507.
University of Wisconsin—Oshkosh, WI 54901. 414-424-4224.

COLLEGES OF MUSIC

University of Wisconsin—Stevens Point, WI 54481. 715–346–3107.
University of Wisconsin—Whitewater, WI 53190. 414–472–1310.
Viterbo College, La Crosse, WI 54601. 608–784–0040.
Wisconsin Conservatory of Music, Milwaukee, WI 53202. 414–276–4350.

WYOMING

University of Wyoming, Laramie, WY 82071. 307–766–5242.

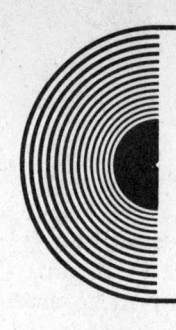

MUSIC BUSINESS AND AUDIO ENGINEERING SCHOOLS

BELMONT COLLEGE
Music Business Department, School of Business, Belmont Boulevard, Nashville, TN 37203. 615-383-7001. Music business program established 1973. Accredited by Southern Association of Schools and Colleges.

Music Business Emphasis—4-year Bachelor of Business Administration program. Tuition: $1,850 per year. Robert E. Mulloy, program director. Courses held on campus at Center for Business and College Recording Studio (16-track). Required courses in language and literature, humanities, social science, and physical education. Music Business courses: Survey of Music Business; Introduction to the Studio; Music Industry Seminar; Copyright; Publishing; Finance; Marketing; Physics of Sound; and others. Recent guest speakers: Jim Fogelson, Vice President, MCA Records; Frances Preston, Vice President, BMI; Larry Gatlin, recording artist; Randy Goodrum, songwriter; Gary Paxton, producer-artist. Courses held throughout the year. Scholarships available—apply to director of Music Business Department, Belmont College. 201 students enrolled last semester; ratio of students to instructors is 14:1. Requirements for admission: ACT or SAT.

BERKLEE COLLEGE OF MUSIC
1140 Boylston Street, Boston, MA 02215. 617-266-1400. Audio Recording program established 1979. Accredited by New England Association of Schools and Colleges.

Audio Recording Major—4-year Bachelor of Music program. Tuition: $2,750 per year. Joe Hostetter, program director. Courses held at main campus, Berklee College of Music. General required courses: Arranging; Harmony; Composition; Counterpoint; Ear Training; History of Music; Conducting; Major Instrument; Ensemble; English; History. Audio Recording courses: Audio Recording 1 and 2; Sound Re-inforcement; Mixdown Lab 1 and 2; Directed Studies 1 and 2; Studio Equipment Maintenance; Basic Electronics; Approved Specified Electives. Courses held throughout the year. No scholarship funds. Standard government education assistance programs available. Requirements for admission: ACT or SAT, high school diploma or equivalent, other musical requirements as described in college catalog.

Audio Recording Major—4-year Professional Diploma program. Content and requirements are essentially the same as for the Bachelor of Music program, but nonmusic courses are deleted. Tuition: $2,620 per year.

BROWN INSTITUTE

3123 East Lake Street, Minneapolis, MN 55406. 612-721-2481. Audio engineering program established 1973. Accredited by National Association of Trade and Technical Schools.

Audio and Recording Technology—2-year Associate in Electronics Technology program (may also be taken as 15-month certificate program). Tuition: $4,600 ($2,875 for certificate program). Bill Johnson, program director. Courses held at Brown Institute. Course titles: Introduction to Electricity & Electronics; to Electronics Technology; Solid State Electronics; Advanced Circuit Analysis; Audio and Recording Technology (also Communications, Computers, Bio-Medical Electronics, or Color Television in degree program). Courses held throughout the year. No scholarship funds. 18 students enrolled last semester; ratio of students to instructors is 18:1. Requirements for admission: high school diploma and electronics aptitude test.

THE BUSINESS ACADEMY OF MUSIC

P. O. Box 4026, Woodbridge, CT 06525. 203-735-5883. Established 1976.

In-depth Study of the Music Industry—20-hour weekend seminar. Tuition: $200. Martin G. Kugell, program director. Classes held in motel conference rooms. Covers songwriting, publishing, copyright, personal management, bookings, recording contracts, and demos. No scholarship funds. Limited to 20 students per class. No admission requirements.

In-studio Course—20-hour weekend seminar. Tuition: $200. Martin G. Kugell, program director. Classes held in various studios in Connecticut. No scholarship funds. Limited to 20 students per class. No admission requirements.

CENTER FOR AUDIO STUDIES

12 Saint John Street, Red Hook, NY 12571. 914-758-5605. Established 1972 (formerly known as Electric Music School). Accredited by State University College of New York and Fredonia as part of its Special Studies program.

Sound Recording Workshop—11-week certificate program, 6 hours daily, 250 total hours, plus 100 hours of access to the studio. Tuition: $450; studio fee: $680. (Graduate students and non-New York residents pay additional tuition surcharges.) David Moulton, program director. Classes held at Dondisound Studios (24-track). Workshop earns 12 credits in Sound Technology. Next scheduled workshop: May 25-August 7, 1981. Scholarships and financial aid available—apply to State University of New York at Fredonia. 24 students enrolled last semester; ratio of students to instructors is 8:1. Requirements for admission: high school diploma, proficiency test, interview.

Tonneister Program—2-year certificate program, 20 hours each week. Tuition: $1,425 per semester (tentative). David Moulton, program director. Courses in studio production, music and acoustics, mathematics and electronics. Scheduled to begin in Fall of 1980. Courses held at Dondisound Studios (24-track). Financial aid available—apply to State University of New York at Fredonia. 25 students projected in initial enrollment; ratio of students to instructors is 10:1. Requirements for admission: high school diploma, proficiency, interview.

COLLEGE FOR RECORDING ARTS

665 Harrison Street, San Francisco, CA 94107. 415-781-6306. Established 1974. Approved by California State Board of Education. Accredited by National Association of Trade and Technical Schools and the NARAS Institute.

The Record/Music Industry—one-year certificate program, 714 total hours. Tuition: $6,190 (includes four optional courses). Leo de Gar Kulka and Jim Economides, program directors. Classes meet at College for Recording Arts, formerly Golden State Recorders (24-track studio). Course titles: Audio Engineering—basic, intermediate, advanced classes; Recording Workshop; Music Production—basic, intermediate, advanced classes; Music Law—basic and intermediate classes; Business and Finance of Music—basic and intermediate classes; Studio Electronics—basic and intermediate classes; Synthesizer Principles—basic and intermediate classes; Disc Mastering; Audio Visual. Recent guest speakers: Rene Hall, songwriter; Fred Catero, record producer. Courses held throughout the year. No scholarship funds. 85 students enrolled last semester; ratio of students to instructors is 17:1. Requirements for admission: high school diploma.

COLORADO AUDIO INSTITUTE

680 Indiana Street, Golden, CO 80401. 303-279-2500. Established 1979 (formerly affiliated with the Recording Institute of America).

Music Business/Audio Engineering Courses—8-12-week program. Tuition varies. David Van Soest, program director. Courses held at Applewood Studios, Golden, CO; Community College of Denver; Sound Labs, Denver, CO. Courses (and tuition): Audio Engineering I ($625); Music Production I ($4450); Live Audio & Stage Production ($250); Legal & Business Aspects of the Music Industry ($30); The Freelance Recording Engineer ($20); Music Publishing for the Songwriter ($20); The New Artist—From Nowhere to National Release ($20); Music Industry Sources ($25); Building a Home Studio ($25). Courses held throughout the year. No scholarships. 45 students enrolled last semester; ratio of students to instructors is 7-15:1. No admission requirements.

FIVE TOWNS COLLEGE

2350 Merrick Avenue, Merrick, NY 11566. 516-379-1400. Music business program established 1976. Accredited by New York State Board of Regents.

Business Management—Music Business—2-year Associate in Applied Science program. Tuition: $2,300 per year. Martin Crafton, program director. Courses held at Five Towns College. Course titles: Introduction to the Music Business; Publishing and Copyright; Music Business Contracts; Audio Recording I, II, & III; Record Promotion and Broadcasting; Principles of Commercial Songwriting; Music Store Management; Manufacture, Distribution, and Marketing of Records; Advanced Problems in the Music Business. Classes meet during fall and spring semesters. Scholarship funds available—apply to Scholarship Committee, Five Towns College. 258 students enrolled last semester; ratio of students to instructors is 9:1. Requirements for admission: high school diploma or equivalent.

GEORGIA STATE UNIVERSITY

College of General Studies, University Plaza, Atlanta, GA 30303. 404-658-3513. Music business program established 1973. Accredited by Southern Association of Colleges and Schools.

Commercial Music/Recording—2-year Associate of Science program. Tuition: $1,235 for Georgia residents, $2,660 for out-of-state students. C. Stephen Weaver, program director. Courses held at Georgia State University campus. Course titles: Structure of the Music Industry; Promotion of Recorded Music; Marketing and Merchandising of Recorded Music; Retailing of Recorded Music; Legal Aspects of the Music Industry; Internship; Survey of American Pop Music; Manufacture and Production of Recorded Music; Recording Artist Representation; The Live Entertainment Industry; Copyright Law; Music Publishing; Selected Topics. Recent guest speakers: Leonard Feist, President, National Music Publishers Association; Atlanta Rhythm Section; Al Berman, President, The Harry Fox Agency; Joe Cohen, Executive Vice President, National Association of Recording Merchandisers. Courses held throughout the year. Scholarships available—apply to Financial Aid Office, Georgia State University. 115 students enrolled last semester; ratio of students to instructors is 25:1. Requirements for admission: ACT or SAT.

HOFSTRA UNIVERSITY

Memorial Hall, Hempstead, NY 11550. 516-560-3371. Music business program established 1976. Accredited by Middle States Association of Colleges.

Music Merchandising—4-year Bachelor of Science in Music, Specialization in Music Merchandising program. Tuition: $3,000 per year. Herbert A. Deutsch, program director. Courses held at main campus, Hofstra University. Required courses in music, English, language, humanities, social sciences, natural science. Music Merchandising courses: Marketing; Management; Finance; Business Law; Accounting; Music Merchandising Seminar. Courses held throughout the year. Scholarships available—apply to department chairman, Music Department, Hofstra University. 21 students enrolled last semester; ratio of students to instructors is 21:1. Requirements for admission: high school diploma, ACT or SAT, interview.

INSTITUTE OF AUDIO RESEARCH

64 University Place, New York, NY 10003. 212-677-7580. Established 1969. Licensed by New York State Education Department.

Elements of Multitrack Recording Technology—one-year certificate program, 261 hours theory, 144 hours practice. Tuition: $2,875. Albert B. Grundy and Philip Stein, program directors. Classes meet at Institute of Audio Research (includes 16-track studio). Course titles: Fundamentals of Audio Technology I; Fundamentals of Audio Technology I—Lab; Studio Synthesizer Techniques; Studio Synthesizer Techniques—Lab; Studio Technology and Practice; Control Room and Console Lab; Digital Logic Design; Fundamentals of Audio Technology II; Audio Systems Design; Practical Disc Recording; Fundamentals of Audio Technology II—Lab; Practical Disc Recording Lab; Recording Studio Workshop. Courses held throughout the year. No scholarships. 130 students enrolled last semester; average ratio of students to instructors is 17:1. Requirements for admission: high school graduate or equivalent background.

Bachelor of Science Degree in Music Technology—4-year program held jointly with New York University. Philip Stein, program director. 28 credits technology, 50–53 credits music. For further information, contact Institute of Audio Research.

KINGSMILL RECORDING STUDIO

1033 Kingsmill Parkway, Columbus, OH 43229. 614–846–4494. Audio engineering program established 1977.

Studio Engineering 100—5-week introductory course. Tuition: $220. Donald H. Spangler, program director. Classes meet at Kingsmill Recording Studio (16-track). Basic console operations, auto-locator, head configurations, studio design, acoustics, and terminology. Courses held throughout the year. No scholarships. Limited to 12 students. No admission requirements.

Studio Engineering 200—8-week intermediate course. Tuition: $380. Donald H. Spangler, program director. Classes meet at Kingsmill Recording Studio (16-track). Recording techniques, miking techniques, electronic alignment, session procedures, mixing, equalization, editing, and peripheral equipment. Courses held throughout the year. No scholarships. Limited to 8 students. No admission requirements.

Studio Engineering 300—16-week advanced course. Tuition: $950. Donald H. Spangler, program director. Classes meet at Kingsmill Recording Studio (16-track). Students assist recording engineer at regularliy-scheduled studio sessions. No scholarships. Limited to 4 students. No admission requirements.

MIDDLE TENNESSEE STATE UNIVERSITY

Box 21, Murfreesboro, TN 37132. 615–898–2813. Music business program established 1974. Accredited by Southeastern Association of Colleges and Schools.

Recording Industry Management—4-year Bachelor of Science program. Tuition: $472 for two regular semesters, Tennessee residents; $1,474 for two regular semesters, nonresidents. Geoffrey Hull, program director. Courses held at Department of Mass Communications, Middle Tennessee State University. Degree requirements include 39 hours university core courses, 24 hours Recording Industry Management courses, and 18 hours mass communications courses. Recording Industry Management courses: Survey of the Recording Industry; Recording Industry Internship; Copyright Law; Career Development for Recording Artists; Promotion of Recordings; Merchandising of Recordings; Technology of Recording; Advanced Technology of Recording; Studio Production; Legal Problems of the Recording Industry; Record Store Operations; Seminar in Current Recording Industry Problems; Survey of American Popular Music. Recent guest speakers: Clive Davis, President, Arista Records; Charlie Daniels, recording artist; Charlie Monck, April/Blackwood Music; Frances Preston, Vice President, BMI; Larry Mundorf, Vice President, Camelot Music; Scott Faragher, Shorty Lavendar Agency. Courses held throughout the year. Scholarships available—apply to University Financial Aid, Middle Tennessee State University. 150 students enrolled last semester; ratio of students to instructors is 15–50:1. Requirements for admission: high school diploma and ACT.

JON MILLER SOUND STUDIOS SCHOOL FOR RECORDING ARTS AND SCIENCES

2524 East Scenic Drive, Bath, PA 18014. 215-837-7550. Established 1976. Charter member of Music Industry Educators Association. Affiliated with NARAS Institute.

Audio Engineering Course—39-week certificate program, 156 total hours. Tuition: $1,200. Jon Miller, program director. Classes meet at Jon Miller Sound Studios (8-track). Course meets throughout the year. No scholarships. 21 students enrolled last semester; ratio of students to instructors is 6:1. Requirements for admission: interest in music and interview.

MUSIC RECORDING SCHOOL

229 Shipley Street, San Francisco, CA 94107. 415-546-6464. Established 1976.

Basic Studio Engineering—10-week program, 65 total hours. Tuition: $500. Vance Frost, program director. Classes meet at Music Recording School and Bear West Studios (8-track). Course covers theory of sound, tape recorders, set-ups, mixing, dynamic range, broadcast sound, disc recording, and remote recording. Course meets throughout the year. No scholarships. 12 students enrolled last semester; ratio of students to instructors is 3-12:1. No admission requirements.

Record Production—8-week program, 50 total hours. Tuition: $425. Ross J. Winetsky, program director. Classes meet at Bear West Studios (24- and 8-track). Course covers functions of a producer, preproduction, engineering and session procedure, postproduction techniques, music business law, record companies, and promotion. Course meets throughout the year. No scholarships. 12 students enrolled last semester; ratio of students to instructors is 3-12:1. No admission requirements.

NEW YORK UNIVERSITY

Department of Music and Music Education, 35 West Fourth Street, New York, NY 10003. 212-598-3493. Music business program established 1976. Accredited by Middle States Association and National Association of Schools of Music.

Music, Business, and Technology—4-year Bachelor of Science program. Tuition: $4,600 per year. Richard Broderick, program director. Courses held at NYU Washington Square Campus and Institute of Audio Research (16-track facility). Required courses in social sciences, humanities, science and mathematics, liberal arts, and music. Music, Business, and Technology courses: Fundamentals of Audio Technology I and II; Studio Synthesizer Technique; Control Room and Console Lab; Digital Logic Design; Fundamentals of Audio Technology; Audio System Design; Practical Disc Recording; Recording Studio Workshop; Principles of Accounting; Corporate Financial Management; Management & Organizational Analysis; Markets & Marketing Methods; Statistics & Business Control; Business Policy; Economic Principles I and II; Introduction to Computers & Programming. Recent guest speakers: Ed Cramer, President, BMI; Alvin Deutsch, attorney; Morton D. Wax, publicist; Tony Bongiovi, record producer; Enoch Light, composer. Courses held throughout the year. Scholarships available—apply to Financial Aid Office, NYU. 40 students enrolled last semester; ratio of students to instructors is 15:1. Requirements for admission: 1,000 combined SAT, academic average of 2.5 or better, and music audition.

OMEGA STUDIOS SCHOOL OF APPLIED RECORDING ARTS AND SCIENCES

10518 Connecticut Avenue, Kensington, MD 20795. 301–946–4686. Established 1976. Approved by Maryland State Board of Higher Education.

Basic Practical Recording Engineering—8-week program, 4 hours each evening, 32 total hours. Tuition: $350. W. Robert Yesbek, program director. Classes meet at Omega Recording Studio (24-track). Course held throughout the year. No scholarships. 28 students enrolled last semester; ratio of students to instructors is no more than 12:1. Requirements for admission: high school diploma or equivalent.

Advanced Recording Engineering—8-week program, 4 hours each evening, 32 total hours. Tuition: $395. W. Robert Yesbek, program director. Classes meet at Omega Recording Studio (24-track). Course held throughout the year. 16 students enrolled last semester; ratio of students to instructors is no more than 12:1. Requirements for admission: Basic Practical Recording Engineering or equivalent in experience and/or education.

ORANGE COAST COLLEGE

2701 Fairview Road, Costa Mesa, CA 92626. 714–556–5523 or 714–556–5629. Music business vocational programs established 1974. Accredited by Western Association of Schools and Colleges,

Music Business Employee—2-year Associate in Arts vocational program. Tuition: free to district residents and California residents with permits; $53 per unit (maximum $795 per semester) for residents less than one year. Howard M. Judkins, program director. Courses held at main campus, Orange Coast College. Required courses: Beginning Instruments; Voice I; Literature and History of Music; Music in America; Instrument Repair; Introduction to Business; Music Store Management; Salesmanship; Retailing. Music Business Employee electives: Classical Guitar 1 and 2; Voice 2; Opera Workshop; Piano 3 and 4; Introduction to Humanities; Marketing and Distribution; Advertising; Buying and Store Operations; Business Ownership; Bookkeeping. Courses held throughout the year. Scholarships available—apply to Office of Student Affairs, Orange Coast College. 24 students enrolled last semester; ratio of students to instructors is 24:1. Admission requirements: high school diploma or over 18.

Instrument Repair—2-year Associate in Arts vocational program. Tuition: free to district residents and California residents with permits; $53 per unit (maximum $795 per semester) for residents less than one year. Howard M. Judkins, program director. Courses held at main campus, Orange Coast College. Required courses: Instrument Repair; Orchestral String Instrument Repair; Woodwind Repair 1 and 2; Fretted String Instrument Repair; Brass Instrument Repair; Instrumental Technique for the Repairman; Bookkeeping; Science of Sound; Music Store Management. Recommended electives: Introduction to Business; Business Law; Business Ownership and Management; Beginning Instruments; Applied Electronics; Piano Repair Tuner; Audio Repair Techniques. Courses held throughout the year. Scholarships available—apply to Office of Student Affairs, Orange Coast College. 24 students enrolled last semester; ratio of students to instructors is 24:1. Admission requirements: high school diploma or over 18.

RECORDING ASSOCIATES

5821 SE Powell Boulevard, Portland, OR 97206. 503-777-4621. Audio engineering program established 1975.

State of the Art Recording Techniques—beginning, intermediate, and advanced training in professional recording methodology. Tuition: $30 for one-day Level One; $95 for 12-hour Level Two; $350 for 30-hour Level Three; $200 for 10-hour Level Four; no tuition for Levels Five and Six, provided students record groups who pay student or regular studio rates. Jay C. Webster, program director. Classes meet at Recording Associates studios (16- and 24-track). Courses held throughout the year. No scholarships. 20 students enrolled last semester; ratio of students to instructors is 15:1. No admission requirements.

RECORDING INSTITUTE OF AMERICA, INC.

15 Columbus Circle, New York, NY 10023. 212-582-0400. Established 1973.

Modern Recording Techniques I—10-week avocational program, one evening per week, 30 total hours. Tuition: $375. Chas Kimbrell, network director. Classes meet at recording studios listed below (8-, 16-, or 24-track—see individual listings). Part theory, part hands-on experience. Courses held throughout the year. No scholarships. Maximum students admitted to each class: 15. No admission requirements.

Modern Recording Techniques II—10-week advanced avocational program, Saturday morning and afternoon, 60 total hours. Tuition: $495. Chas Kimbrell, network director. Classes meet at recording studios listed below (8-, 16-, or 24-track—see individual listings) subject to meeting minimum enrollment. No theory; complete hands-on experience. Courses held throughout the year. No scholarships. Maximum students admitted to each class: 12. Admission requirements: Modern Recording Techniques I or equivalent.

RIA NETWORK:

Ames, Iowa
A&R Recording Studio (16-track)
2700 Ford Street
Ames, IA 50010
515-232-2991

Atlanta, Georgia
Apogee Recording Studio (24-track)
125 Simpson Street NW
Atlanta, GA 30313
404-522-8460

Richmond, Virginia
Alpha Audio (24-track)
2049 West Broad Street
Richmond, VA 23220
804-358-3852

Santee/San Diego, California
Natural Sound (16-track)
8951 Prospect Avenue
Santee, CA 92071
714-448-6000

Seattle, Washington
Holden, Hamilton, Roberts (16-track)
2227 North 56
Seattle, WA 98103
206-632-8300

Tulsa/Oklahoma City, Oklahoma
Ford Audio (16-track)
1815 Classen Boulevard
Oklahoma City, OK 73106
405-525-3343

MUSIC BUSINESS SCHOOLS

Burlington, Vermont
Starbuck/Ashley Recording (8-track)
79 College Street
Burlington, VT 05401
802–658–4616

Jacksonville Beach, Florida
Cypress Recording (16-track)
P. O. Box 51067
Jacksonville Beach, FL
904–246–8222

Easley, South Carolina
The Sounding Board (16-track)
P. O. Box 888
Easley, SC 29640
803–269–7012

Honolulu, Hawaii
Audissey (16-track)
679 Auahi Street
Honolulu, HI 96813
808–521–6792

Houston, Texas
Wells Sound Studio (16-track)
2036 Pasket
Houston, TX 77092
713–688–8067

Knoxville, Tennessee
Thunderhead Sound (16-track)
112 17 Street
Knoxville, TN 37916
615-546-8006

Los Angeles/Orange County, California
United Audio Corp. (24-track)
1519 South Grand Avenue
Santa Ana, CA 92705
714-547-5466

New Haven, Connecticut
Trod Nossel Productions (16-track)
10 George Street
Wallingford, CT 06492
203–269–4465

Philadelphia, Pennsylvania
Starr Recording Inc. (24-track)
201 St. James Place
Philadelphia, PA 19106
215–925–5265

Phoenix and Tucson, Arizona
Lee Furr's Recording (24-track)
25 East Glenn
Tucson, AZ 85705
602–792–3470

Pittsburgh, Pennsylvania
Audio Innovators (24-track)
216 Boulevard of the Allies
Pittsburgh, PA 15222
412–471–6220

Baltimore, Maryland
Sheffield Recording Ltd. (24-track)
13816 Sunny Brook Road
Phoenix, MD 21131
301–628–7260

Birmingham, Alabama
Solid Rock Sound (16-track)
P. O. Box 9482
Birmingham, AL 35215
205–854–4160

Charlotte, North Carolina
Reflection Sound Studio (24-track)
1018 Central Avenue
Charlotte, NC 28204
704–377–4596

Cleveland, Ohio
Agency Recording Studio (16-track)
1730 East 24 Street
Cleveland, OH 44114
216-621-0810

Columbus, Ohio
Mus–I–Col Recording (16-track)
780 Oakland Park Avenue
Columbus, OH 43224
614–267–3133

Dallas, Texas
Sound One Recording (16-track)
2517 Carlisle
Dallas, TX 75201
214-742-2341

Detroit, Michigan
Recording Institute (16-track)
14611 East Nine Mile Road
East Detroit, MI 48021
313–779–1380

THE RECORDING WORKSHOP

455 Massieville Road, Chillicothe, OH 45601. 614–663–2544. Established 1971. Accredited by the State of Ohio.

Recording Engineer Apprentice—4-week certificate program, 6–8 hours daily, 150–160 total hours. Tuition: $1,200. Joseph Waters, program director; Guruka Singh Khalsa, head instructor. Classes meet at the Recording Workshop Complex (2-, 4-, 8-, 16-, and 24-track recording studios). Individual course titles: Creative Record Production; Audio Engineering; The Business of Music; Sound Reinforcement. Recent guest speakers: M. William Krasilovsky, attorney; Billy Cobham, artist; Wally Gold, Vice President, Kirschner Records; Robert Runstein, author, *Modern Recording Techniques*. Courses held throughout the year. 60 students enrolled last semester; ratio of students to instructors is 8:1. No admission requirements.

SHERWOOD OAKS EXPERIMENTAL COLLEGE

6353 Hollywood Boulevard, Hollywood, CA 90028. 213–462–0669. Established 1972.

Introduction to Record Engineering—10-week 30-hour course. Tuition: $250. Classes meet at Sherwood Oaks Experimental College and Hit City Recording Studio (24-track).

Beginning Record Engineering Workshop—10-week 30-hour course. Tuition: $600. Classes meet at Hit City Recording Studio (24-track).

Intermediate Record Engineering Workshop—10-week 30-hour course. Tuition: $600. Classes meet at Hit City Recording Studio (24-track).

Advanced Record Engineering Workshop—10-week 30-hour course. Tuition: $600. Classes meet at Hit City Recording Studio (24-track).

Courses held throughout the year. No scholarships, but work/study programs available. 75 students enrolled last semester; ratio of students to instructors is 8–40:1. Admission requirements: none for Introduction to Record Engineering, experience and/or Introduction to Record Engineering for more advanced courses.

SOUND MASTER RECORDING ENGINEER SCHOOL

P. O. Box 8327, Universal City, CA 91608. 213–650–8000. Established 1973. Accredited by California State Department of Education.

Record Engineering Program—1-year certificate program. Tuition: $4,090. Brian Ingoldsby, program director. Classes meet at 24-track professional recording studios. Course titles: Basic Theory; Beginning Workshop; Advanced Theory; Advanced Workshop; Disc Mastering; Sound Reinforcement; Producer Workshop; Advanced Principles of Disc Mastering. Courses held throughout the year. No scholarships. Ratio of students to faculty is 12:1. Admission requirements: high school diploma or equivalent.

SYRACUSE UNIVERSITY

School of Music, Syracuse, NY 13210. 315–423–2191. Music industry program established 1974. Approved by Middle States Association of College and Secondary Schools.

Music Industry—4-year Bachelor of Music/Music Industry degree program. Tuition: $4,500 per year. Stephen Marcone, program director. Courses held at main campus, Syracuse University. Required courses in major instrument, ensemble, English, psychology, sociology, management, and academic electives. Music Industry courses: Survey of Music Industry; Selected Topics in Music Industry; Music Industry and the Media; Law and Ethics in the Music Industry; Current State of the Music Industry; Music Performance and the Media; Music Industry Practicum; Scoring and Arranging. Recent guest speakers: Seymour Leslie, founder, Pickwick International; Clive Davis, President, Arista Records; Ed Cramer, President, BMI; James Taylor, recording artist. Courses held throughout the year. Scholarships available—apply to Office of Financial Aids, Syracuse University. 25 full-time and 12 part-time students enrolled last semester; ratio of students to instructors is 20:1. Requirements for admission: ACT or SAT and music audition.

UNIVERSITY OF COLORADO AT DENVER

College of Music, 1100 14 Street, Denver, CO 80202. 303-629-2727. Music management and recording technology programs established 1974. Accredited by North Central Association of Colleges and Secondary Schools.

Music Management—4-year Bachelor of Science in Music and Media degree program. Tuition: $498 per year for Colorado residents, $1,886 per year for nonresidents. David Baskerville, program director. Courses held at University of Colorado at Denver campus. Required courses in English, social science, humanities, theory and musicianship, instrumentation, piano, music history, communications, the music business, and broadcasting. Music Management courses: Music and Media; Introduction to Financial Accounting; Introduction to Management and Organization; Principles of Marketing; Field Work. Recent guest speakers: Jim Progris, Executive Director, NARAS; Vladimir Ussachevsky, composer. Courses held during fall and spring semesters. Limited scholarships—apply to Associate Dean of College of Music. 12 students enrolled last semester; ratio of students to instructors is 12:1. Requirements for admission: 1,000 combined SAT, theory placement test, and music audition.

Sound Synthesis and Recording Technology—4-year Bachelor of Science in Music and Media degree program. Tuition: $498 per year for Colorado residents, $1,886 per year for nonresidents. Roy Pritts, program director. Courses held at University of Colorado at Denver campus. Required courses in English, social science, humanities, theory and musicianship, intrumentation, piano, music history, communications, the music business, and broadcasting. Sound Synthesis and Recording Technology courses: Sound Reinforcement & Recording I and II; Electronic Music; Sound and Music; Synthesis Proseminar; Applied Synthesizer; Electrical Engineering; Acoustics. Recent guest speakers: James William Guercio, record producer; Phil Ramone, record producer. Courses held during fall and spring semesters. Limited scholarships—apply to Associate Dean of College of Music. 58 students enrolled last semester; ratio of students to instructors is 11:1. Requirements for admission: 1,000 combined SAT, theory placement test, and music audition.

UNIVERSITY OF MIAMI

School of Music, Box 248165, Coral Gables, FL 33124. 305-284-2433. Music merchandising program established 1965; audio engineering program established 1975. Accredited by Southern Association of Schools and Colleges and NARAS Institute.

Music Merchandising—4-year Bachelor of Music degree program. Tuition: $3,700 per year. Alfred Reed, program director. Required courses: English; History; Music Theory; Economics; Accounting; Music Merchandising and Usages; Music Publishing; Copyright; Distribution; Music and the Mass Media; Record Industry Operations; Advanced Copyright and Contract Problems; Survey of Broadcasting; Survey of Motion Pictures; Effects of Mass Media; Advertising; Marketing Foundations; Basic Management. Elective courses: Basic Audio Recording Techniques; Audio Engineering. Recent guest speakers: David Rothfeld, record buyer, Korvette's; Bernard Korman, Vice President, SESAC. Courses held throughout the year. Scholarships available—apply to Office of Financial Aid, University of Miami. 85 students enrolled last semester; ratio of students to instructors is 17:1. Requirements for admission: ACT or SAT and music audition.

Music Engineering Technology—4-year Bachelor of Music degree program. Tuition: $3,700 per year. Billy R. Porter, program director. Required courses: English; Calculus; Physics of Music; Music Theory; Psychology; Electrical Circuit Theory; Communications; Introduction to Audio Recording; Audio Engineering—Microphone and Mixing Techniques; Recording Studio Equipment and Practices; Advanced Audio Recording Techniques; Internship in Music Engineering. Recent guest speakers: Mack Emerman, President, Criteria Recording Studios; John Woram, President, Woram Audio Associates. Courses held throughout the year. Scholarships available—apply to Office of Financial Aid, University of Miami. 90 students enrolled last semester; ratio of students to instructors is 17:1. Requirements for admission: ACT or SAT, strong math background, and music audition.

UNIVERSITY OF NORTH ALABAMA
Wesleyan Avenue, Florence, AL 35603. 205-381-1455. Commercial music program established 1975. Accredited by Southern Association of Schools and National Council of Accreditation of Teacher Education.

Commercial Music Curriculum—4-year Bachelor of Arts or Bachelor of Science program. Tuition: $580 for two semesters. Kevin Lamb, program director. Classes held at University of North Alabama and Wishbone Recording Studio (24-track). Required courses: Music Theory; Music Publishing; The Record Company; Music of the Twentieth Century; Studio Techniques; Production; Commercial Music Practicum; Music Activities; Class and/or Applied Music; Accounting; Business Law; Major Instrument; Marketing; Finance; Management; General Business; General Electives. Recent guest speakers: Roy Orbison, artist; John Kay, artist; Tony Brown, A&R executive, Free Flight Records. Courses held throughout the year. Scholarships available—apply to Financial Aid Department, University of North Alabama. 45 students enrolled last semester; ratio of students to instructors is 50:1. Requirements for admission: high school diploma or equivalent and ACT.

UNIVERSITY OF SOUND ARTS
6671 Sunset Boulevard, Suite 1508, Los Angeles, CA 90029. 213-467-5256. **Laguna Beach location:** 301 Forest Avenue, Suite 1A, Laguna Beach, CA 92651. 714-497-1725. Established 1976. Accredited California State Board of Education.

Recording Engineering—1-year certificate program. Tuition: $3,160. Raghu Gadhoke, program director. Classes meet at University of Sound Arts and professional recording studios. Course titles: Basic Electronics; Basic Engineering Theory; Basic Recording Techniques; Overview of the Recording Industry; Physics of Music; Intermediate Engineering Theory; Basic Recording Techniques; Overview of the Recording Industry; Physics of Music; Intermediate Engineering Theory; Intermediate Recording Techniques; Music Theory for Engineers; Audio Editing Techniques; Advanced Engineering Theory; Advanced Recording Techniques; Digital Recording Techniques; Studio Business & Management; Disc Mastering Techniques. Recent guest speakers: Richard Shulenberg; Bobby Colomby.

Recording Studio Maintenance Engineer—1-year certificate program. Tuition: $2,395. Raghu Gadhake program director. Classes meet at University of Sound Arts and professional recording studios. Course titles: Basic Electronics; Basic Engineering Theory; Basic Recording Techniques; Algebra & Trigonometry; Acoustic Design; Recording Studio Maintenance I, II, and III; Theory & Lab; Physics of Music; Electronic Drafting; Audio Systems; Theory of Disc Recording; Digital Techniques.

Record Production—1-year certificate program. Tuition: $2,190. Raghu Gadhoke, program director. Courses held at University of Sound Arts and professional recording studios. Course titles: Overview of the Recording Industry; Basic Engineering Theory; Basic Recording Techniques; USC/USA Speaker Series—"Business Aspects of the Recording Industry"; Record Production I and II; Music Theory for Engineers; Physics of Music; Record Appreciation; Music Law; Electronic Music; A&R Procedures & Personal Management; International Music; Psychology of Dealing with Record Industry Personnel.

Secretarial and Official Skills—6-month certificate program. Tuition: $860. Raghu Gadhoke, program director. Classes meet at University of Sound Arts. Course titles: Overview of the Recording Industry; Music Law I; Production Assistant Seminar I and II; Record Publishing; A&R Procedures & Personal Management. Courses held throughout the year. No scholarships. 175 students enrolled last semester; ratio of students to instructors is 10:1. Requirements for admission: aptitude test.

MUSIC BUSINESS CONTRACTS

ARTIST RECORDING AGREEMENT

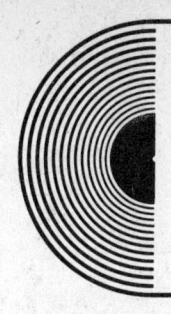

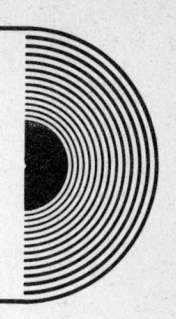

The artist recording agreement* sets forth the terms and conditions under which an artist agrees to render services as a performing artist to a record company, and the company agrees to record such performances and, thereafter, release and sell phonograph records embodying those performances. The artist recording agreement should be comprehensive enough to include provisions which address the following topics: term (number of years) of the contract; nature and scope of services to be provided by artist to record company (and vise versa); recording commitments; recording procedure; selection of material, producer(s) and studio(s); recording costs; advances to artist; grant of rights to record company; calculation and payment of royalties; accountings; mechanical licenses; warranties, representations and indemnities; and breach or default.

KAM

AGREEMENT made this .... day of .... 198.. between .... (hereinafter "you") and Record Company.

1. TERM

1.01 This agreement shall commence as of .... and shall continue in force for a term which shall consist of an initial period ending .... (unless extended or suspended as provided herein) and the additional period or periods, if any, for which such term may be extended through Record Company's exercise of one or more of the options granted to Record Company below.

1.02. You grant Record Company .... consecutive options to extend the term of this agreement for additional periods of one (1) year each ("Option Periods") upon all the terms and conditions herein contained. Record Company may exercise each such option by giving you notice in writing at least thirty (30) days prior to the expiration of the then current Contract Period.

2. SERVICES

2.01. During the term of this agreement you will render your services as a performing artist for the purpose of making Phonograph Records as provided in article 3.

---

*The contracts printed here are intended to be used *for reference purposes only*. It is recommended that all parties seek counsel of an experienced music business attorney when negotiating agreements.

3. RECORDING COMMITMENT

3.01. The Minimum Recording Commitment in respect of each Contract Period shall be as follows:

    Initial Period
    First Option Period
    Second Option Period
    Third Option Period
    Fourth Option Period

3.02. If the Minimum Recording Commitment for the Contract Period concerned is one Album or less, the entire Minimum Recording Commitment will be completed within the first seven (7) months of the Contract Period. If the Minimum Recording Commitment is more than one Album, one-half of the Minimum Recording Commitment will be completed during the first half of the Contract Period, and the balance will be completed not later than ninety (90) days before the end of the Contract Period.

3.03. (a) During each Contract Period, Record Company shall have the option to increase the Recording Commitment for such Period by Recordings constituting not more than one additional Album or the equivalent. Said option is referred to below as the "Overcall Right," and the additional Recordings which may be required hereunder are referred to as "Overcall Recordings."

(b) The Overcall Right shall be exercisable at any time before whichever of the following dates occur later: (1) the date ninety (90) days before the end of the Contract Period concerned; or (2) the date sixty (60) days after the completion of the Minimum Recording Commitment for that Contract Period.

(c) The Overcall Recordings will be Delivered to Record Company within ninety (90) days after the date of Record Company's exercise of the Overcall Right. If Record Company exercises the Overcall Right: (1) Record Company will have the further option, exercisable by notice to you before the end of the current Contract Period, to extend that Period until the date sixty (60) days after the Delivery of the Overall Recordings; and (2) Record Company's option to extend the term of this agreement for the next Option Period under paragraph 1.02 will be exercisable at any time before the expiration of the current Contract Period.

3.04. Only Master Recordings consisting of Compositions not previously recorded by you shall apply in reduction of the Recording Commitment.

3.05. You shall not be required to perform hereunder together with any other royalty artist without your consent. Record Company shall not be deemed to be unreasonable in rejecting any request by you to record with another royalty artist.

4. RECORDING PROCEDURE

4.01. The following matters will be determined, in the order set forth below, by mutual agreement between Record Company and you:

(a) Selection of material, including the number of Compositions, to be recorded. Record Company shall not be deemed to be unreasonable in rejecting any request to record an Album consisting of more than one twelve-inch 33⅓ rpm Record. You shall advise Record Company of the content of all medleys prior to the recording thereof.

(b) Selection of dates of recording and studios where recording is to take place, including the cost of recording therein, and formulation of the recording budget. Record Company will not be deemed to be unreasonable in rejecting any request to begin recording any Album which is a part of the Minimum Recording Commitment hereunder within three (3) months after the acceptance of a prior Album hereunder. The scheduling and booking of all studio time will be done by Record Company. Record Company's facilities and the services of its engineers will be used for all Recordings made hereunder.

4.02. You shall timely supply Record Company with all of the information it needs in order: (1) to make payments due in connection with the Recordings to be made hereunder;

(2) to comply with any other obligations Record Company may have in connection with the making of such Recordings; and (3) to prepare to release Phonograph Records derived from such Recordings.

4.03. (a) Each Master Recording made hereunder shall be subject to Record Company's approval as satisfactory for its manufacture and sale of Phonograph Records.

(b) No "live" Recording or Recording not made in full compliance with the provisions of this agreement will apply in fulfillment of your Recording Commitment, nor will Record Company be required to make any payment in connection with any such Recording, unless Record Company so agrees in writing or such Recording is actually released by Record Company. No Joint Recording will apply in fulfillment of your Recording Commitment, nor will Record Company be required to make any payments in connection with any such Joint Recording other than royalties due you hereunder, even if such Joint Recording is actually released by Record Company.

(c) No Recordings shall be made by unauthorized dubbing.

4.04. Nothing in this agreement shall obligate Record Company to continue or permit the continuation of any recording session or project, even if previously approved hereunder, if Record Company reasonably anticipates that the Recording Costs will exceed those specified in the approved budget or that the Recordings being produced will not be satisfactory.

5. RECORDING COSTS

5.01. Record Company will pay all union scale payments required to be made to you in connection with Recordings made hereunder, all costs of instrumental, vocal and other personnel and arrangements and copying specifically approved by Record Company in respect of the recording of such Master Recordings, and all other amounts required to be paid by Record Company pursuant to any applicable law or any collective bargaining agreement between Record Company and any union representing persons who render services in connection with such Master Recordings.

5.02. All amounts described in paragraph 5.01 above plus all other amounts representing direct expenses paid by Record Company, or incurred in connection with the recording of Master Recordings hereunder (including, without limitation, advances to producers and all studio and engineering charges, in connection with Record Company's facilities and personnel or otherwise) are herein sometimes called "Recording Costs" and shall constitute Advances. The cost of metal parts, and payments to the AFM Special Payments Fund and the Music Performance Trust Fund based upon record sales (so-called "per-record royalties"), shall not constitute Advances. Any Recording Costs in excess of the amount approved by Record Company will be your sole responsibility and will be promptly paid by you (or reimbursed by you if paid by Record Company).

5.03. In determining the portion of the Recording Costs (other than payments to you) applicable to any Joint Recording which shall be charged against your royalties, such portion shall be computed by multiplying the aggregate amount of such Recording Costs by the same fraction used in determining the royalties payable to you in respect of such Joint Recording.

6. ADDITIONAL ADVANCES

6.01. All monies paid to you or on your behalf during the term of this agreement, other than royalties paid pursuant to Articles 9 and 12 hereof, shall constitute Advances unless otherwise expressly agreed in writing by an authorized officer of Record Company.

7. GRANT OF RIGHTS

7.01. All Master Recordings recorded hereunder from the Inception of Recording thereof, and all Matrices and Phonograph Records manufactured therefrom, together with the performances embodied thereon, shall be the sole property of Record Company, free from any claims whatsoever by you or any other Person; and Record Company shall have the exclusive right to copyright such Master Recordings in its name as the owner and author thereof and to secure any and all renewals and extensions of such copyright.

7.02. Without limiting the generality of the foregoing, Record Company and any Person authorized by Record Company have the unlimited right to manufacture Phonograph Records by any method now or hereafter known, derived from the Master Recordings made hereunder, and to sell, transfer or otherwise deal in the same under any trademarks, trade names and labels, or to refrain from such manufacture, sale and dealing, throughout the world.

7.03. Record Company and any licensee of Record Company each shall have the right and may grant to others the right to reproduce, print, publish, or disseminate in any medium your name (including, without limitation, all professional, group, and other assumed or fictitious names used by you), your portraits, pictures and likeness, and biographical material concerning you, as news or information, for the purposes of trade, or for advertising purposes. No direct endorsement by you of any product or service shall be used without your written consent. During the term of this agreement you shall not authorize any Party other than Record Company to use your name or likeness (or any professional, group, or other assumed or fictitious name used by you in connection with the advertising or sale of Phonograph Records.

8. COUPLING

8.01. During the term of this agreement, in respect of Records manufactured for sale in the United States, Record Company will not, without your consent and notwithstanding anything in Article 9:

    (a) couple Master Recordings made hereunder with Recordings not embodying your performances on "pop singles"; or

    (b) so couple more than two Master Recordings made hereunder on any other disc Record, except promotional Records and programs for use on public transportation carriers and facilities.

9. ROYALTIES

You will be paid royalties on Net Sales of Records as hereinafter set forth:

9.01. Record Company will pay you a basic royalty computed at the applicable percentage, indicated below, of the applicable Royalty Base Price in respect of Net Sales of Phonograph Records consisting entirely of Master Recordings recorded hereunder and sold by Record Company or its Licensees through Normal Retail Channels for distribution in the United States:

    (a) *On Albums:* ....%.
    (b) *On "single" Records:* ....%.

9.02. The royalty rate on Phonograph Records sold through any Club Operation shall be determined by multiplying the otherwise applicable royalty rate by a fraction, the numerator of which is 5 and the denominator of which is the basic royalty fixed in paragraph 9.01, and such royalties shall be computed on the basis of 90% of Net Sales of such Records. Notwithstanding the foregoing, no royalty shall be payable to you with respect to (a) Phonograph Records received by members of any such Club Operation in an introductory offer in connection with joining it or upon recommending that another join it or as a result of the purchase of a required number of Records including, without limitation, records distributed as "bonus" or "free" Records, or (b) Phonograph Records for which such Club Operation is not paid.

9.03. In respect of catalog Phonograph Records sold by Record Company special products operations (hereinafter, "SP") to educational institutions or libraries or to other SP clients for their promotion or sales incentive purposes (but not for sale to the general public through normal retail channels), the royalty shall be one-half (½) of the royalty rate otherwise payable. In respect of non-catalog Phonograph Records created on a custom basis for clients of SP, the royalty rate shall be one-half (½) of the royalty rate otherwise payable and shall be computed on the basis of SP's actual sales price therefor (less all taxes and container charges). In respect of any Master Recording leased by Record Company to others for their distribution of Phonograph Records in the United States, Record

Company will pay you 50% of Record Company's net receipts therefrom after deduction of all copyright, AFM and other applicable third party payments; if another artist, a producer, or any other Person is entitled to royalties in respect of such Records, said payment will be divided among you in the same ratio as that among your respective basic royalty percentage rates.

9.04. In respect of Phonograph Records sold in the form of pre-recorded tape, the royalty rate payable to you therefor shall be three-fourths (¾) of the applicable royalty rate which would have been payable to you if such Records were sold in disc form.

9.05. The royalty rate on any Budget Record, Record bearing a Reissue Label, twelve-inch "disco single," or Multiple Record Set shall be one-half (½) of the otherwise applicable royalty rate.

9.06. In respect of Phonograph Records sold by Record Company or its Licensees for distribution outside of the United States of America, the royalty rate payable to you therefor shall be equal to one-half (½) of the applicable royalty rate which would have been payable to you therefor if such Records had been sold for distribution in the United States; and such royalties shall be computed on the basis of 90% of Net Sales of such Records.

9.07. In respect of Phonograph Records derived from Master Recordings leased or otherwise furnished by Record Company's Licensees to others for their manufacture and distribution of Records outside the United States, Record Company will pay you one-half (½) of the amount which would otherwise be payable to you if Record Company or its Licensees manufactured and distributed such Records.

10. MISCELLANEOUS ROYALTY PROVISIONS

Notwithstanding anything to the contrary contained in Article 9 hereof:

10.01. In respect of Joint Recordings, the royalty rate to be used in determining the royalties payable to you shall be computed by multiplying the royalty rate otherwise applicable thereto by a fraction, the numerator of which shall be one and the denominator of which shall be the total number of royalty artists whose performances are embodied on a Joint Recording.

10.02. With respect to Phonograph Records embodying Master Recordings made hereunder together with other Master Recordings, the royalty rate payable to you shall be computed by multiplying the royalty rate otherwise applicable by a fraction, the numerator of which is the number of Sides contained thereon embodying Master Recordings made hereunder and the denominator of which is the total number of Sides contained on such Record.

10.03. No royalties shall be payable to you in respect of Phonograph Records sold or distributed by Record Company or its Licensees for promotional purposes, as cutouts after the listing of such Records has been deleted from the catalog of Record Company or the particular Licensee, as "free," "no charge" or "bonus" Records (whether or not intended for resale), or to radio stations. No royalties will be payable to you on "sampler" Records in tape form intended for free distribution to automobile purchasers and containing not more than one Recording made under this agreement.

11. ROYALTY ACCOUNTINGS

11.01. Record Company will compute royalties payable to you hereunder as of June 30th and December 31st for each preceding six-month period during which Records as to which royalties are payable hereunder are sold, and will render a statement and pay such royalties, less any unrecouped Advances, prior to each succeeding September 30th and March 31st, respectively.

11.02. Royalties for Records sold for distribution outside of the United States ("foreign sales") shall be computed in the national currency in which Record Company is paid by its Licensees and shall be paid to you at the same rate of exchange at which Record Company is paid. For accounting purposes, foreign sales shall be deemed to occur in the same semi-annual accounting periods in which Record Company's Licensees account to Record Company therefore. If Record Company is unable, for reasons beyond its control, to receive payment for such sales in United States dollars in the United States, royalties therefor shall not be credited to your account during the continuance of such inability; if any accounting rendered to you hereunder during the continuance of such inability requires the payment of royalties to you, Record Company will, at your request and if Record Company is able to do so, deposit such royalties to your credit in such foreign currency in a foreign depository, at your expense.

11.03. At any time within eighteen (18) months after any royalty statement is due you hereunder you shall have the right to give Record Company written notice of your intention to examine Record Company's books and records with respect to such statement. Such examination shall be commenced within thirty (30) days after the date of such notice, at your sole cost and expense, by any certified public accountant or attorney designated by you provided he is not then engaged in an outstanding examination of Record Company's books and records on behalf of a Person other than you. Such examination shall be made during Record Company's usual business hours at the place where Record Company maintains the books and records which relate to you and which are necessary to verify the accuracy of the statement or statements specified in your notice to Record Company and your examination shall be limited to the foregoing.

11.04. Your sole right to inspect Record Company's books and records shall be as set forth in subparagraph 11.03 hereof, and Record Company shall have no obligation to produce such books and records more than once with respect to each statement rendered to you. Without limiting the generality of the foregoing, Record Company shall have no obligation to furnish you with any records that do not specifically show sales or gratis distributions of Phonograph Records as to which royalties are payable hereunder.

11.05. Unless notice shall have been given to Record Company as provided in paragraph 11.03 hereof, each royalty statement rendered to you shall be final, conclusive and binding on you and shall constitute an account stated. You shall be foreclosed from maintaining any action, claim or proceeding against Record Company in any forum or tribunal with respect to any statement or accounting due hereunder unless such action, claim or proceeding is commenced against Record Company in a court of competent jurisdiction within three years after the due date of such statement or accounting.

12. MECHANICAL LICENSES

12.01. (a) Each Controlled Composition is hereby licensed to Record Company, for the United States and Canada, at the royalty rate equal to the minimum compulsory license rate applicable under the copyright law of the country concerned at the time of recording (2.75¢ in the United States and 2¢ in Canada, as of January 1, 1978), on the basis of Net Sales of Phonograph Records, except that no copyright royalties shall be payable with respect to Records described in paragraph 10.03. The royalty rate with respect to Records described in paragraph 9.05 or distributed through a Club Operation shall be three-fourths (¾) of said rate, and arranged versions of public domain Compositions which are claimed by you to be Controlled Compositions shall be licensed to Record Company at one-half (½) of said rate.

(b) Notwithstanding the foregoing, Record Company shall not be required to pay an aggregate copyright royalty in excess of ten times the rate provided in the first sentence of subparagraph 12.01(a) for any Album or twice that rate for any single Record consisting of Recordings made hereunder.

(c) Accountings for such royalties shall be rendered quarter-annually, within forty-five days after the end of each calendar quarter.

12.02. Any assignment made of the ownership or copyright in, or right to license the use of, any Controlled Compositions referred to in this paragraph shall be made subject to the provisions hereof.

12.03. The provisions of this Article 12 shall constitute and are accepted by you, on your own behalf and on behalf of any other owner of any Controlled Compositions or any rights therein, as full compliance by Record Company with all of its obligations, under the compulsory license provisions of the Copyright Law, as the same may be amended, or otherwise, arising from any use by Record Company of Controlled Compositions as provided herein.

12.04. If any Recordings made hereunder contain one or more Compositions (other than Controlled Compositions), not available to Record Company under compulsory license, you will obtain, at Record Company's election and for Record Company's benefit, mechanical licenses covering such Compositions on the same terms applicable to Controlled Compositions pursuant to this Article 12.

13. WARRANTIES; REPRESENTATIONS; RESTRICTIONS; INDEMNITIES

13.01. You warrant and represent:

(a) You have the right and power to enter into and fully perform this agreement.

(b) Record Company shall not be required to make any payments of any nature for, or in connection with, the acquisition, exercise or exploitation of rights by Record Company pursuant to this agreement except as specifically provided in this agreement.

(c) You are or will become and will remain to the extent necessary to enable the performance of this agreement, a member in good standing of all labor unions or guilds, membership in which may be lawfully required for the performance of your services hereunder.

(d) No Materials, as hereinafter defined, or any use thereof, will violate any law or infringe upon or violate the rights of any Person. "Materials," as used in this Article, means: (1) all Controlled Compositions, (2) each name used by you in connection with Recordings made hereunder, and (3) all other musical, dramatic, artistic and literary materials, ideas, and other intellectual properties, furnished or selected by you and contained in or used in connection with any Recordings made hereunder or the packaging, sale, distribution, advertising, publicizing or other exploitation thereof.

13.02. During the term of this agreement, you will not enter into any agreement which would interfere with the full and prompt performance of your obligations hereunder, and you will not perform or render any services for the purpose of making Phonograph Records or master Recordings derived from your performances for any Person other than Record Company. After the expiration of the term of this agreement, for any reason whatsoever, you will not perform any Composition which shall have been recorded hereunder for any Person other than Record Company for the purpose of making Phonograph Records or Master Recordings prior to whichever of the following dates shall be later: (a) the date five (5) years subsequent to the date such Composition is recorded hereunder, or (b) the date two (2) years subsequent to the expiration date of the term of this agreement. You will not authorize or knowingly permit your performances to be recorded for any purpose without an express written agreement prohibiting the use of such Recording on Phonograph Records in violation of the foregoing restrictions.

13.03. If you shall become aware of any unauthorized recording, manufacture, distribution or sale by any third party contrary to the foregoing re-recording restrictions, you shall notify Record Company thereof and shall cooperate with Record Company in the event that Record Company commences any action or proceeding against such third party.

13.04. Your services are unique and extraordinary, and the loss thereof cannot be adequately compensated in damages, and Record Company shall be entitled to injunctive relief to enforce the provisions of this agreement.

13.05. You will at all times indemnify and hold harmless Record Company and any Licensee of Record Company from and against any and all claims, damages, liabilities, costs and expenses, including legal expenses and reasonable counsel fees, arising out of any breach by you of any warranty or agreement made by you herein. You will reimburse Record Company and/or its Licensees on demand for any payment made at any time after the date hereof in respect of any liability or claim in respect of which Record Company or its Licensees are entitled to be indemnified.

14. DEFINITIONS

As used in this agreement the following terms shall have the meanings set forth below:

14.01. *"Master Recording"*—every recording of sound, whether or not coupled with a visual image, by any method and on any substance or material, whether now or hereafter known, which is used or useful in the recording, production and/or manufacture of phonograph records.

14.02. *"Inception of Recording"*—the first recording of performances and/or other sounds with a view to the ultimate fixation of a Master Recording, etc.

14.03. *"Matrix"*—any device now or hereafter used, directly or indirectly, in the manufacture of Phonograph Records and which is derived from a Master Recording;

14.04. *"Person"* and *"Party"*—any individual, corporation, partnership, association or other organized group of persons or legal successors or representatives of the foregoing;

14.05. *"Records"* and *"Phonograph Records"*—all forms of reproductions, now or hereafter known, manufactured or distributed primarily for home use, school use, juke box use, or use in means of transportation, embodying (a) sound alone or (b) sound coupled with images, e.g. "sight and sound" devices;

14.06. *"Wholesale Price"*—(a) With respect to Records sold for distribution in the United States or Canada: (1) the average net price received by Record Company from independent distributors for Phonograph Records during the six-month period immediately preceding the accounting period concerned, calculated separately for each separately priced Record series manufactured and sold by Record Company; or (2) if there are no applicable independent distributors, Record Company's published subdistributor price in effect as of the commencement of the accounting period concerned, less ten percent. (b) With respect to Records sold for distribution outside of the United States and Canada, one-half of the suggested or applicable retail list price in the country of sale;

14.07. *"Royalty Base Price"*—the applicable Wholesale Price of Phonograph Records less all taxes and less the applicable container charge;

14.08. *"Container Charge"*—(a) with respect to disc Phonograph Records, 10 percent of the applicable Wholesale Price of such Phonograph Records; and (b) with respect to Phonograph Records in non-disc configurations, 25% of the applicable Wholesale Price of such Phonograph Records.

14.09. *"Net Sales"*—gross sales less returns and credits;

14.10. *"Club Operation"*—any direct sales to consumers conducted on a mail order basis by Record Company or its Licensees, e.g. the XYZ Record Club;

14.11. *"Contract Period"*—the initial period, or any option period, of the term hereof (as such periods may be suspended or extended as provided herein).

14.12. *"Advance"*—amount recoupable by Record Company from royalties to be paid to you or on your behalf pursuant to this or any other agreement.

14.13. *"Composition"*—a single musical composition, irrespective of length, including all spoken words and bridging passages and including a medley.

14.14. *"Controlled Composition"*—a composition written, owned or controlled by you and/or any Person in which you have a direct or indirect interest.

14.15. *"Album"*—one or more twelve-inch 33⅓ rpm records, or the equivalent thereof, sold in a single-package, including all Sides, whether or not released, which are recorded in connection with a specific album project, but not including Sides which were recorded in connection with any other album project. (A "disco single" shall not be deemed an Album.)

14.16. *"Side"*—a Recording of sufficient playing time to constitute one side of a 45 rpm record, but not less than two and one-quarter minutes of continuous sound;

14.17. *"Joint Recording"*—any Master Recording embodying your performance, together with the performance of another artist(s) with respect to which Record Company is obligated to pay royalties.

14.18. *"Sales through Normal Retail Channels in the United States"*—sales other than as described in paragraphs 9.02, 9.03, 9.05, 9.06, and 9.07 hereof.

14.19. *"Licensees"*—includes, without limitation, subsidiaries, wholly or partly owned, and other divisions of Record Company Inc.

14.20. *"Delivery" or "Delivered"*—when used with respect to Master Recordings, means the actual receipt by Record Company of fully mixed and edited Master Recordings, satisfactory to Record Company and ready for Record Company's manufacture of Phonograph Records, and all necessary licenses and applicable approvals and consents.

14.21. *"Reissue Label"*—a label, used primarily for reissues of recordings released previously.

14.22. *"Budget Record"*—a record bearing a suggested retail list price at least $2.00 lower than the suggested retail list price used for the top line Phonograph Records embodying performances of pop artists released by Record Company or its Licensees in the territory concerned.

14.23. *"Multiple Record Set"*—an Album containing two or more 12-inch 33⅓ rpm Records packaged as a single unit, or the equivalent.

15. SUSPENSION AND TERMINATION

15.01. If at any time you fail, except solely for Record Company's refusal without cause to allow you to perform, to fulfill your Recording Commitment within the times set forth herein, then, without limiting Record Company's rights, Record Company shall have the option, exercisable by notice to you, to:

(a) suspend the running of the then current Period of the term of this agreement (and extend its expiration date) for the period of the default plus such additional time as is necessary so that Record Company shall have not less than one hundred and eighty (180) days after completion of your Recording Commitment within which to exercise its option, if any, to extend the term for the next Contract Period, and/or to suspend Record Company's obligation to make payments to you hereunder during such suspension; or

(b) increase the Recording Commitment in any subsequent Contract Period by the number of uncompleted Master Recordings, in addition to the otherwise applicable Recording Commitment under paragraphs 3.01 and 3.03 above. The payments due for such Recordings shall be the payments that would have been due had the Recordings been Delivered during the Contract Period in which they were originally required to be Delivered.

15.02. If Record Company refuses to allow you to fulfill your Recording Commitment for any Contract Period and if, within thirty (30) days after the expiration date of the Contract Period you notify Record Company of your desire to fulfill such Recording Commitment, then Record Company shall permit you to fulfill said Recording Commitment by notice to you to such effect within sixty (60) days of Record Company's receipt of your notice. Should Record Company fail to give such notice, you shall have the option to terminate the term of this agreement by notice given to Record Company within thirty (30) days after the expiration of said sixty-day period; on receipt by Record Company of such notice the term of this agreement shall terminate and all parties will be deemed to have fulfilled all of their obligations hereunder except those obligations which survive the end of the term (e.g., warranties, re-recording restrictions and obligation to pay royalties), at which time Record Company shall pay you at the rate of union scale in full settlement of its obligation in connection therewith, which payment shall constitute an Advance. In the event you fail to give Record Company either notice within the period specified therefor, Record Company shall be under no obligation to you for failing to permit you to fulfill such Recording Commitment.

15.03. If because of: act of God; inevitable accident; fire; lockout, strike or other labor dispute; riot or civil commotion; act of public enemy; enactment, rule, order or act of any government or governmental instrumentality (whether federal, state, local or foreign); failure of technical facilities; failure or delay of transportation facilities; illness or incapacity of any performer or producer; or other cause of a similar or different nature not reasonably within Record Company's control; Record Company is materially hampered in the recording, manufacture, distribution or sale of records; then, without limiting Record Company's rights, Record Company shall have the option by giving you notice to suspend the then current Contract Period for the duration of any such contingency plus such additional time as is necessary so that Record Company shall have no less than thirty (30) days after the cessation of such contingency in which to exercise its option, if any, for the next following option period. Any such extension of the then current Contract Period due to a labor controversy or adjustment thereof which involves only Record Company Records shall be limited to a period of six (6) months.

16. AGREEMENTS, APPROVAL & CONSENT

16.01. As to all matters treated herein to be determined by mutual agreement, or as to which any approval or consent is required, such agreement, approval or consent shall not be unreasonably withheld.

16.02. Your agreement, approval or consent, whenever required, shall be deemed to have been given unless you notify Record Company otherwise within ten (10) days following the date of Record Company's written request therefor.

17. ASSIGNMENT

17.01. Record Company may assign its rights hereunder in whole or in part to any subsidiary, affiliated or controlling corporation or to any Person owning or acquiring a substantial portion of the stock or assets of Record Company, and such rights may be assigned by any assignee thereof; provided, however, that any such assignment shall not relieve Record Company of any of its obligations hereunder. Record Company may also assign its rights hereunder to any of its Licensees to the extent necessary or advisable in Record Company's sole discretion to implement the license granted.

18. NOTICES

18.01. Except as otherwise specifically provided herein, all notices hereunder shall be in writing and shall be given by personal delivery, registered or certified mail or telegraph (prepaid), at the respective addresses hereinabove set forth, or such other address or addresses as may be designated by either Party. Such notices shall be deemed given when mailed or delivered to a telegraph office, except that notice of change of address shall be effective only from the date of its receipt. Each notice sent to Record Company shall be directed to its Vice-President, Business Affairs, and a copy of each such notice shall be sent simultaneously to Managing Attorney, Record Company Law Department, Address.

19. MISCELLANEOUS

19.01. You will, prior to the release of the first Album hereunder, prepare an act of professional quality and will, during the term of this agreement, actively pursue your career as an entertainer in the live engagement field.

19.02. This agreement contains the entire understanding of the Parties hereto relating to the subject matter hereof and cannot be changed or terminated except by an instrument signed by an officer of Record Company. A waiver by either Party of any term or condition of this agreement in any instance shall not be deemed or construed as a waiver of such term or condition for the future, or of any subsequent breach thereof. All remedies, rights, undertakings, obligations, and agreements contained in this agreement shall be cumulative and none of them shall be in limitation of any other remedy, right, undertaking, obligation or agreement of either Party.

19.03. Those provisions of any applicable collective bargaining agreement between Record Company and any labor organization which are required, by the terms of such agreement, to be included in this agreement shall be deemed incorporated herein.

19.04. Each option and/or election granted to Record Company hereunder including, without limitation, to suspend the running of one or more periods of time specified in this agreement, to extend the term of this agreement, to acquire the direct and individual services of a leaving member (if a group artist is involved), or otherwise, is separate and distinct, and the exercise of any such option or election shall not operate as a waiver of any other option or election unless specifically so stated by Record Company in its notice of exercise of such option or election.

19.05. You shall not be entitled to recover damages or to terminate the term of this agreement by reason of any breach by Record Company of its material obligations hereunder, unless Record Company has failed to remedy such breach within a reasonable time following receipt of your notice thereof.

19.06. This agreement has been entered into in the State of ...., and the validity, interpretation and legal effect of this agreement shall be governed by the laws of the State of .... applicable to contracts entered into and performed entirely within the State of ...., with respect to the determination of any claim, dispute or disagreement which may arise out of the interpretation, performance, or breach of this agreement. Any process in any action or proceeding commenced in the courts of the State of .... or elsewhere arising out of any such claim, dispute or disagreement, may among other methods, be served upon you by delivering or mailing the same, via registered or certified mail, addressed to you at the address first above written or such other address as you may designate pursuant to Article 18 hereof. Any such delivery or mail service shall be deemed to have the same force and effect as personal service within the State of   or the jurisdiction in which such action or proceeding may be commenced.

19.07. In entering into this agreement, and in providing services pursuant hereto, you have and shall have the status of an independent contractor and nothing herein contained shall contemplate or constitute you as Record Company's agent or employee.

19.08. This agreement shall not become effective until executed by all proposed Parties hereto.

19.09. Any and all riders annexed hereto together with this basic document shall be taken together to constitute the agreement between you and Record Company.

....

Record Company

By ....

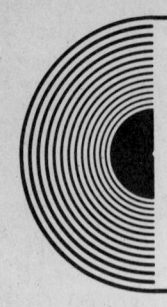

EXCLUSIVE SONGWRITER AGREEMENT

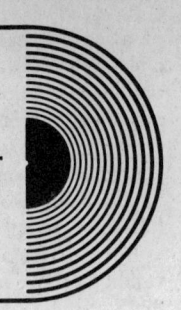

The exclusive songwriter agreement generally provides that the writer agrees to assign, sell or transfer to the publisher a collection of songs either composed or to be composed during the term of the agreement. Under this form of agreement, the writer is bound exclusively to the publisher, and unless otherwise provided, all compositions written during the term of the agreement are automatically assigned to the publisher for the full term of the copyright. Another form of songwriter's agreement provides for the publishing and exploitation of one or more specifically designated compositions. Agreements of this variety are exclusive only as to the songs which are the subject of the contract. The following issues should be given special consideration when negotiating a songwriter's agreement: scope of rights granted; calculation of royalties; reversion of rights to the writer; term (number of years) of the contract; representations by writer; indemnification of publisher by writer; frequency and thoroughness of royalty statements; and breach or default by either party.

KAM

EXCLUSIVE SONGWRITER AGREEMENT

Dated: ....

TO:

Re: Exclusive Songwriter's Agreement
between ....
and ....

Dear Sir:

This will confirm the understanding between you (as Writer) and the undersigned (as Publisher) whereby you and the undersigned have this day entered into an exclusive songwriter's contract, terms of which are embodied upon the annexed form which has been signed by you and the undersigned. The insertions in said annexed form have been agreed to be:

1. (a) Schedule "A" of "Prior Compositions" (Paragraph 3) (b) Rider attached for additional terms
2. Maximum Term of Contract: (Paragraph 8) Five Years

3. Royalties for Sheet Music and Dance Orchestrations: 7.5 cents (Paragraph 13 (a))
4. Royalties for Other Printed Editions: (Paragraph 13 (b)) Five Percent (5%)
5. Writer's Performing Rights Society: (Paragraph 13 (e)) as set forth

This agreement shall not be binding on the undersigned until this document and the annexed form have been fully executed by you and the undersigned.

Very truly yours,

By:......................................

ACCEPTED AND AGREED:

....
Writer

TERMS OF EXCLUSIVE SONGWRITERS' AGREEMENT

BY AND BETWEEN .... AS WRITER AND .... MUSIC CORP. AS PUBLISHER.

1. Publisher employs Writer to render his exclusive services as an author, composer, arranger and adaptor of musical compositions and of related works and Writer accepts such exclusive employment. Writer agrees not to write, compose, arrange or adapt musical compositions or related works for anyone other than Publisher during the term of this agreement. Writer further agrees to devote Writer's best efforts and the necessary time, attention, skill and energy to the employment hereunder and to render services diligently and to the best of Writer's ability in connection with said employment.

2. All musical compositions and related works, including without limitation, all lyrics, music, titles and characters thereof, written, composed, arranged or adapted, in whole or in part, by Writer during the term of this agreement, (herein jointly and severally referred to as the "Compositions") upon the creation thereof, shall be the sole and exclusive property of Publisher together with all copyrights and all renewals and extensions of copyright throughout the world, and together with all other rights of whatsoever nature therein, whether now in existence or hereafter to come into existence.

3. Schedule "A" contains a list of all musical compositions (herein jointly and severally referred to as the "Prior Compositions"), which Writer warrants is a list of all musical compositions written and composed by Writer individually or in collaboration with another or others prior to the term hereof, as to which neither Writer nor such collaborator (if any) has heretofore executed any songwriter's agreements with any Publisher. Writer hereby grants to Publisher all the rights, and Publisher hereby assumes as to the Prior Compositions, all of the obligations as are set forth herein with respect to the Compositions. The Compositions and the Prior Compositions are herein jointly and severally referred to as the "Musical Compositions".

4. Without limitation of the grant of rights set forth in Paragraphs 2 and 3 of this agreement, it is specifically understood that:

(A) Writer authorizes and empowers Publisher and appoints Publisher as Writer's true and lawful attorney to obtain and to renew for Publisher's benefit and in Publisher's name the copyrights and renewal copyrights in the Musical Compositions throughout the world and to execute in Writer's name all documents and instruments necessary or desirable to accomplish such grant of rights or to evidence Publisher's proprietary interest therein. This power is acknowledged by Writer to be coupled with an interest and to be irrevocable.

(B) Writer authorizes and empowers Publisher, in Publisher's sole discretion, to make or authorize changes, adaptations, arrangements, translations, transpositions, or dramatizations of the Musical Compositions or to set or re-set words to music or music to words or to title or re-title any Musical Composition.

(C) Writer authorizes and empowers Publisher throughout the world to exploit, market, distribute, or use the Musical Composition or to authorize the exploitation, marketing, distribution or use of the Musical Compositions in any or all ways and by any or all means (whether now known or hereafter devised) and upon such terms or conditions as are chosen by Publishers in its sole discretion, or to refrain therefrom.

5. (A) Writer shall prepare and deliver to Publisher completed lead sheets of each Composition immediately upon completion thereof and shall prepare and deliver to Publisher completed lead sheets of each Prior Composition, within a reasonable time after the execution of this agreement. Notwithstanding the foregoing, Publisher will accept demonstration recordings of Compositions and/or Prior Compositions in lieu of such lead sheets. One-half of any cost incurred by Publisher in connection with such recordings or in connection with any demonstration records made by Publisher or in connection with any lead sheets made by Publisher of any of the Musical Compositions shall be deemed advances against Writer's royalties and shall be recoupable from out of such royalties due Writer hereunder.

(B) Writer shall execute and deliver to Publisher such documents and instruments with respect to any Musical Composition which Publisher, in its judgment, may deem necessary or desirable to effectuate the intent and purpose of this agreement or to evidence Publisher's ownership of the rights granted to it herein. If Writer fails or is unable to execute any such document or instrument, it is understood that Publisher is empowered to execute such in Writer's name and on Writer's behalf as the attorney-in-fact of the Writer.

6. During the term of this agreement, Writer shall not collaborate as an author, composer, arranger or adapter of any musical compositions or related work with any person unless such collaboration is specifically approved by Publisher in writing prior thereto. Publisher may impose any conditions or terms upon any such collaboration as it alone may determine in its sole discretion or may refuse to approve same in its sole discretion.

7. Publisher shall have the right to use and to allow others to use Writer's name, pseudonym, tradename, assumed name (whenever adopted), likeness, or biographical material concerning Writer in connection with any permitted use, promotion or exploitation of the Musical Compositions.

8. (A) The term of this agreement shall commence on the date hereof and shall end three months thereafter. Said term, however, shall automatically be extended for successive and consecutive periods of three months each unless Publisher shall mail written notice of termination to Writer no less than ten days prior to the end of any such period or prior to the end of the initial period, in which event, this agreement shall terminate at the end of the three month period during which such notice is mailed. In no event shall this agreement continue for longer than five years from the date hereof. It is understood that no termination of this agreement shall diminish, alter or affect any right of Publisher to any Musical Composition acquired by Publisher hereunder.

(B) In any event this agreement shall be co-terminus with Writer's recording contract with Music Corp. entered into simultaneously herewith.

9. Writer's services hereunder are unique and extraordinary. Writer acknowledges that Publisher shall be entitled to equitable relief (in addition to all other available rights and remedies) to enforce the provisions of this agreement.

10. Writer warrants and represents:

(A) The Musical Compositions are or will be new and original and will not infringe upon any other works, compositions, arrangements or materials and will not violate, invade, infringe upon or interfere with any rights of any third party;

(B) Writer has the full right, power and authority to make this agreement, to perform its terms and conditions, to grant the rights herein granted to Publisher, to furnish his services, to render full performance hereunder, and to vest in Publisher all the rights granted Publisher in this agreement, free and clear of all claims, rights and obligations whatsoever;

(C) There does not now and there will not hereafter to Writer's knowledge exist any claim by a third party in or to any of the Musical Compositions or to any rights therein and no third party has or will have to Writer's knowledge any conflicting rights in or to any of the Musical Compositions or to any rights therein.

11. (A) Writer shall indemnify, save and hold Publisher harmless from any loss, liability, damage or expense (including reasonable attorney's fees) arising out of or connected with any adjudicated or settled claim, action or proceeding in which any assertion is made which is inconsistent with any of the warranties, representations, covenants or agreements made by Writer. Publisher may not settle any of the foregoing without Writer's consent.

(B) The decision as to whether any claim shall be made or any legal proceeding shall be brought against any alleged infringer upon any right of Publisher or upon any copyright in any Musical Composition shall be made solely by Publisher. Writer shall fully cooperate with Publisher in connection with any such claim or proceeding prosecuted by Publisher. Fifty (50%) Percent of the net recovery received by Publisher by reason of any such claim or proceeding shall be paid to Writer and the remainder shall be retained by Publisher. Such net recovery shall be the gross recovery therefrom less all expenses and costs (including reasonable attorney's fees) paid by Publisher in connection with such claim or proceeding.

(C) If a claim, action or proceeding is instituted against Publisher or any privee of Publisher in which any assertion is made which is inconsistent with any of the warranties, representations, covenants or agreements made by Writer herein, Publisher shall notify Writer of such claim or proceeding and Writer, at his sole cost and expense, may participate in the defense of any such claim, action or proceeding. Publisher shall have the right to control the defense thereof and to settle or otherwise dispose of such claims, actions and proceedings subject to Writer's consent not to be unreasonably withheld. Without limiting any of the rights Publisher may have, until the claim, action or proceeding has been finally adjudicated or settled, Publisher may withhold any and all monies due and payable to Writer hereunder, and such monies may, at Publisher's option and to the extent necessary, be applied in satisfaction of the indemnity contained in Paragraph 11(A).

12. Neither this agreement, Writer's obligations nor his rights hereunder shall be assignable by him. Publisher shall have the right to assign this agreement only upon the express written provision that Publisher's assignee agrees to be bound by all of the obligations undertaken by Publisher hereunder. Upon any such assignment by Publisher and such assumption by Publisher's assignee, Publisher shall thereafter be relieved of any further obligations hereunder to Writer and Publisher's assignee alone shall be responsible to Writer hereunder.

13. Publisher agrees to pay the following royalties to Writer with respect to each of the Musical Compositions:

(A) 7.5 cents per copy for each regular piano-forte copy thereof and for each dance orchestration thereof printed singly and not together with any other work and which is sold by Publisher (and not pursuant to a license from Publisher) and for which Publisher receives payment.

(B) Five Percent (5%) of the retail selling price of each printed copy or arrangement or edition thereof (other than those referred to in paragraph 13(A) published and sold by Publisher (and not pursuant to a license from Publisher) and for which Publisher receives payment, except that in the event that any of the Musical Compositions shall be printed in whole or in part together with one or more other works in a folio or album, the Writer shall receive that proportion of said royalties which said copyrighted Musical Compositions shall bear to the total number of copyrighted works contained in such folio or album.

(C) Fifty Percent (50%) of all net sums actually received by Publisher or credited to its account by reason of the sale of any printed editions of the Musical Compositions by licensees of Publisher.

(D) Fifty Percent (50%) of any and all net sums actually received by Publisher or credited to its account by reason of the exploitation of the mechanical rights, electrical transcription and reproducing rights, "commercial use" rights, motion picture synchronization and television rights and all other rights not specified in any subparagraph of this paragraph 13 (excepting public performing rights therein).

(E) The Writer shall receive public performance royalties throughout the world exclusively and directly from the performing rights society with which Writer is affiliated and shall have no claim whatsoever against the Publisher for any royalties received by the Publisher as a distribution from any performing rights society which makes payment directly to writers, authors and/or composers. Writer represents that he is now and will continue to be affiliated with (performing rights society).

(F) Fifty Percent (50%) of any and all net sums actually received by Publisher from sales and uses of the Musical Compositions in countries outside of the United States and Canada.

(G) Publisher (if it receives no payment) shall not be required to pay any royalties on professional or complimentary copies or any copies which are distributed gratuitously to performing artists or orchestra leaders or for advertising or exploitation purposes.

(H) In the event that Publisher shall agree in writing pursuant to Paragraph 6 hereof, that Writer may collaborate with any composer in the creation of any Musical Composition, such royalties shall be paid to Writer and such collaborator in the proportions specified by Publisher in the written agreement of Publisher with writer and such collaborator. In the event that pursuant to paragraph 4(B) hereof, some other composer shall adapt, change, arrange, translate, transpose or dramatize any Musical Composition, such other composer shall share in said royalties in a proportion specified by Publisher.

14. Publisher agrees that within forty-five (45) days after the last days of June and December, it will prepare and furnish statements to Writer of all royalties earned and/or payable hereunder. Each such statement shall be accompanied by payment of any sums shown by such statement to be due to Writer. From time to time Publisher may change the dates upon which royalties shall be paid and accompanying statements rendered hereunder, but in no event shall such statements be rendered and royalties paid less often than semi-annually. All statements shall be conclusively binding upon Writer and not subject to question unless Publisher shall receive written specifications of any objections thereto within one year after such statement is rendered, in which case such statement shall be binding in all respects not specified in such written objections. Writer may, upon written notice to Publisher, cause a certified public accountant designated by Writer to inspect Publisher's books and records respecting such statements at Publisher's office during regular business hours.

15. It is agreed that as a condition precedent to any assertion by Writer or Publisher that the other is in default in performing any obligation contained herein, the party alleging the default must advise the other in writing of the specific facts upon which it is claimed that the other is in default and the said other party shall be allowed a period of thirty (30) days after receipt of such written notice, within which to cure such default. The parties agree that no breach of the terms hereof will be deemed incurable.

16. This agreement shall be governed by and shall be construed and enforced in accordance with the laws of the State of New York applicable to agreements made and to be wholly performed therein.

17. This agreement and the rider attached sets forth the entire understanding between the parties, and no modification, amendment, waiver, termination or discharge of this agreement or any provisions thereof including said rider shall be binding unless confirmed by a written instrument signed by both parties hereto. No waiver of any provision of or default under this agreement or rider attached shall affect Publisher's right thereafter to enforce such provision or to exercise any right or remedy in the event of any other similar or dissimilar default.

IN WITNESS WHEREOF, the parties hereto have caused this agreement to be executed on the date first indicated above.

....
Writer

By: ....
Publisher

RIDER TO EXCLUSIVE SONGWRITER'S AGREEMENT
BETWEEN .... MUSIC CORP. (as Publisher)
AND .... (as Writer)

In addition to the royalties specified in paragraph 13 hereof and as to each of the Musical Compositions, the Publisher agrees to pay Writer 50% of the "Publisher's share of income" derived therefrom.

(A) As used herein, "Publisher's share of income" is intended to refer to all of the following income actually received by the Publisher or credited to its account as to each of the Musical Compositions after deducting in each instance all royalties due and owing to authors and composers of such Musical Compositions (including Writer) and after deduction in each instance of an administration fee of 15% of all the following income:

(i) Mechanical royalties received pursuant to any license or variance at any time granted (by operation of law or otherwise) less only collection fees paid, if any, which fees shall not be in excess of those customarily paid to agencies.

(ii) Royalties received pursuant to any synchronization license at any time granted less only collection fees paid, if any, which fees shall not be in excess of those customarily paid to agencies.

(iii) Public performance royalties paid by any performing rights society to Publisher.

(iv) Royalties received from licensees by reason of the sale of printed copies.

(v) Net receipts by Publisher (other than its royalties) by reason of the sale of printed copies of such Musical Compositions by Publisher less only its direct costs of printing, distribution, arranging and preparation of such printed copies and such Musical Compositions and sales commissions paid.

(vi) Any recovery received in connection with any claim or proceeding brought in connection with any Musical Composition less only reasonable attorney's fees, costs and expenses and other fees and disbursements paid by Publisher in connection with such claim or proceeding.

(vii) Sums received and not otherwise specified herein, such as payments on account of uses of any Musical Composition in connection with commercials.

(B) Publisher exclusively shall administer the exploitation of the Musical Compositions and of all copyrights therein, will issue all licenses and sub-publication agreements and all other contracts concerning the Musical Compositions, shall collect all considerations payable with respect to the exploitation of the Musical Compositions and shall institute, defend and control all claims and proceedings brought in connection with the Musical Compositions in accordance with the provisions hereof.

MUSIC CORP.

By: ....
Publisher

By: ....
Writer

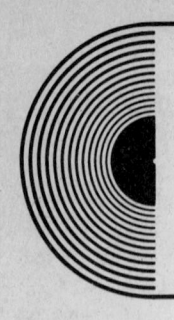

ARTIST–PRODUCER EXCLUSIVE RECORDING AGREEMENT

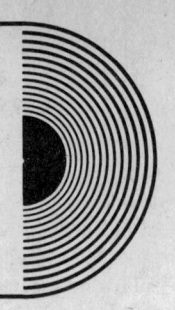

The recording agreement between a producer and an artist sets forth the terms and conditions under which a producer contracts the services of an artist to perform for the purpose of making phonograph records. Principal components of the producer-artist recording agreement include: producer's ability to secure a recording contract with a major distributor; term (number of years) of the contract; exclusivity of artist's services; minimum recording commitment; suspension (or extension) of the agreement; calculation and payment of royalties, advances to artist; accountings; grant of rights to producer; assignment; and breach or default by either party.

KAM

EXCLUSIVE RECORDING AGREEMENT

This Agreement is made as of the .... day of ...., 19.., by and between ....
....
(hereinafter referred to as "Producer") and ....
....
(hereinafter referred to as "Artist").

WITNESSETH as follows:

1. Producer hereby employs Artist as an exclusive recording artist and musician for the purpose of making master recordings from which phonograph records will be produced which embody the recorded performances of Artist, and for such purposes as are normally incidental thereto. Artist hereby accepts such employment, upon all the terms and conditions of this agreement.

2. This agreement is conditioned upon Producer entering into a recording contract with a major United States distributor of phonograph records for records to be made hereunder by the earlier of the following dates:

    (i) one year from ....
    (ii) one year from January 1, 19...

The term of this agreement shall consist of an Initial Period, commencing on the date hereof and continuing until a date one year after the earlier of the said two dates (referred to in the preceding sentence), together with the Periods required for completion of all performances hereunder pursuant to the Options herein granted. Subject to such aforementioned recording contract having been entered into, Artist hereby grants to Producer four (4) consecutive irrevocable Options to extend the term hereof for four (4) additional Periods of one year each. (Each of the said five (5) Periods is sometimes hereinafter referred to as a "Contract Period".)

Each such option shall be exercisable by Producer giving Artist a written notice not less than 30 days before the expiration of the then current Contract Period of its intention to exercise such option. All terms and conditions herein contained shall be applicable during such option periods excepting to the extent the Producer's distribution deal provides otherwise. If Producer can obtain such a commitment from the record distributor, at least one album hereunder will be released each year during the term hereof.

3. During the Contract Periods, and any extensions or renewals thereof, Artist shall not perform for the purpose of making master recordings or phonograph records for any person, firm or corporation other than Producer. For a period of five (5) years subsequent to the recording or two (2) years following the termination or expiration of this agreement, whichever is later, Artist shall not perform for such purposes (for anyone other than Producer) any musical composition or other material recorded hereunder.

4. If during the term of this agreement, Artist performs for the purpose of making any recording for any medium other than phonograph records, Artist agrees and guarantees that the contract pursuant to which such performances are rendered will expressly provide that neither such performance nor any master recording thereof shall be used to manufacture phonograph records (as "phonograph records" are defined herein) and Artist shall promptly furnish Producer with a copy of said contract.

5. Artist will render services at recording sessions scheduled at times and places designated by Producer. Producer and Artist shall mutually select the musical compositions, arrangements and works to be performed by Artist and shall also determine the number and identity of the musicians, vocalists and other performers (if any) to be recorded at such sessions. Upon Producer's request (exercisable in its sole discretion), Artist shall repeat any performance recorded hereunder, but only for the purpose of obtaining a satisfactory master recording.

6. Artist agrees to record a minimum of two (2) albums during the initial term of this agreement and during such subsequent option periods. Notwithstanding the foregoing, Artist shall record additional record sides at Producer's request, not to exceed two albums in any one year.

7. If, during the Initial Term of this agreement or any Contract Period, the Minimum Recording Commitments as set forth above are not recorded by reason of Artist's failure or refusal to record required record sides, or if Artist fails or refuses to render services at any recording session scheduled by Producer, or if Artist breaches any other obligation to Producer, Producer may elect to suspend the obligations of Producer hereunder and to extend the initial term of this agreement or the Contract Period during which such failure or refusal occurs, as the case may be, until such required Albums or record sides are recorded by Artist or until Artist renders such services or until such breach is fully cured. Written notice of Producer's election to extend this agreement pursuant hereto shall be mailed to Artist by certified mail, not more than thirty (30) days prior to the expiration of the Initial Period or Option Period, as the case may be.

8. (a) Artist acknowledges that the services to be rendered by him hereunder are unique and extraordinary and that the breach of this agreement by Artist will cause such irreparable damage to Producer as will justify Producer's application for equitable relief in addition to any other available remedies.

(b) Phonograph records manufactured from master recordings made hereunder shall be distributed and offered for sale under such trademarks, trade names or labels and by such distributors and licensees as Producer alone may determine. But these records shall be released initially under the top-line label for not less than two (2) years.

(c) Producer and Artist shall have the right to determine which of Artist's performances shall be coupled with other performances of Artist upon phonograph records of such sizes and speeds as the Producer and Artist shall determine.

(d) Producer shall have the right with Artist's consent (not to be unreasonably withheld) to couple performances rendered by Artist with performances rendered by others upon phonograph records of such sizes and speeds as Producer alone shall determine.

9. Producer agrees to pay or cause to be paid all costs of recording sessions hereunder, including without limitation the costs of arrangers, musicians, copyists, vocalists, payments due to any union pension and welfare fund, payroll taxes and recording costs (such as

studio time, equipment and personnel charges and mastering costs). All such payments and costs shall be considered non-returnable advances to Artist which shall be recouped from any royalties or other payments due to Artist under this agreement or the Management Agreement between Artist and .... or the Publishing Agreement between Artist and .... Music Corp. Any costs or expenses which are incurred by Producer by reason of Artist's failure to appear or tardiness in appearing at a recording session scheduled by Producer shall be paid by Artist to Producer as Artist's absolute liability without reference to any royalties due and payable to Artist, and Producer, at its option, may deduct such costs or expenses from such royalties. But the failure by Artist to make such payments shall not be deemed to be a breach of contract.

10. Producer shall pay or cause to be paid to Artist, as an additional nonreturnable adcance against the royalties due and payable hereunder, an amount equal to the applicable AFTRA and/or A.F. of M. minimum scale (or the minimum scale of any other union properly having jurisdiction in the event that AFTRA or A.F. of M. ceases to have jurisdiction) for each phonograph record side recorded hereunder. Each such payment shall be made within fourteen (14) days following the recording session at which the side(s) in question were recorded. The foregoing shall not be applicable to recording sessions held prior to the time when Artist becomes a member in good standing of the union properly having jurisdiction.

11. Subject to the provisions of subparagraphs (e), (f) and (g) hereof, Producer agrees to pay to Artist in consideration of the services to be rendered by Artist hereunder a royalty equal to fifty (50%) percent of the gross receipts of Producer from any distributor of phonograph records by reason of the sale, use, license or other exploitation of phonograph records manufactured from master recordings made hereunder (which receipts by Producer shall be based upon all royalty statements and flat fee payments received by Producer or credited to its account of records sold by such distributor) or the total of the following royalties, whichever is greater. The determination of which said royalty is greater shall be made solely by comparing the basic royalty rate agreed to be paid Producer by such a distributor (multiplied by one-half) for retail sales in the United States of disc phonograph records embodying Artist's performances with the basic royalty rate hereinafter stated for such sales. If said basic rate to be paid Producer by such distributor is based upon wholesale prices of such records, the basic rate hereinafter stated shall be multiplied by two (2) before such comparison is made. If the basic rate to be paid Producer by such distributor is based upon 90% of disc records sold, the basic rates herein stated shall be multiplied by 9/10 before said comparison is made.

(a) Such 50% of Producer's gross receipts shall not be less than the royalties which would result if based upon a royalty to Producer of not less than 24% nor more than 26% of the suggested wholesale list price (exclusive of all sales and excise taxes and duties and less the portion of such price allocated and charged the Producer for containers or packaging) for ninety (90%) percent of all phonograph records (exclusive of prerecorded tapes) sold at retail within the United States under the authority of Producer on both sides of which are embodied only performances recorded hereunder, and which are paid for and not returned, and one-half (½) of such royalty with respect to prerecorded tapes (contained in cartridges or otherwise) sold at retail within the United States under the authority of Producer embodying only performances recorded hereunder which are paid for and not returned; however, if Producer's distribution deal provides for a greater or full royalty on tape sales, Artist will also receive such greater or full royalty.

(b) With respect to phonograph records sold at retail outside of the United States under the authority of Producer which contain only performances rendered by Artist hereunder, Producer will pay to Artist a royalty equal to one-half (½) of the royalty specified in subdivision (a) of this paragraph; however, if Producer's distribution deal provides for a greater or full royalty on foreign sales, Artist will also receive such greater or full royalty. Such royalties shall be based upon the suggested retail list price of such records as royalties paid to Producer are calculated. Artist shall be paid at the same rate of exchange as Producer is paid, provided, however, that royalties on such sales shall not be due and payable until payment therefor has been received by Producer in the United States of America or credited to Producer's own bank account anywhere else in the world.

(c) In the event that phonograph records embodying any of Artist's performances recorded hereunder are sold at retail through any direct, mail-order operation, including but not limited to record clubs, and with respect to long-playing albums on which the suggested retail list price is three ($3.00) dollars or less per record or the equivalent thereof in foreign currency, the royalty payable to Artist shall be one-half (½) of the royalty otherwise due and payable as herein provided. No royalties shall be payable to Artist with respect to phonograph records distributed to subscribers to such operation by reason of the purchase of a specified number of phonograph records or by reason of distributions to subscribers of "bonus" or "free" records, limited, however, to two free albums for every ten albums sold and to three free singles for every ten singles sold, unless the distribution deal is more favorable.

(d) No royalties shall be payable on "disc jockey" or "promotional" copies of records distributed and no royalties shall be payable on phonograph records which are sold or distributed as premiums or as distress merchandise or which are sold for less than 50% of the full wholesale price therefor (as such price is established from time to time prior to the calculation of any discounts, allowances or commissions deductible therefrom.

(e) In the event any performance rendered by Artist hereunder is coupled on a phonograph record with any performance rendered by another artist, it is agreed that as to such record, the royalty payable to Artist shall be multiplied by a fraction, the numerator of which shall be the number of Artist's performances coupled thereon and the denominator of which shall be the total number of performances (including Artist's) coupled thereon.

(f) In the event that any master recording made hereunder embodies Artist's performances together with the performance of another artist or artists to whom Producer is obligated to pay a royalty, it is agreed that the royalty payable to Artist (as herein provided) with respect to phonograph records made from such master recording shall be multiplied by a fraction, the numerator of which shall be one and the denominator of which shall be the total number of such royalty artists (including Artist) and the costs of recording chargeable to Artist pursuant to Paragraph 3 hereof shall be multiplied by the same fraction.

(g) No royalties shall be payable to Artist until Producer has fully recouped all nonreturnable advance payments and all other charges against Artist's royalties pursuant to this agreement.

12. Royalties herein stated to be due and payable to Artist, less non-returnable advances, charges, expenses and other recoupable items properly deductible therefrom, will be computed for the preceding six (6) calendar month period within forty-five (45) days after June 30 and December 31 of each year so long as phonograph records embodying Artist's performances recorded hereunder are sold and paid for, it being expressly understood and agreed that Producer may base such computation on statements received from those third parties which distribute phonograph records embodying performances recorded hereunder, provided they are in accordance with the provisions hereof. Such royalties will be paid to Artist within such forty-five (45) day period and will be accompanied by appropriate royalty statements. From time to time Producer may change the dates upon which royalties shall be paid and accounting statements rendered hereunder, but in no event shall such statement be rendered and royalties (if any are due) be paid less than semiannually. All royalty statements and all other accounts rendered by Producer to Artist will be binding upon Artist and not subject to any objections by Artist for any reason unless specific objection in writing, stating the basis thereof, is received by Producer within one (1) year from the date rendered, in which event such statements shall be binding in all respects except for those specifically stated in such written objections. Artist shall have the right, by the use of a Certified Public Accountant during regular business hours, to audit Producer's books and accounts relating to such royalties hereunder, but not more than once in any twelve-month period.

13. Producer shall have the right to use and permit others to use Artist's name, likeness,

biographical material, pseudonym or assumed name (whenever adopted by Artist) and/or facsimile signature for advertising and trade purposes in connection with the manufacture, distribution, sale and exploitation of all phonograph records embodying Artist's performances recorded hereunder.

14. Artist acknowledges that Artist is engaged in the business of musical entertainment and that this agreement is reasonable and provident. Artist hereby represents and warrants that Artist is free to enter into this agreement and that Artist is under no disability, restriction, or prohibition which will interfere in any manner with Artist's full compliance with and performance under this agreement. Artist also warrants and represents that no performance recorded by Producer hereunder will infringe or violate any right of any person or firm and that Producer may exploit such master recordings made hereunder without liability or obligation to any person or firm. Artist agrees to indemnify, save and hold Producer harmless from any loss, damage or expense (including attorney's fees) arising out of or connected with any claim or proceeding which is inconsistent with the warranties, covenants or representations made by Artist in this agreement or arising out of any claim or proceeding instituted against Artist in which it is claimed that Artist has breached his obligations to Producer, provided such loss, damage or expenses is the result of an adjudicated breach or a settlement made with Artist's consent.

15. All master recordings made hereunder, as well as all performances embodied therein and all phonograph records derived therefrom and all rights throughout the world in such performances, master recordings and phonograph records, will be the exclusive property of Producer free of any claim whatsoever by Artist or by anyone deriving rights from Artist. Without limiting the generality of the foregoing, Producer shall have the exclusive right throughout the world, in its sole discretion and at any time, to manufacture, advertise, sell, lease, license, distribute or otherwise exploit said property, including the public performance thereof, and to authorize others to do so or to refrain from doing so. In addition, Producer shall be the sole and exclusive owner of any and all worldwide copyrights and copyright renewals in such master recordings, performances and phonograph records and Artist shall be deemed the employee-for-hire of Producer with respect to such copyrights and copyright renewals. Producer is not obligated to make or sell records manufactured from the master recordings made hereunder or to license such master recordings or to have Artist record the minimum number of record albums referred to above. If Producer fails to have Artist record said minimum number of record albums, the Artist may terminate on 30 days' notice to Producer.

16. Producer, in its sole discretion, may assign this agreement or any of Producer's rights hereunder to any major U.S. record manufacturer or distributor, provided the assignee assumes in writing all of Producer's obligations hereunder, whereupon Producer shall be relieved of the same. Without limiting the generality of the foregoing, Artist acknowledges and agrees that Producer may enter into agreement(s) for the distribution of phonograph records embodying performances recorded hereunder, which agreement(s) may be with such parties and may contain such terms and conditions as Producer, in its sole discretion, deems advisable, providing it is no less favorable to the Artist than is this agreement. Artist agrees to execute all documents, confirmations or assents which any such distributor of phonograph records embodying performances recorded hereunder deems necessary to be executed by Artist. Artist agrees that upon the assignment of this agreement to a corporation of which Producer is at least a fifty percent (50%) owner and upon the written agreement of such corporation to assume all obligations of Producer to Artist hereunder, Producer shall be relieved of any and all further obligations to Artist.

17. If, due wholly or partially to any labor controversy or adjustment thereof or to any cause not entirely within Producer's control or which Producer could not by reasonable diligence have avoided, Producer is prevented from recording, manufacturing, distributing or selling phonograph records or Producer's normal business operations become commercially impractical, then for the duration of such contingency and without liability and without waiving any other rights to which Producer may be entitled, Producer may suspend the obligations of Producer hereunder and the initial term of this agreement or the

option period during which such contingency occurs, as the case may be, for the duration of such contingency. Written notice of Producer's election to exercise Producer's rights hereunder shall be mailed to Artist by certified mail, no less than 30 days after the commencement of such contingency.

18. As a condition precedent to any assertion by Producer or Artist that the other is in default in performing any obligation contained herein, the party alleging the default must advise the other in writing of the specific facts upon which it is claimed that the other is in default and of the specific obligations which it is claimed has been breached and said other party shall be allowed a period of thirty (30) days after receipt of such written notice within which to cure such default. The parties agree that no breach of any obligation shall be deemed to be incurable during such thirty (30) day period.

19. For the purpose of this agreement:

(a) "Master Recording" whenever referred to herein is intended to mean any original recording of sound, whether on magnetic recording tape or wire, lacquer or wax disc, or any other substance or material, whether now known or unknown, which is used in the manufacture of phonograph records. "Sound recordings" within the meaning of the United States Copyright Act as amended at any time shall be deemed to be master recordings within the meaning of this agreement.

(b) "Performance" whenever referred to herein is intended to mean any musical or vocal rendition or artistic service in connection with the production of a master recording, including, but not limited to, arranging, conducting, singing, producing, accompanying or supervising such rendition or the playing of any instrument.

(c) "Phonograph record", "record" or "phonograph recording" whenever referred to is intended to mean any and all objects (whether now known or hereafter devised) manufactured in whole or in part from master recordings and which are intended to reproduce sound, including but not limited to wire, disc, film, cylinder and (except where otherwise expressly stated) tape, whether embodying sound alone or sound synchronized with visual images, e.g., audio-visual devices.

20. Subject to prior professional commitments of Artist, and upon the request of Producer, Artist shall perform all services reasonably desirable to promote the sale of phonograph records embodying Artist's performances, which services shall be without compensation to Artist. But Producer will pay the out-of-pocket costs thereof, which shall not be deemed a recoupable advance.

21. This agreement sets forth the entire agreement between the parties with respect to the subject matter hereof, and no modification, amendment, waiver, termination or discharge of this agreement or any provision thereof shall be binding upon Producer or Artist unless confirmed by a written instrument signed by both parties. No waiver of any provision of or default under this agreement shall affect either party's right thereafter to enforce such provision or to exercise any right or remedy in the event of any other default, whether or not similar. The validity, construction and effect of this agreement, and all extensions and modifications thereof shall be construed in accordance with the laws of the State of New York applicable to agreements wholly to be performed therein.

22. If the Producer gets a Recording Fund from the Record Distributor, and if the cost of recording an album turns out to be less than the Recording Fund, the difference shall be divided 50%-50% between Producer and Artist, and the Artist's share shall be deemed an advance against Artist's royalties under this agreement.

IN WITNESS WHEREOF, the parties hereto have caused this agreement to be executed as of the date and year first indicated above.

....
Artist

By ....
(Producer)

MANAGEMENT AGREEMENT

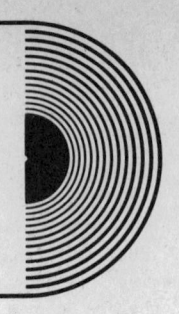

The management agreement is the written agreement which sets forth the expectations, duties, and obligations between a manager and artist. A well drafted agreement will take into account the experience, resources and professional capabilities of the manager and the needs and status of the artist. Particular attention should be given to the provisions in the agreement which address such topics as: services to be rendered by the manager; exclusivity or nonexclusivity of the manager's services; compensation of the manager; term (number of years) of the contract; power of attorney; mutual representations; responsibility for the payment of expenses; and breach or default by either party.

KAM

MANAGEMENT AGREEMENT

AGREEMENT made this .... day of ...., 19.. by and between .... (hereinafter referred to as "MANAGER") and .... of .... (hereinafter referred to as "ARTIST").

WITNESSETH:

WHEREAS, Artist wishes to obtain advice, guidance, counsel and direction in the development and furtherance of Artist's career as a musician, composer, arranger, publisher, actor, writer, producer, director, author, and performing artist and in such new and different areas as Artist's artistic talents can be developed and exploited, and

WHEREAS, Manager, by reason of Manager's contacts, experience and background, is qualified to render such advice, guidance, counsel and direction to Artist:

NOW, THEREFORE, in consideration of the mutual promises herein contained, it is agreed and understood as follows:

1. Manager agrees to render such advice, guidance, counsel, direction and other services as Artist may reasonably require to further Artist's career as a musician, author, composer, arranger, publisher, actor, writer, producer, director and performing artist and to develop new and different areas within which Artist's artistic talents can be developed and exploited, including, but not limited to the following services:

(a) to represent Artist and act as Artist's negotiator, to fix in Artist's best interests the terms governing all manner of disposition, use, employment or exploitation of Artist's talents and the products thereof; and

(b) to supervise Artist's professional employment and, on Artist's behalf, to consult with employers and prospective employers so as to assure the proper use and continued demand for Artist's services; and

(c) to be available at reasonable times and places to confer with Artist in connection with all matters concerning Artist's professional career, business interests, employment and publicity; and

(d) to exploit Artist's personality in all media, and in connection therewith to approve and permit, for the purpose of trade, advertising and publicity, the use, dissemination, reproduction or publication of Artist's name, photographic likeness, voice and artistic and musical materials; and

(e) subject to Artist's prior reasonable consent, to engage, discharge and/or direct such theatrical agents, booking agencies, and employment agencies as well as other firms, persons or corporations who may be retained for the purpose of securing contracts, engagements or employment for Artist. It is understood, however, that Manager is not a booking agent but rather shall represent Artist with all such agencies. Manager is not obligated to and shall not render any services or advice which would require Manager to be licensed as an employment agency in any jurisdiction; and

(f) to represent Artist in all dealings with any union; and

(g) to exercise all powers granted to Manager pursuant to paragraph "4" hereof.

2. Manager is not required to render exclusive services to Artist or to devote the entire time of Manager or the entire time of any of Manager's employees to Artist's affairs. Nothing herein shall be construed as limiting Manager's rights to represent other persons whose talents may be similar to or who may be in competition with Artist or to have and pursue business interests which may be similar to or may compete with those of Artist. Manager shall have the right to delegate management powers and responsibilities to others and to assign such management powers and responsibilities as well as to assign or sell this agreement to an individual who is a stockholder of Manager, or to a partnership at least one of whose partners is a stockholder of Manager, or to another corporation which acquires all or substantially all of Managers' assets, in which event Manager shall be relieved of its obligations hereunder.

3. Artist hereby appoints Manager as Artist's sole and exclusive personal manager in all matters usually and normally within the jurisdiction and authority of personal managers, including but not limited to the advice, guidance, counsel and direction specifically referred to in paragraph "1" hereof. Artist agrees to seek such advice, guidance, counsel and direction from Manager solely and exclusively and agrees that Artist will not engage any other agent, representative or manager to render similar services, and that Artist will not perform said services on his own behalf and Artist will not negotiate, accept or execute any agreement, understanding or undertaking concerning Artist's career without Manager's express prior consent.

4. (a) Artist hereby irrevocably appoints Manager for the term of this agreement and any extensions hereof as Artist's true and lawful attorney-in-fact to sign, make, execute and deliver any and all personal appearance contracts in Artist's name subject to Artist's prior reasonable consent, and to make, execute, endorse, accept, collect and deliver any and all bills of exchange, checks and notes as Artist's said attorney; to demand, sue for, collect, recover, and receive all goods, claims, money, interest or other items that may be due to Artist or belong to Artist; and to make, execute and deliver receipts, releases or other discharges therefor under sale or otherwise and to defend, settle, adjust, compound, submit to arbitration and compromise all actions, suits, accounts, reckonings, claims and demands whatsoever that are or shall be pending in such manner and in all respects as Manager in Manager's sole discretion shall deem advisable; and without in any way limiting the foregoing, generally to do, execute and perform any other act, deed or thing whatsoever that reasonably ought to be done, executed and performed of any and every nature and kind as fully and effectively as Artist could do if personally present; and Artist hereby ratifies and affirms all acts performed by Manager by virtue of this power of attorney.

(b) Artist expressly agrees that he will not on Artist's own behalf exert any of the powers herein granted to Manager by the foregoing power of attorney without the express prior written consent of Manager and that all sums and considerations paid to Artist by reason of Artist's artistic endeavors shall be paid to Manager on his behalf.

(c) It is expressly understood that the foregoing power of attorney is limited to matters reasonably related to Artist's career as musician, author, composer, arranger, publisher, actor, writer, producer, director, and performing artist and such new and different areas within which Artist's artistic talents can be developed and exploited.

(d) Artist agrees and understands that the power of attorney granted to Manager is coupled with an interest which Artist irrevocably grants to Manager in the career of Artist, in the artistic talents of Artist, in the products of said career and talents and in the earnings of Artist, arising by reason of such career, talents and products.

5. (a) As compensation for the services to be rendered to Artist by Manager hereunder, Manager shall receive from Artist (or shall retain from Artist's "gross monthly earnings") at the end of each calendar month during the term hereof, a sum of money equal to Twenty (20%) Percent of Artist's gross monthly earnings. Artist hereby assigns to Manager an interest in such earnings to the extent of Twenty (20%) Percent thereof. Said assignment is intended by Artist to create an assignment coupled with an interest.

(b) The term "gross monthly earnings", as used herein, refers to the total of all earnings, which shall not be accumulated or averaged (whether in the form of salary, bonuses, royalties (or advances against royalties), interests, percentages, shares of profits, merchandise, shares in ventures, products, properties, or any other kind or type of income which is reasonably related to Artist's career in the entertainment, amusement, music, recording, motion picture, television, radio, literary, theatrical and advertising fields and all similar areas whether now known or hereafter devised, in which Artist's artistic talents are developed and exploited), received during any calendar month by Artist or by any of Artist's heirs, executors, administrators, assigns, or by any person, firm or corporation (including Manager) on Artist's behalf. It is understood that, for the purpose hereof, no expense, cost or disbursement incurred by Artist in connection with the receipt of "gross monthly earnings" (including salaries, shares of profits or other sums paid to artists participating in Artist's presentation) shall be deducted therefrom prior to the calculation of Manager's compensation hereunder.

(c) The compensation agreed to be paid to Manager shall be based upon gross monthly earnings (as herein defined) of Artist accruing to or received by Artist during the term of this agreement or subsequent to the termination of this agreement as a result of: (i) any services performed by Artist during or prior to the term hereof, or (ii) any contract negotiated during or prior to the term hereof and any renewal, extension (by exercise of option or otherwise) modification or substitution of such contract, or (iii) any product of Artist's services or talents or of any property created by Artist in whole or in part during or prior to the term hereof.

(d) In the event that Artist utilizes an existing corporation or forms a corporation during the term hereof for the purpose of furnishing and exploiting Artist's artistic talents, Artist agrees that said corporation shall offer to enter into a management contract with Manager identical in all respects to this agreement (except as to the parties thereto).

(i) In the event that Manager accepts such offer, then the gross monthly earnings of such corporation prior to the deduction of any corporate income taxes and of any corporate expenses or other deductions shall be included as part of Artist's gross monthly earnings as herein defined, and any salary paid to Artist by such corporation shall be excluded from Artist's gross monthly earnings for the purpose of calculating the compensation due to Manager hereunder.

(ii) In the event the Manager refuses such offer, then the gross monthly earnings of such corporation prior to deduction of any corporate income taxes and any other corporate expenses or deduction shall be excluded from Artist's gross monthly earnings as defined hereunder, and such salary as is paid to Artist by such corporation shall be included as part of Artist's gross monthly earnings as herein defined.

(e) Artist agrees that all gross monthly earnings as herein defined shall be paid directly to Manager by all persons, firms or corporations and shall not be paid by such persons, firms or corporations to Artist, and that Manager may withhold Manager's compensation therefrom and may reimburse itself therefrom for any fees, costs or expenses advanced or incurred by Manager pursuant to paragraph "6" hereof. In the event that Artist nevertheless receives gross monthly earnings directly, Artist shall be deemed to hold in trust for Manager that portion of Artist's gross monthly earnings which equals Manager's compensation hereunder and such disbursements incurred by Manager on behalf of Artist.

6. Artist shall as between Artist and Manager be solely responsible for payment of all booking agencies' fees, union dues, publicity costs, promotion or exploitation costs, long distance telephone expenses, travelling expenses and wardrobe expenses and all other expenses, fees and costs incurred by Artist. In the event that Manager advances any of the foregoing fees, costs or expenses on behalf of Artist, or incurs any other reasonable costs, fees or expenses in direct connection with Artist's professional career or with the performance of Manager's services hereunder, Artist shall promptly reimburse Manager for such fees, costs and expenses. Without limiting the foregoing, such direct expenses, costs or fees incurred by Manager shall include long distance telephone expenses, legal fees, accounting fees and bookkeeping expenses, incurred on Artist's behalf, promotion and publicity expenses and economy travel and living accommodation expenses and costs whenever Manager, in Manager's opinion, and agreed to by Artist, shall deem it advisable to accompany Artist outside of New York City.

7. Artist warrants that he is under no disability, restriction or prohibition with respect to Artist's right to execute this agreement and perform its terms and conditions. Artist warrants and represents that no act or omission by Artist hereunder will violate any right or interest of any person or firm or will subject Manager to any liability, or claim of liability to any person. Artist agrees to indemnify Manager and to hold Manager harmless against any damages, costs, expenses, fees (including attorneys' fees) incurred by Manager in any claim, suit or proceeding instituted by or against Manager in any claim, suit or proceeding instituted by or against Manager in which any assertion is made which is inconsistent with any warranty, representation or covenant of Artist. Artist agrees to exert Artist's best efforts to further Artist's professional career during the term of this agreement and to cooperate with Manager to the fullest extent in the interest of promoting Artist's career.

8. The initial term of this agreement shall be for a period of one (1) year from the date hereof. This agreement shall automatically renew itself for two (2) additional periods of one (1) year each, unless Manager gives Artist notice of Manager's desire not to continue to represent Artist ten (10) days before the time this agreement would otherwise expire.

9. Manager agrees to maintain accurate books and records of all transactions concerning Artist, which books and records may be inspected by a certified public accountant designated by Artist, at Artist's expense, upon reasonable written notice to Manager, at Manager's office in New York City and during regular business hours.

10. There shall be no change, amendment or modification of this agreement unless it is reduced to writing and signed by all parties hereto. No waiver of any breach of this agreement shall be construed as a continuing waiver or consent to any subsequent breach thereof.

11. It is agreed that as a condition precedent to any assertion by Artist or Manager that the other is in default in performing any obligation contained herein, the party alleging the default must advise the other in writing of the specific facts upon which it is claimed that the other is in default and of the specific facts upon which it is claimed that the other is in default and the said other party shall be allowed a period of thirty (30) days after receipt of such written notice, within which to cure such default. The parties agree that no breach of the terms hereof will be deemed incurable.

12. Artist acknowledges and agrees that Manager's right to represent Artist as Artist's sole and exclusive personal manager and Artist's obligation to solely and exclusively use Manager in such capacity are unique, irreplaceable and extraordinary rights and obligations and that any breach or threatened breach by Artist thereof shall be material and shall cause Manager immediate and unavoidable damages which cannot be adequately compensated for by money judgment. Accordingly, Artist agrees that in addition to all other forms of relief and all other remedies which may be available to Manager in the event of any such breach or threatened breach by Artist, Manager (subject to the notice provision contained in paragraph "11") shall be entitled to seek and obtain injunctive relief against Artist.

13. This agreement does not and shall not be construed to create a partnership or joint venture between the parties hereto.

14. This agreement shall be construed in accordance with the laws of the State of New York governing contracts wholly executed and performed therein, and shall be binding

upon and inure to the benefit of the parties' respective heirs, executors, administrators, and successors.

15. In the event any provision hereof shall be for any reason illegal or unenforceable, the same shall not affect the validity or enforceability of the remaining provisions hereof.

16. Artist acknowledges that this agreement is executed as an arms-length transaction and that Artist is free to use independent legal counsel to advise Artist with respect to Artist's and Manager's rights and obligations under this agreement.

IN WITNESS WHEREOF, the parties have caused this agreement to be executed as of the date first indicated above.

By: ....
(Manager)

By: ....
(Artist)

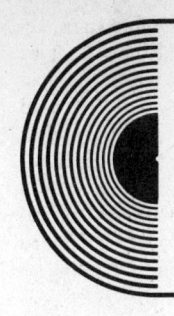

PRODUCTION AGREEMENT

There are several varieties of production agreements pursuant to which a production company agrees to provide to a record company the services of an artist or the services of an independent producer in connection with master recordings of performances by an artist. While the agreements may vary slightly in form, the purpose and the final result (finished master recordings of an artist's performances) are similar. The following summarizes several of the principal considerations and topics covered in a typical production agreement: nature of services to be furnished by the producer (or production company); recording procedure and commitment; recording costs; advances to producer; grant of rights by producer; calculation and payment of royalties; accountings; term (number of years) of the contract; mechanical licenses; warranties, representations, restrictions and indemnities; breach or default. Production agreements are, from time to time, coupled with an inducement rider pursuant to which the independent producer or artist agrees to be bound by the terms and conditions of the principal production agreement.

KAM

AGREEMENT made this .... day of ...., 198.. between .... (hereinafter "you") and Record Company.

1. TERM

1.01. This agreement shall commence as of and shall continue in force for a term which shall consist of an initial period ending .... (unless extended or suspended as provided herein) and the additional period or periods, if any, for which such term may be extended through Record Company's exercise of one or more of the options granted to Record Company below.

1.02. You grant Record Company ...... consecutive options to extend the term of this agreement for additional periods of one (1) year each ("Option Periods") upon all the terms and conditions herein contained. Record Company may exercise each such option by giving you notice in writing at least thirty (30) days prior to the expiration of the then current Contract Period.

2. SERVICES

2.01. During the term of this agreement you will furnish the services of .... (hereinafter referred to as the "Artist") to perform for the purpose of making Phonograph Records as provided in Article 3.

2.02. You shall furnish the services of producers in connection with the Master Recordings to be made by the Artist hereunder (hereinafter, "Producers"), and you shall be solely responsible for engaging and paying them. If, however, the producers whose services are rendered in connection with any Recordings made hereunder are engaged by Record Company: (a) your royalty account and the production budget for the recording project concerned will be charged with a Recording Cost item of $10,000 (or such higher fixed amount, if any, which Record Company is obligated to pay to the producers in connection with the project); and (b) the royalty otherwise payable to you in respect of those Recordings will be reduced by the amount of a royalty computed under this agreement, calculated at a basic rate of 6% under paragraph 9.01 and adjusted as provided elsewhere herein.

3. RECORDING COMMITMENT

3.01. The Minimum Recording Commitment in respect of each Contract Period shall be as follows:

    Initial Period
    First Option Period
    Second Option Period
    Third Option Period
    Fourth Option Period

3.02. If the Minimum Recording Commitment for the Contract Period concerned is one Album or less, the entire Minimum Recording Commitment will be completed within the first seven (7) months of the Contract Period. If the Minimum Recording Commitment is more than one Album, one-half of the Minimum Recording Commitment will be completed during the first half of the Contract Period, and the balance will be completed not later than ninety (90) days before the end of the Contract Period.

3.03. (a) During each Contract Period, Record Company shall have the option to increase the Recording Commitment for such Period by Recordings constituting not more than one additional Album or the equivalent. Said option is referred to below as the "Overcall Right," and the additional Recordings which may be required hereunder are referred to as "Overcall Recordings."

(b) The Overcall Right shall be exercisable at any time before whichever of the following dates occurs later: (1) the date ninety (90) days before the end of the Contract Period concerned; or (2) the date sixty (60) days after the completion of the Minimum Recording Commitment for that Contract Period.

(c) The Overcall Recordings will be Delivered to Record Company within ninety (90) days after the date of Record Company's exercise of the Overcall Right. If Record Company exercises the Overcall Right: (1) Record Company will have the further option, exercisable by notice to you before the end of the current Contract Period, to extend that Period until the date sixty (60) days after the Delivery of the Overcall Recordings; and (2) Record Company's option to extend the term of this agreement for the next Option Period under paragraph 1.02 will be exercisable at any time before the expiration of the current Contract Period.

3.04. Only Master Recordings consisting of Compositions not previously recorded by the Artist shall apply in reduction of the Recording Commitment.

3.05. The Artist shall not be required to perform hereunder together with any other royalty artist without the Artist's consent. Record Company shall not be deemed to be unreasonable in rejecting any request for the Artist to record with another royalty artist.

4. RECORDING PROCEDURE

4.01. You will follow the procedure set forth below in connection with Master Recordings made hereunder:

    (a) Except as expressly noted otherwise in this agreement, prior to the commencement of recording in each instance you shall obtain the approval of Record Company of each of the following, in order, before proceeding further:

(1) Selection of Producer

(2) Selection of material, including the number of Compositions to be recorded. Record Company shall not be deemed to be unreasonable in rejecting any request to record an Album consisting of more than one twelve-inch 33⅓ rpm Record. You shall advise Record Company of the content of all medleys prior to the recording thereof.

(3) Specification of accompaniment, arrangement and copying services.

(4) Selection of dates of recording and studios where recording is to take place, including the cost of recording therein. Record Company will not be deemed to be unreasonable in rejecting any request to begin recording any Album which is a part of the Minimum Recording Commitment hereunder within three (3) months after the acceptance of a prior Album hereunder. The scheduling and booking of all studio time will be done by Record Company. Record Company's facilities and the services of its engineers will be used in all recordings made hereunder.

(5) A proposed budget (which you will submit to Record Company sufficiently in advance of the planned commencement of recording to give Record Company a reasonable time to review and approve or disapprove it at least 14 days before the planned commencement of recording).

(b) You shall notify the appropriate Local of the American Federation of Musicians in advance of each recording session.

(c) As and when required by Record Company, you shall allow Record Company's representatives to attend any or all recording sessions hereunder.

(d) You shall timely supply Record Company with all of the information it needs in order: (1) to make payments due in connection with such Recordings; (2) to comply with any other obligations Record Company may have in connection with the making of such Master Recordings; and (3) to prepare to release Phonograph Records derived from such Master Recordings. Without limiting the generality of clause (2) of the preceding sentence, you shall furnish Record Company with all information it requires to comply with its obligations under its union agreements, including, without limitation, the following:

(i) If a session is held to record new tracks intended to be mixed with existing tracks (and if such information is requested by the American Federation of Musicians), the dates and places of the prior sessions at which such existing tracks were made, and the AFM Phonograph Recording Contract (Form "B") number(s) covering such sessions.

(ii) Each change of title of any composition listed in an AFM Phonograph Recording Contract (Form "B").

(iii) A listing of all the musical selections contained in recordings made at location sessions and delivered to Record Company hereunder.

(e) You shall submit to Record Company fully edited Master Recordings, satisfactory for its manufacture and sale of Phonograph Records, and deliver to Record Company all original and duplicate Master Recordings of the material recorded, together with all necessary licenses and appropriate permissions.

4.02. No "live" Recording or Recording not made in full compliance with the provisions of this agreement will apply in fulfillment of your Recording Commitment, nor will Record Company be required to make any payment in connection with any such Recording, unless Record Company so agrees in writing or such Recording is actually released by Record Company. No Joint Recording will apply in fulfillment of your Recording Commitment, nor will Record Company be required to make any payments in connection with any such Joint Recording other than royalties due you hereunder, even if such Joint Recording is actually released by Record Company. No Recordings shall be made by unauthorized dubbing.

4.03. Nothing in this agreement shall obligate Record Company to continue or permit the continuation of any recording session or project, even if previously approved hereunder, if Record Company reasonably anticipates that the Recording Costs will exceed those specified in the approved budget or that the Recordings being produced will not be satisfactory.

5. RECORDING COSTS

5.01. Record Company will pay all union scale payments required to be made to Artist in connection with Recordings made hereunder, all costs of instrumental, vocal and other personnel and arrangements and copying specifically approved by Record Company in respect of the recording of such Master Recordings, and all other amounts required to be paid by Record Company pursuant to any applicable law or any collective bargaining agreement between Record Company and any union representing persons who render services in connection with such Master Recordings.

5.02. All amounts described in paragraph 5.01 above plus all other amounts representing direct expenses paid by Record Company, or incurred in connection with the recording of Master Recordings hereunder (including, without limitation, advances to producers and all studio and engineering charges, in connection with Record Company's facilities and personnel or otherwise) are herein sometimes called "Recording Costs" and shall constitute Advances. The cost of metal parts, and payments to the AFM Special Payments Fund and the Music Performance Trust Fund based upon record sales (so-called "per-record royalties"), shall not constitute Advances. Any Recording Costs in excess of the amount approved by Record Company will be your sole responsibility and will be promptly paid by you (or reimbursed by you if paid by Record Company).

5.03. In determining the portion of the Recording Costs (other than payments to the Artist) applicable to any Joint Recording which shall be charged against your royalties, such portion shall be computed by multiplying the aggregate amount of such Recording Costs by the same fraction used in determining the royalties payable to you in respect of such Joint Recording.

6. ADDITIONAL ADVANCES

6.01. All monies paid to or on behalf of you or Artist during the term of this agreement at your or Artist's request, other than royalties paid pursuant to Articles 9 and 12 hereof, shall constitute Advances unless otherwise expressly agreed in writing by an authorized officer of Record Company.

7. GRANT OF RIGHTS

7.01. All Master Recordings recorded hereunder from the Inception of Recording thereof, and all Matrices and Phonograph Records manufactured therefrom, together with the performances embodied thereon, shall be the sole property of Record Company, free from any claims whatsoever by you or any other Person; and Record Company shall have the exclusive right to copyright such Master Recordings in its name as the owner and author thereof and to secure any and all renewals and extensions of such copyright.

7.02. Without limiting the generality of the foregoing, Record Company and any Person authorized by Record Company shall have the unlimited right to manufacture Phonograph Records by any method now or hereafter known, derived from the Master Recordings made hereunder, and to sell, transfer or otherwise deal in the same under any trademarks, trade names and labels, or to refrain from such manufacture, sale and dealing, throughout the world.

7.03. Record Company and any Licensee of Record Company each shall have the right and may grant to others the right to reproduce, print, publish, or disseminate in any medium your name, the names, portraits, pictures and likenesses of the Artist and Producer(s) and all other persons performing services in connection with the recording of such Master Recordings (including, without limitation, all professional, group, and other assumed or fictitious names used by them), and biographical material concerning them, as news or information, for the purposes of trade, or for advertising purposes. No direct endorsement by any such Person of any product or service shall be used without his written consent. During the term of this agreement neither you nor Artist shall authorize any Party other than Record Company to use the name or likeness of Artist (or any professional, group, or other assumed or fictitious name used by Artist) in connection with the advertising or sale of Phonograph Records.

8. COUPLING

8.01. During the term of this agreement, in respect of Records manufactured for sale in the United States, Record Company will not, without your consent and notwithstanding anything in Article 9:

(a) couple Master Recordings made hereunder with Recordings not embodying the Artist's performances on "pop singles"; or

(b) so couple more than two Master Recordings made hereunder on any other disc Record, except promotional Records and programs for use on public transportation carriers and facilities.

9. ROYALTIES

You will be paid royalties on Net Sales of Records as hereinafter set forth:

9.01. Record Company will pay you a basic royalty computed at the applicable percentage, indicated below, of the applicable Royalty Base Price in respect of Net Sales of Phonograph Records consisting entirely of Master Recordings recorded hereunder and sold by Record Company or its Licensees Through Normal Retail Channels for distribution in the United States:

(a) *On Albums*: 26%.

(b) *On "single" Records*: 22%.

9.02. The royalty rate on Phonograph Records sold through any Club Operation shall be determined by multiplying the otherwise applicable royalty rate by a fraction, the numerator of which is 7 and the denominator of which is the basic royalty fixed in paragraph 9.01, and such royalties shall be computed on the basis of 90% of Net Sales of such Records. Notwithstanding the foregoing, no royalty shall be payable to you with respect to (a) Phonograph Records received by members of any such Club Operation in an introductory offer in connection with joining it or upon recommending that another join it or as a result of the purchase of a required number of Records including, without limitation, records distributed as "bonus" or "free" Records, or (b) Phonograph Records for which such Club Operation is not paid.

9.03. In respect of catalog Phonograph Records sold by Record Company special products operations (hereinafter, "SP") to educational institutions or libraries or to other SP clients for their promotion or sales incentive purposes (but not for sale to the general public through normal retail channels), the royalty shall be one-half ($\frac{1}{2}$) of the royalty rate otherwise payable. In respect of non-catalog Phonograph Records created on a custom basis for clients of SP, the royalty rate shall be one-half ($\frac{1}{2}$) of the royalty rate otherwise payable and shall be computed on the basis of SP's actual sales price therefor (less all taxes and container charges). In respect of any Master Recording leased by Record Company to others for their distribution of Phonograph Records in the United States, Record Company will pay you 50% of Record Company's net receipts therefrom after deduction of all copyright, AFM and other applicable third party payments; if another artist, a producer, or any other Person is entitled to royalties in respect of such Records, said payment will be divided among you in the same ratio as that among your respective basic royalty percentage rates.

9.04. In respect of Phonograph Records sold in the form of pre-recorded tape, the royalty rate payable to you therefor shall be three-fourths ($\frac{3}{4}$) of the applicable royalty rate which would have been payable to you if such Records were sold in disc form.

9.05. The royalty rate on any Budget Record, Record bearing a Reissue Label, twelve-inch "disco single," or Multiple Record Set shall be one-half ($\frac{1}{2}$) of the otherwise applicable royalty rate.

9.06. In respect of Phonograph Records sold by Record Company or its Licensees for distribution outside of the United States of America, the royalty rate payable to you therefor shall be equal to one-half (½) of the applicable royalty rate which would have been payable to you therefor if such Records had been sold for distribution in the United States; and such royalties shall be computed on the basis of 90% of Net Sales of such Records.

9.07. In respect of Phonograph Records derived from Master Recordings leased or otherwise furnished by Record Company's Licensees to others for their manufacture and distribution of Records outside the United States, Record Company will pay you one-half of the amount which would be payable to you if Record Company or its Licensees manufactured and distributed such Records.

10. MISCELLANEOUS ROYALTY PROVISIONS
Notwithstanding anything to the contrary contained in Article 9 hereof:

10.01. In respect of Joint Recordings, the royalty rate to be used in determining the royalties payable to you shall be computed by multiplying the royalty rate otherwise applicable thereto by a fraction, the numerator of which shall be one and the denominator of which shall be the total number of royalty artists whose performances are embodied on a Joint Recording.

10.02. With respect to Phonograph Records embodying Master Recordings made hereunder together with other Master Recordings, the royalty rate payable to you shall be computed by multiplying the royalty rate otherwise applicable by a fraction, the numerator of which is the number of Sides contained thereon embodying Master Recordings made hereunder and the denominator of which is the total number of Sides contained on such Record.

10.03. No royalties shall be payable to you in respect of Phonograph Records sold or distributed by Record Company or its Licensees for promotional purposes, as cutouts after the listing of such Records has been deleted from the catalog of Record Company or the particular Licensee, as "free," "no charge" or "bonus" Records (whether or not intended for resale), or to radio stations. No royalties will be payable to you on "sampler" Records in tape form intended for free distribution to automobile purchasers and containing not more than one Recording made under this agreement.

11. ROYALTY ACCOUNTINGS

11.01. Record Company will compute royalties payable to you hereunder as of June 30th and December 31st for each preceding six-month period during which Records as to which royalties are payable hereunder are sold, and will render a statement and pay such royalties, less any unrecouped Advances, prior to each succeeding September 30th and March 31st, respectively.

11.02. Royalties for Records sold for distribution outside of the United States ("foreign sales") shall be computed in the national currency in which Record Company is paid by its Licensees and shall be paid to you at the same rate of exchange at which Record Company is paid. For accounting purposes, foreign sales shall be deemed to occur in the same semi-annual accounting periods in which Record Company's Licensees account to Record Company Records therefor. If Record Company is unable, for reasons beyond its control, to receive payment for such sales in United States dollars in the United States, royalties therefor shall not be credited to your account during the continuance of such inability; if any accounting rendered to you hereunder during the continuance of such inability requires the payment of royalties to you, Record Company will, at your request and if Record Company is able to do so, deposit such royalties to your credit in such foreign currency in a foreign depository, at your expense.

11.03. At any time within eighteen (18) months after any royalty statement is due you hereunder you shall have the right to give Record Company written notice of your intention to examine Record Company's books and records with respect to such statement. Such examination shall be commenced within thirty (30) days after the date of such notice, at your sole cost and expense, by any certified public accountant or attorney designated by you provided he is not then engaged in an outstanding examination of Record Company's books and records on behalf of a Person other than you. Such examination shall be made during Record Company's usual business hours at the place where Record Company maintains the books and records which relate to you and which are necessary to verify the accuracy of the statement or statements specified in your notice to Record Company and your examination shall be limited to the foregoing.

11.04. Your sole right to inspect Record Company's books and records shall be as set forth in subparagraph 11.03 hereof, and Record Company shall have no obligation to produce such books and records more than once with respect to each statement rendered to you. Without limiting the generality of the foregoing, Record Company shall have no obligation to furnish you with any records that do not specifically show sales or gratis distributions of Phonograph Records as to which royalties are payable hereunder.

11.05. Unless notice shall have been given to Record Company as provided in paragraph 11.03. hereof, each royalty statement rendered to you shall be final, conclusive and binding on you and shall constitute an account stated. You shall be foreclosed from maintaining any action, claim or proceeding against Record Company in any forum or tribunal with respect to any statement or accounting due hereunder unless such action, claim or proceeding is commenced against Record Company in a court of competent jurisdiction within three years after the due date of such statement or accounting.

12. MECHANICAL LICENSES

12.01. (a) Each Controlled Composition is hereby licensed to Record Company, for the United States and Canada, at the royalty rate equal to the minimum compulsory license rate applicable under the copyright law of the country concerned at the time of recording (2.75¢ in the United States and 2¢ in Canada as of January 1, 1978), on the basis of Net Sales of Phonograph Records, except that no copyright royalties shall be payable with respect to Records described in paragraph 10.03. The royalty rate with respect to Records described in paragraph 9.05 or distributed through a Club Operation shall be three-fourths (¾) of said rate, and arranged versions of public domain Compositions which are claimed by you to be controlled Compositions shall be licensed to Record Company at one-half (½) of said rate.

(b) Notwithstanding the foregoing, Record Company shall not be required to pay an aggregate copyright royalty in excess of ten times the rate provided in the first sentence of subparagraph 12.01(a) for any Album or twice that rate for any single Record consisting of Recordings made hereunder.

(c) Accountings for such royalties shall be rendered quarter-annually, within forty-five days after the end of each calendar quarter.

12.02. Any assignment made of the ownership or copyright in, or right to license the use of, any Controlled Compositions referred to in this paragraph shall be made subject to the provisions hereof.

12.03. The provisions of this Article 12 shall constitute and are accepted by you, on your own behalf and on behalf of any other owner of any Controlled Compositions or any rights therein, as full compliance by Record Company with all of its obligations, under the compulsory license provisions of the Copyright Law, as the same may be amended, or otherwise, arising from any use by Record Company of Controlled Compositions as provided herein.

12.04. If any Recordings made hereunder contain one or more Compositions (other than Controlled Compositions), not available to Record Company under compulsory license, you will obtain, at Record Company's election and for Record Company's benefit, mechanical licenses covering such Compositions on the same terms applicable to Controlled Compositions pursuant to this Article 12.

13. WARRANTIES; REPRESENTATIONS; RESTRICTIONS; INDEMNITIES

13.01. You warrant and represent:
(a) You have the right and power to enter into and fully perform this agreement.
(b) Record Company shall not be required to make any payments of any nature

for, or in connection with, the acquisition, exercise or exploitation of rights by Record Company pursuant to this agreement except as specifically provided in this agreement.

(c) Artist is or will become and will remain to the extent necessary to enable the performance of this agreement, a member in good standing of all labor unions or guilds, membership in which may be lawfully required for the performance of Artist's services hereunder.

(d) No Materials, as hereinafter defined, or any use thereof, will violate any law or infringe upon or violate the rights of any Person. "Materials," as used in this Article, means: (1) all Controlled Compositions, (2) each name used by the Artist, individually or as a group, in connection with Recordings made hereunder, and (3) all other musical, dramatic, artistic and literary materials, ideas, and other intellectual properties, furnished or selected by you, the Artist or any Producer and contained in or used in connection with any Recordings made hereunder or the packaging, sale, distribution, advertising, publicizing or other exploitation thereof.

13.02. During the term of this agreement, neither you nor the Artist will enter into any agreement which would interfere with the full and prompt performance of your obligations hereunder, and neither you nor the Artist will perform or render any services for the purpose of making Phonograph Records or Master Recordings derived from the Artist's performances for any Person other than Record Company. After the expiration of the term of this agreement, for any reason whatsoever, the Artist will not perform any Composition which shall have been recorded hereunder for any Person other than Record Company for the purpose of making Phonograph Records or Master Recordings prior to whichever of the following dates shall be later: (a) the date five (5) years subsequent to the date such Composition is recorded hereunder, or (b) the date two (2) years subsequent to the expiration date of the term of this agreement. Neither you nor the Artist shall authorize or knowingly permit Artist's performances to be recorded for any purpose without an express written agreement prohibiting the use of such recording on Phonograph Records in violation of the foregoing restrictions.

13.03. If you or Artist shall become aware of any unauthorized recording, manufacture, distribution or sale by any third party contrary to the foregoing re-recording restrictions, you and Artist shall notify Record Company thereof and shall cooperate with Record Company in the event that Record Company commences any action or proceeding against such third party.

13.04. The services of the Artist are unique and extraordinary, and the loss thereof cannot be adequately compensated in damages, and Record Company shall be entitled to injunctive relief to enforce the provisions of this agreement.

13.05. You will at all times indemnify and hold harmless Record Company and any Licensee of Record Company from and against any and all claims, damages, liabilities, costs and expenses, including legal expenses and reasonable counsel fees, arising out of any breach by you of any warranty or agreement made by you herein. You will reimburse Record Company and/or its Licensees on demand for any payment made at any time after the date hereof in respect of any liability or claim in respect of which Record Company or its Licensees are entitled to be indemnified.

14. DEFINITIONS

As used in this agreement the following terms shall have the meanings set forth below:

14.01. *"Master Recording"*—every recording of sound, whether or not coupled with a visual image, by any method and on any substance or material, whether now or hereafter known, which is used or useful in the recording, production and/or manufacture of phonograph records;

14.02. *"Inception of Recording"*—the first recording of performances and/or other sounds with a view to the ultimate fixation of a Master Recording;

14.03. *"Matrix"*—any device now or hereafter used, directly or indirectly, in the manufacture of Phonograph Records and which is derived from a Master Recording;

14.04. *"Person" and "Party"*—any individual, corporation, partnership, association or other organized group of persons or legal successors or representatives of the foregoing;

14.05. *"Records" and "Phonograph Records"*—all forms of reproductions, now or hereafter known, manufactured or distributed primarily for home use, school use, juke box use, or use in means of transportation, embodying (a) sound alone or (b) sound coupled with visual images, e.g., "sight and sound" devices;

14.06. *"Wholesale Price"*—(a) With respect to Records sold for distribution in the United States or Canada: (1) the average net price received by Record Company from independent distributors for Phonograph Records during the six-month period immediately preceding the accounting period concerned, calculated separately for each separately priced Record series manufactured and sold by Record Company; or (2) if there are no applicable independent distributors, Record Company's published subdistributor price in effect as of the commencement of the accounting period concerned, less ten percent. (b) With respect to Records sold for distribution outside of the United States and Canada, one-half of the suggested or applicable retail list price in the country of sale.

14.07. *"Royalty Base Price"*—the applicable Wholesale Price of Phonograph Records less all taxes and less the applicable container charge;

14.08. *"Container Charge"*—(a) with respect to disc Phonograph Records, 10% of the applicable Wholesale Price of such Phonograph Records; and (b) with respect to Phonograph Records in non-disc configurations, 25% of the applicable Wholesale Price of such Phonograph Records.

14.09. *"Net Sales"*—gross sales less returns and credits;

14.10. *"Club Operations"*—any direct sales to consumers conducted on a mail order basis by Record Company or its Licensees.

14.11. *"Contract Period"*—the initial period, or any option period, of the term hereof (as such periods may be suspended or extended as provided herein).

14.12. *"Advance"*—amount recoupable by Record Company from royalties to be paid to or on behalf of you or Artist pursuant to this or any other agreement.

14.13. *"Composition"*—a single musical composition, irrespective of length, including all spoken words and bridging passages and including a medley.

14.14. *"Controlled Composition"*—a composition written, owned or controlled by you, the Artist and/or Producer and/or any person in which you, the Artist and/or the Producer has a direct or indirect interest.

14.15. *"Album"*—one or more twelve-inch 33⅓ rpm records, or the equivalent thereof, sold in a single package, including all Sides, whether or not released, which are recorded in connection with a specific album project, but not including Sides which were recorded in connection with any other album project. (A "disco single" shall not be deemed an Album.)

14.16. *"Side"*—a Recording of sufficient playing time to constitute one side of a 45 rpm record, but not less than two and one-quarter minutes of continuous sound;

14.17. *"Joint Recording"*—any Master Recording embodying the Artist's performance, together with the performance of another artist(s) with respect to which Record Company is obligated to pay royalties.

14.18. *"Sales Through Normal Retail Channels in the United States"*—sales other than as described in paragraphs 9.02, 9.03, 9.05, 9.06, and 9.07 hereof.

14.19. *"Licensees"*—includes, without limitation, subsidiaries, wholly or partly owned, and other divisions of Record Company Inc.

14.20. *"Delivery" or "Delivered,"* when used with respect to Master Recordings, means the actual receipt by Record Company of fully mixed and edited Master Recordings, satisfactory to Record Company and ready for Record Company's manufacture of Phonograph Records, and all necessary licenses and applicable approvals and consents.

14.21. *"Reissue Label"*—a Label, such as the .... label, used primarily for reissues of recordings released previously.

14.22. *"Budget Record"*—A record bearing a suggested retail list price at least $2.00 lower than the suggested retail list price used for the top line Phonograph Records embodying performances of pop artists released by Record Company or its Licensees in the territory concerned.

14.23. *"Multiple Record Set"*—An Album containing two or more 12-inch 33⅓ rpm Records packaged as a single unit, or the equivalent.

15. SUSPENSION AND TERMINATION

15.01. If at any time you fail, except solely for Record Company's refusal without cause to allow you to perform, to fulfill your Recording Commitment within the times set forth herein, then, without limiting Record Company's rights, Record Company shall have the option, exercisable by notice to you, to:

(a) suspend the running of the then current Period of the term of this agreement (and extend its expiration date) for the period of the default plus such additional time as is necessary so that Record Company shall have not less than one hundred and eighty (180) days after completion of your Recording Commitment within which to exercise its option, if any, to extend the term for the next Contract Period, and/or to suspend Record Company's obligation to make payments to you hereunder during such suspension; or

(b) increase the Recording Commitment in any subsequent Contract Period by the number of uncompleted Master Recordings, in addition to the otherwise applicable Recording Commitment under paragraphs 3.01 and 3.03. above. The payments due for such Recordings shall be the payments that would have been due had the Recordings been Delivered during the Contract Period in which they were originally required to be Delivered.

15.02. If Record Company refuses to allow you to fulfill your Recording Commitment for any Contract Period and if, within thirty (30) days after the expiration date of the Contract Period you notify Record Company of your desire to fulfill such Recording Commitment, then Record Company shall permit you to fulfill said Recording Commitment by notice to you to such effect within sixty (60) days of Record Company's receipt of your notice. Should Record Company fail to give such notice, you shall have the option to terminate the term of this agreement by notice given to Record Company within thirty (30) days after the expiration of said sixty-day period; on receipt by Record Company of such notice the term of this agreement shall terminate and all parties will be deemed to have fulfilled all of their obligations hereunder except those obligations which survive the end of the term (e.g., warranties, re-recording restrictions and obligation to pay royalties), at which time Record Company shall pay you at the rate of union scale in full settlement of its obligation in connection therewith, which payment shall constitute an Advance. In the event you fail to give Record Company either notice within the period specified therefor, Record Company shall be under no obligation to you for failing to permit you to fulfill such Recording Commitment.

15.03. If because of: act of God; inevitable accident; fire; lockout, strike or other labor dispute; riot or civil commotion; act of public enemy; enactment, rule, order or act of any government or governmental instrumentality (whether federal, state, local or foreign); failure of technical facilities; failure or delay of transportation facilities; illness or incapacity of any performer or producer; or other cause of a similar or different nature not reasonably within Record Company's control; Record Company is materially hampered in the recording, manufacture, distribution or sale of records, then, without limiting Record Company's rights, Record Company shall have the option by giving you notice to suspend the then current Contract Period for the duration of any such contingency plus such additional time as is necessary so that Record Company shall have no less than thirty (30) days after the cessation of such contingency in which to exercise its option, if any, for the next following option period. Any such extension of the then current Contract Period, due to a labor controversy or adjustment thereof which involves only Record Company Records, shall be limited to a period of six (6) months.

16. AGREEMENTS, APPROVAL & CONSENT

16.01. As to all matters treated herein to be determined by mutual agreement, or as to which any approval or consent is required, such agreement, approval or consent will not be unreasonably withheld.

16.02. Your agreement, approval or consent, whenever required, shall be deemed to have been given unless you notify Record Company otherwise within ten (10) days following the date of Record Company's written request therefor.

17. ASSIGNMENT

17.01. Record Company may assign its rights hereunder in whole or in part to any subsidiary, affiliated or controlling corporation or to any Person owning or acquiring a substantial portion of the stock or assets of Record Company, and such rights may be assigned by any assignee thereof; provided, however, that any such assignment shall not relieve Record Company of any of its obligations hereunder. Record Company may also assign its rights hereunder to any of its Licensees to the extent necessary or advisable in Record Company's sole discretion to implement the license granted.

18. NOTICES

18.01. Except as otherwise specifically provided herein, all notices hereunder shall be in writing and shall be given by personal delivery, registered or certified mail or telegraph (prepaid), at the respective addresses hereinabove set forth, or such other address or addresses as may be designated by either Party. Such notices shall be deemed given when mailed or delivered to a telegraph office, except that notice of change of address shall be effective only from the date of its receipt. Each notice sent to Record Company shall be directed to its Vice-President, Business Affairs, and a copy of each such notice shall be sent simultaneously to Managing Attorney, Record Company Law Department.

19. EVENTS OF DEFAULT

19.01. In the event of your dissolution or the liquidation of your assets, or the filing of a petition in bankruptcy or insolvency or for an arrangement or reorganization, by, for or against you, or in the event of the appointment of a receiver or a trustee for all or a portion of your property, or in the event that you shall make an assignment for the benefit of creditors or commit any act for, or in, bankruptcy or become insolvent, or in the event you shall fail to fulfill any of your material obligations under this agreement for any other reason, then at any time after the occurrence of any such event, in addition to any other remedies which may be available, Record Company shall have the option by notice to require that the Artist render his personal services directly to it for the remaining balance of the term of this agreement, including any extensions thereof, for the purpose of making phonograph records, upon all the same terms and conditions as are herein contained, including, without limitation, the provisions of Articles 3 and 9 hereof. In such event the Artist shall be deemed substituted for you as a Party to this agreement, effective from and after the date of Record Company's exercise of such option, and, in respect of Phonograph Records embodying the Artist's performances recorded subsequently, the royalty and any Advances payable hereunder shall be payable to the Artist, subject to recoupment of all Advances.

20. MISCELLANEOUS

20.01. The Artist will, prior to the release of the first Album hereunder, prepare an act of professional quality and will, during the term of this agreement, actively pursue his career as an entertainer in the live engagement field.

20.02. This agreement contains the entire understanding of the Parties hereto relating to the subject matter hereof and cannot be changed or terminated except by an instrument signed by an officer of Record Company. A waiver by either Party of any term or condition of this agreement in any instance shall not be deemed or construed as a waiver of such term or condition for the future, or of any subsequent breach thereof. All remedies, rights, undertakings, obligations, and agreements contained in this agreement shall be cumulative and none of them shall be in limitation of any other remedy, right, undertaking, obligation or agreement of either Party.

20.03. Those provisions of any applicable collective bargaining agreement between Record Company and any labor organization which are required, by the terms of such agreement, to be included in this agreement shall be deemed incorporated herein.

20.04. Each option and/or election granted to Record Company hereunder including, without limitation, to suspend the running of one or more periods of time specified in this agreement, to extend the term of this agreement, to acquire the direct and individual services of a leaving member (if a group artist is involved), or otherwise, is separate and distinct, and the exercise of any such option or election shall not operate as a waiver of any other option or election unless specifically so stated by Record Company in its notice of exercise of such option or election.

20.05. You shall not be entitled to recover damages or to terminate the term of this agreement by reason of any breach by Record Company of its material obligations hereunder, unless Record Company has failed to remedy such breach within a reasonable time following receipt of your notice thereof.

20.06. This agreement has been entered into in the State of ...., and the validity, interpretation and legal effect of this agreement shall be governed by the laws of the State of .... applicable to contracts entered into and performed entirely within the State of ...., with respect to the determination of any claim, dispute or disagreement which may arise out of the interpretation, performance, or breach of this agreement. Any process in any action or proceeding commenced in the courts of the State of .... or elsewhere arising out of any such claim, dispute or disagreement, may among other methods, be served upon you by delivering or mailing the same, via registered or certified mail, addressed to you at the address first above written or such other address as you may designate pursuant to Article 18 hereof. Any such delivery or mail service shall be deemed to have the same force and effect as personal service within the State of .... or the jurisdiction in which such action or proceeding may be commenced.

20.07. In entering into this agreement, and in providing services pursuant hereto, you and the Artist have and shall have the status of independent contractors and nothing herein contained shall contemplate or constitute you or the Artist as Record Company's agents or employees.

20.08. This agreement shall not become effective until executed by all proposed Parties hereto.

20.09. Any and all riders annexed hereto together with this basic document shall be taken together to constitute the agreement between you and Record Company.

By ....

Record Company

By ....

In order to induce Record Company Records to enter into the foregoing agreement (........................) with .... dated ...., the undersigned hereby assents to the execution of such agreement and agrees to be bound by the terms and conditions thereof including, without limitation, any provisions of such agreement relating to the undersigned and restrictions imposed upon the undersigned in accordance with the provisions of such agreement. The undersigned hereby acknowledges that Record Company Records shall be under no obligation to make any payments whatsoever to the undersigned, except as specifically provided in paragraph 5.01 and Article 19 of such agreement, in connection with the services rendered by the undersigned and/or the fulfillment of the undersigned's obligations pursuant to the foregoing agreement.

....

BOOKING AGENCY AGREEMENT

The booking agency-artist agreement sets forth the duties and obligations undertaken by an agency in seeking employment (personal appearances) for an artist. The principal components embodied in the booking agency-artist agreement are as follows: scope of agency and duties and compensation of agent; minimum compensation for artist; assignability of the agreement; and the term (number of years) of the contract.

KAM

EXCLUSIVE AGENCY ARTIST AGREEMENT

MADE AND ENTERED INTO THIS .... day of .... 19.., by and between .... (hereinafter referred to as "Agent"), and .... individually and collectively performing professionally as .... (hereinafter referred to as "Artist");

IN CONSIDERATION of the services to be provided and the mutual conditions to be performed, as provided herein, the parties agree as follows:

1. SCOPE OF AGREEMENT

Artist hereby engages Agent and Agent hereby accepts employment as Artist's exclusive booking agent and representative throughout the world with respect to Artist's services, appearances and endeavors as a performing artist, for the term of this agreement and any renewals hereof. As used in this agreement "Artist" refers to the undersigned vocalist/musician and to artists performing with any band or group which Artist leads or conducts and whom Artist shall make subject to the terms of this agreement.

2. DUTIES OF AGENT

(a) Agent agrees to use reasonable efforts in the performance of the following duties: assist Artist in obtaining, obtain offers of, and negotiate, engagements for Artist; advise, aid, counsel and guide Artist with respect to Artist's professional career; promote and publicize Artist's name and talents; carry on business correspondence in Artist's behalf relating to Artist's professional career; cooperate with duly constituted and authorized representatives of Artist in the performance of such duties.

(b) Agent will maintain office, staff and facilities reasonably adequate for the rendition of such services.

(c) Agent will not accept any engagements for Artist without Artist's prior approval which shall not be unreasonable withheld.

(d) Agent shall fully comply with all applicable laws, rules and regulations of governmental authorities and secure such licenses as may be required for the rendition of service hereunder.

(e) Agent shall furnish Artist with monthly statements setting forth (1) all income received by Artist with respect to appearances, services and endeavors by Artist, and (2) itinerary of Artist for the coming month.

3. COMPENSATION OF AGENT

(a) In consideration of the services to be rendered by Agent hereunder, Artist agrees to pay to Agent a commission of ten percent (10%) of the gross compensation received by Artist, directly or indirectly, for each engagement obtained for Artist by or through Agent, or as a result of Agent's endeavors.

(b) Commissions shall become due and payable to Agent immediately following the receipt thereof by Artist or by anyone else in Artist's behalf.

(c) No commissions shall be payable on any engagement if Artist is not paid for such engagement regardless of the reasons for such non-payment by reason of the fault of Artist. This shall not preclude the awarding of damages to Agent to compensate Agent for actual expenses incurred as the direct result of the cancellation of an engagement when such cancellation was the fault of Artist.

(d) Agent's commissions shall be payable on all monies or other considerations received by Artist pursuant to contracts for engagements negotiated or entered into during the term of this agreement.

(e) As used in this agreement the term "gross compensation" shall mean the gross amounts received by Artist for each engagement less costs and expenses incurred in collecting amounts due for any engagement, including costs of arbitration, litigation and attorney's fees.

(f) By agreement in writing, the parties may revise the commission rate or fee due to Agent for any particular engagement, but any such revision shall be for the specified engagement(s) only.

4. RIGHTS OF AGENT

(a) Agent may render similar services to others and may engage in other businesses and ventures.

(b) Artist will promptly refer to Agent all communications, written or oral, received by or on behalf of Artist relating to the services and appearances by Artist.

(c) Without Agent's written consent, Artist will not engage any other person, firm or corporation to perform the services to be performed by Agent hereunder (except that Artist may employ a personal and/or business manager) nor will Artist perform or appear professionally or offer so to do except through Agent.

(d) Agent may publicize the fact that Agent is the exclusive booking agent and representative for Artist.

(e) Agent shall have the right to use or to permit others to use Artist's name and likeness in advertising or publicity relating to Artist's services and appearances but without cost or expense to Artist unless Artist shall otherwise specifically agree in writing.

(f) In the event of Artist's breach of this agreement, Agent's sole right and remedy for such breach shall be the receipt from Artist of the commissions specified herein, but only as and when Artist actually receives monies or other considerations on which Agent's commissions are payable hereunder.

5. DURATION AND TERM OF AGREEMENT

The initial term of this agreement shall be for a term of one (1) year, commencing on ...., 19.., and terminating on ...., 19...

This agreement may be terminated by either party, by written notice, if Artist is unemployed for four (4) consecutive weeks at any time during the term hereof.

6. ENTIRE AGREEMENT

This writing constitutes the complete agreement between the parties hereto, and no verbal representations by any party, or modifications, revisions or amendments hereto shall be of any effect other than by way of a supplemental agreement, in writing, making reference hereto, and signed by all parties.

7. NO ASSIGNMENT

This agreement shall be personal to the parties and shall not be transferable or assignable by operation of law or otherwise without the prior written consent of the Artist.

The Artist may terminate this agreement at any time within ninety (90) days after the transfer of a controlling interest in the Agent.

8. MINIMUM COMPENSATION

Artist shall not be obligated to accept any performances or appearances, or render any services of whatsoever nature wherein the compensation to be paid Artist for the rendition of such services shall be less than ....

IN WITNESS WHEREOF, the parties hereto have executed this agreement the .... day of ...., 19...

By: ....
   Title or Capacity   *Artist*

              ....
              Residence Address

              ....
            City   *State*   *Zip Code*

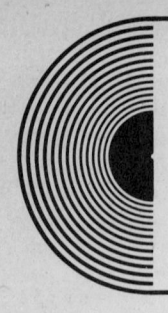

CO-PUBLISHING AGREEMENT

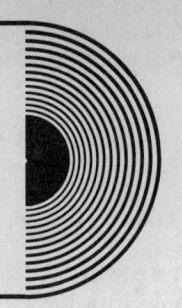

The co-publishing agreement establishes the contractual relationship between two publishers for the exploitation of musical compositions. Such agreements generally provide for the sharing of copyrights in the compositions and appoint one publisher to act in the capacity of an administrator. Attention should be given to the following considerations, among others, when negotiating a participation agreement: division of the copyrights; name(s) in which the copyrights will be registered; royalty statements and accountings; transfer or other disposition of interests in the copyrights; administration fee; term (number of years) of the contract; and breach or default by either party.

KAM

THIS AGREEMENT made this .... day of .... 19.., by and between .... (hereinafter referred to as "Company") and .... (hereinafter referred to as "Participant").

WITNESSETH:

WHEREAS, it is the intention of Company and Participant that they shall jointly own, in equal shares, the musical compositions (hereinafter collectively referred to as the "Composition") listed or described below, so that 50% of the entire world-wide right, title and interest, including the copyright, the right to copyright and the renewal right, in and to the Composition shall be owned by Company and 50% and/or thereof shall be owned by Participant: which shall be divided as indicated below:

Songtitles   *Publishers*

WHEREAS, the Composition(s) has been or shall be registered for copyright in the names of Company and Participant in the Copyright Office of the United States of America:

NOW, THEREFORE, for good and valuable consideration the receipt of which is hereby acknowledged by each party hereto, it is agreed as follows:

1. Company and Participant shall jointly own the Composition(s), in equal shares, including all of the world-wide right, title and interest, including the copyrights, the right to copyright and the renewal rights, therein and hereto.

2. The Composition(s) shall be registered for copyright by Company in the names of Company and Participant in the office of the Register of Copyrights of the United States of America. If the Composition(s) has heretofore been registered for copyright in the name of Company or Participant, such party shall simultaneously herewith deliver to the other party an assignment of a one-half (½) interest therein, in form acceptable to the other party.

3. Company shall have the right to exploit the Composition(s) and to administer, print, publish, sell, use and license the use of our respective shares of the Composition(s) throughout the world, and to execute in our own names and all licenses and agreements affecting or respecting the Composition(s), including but not limited to licenses for mechanical reproduction, public performance, subpublication, merchandising and advertising, and to assign or license such right to others. Licenses for synchronization uses shall be consented by Company.

4. Company shall be entitled to receive and shall receive and collect, directly from the source, all respective shares of all gross receipts derived from the Composition(s). "Gross receipts", as used herein, shall mean any and all revenue, income and sums derived from the Composition(s).

5. Company acknowledges that it will be responsible for royalty payments to the writer(s) pursuant to the terms of the songwriter's agreement(s) between Company and its writer(s). Company acknowledges that it will be responsible for royalty payments to Participant pursuant to this agreement between Participant and Company.

6. Small performing rights in the Composition(s), to the extent permitted by law, shall be assigned to and licensed by .... and .... and hereby is authorized to collect and receive all monies earned from the public performance of the Composition(s) and to pay directly to Company 50% and to Participant its share (as indicated on Page 1) of the amount allocated by .... as the publisher's share of public performance fees.

7. Mechanical royalties for the Composition(s) for the United States shall be collectible by the .... and in the territory of Canada by the Canadian Musical Reproduction Rights Association (CMRRA) if so desired by Company. Said agencies shall be and hereby are authorized to pay directly to Company one hundred percent (100%) (less any costs for collection) of any such mechanical royalties.

8. Company shall remit 50% or 25% (as indicated on Page 1 of this agreement) less fees of 15% to Participant and statements shall be accompanied by appropriate payments.

9. Each party hereto shall give the other the equal benefits of any warranties or representations which it obtained or shall obtain under any agreements affecting the Composition(s).

10. Company shall have the right to prosecute, defend, settle and compromise, with the consent of the other party, such consent not to be unreasonably withheld, all suits, claims, and actions respecting the Composition(s), and generally to do and perform all things necessary concerning the same and the copyrights therein, to prevent and restrain the infringement of copyrights or other rights with respect to the Composition(s). In the event of the recovery by Company of any monies as a result of a judgment or settlement, such monies, less an amount equal to the expense of obtaining said monies, including counsel fees, shall be deemed additional gross receipts hereunder.

11. Company shall not sell, transfer, assign, or otherwise dispose of any interest in the copyright of any Composition(s) without first offering to the other party the right to buy or acquire such interest in the copyrights of such Composition(s) at the same bona fide price and pursuant to the same bona fide terms as may be offered to the party desirous of disposing of its interest by any responsible, prospective and unrelated third party, which terms, may, however, only provide for one payment of cash in lump sum or installments. Such disposing party agrees to give the other party written notice, by certified mail, (which notice shall set forth the name of the prospective buyer, the price and all other terms contained in such offer) of any such bona fide and acceptable offer as described above, and the other party shall have thirty (30) days after actual receipt of such notice in which to notify the disposing party as to whether or not it desires to acquire any interest in said copyrights of the said Composition(s) at the price and pursuant to the terms set forth in said notice. In the event said party fails to give the disposing party notice within the said thirty (30) day period that it is exercising its option to buy or acquire the interest in the said copyrights, then the disposing party shall have the right to accept the bona fide offer by the prospective purchaser, but only as set forth in the disposing party's notice to the other party: provided, however, if Participant does not accept the bona fide offer from a prospec-

tive buyer within sixty (60) days after expiration of the said thirty (30) day period, then the procedure set forth in this paragraph shall once again be followed by the disposing party before same may have disposed of any interest in any copyright of a Composition(s) subject to this agreement.

12. The rights of the parties hereto in and to the Composition(s) shall extend for the term of the copyright of the Composition(s) and of any derivative copyrights therein in the United States of America and throughout the rest of the world and for the terms of any renewals of extensions thereof in the United States of America and throughout the rest of the world.

13. This agreement sets forth the entire understanding between the parties, and cannot be changed, modified or cancelled except by an instrument signed by the party sought to be bound. This agreement shall be governed by and consued under the laws of the State of .... applicable to agreements wholly performed therein.

14. Company hereby warrants and represents that they have the right to enter into this agreement and to grant all of the rights granted herein, and that the exercise by Company of any and all of the rights granted in this agreement will not violate or infringe upon any common law or statutory rights of any person, firm or corporation, including, without limitation, contractual rights, copyrights and rights of privacy. The rights granted herein are free and clear of any claims, demands, liens or encumbrances. Company agrees to and do hereby indemnify, save and hold each other, their assigns, licenses, and their directors, officers, shareholders, agents and employees harmless from any and all liabilities, claims, demands, loss and damage (including attorney's fees and court costs) arising out of or connected with any claim by a third party which is inconsistent with any of the warranties, representations, covenants, or agreements made by Company herein.

15. All notices, statements or other documents which either party shall be required or shall desire to give to the other hereunder must be in writing and shall be given by the parties hereto only in one of the following ways: (1) by personal delivery; or (2) by addressing them as indicated below, and by depositing them postage prepaid, in the United States mail; or (3) by delivering them toll prepaid to a telegraph or cable company. If so delivered, mailed, telegraphed or cabled, each such notice, statement or other document shall, except as herein expressly provided, be conclusively deemed to have been given when personally delivered or on the date of delivery to the telegraph or cable company or 48 hours after the date of mailing, as the case may be. The addresses of the parties shall be those of which the other party actually receives written notice and until further notice are:

"COMPANY"   "PARTICIPANT"

16. This agreement shall not be deemed to give any right or remedy to any third party whatsoever unless said right or remedy is specifically granted to such third party by the terms hereof.

17. The parties hereto shall execute any further documents, including, without limitation, assignments of copyrights, and do all acts necessary to fully effectuate the terms and provisions of this agreement.

18. Company may enter into subpublishing agreements with, or assign or license any of their respective rights hereunder to one or more other countries of the world. In the event Company enters into a subpublishing or administration agreement for any country of the world with a company affiliated with or otherwise related to Company, such agreement shall be deemed to have been made with an independent third party. Each party hereto acknowledges that the other party has the right to administer and publish compositions other than the Composition.

IN WITNESS WHEREOF, the parties hereto have executed this agreement the day and year above set forth.

Agreed and Accepted   Agreed and Accepted

By: ....   By: ....

RIDER TO THE PARTICIPATION AGREEMENT
Agreement dated ....

NOTWITHSTANDING anything to the contrary contained in said agreement, Company will administer one hundred percent (100%) and own fifty percent (50%) each of the copyrights referred to in the basic agreement in perpetuity.

Company will re-assign all rights, title and interest in any tune not recorded and commercially released within twelve months from the date of the basic agreement.

Agreed and Accepted   Agreed and Accepted

By: ....   By: ....

MASTER PURCHASE AGREEMENT

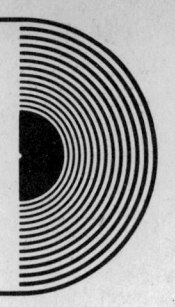

The master purchase agreement provides a vehicle pursuant to which a producer, artist, record company or other party with an interest in a master recording can purchase such master, together with the performances thereon, from its owner. The master purchase agreement enables the purchaser to acquire master recordings of an artist's performances, generally for the purpose of manufacturing, distributing and selling of phonograph records. Particular components of the master purchase agreement which deserve special consideration are: scope of assignment of rights to purchaser; advances to seller; calculation and payment of royalties; mechanical rights and licenses; warranties, representations and indemnities.

KAM

AGREEMENT made .... between ....
.... (hereinafter "you") and Record Company.

1. MASTER RECORDINGS
1.01. You warrant and represent that you are the sole and exclusive owner of Master Recordings (hereinafter referred to as the "Masters") in the form of acetate safety discs, magnetic recording tapes and/or metal parts, embodying performances by ....
.... (hereinafter referred to as the "Artist") of the musical compositions listed in Schedule A attached, and all rights in the Masters, perpetually and throughout the world, free of encumbrances.

2. MASTER PURCHASE
2.01. You hereby sell, transfer and assign to Record Company the Masters and all right, title and interest therein.

2.02. Without limiting the generality of the foregoing:

(a) The Masters and all Matrices and Phonograph Records manufactured therefrom, together with the performances embodied thereon, shall be the sole property of Record Company, free from any claims whatsoever by you or any other Person; and Record Company shall have the exclusive right to copyright the Masters in its name as the owner and author thereof and to secure any and all renewals and extensions of such copyrights, throughout the world.

(b) Record Company and its Licensees shall have the unlimited right to manufacture Phonograph Records derived from the Masters by any method now or hereafter known, and to sell, transfer or otherwise deal in the same under any trademarks, trade names and labels, or to refrain from such manufacture, sale and dealing, throughout the world.

NOTE: If none of the music is copyrighted, revise 5.03, 9.01(c)(iii), and 9.01(d), and delete Article 8 and paragraph 10.12.

(c) Record Company and its Licensees shall have the right and may grant to others the right to reproduce, print, publish, or disseminate in any medium your name and the name, portrait, picture and likeness of the Artist and all other Persons performing services in connection with the recording of the Masters (including, without limitation, all professional, group, and other assumed or fictitious names used by them), and biographical material concerning them, as news or information, for the purposes of trade, or for advertising purposes. No direct endorsement by any such Person of any product or service shall be used without his written consent.

3. DELIVERY

3.01. You will Deliver the Masters to Record Company, in the form of fully edited stereophonic Master Recordings satisfactory to Record Company for its manufacture and sale of Phonograph Records, at its .... in .... on or before ...., ..., together with all other original and duplicate Master Recordings of the performances recorded in the Masters, and all necessary licenses and permissions in connection therewith. If the Masters have not been so Delivered by that date Record Company shall have the right to terminate this agreement, at its election and without limiting its rights.

3.02. You will execute, acknowledge and deliver to Record Company such further instruments and documents and will otherwise cooperate with Record Company as it shall request at any time for the purpose of establishing or evidencing the rights granted to Record Company herein, or otherwise to implement the intent of this agreement.

4. ADVANCE

4.01. Promptly after the completion of Delivery of the Masters as provided in paragraph 3.01, Record Company will make an Advance to you in the amount of ....

5. ROYALTIES

You will be paid royalties on Net Sales of Records derived from the Masters as hereinafter set forth:

5.01. Record Company will pay you a basic royalty computed at the applicable percentage, indicated below, of the applicable Royalty Base Price in respect of Net Sales of Phonograph Records consisting entirely of the Masters and sold by Record Company or its Licensees Through Normal Retail Channels for distribution in the United States:
(a) On Albums: ......%.
(b) On "single" Records: ......%.

5.02. The royalty rate on Phonograph Records sold through any Club Operation shall be determined by multiplying the otherwise applicable royalty rate by a fraction, the numerator of which is 7 and the denominator of which is the basic royalty fixed in paragraph 5.01, and such royalties shall be computed on the basis of 90% of Net Sales of such Records. Notwithstanding the foregoing, no royalty shall be payable to you with respect to (a) Phonograph Records received by members of any such Club Operation in an introductory offer in connection with joining it or upon recommending that another join it or as a result of the purchase of a required number of Records including, without limitation, records distributed as "bonus" or "free" Records, or (b) Phonograph Records for which such Club Operation is not paid.

5.03. In respect of catalog Phonograph Records sold by Record Company's special products operations (hereinafter, "SP") to educational institutions or libraries or to other SP clients for their promotion or sales incentive purposes (but not for sale to the general public through normal retail channels), the royalty shall be one-half (½) of the royalty rate otherwise payable. In respect of non-catalog Phonograph Records created on a custom basis for clients of SP, the royalty rate shall be one-half (½) of the royalty rate otherwise payable and shall be computed on the basis of SP's actual sales price therefor (less all taxes and container charges). If the Masters are leased by Record Company to others for their distribution of Phonograph Records in the United States, Record Company will pay you 50% of Record Company's net receipts therefrom after deduction of all AFM, copyright, and other applicable third party payments.

5.04. The royalty rate on Phonograph Records sold in the form of pre-recorded tape shall be three-fourths (¾) of the applicable royalty rate which would have been payable to you if such Records were sold in disc form.

5.05. The royalty rate on any Budget Record, Record bearing a Reissue Label, twelve-inch "disco single," or Multiple Record Set shall be one-half (½) of the otherwise applicable royalty rate.

5.06. The royalty rate on Phonograph Records sold by Record Company or its Licensees for distribution outside of the United States of America shall be one-half (½) of the applicable royalty rate which would have been payable to you if such Records were sold for distribution in the United States; and such royalties shall be computed on the Basis of 90% of Net Sales of such Records.

5.07. In respect of Phonograph Records derived from Masters leased or otherwise furnished by Record Company's Licensees to others for their manufacture and distribution of Records outside the United States, Record Company will pay you one-half (½) of the amount of which would otherwise be payable to you if Record Company or its Licensees manufactured and distributed such Records.

6. MISCELLANEOUS ROYALTY PROVISIONS

Notwithstanding anything to the contrary in Article 5:

6.01. The royalty payable to you on Phonograph Records containing the Masters and other Master Recordings will be computed by multiplying the royalty rate otherwise applicable by a fraction, the numerator of which is the number of Sides embodying the Masters contained on the Records concerned, and the denominator of which is the total number of Sides on such Records.

6.02. No royalties shall be payable to you in respect of Phonograph Records sold or distributed by Record Company or its Licensees for promotional purposes, as cutouts after the listing of such Records has been deleted from the catalog of Record Company or the particular Licensee, as "free," "no charge" or "bonus" Records (whether or not intended for resale), or to radio stations. No royalties will be payable to you on "sampler" Records in tape form intended for free distribution to automobile purchasers and containing not more than one Recording made under this agreement.

7. ROYALTY ACCOUNTINGS

7.01. Record Company will compute royalties payable to you hereunder as of June 30th and December 31st for each preceding six-month period during which Records as to which royalties are payable hereunder are sold, and will render a statement and pay such royalties, less any unrecouped Advances, prior to each succeeding September 30th and March 31st, respectively.

7.02. Royalties for Records sold for distribution outside of the United States ("foreign sales") shall be computed in the national currency in which Record Company is paid by its Licensees and shall be paid to you at the same rate of exchange at which Record Company is paid. For accounting purposes, foreign sales shall be deemed to occur in the same semi-annual accounting periods in which Record Company's Licensees account to Record Company Records therefor. If Record Company is unable, for reasons beyond its control, to receive payment for such sales in United States dollars in the United States, royalties therefor shall not be credited to your account during the continuance of such inability; if any accounting rendered to you hereunder during the continuance of such inability requires the payment of royalties to you, Record Company will, at your request and if Record Company is able to do so, deposit such royalties to your credit in such foreign currency in a foreign depository, at your expense.

7.03. At any time within eighteen (18) months after any royalty statements due you hereunder you shall have the right to give Record Company notice of your intention to examine Record Company's books and records with respect to such statement. Such examination shall be commenced within thirty (30) days after the date of such notice, at your sole cost and expense, by any certified public accountant or attorney designated by you provided he is not then engaged in an outstanding examination of Record Company's books and records on behalf of a person other than you. Such examination shall be made during Record Company's usual business hours at the place where Record Company maintains the books and records which relate to you and which are necessary to verify the accuracy of the statement or statements specified in your notice to Record Company and your examination shall be limited to the foregoing.

7.04. Your sole right to inspect Record Company's books and records shall be as set forth in subparagraph 7.03 hereof, and Record Company shall have no obligation to produce such books and records more than once with respect to each statement rendered to you. Without limiting the generality of the foregoing, Record Company shall have no obligation to furnish you with any records that do not specifically show sales or gratis distributions of Phonograph Records as to which royalties are payable hereunder.

7.05. Unless notice shall have been given to Record Company as provided in paragraph 7.03, each royalty statement rendered to you shall be final, conclusive and binding on you and shall constitute an account stated. You shall be foreclosed from maintaining any action, claim or proceeding against Record Company in any forum or tribunal with respect to any statement or accounting due hereunder unless such action, claim or proceeding is commenced against Record Company in a court of competent jurisdiction within three years after the due date of such statement or accounting.

8. MECHANICAL LICENSES

8.01. (a) Each Controlled Composition is hereby licensed to Record Company, for the United States and Canada, at the royalty rate of 2.75¢ in the United States and 2¢ in Canada, on the basis of Net Sales of Phonograph Records, except that no copyright royalties shall be payable with respect to Records described in paragraph 6.02. The royalty rate with respect to Records described in paragraph 5.05 or distributed through a Club Operation shall be three-fourths (¾) of the applicable rate prescribed in the first sentence of this paragraph, and arranged versions of public domain Compositions which are claimed by you to be Controlled Compositions shall be licensed to Record Company at one-half (½) of said rate.

(b) Notwithstanding the foregoing, Record Company shall not be required to pay an aggregate copyright royalty in excess of ten times the rate provided in the first sentence of subparagraph 8.01(a) for any Album or twice that rate for any single Record consisting of the Masters.

(c) Accountings for such royalties shall be rendered quarter-annually, within forty-five days after the end of each calendar quarter.

8.02. Any assignment made of the ownership or copyright in, or right to license the use of, any Controlled Compositions referred to in this paragraph shall be made subject to the provisions hereof.

8.03. The provisions of this Article 8 shall constitute and are accepted by you, on your own behalf and on behalf of any other owner of any Controlled Compositions or any rights therein, as full compliance by Record Company with all of its obligations, under the compulsory license provisions of the Copyright Law, as the same may be amended, or otherwise, arising from any use by Record Company of Controlled Compositions as provided herein.

8.04. If any of the Masters contains Compositions (other than Controlled Compositions), not available to Record Company under compulsory license, you will obtain, at Record Company's election and for Record Company's benefit, mechanical licenses covering such Compositions on the same terms applicable to Controlled Compositions pursuant to this Article 8.

9. ADDITIONAL WARRANTIES AND REPRESENTATIONS; RESTRICTIONS; INDEMNITIES

9.01. You warrant and represent (without limiting the generality of paragraph 1.01):

(a) You have the right and power to enter into and fully perform this agreement.

(b) No Phonograph Records have been manufactured from the Masters by you or any other Person, and none of the musical compositions performed in the Masters has been performed by the Artist for the making of any other Master Recordings.

(c) (i) Each Person who rendered any service in connection with, or who otherwise contributed in any way to the making of the Masters, or who granted to you your rights referred to in this agreement, had the full right and power to do so, and was not bound by any agreement which would restrict him from rendering such services or granting such rights.

(ii) All costs and expenses with respect to the making of the Masters have been paid.

(iii) All necessary licenses for the recording of the compositions performed on the Masters have been obtained from the copyright owners, and all moneys payable under such licenses or otherwise by reason of such recording have been paid. (The preceding sentence does not apply with respect to any fees or royalties payable to the copyright owners in connection with the manufacture or sale of phonograph records derived from the Masters.)

(iv) All the Masters were made in accordance with the rules and regulations of the American Federation of Musicians ("AFM"), the American Federation of Television and Radio Artists ("AFTRA"), and all other unions having jurisdiction. Without limiting the generality of the preceding sentence: (1) the requirements of paragraph 18 of the Phonograph Record Labor Agreement between the AFM and Record Company Records, effective as of November, 1975, have been satisfied (which warranty and representation is included herein for the benefit of the AFM, among others, and may be enforced by the AFM or by such person or persons as it may designate); and (2) all artists whose performances embodied on the Masters were recorded in the United States of America have been paid the minimum rates specified in the AFTRA Code of Fair Practice for Phonograph Recordings or the applicable Code then in effect at the time the Masters were made, and all payments due to the AFTRA Pension and Welfare Funds have been made.

(d) Record Company shall have the sole and exclusive rights to manufacture, advertise, distribute, sell and otherwise exploit and deal in the Masters and phonograph records and other reproductions derived therefrom, free from any liability or obligation to make any payments except: (1) payments becoming due to the Music Performance Trust Fund or Special Payments Fund based upon sales of Phonograph Records (so-called "per-record royalties"), (2) the royalties payable to you pursuant to Article 5, and (3) mechanical royalties in accordance with Article 8.

(e) Neither Record Company nor its Licensees will incur any liability for violation of any law or for infringement or violation of the rights of any Person in connection with the Masters, any use thereof, or any other exercise of rights granted to Record Company in this agreement.

9.02. The Artist will not perform any composition recorded in the Masters for any person other than Record Company, for the purpose of making Phonograph Records or Master Recordings, during the period commencing on the date of this agreement and ending five (5) years after the date of Delivery of the Masters in accordance with paragraph 3.01. Neither you nor the Artist shall authorize or knowingly permit the Artist's performances to be recorded for any purpose without an express written agreement prohibiting the use of such recording on Phonograph Records in violation of the foregoing restrictions.

9.03. If you or Artist shall become aware of any unauthorized recording, manufacture, distribution or sale by any third party contrary to the foregoing re-recording restrictions, you and the Artist shall notify Record Company thereof and shall cooperate with Record

Company in the event that Record Company commences any action or proceeding against such third party.

9.04. Record Company shall be entitled to injunctive relief to enforce the provisions of this agreement.

9.05. You will at all times indemnify and hold harmless Record Company and any Licensee of Record Company from and against any and all claims, damages, liabilities, costs and expenses, including legal expenses and reasonable counsel fees, arising out of any breach by you of any warranty, representation or agreement made by you herein. You will reimburse Record Company and/or its Licensees on demand for any payment made at any time after the date hereof in respect of any liability or claim in respect of which Record Company or its Licensees are entitled to be indemnified.

10. DEFINITIONS

As used in this agreement the following terms shall have the meanings set forth below:

10.01. *"Master Recording"*—shall include every recording of sound, whether or not coupled with a visual image, by any method and on any substance or material, whether now or hereafter known, which is used or useful in the recording, production and/or manufacture of Phonograph Records;

10.02. *"Matrix"*—any device now or hereafter used, directly or indirectly, in the manufacture of Phonograph Records and which is derived from a Master Recording;

10.03. *"Person"* and *"Party"*—any individual, corporation, partnership, association or other organized group of persons or legal successors or representatives of the foregoing;

10.04. *"Records"* and *"Phonograph Records"*—all forms of reproductions, now or hereafter known, manufactured or distributed primarily for home use, school use, juke box use, or use in means of transportation, embodying (a) sound alone or (b) sound coupled with visual images, e.g., "sight and sound" devices;

10.05. *"Wholesale Price"*—(a) With respect to Records sold for distribution in the United States or Canada: (1) the average net price received by Record Company from independent distributors for Phonograph Records during the six-month period immediately preceding the accounting period concerned, calculated separately for each separately priced Record series manufactured and sold by Record Company; or (2) if there are no applicable independent distributors, Record Company's published subdistributor price in effect as of the commencement of the accounting period concerned, less ten percent. (b) With respect to Records sold for distribution outside of the United States and Canada, one-half of the suggested or applicable retail list price in the country of sale;

10.06. *"Royalty Base Price"*—the applicable Wholesale Price of Phonograph Records less all taxes and less the applicable container charge;

10.07. *"Container Charge"*—(a) with respect to disc Phonograph Records, 10% of the applicable Wholesale Price of such Phonograph Records; and (b) with respect to Phonograph Records in non-disc configurations, 25% of the applicable Wholesale Price of such Phonograph Records.

10.08. *"Net Sales"*—gross sales less returns and credits;

10.09. *"Club Operation"*—any direct sales to consumers conducted on a mail order basis by Record Company or its Licensees.

10.10. *"Advance"*—amount recoupable by Record Company from royalties to be paid to or on behalf of you or Artist pursuant to this or any other agreement.

10.11. *"Composition"*—a single musical composition, irrespective of length, including all spoken words and bridging passages and including a medley.

10.12. *"Controlled Composition"*—a composition written, owned or controlled by you or the Artist, or any Person in which you or the Artist has a direct or indirect interest.

10.13. *"Sales Through Normal Retail Channels in the United States"*—sales other than as described in paragraphs 5.02, 5.03, 5.05, 5.06, and 5.07 hereof.

10.14. *"Licensees"*—includes, without limitation, subsidiaries, wholly or partly owned, and other divisions of Record Company Inc.

10.15. *"Reissue Label"*—A label, such as the .... label, used primarily for reissues of recordings released previously.

10.16. *"Budget Record"*—A record bearing a suggested retail list price at least $2.00 lower than the suggested retail list price used for the top line Phonograph Records embodying performances of pop artists released by Record Company or its Licensees in the territory concerned.

10.17. *"Side"*—a Recording of sufficient playing time to constitute one side of a 45 rpm record, but not less than two and one-quarter minutes of continuous sound.

10.18. *"Multiple Record Set"*—An Album containing two or more 12-inch 33⅓ rpm Records packaged as a single unit, or the equivalent.

11. ASSIGNMENT

11.01. Record Company may assign its rights hereunder in whole or in part to any subsidiary, affiliated or controlling corporation or to any Person owning or acquiring a substantial portion of the stock or assets of Record Company, and such rights may be assigned by any assignee thereof; provided, however, that any such assignment shall not relieve Record Company of any of its obligations hereunder. Record Company may also assign its rights hereunder to any of its Licensees to the extent necessary or advisable in Record Company's sole discretion to implement the license granted.

12. NOTICES

12.01. Except as otherwise specifically provided herein, all notices hereunder shall be in writing and shall be given by personal delivery, registered or certified mail or telegraph (prepaid), at the respective addresses hereinabove set forth, or such other address or addresses as may be designated by either Party. Such notices shall be deemed given when mailed or delivered to a telegraph office, except that notice of change of address shall be effective only from the date of its receipt. Each notice sent to Record Company shall be directed to its Vice-President, Business Affairs, and a copy of each such notice shall be sent simultaneously to Managing Attorney, Record Company Law Department, Address.

13. MISCELLANEOUS

13.01. This agreement contains the entire understanding of the Parties hereto relating to the subject matter hereof and cannot be changed except by an instrument signed by an officer of Record Company. A waiver by either Party of any term or condition of this agreement in any instance shall not be deemed or construed as a waiver of such term or condition for the future, or of any subsequent breach thereof. All remedies, rights, undertakings, obligations, and agreements contained in this agreement shall be cumulative and none of them shall be in limitation of any other remedy, right, undertaking, obligation or agreement of either Party.

13.02. Those provisions of any applicable collective bargaining agreement between Record Company and any labor organization which are required, by the terms of such agreement, to be included in this agreement shall be deemed incorporated herein.

13.03. No breach by Record Company of its material obligations hereunder will entitle you to recover damages, or affect any of your obligations hereunder, unless Record Company has failed to remedy such breach within a reasonable time following receipt of your notice thereof.

13.04. This agreement has been entered into in the State of ...., and the validity, interpretation and legal effect of this agreement shall be governed by the laws of the State of .... applicable to contracts entered into and performed entirely within the State of ...., with respect to the determination of any claim, dispute or disagreement which may arise out of the interpretation, performance, or breach of this agreement. Any process in any action or proceeding commenced in the courts of the State of .... or elsewhere arising out of any such claim, dispute or disagreement, may among other methods, be served upon you by delivering or mailing the same, via registered or certified mail, addressed to you at the address first above written or such other address as you may designate pursuant to Article 12 hereof. Any such delivery or mail service shall be deemed to have the same force and effect as personal service within the State of .... or the jurisdiction in which such action or proceeding may be commenced.

13.05. This agreement shall not become effective until executed by you and by Record Company.

....

Record Company

By ....

In order to induce Record Company Records to enter into the foregoing agreement (...................) with .... dated ...., I hereby assent to the execution of such agreement and agree to be bound by the terms and conditions thereof including, without limitation, any provisions of such agreement relating to me and restrictions imposed upon me in accordance with the provisions of such agreement. I hereby acknowledge that Record Company Records shall be under no obligation to make any payments whatsoever to me in connection with the fulfillment of my obligations pursuant to the foregoing agreement.

....

INSIDE
THE ROCK BUSINESS

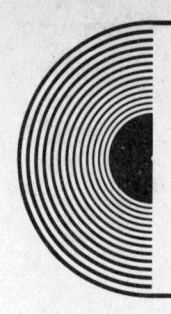

PACESETTING RADIO STATIONS

Top 40 Stations

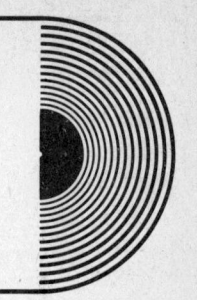

NORTHEASTERN REGION—Primary Markets

Baltimore
WFBR 1300 AM. 13 East 20 Street, Baltimore, MD 21218. 301-685-1300.
WCAO 600 AM. 8001 Park Heights Avenue, Baltimore, MD 21208. 301-685-0600 or 301-484-2300.

Boston
WRKO 680 AM. RKO General Building, Government, Boston, MA 02114. 617-725-2700.
WVBF 105.7 FM. Fairbanks Broadcasting Co., Inc., 100 Mt. Wayte Avenue, Framingham, MA 01701. 617-879-2222.

Buffalo
WKBW 1520 AM. 1430 Main Street, Buffalo, NY 14209. 716-884-5101.
WYSL 1400 AM. 425 Franklin Street, Buffalo, NY 14202. 716-885-1400.

New York
WABC 770 AM. 1330 Avenue of the Americas, New York, NY 10019. 212-887-7777.
WNBC 660 AM. 30 Rockefeller Plaza, New York, NY 10020. 212-664-4444.

Philadelphia
WFIL 560 AM. 4100 City Line, Philadelphia, PA 19131. 215-879-1600.
WIFI 92.5 FM. One Bala Cynwyd Plaza, Bala Cynwyd, PA 19004. 215-839-0900.

Pittsburgh
WKTQ 1320 AM. Broadcast Plaza, Crane Avenue, Pittsburgh, PA 15220. 412-531-9500.
WPEZ 94.5 FM. One Allegheny Square, Pittsburgh, PA 15212. 412-323-5300.

Washington, DC
WPGC 1580 AM. P. O. Box 8550, Washington, DC 20027. 202-779-2100.

NORTHEASTERN REGION—Secondary Markets

Albany
WPTR   1540 AM. 4243 Albany Street, Albany, NY 12205. 518-456-1144.
WTRY   980 AM. 1054 Albany-Schenectady Road, Latham, NY 12110. 518-785-9800.

Bangor
WGUY   1250 AM. Bangor Broadcasting Corp., 7 Main Street, Bangor, ME 04401. 207-947-7354.

Erie
WJET   1400 AM. 1635 Ash Street, Erie, PA 16503. 814-455-2741.
WCCK   103.7 FM. 212 Commerce Building, Erie, PA 16501. 814-456-7078.

Fall River
WSAR   1480 AM. P. O. Box 927, Fall River, MA 02722. 617-677-9477.

Frederick
WZYQ   1370 AM. Box 311A, Route 12, Frederick, MD 21701. 301-662-2148.

Hartford
WDRC   1360 AM. 869 Blue Hills Avenue, Bloomfield, CT 06002. 203-278-1115.

New Haven
WAVZ   1300 AM. 152 Temple Street, New Haven, CT 06510. 203-777-4761.

Providence
WPRO   92.3 FM. 1502 Wampanoag Trail, East Providence, RI 02915. 401-433-4200.
WPJB   105.1 FM. 10 Dorrance Street, Suite 940, Providence, RI 02903. 401-277-7411.

Richmond
WLEE   1480 AM. P. O. Box 8477, Richmond, VA 23226. 804-288-2835.
WRVQ   94.5 FM. P. O. Box 1394, Richmond, VA 23212. 804-649-9151.

Roanoke
WROV   1240 AM. Fifteenth and Cleveland Avenue, Roanoke, VA 24015. 703-343-4444.

Rochester
WBBF   950 AM. 850 Midtown Tower, Rochester, NY 14604. 716-232-7550.
WWWG   1460 AM. 50 Chestnut Plaza, Rochester, NY 14604. 716-546-2325.

Syracuse
WOLF 1490 AM. Box 1490, Syracuse, NY 13201. 315-422-7211.
WNDR 1260 AM. Box 1212, Syracuse, NY 13201. 315-446-1515.

Wheeling
WKWK 1400 AM. 1201 Main Street, Wheeling, WV 26003. 304-232-2250.

Wilmington
WAMS 1380 AM. Owls Nest and Pylesford Roads, Wilmington, DE 19807. 302-654-8881.

Worcester
WORC 1310 AM. 8 Portland Street, Worcester, MA 01608. 617-799-0581.

SOUTHERN REGION—Primary Markets

Atlanta
WQXI 790 AM. 3340 Peachtree Road NE, Atlanta, GA 30326. 404-261-2970.
WZGC 92.9 FM. 603 West Peachtree Street, Atlanta, GA 30308. 404-881-0093.

Dallas
KLIF 1190 AM. 2120 Commerce, Dallas, TX 75201. 214-747-9311.
KNUS 98.7 FM. 1917 Elm Street, Dallas, TX 75201. 214-651-1010.

Fort Worth
KFJZ 97.1 FM. P. O. Box 1317, Fort Worth, TX 76101. 817-731-6301.

Houston
KILT 610 AM. 500 Lovett, Houston, TX 77006. 713-526-3461.
KRBE 104.1 FM. 2500 West Loop S, Fifth Floor, Houston, TX 77027. 713-960-0123.

Louisville
WKLO 1080 AM. 307 West Walnut, Louisville, KY 40202. 502-589-4800.

Memphis
WHBQ 560 AM. 485 South Highland, Memphis, TN 38111. 901-458-0056.
WMPS 680 AM. 112 Union Avenue, Memphis, TN 38103. 901-525-6868.

Miami/Ft. Lauderdale
WHYI 100.7 FM. 2741 North 29 Avenue, Hollywood, FL 33020. 305-944-1956.

New Orleans
WNOE 101.1 FM. 529 Bienville, New Orleans, LA 70130. 504-529-1212.
WTIX 690 AM. 332 Carondelet Street, New Orleans, LA 70130. 504-561-0001.

Oklahoma City
WKY   930 AM. 400 East Britton Road, Oklahoma City, OK 73114. 405-478-2930.
KOMA   1520 AM. 820 South Fourth Moore, Oklahoma City, OK 73101. 405-794-1573.

Tampa
WRBQ   104.7 FM. Box 24897, Tampa, FL 33623. 813-879-1420.
WLCY   1380 AM. 11450 Gandy Building, St. Petersburg, FL 33702. 803-577-1111.

Tulsa
KAKC   970 AM. Box 970, Tulsa, OK 74101. 918-743-9877.
KELI   1430 AM. P. O. Box 52185, Tulsa, OK 74152. 918-622-1430.

SOUTHERN REGION—Secondary Markets

Albany
WALG   1590 AM. P. O. Box W, Albany, GA 31702. 912-436-7233.

Asheboro
WZOO   710 AM. P. O. Box 460, Asheboro, NC 27203. 919-672-0985.

Asheville
WISE   1310 AM. 90 Lookout Road, Asheville, NC 28804. 704-253-5381.

Athens
WRFC   960 AM. 255 South Milledge Avenue, Athens, GA 30605. 404-549-6222.

Austin
KHFI   98.3 FM. P. O. Box 490, Austin, TX 78767. 512-476-3636.
KNOW   1490 AM. Box 2197, Austin, TX 78768. 512-477-9841.

Bainbridge
WJAD   97.3 FM. Box 706, Bainbridge, GA 31717. 912-246-1650.

Baton Rouge
WAIL   1260 AM. 5700 Florida Boulevard, Suite 604, Baton Rouge, LA 70806. 504-926-7600.

Beaumont
KAYC   1450 AM. 3130 Blanchette, Beaumont, TX 77704. 713-833-9421.

PACESETTING RADIO STATIONS — TOP 40

Birmingham
WKXX   106.9 FM. 1729 North Second Avenue, Birmingham, AL 35202. 205-252-3171.
WSGN   610 AM. The Penthouse City Federal Building, Birmingham, AL 35203. 205-322-3434.

Charlotte
WAYS   610 AM. 400 Radio Road, Charlotte, NC 28216. 704-392-6191.

Chattanooga
WFLI   1070 AM. O'Grady Drive, Chattanooga, TN 37409. 615-821-3555.
WGOW   1150 AM. P. O. Box 4704, Chattanooga, TN 37405. 615-756-6141.

Cocoa Beach
WRKT   104.1 FM. Box 3845, Cocoa, FL 32922. 305-632-1300.

Columbus
WCGQ   107.3 FM. Box 1537, Columbus, GA 31906. 404-327-1217.

Corpus Christi
KEYS   1440 AM. 441 Laguna, Corpus Christi, TX 78403. 512-882-7411.

Daytona Beach
WMFJ   1450 AM. Box 5606, Daytona Beach, FL 32018. 904-255-1456.

El Paso
KINT   1590 AM. 5959 Gateway West, Suite 120, El Paso, TX 79925. 915-779-6454.
KELP   920 AM. 4171 North Mesa, El Paso, TX 79902. 915-544-7980.

Fayetteville
WFLB   1490 AM. Box 530, Fayetteville, NC 28302. 919-323-0925.

Greenville
WQOK   1440 AM. Drawer 7777, Greenville, SC 29610. 803-246-8960.

Gulfport
WROA   1390 AM. Box 2639, Gulfport, MS 39503. 601-832-5111.

Jackson
WJDX   620 AM. Box 2171, Jackson, MS 39205. 601-982-1062.

Jacksonville
WAPE   690 AM. P. O. Box 486, Orange Park, FL 32023. 904-264-4523.
WIVY   103 FM. 3100 University Boulevard, Jacksonville, FL 32216. 904-721-9111.

PACESETTING RADIO STATIONS — TOP 40

Lakeland
WQPD 1430 AM. Box 827, Lakeland, FL 33802. 813-682-3143.

Lexington
WVLK 590 AM. P. O. Box 1559, Lexington, KY 40501. 606-254-1151.

Little Rock
KAAY 1090 AM. 2400 Cottendale Lane, Little Rock, AR 72203. 501-661-1090.

Lubbock
KLBK 1340 AM. 7400 South University, Lubbock, TX 79408. 806-745-2345.
KSEL 950 AM. 904 East Broadway, Lubbock, TX 79408. 806-747-2555.

Marietta
WFOM 1230 AM. 835 South Cobb Drive, Marietta, GA 30060. 404-428-3396.

Mobile
WABB 97.5 FM. 1551 Springhill, Mobile, AL 36604. 205-432-5572.

Montgomery
WHHY 1440 AM. P. O. Box 2744, Montgomery, AL 36105. 205-264-2288.
WAAY 1550 AM. Box 2041, Huntsville, AL 35804. 205-533-9190.

Nashville
WLAC 1510 AM. 159 Fourth Avenue N, Nashville, TN 37219. 615-256-0161.
WZEZ 92.9 FM. 1617 Lebanon Road, Nashville, TN 37210. 615-889-1960.

Orlando
WBJW 105.1 FM. P. O. Box 7475, Orlando, FL 32854. 305-425-6633.
WLOF 950 AM. 405 Ring Road, Orlando, FL 32808. 305-293-2431.

Panama City
WDLP 590 AM. Box 759, Panama City, FL 32401. 904-763-1777.

Raleigh
WKIX 850 AM. P. O. Box 12526, Raleigh, NC 27605. 919-851-2711.

San Antonio
KTSA 550 AM. 4050 Eisenhauer, San Antonio, TX 78218. 512-655-5500.

Sarasota
WYND 1280 AM. P. O. Box 3618, Sarasota, FL 33578. 813-365-0700.

Savannah
WSGA 1400 AM. 206 East Broughton Street, Savannah, GA 31401. 912-233-8807.

Shreveport
KEEL   710 AM. P. O. Box 20007, Shreveport, LA 71120. 318-425-8692.
KROK   94.5 FM. 425 Edwards, Shreveport, LA 71120. 318-222-8711.

Spartanburg
WORD   910 AM. Box 3257, Spartanburg, SC 29302. 803-583-2711.

Tallahassee
WGLF   104.1 FM. P. O. Box 1815, Tallahassee, FL 32302. 904-224-1227.

Tyler
KDOK   1490 AM. P. O. Box 6340, Tyler, TX 75711. 214-593-2519.

Vidalia
WTCQ   97.7 FM. Box 900, Vidalia, GA 30474. 912-537-9202.

West Palm Beach
WIRK   1290 AM. P. O. Box 3828, West Palm Beach, FL 33402. 305-965-9211.

Witchita Falls
KTRN   1290 AM. P. O. Box 5005, Wichita Falls, TX 76307. 817-855-3555.

Winston-Salem
WAIR   1340 AM. 986 Hutton Street, Winston-Salem, NC 27103. 919-722-1347.

MIDWESTERN REGION—Primary Markets

Chicago
WEFM   99.5 FM. 120 West Madison, Chicago, IL 60602. 312-558-9332.
WLS   890 AM. 360 North Michigan Avenue, Chicago, IL 60601. 312-782-2002.

Cincinnati
WKRQ   101.9 FM. 1906 Highland Avenue, Cincinnati, OH 45219. 513-381-5500.

Cleveland
WGCL   98.5 FM. 1500 Chester Avenue, Cleveland, OH 44114. 216-861-0100.
WZZP   106.5 FM. One Radio Lane, Cleveland, OH 44114. 216-696-4444.

Columbus
WNCI   98 FM. 4900 Sinclair Road, Columbus, OH 43229. 614-846-3698.

Detroit
CKLW   800 AM. P. O. Box 282, Southville, MI 48037. 313-353-6200.

Indianapolis
WNDE 1260 AM. 6161 Fall Creek Road, Indianapolis, IN 46220. 317-257-7565.

Kansas City
KBEQ 104.3 FM. 3100 Broadway, Suite 111, Kansas City, MO 64111. 816-531-2535.
WHB 710 AM. 106 West 14 Street, Kansas City, MO 64105. 816-221-0688.

Milwaukee
WOKY 920 AM. 3500 North Sherman Boulevard, Milwaukee, WI 53216. 414-442-0150.
WZUU 1290 AM. 520 West Capitol Drive, Milwaukee, WI 53212. 414-964-8300.

Minneapolis/St. Paul
KDWB 630 AM. P. O. Box 7630, St. Paul, MN 55119. 612-739-4000.
KSTP 1500 AM. 3415 University Avenue, Minneapolis, MN 55414. 612-645-2724.

St. Louis
KXOX 630 AM. 7777 Bonhomme Avenue, St. Louis, MO 63105. 314-727-6500.
KSLQ 98.1 FM. 111 South Bemiston, Clayton, MO 63105. 314-725-9814.

MIDWESTERN REGION—Secondary Markets

Akron
WCUE 1150 AM. 424 Sackett Avenue, Akron, OH 44313. 216-923-9761.

Bismark
KFYR 550 AM. Box 1738, Bismark, ND 58501. 701-223-0900.

Canton
WINW 1520 AM. Box 9217, Canton, OH 44705. 216-492-5630.

Cedar Rapids
KLWW 1450 AM. P. O. Box 876, Cedar Rapids, IA 52406. 319-363-8265.

Davenport
KSTT 1170 AM. P. O. Box 3788, Davenport, IA 52808. 319-326-2541.

Dayton
WING 1410 AM. 717 East David Road, Dayton, OH 45429. 513-294-5858.

Des Moines
KIOA 940 AM. 215 Keo Way, Suite 132, Des Moines, IA 50309. 515-247-4533.
KGGO 94.9 FM. 3900 NE Broadway, Des Moines, IA 50317. 515-265-6181.

Duluth
WEBC 560 AM. 1001 East Ninth Street, Duluth, MN 55805. 218-728-4484.
WAKX 970 AM. 410 West Superior Street, Duluth, MN 55802. 218-727-8681.

Eau Claire
WEAQ 790 AM. P. O. Box 1, Eau Claire, WI 54701. 715-832-3463.

Fargo
KVOX 99.9 FM. 4000 South Eighth Street, Moorhead, MN 56560. 218-233-1522.
KQWB 1550 AM. Old Highway 75 N. Moorhead, MN 56560. 218-236-7800.

Flint
WTAC 600 AM. Box 600, Flint, MI 48501. 313-694-4146.

Grand Rapids
WGRD 1410 AM. 122 Lyon NW, Grand Rapids, MI 49503. 616-459-4111.
WZZR 95.7 FM. Box 96, Grand Rapids, MI 49501. 616-364-9551.

Lafayette
WAZY 1410 AM. Box 1410, Lafayette, IN 47902. 317-474-1410.

Madison
WISM 1480 AM. P. O. Box 2058, Madison, WI 53701. 608-271-1484.

Minot
KKOA 1390 AM. Box 10, Minot, ND 58701. 701-852-4646.

Omaha
KOIL 1290 AM. 8901 Indian Hills Drive, Omaha, NE 68114.
WOW 590 AM. 11128 John Galt Boulevard, Omaha, NE 68137. 402-592-3500.

Peoria
WIRL 1290 AM. Box 3335, Peoria, IL 61614. 309-694-6262.

Rapid City
KKLS 920 AM. Box 460, Rapid City, SD 57709. 605-343-6161.
KTOQ 1340 AM. Box 8250, Rapid City, SD 57701. 605-343-0888.

Rochester
KWEB 1270 AM. Box 6428, Rochester, MN 55901. 507-288-3888.

Rockford
WROK   1440 AM. 1100 Tamarack Lane, Rockford, IL 61125. 815–399–2233.

Saginaw
WSAM   1400 AM. 2000 Whittier, Saginaw, MI 48601. 517–752–8161.

St. Cloud
WJON   1240 AM. Box 220, St. Cloud, MN 56301. 612–251–4422.

Stevens Point
WSPT   97.9 FM. Box 247, Stevens Point, WI 54481. 715–341–1300.

Waterloo
KWWL   1330 AM. East Fourth and Franklin Streets, Waterloo, IA 50703. 319–235–1716.

Wichita
KLEO   1480 AM. 5610 East 29 N, Wichita, KS 67220. 316–685–0261.
KEYN   104 FM. 3829 North Salina, Wichita, KS 67204. 316–838–7744.

Youngstown
WHOT   1330 AM. 401 North Blaine Avenue, Youngstown, OH 44505. 216–746–8464.
WFMJ   1390 AM. 101 West Boardman Street, Youngstown, OH 44503. 216–744–5115.

WESTERN REGION—Primary Markets

Denver
KIMN   950 AM. 5350 West 20 Avenue, Denver, CO 80214. 303–234–9500.
KTLK   1280 AM. 1165 Delaware Street, Denver, CO 80204. 303–573–1280.

Los Angeles
KFI   640 AM. 610 South Ardmore Street, Los Angeles, CA 90005. 213–385–0101.
KHJ   930 AM. 5515 Melrose Avenue, Los Angeles, CA 90038. 213–462–2133.
KEZY   1190 AM. 1190 East Ball Road, Anaheim, CA 92804. 714–776–1191.
KIQQ   100.3 FM. 6430 Sunset Boulevard, Suite 1102, Hollywood, CA 90028. 213–469–1631.
KKIQ   101.7 FM. 1603 Barcelona Street, Livermore, CA 94550. 415-4

Portland
KGW   620 AM. 1501 SW Jefferson, Portland, OR 97201. 503–226–5055.

Salt Lake City
KCPX 1320 AM. 1760 Fremont Drive, Salt Lake City, UT 84104. 801–972–3030.
KRSP 1060 AM. Box 7760, Salt Lake City, UT 84107. 801–262–5541.

San Diego
KFMB 100.7 FM. 7677 Engineer Road, San Diego, CA 92020. 714–292–5362.

San Francisco
KFRC 610 AM. 415 Bush Street, San Francisco, CA 94108. 415–986–6100.
KYA 1260 AM. One Nob Hill Circle, San Francisco, CA 94108. 415–397–2500.

Seattle
KJR 950 AM. P. O. Box 3726, Seattle, WA 98124. 206–937–5100.
KING 1090 AM. 320 Aurora Avenue North, Seattle, WA 98109. 206–223–5226.

Tacoma
KTAC 850 AM. 2000 Tacoma Mall Office Building, Tacoma, WA 98411. 206–473–0085.

WESTERN REGION—Secondary Markets

Albuquerque
KQEO 920 AM. 2000 Indian School Road NW, Albuquerque, NM 87105. 505–243–6791.
KRKE 610 AM. 1410 Coal Avenue SW, Albuquerque, NM 87103. 505–765–5600.

Bakersfield
KERN 1410 AM. P. O. Box 2700, Bakersfield, CA 93303. 805–832–1410.
KAFY 550 AM. Box 6128, Bakersfield, CA 93306. 805–366–4411.

Boise
KFXD 580 AM. P. O. Box 107, Boise, ID 83701. 208–345–8812.

Eugene
KBDF 1280 AM. P. O. Box 506, Eugene, OR 97401. 503–345–4304.

Fresno
KYNO 1300 AM. 2125 North Barton, Fresno, CA 93706. 209–255–8383.

Great Falls
KEIN 1310 AM. P. O. Box 1239, Great Falls, MT 59403. 406–761–1310.

PACESETTING RADIO STATIONS — TOP 40

Las Vegas
KENO   1460 AM. 4660 South Decatur, Las Vegas, NV 89103. 702–876–1460.

Lewiston
KOZE   1300 AM. Box 936, Lewiston, ID 83501. 208–743–2502.

Monterey
KMBY   1240 AM. 651 Cannory Row, Monterey, CA 93940. 408–373–1234.

Moscow
KRPL   1400 AM. Box 8849, Moscow, ID 83843. 208–882–2551.

Oxnard
KACY   1520 AM. P. O. Box 1520, Oxnard, CA 93034. 805–488–3551.

Phoenix
KRIZ   1230 AM. 2345 West Buckeye Road, Phoenix, AZ 85009. 602–258–6717.

Sacramento
KNDE   1470 AM. 355 Commerce Circle, Sacramento, CA 95815. 916–922–8851.
KROY   1240 AM. 1019 Second Street, Sacramento, CA 95814. 916–441–4950.

Salem
KBZY   1490 AM. Box 14900, Salem, OR 97309. 503–364–6748.

San Bernardino
KFXM   590 AM. 666 Fairway Drive, San Bernardino, CA 92408. 714–825–5555.

San Jose
KLIV   1590 AM. Box 995, San Jose, CA 95108. 408–293–8030.

San Luis Obispo
KSLY   1400 AM. Box 1400, San Luis Obispo, CA 93406. 805–543–9400.

Santa Barbara
KIST   1340 AM. 735 State Street, Santa Barbara, CA 93101. 805–966–3981.

Spokane
KJRB   790 AM. P. O. Box 8007, Spokane, WA 99203. 509–448–1000.
KREM   970 AM. 4103 South Regal, Spokane, WA 99203. 509–534–0423.

Stockton
KJOY   1280 AM. 110 North El Dorado, Stockton, DA 95201. 209–466–2844.
KSTN   1420 AM. 2171 Ralph Avenue, Stockton, CA 95206. 209–948–5786.

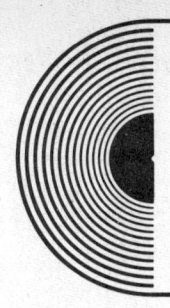

ROCK ALBUM-ORIENTED STATIONS

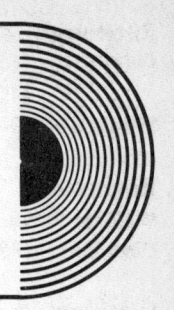

NORTHEASTERN REGION—Primary Markets

Baltimore
WKTX   105.7 FM. 5200 Moravia Road, Baltimore, MD 21206. 301–485–2400.
WIYY   97.9 FM. 3800 Hooper Avenue, Baltimore, MD 21211. 301–889–0098.

Boston
WCOZ   94.5 FM. 441 Stuart Street, Boston, MA 02116. 617–247–2020.
WBCN   104.1 FM. 5005 Prudential Tower, Boston, MA 02199. 617–266–1111.

Buffalo
WGRQ   96.9 FM. 59 Virginia Place, Buffalo, NY 14202. 716–881–4555.
WBUF   92.9 FM. 1233 Main Street, Buffalo, NY 14209. 716–882–4300.

Hartford
WCCC   106.9 FM. 11 Asylum Street, Hartford, CT 06103. 203–549–3456.
WHCN   106 FM. 60 Washington Street, Hartford, CT 06106. 203–247–1060.

New Haven
WPLR   99.1 FM. 1294 Chapel Street, New Haven, CT 06510. 203–777–6617.

New York
WNEW   102.7 FM. 565 Fifth Avenue, New York, NY 10017. 212–986–8844.
WPLJ   95.5 FM. 1330 Avenue of the Americas, New York, NY 10019. 212–887–7777.
WPIX   101.9 FM. 220 East 42 Street, New York, NY 10017. 212–949–2102.

Philadelphia
WMMR   93.3 FM. Nineteenth and Walnut Streets, Philadelphia, PA 19103. 215–561–0933.
WYSP   94.1 FM. One Bala Cynwyd Plaza, Bala Cynwyd, PA 19004. 215–839–7625.
WIOQ   102 FM. Two Bala Cynwyd Plaza, Bala Cynwyd, PA 19004. 215–835–6100.

Pittsburgh
WDVE   102 FM. Chamber of Commerce Building, Pittsburgh, PA 15219. 412-562-5900.
WYDD   104.7 FM. Box 7050, Pittsburgh, PA 15212. 412-362-2144.

Rochester
WCMF   96.5 FM. 129 Leighton Avenue, Rochester, NY 14609. 716-288-3200.
WSAY   1370 AM. 250 East Avenue, Rochester, NY 14604. 716-232-5580.

Washington, DC
WWDC   101.1 FM. 8800 Brookville Road, Silver Spring, MD 20910. 301-589-7100.
WHFS   102.3 FM. 4853 Cordell Avenue, Bethesda, MD 20014. 301-656-0600.
WAVA   780 AM. 1901 North Fort Myer Drive, Arlington, VA 22209. 703-522-1111.

NORTHEASTERN REGION—Secondary Markets

Albany
WQBK   104 FM. Box 1300, Albany, NY 12201. 518-462-5555.

Allentown
WSAN   1470 AM. 1183 Mickley Road, Whitehall, PA 18052. 215-434-9511.
WEZV   95.1 FM. 428 Brodhead Avenue, Bethlehem, PA 18015. 215-694-0511.

Hagerstown
WQCM   96.7 FM. 1250 Downsville Pike, Hagerstown, MD 21740. 301-797-7300.

Harrisburg
WRHY   92.7 FM. RD 1, Mt. Wolf, PA 17347. 717-266-6606.
WSFM   99.3 FM. Box 3433, Harrisburg, PA 17105. 717-234-3005.

Lewiston
WBLM   107.5 FM. Box 478, Lewiston, ME 04240. 207-375-4208.

Long Island
WLIR   92.7 FM. 175 Fulton Avenue, Garden City, NY 11550. 516-485-9200.

Utica
WOUR   96.9 FM. 288 Genessee Street, Utica, NY 13502. 315-797-0803.

Worcester
WAAF   107.3 FM. 34 Mechanic Street, Worcester, MA 01608. 617-752-5611.

SOUTHERN REGION—Primary Markets

Atlanta
WKLS   96.1 FM. 100th Tenth Street, Atlanta, GA 30309. 404–892–9557.
WRAS   88.5 FM. Georgia State University, University Place, Atlanta, GA 30303. 404–658–2240.

Dallas
KFWD   102.1 FM. 3626 North Hall Street, Dallas, TX 75219. 214–528–5500.
KZEW   97.9 FM. Communications Center, Dallas, TX 75202. 214–748–9898.

Houston
KLOL   101.1 FM. 510 Lovett, Houston, TX 77066. 713–526–4591.

Jacksonville
WAIV   96.9 FM. 6869 Lenox Avenue, Jacksonville, FL 32205. 904–783–3697.

Memphis
WZXR   102.7 FM. Box 2099, Memphis, TN 38101. 901–726–0060.

Miami/Fort Lauderdale
WINZ   94.9 FM. 4330 NW 207 Drive, Opa Locka, FL 33055. 305–371–6641.
WSHE   103.5 FM. 3000 SW 60 Avenue, Fort Lauderdale, FL 33314. 305–581–1580.

Nashville
WKDF   103.3 FM. 1202 Stahlman Building, Nashville, TN 37201. 615–254–0511.

New Orleans
WNOE   1060 AM. 529 Bienville, New Orleans, LA 70130. 504–529–1212.
WRNO   99.5 FM. 3400 North Causeway Boulevard, New Orleans, LA 70114. 504–837–2424.

Oklahoma City
KATT   100 FM. Box 25787, Oklahoma City, OK 73125. 405–631–8881.

Orlando
WORJ   107 FM. 2001 Mercy Drive, Orlando, FL 32808.
WDIZ   100.3 FM. Southland Building, Suite 470, Lee Road, Winter Park, FL 32789. 305–645–1802.

San Antonio
KMAC   630 AM. World Savings Building, 1100 North Main Avenue, San Antonio, TX 78212. 512–223–6211.

Tampa
WQSR 102.5 FM. Box 7700, Sarasota, FL 33578. 813-366-0424.
WQXM 97.9 FM. 8320 Starkey Road, Seminole, FL 33542. 813-391-9988.

Tulsa
KMOD 97.5 FM. 5350 East 31 Street, Tulsa, OK 74135. 918-664-2810.

SOUTHERN REGION—Secondary Markets

Austin
KLBJ 93.7 FM. P. O. Box 1209, Austin, TX 78767. 512-474-6543.

Baton Rouge
WFMF 102.5 FM. P. O. Box 496, Baton Rouge, LA 70821. 504-383-5271.

Beaumont
KHYS 98.5 FM. P. O. Box 968, Port Arthur, TX 77640. 713-963-1276.

Birmingham
WVOK 99.5 FM. P. O. Box 1926, Birmingham, AL 35201. 205-785-5111.

Charleston, SC
WWWZ 93.5 FM. P. O. Box 3437, Charleston, SC 29407. 803-766-6584.
WKTM 102.5 FM. Box 5758, Charleston, SC 29406. 803-554-7154.

Charleston, WV
WVAF 100 FM. 4110 McCorkle Avenue, Charleston, WV 25304. 304-925-7829.

Charlotte
WROQ 95.1 FM. 400 Radio Road, Charlotte, NC 28216. 704-392-6191.
WRPL 1540 AM. 1402 East Morehead Street, Charlotte, NC 28204.

Corpus Christi
KZFM 95.5 FM. 600 Broadway Building, Corpus Christi, TX 78401. 512-883-5316.
KNCN 101.3 FM. 3817 South Alameda, Corpus Christi, TX 78411. 512-855-4641.

El Paso
KINT 1590 AM. 5959 Gateway West, Suite 120, El Paso, TX 79925. 915-779-6454.
KPAS 93.9 FM. 3901 North Mesa, El Paso, TX 79902. 915-533-8211.

Gainesville
WGVL 105.3 FM. 7120 SW 20 Avenue, Gainesville, FL 32601. 904-378-3806.

Greensboro
WRQK 98.7 FM. P. O. Box 950, Greensboro, NC 27402. 919-275-9895.

Jackson
WZZQ 102.9 FM. P. O. Box 2171, Jackson, MS 39205. 601-982-1062.

Lafayette
KSMB 94.5 FM. P. O. Box 3345, MPO, Lafayette, LA 70502. 318-232-1311.
KPEL 1420 AM. 319 Audobon, Lafayette, LA 70505. 318-233-7003.

Lake Charles
KGRA 104 FM. 326 Pujo Street, Lake Charles, LA 70601. 318-433-0700.

Lexington
WKQQ 98.1 FM. Box 100, Lexington, KY 40590. 606-252-6694.

Mobile
WABB 97.5 FM. 1551 Springhill, Mobile, AL 36604. 205-432-5572.

Norfolk
WNOR 98.7 FM. 700 Monticello Avenue, Suite 555, Norfolk, VA 23510. 804-623-9667.
WMYK 93.7 FM. Box 269, Moyock, NC 27958. 804-421-9695.

Raleigh
WQDR 94.7 FM. P. O. Box 1511, Raleigh, NC 27602. 919-832-8311.

Roanoke
WROV 1240 AM. Fifteenth and Cleveland Avenue, Roanoke, VA 24015. 703-343-4444.

Shreveport
KROK 94.5 FM. 425 Edwards, Shreveport, LA 71120. 318-222-8711.

Wheeling
WOMP 1290 AM. Box 448, Woodmont Hill, Bellaire, OH 43906. 614-676-5661.

Winston-Salem
WKLZ 107.5 FM. Box 11967, Winston-Salem, NC 27106. 919-767-3705.

MIDWESTERN REGION—Primary Markets

Chicago
WMET 95.5 FM. 440 North Michigan Avenue, Chicago, IL 60611. 312-346-5411.

ROCK ALBUM ORIENTED

WKQX   101.1 FM. Merchandise Mart, Chicago, IL 60654. 312-861-5555.
WXRT   93.1 FM. 4949 West Belmont Avenue, Chicago, IL 60641. 312-777-1700.
WLUP   97.9 FM. 875 North Michigan Avenue, Chicago, IL 60611. 312-440-5270.

Cincinnati
WEBN   102.7 FM. 2724 Erie Avenue, Cincinnati, OH 45208. 513-871-8500.

Cleveland
WMMS   100.7 FM. The Cleveland Plaza, Euclid Avenue at East Twelfth Street, Cleveland, OH 44115. 216-781-9667.
WWWM   105.7 FM. 3940 Euclid Avenue, Cleveland, OH 44115. 216-391-1260.

Columbus
WLVQ   96.3 FM. 42 East Gay Street, Columbus, OH 43215. 614-224-1271.

Detroit
WRIF   101 FM. 20777 West 10 Mile Road, Southfield, MI 48075. 313-444-1010.
WABX   99.5 FM. 20760 Coolidge, Detroit, MI 48237. 313-398-1100.
WWWW   106.7 FM. 2930 East Jefferson, Detroit, MI 48207. 301-259-4323.

Indianapolis
WIFE   1310 AM. 1440 North Meridian Street, Indianapolis, IN 46202. 317-736-1375.
WNAP   93.1 FM. 2835 North Illinois Street, Indianapolis, IN 46208. 317-924-5211.
WFBQ   94.7 FM. 6161 Fall Creek Road, Indianapolis, IN 46220. 317-257-7565.

Kansas City
KYYS   102.1 FM. 3030 Summit, Kansas City, MO 64108. 816-753-4567.
KWKI   93.3 FM. 1722 Main, Kansas City, MO 64108. 816-474-6400.

Louisville
WLRS   102.3 FM. 800 South Fourth Street, Louisville, KY 40203. 502-585-5178.

Milwaukee
WZMF   98.3 FM. Box 216, Menomenee Falls, WI 53051. 414-251-7070.
WQFM   93.3 FM. 606 West Wisconsin Avenue, Milwaukee, WI 53203. 414-276-2040.

Minneapolis
KQRS   1440 AM. 917 North Lilac Drive, Golden Valley, MN 55422. 612-545-5601.

St. Louis
KADI   96.3 FM. 7530 Forsyth Boulevard, Clayton, MO 63105. 314-721-2323.
KSHE   94.7 FM. 9434 Watson Road, St. Louis, MO 63126. 314-842-1111.

MIDWESTERN REGION—Secondary Markets

Akron
WKDD   96.5 FM. 424 Sackett Avenue, Akron, OH 44313. 216–923–9761.

Ann Arbor
WIQB   102.9 FM. Box 5, Ann Arbor, MI 48107. 313–662–2881.

Des Moines
KCBC   1390 AM. 6967 University, Des Moines, IA 50305. 515–277–4483.

Flint
WWCK   105.5 FM. 3217 Lapeer Street, Flint, MI 48503. 313–744–1570.

Grand Rapids
WLAV   96.9 FM. 101C Waters Building, Grand Rapids, MI 49502. 616–456–5461.

Lincoln
KFMQ   101.9 FM. Terminal Building, Tenth and O Streets, Lincoln, NE 68508. 402–432–8565.

Madison
WIBA   101.5 FM. P. O. Box 99, Madison, WI 53701. 608–274–5450.
WYXE   92.1 FM. Box 3470, Madison, WI 53704. 608–837–8592.

Omaha
KQKQ   98.5 FM. P. O. Box 586, Council Bluffs, IA 51501. 712–322–4041.

Peoria
WWCT   105.7 FM. 100 SW Adams, Peoria, IL 61602. 309–674–2000.

Rockford
WYFE   95.3 FM. 1901 Shaw Road, Rockford, IL 61111. 815–877–3075.

Toledo
WIOT   104.7 FM. 604 Jackson Street, Toledo, OH 43604. 419–248–3377.
WMHE   92.5 FM. 4665 West Bancroft Street, Toledo, OH 43615. 419–531–1681.

WESTERN REGION—Primary Markets

Denver
KBPI   105.9 FM. 4460 Morrison Road, Denver, CO 80214. 303–936–2313.

Long Beach
KNAC   105.5 FM. 320 Pine Avenue, Long Beach, CA 90802. 213-437-0366.

Los Angeles
KWST   106 FM. 8833 West Sunset Boulevard, Los Angeles, CA 90069. 213-657-6130.
KMET   94.7 FM. 5764 Sunset Boulevard, Los Angeles, CA 90028. 218-464-5638.
KLOS   95.5 FM. 3321 South LaCienega Boulevard, Los Angeles, CA 90016. 213-663-3311.

Phoenix
KDKB   93.3 FM. 146 South Country Club, Mesa, AZ 85202. 602-833-8888.

Portland
KGON   92.3 FM. Box 22125, Portland, OR 97222. 503-655-9181.
KVAN   1480 AM. 1300 SW 5 Street, Suite 3231, Portland, OR 97201. 503-223-6328.
KINK   102 FM. 1501 SW Jefferson, Portland, OR 97201. 503-226-5080.

San Diego
KPRI   106.5 FM. 5252 Balboa Avenue, San Diego, CA 92117. 714-565-6006.
KCBQ   1170 AM. 9416 Mission Gorge Road, Santee, CA 90271. 714-286-1170.
KGB   101.5 FM. 4141 Pacific Highway, San Diego, CA 92110. 714-297-2201.

San Francisco
KSAN   94.9 FM. 345 Sansome Street, San Francicso, CA 94104. 415-986-2825.
KMEL   106.1 FM. 2300 Stockton, San Francisco, CA 94133. 415-391-9400.

Seattle
KISW   99.9 FM. Box 21449, Seattle, WA 98111. 206-937-5100.
KZOK   102.5 FM. 1426 Fifth Avenue, Seattle, WA 98101. 206-223-3911.
KZAM   92.5 FM. 10245 Main Street, Bellevue, WA 98004. 206-454-1540.

WESTERN REGION—Secondary Markets

Albuquerque
KRKE   610 AM. 1410 Coal Avenue SW, Albuquerque, NM 87103. 505-765-5600.
KRST   2405 Quincy NE, Albuquerque, NM 87190. 505-266-7946.

Anaheim
KEZY   95.9 FM. 1190 East Ball Road, Anaheim, CA 92805. 714-776-3696.

Colorado Springs
KKFM   96.5 FM. 225 South Academy Boulevard, Colorado Springs, CO 80910. 303-596-5536.

Eugene
KZEL   96.1 FM. P. O. Box 10527, Eugene, OR 97440. 503-747-1221.

Fresno
KYNO   96 FM. 2125 North Barton, Fresno, CA 93706. 209-255-8383.

Sacramento
KZAP   98.5 FM. 924 Ninth Street, Sacramento, CA 95803. 916-444-2806.
KSFM   102.5 FM. 937 Enterprise Drive, Sacramento, CA 95825. 916-929-5467.

San Bernardino
KOLA   99.9 FM. 3616 Main Street, Riverside, CA 92501. 714-684-9992.

San Luis Obispo
KZOZ   93.3 FM. 341 South Higuera, San Luis Obispo, CA 93401. 805-544-5093.

San Rafael
KTIM   100.9 FM. 1040 B Street, San Rafael, CA 94901. 415-456-1510.

Santa Barbara
KTYD   99.9 FM. 1216 State Street, Santa Barbara, CA 93101. 805-963-1601.
KTMS   97.5 FM. P. O. Drawer NN, News Press Building, Santa Barbara, CA 93102. 805-963-1975.

Santa Maria
KXFM   99.1 FM. Box 1964, Santa Maria, CA 93454. 805-922-2156.

Spokane
KREM   92.9 FM. 4103 South Regal Street, Spokane, WA 99203. 509-448-2000.

Tacoma
KLAY   106.1 FM. 215 Tacoma Avenue South, Tacoma, WA 98402. 206-627-3138.

Tucson
KWFM   92.9 FM. Box 13, Lawyers Title Building, Tucson, AZ 85702. 602-624-5588.

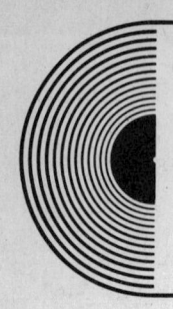

CONCERT PROMOTERS
(*in alphabetical order*)

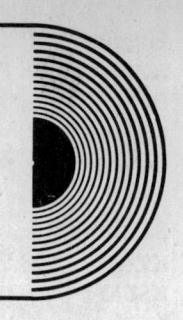

Avalon Attractions, 233 Wilshire Boulevard, Suite 940, Santa Monica, CA 90401. 213-393-9251.

John Bauer Concert Co., 2500 116 Avenue NE, Bellevue, WA 98004. 206-828-3576.

Beach Club Booking, 2507 North Broad Street, Camden, SC 29020. 803-432-6134.

Beaver Productions, 323 Dauphine Street, New Orleans, LA 70112. 504-821-8211.

Belkin Productions, 28001 Chagrin Boulevard, Cleveland, OH 44122. 216-464-5990.

Brass Ring Productions, 496 West Ann Arbor Trail, Suite 204, Plymouth, MI 48170. 313-459-5520.

Celebration Productions, Inc., 505 North Lakeshore Drive, Chicago, IL 60611. 312-644-7360.

Cellar Door Concerts, 2190 South East 17 Street, Ft. Lauderdale, FL 33316. 305-761-1200.

Concert Productions International Ltd., 2400 Eglington Avenue West, M6M 1S6 Toronto, Canada, 416-653-8603.

Contemporary Productions, 680 Craig Road, St. Louis, MO 63141. 314-567-9650.

Alex Cooley Associates, P.O. Box 77123, Atlanta, GA 30357. 404-873-4081.

Cross-Country Concerts Corporation, 527 Madison Avenue, New York, NY 10022. 212-758-6211.

DiCesare-Engler Productions, 207 Seventh Street, Pittsburgh, PA 15222. 412-281-3700.

Donald K. Donald Productions, 354 Youville Street, Montreal, H2Y 2C3, Quebec, Canada, 514-284-1010.

Electric Factory Concerts, 18 Street and Lombard Streets, Philadelphia, PA 19146. 215-732-3111.

Entertainment Amusement Company Entam, 901 Quarrier Street, Suite 407, Charleston, WV 25301. 304-345-8100.

Festival East Concerts, Statler Hilton Hotel, Buffalo, NY 14202. 716-854-7175.

Feyline Presents Inc., 8933 East Union, Englewood, CO 80110. 303-773-6000.

Friends Productions, 4447 North Central Expressway, Dallas, TX 75205. 214-522-6001.

Chris Fritz and Co., P. O. Box 8111, Kansas City, MO 64112. 816-531-1665.

Gemini Concerts Inc., Johnston, RI 02903. 401-231-3833.

Bil Graham Presents, 201 Eleventh Street, San Francisco, CA 94103. 415-864-0815.

Harvey & Corky Productions, c/o Buffalo Memorial Auditorium, Main and Terrace Streets, Buffalo, NY 14202. 716-854-0545.

JAM Productions, 360 North Michigan Avenue, Chicago, IL 60601. 312-726-6262.

CONCERT PROMOTERS

Jet Set Enterprises, 4031 Cordova Avenue, Jacksonville, FL 32201. 904-398-3786.

KMR Productions, 5553 Pia Street, Honolulu, HI 96821. 808-377-5422.

Danny Kresky Enterprises, 3100 Banksville Road, Pittsburgh, PA 15216. 412-343-7405.

Cedric Kushner Productions, 250 West 57 Street, New York, NY 10019. 212-489-6750.

Lewis Grey Productions, 9454 Wilshire Boulevard, Beverly Hills, CA 90212. 213-550-1065.

Mid-South Concerts, 143 Stonewall, Memphis, TN 38104. 901-726-5385.

Monarch Entertainment Bureau, Inc., 412 Pleasant Valley Way, West Orange, NJ 07052. 201-736-9828.

James Nederlander Associates, 9255 Sunset Boulevard, Hollywood, CA 90069. 213-278-9087.

New England Productions, 31 Fresh Pond Parkway, Cambridge, MA 02138. 617-547-0620.

Pace Concerts Inc., 3003 West Alabama, Houston, TX 77098. 713-526-7666.

Teddy Powell Entertainments, 114 East Fifty-Fifth Street, New York, NY 10022. 212-935-1050.

Schon Productions, 100 North Seventh Street, Minneapolis, MN 55403. 612-332-6575.

Tony Ruffino & Larry Vaughn Productions Ltd., 131 Jericho Turnpike, Penthouse 5, Jericho, NY 11753. 516-997-3710.

Sound Seventy Productions, 210 25 Avenue North, Nashville, TN 37203. 615-327-1711.

Stardate Productions Ltd., 1845 North Farwell Avenue, Suite 208, Milwaukee, WI 53202. 414-765-0133.

Stone City Attractions, 4415 Piedras Drive West, Suite 253, San Antonio, TX 78228. 512-732-1101.

Sunshine Promotions, 6502 Westfield Boulevard, Indianapolis, IN 46220. 317-257-7333.

Taurus Productions, P.O. Box 42439, Atlanta, GA 30311. 404-755-1676.

Tiger Flower and Co. Inc., 715 G Street Northwest, Washington, DC 20001. 202-347-7234.

United Concerts, 731 E. S. Temple, Salt Lake City, UT 84102. 801-328-4801.

Wolf and Rissmiller, 292 S. LaCienga, Beverly Hills, CA 90211. 213-659-8000.

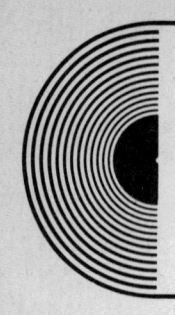

CONCERT FACILITIES

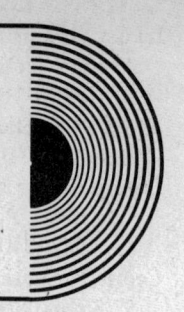

ALABAMA

Auburn Memorial Coliseum, c/o Auburn University, Auburn, AL 36830. 205–826–4564. Owned by State of Alabama. Tom Sparrow, facility and booking manager.
    Seats 13,239. Tickets normally $5-7. Rent: $1,000 v. 10 percent gross receipts. 10 concerts in 1978, 12-15 in 1979.

Birmingham-Jefferson Civic Center, One Civic Center Plaza, Birmingham, AL 35203. 205–328–8160. Owned by People of Birmingham and Jefferson Counties. E. A. "Casey" Jones, facility manager; Phoebe Howell, booking manager.
    COLISEUM seats 16,500-19,000. CONCERT HALL seats 800-1,000. Ticket prices vary. Rent: call Phoebe Howell, ext. 25. 105 concerts in 1978, 105 in 1979.

Mobile Municipal Auditorium, 401 Auditorium Drive, P. O. Box 369, Mobile, AL 36601. 205–438–7261. Owned by City of Mobile. W. C. Clewis, facility manager; Geurge D. Juzang and David Gwin, booking managers.
    Seats 10,500-14,000. Tickets normally $5-10. Rent: $1,250 v. 10 percent gross receipts. 38 concerts in 1978, 49 in 1979.

Montgomery Civic Center, 300 Bibb Street, P. O. Box 4037, Montgomery, AL 36101. 205–263–3886. Owned by City of Montgomery. Charlie F. Kinsaul, facility and booking manager.
    Seats 6,300. Tickets normally $6 and $7. Rent: $1,000 v. 10 percent gross receipts. 20 concerts in 1978, 20 in 1979.

Von Braun Civic Center, 700 Monroe Street, Huntsville, AL 35801. 205–533–1953. Owned by City of Huntsville. Cliff Wallace, facility and booking manager.
    ARENA seats 8,738. Tickets normally $5.50-8. Rent: $1,500 v. 12 percent gross receipts. CONCERT HALL seats 2,171. Tickets normally $5.50-8. Rent: $500 v. 12 percent gross receipts. PLAYHOUSE seats 502. Tickets normally $5.50-8. Rent: $200. 60 concerts in 1978, 60 in 1979.

*Four-wall deal information does not include equipment, labor and house expenses; insurance; and amusement/sales taxes; unless otherwise noted.

ARIZONA

Arizona Veterans' Memorial Coliseum, 1826 West McDowell, P.O. Box 6715, Phoenix, AZ 85005. 602–252–6771. Owned by State of Arizona. Thomas E. Clark, executive director; Richard J. Bjorklund, booking manager.

Seats 13,400. Tickets normally $7 and $8. Rent: approximately $20,000, including concessions and parking. 12 concerts in 1978, 4 in 1979.

Phoenix Civic Plaza, 225 East Adams, Phoenix, AZ 85004. 602–262–6225. Owned by City of Phoenix. Edward J. Allen, facility manager; Denny Maus, booking manager.

EXHIBIT HALL seats 6,000. Tickets normally $5.50, $6.50, $7.50. Rent: $1,500 v. 10 percent gross receipts. SYMPHONY HALL seats 2,500. Tickets normally $5.50, $6.50, $7.50. Rent: $700.

Yuma Civic & Convention Center, P. O. Box 5653, Yuma, AZ 85364. 602–344–3800. Owned by City of Yuma. Paul T. Whitehead, facility manager; Thomas A. Robinson, booking manager.

Seats 2,200. Tickets normally $7 and $8. Rent: $350 v. 10 percent gross receipts. 19 concerts in 1978, 35 in 1979.

ARKANSAS

T. H. Barton Coliseum, P. O. Box 907, Little Rock, AR 72203. 501–372–8341. Owned by State of Arkansas. John R. Holmes, facility manager; Gloria C. Chappelle, booking manager.

Seats 10,000. Tickets normally $6-9. Rent: $1,000 v. 12 percent gross receipts. 9 concerts in 1978, 20-25 in 1979.

El Dorado Municipal Auditorium, 100 West 8 Street, El Dorado, AR 71730. 501–862–1387. Owned by City of El Dorado. John R. Alley, facility and booking manager.

Seats 1,872. Tickets normally $2-10. Rent: $150-300 or 20 percent gross receipts (open date plan). 75 concerts in 1978, 100 in 1979.

Little Rock Convention Center, Markham and Broadway, P. O. Box 3232, Little Rock, AR 72203. 501–376–4781. Owned by City of Little Rock. Delores J. Waller, facility manager; Phyllis Griffith, booking manager.

Seats 2,645. Tickets normally $5-10. Rent: $500 v. 7 percent gross receipts on first $9,000, 10 percent over $9,000 (maximum rent: $1,200). 27 concerts in 1978, 30 in 1979.

CALIFORNIA

Bakersfield Civic Auditorium, 1001 Truxtun Avenue, Bakersfield, CA 93301. 805-327-7553. Owned by City of Bakersfield. Charles P. Graviss, facility manager; Charles P. Graviss or Bob Quintella, booking managers.
   Seats 3,041 reserved, 6,000 festival. Tickets normally $5.50, $6.50, $7.50. Rent: $750 v. 10 percent gross receipts. 40 concerts in 1978, 35 in 1979.

Century City Playhouse, 10508 West Pico Boulevard, Los Angeles, CA 90064. 213-839-3322. Ivan Spiegel, facility manager; Lee Kaplan, booking manager.
   Seats 95. Tickets normally $3. Rental: $75. 35 concerts in 1978, 35 in 1979.

Circle Star Theatre, 1717 Industrial Road, San Carlos, CA 94070. 415-364-2550. Owned by Marquee Enterprises. Jack Medlevine, faculty manager; B. Stroum, booking manager.
   Seats 3,700. Tickets normally $7.75, $8.75. Rent: 10 percent gross receipts. 46 concerts in 1978, 46 in 1979.

Civic Auditorium, 307 Church Street, Santa Cruz, CA 95060. 408-429-3655. Owned by City of Santa Cruz. Robert W. Bolls, facility manager; Donald Ricker, booking manager.
   Seats 1,952. Tickets normally $3.50-8.50. Rent: approximately $200 plus 10 percent gross receipts. 30-40 concerts in 1978, 60-80 in 1979.

Civic Memorial Auditorium, 525 North Center Street, Stockton, CA 95202. 209-944-8223. Owned by City of Stockton. Leo P. Burke, facility and booking manager.
   Seats 3,600. Tickets normally $4.50-10. Rent: $300 v. 10 percent gross receipts. 13 concerts in 1978, 10 in 1979.

Concord Pavilion, 2000 Kirker Pass Road, Concord, CA 94523. 415-671-3270. Owned by City of Concord. John Toffoli, Jr., facility manager; Jay Bedecarre, booking manager.
   Seats 8,500. Tickets normally $5-15. Rent: limited availability—call Jay Bedecarre. 65 concerts in 1978, 65 in 1979.

Cow Palace, Geneva Avenue, P. O. Box 34206, San Francisco, CA 94134. 415-584-2480. Owned by State of California. John S. Root, facility manager; Dana Lewis, booking manager.
   Seats 14,706. Tickets normally $6.50-15. Rent: $1,500 v. 10 percent gross receipts. 18 concerts in 1978, 22 in 1979.

Dodger Stadium, 1000 Elysian Park Avenue, Los Angeles, CA 90012. 213-224-1500 or 213-224-1351. Privately owned facility. Bob Smith, facility and booking manager.
   Seats 56,000-60,000. Tickets normally $10-12.50. Rent: flat rate—no percentages. No concerts in 1978, 1 in 1979.

CONCERT FACILITIES 651

The Forum, 3900 West Manchester, Inglewood, CA 90306. 213–674–6000. Owned by Dr. Jerry H. Buss. Claire Rothman, facility and booking manager.
    Seats 18,649. Tickets normally $7.75, $8.75, $9.75. Rent: call Claire Rothman. 50 concerts in 1978, 50 in 1979.

Fresno Convention Center, 700 M Street, Fresno, CA 93721. 209–488–1511. Owned by City of Fresno. Robert A. Schoettler, facility manager; Jerry Cutright, booking clerk.
    ARENA seats 7,330. THEATRE seats 2,351. Tickets normally $7.50-10. Rent: flat rate v. 10 percent gross receipts. 36 concerts in 1978, 45 in 1979.

Greek Theatre, 2700 North Vermont, Los Angeles, CA 90027. 213–660–6302. Operated by James Nederlander. Robert W. McTyre, general manager; Alan Bregman and Jeff Greenberg, booking agents.
    Seats 4,600. Tickets normally $7-12.50. Rent: call Alan Bregman or Jeff Greenberg.

Hollywood Palladium, 6215 Sunset Boulevard, Hollywood, CA 90028. 213–466–4311. Owned by Montgomery Ward & Co. Fred Otash, facility and booking manager.
    Seats 2,200. Tickets normally $8-15. Rent: $2,500-5,000 v. 15 percent gross receipts. 24 concerts in 1978, 30 in 1979.

Hughes Stadium, 3835 Freeport Boulevard, Sacramento, CA 95822. 916–442–0783. Owned by Los Rios Community College District. Roy Tamm, facility and booking manager.
    Seats 30,000. Tickets normally $7-10. Rent: $2,500 v. 7 percent gross receipts. 1 concert in 1978, none in 1979.

Ben Lewis Hall at Raincross Square, 3443 Orange Street, Riverside, CA 92501. 714–787–7950. Owned by City of Riverside. George Brodeur, facility and booking manager.
    Seats 2,724. Tickets normally $7.50 and $8.50. Rent: $500 v. 10 percent gross receipts. 20 concerts in 1978, 25 in 1979.

Los Angeles Coliseum, 3911 South Figueroa, Los Angeles, CA 90037. 213–747–7111. Owned by City of Los Angeles, County of Los Angeles, and State of California. James F. Hardy, facility and booking manager.
    Seats 90,000. Tickets normally $10-15. Rent: $5,000 v. 10 percent gross receipts. 3 concerts in 1978, 5 in 1979.

Los Angeles Sports Arena, 3939 South Figueroa, Los Angeles, CA 90037. 213–748–6131. Owned by City of Los Angeles, County of Los Angeles, and State of California, James F. Hardy, facility and booking manager.
    Seats 20,000. Tickets normally $8-15. Rent: $3,000 v. 10 percent gross receipts. 8 concerts in 1978, 12 in 1979.

CONCERT FACILITIES

Long Beach Convention and Entertainment Center, 300 East Ocean Boulevard, Long Beach, CA 90802. 213-436-3636. Owned by City of Long Beach. Richard H. Shaff, facility manager; Margie Garvin, booking coordinator.

    ARENA seats 6,200, 9,200, or 13,933. Tickets normally $6.50-9.75. Rent: $2,650 v. 10 percent gross receipts. TERRACE THEATER seats 3,141. Tickets normally $6.50-12.50. Rent: $1,000 v. 10 percent gross receipts. 52 concerts in 1978, 25 in 1979 (through July).

Oakland-Alameda County Coliseum, Nimitz Freeway and Hegenberger Road, Oakland, CA 94621. 415-569-2121. Owned by City of Oakland and County of Alameda. Bill Cunningham, facility and booking manager.

    STADIUM seats 60,000. ARENA seats 14,200. Ticket prices vary. Rent: negotiable. 30 concerts in 1978, 25 in 1979.

Oxnard Civic Auditorium, 800 Hobson Way, Oxnard, CA 93030. 805-486-2424. Owned by City of Oxnard. Jack C. Lavin, facility and booking manager.

    Seats 1,604. Tickets normally $4.50 and $7.50. Rent: $450 v. 10 percent gross receipts. 80 concerts in 1978, 88 in 1979.

La Paloma, P. O. Box 41, Encinitas, CA 92024. 714-436-7788. Owned by Edward A. Seykota. Roanne Withers, facility and booking manager.

    Seats 325. Tickets normally $8.25. Rent: $700-1,000—percentage deals possible. 15 concerts in 1978, 30 in 1979.

Paramount Theatre, 2025 Broadway, Oakland, CA 94612. 415-893-2300. Owned by City of Oakland. Peter J. Botto, general manager.

    Seats 2,998. Tickets normally $7.50 and $9.50. Rent: $575 plus 5 percent gross receipts over $3,000. 20 concerts in 1978, 20 in 1979.

Pasadena Civic Auditorium, 300 East Green Street, Pasadena, CA 91101. 213-577-4343. Owned by City of Pasadena. Doris G. Stovall, facility and booking manager.

    Seats 2,965. Tickets normally $8.50, $10, $12.50. Rent: $750 v. 10 percent gross receipts. 8 concerts in 1978, 13 in 1979.

Sacramento Community/Convention Center, 1100 Fourteenth Street, Sacramento, CA 95814. 916-449-5291. Owned by City of Sacramento. Sam J. Burns, facility manager; Leonard Zerilli, assistant manager.

    EXHIBIT HALL seats 7,000. MEMORIAL AUDITORIUM seats 2,452. Tickets normally $7.50, $8.50, $9.50. Rent: 10 percent gross receipts. 130 concerts in 1978, 150 in 1979.

San Diego Sports Arena, 3500 Sports Arena Boulevard, San Diego, CA 92110. 714-224-4171. Owned by San Diego Arena Lease Co. Philip R. Quinn, facility and booking manager.

    Seats 14,585. Tickets normally $5.75-12.75. Rent: percentage of gross receipts. 39 concerts in 1978, 43 in 1979.

San Diego State University Open Air Amphitheatre, c/o San Diego State University, San Diego, CA 92182. 714-286-6555. Owned by San Diego State University. Jim Carruthers, facility manager; Russell Wright, booking manager.

Seats 3,800. Tickets normally $7.75-9.75. Rent: $1,200-1,800 plus percentage of gross receipts when appropriate. 25 concerts in 1978, 30 in 1979 (summer only).

San Francisco Civic Auditorium, 99 Grove Street, San Francisco, CA 94102. 415-558-5065. Owned by City and County of San Francisco. Joseph F. Balzer, facility manager; Joseph F. Balzer or Frank Cox, booking managers.

Seats 7,500. Tickets normally $4-12.50. Rent: $1,260 v. 10 percent gross receipts. 4 concerts in 1978, 6 in 1979.

Santa Barbara County Bowl, 1122 North Milpas, Santa Barbara, CA 93102. 805-963-8634. Owned by Santa Barbara County. Sam Scranton, facility and booking manager.

Seats 4,788. Tickets normally $6.50, $7.50, $8.50. Rent: 15 percent gross receipts. 18 concerts in 1978, approximately 25 in 1979.

Santa Monica Civic Auditorium, 1855 Main Street Santa Monica, CA 90401. 213-451-1578. Owned by City of Santa Monica. Jeremy B. Ferris, facility and booking manager.

Seats 3,000. Tickets normally $7.50 and $8.50. Rent: $675 plus 10 percent gross receipts ($1,500 maximum). 100 concerts in 1978, 110 in 1979.

Universal Amphitheatre, 100 Universal City Plaza, Universal City, CA 91608. 213-980-9421. Owned by MCA Inc. Stu Adelson, facility manager; Danny Bramson, booking manager.

Seats 5,300. Tickets normally $8.50-17.50. Rent: call Danny Bramson. No concerts in 1978, 1 in 1979.

CONNECTICUT

Bushnell Memorial Hall, 166 Capitol Avenue, Hartford, CT 06106. 203-527-3123. Privately owned facility. Leland S. Jamieson, facility manager; Murray H. Cohen, booking manager.

Seats 2,728. Ticket prices vary. Rent: sliding scale depending upon day of the week. 138 concerts in 1978, 175 in 1979.

Hartford Civic Center, One Civic Center Plaza, Hartford, CT 06103. 203-566-6588. Owned by City of Hartford. Frank E. Russo, Jr., facility and booking manager; Lucy Skolnick, booking assistant.

Seats 16,400. Tickets normally $7.50 and $8.50. Rent: $2,500 v. 12½ percent gross receipts. 40 concerts in 1977. Roof collapsed, January 1978—scheduled to reopen in January 1980.

Hartford Jai Alai Fronton, Hartford, CT 203-566-6588. Owned by World Jai Alai of Miami. Patrick Levine, facility; Frank E. Russo, Jr., booking manager of all non-jai alai events.
    Seats 4,235-4,800. Tickets normally $7.50 and $8.50. Rent: $2,000. 15 concerts in 1978, 18 in 1979.

New Haven Veterans Memorial Coliseum, 275 South Orange, New Haven, CT 06508. 203-772-4200. Owned by New Haven Veterans Memorial Coliseum Authority. Tony Tavares, facility and booking manager.
    Seats 11,099. Tickets normally $6.50-8.50. Rent: $1,850 v. 12½ percent gross receipts. 45 concerts in 1978, 45 in 1979.

DELAWARE

Grand Opera House, 818 Market Street Mall, Wilmington, DE 19801. 302-658-7897. Owned by Grand Opera House, Inc. Robert B. Dustman, III, executive director and booking manager.
    Seats 1,100. Tickets average $9.50. Rent: $1,400 plus 10 percent gross receipts. 60 concerts in 1978, 50 in 1979.

DISTRICT OF COLUMBIA

Robert F. Kennedy Memorial Stadium, 2001 East Capitol Street, Washington, DC 20003. 202-543-6465. Operated by D.C. Armory Board. Robert H. Sigholtz, general manager; Kenneth C. Hopkins, stadium manager.
    Seats 55,000. Tickets normally $8-15. Rent: $2,500 v. 15 percent gross receipts. 1 concert in 1978, none in 1979.

Warner Theatre, 513 Thirteenth Street NW, Washington, DC 20004. 202-347-7801. Owned by Sam L'Hommedieu. David Anderson, facility and booking manager.
    Seats 2,000. Ticket prices vary. Rent: negotiable. 100 concerts produced in 1978, a few concerts in 1979 (used primarily for legitimate theatre).

FLORIDA

Bayfront Center, 400 First Street South, St. Petersburg, FL 33701. 813-893-7251. Owned by City of St. Petersburg. Al Leggat, facility manager; Phil Scott, booking manager.
    ARENA seats 8,400. Tickets normally $6.50 and $7.50. Rent: $1,000 v. 12½ percent. THEATRE seats 2,287. Tickets normally $6.50 and $7.50. Rent: $800 v. 8 percent gross receipts. 75 concerts in 1978, 75 in 1979.

Mayor Bob Carr Municipal Auditorium, 401 West Livingston Street, Orlando, FL 32801. 305-849-2185. Owned by City of Orlando. Miles C. Wilkin, facility manager.
Seats 2,542. Tickets normally $5.50-13.95. Rent: $600 v. 10 percent gross receipts. 180 show days during 1978-79 season.

Dade County Auditorium, 2901 West Flagler Street, Miami, FL 33135. 305-547-5414 or 305-547-5412. Owned by Dade County. Ralph Gilman, facility and booking manager.
Seats 2,501. Tickets normally $5-25. Rent: $600 plus 5 percent gross receipts. 200 concerts in 1978, 200 in 1979.

Maurice Gusman Cultural Center, 174 East Flagler Street, Miami FL 33131. 305-374-2444. Owned by City of Miami. Ronald Wayne, facility and booking manager.
Seats 1,883. Tickets normally $7.50 and $8.50. Rent: $650 v. 8 percent gross receipts. 150 concerts in 1978, 200 in 1979.

Jacksonville Veterans Memorial Coliseum, 1145 East Adams Street, Jacksonville, FL 32202. 904-633-2350. Owned by City of Jacksonville. Jerry Young, facility manager; Ken Parton, booking manager.
Seats 7,828-10,428. Tickets normally $7 and $8. Rent: $1,000 v. 12 percent gross receipts.

Lakeland Civic Center, 700 West Lemon, P. O. Drawer Q, Lakeland, FL 33802. 813-686-7126. Owned by City of Lakeland. Jerry MacDonald, facility and booking.
ARENA seats 8,136. Tickets normally $7-9. Rent: $800 v. 12 percent gross receipts. THEATRE seats 2,282. Tickets normally $7-9. Rent: $450 v. 9 percent gross receipts. 61 concerts in 1978, 75 in 1979.

Miami Beach Convention Center, 1901 Convention Drive, Miami Beach, FL 33140. 305-673-7311. Owned by City of Miami Beach. Norman Litz, facility and booking manager.
NORTH HALL seats 15,000. Tickets normally $4-15.50. Rent: $2,500 v. 12 percent gross receipts. SOUTH HALL seats 10,000. Tickets normally $4-15.50. Rent: $2,500 v. 12 percent gross receipts. THEATER OF THE PERFORMING ARTS seats 3,000. Tickets normally $4-15.50. Rent: $1,000 v. 12 percent gross receipts. 28 concerts in 1978, 25 in 1979.

Miami Jai-Alai Fronton, 3500 Northwest 37 Avenue, Miami, FL 33142. 305-633-6400. Owned by World Jai-Alai. Steve Shuart, facility and booking manager.
Seats 6,000. Tickets normally $6.50-9. Rent: $4,000 v. $.85 per person. 40 concerts in 1978, 40 in 1979.

Orlando Sports Stadium, 2285 North Econ Trail, Orlando, FL 32807. 305-277-8000. Owned by Pete Ashlock. Barbara Ashlock, facility and booking manager.
Seats 8,000-10,000. Tickets normally $4-8. Rent: $2,000 v. 15 percent gross receipts. 15 concerts in 1978, 5 in 1979.

Palm Beach Fairgrounds Speedway, 9067 Southern Boulevard, West Palm Beach, FL 33406. 305-793-0551. Owned by South Florida Fair & Exposition Corp. Buford Seals, facility manager; Danny Taylor, booking manager.
  Seats 5,000. Tickets normally $5 for adults, $2 for children under 12. Rent: $2,500. 2 concerts in 1978, 4 in 1979.

The Sportatorium, 16661 Hollywood Boulevard, P. O. Box 7029, Hollywood, FL 33021. 305-431-5901. Owned by Stephen Calder Estate. Bruce Johnson, facility and booking manager.
  Seats 15,500. Tickets normally $8-10. Rent: $5,000 v. 15 percent gross receipts. 25 concerts in 1978, 13 in 1979 (as of July).

Swisher Gym, c/o Jacksonville University, 2800 University Boulevard North, Jacksonville, FL 32211. 904-744-3950. Owned by Jacksonville University. Judson Harris, facility manager; Steve Crandall, booking manager.
  Seats 1,500-2,500. Tickets normally $5-7. Rent: $500 or free, provided accommodation is made for university students. 4 concerts in 1978, 4 in 1979.

Tampa Stadium, 4201 North Dale Mabry Highway, Tampa, FL 33607. 813-872-7977. Owned by Tampa Sports Authority. Robert J. Pierce, stadia manager; Edward W. Hamp, event coordinator.
  Seats 50,000. Ticket prices vary. Rent: $30,000 plus 15 percent gross receipts. Two concerts in 1977. Self-imposed moratorium on concerts since July 11, 1977, following abortive Led Zeppelin concert—ban lifted June 26, 1978.

Tangerine Bowl, 400 West Livingston Street, Orlando, FL 32801. 305-849-2185. Owned by City of Orlando. Miles Wilkin, facility manager.
  Seats 60,000. Tickets normally $10, $12.50, $15. Rent: $25,000 v. 10 percent gross receipts. 3 concerts in 1978, 3 in 1979.

GEORGIA

Fox Theatre, 660 Peachtree Street NE, Atlanta, GA 30308. 404-892-5685. Owned by Atlanta Landmarks, Inc. Alan McCracken, facility and booking manager.
  Seats 3,933. Tickets normally $6.50-8.75. Rent: call Alan McCracken.

Macon Coliseum, 200 Coliseum Drive, Macon, GA 31201. 912-742-0901. Owned by Middle Georgia Coliseum Authority; leased to City of Macon. Bill H. Lavery, facility and booking manager.
  Seats 10,242. Tickets normally $7.50 and $8.50. Rent: $750 v. 10 percent gross receipts. 34 concerts in 1978, 48 in 1979.

Maddox Hall, c/o Atlanta Civic Center, 395 Piedmont Avenue NE, Atlanta, GA 30308. 404-523-6275. Owned by City of Atlanta. Al Leiker, facility and booking manager.
  Seats 4,600. Tickets normally $6-8. Rent: $1,400. 154 concerts in 1978, 154 in 1979.

The Omni, 100 Techwood Drive NW, Atlanta, GA 30303. 404-681-2100. Owned by City of Atlanta. Robert H. Kent, facility manager; Robert W. Dhue, booking manager.
    Seats 16,500. Tickets normally $5-15. Rent: $6,000 v. 16½ percent gross receipts.

Savannah Civic Center, Orleans Square, P. O. Box 726, Savannah, GA 31402. 912-236-4275. Owned by City of Savannah. John Tidwell, executive director; Mike Finocchiaro, booking manager.
    ARENA seats 8,000. Tickets normally $7.50 and $8.50. Rent: $300 v. 9 percent gross receipts. JOHNNY MERCER THEATER seats 2,566. Tickets normally $7.50 and $8.50. Rent: $600 v. 10 percent gross receipts.

HAWAII

Aloha Stadium, P. O. Box 30666, Honolulu, HI 96820. 808-487-3838. Owned by State of Hawaii. Mackay Yanagisawa, facility and booking manager.
    Seats 40,000-50,000. Tickets normally $7.50-10. Rent: 10 percent gross receipts. No concerts in 1978, 4 in 1979.

IDAHO

Idaho State University Minidome, Campus Box 8098, Pocatello, ID 83221. 208-236-2831. Owned by Idaho State University. Ray Ritari, facility and booking manager.
    Seats 17,000. Tickets normally $6.50 and $7.50. Rent: $1,400 v. 12 percent gross receipts. 6 concerts in 1978, 10 in 1979.

ILLINOIS

Chicago Stadium, 1800 West Madison, Chicago, IL 60612. 312-733-5300. Owned by Arthur M. Wirtz. John Fett, facility manager.
    Seats 19,000. Tickets normally $10-15. Rent: call Arthur M. Wirtz. 25 concerts in 1978, 25 in 1979.

Comiskey Park, 324 West 35 Street, Chicago, IL 60616. 312-924-1000. Owned by the Chicago White Sox, Inc. David Schaffer, facility manager; Michael Veeck, booking manager.
    Seats 60,000. Tickets normally $10-15. Rent: negotiated percentage of gross receipts. 2 concerts in 1978, 4 in 1979.

CONCERT FACILITIES

International Amphitheatre, 4300 South Halsted Street, Chicago, IL 60609. 312-927-5580. Owned by International Amphitheatre Company. Larry P. Caine, facility and booking manager.
 Seats 12,000. Tickets normally $7.50, $8.50, $9.50. Rent: approximately $6,000. 26 concerts in 1978, 30 in 1979.

Orchestra Hall, 200 South Michigan Avenue, Chicago, IL 60604. 312-435-8122. Owned by The Orchestra Association (Chicago Symphony Orchestra). Michael M. Brotman, facility manager; Carolyn Bean, booking manager.
 Seats 2,566. Tickets normally $6-30. Rent: $2,200. 59 concerts in 1978, 60 in 1979.

Park West, 322 West Armitage, Chicago, IL 60614. 312-929-1322. Owned by Dale Neidermaier. Coleman, facility manager; Arny Granat (Jam Productions), booking manager.
 Seats 750-1,000. Tickets normally $8.50. Rent: call Arny Granat. 150 concerts in 1978, 200 in 1979.

Soldier Field, 425 East McFetridge, Chicago, IL 60605. 312-294-2309. Owned by Chicago Park District. Charles Fabiano, facility and booking manager.
 Seats 70,000. Ticket prices vary. Rent: 15 percent gross receipts. 2 concerts in 1978, none in 1979.

INDIANA

Clowes Memorial Hall, 4600 Sunset Avenue, Indianapolis, IN 46208. 317-924-6321. Owned by Butler University. T. H. Hollingsworth; Theater Management, booking agency.
 Seats 2,182. Tickets normally $10, $11, $12, $13, $14, $15. Rent: $1,000 for one performance, $1,500 for two performances, plus 15 percent gross receipts above specified amount. 64 concerts in 1978, 70 in 1979.

Hammond Civic Center, 5825 Sohl Avenue, Hammond, IN 46230. 219-853-6378. Owned by City of Hammond, Indiana. Michael Bicanic, facility and booking manager.
 Seats 5,170. Tickets normally $3-8.50. Rent: $4,200 for rock events, $2,000 for country. 10 concerts in 1978, 8 in 1979.

Hulman Civic University Center, Ninth and Cherry Streets, Terre Haute, IN 47809. 812-232-6311, ext. 2757. Owned by Indiana State University. Cliff Lambert, facility and booking manager.
 Seats 10,000. Tickets normally $5 and $10. Rent: 15 percent gross receipts. 14 concerts in 1978, 16 in 1979.

Market Square Arena, 300 East Market Street, Indianapolis, IN 46204. 317-639-6411. Owned by City of Indianapolis. E. B. Sumerlin, executive director; Charles A. Ross, marketing director and booking manager.
 Seats 18,250. Tickets normally $6.50-15. Rent: $5,000 v. 15 percent gross receipts. 34 concerts in 1978, 42 in 1979.

Morris Civic Auditorium, 211 North Michigan Street, South Bend, IN 46601. 219-232-6954. Owned by City of South Bend. Floyd M. Jessup, facility and booking manager.
    Seats 2,486. Tickets normally $3.50-12. Rent: $600 plus 5 percent gross receipts above $12,500. 98 concerts in 1978, 98 in 1979.

IOWA

Five Seasons Center, 370 First Avenue NE, Cedar Rapids, IA 52401. 319-398-5211. Owned by City of Cedar Rapids. H. Michael Gebauer, facility manager; Jim Brown, booking manager.
    Seats 10,000. Tickets normally $7-10. Rent: $1,500 v. 12 percent gross receipts. 35 concerts in 1979.

James H. Hilton Coliseum, c/o Iowa State Center, Ames, IA 50011. 515-294-3347. Owned by Iowa State University. Richard Snyder, facility manager; Robert Dagitz, booking manager.
    Seats 15,000. Tickets average $8. Rent: call Robert Dagitz. 12 concerts in 1978, 9 in 1979.

Masonic Temple Auditorium, 115 West 7 Street, P. O. Box 3627, Davenport, IA 52808. 319-323-1874. Owned by Masonic Temple Association, Inc. Herbert F. Maley, facility and booking manager.
    Seats 2,700. Tickets normally $5-8. Rent: $600 for one performance, $1,000 for two performances, plus 15 percent commission on souvenir program sales and 25 percent commission on record and tape sales. 16 concerts in 1978, 18 in 1979.

McElroy Auditorium, P. O. Box 622, Waterloo, IA 50704. 319-291-4551. Owned by City of Waterloo. Richard Byrum, facility and booking manager.
    Seats 7,200. Tickets normally $6-8. Rent: 10 percent gross receipts. 5 concerts in 1978, 2 in 1979.

Orpheum Theatre, 116 East Third Street, Davenport, IA 52801. 319-323-5314. Owned by Verid Corporation. Harold Denton, facility manager; Wilford J. Huebner, booking manager.
    Seats 2,708. Tickets normally $8, $10, $12. Rent: $2,000.

Sioux City Auditorium, 401 Gordon Drive, Sioux City, IA 51101. 712-279-6157. Owned by City of Sioux City. Harold C. Hansen, facility manager; Roberta G. Morgan, business manager; Joe Romano, technical director.
    Seats 4,781-5,000. Tickets normally $4-9. Rent: $575 v. 10 percent gross receipts. 7 concerts in 1978, 10 in 1979.

KENTUCKY

Commonwealth Convention Center, 221 River City Mall, Louisville, KY 40202. 502–588–4381. Owned by Commonwealth of Kentucky. Taskel H. Ross, facility manager; Roger A. Dixon, booking manager.
    Variable seating: 3,000-5,000-8,250. Tickets normally $4.50-8.50. Rent: $450-750 v. 10 percent gross receipts. 23 concerts in 1978, 8 in 1979.

Kentucky Fair & Exposition Center, Phillips Lane at Freedom Way, P. O. Box 21179, Louisville, KY 40221. 502–366–9592. Owned by Commonwealth of Kentucky. A. C. Chapman, deputy director; Thomas Zimmerman, booking manager.
    Seats 19,400. Tickets normally $7.50 and $8.50. Rent: $2,400 v. 10 percent gross receipts. 22 concerts in 1978, 20-25 in 1979.

Louisville Gardens, 525 West Muhammad Ali Boulevard, Louisville, KY 40202. 502–582–2601. Owned by Jefferson County Fiscal Court; leased to Louisville Gardens. Al Antee, facility and booking manager.
    Seats 6,600. Tickets normally $6.50 and $7.50. Rent: $1,000 v. 10 percent gross receipts. 36 concerts in 1978, 40 in 1979.

Owensboro Sportscenter, Twelfth and Hickman Avenue, Owensboro, KY 42301. 502–683–7347. Owned by City of Owensboro. Cissy Gregson, facility and booking manager.
    Seats 5,600. Tickets normally $3.50-6.50. Rent: $300 v. 10 percent gross receipts. 8 concerts in 1978, 4 in 1979.

LOUISIANA

Hirsch Memorial Coliseum, Louisiana State Fair Grounds, P. O. Box 9100, Shreveport, LA 71109. 318–635–1361. Owned by Louisiana State Fair. Henry M. Sheffield, facility and booking manager.
    Seats 10,359. Tickets normally $7.50 and $8.50. Rent: $1,000 v. 10 percent gross receipts. 26 concerts in 1978, 28 in 1979.

LSU Assembly Center, c/o Louisiana State University, Baton Rouge, LA 70803. 504–388–8205. Owned by Louisiana State University. Dr. William H. Bankhead, facility and booking manager.
    Seats 15,000. Tickets normally $6, $7, $8. Rent: 10 percent gross receipts. 22 concerts in 1978, 20 in 1979.

New Orleans Cultural Center, 1201 St. Peter Street, New Orleans, LA 70116. 504–586–4203. Owned by the City of New Orleans. James Campbell, manager; Pauline B. Morton, coordinator of schedules and booking.
    AUDITORIUM seats 2,700-8,300. THEATRE seats 2,379. Ticket prices vary. Rent: $1,200 v. 10 percent gross receipts. Over 700 "event days" in 1978.

Rapides Parish Coliseum, 5600 Highway 28 West, Alexandria, LA 71301. 318-442-9581. Owned by Rapides Parish. Terry O. Pullig, facility manager; Susen Kerry, booking manager.
    Seats 10,092. Tickets normally $5-8. Rent: $600 v. 10 percent gross receipts. 20 concerts in 1978, 32 in 1979.

Thibodaux Civic Center, P. O. Box 1178, Thibodaux, LA 70301. 504-446-1570. Owned by City of Thibodaux. Candy Clement, facility and booking manager.
    Seats 4,500. Tickets normally $7. Rent: $500 v. 10 percent gross receipts. 14 concerts in 1978, 50 in 1979.

The Warehouse, 1820 Tchoupitoulas Street (mailing address: 323 Dauphine Street, New Orleans, LA 70112). 504-821-8211. Owned by Beaver Productions, Inc. Clayton Faught, facility manager; Barry Leff, booking manager.
    Seats 3,500. Tickets normally $7.50-9.50. Rent: $1,500 v. 10 percent gross receipts. 30 concerts in 1978, 30 in 1979.

MAINE

Augusta Civic Center, Community Drive, Augusta, ME 04330. 207-622-4771. Owned by City of Augusta. Lionel J. Dubay, facility and booking manager.
    Seats 7,240 reserved, 8,000 festival. Tickets normally $7.50 and $8.50. Rent: 10 percent gross receipts. 12 concerts in 1978, 12 in 1979.

Cumberland County Civic Center, One Civic Center Square, Portland, ME 04101. 207-775-3481. Owned by Cumberland County. Jack Nicholson, facility and booking manager.
    Seats 9,300. Tickets normally $6.50, $7.50, $8.50. Rent: $1,500 v. 12½ percent gross receipts. 35 concerts in 1978, 40 in 1979.

MARYLAND

Baltimore Civic Center, 201 West Baltimore Street, Baltimore, MD 21201. 301-837-0903. Owned by City of Baltimore; managed by Hyatt Management Corp. Charles Heustadt, executive director; John Scollan, marekting director.
    ARENA seats 12,420. Tickets normally $5-8.50. Rent: $1,500 v. 12½ percent gross receipts. MINI II seats 6,462. Tickets normally $5-8.50. Rent: $1,500 v. 10 percent gross receipts. MINI I seats 4,312. Tickets normally $5-8.50. Rent: $1,500 v. 8 percent gross receipts. 20 concerts in 1978, 11 in 1979 (as of August).

Capital Centre, 1 Harry S. Truman Drive, Landover, MD 20786. 301-350-3400. Owned by Abe Pollin. Jerry Sachs, president; Pat Darr, director of events.
    Seats 18,787. Tickets normally $7.70-15.60. Rent: $10,000 v. 25 percent gross receipts. 53 concerts in 1978, 59 in 1979.

CONCERT FACILITIES

Cole Field House, c/o University of Maryland, College Park, MD 20742. 301-454-4546. Owned by University of Maryland. Robert Wall, facility manager; Michael Jaworek, booking manager.
    Seats 14,500. Tickets normally $7.50 and $8.50. Rent: 12½ percent gross receipts. 6 concerts in 1978, 24 in 1979.

Towson Center, Towson, MD 21204. 301-321-2743. Owned by Towson State University. Robert L. Riley, Jr., facility manager; David Nevins, booking manager.
    Seats 5,500. Tickets normally $6.50 and $7.50. Rent: $1,200 v. 11½ percent gross receipts. 17 concerts in 1978, 23 in 1979.

MASSACHUSETTS

Berklee Performance Center, 1140 Boylston Street, Boston, MA 02215. 617-266-7455. Owned by Berklee College of Music. James T. Mavrikos, facility and booking manager.
    Seats 1,226. Tickets normally $7.50 and $8.50. Rent: approximately $1,300. 54 concerts in 1978, 60 in 1979.

Boston Garden, Causeway Street, Boston, MA 02114. 617-227-3204. Owned by Sportsystem of Buffalo. Paul A. Mooney, president; Steve Nazro, director of events.
    Seats 15,509. Tickets normally $8.50 and $9.50. Rent: call Steve Nazro. 28 concerts in 1978, 22 in 1979.

Music Hall Theatre, 268 Tremont Street, Boston, MA 02116. 617-423-3300. Owned by New England Medical Center. A. Terban, facility and booking manager.
    Seats 4,225. Tickets normally $9 and $10. Rent: call A. Terban.

The Music Inn, Lenox, MA 01240. 413-637-2200. Owned by New Music Barn, Inc. Al Dotoly, facility manager; Frank J. Russo, booking manager.
    Seats 10,000. Tickets normally $7.50-10.50. Rent: 10 percent gross receipts. 8 concerts in 1979.

New England Life Hall, 225 Clarendon Street, Boston, MA 02117. 617-266-7262 or 617-266-7660. Owned by New England Life Insurance Co. George W. Johnson, facility and booking manager.
    Seats 685. Ticket prices vary. Rent: $275. 20 concerts in 1978, 20 in 1979.

Springfield Civic Center, 1277 Main Street, Springfield, MA 01103. 413-781-7080. Owned by City of Springfield. Kerry P. Felsky, facility manager; Jim Mandrus, assistant facility manager.
    Seats 7,459. Tickets normally $7.50 and $8.50. Rent: $1,000 v. 12½ percent gross receipts. 35 concerts in 1978, 34 in 1979.

MICHIGAN

Aquinas College Fieldhouse, 1607 Robinson Road SE, Grand Rapids, MI 49506. 616–459–8281. Owned by Aquinas College. Terry Bocian, facility director; John J. Nichols, booking manager.
    Seats 4,500-5,000. Tickets normally $5.50, $6.50, $7.50. Rent: $900. 1 concert in 1978, 5 in 1979.

Henry and Edsel Ford Auditorium, 20 Auditorium Drive, Detroit, MI 48226. 313–224–1055. Owned by City of Detroit. Lee I. Schulte, facility manager; Richard M. Zimmerman, booking manager.
    Seats 2,872. Tickets normally $5.50, $6.50, $7.50. Rent: $750 v. 12 percent gross receipts. 230 concerts in 1978, 250 in 1979.

Marquette Lakeview Arena, 301 East Fair Avenue, Marquette MI 49855. 906–228–7530. Owned by City of Marquette. Robert Lister, facility and booking manager.
    Seats 5,400. Tickets normally $6.50 and $7.50. Rent: $500 v. 12 percent gross receipts. 30 concerts in 1978, 30 in 1979.

Masonic Temple Auditorium, 500 Temple Avenue, Detroit, MI 48201. 313–832–7100. Owned by Masonic Temple Association. John Langs, president; Richard Carlson, booking manager.
    Seats 4,865. Tickets normally $6-10. Rent: $1,700 plus 10 percent gross receipts above $15,000. 45 concerts in 1978, 45 in 1979.

Orchestra Hall/The Paradise Theater, 3711 Woodward, Detroit, MI 48201. 313–833–3700. Owned by Save Orchestra Hall, Incorporated. Sandor Kallai, executive director; Harold West, booking manager.
    Seats 1,100 (2,200 after restoration is completed). Tickets normally $5-9. Rent: $500-650 plus 6 percent net receipts. 100 concerts in 1978, 125 in 1979.

Pontiac Silverdome, 1200 Featherstone, Pontiac, MI 48057. 313–857–7700. Owned by City of Pontiac. Charles H. McSwigan, Jr., executive director; Gerald W. Baron, director of promotions and publicity.
    Seats 15,000-76,000. Tickets normally $8-12.50. Rent: call Gerald W. Baron. 8 concerts in 1978, 5 in 1979.

Saginaw Civic Center, 303 Johnson Street, Saginaw, MI 48607. 517–776–1320. Owned by City of Saginaw. Sid Morse, facility and booking manager.
    Seats 7,200. Tickets normally $8 or $8.50. Rent: $950 v. 10 percent gross receipts. 36 concerts in 1978, 20 in 1979 (through August).

MINNESOTA

Duluth Arena-Auditorium, 350 South 5 Avenue West, Duluth, MN 55802. 218-722-5573. Owned by City of Duluth. Joseph C. Sturckler, facility manager; Joyce Benedict, booking manager.
    ARENA seats 8,000. Tickets normally $6-8.50. Rent: $850 v. 12 percent gross receipts. AUDITORIUM seats 2,400. Tickets normally $6-8.50. Rent: $700 v. 10 percent gross receipts. 18 concerts in 1978, 15 in 1979.

The Guthrie Theater, Vineland Place, Minneapolis, MN 55403. 612-377-2824. Owned by The Guthrie Theater Foundation. Donald M. Schoenbaum, facility manager; Dennis A. Babcock, booking manager.
    Seats 1,441. Tickets normally $7.50 and $8.50. Rent: contact Dennis A. Babcock—available only to nonprofit organizations. 30 concerts in 1978, 40 in 1979.

Mayo Civic Auditorium Arena, 30 SE Second Avenue, P. O. Box 895, Rochester, MN 55901. 507-288-8475. Owned by City of Rochester. Cal Smith, facility and booking manager.
    Seats 4,000. Tickets normally $3.50-7.50. Rent: $550.

Met Center, 7901 Cedar Avenue South, Bloomington, MN 55420. 612-854-4411. Owned by State of Minnesota; operated by Northstar Financial Corp. Bob Reid, facility and booking manager.
    Variable seating: 5,000-7,550—10,000—17,000. Tickets normally $7.50 and $8.50. Rent: $1,000-6,000. 21 concerts in 1978, 35-40 in 1979.

Minneapolis Auditorium & Convention Hall, 1403 Stevens Avenue South, Minneapolis, MN 55403. 612-870-4436. Owned by City of Minneapolis. Gary Dorrian, facility and booking manager.
    Seats 8,686. Tickets normally $6.50-8.50. Rent: $950 v. 10 percent gross receipts. 15 concerts in 1978, 12 in 1979.

Northrop Memorial Auditorium, 84 Church Street SE, Minneapolis, MN 55455. 612-376-8378. Owned by University of Minnesota. Dale Schatzlein, facility and booking manager.
    Seats 4,810. Tickets normally $7.50, $8.50, $9.50. Rent: $1,500 v. 10 percent gross receipts. 20 concerts in 1978, 25 in 1979.

Orchestra Hall, 1111 Nicolett Mall, Minneapolis, MN 55403. 612-371-5600. Owned by Minnesota Orchestra Association. Jeff Prauer, operations manager; Russ Bursch, artistic administrator; Kim Holmberg, hall facilities administrator.
    Seats 2,543. Tickets normally $4-10. Rent: $1,200 v. 10 percent gross receipts. 51 concerts in 1978, 51 in 1979.

Orpheum Theater, 910 Hennepin Avenue, Minneapolis, MN 55403. 612-338-7968. Owned by Orpheum Theater Corporation. Gary Tassone, facility manager; Fred Krohn, booking manager.
    Seats 2,769. Tickets normally $7.50, $8.50, $9.50. Rent: unavailable to outside promoters. No concerts in 1978, 8 in 1979.

St. Paul Civic Center, I. A. O'Shaughnessy Plaza, St. Paul, MN 55102. 612-224-7361. Owned by City of St. Paul. John Friedmann, director; Russ Grimes, deputy director.
    Seats 5,000-17,500. Tickets normally $6-15. Rent: $2,000 v. 10 percent gross receipts. 49 concerts in 1978, 20 in 1979.

MISSISSIPPI

Humphrey Coliseum, P. O. Drawer HY, Mississippi State, MS 39762. 601-325-2743. Owned by Mississippi State University. Gaddis Hunt, facility manager; Michael Marion, booking manager.
    Seats 11,000. Tickets normally $5-9. Rent: $2,000-5,000. 12 concerts in 1978, 12 in 1979.

Mississippi Coast Coliseum and Convention Center, 3800 West Beach Boulevard, P. O. Box 4676, Biloxi, MS 39531. 601-388-8010. Owned by State of Mississippi and Harrison County. W. Gene Lambert, facility manager; W. Gene Lambert and William F. Holmes, booking managers.
    Seats 11,517 reserved, 14,000 festival. Tickets normally $7.50-12.50. Rent: $1,500 v. 10 percent gross receipts. 30 concerts in 1978, 40 in 1979.

MISSOURI

Arrowhead Stadium, 1 Arrowhead Drive, Kansas City, MO 64129. 816-924-9300. Owned by Jackson County Taxpayers. Bob Wachter, facility manager; Russ Cline, booking manager.
    Seats 60,000. Tickets normally $12 and $15. Rent: 15 percent gross receipts. 3 concerts in 1978, 2 in 1979.

Checkerdome, 5700 Oakland Avenue, St. Louis, MO 63110. 314-644-0900. Owned by Ralston Purina Co. Charles G. Mancuso, facility and booking manager.
    Seats 19,230. Tickets normally $7.50 and $8.50. Rent: 13 percent gross receipts. 18 concerts in 1978, 34 in 1979.

Kansas City Convention Center, 301 West 13 Street, Kansas City, MO 64105. 816-421-8000. Owned by City of Kansas City. Jim Abel, facility and booking manager.
    MUNICIPAL AUDITORIUM seats 9,200. Tickets normally $4-15. Rent: $1,000 plus 12½ percent gross receipts above $10,000. MUSIC HALL seats 2,500. Tickets normally $4-15. Rent: $400 v. 9 percent gross receipts. 34 concerts in 1978, 27 in 1979.

Kemper Arena, 1800 Genessee Street, Kansas City, MO 64102. 816-421-6460. Owned by City of Kansas City. Stephen Scherbenske, facility manager; Robert Hodge, assistant facility manager.
    Seats 17,614. Tickets normally $7.50-12. Rent: $3,500 v. 12 percent gross receipts.

Jack Lawton Webb Convention Center, 5400 South Range Line Road, Joplin, MO 64801. 417-781-4000. Owned by Jack Lawton Webb, Jr. Joe H. Burtrum, Jr., facility manager; Jack Lawton Webb, Jr. or Joe H. Burtrum, Jr., booking managers.
    Seats 3,000. Tickets normally $2-10. Rent: $500. 36 concerts in 1978, 36 in 1979.

Memorial Hall, 212 West 8 Street, Joplin, MO 64801. 417-623-3254. Owned by City of Joplin. Clarke Johnson, facility and booking manager.
    Seats 3,000. Tickets normally $7 and $8. Rent: $305. 23 concerts in 1978, 23 in 1979.

Royal Stadium, P. O. Box 1969, Kansas City, MO 64129. 816-921-8000. Owned by Jackson County Taxpayers. Herk Robinson, facility and booking manager.
    Seats 40,000. Tickets normally $12 and $15. Rent: 15 percent gross receipts. 2 concerts in 1978, 2 in 1979.

NEBRASKA

Omaha Civic Auditorium, 1804 Capitol Avenue, Omaha, NE 68102. 402-346-1323. Owned by City of Omaha. Terry G. Forsberg, facility and booking manager.
    Seats 11,300. Tickets normally $7.50, $8.50, $9.50. Rent: 10 percent gross receipts. 60 concerts in 1978, 65 in 1979.

NEVADA

Pioneer Theater Auditorium, 100 South Virginia Street, P. O. Box 837, Reno, NV 89504. 702-786-5105. Owned by Reno-Sparks Convention Authority. Bob Thornbury, facility manager; Norma Gasser, booking manager.
    Seats 1,428. Tickets normally $3.50-7.50. Rent: $430 v. 10 percent gross receipts. 78 concerts in 1978, 85 in 1979.

NEW JERSEY

The Capitol Theatre, 326 Monroe Street, Passaic, NJ 07055. 201-778-2888. Owned by Capitol Rock, Inc. John Scher, facility and booking manager.
    Seats 3,247. Tickets normally $7.50, $8.50, $9.50. Rent: call John Scher. 50 concerts in 1978, 50 in 1979.

Garden State Arts Center, Box 116, Holmdel, NJ 07733. 201-264-9039. Owned by New Jersey Highway Authority. John Larson, general manager.
   Seats 9,500. Tickets normally $4.50-9.50. Rent: call John Larson. 68 concerts in 1978, 68 in 1979.

Giants Stadium, c/o New Jersey Sports Complex—The Meadowlands, East Rutherford, NJ 07073. 201-935-8500. Owned by New Jersey Sports and Exposition Authority. Robert G. Harter, executive director; Loris F. Smith, general manager.
   Seats 65,000. Ticket prices vary. Rent: $25,000 v. 15 percent gross receipts. 3 concerts in 1978, 2 in 1979.

NEW YORK

Brooklyn Academy of Music, Inc., 30 Lafayette Avenue, Brooklyn, NY 11217. 212-636-4100. Owned by City of New York. Harvey Lichtenstein, president; John Miller, booking manager.
   OPERA HOUSE seats 2,000. Tickets normally $5.50, $7.50, $10.50. Rent: $4,000-4,500. PLAYHOUSE seats 1,078. Tickets normally $5.50, $7.50, $10.50. Rent: $3,000-3,500. LEPERCQ SPACE seats 600. Tickets normally $5.50, $7.50, $10.50. Rent: $2,000-2,500. 8 concerts in 1978, 6 in 1979.

Broome County Veterans Memorial Arena, One Stuart Place, Binghamton, NY 13902. 607-772-2611. Owned by Broome County. Paul Gamsby, facility and booking manager.
   Seats 7,200. Ticket prices vary. Rent: $1,250 v. 12½ percent gross receipts. 122 concerts in 1978, 130 in 1979.

Buffalo Convention Center, Convention Center Plaza, Buffalo, NY 14202. 716-855-5555. Owned by City of Buffalo. Glenn Arnette III, director; Nita Lineberger, deputy director and booking manager.
   Seats 8,000. Tickets normally $4, $5, $6, $7. Rent: $1,000 v. 10 percent gross receipts. 5 concerts in 1978, 10 in 1979.

Buffalo Memorial Auditorium, Main and Terrace Streets, Buffalo, NY 14202. 716-856-4200, ext. 364. Owned by City of Buffalo. Joseph D. Figliola, facility and booking manager.
   Seats 18,100. Tickets normally $8 and $9. Rent: $1,000 v. 12½ percent gross receipts. 35 concerts in 1978, 40 in 1979.

Carnegie Hall/Carnegie Recital Hall, 881 Seventh Avenue, New York, NY 10019. 212-397-8750. Owned by City of New York. George Cree, house manager; Gilda Weissberger, booking manager.
   MAIN HALL seats 2,800. Tickets normally $4-20. Rent: $1,625. RECITAL HALL seats 250. Tickets normally $4-20. Rent: $275. 312 concerts during 1978-79 season.

CONCERT FACILITIES

City Center, 131 West 55 Street, New York, NY 10019. 212-247-0430. Owned by City of New York. Gail Harper, executive director; Ting Barrow, associate director.
    Seats 2,932. Tickets normally $8-15. Rent: varies.

Civic Center of Onondaga County, 411 Montgomery Street, Syracuse, NY 13202. 315-425-2155. Owned by County of Onondaga. Joseph Golden, booking manager; Carol T. Jeschke, booking manager.
    Seats 2,117. Tickets normally $6.50-10.50. Rent: $1,200. 100 concerts in 1978, 150 in 1979.

Dome Center—Monroe County Fair & Recreation Association, Inc., Box 22848, Rochester, NY 14692. 716-334-4000. Owned by Monroe County Fair & Recreation Association, Inc. G. Robert Alhart, facility and booking manager.
    Seats 4,700 reserved, 5,600 festival. Tickets normally $7.50, $8.50, $9.50. Rent: $1,000 v. 12 percent gross receipts. 13 concerts in 1978, 15 in 1979.

Entermedia Theatre, 187 Second Avenue, New York, NY 10003. 212-777-6230. Owned by Entermedia Inc. Joseph Asaro, executive director and booking manager.
    Seats 1,143. Tickets normally $5-12. Rent: $2,000-2,500 v. 20-25 percent gross receipts. 30 concerts in 1978, 75 in 1979.

Avery Fisher Hall, Lincoln Center Plaza, New York, NY 10023. 212-580-8700. Owned by Lincoln Center for the Performing Arts, Inc. Delmar D. Hendricks, booking manager.
    Seats 2,720. Ticket prices vary. Rent: $1,900-2,250.

Madison Square Garden Center, 4 Penn Plaza, New York, NY 10001. 212-563-8000. Owned by Madison Square Garden Corp. Michael Burke, president; Robert Franklin, booking manager.
    Seats 19,680. Tickets normally $8.50-12.50. Rent: call Robert Franklin. 47 concerts in 1978, 60 in 1979.

Max's Kansas City, 213 Park Avenue South at 17 Street, New York, NY 10003. 212-777-7870. Owned by Tommy and Laura Dean. Ivan Bernstein, facility manager; Peter Crowley, booking manager.
    Seats 250. Tickets normally $4-6. Rent: flat fee or percentage. 300 concerts in 1978, 300 in 1979.

Palladium, 126 East 14 Street, New York, NY 10003. 212-249-8870. Ron Delsener, facility and booking manager.
    Seats 3,387. Tickets normally $7.50 and $8.50. Rent varies. 70 concerts in 1978, 70 in 1979.

Radio City Music Hall Entertainment Center, 1260 Avenue of the Americas, New York, NY 10020. 212-246-4600. Owned by Rockefeller Center, Inc. Robert F. Jans, president, Nance Slemmons, booking manager.
    Seats 5,883. Tickets normally $8.50-15. Rent: call Nance Slemmons. 6 concerts in 1978, 6 in 1979.

Rochester Community War Memorial, 100 Exchange Street, Rochester, NY 14614. 716–546–2030. Owned by City of Rochester. Bernard A. Hoepfl, facility and booking manager.
    Seats 9,200. Tickets normally $6.50, $7.50, $8.50. Rent: $3,000 v. 15 percent gross receipts. 70 concerts in 1978, 75 in 1979.

Utica Memorial Auditorium, 400 Oriskany Street West, Utica, NY 13502. 315–798–3356. Owned by City of Utica. Joseph P. Critelli, facility and booking manager.
    Seats 6,000. Tickets normally $7.50 and $8.50. Rent: $425 v. 12 percent gross receipts. 12 concerts in 1978, 24 in 1979.

NORTH CAROLINA

Greensboro Coliseum Complex, 1921 West Lee Street, Greensboro, NC 27403. 919–294–2140. Owned by City of Greensboro. James F. Oshust, facility and booking manager.
    Seats 15,800. Tickets normally $7-10. Rent: $2,500 v. 12 percent gross receipts. 35 concerts in 1978, 30-35 in 1979.

OHIO

Blossom Music Center, 1145 West Steels Corners Road, Cuyahoga Falls, OH 44223. 216–929–3048. Owned by Music Arts Association. J. Christopher Fahlman, facility and booking manager.
    Seats 18,140. Tickets normally $6-9. Self-promoted facility—not available for rental. 65 concerts in 1978, 65 in 1979.

Cincinnati Music Hall, 1243 Elm Street, Cincinnati, OH 45210. 513–621–1919. Owned by City of Cincinnati. David P. Curry, facility and booking manager.
    Seats 3,631. Tickets normally $5.50-9.50. Rent: $2,200. 30 concerts in 1978, 25-35 in 1979.

The Coliseum in Richfield, 2923 Streetsboro Road, Richfield, OH 44286. 216–659–9100. Owned by Sanford Greenburg. Stuart Giller, president; Robbie Braessler, booking director.
    Seats 20,000. Tickets normally $8 and $9. Rent: call Robbie Braessler. 45 concerts in 1978, 50 in 1979.

Akron Civic Theatre, 182 South Main Street, Akron, OH 44308. 216–535–3178. Owned by Community Hall Foundation, Inc. Randall J. Hemming, facility and booking manager.
    Seats 2,918. Tickets normally $7 and $8. Rent: $1,000 v. 12 percent gross receipts. 25 concerts in 1978, 50 in 1979.

Ohio Theatre, 29 East State Street, Columbus, OH 43215. 614–469–1045. Owned by Columbus Association for the Performing Arts. Donald R. Streibig, facility and booking manager.
    Seats 2,897. Tickets normally $10 and $12. Rent: $1,100. 20 concerts in 1978, 28 in 1979.

H. H. Stambaugh Auditorium, 1000 Fifth Avenue, Youngstown, OH 44504. 216–747–5175. Owned by H. H. Stambaugh Auditorium Association. William E. Melody, facility and booking manager.
    Seats 2,600. Tickets normally $6, $8, $9. Rent: $500.

Toledo Masonic Auditorium, 4645 Heather Downs Boulevard, Toledo, OH 43614. 419–381–8851. Robert S. Moffat, facility and booking manager.
    Seats 2,520. Ticket prices vary. Rent: $1,050.

OKLAHOMA

Comanche County Fairgrounds, c/o Great Plains Coliseum, 920 South Sheridan Road, P. O. Box 584, Lawton, OK 73501. 405–357–1483. Owned by County of Lawton. Ronnie Rimer, facility and booking manager.
    Seats 3,500. Tickets normally $5. Rent: $400 v. 10 percent gross receipts. 13 concerts in 1978, 15 in 1979.

Mabee Center, 8100 South Lewis, Tulsa, OK 74171. 918–492–7545. Owned by Oral Roberts University. Dexter King, facility manager; Collinn Steele, booking manager.
    Seats 11,575. Tickets normally $6.50-15. Rent: $1,500 v. 10 percent gross receipts. 47 concerts in 1978, 65 in 1979.

Muskogee Civic Assembly Center, 425 Boston, Muskogee, OK 74401. 918–682–9131. Owned by City of Muskogee. Ron Hendrix, facility manager; Betty Wolfe, booking manager.
    Seats 3,710. Tickets normally $4-8. Rent: $330 v. 10 percent gross receipts.

Myriad Convention Center, 1 Myriad Gardens, Oklahoma City, OK 73102. 405–232–8871. Owned by City of Oklahoma City. John Ziegler, executive director.
    Seats 15,600. Tickets normally $7.50-15. Rent: $1,200 v. 12½ percent gross receipts.

Tulsa Performing Arts Center, Second and Cincinnati, Tulsa, OK 74103. 918–581–5641. Owned by City of Tulsa. Terry L. Schell, facility manager; Robert Mayer, booking manager.
    Seats 2,450. Tickets normally $4-10. Rent: $1,000 v. 10 percent gross receipts ($1,400 maximum). 29 concerts in 1978, 35 in 1979.

OREGON

Memorial Coliseum Complex, P. O. Box 2746, Portland, OR 97208. 503–235–8771. Owned by City of Portland. Richard C. Reynolds, general manager; Tim A. Parrott, sales/public relations manager.
    Seats 13,000. Tickets normally $7-15. Rent: $1,500 v. 12 percent gross receipts. 18 concerts in 1978, 25 in 1979.

Paramount Theatre, 1037 SW Broadway, Portland, OR 97205. 206–682–1414 (business phone in Seattle, WA). Owned by West Coast Theatre Corporation. Michael McManus, facility manager; Claudia Redner, leasing director.
    Seats 2,958. Tickets normally $7, $8, $9. Rent: $1,000 v. 10 percent gross receipts. 125 concerts in 1978, 150 in 1979.

PENNSYLVANIA

Academy of Music, Broad and Locust Streets, Philadelphia, PA 19102. 215–893–1935. Owned by Philadelphia Orchestra Association. Hugh F. Walsh, Jr., facility and booking manager.
    Seats 2,929. Tickets normally $6.50, $8.50, $9.50, $10.50. Rent: $1,750. 100 concerts in 1978, 100 in 1979.

Agricultural Hall, Chew and 17 Streets, Allentown, PA 18104. 215–433–7541. Owned by Lehigh County Agricultural Society. Martin H. Ritter, facility and booking manager.
    Seats 5,000. Tickets normally $7.50 and $8.50. Rent: $1,200 v. 5 percent gross receipts. 4 concerts in 1978, 4 in 1979.

Civic Arena, Gate 8 Auditorium Place, Pittsburgh, PA 15219. 412–391–4545. Owned by Public Auditorium Authority of Pittsburgh and Allegheny County. Charles W. Strong, facility manager; Jack Mathison, booking manager.
    Seats 17,735. Tickets normally $6.50-8.75. Rent: $2,500 v. 12½ percent gross receipts. 36 concerts in 1978, 36 in 1979.

Hersheypark Arena, Hershey, PA 17033. 717–534–3900. Owned by HERCO Inc. Paul L. Serff, general manager; Cyril J. Little, entertainment and booking manager.
    Seats 6,700-10,000. Tickets normally $6, $7, $8. Rent: $2,000 v. 12½ percent gross receipts. 10 concerts in 1978, 15 in 1979.

John F. Kennedy Stadium, Broad Street and Terminal Avenue, Philadelphia, PA 19148. 215–561–5100, ext. 84200. Owned by City of Philadelphia. Joel Ralph, facility and booking manager.
    Seats 90,000. Tickets normally $12.50. Rent: $100,000 per day. 2 concerts in 1978, none in 1979.

Philadelphia Civic Center, Civic Center Boulevard at 34 Street, Philadelphia, PA 19104. 215–823–7031. Owned by Department of Commerce, City of Philadelphia. John Pierron, facility manager; Francis Herbert, booking manager.

    CONVENTION HALL seats 11,500. Tickets normally $8, $10.50, $12.50. Rent: $1,500 v. 12 percent gross receipts. PENNSYLVANIA HALL seats 4,500. Tickets normally $8, $10.50, $12.50. Rent: $1,200 v. 12 percent gross receipts. 5 concerts in 1978, 6 in 1979.

Spectrum, Philadelphia, PA 19148. 215–336–3600. Privately owned facility. Allen B. Flexer, president; Steve Greenberg, vice president of productions; Mich Sauers, director of productions.

    Seats 19,500. Tickets normally $6.50, $7.50, $8.50, $9.50. Rent: call Mich Sauers. 57 concerts in 1978, more than 60 in 1979.

Stanley Theatre, 207 Seventh Street, Pittsburgh, PA 15222. 412–261–2800. Owned by Stanley Theatre Corp. Gene Ciavarra, facility and booking manager.

    Seats 3,500. Tickets normally $7.75-12.75. Rent: $1,500-3,500 v. 10 percent net receipts. 115 concerts in 1978, 55 in 1979.

Three Rivers Stadium, 700 Stadium Circle, Pittsburgh, PA 15212. 412–323–5000. Owned by Stadium Authority of the City of Pittsburgh. Walter E. Golby, facility and booking manager.

    Seats 55,000-60,000. Tickets normally $10-12.50. Rent: 10 percent gross receipts. 1 concert in 1978, none in 1979 due to field repair.

Tower, Theatre, South 69 Boulevard and Ludlow Street, Upper Darby, PA 19082. 215–352–0313. Owned by Electric Factory Concerts. Sid Payne, facility manager; Larry Magid, booking manager.

    Seats 3,000. Tickets normally $4.50-8.50. Rent: call Larry Magid.

RHODE ISLAND

Leroy Concert Theatre, 66 Broad Street, Pawtucket, RI 02840. 401–723–4745. Owned by Associates Realty, Inc. Al Dotoly, facility manager; Frank J. Russo, booking manager.

    Seats 2,400. Tickets normally $7.50 and $8.50. Rent: $1,250. 27 concerts in 1978, 30 in 1979.

Ocean State Performing Arts Center, 220 Weybosset Street, Providence, RI 02903. 401–421–2997. Owned by O.S.P.A.C., Inc. T. E. Stevens, facility and booking manager.

    Seats 3,232. Tickets normally $8, $10, $12. Rent: call T. E. Stevens. 5 concerts in 1978, 30 in 1979.

Providence Civic Center, One LaSalle Square, Providence, RI 02903. 401–331–0700. Owned by City of Providence. Charles J. Toomey, facility and booking manager.

    Seats 13,500. Tickets normally $8.50 and $9.50. Rent: $3,000 v. 12½ percent gross receipts. 60 concerts in 1978, 60 in 1979.

SOUTH CAROLINA

Carolina Coliseum, P. O. Box 11515, Columbia, SC 29211. 803-777-5113. Owned by University of South Carolina. Robert Horning, facility and booking manager.
　　Seats 12,800. Tickets normally $6.50-15. Rent: 12 percent gross receipts. 35 concerts in 1978, 38 in 1979.

Spartanburg Memorial Auditorium, 385 North Church Street, P. O. Box 1410, Spartanburg, SC 29304. 803-582-8107. Publicly owned. G. Michael Abington, facility and booking manager.
　　Seats 3,406. Tickets normally $4.50-8.50. Rent: $450 v. 10 percent gross receipts. 17 concerts in 1978, 17 in 1979.

Textile Hall, P. O. Box 5823, Greenville, SC 29606. 803-233-2562. Owned by Textile Hall Corporation. Ronald D. Plemmons, facility manager; Butler B. Mullins, booking manager.
　　Seats 4,000. Ticket prices vary. Rent: $750-1,000. No concerts in 1978, none in 1979.

The Township, 1703 Taylor Street, Columbia, SC 29201. 803-252-2032. Owned by Richland County. Lee Herbert, executive director; Lee Herbert, J. R. Felts, and Maryjac Adams, booking managers.
　　Seats 3,200. Tickets normally $5-8. Rent: $450 v. 10 percent gross receipts. 200 concerts in 1978, more than 250 in 1979.

SOUTH DAKOTA

Rushmore Plaza Civic Center, 444 Mt. Rushmore Road, Rapid City, SD 57701. 605-394-4115. Owned by City of Rapid City. Joe Floreano, facility and booking manager.
　　ARENA seats 11,219. Tickets normally $7 and $8. Rent: $850-4,000. THEATER seats, 1,774. Tickets normally $7 and $8. Rent: $500 v. 5 percent gross receipts. 21 concerts in 1978, 25 in 1979.

Sioux Falls Arena, 1201 West Avenue North, Sioux Falls, SD 57104. 605-336-3711. Owned by City of Sioux Falls. Bob Kunkel, facility and booking manager.
　　Seats 8,000. Tickets normally $7.50 and $8.50. Rent: $750 plus 5 percent adjusted gross receipts. 30 concerts in 1978, 30 in 1979.

TENNESSEE

Freedom Hall Civic Center, P. O. Box 3826 CRS, Johnson City, TN 37601. 615-929-1171. Owned by City of Johnson City. Lynn M. Jantuolo, facility and booking manager.
　　Seats 8,500. Tickets normally $7 and $8. Rent: $1,800 v. 11 percent gross receipts. 3 concerts in 1978, 3 in 1979.

Jackson Civil Center, 400 South Highland Avenue, Jackson, TN 38301. 901–423–9404. Owned by City of Jackson, Tennessee. William J. Gist, facility and booking manager.

Seats 2,200. Tickets normally $7. Rent: $700-1,200 v. 5 percent gross receipts. 6 concerts in 1978, 10 in 1979.

Mid-South Coliseum, Mid-South Fairgrounds, Memphis, TN 38104. 901–274–3982. Owned by City and County of Memphis. Edward E. Bland, facility and booking manager.

Seats 12,000. Tickets normally $6, $7, $8. Rent: $1,200 v. 12 percent gross receipts. 58 concerts in 1978, 18 in 1979 (as of June).

Nashville Municipal Auditorium, 417 Fourth Avenue North, Nashville, TN 37219. 615–259–5367. Owned by Metropolitan Government of Davidson County. Robert E. Highsmith, facility manager; Robert C. Skoney, assistant manager.

Seats 9,654. Tickets normally $6.50, $7.50, $8.50. Rent: $1,000 v. 12½ percent gross receipts. 32 concerts in 1978, 45 in 1979.

TEXAS

Amarillo Civic Center, P. O. Box 1971, Amarillo, TX 79186. 806–378–3000, ext. 2145. Owned by City of Amarillo. David DeWald, facility manager; Millie Goodson, booking manager.

COLISEUM seats 7,037. AUDITORIUM seats 2,434. Tickets normally $7 and $8. Rent: call Millie Goodson. 25 concerts in 1978, 30 in 1979.

Astrodome, P. O. Box 288, Houston, TX 77001. 713–749–9500. Privately owned. Jimmie D. Fore, executive vice president and booking manager for non-baseball events.

ASTRODOME seats 66,000. Ticket prices vary. Rent: $12,500 v. 17½ percent gross receipts. ASTROARENA seats 8,000. Ticket prices vary. Rent: $1,500 v. 10 percent gross receipts. 1 concert in 1978, 1 in 1979.

Celebrity Circle Theatre, 7326 Southwest Freeway, Houston, TX 77074. 713–626–3520. Owned by Texas Limited Partnership. Diane Smith, facility manager; George Apolzon, booking manager.

Seats 2,860. Tickets normally $8.75 and $9.75. Rent: $500. 2 concerts in 1979.

Corpus Christi Memorial Coliseum & Exposition Hall, 402 South Shoreline Drive, Corpus Christi, TX 78048. 512–884–8228. Owned by City of Corpus Christi. Charles D. Randall, facility and booking manager.

Seats 6,000. Tickets normally $6.50-8. Rent: $345 v. 10 percent gross receipts. 13 concerts in 1978, 9 in 1979 (through July).

Cotton Bowl, Fair Park, Dallas, TX 75226. 214–565–9931. Owned by City of Dallas; operated by State Fair of Texas. Arthur Hale, facility manager; Bob Halford, booking manager.

Seats 72,000-82,000. Tickets normally $3-15. Rent: $20,000-30,000 v. 15 percent gross receipts. 6 concerts in 1978, 4 in 1979.

CONCERT FACILITIES 675

Dallas Convention Center, 650 South Griffin, Dallas, TX 75202. 214-658-7000. Owned by City of Dallas, J. M. Barshop, director.
> ARENA seats 9,816. Tickets normally $6-9. Rent: $1,500 v. 10 percent gross receipts (maximum $5,000). THEATER seats 1,770. Tickets normally $6-9. Rent: $500. 50 concerts in 1978, 50 in 1979.

El Paso County Coliseum, Piasano and Boone Street, P. O. Box 10697, El Paso, TX 79997. 915-543-2961. Owned by County of El Paso. Robert C. Skinner, facility manager; Pamela Haynes, booking manager.
> Seats 10,500. Tickets normally $6.50-8. Rent: $350 v. 5 percent gross receipts. 30 concerts in 1978, 50 in 1979.

Houston Civic Center, 615 Louisiana, P. O. Box 61469, Houston, TX 77208. 713-222-3561. Owned by City of Houston. Jerry Lowery, director; Ruby Black, booking supervisor.
> COLISEUM seats 12,000. Tickets normally $8.50-12.50. Rent: $1,200. MUSIC HALL seats 3,005. Tickets normally $8.50-12.50. Rent: $700. 67 concerts in 1978, 23 in 1979 (through June).

Laurie Auditorium, c/o Trinity University, 715 Stadium Drive, San Antonio, TX 78284. 512-736-8119. Owned by Trinity University. John McFadden, facility and booking manager.
> Seats 2,965. Tickets normally $5-10. Rent: $750. 50 concerts in 1978, 50 in 1979.

Lubbock Memorial Civic Center, 1501 Sixth Street, Lubbock, TX 79413. 806-762-6411. Owned by City of Lubbock. Dottie Townsend, facility and booking manager.
> EXHIBIT HALL seats 5,047. Tickets normally $5.50-8.50. Rent: $850 v. 10 percent gross receipts. THEATRE seats 1,400. Tickets normally $5.50-8.50. Rent: $450 v. 10 percent gross receipts. 15 concerts in 1978, approximately 20 in 1979.

Memorial Auditorium, 1300 Seventh Street, Wichita Falls, TX 76307. 817-322-5611, ext. 206. Owned by City of Wichita Falls. Donald M. Burkman, facility manager.
> Seats 2,717. Tickets normally $6.50 and $7.50. Rent: $750 for one performance, $950 for two performances. 80 concerts in 1978, 80 in 1979.

Paramount Theatre for the Performing Arts, 713 Congress, Austin, TX 78701. 512-472-5411. Owned by Paramount Theatre, Inc. Frederick C. Jarmon, facility manager; John Bernardoni, booking manager.
> Seats 1,319. Tickets normally $6.50 and $7.50. Rent: $500. 40 concerts in 1978, 5 in 1979 (closed for restoration).

Reunion Arena, c/o Dallas Chamber of Commerce, 1507 Pacific Avenue, Dallas, TX 75201. 214-651-1020. Owned by City of Dallas. Jack Beckman, facility manager; Gordon Rea, booking manager.
> Seats 20,000. Ticket prices vary. Rent: $3,500 v. 12 percent gross receipts. Scheduled for April, 1980 opening.

San Antonio Convention Center, Market at Alamo Streets, P. O. Box 1898, San Antonio, TX 78297. 512-225-6351. Owned by City of San Antonio. Francis W. Vickers; Solomon Wolf, booking manager.
    Seats 16,000. Tickets normally $3.50-15. Rent: $4,500.

The Summit, 10 Greenway Plaza, Houston, TX 77046. 713-627-9470. Owned by City of Houston. Burnell Cohen, president; Annette Miller, booking manager.
    Seats 17,094. Tickets normally $8.35 and $9.35. Rent: $5,000 v. 17½ percent gross receipts. 52 concerts in 1978, 60 in 1979.

Tarrant County Convention Center, 1111 Houston Street, Fort Worth, TX 76102. 817-332-9222. Owned by Tarrant County Taxpayers. Louis C. Owen, CFE, executive director; Wm. F. Hemphill, CFE, booking manager.
    ARENA seats 13,956. Tickets normally $10. Rent: $1,200 v. 12 percent gross receipts. THEATRE seats 3,054. Tickets normally $8.50. Rent: $700 for one performance, $1,000 for two performances (or all day). 237 concerts in 1978, 279 in 1979.

UTAH

Capitol Theatre—Salt Palace Center, 50 West 200 South, Salt Lake City, UT 84101. 801-535-7916 or 801-535-7912. Owned by Salt Lake County. Douglas S. Borg, general manager; Steven H. Horton, assistant manager and booking director.
    SYMPHONY HALL seats 2,810. Tickets normally $4.50-15.50. Rent: $1,300-1,900. THEATRE seats 1,946. Tickets normally $4.50-15.50. Rent: $700-1,300. 2 concerts in 1978 (facility just opened), 20 in 1979.

VIRGINIA

Hampton Coliseum, 1000 Coliseum Drive, P. O. Box 7309, Hampton, VA 23666. 804-838-5650. Owned by City of Hampton. Andrew D. Greenwell, facility and booking manager.
    Seats 11,111 reserved, 13,800 festival. Tickets normally $7.50, $8.50, $9.50. Rent: $1,200 v. 12 percent gross receipts. 34 concerts in 1978, 35 in 1979.

Mosque Theatre, 6 North Laurel Street, Richmond, VA 23220. 804-780-8226. Owned by City of Richmond. D. Carmen Barefoot, facility and booking manager.
    Seats 3,732. Tickets normally $6.50 and $7.50. Rent: $500 v. 10 percent gross receipts. 76 concerts in 1978, 58 in 1979.

Roanoke Civic Center, 710 Williamson Road NE, P. O. Box 13005, Roanoke, VA 24030. 703-981-2241. Owned by City of Roanoke. Bob Chapman, facility and booking manager.
    Seats 11,000. Tickets normally $8.50. Rent: $975 v. 12 percent gross receipts. 60 concerts in 1978, 60 in 1979.

Scope Convention Hall, P. O. Box 1808, Norfolk, VA 23501. 804–441–2764. Owned by City of Norfolk. C. E. Bell, facility manager; C. E. Gilbert, booking manager.
> Seats 12,000-13,000. Tickets normally $5-8.50. Rent: $1,500 v. 9 percent gross receipts (maximum $5,000). 33 concerts in 1978, 25 in 1979.

WASHINGTON

The Kingdome, 201 South King Street, Seattle, WA 98104. 206–628–3663. Owned by King County. E. O. Ted Bowsfield, facility manager; Jay Green, booking manager.
> Seats 30,000-70,000. Tickets normally $8-12. Rent: $15,000-25,000 v. 13 percent gross receipts. No concerts in 1978, 1 in 1979.

Paramount Northwest, 901 Pine Street, Seattle, WA 98101. 206–682–1414. Owned by West Coast Theatre Corp. Pat McManus, facility manager; Claudia Redner, leasing director.
> Seats 2,976. Tickets normally $7, $8, $9. Rent: $1,000 v. 10 percent gross receipts. 125 concerts in 1978, 150 in 1979–

Seattle Center, 305 Harrison Street, Seattle, WA 98109. 206–625–4254. Owned by City of Seattle. John W. Fearey, CFE, executive director; Bob Days, booking agent.
> COLISEUM seats 15,000. Tickets normally $5.50-15. Rent: $1,800 v. 12 percent gross receipts. ARENA seats 6,100. Tickets normally $5.50-15. Rent: $900 v. 10 percent gross receipts. 52 concerts in 1978, 60 in 1979.

Spokane Riverpark Center Opera House, W. 334 Spokane Falls Boulevard, Spokane, WA 99201. 509–456–6000. Owned by City of Spokane. Michael D. Kobluk, facility manager; Kevin J. Twohig, booking manager.
> Seats 2,700. Tickets normally $3-13.50. Rent: $950. 100 concerts in 1978, 120 in 1979.

WEST VIRGINIA

Memorial Field House, Fifth Avenue and 26 Street, P. O. Box 5455, Huntington, WV 25703. 304–529–4124. Owned by Cabell County, West Virginia. Glenn Verbage, facility and booking manager.
> Seats 7,200. Tickets normally $6.50 and $7.50. Rent: $600 v. 10 percent gross receipts. 15 concerts in 1978, 15 in 1979.

WISCONSIN

Brown County Veterans Memorial Arena, 1901 South Oneida Street, P. O. Box 3306, Green Bay, WI 54303. 414–494–3404. Owned by Brown County. John Dederich, facility and booking manager.
> Seats 6,532. Tickets normally $7.50 and $8.50. Rent: $1,550 plus 3 percent net receipts. 20 concerts in 1978, 20 in 1979.

Dane County Memorial Coliseum, 1881 Expo Mall East, Madison, WI 53713. 608–257–5681. Owned by Dane County. Roy H. Gumtow, facility manager; Roy H. Gumtow or Joyce Poole, booking managers.

Seats 4,171-10,100. Tickets normally $4.50-9.50. Rent: $2,000-2,700. 36 concerts in 1978, 40-45 in 1979.

Milwaukee Exposition & Convention Center & Arena (MECCA), 500 West Kilbourn Avenue, Milwaukee, WI 53202. 414–271–4000. Owned by City of Milwaukee. Robert O. Ertl, president; Fred A. Muth, vice president operations and booking manager.

ARENA seats 12,100. Tickets normally $7.50 and $8.50. Rent: $2,750 v. 12 percent gross receipts. AUDITORIUM seats 6,100. Tickets normally $7.50 and $8.50. Rent: $1,800 v. 12 percent gross receipts. 25 concerts in 1978, 40 in 1979.

Milwaukee Summerfest Grounds, 200 North Harbor Drive, Milwaukee, WI 53202. 414–273–2680. Owned by City of Milwaukee. James T. Butler, executive director; Robert Babisch, facility manager.

Seats 18,700. Tickets normally $2.50 and $3. Rent: $5,000 v. 10 percent gross receipts. 155 concerts in 1978, 170 in 1979.

Performing Arts Center of Milwaukee, 929 North Water Street, Milwaukee, WI 53202. 414–273–7121. Owned by Milwaukee County. Archie A. Sarazin, managing director.

Seats 2,331. Tickets normally $6.50, $8, $9.50. Rent: $1,172-1,420.

ROCK CLUBS

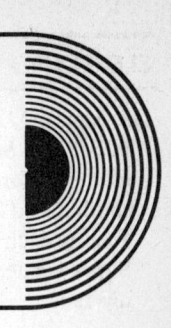

ATLANTA

The Agora, 655 Peachtree. 404–881–1301. Seats 1,296; owned by Hank LoConti. A real good venue for the toned-down, Jackson Browne-type artist. Large and sophisticated.

Great Southeast Music Hall, Broadview Plaza. 404–261–2345. Seats 750; owned by Jack Tarber. Though traditionally a country/country-rock venue for artists like Earl Scruggs and Eric Anderson, Weather Report has played here, too.

The Capri, 3110 Roswell Road. 404–281–9966. Seats 900; owned by Alex Cooley. Excellent sound, spectacular lights, and a bar area that doesn't interfere with what's happening onstage. A fine showcase for a new artist.

BOSTON

The Paradise Club, 967 Commonwealth Avenue. 617–254–2052. Seats 500; booked by Don Law. Very influential venue due to Don Law's power as a promoter in Boston and the Northeast. Suitable for bands from jazz progressive to country.

Passim's, 47 Palmer Street, Cambridge. 617–492–7679. Seats 150; owned by Bob Donlin. Coffeehouse setting for the folk-oriented artist who plays solo piano or guitar, or who has a small backup group.

Modern Theatre, 523 Washington Street. 617–426–8445. Seats 628; booked by David Archer and Bill Packard. Good all-purpose club.

CHICAGO

Park West, West Armitage Avenue. 312–929–5959. Seats 750; owned by Dale Niedermaier; booked by Jam Productions. Beautifully laid-out club which packs a terrific media wallop. Acts that could sell out a 3,000-seater in Chicago would be much better off playing here to a huge turn-away crowd.

B'ginnings, 1227 East Gulf Road, Shaumburg. Seats 1,200. Owned by Danny Seraphine, the drummer in Chicago, this club is a very popular press hang-out.

Gaspar's, 3159 Southport. 312–871–6680. Seats 200; owned by Jim Macnamara. Chicago's intimate "in" spot.

CINCINNATI

Bogart's, 2621 Vine Street. 513–281–8400. Seats 350-600. Owned by Al Porkolab; booked by Cal Levey of Electric Factory Concerts. Particularly good cooperative situation. Clubowner works very closely with the artist's record company, agency, and local WEBN-FM.

CLEVELAND

The Agora, 1730 East 24 Street. 216-696-8833. Seats 1,000; owned by Hank LoConti. Springsteen, Aerosmith, Meat Loaf, and Southside Johnny each broke from the Agora. Super venue, super cooperation, super-hip fans.

DALLAS

The Palladium Ballroom, 6532 East Northwest Highway. 214-363-4455. Seats 800; booked by Jimmy Page, Danny Eaton, and David Hickey. Dyre Straits, Carrs, and Kinks each sold out here. Fine place for medium-priced rock 'n roll bands.

DETROIT

Center Stage, 39940 Ford Road, Canton. 313-455-3010. Seats 1,500; booked by Rick Kay of Brass Ring Productions. Similar to New York's Bottom Line, but three times the size. Used not only for rock groups but as a disco.

DENVER

The Rainbow Music Hall, 6358 East Evan. 303-753-1252. Seats 1,400; owned by Barry Fey. One of the nicest clubs in the U.S. Clubowner Barry Fey carries a lot of weight at radio stations, and can offer and act a number of other showcase opportunities in the West.

The Blue Note, 116 Pearl, Boulder. 303-443-0523. Seats 300. Good all-purpose club.

DISTRICT OF COLUMBIA

The Cellar Door, 1201 34 Street NW. 202-337-3389. Seats 400; owned by Jack Boyle. Everyone from Cat Stevens to the Cuban group Irakere has played this legendary club. Small, terrific, and the press really turn out here.

The Bayou, 3135 Kaye Street. 202-333-2898. Seats 500; owned by Mike Schriebman. Rather shabby on the inside, this club is used mainly for rock attractions.

HARTFORD

Hard Rock Cafe, 165 Dexter Avenue. 203-246-2602. Seats 1,000 (3,000 with adjoining room open). Used to stage sneak press previews and break in an act's live show. A must club if you're touring the Northeast.

Toad's Place, 300 York Street, New Haven. 203-777-7431. Seats 600; owned by Mike Spoerandle. Good all-purpose club.

HOUSTON

Texas Opry House, 1416 Richmond Avenue. 713-524-4646. Seats 700; owned by Foster and Robert Taylor. Feels like the Bottom Line, but not as nice as the Palladium. The place to play in Houston for medium-priced rockers.

LOS ANGELES

The Roxy, 9009 Sunset Boulevard. 213-878-2222. Seats 500; owned by Elmer Valentine. Good service, quick drinks, and a star-studded audience. When you sell out the Roxy for two consecutive nights, you're ready for great big things in your career.

The Whiskey, 8901 Sunset Boulevard. 213-652-4202. Seats 400; owned by

Elmer Valentine; booked by David Forest. One of the more alert, hip, glitterized, flamboyant crowds anywhere. David Forest makes sure things come off with a special flair.

The Golden Bear, 306 Pacific Coast Highway Huntington Beach. 714–536–3192. Seats 350; owned by Rick Babaraki. Nice place to warm up an act or pick up some extra money before or after playing L.A.

The Starwood, 8151 Santa Monica Boulevard. 213–656–2200. Seats 600; managed by Gary Fontenot; booked by David Night. Terrific kick-in-the-ass club for heavy metal bands and acts like Peter Tosh. Aerosmith played a surprise club date here recently.

The Palomino, 6907 Lankershim Boulevard. 213–765–9256. Seats 400; booked by Tommy Thomas. Basically a country-western and progressive country club, Elvis Costello's recent gig provoked a tremendous media reaction.

MINNEAPOLIS

The Longhorn, 14 South 5 Street. 612–333–8108. Seats 400; owned by Hartley Frank. Boomtown Rats, Rachel Sweet, and Jules & the Polar Bears showcased here.

Thumpers North, 2020 North Dale Boulevard. 612–757–1720. Seats 855.

Thumpers South, 7884 Court House Boulevard. 612–457–2695. Seats 1,800. Owned by Nicky Sezanski; booked by Sue McLean. Good all-purpose clubs.

NASHVILLE

Exit/In, 2208 Elliston Place. 615–327–2784. Seats 248; managed and booked by Jack Denett. Everyone who's important shows up here, including superstars who will jump onstage to jam with their old friends.

NEW YORK

The Bottom Line, 15 West 4 Street. 212–228–6300. Seats 400; Stanley Snadowsky and Alan Pepper, owners. The most important New York media venue. Playing New York's other clubs leads up to this club, where superstardom (e.g., Patti Smith, Bruce Springsteen) can seemingly occur instantaneously.

The Other End, 149 Bleeker Street. 212–745–5120. Seats 200; owned by Paul Colby. Formerly known as the Bitter End. Artists like Steve Forbert have used this venue to develop their audience.

My Father's Place, 19 Bryant Avenue, Roslyn. 516–621–3830. Seats 400; owned by Michael Epstein. Epstein, better known as Eppie, has a fine working relationship with WLIR Radio. Artists play here before they hit N.Y.

Trax, 100 West 72 Street. 212–799–1448. Seating capacity varies. Club-owner Jimmy Pullis, who also owns JP's on First Avenue, features freak-o punk bands one evening and occasional superstars the next. People feel very comfortable here.

Hurrah, 36 West 62 Street. 212–586–2636. Seating capacity varies. Artists like the Knack are featured in addition to rock 'n roll disco. Very freaky crowd with an aggressive young owner who is willing to take chances.

CBGB's, 315 Bowery. 212–473–9763. Seats 350; booked by Hilly Crystal. Tremendously influential club, particularly in the punk/new wave area. Its legendary reputation is well deserved.

ROCK CLUBS

Great Gildersleeves, 331 Bowery. 212-533-3940. Seats 500; owned by Tim Finnegan. A basic rock 'n roll bar-club. Often used to audition a band or see how the act plays in front of an audience.

Le Mudd Club, 77 White Street. Phone number is unlisted. Seating capacity varies; managed by Glenn McDermott. One of the funnier, exciting places in America. Things start cooking around two o'clock in the morning, with unusual happenings as late as daybreak.

PHILADELPHIA

The Bijou, 1409 Lombard Street. 215-735-4444. Seats 250; booked by Larry Magid. Philadelphia's major promoter runs a very classy operation. Preferred place for a new or struggling band to improve its stage show.

Starrs Nightclub, 626 South Second Street. 215-627-8033. Seats 200; owned by Steven Starr. Good all-purpose club.

PHOENIX

Doolie's, 1216 East Appache. 602-968-2448. Seats 650. Similar to the Palladium Ballroom in Dallas. Best local venue before advancing to larger cities.

SAN FRANCISCO

The Boarding House, 960 Bush. 415-441-4333. Seats 280; owned by David Johanson. Doesn't have a liquor license and it's not clean inside, but Steve Martin and the Tubes started there.

The Old Waldorf, 2801 California. 415-921-3050. Seats 600. Bigger club for oversized bands, such as Toto or Dire Straits. Steady hang out of press and radio personnel.

Great American Music Hall, 859 O'Farrell. 415-855-0750. Seats 400. Good all-purpose club.

AA

Park West Club, Chicago

The Bottom Line, New York City

ROCK TRAVEL: 20 MAJOR US CITIES

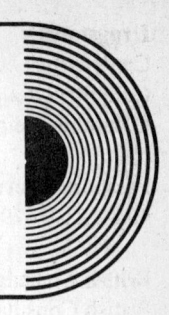

ATLANTA

Airport
Hartsfield International (ATL), 8 miles SW of city

Airlines
Braniff 404–577–7700
Delta 404–765–5000
Eastern 404–435–1111
Frontier 404–523–5487
North Central 404–524–0057
Northwest 404–577–3271
Ozark 404–763–3500
Piedmont 404–681–3100
Sabena 800–645–3790
Southern 404–762–5561
TWA 404–522–5738
United 404–394–2234

Air Freight
Braniff 404–766–1678
Delta 404–765–2851
Eastern 404–432–4281
Frontier 404–768–9105
North Central 404–768–1681
Northwest 404–767–9756
Ozark 404–768–7411
Piedmont 404–766–7879
Sabena 404–524–1151
Southern 404–766–3562
TWA 800–528–0466
United 404–761–8811

Aircraft Charter
Aztec Charter 404–455–3456
Planes Inc. 404–691–7825
Jet Air Inc. 404–892–3166

Bus Charters
Greyhound 404–522–5380
Trailways 404–577–2325

Car Rentals
Avis 404–768–3400
Hertz 404–763–2611
National 404–766–5337

Truck Rentals
Avis 404–351–5330
Hertz 404–938–7691

Train
Amtrack 800–874–2800
Passenger Station—Peachtree Station, 1688 Peachtree NW. 404–872–9815

Package Express
Emery Air Freight 404–762–1611
Federal Express 404–768–8656

Hotels
Peachtree Plaza, Peachtree & International. 404–659–1400
Atlanta Hilton, 255 Courtland Street. 404–659–2000

Drugstores
Can's Drugs 404–938–3144
Colquitt Rexall 404–256–2914
Columbia Heights 404–289–6332

Passport Information
404–221–1479

British Consulate
British Consulate-General
Suite 912, 225 Peachtree Street, NE
Atlanta, GA 30303
404–524–5856

Nearest Australian Consulate
Australian Embassy
1606 Massachusetts Ave.
Washington, D. C. 20036
202–797–3000

American Civil Liberties Union
404–523–5398

AAA
404–875–7171

Suicide Prevention
404–422–0202

VD Information
404–572–2201

Legal Drinking Age
18

Marijuana Laws
0-1 year imprisonment and $1,000 fine for possession of 1 ounce or less; 1-10 years imprisonment for possession or selling more than 1 ounce.

BOSTON

Airport
Logan International (BOS), 3 miles NE of city

Airlines
Aer Lingus 800–223–6270
Air Canada 617–482–4300
Air New England 617–569–5510
Alitalia 617–542–9060
Allegheny 617–482–3160
American 617–542–6700
Braniff 617–423–2100
British Airways 617–426–4105
Caribbean Airways 800–638–5000
Delta 617–567–4100
Eastern 617–262–3700
Lufthansa 800–645–3860
National 617–269–4120
North Central 617–482–4332
Northwest 617–267–4885
Piedmont 617–523–1100
Swissair 800–221–6030
TAP 800–221–2001

TWA 617–742–8800
United 617–482–7900

Air Freight
Aer Lingus 617–569–2434
Air Canada 617–567–4665
Air New England 617–569–4770
Allegheny 617–569–3210
American 617–567–7700
British Airways 617–569–0323
Delta 617–567–7300
Eastern 617–569–3323
El Al 617–267–9220
Japan 617–262–1810
Lufthansa 617–567–4620
National 617–567–7600
Nor East Commuter Airlines 617–569–7880
North Central 617–569–7621
Northwest Orient 617–482–9137
Pan Am 617–569–5460
Qantas 800–227–0290

SAS 800-221-7897
Swissair 617-569-4956
TWA 617-567-4800
United 617-567-4500
World Airways 617-357-9080

Aircraft Charter
Aerotransit 617-777-3250
Boston Air Taxi 617-922-4177
Comerford Airways 617-274-7730

Bus Charters
Greyhound 617-542-4300
Trailways 617-426-5300

Car Rentals
Avis 617-569-3300
Hertz 617-569-5930
National 617-569-6700

Truck Rentals
Avis 617-426-0214
Hertz 617-442-7000

Train
Amtrack 1-800-523-5720

Package Express
Emery Air Freight 617-569-7760
Federal Express 617-274-0250

Hotels
Ritz Carlton, Arlington & Newbury.
  617-536-5700
Copley Plaza, 138 St. James Avenue.
  617-267-5300
Hyatt Cambridge, 575 Memorial Drive,
  Cambridge. 617-492-1234
Treadway Cambridge, 110 Mt. Auburn
  Street, Cambridge. 617-864-5200

Drugstores
Phillips Drug Co. Inc. 617-523-1028
Alan Drug 617-864-7234
Maida Pharmacy Inc. 617-643-7840

Passport Information
617-223-3831

British Consulate
British Consulate—General
Suite 4740, Prudential Tower
Prudential Center
Boston, MA 02199
617-261-3060

Nearest Australian Consulate
Australian Consulate—General
International Building
636 Fifth Avenue
New York, NY 10020
212-245-4000

American Civil Liberties Union
617-742-8020

AAA
617-482-8031

Suicide Prevention
617-247-0220

VD Information
Public Health MA
  617-727-2688

Legal Drinking Age
18

Marijuana Laws
0-6 months imprisonment and $500 fine for possession; 0-2 years imprisonment and $5,000 fine for selling marijuana.

CHICAGO

Airports
O'Hare International (ORD), 19 miles NW of city
Midway (MDW), 10 miles SW of city
Meigs (CGX), 1 mile east of city

Airlines
Aer Lingus 800-223-6292
Air Canada 312-527-3900
Air France 312-782-6181
Air Jamaica 312-527-3923
Air Wisconsin 312-686-7424
Allegheny 312-726-1201
American 312-372-8000
Braniff 312-372-8900
British Airways 312-332-7744
Continental 312-686-6500
Delta 312-346-5300
Eastern 312-467-2900
Frontier 312-236-3790
KLM 312-346-3635
Lufthansa 800-645-3880
Mexicana 800-421-8301
Mississippi Valley 312-686-7400
North Central 312-346-9860
Northwest 312-346-4900
Ozark 312-726-4680
Piedmont 312-263-3656
SAS 800-221-2350
Southern 312-726-6273
Swissair 800-221-6030
TWA 312-332-7600
United 312-569-3000

Air Freight
Aer Lingus 312-686-6010
Air Canada 312-686-3614
Air France 312-686-4521
Air Jamaica 312-686-4558
Air Wisconsin 312-686-7690
Allegheny 312-686-7150
American 312-686-4100
Braniff 312-686-4630
British Airways 312-686-5720
China Airlines 312-686-6850
Continental 312-686-4720
Delta 312-686-4900
Eastern 312-686-5400
Frontier 312-686-6290
KLM 641-5775
Mexicana 312-686-6052
Northwest Orient 312-686-5520
Ozark 312-686-3821
Pan Am 312-686-3760
Piedmont 312-686-4690
Qantas 800-227-0290
SAS 312-686-5900
Seaboard 312-298-1420
Skystream 800-348-2040
Southern Airways 312-686-7086
Swissair 312-686-7335
Trans International 312-332-0411
TWA 312-686-5000
United 312-686-3500
World Airways 312-663-5433

Aircraft Charter
Hartzog Aviation 312-226-5065
Aviation Center Enterprises 312-529-7321
Mid-Continent Air Service 312-284-2313

Bus Charters
Greyhound 312-781-2890
Trailways 312-782-6372

Car Rentals
Avis 312-694-2222
Hertz 312-686-7272
National 312-686-7722

Truck Rentals
Avis 312-427-6184
Hertz 312-489-6200

Train
Amtrack 312-786-1333

Package Express
Emery Air Freight 312-686-7315
Federal Express 312-593-3290

Hotels
Whitall, 105 East Delaware. 312–944–6300
Continental Plaza, 909 North Michigan Avenue. 312–943–7200
Blackstone, 636 South Michigan Avenue. 312–427–4300.
O'Hare Hyatt, 9300 Bryn Mawr, Rosemont. 312–696–1234
Holiday Inn, 644 North Lakeshore Drive. 312–943–9200

Drugstores
Modern Rexall Pharmacy 312–842–5131
Strickland Drugs 312–873–5900
Musket & Henrikson 312–338–8400

Passport Information
312–353–5426

British Consulate
British Consulate—General
33 North Dearborn Street
Chicago, IL 60602
312–346–1810

Australian Consulate
Australian Consulate—General
Suite 2212—One Illinois Centre
111 East Wacker Drive
Chicago, IL 60601
312–329–1740

American Civil Liberties Union
5 South Wabash Avenue, Suite 1516
Chicago, IL
312–236–5564

AAA
Chicago Motor Club 312–372–1818

Suicide Prevention
312–794–3609

VD Information
312–638–3365

Legal Drinking Age
19 for beer and wine, 21 for hard liquor

Marijuana Laws
0-30 days imprisonment and $500 fine for possession of 2.5 grams or less; 0-6 months imprisonment and $500 fine for possession of 2.5-10 grams; 0-1 year imprisonment and $1,000 fine for possession of 10-30 grams; 1-3 years imprisonment and $10,000 fine for possession of 30-500 grams; 1-10 years imprisonment and $10,000 fine for possession of more than 500 grams; 0-6 months imprisonment and $500 fine for selling 2.5 grams or less; 0-1 year imprisonment and $1,000 fine for selling 2.5-10 grams; 1-3 years imprisonment and $10,000 fine for selling 10-30 grams; 1-10 years imprisonment and $10,000 fine for selling 30-500 grams; 1-20 years imprisonment and $10,000 fine for selling more than 500 grams.

CLEVELAND

Airports
Hopkins International (CLE), 12.5 miles SW of city
Lakefront (BKL), 1 mile North of city

Airports
Air Canada 216–861–3757
Allegheny 216–696–8050
American 216–696–8500
Braniff 216–861–2300
Delta 216–781–8800
Eastern 216–861–7300
North Central 216–861–4815
Northwest 216–267–0515
TWA 216–781–2700
United 216–356–1311
Wright 216–781–9500

Air Freight
Air Canada 216–265–6900
Allegheny 216–267–0230
American 216–265–6660
Delta 216–433–4242
Eastern 216–267–3970
North Central 216–267–1585
Northwest 216–265–6565
United 216–267–0135

Aircraft Charter
Air North Inc. 216–621–3166
Sundorph 216–267–3450
Mercury Aviation 216–261–5900

Bus Charters
Greyhound 216–241–6155
Trailways 216–861–3161

Car Rentals
Avis 216–267–3060
Hertz 216–267–8900
National 216–267–0060

Truck Rentals
Avis 216–432–2323
Hertz 216–391–8070

Train
Amtrack 1–800–621–0317
Passenger Station—200 Cleveland Memorial, Shoreway, N.E.
216–696–5115

Package Express
Emery Air Freight 216–243–8805
Federal Express 216–433–1774

Hotels
Swingo's Celebrity Hotel, 1800 Swingo's Center. 216–861–5501
Holiday Inn, 4742 Brecksville Road. 216–659–6151

Drugstores
Cunningham Drug Stores 216–732–8060
Hoefer Drug Company 216–961–3200
Creem-Leader Drug 216–391–6310

Passport Information
216–522–4240

British Consulate
British Consulate-General
1828 Illuminating Building
55 Public Square
Cleveland, OH 44113
216–621–7674

Nearest Australian Consulate
Australian Consulate-General
Suite 2212
One Illinois Centre
111 East Wacker Drive
Chicago, IL 60601
312–329–1740

American Civil Liberties Union
1223 West 6th Street, 2nd Fl.
Cleveland, OH
216–781–6276

AAA
216–881–6000

Suicide Prevention
216–229–4545

VD Information
216–621–2191

Legal Drinking Age
18 for 3.2 percent beer, 21 for 6 percent liquor

Marijuana Laws
$0-100 fine for possession of 100 grams or less; 0-30 days imprisonment and $250 fine for possession of 100-200 grams; 6 months-5 years imprisonment and $2,500 fine for possession of 200-600 grams; 1-10 years imprisonment and $5,000 fine for possession of more than 600 grams; 6 months-5 years imprisonment and $2,500 fine for selling 200 grams or less; 1-10 years imprisonment and $5,000 fine for selling 200-600 grams; 2-15 years imprisonment and $7,500 for selling more than 600 grams.

DALLAS

Airports
Dallas/Ft. Worth (DFW), 17 miles West of city
Love (DAL), 7 miles North of city

Airlines
Air Canada 800-261-6464
American 214-267-1151
Braniff 214-357-9511
Continental 214-647-2910
Delta 214-630-3200
Eastern 214-453-0231
Frontier 214-453-0123
Mexicana 800-421-8301
Ozark 214-647-8013
Texas Intl 214-267-8141

Air Freight
American 214-574-3520
Braniff 214-574-2511
Continental 214-574-4870
Delta 214-574-2200
Eastern 214-574-3266
Japan 214-630-4661
Korean 214-744-5981
Ozark 214-574-3366
Pan Am 800-392-2080
Seaboard 214-453-0554
TWA 214-630-1161
Texas Intl. 214-574-4603

Aircraft Charter
Dallas Flight Center 214-351-5386
Executive Express 214-233-1784
Alpha Aviation 214-352-4801

Bus Charter
Greyhound 1-800-528-0369
Trailways 214-655-7872

Car Rentals
Avis 214-574-4100
Hertz 214-574-2000
National 214-574-3400

Truck Rentals
Hertz 214-638-2680
National 214-631-7700

Train
Amtrack 800-421-8320
Passenger Station—400 S. Houston
   214-653-1101

Bus Charter
Greyhound 1-800-528-0369
Trailways 214-655-7872

Package Express
Emery Air Freight 214-574-6310
Federal Express 214-357-9141

Hotels
Fairmont, Ross & Akard 214-748-5454

Drugstores
Sun Rexall Drugs 214-824-4539
Eckerd Drugs 214-391-2151
Lantrip's Marsh Lane Pharmacy—
   214-352-7559

Passport Information
214-749-8691

British Consulate
British Consulate
813 Stemmons Tower West
2730 Stemmons Freeway
Dallas, TX 75207
214-637-3600

Nearest Australian Consulate
Australian Embassy
1606 Massachusetts Ave.
Washington, D.C. 20036
202-797-3000

American Civil Liberties Union
P.O. Box 12371
Dallas, TX 75225
214-387-0072

AAA
214-526-7911

Suicide Prevention
214-521-5531

VD Information
Crisis Center 214-783-0008

Legal Drinking Age
18

Marijuana Laws
0-6 months imprisonment and $1,000 fine for possession of 2 ounces or less; 0-1 year imprisonment and $2,000 fine for possession of 2-4 ounces; 2-10 years imprisonment and $5,000 fine for possession of more than 4 ounces; 2-10 years imprisonment and $5,000 fine for selling marijuana.

DETROIT

Airports
Metro (DTW), 20 miles SW of city
City (DET), 5 miles NE of city

Airlines
Air Wisconsin 313-942-0400
Allegheny 313-963-8340
American 313-965-1000
British Airways 313-965-7850
Delta 313-355-3200
Eastern 313-965-8200
North Central 313-283-8910
Northwest 313-962-2002
Ozark 313-961-1200
Pan Am 313-354-0500
Southern 313-964-2323
TWA 313-962-8650
United 313-336-9000
Wright 313-372-3300

Air Freight
Air Wisconsin 313-942-0400
Allegheny 313-941-2900
American 313-291-7550
British Airways 313-965-7850
Delta 313-274-1500
Eastern 313-964-5200
North Central 313-562-5511
Northwest 313-562-3414
Pan American 313-721-9000
Southern 313-562-8717
TWA 313-565-4500
United 313-942-9100
Wright 313-372-4772

Aircraft Charter
Executive Express 313-569-6699
Jet Aviation 313-481-1404
Jet Way 313-482-6600

Bus Charters
Greyhound 313-961-4050
Trailways 313-963-1322

Car Rentals
Avis 313-941-5796
Hertz 313-729-5200
National 313-941-5030

Truck Rental
Avis 313-584-7000
Hertz 313-933-6850

Train
Amtrack 800-621-0353
Passenger Station 313-965-0314

Package Express
Emery Air Freight 313-942-0600
Federal Express 313-941-7822

Hotels
Detroit Plaza, Renaissance Center.
313-568-8000
Ponchartrain, 2 Washington Boulevard.
313-965-0200
St. Regis, 3071 West Grand Boulevard.
813-873-3000

Drugstores
Richardson's 313–LO2–4700
Merit-Woods 313–882–0922
Pugh's Prescription Pharmacy
  313–897–7644

Passport Information
313–381–1047

British Consulate
British Consulate-General
2200 Detroit Bank and Trust Building
211 Fort Street West
Detroit, MI 48226
313–962–4776

Nearest Australian Consulate
Australian Consulate-General
Suite 2212, One Illinois Centre
111 East Wacker Drive
Chicago, IL 60601
312–329–1740

American Civil Liberties Union
313–961–4662

AAA
313–336–1000

Suicide Information
313–875–5466

VD Information
313–494–4242

Legal Drinking Age
18

Marijuana Laws
0-1 year imprisonment and $1,000 for possession of any amount; 0-4 years imprisonment and $2,000 fine for selling marijuana.

DISTRICT OF COLUMBIA

Airports
National (DCA), 3 miles south of Washington
Dulles (IAD), 26 miles west of Washington
Baltimore Washington Intl. (BAL), 32 mlies NE of Washington, 10 mlies SW of Baltimore

Airlines
Aeroflot 202–296–0077
Air Florida 800–327–2971
Air France 202–337–8711
Allegheny 202–783–4500
American 202–393–2345
British Airways 202–393–5300
Caribbean Airways 800–638–5000
Continental 202–628–6666
Delta 202–920–5500
Eastern 202–393–4000
National 202–549–7633
North Central 202–347–0448
Northwest 202–337–0611
Ozark 202–347–4744

Pan American 202–833–1000
Piedmont 202–347–1800
Southern 202–628–9032
TWA 202–893–3400
United 202–893–3400

Air Freight
Allegheny 202–892–7381
American 202–892–5100
British Airways 202–471–9071
Delta 202–521–4600
Eastern 202–737–6877
National 202–892–5420
Northwest 202–783–9014
Ozark 202–471–9290
Pan American 202–471–9650
Southern 202–471–4341
TWA 202–892–4550
United 202–892–7500

Aircraft Charter
Federal Airways 202–684–7400
Class 1 Aviation 202–393–5800
Baltimore Airways 301–768–0331

Bus Charters
Greyhound 202–833–3380
Trailways 202–347–4200

Car Rentals
Avis 703–684–8682
Hertz 703–979–0900
National 703–783–1590

Truck Rentals
Avis 202–526–5400
Hertz 202–832–1600

Train
Amtrack 800–523–5720

Package Express
Emery Air Freight 202–836–5180
Federal Express 202–659–4297

Hotels
Watergate, 2650 Virginia Avenue NW. 202–965–2300
Georgetown Inn, 1310 Wisconsin Avenue NW. 202–333–8900
Georgetown Dutch Inn, 1075 Thomas Jefferson Street NW. 202–337–0900
Ramada Inn, Princess Garden Parkway, Landover. 301–459–1000

Drugstores
Rodman's 202–363–3466
Ethical 202–387–6881
Professional 202–234–0844

Passport Information
202–783–8200

British Consulate
British Embassy
3100 Massachusetts Avenue, NW
Washington, D.C. 20008
202–HO2–1340

Australian Consulate
Australian Embassy
1606 Massachusetts Ave.
Washington, D.C. 20036
202–797–3000

American Civil Liberties Union
202–544–1076

Suicide Prevention
202–727–3622

VD Information
202–832–7000

AAA
202–222–6000

Legal Drinking Age
18

Marijuana Laws
0-1 year imprisonment and $100-1,000 fine for possession or selling marijuana.

HOUSTON

Airports
Intercontinental (IAH), 20 miles North of city
Hobby (HOU), 10 miles SE of city

Airlines
Aeromexico 713–691–3071
Air Canada 800–261–6464
Air France 800–221–2110
American 713–222–9873
Br. Caledonian 713–445–3501
Braniff 713–621–3111
Cayman Airways 800–327–2864
Continental 713–780–3344
Delta 713–623–6000
Eastern 713–621–8100
KLM 713–658–1781
National 713–224–9011
Pan American 713–659–3333
Texas Intl. 713–443–8900
Viasa 713–877–8223

Air Freight
Ace 713-666-2544
Aeromexico 713-443-4661
American 713-228-5237
Braniff 713-443-4211
British Airways 713-443-4186
Continental 713-443-4241
Delta 713-443-4111
Eastern 713-225-2061
Japan Airlines 713-223-3833
National 713-443-4343
Pan Am 713-443-0820
Seaboard 713-688-9200
Texas Intl. 713-443-4311
Trans International 713-627-7201

Aircraft Charter
Aviation Charter Inc. 713-644-2037
Western Jet Corp. 713-641-6153
Space City 713-645-3269

Bus Charters
Greyhound 1-800-528-0369
Trailways 713-759-6510

Car Rentals
Avis 713-443-2130
Hertz 713-443-0800
National 713-443-8850

Truck Rentals
Avis 713-659-1205
Hertz 713-691-1256

Train
Amtrack 1-800-421-8320
Passenger Station, 902 Washington
 713-224-1577

Package Express
Emery Air Freight 713-443-0930
Federal Express 713-641-0261

Hotel
Whitehall, 1700 Smith. 713-659-5000

Drugstores
Hillcroft Pharmacy 713-774-5806

Almeda Square Metro Pharmacy
 713-946-2604
Bissonnet Pharmacies 713-772-1902

Passport Information
713-226-5575

British Consulate
British Consulate-General
Suite 2250
601 Jefferson
Houston, TX 77002
713-659-6270

Nearest Australian Consulate
Australian Embassy
1606 Massachusetts Ave.
Washington, D.C. 20036
202-797-3000

American Civil Liberties Union
1236 W. Gray
Houston, TX
713-524-5925

AAA
713-524-1851

Suicide Prevention
713-488-7222

VD Information
713-790-9277

Legal Drinking Age
18

Marijuana Laws
0-6 months imprisonment and $1,000
 fine for possession of 2 ounces or less;
 0-1 year imprisonment and $2,000 fine
 for possession of 2-4 ounces; 2-10
 years imprisonment and $5,000 fine
 for possession of more than 4 ounces;
 2-10 years imprisonment and $5,000
 fine for selling marijuana.

KANSAS CITY

Airports
International (MCI), 18 miles NW of city
Municipal (MKC), 2 miles North of city

Airlines
Air Midwest 816-474-5150
Braniff 816-753-1740
Continental 816-471-3700
Delta 816-471-1828
Frontier 816-383-3300
Mexicana 800-421-8301
North Central 816-243-7400
Ozark 816-471-7383
Texas International 816-474-3377
TWA 816-842-4000
United 816-471-6060

Air Freight
Braniff 816-243-2121
Continental 816-243-6000
Delta 816-243-5300
Frontier 816-243-2666
Mexicana 816-243-6540
North Central 816-243-7403
Ozark 816-243-7011
Texas Intl. 816-243-5511
TWA 816-243-4111
United 816-243-6520

Aircraft Charter
Corporate Charter Services
   816-474-8226
Perkins & Assoc. 816-842-1985
Royal Air 816-474-7093

Bus Charter
Greyhound 1-800-528-0369

Car Rentals
Avis 816-243-5760
Hertz 816-243-5765
National 816-243-5770

Truck Rentals
Avis 816-321-1717
Hertz 816-321-5105

Train
Amtrack 1-800-621-0317
Passenger Station, 30 W. Pershing Road
   816-421-3622

Package Express
Emery Air Freight 816-891-8422
Federal Express 816-471-7110

Hotels
The Crown Center, 1 Pershing Road.
   816-474-4400
The Granada Royale, 220 West 43.
   816-756-1720

Drugstores
Mid-City 816-921-4482
Wooten Drugs 816-381-3300
Valle Vista Rexall Drugs 816-524-4747

Passport Information
816-374-6458

Nearest British Consulate
British Consulate-General
Gateway Tower
Suite 700, 1 Memorial Drive
St. Louis, MO 63102
314-621-4688

Nearest Australian Consulate
Australian Consulate-General
Suite 2212, One Illinois Centre
111 East Wacker Drive
Chicago, IL 60601
312-329-1740

American Civil Liberties Union
816-421-1875

AAA
816-421-4177

Suicide Prevention
816-471-3000

VD Information
816–274–1381

Legal Drinking Age
21

Marijuana Laws
0-1 year imprisonment and $1,000 fine for possession of 35 grams or less; 0-5 years imprisonment and $1,000 fine for possession of more than 35 grams; 5 years-life imprisonment for selling marijuana.

LOS ANGELES

Airports
International (LAX), 15 miles SW of city
Burbank Airport (BUR), 15 miles NW of city
Ontario (ONT), 52 miles East of city

Airlines
Aerolineas Argentinas 213–683–1633
Aeromexico 213–380–6030
Aeroperu 800–327–4363
Air California 714–983–2743
Air Canada 213–776–7000
Air France 213–625–7171
Air New Zealand 213–629–5454
Air Panama 213–488–1065
American 213–937–6811
Avianca 800–221–2200
Braniff 213–680–2202
British Airways 213–272–8866
China 213–624–1161
Continental 213–772–6000
CP Air 800–426–7000
Delta 213–386–5510
Eastern 213–380–2070
Golden West 213–930–2200
Hughes Airwest 213–772–5100
Japan 213–620–9580
KLM 800–231–2164
Korean 213–484–1900
Laker Airway Ltd. 213–646–9600
Mexicana 213–487–6950
National 213–381–5777
Northwest 213–380–1511
Pacific Southwest 213–776–0125
Pan American 213–629–3292
SAS 213–652–8600
Swift Air Lines 800–592–5900
Texas Intl. 213–680–1150

TWA 213–483–1100
United 213–482–2000
UTA 213–625–7171
Varig 800–223–5720
Western 213–776–2311

Air Freight
Aeroperu 213–646–9216
Air Canada 213–646–3921
Air France 213–646–3620
Air New Zealand 800–262–1328
American 213–776–2520
Avianca 213–776–6088
Braniff 213–646–9281
Continental 213–776–2421
CP Air 213–646–9484
Delta 213–776–0423
Eastern 213–646–7370
Golden West 213–646–3958
Hughes Airwest 213–646–6800
Japan 213–646–2353
National 213–646–4611
Northwest 213–646–7700
SAS 213–646–5180
TWA 213–646–5400
United 213–776–2000
Western 213–776–2222

Aircraft Charter
ChartAir 213–649–0707
Golden Jet Airways 213–670–1976
Gunnell Aviation 213–391–6355

Bus Charters
Greyhound 213–629–8415
Trailways 213–742–1231

Car Rentals
Avis 213-646-5600
Hertz 213-646-2851
National 213-645-4500

Truck Rentals
Avis 213-748-8601
Hertz 213-628-1255

Train
Amtrack 213-624-0171

Package Express
Emery Air Freight 213-776-2511
Federal Express 213-776-1800

Hotels
Continental Hyatt, 8401 Sunset Boulevard. 213-656-4101
Airport Marriott, 13480 Maxella Drive, Marina Del Ray. 231-822-8555
Beverly Rodeo, 360 North Rodeo Drive. 213-273-0300
Sunset Marquee, 1200 North Alta Loma Road. 213-657-1333

Drugstores
Thrifty Drugstore 213-295-8478
Family Pharmacy Service 213-653-4070

Passport Information
213-688-3283

British Consulate
British Consulate-General
Ahmanson Center E. Building
(Suite 312)
3701 Wilshire Blvd.
Los Angeles, CA 90010
213-385-7381

Australian Consulate
Australian Consulate-General
3550 Wilshire Boulevard
Los Angeles, CA 90010
213-387-9102

American Civil Liberties Union
213-487-1720

AAA
213-741-3111

Suicide Prevention 213-381-5111

VD Information
Hotline 213-588-5221
LA Free Clinic 213-653-1990

Legal Drinking Age
21

Marijuana Laws
$0-100 fine for possession of 1 ounce or less; 0-6 months imprisonment and $500 fine for possession of more than 1 ounce; 2-4 years imprisonment for selling marijuana.

LOUISVILLE

Airport
Standiford Field (SDF), 5 miles South of city

Airlines
Allegheny 502-584-0354
American 502-589-3730
Delta 502-584-6151
Eastern 502-587-7551
Ozark 502-366-4541
Piedmont 502-583-0691
TWA 502-584-8101

Air Freight
Burlington Northern Air Freight
  502-367-0151
American 502-368-1666
Delta 502-363-3544
Eastern 502-368-1646
Ozark 502-361-2361

Piedmont 502-361-5443
TWA 502-368-2566

Aircraft Charter
Sprite-Flite Jets Inc. 606-253-2681
Corporate Air Fleet 800-251-1225
River City Aviation 502-454-5184

Bus Charters
Greyhound 502-587-6831
Trailways 502-584-5336

Car Rentals
Avis 502-368-5851
Hertz 502-361-0181
National 502-361-2515

Truck Rentals
Avis 502-366-0331
Hertz 502-584-5275

Train
Amtrack 502-367-2231
Passenger Station, 7727 National Turnpike

Package Express
Emery Air Freight 502-361-4481
Federal Express 1-800-238-5355

Hotels
Galt House, Fourth Street at River. 502-589-5200
Hyatt Regency, 320 West Jefferson. 592-587-3434

Drugstores
Wagner's Pharmacy 502-637-3678
Myles Drugs 502-425-2531
Drug World 502-426-5500

Passport Information
502-582-5492

Nearest British Consulate
British Consulate-General
Gateway Tower
Suite 700, 1 Memorial Drive
St. Louis, MO 63102
314-621-4688

Nearest Australian Consulate
Australian Consulate-General
Suite 2212, One Illinois Centre
111 East Wacker Drive
Chicago, IL 60601
312-329-1740

American Civil Liberties Union
502-895-0279

AAA
502-582-3311

Suicide Prevention
Crisis & Info Center 502-589-4313

VD Information
502-587-3895

Legal Drinking Age
21

Marijuana Laws
0-90 days imprisonment and $250 fine for possession; 0-1 year imprisonment and $500 fine for selling marijuana.

MIAMI

Airport
International (MIA), 6 miles NW of city

Airlines
Aerocondor 305-885-2121
Aerolineas Argentinas 305-377-3605
Aeromexico 1-800-231-6550
Aeroperu 305-373-7361
Air Canada 305-371-9026
Air Florida 305-592-8010
Air France 1-800-221-2110
Air Jamaica 305-358-1121

Air Panama 305-526-5935
American 305-358-6800
Avianca 1-800-221-2200
Aviateca 305-373-1080
Bahamas Air 305-442-8585
Belize Airways 305-592-1134
Braniff 305-358-9400
British Airways 305-377-2051
BWIA 305-371-2947
Continental 305-371-8421
Delta 305-448-7000
Dominicana 305-358-5355
Eastern 305-873-3000
Equatoriana 305-526-5734
Iberia 1-800-221-9741
Lacsa 305-445-8737
Lan Chile 305-377-8306
Lanica 305-358-6444
Mexicana 1-800-421-8301
National 305-874-5000
Northwest 305-377-0311
Ozark 305-358-7582
Pan American 305-637-6444
Piedmont 305-358-3396
Southern 305-379-7501
TACA 305-358-0066
TAN 305-526-4300
TWA 305-371-7471
United 305-377-3461
Varig 1-800-223-5720
Viasa 305-374-5000
Western 305-526-6700

Air Freight
Aerocondor 305-371-0671
Aerolineas Argentinas 305-526-6983
Aeromexico 305-526-5870
Aeroperu 305-871-1893
Air Canada 305-526-5433
Air Panama 305-526-5933
Avianca 305-871-6720
Bahamas Air 305-526-5559
Braniff 305-526-4211
British Airways 305-526-5242
BWIA 305-526-6880
Continental 305-526-5514
Delta 305-526-4700
Dominicana 305-526-3925
Eastern 305-871-4600

Equatoriana 305-526-5875
Lanica 305-526-5510
Mexicana 305-526-6204
National 305-874-3700
Northwest 305-526-4020
Pan American 305-637-6911
Southern 305-526-6562
TAN 305-526-4400
TWA 305-526-4120
United 305-526-4521
Varig 305-526-6583
Viasa 305-871-1580
Western 305-526-6700

Aircraft Charter
Key West Airlines 305-526-6503
Northeast Jet Company 305-964-0134
Miami Airways Inc. 305-443-3869

Bus Charters
Greyhound 1-800-241-0396
Trailways 305-373-6561

Car Rentals
Avis 800-331-1212
Hertz 305-526-5645
National 305-526-5200

Truck Rentals
Hertz 305-945-3840
National 305-885-1444

Train
Amtrack 800-342-2520

Package Express
Emery Air Freight 305-592-5570
Federal Express 305-940-6893

Hotels
Coconut Grove Hotel, 2649 South
  Bayshore Drive. 305-858-2500
Holiday Inn Country Club, 14800
  Hollywood Boulevard, Hollywood,
  305-431-8800

Drugstores
Robert's 305-545-0533

Sunset Drug Store 305-667-7577
Penine Center Pharmacy 305-238-3641

Passport Information
305-350-4681

Nearest British Consulate
British Consulate-General
Suite 912
225 Peachtree Street, NE
Atlanta, GA 30303
404-524-5856

Nearest Australian Consulate
Australian Embassy
1606 Massachusetts Ave.
Washington, D.C. 20036
202-797-3000

American Civil Liberties Union
305-666-2950

AAA
305-573-5611

Suicide Prevention
305-358-4357

VD Information
305-325-2550

Legal Drinking Age
18

Marijuana Laws
0-1 year imprisonment for possession of 5 grams or less; 0-5 years imprisonment and $5,000 fine for possession of more than 5 grams; 0-5 years imprisonment and $5,000 fine for selling marijuana.

NEW ORLEANS

Airports
International (MSY), 14 miles NW of city
Lakefront (NEW), 5 miles SW of city

Airlines
American 504-523-2188
Aviateca 800-327-7937
Braniff 504-523-9011
Continental 504-522-2161
Delta 504-529-2431
Eastern 504-524-4211
National 504-529-5192
Northwest 504-566-1100
Sahsa 504-524-3318
Southern 504-525-0423
Taca 504-729-4551
Texal Intl. 504-721-6263
United 504-525-2255

Air Freight
American 504-466-1114
Aviateca 504-729-4421

Braniff 504-729-3411
Continental 504-721-7666
Delta 504-729-5563
Eastern 504-729-3601
National 504-729-3616
Northwest 504-721-0922
Sahsa 504-721-0234
Southern 504-721-3429
Taca 504-729-4551
Texas Intl. 504-721-6803
United 504-729-3500

Aircraft Charter
Pan Air Corporation 504-245-1707
Gulf Coast 504-729-1041
Airtaix Aviation Inc. 504-242-3214
Pelican Aviation Corp. 318-365-5451

Bus Charters
Greyhound 504-524-1261
Trailways 504-525-4201

Car Rentals
Avis 504–729–8421
Hertz 504–443–6513
National 504–729–6447

Truck Rentals
Avis 504–524–7567
Hertz 504–837–5770

Train
Amtrack 504–586–0027
Passenger Station, 1001 Loyola Avenue

Package Express
Emery Air Freight 504–722–1333
Federal Express 504–486–5838

Hotels
Marie Antoinette, 827 Toulouse Street. 504–525–2300
Hyatt Regency, Poydras Plaza & Loyola Avenue. 504–561–1234

Drugstores
Waterbury's Rexall 504–525–0321
Patio Drugs 504–887–1310
Merhoff & Reine Drugs 504–254–9521

Passport Information
504–589–6728

Nearest British Consulate
British Consulate-General
Suite 2250, 601 Jefferson
Houston, TX 77002
713–659–6270

Nearest Australian Consulate
Australian Embassy
1606 Massachusetts Ave.
Washington, DC 20036
202–797–3000

American Civil Liberties Union
504–522–0617

AAA
504–837–1080

Suicide Prevention
504–523–2673

VD Information
504–586–8383

Legal Drinking Age
18

Marijuana Laws
0-6 months imprisonment and $500 fine for possession; 0-10 years imprisonment and $15,000 fine for selling marijuana.

NEW YORK

Airports
Kennedy International (JFK), 15 miles SE of city
LaGuardia (LGA), 8 miles NE of city
Newark (EWR), 10 miles SW of city

Airlines
Aer Lingus 212–557–1110
Aeroflot 212–661–4050
Aerolineas Argentinas 212–757–6400
Aeromexico 212–391–2900
Aeroperu 800–327–4363
Air Afrique 212–759–9000
Air Canada 212–421–8000
Air France 212–247–0100
Air India 212–751–6200
Air Jamaica 212–421–9750
Air New England 800–225–3640
Air Panama 212–246–4060
Alia 212–949–0050
Alitalia 212–582–8900
Allegheny 212–736–3200
Alm-Antillean 212–459–6900
American 212–661–4242
Avianca 212–586–6040
Braniff 212–687–8200

British Airways 212-687-1600
BWIA 212-581-3200
Czechoslovak 212-682-5833
Delta 212-239-0700
Dominicana 212-757-9305
Eastern 212-986-5000
Ecuatoriana 800-327-1337
El Al 212-486-2600
Finnair 212-889-7070
Iberia 212-793-3300
Icelandic 212-757-8585
Japan 212-759-9100
KLM 212-759-3600
Laker Airways Ltd. 212-459-6092
Lufthansa 212-357-8400
National 212-697-9000
New York Airways 212-661-5100
North Central 212-581-8851
Northwest 212-564-2300
Olympic 212-656-6215
Ozark 212-586-3612
Pakistan 212-949-0488
Pan Am 212-973-4000
Piedmont 212-489-1460
Royal Air Maroc 212-974-3854
Sabena 212-961-6200
SAS 212-657-7700
South African 212-826-1245
Southern 212-765-4210
Swissair 212-995-8400
TAP 212-421-8500
Tarom 212-687-6013
TWA 212-695-6000
United 212-867-3000
Varig 212-682-3100
Viasa 212-421-7722
Yugoslav 212-757-9676

Air Freight
Aer Airlines 212-995-4340
Aer Lingus 212-575-8400
Aerolineas Argentinas 212-632-1737
Aeromexico 212-656-6444
Air Canada 212-656-3440
Air France 212-758-6300
Air India 212-632-0134
Air New England 212-779-6536
ALIA 212-656-3570
Alitalia 212-656-2720

Allegheny 212-656-2107
Altair 914-428-5727
American 212-656-3329
Argentine Airlines 212-632-1737
Avianca 212-632-1460
Belize 800-327-9838
Braniff 212-632-1500
British Airways 212-995-3100
China Airlines 212-656-5545
Delta Airlines 212-632-1400
Eastern 212-656-7020
Ecuatorian 800-327-1348
El Al 212-486-2601
Finnair 212-656-7520
Iberia Air Lines 212-632-1240
Icelandic 212-656-2630
Japan 212-656-2345
KLM 212-759-2400
Korean 212-656-7367
Lufthansa 212-995-8300
National 212-656-8130
Northwest Orient 212-632-3300
Olympic 212-656-5565
Ozark 212-651-0659
Pan Am 212-632-5800
Qantas 800-227-0290
Sabena 212-632-1050
SAS 212-995-9400
Seaboard World Airlines 212-632-7400
Southern Airways 212-335-1211
Swissair 212-995-3800
TAP 212-656-7455
TWA 212-995-9700
United 212-656-7300
Varig 212-632-0831
Viasa Airways 212-656-7092
World Airways 212-661-3423

Aircraft Charter
Air Charter Executive Service 212-639-9100
Sound Air Aviation 212-476-0200
Island Helicopter 212-895-5372

Bus Charters
Greyhound 212-594-2000
Trailways 212-563-9650

Car Rentals
Avis 800–331–1212
Hertz 800–654–3131
National 800–328–4567

Truck Rentals
Avis 212–255–0150
Hertz 212–427–6912

Train
Amtrack 212–736–4545

Package Express
Emery Air Freight 212–995–6400
Federal Express 212–361–8811

Hotels
Pierre Hotel, Fifth Avenue and 61 Street, 212–838–8000
Plaza Hotel, Fifth Avenue and 59 Street. 212–759–3000
Navarro Hotel, 112 Central Park South. 212–757–1900
St. Regis Hotel, Fifth Avenue and 55 Street. 212–753–4500
Waldorf Astoria, Park Avenue and 50 Street. 212–355–3000
Loews Warwick Hotel, 54 Street and Avenue of the Americas. 212–247–2700
Sherry-Netherland Hotel, 781 Fifth Avenue. 212–355–2800
Gramercy Park Hotel, 2 Lexington Avenue. 212–475–4320

Drugstores
Kaufman Pharmacy 212–PL5–2266
Martin's Drug Store 212–MU5–5230
Caswell-Massey Co. Ltd. 212–PL5–2254

Passport Information
212–541–7700

British Consulate
British Consulate-General
150 East 58th Street
NY, NY 10022
212–593–2258

Australian Consulate
Australian Consulate-General
International Building
636 Fifth Avenue
NY, NY 10020
212–245–4000

American Civil Liberties Union
212–725–1222

AAA
212–695–8311

Suicide Prevention
212–462–3322

VD Information
212–269–5300

Legal Drinking Age
18

Marijuana Laws
$0-100 fine for possession of 25 grams or less; 0-3 months imprisonment and $500 fine for possession of more than 25 grams; 0-1 year imprisonment and $1,000 fine for possession of more than 4 ounces; 0-4 years imprisonment for possession of more than 8 ounces; 0-7 years imprisonment for possession of more than 16 ounces; 0-15 years imprisonment for possession of more than 1 pound; 0-1 year imprisonment and $1,000 fine for selling less than 25 grams; 0-4 years imprisonment for selling 25 grams-4 ounces; 0-7 years imprisonment for selling 4-16 ounces; 0-15 years imprisonment for selling more than 1 pound.

PHILADELPHIA

Airports
International (PHL), 7 miles SW of city
North Philadelphia (PNE), 12 miles NE of city

Airlines
Air Florida 800-327-2971
Air Jamaica 215-567-7560
Alitalia 215-568-5444
Allegheny 215-563-8055
Altair Airlines 215-521-4300
American 215-568-3600
Braniff 215-492-3477
British Airways 215-568-5070
Delta 215-927-1700
Eastern 215-923-3500
Lufthansa 800-645-3860
National 215-923-1860
North Central 215-563-7501
Northwest 215-922-2900
Ozark 215-922-7350
TWA 215-923-2000
United 215-568-2800

Air Freight
Allegheny 215-365-7300
American 215-492-3500
British Airways 215-492-2465
Delta 215-492-3600
Eastern 215-365-6056
National 215-492-2400
Pan Am 215-492-2700
Seaboard 215-365-8228
Summit Air Lines 215-492-2775
TWA 215-492-2200
United 215-492-3711

Aircraft Charter
VIP Air Inc. 215-698-7926
Wing's Airways 215-MI 6-1800
American Jet Charter Service 800-325-4256

Bus Charters
Greyhound 800-223-0188
Trailways 215-972-3309

Car Rentals
Avis 215-492-3350
Hertz 215-492-2900
National 215-492-2750

Truck Rentals
Avis 215-467-7800
Hertz 215-831-4500

Train
Amtrack 215-824-4600
Passenger Station, 30th & Market 215-387-5911

Package Express
Emery Air Freight 215-LE2-6300
Federal Express 800-238-5355

Hotels
Barclay, 237 South 18 Street. 215-545-0300
Stadium Hilton, Tenth & Packer. 215-755-9500
Fairmont Hotel, Broad Street & Walnut. 215-093-1776

Drugstores
Corson's Pharmacy 215-PE5-1386
Haussmann's Pharmacy 215-MA7-7707
Esquire Prescriptions 215-HA4-7400

Passport Information
215-597-7482

British Consulate
British Consulate-General
12 South 12th Street
Philadelphia, PA 19107
215-WA5-2430

Nearest Australian Consulate
Australian Consulate-General
International Building
636 Fifth Avenue
NY, NY 10020
212-245-4000

American Civil Liberties Union
260 S. 15th Street
Philadelphia, PA
215-735-7103

AAA
Keystone Automobile Club
215-864-5000

Suicide Prevention
215-831-8855

VD Information
215-546-0141

Legal Drinking Age
21

Marijuana Laws
0-30 days imprisonment and $500 fine for possession of 30 grams or less; 0-1 year imprisonment and $5,000 fine for possession of more than 30 grams; 0-5 years imprisonment and $15,000 fine for selling marijuana.

PORTLAND

Airport
International (PDX), 9 miles NE of city

Airlines
Braniff 503-224-5030
Continental 503-224-4560
Eastern 503-224-7550
Hughes Airwest 503-224-5252
Northwest 503-226-3211
United 503-226-7211
Western 503-225-0830

Air Freight
Air Oregon 503-249-4130
Braniff 503-249-4890
Cascade 503-249-4920
Columbia-Pacific 503-249-4495
Continental 503-249-4626
Eastern 503-249-4010
Hughes Airwest 503-249-4730
Northwest Orient 503-249-4826
Pan Am 503-249-4995
United 503-249-4300

Aircraft Charter
Flightcraft 503-249-4400
Executive Flight Services Inc.
 503-249-4480
Horizon Aviation 503-682-2811

Bus Charter
Greyhound 503-243-2340
Trailways 503-248-9700

Car Rentals
Avis 503-249-4950
Hertz 503-249-4080
National 503-249-4900

Truck Rental
Hertz 503-226-7971

Train
Amtrack 1-800-421-8320
Passenger Station, 800 NW 6th
 503-248-1146

Package Express
Emery Air Freight 503-255-8970
Federal Express 503-287-4364

Hotels
The Benson, SW Broadway at Oak.
 503-228-9611
Hilton Hotel, 921 SW Sixth Avenue.
 503-226-1611

Drugstores
Phoenix Rexall Drug 503-774-3239
Gorden Home Pharmacy 503-246-1432
Monarch Rexall Pharmacy
 503-236-4103

Passport Information
503-248-3800

Nearest British Consulate
British Consulate-General
1216 Norton Building
2nd Avenue and Columbia Street
Seattle, WA 98104
206–622–9253

Nearest Australian Consulate
Australian Consulate-General
Quantas Building
360 Post Street
San Francisco, CA 94108
415–362–6160

American Civil Liberties Union
534 SW 3rd
Portland, OR
503–227–3186

AAA
503–222–6777

Suicide Prevention
503–227–0403

VD Information
503–248–3700

Legal Drinking Age
21

Marijuana Laws
$0-100 fine for possession of 1 ounce or less; 0-10 years imprisonment and $2,500 fine for possession of more than 1 ounce; 0-10 years imprisonment and $2,500 fine for selling marijuana.

ST. LOUIS

Airports
Lambert Intl. (STL), 15 miles West of city
Spirit of St. Louis (SUS), 20 miles West of city

Airlines
Allegheny 314–421–1018
American 314–231–9505
Braniff 314–436–6500
Delta 314–421–2600
Eastern 314–621–8900
Frontier 314–436–6650
Mexicana 800–421–8301
Northwest 314–241–2151
Ozark 314–436–1900
Southern 314–621–9177
TWA 314–291–7500

Air Freight
Allegheny 314–423–3313
American 314–426–5522
Braniff 314–426–7577
Delta 314–426–7660
Eastern 314–426–4030
Frontier 314–426–1010
Ozark 314–426–2770

Southern Airways 314–429–7524
TWA 314–436–3600

Aircraft Charter
Tri-Star Ltd. 314–727–1213
Walston Aviation 314–741–6700
Sisk Aviation Activities 314–337–5024

Bus Charters
Greyhound 314–231–7277
Trailways 314–621–6242

Car Rentals
Avis 314–426–7766
Hertz 314–426–7555
National 314–426–6272

Truck Rentals
Hertz 314–371–5400
National 314–621–0060

Train
Amtrack 1–800–621–0317
Passenger Station, 1820 Market
    314–231–0061

Package Express
Emery Air Freight 314-423-4470
Federal Express 314-426-0117

Hotels
Marriott Pavillion, 1 Broadway
 314-421-1776.

Drugstores
Creve Coeur Pharmacy 314-872-9107
Weipert's 314-241-8253
Ross Pharmacy 314-868-2343

Passport Information
314-425-3054

British Consulate
British Consulate-General
Gateway Tower
Suite 700, 1 Memorial Drive
St. Louis, MO 63102
314-621-4688

Nearest Australian Consulate
Australian Consulate-General
Suite 2212
One Illinois Centre
111 East Wacker Drive
Chicago, IL 60601
312-329-1740

American Civil Liberties Union
314-721-1215

AAA
Auto Club of Missouri 314-576-7373

Suicide Prevention
314-868-6300

VD Information
314-361-7575

Legal Drinking Age
21

Marijuana Laws
0-1 year imprisonment and $1,000 fine for possession of 35 grams or less; 0-5 years imprisonment and $1,000 fine for possession of more than 35 grams; 5 years-life imprisonment for selling marijuana.

SAN FRANCISCO

Airports
International (SFO), 15 miles South of city
International (OAK), 7 miles SE of city

Airlines
Air California 415-433-2660
CP Air 415-391-0880
Delta 415-552-5700
Eastern 415-474-5858
Hughes Airwest 415-397-3121
Japan 415-982-8141
Mexicana National 800-262-1309
Northwest 415-391-8440
Pacific Southwest 415-761-0818
Pan Am 415-397-5200
Philippine 415-391-0470
Qantas 415-445-6666
TWA 415-626-5600
United 415-397-2100
Western 415-761-3300

Air Freight
Air California 415-877-0113
CP Air 415-877-5960
Delta 415-761-1727
Hughes Airwest 415-761-1150
Japan 415-877-3311
Northwest 415-761-4617
Pacific Southwest 415-761-4061
Pan Am 415-761-4242
Philippine 415-391-3400

Qantas 800–632–4711
TWA 415–877–4000
United 415–761–4212
Western 415–877–1414

Aircraft Charter
EAS 415–756–8288
California Air Commuter 800–772–1450
Jet Associates 408–649–3545

Bus Charters
Greyhound 415–495–1234
Trailways 415–982–9021

Car Rentals
Avis 800–331–1212
Hertz 415–877–1600
National 415–877–4745

Truck Rentals
Avis 415–285–3500
Hertz 415–873–5443

Train
Amtrack 800–648–3850
Passenger Station 415–556–8287

Package Express
Emery Air Freight 415–877–1812
Federal Express 415–568–6612

Hotels
Mikako, 1625 Post Street. 415–922–3200
Fairmont, California and Mason.
    415–772–5000
Oakland Hyatt House, 455 Hegenberger
    Road, Oakland. 415–562–6100
Mark Hopkins, One Nob Hill.
    415–392–3434
San Francisco Hyatt, 345 Stockton
    Street. 415–398–1234

Drugstores
Day-Walsh Owl Rexall 415–421–6566
Hub Pharmacy 415–431–0068
Geary Drug 415–751–4539

Passport Information
415–556–4516

British Consulate
British Consulate-General
Equitable Life Building
120 Montgomery Street
San Francisco, CA 94104
415–981–3030

Australian Consulate
Australian Consulate-General
Qantas Building
360 Post Street
San Francisco, CA 94108
415–362–6160

American Civil Liberties Union
415–777–4545

AAA
415–565–2012

Suicide Prevention
415–221–1423

VD Information
415–558–3804

Legal Drinking Age
21

Marijuana Laws
$0-100 fine for possession of 1 ounce or less; 0-6 months imprisonment and $500 fine for possession of more than 1 ounce; 2-4 years imprisonment for selling marijuana.

SEATTLE

Airports
Seattle/Tacoma Intl. (SEA), 12 miles from city
Lake Union (LKE), 21 miles North of city
Boeing Field (BFI), 5 miles south of city

Airlines
Airwest Airlines 206–682–8110
Alaska Airlines 206–433–3100
Braniff 206–623–2390
Continental 206–624–1740
Eastern 206–622–1881
Hughes Airwest 206–285–1234
Northwest 206–433–3500
Pacific Western 206–433–5088
Pan American 206–624–2121
SAS 800–421–0850
United 206–682–3700
Western 206–433–4711

Air Freight
Alaska Airlines 206–433–3100
Braniff 206–433–5095
Container Air Freight 206–762–5717
Eastern 206–433–5003
Hughes Airwest 206–433–3033
Northern Air Freight 206–433–6066
Northwest Orient 206–433–3747
Pan Am 206–433–4571
Seattle Transfer & Storage 206–433–5365
United 206–433–4000
Western 206–433–4900

Aircraft Charter
Aero-Copters 206–763–2177
Corporate Jets Northwest 206–763–2123
Cliff Howard's Aviation 206–762–2050

Bus Charters
Greyhound 206–628–5510
Trailways 206–624–5330

Car Rentals
Avis 206–433–5231
Hertz 206–433–5262
National 206–433–5500

Truck Rentals
Hertz 206–246–7600
National 206–763–2144

Train
Amtrack 800–421–8320
Passenger Station, 3rd & S. Jackson 206–624–3195

Package Express
Emery Air Freight 206–433–5060
Federal Express 206–762–5811

Hotels
Hilton Hotel, Sixth and University Street. 206–624–0500

Drugstores
Crown Hill Pharmacy 206–784–0759
Jordan Drug & Grocery Center 206–322–3050
Craigen Rexall Pharmacy 206–525–4411

Passport Information
206–442–7941

British Consulate
British Consulate-General
1216 Norton Building
2nd Avenue and Columbia Street
Seattle, WA 98104
206–622–9253

Nearest Australian Consulate
Australian Consulate-General
Qantas Building
360 Post Street
San Francisco, CA 94108
415–362–6160

American Civil Liberties Union
2101 Smith Tower
Seattle, WA
206–624–2180

AAA
206–292–5409

Suicide Prevention
206–325–5550

VD Information
206–625–2134

Marijuana Laws
0-90 days imprisonment and $250 fine for possession of 40 grams or less; 0-5 years imprisonment and $10,000 fine for possession of more than 40 grams; 0-5 years imprisonment and $10,000 fine for selling marijuana.

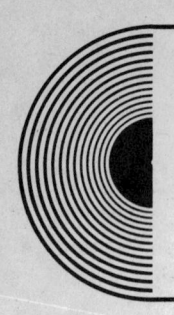

AMERICAN FEDERATION OF MUSICIANS (AFM) LOCALS

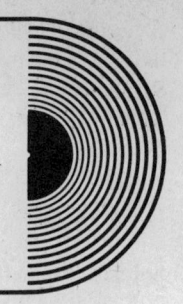

ALABAMA

Birmingham, Local 256-733
 205–786–1201
Mobile, Local 407–613   205–432–2934
Montgomery, Local 479–718
 205–288–1064
Tuscaloosa, Local 435   205–553–0645

ALASKA

Anchorage, Local 650   907–279–3415
Fairbanks, Local 481   907–456–3199
Juneau, Local 672   907–789–9419

ARIZONA

Phoenix, Local 586   602–254–8838
Tucson, Local 771   602–624–4556

ARKANSAS

Fayetteville, Local 273   501–442–4100
Fort Smith, Local 385   501–474–3330
Little Rock, Local 266   501–375–4911

CALIFORNIA

Bakersfield, Local 263   805–325–1650
Chico, Local 508   916–343–4508
Eureka, Local 333   707–442–3375
Fresno, Local 210   209–485–3600
Imperial Valley, Local 347
 714–353–4224
Long Beach, Local 353   213–421–4747
Los Angeles, Local 47   213–462–2161
Marysville, Local 158   916–742–8424
Merced, Local 454   209–722–9371
Modesto, Local 652   209–522–8015
Monterey, Local 616   408–375–6166
Napa, Local 541   707–255–7533
Redding, Local 113   916–241–2441
Richmond, Local 424   415–758–2336
Sacramento, Local 12   916–444–6660
San Bernardino, Local 167
 714–824–1450
San Diego, Local 325   714–276–4324
San Francisco, Local 6   415–775–8118
San Jose, Local 153   408–286–8602
San Leandro, Local 510   415–483–5470
San Luis Obispo, Local 305
 805–937–2694
Santa Ana, Local 7   714–546–8166
Santa Barbara, Local 308
 805–687–3519
Santa Cruz, Local 346   408–426–1776
Santa Rosa, Local 292   707–545–1434
Stockton, Local 189   209–464–4016
Vallejo, Local 367   707–642–6152
Ventura, Local 581   805–643–9953

COLORADO

Boulder, Local 275   303–530–1912
Colorado Springs, Local 154
 303–632–5033
Denver, Local 20–623   303–861–1112
Grand Junction, Local 164
 303–242–0722
Greeley, Local 396   303–352–5276

Leadville, Local 28   303–486–0252
Pueblo, Local 69   303–544–4725

West Palm Beach, Local 806
305–655–3337

CONNECTICUT

Bridgeport, Local 63–549
   203–333–2017
Bristol, Local 432   203–583–0209
Danbury, Local 87   203–743–1666
Hartford, Local 400   203–563–1501
Meriden, Local 55   203–238–0321
Middletown, Local 499   203–347–7805
New Britain, Local 440   203–229–4037
New Haven, Local 234–486
   203–387–4765
New London, Local 285   203–536–7362
Norwalk, Local 52   203–866–9368
Stamford, Local 626   203–938–3406
Torrington, Local 514   203–482–4097
Waterbury, Local 186   203–755–1281
Willimantic, Local 403   203–423–0354

DELAWARE

Wilmington, Local 311–641
   302–798–6060

DISTRICT OF COLUMBIA

Washington, Local 161–710
   202–244–8833

FLORIDA

Clearwater, Local 729   813–441–9447
Daytona Beach, Local 601
   904–252–6333
Fort Myers, Local 730   813–334–3423
Jacksonville, Local 444   904–398–9735
Key West, Local 202   305–296–2276
Miami, Local 655   355–633–3235
Orlando, Local 389   305–894–8666
Panama City, Local 448   904–785–5655
Pensacola, Local 284   904–456–1643
St. Petersburg, Local 427
   813–894–5059
Tampa, Local 721   813–254–0191

GEORGIA

Augusta, Local 488   803–648–7276
Atlanta, Local 148–462
   404–873–2033
Brunswick, Local 420   912–265–1628
Columbus, Local 331   404–323–0515
Macon, Local 359   912–746–6035
Savannah, Local 447–704
   912–352–9470

HAWAII

Honolulu, Local 677   808–521–1881

IDAHO

Boise, Local 537   208–345–0537
Coeur d'Alene, Local 225
   208–667–0891
Lewiston, Local 664   208–843–2486
Nampa, Local 423   208–459–7503
Pocatello, Local 295   208–233–3483
Rexburg, Local 371   208–624–7073
Sun Valley, Local 474   208–788–4358

ILLINOIS

Alton, Local 282   618–463–1179
Aurora, Local 181   312–897–6894
Belleville, Local 29   618–233–0525
Benld, Local 88   217–835–4377
Bloomington, Local 102   309–963–4217
Canton, Local 304   309–647–1499
Centralia, Local 681   618–548–1744
Champaign, Local 196   217–356–4151
Chicago, Local 10–208   312–782–0063
Chicago Heights, Local 386
   312–755–8144
Coal City, Local 323   815–942–0502
Collinsville, Local 350   618–344–3197
Danville, Local 90   217–446–4806
Decatur, Local 89   217–423–9157
DeKalb, Local 572   815–758–3952

Dixon, Local 525   815-284-7655
East St. Louis, Local 717
   618-397-0198
Edwardsville, Local 98   618-656-4169
Elgin, Local 48   312-742-3757
Freeport, Local 340   815-233-1040
Galesburg, Local 178   309-342-9233
Herrin, Local 280   618-985-4704
Hillsboro, Local 516   217-532-3862
Jacksonville, Local 128   217-245-9723
Joilet, Local 37   815-723-1645
Kankakee, Local 288   815-933-2733
Kewanee, Local 100   309-852-3252
LaSalle, Local 307   815-223-4793
Lincoln, Local 268   217-732-6182
Macomb, Local 330   217-322-6428
Mattoon, Local 224   217-234-6464
Mt. Vernon, Local 465   618-242-7613
Murphysboro, Local 697
   618-684-2736
Ottawa, Local 391   815-434-0807
Pekin, Local 301   309-347-2350
Peoria, Local 26   309-682-7517
Pontiac, Local 759   815-844-3333
Princeton, Local 431   309-895-2544
Quincy, Local 265   217-222-0941
Rockford, Local 24   815-965-2132
Springfield, Local 19-675
   217-546-6260
Sterling, Local 329   815-625-1380
Streator, Local 131   815-672-7431
Taylorville, Local 798   217-824-4047
Trenton, Local 175   618-224-9460
Virden, Local 354   217-965-3433
Waukegan, Local 284   312-662-4738

INDIANA

Anderson, Local 32   317-778-3978
Decatur, Local 607   219-724-7670
Elkhart, Local 192   219-293-2998
Evansville, Local 35   812-422-0366
Fort Wayne, Local 58   219-483-7778
Frankfort, Local 352   317-654-8209
Hammond, Local 203   219-845-0666
Indianapolis, Local 3   317-636-3595
Kokomo, Local 141   317-457-3996
Lafayette, Local 162   317-447-2051
LaPorte, Local 421   219-324-0332

Logansport, Local 53   219-753-6781
Marion, Local 45   317-674-5710
Michigan City, Local 578
   219-872-9839
Muncie, Local 245   317-282-2134
Richmond, Local 388   317-962-6917
South Bend, Local 278   219-233-8111
Terre Haute, Local 25   812-234-6750
Valparaiso, Local 732   219-462-8611

IOWA

Boone, Local 574   515-432-2007
Burlington, Local 646   319-754-4705
Cedar Rapids, Local 137
   319-362-7902
Clinton, Local 79   319-242-6257
Davenport, Local 67   319-324-7088
Des Moines, Local 75   515-244-2058
Dubuque, Local 289   319-583-8434
Fort Dodge, Local 504   515-576-3452
Iowa City, Local 450   319-643-2347
Marshalltown, Local 176
   515-752-0247
Mason City, Local 230   515-424-2384
Muscatine, Local 551   319-263-0649
Oelwein, Local 483   319-427-3485
Ottumwa, Local 64   515-684-4439
Sioux City, Local 254   712-276-7594
Spencer, Local 405   712-262-6488
Waterloo, Local 334   319-234-0357

KANSAS

Coffeyville, Local 449   316-251-4274
Fort Scott, Local 755   316-233-4424
Hutchinson, Local 110   316-663-9881
Lawrence, Local 512   913-843-4966
Manhattan, Local 169   915-537-1928
Parsons, Local 250   316-421-2782
Pittsburgh, Local 452   316-231-5220
Salina, Local 207   913-827-9975
Topeka, Local 36-665   913-272-7052
Wichita, Local 297   316-684-1311

KENTUCKY

Ashland, Local 691   606-739-4927

Lexington, Local 554–635
606–255–4721
Louisville, Local 11–637
502–451–7509
Paducah, Local 200   618–524–8733

LOUISIANA

Baton Rouge, Local 538   504–926–5088
Monroe, Local 425   318–387–5030
New Orleans, Local 174–496
504–947–1700
Shreveport, Local 116   318–222–5183

MAINE

Bangor, Local 768   207–947–8027
Biddeford, Local 408   207–282–2437
Lewiston, Local 409   207–782–0029
Portland, Local 364   207–774–6757

MARYLAND

Baltimore, Local 40–543   301–728–4500
Cumberland, Local 787   301–722–2875
Hagerstown, Local 770   301–791–1551
Salisbury, Local 44   301–749–6372

MASSACHUSETTS

Boston, Local 9–535   617–536–2486
Brockton, Local 138   617–583–0192
Fall River, Local 216   617–679–6235
Fitchburg, Local 173   617–345–7191
Framingham-Marlboro, Local 393
617–295–8888
Greenfield, Local 621   413–773–9769
Haverhill, Local 302   617–373–0525
Holyoke, Local 144   413–533–5235
Hyannis, Local 155   617–394–4155
Lawrence, Local 372   617–686–2744
Lowell, Local 83   617–453–5621
Lynn, Local 126   617–581–3550
Milford, Local 319   617–473–0473
New Bedford, Local 214   617–994–3049
Newburyport, Local 378   617–462–2276
North Adams, Local 96   413–664–6216

Northampton, Local 220   413–527–4094
Norwood, Local 343   617–326–9141
Pittsfield, Local 109   413–448–8541
Plymouth, Local 281   617–746–2247
Southbridge, Local 494   617–764–4652
Springfield, Local 171   413–594–4170
Taunton, Local 231   617–822–0009
Worcester, Local 143   617–852–3244

MICHIGAN

Ann Arbor, Local 625   313–668–8041
Battle Creek, Local 594   616–962–3063
Bay City, Local 127   517–684–8208
Benton Harbor, Local 232
616–429–8777
Detroit, Local 5   313–345–6200
Escanaba, Local 663   906–786–0271
Flint, Local 542   313–235–3708
Grand Rapids, Local 56   616–874–7421
Iron Mountain, Local 249
906–774–9629
Jackson, Local 387   517–784–3784
Kalamazoo, Local 228   616–344–0049
Lansing, Local 303   517–484–4461
Marquette, Local 218   906–387–2123
Menominee, Local 39   906–863–2073
Muskegon, Local 252   616–733–2227
Pontiac, Local 784   313–333–7177
Port Huron, Local 33   313–982–8390
Saginaw, Local 57   517–793–1877
Sault Ste. Marie, Local 593
906–632–6226
Stambaugh, Local 523   906–265–3600

MINNESOTA

Albert Lea, Local 567   507–373–4310
Austin, Local 766   507–433–8373
Brainerd, Local 487   218–764–2275
Duluth, Local 18   218–728–1990
Faribault, Local 565   507–334–6668
Hibbing, Local 612   218–262–2941
International Falls, Local 156
218–283–3734
Mankato, Local 477   507–625–3339
Minneapolis, Local 73   612–333–8205
New Prague, Local 602   612–758–2227

New Ulm, Local 513   507-354-6807
Owatonna, Local 490   no telephone number.
Rochester, Local 437   507-288-1519
St. Cloud, Local 536   612-253-6981
St. Paul, Local 30   612-698-0877
Virginia, Local 459   218-741-4935
Winona, Local 453   507-452-4885

MISSISSIPPI

Hattiesburg, Local 568   601-544-2834
Jackson, Local 579   601-924-9313

MISSOURI

Cape Girardeau, Local 818
  314-334-2727
Jefferson City, Local 217
  314-636-4514
Joplin, Local 620   417-624-1892
Kansas City, Local 34-627
  816-221-6934
St. Joseph, Local 50   816-232-7592
St. Louis, Local 2-197   314-781-6612
Sedalia, Local 22   816-826-7334
Springfield, Local 150   417-869-5226

MONTANA

Anaconda, Local 81   406-563-3385
Billings, Local 439   406-252-1658
Bozeman, Local 709   406-586-6248
Butte, Local 241   406-792-3272
Deer Lodge, Local 555   406-846-1522
Great Falls, Local 365   406-452-3962
Helena, Local 642   406-933-5985
Kalispell, Local 552   406-857-3560
Livingston, Local 358   406-222-1274
Miles City, Local 429   406-232-2247
Missoula, Local 498   406-728-3473

NEBRASKA

Grand Island, Local 777
  308-382-7932
Lincoln, Local 463   402-474-3868

North Platte, Local 609   308-532-5037
Omaha, Local 70-558   402-571-2722

NEVADA

Las Vegas, Local 369   702-739-9369
Reno, Local 368   702-323-2116

NEW HAMPSHIRE

Concord, Local 374   603-228-8254
Keene, Local 634   603-353-1565
Manchester, Local 349   603-622-9084
Portsmouth, Local 376   603-436-3893

NEW JERSEY

Asbury Park, Local 399   201-477-9668
Atlantic City, Local 661-708
  609-345-4661
Burlington, Local 336   609-499-0569
Dover, Local 237   201-845-7426
Elizabeth, Local 151   201-789-0109
Jersey City, Local 526   201-653-0750
Morristown, Local 177   201-539-2619
Newark, Local 16   201-675-1333
New Brunswick, Local 204
  201-572-2832
Paterson, Local 248   201-274-8265
Perth Amboy, Local 373   201-634-0750
Plainfield, Local 746   201-647-3773
Trenton, Local 62   609-586-0022
Vineland, Local 595   609-692-3070

NEW MEXICO

Albuquerque, Local 618   505-255-2069
Roswell, Local 640   505-622-7125

NEW YORK

Albany, Local 14   518-436-1909
Amsterdam, Local 133   518-883-5713
Auburn, Local 239   315-253-3345
Batavia, Local 575   716-343-1812
Binghamton, Local 380   607-724-3866

AFM LOCALS

Buffalo, Local 92   716–873–1275
Cortland, Local 528   607–753–0742
Dunkirk, Local 108   716–673–1118
East Aurora, Local 366   716–886–5902
Elmira, Local 314   607–562–8114
Fulton, Local 267   315–592–4347
Geneva, Local 570   315–789–5441
Glens Falls, Local 129   518–793–4801
Gloversville, Local 163   518–725–1256
Hamburg, Local 649   716–649–5775
Hornell, Local 416   607–324–1370
Hudson, Local 676   518–851–7743
Ithaca, Local 132   607–272–8170
Jamestown, Local 134   716–665–3458
Kingston, Local 215   914–679–6227
Larchmont, Local 38   914–834–0823
Lockport, Local 97   716–434–2229
Medina, Local 312   716–589–7760
Middletown, Local 809   914–343–5578
Newburgh, Local 291   914–562–3968
New York City, Local 802
   212–757–7722
Niagara Falls, Local 106
   716–284–6247
Olean-Salamanca, Local 115–614
   716–945–4667
Oneonta, Local 443   607–432–7162
Ossining, Local 398   914–762–0877
Oswego, Local 441   315–343–0557
Port Jervis, Local 667   914–856–5612
Poughkeepsie, Local 238
   914–471–2305
Rochester, Local 66   716–546–7633
Rome, Local 313   315–336–3534
Saratoga Springs, Local 506
   518–584–7835
Schenectady, Local 85   518–346–2086
Syracuse, Local 78   315–472–3056
Tonawanda, Local 209   716–692–7109
Troy, Local 13   518–785–8275
Utica, Local 51   315–896–2514
Watertown, Local 734   315–788–4583
Yonkers, Local 402   914–478–0402

NORTH CAROLINA

Charlotte, Local 342   704–377–2764
Greensboro, Local 332   919–855–1333
Raleigh, Local 500   919–872–0702

NORTH DAKOTA

Bismarck, Local 229   701–258–7777
Fargo, Local 382   701–235–4991
Grand Forks, Local 485
   701–775–9843
Minot, Local 656   701–852–2769

OHIO

Akron, Local 24   216–376–8174
Alliance, Local 68   216–821–2761
Ashtabula, Local 107   216–992–0970
Cambridge, Local 415   614–432–2397
Canton-Massillon, Local 111
   216–454–7430
Cincinnati, Local 1   513–241–0900
Cleveland, Local 4   216–771–1802
Columbus, Local 103   614–261–9826
Coshocton, Local 478   614–545–6121
Dayton, Local 101–473   513–253–2791
East Liverpool, Local 172
   216–385–0637
Fostoria, Local 121   419–435–5437
Greenville, Local 599   513–548–6714
Hamilton, Local 31   513–892–7922
Lancaster, Local 683   614–654–1560
Lima, Local 320   419–227–1372
Lorain and Elyria, Local 146
   216–967–3023
Mansfield, Local 159   419–529–2754
Marietta, Local 179   614–373–6322
Marion, Local 531   614–389–4226
Mentor, Local 657   216–25 –2628
Middletown, Local 321   513–423–8049
Mt. Vernon, Local 338   614–668–4772
Newark, Local 122   614–366–1757
New Philadelphia-Dover, Local 404
   216–343–0266
Piqua, Local 576   513–773–2665
Portsmouth, Local 482   614–574–6796
Salem, Local 222   216–332–1281
Sandusky, Local 573   419–625–1499
Springfield, Local 160   513–390–2351
Steubenville, Local 223   614–282–5212
Toledo, Local 15–286   419–243–2017
Warren, Local 118   216–369–6745
Youngstown, Local 86–242
   216–788–8451

Zanesville, Local 54   614–453–6112

OKLAHOMA

Bartlesville, Local 316   918–333–2054
Oklahoma City, Local 375
    405–235–5079
Tulsa, Local 94   918–742–5097

OREGON

Astoria, Local 608   503–458–5150
Coos Bay, Local 520   503–888–5658
Eugene, Local 689   503–343–9329
Klamath Falls, Local 495
    503–884–8183
Medford, Local 597   503–772–2431
Pendleton, Local 560   503–276–0447
Portland, Local 99   503–235–8791
Roseburg, Local 539   503–672–4502

PENNSYLVANIA

Allentown, Local 561   215–433–8435
Altoona, Local 564   814–943–3230
Beaver Falls, Local 82   412–774–6715
Berwick, Local 727   717–752–5115
Bethlehem, Local 411   215–866–8131
Bradford, Local 84   814–368–7421
Butler, Local 188   412–287–1591
Canonsburg, Local 509   412–745–2814
Carbondale, Local 130   717–282–3155
Charleroi, Local 592   412–785–5534
Chester, Local 484   215–874–7158
Columbia, Local 296   717–426–3242
Connellsville, Local 417   412–628–1530
Easton, Local 379   215–253–0164
Ellwood City, Local 545   412–728–3975
Erie, Local 17   814–864–5846
Freeland, Local 557   717–636–0600
Glen Lyon, Local 696   717–735–1338
Greensburg, Local 339   412–834–5596
Greenville, Local 460   412–588–7604
Hanover, Local 49   717–632–7272
Harrisburg, Local 269   717–234–8400
Hazleton, Local 139   717–455–5160
Indiana, Local 251   412–463–0814
Johnstown, Local 41   814–255–5033

Kittanning, Local 603   412–543–2607
Lancaster, Local 294   717–733–3410
Lansford, Local 436   717–645–5527
Lebanon, Local 750   215–376–7038
Lehighton, Local 659   215–377–2350
Mahanoy City, Local 170
    717–462–3075
Meadville, Local 344   814–335–6254
New Castle, Local 27   412–654–5182
New Kensington, Local 630
    412–335–6651
Norristown, Local 341   215–272–6210
Oil City, Local 61   814–432–5518
Philadelphia, Local 77   215–567–1071
Pittsburgh, Local 60–471
    412–281–1822
Pottstown, Local 211   215–323–3136
Pottsville, Local 515   717–622–8784
Punxsutawney, Local 624
    814–938–5854
Quakertown, Local 569   215–282–4476
Reading, Local 135   215–779–1651
Reinerton, Local 401   717–647–2876
Ridgway, Local 317   814–776–1203
Sayre, Local 645   717–882–7953
Scranton, Local 120   717–342–4366
Shamokin, Local 456   717–648–0883
Sharon, Local 187   412–981–5760
Sunbury, Local 605   717–286–9449
Tyrone, Local 660   814–237–4344
Uniontown, Local 596   412–438–7587
Vandergrift, Local 476   412–845–7273
Washington, Local 277   412–225–9790
Wilkes-Barre, Local 140   717–822–4426
Williamsport, Local 761   717–368–2977
York, Local 472   717–764–5807

RHODE ISLAND

Newport, Local 529   501–849–3070
Providence, Local 198–457
    401–421–0460
Woonsocket, Local 262   401–762–5146

SOUTH CAROLINA

Charleston, Local 502   803–795–6232
Greenville, Local 694   803–244–5832

SOUTH DAKOTA

Huron, Local 693 605–352–4323
Mitchell, Local 773 605–996–5467
Rapid City, Local 686 605–348–3106
Sioux Falls, Local 114 605–338–5818
Yankton, Local 255 605–665–2488

TENNESSEE

Bristol, Local 556 615–968–3102
Chattanooga, Local 80 615–266–1725
Jackson, Local 639 901–427–8348
Knoxville, Local 546 615–687–8350
Memphis, Local 71 901–272–1746
Nashville, Local 257 615–244–9514

TEXAS

Amarillo, Local 532 806–383–6232
Austin, Local 433 512–476–6798
Beaumont-Port Arthur, Local 464–615
  713–727–7645
Corpus Christi, Local 644
  512–855–1741
Dallas, Local 146 214–742–5868
El Paso, Local 466 915–859–7982
Fort Worth, Local 72 817–927–8478
Galveston, Local 74 713–763–3754
Houston, Local 65 713–236–8676
San Angelo, Local 361 915–653–2690
San Antonio, Local 23 512–227–3582
Waco, Local 306 817–772–7929
Wichita Falls, Local 688 817–766–0859

UTAH

Ogden, Local 356 801–782–9564
Provo, Local 272 801–377–0857
Salt Lake City, Local 104
  801–581–8707

VERMONT

Burlington, Local 351 802–862–0153

VIRGINIA

Covington, Local 674 703–962–3346
Lynchburg, Local 157 703–845–2383
Newport News, Local 199
  804–380–1022
Norfolk, Local 125 804–622–8095
Richmond, Local 123 804–285–0114
Roanoke, Local 165 703–342–8933

WASHINGTON

Aberdeen, Local 236 206–532–1848
Anacortes, Local 461 206–855–1169
Bellingham, Local 451 206–733–2850
Centralia, Local 505 206–736–1474
Everett, Local 184 206–259–3802
Kelso-Longview, Local 668
  206–423–5010
Moses Lake, Local 397 509–765–3267
Olympia, Local 124 206–491–1680
Port Angeles, Local 395 206–457–0545
Pasco, Local 524 509–547–6698
Renton-Auburn, Local 360
  206–852–6695
Seattle, Local 76 206–623–0025
Spokane, Local 105 509–624–3102
Tacoma, Local 117 206–272–1177
Walla Walla, Local 501 509–529–1843
Wenatchee, Local 233 509–663–4555
Yakima, Local 442 509–452–0802

WEST VIRGINIA

Bluefield, Local 419 304–327–8743
Charleston, Local 136 304–346–9693
Clarksburg, Local 580 304–842–3088
Fairmont, Local 507 304–366–1635
Grafton, Local 684 304–457–3524
Huntington, Local 362 304–453–2438
Morgantown, Local 562 304–599–0793
Moundsville, Local 492 304–845–2225
Parkersburg, Local 259 304–422–1331
Wheeling, Local 142 304–233–0620

WISCONSIN

Abbotsford, Local 194 715–748–4482

Antigo, Local 638   no telephone number
Appleton, Local 337   414-734-0021
Baraboo, Local 327   608-522-4486
Beaver Dam, Local 422   414-887-2984
Beloit, Local 183   608-362-8356
Eau Claire, Local 345   715-832-1937
Elkhorn, Local 680   414-723-4186
Fond du Lac, Local 309   414-921-9248
Green Bay, Local 205   414-432-1340
Janesville, Local 328   608-754-7474
Kenosha, Local 59   414-658-8789
Kewaunee, Local 604   414-468-5116
LaCrosse, Local 201   608-788-6592
Madison, Local 166   608-238-3420
Manitowoc, Local 195   414-684-4104
Marchfield, Local 270   715-384-9942
Milwaukee, Local 8   414-444-5234
Monroe, Local 243   608-439-5563
Neenah and Menasha, Local 182
   414-235-7088
New London, Local 300   414-779-6564
Oconto Falls, Local 648   414-834-5153

Oshkosh, Local 46   414-235-3461
Racine, Local 42   414-634-2839
Rhinelander, Local 489   715-362-2787
Shawano, Local 227   715-758-8812
Sheboygan, Local 95   414-452-4435
Stevens Point, Local 213   715-344-2099
Sturgeon Bay, Local 654   414-743-6319
Superior, Local 260   715-394-3235
Watertown, Local 469   414-925-3749
Waukesha, Local 193   414-542-2425
Wausau, Local 480   715-359-2505
Wisconsin Rapids, Local 610
   715-423-3050

WYOMING

Casper, Local 381   307-237-8616
Cheyenne, Local 590   307-632-1057
Rock Springs, Local 470   307-362-3383
Sheridan, Local 348   307-674-7030

AMERICAN FEDERATION OF TELEVISION AND RADIO ARTISTS (AFTRA) LOCALS

Albany, NY   518–436–4841
Atlanta, GA   404–237–0831;
   404–237–9961
Binghamton, NY   607–723–7311
Boston, MA   617–742–0208;
   617–742–2688
Buffalo, NY   716–854–6495
Chicago, IL   312–372–8081
Cincinnati, OH   513–241–7332
Cleveland, OH   216–781–2255
Columbus-Dayton, OH   614–261–7952
Dallas-Fort Worth, TX   214–522–2080
Denver, CO   303–388–4287
Detroit, MI   313–354–1774
District of Columbia   202–657–2560
Fresno, CA   209–224–8929
Indianapolis, IN   317–636–5425
Kansas City-Omaha, NE   816–753–4557
Los Angeles, CA   213–461–8111
Louisville, KY   502–584–6594

Miami, FL   305–759–4121
Minneapolis, MN   612–871–2404
Nashville, TN   615–256–0155
New Orleans, LA   504–524–9903
New York, NY   212–265–7700
Peoria, IL   309–699–3961
Philadelphia, PA   215–732–0507
Phoenix, AZ   602–957–9789
Pittsburgh, PA   412–281–6767
Portland, OR   503–222–9111
Rochester, NY   716–325–3175
Sacramento-Stockton, CA
   916–441–2196
St. Louis, MO   314–231–8410
San Diego, CA   714–222–1161
San Francisco, CA   415–391–7510
Schenectady, NY   518–385–1385
Seattle, WA   206–624–7340
South Bend, IN   219–232–9553
Stamford, CT   203–327–1400

PUBLICITY FIRMS AND THEIR CLIENTS

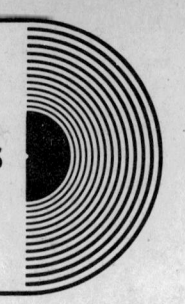

FIRM	ACCOUNT EXECUTIVES	CLIENTS
American-International Attractions, Inc., 300 Tideway Drive, Ballena Bay Harbor, Alameda, CA 94510. 415-522-2020.	E. Weiss; L. H. Jacobs; L. Baker; J. Holko; M. Tanner; M. Margulis; K. Foster; M. Rosen; B. Meyers; A. R. Khan; N. Akim-Nara; S. D. Bauenmeyer; N. Vanderslice; J. Rountree.	Firm did not wish to disclose names of clients.
Benjamin Ashburn Associates, 39 West 55 Street, Penthouse South, New York, NY 10019. 212-246-0385. *Los Angeles office:* c/o Commodores Entertainment Corporation, 6255 Sunset Boulevard, Los Angeles, CA 90028. 213-468-3782.	Benjamin Ashburn, president. East Coast: Karolyn Ali; West Coast: JoAnn Geffen.	Commodores; Platinum Hook; Three Ounces of Love.
Ken Baker Publicity Services, 4034 Twentieth Street, San Francisco, CA 94114. 415-864-2333.	Ken Baker; John Glodow; Brad Schulenberg; Linda Stokely.	Beserkley Records; Greg Kihn Band; Jonathan Richman; The Rubinoos; Earth Quake; The Tyla Gang; David Rubinson & Friends; Capt. Beefheart & the Magic Band; Ozark Mountain Daredevils; Stanford University Concert Series; Bay Area Music Awards (the Bammies); Herbie Hancock.
Bob Bank Publicity, 3025 Ocean Avenue, Brooklyn, NY 11235. 212-646-0352.	Bob Bank; Sheryl Krackow.	Charlie Calello; William Oz; Sound Labs Studios.

PUBLICITY FIRMS AND THEIR CLIENTS

FIRM	ACCOUNT EXECUTIVES	CLIENTS
Howard Bloom Organization, Ltd., 135 East 55 Street, New York, NY 10022. 212-751-9852.	Howard Bloom, president. Ellen Smith; Gayle Roffis; Joan Tarshis; Darryl Minger; Ida F. Langsam; Andrea Zax; Laurie Hersch.	RFC Records recording artists; Island Records recording artists; Anne Murray; Herman Brood; Randy Vanwarmer; REO Speedwagon; Triumph; Ron Dante; Cameo; Billy Falcon; Brand X; Jem Records recording artists; Larry Fast; ZZ Top; Melba Moore; Grace Jones.
Bollinger Public Relations, 9200 Sunset Boulevard, Suite 601, Los Angeles, CA 90069. 213-274-8483.	Henri Bollinger.	Firm did not wish to disclose names of clients.
Brokaw-Gangwisch (in association with The Brokaw Company), 207 Westport Road, Kansas City, MO 64111. 816-931-8000. *Los Angeles office:* 9255 Sunset Boulevard, Hollywood, CA 90069. 213-273-2060.	Kathy Gangwisch; David Brokaw; Sandy Brokaw.	Roy Clark; Bill Cosby; John Davidson; The Emotions; Freddy Fender; Gallagher; The Jim Halsey Company; Mickey Gilley; The Kendalls; Loretta Lynn; The Oak Ridge Boys; Tony Orlando; Ron Palillo; Freda Payne; Ray Price; Lou Rawls; Earl Scruggs; Doc Severinson; T. G. Sheppard; Dottie West; Don Williams.
C&S Associates, Inc., 8715 First Avenue, Suite 1008, Silver Springs, MD 20910. 301-565-2148.	Ilya Chamberlain; Clayborne E. Chavers; Steven E. Murray; Leonard Schnurmacher; Michael Shulman.	Howard Koch; Bernie McCane.
Maggie Cavender Enterprises, 25 Music Square West, Nashville, TN 37203. 615-254-5721.	Maggie Cavender; Dot Thornton.	The Nashville Songwriters Association, International; The Nashville Association of Talent Directors; Billy Deaton Talent Agency.

PUBLICITY FIRMS AND THEIR CLIENTS

FIRM	ACCOUNT EXECUTIVES	CLIENTS
Gary Crawford Associates, P. O. Box 767, Encino, CA 91316. 213-881-7323.	Gary L. Crawford.	Joey Gee; Sabu; Shout!
Shelly Field Organization, 25 Landfield Avenue, Monticello, NY 12701. 914-794-7312 or 914-794-8182.	Shelly Field.	Firm did not wish to disclose names of clients.
Gregory Joseph Foster, Jr., Inc., 175 Fulton Avenue, Suite 1218, Hempstead, NY 11550. 516-486-0500.	Gregory Joseph Foster, Jr., president. Gabrielle Lisa Brand.	Yvonne Hodge; Steven Duncan; Gregory Burge.
Freeman & Doff, Inc., 8732 Sunset Boulevard, Suite 250, Los Angeles, CA 90069. 213-659-4700.	Mickey Freeman; Red Doff; Adrienne Anderson.	Tennessee Ernie Ford; Cristy Lane, Jehry Miller; Lettermen.
The Garrett/Simes Company, 8732 Sunset Boulevard, Suite 220, Los Angeles, CA 90069. 213-657-1711.	Don Garrett; John Simes; Timothy Barker.	Isaac Hayes; Dionne Warwick; DeWayne Jessie; Peggy Lee; Bobby Short (West Coast).
Richard Gersh Associates, Inc., 200 West 57 Street, New York, NY 10019. 212-757-1101.	Bonnie Zucker; Janet Peperny; Arlene Gersh.	Van McCoy; Meat Loaf; The Sylvers; Lonnie Liston Smith; Charles Aznavour; Dick Clark; Bill Quateman; Tycoon; Kal Rudman.
Walt Gollender Enterprises, 12 Marshall Street, Penthouse Am, Irvington, NJ 07111. 201-373-6050.	Walt Gollender.	Irwin Levine (songwriter).
Ren Grevatt Associates Ltd., 200 West 57 Street, Suite 907, New York, NY 10019. 212-582-0252.	Ren Grevatt, president.	The Grateful Dead; David Bromberg Band; Fantasy Records.
Henderson, Kelley & Ward Inc., 3716 Hillsboro Road, Nashville, TN 37215. 615-383-0424.	David L. Ward.	Yongestreet Productions (*Hee Haw*).

FIRM	ACCOUNT EXECUTIVES	CLIENTS
Bill Hudson & Associates, Inc., 1514 South Street, Box 120339, Nashville, TN 37212. 615-244-8872.	Bill Hudson, president. Betty Hofer, PR director.	Country Music Foundation; Grand Ole Opry; Ronnie McDowell; Tree International; Soundship Recording Studios.
Judy Jernudd & Associates, 8101 Melrose Avenue, Suite 203, Los Angeles, CA 90046. 213-653-6950.	Jan Brown.	Firm did not wish to disclose names of clients.
Jolly Public Relations, 6605 Hollywood Boulevard, Suite 309, Hollywood, CA 213-469-4631.	Richard Bernstein, president. Stuart Needman.	Motivation Records; Barry Records; Seven Arts Press; Pacific Global Film Distributors; Anne Gaybis; Guich Koock; Peggy Arpa; Sabrina; Stephen Morrell; Tom Hernandez; Aldo Sanbrell; Joey Green; Bruce M. Fischer; Dean Selmier; Thomas Hilliard; Maxim Productions; Talent World Productions; Russ Fisher; Lea Lander, Pete Willcox; TransWorld Film Enterprises; Joseph Michael Cala; Thor Nielsen; Benn Squires; George Jammal; Russell Elliott; Tiffany Peters; Thelma Pelish; Albert Cole.
KLS Management, Ltd., 853 Broadway, New York, NY 10003. 212-982-0615.	Kaylynn Sullivan; Carolelinda Dickey.	Meredith Monk; Meredith Monk & Ensemble; Michael Nyman Band.
Laura Kaufman, c/o Leber-Krebs, Inc., 65 West 55 Street, New York, NY 10019. 212-765-2600.	Laura Kaufman; Trudi Hunter; Jules Solo.	Ted Nugent; Aerosmith; Beatlemania; Russ Ballard; Golden Earring; Max's Kansas City; Rex Smith.

PUBLICITY FIRMS AND THEIR CLIENTS

FIRM	ACCOUNT EXECUTIVES	CLIENTS
Levinson Associates, Inc., 927 North LaCienega Boulevard, Los Angeles, CA 90069. *New York office:* 10 West 66 Street, Suite 12B, New York, NY 10023. 212-595-3336.	West Coast: Robert Levinson; Eve Joffee; Chris Van Ness. East Coast: Beth Wernick; Patricia Ravalgi; Mark Stern; Jed Leland. Jr.	Firm did not wish to disclose names of clients.
Peter Levinson Communications, 75 East 55 Street, Suite 803, New York, NY 10022. 212-935-1036.	Peter Levinson; Deborah Horton.	Dave Brubeck; Maynard Ferguson; Billy Taylor; Woody Herman; Ramsey Lewis.
Lone Star Country Music Company, 4724 Ninth Avenue NE, Seattle, WA 98105. 206-632-1671.	Theodore Alvy; Stoney Walker.	Buck Rivets; The Redwood Roughcuts.
E. Magwood & Associates, Inc., 2600 Nonconnah Boulevard South, Suite 223, Memphis, TN 38132. 901-345-6834.	Fred Jones; Gloria Rankin; Claudette Galigher.	The Isley Brothers.
Mahoney/Wasserman & Associates, 510 Madison Avenue, Suite 601, New York, NY 10022. 212-751-2060. *Los Angeles office:* 117 North Robertson, Los Angeles, CA 90048. 213-550-3922.	Larry Eisenberg.	The Rolling Stones; Neil Diamond; James Taylor; Carly Simon; Paul Simon; Linda Ronstadt; Peter Tosh.
Manquin, 4423 Ledge Avenue, Toluca Lake, CA 91602. 213-985-8284.	Quint Benedetti; Manuel Rodriguez.	Agnes Moorehead; Amicus Corporation; Ruby Hillyer; Quinto Records.
The Merlin Group Ltd., 1560 Broadway, Suite 1515, New York, NY 10036. 212-575-9680.	Cheryl Sue Dolby; Sandra Manley; Becky Flora; Bob Pontarelli.	RFC Records.
David Mirisch Enterprises, 9911 West Pico Boulevard, Suite 650, Los Angeles, CA 90035. 213-277-3621.	David Mirisch.	Trini Lopez; Pat Boone; Debby Boone; Tom Sullivan; The Hudson Brothers; Buddy Greco.
The Music Agency Ltd., 135 West 50 Street, New York, NY 10020. 212-765-1616.	Jay Leipzig, president; Joel Borowka; Steve Sussman.	United Artists Music Publishing.

PUBLICITY FIRMS AND THEIR CLIENTS

FIRM	ACCOUNT EXECUTIVES	CLIENTS
Network Talent International, 98 Cuttermill Road, Suite 342A, Box 82, Great Neck, NY 11021. 516-482-4677. *Los Angeles office:* 9200 Sunset Boulevard, Suite 808, Los Angeles, CA 90069. 213-988-0644.	Richard Dostal; Dave Kuck.	James Brown; Judy Collins; Guess Who; Iron Butterfly; John Kay; Rare Earth; Steppenwolf; Wild Cherry.
Northcoast Design, 4724 Ninth Avenue NE, Seattle, WA 98105. 206-632-1671.	Ted Alvy.	Madshadows; The Jitters; William Earl Harkleroad.
Myrna Post Associates, 9 East 53 Street, 5th Floor, New York, NY 10022. 212-935-7122.	Myrna Post, president. Merle Frimark; Linda Wimbs; Pierre Lehu.	Theatrical personalities and recording artists.
The Press Office Ltd., 555 Madison Avenue, New York, NY 10022. 212-935-9041. *Los Angeles office:* 552½ Norwich Avenue, Los Angeles, CA 90048. 213-659-8987.	Carol Ross, president; Hariette Vidal, vice president. East Coast: Raleigh Pinskey; Julie Steigman; Beth Landamn; Lori Cohen; Didi Palmer (receptionist); Peter Crescenti. West Coast: Nancee Parkinson; Steve Sterling.	Paul McCartney and Wings; Kiss; Blondie; Samantha Sang; Amii Stewart; Ariola Records; Millennium Records; Love-Zager Productions; Electric Lady Recording Studios; New York Music Task Force; The Gizmatron; *Rust Never Sleeps* (Neil Young film) [partial list].
Rogers & Cowan, Inc., 9665 Wilshire Boulevard, Suite 200, Beverly Hills, CA 90212. 213-275-4581. *New York office:* 3 East 54 Street, New York, NY 10022. 212-486-7100.	Paul Bloch, president, music division; Sandy Friedman, senior vice president, music division; Phil Symes, international director, music division. East Coast: Joe Dera.	Bee Gees; Peter Frampton; Natalie Cole; George Benson; Olivia Newton-John; Kenny Rogers; Bette Midler; The Beach Boys; The Village People; The Carpenters.
Solters and Roskin, Inc., 62 West 45 Street, New York, NY 10036. 212-840-3500. *Los Angeles office:* 9255 Sunset Boulevard, Los Angeles, CA 90069. 213-278-5692.	East Coast: Sari Becker; Eric Rudolph; Katie Valk; Diana Parker. West Coast: Beverly Magid; Ian Dove; Eliot Sekular; Mitchell Schneider.	Eagles; John Denver; Dolly Parton; Charley Pride; Alice Cooper; Teddy Pendergrass; Paul Anka; Melissa Manchester; Leif Garrett; Mac Davis; Alive Enterprises; Barbra Streisand;

PUBLICITY FIRMS AND THEIR CLIENTS

FIRM	ACCOUNT EXECUTIVES	CLIENTS
		Frank Sinatra; Barry Manilow; Eddie Rabbitt; Butterfly Records; NARAS; Pink Lady; Blackjack.
Steinberg, Lipsman and Associates Public Relations, 8961 Sunset Boulevard, Los Angeles, CA 90069. 213-278-3838.	David Steinberg; Sari Steinberg; Arnold Lipsman; Mike Harris; Robin Rinehart; Pamela Turski.	The Crusaders; Sammy Davis, Jr.; Peter Sellers; Martin Mull; Cindy Williams.
W3 Public Relations, 8285 Sunset Boulevard, Suite 8, Los Angeles, CA 90046. 213-650-6535.	Sharon Weisz.	Fleetwood Mac; Climax Blues Band; Bob Welch; Amazing Rhythm Aces; Muscle Shoals Sound Studios.
The Wartoke Concern, Inc., 250 West 57 Street, New York, NY 10019. 212-245-5587.	Jane Friedman; Tom Murrin; Bob Laul.	Frank Zappa; John Cale; The Police; Squeeze; The The; Chelsea; Alternative; TV; The Cramps.
Harriet Wasser, 250 West 57 Street, Suite 1527, New York 10019. 212-582-1960.	Harriet Wasser.	Sid Woloshin Inc.; Al Ham Productions, Inc.; Rapp/Metz Management; Coco Records; Charles Fox; Carlos Franzetti; Big Boro Records.
Morton Dennis Wax and Associates, 1650 Broadway, New York, NY 10019. 212-247-2159.	Morton Dennis Wax; Jessica Josell; Elaine Wohl; Martin Folkman; Claudia Simon; Tom Gilbert; Fred Rosen.	Robert Stigwood Organisation; RSO Records; Xenon; CAM Productions; Famous Music; Screen Gems-EMI Music; M. Hohner, Inc.; Buddah Records; Chappell Music; Midsong International; Spring Records; Millie Jackson; Joe Simon; Fatback Band; Hugo & Luigi; Steve Karmen; David Lucas —Tom McFaul; RBR

FIRM	ACCOUNT EXECUTIVES	CLIENTS
		Communications; Radio Band of America.
Norman Winter Associates, 6255 Sunset Boulevard, Suite 714, Los Angeles, CA 90028. 213–462–7453.	Ron Baron, vice president; Sandy Wardlow; Justin Pierce.	Pickwick International; Windsong Records; Interworld Music; Welk Music; Solar Records; Gloria Jones.
Paul Wolfe Associates, P. O. Box 262, Carteret, NJ 07008. 201–541–9422.	Paul Wolfe, Jr.; Gary U. S. Hills; Barbara Hills; Diane Klosowski; Tony Grova; Susan Liss; Bobbi Lewis.	Memories of Elvis Show; Sonny Ray and the Delrays; Friends of Jackie Wilson.

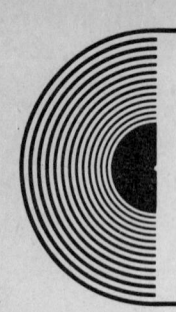

FAN CLUBS

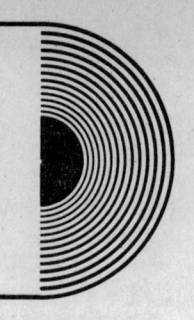

Aerosmith Productions, Inc., P. O. Box 1108 Radio City Station, New York, NY 10019.

Joan Baez Fan Club, c/o CBS Records, 1801 Century Park West, Los Angeles, CA 90067.

Official Bee Gees Fan Club, P. O. Box 9488, North Hollywood, CA 91606.

Best of Bette (Midler), P. O. Box 1010, Bayonne, NJ 07002.

The Boyzz Fan Club, c/o Cleveland International Records, P. O. Box 783, Willoughby, OH 44095.

Jimmy Buffett Fan Club, c/o Front Line Management, 8380 Melrose Avenue, Los Angeles, CA 90069.

Captain & Tennille Fan Club, c/o Moonlight & Magnolias Fan Club, Inc., P. O. Box 1050, Woodland Hills, CA 91365.

Carpenters Fan Club, P. O. Box 1084, Downey, CA 90240.

Lynda Carter International Fan Club, P. O. Box 1235, Beverly Hills, CA 90213.

Valerie Carter Fan Club, c/o ARC Records, 9885 Charleyville Boulevard, Beverly Hills, CA 90212.

House of Cash, P. O. Box 508, Hendersonville, TN 37075.

Shaun Cassidy Fan Club, P. O. Box 750, Medina, OH 44256.

Cheap Trick International Fan Service, P. O. Box 4321, Madison, WI 53711.

Commodores Fan Club, P. O. Box 784, Radio City Station, New York, NY 10019.

Earth Quake Fan Club, P. O. Box 589, Berkeley, CA 94701.

Earth, Wind & Fire, c/o ARC Records, 9885 Charleyville Boulevard, Beverly Hills, CA 90212.

The Emotions Fan Club, c/o ARC Records, 9885 Charleyville Boulevard, Beverly Hills, CA 90212.

Fania All-Stars Fan Club, c/o Fania Records, 888 Seventh Avenue, New York, NY 10019.

Fleetwood Mac Fan Club, c/o Winterland Productions, 890 Tennessee Street, San Francisco, CA 94107.

Grateful Dead, Box 1073, San Rafael, CA 94901.

Friends of Elvis Fan Club, P. O. Box 16969, Memphis, TN 38116.

Daryl Hall & John Oates Fan Club, P. O. Box 1760, Grand Central Station, New York, NY 10017.

Isley Brothers Fan Club, P. O. Box 958, Radio City Station, New York, NY 10019.

Bob James Fan Club, c/o Tappan Zee Records, 888 Seventh Avenue, New York, NY 10019.

FAN CLUBS 729

Sonny James & Friends Association, Route 1, Box 207-A, Kilgore, TX 75662.

KC & the Sunshine Band Fan Club, P. O. Box 1780, Hialeah, FL 33011.

Greg Kihn Band Fan Club, P. O. Box 589, Berkeley, CA 94701.

Loretta Lynn International Fan Club, P. O. Box 177, Wild Horse, CO 80862.

Barbara Mandrell Fan Club, P. O. Box 800, Hendersonville, TN 37075.

Steve Martin, "A Wild & Crazy Guy," P. O. Box 77505, San Francisco, CA 94107.

Jimmy McNichol Fan Club, P. O. Box 760, Medina, OH 44256.

Kristy McNichol Fan Club, P. O. Box 760, Medina, OH 44256.

Ronnie Milsap Fan Club, P. O. Box 23109, Nashville, TN 37202.

Eddie Money Fan Club, 890 Tennessee Street, San Francisco, CA 94107.

Willie Nelson Fan Club, P. O. Box 571, Danbury, CT 06810.

Olivia Newton-John Fan Club, P. O. Box 730, Medina, OH 44256.

Kenny Nolan International Fan Club, 211 South Beverly Drive, Beverly Hills, CA 90212.

The O'Jays, c/o Philadelphia International Records, 309 South Broad Street, Philadelphia, PA 19107.

Pablo Cruise Fan Club, P. O. Box 779, Mill Valley, CA 94941.

Dolly Parton Enterprises, Box 8099, Nashville, TN 37207.

Freda & Scherrie Payne International Fan Club, P. O. Box 451, Lake Zurich, IL 60047.

Tom Petty and the Heartbreakers Fan Club, c/o Taylormade Productions, P. O. Box 6233, San Rafael, CA 94903.

Pockets Fan Club, c/o ARC Records, 9885 Charleyville Boulevard, Beverly Hills, CA 90212.

The Official International Queen Fan Club, 13/14 Cornwall Terrace, Allsop Place, London, NW1 4QP.

Jonathan Richman Fan Club, P. O. Box 589, Berkeley, CA 94701.

Rolling Stones Office, P. O. Box 2801502, Copenhagen V, Denmark.

Rubinoos Fan Club, P. O. Box 589, Berkeley, CA 94701.

Mongo Santamaria Fan Club, c/o Tappan Zee Records, 888 Seventh Avenue, New York, NY 10019.

Santana International Fan Club, P. O. Box 26671, San Francisco, CA 94126.

Neil Sedaka Fan Club, 1370 Avenue of the Americas, New York, NY 10019.

Lonnie Liston Smith Fan Club, P. O. Box 997, Radio City Station, New York, NY 10019.

Patti Smith Group, c/o Radio Ethopia, P. O. Box 188, Mantua, NJ 08051.

Rex Smith Fan Club, c/o Leber-Krebs Inc., 65 West 55 Street, New York, NY 10019.

Barbra Streisand International Fan Club, 521 Fifth Avenue, New York, NY 10017.

Synergy, P. O. Box 362, South Plainfield, NJ 07080.

Mel Tillis Fan Club, P. O. Box 12146, Nashville, TN 37212.

Weather Report, c/o ARC Records, 9885 Charleyville Boulevard, Beverly Hills, CA 90212.

Deniece Williams Fan Club, c/o ARC Records, 9885 Charleyville Boulevard, Beverley Hills, CA 90212.

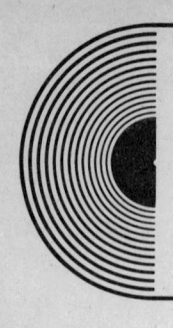

ATTORNEYS AND THEIR CLIENTS

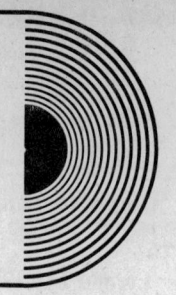

CALIFORNIA

FIRM	ATTORNEY(S)	CLIENTS
Law Office of Larry Allman, 1033 Gayley Avenue, Suite 108, Los Angeles, CA 90024. 213-277-4081.	Larry Allman.	James Burton; Don Williams Music Organization; A. Louis Bramy; Gregory Nelson.
Michael R. Ashburne, 950 Battery Street, Suite 300B, San Francisco, CA 94111. 415-421-8160.	Michael R. Ashburne.	Richard Pryor; Taj Mahal; Street Corner Symphony; Lonette McKee; Ken Nash.
Bernstein, Zerbe, and Buck Professional Corporation, 721 Lighthouse Avenue, P. O. Box 607, Pacific Grove, CA 93950. 408-373-0703.	Edward G. Bernstein; Gwendolen S. Buck.	Firm did not wish to disclose names of clients.
Law Offices of Stephen M. Baron, 10100 Santa Monica Boulevard, Century City North, 25th Floor, Los Angeles, CA 90067. 213-553-8200.	Stephen M. Baron.	Attorney did not wish to disclose names of clients.
Robert Brenner, 9200 Sunset Boulevard, Suite 404, Los Angeles, CA 90069. 213-462-2655.	Robert Brenner.	Attorney did not wish to disclose names of clients.
Cohen and Steinhart, 6430 Sunset Boulevard, Suite 1500, Los Angeles, CA 90028. 213-463-1151.	Martin Cohen; Terry Steinhart; Fredric Ansis.	Tom Waits; John Mayall; Robin Trower; UFO; Glenn Yarbrough; The Crusaders; George Duke; Discreet Records; Association of Independent Music Publishers (A.I.M.P.).

ATTORNEYS AND THEIR CLIENTS

FIRM	ATTORNEY(S)	CLIENTS
Cooper, Epstein & Hurewitz, 9465 Wilshire Boulevard, Suite 800, Beverly Hills, CA 90212. 213–278–1111.	Jay L. Cooper; Alan L. Grodin; Phalen G. Hurewitz; Daniel Webb Lang; Michael A. Painter; Ross T. Schwartz; Ronnie June Wasson.	Firm did not wish to disclose names of clients.
Kenneth B. Dusick, Attorney at Law, 8447 Wilshire Boulevard, Suite 409, Beverly Hills, CA 90211. 213–653–2123.	Kenneth B. Dusick.	Attorney did not wish to disclose names of clients.
Eric Eisner, Esq., 9885 Charleville Boulevard, Beverly Hills, CA 90212. 213–277–8148.	Eric Eisner.	Attorney did not wish to disclose names of clients.
Fischbach & Fischbach, A Professional Corporation, 2029 Century Park East, Suite 1370, Los Angeles, CA 90067. 213–556–1956.	Gregory E. Fischbach; Bernard J. Fischbach; Gerald B. Weiner.	Firm did not wish to disclose names of clients.
Goller, Gillin, Gottesman & Menes, 1901 Avenue of the Stars, Suite 1240, Los Angeles, CA 90067. 213–277–4895.	Phil Gillin; Joel Turtle; Eugene Gratz; Barry Menes.	Harvey Mason; SeaWind; Lee Ritenour; Friendship; JVC Corporation; Victor Publishing of Japan; Inphasion Records; Merv Griffin Productions (West Coast counsel for Roy Blakeman, Esq.); B-Line Productions & Management.
Gordon & Hodge, 544 Pacific Avenue, San Francisco, CA 94133. 415–391–4550.	Robert E. Gordon; Richard A. Hodge.	Firm did not wish to disclose names of clients.
Green and Hayes, 2029 Century Park East, Suite 600, Los Angeles, CA 90067. 213–277–8337.	William K. Hayes; Paul A. Green.	Firm did not wish to disclose names of clients.
Donald L. Hambrick, Attorney at Law, 9465 Wilshire Boulevard, Suite 730, Beverly Hills, CA 90210. 213–278–4782.	Donald L. Hambrick	Attorney did not wish to disclose names of clients.
Irell & Manella, 1800 Avenue of the Stars, Suite 900, Los Angeles, CA 90067. 213–277–1010 or 213–879–2600.	Arthur Manella; Werner F. Wolfen; Ronald L. Blanc; Richard D. Kirshberg; Peter M. Hoffman; Harley J. Williams.	Firm did not wish to disclose names of clients.

ATTORNEYS AND THEIR CLIENTS

FIRM	ATTORNEY(S)	CLIENTS
Kelly, Knapp & Cogan, 6399 Wilshire Boulevard, Penthouse Suite, Los Angeles, CA 90048. 213-651-5130.	Stephen R. Knapp.	Established and unestablished artists, producers, songwriters, record companies, and music publishers.
Leonard Korobkin Esq., 1801 Avenue of the Stars, Suite 310, Los Angeles, CA 90067. 213-277-8200.	Leonard Korobkin.	Johnny Cash; Freddy Fender; Roy Head; Curtis Mayfield; John Brimhall; Bob Monaco; Ariola Records; Cachet Records; Kidsname Records; Lakeshore Music; Music Enterprises; Starflite Records; Ziv International.
J. H. Kushnick, 9100 Wilshire Boulevard, Beverly Hills, CA 90212. 213-274-8805.	J. H. Kushnick.	Attorney did not wish to disclose names of clients.
Lenoir and Shaw, 6255 Sunset Boulevard, Penthouse Suite 2205, Hollywood, CA 90028. 213-464-8424.	Curtis M. Shaw.	Marvin Gaye; Bobby Womack; Gloria Lynne; Dennis Edwards.
Loeb & Loeb, 10100 Santa Monica Boulevard, Los Angeles, CA 90067. 213-552-7700.	M. Kenneth Suddleson; John T. Frankenheimer; Keith Zajic; Gerald Offsay; Mario Gonzalez; Karen Fairbanks.	Steve Martin; Andy Gibb; Michael Jackson; John Klemmer; Little Feat; Pure Prairie League; Elvin Bishop; Le Roux; Shelter Records; Bob Esty; Chris Kimsey; Val Garay.
Manatt, Phelps, Rothenberg & Tunney, 1888 Century Park East, Second Floor, Los Angeles, CA 90067. 213-556-1500.	L. Lee Phillips; George D. Kieffer; Deborah B. Reinberg.	Firm did not wish to disclose names of clients.
Manning, Reynolds & Roberts, 1900 Avenue of the Stars, Suite 2840, Los Angeles, CA 90067. 213-277-4796.	Virgil Roberts; Harry Reynolds.	Norman Whitfield; Whitfield Records; Solar Records; The Whispers.
Mason and Sloane, Professional Corporations, 9200 Sunset Boulevard, Los Angeles, CA 90069. 213-273-8351.	Owen J. Sloane; John E. Mason, Jr., Gary L. Gilbert; Evanne L. Levin.	Firm did not wish to disclose names of clients.
Law Offices of N. Dann Moss, 9220 Sunset Boulevard, Suite 306, Los Angeles, CA 90069. 213-278-8090.	N. Dann Moss.	Attorney did not wish to diclose names of clients.

ATTORNEYS AND THEIR CLIENTS

FIRM	ATTORNEY(S)	CLIENTS
Pacht Ross Warne Bernhard & Sears, Inc., 1800 Avenue of the Stars, Suite 500, Century City, Los Angeles, CA 90067. 213-277-1000.	Edward Blau; Ed Barton.	Firm did not wish to disclose names of clients.
Rosenfeld, Kassoy & Kraus, 270 North Canon Drive, Beverly Hills, CA 90212. 213-858-7788.	Michael Rosenfeld; Arnold Kassoy; Ken Kraus; David Alfschul.	Firm did not wish to disclose names of clients.
Law Offices of Barry K. Rothman, A Professional Corporation, 9200 Sunset Boulevard, Suite 509, Los Angeles, CA 90069. 213-550-6166.	Barry K. Rothman; John E. David; Eric R. Greenspan.	Dave Mason; Ron Wood; Ian McLagan; The Emotions; Les Dudek; Mike Finnigan; Jim Krueger; Ron Nevison; Jason Cooper; Jabre Inc.
Richard M. Rosenthal, P.C., 12301 Wilshire Boulevard, Suite 610, Los Angeles, CA 90025. 213-820-8585. **New York office:** 425 Park Avenue, 5th Floor, New York, NY 10022. 212-758-0809.	Richard M. Rosenthal; Thomas J. Wiley.	Ron Dante; Eleanor Greenwich; Tom Moulton; David Naughton; Susan Collins.
Schitty Hirsch & Schreiber, 9777 Wilshire Boulevard, Suite 800, Beverly Hills, CA 90212. 213-278-1500.	Ronald J. Bass; Paul L. Brindze.	Tim Weisberg; Dick Clark; Johnny Sandlin; Dennis Zeitlin.
Schlesinger and Guggenheim, 6255 Sunset Boulevard, Suite 1214, Hollywood, CA 90028. 213-462-6011.	Alfred W. Schlesinger; Alfred Kim Guggenheim.	Firm did not wish to disclose names of clients.
Schulenberg & Warren, A Professional Corporation, 10100 Santa Monica Boulevard, 25th Floor, Los Angeles, CA 90067. 213-553-8200.	Richard Schulenberg.	Firm did not wish to disclose names of clients.
Shahin Wawro & Lorimer, 1801 Century Park East, Los Angeles, CA 90067. 213-556-0200.	Walter L. M. Lorimer; Robert Shahin.	Firm did not wish to disclose names of clients.
Shapiro & Steinberg, P.C., 315 South Beverly Drive, Suite 210, Beverly Hills, CA 90212. 213-553-1601.	Michael R. Shapiro; Steven P. Steinberg; Mark B. Sandground; Steven E. Mangel.	Fleetwood Mac; Bob Welch; Kinks; Stan Getz; Al DiMeola; Alan Parsons; Mick Taylor; Vapour Trails; Sniff 'N' The Tears.

FIRM	ATTORNEY(S)	CLIENTS
Albert Spevak, Esq., 8748 Holloway Drive, Los Angeles, CA 90069. 213-855-1010.	Albert Spevak.	Boutwell/Miocua (artist merchandizing).
Strote & Whitehouse Professional Corporation, 280 South Beverly Drive, Beverly Hills, CA 90212. 213-858-8816.	Joel R. Strote; Richard W. Whitehouse; S. D. Ashley.	Motown Record Corporation; Warner/Curb Records; AVI Records; Alive Enterprises, Inc.; Liberace; Santa Esmeralda; Rick James; Freddie Perren; MVP Records; Grand Slam Productions; Perren Vibes Music; Jerry Lee Lewis; Chuck Berry; Commodores, Mike Curb Productions, Inc.; Jeff Lane; Hometown Productions; Ken Mansfield.
Larry A. Thompson, Esq., 1888 Century Park East, Suite 622, Los Angeles, CA 90067. 213-553-1555.	Larry A. Thompson.	Barry White; Unlimited Gold Records; Love Unlimited; Love Unlimited Orchestra; Sonny Bonc; Jim Nabors; Gloria Loring; Kay Starr; Johnny Brown.
David W. Williams, 9701 Wilshire Boulevard, Suite 900, Beverly Hills, CA 90212. 213-858-8051.	David W. Williams.	Attorney did not wish to disclose names of clients.

DISTRICT OF COLUMBIA

FIRM	ATTORNEY(S)	CLIENTS
Hayes & White, 1220 Nineteenth Street, Suite 503, Washington, DC 20036. 202-452-1320.	Edward Hayes, Jr.; Curtis T. White; Larisa Dobriansky.	Firm did not wish to disclose names of clients.
Albert R. Hopkins, Jr., Esq., 1850 K Street NW, Suite 880, Washington, DC 20006. 202-223-3947.	Albert R. Hopkins	Firm did not wish to disclose names of clients.
Raphael E. Tisdale, 2020 K Street NW, Suite 410, Washington, DC 20006. 202-466-6480.	Raphael E. Tisdale.	Frank E. Wilson.

FLORIDA

FIRM	ATTORNEY(S)	CLIENTS
Law Offices of Jason M. Chapnick, 726 NW 8 Avenue, Suite C, Gainesville, FL 32601. 904-373-2500.	Jason M. Chapnick.	Axe; Stardate International.

FIRM	ATTORNEY(S)	CLIENTS

GEORGIA

Robert A. Falanga, Attorney at Law, 1401 West Paces Ferry Road NW, Suite D-110, Atlanta, GA 30327. 404–231–0993.	Robert A. Falanga.	Mother's Finest; Dixie Dregs; Nohab Records.
David M. Franklin & Associates, 1290 South Omni International, Atlanta, GA 30303. 404–688–2233.	David M. Franklin.	Attorney did not wish to disclose names of clients.
Katz & Weissman, P.C., 5775 Peachtree Dunwoody Road NE, Suite B-130, Atlanta, GA 30342. 404–252–6600.	Joel A. Katz; Donald A. Weissman.	Willie Nelson; B. J. Thomas; The Outlaws; Sea Level; Hamilton Bohannon; Mylon LeFevre; William Bell; Paragon Agency; Rodgers Agency.
Ranson & Axam, 1290 South Omni International, Atlanta, GA 30303. 404–688–2233.	Philip F. Ransom.	Peabo Bryson; Anita Ward.

ILLINOIS

Carlins and Marrinson, Ltd., 180 North LaSalle Street, Suite 1810, Chicago, IL 60601. 312–726–9710.	Joel M. Carlins.	Styx; Frannie Goldie; Greg Clemmens; Gambler; Peter McIan; Full Power Records; Chicago Academy of Recording Arts and Sciences.

MASSACHUSETTS

Budd, Reilly & Wiley, 47 Winter Street, Suite 800, Boston, MA 02108. 617–542–1211.	Fletcher H. Wiley; Wayne A. Budd; Thomas F. Reilly.	Firm did not wish to disclose names of clients.
Esdaile, Barrett & Esdaile, 75 Federal Street, Boston, MA 02110. 617–482–0333.	Norman I. Jacobs.	Aerosmith; Webster Lewis.

ATTORNEYS AND THEIR CLIENTS

FIRM	ATTORNEY(S)	CLIENTS

MARYLAND

Days and McCants, 8730 Georgia Avenue, Suite 600, Silver Spring, MD 20910. 301–588–1850.

John Wesley Days.

Firm did not wsh to disclose names of clients.

Hadley, Hause & Tjanden, 8401 Connecticut Avenue, Suite 1212, Chevy Chase, MD 20015. 301–654–1181.

Clayborne E. Chavers; Steven E. Murray.

Howard Koch.

MICHIGAN

Law Offices of Gregg Reed & Associates, 225 Garfield Avenue, Detroit, MI 48201. 313–962–0088.

Gregg Reed

Firm did not wish to disclose names of clients.

Robert G. Weed, P.C., 241 East Saginaw Highway, 241 Building, Suite 515, East Lansing, MI 48823. 517–332–7602.

Robert G. Weed.

Ted Nugent; Amboy Dukes.

NEW JERSEY

Wright and Brennan, 167 North Avenue, Plainfield, NJ 07061. 201–561–5511. **East Orange office:** 604 Central Avenue, East Orange, NJ 07018. 201–676–5700.

Robert B. Brennan; William Wright, Jr.

Firm did not wish to disclose names of clients.

NEW YORK

Arrow Edelstein Gross & Margolis, P.C., 1370 Avenue of the Americas, New York, NY 10019. 212–586–1451.

Allen H. Arrow; Gerald F. Edelstein; John M. Gross; Gerald A. Margolis; Paul Truss; Clair Burrill.

Neil Sedaka; Bay City Rollers; Foreigner; Bette Midler.

ATTORNEYS AND THEIR CLIENTS

FIRM	ATTORNEY(S)	CLIENTS
Becker & London, 15 Columbus Circle, New York, NY 10023. 212-541-7070.	Mortimer Becker; Jack London; Daniel H. Kossow; Irwin J. Tenenbaum.	Firm did not wish to disclose names of clients.
Beldock Levine & Hoffman, 565 Fifth Avenue, New York, NY 10017. 212-490-0400.	Elliot L. Hoffman; Lawrence S. Levine; Myron Beldock; Bruce E. Trauner; Elliot G. Sagor; Jon B. Levison; Peter S. Matorin; Cynthia Rollings; Marc Bailin; Helene Fromm.	Firm declined to disclose names of clients except to report representation of record companies, artists, publishers, agents, managers, promoters, and producers (music, concert, film, stage, and television).
Alan Brutten, 1290 Avenue of the Americas, Suite 3710, New York, NY 10019. 212-581-1522.	Alan Brutten.	Attorney did not wish to disclose names of clients.
Burns Jackson Miller Summit & Jacoby, 445 Park Avenue, New York, NY 10022. 212-980-3200.	Herbert Jacoby; John L. Amabile; Jeffrey A. Moross; Arthur H. Schwartz; Arnold I. Burns; Kendall A. Minter.	Firm did not wish to disclose names of clients.
Casper & Epstein, P.C., 1780 Broadway, New York, NY 10019. 212-765-5038.	Robert L. Casper; Robert J. Epstein.	Firm did not wish to disclose names of clients.
Cohen Grossberg & Zinkin, 505 Park Avenue, New York, NY 10022. 212-688-6940.	Irving Cohen; David Grossberg; Benjamin Zinkin.	Firm did not wish to disclose names of clients.
Colton, Weissberg, Hartnick & Yamin, 505 Park Avenue, New York, NY 10022. 212-371-4350.	Edward E. Colton; Franklin R. Weissberg; Marsha S. Brooks; Ronald E. Feiner.	Firm did not wish to disclose names of clients.
Cowan and Cowan, 1350 Avenue of the Americas, New York, NY 10019. 212-246-2060.	A. Halsey Cowan; Philip M. Cowan.	Firm did not wish to disclose names of clients.
Dumler & Giroux, 575 Madison Avenue, New York, NY 10022. 212-759-4580.	John A. Giroux; Egon Dumler.	Firm did not wish to disclose names of clients.
Donald C. Farbes, 800 Third Avenue, New York, NY 10022. 212-688-7008.	Donald C. Farbes.	Attorney did not wish to disclose names of clients.

ATTORNEYS AND THEIR CLIENTS

FIRM	ATTORNEY(S)	CLIENTS
Feig & Taubman, 159 West 53 Street, New York, NY 10019. 212-586-6380.	Joseph Taubman; Seymour Feig.	Gunther Schuller; Harvey Phillips; John Lewis; Margun Music, Inc. MJQ Music, Inc.; Richard Peaslee; Sanga Music, Inc.; Pete Seeger; Harold Leventhal Management, Inc.; Folklore Productions, Inc. Doc Watson; Stefan Grossman.
Feinman and Krasilovsky, P.C., 424 Madison Avenue, New York, NY 10017. 212-421-8787.	Andrew J. Feinman; M. William Krasilovsky.	Paul Anka; Burt Bacharach; Billboard Publications; Chuck Berry; C.A.M.-U.S.A., Inc.; Jack Clement; Aretha Franklin; Bobbi Humphrey; Estate of Sergai Rachmaninoff; Allen Reynolds; Fats Waller; Music for Unicef.
John R. Fernbach, 1370 Avenue of the Americas, New York, NY 10019. 212-246-2060.	John R. Fernbach.	Attorney did not wish to disclose names of clients.
Franklin Weinrib Rudell & Vassallo, 950 Third Avenue, New York, NY 10022. 212-935-5500.	Leonard Franklin; Michael Rudell; John Vassallo.	Firm did not wish to disclose names of clients.
Goldschmidt, Fredericks, Kurzman & Oshatz, 655 Madison Avenue, New York, NY 10021. 212-838-2424.	Barry I. Fredericks; Mark P. Hirschhorn.	Firm did not wish to disclose names of clients.
Grubman & Indursky P.C., 65 East 55 Street, New York, NY 10022. 212-688-6470.	Allen Grubman; Arthur Indursky; Paul Schindler; Stephen Kopitko.	Village People; Hall & Oates; T. K. Records; K-tel International; American Talent International; Salsoul Records; Millennium Records; Jacques Morali; Albhy Galuten & Karl Richardson; Entertainment Company; Tommy Mottola; Hit Factory; Criteria Recording Studio; Millie Jackson.
Herman & Beinin, Esqs., 110 East 50 Street, New York, NY 10022. 212-758-3102.	Mark D. Herman.	Firm did not wish to disclose names of clients.
Walter Hofer, 221 West 57 Street, New York, NY 10019. 212-582-5030.	Milton I. Rothman; Alan N. Skiena.	Firm did not wish to disclose names of clients.

ATTORNEYS AND THEIR CLIENTS 739

FIRM	ATTORNEY(S)	CLIENTS
Howard & Holland, 10 Columbus Circle, Suite 1503, New York, NY 10019. 212–265–3340.	Edward O. Howard.	Dizzy Gillespie; Max Roach; Johnny Hartman; Estate of Jimi Hendrix; The O'Jays.
Jones, Michael & Cherot, 888 Seventh Avenue, New York, NY 10019. 212–541–6900.	Louise C. West	Firm did not wish to disclose names of clients.
N. Dennis Kaplan, 635 Madison Avenue, New York, NY 10022. 212–421–1620.	N. Dennis Kaplan.	Attorney did not wish to disclose names of clients.
Karpatkin, Pollet & LeMoult, 1345 Avenue of the Americas, New York, NY 10019. 212–765–2700.	Marshall Beil.	Firm did not wish to disclose names of clients.
Dennis Katz, P.C., 110 East 59 Street, New York, NY 10022. 212–758–1433.	Dennis Katz.	Bruce Johnston; Jan and Dean; Michael Nesmith; Pacific Arts Records; MK Dance Promotions; Ocean Records; Xenon (discotheque); The Monkees.
Kaye, Scholer, Fierman, Hays & Handler, 425 Park Avenue, New York, NY 10022. 212–759–8400.	David Goldberg; William M. Borchard.	CBS Records; The Decca Record Company Limited (U.K.); London Records; Peer-Southern Music Publishing Co.; RCA Records; Recording Industry Association of America; Estate of Igor Stravinsky.
Kazdin & Weinstein, P.C., Two Pennsylvania Plaza, New York, NY 10001. 212–564–3377.	Richard I. Bier.	Firm did not wish to disclose names of clients.
Law Offices of Eric Kronfeld, 1501 Broadway, 30th Floor, New York, NY 10036. 212–840–2200.	Eric Kronfeld.	Glyn Johns; Charlie Daniels; Cheryl Lynn; Lou Reed; Bob Johnston; Charles Brusco; Ronco Teleproducts, Inc.; Alan Walden.
Law Offices of Jules I. Kurz, 161 West 54 Street, New York, NY 10019. 212–489–7095.	Robert Flax.	Phonogram International B.V.; Intersong International GMBH; Sam Records; Midland Records; Grace Jones; E. G. Records, Inc.
Peter Lane, Esq., 60 East 42 Street, New York, NY 10017. 212–986–0086.	Peter Lane.	Attorney did not wish to disclose names of clients.

740 ATTORNEYS AND THEIR CLIENTS

FIRM	ATTORNEY(S)	CLIENTS
Leber-Krebs, Inc., 65 West 55 Street, Room 306, New York, NY 10019. 212–765–2600.	Robert Edward Donnelly; Eugene Fischer; David Krebs.	Leber-Krebs, Inc.
Levine & Thall, 485 Madison Avenue, New York, NY 10022. 212–980–0120.	Robert F. Levine; Peter M. Thall; Owen M. Epstein.	Firm did not wish to disclose names of clients.
Levy, Gutman, Goldberg & Kaplan, 363 Seventh Avenue, New York, NY 10001. 212–736–2226.	Jeremiah S. Gutman.	Desmar Music, Inc.; Euroclass Record Distributors, Ltd.; Improvising Artists Incorporated; Symphony of the New World.
Lawrence Lighter, 1350 Avenue of the Americas, New York, NY 10019. 212–582–5250.	Lawrence Lighter.	Roulette Records; AVI Records; Glori Records; Sweet City Records; Big Seven Music Corp.; Belkin-Maduri Organization; Inspirational Sounds.
Linden and Deutsch, 110 East 59 Street, New York, NY 10022. 212–758–1100.	David Blasband; Joseph Calderon; Alvin Deutsch; Mary Drugan; Frederick F. Greenman, Jr.; Edward Klagsbrun; Bella L. Linden; William K. Sheehy; Donna M. Crisalli; Bernard G. Schneider; Richard A. Whitney; Jules D. Zalon.	American Guild of Authors and Composers; CLEF; G. Schirmer, Inc.; Editions Solabert, Inc.
Machat & Machat, 1501 Broadway, New York, NY 10036. 212–840–2200. **Los Angeles office:** 2049 Century Park East, Suite 2717, Los Angeles, CA 90067. 213–553–8715.	Martin J. Machat; Steven E. Machat; John Lehr.	Electric Light Orchestra; Jet Records; Cerrone; Black Sabbath; Leonard Cohen; Phil Spector; Eugene Record; Pavillion Records; John Luongo; Jeremy Spencer; Status Quo; Real Thing; Space; Call Me Music; Helen Lowe, All-American Productions; Shel Talmy.
Moses & Singer, 1271 Avenue of the Americas, New York, NY 10021. 212–246–3700.	Stanley Rothenberg.	Golden Bell Songs; Maya Productions, Ltd.; Halrone Music.
Harold Orenstein P.C., 110 West 57 Street, New York, NY 10019. 212–247–6460.	Harold Orenstein; William Calderwood.	Gordon Lightfoot; Ray Stevens; Carole Bayer Sager; Acuff-Rose Publications; Frank Loesser Estate; Al Gallico; Johnny Paycheck.

… ATTORNEYS AND THEIR CLIENTS

FIRM	ATTORNEY(S)	CLIENTS
Parcher & Herbert, P.C., 10 East 40 Street, New York, NY 10016. 212-689-5606.	L. Peter Parcher; Peter A. Herbert.	Firm did not wish to disclose names of clients.
Barry H. Platnick, 250 West 57 Street, New York, NY 10019. 212-757-4315.	Barry H. Platnick; Henry B. Goldstein.	David Bowie; Michael Zager; Cissy Houston; Narada Michael Walden; Kleeer; Love/Zager Productions; Trax; JP's; Studio Instrument Rentals; Cowbell Agency; Electric Lady Productions; Patrick Stansfield Associates, Inc.; Keith Kevan Associates, Inc.; Jimmy Douglass; Dennis King; Iggy Pop.
Pryor, Cashman, Sherman & Flynn, 410 Park Avenue, New York, NY 10022. 212-421-4100.	Saul P. Pryor; Gideon Cashman; Paul J. Sherman; Alan H. Siegel; Howard Siegel; Lawrence Erbst; Ronald Kreidman; Stephen B. Rodner; Bradley Wechsler.	Tony Orlando; Gloria Gaynor; Petula Clark; Todd Rundgren; Melba Moore; Isley Brothers; Albert Grossman; Orleans; Spyro Gyra; Lenny White; Lonnie Liston Smith; Ashford & Simpson; Milt Okun; Teresa Brewer; Gordon Lightfoot; Laura Nyro; Patrick Moraz; Connie Francis; Arthur Blythe; A. A. Records; Private Stock Records; Buddah Records; Spring Records; Guardian Records.
Steven R. Rand, 1290 Avenue of the Americas, Suite 3232, New York, NY 10019. 212-541-4655.	Steven R. Rand.	Attorney did not wish to disclose names of clients.
Ressa, Nappi & Weinig, P. O. Box 1060, 33 Main Street, Port Washington, NY 11050. 516-767-5800.	Harvey Weinig.	Firm did not wish to disclose names of clients.
Roermer & Nadler, 605 Third Avenue, Suite 1501, New York, NY 10016. 212-972-1100.	Richard H. Roemer; Myron R. Nadler; Howard Krantz, of counsel.	Firm did not wish to disclose names of clients.
Richard D. Savitsky, 50 East 42 Street, New York, NY 10017. 212-697-8689.	Gary Richard Miller.	Firm did not wish to disclose names of clients.

ATTORNEYS AND THEIR CLIENTS

FIRM	ATTORNEY(S)	CLIENTS
Shaw & Stedina, 350 Madison Avenue, New York, NY 10017. 212-682-2233.	Leon Baer Borstein.	American Talent International Ltd.; Millennium Records; Delite Recorded Sound; Roulette Records; Adam VIII Ltd.; Big Seven Music Publishing.
Martin E. Silfen, P.C., 595 Fifth Avenue, New York, NY 10017. 212-986-0890.	Martin E. Silfen.	Attorney did not wish to disclose names of clients.
Silverman & Shulman P.C., 136 East 57 Street, New York, NY 10022. 212-758-2020.	Noel L. Silverman; Alan L. Shulman; Barry I. Slotnick; Linda S. Rein.	The Harry Fox Agency, Inc.; National Music Publishers Association (NMPA); Hal Leonard Publishing Corporation; Estate of Paul Desmond; Stan Getz; Jim Hall; Estate of Charles Mingus; Gerry Mulligan.
Barry M. Smith, Esq., 110 East 59 Street, Suite 1407, New York, NY 10022. 212-838-7970.	Barry M. Smith.	Attorney did not wish to disclose names of clients.
Stanley Snadowsky, 15 West 4 Street, New York, NY 10012. 212-228-6300.	Stanley Snadowsky.	The Bottom Line Theater Cabaret, Inc.; Capitol Theater; John Scher.
Michael W. Stout Law Offices, 375 Park Avenue, New York, NY 10022. 212-PL 9-4300.	Jeramy Berman.	Attorney did not wish to disclose names of clients.
Michael F. Sukin, P.C., 919 Third Avenue, New York, NY 10022. 212-838-6044.	Michael F. Sukin.	Attorney did not wish to disclose names of clients.
Taft & Kaminsky, 18 West 55 Street, New York, NY 10019. 212-586-8844.	Ronald S. Taft.	Firm did not wish to disclose names of clients.
Robert M. Urband, 641 Lexington Avenue, New York, NY 10024. 212-421-6190.	Robert M. Urband.	Attorney did not wish to disclose names of clients.
Jon M. Waxman, Esq., 65 West 55 Street, New York, NY 10019. 212-977-9340.	Jon M. Waxman.	Attorney did not wish to disclose names of clients.
Weiss Meibach & Shukat, 888 Seventh Avenue, New York, NY 10019. 212-765-4936.	Nathan Weiss; Ina Lea Meibach; Peter Shukat.	Firm did not wish to disclose names of clients.

ATTORNEYS AND THEIR CLIENTS

FIRM	ATTORNEY(S)	CLIENTS
Weissberger & Harris, 120 East 56 Street, New York, NY 10022. 212-758-0800.	L. Arnold Weissberger; Jay S. Harris.	Samantha Sang; Burton Lane.
Zissu, Stein, Bergman, Couture & Mosher, 270 Madison Avenue, New York, NY 10016. 212-683-5320.	Leonard Zissu; Alan J. Stein; Jerold L. Couture; Alan S. Bergman; James W. Mosher; George N. Stein.	Firm did not wish to disclose names of clients.

PENNSYLVANIA

FIRM	ATTORNEY(S)	CLIENTS
Barsky Golden & Remick P.C., 1529 Walnut Street, 6th Floor, Philadelphia, PA 19102. 215-568-0500.	Lloyd Zane Remick; Jeff D. Servin.	Grover Washington, Jr.; Phil Hurtt; Bunny Sigler; Karen Young; Richie Rome; Michael Pedicin, Jr.; Victor Carstarphen.
Bloom Ocks & Fisher, 1822 Spruce Street, Philadelphia, PA 19103. 215-KI 6-7100.	John Anderson.	Firm did not wish to disclose names of clients.
Steinberg, Greenstein, Gorelick & Price, 818 Widener Building, 1339 Chestnut Street, Philadelphia, PA 19107. 215-LO 4-3880.	David J. Steinberg.	Eric Records; Philadelphia International Records; Mighty Three Music; Bob Marley Music; Six Strings Music; Bob Marley; The Spinners; The Trammps; T-Connection; The Imperials; Bell and James; BHY; AKB; Gamble-Huff Productions; Baker, Harris, Young Productions; Bellboy Productions; Norman Harris—The Harris Machine; Thom Bell; Kenneth Gamble; Bernard Lowe; Leon Huff; Joe Jefferson; Charles Simmons; Linda Creed; Casey James; Leroy Bell; Record Museum; Ron Baker; Earl Young; Leroy Green; Ron Tyson; Jimmy Cliff; Jack Faith; Don Taylor Management; Lost-Nite Records.

744 ATTORNEYS AND THEIR CLIENTS

FIRM	ATTORNEY(S)	CLIENTS
Wolov and Rosenberg, 215 South Broad Street, 7th Floor, Philadelphia, PA 19107. 215-735-9690.	Malcolm Pierce Rosenberg.	Friday Morning Quarterback; Kal Rudman; Bill Hard; Inside Radio; Jerry Del Colliano; Sigma Sound Studios; Joe Tarsia; Independent Promotion Network; Fred DiSipio.

TENNESSEE

FIRM	ATTORNEY(S)	CLIENTS
Seymour S. Rosenberg, c/o Sy Rosenberg, Org., 3681 Summer Avenue, Memphis, TN 38122. 901-454-1393.	Seymour S. Rosenberg.	Sy Rosenberg, Org.; Wilson Bros.; Wilson Bros. Publishing; Lee Moore; Bagdad Publishing.
Benson & Ellis, 112 Twenty-First Avenue South, Suite 205, Nashville, TN 37203. 615-327-3334.	Craig B. Benson; Fred O. Ellis, Jr.	Firm did not wish to disclose names of clients.
Harris & Leach, 2 Music Circle South, Nashville, TN 37203. 615-259-4507.	James H. Harris III; Charles A. Leach.	Firm did not wish to disclose names of clients.
Martin & Cochran, 226 Third Avenue North, Nashville, TN 37201. 615-327-3000.	John D. Lentz.	Tom T. Hall; Tammy Wynette; Johnny Rodriguez; Charly McClain; BMI; Lavender-Blake Agency, Inc.

TEXAS

FIRM	ATTORNEY(S)	CLIENTS
Jerry R. Bonney, Attorney at Law, 201 Main Street, Suite 700, Houston, TX 77002. 713-224-7737.	Jerry R. Bonney.	Archie Bell and the Drells; Justice.
Lastelick, Anderson & Hilliard, 2612 Mercantile Bank Building, Dallas, TX 75201. 214-742-3941.	Jerry Lasterlick.	Charley Pride; Johnny Duncan; Pi-Gem Music; Chess Music; Roz Tense Music; Cecca Music; Chardon (booking agency).

Louis C. Owen, president; Gay Gelman, executive director.

Music Critics Association Inc., 6201 Tuckerman Lane, Rockville, MD 20852. 301–530–9527. Richard D. Free, executive secretary.

Music Educators National Conference, 1902 Association Drive, Reston, VA 22091. 703–860–4000. Dr. James A. Mason, president; Dr. A. Theodore Tellstrom, executive director.

Music Performance Trust Fund (MPTF), 1501 Broadway, New York, NY 10036. 212–239–8550. Martin A. Paulson, trustee.

National Academy of Recording Arts & Sciences (NARAS), 4444 Riverside Drive, Suite 202, Burbank, CA 91505. 213–848–8233. Christine M. Farnon, national executive director.

National Association of Broadcasters (NAB), 1771 N Street NW, Washington, DC 20036. 202–293–3516. Vincent T. Wasilewski, president.

National Association of Recording Merchandisers Inc. (NARM), 1060 Kings Highway N, Suite 200, Cherry Hill, NJ 08034. 609–795–5555. Joseph Cohen, executive vice president.

National Association of Schools of Music (NASM), 11250 Roger Bacon Drive, No. 5, Reston, VA 22090. 703–437–0700. Warner Imig, president; Samuel Hope, executive director.

National Entertainment & Campus Activities Association (NECAA), P. O. Box 11489, Columbia, SC 29211. 803–799–0768. Gary English, executive director.

National Federation of Music Clubs, 310 South Michigan Avenue, Suite 1936, Chicago, IL 60604. 312–427–3683. Mrs. Jack C. Ward, president.

National Music Council, 250 West 57 Street, New York, NY 10019. 212–265–8132. Merle Montgomery, president; Doris O'Connell, executive secretary.

National Music Publishers Association (NMPA), 110 East 59 Street, New York, NY 10022. 212–751–1930. Leonard Feist, president.

Recording Industry Association of America (RIAA), 1633 Broadway, New York, NY 10019. 212–765–4330. Stan Gortikov, president; Henry Brief, executive director.

PRINT AND FILM

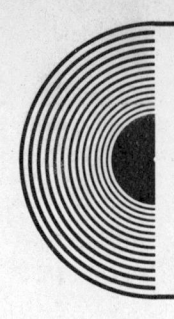

DIRECTORY OF MUSIC MAGAZINES

Ad rates quoted are one-time national rates. Virtually all music magazines accept a 15 percent agency discount for camera-ready copy.

The Album Network—sold only through subscription; tip sheet directed at album rock radio programmers, recording executives, retailers, managers, producers, and the press. 9000 Sunset Boulevard, Suite 1000, Hollywood, CA 90069. 213-550-3988.
   Published once each week. Subscription: $150 for 52 issues; unaudited circulation: 1,500. 42 pages, 8¼" wide, 14" high. No free-lance stories or photographs. Full-page black and white ad costs $1,000; full-page color ad costs $1,240. Fiedel-Antoon Enterprises, publisher; Don McGregor, managing director; Steve Smith, editor. Established 1978.

Allegro—free to members of Local 802, American Federation of Musicians; stories intended for professional musicians in New York City. 261 West 52 Street, New York, NY 10019. 212-PL 7-7722.
   Published once each month. Subscription: $3.30 for issues; unaudited circulation: 26,000. 18 pages, 11" wide, 15¾" high. Free-lance stories and photographs accepted. Recent features: "Man in the Street;" "Musical Rape;" "Brass Conference." Full-page black and white ad costs $650; no color ads. Local 802, American Federation of Musicians, publisher; Lester Salomon, editor. Established 1921.

Ampersand—free to affiliated student bodies; music and entertainment magazine distributed on campus by college newspapers. 1680 Vine Street, Suite 201, Hollywood, CA 90028. 213-462-7175.
   Published once each during school year. Subscription: $5 for 9 issues; unaudited circulation: 800,000. 32 pages, 8¼" wide, 13½" high. Free-lance stories and photographs accepted. Recent features: "Rickie Lee Jones Is Whiskey Basted and Nearly Wasted;" "John Klemmer—Pop Goes the Jazz Man;" "Zombies for Fun & Profit and Social Commentary." Full-page black and white ad costs $9,120; full-page color ad costs $13,200. Durand W. Achee, publisher; Judith Sims, editor; Byron Laursen, music editor. Established 1977.

Amusement Business—$2 at newstands; newsweekly providing attendance, grosses, and concession reports on mass entertainment events such as concerts, fairs, carnivals, and theme parks. Box 24970, Nashville, TN 37202. 615-748-8120.
   Published once each week. Subscription: $35 for 52 issues; total circulation (ABC): 15,000. 34 pages, 11-5/16" wide, 14" high. Free-lance stories and photographs accepted. Full-page black and white ad costs $1,641; full-page color ad costs $2,116. Walter J. Heeney, publisher; Tom Powell, editor.

ASCAP in Action—free to members of ASCAP, the music trade, schools, and libraries. One Lincoln Plaza, New York, NY 10023. 212-595-3050.

Published once every three months. 48 pages, 8⅜″ wide, 11″ high. Free-lance stories and photographs accepted. Recent features: "Billy Joel;" "Freddie Perren;" "Women in Theatre Music." No advertising. ASCAP, publisher; Merry Aronson, editor. Established 1979.

Audio Magazine—$1.25 at newstands; covers design and theory of current hi-fi equipment, record and tape reviews, and new product ratings. 401 North Broad Street, Philadelphia, PA 19107. 215-574-9600.

Published once each month. Subscription: $12 for 12 issues. 120 pages, 8-3/16″ wide, 10⅞″ high; total circulation (ABC): 130,000. Free-lance stories and photographs accepted. Recent features: "Build a Headphone Amp;" "Tweaking Your Turntable;" "Install Your Own Car Speakers." Full-page black and white ad costs $3,565; full-page color ad costs $4,290. Jay L. Butler, publisher; Eugene Pitts III, editor. Established 1947.

BAM, The California Music Magazine—free at record stores, music stores, and clubs; covers the California music scene in depth. 5951 Canning Avenue, Oakland, CA 94609. 415-652-3810.

Published twice each month. Subscription: $20 for 24 issues; unaudited circulation: 93,000. 72 pages, 11″ wide, 13½″ high. Free-lance stories and photographs accepted. Recent features: "The Big Knack Attack;" "Charles Mingus—An Immortal Legacy;" "California Studios—A Directory." Full-page black and white ad costs $1,045; full-page color ad costs $1,745. Dennis Erokan, publisher and editor; Blair Jackson, managing editor. Established 1976.

Backstage—$.50 at newsstands; production and postproduction coverage of the TV commercial, videotape, theatrical, and nontheatrical film industries. 165 West 46 Street, New York, NY 10036. 212-581-1080.

Published once each week. Subscription: $22 for 52 issues; unaudited circulation: 22,000. Free-lance stories and photographs accepted. Full-page black and white ad costs $630; full-page color ad costs $830. Ira Eaker and Allen Zwerling, publishers; Allen Zwerling, editor.

Billboard—$3 at newsstands; business weekly covering national and international developments in the photograph record, tape, audio, and audiovisual industries. 1515 Broadway, New York, NY 10036. 212-764-7300.

Published once each week. Subscription: $110 for 52 issues; total circulation (ABC): 46,679. 86 pages, 11″ wide, 14½″ high. Free-lance articles and photographs accepted on limited basis. Full-page black and white ad costs $3,683; full-page color ad costs $4,520. Lee Zhito, publisher and editor-in-chief; Eliot Tiegel, managing editor. Established 1894.

BOMP!—$1.50 at newsstands; covers rock history, new music, local bands, and pop culture. Box 7112, Burbank, CA 91510. 213-227-4141.

Published once every two months. Subscription: $8 for 8 issues; unaudited circulation: 39,000. 48 pages, 8½″ wide, 11″ high. Free-lance stories and photographs accepted. Recent features: "Talking Heads;" "More Songs from the Electronic Garage;" "Greg Kihn—The Lazy Man's Rock Star." Full-page black and white ad costs $880; full-page color ad costs $1,320. Greg Shaw, publisher and editor. Established 1970.

Buddy, the Original Texas Music Magazine—$.50 at newsstands; covers all facets of the music business. P. O. Box 8366, Dallas, TX 75205. 214-526-6049.
Published twice each month. Subscription: $10 for 22 issues; unaudited circulation: 89,000. 32 pages, 7" wide, 10⅞" high. Free-lance stories pay $.03 per word minimum, photos $5 minimum. Recent feature: "Sex and the Album Cover." Full-page black and white ad costs $1,455; full-page color ad costs $2,655. Stoney Burns, publisher; Kirby Warnock, editor. Established 1973.

Cashbox—$1.95 at newsstands; weekly trade magazine aimed at both the creative and business areas of the music industry. 6363 Sunset Boulevard, Suite 930, Hollywood, CA 90028. 213-464-8241.
Published once each week. Subscription: $80 for 52 issues; unaudited circulation: 25,000. 60 pages, 10" wide, 13½" high. No free-lance stories or photographs. Full-page black and white ad costs $2,555; full-page color ad costs $3,045. George Albert, publisher; Dave Fulton, editor-in-chief. Established 1942.

Circus Weekly Magazine—$1.25 at newsstands; music, news and entertainment, with emphasis on rock 'n roll, for teenagers and young adults. 115 East 57 Street, New York, NY 10022. 212-832-1626.
Published once each week. Subscription: $26 for 52 issues [**Circus**, P.O. Box 265, Mt. Morris, IL 61054]; total circulation (ABC): 134,707. 56 pages, 8⅜" wide, 10⅞" high. No free-lance stories. Recent features: "Rockers and Drugs;" "American World Music Festival;" "The New Military Draft." Full-page black and white ad costs $2,475; full-page color ad costs $3,300. Gerald Rothberg, publisher and editor. Established 1969.

The Complete Buyer's Guide to Stereo/Hi Fi Equipment—$2.50 at newsstands; information, critical analysis, and manufacturer's specs on everything for the beginning and semiprofessional audio enthusiast. 50 Rockefeller Plaza, New York, NY 10020. 212-586-6030.
Published once every three months. No subscriptions. Total circulation (ABC): 65,000. 176 pages, 8⅛" wide, 10⅞" high. Free-lance stories and photographs accepted. Recent features: "FM Antennas—Your Best Bet for Best Reception;" "Audio & Video—A Look toward the Future;" "Special Section on Phonograph Records." Full-page black and white ad costs $2,475; full-page color ad costs $3,475. Joyce K. Fuchs, publisher; David Drucker, editor. Established 1974.

The Confidential Report—sold only through subscription; consulting service to the radio and recording industries. 9000 Sunset Boulevard, Suite 1000, Hollywood, CA 90069. 213-550-3988.
Published once each week. Subscription: $150 for 52 issues; total circulation (Eli Bird): 1,500. 38 pages, 8½" wide, 14" high. No free-lance stories or photographs. Full-page black and white ad costs $1,250; full-page 2-color ad costs $1,310. Fiedel-Antoon Enterprises, publisher; Barry Fiedel and John Antoon, editors. Established 1977.

Contemporary Keyboard—$1.25 at newsstands; aimed at professional and serious amateur keyboardists. 20605 Lazaneo, Cupertino, CA 95014. 408–446–1105.

Published once each month. Subscription: $15 for 12 issues; total circulation (SRDS): 57,200. 80 pages, 8⅜″ wide, 10¾″ high. Free-lance stories pay $70-150, black and white photos $35-50, color-cover photos $100-150. Recent features: "Suzanne Ciani—Leading N.Y. Studio Synthesist;" "Dr. John—Legendary New Orleans Piano Rocker;" "Lorin Hollander—The Classical Pianist as Philosopher." Full-page black and white ad costs $920; full-page color ad costs $1,191. Jim Crockett, publisher; Tom Darter, editor. Established 1975.

Country Music Magazine—$1.25 at newsstands; general interest coverage of country music. 475 Park Avenue South, New York, NY 10016. 212–685–8200.

Published once each month. Subscription: $9.95 for 12 issues [**Country Music Magazine**, P.O. Box 2560, Boulder, CO 80302]; total circulation (ABC): 334,000. 74 pages, 8¼″ wide, 10⅞″ high. Free-lance stories pay $25-400; photographs accepted. Recent features: "Tammy Wynette—Sad-eyed Lady;" "Johnny Cash Regains His Freedom;" "Willie Nelson—The Gypsy Cowboy Goes Hollywood." Full-page black and white ad costs $3,000; full-page color ad costs $3,900. John Killion, publisher; Russell Barnard, editor. Established 1972.

Countrystyle—$1 at newsstands; lifestyle newspaper of country music. 11058 West Addison Street, Franklin Park, IL 60131. 312–455–7178.

Published once each month. Subscription: $6.95 for 12 issues; total circulation (ABC): 82,000. 48 pages, 10⅞″ wide, 11½″ high. Free-lance stories and photographs accepted. Recent features: "Kenny Rogers—Newest Superstar;" "Loretta Lynn's Haunted House;" "Freddy Fender—Dreams Come True." Full-page black and white ad costs $795; full-page color ad costs $1,095. Vincent Sorren, publisher; Ray Bachar, editor. Established 1976.

Creem Magazine—$1.25 at newsstands; fan-oriented magazine featuring news, interviews, stereo products, and record and concert reviews. 187 South Woodward Avenue, Suite 211, Birmingham, MI 48011.

Published once each month. Subscription: $6 for 12 issues [**Creem Magazine,** 10 Pelham Parkway, Pelham Manor, NY 10803]; total circulation (ABC): 160,000. 70 pages, 8⅛″ wide, 10⅞″ high. Free-lance stories pay $35-100; photographs accepted. Recent features: "Blondie's Dark Roots—An Intimate Interview with Debby Harry;" "Cheap Trick's Group Therapy;" "History of Punk—The Good, Bad, and Ugly." Full-page black and white ad costs $1,950; full-page color ad costs $2,850. Barry Kramer, publisher; Susan Whitall, editor. Established 1969.

CUE New York—$1.50 at newsstands; entertainment and leisure magazine for upscale New York metropolitan audience interested in the arts. 545 Madison Avenue, New York, NY 10022. 212–371–6900.

Published twice each month. Subscription: $18 for 26 issues [**CUE New York** Subscriptions, 401 North Broad Street, Philadelphia, PA 19108; total circulation (ABC); 245,000. 140 pages, 8⅛″ high, 10⅞″ high. Free-lance stories and photographs accepted. Recent features: "Summer Music;" "Cheers for Chamber Music;" "Einstein on the Turntable—Philip Glass." Full-page black and white ad costs $3,970; full-page color ad costs $5,590. Stephen M. Blacker, publisher; Nancy Love, editor-in-chief. Established 1932.

The Fugue—$2 at newsstands; Florida's magazine of the arts and music. 2951 South Bayshore Drive, Miami, FL 33133. 305-443-5251.

Published once each month. Subscription: $15 for 12 issues; total circulation (USPS): 10,000. 64 pages, 8½" wide, 11" high. Free-lance stories and photographs accepted. Recent features: "Music and Sex—How Helpful to Each Other?" "What Tempo Jogging?" "Ecumenical Piracy—Church Music at Home." Full-page black and white ad costs $500; full-page color ad costs $800. Marlin Ltd. Partnership, publisher; Larry Litt, editor.

The Gavin Report—sold only through subscription; oldest continuing weekly radio programming guide for record companies, radio stations, and producers. One Embarcadero Center, Suite 220, San Francisco, CA 94111. 415-392-7750.

Published once each week. Subscription: $200 for 52 issues; unaudited circulation: confidential. 32 pages, 7" wide, 10½" high. No free-lance stories or photographs. No advertising. Bill Gavin, publisher and editor; Gary Taylor, managing editor. Established 1958.

Goldmine Magazine—$1.50 at newsstands; international information center for collectors of rare phonograph recordings. P. O. Box 187, 31900 Utica Road, Suite 4, Fraser, MI 48026. 313-296-0185.

Published once each month. Subscription: $12 for 12 issues; unaudited circulation: 10,000. 100 pages, 8½" wide, 11" high. Free-lance stories pay $5-25. Recent features: "John Koenig Talks to Dennis Thompson about the MC-5;" "Lesley Gore —Changing with the Times;" "John Stewart—Survivor." Full-page black and white ad costs $130; full-page color ad costs $450. Arena Magazine Co., publisher; Rick Whitesell, editor. Established 1974.

Good Times—free at record stores, music stores, and clubs; entertainment and lifestyle magazine for the 18-40 market. 1619 East Sunrise Boulevard, Fort Lauderdale, FL 33304. 305-761-3401.

Published twice each month. Subscription: $8 for 27 issues; unaudited circulation: 18,000. 32 pages, 11" wide, 14" high. Free-lance stories and photographs accepted. Recent features: "John Wayne—The Last American Hero;" "Cheap Trick—Zeroing In on the American Front;" "The Cichlids—Splashy Past and a Lot of Future." Full-page black and white ad costs $425; full-page color ad costs $925. Richard Branciforte, publisher; Paul Beeman, managing editor. Established 1976.

Good Times, Long Island edition. 230 Arlington Circle, East Hills, NY 11548. 516-484-4477.

Published twice each month. Subscription: $8 for 27 issues; unaudited circulation: 32,000. 88 pages, 11" wide, 14" high. Free-lance stories and photographs accepted. Recent features: same as **Good Times** Fort Lauderdale edition. Full-page black and white ad costs $960; full-page color ad costs $1,460. Richard Branciforte, publisher and editor. Established 1968.

Goodphone Weekly—sold only through subscription; a communique to radio programmers of music and talk containing facts, theories, and airplay data. 4565 Sherman Oaks Avenue, Sherman Oaks, CA 91403. 213-995-6363.

Published once each week. Subscription: $120 for 50 issues; unaudited circulation: 3,000. 52 pages, 8" wide, 13½" high. Free-lance stories accepted. Recent features:

"Minorities Mix and the Mass Is a Conglomerate;" "There Is No Longer a Distinct and Separate Counter-culture;" "There's a Growing Market Out There for Intelligent Radio." Full-page black and white ad costs $1,000; no color ads. Goodphone Communications, Inc., publisher. Established 1978.

Grooves—$1.95 at newsstands; full-service periodical featuring interviews, gossip, and record reviews of rock, R&B, and disco music. 801 Second Avenue, New York, NY 10017. 212–986–5100.

Published once each month. Subscription: $14.95 for 12 issues; unaudited circulation: 350,500. 82 pages, 8⅛" wide, 10⅞" high. Free-lance stories and photographs accepted. Recent features: "Bruce Springsteen—Frenzied Flight, Glorious Landing;" "Meat Loaf's Rock Opera;" "Parliament Funks the Placebo Syndrome." Full-page black and white ad costs $1,900; full-page color ad costs $2,500. John Shelton Ivany, publisher and editor. Established 1978.

Guitar Player Magazine—$1.50 at newsstands; for professional and amateur guitarists. 20605 Lazaneo Drive, Cupertino, CA 95014. 408–446–1105.

Published once each month. Subscription: $18 for 12 issues; total circulation (ABC): 136,500. 172 pages, 8⅜" wide, 10¾" high. Free-lance stories pay $50-200, black and white photos $25-50, color photos $150. Recent features: "Larry Carlton—Studio Legend, Virtuoso Solo Guitarist;" "Howard Roberts—A Renaissance Man of Electric Guitar;" "George Benson—Pop Ambassador of Jazz Guitar." Full-page black and white ad costs $1,699; full-page color ad costs $2,370. Jim Crockett, publisher; Don Menn, editor. Established 1966.

The Harmonizer—sold only through subscription; published in the interests of Barber-Shop-quartet Harmony by the Society for the Preservation and Encouragement of Barber Shop Quartet Singing in America, Inc. 6315 Third Avenue, Kenosha, WI 53141. 414–654–9111.

Published once every two months. Subscription: $3.50 for 6 issues; unaudited circulation: 40,000. 32 pages, 8½" wide, 11" high. No free-lance stories. Recent features: "How to Produce a Hit Record (and Lose Your Job);" "Workers of the Society, Unite!" "A Battle of Songs." Full-page black and white ad costs $415; full-page color ad costs $1,240. Society for the Preservation and Encouragement of Barber Shop Quartet Singing in America (SPEBSQSA), publisher; Leo W. Fobart, editor. Established 1942.

High Fidelity—$1.50 at newsstands; news and articles about popular and classical music, consumer and semiprofessional audio and video equipment, and critical reviews of records and equipment. The Publishing House, Great Barrington, MA 01230. 413–528–1300.

Published once each month. Subscription: $11.95 for 12 issues [**High Fidelity**, 1 Sound Avenue, Marion, OH 43302]; total circulation (ABC): 360,000. 140 pages, 8½" wide, 11" high. Free-lance stories and photographs accepted. Recent features: "Recording Technology's Quantum Leap;" "Audio Heads into the 80's;" "Fred Astaire the Musician—Not Just a Pair of Dancing Feet." Full-page black and white ad costs $8,530; full-page color ad costs $10,800. Warren B. Syer, publisher; Leonard Marcus, editor. Established 1951.

Hollywood Reporter—$.50 at newsstands; business and entertainment daily for people in the motion picture, television and music industries. 6715 Sunset Boulevard, Hollywood, CA 90028. 213-464-7411.
  Published once each day, Monday through Friday. Subscription: $55 for 52 weeks; total circulation (ABC): 15,000. 24 pages, 8¼" wide, 11" high. No free-lance stories or photographs. Full-page black and white ad costs $787; full-page color ad costs $1,787. Tichi Wilkerson Miles, publisher; Martin Kent, editor; Cynthia Wilkerson Miles, managing editor. Established 1930.

Hit Parader—$1.25 at newsstands; in-depth interviews and stories about leading rock stars, plus lyrics of the top rock songs. Charlton Publications, Inc., Charlton Building, Derby, CT 06418. 203-735-3381.
  Published once each month. Subscription: $10 for 12 issues; unaudited circulation: 250,000. 64 pages, 8" wide, 10¾" high. Free-lance stories and photographs accepted on limited basis. Recent features: "Exclusive Peter Frampton at Home Interview and Pix;" "Kiss—New Show, New Look, New Music;" "The Cars—Stick-Shifting." Full-page black and white ad costs $1,250; full-page color ad costs $2,000. John Santangelo, Jr., publisher; Lisa Robinson, editor. Established 1943.

Illinois Entertainer—free at record stores, music stores, and clubs; includes reviews, interviews, feature stories, and photographs dealing with music and the entertainment industry, P. O. Box 356, Mt. Prospect, IL 60056. 312-298-9333.
  Published once each month. Subscription: $20 for 12 issues; unaudited circulation: 60,400. 72 pages, 10" wide, 15" high. Free-lance stories pay $.02 per word, photos $10. Recent features: "A Blazing Firefall in the Night;" "Kayak Sails the Phantom Seas;" "Nugent Flips Out over Pinball." Full-page black and white ad costs $700; full-page color ad costs $1,150. Ken Voss, publisher; Guy C. Arnston, editor. Established 1973.

International Musician—sold only through subscription; official journal of the American Federation of Musicians with articles on rock, jazz, country, and classical music and union news. 1500 Broadway, New York, NY 10036. 212-869-1330.
  Published once each month. Subscription: $.60 for 12 issues to AFM members, $6 for 12 issues to non-members; unaudited circulation: 305,000. 32 pages, 11¾" wide, 15" high. Free-lance stories and photographs accepted. Recent features: "Music Industry Declares War on Recording Pirates;" "Congress of Strings Is a Catalyst in a Young Musician's Career;" "Sylvan Levin—Perpetual Energy." Full-page black and white ad costs $1,881; no color ads. J. Martin Emerson, publisher and editor. Established 1898.

International Radio Report—sold only through subscription; weekly features and news articles dealing with the radio and music industries. 7011 Sunset Boulevard, Los Angeles, CA 90028. 213-462-0797.
  Published once each week. Subscription: $130 for 52 issues; total circulation (Haskin & Sells): 1,500. 64 pages, 8½" wide, 11" high. No free-lance stories or photographs. Recent features: "Contemporary Radio Delivers $$$$ Power;" "How to Handle a 'Personality';" "Bill Meeks—The Man Who Put Jingles on the Radio." Full-page black and white ad costs $1,200; 2-color ads available. Claude Hall, publisher; Judith Moorhead, managing editor. Established 1978.

Jazz Magazine—$2.50 at newsstands; devoted exclusively to jazz. 11 Bayview Avenue, Northport, NY 11768. 516-261-5901.

Published once every three months. Subscription: $10 for 4 issues; unaudited circulation: 20,000. 90 pages, 8¼" wide, 11" high. Free-lance stories and photographs accepted. Recent features: "Exploring the Contours of Gary Burton;" "Photo Tribute and Memories of Mingus." Full-page black and white ad costs $460; full-page color ad costs $710. C. Thomas Stites, publisher and editor. Established 1976.

Journal of Music Therapy—sold only through subscription; comprehensive periodical devoted to articles on music therapy research, new techniques, and activities of the National Association for Music Therapy, Inc. P. O. Box 610, Lawrence, KS 66044. 913-842-1909.

Published once every three months. Subscription: $12 for 4 issues; circulation (National Association for Music Therapy Editorial Committee): 4,000. 56 pages, 6" wide, 9" high. Free-lance stories accepted. Recent features: "The Effect of Interrupted Music and Incompatible Responses on Bodily Movement and Music Attentiveness;" "A Report on the First World Congress on Future Special Education." No advertising. National Association for Music Therapy, publisher; Janet Gilbert, editor. Established 1964.

Keyboard World Magazine—sold only through subscription; instruction, sheet music, artists' profiles, and stories of interest to keyboard players. P. O. Box 4399, Downey, CA 90241. 213-923-0331.

Published once each month. Subscription: $14.50 for 12 issues; total circulation (Ron Worrall): 17,000. 52 pages, 8½" wide, 11" high. Free-lance stories accepted; photos pay $7.50 each. Recent features: "Liberace Talent Search;" "Multi-talented Chuck Mangione;" "Harold Rhodes—His Piano Idea Was a Quarter-century Struggle." Full-page black and white ad costs $760; full-page color ad costs $1,010. Bill Worrall, publisher; Jean Garland, editor. Established 1972.

Latin N. Y. Magazine—$1 at newsstands; extensive coverage of Salsa and disco music in New York City. 419 Park Avenue South, New York, NY 10016. 212-686-6036.

Published once each month. Subscription: $10 for 12 issues; total circulation (ABC): 44,500. 84 pages, 8" wide, 10¾" high. Free-lance stories pay $25-75, photos $5-20. Recent features: "Birth of Disco;" "Roots of Charanga & Salsa;" "Sunday's Radio Battle—WRVR, WBLS & WKTU Fight for Latin Audience." Full-page black and white ad costs $600; full-page color ad costs $1,400. Izzy Sanabria, publisher; Anne Saxon, editor. Established 1973.

The Many Worlds of Music—free to BMI affiliates, qualified educational institutions, and the general press; deals with the writers and publishers of music licensed by Broadcast Music, Inc. (BMI).

Published once every three months. 48 pages, 8½" wide, 11" high. No free-lance stories or photographs. Recent features: "Women in Music;" "The History of Salsa;" "The BMI Payment System." No advertising. Broadcast Music, Inc., publisher; Russ Sanjek, editor. Established 1958.

Modern Recording—$1.50 at newsstands; designed for the creative recordist and musician who is actively involved in sound reproduction on a professional or semi-pro level. 14 Vanderventer Avenue, Port Washington, NY 11050. 516-883-5705.

Published once each month. Subscription: $12 for 12 issues; unaudited circulation: 85,200. 96 pages, 8¼" wide, 10¾" high. Free-lance stories and photographs accepted. Recent features: "A Session with Kansas;" "Studio Special Effects for Musicians;" "Profile—Cheap Trick's Producer Tom Werman." Full-page black and white ad costs $1,595; full-page color ad costs $2,205. Vincent P. Testa, publisher; H. G. La Torre, editor. Established 1975.

Music City News—$1 at newsstands; country music tabloid with news, interviews, and stories about Nashville's music industry. P. O. Box 22975, Nashville, TN 37202. 615-244-5187.

Published once each month. Subscription: $9 for 12 issues; total circulation (J. Alan Hopper & Co.): 172,000. 36 pages, 10¾" wide, 14" high. Free-lance stories pay $3 per 20-pica column inch; photographs accepted. Recent features: "On the Road with Mel Tillis);" "Kenny Rogers Becomes Music City Landlord;" "Loretta Lynn Predicts She'll Quit Road, May Go into Movies." Full-page black and white ad costs $1,500; full-page 2-color ad costs $1,650. Music City News Publishing Company, Inc., publisher; Lee Rector, editor. Established 1963.

The Music Connection—$.75 at newsstands; business news, articles, and reviews plus free classified ads and up-to-date gig guide. 6381 Hollywood Boulevard, Hollywood, CA 90028. 213-462-5772.

Published twice each month. Subscription: $15 for 26 issues; unaudited circulation: 27,000. 26 pages, 8½" high, 11" high. Free-lance stories pay $5-30; photographs accepted. Recent features: "All-star Producer Ken Scott—Creative Wizard and Technical Perfectionist in the Studio;" "Demo Tapes Flood L.A. Radio Stations as Unsigned Local Acts Scramble for Airplay." Full-page black and white ad costs $420; full-page color ad costs $670. J. Michael Dolan, publisher and editor. Established 1977.

Music Programmers Guide—sold only through subscription; national tip sheet with radio research, record charts, promotion priorities, and gossip. 233 East Erie Street, Chicago, IL 60611. 312-943-3900.

Published once each week. Subscription: $150 for 52 issues; unaudited circulation: 1,500. 34 pages, 8½" wide, 11" high. No freelance stories or photographs. Full-page black and white ad costs $950; full-page color ad costs $2,200. Howard Bedno, publisher; Peter H. Wright, editor. Established 1978.

Music Retailer—sold only through subscription; trade magazine for distributors and retailers of records, tapes, and sheet music. 210 Boylston Street, Chestnut Hill, MA 02167. 617-964-5100.

Published once each month. Subscription: $16 for 12 issues; total circulation (BPA): 21,000. 72 pages, 8¼" wide, 11¼" high. Free-lance stories pay $150-250; photographs accepted. Recent features: "Sheet Music Report;" "Black Music Merchandising." Full-page black and white ad costs $1,900; full-page color ad costs $2,400. Larkin Publications, publisher; Sidney L. Davis, editor.

Musical America—sold primarily through subscription; classical music journal. 825 Avenue of the Americas, New York, NY 10019. 212-265-8360.

Published once each month. Subscription: $24 for 12 issues [**Musical America**, 1 Sound Avenue, Marion, OH 43302]; total circulation (ABC): 25,000. 40 pages, 8½" wide, 11" high. Free-lance stories pay $100. Recent features: "The NEA and Education—An Overdue Truce;" "A Florida Bach Festival;" "A Russian Critic Defects." Full-page black and white ad costs $775; color available. Warren Syer, publisher; Shirley Fleming, editor. Established 1896.

Musicians' Insider—free at record stores, music stores, and clubs; trade-oriented tabloid geared to the Upper Midwest United States, forcusing primarily on rock 'n roll, jazz, and blues. 2882 Humboldt Avenue South, Minneapolis, MN 55408. 612-822-2131.

Published once each month; combined issue for January and February. Subscription: $10 for 11 issues; unaudited circulation: 40,000. 40 pages, 13" wide, 23" high. Free-lance stories pay $1.55 per inch, photos $25-110. Recent features: "Under the Influence—Alcoholism and Musicians;" "NNB—Modern Band Takes Big Risks for Freedom;" "People as Product—Live Disco Bands." Full-page black and white ad costs $924; full-page color ad costs $1,224. Dean J. Seal, publisher; Leslie Fugate, editor. Established 1978.

New on the Charts—sold only through subscription; information service, exclusively for professionals, listing important new songs, LPs, addresses, and phone numbers for the artists, producers, managers, agents, record companies, and publishers involved. 1501 Broadway, New York, NY 10036. 212-921-0165.

Published once each month. Subscription: $75 for 12 issues; unaudited circulation: 1,000. 32 pages, 8½" wide, 11" high. No free-lance stories or photographs. Full-page black and white ad costs $450; full-page color ad costs $1,000. Music Business Reference, Inc., publisher; Leonard Kalikow, editor. Established 1976.

New Music Literary Journal—$1 at newsstands; articles, information, announcements, and musical scores for aficionados of new music and literature. 26 Second Avenue, Suite 2B, New York, NY 10003. 212-966-5842 or 212-777-6787.

Published 5 times each year. Subscription: $10 for 5 issues; total circulation (New Wilderness Foundation): 3,000. 14 pages, 10" wide, 17" high. Free-lance stories and photographs accepted. Recent features: **"Satyagraha—An Opera, by Philip Glass;" "Orderly Thoughts, by Daniel Goode;" "On Something (To Do) Doing,** by Doris Hays." Full-page black and white ad costs $150; no color ads. New Wilderness Foundation, publisher; Beth Anderson, Michael Cooper, Richard Hayman, David Feldman, Peter Wetzler, Larry Kuharz, and Charlie Morrow, editors. Established 1973.

New York Rocker—$1.25 at newsstands; feature stories, interviews, record reviews, and unusual photographs in a tabloid format. 166 Fifth Avenue, New York, NY 10010. 212-243-4814.

Published once every 6 weeks. Subscription: $7 for 6 issues; unaudited circulation: 20,000. 56 pages, 10" wide, 15½" high. Free-lance stories pay $10-25, photos $5-15. Recent features: "Clash-mania—Joe Strummer Speaks Out;" "Elvis—The Story He Won't Tell;" "Author Richard Price—From Co-op City to Silver Screen." Full-page black and white ad costs $600; full-page 2-color ad costs $650. Andrew Schwartz, publisher and editor. Established 1976.

Paid My Dues: Journal of Women & Music—$2.75 at newsstands; feminist publication devoted to women who write, play, conduct, and care about music. P. O. Box 6517, Chicago, IL 60680. 312-929-5592.

Published once every three months. Subscription: $10 for 4 issues; unaudited circulation: 3,000. 44 pages, 8¼" wide, 11" high. Free-lance stories pay $10 per thousand words, photos $5. Recent features: "Writing Topical Songs;" "Ruth Crawford Seeger—An Introduction;" "Getting There Is Part of the Job—An Interview with Tyson and Abod." Full-page black and white ad costs $225; no color ads. Calliope Publishing, publisher; K. Corti, M. K. Gohl, editors. Established 1974.

Pop Top, "The Record Buyer's Guide"—free at record stores, music stores, and clubs; artist profiles, record reviews, collectors reviews and discographies covering pop, rock, jazz, R&B, disco, and country music. 909 Beacon Street, Boston, MA 02215. 617-536-8807.

Published once each month. Subscription: $6 for 12 issues; total circulation: 242,400. 24 pages, 9¾" wide, 12" high. Free-lance stories pay $25-50; photographs accepted. Recent features: "Lake—Fairly Smooth Sailing;" "Living Chicago Blues;" "Sylvester—Putting the Lid on Camp." Full-page black and white ad costs $1,500; full-page color ad costs $2,000. Barry Glovsky, publisher; Jim Mentel, editor. Established 1975.

Popular Music and Society—sold only through subscription; eclectic magazine featuring stories on music, the music business, music education, and the influence of music on modern civilization. Bowling Green State University, Department of Sociology, Bowling Green, OH 43403. 419-372-2294.

Published once every three months. Subscription: $7 for 4 issues; unaudited circulation: 5,000. 90 pages, 6" wide, 8" high. Free-lance stories and photographs accepted. Recent features: "From ASCAP to Alan Freed;" "ASCAP v. BMI;" "Tom Paxton Interview." Full-page black and white ad costs $100; no color ads. R. Serge Denisoff, publisher and editor. Established 1972.

Pro Sound News—free to recording engineers, studio personnel, and sound reinforcement companies; news tabloid, strictly for the recording and sound professional. 15 Columbus Circle, New York, NY 10023. 212-582-3680.

Published once each month. Subscription: $15 for 12 issues; circulation: 12,000. 32 pages, 11" wide, 14½" high. No free-lance stories or photographs. Recent features: "Banking Circles Respond Favorably to Studio Needs;" "NEVE Introduces Largest Standard Studio Console;" "Maintenance Engineers Are New Superstars." Full-page black and white ad costs $1,345; full-page color ad costs $1,870. Professional Recording & Sound Publications, Inc., publisher; Paul G. Gallo, associate publisher; Judi Bernstein-Cohen, editor. Established 1978.

Punk Publications Inc.—$1.25 at newsstands; music, cartoons, entertainment, and features covering the punk scene worldwide. 225 Lafayette Street, Room 1212, New York, NY 10012. 212-226-7849.

Published twice each month. Subscription: $13 for 12 issues [**Punk Publications Inc.,** P. O. Box 675, New York, NY 10009]; circulation: 25,000. 44 pages, 8½" wide, 11" high. Free-lance stories and photographs accepted. Recent features: "Sid Vicious and Nancy Spungen Tell All;" "CLASH;" "Rock 'n Roll High School." Full-page black and white ad costs $750; full-page color ad costs $1,150. John Spaceley, publisher; John Holmstrom, editor. Established 1974.

Radio & Records—sold only through subscription; newspaper covering recent trends within the radio and record industries, and providing up-to-date airplay information on current records in all important music radio formats. 1930 Century Park West, Los Angeles, CA 90067. 213-553-4330.

Published once each week. Subscription: $140 for 50 issues; circulation: 6,300. 80 pages, 9¾" wide, 13½" high. No free-lance stories or photographs. Full-page black and white ad costs $2,485. Bob Wilson, publisher; Ken Barnes, John Leader, Mike Kasabo, Bill Speed, Jeff Gelb, Jim Duncan, Pam Bellamy, and Gail Mitchell, editors. Established 1973.

Radio Free Jazz—$1 at newsstands; the newspaper of jazz professionals. 3212 Pennsylvania Avenue SE, Washington, DC 20020. 202-582-2000.

Published once each month. Subscription: $10 for 12 issues; circulation: 45,000. 32 pages, 10" wide, 14" high. Free-lance stories and photographs accepted. Recent features: "Newport Jazz Festival New York—A Complete Review of the Year's Most Important Festival;" "National Jazz Survey;" "Jazz Director." Full-page black and white ad costs $946; full-page color ad costs $1,400. Ira Sabin, publisher; Karen Fitchett, editor. Established 1968.

Radio Free Rock—free at retail outlets; magazine showcasing artists and music heard infrequently on popular radio stations. P. O. Box 68477, Indianapolis, IN 46268. 317-257-4615.

Published once each month. Subscription: $6 for 12 issues; circulation: 10,400. 16 pages, 8" wide, 11¾" high. Free-lance stories pay $2-20; photographs accepted. Recent features: "Elvis Costello—Armed & Ready;" "Peter Hammill—The Future Now?" "Rickie Lee Jones—The Return of Cool." Full-page black and white ad costs $460; no color ads. Media Maniax, publisher; David Myers, editor. Established 1976.

Radio Music Report—sold only through subscription; national tip sheet covering top 40 singles, single breakouts, new singles reviews, top 50 album cuts, disco reviews, general news, and job opening at radio stations. 6445 Powers Ferry Road, Suite 210, Atlanta, GA 30339. 404-953-1925.

Published once each week. Subscription: $120 for 52 issues [**Radio Music Report,** P. O. Box 502, Marietta, GA 30061]; circulation: 1,400. 76 pages, 8½" wide, 11" high. No free-lance stories or photographs. Full-page black and white ad costs $750; no color ads. Ron Brandon, publisher; Chuck Dunaway, editor. Established 1963.

Record World—$2.25 at newsstands; music and phonograph record trade publication. 1700 Broadway, New York, NY 10019. 212-765-5020.

Published once each week. Subscription: $95 for 52 issues [**Record World,** 1697 Broadway, New York, NY 10019]; circulation (L. Orenstein Associates): 18,000. 68 pages, 9⅝" wide, 12¾" high. Free-lance stories and photographs accepted. Full-page black and white ad costs $2,898; full-page color ad costs $3,548. Bob Austin, publisher; Mike Sigman, editor. Established 1964.

Relix Magazine—$1.75 at newsstand; rock 'n roll news reported from the audiences' point of view. P. O. Box 94, Brooklyn, NY 11229. 212-998-2039.

Published once every two months. Subscription: $7.75 for 5 issues and special photo issue; circulation: 20,000. 60 pages, 8½" wide, 11" high. Free-lance stories pay $.75-1.25 per column inch, black and white photos $5-30, color-cover photos $125. Recent features: "Grateful Dead in Egypt;" "Blues Brothers;" "The Who." Full-page black and white ad costs $525; full-page color ad costs $1,000. Leslie D. Kippel, publisher; Jeff Tamarkin, Steve Kraye, and Clark Peterson, editors. Established 1974.

Rock Love—$1.50 at newsstands; exclusive interviews and full-color photographs documenting the lifestyles, loves, and music of rock 'n roll superstars. 515 Hempstead Turnpike, West Hempstead, NY 11552. 516-292-8585.

Published once every two months. No subscriptions; circulation: 175,000. 76 pages, 8⅛" wide, 10¾" high. Free-lance stories and photographs accepted. Recent features: "Billy Joel—The Woman Who Changed His Life;" "John Belushi—Madman in the Animal House;" "Elvis and Travolta—Their Secret Shared." Full-page black and white ad costs $1,395; full-page color ad costs $2,095. Target Publishing Corp., publisher; Paul Trolio and Leslie Groher, editors. Established 1979.

Rockingchair—sold only through subscription; record reviews, book reviews, and discographics for all types of music except classical and jazz. P. O. Box 27, Philadelphia, PA 19105. 215-WA 5-3673.

Published once each month. Subscription: $11.95 for 12 issues; circulation: 1,113. 16 pages, 6" wide, 8½" high. Free-lance reviews accepted. No feature stories. No advertising. Cupola Productions, publisher; John Politis, editor. Established 1977.

Rock Scene—$1.25 at newsstands; fan-oriented magazine containing over 160 photographs each issue plus reviews, musical instrument department, and tips on buying and collecting records. 358 Fairwood Road, Bethany, CT 06525. 203-393-3082.

Published once every two months. Subscription: $6 for 6 issues; circulation: 105,850. 68 pages, 8⅛" wide, 10⅞" high. No free-lance stories or photographs. Recent features: "Rick Derringer's Electric Rock;" "Unofficial History—The Aerosmith Story;" "Bruce Bolen's Guitar Seminar." Full-page black and white ad costs $1,300; full-page color ad costs $2,000. Four Seasons Publications, Inc., publisher; Richard Robinson, editor. Established 1973.

Rolling Stone Magazine—$1.25 at newsstands; periodical with extended music coverage and features of a timely nature. 745 Fifth Avenue, New York, NY 10022. 212-PL 8-3800.

Published twice each month. Subscription: $15.95 for 26 issues [**Rolling Stone Magazine,** Box 2983, Boulder, CO 80302]; circulation (ABC): 650,000. 104 pages, 9⅞" wide, 12" high. Free-lance stories and photographs accepted. Recent features: "The Rolling Stone Interview with Johnny Carson;" "The Shroud of Turin;" "Skating on Thin Ice with Don Murdoch." Full-page black and white ad costs $7,985; full-page color ad costs $12,370. Jann S. Wenner, publisher and editor. Established 1967.

Schwann 1—$1.25 at retail outlets; monthly listing of records, 8-track, and cassette tapes (including direct-to-disc and digital recordings) under rock, jazz, country, classical, musical shows, electronic, folk blues, and specialty headings. P. O. Box 550, Great Barrington, MA 01230. 413-528-1300.

Published once each month. Subscription: $25 for 12 issues (includes 2 issues of **Schwann-2** and **Schwann Children's and Christmas Catalog**); circulation (SRDS): 46,500. 275 pages, 5¼" wide, 8" high. No free-lance stories or photographs. No feature articles. Full-page black and white ad costs $1,355; color rates available upon request. ABC Schwann Publications, Inc., publisher; William Schwann and Robert Clark, editors. Established 1949.

Schwann-2—$1.25 at retail outlets; semiannual listing of pop and rock recordings more than two years old; classical and jazz recordings of the prestereo era; and spoken, educational, religious, and international pop and folk music released on domestic labels. P. O. Box 550, Great Barrington, MA 01230. 413-528-1300.

Published twice each year. Subscription: $25 for 2 issues (includes 12 issues of **Schwann-1** and **Schwann Children's and Christmas Catalog**); circulation (SRDS): 46,500. 130 pages, 5¼" wide, 8" high. No free-lance stories or photographs. No feature articles. Ad rates available upon request. ABC Schwann Publications, Inc., publisher; William Schwann and Robert Clark, editors.

Schwann Children's and Christmas Catalog—$1.25 at retail outlets; listing of musical recordings and tapes for young people (preschool through high school) and Christmas guide for parents, librarians, teachers, and music educators. 137 Newbury Street, Boston, MA 02116. 617-261-3143.

Published once each year. Subscription: $25 for 1 issue (includes 12 issues of **Schwann-1** and 2 issues of **Schwann-2**); circulation (SRDS): 10,000. 20 pages, 5¼" wide, 8" high. No free-lance stories or photographs. No feature articles. Ad rates available upon request. ABC Schwann Publications, Inc., publisher; William Schwann and Robert Clark, editors.

The Sensible Sound—$4 at newsstands; an equipment and record review magazine that helps readers obtain the best-sounding home audio system at a reasonable price. 403 Darwin Drive, Snyder, NY 14226.

Published once every three months. Subscription: $14 for 4 issues; circulation: 6,520. 60 pages, 5½" wide, 8½" high. Free-lance stories and photographs accepted. Recent features: "Loudspeakers and the Laws of Physics and Acoustics;" "The New Hype—Same as the Old Hype;" "Considerations on Phono Cartridge Capacitive Loading." Full-page black and white ad costs $450; no color ads. John A. Horan, publisher and editor. Established 1977.

Songwriter—$1.50 at newsstands; special interest magazine devoted to the art and craft of songwriting, with how-to articles, features, interviews, industry news, and departments. P. O. Box 3510, Hollywood, CA 90028. 213-464-SONG.

Published once each month. Subscription: $14 for 12 issues; circulation: 50,000. 68 pages, 8⅜" wide, 10⅞" high. Free-lance stories and photographs accepted. Recent features: "Richard Kerr—He Writes the Melodies for Manilow;" "How to Build and Equip Your Own Studio;" "The Copyright Tribunal—How It Affects You." Full-page black and white ad costs $850; full-page color ad costs $1,200. Len Latimer, publisher; Rich Wiseman, editor. Established 1975.

Soul—$.75 at newsstands; black entertainment tabloid. 8271 Melrose Avenue, Suite 208, Los Angeles, CA ..... 213-653-7775.

Published twice each month. Subscription: $12 for 24 issues; circulation: 175,000.

24 pages, ... Free-lance stories pay $10-100; photographs accepted. Recent features: "Michael Jackson Turns 21;" "Doobie Brothers;" "Bootsy Collins." Full-page black and white ad costs $1,800; full-page color ad costs $3,240. Regina Jones, publisher; Leonard Pitts, editor. Established 1966.

Sound Arts Merchandising Journal—sold only through subscription; technical and merchandising articles for retailers of electronic music instruments and creative audio equipment. 14 Vanderventer Avenue, Port Washington, NY 11050. 516-883-5705.
Published once each month. Subscription: $18 for 12 issues; circulation: 14,600. 72 pages, 8¼" wide, 11" high. Free-lance stories and photographs accepted. Recent features: "Do's and Don'ts of Equalization;" "Building Sales with In-store Displays;" "Computer Technology and Music." Full-page black and white ad costs $1,165; full-page color ad costs $1,715. Vincent P. Testa, publisher; Judith Morrison Lipton, editor. Established 1978.

Sweet Potato—free at retail outlets; feature-oriented music magazine dealing with rock, blues, jazz, classical, and bluegrass subjects. P. O. Box B, Astor Station, Boston, MA 02123. 617-536-2060.
Published once each month. Subscription: $5 for 12 issues; circulation: 85,300. 36 pages, 10-3/16" wide, 13½" high. Free-lance stories pay $20-75, photos $5-25. Recent features: "The Thorogood Tapes;" "Dire Straits;" "The Police." Full-page black and white ad costs $1,100 ($700 for Boston-only edition); full-page color ad costs $1,200 ($800 for Boston-only edition). David S. Wright, publisher; Dean Johnson and Ryan W. Wright, editors. Established 1976.

Teen Beat's Rock Stars—$1.50 at newsstands; photographs, interviews with rock 'n roll superstars, gossip, stories about new performers, and contest information. 2 Park Avenue, New York, NY 10016. 212-683-4200.
Published once every two months. No subscriptions. Circulation: 300,000. 72 pages, 8⅛" wide, 10⅞" high. Free-lance stories pay $50, black and white photos $25, color $50 and up. Recent features: "Spend a Day with the Bee Gees—Exclusive Pix, Their Homes, Boats, Private Lives!" "Aerosmith's Steven Tyler Tells All— What the Group Is Really Like!" "Gene, Paul, Peter & Ace Reveal 'The Truth about Kiss and Our Special Plans for the Future'." Full-page black and white ad costs $600; full-page color ad costs $975. Phil Hirsch, publisher; Sheila Steinbach, editor. Established 1978.

Thunder Road—$1.50 at newsstands; fanzine dealing primarily with Bruce Springsteen, Southside Johnny, and rock 'n roll subjects. P. O. Box 171 Bogota, NJ 07603. 201-772-4188. **California office:** P. O. Box 861, Cypress, CA 90630. 714-527-1273.
Published once every three months. Subscription: $5 for 4 issues; circulation (Balon & Ganseret): 5,000. 40 pages, 10-3/16" wide, 13½" high. Free-lance stories pay $20-75, photos $5-25. Recent features: "Cannon Blast;" Lightning Flashed— The Mighty Max Interview;" "Lyrics to 'The Wild, Innocent & the E Street Shuffle'." Full-page black and white ad costs $300; no color ads. Ken Viola and Lou Cohan, publishers and editors.

Tiger Beat Magazine—$1.25 at newsstands; fanzine aimed at teenage girls featuring stories and pictures of record, movie, and television stars of interest to them. 7060 Hollywood Boulevard, Suite 800, Hollywood, CA 90028. 213-467-3111.

Published once each month. Subscription: $10 for 12 issues [**Tiger Beat Magazine**, Drawer L, Hollywood, CA 90028]; circulation (ABC): 525,000. 98 pages, 8⅛" wide, 10⅞" high. Free-lance stories pay $25-200, photos $25-200. Recent features: "Tony Danza—Part-time Dad;" "Catching Up to Shaun;" "Erik—Two Wheels or Four?" Full-page black and white ad costs $2,495; full-page color ad costs $3,900. Ralph Benner, publisher; Kathy Kirkland, editor. Established 1964.

Time Barrier Express—$1.75 at newsstands; magazine focusing on the history of rock 'n roll. P. O. Box 206, Yonkers, NY 10710. 914-337-8050.

Published once every two months. Subscription: $9 for 6 issues; circulation: .... 56 pages, 8½" wide, 11" high. Free-lance stories and photographs accepted. Recent features: "Carl Perkins Then and Now;" "Jan & Dean: Back from Dead Man's Curve;" "Jackie Wilson—A Forgotten Man's Lonely Teardrops." Full-page black and white ad costs $450; full-page color ad costs $1,100. Time Barrier Enterprises, Inc., publisher; Ralph M. Newman, editor. Established 1974.

Trouser Press—$1.25 at newsstands; high-quality features and reviews of new wave and progressive music for rock fans who like to read. 147 West 42 Street, New York, NY 10036. 212-354-4376.

Published once each month. Subscription: $12 for 12 issues; circulation: 41,500. 60 pages, 8⅜" wide, 10⅞" high. Free-lance stories pay $25-50, photos $10. Recent features: "Cheap Trick—The Band Nobody Really Knows;" "Who Film Preview—'The Kids Are Alright';" "John Lennon in Limbo." Full-page black and white ad costs $725; full-page color ad costs $975. Ira A. Robbins, publisher; Dave Schulps, editor. Established 1974.

Trouser Press Collectors' Magazine—$.75 at newsstands; tabloid listing recent British record releases and U.S. record auctions. P. O. Box 2450, Grand Central Station, New York, NY 10017.

Published once every two months. Subscription: $4 for 6 issues; circulation: 3,500. 24 pages, 11½" wide, 15¼" high. Free-lance stories pay 0-$25. Recent features: "Bubblerock—Ageless Artifice;" "Back Page and the Yardbirds." Full-page black and white ad costs $150; no color ads. Ira A. Robbins, publisher; Jim Green and Dave Schulps, editors.

Unicorn Times—free at retail outlets; tabloid concentrating on performing arts in the Washington, DC/Baltimore area. 2025 R Street NW, Washington, DC 20009. 202-332-2800.

Published once each month. Subscription: $7 for 12 issues; circulation: 77,000. 80 pages, 10¼" wide, 12-9/16" high. Free-lance stories pay $15-100; photographs accepted. Recent features: "Waiting for Brian;" "The Silent Clowns—A Summer Tribute to Comic Genius;" "Anthems for the Faithful." Full-page black and white ad costs $600; color rates available upon request. Elliot Ryan, publisher; Richard Harrington, editor. Established 1973.

Up Beat—sold only through subscription; business of music magazine aimed at the music retailer. 222 West Adams Street, Chicago, IL 60606. 312-346-7820.

Published 9 times a year. Subscription: $8.50 for 9 issues; circulation: 11,080. 72 pages, 8⅜" wide, 10⅞" high. Free-lance stories and photographs by assignment. Recent features: "Inventory Loan Can Be Risky;" "Banker Profits from Sound;"

"How to Buy and Sell in a Weak Economy." Full-page black and white ad costs $659; full-page color ad costs $954. Chuck Suber, publisher; Tim Schneckloth, editor. Established 1978.

Variety—$1 at newsstands; entertainment industry trade publication. 154 West 46 Street, New York, NY 10036. 212-582-2700.
   Published once each week. Subscription: $40 for 52 issues; circulation: 52,000. 116 pages, 11⅜" wide, 16" high. No free-lance stories or photographs. Full-page black and white ad costs $1,395. Syd Silverman, publisher and editor. Established 1905.

Walrus—sold only through subscription; national album tip sheet, half research and half feature stories. Box 35, Narberth, PA 19072. 215-667-9788.
   Published twice each month. Subscription: $125 for 26 issues; circulation: 1,400. 36 pages, 11¼" wide, 14¾" high. Free-lance stories and photographs accepted. Full-page black and white ad costs $1,500; full-page color ad costs $1,950. George B. Meier, publisher and editor. Established 1969.

CONTEMPORARY MUSIC BIBLIOGRAPHY

Adler, Irene. *Peter Frampton.* New York: Quick Fox, 1979.
Alphabeat. *Who's Who in Pop.* London: Century 21 Publishing, Ltd., 1969.
Anderson, Craig. *Home Recording for Musicians.* New York: Guitar Player Books, 1978.
Armitage, A. and Tudor, Dean (editors). *Annual Index to Popular Music Record Reviews,* 1972. Metuchen, New Jersey: Scarecrow, 1973.
Baez, Joan. *Daybreak.* New York: Avon Books, 1969.
Baker, Robb. *Bette Midler.* New York: Popular Library, 1975.
Bane, Michael. *The Outlaws: Revolution in Country Music.* New York: Country Music Magazine Press, 1978.
Baral, Robert. *Revue: The Great Broadway Period.* Revised Edition. New York: Fleet Press Corporation, 1970.
Barnes, Ken (editor). *Sinatra and the Great Song Stylists.* London: Allan, 1972.
Baskerville, David. *Music Business Handbook.* Denver: The Sherwood Company, 1979.
Batcheller, John. *Music in Recreation and Leisure.* Dubuque, Iowa: W. C. Brown Company, 1972.
Belz, Carl. *The Story of Rock.* Second Edition. New York: Oxford University Press, 1972.
Boeckman, Charles. *And the Beat Goes On: A Survey of Pop Music in America.* Washington, D. C.: Robert B. Luce, Inc., 1972.
Boyce, Tommy. *How to Write a Hit Song and Sell It.* Alhambra, California: Wilshire, 1975.
Braun, D. Duane. *Toward a Theory of Popular Culture: The Sociology and History of American Music and Dance, 1920-1968.* Ann Arbor, Michigan: Ann Arbor Publishers, 1969.
Braun, Michael. *Love Me Do: The Beatles' Progress.* London: Penguin Books, 1964.
Brand, Oscar. *The Ballad Mongers: Rise of the Modern Folk Song.* New York: Funk and Wagnalls, 1967.
Brohaugh, William (editor). *1979 Songwriter's Market.* Cincinnati, Ohio: Writer's Digest Books, 1978.
Bronson, Bertrand Harris. *The Ballad as Song.* Berkeley, California: University of California Press, 1969.
Brown, Len and Friedrich, Gary. *Encyclopedia of Rock and Roll.* New York: Tower Publications, 1970.
Burt, Jesse and Ferguson, Bob. *So You Want to Be in Music!* Nashville, Tennessee: Abingdon Press, 1970.

Burton, Jack. *The Blue Book of Broadway Musicals.* Third Edition. Watkins Glen, New York: Century House, 1976.
———. *The Blue Book of Hollywood Musicals.* Watkins Glen, New York: Century House, 1953.
———. *The Blue Book of Tin Pan Alley: A Human Interest Encyclopedia of American Popular Music.* Second Edition. Watkins Glen, New York: Century House, 1962-1965.
Carpozi, Jr., George. *The Johnny Cash Story.* New York: Pyramid Books, 1970.
Carr, Roy and Clarke, Steve. *Fleetwood Mac: Rumours 'n Fax.* New York: Harmony, 1978.
Carr, Roy and Tyler, Tony. *The Beatles Illustrated Record.* New York: Harmony, 1975.
Caserta, Peggy. *Going Down with Janis.* New York: Dell, 1973.
Cash, Anthony. *Anatomy of Pop.* London: British Broadcasting Corporation, 1970.
Cash, Johnny. *Man in Black.* Grand Rapids, Michigan: Zondervan, 1975.
Chapple, Steve and Garofalo, Reebee. *Rock 'n Roll Is Here to Pay: The History and Politics of the Music Industry.* Chicago: Nelson-Hall, 1977.
Christgau, Robert. *Any Old Way You Choose It: Rock and Other Pop Music, 1967-1973.* Baltimore: Penguin Books, 1973.
Claire, Vivian. *David Bowie.* New York: Flash, 1967.
———. *Linda Ronstadt.* New York: Flash, 1978.
Cohn, Nik. *Rock from the Beginning.* New York: Stein and Day, 1969.
Cole, Maria and Robinson, Louie. *Nat King Cole.* New York: William Morrow, 1971.
Conn, Charles P. *The New Johnny Cash.* Old Tappan, New Jersey: Spire Books, 1973.
Connor, D. Russell and Hicks, Warren W. *BG on the Road: A Bio-discography of Benny Goodman.* New Rochelle, New York: Arlington House, 1969.
Coon, Caroline. *1988: The New Wave Punk Rock Explosion.* London: Orbach & Chambers, 1977.
Cromelin, Richard. *Rod Stewart.* New York: Chappell & Co., 1976.
Csida, Joseph. *The Music/Record Career Handbook.* New York: Billboard Publications, 1975.
Cummings, Tony. *The Sound of Philadelphia.* London: Methuen, 1975.
Dachs, David. *American Pop.* New York: Scholastic Books, 1969.
———. *Anything Goes: The World of Popular Music.* New York: Bobbs-Merrill, 1964.
———. *Encyclopedia of Pop/Rock.* New York: Scholastic Book Service, 1972.
Dallas, Karl. *Singers of an Empty Day.* London: Kahn and Averill, 1971.
Dalton, David. *Janis.* New York: Simon and Schuster, 1971.
———. *Rolling Stones.* New York: Quick Fox, 1979.
——— (editor). *Rolling Stones: An Unauthorized Biography in Words, Pictures, and Music.* New York: Amsco Music Publishing, 1972.
Daly, Marsha. *Peter Frampton.* New York: Tempo, 1978.
Daufouy, Phillippe and Sarton, Jean-Pierre. *Pop Music/Rock.* Paris: Editions Champ Libre, 1972.
Davies, Hunter. *The Beatles.* New York: McGraw-Hill, 1965.
Davis, Clive. *Clive: Inside the Record Business.* New York: William Morrow, 1975.
Demorest, Steve. *Alice Cooper.* New York: Popular Library, 1974.
Denisoff, R. Serge. *Great Day Coming: Folk Music and the American Left.* Urbana: University of Illinois Press, 1971.

———. *Sing a Song of Social Significance.* Bowling Green, Ohio: Bowling Green University Popular Press, 1972.

———. *Solid Gold: The Record Industry, Its Friends and Enemies.* New York: Transaction Books, 1975.

———. *Songs of Protest—War and Peace: A Bibliography and Discography.* Santa Barbara, California: American Bibliographical Center-Clio Press, 1973.

Denisoff, R. Serge and Peterson, Richard A. *The Sounds of Social Change: Studies in Popular Culture.* Chicago: Rand McNally, 1972.

DeTurk, David A. and Poulin, Jr., A. (editors). *The American Folk Scene.* New York: Dell, 1967.

DiFranco, J. Philip (editor). *The Beatles: A Hard Day's Night.* London: Penguin Books, 1977.

Dilello, Richard. *The Longest Cocktail Party: A Personal History of Apple.* Chicago: Playboy, 1972.

Dimmick, Mary Laverne. *The Rolling Stones: An Annotated Bibliography.* Pittsburgh, Pennsylvania: Graduate School of Library and Information Science, University of Pittsburgh, 1979.

Douglas, David. *Presenting David Bowie.* New York: Pinnacle Books, 1975.

Doukas, James N. *Electric Tibet.* Hollywood: Dominican Publishing Company, 1969.

Dunn, Lloyd. *On the Flip Side.* New York: Billboard, 1975.

Dunn, Paul H. *The Osmonds.* Salt Lake City, Utah: Bookcraft, Inc., 1975.

Dutton, David and Kaye, Lenny. *Rock 100.* New York: Grosset and Dunlap, 1977.

Eisen, Jonathan (editor). *The Age of Rock.* New York: Random House, 1969.

———. *The Age of Rock, 2.* New York: Random House, 1970.

Eliot, Marc. *Death of a Rebel Starring Phil Ochs.* Garden City, New York: Anchor Press/Doubleday, 1979.

Elmlark, Walli and Beckley, Timothy G. *Rock Raps of the 70s.* New York: Drake Publishers, Inc., 1972.

Elsner, Constance. *Stevie Wonder.* New York: Popular Library, 1977.

Emerson, Lucy. *The Gold Record.* New York: Fountain, 1978.

Engel, Lehman. *The American Musical Theater.* Revised Edition. New York: Macmillan, 1975.

Epstein, Brian. *A Cellarful of Noise.* New York: Doubleday, 1964.

Errigo, Angie. *The Illustrated History of Rock Album Art.* London: Octopus/Mayflower, 1979.

Escott, Colin and Hawkins, Martin. *Catalyst: The Story of Sun Records.* London: Aquarius, 1975.

Ewen, David. *All the Years of American Popular Music.* Englewood Cliffs, New Jersey: Prentice-Hall, 1977.

———. *Great Men of American Popular Song.* Englewood Cliffs, New Jersey: Prentice-Hall, 1970.

———. *History of Popular Music.* New York: Barnes and Noble, 1961.

Fast, Julius. *The Beatles: The Real Story.* New York: Berkley Medalion, 1968.

Fawcett, Anthony. *John Lennon: One Day at a Time.* New York: Grove, 1976.

Ferlingere, Robert D. *A Discography of Rhythm and Blues and Rock and Roll Vocal Groups, 1945-1965.* Pittsburg, California: The Author (P. O. Box 1695), 1976.

Field, James J. *American Popular Music, 1950-1975.* Philadelphia, Pennylvania: Musical Americana, 1956.

Flattery, Paul. *The Illustrated History of British Pop.* New York: Drake Publishers, Inc., 1975.

Flippo, Chet. "Rock Journalism and Rolling Stone." M. A. Thesis, University of Texas at Austin, 1974.
Flower, John. *Moonlight Serenade: A Bio-discography of the Glenn Miller Civilian Band*. New Rochelle, New York: Arlington House, 1972.
Fong-Torres, Ben (editor). *The Rolling Stone Rock 'n Roll Reader*. New York: Bantam Books, 1974.
Frascogna, Jr., Xavier, M. and Hetherington, H. Lee. *Successful Artist Management*. New York: Billboard Publications, 1978.
Fredericks, Vic (editor). *Who's Who in Rock 'n Roll*. New York: Frederick Fell, 1958.
Friedman, Myra. *Buried Alive: The Biography of Janis Joplin*. New York: William Morrow, 1973.
Friedman, Rick. *The Beatles: Words without Music*. New York: Grosset and Dunlap, 1968.
Gabree, John. *The World of Rock*. Greenwich, Connecticut: Fawcett Publications, 1968.
Gaines, Steve. *Who's Who in Rock 'n Roll*. New York: Popular Library, 1975.
Gambaccini, Paul. *Paul McCartney in His Own Words*. New York: Flash, 1976.
———. *A Conversation with Elton John & Bernie Taupin*. New York: Flash, 1975.
———. *Bruce Springsteen*. New York: Jove, 1979.
———. *Rock Critics Choice: The Top 200 Albums*. New York: Quick Fox, 1978.
Garland, Phyl. *The Sound of Soul*. Chicago: Henry Regnery Company, 1969.
Gelatt, Ronald. *The Fabulous Phonograph, 1877-1977*. New York: Collier Books, 1977.
Gersohn, Fredric B. (editor). *Counseling Clients in the Performing Arts*. New York: Practising Law Institute, 1975.
Gillett, Charlie. *Making Tracks: The Story of Atlantic Records*. New York: Outerbridge and Lazard, 1973.
———. *The Sound of the City: The Rise of Rock 'n Roll*. New York: Dell, 1972.
———. (editor). *Rock File*. London: New English Library, 1972.
Gillett, Charlie and Nugent, Stephen. *Rock Almanac*. Garden City, New York: Ancho Press/Doubleday, 1976.
Gleason, Ralph J. *The Jefferson Airplane and the San Francisco Sound*. New York: Ballantine Books, 1969.
Goldman, Albert H. *The Freakshow*. New York: Antheneum, 1971.
Goldrosen, John. *Buddy Holly: His Life and Music*. Bowling Green, Ohio: Popular Press, 1975.
Goldstein, Richard. *Goldstein's Greatest Hits*. Englewood Cliffs, New Jersey: Prentice-Hall, 1970.
Goodgold, Ehwin and Carlinsky, Dan. *The Compleat Beatles Quiz Book*. New York: Warner Books, 1975.
Govoni, Albert. *A Boy Named Cash*. New York: Lancer Books, 1970.
Graham, Samuel. *Fleetwood Mac: The Authorized History*. New York: Warner Books, 1978.
Gray, Michael. *Song and Dance Man: The Art of Bob Dylan*. London: Abacus, 1973.
Greene, Bob. *Billion Dollar Baby*. New York: Signet, 1975.
Greenfield, Robert. *S.T.P.: A Journey through America with the Rolling Stones*. New York: E. P. Dutton, 1974.
Gregory, James. *David, David, David*. New York: Curtis Books, 1972.

Groia, Philip. *They All Sang on the Corner: New York City's Rhythm & Blues Vocal Groups of the 1950s*. New York: Edmond, 1973.
Gross, Michael. *Bob Dylan: An Illustrated History*. New York: Grosset & Dunlap, 1978.
Hall, Douglas K. and Clark, Sue C. *Rock: A World Bold as Love*. Chicago: Regnery, 1970.
Hallowell, John. *Inside Creedence*. New York: Bantam Books, 1971.
Haralambos, Michael. *From Blues to Soul in Black America*. New York: Drake Publishers, Inc., 1975.
Harris, Herby and Farrar, Lucien. *How to Make Money in Music*. New York: Arco, 1978.
Hasegawa, Sam. *Stevie Wonder*. Mankato, Minnesota: Creative Educational Society, Inc., 1974.
Haskins, James. *The Story of Stevie Wonder*. New York: Dell, 1976.
Herman, Gary. *The Who*. London: Studio Vista, 1971.
Hirsch, Paul. *The Structure of the Popular Music Industry: The Filtering Process by Which Records Are Pre-Selected for Consumption*. Ann Arbor, Michigan: University of Michigan, Institute for Social Research, 1969.
Hopkins, Jerry. *Festival*. New York: Macmillan, 1971.
―――. *Elvis: A Biography*. New York: Simon and Schuster, 1971.
―――. *The Rock Story*. New York: Signet, 1970.
Horn, David. *The Literature of American Music in Books and Folk Music Collections: A Fully Annotated Bibliography*. Metuchen, New Jersey: Scarecrow, 1977.
Howard, John Tasker and Bellows, George Kent. *A Short History of Music in America*. New York: Crowell, 1967.
Hudson, James A. *Fillmore East and West*. New York: Scholastic Book Services, 1970.
―――. *Johnny Cash Close-Up*. New York: Scholastic Book Services, 1971.
―――. *Meet David Cassidy*. New York: Scholastic Book Services, 1972.
Hutchinson, Larry. *Rock and Roll Songwriter's Handbook*. New York: Scholastic Book Services, 1972.
Jahn, Mike. *Jim Morrison and the Doors*. New York: Grune and Stratton, 1969.
―――. *Rock: From Elvis Presley to the Rolling Stones*. New York: Quadrangle/New York Times Book Company, 1973.
Jasper, Tony. *Understand Pop*. London: S.C.M. Press, 1972.
―――. *Today's Sound*. Great Yarmouth, Great Britain: Galliar, 1970.
Jenkinson, Philip and Warner, Alan. *Celluloid Rock: Twenty Years of Movie Rock*. London: Lorrimer, 1974.
Jones, Peter. *Elvis*. New Jersey: Chartwell Books, 1977.
―――. *Tom Jones*. Chicago: Henry Regnery Company, 1970.
Kasak, Richard (editor). *Jim Croce: His Life and Music*. Secaucus, New Jersey: Deribooks, 1975.
Katz, Susan. *Superwomen of Rock*. New York: Tempo, 1978.
Kaufman, Murry. *Murry the K Tells It Like It Is, Baby*. New York: Holt, Rinehart and Winston, 1966.
Kinkle, Roger D. *The Complete Encyclopedia of Popular Music and Jazz, 1900-1950*. New Rochelle, New York: Arlington House, 1974.
Knight, Curtis. *Jimi*. New York: Praeger, 1974.
Kooper, A. and Edmonds, Ben. *Nothing Personal: Reliving Rock in the Sixties*. New York: Stein and Day, 1975.

Kramer, Daniel. *Bob Dylan.* New Jersey: Castle Books, 1967.
Kramer, Freda. *The Glen Campbell Story.* New York: Pyramid Books, 1970.
Laing, Dave. *Buddy Holly.* London: Studio Vista, 1971.
——. *The Sound of Our Time.* Chicago: Quadrangle Books, 1970.
—— (editor). *The Electric Muse: The Story of Folk into Rock.* London: Methuen, 1975.
Lambert, Dennis with Zalkind, Ronald. *Producing Hit Records.* A Zadoc Book. New York: Schirmer Books, 1980.
Landau, Jon. *It's Too Late to Stop Now: A Rock 'n Roll Journal.* San Francisco: Straight Arrow Books, 1972.
Larkin, Rochelle. *Soul Music.* New York: Lancer Books, 1970.
Laufe, Abe. *Broadway's Greatest Musicals.* New York: Funk and Wagnalls, 1973.
Lawrence, Sharon. *So You Want to Be a Rock and Roll Star.* New York: Dell, 1976.
Leaf, David. *The Beach Boys and the California Myth.* New York: Grosset & Dunlap, 1978.
Lee, Edward. *Music of the People: A Study of Popular Music in Great Britain.* London: Barrie and Jenkins, 1970.
Leigh, Spencer. *Paul Simon: Now and Then.* Liverpool: Raven Books, 1973.
Leisy, James F. *Hootennany Tonight.* Greenwich, Connecticut: Fawcett Publications, 1964.
Lewine, Richard and Simon, Alfred. *Encyclopedia of Theatre Music.* New York: Random House, 1961.
Lewine, Richard et al. *Songs of the American Theater: A Comprehensive Listing of More than 12,000 Songs.* New York: Dodd, Mead and Company, Inc., 1973.
Lieber, Leslie. *How to Form a Rock Group.* New York: Grosset and Dunlap, 1968.
Limbacher, James L. *Film Music: From Violins to Video.* Metuchen, New Jersey: Scarecrow, 1974.
Logan, Nick and Woffinden, Bob. *The Illustrated Encyclopedia of Rock.* New York: Harmony Books, 1977.
Luce, Philip C. *The Stones.* London: Howard Baker, 1970.
Lydon, Michael. *Boogie Lightnin'.* New York: Dial, 1974.
——. *Rock Folk: Portraits from the Rock 'n Roll Pantheon.* New York: Dial, 1971.
Mabey, Richard. *Behind the Scene.* London: Penguin Books, 1968.
——. *The Pop Process.* London: Hutchinson, 1969.
Marchbank, Pearce and Miles. *The Illustrated Rock Almanac.* New York: Paddington Press, 1977.
Marks, J. *Mick Jagger.* New York: Curtis Books, 1973.
May, Chris and Phillips, Tim. *British Beat.* London: Socion Books, n.d.
McCabe, Peter and Schonfeld, D. R. *Apple to the Core.* New York: Pocket Books, 1972.
McCarthy, Albert. *Big Band Jazz.* New York: G. P. Putnam's, 1974.
——. *The Dance Band Era: The Dancing Decades from Ragtime to Swing, 1910-1950.* Philadelphia: Chilton, 1972.
McGregor, Craig. *Bob Dylan: A Retrospective.* New York: Doubleday, 1972.
McNeel, Kent and Luther, Mark. *How to Be a Successful Songwriter.* New York: St. Martins Press, 1978.
Marcus, Greil. *Mystery Train: Images of America in Rock 'n Roll Music.* New York: Dutton, 1975.
——. *Rock and Roll Will Stand.* Boston: Beacon Press, 1969.

Marsh, Dave. *Born to Run: The Bruce Springsteen Story.* Garden City, New York: Doubleday, 1979.

———. (Editor with John Swenson). *The Rolling Stone Record Guide.* New York: A Random House/Rolling Stone Press Book, 1979.

Mattfield, Julius. *Variety Music Cavalcade.* Third Edition. Englewood Cliffs, New Jersey: Prentice-Hall, 1971.

Mellers, Wilfrid. *Music in a New Found Land.* London: Barrie and Rockliff, 1964.

———. *Twilight of Gods.* London: Faber and Faber, 1973.

Melly, George. *Revolt into Style: The Pop Arts in Britain.* London: Allen Lane, 1970.

Meltzer, Richard. *The Aesthetics of Rock.* New York: Something Else Press, 1970.

Middleton, Richard. *Pop Music and the Blues: A Study of the Relationship and Its Significance.* London: Victor Gollancz, Ltd., 1972.

Miles (compiler). *Beatles in Their Own Words.* New York: Quick Fox, 1978.

Millar, Bill. *The Drifters: The Rise and Fall of the Black Vocal Group.* New York: Macmillan, 1972.

Miller, Jim (editor). *Rolling Stone Illustrated History of Rock & Roll.* New York: Rolling Stone Press/Random House, 1976.

Miron, Charles. *Rock Gold, 1955-1976.* New York: Drake, 1977.

Moore, Maury Ellen. *The Linda Ronstadt Scrapbook.* New York: Sunridge, 1978.

Morse, David. *Motown and the Arrival of Black Music.* New York: Macmillan, 1972.

The Music Yearbook: A Survey and Directory with Statistics and Reference Articles. New York: St. Martin's Press, 1973.

The Musician's Guide, 1976. New York: Music Information Service. (available every four years)

Nanry, Charles (editor). *American Music: From Storyville to Woodstock.* New Brunswick, New Jersey: Transaction Books, 1972.

Nite, Norm N. *Rock On: The Illustrated Encyclopedia of Rock 'n Roll for the Solid Gold Years.* New York: Thomas Y. Crowell, 1974.

———. *Rock On: The Illustrated Encyclopedia of Rock 'n Roll, Volume II—The Modern Years, 1964-Present.* New York: Thomas Y. Crowell, 1978.

O'Donnell, Jim. *The Rock Book.* New York: Pinnacle Books, 1975.

Osborne, Jerry and Hamilton, Bruce (editors). *Record Album Price Guide, 1948-1978.* Phoenix, Arizona: O'Sullivan, Woodside & Co., 1978.

Passman, Arnold. *The Dee Jays.* New York: Macmillan, 1971.

Paul, Elliot. *That Crazy American Music.* Port Washington, New York: Kennikat Press, 1970.

Pleasants, Henry. *The Great American Popular Singers.* New York: Simon and Schuster, 1974.

Pickering, Stephen. *Bob Dylan Approximately.* New York: David McKay, 1975.

Pincus, Lee. *The Songwriters Success Manual.* New York: Music Press, 1974.

Popular Music Periodicals Index, 1973. Metuchen, New Jersey: Scarecrow, 1974.

Preiss, Byron. *The Beach Boys.* New York: Ballantine, 1979.

Propes, Steve. *Golden Goodies: A Guide to 50s and 60s Popular Rock and Roll Record Collecting.* Philadelphia, Pennsylvania: Chilton, 1975.

———. *Golden Oldies: A Guide to 60s Record Collecting.* Philadelphia, Pennsylvania: Chilton, 1974.

———. *Those Oldies but Goodies: A Guide to 50s Record Collecting.* New York: Macmillan, 1973.

Rachlin, Harvey. *The Songwriters Handbook.* New York: Funk & Wagnalls, 1978.

Redd, Lawrence N. *Rock Is Rhythm and Blues: The Impact of Mass Media*. East Lansing: Michigan State University Press, 1974.

Reggero, John. *Elvis in Concert*. New York: Delta/Lorelei, 1979.

Ribakove, Sy and Ribakove, Barbara. *Folk Rock—The Bob Dylan Story*. New York: Dell, 1966.

Rinzler, Alan. *Bob Dylan*. New York: Harmony Books, 1978.

Rivelli, Pauline and Levin, Robert (editors). *The Rock Giants*. New York: World, 1971.

Robinson, Richard. *Pop, Rock, and Soul*. New York: Pyramid Books, 1972.

———. *The Osmond Brothers and the New Pop Scene*. New York: Pyramid Books, 1972.

Robinson, Richard and Zwerling, Andy. *The Rock Scene*. New York: Pyramid Books, 1971.

Rodnitzky, Jerome. *Minstrels of the Dawn: The Folk-Protest Singer as a Cultural Hero*. New York: Nelson-Hall, 1976.

Rohde, H. Kandy. *The Gold of Rock and Roll: 1955-1967*. New York: Arbor House, 1970.

Rolling Stone. *Knockin' on Dylan's Door: On the Road in '74*. New York: Pocket Books, 1974.

———. *The Rolling Stone Interviews*. New York: Paperback Library, 1971.

———. *The Rolling Stone Interviews, Volume 2*. New York: Paperback Library, 1973.

———. *The Rolling Stone Reader*. New York: Warner Paperback Library, 1974.

Rosenbaum, Halen. *Rolling Stones Trivia Quiz Book*. New York: Signet, 1979.

———. *The Beatles Trivia Quiz Book*. New York: Signet, 1978.

Roxon, Lillian. *Rock Encyclopedia*. New York: Grosset and Dunlap, 1969.

Rublowsky, John. *Popular Music*. New York: Basic Books, 1967.

Rust, Brian. *The American Dance Band Discography, 1917-1942*. New Rochelle, New York: Arlington House, 1975 (2 volumes).

———. *The Complete Entertainment Discography: From the Mid 1890s to 1942*. With Debus, Allen G. New Rochelle, New York: Arlington House, 1973.

———. *The Dance Bands*. London: Ian Allan, 1972.

———. *Jazz Records, A-Z, 1897-1942*. Fourth edition. New Rochelle, New York: Arlington House, 1978 (2 volumes).

———. *The Victor Master Book, Volume 2 (1925-1936)*. Hatch End, Middlesex: The Author, 1969.

Salek, Dennis (editor). *Rock Art*. New York: Comma Books/Ballantine Books, 1977.

Salem, James M. *A Guide to Critical Reviews, Part II: The Musical from Rodgers and Hart to Lerner and Loew*. Metuchen, New Jersey: Scarecrow, 1967.

Sanders, Ellen. *Trips: Rock Life in the Sixties*. New York: Scribner, 1973.

Sarlin, Bob. *Turn It Up! (I Can't Hear the Words): The Best of the New Singer/Songwriters*. New York: Simon and Schuster, 1974.

Scaduto, Anthony. *The Beatles*. New York: Signet Books, 1968.

———. *Bob Dylan: An Intimate Biography*. New York: W. H. Allen, 1972.

———. *Mick Jagger: Everybody's Lucifer*. New York: David McKay, 1974.

Schafer, William J. *Rock Music: Where It's Been, What It Means, Where It's Going*. Minneapolis, Minnesota: Augsburg Publishing, 1972.

Schicke, C. A. *Revolution in Sound: A Biography of the Recording Industry*. Boston: Little, Brown, 1974.

Scott, John Anthony. *The Ballad of America: The History of the United States in Song and Story*. New York: Grosset and Dunlap, 1967.
Schaffner, Nicholas. *The Beatles Forever*. New York: McGraw-Hill, 1977.
Shaw, Arnold. *Honkers and Shouters*. New York: Macmillan, 1978.
———. *The Rock Revolution*. New York: Crowell-Collier, 1969.
———. *Sinatra*. New York: W. H. Allen, 1968.
———. *The Rockin' 50s: The Decade That Transformed the Pop Music Scene*. New York: Hawthorn, 1974.
———. *The World of Soul*. New York: Paperback Library, 1971.
Shapiro, Nat (editor). *Popular Music: An Annotated Index of American Popular Songs (Volumes 1-6)*. New York: Adrian Press, 1964.
Shemel, Sidney and Krasilovsky, M. William. *This Business of Music*. Fourth edition. New York: Billboard Publications, 1978.
———. *More about This Business of Music*. Third edition. New York: Billboard Publications, 1978.
Shepard, Sam. *Rolling Thunder Logbook*. New York: Viking Press, 1977.
Shepherd, Billy. *The True Story of the Beatles*. New York: Bantam Books, 1964.
Shipper, Mark. *Paperback Writer*. New York: Grosset & Dunlap, 1977.
Simon, George T. *The Best of the Music Makers*. New York: Doubleday, 1979.
———. *The Big Bands*. Second edition. New York: Macmillan, 1971.
———. *Simon Says: The Sights and Sounds of the Swing Era, 1935-1955*. New Rochelle, New York: Arlington House, 1971.
Sinclair, John and Levin, Robert. *Music and Politics*. New York: World Publishing, 1971.
Sloman, Larry. *On the Road with Bob Dylan*. New York: Bantam Books, 1978.
Smith, Cecil. *Musical Comedy in America*. New York: Theatre Arts Books, 1950.
Smolian, Steven (editor). *A Handbook of Film, Theatre, and Television Music on Record, 1948-1969*. New York: Record Undertaker (P. O. Box 437, New York, NY 10023), 1970.
Solomon, Clive (compiler). *Record Hits* (index of U. K. singles, 1954-76). London: Omnibus Press, n.d.
Somma, Robert (editor). *No One Waved Goodbye: A Casualty Report on Rock and Roll*. New York: Outerbridge and Dienstfrey, 1971.
Southern, Terry. *The Rolling Stones on Tour*. France: Dragon Dream, 1978.
Spiegel, Irwin O. and Cooper, Jay L. *Record and Music Publishing Forms of Agreement in Current Use*. New York: Law-Arts Publishers, 1971.
Stambler, Irwin. *Encyclopedia of Pop, Rock and Soul*. New York: St. Martin's Press, 1975.
———. *Encyclopedia of Popular Music*. New York: St. Martin's Press, 1965.
———. *Guitar Years: Pop Music from Country and Western to Hard Rock*. Garden City, New York: Doubleday, 1970.
Staulcup, Jack. *Today's Teenager and Dance Music*. Illinois: Metropolis Printing Service, 1964.
Stearns, Marshall and Stearns, Jean. *Jazz Dance: The Story of American Vernacular Dance*. New York: Macmillan, 1968.
Stein, Howard with Zalkind, Ronald. *Promoting Rock Concerts*. A Zadoc Book. New York: Schirmer Books, 1979.
Stein, Jeff and Johnston, Chris. *The Who*. New York: Stein and Day, 1973.

Stevens, Kim. *The Bee Gees: A Photo Bio*. New York: Jove, 1978.
Stokes, Geoffrey. *Starmaking Machinery*. New York: The Bobbs-Merrill Company, Inc., 1976.
Swann, P. *Encyclopedia of Rock*. New York: Tempo Books, 196?.
Swenson, John. *Kiss*. New York: Ace Books, 1978.
Taubman, Howard (editor). *The New York Times Guide to Listening Pleasure*. New York: Macmillan, 1968.
Taylor, Derek. *As Time Goes By*. London: Davis-Poynter, 1973.
Taylor, John Russell. *The Hollywood Musical*. New York: McGraw-Hill, 1971.
Thompson, Toby. *Positively Main Street: An Unorthodox View of Bob Dylan*. New York: Coward-McCann, 1971.
Thomas, Tony. *Music for the Movies*. New York: A. S. Barnes, 1973.
Tudor, Dean and Tudor, Nancy. *Contemporary Popular Music*. Littleton, Colorado: Libraries Unlimited, Inc., 1979.
―――. *Grass Roots Music*. Littleton, Colorado: Libraries Unlimited, Inc., 1979.
Tremlett, George. *The David Bowie Story*. New York: Warner Paperback Library, 1975.
―――. *The Osmond Story*. New York: Warner Paperback Library, 1975.
―――. *The Rolling Stones*. New York: Warner Books, 1974.
Uslan, Michael and Soloman, Bruce. *The Rock & Roll Trivia Quiz*. New York: Simon and Schuster, 1978.
Van Der Horst, Brian. *Rock Music*. New York: Watts, 1973.
Vassal, Jacques. *Electric Children: Roots and Branches of Modern Folk-Rock*. (Translated from French by Paul Barnett.) New York: Taplinger, 1975.
Vernon, Paul. *The Sun Legend*. London: Steve Lane, 1969.
Vinson, Lee. *Encyclopedia of Rock*. New York: Drake Publishers, Inc., 1976.
Walley, David. *No Commercial Potential: The Saga of Frank Zappa and the Mothers of Invention*. New York: Outerbridge, 1972.
Warner, Jay. *How to Have Your Hit Song Published*. Murphys, California: Music Bank Publications, 1978.
Weissman, Dick. *The Music Business: Career Opportunities and Self Defense*. New York: Crown Publishers, 1979.
Welch, Chris. *Hendrix*. New York: Flash Books, 1973.
Whitburn, Joel. Record Research Collection (includes *Top Pop [Hot 100] 1955-72; Top Pop 1940-55; Top LPs 1945-72; Top Country 1949-71; Top R&B 1949-71; Top Easy Listening 1961-74;* plus yearly supplements. Menomenee Falls, Wisconsin: Record Research, 1975.
Whitcomb, Ian. *After the Ball*. London: Allen Lane, 1972.
―――. *Tin Pan Alley: A Pictorial History, 1919-1939*. New York: Continents, 1975.
Wilder, Alec. *American Popular Song: The Great Innovators, 1900-1950*. New York: Oxford University Press, 1972.
Wilk, Max. *They're Playing Our Song*. New York: Atheneum, 1973.
Williams, Allan and Marshall, William. *The Man Who Gave the Beatles Away*. New York: Macmillan, 1975.
Williams, John R. *This Was Your Hit Parade: 1935-1950*. Rockland, Maine: Courier-Gazette, 1973.
Williams, Paul. *Outlaw Blues: A Book of Rock Music*. New York: Dutton, 1969.

Williams, Richard. *Out of His Head: The Sound of Phil Spector.* New York: Outerbridge and Lazard, 1972.

Wise, Herbert H. (editor). *Professional Rock and Roll.* New York: Collier Books, 1967.

Wood, Graham. *An A-Z of Rock and Roll.* London: Studio Vista, 1971.

Wren, Christopher S. *Winner Got Scars Too: The Life and Legends of Johnny Cash.* New York: Ballantine, 1974.

Young, Jean and Lang, Michael. *Woodstock Festival Remembered.* New York: Ballantine, 1979.

Zalkind, Ronald (Editor). *Contemporary Music Almanac 1980.* New York: Schirmer Books, 1980.

――――. *Getting Ahead in the Music Business.* New York: Schirmer Books, 1979.

Zalkind, Ronald and Goldstein, Toby. *All about the Music Business: A Career Guidebook.* New York: Practical Learning for the Arts, Inc., 1978.

RSD

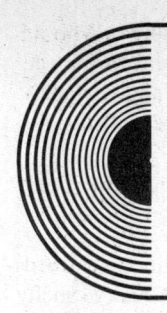

MUSIC BOOKS 1979

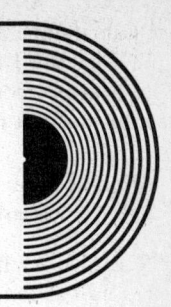

American Singers, by Whitney Balliett. New York: Oxford University Press, 1979.

This latest book by Whitney Balliett, jazz critic for *The New Yorker,* is about fourteen of America's popular and jazz stylists, some famous (Tony Bennett, for example), some known only to a loyal coterie of fans. There are renowned blues and jazz singers: Ray Charles, Joe Turner, Alberta Hunter, Helen Humes; disciples of Mabel Mercer's cabaret singing style: Bobby Short, Hugh Shannon, Blossom Dearie; and several women who bridge the gap between jazz singing and the cabaret style—Sylvia Syms, Anita Ellis, Teddi Kind, Mary Mayo, and Barbara Lea. Balliett lets each singer tell his or her own story and adds his own perceptive comments, linking them to the music scene in general.

FROM THE BOOK:

Mabel Mercer

By the thirties, I had settled pretty much into Bricktop's, and it was a lovely era. Bricktop's was very chic, and money was plentiful. There were banquettes around the walls, lit from behind, and an orchestra and a small dance floor. I'd sit right at people's tables and sing to them. That sort of intimate singing is tricky, you know. You can't *look* at the people you are singing to. They get embarrassed. So you look at the ceiling or the far corner of the room, and then they can stare at you and know that you won't look down and catch them.

Tony Bennett

"All kinds of things go through my head when I'm singing. I think of Joanna [Bennett's wife] a lot. I think of things from my past; I even *see* them. If I'm working in a beautiful place like Festival Hall, in London, I think of the great lighting, the great clusters of light, and they inspire me. If a song is truly believable, it becomes a self-hypnosis thing. And when that happens I automatically start thinking a line ahead, like when I serve at tennis and am already thinking of the next shot. My concentration becomes heavy, so that if I forget the words I can do what Harold Arlen told me: 'Just make up new words in the right spirit and don't let anybody know, and you'll be all right.'

Ray Charles

"I can't give any reasons why the public likes me. Of course, one time I might be up and the public might not feel a thing, and another time they might cry and I might consider myself down. The only thing is I have tried to be honest and I cannot be a disappointment to myself. I've felt that way all my life. I've often wondered. Who am I? What am I that people would spend the money to come out and stand in the rain to hear me, come out and spend the money on tickets and baby-sitters and carfare to hear me? But if I can tell myself I did my best, I know in my heart I feel satisfied."

Straight Life: The Story of Art Pepper, by Art and Laurie Pepper. New York: Schirmer Books, A Division of Macmillan Publishing Co., 1979.

Regarded by many as the foremost living jazz altoist, Art Pepper in his own words (as well as those of relatives, friends, and such contemporaries as June Christy, Shelly Manne, and Don Menza), chronicles his career, which began in his teens and included years on the road with Stan Kenton and others. Heroin addiction paralleled his musical success and Pepper candidly—often in harrowing detail—talks about his years as an artist-junkie. Through it all, his musical talent has held him together and he has bounced back to perform to rave reviews. A story of the ongoing rebirth of an artist and a portrait of a man intent on living life to the fullest.

FROM THE BOOK:

I remember one time when I was playing at the Black Hawk in San Francisco. I forget the date, but Sonny Stitt was touring with Jazz At The Philharmonic. He came in, and he wanted to jam with me. He came in, and he says, "Can I blow?" I said, "Yeah, great" We *both* play alto, which is . . . It really makes it a contest. But Sonny is one of those guys, that's the *thing* with him. It's a communion. It's a battle. It's an ego trip. It's a testing ground. And that's the beautiful part of it. It's like two guys that play great pool wanting to play pool togeher or two great football teams or two magnificent basketball teams, and just the joy of playing with someone great, being with someone great.

I said, "What do you want to play?" Sonny says, "Let's play 'Cherokee.' " That's a song jazz musicians used to play. The bridge, which is the middle part, has all kinds of chord changes in it. It's very difficult. If you can play that . . . If some kid came around, and he wanted to play, you'd say "Let's play 'Cherokee,' " and you'd count it off real fast. I said, "Well, beat it off." He went, "One-two, one-two;" he was flying. We played the head, the melody, and then he took the first solo. He played, I don't know, about forty choruses. He played for an hour maybe, did everything that could be done on a saxophone, everything you could play, as much as Charlie Parker could have played if he'd been there. Then he stopped. And he looked at me. Gave me one of those looks, "All right, suckah, your turn." And it's my job; it's my gig. I was strung out. I was hooked. I was drunk. I was having a hassle with my wife, Diane, who'd threatened to kill herself in our hotel room next door. I had marks on my arm. I thought there were narcs in the club, and I all of a sudden realized that it was me. He'd done all those things, and now I had to put up or shut up or get off or forget it or quit or kill myself or do *something*.

I forgot everything, and everything came out. I played way over my head. I played completely different than he did. I searched and found my own way, and what I said reached the people. I played myself, and I knew I was right, and the people loved it, and they felt it. I blew and I blew, and when I finally finished I was shaking all over; my heart was pounding; I was soaked in sweat, and the people were screaming; the people were clapping, and I looked at Sonny, but I just kind of nodded, and he went, "All *right*." And that was it. That's what it's all about.

As It Happened: A Memoir by William S. Paley. New York: Doubleday, 1979.

Founder and Chairman of CBS William Paley reminisces about his personal life and his life with CBS—from the celebrities of the entertainment world to the business and political leaders of America. Paley has always had an uncanny eye for a good business venture. In 1938, sensing that a boom in the record industry was at hand, he bought the American Record Corporation— this company evolved into CBS Records, and the acquisition turned out to be one of Paley's most profitable deals. Examples of other successes abound: Paley foresaw the enormous impact of radio and, later, television; he discovered such greats as Bing Crosby, Kate Smith, and Frank Sinatra; he lured to CBS stars such as Jack Benny, George Burns, Red Skelton, and scores of others. A look at radio and television history—and at the tastes and trends of our times—by one of most important people in the industry. Illustrated.

FROM THE BOOK:
In the same vein, many people thought I was overpaying when CBS bought the American Record Corporation, whose chief asset was the Columbia Phonograph Company, for about $700,000 in 1938. Some people at the time may have attributed our purchase to sentiment, for the same Columbia Phonograph Company had been the largest stockholder in CBS for a short time back in 1927. But sentiment had nothing to do with it. The whole recording industry had been in a slump during the Depression years and yet I felt bullish about its future. Radio had introduced a great many people to the enjoyment of music and with radio then starting to turn to variety, drama, and comedy programs in place of music, I felt the record business was on its way to making a comeback. Negotiating the purchase was not difficult at all. The owner of American Record thought he had a lemon on his hands, a company that was draining him and, I think, he was happy at the time to get rid of it at that price.
It turned out to be the best deal I ever made, except for buying CBS itself. We gave the company a new name, Columbia Recording Corporation, and it has evolved into what is known today as Columbia Records, which is part of our CBS/Records Group. In its first full year as part of CBS, the new company lost $73,000, and from that tiny operation in red ink in 1939, we developed it into one of the largest record companies in the world, as well as CBS's largest non-broadcasting operation.
At the very start, we engaged Edward Wallerstein, who had then been the general manager of Victor, the record division of RCA, as the first president of Columbia Records. Later in that first year, we hired a young, struggling composer, as the assistant to the director of the Masterworks Division of Columbia Records at $50 a week. That was Goddard Lieberson, the son of an English manufacturer and a graduate of the Eastman School of Music, who rose to become the brilliant president of Columbia Records and a legend in his time.

Bee Gees: The Authorized Biography, by Barry, Robin, and Maurice Gibb as told to David Leaf. New York: Delta Books, Dell Publishing Co., Inc., 1979.

In their own words, Barry, Robin, and Maurice Gibb tell their life story: from childhood in England through their life in Australia to the dramatic development of their musical talents. The book also relates the legendary London meeting with Robert Stigwood, the Bee Gees' breakup and reconciliation, the phenomenal success of "Saturday Night Fever," and all that has happened since. Over 3,000 photographs show the Bee Gees on stage as small children, in intimate family scenes, and performing in concerts and films. A big bonus for the dedicated fan is a full-color pull-out poster of the group. Also included: complete Bee Gees discography, filmography, and list of awards.

FROM THE BOOK:
The brothers' debut in Australia was quite auspicious, and they became regulars at the track. During one of their earliest performances, a racing driver named Bill Goode heard a lot of commotion from the crowd and left the racing pits to find out what was happening. He heard three kids singing, and was impressed enough to find out where they lived and let them know he wanted to talk to their parents. None of the Gibbs remembers the exact time of Bill Goode's discovery. Barbara recalls that "it was weeks before I found out what they were doing. I thought they were just going to watch the races. Until one night they came home with the pockets of their jeans stuffed with pennies. They couldn't walk. And they were complaining, 'Nobody's discovered us yet.'" So it was probably late in 1959 that Bill Goode noticed the brothers singing. Barbara remembers the "night after Bill Goode had heard them. They never met Goode, but one of the boys who worked in the pits came over to them and said, 'Tell your mum to ring this number. It's to do with recording.' So Barry says, 'How much money will we get?'" And the man told the brothers £2,000. Actually, the man told them they might earn as much as £2,000, but when the kids got home they said, "Mommy, you ring this number in the morning and we're going to get £2,000."

When Mrs. Gibb called the next day, she found out that a number of people were interested in helping the boys' career along. Bill Goode had a friend, Bill Gates, who was a DJ in Brisbane. Goode brought Gates to the Gibb's home to hear the boys sing. Hugh was still out working in the bush country, and Barbara didn't want to be the only adult representing her sons. So Barbara's cousin came over from his nearby home to be there when the important visitors arrived. As Barbara remembers, "they came and listened to the boys, and they were absolutely knocked out." Bill Gates points out that "the raw talent of the Bee Gees was apparent. The harmonies were fantastic. Barry was able to write a new song in five minutes."

Fight Back! And Don't Get Ripped Off, by David Horowitz. San Francisco: Harper & Row, 1979.

One of America's leading consumer experts David Horowitz tells how to avoid getting ripped off when purchasing goods or services. What he has to say about buying records and stereo equipment is useful, common sense advice and he lets you in on how record manufacturers and record stores sometimes try to cheat the consumer. Other topics discussed range from oranges to autos and include restaurants, mail order, doctors, lawyers and other professionals, and deceptive advertising practices. The appendices alone are worthwhile—you'll learn how to write a complaint letter that gets results and find lists of state government agencies, consumer groups, and other organizations devoted to the buyer's interests.

FROM THE BOOK:

Buying Records

Record manufacturers and record stores sometimes conspire to rip us off. Record industry insiders admit that as many as 50 percent of the record albums pressed from the master cut are bad reproductions, are warped, or are technically defective. But they're shipped to record stores anyway. Customers often blame the poor sound on their record player if they notice it at all. Those who take back the record get a new one or their money back but the bum record isn't always returned to the manufacturer for credit. Why? Because the record labels will only give return credit on 10 percent of the albums they ship to a store in a given year. What happens to the other 90 percent? You better believe the retailer doesn't eat them. The retailer simply recycles the defective record until he finds a consumer who is either too timid, or who ignores or doesn't hear the obvious defects. The record stores re-shrinkwrap the returned album and put it back on the shelf—so look out.

To save the next consumer from getting cheated, ask the store clerk to write the word *defective* on the record label and the record packet when you return an album. That way, they can't rewrap it as if it were brand new. But don't you try and rip off the record store. Retailers complain that some customers buy an album, take it home and record it onto a cassette tape, then bring the record back, claiming it was defective, and exchange it for an entirely different recording. Using the record store's refund or exchange policy to build your personal tape library is petty thievery.

Buying Stereo Equipment

This warning doesn't belong in the advertising chapter but since it was an ad that pulled you into the store, I want to stress this one point: You must be careful not to get razzle-dazzled into spending more on a stereo outfit than your budget allows. Retailers call this point-of-purchase pressure and it often works. As one former stereo store manager told me, "Don't buy stereo equipment with the most knobs, switches, and dials just to impress your friends with its appearance. Unfortunately, many people do just that. Settle on a dollar figure and tell the salesperson flat out that's all you are going to spend and you'll walk out before you spend a dime more."

The Golden Age of Jazz, by William P. Gottlieb. New York: Simon and Schuster, 1979.

The golden years of jazz are captured in these photographs of more than 200 outstanding musicians of the late 1930s and '40s. A writer-photographer for *The Washington Post* and *Down Beat,* Gottlieb was at the center of the jazz scene with the great names: Satchmo, Billie Holiday, Ella Fitzgerald, Thelonius Monk, Miles Davis, and scores of others. The photographs are superb and they are accompanied by Gottlieb's own fascinating stories of the people he photographed. For jazz fans—and for anyone who wants to discover the visual magic of jazz—this is an excellent collection.

FROM THE BOOK:

Louis "Satchmo" Armstrong

During much of the Golden Age, Louis Armstrong shifted from serious musician to amusing entertainer. He clowned . . . showed off spectacular high notes . . . sang sticky pop songs . . . became a movie star. But he never could completely conceal his musical talent. Satchmo's most banal performances were peppered with flecks of his genius.

Despite his lofty perch, Satch was easily approached and as genial offstage as on. Almost everyone wtih whom he had much contact regarded this open, earthy man as a friend, even though he often couldn't remember names and called most everyone Pops. (In turn, almost everyone called *him* Pops, though he also answered to Louis, Satch, Satchmo—the last two being diminutives of Satchelmouth.)

Satch, like so many ordinary humans, had a weight problem and had both fat periods and lean. As a prodigious consumer of red beans and rice (he often ended his many amusing letters with "Red beans and ricely yours"), Louis was more often fat than lean.

Louis had a personal diet that he touted. It was heavy on Pluto Water, a patented laxative that was popular years ago. Genial Satch kept in his inside jacket pocket copies of the diet, which he liked to hand out to friends who he thought needed it.

Louis and I happened to have the same dentist. A few months before Louis died, I found him entering the dentist's office as I was about to leave. The great man's famous chops were hurting and, from the way he looked, so were many other parts of him.

Bad as Satch must have felt, he was his usual gracious self. We chatted about old times until it was time for me to depart. Just before I was about to disappear through the door, he called out, "Hey, Pops, wait!" I turned toward him and could see that he had been sizing up my hulk. He then pulled a sheet of paper from his inside jacket pocket and handed it to me. "There's this diet, man. The greatest. Try it."

And I might have. But I just couldn't find a store that still sold Pluto Water.

Great Rock Musicals, edited with an introduction and notes by Stanley Richards. New York: Stein and Day, 1979.

This book by noted playwright and anthologist Stanley Richards presents eight of the most popular rock musicals—productions that have won Tony's, New York Drama Critics' Circle Awards, and Drama Desk Awards. Included are "The Wiz," "Two Gentlemen of Verona," "Grease," "Jesus Christ Superstar," "Your Own Thing," "Tommy," "Promenade," and of course "Hair." For each production, Richards provides not only script and lyrics but also cast listings and opening night credits; background and production history; critics' quotes; biographical sketches of librettists, lyricists, and composers; and photos from the original productions.

FROM THE BOOK:
While the rock musical was nurtured in the environs of Off-Broadway, it soon moved uptown to more affluent Broadway, where it was enthusiastically greeted with cheers and huge patronage by the theatregoing public. To consider some figures: seven of the musicals included in this volume totaled 8,050 performances in their initial engagements. (Two—*The Wiz* and *Grease,* as of this writing—are still playing to packed houses and are approaching long-run records.) What went beyond—with countless revivals, road, stock, concert, and amateur performances—only God and the musicals' copyright holders can determine.

How does the rock musical differ from the traditional musical? It is more freewheeling, less confined, and even when set in a specific period, manages to evoke an expressive topicality, an implied contemporaneousness. Frequently, it is also more generous in its utilization of lights and audiovisuals and, of course, there is the beat and the amplified sound. (It might be of interest to point out here that even in the more traditional musicals and revivals produced today, the amplification is souped-up to give them a more modern sound.)

A Guide to Music Festivals, by Carol Price Rabin. Stockbridge, Massachusetts: The Berkshire Traveller Press, 1979.

This selective guide to over 120 music festivals in 39 states includes festivals of classical, opera, folk, jazz, pop, bluegrass, country, and old-time fiddlers' music, arranged by category of music and by state. Each listing includes the type of music performed, a brief history of the festival, a sampling of the artists who have performed, and a description of the festival's setting. Most helpful to festival-goers is the comprehensive information provided on locations, dates, and where to write or phone for tickets and accommodations. Engaging pen-and-ink sketches accompany some of the descriptions, and convey a sense of the festival atmosphere.

FROM THE BOOK:

Monterey Jazz Festival
MONTEREY, CALIFORNIA
Third weekend in September for three days

Jimmy Lyons, a widely respected disc jockey on the West Coast is credited with starting the first festival in Monterey in 1958. During the first two decades, there were many memorable concerts—Dizzy Gillespie was frequently featured displaying his genius as the greatest of all contemporary trumpet players; one Sunday, six different symphonic brass ensembles performed a number of premiere compositions; Jimmy Witherspoon made his first appearance in 1959 and the Teagarden family—Jack, Charlie, Norma, and their mother were there in 1963. There were many world premieres at the festival—Jon Hendrick's *Evolution of the Blues Song,* Duke Ellington's *Suite Thursday,* Lalo Schifrin's Gillespiana, J. J. Johnson's *Perceptions.* Charles Mingus' *Meditations on Monterey,* and Gil Fuller's *On the Road to Monterey* are a few of the many performed. Much of the musical fare is devoted to jazz-as-before, but there are also many programs presenting new bands and new faces. Whatever the jazz style, Monterey has always enlisted talented jazz artists each year. Some of these well-known performers are Ruth Brown, Ron Carter, Benny Carter, Ornette Coleman, Red Garland, Dizzy Gillespie, Vince Guaraldi, Milt Jackson, Woody Herman, Carmen McRae, Thelonious Monk, Gerry Mulligan, Odetta, Sonny Rollins, Pee Wee Russell, Bola Sete, and many, many more jazz greats.

The performances are held in an open arena at the Monterey Fairgrounds, one mile from the city of Monterey, located on the northern California coast, 120 miles south of San francisco. There is seating for 7,000 fans, and a carnival-like atmosphere prevails during afternoon performances with booths lining the outside of the arena selling everything from sweet potato pies to tacos to beef teriyaki. The September weather on the Monterey Peninsula is usually ideal for the festival, with warm days and cool evenings. But there is always the possibility of the Monterey fog rolling in, so it is best to come prepared with a blanket or a warm coat!

The list of loyal fans and artists that keeps growing with every year, proves the theme of the Monterey Jazz Festival, "Keepin' the faith," is still working.

For information write to: Monterey Jazz Festival, P. O. Box Jazz, Monterey, California 93940. Telephone: (408) 373-3366.

For accommodations write to: Monterey Peninsula Chamber of Commerce, P. O. Box 1770, Monterey, California 93940. Telephone: (408) 649-3200.

Home Computers: A Manual of Possibilities, by Richard M. Koff. New York: Harcourt Brace Jovanovich, 1979.

This comprehensive guide to understanding, buying, and using the home computer (undoubtedly the next electronic product that will revolutionize the home) includes a section on music and voice that describes the many possibilities for creating and performing music with computers. Computers can also figure income tax, store personal data, and turn your TV set into a game center, and this book tells how to perform these and dozens more useful tasks. It also presents the basic concepts necessary to understand computers.

FROM THE BOOK:
Music synthesizers have a keyboard like a piano, except that under every key is a simple switch like the contacts under the computer keyboard. Each such key is connected to a circuit that will produce a desired base frequency. Volume or intensity is controlled by a pedal. A series of knobs or slides permits you to add different amounts of the higher frequencies, the harmonics, to change the character of the sound but not its base note.

Enter the computer. Now note selection, higher frequency additions, volume, and all the other variables can be preset. The programming time is separated from running or playing time. You can ask for a sequence of notes to be played at a speed faster than any human hands could possibly play them. You can make frequency jumps that go well beyond the limits of any given instrument. You can simulate the human voice and at pitches no human voice could ever produce. You can add more and more instruments to your orchestra without rehearsal or concern about how large the stage needs to be to include them all.

You are writing the music at your own pace, adding whatever complexity you want to the combination of notes, their timing, build-up, and fade-out patterns. Then, when you run the program, it "plays" the music through an audio amplifier and speaker after being processed by a digital-to analog converter at the output because audio amplifiers are analog devices.

Music creation and performance by computers is a fascinating subject that involves considerable technical knowledge at this stage of its development. No completely satisfactory method has been developed to program the sounds—but that is only a matter of time. The fact that computers will free composers from the limitations of instruments and performers means we are going to hear very different music in the near future. A composer can write his music (program it), play, edit, modify it, add to it, play it again, and so on, knowing that each time he plays it the music will be exactly as he last programmed it. He is in total control of his medium. Not many art forms offer that much freedom.

Jammin': Bill Butler's Complete Guide to Roller Disco, by Bill Butler and Elin Schoen. New York: Pocket Books, 1979.

Jammin' tells what you need to know to learn disco-on-wheels. Step by step, from the first moment you strap on a pair of skates to the ultimate accomplishment of mastering The Jam (roller disco's answer to The Hustle), Bill Butler teaches how to roller skate to jazz, R&B, or disco music. Included are tips on skates and how to care for them, warming up, choosing the right clothes to wear, safety rules, and what skating does for your body. The fundamentals of skating are clearly presented: how to fall, how to stop, how to do the different regional styles of skating. And, there are precise directions for performing the simple and fancy footwork for all the latest roller dances. Featuring many instructional diagrams and photographs supplemented with a clear, simple text, *Jammin'* is geared to both the beginner and the advanced skater.

FROM THE BOOK:

Jacob's Ladder

This is a series of sideways pivots, tracing a herringbone pattern on the floor. Lift your left leg, the toe pointing slightly inward. The right foot points inward also (so you're pigeon-toed). Bend your right knee. Then, raising the right knee a little for motivation, swivel the right foot to the right, pressure on the back wheels, so that it's turned out. At the same time, turn the left foot out (so it's pointing left). Then, without pausing, put your weight on the front wheels of the right foot and turn it inward again, turning the left foot inward at the same time. Continue the pattern as many times as you want (or for as long as you're capable of swiveling along). The total picture should be a smooth, quick X-ing to the side.

Jacob's Ladder can also be done with both feet on the floor, remaining parallel, applying pressure on the heels when turning the toes right and on the toes when pointing the toes to the left. But keep all your wheels on the floor at all times. Simply putting pressure on the front wheels frees the back wheels to swivel sideways, and vice-versa.

Back-Pedal

The purpose of this move is to interrupt your (Detroit) stride to avoid an oncoming skater tripping over your extended foot—to swerve out of the way, in other words, without losing the beat. It occurs at the point in the stride when you are about to bring your back foot forward. Instead of bringing it to the instep of the foot you're rolling on, put it down on the floor, front wheels first, behind you, and glide on it, forward on all four wheels, from that position.

Scissors Jump

This is like overdrive, like putting your car in second gear, a power play to get more force, more speed—by taking a stride in the air. As you bring your back foot forward to stride, you don't bring it down immediately. You propel yourself in the air with the foot that was rolling. In other words, you leap up and forward in the same position in which you were striding. Land on eight wheels, the foot that was rolling still behind the other. Then you resume the stride, pumping forward with most of your weight on the back foot. If you can switch your legs in the air while in the leap, the more power to you.

The Official Price Guide to Collectible Rock Records, by Randal C. Hill. Orlando, Florida: House of Collectibles, 1979.

Today, a recording of Elvis Presley's "That's All Right" is worth up to $200 and his "Mystery Train" should bring up to $120. Not all old records command such prices, but many are valued at many times their original price and no in-demand rock record will ever depreciate in value. This guide lists the current buying and selling prices of over 25,000 of the most collectible singles, EPs, and albums. Included are over 12,000 song titles recorded by more than 500 artists. The author provides practical tips on starting a collection, investing, and proper storage and display techniques. In addition to the listings, the book is studded with photographs and 100 capsule biographies of the most famous recording artists in rock 'n roll.

FROM THE BOOK:

Condition

By actual definition, a record is Mint *only* if it has never been played. Unless you are dealing in store-stock merchandise, this definition has been stretched (out of necessity) by nearly every collector.

This book deals with prices for two grades:

MINT—unplayed or played a minimum of times so as to produce no scratches, label blemishes or audible surface noise.

VG (Very Good)—a well-cared-for record, usually stored in a sleeve or jacket since first bought, with *some* scratches and surface noise but not enough to retract aurally or visually. More specific grading uses the symbols + and −. (For example, a M − record is slightly better than a VG + one.)

Grading with any record less than unplayed (mint) is subjective. Practice in grading discs doesn't make perfect but experience *is* the best teacher. Be particular in buying and honest in selling. An unhappy customer warrants an immediate refund. If you're the seller, it is better to undergrade than to label a record's condition better than it really it.

ISSUE #	LABEL	ARTIST/TITLE	VG	MINT
		FATS DOMINO		
5058	Imperial	The Fat Man/Detroit City Blues	15.00	25.00
5065		Boogie Woogie Baby/Little Bee	15.00	25.00
5077		She's My Baby/Hideaway Blues	15.00	25.00
5085		He La Bas Boogie/Brand New Baby	15.00	25.00
		(The first four releases were issued only on 78 RPM. The following reflect prices for 45 RPM discs.)		
5099		Korea Blues/Every Night About This Time	20.00	30.00
5114		Tired of Crying/What's The Matter, Baby?	15.00	25.00
5123		Don't You Lie To Me/Sometimes I Wonder	15.00	25.00
5138		No, No Baby/Right From Wrong	12.00	22.00
5145		Rockin' Chair/Careless Love	12.00	20.00
5167		You Know I Miss You/I'll Be Gone	10.00	18.00
5180		Goin' Home/Reeling and Rocking	12.00	20.00
5197		Poor Poor Me/Trust In Me	10.00	18.00
5209		How Long?/Dreaming	8.00	15.00
5220		Nobody Loves Me/Cheatin'	7.00	12.00
5231		Going To The River/Mardi Gras in New Orleans	7.00	12.00
5240		Please Don't Leave Me/The Girl I Love	6.00	10.00
5251		Rose Mary/You Said You Loved Me	6.00	10.00
5262		Don't Leave Me This Way/Something's Wrong	6.00	10.00
5272		Little School Girl/You Done Me Wrong	6.00	10.00
5283		Baby, Please/Where Did You Stay?	6.00	10.00
5301		You Can Pack Your Suitcase/I Lived My Life	6.00	10.00
5313		Don't You Hear Me Calling You/Love Me	5.00	8.00
5323		I Know/Thinking Of You	4.00	7.00

ISSUE #	LABEL	ARTIST/TITLE	VG	MINT
5340		Don't You Know/Helping Hand	3.50	6.00
5348		Ain't It A Shame/La La (16)	3.00	5.00
5357		All By Myself/Troubles Of My Own	3.50	6.00
5369		Poor Me/I Can't Go On	3.00	5.00
5375		Bo Weevil/Don't Blame It On Me (35)	2.50	4.00
5386		I'm In Love Again/My Blue Heaven (5)	2.00	4.00
5396		When My Dreamboat Comes Home/So-Long (22)	2.50	4.00
5407		Blueberry Hill/Honey Chile (4)	2.00	3.00

Up and Down With the Rolling Stones, by Tony Sanchez. New York: William Morrow and Company, Inc., 1979.

This insider's account takes you through two stormy decades in the lives of the most notorious of the Rolling Stones and their spectacular women. Here are Brian Jones, who originated the style of arrogant hedonism and virtually created the Stones; Keith Richards; Mick Jagger; Anita Pallenberg; Marianne Faithful; and Bianca Jagger. Tony Sanchez, an employee of Keith Richards, was there, and he records the events of those years: racing fast cars on the Cote d'Azur, murder at Altamont, and Mick's stream of girlfriends, culminating in Bianca and the wedding in France with half the rock world present. Sanchez doesn't spare himself; he finally left the Stones to enter a drug rehabilitation program. With over one hundred photographs by the author.

FROM THE BOOK:
Bianca was flattered by Jagger's attentions and pleased that the whole room stared at them when they danced. It had been the same when she had lived with actor Michael Caine. People had admired her, treated her with respect because she was the woman of a rich, powerful and famous man. Jagger was fastidiously polite to her, treating her in a slightly awed, little-boy way—like a princess. He suggested an intimate club where they could meet later, and she slipped away without a word to Eddie Barclay. Jagger followed her half an hour later, enormously flattered that she had dropped her fiancé to be with him. It appeared that she had fallen as instantly for him as he had for her. Only later was Mick to discover that Bianca was insecure and needed constant reassurance of her charm and power to attract beautiful men who were not lways prepared to put up with her selfish ways, and that, in the future, she would feel as little compunction about humiliating Mick as she had felt about walking out on Eddie Barclay.

"I'm a bit destructive," she was to admit later in an interview. "I used to be destructive in a relationship because I was scared of it getting out of hand. It was not really to destroy other people but to protect myself."
But on that balmy September evening it seemed to Mick that he had at last met the mystery woman of his dreams. She was a perfect lady, refusing to sleep with him at first, but telling him that yes, she too had never been quite so happy in her life. He had a few days to spare before the next gig, in Vienna, so they spent every second together, dining in candlelit restaurants, walking around the fairy-tale gardens of Versailles together, holding hands like kids. Mick offered her a little coke, and she snorted it so clumsily that he thought she had probably never tried the drug before, but he said nothing, thinking only how different she was from the other girls he had known.

But still, they didn't make love, and Jagger was more entranced than ever. Bianca was holding back, making excuses, letting him know that he hadn't totally captured her, and he was as aroused and intrigued by her as he had originally been by Marianne. The Stones flew to Vienna for the next gig, and he arranged for her to fly to Rome a couple of days later, when they played there. He sent a limousine to the airport to meet her and arranged a separate room for her. "This," said Keith, "has got to be the real thing."

A Generation in Motion: Popular Music and Culture in the Sixties, by David Pichaske. New York: Schirmer Books, A Division of Macmillan Publishing Co., 1979.

From the Beatles to Bob Dylan, the songs of the 60s created a new mythology for an entire generation. This book, is a clear-eyed look at the words and music that turned on a generation and a hard look at the forces that carried it from innocence to anger to despair. Pichaske interprets what really happened in the 60s, and why. An intelligent book that captures the idealism and pioneer spirit of a volatile time.

FROM THE BOOK:
The sixties, like other periods of social and political unrest, were also a time of great artistic flowering. In print, in theater, in film, art flourished, but most of all in music, the chosen medium of the decade. The Beatles, the Stones, the Who, the Doors, Bob Dylan, Paul Simon and a dozen other artists (both popular and fine) turned folk music, rock, rhythm and blues, even country music into a form of protest more refined than the topical ballads of the protest singers, infinitely more to the moral and social point than the cotton candy of Tin Pan Alley or *American Bandstand*. This protest has weathered the intervening years much better than the songs that tied themselves more closely to civil rights or the war. Art always does. In fact, some of it speaks as much to the seventies as it did to the sixties, both the fine art and the pop art.

The most important work in the latter category is unquestionably the Beatles' *Sgt. Pepper's Lonely Hearts Club Band*, released in June 1967 (and resurrected eleven years later as a purely shlock piece of nostalgia). This album was in many respects the most remarkable of the decade: in its production, instrumentation, lyrics, and conceptualization it was a musical revolution. It virtually created the concept album. It introduced multitrack recording technique. It turned rock into art, completing a process begun with Bob Dylan's *Bringing It All Back Home* and the Beatles' own *Rubber Soul* (both 1965). It was a terrific head album and did much to promote the use of dope by giving heads something rich and complex to listen to while stoned. It contained one great song after another, so that whether you picked up on the words or not (and many folks didn't although the lyrics were printed on the back of the album packet—a pretty good indication that the Beatles were trying to tell us something), the album tended to get inside you.

And it made a remarkably coherent statement on modern society and on the pervasive emptiness of all our lives and on the assorted methods we use to cope with that emptiness.

ASCAP-DEEMS TAYLOR AWARDS
For literary excellence in the field of music.

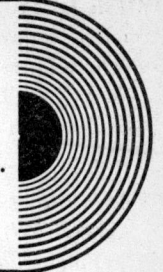

BOOKS

1968

The Big Bands, George T. Simon (Macmillan)
More about This Business of Music, Sidney Shemel and M. William Krasilovsky (Billboard)
The Life That Late He Led, George Eells (G. P. Putnam's Sons)

1969

Early Jazz, Gunther Schuller (Oxford University Press)
My Music, My Life, Ravi Shankar (Simon and Schuster)
Exploring Twentieth-Century Music, Dr. Otto Deri (Holt, Rinehart and Winston)

1970

Music: Mirror of the Arts, Alan Rich (Praeger Publishers and Ridge Press)
The Continuity of Music, Irving Kolodin (Alfred A. Knopf)
The Music Merchants, Milton Goldin (Macmillan)

1971

Legal Protection for the Creative Musician, Lee Eliot Berk (Berklee Press)
Critical Affairs—A Composer's Journal, Ned Rorem (George Braziller)
The Singer and His Art, Aksel Schiotz (Harper & Row)

1972

The Classical Style: Haydn, Mozart, Beethoven, Charles Rosen (Viking)
The Music of Black Americans, A History, Dr. Eileen Southern (W. W. Norton)
Pops Foster—The Autobiography of a New Orleans Jazzman, Tom Stoddard (University of California Press)
The Jazz Tradition, Martin Williams (Oxford University Press)

1973

And Music at the Close: Stravinsky's Last Years, Lillian Libman (W. W. Norton)
American Popular Song—The Great Innovators, 1900-1950, Alec Wilder (Oxford University Press)
Sounds of Social Change, Richard A. Peterson and R. Serge Denisoff (Rand McNally)
Music and Musical Life in Soviet Russia 1917-1970, Boris Schwarz (Macmillan)

1974

Mahler, Henry-Louis de La Grange (Doubleday)
They're Playing Our Song, Max Wilk (Atheneum)
Buried Alive, Myra Friedman (Wm. Morrow)

Music Is My Mistress, Duke Ellington (Doubleday)
Orpheus in the New World, Philip Hart and Claire Brook (W. W. Norton)

1975

The Music of Africa, J. H. Kwabena Nketia (W. W. Norton)
The Finali Diary, Ned Rorem (Holt, Rinehart and Winston)
The Composer's Voice, Edward T. Cone (University of California Press)
Dancing in the Dark, Howard Dietz (Quadrangle)
Raise Up off Me, Hampton Hawes and Don Asher (Coward, McCann & Geoghegan)

1976

Music for Patriots, Politicians, and Presidents, Vera Brodsky Lawrence (Macmillan)
American Labor Songs of the Nineteenth Century, Philip S. Foner (University of Illinois Press)
Charles Ives & His America, Frank R. Rossiter (Liverright)
Style and Idea, Leonard Stein (St. Martin's Press)
Arnold Schoenberg, Charles Rosen (Viking)

1977

Jazz People, Dan Morgenstern, Harry N. Abrams)
Stomping the Blues, Albert Murray (McGraw Hill)
The Folk Music Sourcebook, Larry Sandberg and Dick Weissman (Alfred A. Knopf)

Starmaking Machinery, Geoffrey Stokes (Bobbs-Merrill)
Gradus, Leo Kraft (W. W. Norton)

1978

John Hammond on Record, John Hammond (Ridge Press)
Josquin des Prez, Edward Lowinsky (Oxford University Press)
A History of the Oratorio, Prof. Howard S. Smither (University of North Carolina Press)
Beethoven, Maynard Solomon (Schirmer Books)
Early Downhome Blues, Jeff Todd Titon (University of Illinois Press)

1979

Haydn: Chronicle and Works, H. C. Robbins Landon (Indiana University Press)
Medieval Music, Richard H. Hoppin (W. W. Norton)
The Soul of Mbira, Paul F. Berliner (University of California Press)
Hucbald, Guido & John on Music—Three Medieval Treatises, Warren Babb, translator, Claude V. Palisca, editor (Yale University Press)
Duke Ellington in Person, Mercer Ellington and Stanley Dance (Houghton Mifflin Co.)
Honkers & Shouters, Arnold Shaw (Macmillan)
Scott Joplin—The Man Who Made Ragtime, James Haskins with Kathleen Benson (Doubleday)

ARTICLES

1968

James Ringo—five reviews published in the American Record Guide
Arnold Shaw—articles published in Cavalier Magazine
Joan Peyser—article published in the Columbia University Forum

1969

Joan Peyser—article published in the New York Times
James Ringo—article published in the American Record Guide
James Lyons—Boston Symphony Orchestra program notes

1970

Ralph J. Gleason—article published in Lithopinion
Alan Rich—article published in New York Magazine
Issachar Miron—article published in the New York Times

1971

Boris E. Nelson—19 articles published in the Toledo Blade
"A Hiatus in American Music History," Dr. Paul Glass, published in Afro-American Studies (Brooklyn College)
"Mozart: His Tragic Life and Controversial Death," Dr. Louis Carp, published in Bulletin of the New York Academy of Medicine

1972

Elliot W. Galkin—articles published in the Baltimore Sun
"Webern's Twelve-Tone Sketches," George Perle, published in The Musical Quarterly
"God Bless Louis Armstrong," Ralph J. Gleason, published in Rolling Stone
Irving Lowens—articles published in the Washington Star

1973

Martin Bernheimer—article published in Los Angeles Times
Alan Rich—article published in New York Magazine
Robert Finn—article published in Cleveland Plain Dealer
Bruce Pollock—article published in Rock Magazine

1974

Jack O'Brian—syndicated columnist
Hubert Saal—Newsweek
Ben Fong Torres—Rolling Stone
Alan Rich—New York Magazine

1975

"American Music: 1918-1960," Richard Franko Goldman (chapter in The New Oxford History of Music—The Modern Age 1890-1960, published by Oxford University Press)
"Farewell to the Duke," Ralph J. Gleason, published in Rolling Stone
Elliott W. Galkin—articles published in the Baltimore Sun
Andrew Porter—articles published in The New Yorker
David Hamilton—articles published in The New Yorker

1976

Robert Commanday—The San Francisco Chronicle
Richard Dyer—The Boston Globe
Robert Finn—Cleveland Plain Dealer
Jack O'Brain—articles for King Features Syndicate
Gary Giddins—articles published in the Village Voice

1977

Paul Baratta—Songwriter Magazine
Gary Giddins—Village Voice
Maureen Orth—Newsweek
Samuel Lipman—Commentary
Karen Monson—Chicago Daily News
Irving Lowens—The Washington Star
Richard Dyer—The Boston Globe
John Ardoin—The Dallas Morning News

1978

Martin Bernheimer—published in Los Angeles Times
Andrew Porter—published in The New Yorker
David Burge—published in Contemporary Keyboard
George Perle—published in the International Alban Berg Society Newsletter
Douglas M. Green—published in the International Alban Berg Society Newsletter
Gene Lees—published in High Fidelity
Joe Klein—published in Rolling Stone

1979

Michael Nelson—article in Baltimore Magazine
Robert Finn—articles in The Cleveland Plain Dealer
Bernard Holland—articles in The Pittsburgher Magazine
David Burge—articles in Contemporary Keyboard
Leighton Kerner—articles in the Village Voice

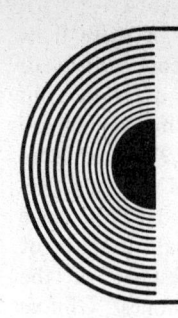

ROCK 'N' ROLL FILMS

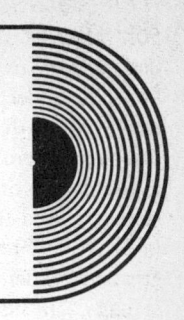

Since Bill Haley and the Comets' "Rock around the Clock" first thrust rock and roll onto the widescreen in 1955 as the opening number of *Blackboard Jungle,* there have been about 300 rock-related movies made in Hollywood and England. It's impossible to estimate the number more accurately, mostly because youth films have never had much cachet with film scholars, but also because some rock-based movies (Brian DePalma's *The Phantom of the Paradise,* Gordon Parks Jr.'s *Superfly*) straddle the lines on one or more genres. Even the definitive at-home film reference book, Leonard Maltin's TV Movies, omits such essential rock flichs as *Performance* and *Rock Rock Rock.*

Because youth films in general have never had much Hollywood prestige, most rock movies have been made either by beginners or exploitation-minded directors. Michael Curtiz' *King Creole,* the 1958 Elvis Presley vehicle, is a rare exception, but by 1958 Curtiz' career was on the downslide. Indeed, the only rock movie made by a director at the height of his show business clout is Martin's Scorsese's 1978 Band documentary, *The Last Waltz.*

More often, the rock film has served as a director's starting point: William Friedkin got his first directing assignment with *Good Times,* the 1967 Sonny and Cher vehicle, then went on to direct *The French Connection* and *The Exorcist.* Similarly John Boorman (*Point Blank, Deliverance*) got his start with a 1965 Animals feature, alternately known as *Catch Us If You Can* and *Having a Wild Weekend.* So did Bob Rafeaison (*Five Easy Pieces*) with the Monkees 1968 starrer, *Head.*

Head, Good Times and *Having a Wild Weekend* are examples of two of the rock film's prominent genres: The former pair are essentially vehicles for a star performer—the quintessential examples of such things are the 38 features Elvis Presley made for Hal Wallis, beginning with *Love Me Tender* and ending, not a moment too soon, with *Charo.* Generally, these were excuses to flaunt a popular face on the big screen in hope of quick return. The Beatles movies, thanks to the quick-cutting brilliance of director Richard Lester, are probably the most transcendent examples of star vehicle movies ever made.

Having a Wild Weekend, on the other hand, was formally a beach party movie, not unlike the ones that William Asher churned out for American International. But Boorman's direction was much more inspired, and rather than the tepid Annette and adenoidal Fabian, he got one of the best early British pop bands in the Dave Clark Five to help him along.

The surfing and beach party movies of the early 60s were, of course, the inheritors of the adolescent rebellion tradition set up by James Dean in *Rebel without a Cause* and Marlon Brando in *The Wild One* during the prerock

50s. Most of the 50s rock movies were descendants of just such social-problem films, as indeed was *Blackboard Jungle* itself. Most of these soon disintegrated into soap opera or worse, with the tamest available performers and plots. But occasionally, even this genre could rise above itself. Alan Freed was Mr. Sincerity, the great defender of rock and all things teenage, in his various movies (which were otherwise little more than an excuse to flaunt some hitmakers). In *Shake, Rattle and Rock*, a 1956 film directed by Edward L. Cahn and featuring not only Fats Domino but Mike ("Touch") Connors, the anti-rock legions really took it on the chin; that film's climactic scene features Sterling Holloway delivering testimony at a Ban the Beat hearing which is so full of double-talk jive that it's actually subtitled.

But most rock films were much more pedestrian. Even the motorcycle films of mid-60s, which gave the back of their hand to conventional morality, always made sure that the bad guys came to an unhappy ending, and took their rock and roll down with them. The psychedelic movies that came along a few years later did the same; even in *Easy Rider*, remember, the hipsters wind up on the short end of the stick.

A Hard Day's Night and *Help!*, Lester's 1964-65 Beatles movies, were among the first to share rock's perspective as well as exploiting its message. But more influential was D. A. Pennebaker's 1967 documentary of a Bob Dylan tour, *Don't Look Back*, which featured Dylan in his natural environment of surrealist putdowns and put-ons. *Don't Look Back* and Pennebaker's 1968 documentary of the Monterey International Pop Festival, *Monterey Pop*, established a trend toward live-action rock movies, which reached its peak with Michael Wadleigh's 1970 *Woodstock*, a four-hour epic of the great event. Since then, almost every major rock band has been somehow documented in a feature-length stage show, although few of these films succeed except for hard-core cultists of the particular group in question. But even these movies often smacked of the old exploitation as the 1976 Led Zeppelin "concert" movie, The Song Remains the Same, which fudged the issue by resorting to long, banal stretches of "fantasy" from each member of the group, or the Rolling Stones' *Gimme Shelter*, which includes rather cynically edited footage of the murder of Meredith Hunter at the climactic Altamont concert. To date, only *Woodstock, Monterey Pop, Don't Look Back* and two more recent entries, *The Kids Are Alright* and *The Last Waltz*, look likely to hold up as nonfiction rock movies.

Rock as fiction hasn't fared much better, unfortunately. Mick Jagger's heralded star turn in *Performance* seems more pretentious and windy with each passing year, and Ken Russell's adaptation of The Who's *Tommy* was cretinous from the start. But both those films made money, and with the added success of blaxploitation films using Seventies soul-funk (*Superfly*) and rock's ascension to the top-grossing entertainment medium position, concessions were made, and the late 70s have seen a flood of footage.

Generally, these pictures have had much more box-office than artistic success. The top example remains, of course, *Saturday Night Fever*, the 1978 disco-flick starring John Travolta, which was rock only narrowly; *Grease*, which had much to do with the early rock milieu in its Broadway incarnation, was almost equally explosive at the gate, but once again, the music veered closer to disco than rock. The former, directed by John Badham, another beginner, was not bad, but *Grease* was insipid, with a cast of 40-year old teens, and dialogue just as authentic. Much the same could be said of *FM*, the disco-exploitation movie *Thank God It's Friday*, and such cheapo bilge as *Americathon* and *The Chicken*

Chronicles, not to mention *Rock and Roll High School,* which wasted the inspired, trashy Ramones.

Rock fiction on film was more successful when it was pinned to nostalgia. George Lucas's *American Graffiti* had one of the best soundtracks in history (Martin Scorsese's *Mean Streets* had the very best), and it captured an aspect of the teenage lifestyle circa 1963. (The sequel missed everything.) *I Wanna Hold Your Hand* missed the excitement of the early Beatles days, wasting some fine acting in the process. More pungent nostalgia was ladled up by Floyd Mutrux's American Hot Wax, a skillful Alan Freed biography, heavily fictionalized but moving nonetheless. But the best rock biopic was *The Buddy Holly Story,* in which Gary Busey came on so convincingly that he made you forget the original (until the lights came up). Busey earned an Oscar nomination for his work.

Significantly all of the films mentioned in the last two paragraphs, with the exception of *American Graffiti* and *Americathon,* were released in 1977-78. By 1979, the pickings were much more slim. Only The Who, with their documentary *The Kids Are Alright,* and an excellent adaptation of *Quadrophenia,* Pete Townshend's second rock opera, seemed to be carrying on with rock movies on any grand scale.

DM

TEN BEST/TEN WORST ROCK 'N' ROLL FILMS

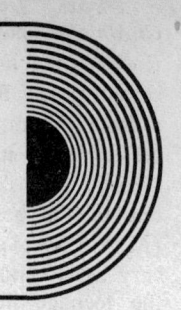

The listings below are, of course, extremely subjective, omitting some of what are ordinarily considered classics (*Performance, Woodstock, Jailhouse Rock*) in favor of lesser known but more substantial fare. In the negative category, I tried to duck genre films, since it would be easy to make a case against the plotless *Beach Party* cycle, but serve no other purpose. The movies listed below are bad to the point of being unwatchable; I've seen them, and I know. Films are presented in chronological order, with director's name and year of release in parentheses. Apologies to Bob Dylan fans, but on one who saw it could deny it—save for fans of Neil Young.

Ten Best Rock 'n' Roll Movies, 1955-79

1. **The Girl Can't Help It** (Frank Tashlin, 1956). Stars Jayne Mansfield, Tom Ewell, with Little Richard, Gene Vincent, Eddie Cochran, Fats Domino, The Platters.

A wacky comedy plot, not far removed from the sort of thing Tashlin later did for Jerry Lewis, but the most spectacular array of rock talent ever assembled for a dramatic picture. Vincent is so young and free, he'll make your heart ache with "Be Bop A Lula." Little Richard looks a choir boy on "Tutti Frutti," and Eddie Cochran tears the house down with "20 Flight Rock." The color photography is iconographic in its beauty.

2. **King Creole** (Michael Curtiz, 1958). Stars Elvis Presley, Carolyn Jones, Dean Jagger, Dolores Hart.

Presley's fourth movie, and one of the few in which he had a fighting chance as an actor. There's a solid plot (based on the Harold Robbins novel, *A Stone for Danny Fisher*), a supporting cast worthy of the name, fine direction from Curtiz (who also did *Casablanca,* among many others), and best of all, a great batch of songs written by Jerry Leiber and Mike Stoller. Shot on location in New Orleans, this ranks above even such acclaimed Elvis epics as *Flaming Star* (directed by *Dirty Harry* auteur Don Siegel) and *Jailhouse Rock* (with brilliant choreography by The King himself, and another fine crop of Leiber-Stoller compositions).

3. **A Hard Days Night** (Richard Lester, 1964). Stars The Beatles, Victor Spinetti.

At the time it was released, this was offered as evidence of the Beatles' inventive genius. But as time goes by, the real source of this film's attraction (and all of the appeal of the sequel, *Help*) lies not at all in the acting of the Liverpool quartet, which is rarely more than mugging, but in Lester's quick-cut directorial debut and a batch of songs as snappy and rocking as any they ever came up with.

4. **The T.A.M.I. Show** (Steve Binder, 1964). Stars James Brown, the Rolling Stones, the Beach Boys, Chuck Berry, Lesley Gore, Marvin Gaye, the Barbarians, Gerry and the Pacemakers, the Supremes, Billy J. Kramer, and the Dakotas.

This was a mind-boggling array of talent then, and it's equally staggering today. For those who never saw the Rolling Stones with Brian Jones, or James Brown at all, it's a must, but the real delights for connosseiurs are Lesley Gore's prefeminist anthem, "You Don't Own Me," and the bad Barbarians, singing "Are You a Boy or Are You a Girl, with their hook-armed drummer, Moulty. The sequel, the 1965 *T.N.T. Show*, despite Phil Spector's front-line involvement, suffered from a much less stellar array of talent: Bo Diddley, Ray Charles, the Ronettes, Ike and Tina Turner, the Byrds and Lovin' Spoonful are great, but who needs Roger Miller, Joan Baez, Petula Clark and David McCallum?

5. **Privilege** (Peter Watkins, 1967). Stars Paul Jones, Jean Shrimpton, Marc London, Max Bacon, Jeremy Child.

The only rock-as-apocalypse movie that works. Jones (the ace former lead vocalist of Manfred Mann) plays a rock star whose career is controlled by a consortium of church, state and private industry interests. This is spooky beyond all reason, with the limpid mod model Shrimpton as the perfect courtesan and a soundtrack of pure foreboding.

6. **Wild in the Streets** (Barry Shear, 1968). Stars Christopher Jones, Diane Varsi, Richard Pryor, Hal Holbrook, Millie Perkins, Ed Begley, Bert Freed.

This could actually have been listed both as one of the best and one of the worst. The premise is perversely insipid: Jones plays America's first teenage president, after securing the 14-year old vote through an LSD campaign. But the acting is so vigorous (catch Pryor in what might be his debut as a one-armed manager-thug), and the score so excellent that this one finally transcends itself.

7. **Beyond the Valley of the Dolls** (Russ Meyer, 1970). Stars Dolly Read, Cynthia Myers, Marcia McBroom, Edy Williams, Michael Blodgett, Erica Gavin, Strawberry Alarm Clock.

Myers' usual total assault on the sexes features Read, Myers, McBroom and Williams as big-busted rock quartet on the make, and Michael Blodgett as a Spector-like transvestite who's running the show. Byzantine plot, lame music, hilariously camp in every respect. Beats the original by a mile. No point in looking for it on TV, though. Myer's specialty is the hardest soft-core porn in existence.

8. **The Buddy Holly Story** (Fred Bauer, 1978). Stars Gary Busey, Charles Martin Smith, Don Stroud.

This muddles the details (gets some wrong, omits others), but Busey's performance in the title role is thoroughly convincing and the broad outline of the story makes almost all the important artistic and personal points about Holly's attenuated career.

9. **The Last Waltz** (Martin Scorsese, 1978). Stars The Band, Bob Dylan, Van Morrison, Neil Young, Joni Mitchell, Muddy Waters, Dr. John, others.

The music here isn't what it's cracked up to be. Only Waters' performance qualifies as a revelation, though it may be interesting in future years to see this gathering of America's late 60s-early 70s rock establishment for one final fling. What makes *The Last Waltz* great, though, is Scorsese, whose approach to shooting live concert footage is spectacular and never intrudes on the players. Scorsese is *the* great rock director: *Mean Streets,* his initial tango with Robert DeNiro, has what might be the best soundtrack of any movie in history, while *Alice Doesn't Live Here Anymore* opens with a helicopter shot set to Mott the Hoople's "All the Way from Memphis" that has pure rock and roll energy transferred to cinematic terms.

10. **The Kids Are Alright** (Jeff Stein, 1979). Stars the Who, Ringo Starr, and the Absence of Ann-Margret.

The only rock documentary that comes close to *The Last Waltz,* this look at fifteen years of Who history misses almost nothing, from orgies of guitar smashing to the band's earliest performance clips and its final stage show with Keith Moon. Because there is no narration, newcomers may become a bit confused at the start, but the heart of the matter-anarchic, powerful, violent, hilarious—comes through cleanly.

Ten Worst Rock 'n' Roll Movies, 1955-78

1. **Blackboard Jungle** (Richard Brooks, 1955). Stars Glenn Ford, Anne Francis, Sidney Poitier, Vic Morrow.

I don't care if this is the beginning, it's still horrid. You want to know why Morrow busted up all of Ford's jazz records? Because they were boring, just like this soap opera, in which the cleanup collar is taken as the equivalent of the greatest virtue.

2. **State Fair** (Jose Ferrer, 1962). Stars Pat Boone, Bobby Darin, Pamela Tiffin, Ann-Margret.

Wastes Darin, in a remake of Walter Lang's far superior 1945 effort. Some of the worst people ever to appear in youth genre movies show up in this total fraud.

3. **The Monkeys Uncle** (Robert Stevenson, 1965). Stars the Beach Boys, Annette Funicello, Tommy Kirk, Frank Faylen.

The beach party movie at its worst. Even a decent song by the Beach Boys can't overcome the lack of a plot—or the cast's lack of talent.

4. **Riot on Sunset Strip** (Arthur Dreifuss, 1967). Stars Aldo Ray, Mimsy Farmer, the Standells.

Ray turned to porno act in 1979, almost exactly a decade too late. No plot, the Standells play lousy, and the photograph is so poor it looks like someone smeared rancid anchovy paste over the lens.

5. **Sympathy for the Devil (One Plus One).** (Jean Luc Godard, 1970).

Godard was the great director, but not in his revolutionary polemic period, of which this is a trenchant example. Shots of the Stones in the studio, cutting the title song, are interspersed with Black Panthers reading from Eldridge Cleaver and the like. Dullsville.

6. **Celebration at Big Sur** (Baird Bryant, Johanna Demetrakas, 1971). Stars Joan Baez, Joni Mitchell, Crosby Stills Nash and Young, John Sebastian, Mimi Farina.

Tiedyed *T.A.M.I. Show,* featuring some of the most pretentious and dis-spirited performances in pop music history. Hippies couldn't even sit through this one.

7. **Journey through the Past** (Neil Young, 1973). Stars Young.

Bloated, self-important exercise in early film school approach to spiritual side of rock. Genuinely incompetent.

8. **Tommy** (Ken Russell, 1975). Stars

Roger Daltrey, Ann-Margret, Oliver Reed, Elton John, Keith Moon, Ringo Starr, Eric Clapton, Robert Powell, Tina Turner, Jack Nicholson, and a blushing Pete Townshend.

Russel's deranged Catholicism meets Townshend's rock opera for a stylistic clash that is pure embarrassment. Ann-Margret alone could have eliminated any possibility of the rock and roll in the original coming through, and the fact that *Tommy* has too little story to work on disc is far more crucial here. A real waste, not only of talent, but of potentially good material.

9. **Renaldo and Clara** (Bob Dylan, Howard Alk, 1978). Stars Bob Dylan, Sam Shepard, Mick Ronson, Ronnie Hawkins, Sarah Rylan, Joan Baez, Joni Mitchell, others.

Fictionalized account of Dylan's 1977 Rolling Thunder Revue, so incompetently performed, photographed and written that it actually makes *Journey through the Past* seem professional. Pretentious and phony, Dylan at his worst, this one bottoms out even below the previous Dylan-Alk collaboration, *Eat the Document*, a 1966 documentary rejected (wisely) by ABC-TV.

10. **Grease** (..........., 1978). Stars John Travolta, Olivia Newton-John, Stockard Channing.

There isn't a teenager under thirty in this whole film with the exception of Travolta, who can't do as much with this flimsy material as he could in the far superior *Saturday Night Fever*. A distortion of 50s youth culture, far less forgivable than the ones Hollywood made at the time—these guys ought to know better by now. Hateful.

DM

ROCK 'N' ROLL FILM DIRECTORY

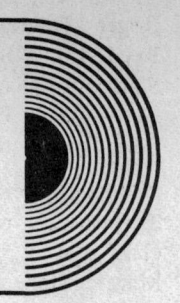

1956

TITLE	FEATURED PERFORMERS	DISTRIBUTOR
Don't Knock the Rock	Bill Haley & the Comets, Little Richard, Dave Appell & His Applejacks, Alan Freed	Columbia
The Girl Can't Help It	Fats Domino, Platters, Little Richard, Gene Vincent, Eddie Cochran	20th Century Fox
Love Me Tender	Elvis Presley	20th Century Fox
Rock around the Clock	Bill Haley & the Comets, Platters	Columbia
Rock Pretty Baby	Sal Mineo, John Saxon	Universal
Shake, Rattle & Rock	Fats Domino, Big Joe Turner	American Intl.

1957

TITLE	FEATURED PERFORMERS	DISTRIBUTOR
April Love	Pat Boone	20th Century Fox
The Big Beat	Del Vikings, Fats Domino, Diamonds	Universal
Bop Girl	Bobby Troup, Nino Tempo	independent dist.
Harlem Rock 'n Roll	Clovers, Joe Turner, Duke Ellington	independent dist.
Jailhouse Rock	Elvis Presley	20th Century Fox
Jamboree	Fats Domino, Jerry Lee Lewis, Carl Perkins, Lewis Lymon & the Teen Chords, Connie Francis	Warner Bros.

Title	Featured Performers	Distributor
Loving You	Elvis Presley	Paramount
Mister Rock 'n' Roll	Frankie Lymon, Little Richard, Clyde McPhatter, Alan Freed	Paramount
Rock All Night	Platters	American Intl.
Rock, Rock, Rock	Moonglows, Chuck Berry, Flamingos, Johnny Burnette, Frankie Lymon, LaVern Baker	independent dist.
Summer Love	Rod McKuen, Shelly Fabares, John Saxon	independent dist.
Untamed Youth	Eddie Cochran	Warner Bros.

1958

TITLE	FEATURED PERFORMERS	DISTRIBUTOR
Hot Rod Gang	Gene Vincent	independent dist.
Country Music Holiday	Jordanaires, Drifting Johnny Miller	Paramount
High School Confidential	Jerry Lee Lewis	MGM
Keep It Cool	Paul Anka, Danny & the Juniors, Royal Teens, Della Reese	independent dist.
Sing Boy Sing	Tommy Sands	20th Century Fox
King Creole	Elvis Presley	Paramount
Mardi Gras	Pat Boone	independent dist.
Rock-a-Bye Baby	Connie Stevens, Gary Lewis	Paramount

1959

TITLE	FEATURED PERFORMERS	DISTRIBUTOR
College Confidential	Conway Twitty, Cathy Crosby, Randy Sparks	Universal
Expresso Bongo	Cliff Richard	independent dist.
Go Johnny Go	Eddie Cochran, Alan Freed, Chuck Berry, Flamingos, Jackie Wilson, Jimmy Clanton	independent dist.

Title	Featured Performers	Distributor
Hound Dog Man	Fabian, Dodie Stevens	20th Century Fox
Juke Box Rhythm	Johnny Otis, Nitwits	independent dist.
Jazz on a Summer Day	Chuck Berry	independent dist.

1960

TITLE	FEATURED PERFORMERS	DISTRIBUTOR
The Alamo	Frankie Avalon	independent dist.
The Beat Generation	Louis Armstrong, Ray Anthony, Cathy Crosby	independent dist.
Wild for Kicks	Adam Faith	independent dist.
Because They're Young	James Darren, Duane Eddy	Columbia
Flaming Star	Elvis Presley	20th Century Fox
Platinum High School	Mickey Rooney, Terry Moore, Conway Twitty	MGM
G.I. Blues	Elvis Presley	20th Century Fox
Girls' Town	Paul Anka	independent dist.

1961

TITLE	FEATURED PERFORMERS	DISTRIBUTOR
Hey Let's Twist	Joey Dee, Teddy Randazzo	Paramount
Swinging Along	Ray Charles, Bobby Vee	20th Century Fox
Teenage Millionaire	Chubby Checker, Jackie Wilson, Dion, Mary Johnson, Jimmy Clanton	independent dist.
Twist around the Clock	Chubby Checker, Dion, Marcels	Columbia
Where the Boys Are	Connie Francis	independent dist.
Come September	Bobby Darin	independent dist.
Wild Country	Elvis Presley	20th Century Fox
The Young Ones	Cliff Richard, Shadows	independent dist.

1962

TITLE	FEATURED PERFORMERS	DISTRIBUTOR
Don't Knock the Twist	Chubby Checker, Gene Chandler, Dovells, Linda Scott	Columbia
Follow the Boys	Connie Francis	independent dist.
It's Trad Dad	Chubby Checker, Gene Vincent, Gary U. S. Bonds, Del Shannon, Gene McDaniel, Chris Barber and His Band	Columbia
Lonely Boy	Paul Anka	independent dist.
Play It Cool	Bill Fury, Bobby Vee, Jimmy Crawford, Paul Jones	Allied Artists
State Fair	Pat Boone, Bobby Darin	20th Century Fox
Girl! Girls! Girls!	Elvis Presley	20th Century Fox
Kid Galahad	Elvis Presley	20th Century Fox
Mix Me a Person	Adam Faith	independent dist.
Two Little Bears	Brenda Lee	independent dist.
Two Tickets to Paris	Joey Dee & the Starliters, Gary Crosby	independent dist.

1963

TITLE	FEATURED PERFORMERS	DISTRIBUTOR
Farewell Performance	Tornadoes, Heinz	independent dist.
Hootenanny Hoot	Johnny Cash, Chris Crosby, Brothers Four	independent dist.
It's All Happening	Tommy Steele, Shane Fenton, Carol Deene	independent dist.
Just for Fun	Bobby Vee, Crickets, Freddy Cannon, Tremeloes	Columbia
Live It Up	Gene Vincent, Kenny Ball, Sounds Inc.	Allied Artists
Young Swingers	Rod Lauren, Gene McDaniels	independent dist.
Bye Bye Birdie	Bobby Rydell	Columbia

| Fun in Acapulco | Elvis Presley | 20th Century Fox |
| What a Crazy World | Joe Brown, Freddie & the Dreamers | independent dist. |

1964

TITLE	FEATURED PERFORMERS	DISTRIBUTOR
Ballad in Blue	Ray Charles	
Beach Party	Frankie Avalon, Annette	independent dist.
Bikini Beach	Frankie Avalon, Stevie Wonder, Pyrimid, Exciters	American Intl.
Ferry Cross the Mersey	Gerry & the Pacemakers, Cilla Black	independent dist.
Get Yourself a College Girl	D.C.S., Animals, Standells	MGM
Hard Day's Night	Beatles	United Artists
It's All Over Town	Hollies, Springfields	independent dist.
Just for You	Peter & Gordon, Freddie & the Dreamers, Merseybeats	Paramount
Monkey's Uncle	Beach Boys	
Muscle Beach Party	Frankie Avalon, Annette	independent dist.
Pajama Party	Noony Rickett Four	independent dist.
Ride the Wild Surf	Fabian, Shelly Fabares	Columbia
T.A.M.I. Show	Rolling Stones, Beach Boys, Chuck Berry, James Brown, Marvin Gaye, Smokey Robinson & the Miracles, Jan & Dean, Lesley Gore, Gerry & the Pacemakers, B. J. Kramer, Supremes, Barbarians	American Intl.
Roustabout	Elvis Presley	20th Century Fox
Surf Party	Bobby Vinton, Jackie DeShannon	

1965

TITLE	FEATURED PERFORMERS	DISTRIBUTOR
Beach Ball	Supremes, Four Seasons, Righteous Brothers, Hondells	Paramount
Be My Guest	Jerry Lee Lewis, Nashville Teens	independent dist.
Bunny Lake Is Missing	Zombies	
Cukoo Patrol	Freddie & the Dreamers	independent dist.
Dateline Diamonds	Small Faces, Kiki Dee, Chantelles	independent dist.
The Girls on the Beach	Crickets, Beach Boys, Lesley Gore	Paramount
Go Go Mania	Animals, Nashville Teens, B. J. Kramer, Honeycombs, Herman's Hermits, Beatles, Spencer Davis Group	American Intl.
Gonks Go Beat	Nashville Teens, Lulu & the Lovers	independent dist.
Having a Wild Weekend	Dave Clark Five	Warner Bros.
Help!	Beatles	United Artists
Hold On	Herman's Hermits	
How to Stuff a Wild Bikini	Annette, Kingsmen Combo	independent dist.
Ski Party	Frankie Avalon, James Brown, Leslie Gore, Hondells	American Intl.
A Swinging Summer	Righteous Brothers, Gary Lewis & the Playboys	independent dist.
When the Boys Meet the Girls	Herman's Hermits, Sam the Sham	independent dist.
Wild on the Beach	Sonny & Cher	20th Century Fox
Girl Happy	Elvis Presley	20th Century Fox
Tickle Me	Elvis Presley	20th Century Fox

1966

TITLE	FEATURED PERFORMERS	DISTRIBUTOR
Charlie Is My Darlin'	Rolling Stones	independent dist.
Chappaqua	Fugs, Ravi Shankar	independent dist.
Fastest Guitar Alive	Roy Orbison	MGM
The Ghost Goes Gear	Spencer Davis Group, Dave Berry	
Out of Sight	Gary Lewis & the Playboys, Turtles, Knickerbockers, Freddie & the Dreamers	independent dist.
Frankie and Johnny	Elvis Presley	20th Century Fox
Legend of Bo Diddley	Bo Diddley	independent dist.
Fugs	Fugs	independent dist.
Paradise Hawaiian Style	Elvis Presley	20th Century Fox
Spinout	Elvis Presley	20th Century Fox
Sting of Death	Neil Sedaka	independent dist.
To Sir with Love	Lulu	

1967

TITLE	FEATURED PERFORMERS	DISTRIBUTOR
Blow Up	Yardbirds	MGM
C'mon Let's Live a Little	Bobby Vee, Jackie DeShannon	Paramount
Don't Look Back	Bob Dylan, Alan Price, Joan Baez, Donovan	independent dist.
Magical Mystery Tour	Beatles	United Artists
Festival	Joan Baez, Bob Dylan, Judy Collins, Donovan, Howlin' Wolf, Peter, Paul & Mary, Pete Seeger, Johnny Cash	independent dist.
For Singles Only	Nitty Gritty Dirt Band, Sunshine Company	independent dist.
Good Times	Sonny & Cher	independent dist.

It's a Bikini World	Animals, Castaways, Toys, Gentrys	independent dist.
Riot on Sunset Strip	Standells, Chocolate Watch Band, Mugwumps	independent dist.
Privilege	Paul Jones, Jean Shrimpton	Universal
Tonight Let's Make Love in London	Rolling Stones, Pink Floyd	independent dist.

1968

TITLE	FEATURED PERFORMERS	DISTRIBUTOR
Monterey Pop	Mamas and the Papas, Jefferson Airplane, The Who, Big Brother & the Holding Company, Otis Redding, Jimi Hendrix, Eric Burdon & the Animals, Ravi Shankar	20th Century Fox
Mrs. Brown You've Got a Lovely Daughter	Herman's Hermits	independent dist.
Psych-out	Strawberry Alarm Clock, Seeds	independent dist.
Sympathy for the Devil	Rolling Stones	independent dist.
Yellow Submarine	Beatles	United Artists
You Are What You Eat	Tiny Tim, Barry McGuire, Paul Butterfield, Electric Flag	American Intl.
The Committee	Paul Jones, Crazy World of Arthur Brown	independent dist.
Cream Last Concert	Cream	independent dist.
The Lone Ranger	Pete Townshend	independent dist.
Pop Down	Zoot Money, Brian Auger & Trinity	independent dist.
Sweet Ride	Moby Grape	20th Century Fox
Speedway	Elvis Presley, Nancy Sinatra	20th Century Fox
Head	Monkees, Frank Zappa	Columbia
Stay Away Joe	Elvis Presley	20th Century Fox
Voices	Rolling Stones	independent dist.
Wild in the Streets	Christopher Jones, Hal Holbrook	American Intl.

ROCK 'N' ROLL FILM DIRECTORY

1969

TITLE	FEATURED PERFORMERS	DISTRIBUTOR
Paint Your Wagon	Nitty Gritty Dirt Band	independent dist.
The Trouble with Girls	Elvis Presley	20th Century Fox
What's Good for the Goose	Pretty Things	independent dist.
Charro	Elvis Presley	20th Century Fox
Rolling Stones Rock and Roll Circus	Rolling Stones, The Who, Marianne Faithfull, Jethro Tull, Darty Mann Band, Taj Mahal	

1970

TITLE	FEATURED PERFORMERS	DISTRIBUTOR
Woodstock	Arlo Guthrie, Sly & the Family Stone, Ten Years After, The Who, Joe Cocker, Crosby, Stills, Nash & Young, Joan Baez, Richie Havens, Jimi Hendrix	Warner Bros.
Gimme Shelter	Rolling Stones, Ike & Tina Turner, Jefferson Airplane, Flying Burrito Brothers	independent dist.
Diary of a Mad Housewife	Alice Cooper Band	independent dist.
Elvis—That's the Way It Is	Elvis Presley, Sweet Inspiration	20th Century Fox
Beyond the Valley of the Dolls	Dolly Read, Cynthia Myers, Marcia McBroom, Edy Williams, Michael Blodgett, Erica Gavin, Strawberry Alarm Clock	20th Century Fox
It's Your Thing	Isley Brothers, Brooklyn Bridge, Five Stair Steps	independent dist.
Jimi Hendrix Plays Berkeley	Jimi Hendrix	independent dist.
Let It Be	Beatles, Billy Preston	United Artists
Performance	Mick Jagger	Warner Bros.
Supershow	Led Zeppelin, Eric Clapton, Jack Bruce, Stephen Stills	independent dist.
Zachariah	Country Joe & the Fish, New York Rock Ensemble	independent dist.

1971

TITLE	FEATURED PERFORMERS	DISTRIBUTOR
Stamping Ground	Santana, Canned Heat, Jefferson Airplane, T-Rex, It's a Beautiful Day, Byrds, Pink Floyd, Dr. John, Family, Flock	independent dist.
Medicine Ball Caravan	B. B. King, Alice Cooper, Delaney & Bonnie	Warner Bros.
Rainbow Bridge	Jimi Hendrix	Warner Bros.
Not Tonight Darling	Thunderclap Newman	independent dist.
Raga	Ravi Shankar, George Harrison	independent dist.
200 Motels	Frank Zappa & the Mothers of Invention, Ringo Starr, Keith Moon	
Celebration at Big Sur	Joan Boaez, Graham Nash, Stephen Stills, Neil Young, David Crosby	20th Century Fox
Ladies and Gentlemen The Rolling Stones (Marquee Club)	Rolling Stones	Universal

1972

TITLE	FEATURED PERFORMERS	DISTRIBUTOR
Fillmore	Santana, Grateful Dead, Hot Tuna, Quicksilver, New Riders of the Purple Sage	20th Century Fox
The Pied Piper	Donovan	Paramount
Superfly	Curtis Mayfield	Warner Bros.
Imagine	John Lennon, Yoko Ono	independent dist.
Creedence in Oakland	Creedence Clearwater Revival	independent dist.
The Concert for Bangladesh	George Harrison, Ringo Starr, Billy Preston, Leon Russell, Bob Dylan, Ravi Shankar, Badfinger	20th Century Fox

ROCK 'N' ROLL FILM DIRECTORY

1973

TITLE	FEATURED PERFORMERS	DISTRIBUTOR
American Graffiti	Flash Cadillac & the Continental Kids, Richard Dreyfus, Ron Howard, Andy Williams	Universal
Born to Boogie	Marc Bolan, T-Rex, Ringo Starr, Elton John	
Catch My Soul	Richie Havens	
Glastonbury Fair	Fairport Convention, Traffic, Melanie, Arthur Brown	
Jimi Hendrix	Jimi Hendrix	Warner Bros.
Let the Good Times Roll	Chuck Berry, Little Richard, Jerry Lee Lewis	Columbia
That'll Be the Day	David Essex, Ringo Starr, Keith Moon	
Wattstax	Isaac Hayes, Carla Thomas, Eddie Floyd, Johnnie Taylor, Rufus Thomas, Staple Singers	Columbia
Ladies and Gentlemen The Rolling Stones (American tour)	Rolling Stones	Universal
Soul to Soul	Wilson Pickett, Santana, Roberta Flack, Ike & Tina Turner	independent dist.

1974

TITLE	FEATURED PERFORMERS	DISTRIBUTOR
Pink Floyd Live at Pompeii	Pink Floyd	independent dist.
Save the Children	Cannonball Adderley, Marvin Gaye, Jackson Five, Main Ingredient, Curtis Mayfield, O'Jays, Temptations, Bill Withers, Gladys Knight & the Pips	Paramount
Stardust	David Essex, Keith Moon, Dave Edmunds	Columbia
Phantom of the Paradise	Paul Williams, Jessica Harper	20th Century Fox
Tommy	The Who, Tina Turner, Elton John, Roger Daltrey	Columbia

1975

TITLE	FEATURED PERFORMERS	DISTRIBUTOR
Carry It On	Joan Baez	independent dist.
Revolution	Steve Miller Band, Quicksilver, Country Joe & the Fish	independent dist.
The Grateful Dead	Grateful Dead	

1976

TITLE	FEATURED PERFORMERS	DISTRIBUTOR
Petulia	Grateful Dead, Big Brother & the Holding Company	Warner Bros.
The Rocky Horror Picture Show	Tim Curry, Barry Bostwick, Meatloaf	20th Century Fox
Journey through the Past	Buffalo Springfield, Crosby, Stills, Nash & Young, Crazy Horse	independent dist.
Yes Song	Yes	

1977

TITLE	FEATURED PERFORMERS	DISTRIBUTOR
The Song Remains the Same	Led Zeppelin	
Saturday Night Fever	John Travolta	Paramount
Trouble Man	Marvin Gaye	20th Century Fox

1978

TITLE	FEATURED PERFORMERS	DISTRIBUTOR
Punk Rock	Sex Pistols, Clash	independent dist.
Grease	John Travolta, Olivia Newton-John, Stockard Channing	Paramount
Thank God It's Friday		Columbia
I Wanna Hold Your Hand	Murray the K	Universal
American Hot Wax		Paramount

The Buddy Holly Story	Gary Busey, Charles Martin Smith, Don Stroud
Renaldo & Clara	Bob Dylan, Sam Shepard, Mick Ronson, Ronnie Hawkins, Sara Dylan, Joan Baez, Joni Mitchell
Sgt. Pepper's Lonely Hearts Club Band	Aerosmith, Peter Frampton, Bee Gees, Earth, Wind & Fire
The Last Waltz	Band, Bob Dylan, Van Morrison, Neil Young, Joni Mitchell, Muddy Waters, Dr. John

1979

TITLE	FEATURED PERFORMERS	DISTRIBUTOR
Rock and Roll High School	Ramones	
F.M.	Martin Mull	Universal
Rust Never Sleeps	Neil Young	
The Kids Are Alright	The Who	independent dist.
The Great Rock 'n Roll Swindle	Sex Pistols	independent dist.

JK

AWARDS

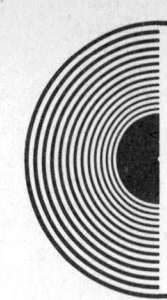

NARM AWARDS*

Boston, Boston (Epic)
Foreigner, Foreigner (Atlantic)
Shaun Cassidy, Shaun Cassidy (Warner-Curb)
Too Hot to Handle, Heat wave (Epic)
Bat out of Hell, Meatloaf (Cleveland International-Epic)
City to City, Gerry Rafferty (United Artists)
The Cars, Cars (Elektra)

SELLING FOLK ARTIST/ VOCAL GROUP

Peter, Paul & Mary (Warner Bros.)
Bob Dylan (Columbia)
Peter, Paul & Mary (Warner Bros.)
Simon & Garfunkel (Columbia)
Bob Dylan (Columbia)
Simon & Garfunkel (Columbia)
Bob Dylan (Columbia)
Bob Dylan (Columbia)
John Denver (RCA)

SELLING INSTRUMENTALIST

Al Hirt (RCA)
Herb Alpert & the Tijuana Brass (A&M)
Henry Mancini (RCA Victor)
Herb Alpert & The Tijuana Brass (A&M)
Herb Alpert & the Tijuana Brass (A&M)
Herb Alpert & the Tijuana Brass (A&M)
Herb Alpert & the Tijuana Brass (A&M)

SELLING ORCHESTRA

Billy Vaughn (Dot)
Billy Vaughn (Dot)
Henry Mancini (RCA Victor)

1965 Henry Mancini (RCA Victor)
1966 Lawrence Welk (Dot)
1967 Ray Conniff (Columbia)
1968 —
1969 Henry Mancini (RCA)
1970 Burt Bacharach (A&M)
1971 Burt Bacharach (A&M)
1972 Burt Bacharach (A&M)
1973 Deodato (CTI)

BEST SELLING MOTION PICTURE SOUNDTRACK ALBUM

1962 *West Side Story* (Columbia)
1963 *West Side Story* (Columbia)
1964 *A Hard Day's Night* (United Artists)
1965 *The Sound of Music* (RCA Victor)
1966 *Dr. Zhivago* (MGM)
1967 *Dr. Zhivago* (MGM)
1968 *The Graduate* (Capitol)
1969 *Romeo & Juliet* (Capitol)
1970 *Woodstock* (Atlantic)
1971 *Shaft* (Enterprise-Stax/Volt)
1972 *Superfly* (Curtom)
1973 *American Graffiti* (MCA)
1974 *The Sting* (MCA)
1975 *Tommy* (Polydor)
1976 *A Star Is Born* (Columbia)
1977 *A Star Is Born* (Columbia)
1978 *Saturday Night Fever* (RSO)

BEST SELLING ORIGINAL CAST ALBUM

1967 *Man of La Mancha* (Kapp)
1968 —
1969 *Hair* (RCA)
1970 *Hair* (RCA)
1971 *Hair* (RCA)
1972 —
1973 —
1974 —
1975 *The Wiz* (Atlantic)
1976 *A Chorus Line* (Columbia)
1977 *A Chorus Line* (Columbia)
1978 *Annie* (Columbia)

BEST SELLING ALBUM

1959 *Inside Shelley Berman*, Shelley Berman (Verve)
   Chipmunks (Liberty)
   Sixty Years of Music (RCA Victor)
1960 *Sixty Years of Music, Vol. II* Victor)
1961 *Blue Hawaii*, Elvis Presley (RCA Victor)
1962 *First Family*, Vaughn Meader (Cadence)
1963 *Peter, Paul & Mary*, Peter, Paul & Mary (Warner Bros.)
1964 *Meet the Beatles*, Beatles (Capitol)
1965 *Whipped Cream & Other Delights*, Herb Alpert & the Tijuana Brass (A&M)
1966 *Monkees*, Monkees (Colgems)
1967 *Sgt. Pepper's Lonely Hearts Club*, Beatles (Capitol)
1968 *The Beatles*, Beatles (Apple)
1969 *Abbey Road*, Beatles (Apple)
1970 *Bridge over Troubled Waters*, Simon & Garfunkel (Columbia)
1971 *Tapestry*, Carole King (Ode)
1972 *Tapestry*, Carole King (Ode)
1973 *You Don't Mess around with Jim*, Jim Croce (ABC)
1974 *Elton John's Greatest Hits*, Elton John (MCA)
1975 *Captain Fantastic and the Brown Dirt Cowboy*, Elton John (MCA)
1976 *Frampton Comes Alive*, Peter Frampton (A&M)
1977 *Rumours*, Fleetwood Mac (Warner Bros.)
1978 *Saturday Night Fever*—motion picture soundtrack (RSO)

BEST SELLING SINGLE

1959 "Battle of New Orleans," Johnny Horton (Columbia)
1960 "Are You Lonesome," Elvis Presley (RCA Victor)
1961 "Big Bad John," Jimmy Dean (Columbia)
1962 "I Can't Stop Loving You," Ray Charles (ABC-Paramount)
1963 "Dominique," Soeur Sourire (Philips)
   "Blue Velvet," Bobby Vinton (Epic)
1964 "I Want to Hold Your Hand," Beatles (Capitol)
1965 "Mrs. Brown, You've Got a Lovely Daughter," Herman's Hermits (MGM)
1966 "I'm a Believer," Monkees (Colgems)
1967 "Daydream Believer," Monkees (Colgems)
1968 "Hey Jude,'" Beatles (Apple)
1969 "Sugar, Sugar," Archies (RCA)
1970 "I Think I Love You," Partridge Family (Bell)

*Given by National Association of Recording Merchandisers, Inc.

1971 "Joy to the World," Three Dog Night (Dunhill)
1972 "American Pie," Don McLean (United Artists)
1973 "Tie a Yellow Ribbon 'round the Ole Oak Tree," Tony Orlando and Dawn (Bell)
1974 "Kung-Fu Fighting," Carl Douglas (20th Century Fox)
1975 "Love Will Keep Us Together," Captain & Tennille (A&M)
1976 "Disco Duck," Rick Dees and His Cast of Idiots (RSO)
1977 "You Light Up My Life," Debby Boone (Warner-Curb)
1978 "Stayin' Alive," Bee Gees (RSO)

BEST SELLING VOCALIST (Female)

1959 Connie Francis (MGM)
1960 Connie Francis (MGM)
1961 Connie Francis (MGM)
1962 Brenda Lee (Decca)
1963 Barbra Streisand (Columbia)
1964 Barbra Streisand (Columbia)
1965 Barbra Streisand (Columbia)
1966 Barbra Streisand (Columbia)
1967 Aretha Franklin (Atlantic)
1968 Aretha Franklin (Atlantic)
1969 Dionne Warwick (Scepter)
1970 Dionne Warwick (Scepter)
1971 Carole King (Ode)
1972 Carole King (Ode)
1973 Helen Reddy (Capitol)

BEST SELLING ALBUM BY FEMALE ARTIST

1974 *If You Love Me Let Me Know*, Olivia Newton-John (MCA)
1975 *Have You Never Been Mellow*, Olivia Newton-John (MCA)
1976 *Hasten Down the Wind*, Linda Ronstadt (Asylum)
1977 *Simple Dreams*, Linda Ronstadt (Asylum)
1978 *Greatest Hits Volume 2*, Barbra Streisand (Columbia)
    Live and More, Donna Summer (Casablanca)

BEST SELLING MALE VOCALIST

1959 Elvis Presley (RCA Victor)
1960 Elvis Presley (RCA Victor)
1961 Elvis Presley (RCA Victor)
1962 Elvis Presley (RCA Victor)
1963 Andy Williams (Columbia)
1964 Andy Williams (Columbia)
1965 Elvis Presley (RCA Victor)
1966 Dean Martin (Reprise)
1967 Dean Martin (Reprise)
1968 Glen Campbell (Capitol)
1969 Tom Jones (Parrot)
1970 Neil Diamond (UNI)
1971 James Taylor (Warner Bros.)
1972 Neil Diamond (UNI)
1973 Jim Croce (ABC)

BEST SELLING ALBUM BY A MALE ARTIST

1974 *Elton John's Greatest Hits*, Elton John (MCA)
1975 *Captain Fantastic and the Brown Dirt Cowboy*, Elton John (MCA)
1976 *Frampton Comes Alive*, Peter Frampton (A&M)
1977 *Silk Degrees*, Boz Scaggs (Columbia)
1978 *The Stranger*, Billy Joel (Columbia)

BEST SELLING VOCAL GROUP/POP VOCAL GROUP/GROUP

1960 Kingston Trio (Capitol)
1961 Mitch Miller & The Gang (Columbia)
1962 Kingston Trio (Capitol)
    Peter, Paul & Mary (Warner Bros.)
1963 Peter, Paul & Mary (Warner Bros.)
1964 Beatles (Atco, Capitol, MGM, United Artists, Vee Jay)
1965 Beach Boys (Capitol)
    Supremes (Motown)
    Beatles (Capitol)
1966 Monkees (Colgems)
    Herman's Hermits (MGM)
    Rolling Stones (London)
1967 Monkees (Colgems)
    Beatles (Capitol)
1968 Beatles (Capitol)
1969 Beatles (Capitol)
1970 Creedence Clearwater Revival (Fantasy)
1971 Chicago (Columbia)
    Carpenters (A&M)
    Partridge Family (Bell)
1972 Moody Blues (Threshold)
1973 Carpenters (A&M)

BEST SELLING ALBUM BY A GROUP

1974 *Bachman-Turner Overdrive II*, Bachman-Turner Overdrive (Phonogram-Mercury)
1975 *One of These Nights*, Eagles (Asylum)
1976 *Their Greatest Hits 1971-75*, Eagles (Asylum)
1977 *Rumours*, Fleetwood Mac (Warner Bros.)
1978 *Double Vision*, Foreigner (Atlantic)

MOST PROMISING FEMALE VOCALIST/BEST SELLING NEW FEMALE ARTIST

1960 Brenda Lee (Decca)
1961 Linda Scott (Canadian American)
1962 Dee Dee Sharp (Cameo)
    Mary Wells (20th Century Fox)
1963 Lesley Gore (Mercury)
    Nancy Wilson (Capitol)
1964 Dusty Springfield
    Dionne Warwick
    Gale Garnett
1965 Petula Clark
1966 Nancy Sinatra
1967 Vicki Carr
1968 —
1969 —
1970 Melanie (Buddah)
1971 Carole King
1972 Carly Simon
1973 Bette Midler

MOST PROMISING VOCALIST/BEST SELLING MALE ARTIST

1960 Bobby Rydell
1961 Chubby Checker
1962 Robert Goulet
1963 John Gary (RCA)
1964 Johnny Rivers
1965 Gary Lewis
1966 Lou Rawls (Capitol)
1967 Engelbert Humperdinck (Parrot)
1968 —
1969 —
1970 James Taylor
1971 Rod Stewart
1972 Don McLean
1973 Jim Croce (ABC)

BEST SELLING NEW

1970 Grand Funk Railroad
1971 Black Sabbath
1972 America (Warner)
1973 Doobie Brothers
1974 —

BEST SELLING ALBUM BY A NEW ARTIST

1975 *Love Will Keep Us Together*, Captain & Tennille

BEST SELLING RHYTHM & BLUES ARTIST/SOUL ARTIST (Female)

1966 Dionne Warwick (Scepter)
1967 Aretha Franklin (Atlantic)
1968 Aretha Franklin (Atlantic)
1969 Diana Ross (Motown)
   Aretha Franklin (Atlantic)
1970 Diana Ross (Motown)
1971 Aretha Franklin (Atlantic)
1972 Roberta Flack (Atlantic)
1973 Gladys Knight & The Pips (Buddah and Soul-Motown)

BEST SELLING ALBUM BY A FEMALE SOUL ARTIST/BLACK FEMALE ARTIST

1974 *Imagination*, Gladys Knight & the Pips (Buddah)
1975 *Inseparable*, Natalie Cole (Capitol)
   Love to Love You Baby, Donna Summer (Oasis-Casablanca)
1976 *Love Trilogy*, Donna Summer (Oasis-Casablanca)
1977 *I Remember Yesterday*, Donna Summer (Casablanca)
1978 *Live and More*, Donna Summer (Casablanca)

BEST SELLING MALE RHYTHM & BLUES ARTIST/MALE SOUL ARTIST

1966 James Brown (King)
1967 Wilson Pickett (Atlantic)
1968 James Brown (King)
   Otis Redding (Atco)
1969 James Brown (King)
1970 Isaac Hayes (Enterprise-Stax/Volt)
1971 Isaac Hayes (Enterprise-Stax/Volt)
1972 Al Green (Hi)
1973 Stevie Wonder (Tamla-Motown)

BEST SELLING ALBUM BY A MALE SOUL ARTIST/BLACK MALE ARTIST

1974 *Can't Get Enough*, Barry White (20th Century Fox)
1975 *Barry White's Greatest Hits*, Barry White (20th Century Fox)
1976 *Songs in the Key of Life*, Stevie Wonder (Tamla-Motown)
1977 *Songs in the Key of Life*, Stevie Wonder (Tamla-Motown)
1978 *Weekend in L.A.*, George Benson (Warner Bros.)

BEST SELLING JAZZ ARTIST

1966 Ramsey Lewis Trio (Cadet)
1967 Wes Montgomery (A&M and Verve)
1968 Sergio Mendes (A&M)
1969 Isaac Hayes (Enterprise-Stax/Volt)
1970 Isaac Hayes (Enteprise-Stax/Volt)
1971 Isaac Hayes (Enterprise-Stax/Volt)
1972 Isaac Hayes (Enterprise-Stax/Volt)
1973 Deodato (CTI)

BEST SELLING JAZZ ALBUM

1974 *Headhunters*, Herbie Hancock (Columbia)
1975 *Mr. Magic*, Grover Washington (Kudu)
1976 *Breezin'*, George Benson (Warner Bros.)
1977 *In Flight*, George Benson (Warner Bros.)
1978 *Feels So Good*, Chuck Mangione (A&M)

BEST SELLING FEMALE COUNTRY & WESTERN ARTIST/BEST SELLING FEMALE COUNTRY ARTIST

1965 Kitty Wells (Decca)
1966 Loretta Lynn (Decca)
1967 Loretta Lynn (Decca)
1968 Tammy Wynette (Epic)
1969 Tammy Wynette (Epic)
1970 Tammy Wynette (Epic)
1971 Lynn Anderson (Columbia)
1972 Donna Fargo (Dot)
1973 Donna Fargo (Dot)

BEST SELLING ALBUM BY A FEMALE COUNTRY ARTIST

1974 *If You Love Me Let Me Know*, Olivia Newton-John (MCA)
1975 *Have You Never Been Mellow*, Olivia Newton-John (MCA)
1976 *Hasten Down the Wind*, Linda Ronstadt (Asylum)
1977 *Simple Dreams*, Linda Ronstadt (Asylum)
1978 *Let's Keep It That Way*, Anne Murray (Capitol)

BEST SELLING MALE COUNTRY & WESTERN ARTIST/BEST SELLING MALE COUNTRY ARTIST

1965 Roger Miller (Smash)
1966 Eddy Arnold (RCA Victor)
1967 Eddy Arnold (RCA Victor)
1968 Glen Campbell (Capitol)
1969 Johnny Cash (Columbia)
1970 Johnny Cash (Columbia)
1971 Charley Pride (RCA)
1972 Charley Pride (RCA)
1973 Charlie Rich (Epic)

BEST SELLING ALBUM BY A MALE COUNTRY ARTIST

1974 *Behind Closed Doors*, Charlie Rich (Epic)
1975 *Before the Next Teardrop Falls*, Freddy Fender (ABC-Dot)
1976 *The Outlaws*, Waylon Jennings, Willie Nelson, Jessi Colter, Tompal Glaser (RCA)
1977 *Moody Blue*, Elvis Presley (RCA)
1978 *Stardust*, Willie Nelson (Columbia)

BEST SELLING CLASSICAL ARTIST

1966 Leonard Bernstein (Columbia)
1967 Leonard Bernstein (Columbia)
1968 Leonard Bernstein and the New York Philharmonic (Columbia)
1969 Leonard Bernstein and the New York Philharmonic (Columbia)
1970 Leonard Bernstein (Columbia)

BEST SELLING CLASSICAL ALBUM

1969 *Switched On Bach*, Walter Carlos (Columbia)
1970 —
1971 *Mass*, Leonard Bernstein (Columbia)
1972 *Switched On Bach*, Walter Carlos (Columbia)
Mass, Leonard Bernstein (Columbia)
1973 *Switched On Bach*, Walter Carlos (Columbia)
1974 *Snowflakes Are Dancing*, Tomita (RCA)
1975 *Mussourgsky: Pictures at an Exhibition*, Isao Tomita (RCA)
1976 *Suite for Flute and Jazz Piano*, Jean-Pierre Rampal and Claude Bolling (Columbia)
1977 *Suite for Flute and Jazz Piano*, Jean-Pierre Rampal and Claude Bolling (Columbia)
1978 *Suite for Flute and Jazz Piano*, Jean-Pierre Rampal and Claude Bolling (Columbia)

BEST SELLING SPECIALTY ARTIST/BEST SELLING COMEDY RECORDING ARTIST

1960 Bob Newhart (Warner Bros.)
1961 Bob Newhart (Warner Bros.)
1962 Rusty Warren (Jubilee)
1963 Smothers Brothers (Mercury)
1964 Smothers Brothers (Mercury)
1965 Bill Cosby (Warner Bros.)
1966 Bill Cosby (Warner Bros.)
1967 Bill Crosby (Warner Bros.)
1968 Bill Cosby (Warner Bros.)
1969 Bill Cosby (Warner Bros. and UNI)
1970 Flip Wilson (Little David)
1971 —

1972 —
1973 Cheech & Chong (Ode)

BEST SELLING COMEDY ALBUM

1971 *All in the Family* (Atlantic)
1972 *Big Bambu*, Cheech & Chong (Ode)
1973 —
1974 *Wedding Album*, Cheech & Chong (Ode)
1975 *Is It Something I Said*, Richard Pryor (Warner Bros.-Reprise)
1976 *Bicentennial Nigger*, Richard Pryor (Warner Bros.)
1977 *Let's Get Small*, Steve Martin (Warner Bros.)
1978 *A Wild and Crazy Guy*, Steve Martin (Warner Bros.)

BEST SELLING CHILDREN'S ALBUM/CHILDREN'S LINE

1961 *101 Dalmations* (Disneyland)
1962 Golden Records
1963 Disneyland Records
1964 Disneyland Records
1965 Disneyland Records
1966 Disneyland Records
1967 Disneyland Records
1968 Disneyland Records
1969 Disneyland Records
1970 Disneyland Records
1971 *Sesame Street* (Columbia)
     Sesame Street 2 (Warner Bros.)
1972 Sesame Street (Columbia)
     Sesame Street 2 (Warner Bros.)
1973 *The Chilling, Thrilling Sounds of the Haunted House* (Disneyland)
1974 *Free to Be You and Me*, Marlo Thomas and Friends (Bell)
1975 *The Mickey Mouse Club* (Disneyland)
1976 —
1977 *The Rescuers* (Disneyland)
1978 *Sesame Street Fever*, Muppetts and Robin Gibb (Sesame Street)

BEST SELLING ECONOMY ALBUM/ECONOMY PRICE LABEL

1959 *Soul of Spain* (Somerset)
1960 *Montovani Showcase* (London)
1961 Bravo Records (Pickwick)
1962 Pickwick International (under $1)
     Camden Records (over $1)
1963 Somerset Stereo Fidelity (under $1)
     Camden Records (over $1)
1964 Somerset Stereo Fidelity (under $1)
     Camden Records (over $1)
1965 Somerset Stereo Fidelity (under $1)
     Camden Records (over $1)
1966 Ambassador Records, Crown Records, Pickwick International (under $1) [tie]
     Camden Records (over $1)
1967 Pickwick International, Camden Records [tie]
1968 Pickwick International
1969 Pickwick International
1970 Pickwick International
1971 *Excerpts from Jesus Christ Superstar* (Pickwick-33 Records)
1972 *Burning Love*, Elvis Presley (RCA Camden)
1973 *Burning Love*, Elvis Presley (RCA Camden)
     Pickwick International
1974 *Piano Rags by Scott Joplin Vol. 1*, Joshua Rifkin (Nonesuch)
1975 *High Water*, Beach Boys (Pickwick)
1976 —
1977 *Christmas Album*, Elvis Presley (Pickwick)
1978 —

PRESIDENTIAL AWARDS

1964 Mitch Miller, Columbia Records
1965 —
1966 Frank Sinatra, Reprise Records
1967 Mantovani, London Records
     George R. Marek, RCA Records

NARM AWARDS

1968 Irwin Tarr (RCA) and Wm. Gallagher (CBS): "Men of the Decade"
1969 Burt Bacharach and Hal David
Dr. Peter C. Goldmark, CBS
1970 —
1971 Herb Alpert and Jerry Moss, A&M Records
1972 Perry Como, RCA Records
Clive J. Davis, Columbia Records
1973 Judy Garland
Ahmet Ertegun, Nesuhi Ertegun, Jerry Wexler (Atlantic Records)
1974 Lou Adler, Ode Records
Russ Regan, 20th Century Fox Records
1975 Joseph Smith, Warner Bros. Records
Mo Ostin, Warner Bros. Records
Stevie Wonder, Tamla Records
1976 Cy Leslie, Pickwick International
Neil Sedaka, Rocket Records
Paul Anka, United Artists Records
1977 Amos and Daniel Heilicher
Neil Bogart, Casablanca Records
1978 —
1979 Robert Stigwood, RSO Records
Bee Gees

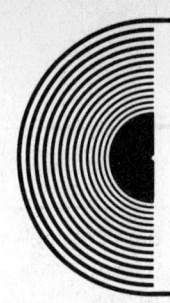

GRAMMY AWARDS

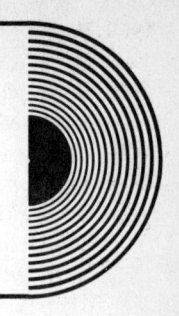

RECORD OF THE YEAR

1958 "Nel Blu Dipinto Di Blu (Volare)," Domenico Modugno (Decca)
1959 "Mack the Knife," Bobby Darin (Atco)
1960 "Theme from a Summer Place," Percy Faith (Columbia)
1961 "Moon River," Henry Mancini (RCA)
1962 "I Left My Heart in San Francisco," Tony Bennett (Columbia)
1963 "The Days of Wine and Roses," Henry Mancini (RCA)
1964 "The Girl from Ipanema," Stan Getz, Astrud Gilberto (Verve)
1965 "A Taste of Honey," Herb Alpert & The Tijuana Brass (A&M)
1966 "Stranger in the Night," Frank Sinatra (Reprise)
1967 "Up, Up and Away," 5th Dimension (Soul City)
1968 "Mrs. Robinson," Simon & Garfunkel (Columbia)
1969 "Aquarius/Let the Sun Shine In," 5th Dimension (Soul City)
1970 "Bridge over Troubled Water," Simon & Garfunkel (Columbia)
1971 "It's Too Late," Carole King (Ode)
1972 "The First Time Ever I Saw Your Face," Roberta Flack (Atlantic)
1973 "Killing Me Softly with His Song," Roberta Flack (Atlantic)
1974 "I Honestly Love You,'" Olivia Newton-John (MCA)
1975 "Love Will Keep Us Together," Captain & Tennille (A&M)
1975 "This Masquerade," George Benson (Warner Bros.)
1977 "Hotel California," Eagles (Asylum)
1978 "Just the Way You Are," Billy Joel (Columbia)

ALBUM OF THE YEAR

1958 *The Music from Peter Gunn,* Henry Mancini (RCA)
1959 *Come Dance with Me,* Frank Sinatra (Capitol)
1960 *Button Down Mind,* Bob Newhart (Warner Bros.)
1961 *Judy at Carnegie Hall,* Judy Garland (Capitol)
1962 *The First Family,* Vaughn Meader (Cadence)
1963 *The Barbra Streisand Album,* Barbra Streisand (Columbia)
1964 *Getz/Gilberto,* Stan Getz, Joao Gilberto (Verve)
1965 *September of My Years,* Frank Sinatra (Reprise)
1966 *Sinatra—A Man & His Music,* Frank Sinatra (Reprise)
1967 *Sgt. Pepper's Lonely Hearts Club Band,* Beatles (Capitol)
1968 *By the Time I Get to Phoenix,* Glen Campbell (Capitol)

*Given by the National Association of Recording Arts and Sciences (NARAS).

1969 *Blood, Sweat & Tears,* Blood, Sweat & Tears (Columbia)
1970 *Bridge Over Troubled Water,* Simon & Garfunkel (Columbia)
1971 *Tapestry,* Carole King (Ode)
1972 *The Concert for Bangladesh,* George Harrison, Ravi Shankar, Bob Dylan, Leon Russell, Ringo Starr, Billy Preston, Eric Clapton, Klaus Voormann (Apple)
1973 *Innervisions,* Stevie Wonder (Tamla-Motown)
1974 *Fulfillingness First Finale,* Stevie Wonder (Tamla-Motown)
1975 *Still Crazy After All These Years,* Paul Simon (Columbia)
1976 *Songs in the Key of Life,* Stevie Wonder (Tamla-Motown)
1977 *Rumours,* Fleetwood Mac (Warner Bros.)
1978 *Saturday Night Fever*—motion picture soundtrack featuring the Bee Gees, David Shire, Yvonne Elliman, Tavares, Kool & the Gang, KC & the Sunshine Band, MFSB, Trammps, Walter Murphy, Ralph MacDonald (RSO)

BEST NEW ARTIST OF THE YEAR

1959 Bobby Darin
1960 Bob Newhart
1961 Peter Nero
1962 Robert Goulet
1963 Swingle Singers
1964 Beatles
1965 Tom Jones
1966 —
1967 Bobbie Gentry
1968 Jose Feliciano
1969 Crosby, Stills & Nash
1970 Carpenters
1971 Carly Simon
1972 America
1973 Bette Midler
1974 Marvin Hamlisch
1975 Natalie Cole
1976 Starland Vocal Band
1977 Debby Boone
1978 A Taste of Honey

SONG OF THE YEAR
(Award to Songwriter)

1958 "Nel Blu Dipinto Di Blu (Volare)," Domenico Modugno (Decca)
1959 "The Battle of New Orleans," Jimmy Driftwood (Columbia)
1960 "Theme from Exodus," Ernest Gold (RCA)
1961 "Moon River," Henry Mancini and Johnny Mercer (RCA)
1962 "What Kind of Fool Am I," Leslie Bricusse and Anthony Newley (London)
1963 "The Days of Wine and Roses," Henry Mancini and Johnny Mercer (RCA)
1964 "Hello, Dolly!" Jerry Herman (Kapp)
1965 "The Shadow of Your Smile (Love Theme from the Sandpiper)," Paul Francis Webster and Johnny Mandel (Mercury)
1966 "Michelle," John Lennon and Paul McCartney (Capitol)
1967 "Up, Up and Away," Jim Webb (Soul City)
1968 "Little Green Apples," Bobby Russell (Columbia)
1969 "Games People Play," Joe South
1970 "Bridge over Troubled Water," Paul Simon (Columbia)
1971 "You've Got a Friend," Carole King (Ode)
1972 "The First Time Ever I Saw Your Face," Ewan MacColl (Atlantic)
1973 "Killing Me Softly with His Song," Norman Gimbel and Charles Fox (Atlantic)
1974 "The Way We Were," Marilyn and Alan Bergman, Marvin Hamlisch
1975 "Send In the Clowns," Stephen Sondheim
1976 "I Write the Songs," Bruce Johnston

1977 "Evergreen," Love Theme from A Star Is Born, Barbra Streisand and Paul Williams (Columbia)
1978 "Just the Way You Are," Billy Joel (Columbia)

BEST VOCAL PERFORMANCE/ BEST SOLO VOCAL PERFORMANCE/BEST CONTEMPORARY POP VOCAL PERFORMANCE (Female)

1958 Ella Fitzgerald, *Ella Fitzgerald Sings the Irving Berlin Song Book* (Verve)
1959 Ella Fitzgerald, *But Not for Me* (Verve)
1960 Ella Fitzgerald, "Mack the Knife" (Verve) (single)
Ella Fitzgerald, *Mack the Knife—Ella in Berlin* (Verve) (album)
1961 Judy Garland, *Judy at Carnegie Hall* (Capitol) (album)
1962 Ella Fitzgerald, *Ella Swings Brightly with Nelson Riddle* (Verve) (album)
1963 Barbra Streisand, *The Barbra Streisand Album* (Columbia) (album)
1964 Barbra Streisand, *"People"* (Columbia) (single)
1965 Barbra Streisand, *My Name Is Barbra* (Columbia) (album)
1966 Eydie Gorme, *"If He Walked into My Life"* (Columbia) (single)
1967 Bobbie Gentry, *"Ode to Billie Joe"* (Capitol) (single)
1968 Dionne Warwick, *"Do You Know the Way to San Jose"* (Scepter) (single)
1969 Peggy Lee, *"Is That All There Is"* (Capitol) (single)
1970 Dionne Warwick, *I'll Never Fall in Love Again* (Scepter) (album)
1971 Carole King, *Tapestry* (Ode) (album)
1972 Helen Reddy, *"I Am Woman"* (Capitol) (single)
1973 Roberta Flack, *"Killing Me Softly with His Song"* (Atlantic) (single)
1974 Olivia Newton-John, *"I Honestly Love You"* (MCA) (single)
1975 Janis Ian, *"At Seventeen"* (Columbia) (single)
1976 Linda Ronstadt, *Hasten Down the Wind* (Asylum) (album)
1977 Barbra Streisand, "Evergreen," Love Theme from *A Star Is Born* (Columbia) (single)
1978 Anne Murray, *"You Needed Me"* (Capitol) (single)

BEST VOCAL PERFORMANCE/ BEST SOLO VOCAL PERFORMANCE/BEST CONTEMPORARY POP VOCAL PERFORMANCE (Male)

1958 Perry Como, *Catch a Falling Star* (RCA Victor) (album)
1959 Frank Sinatra, *Come Dance with Me* (Capitol) (album)
1960 Ray Charles, "Georgia on My Mind" (ABC) (single)
Ray Charles, *Genius of Ray Charles* (ABC) (album)
1961 Jack Jones, "Lollipops and Roses" (Kapp) (single)
1962 Tony Bennett, *I Left My Heart in San Francisco* (Columbia) (album)
1963 Jack Jones, "Wives and Lovers" (Kapp) (single)
1964 Louis Armstrong, "Hello, Dolly!" (Kapp) (single)
1965 Frank Sinatra, "It Was a Very Good Year" (Reprise) (single)
1966 Frank Sinatra, "Strangers in the Night" (Reprise) (single)
1967 Glen Campbell, "By the Time I Get to Phoenix" (Capitol) (single)
1968 Jose Feliciano, "Light My Fire" (RCA) (single)
1969 Harry Nilsson, "Everybody's Talkin' " (United Artists) (single)
1970 Ray Stevens, "Everything Is Beautiful" (Barnaby) (single)

1971 James Taylor, "You've Got a Friend" (Warner Bros.) (single)
1972 Harry Nilsson, "Without You" (RCA) (single)
1973 Stevie Wonder, "You Are the Sunshine of My Life" (Tamla-Motown) (single)
1974 Stevie Wonder, *Fulfillingness First Finale* (Tamla-Motown) (album)
1975 Paul Simon, *Still Crazy after All These Years* (Columbia) (album)
1976 Stevie Wonder, *Songs in the Key of Life* (Tamla-Motown) (album)
1977 James Taylor, "Handy Man" (Columbia) (single)
1978 Barry Manilow, "Copacabana (at the Copa)" (Arista) (single)

BEST PERFORMANCE BY A VOCAL GROUP/BEST POP VOCAL PERFORMANCE BY A DUO, GROUP OR CHORUS

1960 Eydie Gorme, Steve Lawrence, *We Got Us* (ABC)
1961 Lambert, Hendricks and Ross, *High Flying* (Columbia)
1962 Peter, Paul & Mary, *If I Had a Hammer* (Warner Bros.)
1963 Peter, Paul & Mary, *Blowin' in the Wind* (Warner Bros.)
1964 Beatles, *A Hard Day's Night* (Capitol)
1965 Anita Kerr Singers, *We Dig Mancini* (RCA)
1966 Anita Kerr Singers, *A Man and a Woman* (Warner Bros.)
1967 5th Dimension, *Up, Up and Away* (Soul City)
1968 Simon & Garfunkel, *Mrs. Robinson* (Columbia)
1969 5th Dimension, *Aquarius/Let the Sun Shine In* (Soul City)
1970 Carpenters, *Close to You* (A&M)
1971 Carpenters, *Carpenters* (A&M)
1972 Roberta Flack, Donny Hathaway, *Where Is the Love* (Atlantic)
1973 Gladys Knight & the Pips, *Neither One of Us (Wants to Be the First to Say Goodbye)* (Soul-Motown)
1974 Paul McCartney & Wings, *Band on the Run* (Apple)
1975 Eagles, *Lyin' Eyes* (Asylum)
1976 Chicago, *If You Leave Me Now* (Columbia)
1977 Bee Gees, *How Deep Is Your Love* (RSO)
1978 Bee Gees, *Saturday Night Fever* (RSO)

BEST PERFORMANCE BY AN ORCHESTRA/BEST INSTRUMENTAL PERFORMANCE/POP INSTRUMENTAL PERFORMANCE

1958 *Billy May's Big Fat Brass*, Billy May (Capitol)
1959 *Like Young*, David Rose and His Orchestra with Andre Previn (MGM)
1960 *Mr. Lucky*, Henry Mancini (RCA)
1961 *Breakfast at Tiffany's*, Henry Mancini (RCA)
1962 *The Colorful Peter Nero*, Peter Nero (RCA)
1963 *Java*, Al Hirt (RCA)
1964 *Pink Panther*, Henry Mancini (RCA)
1965 *A Taste of Honey*, Herb Alpert & the Tijuana Brass (A&M)
1966 *What Now My Love*, Herb Alpert & the Tijuana Brass (A&M)
1967 *Chet Atkins Picks the Best*, Chet Atkins (RCA)
1968 *Classical Gas*, Mason Williams (Warner Bros.-7 Arts)
1969 *Variations on a Theme by Eric Satie*, Blood, Sweat & Tears (Columbia)
1970 *Theme from "Z" and Other Film Music*, Henry Mancini (RCA)
1971 *Smackwater Jack*, Quincy Jones (A&M)
1972 "Outa-Space," Billy Preston (A&M)
1973 *Also Sprach Zarathustra* (theme from *2001: A Space Odyssey*), Eumir Deodato (CTI)
1974 "The Entertainer," Marvin Hamlisch (MCA)

1975 "The Hustle," Van McCoy and the Soul City Symphony (Avco)
1976 Breezin', George Benson (Warner Bros.)
1977 Star Wars, John Williams conducting London Symphony Orchestra (20th Century Fox)
1978 Children of Sanchez, Chuck Mangione Group (A&M)

BEST RHYTHM AND BLUES PERFORMANCE

1958 Tequila, The Champs (Challenge)
1959 What a Diff'rence a Day Makes, Dinah Washington (Mercury)
1960 Let the Good Times Roll, Ray Charles (Atlantic)
1961 Hit the Road Jack, Ray Charles (ABC-Paramount)
1962 I Can't Stop Loving You, Ray Charles (ABC)
1963 Busted, Ray Charles (ABC-Paramount)
1964 How Glad I Am, Nancy Wilson (Capitol)
1965 Papa's Got a Brand New Bag, James Brown (King)
1966 Crying Time, Ray Charles (ABC-Paramount)

BEST RHYTHM AND BLUES VOCAL PERFORMANCE (Female)

1967 Aretha Franklin, Respect (Atlantic)
1968 Aretha Franklin, Chain of Fools (Atlantic)
1969 Aretha Franklin, Share Your Love with Me (Atlantic)
1970 Aretha Franklin, Don't Play That Song (Atlantic)
1971 Aretha Franklin, Bridge over Troubled Water (Atlantic)
1972 Aretha Franklin, Young, Gifted & Black (Atlantic)
1973 Aretha Franklin, Master of Eyes (Atlantic)
1974 Aretha Franklin, Ain't Nothing Like the Real Thing (Atlantic)
1975 Natalie Cole, This Will Be (Capitol)
1976 Natalie Cole, Sophisticated Lady (She's a Different Lady) (Capitol)
1977 Thelma Houston, Don't Leave Me This Way (Motown)
1978 Donna Summer, Last Dance (Casablanca)

BEST RHYTHM AND BLUES VOCAL PERFORMANCE (Male)

1967 Lou Rawls, Dead End Street (Capitol)
1968 Otis Redding, (Sittin' on) The Dock of the Bay (Volt)
1969 Joe Simon, The Chokin' Kind (Sound Stage 7)
1970 B. B. King, The Thrill Is Gone (ABC)
1971 Lou Rawls, A Natural Man (MGM)
1972 Billy Paul, Me & Mrs. Jones (Phila. Intl.)
1973 Stevie Wonder, Superstition (Tamla-Motown)
1974 Stevie Wonder, Boogie on Reggae Woman (Tamla-Motown)
1975 Ray Charles, Living for the City (Crossover)
1976 Stevie Wonder, I Wish (Tamla-Motown)
1977 Lou Rawls, Unmistakably Lou (Phila. Intl.)
1978 George Benson, On Broadway (Warner Bros.)

BEST RHYTHM AND BLUES GROUP PERFORMANCE (Two or More), VOCAL OR INSTRUMENTAL

1966 Ramsey Lewis, Hold It Right There (Cadet)
1967 Sam & Dave, Soul Man (Stax)
1968 Temptations, Cloud Nine (Soul-Gordy)
1969 Isley Brothers, It's Your Thing (T-Neck)

GRAMMY AWARDS

1970 Delfonics, *Didn't I (Blow Your Mind This Time)* (Philly Groove)
1971 Ike and Tina Turner, *Proud Mary* (United Artists)
1972 Temptations, *Papa Was a Rolling Stone* (Motown)
1973 Gladys Knight & the Pips, *Midnight Train to Georgia* (Buddah)
1974 Rufus, *Tell Me Something* (ABC)
1975 Earth, Wind & Fire, *Shining Star* (Columbia)
1976 Marilyn McCoo & Billy Davis, Jr., *You Don't Have to Be a Star (to Be in My Show)* (ABC)
1977 Emotions, *Best of My Love* (Columbia)
1978 Earth, Wind & Fire, *All 'N All* (Columbia)

BEST RHYTHM AND BLUES INSTRUMENTAL PERFORMANCE

1969 King Curtis, *Games People Play* (Atco)
1970 —
1971 —
1972 Temptations, *Papa Was a Rolling Stone* (Motown)
1973 Ramsey Lewis, *Hang on Sloopy* (Columbia)
1974 MFSB, *TSOP (The Sound of Philadelphia)* (Phila. Intl.)
1975 Silver Convention, *Fly, Robin, Fly* (Midland International-RCA)
1976 George Benson, *Theme from Good King Bad* (CTI)
1977 Brothers Johnson, *Q* (A&M)
1978 Earth, Wind & Fire, *Runnin'* (Columbia)

BEST RHYTHM AND BLUES SONG (Award to Songwriter)

1968 "(Sittin' on) The Dock of the Bay," Otis Redding and Steve Cropper (Volt)
1969 "Color Him Father," Richard Spencer
1970 "Patches," Ronald Dunbar and General Johnson (Atlantic)
1971 "Ain't No Sunshine," Bill Withers (Sussex)
1972 "Papa Was a Rolling Stone," Barrett Strong and Norman Whitfield
1973 "Superstition," Stevie Wonder (Tamla-Motown)
1974 "Living for the City," Stevie Wonder (Tamla-Motown)
1975 "Where Is the Love," Harry Wayne Casey, Richard Finch, Willie Clarke, Betty Wright
1976 "Lowdown," Boz Scaggs, David Paich (Columbia)
1977 "You Make Me Feel Like Dancing," Leo Sayer and Vini Poncia
1978 "Last Dance," Paul Jabara

BEST COUNTRY VOCAL PERFORMANCE (Female)

1964 Dottie West, *Here Comes My Baby* (RCA)
1965 Jody Miller, *Queen of the House* (Capitol)
1966 Jeannie Seely, *Don't Touch Me* (Monument)
1967 Tammy Wynette, *I Don't Wanna Play House* (Epic)
1968 Jeannie C. Riley, *Harper Valley PTA* (Plantation)
1969 Tammy Wynette, *Stand By Your Man* (Epic)
1970 Lynn Anderson, *Rose Garden* (Columbia)
1971 Sammi Smith, *Help Me Make It through the Night* (Mega)
1972 Donna Fargo, *Happiest Girl in the U.S.A.* (Dot)
1973 Olivia Newton-John, *Let Me Be There* (MA)
1974 Anne Murray, *Love Song* (Capitol)
1975 Linda Ronstadt, *I Can't Help It (if I'm Still in Love with You)* (Capitol)

1976 Emmylou Harris, *Elite Hotel* (Warner Bros.-Reprise)
1977 Crystal Gayle, *Don't It Make My Brown Eyes Blue* (United Artists)
1978 Dolly Parton, *Here You Come Again* (RCA)

BEST COUNTRY VOCAL PERFORMANCE (Male)

1964 Roger Miller, *Dang Me* (Smash)
1965 Roger Miller, *King of the Road* (Smash)
1966 David Houston, *Almost Persuaded* (Epic)
1967 Glen Campbell, *Gentle on My Mind* (Capitol)
1968 Johnny Cash, *Folsom Prison Blues* (Columbia)
1969 Johnny Cash, *A Boy Named Sue* (Columbia)
1970 Ray Price, *For the Good Times* (Columbia)
1971 Jerry Reed, *When You're Hot, You're Hot* (RCA)
1972 Charley Pride, *Charley Pride Sings Heart Songs* (RCA)
1973 Charlie Rich, *Behind Closed Doors* (Epic)
1974 Ronnie Milsap, *Please Don't Tell Me How the Story Ends* (RCA)
1975 Willie Nelson, *Blue Eyes Crying in the Rain* (Columbia)
1976 Ronnie Milsap, *(I'm a) Stand by My Woman Man* (RCA)
1977 Kenny Rogers, *Lucille* (United Artists)
1978 Willie Nelson, *Georgia on My Mind* (Columbia)

BEST COUNTRY PERFORMANCE BY A DUO OR GROUP/BEST COUNTRY VOCAL PERFORMANCE BY A DUO OR GROUP

1969 Waylon Jennings & the Kimberleys, *MacArthur Park* (RCA)
1970 Johnny Cash & June Carter, *If I Were a Carpenter* (Columbia)
1971 Conway Twitty and Loretta Lynn, *After the Fire Is Gone* (Decca)
1972 Statler Brothers, *Class of '57* (Mercury)
1973 Kris Kristofferson, Rita Coolidge, *From the Bottle to the Bottom* (A&M)
1974 Pointer Sisters, *Fairytale* (Blue Thumb)
1975 Kris Kristofferson, Rita Coolidge, *Lover Please* (Monument)
1976 Amazing Rhythm Aces, *The End Is Not in Sight (The Cowboy Tune)* (ABC)
1977 Kendalls, *Heaven's Just a Sin Away* (Ovation)
1978 Waylon Jennings & Willie Nelson, *Mamas Don't Let Your Babies Grow Up to Be Cowboys* (RCA)

BEST COUNTRY INSTRUMENTAL PERFORMANCE

1967 Johnny Cash, June Carter, *Jackson* (Columbia)
1968 Flatt & Scruggs, *Foggy Mountain Breakdown* (Columbia)
1969 Danny Davis & the Nashville Brass, *The Nashville Brass Featuring Danny Davis Play More Nashville Sounds* (RCA)
1970 Chet Atkins & Jerry Reed, *Me & Jerry* (RCA)
1971 Chet Atkins, *Snowbird* (RCA)
1972 Charlie McCoy, *Charlie McCoy/ The Real McCoy* (Monument)
1973 Eric Weissberg, Steve Mandell, *Dueling Banjos* (Warner Bros.)
1974 Chet Atkins & Merle Travis, *The Atkins-Travis Traveling Show* (RCA)
1975 Chet Atkins, *The Entertairner* (RCA)
1976 Chet Atkins, Les Paul, *Chester & Lester* (RCA)
1977 Hargus "Pig" Robbins, *Country Instrumentalist of the Year* (Elektra)
1978 Asleep at the Wheel, *One O'clock Jump* (Capitol)

BEST COUNTRY SONG
(Award to Songwriter)

1964 "Dang Me," Roger Miller (Smash)
1965 "King of the Road," Roger Miller (Smash)
1966 "Almost Persuaded," David Houston (Epic)
1967 "Gentle on My Mind," John Hartford (RCA)
1968 "Little Green Apples," Bobby Russell (Smash)
1969 "A Boy Named Sue," Shel Silverstein (Columbia)
1970 "My Woman, My Woman, My Wife," Marty Robbins (Columbia)
1971 "Help Me Make It Through the Night," Kris Kristofferson
1972 "Kiss an Angel Good Mornin'," Ben Peters
1973 "Behind Closed Doors," Kenny O'Dell
1974 "A Very Special Love Song," Norris Wilson and Billy Sherrill
1975 ("Hey Won't You Play) Another Somebody Done Somebody Wrong Song," Chips Moman and Larry Butler
1976 "Broken Lady," Larry Gatlin
1977 "Don't It Make My Brown Eyes Blue," Richard Leigh (United Artists)
1978 "The Gambler," Don Schlitz (United Artists)

BEST GOSPEL OR OTHER RELIGIOUS RECORDING/BEST GOSPEL PERFORMANCE (Other than Soul Gospel)/BEST GOSPEL PERFORMANCE, TRADITIONAL

1961 *Every Time I Feel the Spirit,* Mahalia Jackson (Columbia)
1962 *Great Songs of Love and Faith,* Mahalia Jackson (Columbia)
1963 *Dominique,* Soeur Sourire (The Singing Nun) (Philips)
1964 *Great Gospel Songs,* Tennessee Ernie Ford (Capitol)
1965 *Southland Favorites,* George Beverly Shea and the Anita Kerr Singers (RCA)
1966 *Grand Old Gospel,* Porter Wagoner & the Blackwood Brothers (RCA)
1967 *More Grand Old Gospel,* Porter Wagoner & the Blackwood Brothers (RCA)
1968 *The Happy Gospel of the Happy Goodmans,* Happy Goodman Family (Word)
1969 *In Gospel Country,* Porter Wagoner & the Blackwood Brothers (RCA)
1970 *Talk about the Good Times,* Oak Ridge Boys (Heart Warming)
1971 *Let Me Live,* Charley Pride (RCA)
1972 *Love,* Blackwood Brothers (RCA)
1973 *Release Me (from My Sin),* Blackwood Brothers (Skylite)
1974 *The Baptism of Jesse Taylor,* Oak Ridge Boys (Columbia)
1975 *No Shortage,* Imperials (Impact)
1976 *Where the Soul Never Dies,* Oak Ridge Boys (Columbia)
1977 *Just a Little Talk with Jesus,* Oak Ridge Boys (Rockland Road)
1978 *Refreshing,* Happy Goodman Family (Canaan)

BEST SOUL GOSPEL PERFORMANCE

1968 Dottie Rambo, *The Soul of Me* (Heartwarming)
1969 Edwin Hawkins Singers, *Oh Happy Day* (Buddah)
1970 Edwin Hawkins Singers, *Every Man Wants to Be Free* (Buddah)
1971 Shirley Caesar, *Put Your Hand in the Hand of the Man from Galilee* (Hob)
1972 Aretha Franklin, *Amazing Grace* (Atlantic)
1973 Dixie Hummingbirds, *Loves Me Like a Rock* (ABC)

1974 James Cleveland and the Southern California Community Choir, *In the Ghetto* (Savoy)
1975 Andrae Crouch and the Disciples, *Take Me Back* (Light)
1976 Mahalia Jackson, *How I Got Over* (Columbia)
1977 Edwin Hawkins & the Edwin Hawkins Singers, *Wonderful!* (Birthright) [contemporary category]
James Cleveland, *James Cleveland Live at Carnegie Hall* (Savoy) [traditional category]
1978 Andrae Crouch and the Disciples, *Live in London* (Light) [contemporary category]
Mighty Clouds of Joy, *Live and Direct* (ABC) [traditional category]

BEST INSPIRATIONAL PERFORMANCE

1977 B. J. Thomas, *Home Where I Belong* (Myrrh-Word)
1978 B. J. Thomas, *Happy Man* (Myrrh-Word)

BEST FOLK PERFORMANCE/ BEST ETHNIC OR TRADITIONAL PERFORMANCE

1959 Kingston Trio, *The Kingston Trio at Large* (Capitol)
1960 Harry Belafonte, *Swing Dat Hammer* (RCA)
1961 Belafonte Folk Singers, *Belafonte Folk Singers at Home and Abroad* (RCA)
1962 Peter, Paul & Mary, *If I Had a Hammer* (Warner Bros.)
1963 Peter, Paul & Mary, *Blowin' in the Wind* (Warner Bros.)
1964 Gale Garnett, *We'll Sing in the Sunshine* (RCA)
1965 Harry Belafonte, Miriam Makeba, *An Evening with Belafonte/Makeba* (RCA)
1966 Cortelia Clark, *Blues in the Street* (RCA)
1967 John Hartford, *Gentle on My Mind* (RCA)
1968 Judy Collins, *Both Sides Now* (Elektra)
1969 Joni Mitchell, *Clouds* (Warner Bros.)
1970 T-Bone Walker, *Good Feelin'* (Polydor)
1971 Muddy Waters, *They Call Me Muddy Waters* (Chess)
1972 Muddy Waters, *The London Muddy Waters Session* (Chess)
1973 Doc Watson, *Then and Now* (United Artists)
1974 Doc & Merle Watson, *Two Days in November* (United Artists)
1975 Muddy Waters, *The Muddy Waters Woodstock Album* (Chess)
1976 John Hartford, *Mark Twang* (Flying Fish)
1977 Muddy Waters, *Hard Again* (Blue Sky-CBS)
1978 Muddy Waters, *I'm Ready* (Blue Sky-CBS)

BEST LATIN RECORDING

1975 *Suns of Latin Music*, Eddie Palmieri (Coco)
1976 *Unfinished Masterpiece*, Eddie Palmieri (Coco)
1977 *Dawn*, Mongo Santamaria (Vaya)
1978 *Homenaje a Beny More*, Tito Puente (Tico)

BEST RECORDING FOR CHILDREN

1958 *The Chipmunk Song*, David Seville (Liberty)
1959 *Peter and the Wolf*, Peter Ustinov, narrator; Herbert von Karajan conducting Philharmonia orchestra (Angel)
1960 *Let's All Sing with the Chipmunks*, David Seville (Ross Bagdasarian) (Liberty)

1961 *Prokofiev: Peter and the Wolf*, Leonard Bernstein conducting New York Philharmonic (Columbia)
1962 *Saint-Saens: Carnival of the Animals/Britten: Young Person's Guide to the Orchestra*, Leonard Bernstein conducting New York Philharmonic (Columbia)
1963 *Bernstein Conducts for Young People*, Leonard Bernstein conducting New York Philharmonic (Columbia)
1964 *Mary Poppins*, Julie Andrews, Dick Van Dyke (Buena Vista)
1965 *Dr. Seuss Presents "Fox in Sox"—"Green Eggs and Ham"*, Marvin Miller (RCA-Camden)
1966 *Dr. Seuss Presents "If I Ran the Zoo" and "Sleep Book"*, Marvin Miller (RCA-Camden)
1967 *Dr. Seuss: How the Grinch Stole Christmas*, Boris Karloff (MGM)
1968 —
1969 *Peter, Paul & Mommy*, Peter, Paul & Mary (Warner Bros.)
1970 *Sesame Street*, Joan Cooney, producer (Columbia)
1971 *Bill Cosby Talks to Kids about Drugs*, Bill Cosby (UNI)
1972 *The Electric Company*, Bill Cosby, Rita Morena, Lee Chamberlin; Christopher Cerf, project director; Joe Raposo, producer and music director (Warner Bros.)
1973 *Sesame Street Live*, Sesame Street Cast; Joe Raposo, producer (Columbia)
1974 *Winnie the Pooh & Tigger To*, Sebastian Cabot, Sterling Holloway, Paul Winchell (Disneyland)
1975 *The Little Prince*, Richard Burton, narrator (PIP)
1976 *Prokofiev: Peter and the Wolf/Saint-Saens: Carnival of the Animals*, Hermione Gingold, Karl Bohm, conductor (Deutsche Gramaphone)
1977 *Aren't You Glad You're You*, Christopher Cerf and Jim Timmens (Sesame Street)
1978 *The Muppet Show*, Jim Henson (Arista)

BEST COMEDY PERFORMANCE

1958 "The Chipmunk Song," David Seville (Liberty)
1959 *Inside Shelley Berman*, Shelley Berman (Verve)
The Battle of Kookamonga, Homer and Jethro (RCA)
1960 *Button Down Mind Strikes Back*, Bob Newhart (Warner Bros.)
Jonathan and Darlene Edwards in Paris, Jonathan and Darlene Edwards (Jo Stafford and Paul Weston) (Columbia)
1961 *An Evening with Mike Nichols and Elaine May*, Mike Nichols and Elaine May (Mercury)
1962 *The First Family*, Vaughn Meader (Cadence)
1963 *Hello Mudduh, Hello Faddah*, Allan Sherman (Warner Bros.)
1964 *I Started Out as a Child*, Bill Cosby (Warner Bros.)
1965 *Why Is There Air?* Bill Cosby (Warner Bros.)
1966 *Wonderfulness*, Bill Cosby (Warner Bros.)
1967 *Revenge*, Bill Cosby (Warner Bros.-7 Arts)
1968 *To Russell, My Brother, Whom I Slept With*, Bill Cosby (Warner Bros.-7 Arts)
1969 *Bill Cosby*, Bill Cosby (UNI)
1970 *The Devil Made Me Buy This Dress*, Flip Wilson (Little David)
1971 *This Is a Recording*, Lily Tomlin (Polydor)
1972 *FM & AM*, George Carlin (Little David)
1973 *Los Cochinos*, Cheech & Chong (Ode)
1974 *That Nigger's Crazy*, Richard Pryor (Partee-Stax)

1975 *Is It Something I Said?* Richard Pryor (Reprise)
1976 *Bicentennial Nigger,* Richard Pryor (Warner Bros.)
1977 *Let's Get Small,* Steve Martin (Warner Bros.)
1978 *A Wild and Crazy Guy,* Steve Martin (Warner Bros.)

BEST SPOKEN WORD OR DRAMA RECORDING

1958 *The Best of the Stan Freberg Shows,* Stan Freberg (Capitol)
1959 *A Lincoln Portrait,* Carl Sandburg (Columbia)
1960 *F.D.R. Speaks,* Robert Bialek, producer (Washington)
1961 *Humor in Music,* Leonard Bernstein conducting New York Philharmonic (Columbia)
1962 *The Story-teller: A Session with Charles Laughton,* Charles Laughton (Columbia)
1963 *Who's Afraid of Virginia Woolf?* Edward Albee (Warner Bros.)
1964 *BBC Tribute to John F. Kennedy,* "That Was the Week That Was" cast (Decca)
1965 *John F. Kennedy—As We Remember Him,* Goddard Lieberson, producer (Columbia)
1966 *Edward R. Murrow—A Reporter Remembers, Vol. I, the War Years,* (Columbia)
1967 *Gallant Men,* Sen. Everett M. Dirksen (Capitol)
1968 *Lonesome Cities,* Rod McKuen (Warner Bros.-7 Arts)
1969 *We Love You, Call Collect,* Art Linkletter & Diane (Word-Capitol)
1970 *Why I Oppose the War in Vietnam,* Dr. Martin Luther King, Jr. (Black Forum)
1971 *Desiderata,* Les Crane (Warner Bros.)
1972 *Lenny,* Bruce Botnick, producer (Blue Thumb)
1973 *Jonathan Livingston Seagull,* Richard Harris (ABC-Dunhill)
1974 *Good Evening,* Peter Cook & Dudley Moore (Island)
1975 *Give 'Em Hell Harry,* James Whitmore (United Artists)
1976 *Great American Documents,* Orson Welles, Henry Fonda, Helen Hayes, James Earl Jones (CBS)
1977 *The Belle of Amherst,* Julie Harris (Credo)
1978 *Citizen Kane* (original motion picture soundtrack), Orson Welles (Mark 56)

BEST INSTRUMENTAL THEME/ BEST INSTRUMENTAL COMPOSITION (Excluding Jazz) (Award to Composer)

1961 "African Waltz," Galt MacDermott (Roulette)
1962 "A Taste of Honey," Bobby Scott and Ric Marlow (Reprise)
1963 "More (theme from *Mondo Cane*), Norman Newell, Nino Oliviero, Riz Ortolani (United Artists)
1964 "The Pink Panther Theme," Henry Mancini (RCA)
1965 —
1966 "Batman Theme," Neal Hefti (RCA)
1967 "Mission: Impossible," Lalo Schifrin (Dot)
1968 "Classical Gas," Mason Williams (Warner Bros.-7 Arts)
1969 "Midnight Cowboy," John Barry
1970 "Airport Love Theme," Alfred Newman (Decca)
1971 "Theme from *Summer of '42*," Michel Legrand (Warner Bros.)
1972 "Brian's Song," Michel Legrand
1973 "Last Tango in Paris," Cato Barbieri
1974 "Tubular Bells" (Theme from ("The Exorcist"), Mike Oldfield
1975 "Images," Michel Legrand
1976 "Bellavia," Chuck Mangione

1977 "Main title from *Star Wars*," John Williams (20th Century Fox)
1978 "Theme from *Close Encounters of the Third Kind*," John Williams (Ansto)

BEST SOUNDTRACK ALBUM OR RECORDING OF MUSIC SCORE FROM MOTION PICTURE OR TELEVISION

1959 *Anatomy of a Murder*, Duke Ellington (Columbia)
1960 *Exodus*, Ernest Gold (RCA)
1961 *Breakfast at Tiffany's*, Henry Mancini (RCA)
1962 —
1963 *Tom Jones*, John Addison (United Artists)
1964 *Mary Poppins*, Richard M. and Robert B. Sherman (Buena Vista)
1965 *The Sandpiper*, Johnny Mandel (Mercury)
1966 *Dr. Zhivago*, Maurice Jarre (MGM)
1967 *Mission: Impossible*, Lalo Schifrin (Dot)
1968 *The Graduate*, Paul Simon (additional music: Dave Grusin) (Columbia)
1969 *Butch Cassidy & the Sundance Kid*, Burt Bacharach (A&M)
1970 *Let It Be*, John Lennon, Paul McCartney, George Harrison, Ringo Starr (Apple)
1971 *Shaft*, Isaac Hayes (Enterprise)
1972 *The Godfather*, Nino Rota (Paramount)
1973 *Jonathan Livingston Seagull*, Neil Diamond (Columbia)
1974 *The Way We Were*, Marvin Hamlisch, Alan and Marilyn Bergman (Columbia)
1975 *Jaws*, John Williams (MCA)
1976 *Car Wash*, Norman Whitfield (MCA)
1977 *Star Wars*, John Williams (20th Century Fox)
1978 *Close Encounters of the Third Kind*, John Williams (Arista)

BEST BROADWAY SHOW ALBUM/ BEST SHOW ALBUM (Original Cast)/BEST SCORE FROM ORIGINAL CAST SHOW ALBUM (Award to Composer since 1961; Award to Composer and Producer since 1967)

1959 *Gypsy*, Ethel Merman (Columbia)
  Redhead, Gwen Verdon (RCA)
1960 *The Sound of Music*, Mary Martin (Columbia)
1961 *How to Succeed in Business without Really Trying*, Frank Loesser (RCA)
1962 *No Strings*, Richard Rodgers (Capitol)
1963 *She Loves Me*, Jerry Bock, Sheldon Harnick (MGM)
1964 *Funny Girl*, Jule Styne, Bob Merrill (Capitol)
1965 *On a Clear Day*, Alan Lerner,
1966 *Mame*, Jerry Herman (Columbia)
1967 *Cabaret*, Fred Ebb & John Kander, composers; Goddard Lieberson, producer (Columbia)
1968 *Hair*, Gerome Ragni, James Rado, Galt MacDermott, composers; Andy Wiswell, producer (RCA)
1969 *Promises, Promises*, Burt Bacharach & Hal David, composers; Henry Jerome, Phil Ramone, producers (Liberty-United Artists)
1970 *Company*, Stephen Sondheim, composer; Thomas Z. Shepard, producer (Columbia)
1971 *Godspell*, Stephen Schwartz, composer and producer (Bell)
1972 *Don't Bother Me, I Can't Cope*, Micki Grant, composer; Jerry Ragavoy, producer (Polydor)
1973 *A Little Night Music*, Stephen Sondheim, composer; Goddard Lieberson, producer (Columbia)
1974 *Raisin*, Judd Woldin & Robert Brittan, composers; Thomas Z. Shepard, producer (Columbia)

1975 *The Wiz*, Charlie Smalls, composer; Jerry Wexler, producer (Atlantic)
1976 *Bubbling Brown Sugar*, various composers; Hugo & Luigi, producers (H&L)
1977 *Annie*, Charles Strouse & Martin Charnin, composers, Larry Morton, Charles Sprouse, producers (Columbia)
1978 *Ain't Misbehavin'*, Thomas Z. Shepard, producer (RCA)

BEST JAZZ PERFORMANCE/ SOLO/SOLO OR SMALL GROUP/ SMALL GROUP OR SOLOIST WITH SMALL GROUP

1958 Ella Fitzgerald, *Ella Fitzgerald Sings the Duke Ellington Song Book* (Verve)
1959 Ella Fitzgerald, *Ella Swings Lightly* (Verve)
1960 Andre Previn, *West Side Story* (Contemporary)
1961 Andre Previn, *Andre Previn Plays Harold Arlen* (Contemporary)
1962 Stan Getz, *Desafinado* (Verve)
1963 Bill Evans, *Conversations with Myself* (Verve)
1964 Stan Getz, *Getz/Gilberto* (Verve)
1965 Ramsey Lewis Trio, *The "In" Crowd* (Cadet)
1966 Wes Montgomery, *Goin' Out of My Head* (Verve)
1967 Cannonball Adderley Quintet, *Mercy, Mercy, Mercy* (Capitol)
1968 Bill Evans Trio, *Bill Evans at the Montreux Jazz Festival* (Verve)
1969 Wes Montgomery, *Willow Weep for Me* (Verve)
1970 Bill Evans, *Alone* (MGM)
1971 Bill Evans, *The Bill Evans Album* (Columbia)
1972 Gary Burton, *Alone at Last* (Atlantic)

BEST JAZZ VOCAL PERFORMANCE

1976 Ella Fitzgerald, *Fitzgerald & Pass...Again* (Pablo)
1977 Al Jarreau, *Look to the Rainbow* (Warner Bros.)
1978 Al Jarreau, *All Fly Home* (Warner Bros.)

BEST JAZZ PERFORMANCE BY A SOLOIST

1973 Art Tatum, *God Is in the House* (Onyx)
1974 Charlie Parker, *First Recordings* (Onyx)
1975 Dizzy Gillespie, *Oscar Peterson and Dizzy Gillespie* (Pablo)
1976 Count Basie, *Basie & Zoot* (Pablo)
1977 Oscar Peterson, *The Giants* (Pablo)
1978 Oscar Peterson, *Montreux '77— Oscar Peterson Jam* (Pablo)

BEST JAZZ PERFORMANCE BY A GROUP/LARGE INSTRUMENTAL GROUP/LARGE GROUP OR SOLOIST WITH LARGE GROUP

1958 Count Basie, *Basie* (Roulette)
1959 Jonah Jones, *I Dig Chicks* (Capitol)
1960 Henry Mancini, *Blues and the Beat* (RCA)
1961 Stan Kenton, *West Side Story* (Capitol)
1962 Stan Kenton, *Adventures in Jazz* (Capitol)
1963 Woody Herman Band, *Encore: Woody Herman, 1963* (Philips)
1964 Laurindo Almeida, *Guitar from Ipanema* (Capitol)
1965 Duke Ellington Orchestra, *Ellington '66* (Reprise)
1966 —
1967 Duke Ellington, *Far East Suite* (RCA)
1968 Duke Ellington, *And His Mother Called Him Bill* (RCA)

1969 Quincy Jones, *Walking in Space* (A&M)
1970 Miles Davis, *Bitches Brew* (Columbia)
1971 Bill Evans Trio, *The Bill Evans Album* (Columbia)
1972 Freddie Hubbard, *First Light* (CTI)
1973 Supersax, *Supersax Plays Bird* (Capitol)
1974 Oscar Peterson, Joe Pass, Niels Pedersen, *The Trio* (Pablo)
1975 Chick Corea and Return to Forever, *No Mystery* (Polydor)
1976 Chick Corea, *The Leprechaun* (Polydor)
1977 Phil Woods, *The Phil Woods Six— Live from the Showboat* (RCA)
1978 Chick Corea, *Friends* (Polydor)

BEST JAZZ PERFORMANCE BY A BIG BAND

1971 Duke Ellington, *New Orleans Suite* (Atlantic)
1972 Duke Ellington, *Toga Brava Suite* (United Artists)
1973 Woody Herman, *Giant Steps* (Fantasy)
1974 Woody Herman, *Thundering Herd* (Fantasy)
1975 Phil Woods with Michel Legrand & His Orchestra, *Images* (Gryphon-RCA)
1976 Duke Ellington, *The Ellington Suites* (Pablo)
1977 Count Basie and His Orchestra, *Prime Time* (Pablo)
1978 Thad Jones and Mel Lewis, *Live in Munich* (Horizon-A&M)

BEST ORIGINAL JAZZ COMPOSITION

1961 "African Waltz," Galt MacDermott (Roulette)
1962 "Cast Your Fate to the Winds," Vince Guaraldi (Fantasy)
1963 "Gravy Waltz," Steve Allen, Ray Brown
1964 "The Cat," Lalo Schifrin (Verve)
1965 "Jazz Suite on the Mass Texts," Lalo Schifrin (RCA)
1966 "In the Beginning God," Duke Ellington (RCA)

BEST ARRANGER/BEST INSTRUMENTAL ARRANGER

1958 Henry Mancini, *The Music from Peter Gunn* (RCA)
1959 Billy May, *Come Dance with Me* (Capitol)
1960 Henry Mancini, *Mr. Lucky* (RCA)
1961 Henry Mancini, *Moon River* (RCA)
1962 Henry Mancini, *Baby Elephant Walk* (RCA)
1963 Quincy Jones, *I Can't Stop Loving You* (Reprise)
1964 Henry Mancini, *Pink Panther* (RCA)
1965 Herb Alpert, *A Taste of Honey* (A&M)
1966 Herb Alpert, *What Now My Love* (A&M)
1967 Burt Bacharach, *Alfie* (A&M)
1968 Mike Post, *Classical Gas* (Warner Bros.)
1969 Henry Mancini, *Love Theme from Romeo & Juliet* (RCA)
1970 Henry Mancini, *Theme from "Z"* (RCA)
1971 Isaac Hayes and Johnny Allen, *Theme from Shaft* (Enterprise)
1972 Don Ellis, *Theme from the French Connection* (Columbia)
1973 Quincy Jones, *Summer in the City* (A&M)
1974 Pat Williams, *Threshold* (Capittol)
1975 Mike Post, Pete Carpenter, *The Rockford Files* (MGM)
1976 Chick Corea, *Leprechauns Dream* (Polydor)
1977 Harry Betts, Perry Botkin, Jr. and Barry De Vorzon, *Nadia's Theme*

(*The Young and the Restless*) (Arista)
1978 Quincy Jones and Robert Freedman, *The Wiz* (MCA)

BEST ALBUM COVER/BEST ALBUM COVER, GRAPHIC ARTS/ BEST ALBUM PACKAGE
(Award to Art Director)

1958 *Only the Lonely*, Frank Sinatra (Capitol)
1959 *Shostakovich Symphony No. 5*, Robert M. Jones (RCA)
1960 *Latin a la Lee*, Marvin Schwartz (Capitol)
1961 *Judy at Carnegie Hall*, Jim Sike (Capitol)
1962 *Lena...Lovely and Alive*, Robert Jones (RCA)
1963 *The Barbra Streisand Album*, John Berg (Columbia)
1964 *People*, Robert Cato, art director; Don Bronstein, photographer (Columbia)
1965 —
1966 *Revolver*, Klaus Voormann (Capitol)
1967 *Sgt. Pepper's Lonely Hearts Club Band*, Peter Blake and Jann Haworth (Capitol)
1968 *Underground*, John Berg and Richard Mantel, art directors; Horn/Griner Studio, photographer (Columbia)
1969 *America the Beautiful*, Evelyn J. Kelbish (painting), David Stahlberg, graphics
1970 *Indianola Mississippi Seeds*, Robert Lockart (cover design), Ivan Nagy (photographer) (ABC)
1971 *Pollution*, Deane O. Torrance and Gene Brownell (Prophesy)
1972 *The Siegel Schwall Band*, Acy Lehman, Harvey Dinnerstein (Wooden Nickel)
1973 *Tommy*, Wilkes & Braun, Inc. (Ode)
1974 *Come & Gone*, Ed Thrasher and Christopher Whorf (Warner Bros.)
1975 *Honey*, Jim Ladwig (Mercury)
1976 *Chicago X*, Jim Berg (Columbia)
1977 *Simple Dreams*, Kosh (Asylum)
1978 *Boys in the Trees*, Johnny Lee and Tony Lane (Elektra)

BEST ALBUM NOTES
(Award to Annotator)

1963 Stanley Dance, Leonard Feather, *The Ellington Era* (Columbia)
1964 Stanton Catlin, Carleton Beals. *Mexico* (*Legacy Collection*) (Columbia)
1965 Stan Cornyn, *September of My Years* (Reprise)
1966 Stan Cornyn, *Sinatra at the Sands* (Reprise)
1967 John D. Loudermilk, *Suburban Attitudes in Country Verse* (RCA)
1968 Johnny Cash, *Johnny Cash at Folsom Prison* (Columbia)
1969 Johnny Cash, *Nashville Skyline* (Columbia) (Columbia)
1970 Chris Albertson, *The World's Greatest Blues Singer* (Columbia)
1971 Sam Samudio, *Sam, Hard and Heavy* (Atlantic)
1972 Tom T. Hall, *Tom T. Hall's Greatest Hits* (Mercury)
1973 Dan Morgenstern, *God Is in the House* (Onyx)
1974 Charles R. Townsend, *For the Last Time* (United Artists)
Dan Morgenstern, *The Hawk Flies* (Milestone)
1975 Pete Hamill, *Blood on the Tracks* (Columbia)
1976 Dan Morgenstern, *The Changing Face of Harlem*, the Savoy Sessions (Savoy)
1977 George T. Simon, *Bing Crosby: A Legendary Performer* (RCA)
1978 Michael Brooks, *A Bing Crosby Collection, Vols. I & II* (Columbia)

BEST ENGINEERED RECORD, OTHER THAN CLASSICAL/BEST ENGINEERING CONTRIBUTION/ BEST ENGINEERED RECORDING OTHER THAN CLASSICAL

1958 Ted Keep, *The Chipmunk Song* (Liberty)
1959 Robert Simpson, *Belafonte at Carnegie Hall* (RCA)
1960 Luis P. Valentin, *Ella Fitzgerald Sings the George and Ira Gershwin Song Book* (Verve)
1961 Robert Arnold, *Judy at Carnegie Hall* (Capitol)
1962 Al Schmitt, *Hatari!* (RCA)
1963 James Malloy, *Charade* (RCA)
1964 Phil Ramone, *Getz/Gilberto* (Verve)
1965 Larry Levine, *A Taste of Honey* (A&M)
1966 Eddie Brackett, Lee Herschberg, *Strangers in the Night* (Reprise)
1967 G. E. Emerick, *Sgt. Pepper's Lonely Hearts Club Band* (Capitol)
1968 Joe Polito, Hugh Davies, *Wichita Lineman* (Capitol)
1969 Geoff Emerick and Phillip McDonald, *Abbey Road* (Apple)
1970 Roy Halee, *Bridge over Troubled Water* (Columbia)
1971 Dave Purple, Ron Capone, Henry Bush, *"Theme from Shaft"* (Enterprise)
1972 Armin Steiner, *Moods* (UNI)
1973 Robert Margouleff and Malcolm Cecil, *Innervisions* (Tamla-Motown)
1974 Geoff Emerick, *Band on the Run* (Apple)
1975 Brooks Arthur, Larry Alexander and Russ Payne, *Between the Lines* (Columbia)
1976 Al Schmitt, *Breezin'* (Warner Bros.)
1977 Roger Nichols, Elliot Scheiner, Bill Schnee and Al Schmitt, *Aja* (ABC)
1978 Roger Nichols, Al Schmitt, *FM ("No Static at All")* (MCA)

BEST PRODUCER OF THE YEAR

1974 Thom Bell
1975 Arif Mardin
1976 Stevie Wonder
1977 Peter Asher
1978 Bee Gees, Albhy Galuten & Karl Richardson

ALBUM OF THE YEAR, CLASSICAL

1961 *Stravinsky Conducts, 1960: Le Sacre du Printemps; Petrouchka,* Igor Stravinsky conducting Columbia Symphony (Columbia)
1962 *Vladimir Horowitz,* Vladimir Horowitz (Columbia)
1963 *Britten: War Requiem,* Benjamin Britten conducting London Symphony Orchestra and Chorus (London)
1964 *Bernstein: Symphony No. 3 ("Kaddish"),* Leonard Bernstein conducting New York Philharmonic (Columbia)
1965 *Horowitz at Carnegie Hall,* Vladimir Horowitz (Columbia)
1966 *Ives: Symphony No. 1 in D Minor,* Morton Gould conducting Chicago Symphony (RCA)
1967 *Berg: Wozzeck,* Pierre Boulez, Paris National Opera (Columbia)
1968 —
1969 *Switched On Bach,* Walter Carlos (Columbia)
1970 *Berlioz: Les Troyens,* Colin Davis, Royal Opera House Orchestra (Philips)
1971 *Horowitz Plays Rachmaninoff,* Vladimir Horowitz (Columbia)
1972 *Mahler: Symphony No. 8,* Georg Solti conducting Chicago Symphony Orchestra, Vienna Boys Choir, Vienna State Opera Chorus,

Vienna Sinverein Chorus and Soloists (London)
- **1973** *Bartok: Concerto for Orchestra,* Pierre Boulez conducting New York Philharmonic (Columbia)
- **1974** *Berlioz: Symphonie Fantastique,* Georg Solti conducting Chicago Symphony (London)
- **1975** *Beethoven: Symphonies (9) Complete,* Sir Georg Solti conducting Chicago Symphony (London)
- **1976** *Beethoven: Five Piano Concertos,* Artur Rubinstein, Daniel Barenboim conducting London Philharmonic (RCA)
- **1977** *Concert of the Century,* Leonard Bernstein, Vladimir Horowitz, Isaac Stern, Mstislav Rostropovich, Dietrich Fischer-Dieskau, Yehudi Menuhin and Lyndon Woodside (Columbia)
- **1978** *Brahms: Concerto for Violin in D Major,* Itzhak Perlman, Carlo Maria Giulini conducting Chicago Symphony (Angel)

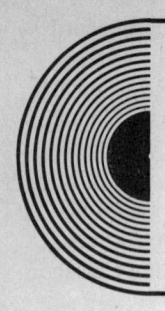

GOLD AND PLATINUM RECORD AWARDS

GOLD RECORD AWARDS—ALBUMS (500,000 units sold)

1958

Oklahoma, Gordon MacRae (Capitol)

1959

Hymns, Ernie Ford (Capitol)
Johnny's Greatest Hits, Johnny Mathis (Columbia)
Music Man—original cast (Capitol)
Sing Along with Mitch, Mitch Miller (Columbia)
South Pacific, Rodgers & Hammerstein (RCA Victor)
Peter Gunn, Henry Mancini (RCA Victor)

1960

Student Prince, Mario Lanza (RCA Victor)
60 Years of Music—honoring 30 great artists (RCA Victor)
Elvis, Elvis Presley (RCA Victor)
Pat's Great Hits, Pat Boone (Dot)
Kingston Trio at Large, Kingston Trio (Capitol)
Kingston Trio, Kingston Trio (Capitol)
More Sing Along with Mitch, Mitch Miller (Columbia)

Heavenly, Johnny Mathis (Columbia)
Warm, Johnny Mathis (Columbia)
Love Is the Thing, Nat King Cole (Capitol)
Here We Go Again, Kingston Trio (Capitol)
From the Hungry i, Kingston Trio (Capitol)
Sound of Music—original cast (Columbia)
Merry Christmas, Johnny Mathis (Columbia)
Christmas Sing Along, Mitch Miller (Columbia)
Still More! Sing Along, Mitch Miller (Columbia)

1961

Calcutta Album, Lawrence Welk
Come Dance with Me, Frank Sinatra (Capitol)
Sold Out, Kingston Trio (Capitol)
Glenn Miller Story, Glenn Miller Orchestra (RCA Victor)
Christmas Carols, Mantovani (London)
Theatre Land, Mantovani (London)
Film Encorse Vol. I, Mantovani (London)
Gems Forever, Mantovani (London)
Strauss Waltzes, Mantovani (London)

*Issued by Recording Industry Association of America, Inc. (RIAA).

Spirituals, Ernie Ford (Capitol)
Elvis' Golden Records, Elvis Presley (RCA Victor)
Belafonte at Carnegie Hall, Harry Belafonte (RCA Victor)
Tchaikovsky Concerto, Van Cliburn (RCA Victor)
Encore—Golden Hits, The Platters (Mercury)
Blue Hawaii, Elvis Presley (RCA Victor)

1962

Holiday Sing Along with Mitch, Mitch Miller (Columbia)
Party Sing Along with Mitch, Mitch Miller (Columbia)
More Johnny's Greatest Hits, Johnny Mathis (Columbia)
West Side Story—original cast (Columbia)
Camelot—original cast (Columbia)
Flower Drum Song—original cast (Columbia)
Theme from a Summer Place, Billy Vaughn (Dot)
Blue Hawaii, Billy Vaughn (Dot)
Sail Along Silvery Moon, Billy Vaughn (Dot)
Bob Newhart Button-down Mind, Bob Newhart (Warner Bros.)
Saturday Night Sing Along with Mitch, Mitch Miller (Columbia)
Memories Sing Along with Mitch, Mitch Miller (Columbia)
Sentimental Sing Along with Mitch, Mitch Miller (Columbia)
Star Carol, Ernie Ford (Capitol)
Nearer the Cross, Ernie Ford (Capitol)
Frank Sinatra Sings for Only the Lonely, Frank Sinatra (Capitol)
Nice 'n' Easy, Frank Sinatra (Capitol)
Songs for Swingin' Lovers, Frank Sinatra (Capitol)
String Along, Kingston Trio (Capitol)
Music, Martinis and Memories, Jackie Gleason (Capitol)
Music for Lovers Only, Jackie Gleason (Capitol)
Judy at Carnegie Hall, Judy Garland (Capitol)
Happy Times Sing Along, Mitch Miller (Columbia)
Memories Are Made of This, Ray Conniff (Columbia)
Concert in Rhythm, Columbia (Ray Conniff (Columbia)
'S Marvelous, Ray Conniff (Columbia)
Modern Sounds in Country & Western Music, Ray Charles (ABC-Paramount)
Breakfast at Tiffany's, Henry Mancini (RCA Victor)
This Is Sinatra, Frank Sinatra (Capitol)
Bouquet, Percy Faith Strings (Columbia)
So Much in Love, Ray Conniff (Columbia)
Faithfully, Johnny Mathis (Columbia)
Swing Softly, Johnny Mathis (Columbia)
Open Fire, Two Guitars, Johnny Mathis (Columbia)
Peter, Paul and Mary, Peter, Paul and Mary (Warner Bros.)
My Son the Folk Singer, Allan Sherman (Warner Bros.)
The First Family, Vaughn Meader (Cadence)

1963

West Side Story—motion picture soundtrack (Columbia)
Glorious Sound of Christmas, Eugene Ormandy and The Philadelphia Orchestra (Columbia)
1812 Overture—Tchaikovsky, Antal Dorati and the Minneapolis Symphony (Mercury)
Exodus—motion picture soundtrack (RCA Victor)
Calypso, Harry Belafonte (RCA Victor)
G.I. Blues, Elvis Presley (RCA Victor)
Season's Greetings from Perry Como, Perry Como (RCA Victor)
VIVA, Percy Faith (Columbia)
The Music Man—motion picture soundtrack (Warner Bros.)
Time Out, Dave Brubeck Quartet (Columbia)

I Left My Heart in San Francisco, Tony Bennett (Columbia)
Elvis' Christmas Album, Elvis Presley (RCA Victor)
Girls, Girls, Girls, Elvis Presley (RCA Victor)
Belafonte Returns to Carnegie Hall, Harry Belafonte (RCA Victor)
Belafonte, Harry Belafonte (RCA Victor)
Jump-Up Calypso, Harry Belafonte (RCA Victor)
Moving, Peter, Paul and Mary (Warner Bros.)
Exodus, Mantovani (London)
Days of Wine and Roses, Andy Williams (Columbia)
Moon River and Other Great Movie Themes, Andy Williams (Columbia)
Handel's Messiah, Eugene Ormandy and The Philadelphia Orchestra (Columbia)
Christmas with Conniff, Ray Conniff (Columbia)
The Lord's Prayer, Mormon Tabernacle Choir (Columbia)
Porgy and Bess—motion picture soundtrack (Columbia)
Folk Song Sing Along, Mitch Miller (Columbia)
In the Wind, Peter, Paul and Mary (Warner Bros.)
Singing Nun, Soeur Sourire (Philips)
The Second Barbra Streisand Album, Barbra Streisand (Columbia)
Hello, Dolly!—original cast (RCA Victor)
Hello, Dolly!, Louis Armstrong (Kapp)
The Wonderful World of Andy Williams, Andy Williams (Columbia)
Christmas Hymns and Carols, Robert Shaw (RCA Victor)
Victory at Sea, Volume I, Robert Russell Bennett (RCA Victor)
Something New, The Beatles (Capitol)
The Best of the Kingston Trio, Kingston Trio (Capitol)
Unforgettable, Nat King Cole (Capitol)
Funny Girl—original cast (Capitol)
Ramblin, New Christy Minstrels (Columbia)
The Barbra Streisand Album, Barbra Streisand (Columbia)
Johnny Horton's Greatest Hits, Johnny Horton (Columbia)
Cotton Candy, Al Hirt (RCA Victor)
The Andy Williams Christmas Album, Andy Williams (Columbia)
Cal Me Irresponsible, Andy Williams (Columbia)
My Fair Lady—motion picture soundtrack (Columbia)
Beatles '65, The Beatles (Capitol)
The Beatles' Story, The Beatles (Capitol)
Mary Poppins—motion picture soundtrack (Vista)

1964

My Fair Lady—original cast
John Fitzgerald Kennedy: A Memorial Album (Premier Albums)
Carousel—motion picture soundtrack (Capitol)
The King and I—motion picture soundtrack (Capitol)
Ramblin' Rose, Nat King Cole (Capitol)
Meet The Beatles! The Beatles (Capitol)
Honey in the Horn, Al Hirt (RCA Victor)
The Beatles' Second Album, The Beatles (Capitol)

1965

Glad All Over, The Dave Clark Five (Epic)
Peter, Paul and Mary in Concert, Peter, Paul and Mary (Warner Bros.)
Everybody Loves Somebody, Dean Martin (Reprise)
Wonderland of Golden Hits, Andre Kostelanetz (Columbia)
Barbra Streisand/The Third Album, Barbra Streisand (Columbia)
Ring of Fire, Johnny Cash (Columbia)
Beach Boys in Concert, The Beach Boys (Capitol)

All Summer Long, The Beach Boys (Capitol)
Sugar Lips, Al Hirt (RCA Victor)
People, Barbra Streisand (Columbia)
The Sound of Music—motion picture soundtrack (RCA Victor)
Trini Lopez at PJ's, Trini Lopez (Warner Bros.)
Getz/Gilberto, Stan Getz (Verve)
Beatles VI, The Beatles (Capitol)
Dear Heart, Andy Williams (Columbia)
Help!, The Beatles (Capitol)
Introducing Herman's Hermits, Herman's Hermits (MGM)
Herman's Hermits on Tour, Herman's Hermits (MGM)
More Encore of Golden Hits, The Platters (Mercury)
Return of Roger Miller, Roger Miller (Smash)
Great Songs from My Fair Lady, Andy Williams (Columbia)
Gunfire Ballads & Trail Songs, Marty Robbins (Columbia)
Look at Us, Sonny and Cher (Atco)
The Beach Boys Today, The Beach Boys (Capitol)
The Pink Panther, Henry Mancini (RCA Victor)
Out of Our Heads, The Rolling Stones (London)
Fiddler on the Roof—original cast (RCA Victor)
Surfer Girl, The Beach Boys (Capitol)
Surfin' USA, The Beach Boys (Capitol)
Sinatra's Sinatra, Frank Sinatra (Reprise)
Welcome to the LBJ Ranch (Capitol)
My Name Is Barbra, Barbra Streisand (Columbia)
The Door Is Still Open to My Heart, Dean Martin (Warner Bros.)
Going Places, Herb Alpert and the Tijuana Brass (A&M)
Whipped Cream & Other Delights, Herb Alpert and the Tijuana Brass (A&M)
Rubber Soul, The Beatles (Capitol)

1966

My Name Is Barbra, Two, Barbra Streisand (Columbia)
The Best of Herman's Hermits, Herman's Hermits (MGM)
December's Children, Rolling Stones (London)
Joan Baez, Vol. 2, Joan Baez (Vanguard)
Joan Baez, Joan Baez (Vanguard)
Joan Baez in Concert, Joan Baez (Vanguard)
September of My Years, Frank Sinatra (Reprise)
A Man and His Music, Frank Sinatra (Reprise)
Summer Days, The Beach Boys (Capitol)
Golden Hits, Roger Miller (Smash)
Ballads of the Green Berets, SSGT. Barry Sadler (RCA Victor)
Ray Orbison's Greatest Hits, Roy Orbison (Monument)
Living Language Spanish (Young People's)
Living Language French (Young People's)
Color Me Barbra, Barbra Streisand (Columbia)
I'm the One Who Loves You, Dean Martin (Reprise)
Big Hits (High Tide and Green Grass), Rolling Stones (London)
Oliver—original cast (RCA Victor)
South of the Border, Herb Alpert and the Tijuana Brass (A&M)
The Lonely Bull, Herb Alpert and the Tijuana Brass (A&M)
What Now My Love, Herb Alpert and the Tijuana Brass (A&M)
Herb Alpert's Tijuana Brass Volume 2, Herb Alpert and the Tijuana Brass (A&M)
My World, Eddy Arnold (RCA Victor)
South Pacific—original cast (Columbia)
If You Can Believe Your Eyes and Ears, The Mama's and the Papa's (Dunhill)
Yesterday and Today, The Beatles (Capitol)

The Best of Jim Reeves, Jim Reeves (RCA Victor)
The Best of The Animals, The Animals (MGM)
Dang Me, Roger Miller (Smash)
Gold Vault of Hits, Four Seasons (Philips)
Aftermath, The Rolling Stones (London)
Dr. Zhivago—motion picture soundtrack (MGM)
Think Ethnic, Smothers Brothers (Mercury)
Strangers in the Night, Frank Sinatra (Reprise)
Revolver, The Beatles (Capitol)
The Dave Clark Five's Greatest Hits, Dave Clark Five (Epic)
Somewhere My Love, Ray Conniff (Columbia)
The Shadow of Your Smile, Andy Williams (Columbia)
The Best of Al Hirt, Al Hirt (RCA Victor)
I Started Out as a Child, Bill Cosby (Warner Bros.)
Wonderfulness, Bill Cosby (Warner Bros.)
Why Is There Air?, Bill Cosby (Warner Bros.)
Bill Cosby Is a Very Funny Fellow, Right?, Bill Cosby (Warner Bros.)
Jeanette MacDonald and Nelson Eddy Favorites, Jeanette MacDonald and Nelson Eddy (RCA Victor)
Perry Como Sings Merry Christmas Music, Perry Como (Camden)
The Monkees, The Monkees (Colgems)
Elvis Presley, Elvis Presley (RCA Victor)
Elvis' Gold Records, Vol. 2, Elvis Presley (RCA Victor)
Elvis' Golden Records, Vol. 3, Elvis Presley (RCA Victor)
Dean Martin Sings Again, Dean Martin (Reprise)
Boots, Nancy Sinatra (Reprise)
Soul and Inspiration, Righteous Brothers (Verve)
The Mamas and the Papas, Mamas and the Papas (ABC-Dunhill)
Bobby Vinton's Greatest Hits, Bobby Vinton (Epic)
Little Deuce Coupe, The Beach Boys (Capitol)
Shut Down—Vol. 2, The Beach Boys (Capitol)
Winchester Cathedral, New Vaudeville Band (Fontana)
Spanish Eyes, Al Martino (Capitol)

1967

Just Like Us, Paul Revere & The Raiders (Columbia)
More of The Monkees, The Monkees (Colgems)
S.R.O., Herb Alpert and the Tijuana Brass (A&M)
Got Live if You Want It, The Rolling Stones (London)
Till, Roger Williams (Kapp)
Songs of the Fabulous Fifties Part 1, Roger Williams (Kapp)
Songs of the Fabulous Fifties Part 2, Roger Williams (Kapp)
Roger Williams' Greatest Hits, Roger Williams (Kapp)
Yakety Sax, Boots Randolph (Monument)
That's Life, Frank Sinatra (Reprise)
Lou Rawls Live! Lou Rawls (Capitol)
The Two Sides of the Smothers Brothers, Smothers Brothers (Mercury)
Between the Buttons, The Rolling Stones (London)
Midnight Ride, Paul Revere & The Raiders (Columbia)
Thoroughly Modern Millie—motion picture soundtrack (Decca)
The Best of Mancini, Henry Mancini (RCA Victor)
An Evening with Belafonte, Harry Belafonte (RCA Victor)
Best of The Beach Boys, The Beach Boys (Capitol)

Winchester Cathedral, Lawrence Welk (Dot)
Spirit of '67, Paul Revere & The Raiders (Columbia)
The Mamas and the Papas Deliver, Mamas and the Papas (Dunhill)
Born Free, Roger Williams (Kapp)
Mame—original cast (Columbia)
Headquarters, The Monkees (Colgems)
My Cup Runneth Over, Ed Ames (RCA Victor)
Stranger on the Shore, Mr. Acker Bilk (Atco)
I Never Loved a Man the Way I Love You, Aretha Franklin (Atlantic)
Sgt. Pepper's Lonely Hearts Club Band, Beatles (Capitol)
Man of La Mancha—original cast (Kapp)
Revenge, Bill Cosby (Warner Bros.)
Parsley, Sage, Rosemary & Thyme, Simon & Garfunkel (Columbia)
Born Free, Andy Williams (Columbia)
The Best of the Lovin' Spoonful, Lovin' Spoonful (Kama Sutra)
Themes for Young Lovers, Percy Faith & His Orchestra (Columbia)
I Walk the Line, Johnny Cash (Columbia)
Surrealistic Pillow, Jefferson Airplane (RCA Victor)
Flowers, Rolling Stones (London)
A Man and a Woman—motion picture soundtrack (United Artists)
Ebb Tide, Earl Grant (Decca)
Blue Midnight, Bert Kaempfert (Decca)
Sounds Like, Herb Alpert & the Tijuana Brass (A&M)
Sergio Mendes and Brasil '66, Sergio Mendes & Brasil '66 (A&M)
Sounds of Silence, Simon & Garfunkel (Columbia)
Paul Revere & the Raiders Greatest Hits, Paul Revere & the Raiders (Columbia)
Blonde on Blonde, Bob Dylan (Columbia)
Highway 61, Bob Dylan (Columbia)
Bringing It All Back Home, Bob Dylan (Columbia)

The Doors, Doors (Elektra)
2nd Vault of Golden Hits, Four Seasons (Philips)
Ode to Billie Joe, Bobbie Gentry (Capitol)
Tony Bennett's Greatest Hits Volume III, Tony Bennett (Columbia)
Pisces, Aquarius, Capricorn and Jones Ltd., Monkees (Colgems)
Sinatra at The Sands, Frank Sinatra (Reprise)
Along Comes The Association, Association (Warner Bros.)
Their Satanic Majesty's Request, Rolling Stones (London)
Release Me, Engelbert Humperdinck (Parrot)
Herb Alpert's Ninth, Herb Alpert & the Tijuana Brass (A&M)
Magical Mystery Tour, The Beatles (Capitol)
Merry Christmas to All, Ray Conniff (Columbia)
The Button-down Mind Strikes Back, Bob Newhart (Warner Bros.)
Insight Out, Association (Warner Bros.)

1968

Jim Nabors Sings, Jim Nabors (Columbia)
Bob Dylan's Greatest Hits, Bob Dylan (Columbia)
Strange Days, Doors (Elektra)
Dream with Dean, Dean Martin (Reprise)
Guantanamera, Sandpipers (A&M)
Farewell to the First Golden Era, Mamas and the Papas (Dunhill)
How Great Thou Art, Elvis Presley (RCA Victor)
Distant Drums, Jim Reeves (RCA Victor)
Blooming Hits, Paul Mauriat and Orchestra (Philips)
Best of Buck Owens, Buck Owens (Capitol)
Doctor Doolittle—motion picture soundtrack (20th Century Fox)

The Byrds' Greatest Hits, The Byrds (Columbia)
Welcome to My World, Dean Martin (Reprise)
Houston, Dean Martin (Reprise)
Are You Experienced, Jimi Hendrix (Reprise)
John Wesley Harding, Bob Dylan (Columbia)
The Graduate—motion picture soundtrack (Columbia)
The Best of Eddy Arnold, Eddy Arnold (RCA Victor)
The Great Caruso, Mario Lanza (RCA Victor)
Modern Sounds in Country and Western Music, Vol. 2, Ray Charles (ABC)
Greatest Hits, Ray Charles (ABC)
Loving You, Elvis Presley (RCA Victor)
Turtles' Greatest Hits, The Turtles (White Whale)
The Birds, The Bees and The Monkees, The Monkees (Colgems)
Gigi—motion picture soundtrack (MGM)
Bookends, Simon & Garfunkel (Columbia)
Somewhere There's a Someone, Dean Martin (Reprise)
Persuasive Percussion, Enoch Light (Command)
Songs I Sing on The Jackie Gleason Show, Frank Fontaine (ABC)
Love, Andy, Andy Williams (Columbia)
Doris Day's Greatest Hits, Doris Day (Columbia)
Disraeli Gears, Cream (Atco)
Merry Christmas, Andy Williams (Columbia)
Glenn Miller and His Orchestra, Glenn Miller (RCA Victor)
To Russell, My Brother, Whom I Slept With, Bill Cosby (Warner Bros.)
The Beat of the Brass, Herb Alpert and the Tijuana Brass (A&M)
Wheels of Fire, Cream (Atco)
Groovin', The Rascals (Atlantic)
Vanilla Fudge, Vanilla Fudge (Atco)
Collections, The Rascals (Atlantic)
Somewhere My Love, Roger Williams (Kapp)
Waiting for the Sun, The Doors (Elektra)
The Good, the Bad and the Ugly—motion picture soundtrack (United Artists)
A Man and His Soul, Ray Charles (ABC)
Lady Soul, Aretha Franklin (Atlantic)
Look Around, Sergio Mendes & Brasil '66 (A&M)
The Young Rascals, The Rascals (Atlantic)
Time Peace—The Rascals Greatest Hits, The Rascals (Atlantic)
Camelot—motion picture soundtrack (Warner Bros.)
Feliciano, Jose Feliciano (RCA Victor)
Axis: Bold as Love, Jimi Hendrix (Reprise)
Cheap Thrills, Janis Joplin with Big Brother and the Holding Company (Columbia)
By the Time I Get to Phoenix, Glen Campbell (Capitol)
Gentle on My Mind, Glen Campbell (Capitol)
My Love Forgive Me, Robert Goulet (Columbia)
Johnny Cash at Folsom Prison, Johnny Cash (Columbia)
Honey, Andy Williams (Columbia)
Purple Onion, Smothers Brothers (Mercury)
Wichita Lineman, Glen Campbell (Capitol)
Electric Ladyland, Jimi Hendrix (Reprise)
The Kinks Greatest Hits, The Kinks (Reprise)
Honey, Bobby Goldsboro (United Artists)
Dean Martin Christmas Album, Dean Martin (Reprise)
Steppenwolf, Steppenwolf (Dunhill)
Aretha Now, Aretha Franklin (Atlantic)

In-a-Gadda-da-Vida, Iron Butterfly (Atco)
Fresh Cream, Cream (Atco)
The Time Has Come, Chambers Brothers (Columbia)
Walt Disney Presents The Jungle Book—motion picture soundtrack (Disneyland)
The Beatles, The Beatles (Apple)
The Christmas Album, Herb Alpert and the Tijuana Brass (A&M)
Harper Valley PTA, Jeannie C. Riley (Plantation)
Funny Girl—motion picture soundtrack (Columbia)
Beggars Banquet, The Rolling Stones (London)
The Sea, San Sebastian Strings (Warner Bros.)

1969

Walt Disney Presents The Story of Mary Poppins—storyteller LP (Disneyland)
Hey Little One, Glen Campbell (Capitol)
The Christmas Song, Nat King Cole (Capitol)
The Lettermen!!!...and "Live", The Lettermen (Capitol)
Wildflowers, Judy Collins (Elektra)
Album 1700, Peter, Paul and Mary (Warner Bros.)
Gentry/Campbell, Bobbie Gentry and Glen Campbell (Capitol)
Dean Martin's Greatest Hits, Volume I, Dean Martin (Reprise)
Yellow Submarine, The Beatles (Apple)
Steppenwolf the Second, Steppenwolf (Dunhill)
Who Will Answer?, Ed Ames (RCA)
Boots with Strings, Boots Randolph (Monument)
Dionne Warwick's Greatest Hits, Dionne Warwick (Scepter)
A Man without Love, Engelbert Humperdinck (Parrot)
The Last Waltz, Engelbert Humperdinck (Parrot)
The Association's Greatest Hits, The Association (Warner Bros.)
Wednesday Morning 3 A.M., Simon & Garfunkel (Columbia)
Wonderland by Night, Bert Kaempfert (Decca)
Bert Kaempfert's Greatest Hits, Bert Kaempfert (Decca)
Drummer Boy, Harry Simeone (20th Century Fox)
200 MPH, Bill Cosby (Warner Bros.)
Hair—original cast (RCA)
It Must Be Him, Ray Conniff (Columbia)
Young Girl, Union Gap (Columbia)
His Hand in Mine, Elvis Presley (RCA)
Blood, Sweat and Tears, Blood, Sweat and Tears (Columbia)
Galveston, Glen Campbell (Capitol)
Freedom Suite, The Rascals (Atlantic)
Goodbye, Cream (Atco)
Donovan's Greatest Hits, Donovan (Epic)
2001: A Space Odyssey—motion picture soundtrack (MGM)
Soulin', Lou Rawls (Capitol)
Best of The Lettermen, The Lettermen (Capitol)
Nashville Skyline, Bob Dylan (Columbia)
Fever Zone, Tom Jones (Parrot)
Help Yourself, Tom Jones (Parrot)
Equinox, Sergio Mendex & Brasil '66 (A&M)
A Day in the Life, Wes Montgomery (A&M)
Fool on the Hill, Sergio Mendes & Brasil '66 (A&M)
The Righteous Brothers Greatest Hits, The Righteous Brothers (Verve)
This Is Tom Jones, Tom Jones (Parrot)
H. William's Greatest Hits, Hank Williams (MGM)
The Very Best of Connie Francis, Connie Francis (MGM)
How the West Was Won—motion picture soundtrack (MGM)
Your Cheatin' Heart, Hank Williams (MGM)

852   GOLD RECORD AWARDS—ALBUMS

The Best of Herman's Hermits Vol. II, Herman's Hermits (MGM)
The Stripper and Other Fun Songs for the Family, David Rose and Orchestra (MGM)
There's a Kind of Hush All Over the World, Herman's Hermits (MGM)
Romeo & Juliet—motion picture soundtrack (Capitol)
Tom Jones Live!, Tom Jones (Parrot)
The Age of Aquarius, 5th Dimension (Soul City)
Elvis TV Special, Elvis Presley (RCA)
Ball, Iron Butterfly (Atco)
Led Zeppelin, Led Zeppelin (Atlantic)
Johnny Cash's Greatest Hits, Johnny Cash (Columbia)
Oliver—motion picture soundtrack (Colgems)
The Soft Parade, The Doors (Elektra)
Johnny Cash at San Quentin, Johnny Cash (Columbia)
Switched On Bach, Walter Carlos (Columbia)
Three Dog Night, Three Dog Night (Dunhill)
Tommy, The Who (Decca)
Blind Faith, Blind Faith (Atco)
Happy Heart, Andy Williams (Columbia)
Gentle on My Mind, Dean Martin (Reprise)
Through the Past, Darkly, The Rolling Stones (London)
The Good, the Bad and the Ugly, Hugo Montenegro (RCA)
A Warm Shade of Ivory, Henry Mancini (RCA)
Glen Campbell—"Live", Glen Campbell (Capitol)
Alice's Restaurant, Arlo Guthrie (Reprise)
Realization, Johnny Rivers (Imperial)
Golden Greats, Gary Lewis (Liberty)
Crosby, Stills & Nash, Crosby, Stills & Nash (Atlantic)
Who Knows Where the Time Goes, Judy Collins (Elektra)
Golden Instrumentals, Billy Vaughn and Orchestra
Jimi Hendrix Smash Hits, Jimi Hendrix (Reprise)
Abbey Road, The Beatles (Apple)
Tom Jones—Live at Las Vegas, Tom Jones (Parrot)
Best of Cream, Cream (Atco)
Best of The Bee Gees, The Bee Gees (Atco)
Led Zeppelin II, Led Zeppelin (Atlantic)
Green Green Grass, Tom Jones (Parrot)
Let It Bleed, The Rolling Stones (London)
The Band, The Band (Capitol)
Santana, Santana (Columbia)
The Child Is Father to the Man, Blood, Sweat & Tears (Columbia)
Kozmic Blues, Janis Joplin (Columbia)
Stand!, Sly and the Family Stone (Epic)
Suitable for Framing, Three Dog Night (Dunhill)
Cycles, Frank Sinatra (Reprise)
Hot Buttered Soul, Isaac Hayes (Enterprise)
From Vegas to Memphis, Elvis Presley (RCA)
Chicago Transit Authority, Chicago Transit Authority (Columbia)
Buddy Holly Story, Buddy Holly and the Crickets (Decca)
Honey, Ray Conniff (Columbia)

1970

Engelbert, Engelbert Humperdinck (Parrot)
Engelbert Humperdinck, Engelbert Humperdinck (Parrot)
Captured Live at the Forum, Three Dog Night (Dunhill)
Easy Rider—motion picture soundtrack (Dunhill)
The Best of Charley Pride, Charley Pride (RCA)
Volunteers, Jefferson Airplane (RCA)

Crown of Creation, Jefferson Airplane (RCA)
From Elvis in Memphis, Elvis Presley (RCA)
Hello, I'm Johnny Cash, Johnny Cash (Columbia)
See What Tomorrow Brings, Peter, Paul and Mary (Warner Bros.)
Alive Alive-O! Jose Feliciano (RCA)
Bridge over Troubled Water, Simon & Garfunkel (Columbia)
Bobby Sherman, Bobby Sherman (Metromedia)
Mantovani's Golden Hits, Mantovani (London)
Try a Little Kindness, Glen Campbell (Capitol)
Get Together, Andy Williams (Columbia)
Morrison Hotel, Doors (Elektra)
Goin' Out of My Head, The Lettermen (Capitol)
Hey Jude, Beatles (Apple)
My Way, Frank Sinatra (Reprise)
The Plastic Ono Band—Live Peace in Toronto, The Plastic Ono Band (Apple)
Monster, Steppenwolf (Dunhill)
Feliciano/10 to 23, Jose Feliciano (RCA)
Deja Vu, Crosby, Stills, Nash & Young (Atlantic)
Up, Up and Away, Fifth Dimension (Soul City)
Warm, Herb Alpert & the Tijuana Brass (A&M)
A Gift from a Flower to a Garden, Donovan (Epic)
Don't Come Home a Drinkin' (with Lovin' on Your Mind), Loretta Lynn (Decca)
Chicago, Chicago (Columbia)
Tammy's Greatest Hits, Tammy Wynette (Epic)
Claudine, Claudine Longet (A&M)
Joe Cocker, Joe Cocker (A&M)
Tom, Tom Jones (Parrot)
A Song Will Rise, Peter, Paul and Mary (Warner Bros.)
McCartney, Paul McCartney (Apple)
Midnight Cowboy—motion picture soundtrack (United Artists)
Fifth Dimension—Greatest Hits, 5th Dimension (Soul City)
Butch Cassidy and the Sundance Kid, Burt Bacharach (A&M)
The Ventures Play Telstar, The Lonely Bull and Others. The Ventures (Dolton)
Golden Greats, The Ventures (Liberty)
American Woman, The Guess Who (RCA)
Let It Be, The Beatles (Apple)
Woodstock (Cotillion)
Band of Gypsys, Jimi Hendrix (Capitol)
Hurt So Bad, Lettermen (Capitol)
Self Portrait, Bob Dylan (Columbia)
Grand Funk, Grand Funk Railroad (Capitol)
Here Comes Bobby, Bobby Sherman (Metromedia)
Blood, Sweat and Tears 3, Blood, Sweat and Tears (Columbia)
Live Steppenwolf, Steppenwolf (Dunhill)
Golden Grass, Grassroots (Dunhill)
It Ain't Easy, Three Dog Night (Dunhill)
Raindrops Keep Fallin' on My Head, B. J. Thomas (Scepter)
To Our Children's Children's Children, Moody Blues (Threshold)
The Devil Made Me Buy This Dress, Flip Wilson (Little David)
Absolutely Live, Doors (Elektra)
Live at Leeds, The Who (Decca)
Here Where There Is Love, Dionne Warwick (Scepter)
Valley of the Dolls, Dionne Warwick (Scepter)
Closer to Home, Grand Funk Railroad (Capitol)
Mountain Climbing, Climbing (Windfall)
Mad Dogs and Englishmen, Joe Cocker (A&M)
Days of Future Passed, Moody Blues (Deram)

GOLD RECORD AWARDS—ALBUMS

On the Threshold of a Dream, Moody Blues (Deram)
Okie from Muskogee, Merle Haggard and the Strangers (Capitol)
Led Zeppelin III, Led Zeppelin (Atlantic)
Edizione D'Oro, Four Seasons (Philips)
On Time, Grand Funk Railroad (Capitol)
Everybody Knows This Is Nowhere, Neil Young with Crazy Horse (Reprise)
Best of Peter, Paul and Mary (Ten) Years Together, Peter, Paul and Mary (Warner Bros.)
Sweet Baby James, James Taylor (Warner Bros.)
Stage Fright, The Band (Capitol)
Paint Your Wagon—motion picture soundtrack (Paramount)
Abraxas, Santana (Columbia)
Sesame Street—original cast (Columbia)
With Love, Bobby, Bobby Sherman (Metromedia)
Get Yer Ya-Ya's Out!, The Rolling Stones (London)
A Question of Balance, Moody Blues (Threshold)
Jimi Hendrix/Otis Redding at Monterey—Monterey Pop Festival soundtrack (Reprise)
After the Gold Rush, Neil Young (Reprise)
Make It Easy on Yourself, Burt Bacharach (A&M)
Close to You, The Carpenters (A&M)
Reach Out, Burt Bacharach (A&M)
With a Little Help from My Friends, Joe Cocker (A&M)
Gold, Neil Diamond (UNI)
Benefit, Jethro Tull (Reprise)
Merry Christmas, Bing Crosby (Decca)
Share the Land, The Guess Who (RCA)
Sly & the Family Stone's Greatest Hits, Sly & the Family Stone (Epic)
Nancy & Lee, Nancy Sinatra and Lee Hazlewood (Reprise)
Frank Sinatra's Greatest Hits, Frank Sinatra (Reprise)
Live Album, Grand Funk Railroad (Capitol)
Stephen Stills, Stephen Stills (Atlantic)
Jim Nabors' Christmas Album, Jim Nabors (Columbia)
Super Session, Bloomfield/Kooper/Stills (Columbia)
Touching You, Touching Me, Neil Diamond (UNI)
In Search of the Lost Chord, Moody Blues (Deram)
New Morning, Bob Dylan (Columbia)
Cosmo's Factory, Creedence Clearwater Revival (Fantasy)
Willy and the Poor Boys, Creedence Clearwater Revival (Fantasy)
Green River, Creedence Clearwater Revival (Fantasy)
Bayou Country, Creedence Clearwater Revival (Fantasy)
Creedence Clearwater Revival, Creedence Clearwater Revival (Fantasy)
All Things Must Pass, George Harrison (Apple)
The Partridge Family Album, The Partridge Family (Bell)
Pendulum, Creedence Clearwater Revival (Fantasy)
The Freewheelin' Bob Dylan, Bob Dylan (Columbia)
John Barleycorn Must Die, Traffic (United Artists)
We Made It Happen, Engelbert Humperdinck (Parrot)
Jesus Christ Superstar—various artists (Decca)
Ladies of the Canyon, Joni Mitchell (Reprise)
Dean Martin's Greatest Hits Vol. II, Dean Martin (Reprise)
Portrait, Fifth Dimension (Bell)
In My Life, Judy Collins (Elektra)

1971

I Who Have Nothing, Tom Jones (Parrot)

GOLD RECORD AWARDS—ALBUMS

Taproot Manuscript, Neil Diamond (UNI)
Plastic Ono Band, John Lennon (Apple)
Love Story—motion picture soundtrack (Paramount)
Chicago III, Chicago (Columbia)
The Worst of Jefferson Airplane, Jefferson Airplane (RCA)
Elton John, Elton John (UNI)
On Stage February 1970, Elvis Presley (RCA)
Charley Pride's 10th Album, Charley Pride (RCA)
Just Plain Charley, Charley Pride (RCA)
Charley Pride in Person, Charley Pride (RCA)
Pearl, Janis Joplin (Columbia)
For the Good Times, Ray Price (Columbia)
The Fightin' Side of Me, Merle Haggard and the Strangers (Capitol)
Gary Puckett and the Union Gap's Greatest Hits, Gary Puckett and the Union Gap (Columbia)
Tumbleweed Connection, Elton John (UNI)
Love Story, Andy Williams (Columbia)
Rose Garden, Lynn Anderson (Columbia)
Up to Date, The Partridge Family (Bell)
The Cry of Love, Jimi Hendrix (Reprise)
Woodstock II (Cotillion)
Friends, Elton John (Paramount)
Whales & Nightingales, Judy Collins (Elektra)
If I Could Only Remember My Name, David Crosby (Atlantic)
Naturally, Three Dog Night (ABC-Dunhill)
Steppenwolf 7, Steppenwolf (ABC-Dunhill)
Golden Bisquits, Three Dog Night (ABC-Dunhill)
Steppenwolf Gold, Steppenwolf (ABC-Dunhill)
Greatest Hits, Herb Alpert and the Tijuana Brass (A&M)

Four Way Street, Crosby, Stills, Nash & Young (Atlantic)
Stoney End, Barbra Streisand (Columbia)
Survival, Grand Funk Railroad (Capitol)
Mud Slide Slim and the Blue Horizon, James Taylor (Warner Bros.)
Greatest Hits, Barbra Streisand (Columbia)
Paranoid, Black Sabbath (Warner Bros.)
Sticky Fingers, The Rolling Stones (Rolling Stones)
Tea for the Tillerman, Cat Stevens (A&M)
Sweetheart, Engelbert Humperdinck (Parrot)
Nantucket Sleigh Ride, Mountain (Windfall)
Love's Lines Angles and Rhymes, 5th Dimension (Bell)
Carpenters, The Carpenters (A&M)
Tapestry, Carole King, (Ode)
Ram, Paul and Linda McCartney (Apple)
Black Sabbath, Black Sabbath (Warner Bros.)
If You Could Read My Mind, Gordon Lightfoot (Warner-Reprise)
The Best of The Guess Who, The Guess Who (RCA)
Hawaii 5–0, The Ventures (UA-Liberty)
Aqualung, Jethro Tull (Reprise)
Aretha Franklin at the Fillmore West, Aretha Franklin (Atlantic)
Burt Bacharach, Burt Bacharach (A&M)
L.A. Woman, The Doors (Elektra)
Every Picture Tells a Story, Rod Stewart (Mercury)
Emerson, Lake & Palmer, Emerson, Lake & Palmer (Cotillion)
B. S. & T. 4, Blood, Sweat and Tears (Columbia)
Layla, Derek & The Dominos (Atco)
Chapter Two, Roberta Flack (Atlantic)
Stephen Stills 2, Stephen Stills (Atlantic)
Songs for Beginners, Graham Nash (Atlantic)

GOLD RECORD AWARDS—ALBUMS

Tarkus, Emerson, Lake & Palmer (Cotillion)
Bark, Jefferson Airplane (Grunt)
Every Good Boy Deserves Favour, Moody Blues (Threshold)
Osmonds, The Osmond Brothers (MGM)
Andy Williams' Greatest Hits, Andy Williams (Columbia)
Poems, Prayers and Promises, John Denver (RCA)
Who's Next, The Who (Decca)
Master of Reality, Black Sabbath (Warner Bros.)
Sound Magazine, The Partridge Family (Bell)
Imagine, John Lennon (Apple)
Santana, Santana (Columbia)
Harmony, Three Dog Night (ABC-Dunhill)
Fiddler on the Roof—motion picture soundtrack (United Artists)
Teaser & the Firecat, Cat Stevens (A&M)
The Allman Brothers Band at Fillmore East, The Allman Brothers (Capricorn)
James Gang Rides Again, James Gang (ABC-Dunhill)
A Partridge Family Christmas Card, The Partridge Family (Bell)
There's a Riot Goin' On, Sly & the Family Stone (Epic)
Live at Carnegie Hall, Chicago (Columbia)
Blue, Joni Mitchell (Reprise)
Grateful Dead, Grateful Dead (Warner Bros.)
Led Zeppelin, Led Zeppelin (Atlantic)
E Pluribus Funk, Grand Funk Railroad (Capitol)
Barbra Joan Streisand, Barbra Streisand (Columbia)
Rainbow Bridge, Jimi Hendrix (Reprise)
A Space in Time, Ten Years After (Columbia)
Carole King Music, Carole King (Ode)
Candles in the Rain, Melanie (Buddah)
All in the Family—original cast (Atlantic))
The Donny Osmond Album, Donny Osmond (MGM)
Live, Fifth Dimension (Bell)
The World of Johnny Cash, Johnny Cash (Columbia)
Dionne Warwick Story—Decade of Gold, Dionne Warwick (Scepter)

1972

American Pie, Don McLean (United Artists)
Bob Dylan's Greatest Hits, Vol. II, Bob Dylan (Columbia)
The Concert for Bangladesh, George Harrison and Friends (Apple)
Aerie, John Denver (RCA)
She's a Lady, Tom Jones (Parrot)
Wildlife, Wings (Apple)
Meaty, Beaty, Big & Bouncy, The Who (Decca)
Stones, Neil Diamond (UNI)
Loretta Lynn's Greatest Hits, Loretta Lynn (Decca)
Homemade, Osmonds (MGM)
Hot Rocks, Rolling Stones (London)
To You with Love, Donny Osmond (MGM)
Killer, Alice Cooper (Warner Bros.)
Blessed Are, Joan Baez (Vanguard)
Any Day Now, Joan Baez (Vanguard)
Leon Russell & the Shelter People, Leon Russell (Shelter)
A Nod Is as Good as a Wing...to a Blind Horse, Faces (Warner Bros.)
Low Spark of High Heeled Boys, Traffic (Island)
Charley Pride Sings Heart Songs, Charley Pride (RCA)
Harvest, Neil Young (Warner-Reprise)
Madman across the Water, Elton John (UNI)
Rockin' the Fillmore, Humble Pie (A&M)
Paul Simon, Paul Simon (Columbia)
Nilsson Schmilsson, Harry Nilsson (RCA)
Baby I'm a Want You, Bread (Elektra)

America, America (Warner Bros.)
Fragile, Yes (Atlantic)
Tom Jones Live at Caesars Palace, Tom Jones (Parrot)
Another Time, Another Place, Engelbert Humperdinck (Parrot)
Eat a Peach, Allman Brothers Band (Capricorn)
Cher, Cher Bono (Kapp)
Pictures at an Exhibition, Emerson, Lake & Palmer (Atlantic)
First Take, Roberta Flack (Atlantic)
Quiet Fire, Roberta Flack (Atlantic)
Young Gifted and Black, Aretha Franklin (Atlantic)
Let's Stay Together, Al Green (Hi)
All I Ever Need Is You, Sonny & Cher (Kapp)
Blood, Sweat and Tears Greatest Hits, Blood, Sweat and Tears (Columbia)
Glen Campbell's Greatest Hits, Glen Campbell (Capitol)
Hello Darlin', Conway Twitty (Decca)
Partridge Family Shopping Bag, The Partridge Family (Bell)
Thick as a Brick, Jethro Tull (Warner-Reprise)
Hendrix in the West, Jimi Hendrix (Warner-Reprise)
Phase III, The Osmonds (MGM)
Exile on Main Street, The Rolling Stones (Rolling Stones)
Graham Nash & David Crosby, Graham Nash & David Crosby (Atlantic)
Manassas, Stephen Stills (Atlantic)
Mark, Don & Mel, Grand Funk Railroad (Capitol)
Mardi Gras, Creedence Clearwater Revival (Fantasy)
Gather Me, Melanie (Neighborhood)
13, The Doors (Elektra)
Joplin in Concert, Janis Joplin (Columbia)
All Day Music, War (United Artists)
Live in Concert, James Gang, (ABC-Dunhill)
Cherish, David Cassidy (Bell)
Simon & Garfunkel's Greatest Hits, Simon & Garfunkel (Columbia)
School's Out, Alice Cooper (Warner Bros.)
A Song for You, The Carpenters (A&M)
Thirds, James Gang (ABC-Dunhill)
History of Eric Clapton, Eric Clapton (Atco)
Amazing Grace, Aretha Franklin (Atlantic)
Roberta Flack & Donny Hathaway, Roberta Flack & Donny Hathaway (Atlantic)
Honky Chateau, Elton John (UNI)
Sonny & Cher Live, Sonny & Cher (Kapp)
Seven Separate Fools, Three Dog Night (ABC-Dunhill)
Never a Dull Moment, Rod Stewart (Mercury)
Cheech & Chong, Cheech & Chong (Ode)
Chicago V, Chicago (Columbia)
Elvis as Recorded at Madison Square Garden, Elvis Presley (RCA)
Carlos Santana & Buddy Miles 'Live', Carlos Santana and Buddy Miles
Their Sixteen Greatest Hits, The Grassroots (ABC-Dunhill)
Donny Hathaway Live, Donny Hathaway (Atco)
Big Bambu, Cheech & Chong (Ode)
Procol Harum 'Live' in Concert with the Edmonton Symphony Orchestra, Procol Harum (A&M)
Love Theme from "The Godfather", Andy Williams (Columbia)
Moods, Neil Diamond (UNI)
Trilogy, Emerson, Lake & Palmer (Cotillion)
Still Bill, Bill Withers (Sussex)
Super Fly—motion picture soundtrack by Curtis Mayfield (Curtom)
Smokin', Humble Pie (A&M)
What You Hear Is What You Get, Ike and Tina Turner (United Artists)
Carney, Leon Russell (Shelter)
FM & AM, George Carlin (Little David)
Phoenix, Grand Funk Railroad (Capitol)
Catch Bull at Four, Cat Stevens (A&M)

GOLD RECORD AWARDS—ALBUMS

The Best of Charley Pride, Charley Pride (RCA)
Easy Loving, Freddie Hart (Capitol)
The London Chuck Berry Session, Chuck Berry (Chess)
Demons and Wizards, Uriah Heep (Mercury)
Close to the Edge, Yes (Atlantic)
Rhymes & Reasons, Carol King (Ode)
The Best of Merle Haggard, Merle Haggard (Capitol)
Rock of Ages, The Band (Capitol)
Machine Head, Deep Purple (Warner Bros.)
Black Sabbath—Vol. IV, Black Sabbath (Warner Bros.)
Love It to Death, Alice Cooper (Warner Bros.)
Stand Up, Jethro Tull (Warner-Reprise)
Living in the Past, Jethro Tull (Chrysalis)
Caravanserai, Santana (Columbia)
Guitar Man, Bread (Elektra)
Seventh Sojourn, Moody Blues (Threshold)
It's a Beautiful Day, It's a Beautiful Day (Columbia)
I'm Still in Love with You, Al Green (Hi)
Chilling, Thrilling Sounds of the Haunted House—motion picture soundtrack (Disneyland)
No Secrets, Carly Simon (Elektra)
Greatest Hits on Earth, 5th Dimension (Bell)
Godspell—original cast (Bell)
The Partridge Family at Home with Their Greatest Hits, The Partridge Family (Bell)
Tommy, London Symphony Orchestra and Chamber Choir with Guest Soloists (Ode)
The World Is a Ghetto, War (United Artists)
Summer Breeze, Seals & Crofts (Warner Bros.)
Europe '72, Grateful Dead (Warner Bros.)
One Man Dog, James Taylor (Warner Bros.)
Homecoming, America (Warner Bros.)
Summer of '42, Peter Nero (Columbia)
An Anthology, Duane Allman (Capricorn)
Manna, Bread (Elektra)
On the Waters, Bread (Elektra)
For the Roses, Joni Mitchell (Asylum)
Hot August Night, Neil Diamond (MCA)
Portrait of Donny, Donny Osmond (MGM)
The Osmonds 'Live', The Osmonds (MGM)
Son of Schmilsson, Harry Nilsson (RCA)
Rocky Mountain High, John Denver (RCA)

1973

Long John Silver, Jefferson Airplane (Grunt)
More Hot Rocks (Big Hits and Fazed Cookies), Rolling Stones (London)
The Magician's Birthday, Uriah Heep (Mercury)
Crazy Horses, Osmonds (MGM)
Too Young, Donny Osmond (MGM)
Creedence Gold, Creedence Clearwater Revival (Fantasy)
The Happiest Girl in the Whole U.S.A., Donna Fargo (Dot)
Loggins & Messina, Loggins & Messina (Columbia)
360 Degrees of Billy Paul, Billy Paul (Phila. Intl.)
Don't Shoot Me I'm Only the Piano Player, Elton John (MCA)
World Wide 50 Gold Award Hits, Vol. I, Elvis Presley (RCA)
Elvis—Aloha from Hawaii via Satellite, Elvis Presley (RCA)
Live Concert at the Forum, Barbra Streisand (Columbia)
The Stylistics, The Stylistics (Avco)
Around the World with Three Dog Night, Three Dog Night (ABC-Dunhill)
I Am Woman, Helen Reddy (Capitol)

GOLD RECORD AWARDS—ALBUMS

Shoot Out at the Fantasy Factory, Traffic (Island)
Dueling Banjos—motion picture soundtrack from *Deliverance*, as performed by Eric Weissberg and Steve Mandel (Warner Bros.)
Baby Don't Get Hooked on Me, Mac Davis (Columbia)
Wattstax—The Living Word—various artists (Stax)
In Concert, Derek & The Dominos (RSO)
Billion Dollar Babies, Alice Cooper (Warner Bros.)
Kenny Rogers & The First Edition Greatest Hits, Kenny Rogers & The First Edition (Warner-Reprise)
Houses of the Holy, Led Zeppelin (Atlantic)
The Best of Bread, Bread (Elektra)
Who Do We Think We Are!, Deep Purple (Warner Bros.)
The Beatles 1962-1966, The Beatles (Apple)
The Beatles 1966-1970, The Beatles (Apple)
The Dark Side of the Moon, Pink Floyd (Harvest)
The Divine Miss M, Bette Midler (Atlantic)
They Only Come Out at Night, Edgar Winter Group (Epic)
Back Stabbers, The O'Jays (Phila. Intl.)
Sittin's In, Loggins & Messian (Columbia)
Yessongs, Yes (Atlantic)
The Yes Album, Yes (Atlantic)
Red Rose Speedway, Paul McCartney & Wings (Apple)
William E. McEuen Presents Will the Circle Be Unbroken, The Nitty Gritty Dirt Band (United Artists)
Can't Buy a Thrill, Steely Dan (ABC-Dunhill)
Made in Japan, Deep Purple (Warner Bros.)
Living in the Material World, George Harrison (Apple)
Curtis, Curtis Mayfield (Curtom)
Back to the World, Curtis Mayfield (Curtom)
Now & Then, The Carpenters (A&M)
Class Clown, George Carlin (Little David)
The Sensational Charley Pride, Charley Pride (RCA)
From Me to You, Charley Pride (RCA)
The Country Way, Charley Pride (RCA)
Round 2, The Stylistics (Avco)
There Goes Rhymin' Simon, Paul Simon (Columbia)
Moving Waves, Focus (Sire)
Diamond Girl, Seals & Crofts (Warner Bros.)
Fantasy, Carole King, (Ode)
Lone Live, Leon Russell (Shelter)
Elvis—That's the Way It Is, Elvis Presley (RCA)
Live at the Sahara Tahoe, Isaac Hayes (Stax)
The Captain and Me, Doobie Brothers (Warner Bros.)
Call Me (Come Back Home), Al Green (London)
Spinners, Spinners (Atlantic)
Chicago VI, Chicago (Columbia)
Dick Clark: 20 Years of Rock 'N Roll—various artists (Buddah)
A Passion Play, Jethro Tull (Chrysalis)
Foreigner, Cat Stevens (A&M)
Cabaret—motion picture soundtrack (ABC-Dunhill)
Fresh, Sly & the Family Stone (Epic)
We're an American Band, Grand Funk Railroad (Capitol)
Brothers and Sisters, The Allman Brothers Band (Capricorn)
Toulouse Street, Doobie Brothers
Killing Me Softly, Roberta Flack (Atlantic)
Farewell Andromeda, John Denver (RCA)
Jesus Christ Superstar—motion picture soundtrack (MCA)
Anticipation, Carly Simon (Elektra)
Deliver the Word, War (United Artists)
Bloodshot, J. Geils Band (Atlantic)
My Best to You, Donny Osmond (Kolob)

Love Devotion Surrender, Carlos Santana and Mahavishnu John McLaughlin (Columbia)
Long Hard Climb, Helen Reddy (Capitol)
Beginnings, The Allman Brothers Band (Atco)
Goats Head Soup, The Rolling Stones (Rolling Stones)
Focus 3, Focus (Sire)
Los Cochinos, Cheech & Chong (Ode)
Goodbye Yellow Brick Road, Elton John (MCA)
Cyan, Three Dog Night (ABC-Dunhill)
Sing It Again Rod, Rod Stewart (Mercury)
Uriah Heep Live, Uriah Heep (Mercury)
Angel Clare, Art Garfunkel (Columbia)
Quadrophenia, The Who (MCA)
Meddle, Pink Floyd (Harvest)
Jonathan Livingston Seagull—motion picture soundtrack by Neil Diamond (Columbia)
The Golden Age of Rock 'n' Roll, Sha Na Na (Kama Sutra)
Life and Times, Jim Croce (ABC)
The Smoker You Drink, The Player You Get, Joe Walsh (ABC-Dunhill)
Imagination, Gladys Knight & The Pips (Buddah)
I've Got So Much to Give, Barry White (20th Century Fox)
Head to the Sky, Earth, Wind & Fire (Columbia)
Ringo, Ringo Starr (Apple)
The Silver Tongued Devil and I, Kris Kristofferson (Monument)
3 + 3, Isley Brothers (T-Neck)
You Don't Mess around with Jim, Jim Croce (ABC-Dunhill)
Behind Closed Doors, Charlie Rich (Epic)
Joy, Isaac Hayes (Stax)
Welcome, Santana (Columbia)
Jesse Was a Capricorn, Kris Kristofferson (Monument)
Mind Games, John Lennon (Apple)
I Got a Name, Jim Croce (ABC-Dunhill)
The Joker, Steve Miller Band (Capitol)
Muscle of Love, Alice Cooper (Warner Bros.)
Full Sail, Loggins & Messina (Columbia)
Time Fades Away, Neil Young (Warner-Reprise)
Band on the Run, Paul McCartney & Wings (Apple)
John Denver's Greatest Hits, John Denver (RCA)
The Singles 1969-1973, The Carpenters (A&M)
Brain Salad Surgery, Emerson, Lake & Palmer (Manticore)
Bette Midler, Bette Midler (Atlantic)
Snowbird, Anne Murray (Capitol)
Dylan, Bob Dylan (Columbia)
American Graffiti—motion picture soundtrack (MCA)

1974

The Early Beatles, The Beatles (Apple)
The Lord's Prayer, Jim Nabors (Columbia)
Ship Ahoy, The O'Jays (Phila. Intl.)
Livin' for You, Al Green (Hi)
Eagles, Eagles (Asylum)
Colors of the Day, Judy Collins (Elektra)
Hot Cakes, Carly Simon (Elektra)
Planet Waves, Bob Dylan (Asylum)
Johnny Winter Live, Johnny Winter (Columbia)
The Pointer Sisters, The Pointer Sisters (Blue Thumb)
Alone Together, Dave Mason (Blue Thumb)
Under the Influence of Love Unlimited, Love Unlimited (20th Century Fox)
Stone Gon', Barry White (20th Century Fox)
Live—Full House, J. Geils Band (Atlantic)
Tales from Topographic Oceans, Yes (Atlantic)
The Way We Were, Barbra Streisand (Columbia)

Court and Spark, Joni Mitchell (Asylum)
Ummagumma, Pink Floyd (Harvest)
Half Breed, Cher (MCA)
Sweet Freedom, Uriah Heep (Warner Bros.)
Laid Back, Greg Allman (Capricorn)
Unborn Child, Seals & Crofts (Warner Bros.)
War Live, War (United Artists)
The Payback, James Brown (Polydor)
Chicago VII, Chicago (Columbia)
Burn, Deep Purple (Warner Bros.)
Sabbath, Bloody Sabbath, Black Sabbath (Warner Bros.)
Tubular Bells, Mike Oldfield (Virgin)
Shinin' On, Grand Funk Railroad (Capitol)
What Were Once Vices Are Now Habits, Doobie Brothers (Warner Bros.)
Buddha and the Chocolate Box, Cat Stevens (A&M)
Love Is the Message, MSFB (Phila. Intl.)
Hard Labor, Three Dog Night (ABC-Dunhill)
The Sting—motion picture soundtrack (MCA)
Very Special Love Songs, Charlie Rich (Epic)
Headhunters, Herbie Hancock (Columbia)
Rhapsody in White, Love Unlimited Orchestra (20th Century Fox)
The Best of the Best of Merle Haggard, Merle Haggard (Capitol)
Bachman-Turner Overdrive II, Bachman-Turner Overdrive (Mercury)
Wild and Peaceful, Kool & The Gang (De-Lite)
Maria Muldaur, Maria Muldaur (Warner-Reprise)
Open Our Eyes, Earth, Wind & Fire (Columbia)
Pretzel Logic, Steely Dan (ABC)
The Way We Were—motion picture soundtrack (Columbia)
Mighty Love, Spinners (Atlantic)
Tres Hombres, Z. Z. Top (London)
Sundown, Gordon Lightfoot (Warner-Reprise)
It's Been a Long Time, The New Birth (RCA)
On the Border, Eagles (Asylum)
Love Song for Jeffrey, Helen Reddy (Capitol)
Claudine—motion picture soundtrack, Gladys Knight & The Pips (Buddah)
Live Rhymin', Paul Simon (Columbia)
Ziggy Stardust, David Bowie (RCA)
On Stage, Loggins & Messina (Columbia)
Back Home Again, John Denver (RCA)
Skin Tight, Ohio Players (Mercury)
Caribou, Elton John (MCA)
The Great Gatsby—motion picture soundtrack (Paramount)
Before the Flood, Bob Dylan and The Band (Asylum)
Workingman's Dead, Grateful Dead (Warner Bros.)
American Beauty, Grateful Dead (Warner Bros.)
Shock Treatment, The Edgar Winter Group (Epic)
There's a Plenty, The Pointer Sisters (Blue Thumb)
Diamond Dogs, David Bowie (RCA)
461 Ocean Boulevard, Eric Clapton (RSO)
Let's Put It All Together, Stylistics (Avco)
Endless Summer, The Beach Boys (Capitol)
Not Fragile, Bachman-Turner Overdrive (Mercury)
Journey to the Centre of the Earth, Rick Wakeman (A&M)
Rags to Rufus, Rufus (ABC)
If You Love Me, Let Me Know, Olivia Newton-John (MCA)
His 12 Greatest Hits, Neil Diamond (MCA)
Bridge of Sighs, Robin Trower (Chrysalis)
Can't Get Enough, Barry White (20th Century Fox)

GOLD RECORD AWARDS—ALBUMS

So Far, Crosby, Stills, Nash & Young (Atlantic)
Welcome Back, My Friends, to the Show That Never Ends—Ladies and Gentlemen, Emerson, Lake & Palmer (Manticore)
Bad Company, Bad Company (Swan Song)
Moontan, Golden Earring (MCA)
Second Helping, Lynyrd Skynyrd (MCA)
Desperado, Eagles (Asylum)
The Souther-Hillman-Furay Band, The Souther-Hillman-Furay Band (Asylum)
Stop and Smell the Roses, Mac Davis (Columbia)
On the Beach, Neil Young (Warner-Reprise)
Reprist)
Santana's Greatest Hits, Santana (Columbia)
The Beach Boys in Concert, The Beach Boys (Warner-Reprise)
Black Oak Arkansas, Black Oak Arkansas (Atco)
Body Heat, Quincy Jones (A&M)
Cheech and Chong's Wedding Album, Cheech & Chong (Ode)
Bachman-Turner Overdrive, Bachman-Turner Overdrive (Mercury)
Let Me Be There, Olivia Newton-John (MCA)
Alice Cooper's Greatest Hits, Alice Cooper (Warner Bros.)
Wrap Around Joy, Carole King, (Ode)
Photographs and Memories, His Greatest Hits, Jim Croce (ABC)
Walls and Bridges, John Lennon (Apple)
There Won't Be Anymore, Charlie Rich (RCA)
Serenade, Neil Diamond (Columbia)
Holiday, America (Warner Bros.)
It's Only Rock 'n' Roll, The Rolling Stones (Rolling Stones)
Live It Up, Isley Brothers (T-Neck)
When the Eagle Flies, Traffic (Island)
David Live, David Bowie (RCA)
Small Talk, Sly & the Family Stone (Epic)
War Child, Jethro Tull (Chrysalis)

Greatest Hits, Elton John (MCA)
I Feel a Song, Gladys Knight & The Pips (Buddah)
Anka, Paul Anka (United Artists)
Mother Lode, Loggins & Messina (Columbia)
Miles of Aisles, Joni Mitchell (Asylum)
I Don't Know How to Love Him, Helen Reddy (Capitol)
This Is the Moody Blues, Moody Blues (Threshold)
Here's Johnny...Magic Moments from The Tonight Show—various artists (Casablanca)
Melodies of Love, Bobby Vinton (ABC)
Odds and Sods, The Who (MCA)
Goodnight Vienna, Ringo Starr (Apple)
Fire, Ohio Players (Mercury)
Dark Horse, George Harrison (Apple)
Verities and Balderdash, Harry Chapin (Elektra)
Me and Bobby McGee, Kris Kristofferson (Monument)
Roadwork, Edgar Winter (Epic)
New and Improved, Spinners (Atlantic)
Relayer, Yes (Atlantic)
Free and Easy, Helen Reddy (Capitol)
All the Girls in the World Beware!!!, Grand Funk Railroad (Capitol)
Pronounced Leh-nerd Skin-nerd, Lynyrd Skynyrd (MCA)
Late for the Sky, Jackson Browne (Asylum)
The Best of Bread: Vol. II, Bread (Elektra)
Rufusized, Rufus (ABC)

1975

Butterfly, Barbra Streisand (Columbia)
Elvis—A Legendary Performer, Vol. I, Elvis Presley (RCA)
Did You Think to Pray, Charley Pride (RCA)
Stormbringer, Deep Purple (Warner Bros.)
Al Green Explores Your Mind, Al Green (Hi)

GOLD RECORD AWARDS — ALBUMS

Average White Band, Average White Band (Atlantic)
Joy to the World—Their Greatest Hits, Three Dog Night (ABC-Dunhill)
So What, Joe Walsh (ABC-Dunhill)
Caught Up, Millie Jackson (Spring)
Heart Like a Wheel, Linda Ronstadt (Capitol)
Dawn's New Ragtime Follies, Dawn (Bell)
Blood on the Tracks, Bob Dylan (Columbia)
An Evening with John Denver, John Denver (RCA)
Dragon Fly, Jefferson Starship (Grunt)
I'm Leaving It All Up to You, Marie and Donny Osmond (MGM)
Have You Never Been Mellow, Olivia Newton-John (MCA)
Something/Anything?, Todd Rundgren (Bearsville)
Energized, Foghat (Bearsville)
Together for the First Time, Bobby Bland/B. B. King (ABC-Dunhill)
Physical Graffiti, Led Zeppelin (Swan Song)
Do It ('Til You're Satisfied), B. T. Express (Scepter)
A Touch of Gold Volume II, Johnny Rivers (Imperial)
Johnny Rivers' Golden Hits, Johnny Rivers (Imperial)
Tommy—motion picture soundtrack (Polydor)
Perfect Angel, Minnie Riperton (Epic)
Chicago VIII, Chicago (Columbia)
Tuneweaving, Tony Orlando & Dawn (Bell)
White Gold, Love Unlimited Orchestra (20th Century Fox)
Just Another Way to Say I Love You, Barry White (20th Century Fox)
That's the Way of the World, Earth, Wind & Fire (Columbia)
Phoebe Snow, Phoebe Snow (MCA)
Get Your Wings, Aerosmith (Columbia)
Spirit of America, The Beach Boys (Capitol)
Styx II, Styx (Wooden Nickel)
Eldorado, Electric Light Orchestra (United Artists)
Nightbirds, LaBelle (Epic)
Straight Shooter, Bad Company (Swan Song)
Katy Lied, Steely Dan (ABC)
Sun Goddess, Ramsey Lewis (Columbia)
Capt. Fantastic and the Brown Dirt Cowboy, Elton John (MCA)
Four Wheel Drive, Bachman-Turner Overdrive (Mercury)
Stampede, Doobie Brothers (Warner Bros.)
Welcome to My Nightmare, Alice Cooper (Atlantic)
Venus & Mars, Wings (Capitol)
Survival, The O'Jays (Phila. Intl.)
Janis Joplin's Greatest Hits, Janis Joplin (Columbia)
Hearts, America (Warner Bros.)
Horizon, Carpenters (A&M)
Live in London, The O'Jays (Phila. Intl.)
Fandango, Z. Z. Top (London)
Nuthin' Fancy, Lynyrd Skynyrd (MCA)
One of These Nights, Eagles (Asylum)
The Heat Is On, Isley Brothers featuring Fight the Power (T-Neck)
To Be True, Harold Melvin & The Blue Notes featuring Teddy Pendergrass (Phila. Intl.)
Young Americans, David Bowie (RCA)
Chocolate Chip, Isaac Hayes (ABC)
Barry Manilow II, Barry Manilow (Bell)
Cut the Cake, Average White Band (Atlantic)
Why Can't We Be Friends?, War (United Artists)
Fire on the Mountain, Charlie Daniels Band (Kama Sutra)
Love Will Keep Us Together, Captain & Tennille (A&M)
Made in the Shade, The Rolling Stones (Rolling Stone)
Toys in the Attic, Aerosmith (Columbia)
The Marshall Tucker Band, The Marshall Tucker Band (Capricorn)
Cat Stevens Greatest Hits, Cat Stevens (A&M)

GOLD RECORD AWARDS—ALBUMS

Honey, Ohio Players (Mercury)
Light of Worlds, Kool & The Gang (De-Lite)
Red Octopus, Jefferson Starship (Grunt)
Don't Cry Now, Linda Ronstadt (Asylum)
Before the Next Teardrop Falls, Freddy Fender (ABC-Dot)
Funny Lady—motion picture soundtrack featuring Barbra Streisand and James Caan (Arista)
Aerosmith, Aerosmith (Columbia)
Between the Lines, Janis Ian (Columbia)
Gorilla, James Taylor (Warner Bros.)
Wish You Were Here, Pink Floyd (Columbia)
Pick of the Litter, Spinners (Atlantic)
Windsong, John Denver (RCA)
Tony Orlando & Dawn's Greatest Hits, Tony Orlando & Dawn (Arista)
Clearly Love, Olivia Newton-John (MCA)
I'll Play for You, Seals & Crofts (Warner Bros.)
Is It Something I Said?, Richard Pryor (Warner-Reprise)
Win, Lose or Draw, The Allman Brothers Band (Capricorn)
Prisoner in Disguise, Linda Ronstadt (Asylum)
For Everyman, Jackson Browne (Asylum)
Blow by Blow, Jeff Beck (Epic)
Born to Run, Bruce Springsteen (Columbia)
Ain't No 'Bout-a-Doubt It, Graham Central Station (Warner Bros.)
Kris & Rita Full Moon, Kris Kristofferson and Rita Coolidge (A&M)
The Six Wives of Henry VIII, Rick Wakeman (A&M)
Rock of the Westies, Elton John (MCA)
Rock Mountain Christmas, John Denver (RCA)
Raunch 'N Roll, Black Oak Arkansas (Atco)
Where We All Belong, The Marshall Tucker Band (Capricorn)
Wind on the Water, David Crosby & Graham Nash (ABC Records/Atlantic Tapes)
Foghat, Foghat (Bearsville)
Extra Texture, George Harrison (Apple)
Sedaka's Back, Neil Sedaka (Rocket)
Diamonds and Rust, Joan Baez (A&M)
Piano Man, Billy Joel (Columbia)
Minstrel in the Gallery, Jethro Tull (Chrysalis)
Still Crazy after All These Years, Paul Simon (Columbia)
Blue Sky—Night Thunder, Michael Murphey (Epic)
Blue Sky—Night Thunder, Michael Murphey (Epic)
Chicago IX—Chicago's Greatest Hits, Chicago (Columbia)
Sheer Heart Attack, Queen (Elektra)
Judith, Judy Collins (Elektra)
History—America's Greatest Hits, America (Warner Bros.)
Helen Reddy's Greatest Hits, Helen Reddy (Capitol)
Alive! Kiss (Casablanca)
The Hissing of Summer Lawns, Joni Mitchell (Asylum)
Seals & Crofts Greatest Hits, Seals & Crofts (Warner Bros.)
Fleetwood Mac, Fleetwood Mac (Warner-Reprise)
Breakaway, Art Garfunkel (Columbia)
Gratitude, Earth, Wind & Fire (Columbia)
Family Reunion, The O'Jays (Epic)
Save Me, Silver Convention (Midland International-RCA)
The Who by Numbers, The Who (MCA)
The Best of Carly Simon, Carly Simon (Elektra)
The Hungry Years, Neil Sedaka (Rocket)
Atlantic Crossing, Rod Stewart (Warner Bros.)
Head On, Bachman-Turner Overdrive (Mercury)
Main Course, The Bee Gees (RSO)
Trying to Get the Feeling, Barry Manilow (Arista)
Rhinestone Cowboy, Glen Campbell (Capitol)
Bay City Rollers, Bay City Rollers (Arista)

1976

High on the Hog, Black Oak Arkansas (Atco)
Wake Up Everybody, Harold Melvin & The Blue Noes featuring Teddy Pendergrass (Phila. Intl.)
Rufus—Featuring Chaka Khan, Rufus featuring Chaka Khan (ABC)
Desire, Bob Dylan (Columbia)
Numbers, Cat Stevens (A&M)
Mona Bone Jakon, Cat Stevens (A&M)
Love to Love You Baby, Donna Summer (Oasis)
No Way to Treat a Lady, Helen Reddy (Capitol)
A Christmas Album, Barbra Streisand (Columbia)
Face the Music, Electric Light Orchestra (United Artists)
Black Bear Road, C. W. McCall (MGM)
Searchin' for a Rainbow, The Marshall Tucker Band (Capricorn)
Bare Trees, Fleetwood Mac (Warner-Reprise)
Run with the Pack, Bad Company (Swan Song)
Inseparable, Natalie Cole (Capitol)
Eagles—Their Greatest Hits 1971-1975, Eagles (Asylum)
M.U.—The Best of Jethro Tull, Jethro Tull (Chrysalis)
Station to Station, David Bowie (RCA)
Frampton Comes Alive!, Peter Frampton (A&M)
The Dream Weaver, Gary Wright (Warner Bros.)
Barry White's Greatest Hits, Barry White (20th Century Fox)
Will O' the Wisp, Leon Russell (Shelter)
A Night at the Opera, Queen (Elektra)
Song of Joy, Captain & Tennille (A&M)
Red Headed Stranger, Willie Nelson (Columbia)
Fool for the City, Foghat (Bearsville)
Bustin' Out, Pure Prairie League (RCA)
Thoroughbred, Carole King (Ode)
Wings at the Speed of Sound, Paul McCartney & Wings (Capitol)
The Outlaws, Waylon Jennings, Willie Nelson, Jessi Colter, Tompall Glaser (RCA)
Brass Construction, Brass Construction (United Artists)
Presence, Led Zeppelin (Swan Song)
Eargasm, Johnnie Taylor (Columbia)
Apostrophé, Frank Zappa (Discreet)
Hair of the Dog, Nazareth (A&M)
City Life, Blackbyrds (Fantasy)
2nd Anniversary, Gladys Knight & The Pips (Buddah)
Lazy Afternoon, Barbra Streisand (Columbia)
Destroyer, Kiss (Casablanca)
Black and Blue, The Rolling Stones (Rolling Stone)
Mothership Connection, Parliament (Casablanca)
Come on Over, Olivia Newton-John (MCA)
You've Never Been This Far Before/Baby's Gone, Conway Twitty (MCA)
Here and There, Elton John (MCA)
Takin' It to the Streets, Doobie Brothers (Warner Bros.)
Look Out for #1, Brothers Johnson (A&M)
Bitches Brew, Miles Davis (Columbia)
Hideaway, America (Warner Bros.)
Rocks, Aerosmith (Columbia)
Souvenirs, Dan Fogelberg (Epic)
All the Love in the World, Mac Davis (Columbia)
Desolation Boulevard, Sweet (Capitol)
Harvest for the World, Isley Brothers (T-Neck)
Breezin', George Benson (Warner Bros.)
Contradiction, Ohio Players (Mercury)
Amigos, Santana (Columbia)
Rock 'n' Roll Music, The Beatles (Capitol)
Twelve Dreams of Dr. Sardonicus, Spirit (Columbia)
Olé ELO, Electric Light Orchestra (United Artists)
Chicago X, Chicago (Columbia)
Beautiful Noise, Neil Diamond (Columbia)
Love Trilogy, Donna Summer (Oasis)

GOLD RECORD AWARDS—ALBUMS

Spitfire, Jefferson Starship (Grunt)
Natalie, Natalie Cole (Capitol)
Sparkle, Aretha Franklin (Atlantic)
Second Childhood, Phoebe Snow (Columbia)
All-time Greatest Hits, Johnny Mathis (Columbia)
A Kind of Hush, The Carpenters (A&M)
Silk Degrees, Boz Scaggs (Columbia)
Ted Nugent, Ted Nugent (Epic)
Fly like an Eagle, Steve Miller Band (Capitol)
Changesonebowie, David Bowie (RCA)
Music, Music, Helen Reddy (Capitol)
Soul Searching, Average White Band (Atlantic)
This One's for You, Barry Manilow (Arista)
Spirit, John Denver (RCA)
Native Sons, Loggins & Messina (Columbia)
All Things in Time, Lou Rawls (Phila. Intl.)
War's Greatest Hits, War (United Artists)
Get Closer, Seals & Crofts (Warner Bros.)
Hasten Down the Wind, Linda Ronstadt (Asylum)
15 Big Ones, The Beach Boys (Warner-Reprise)
Dreamboat Annie, Heart (Mushroom)
Wild Cherry, Wild Cherry (Epic-Sweet City)
Peter Frampton, Peter Frampton (A&M)
Wired, Jeff Beck (Epic)
Royal Scam, Steeley Dan (ABC)
Children of the World, The Bee Gees (RSO)
Best of BTO (So Far), Bachman-Turner Overdrive (Mercury)
Hard Rain, Bob Dylan (Columbia)
Abandoned Luncheonette, Daryl Hall & John Oates (Atlantic)
Spirit, Earth, Wind & Fire (Columbia)
Dave Mason, Dave Mason (Columbia)
The Manhattans, The Manhattans (Columbia)
Happiness Is Being with the Spinners, Spinners (Atlantic)
Whistling Down the Wire, David Crosby & Graham Nash (ABC Records/Atlantic Tapes)
The Clones of Dr. Funkenstein, Parliament (Casablanca)
In the Pocket, James Taylor (Warner Bros.)
A Night on the Town, Rod Stewart (Warner Bros.)
Message in the Music, The O'Jays (Phila. Intl.)
Barry Manilow I, Barry Manilow (Arista)
A New World Record, Electric Light Orchestra (United Artists)
One More for From the Road, Lynyrd Skynyrd (MCA)
Agents of Fortune, Blue Oyster Cult (Columbia)
Boston, Boston (Epic)
A Fifth of Beethoven, Walter Murphy Band (Private Stock)
Summertime Dream, Gordon Lightfoot (Warner-Reprise)
Free to Be You and Me, Marlo Thomas and Friends (Arista-Bell)
Blue Moves, Elton John (Rocket-MCA)
For Earth Below, Robin Trower (Chrysalis)
The Song Remains the Same, Led Zeppelin (Swan Song)
Firefall, Firefall (Atlantic)
Bigger than Both of Us, Daryl Hall & John Oates (RCA)
Rock and Roll Outlaws, Foghat (Bearsville)
Mystery to Me, Fleetwood Mac (Warner-Reprise)
Over-Nite Sensation, The Mothers (Discreet)
Rock and Roll Over, Kiss (Casablanca)
Four Seasons of Love, Donna Summer (Oasis)
Free for All, Ted Nugent (Epic)
Brass Construction II, Brass Construction (United Artists)

The Pretender, Jackson Browne (Asylum)
Times of Your Life, Paul Anka (United Artists)
Jackson Browne, Jackson Browne (Asylum)
Ol' Blue Eyes Is Back, Frank Sinatra (Warner-Reprise)
Moondance, Van Morrison (Warner Bros.)
Best of the Doobies, Doobie Brothers (Warner Bros.)
Alice Cooper Goes to Hell, Alice Cooper (Warner Bros.)
And I Love You So, Perry Como (RCA)
Nights Are Forever, England Dan & John Ford Coley (Big Tree)
Bicentennial Nigger, Richard Pryor (Warner Bros.)
Don't Stop Believin', Olivia Newton-John (MCA)
Greatest Hits, Linda Ronstadt (Asylum)
That Christmas Feeling, Glen Campbell (Capitol)
Best of the Beach Boys Volume 2, The Beach Boys (Capitol)
Hotel California, Eagles (Asylum)
Long Misty Days, Robin Trower (Chrysalis)
Wings over America, Wings (Capitol)
Daryl Hall & John Oates, Daryl Hall & John Oates (RCA)
Dr. Buzzard's Original Savannah Band, Dr. Buzzard's Original Savannah Band (RCA)
Car Wash—motion picture soundtrack featuring Rose Royce (MCA)
James Taylor's Greatest Hits, James Taylor (Warner Bros.)
Live Bullet, Bob Seger and the Silver Bullet Band (Capitol)
Hejira, Joni Mitchell (Asylum)
A Star Is Born, Barbra Streisand and Kris Kristofferson (Columbia)
Donny and Marie Featuring Songs from Their Television Show, Donny and Marie Osmond (Polydor)
Occupation: Foole, George Carlin (Little David)
A Day at the Races, Queen (Elektra)
The Best of Leon Russell, Leon Russell (Shelter)
Greatest Hits, ABBA (Atlantic)

1977

After the Lovin', Engelbert Humperdinck (Columbia)
Long May You Run, Stills & Young Band (Warner-Reprise)
Year of the Cat, Al Stewart (GRT-Janus)
Tejas, Z. Z. Top (London)
Thirty-Three & ⅓, George Harrison (Warner-Dark Horse)
Ohio Players Gold, Ohio Players (Phonogram-Mercury)
Leftoverture, Kansas (Columbia-Kirshner)
Night Moves, Bob Seger and the Silver Bullet Band (Capitol)
Flowers, Emotions (Columbia)
Ask Rufus, Rufus featuring Chaka Khan (ABC)
You Are My Starship, Norman Connors (Buddah)
Night Shift, Foghat (Warner-Bearsville)
Animals, Pink Floyd (Columbia)
Rumours, Fleetwood Mac (Warner Bros.)
The Best of George Harrison, George Harrison (Capitol)
Songs from the Wood, Jethro Tull (Chrysalis)
Lost without Your Love, Bread (Elektra)
Southern Comfort, Crusaders (ABC-Blue Thumb)
I Hope We Get to Love in Time, Marilyn McCoo & Billy Davis, Jr.
...Roots, Quincy Jones (A&M)
Dressed to Kill, Kiss (Casablanca)
Love at the Greek, Neil Diamond (Columbia)
24 Greatest Hits, Hank Williams (Polydor-MGM)
Unpredictable, Natalie Cole (Capitol)

GOLD RECORD AWARDS—ALBUMS

This Is Niecy, Deniece Williams (Columbia)
The Best of the Statler Brothers, Statler Brothers (Phonogram-Mercury)
Burnin' Sky, Bad Company (Swan Song)
In Flight, George Benson (Warner Bros.)
Dreaming My Dreams, Waylon Jennings (RCA)
Queen, Queen (Elektra)
Works, Vol. I, Emerson, Lake & Palmer (Atlantic)
In the Court of the Crimson King/An Observation, King Crimson (Atlantic)
John Denver's Greatest Hits, Vol. II, John Denver (RCA)
Arrival, ABBA (Atlantic)
The Roaring Silence, Manfred Mann's Earth Band (Warner Bros.)
The Jacksons, The Jacksons (Epic)
Come In from the Rain, Captain & Tennille (A&M)
A Rock and Roll Alternative, Atlanta Rhythm Section (Polydor)
Unfinished Business, The Blackbyrds (Fantasy)
Montrose, Montrose (Warner Bros.)
Ahh...The Name Is Bootsy, Baby, Bootsy's Rubber Band (Warner Bros.)
Go for Your Guns, Isley Brothers (T-Neck)
Gord's Gold, Gordon Lightfoot (Warner-Reprise)
Rocky—motion picture soundtrack (United Artists)
Endless Flight, Leo Sayer (Warner Bros.)
Festival, Santana (Columbia)
The Wild, the Innocent, and the E Street Shuffle, Bruce Springsteen (Columbia)
The Beatles at the Hollywood Bowl, The Beatles (Capitol)
The Best of Friends, Loggins & Messina (Columbia)
Book of Dreams, Steve Miller Band (Capitol)
Foreigner, Foreigner (Atlantic)
Toldeo Window Box, George Carlin (Little David)
Person to Person, Average White Band (Atlantic)
Teddy Pendergrass, Teddy Pendergrass (Phila. Intl.)
Right on Time, Brothers Johnson (A&M)
Little Queen, Heart (Portrait)
Ain't That a Bitch, Johnny Guitar Watson (DJM)
A Real Mother for Ya, Johnny Guitar Watson (DJM)
Carolina Dreams, The Marshall Tucker Band (Warner-Reprise)
Kiss, Kiss (Casablanca)
Parliament Live/P Funk Earth Tour, Parliament (Casablanca)
Izitso, Cat Stevens (A&M)
I'm in You, Peter Frampton (A&M)
Ol' Waylon, Waylon Jennings (RCA)
Slave, Slave (Atlantic-Cotillion)
Barry Manilow Live, Barry Manilow (Arista)
Changes in Latitudes, Changes in Attitudies, Jimmy Buffett (ABC)
Superman, Barbra Streisand (Columbia)
Hotter Than Hell, Kiss (Casablanca)
Here at Last...Bee Gees...Live, The Bee Gees (RSO)
Melissa, Melissa Manchester (Arista)
CSN, Crosby, Stills & Nash (Atlantic)
Love Gun, Kiss (Casablanca)
J.T., James Taylor (Columbia)
Unmistakably Lou, Lou Rawls (Phila. Intl.)
Beethoven: The 9 Symphonies, Herbert von Karajan and the Berlin Philharmonic Orchestra (Deutsche Grammaphon-Polydor)
Cat Scratch Fever, Ted Nugent (Epic)
Rejoice, Emotions (Columbia)
Travelin' at the Speed of Thought, The O'Jays (Columbia)
Even in the Quietest Moments..., Supertramp (A&M)
I Remember Yesterday, Donna Summer (Casablanca)
On Your Feet or On Your Knees, Blue Oyster Cult (Columbia)
Star Wars—motion picture soundtrack (20th Century Fox)
Alleluia—Praise Gathering for Believers—various artists (Benson-Impact)

GOLD RECORD AWARDS—ALBUMS

The Floaters, The Floaters (ABC)
Are You Ready for the Country, Waylon Jennings (RCA)
Maze, Featuring Frankie Beverly, Maze (Capitol)
Going for the One, Yes (Atlantic)
Crime of the Century, Supertramp (A&M)
Nether Lands, Dan Fogelberg (Epic)
You Get What You Play For, REO Speedwagon (Epic)
Shaun Cassidy, Shaun Cassidy (Warner Bros.)
Kenny Rogers, Kenny Rogers (United Artists)
Platinum Jazz, War (United Artists-Blue Note)
A New Life, The Marshall Tucker Band (Warner Bros.)
It's a Game, Bay City Rollers (Arista)
Anytime...Anywhere, Rita Coolidge (A&M)
A Place in the Sun, Pablo Cruise (A&M)
Equinox, Styx (A&M)
Ozark Mountain Daredevils, Ozark Mountain Daredevils (A&M)
Pure Gold, Elvis Presley (RCA)
Livin' on the Fault Line, Doobie Brothers (Warner Bros.)
I Robot, Alan Parsons (Arista)
Chicago XI, Chicago (Columbia)
Beauty on a Back Street, Daryl Hall & John Oates (RCA)
Simple Dreams, Linda Ronstadt (Asylum)
Celebrate Me Home, Kenny Loggins (Columbia)
The Outlaws, The Outlaws (Arista)
Barry White Sings for Someone You Love, Barry White (20th Century Fox)
Simple Things, Carole King (Capitol)
Star Wars and Other Galactic Funk, Meco (Millennium)
Elton John's Greatest Hits, Vol. II, Elton John (MCA)
Welcome to My World, Elvis Presley (RCA)
Luna Sea, Firefall (Atlantic)
Love You Live, The Rolling Stones (Rolling Stones)
Aja, Steely Dan (ABC)
In Full Bloom, Rose Royce (Warner-Whitfield)
Southern Nights, Glen Campbell (Capitol)
From Elvis Presley Boulevard, Memphis, Tennessee, Elvis Presley (RCA)
Too Hot to Handle, Heatwave (Epic)
Point of Know Return, Kansas (Columbia-Kirshner)
Foghat Live, Foghat (Bearsville)
American Stars 'n' Bars, Neil Young (Bearsville)
The Grand Illusion, Styx (A&M)
Jailbreak, Thin Lizzy (Phonogram-Mercury)
Greatest Hits, Olivia Newton-John (MCA)
Love Songs, The Beatles (Capitol)
Elvis—A Legendary Performer, Vol. II, Elvis Presley (RCA)
The Johnny Cash Portrait/His Greatest Hits, Vol. II, Johnny Cash (Columbia)
You Light Up My Life, Debby Boone (Warner Bros.)
Rock & Roll Love Letter, Bay City Rollers (Arista)
Eric Carmen, Eric Carmen (Arista)
Street Survivors, Lynyrd Skynyrd (MCA)
You Light Up My Life—motion picture soundtrack (Arista)
Captured Angel, Dan Fogelberg (Epic)
Let It Flow, Dave Mason
Elvis Sings the Wonderful World of Christmas, Elvis Presley (RCA)
Anthology, Steve Miller Band (Capitol)
Something to Love, L.T.D. (A&M)
We Must Believe in Magic, Crystal Gayle (United Artists)
Out of the Blue, Electric Light Orchestra (Jet-United Artists)
News of the World, Queen (Elektra)
2112, Rush (Phonogram)
A Farewell to Kings, Rush (Phonogram)
All the World's a Stage, Rush (Phonogram)
I'm Glad Your'e Here with Me Tonight, Neil Diamond (Columbia)
All 'N All, Earth, Wind & Fire (Columbia)

Down Two Then Left, Boz Scaggs (Columbia)
Greatest Hits, Etc., Paul Simon (Columbia)
In City Dreams, Robin Trower (Chrysalis)
Saturday Night Fever—motion picture soundtrack (RSO)
Flowing Rivers, Andy Gibb (RSO)
Foot Loose & Fancy Free, Rod Stewart (Warner Bros.)
Born Late, Shaun Cassidy (Warner Bros.)
Dedication, Bay City Rollers (Arista)
Kiss Alive II, Kiss (Casablanca)
Galaxy, War (MCA)
The Turning Point, John Mayall (Polydor)
Let's Get Small, Steve Martin (Warner Bros.)
Moonflower, Santana (Columbia)
The Stranger, Billy Joel (Columbia)
I Want to Live, John Denver (RCA)
His Hand in Mine, Elvis Presley (RCA)
Elvis Country, Elvis Presley (RCA)
The Story of Star Wars—original cast with narration by Roscoe Lee Browne (20th Century Fox)
Bay City Rollers/Greatest Hits, Bay City Rollers (Arista)
Draw the Line, Aerosmith (Columbia)
French Kiss, Bob Welch (Capitol)
Once upon a Time, Donna Summer (Casablanca)
Friends & Strangers, Ronnie Laws (United Artists-Blue Note)
Greatest Hits, Captain & Tennille (A&M)
Tupelo Honey, Van Morrison (Warner Bros.)
Daytime Friends, Kenny Rogers (United Artists)
Viva Terlingua, Jerry Jeff Walker (MCA)
Masque, Kansas (Columbia-Kirshner)
A Chorus Line—original cast (Columbia)
Feelin' Bitchy, Millie Jackson (Spring)
Thankful, Natalie Cole (Capitol)

Here You Come Again, Dolly Parton (RCA)
Action, Blackbyrds (Fantasy)
Running on Empty, Jackson Browne (Asylum)
Works, Vol. II, Emerson, Lake & Palmer (Atlantic)
Best of Z.Z. Top, Z.Z. Top (London)

1978

Bee Gees Gold, Volume I, Bee Gees (RSO)
Brass Construction III, Brass Construction (United Artists)
Close Encounters of the Third Kind—motion picture soundtrack (Arista)
Diamantina Cocktail, Little River Band (Capitol-Harvest)
Funkentelechy vs. Placebo Syndrome, Parliament (Casablanca)
New Season, Donny & Marie Osmond (Polydor)
Waylon Live, Waylon Jennings (RCA)
Reach for It, George Duke (Epic)
Spectres, Blue Oyster Cult (Columbia)
Little Criminals, Randy Newman (Warner Bros.)
Slowhand, Eric Clapton (RCO)
Leif Garrett, Leif Garrett (Atlantic)
Waylon & Willie, Waylon Jennings and Willie Nelson (RCA)
It Was Almost Like a Song, Ronnie Milsap (RCA)
Don Juan's Reckless Daughter, Joni Mitchell (Asylum)
Double Live Gonzo, Ted Nugent (Epic)
When You Hear Lou, You've Heard It All, Lou Rawls (Phila. Intl.)
Even Now, Barry Manilow (Arista)
Ten Years of Gold, Kenny Rogers (United Artists)
Street Player, Rufus (ABC)
Blue Lights in the Basement, Roberta Flack (Atlantic)
A Weekend in L.A., George Benson (Warner Bros.)
Earth, Jefferson Starship (RCA-Grunt)

GOLD RECORD AWARDS — ALBUMS

Watermark, Art Garfunkel (Columbia)
Countdown to Ecstasy, Steely Dan (ABC)
Bootsy? Player of the Year, Bootsy's Rubber Band (Warner Bros.)
The Album, ABBA (Atlantic)
Golden Time of Day, Maze (Capitol)
It Feels So Good, Manhattans (Columbia)
Longer Fuse, Dan Hill (20th Century Fox)
London Town, Paul McCartney & Wings (Capitol)
Feels So Good, Chuck Mangione (A&M)
Emotion, Samantha Sang (Private Stock)
Chic, Chic (Atlantic)
Carole King...Her Greatest Hits, Carole King (CBS-Ode)
Son of a Son of a Sailor, Jimmy Buffett (ABC)
Central Heating, Heatwave (Epic)
Showdown, Isley Brothers (T-Neck)
Champagne Jam, Atlanta Rhythm Section (Polydor)
Excitable Boy, Warren Zevon (Asylum)
Heavy Horses, Jethro Tull (Chrysalis)
FM—motion picture soundtrack (MCA)
Player, Player (RSO)
Endless Wire, Gordon Lightfoot (Warner Bros.)
Rock 'n' Roll Animal, Lou Reed (RCA)
Grease—motion picture soundtrack (RSO)
Together Forever, Marshall Tucker Band (Capricorn)
You Light Up My Life, Johnny Mathis (Columbia)
So Full of Love, O'Jays (Phila. Intl.)
Infinity, Journey (Columbia)
The Sound in Your Mind, Willie Nelson (Columbia)
Secrets, Con Funk Shun (Polydor-Mercury)
Flying High on Your Love, Bar-Kays (Polydor-Mercury)
Boys in the Trees, Carly Simon (Elektra)
Warmer Communications, Average White Band (Atlantic)
Double Platinum, Kiss (Casablanca)
Thank God It's Friday—motion picture soundtrack (Casablanca)
Menagerie, Bill Withers, (Columbia)
Bat Out of Hell, Meatloaf (Cleveland Intl.)
Van Halen, Van Halen (Warner Bros.)
The Best of Rod Stewart, Rod Stewart (Polydor-Mercury)
City to City, Gerry Rafferty (United Artists)
Shadow Dancing, Andy Gibb (RSO)
Stranger in Town, Bob Seger and the Silver Bullet Band (Capitol)
And Then There Were Three, Genesis (Atlantic)
Songbird, Barbra Streisand (Columbia)
Disco Inferno, Tramps (Atlantic)
But Seriously, Folks, Joe Walsh (Asylum)
Magazine, Heart (Mushroom)
Greatest Stories—Live, Harry Chapin (Elektra)
Don't Let Me Be Misunderstood, Santa Esmeralda starring Leroy Gomez (Casablanca)
The Best of Dolly Parton, Dolly Parton (RCA)
Some Girls, The Rolling Stones (Rolling Stones)
Life Is a Song Worth Singing, Teddy Pendergrass (Phila. Intl.)
Darkness on the Edge of Town, Bruce Springsteen (Columbia)
Octave, Moody Blues (London)
Double Vision, Foreigner (Atlantic)
Send It, Ashford & Simpson (Warner Bros.)
Love Me Again, Rita Coolidge (A&M)
Worlds Away, Pablo Cruise (A&M)
Stone Blue, Foghat (Bearsville)
Sounds...and Stuff Like That, Quincy Jones (A&M)
Togetherness, L.T.D. (A&M)
You Can Tune a Piano, but You Can't Tuna Fish, REO Speedwagon (Epic)
Street Legal, Bob Dylan (Columbia)
It's a Heartache, Bonnie Tyler (RCA)
Eddie Money, Eddie Money (Columbia)

GOLD RECORD AWARDS—ALBUMS

You're Gonna Get It, Tom Petty and the Heartbreakers (ABC-Shelter)
Natalie Live, Natalie Cole (Capitol)
Sgt. Pepper's Lonely Hearts Club Band—motion picture soundtrack (RSO)
That's What Friends Are For, Johnny Mathis and Deniece Williams (Columbia)
Stardust, Willie Nelson (Columbia)
Pyramid, Alan Parsons Project (Arista)
Elite Hotel, Emmylou Harris (Warner Bros.-Reprise)
Blam, Brothers Johnson (A&M)
A Taste of Honey, A Taste of Honey (Capitol)
Under Wraps, Shaun Cassidy (Warner Bros.)
Macho Man, Village People (Casablanca)
Heartbreaker, Dolly Parton (RCA)
Reaching for the Sky, Peabo Bryson (Capitol)
Natural High, Commodores (Motown)
Come Get It, Rick James (Motown)
Who Are You, The Who (MCA)
Don't Look Back, Boston (Epic)
Loveshine, Con Funk Shun (Polydor-Mercury)
Get It Out 'Cha System, Millie Jackson (Polydor-Spring)
Sleeper Catcher, Little River Band (Capitol-Harvest)
Smooth Talk, Evelyn "Champagne" King (RCA)
Skynyrd's First and...Last, Lynyrd Skynyrd (MCA)
Do What You Wanna Do, Dramatics (ABC)
Sunbeam, Emotions (Columbia-ARC)
Mariposa de Oro, Dave Mason (Columbia)
Nightwatch, Kenny Loggins (Columbia)
Live and More, Donna Summer (Casablanca)
When I Dream, Crystal Gayle (United Artists)
Love or Something Like It, Kenny Rogers (United Artists)
Village People, Village People (Casablanca)

Flat as a Pancake, Head East (A&M)
Rose Royce Strikes Again, Rose Royce (Warner Bros.-Whitfield)
Raydio, Raydio (Arista)
Living in the U.S.A., Linda Ronstadt (Asylum)
I've Always Been Crazy, Waylon Jennings (RCA)
Dog and Butterfly, Heart (Portrait)
Twin Sons of Different Mothers, Dan Fogelberg and Tim Weisberg (Epic-Full Moon)
The Wiz—original soundtrack (MCA)
Bursting Out, Jethro Tull (Chrysalis)
Kiss—Peter Criss, Peter Criss (Casablanca)
Kiss—Ace Frehley, Ace Frehley (Casablanca)
Kiss—Gene Simmons, Gene Simmons (Casablanca)
Kiss—Paul Stanley, Paul Stanley (Casablanca)
One Nation under a Groove, Funkadelic (Warner Bros.)
Sunburn, Sun (Capitol)
Is It Still Good to Ya, Ashford & Simpson (Warner Bros.)
Hot Streets, Chicago (Columbia)
Images, Crusaders (ABC-Blue Thumb)
Mixed Emotions, Exile (Warner-Curb)
Children of Sanchez, Chuck Mangione (A&M)
Pieces of Eight, Styx (A&M)
Tormato, Yes (Atlantic)
Let's Keep It That Way, Anne Murray (Capitol)
Only One Love in My Life, Ronnie Milsap (RCA)
Cruisin', Village People (Casablanca)
The Cars, Cars (Elektra)
Elan, Firefall (Atlantic)
Danger Zone, Player (RSO)
52nd Street, Bill Joel (Columbia)
A Single Man, Elton John (MCA)
Along the Red Ledge, Daryl Hall & John Oates (RCA)
Time Passages, Al Stewart (Arista)
What Ever Happened to Benny Santini? Chris Rea (United Artists)
Inner Secrets, Santana (Columbia)

Weekend Warriors, Ted Nugent (Epic)
Marshall Tucker Band's Greatest Hits, Marshall Tucker Band (Capricorn)
Live Bootleg, Aerosmith (Columbia)
A Wild and Crazy Guy, Steve Martin (Warner Bros.)
Goin' Coconuts, Donny & Marie Osmond (Polydor)
Brother to Brother, Gino Vannelli (A&M)
Feel the Need, Leif Garrett (Atlantic) Scotti Bros.)
Songs of Kristofferson, Kris Kristofferson (Columbia)
You Had to Be There, Jimmy Buffett (ABC)
Crystal Ball, Styx (A&M)
A Retrospective, Linda Ronstadt (Capitol)
Backless, Eric Clapton (RSO)
Chaka, Chaka Khan (Warner Bros.-Tattoo)
Totally Hot, Olivia Newton-John (MCA)
Two for the Show, Kansas (CBS-Kirshner)
Barbra Streisand's Greatest Hits, Volume II, Barbra Streisand (Columbia)
In the Night-Time, Michael Henderson (Arista-Buddah)
Sesame Street Fever, Muppets and Robin Gibb (Sesame Street)
Greetings from Asbury Park, New Jersey, Bruce Springsteen (Columbia)
Comes a Time, Neil Young (Warner-Reprise)
Greatest Hits, Barry Manilow (Arista)
The Steve Miller Band's Greatest Hits 1974-78, Steve Miller Band (Capitol)
C'est Chic, Chic (Atlantic)
Jazz, Queen (Elektra)
The Gambler, Kenny Rogers (United Artists)
Wings Greatest, Wings (Capitol)
Bish, Stephen Bishop (ABC)
You Don't Bring Me Flowers, Neil Diamond (Columbia)
The Best of Earth, Wind & Fire, Volume I, Earth, Wind & Fire (Columbia-ARC)

Steely Dan's Greatest Hits, Steely Dan (ABC)
Toto, Toto (Columbia)
Motor-Booty Affair, Parliament (Casablanca)
Blondes Have More Fun, Rod Stewart (Warner Bros.)
Hemispheres, Rush (Mercury)
Tanya Tucker's Greatest Hits, Tanya Tucker (Columbia)
A Legendary Performer—Elvis, Volume 3, Elvis Presley (RCA)
Take This Job and Shove It, Johnny Paycheck (Epic)
Entertainers...on and off the Record, Statler Brothers (Mercury)
Briefcase Full of Blues, Blues Brothers (Atlantic)
Barry White, the Man, Barry White (20th Century Fox)
Minute by Minute, Doobie Brothers (Warner Bros.)
The Last Farewell and Other Hits, Roger Whittaker (RCA)

1979

Heaven Tonight, Cheap Trick (Epic)
Spark of Love, Lenny Williams (ABC)
10th Anniversary of Golden Piano Hits, Ferrante & Teicher (United Artists-Liberty)
John Denver, John Denver (RCA)
Life for the Taking, Eddie Money (Columbia)
Love Beach, Emerson, Lake & Palmer (Atlantic)
Spirits Having Flown, Bee Gees (RSO)
Love Tracks, Gloria Gaynor (Polydor)
New Kind of Feeling, Anne Murray (Capitol)
Sanctuary, J. Geils Band (EMI America)
Gold, Jefferson Starship (RCA-Grunt)
Willie & Family Live, Willie Nelson (Columbia)
Step II, Sylvester (Fantasy)
Energy, Pointer Sisters (Plant-EA)
2 Hot! Peaches & Herb (Polydor)
Dire Straits, Dire Straits (Warner Bros.)

GOLD RECORD AWARDS—ALBUMS

Armed Forces, Elvis Costello (Columbia)
Cheryl Lynn, Chery Lynn (Columbia)
TNT, Tanya Tucker (MCA)
Three Hearts, Bob Welch (Capitol)
Knock on Wood, Amii Stewart (Ariola America)
Crosswinds, Peabo Bryson (Capitol)
Nicolette, Nicolette Larson (Warner Bros.)
Enlightened Rogues, Allman Brothers Band (Capricorn)
Wanted Live in Concert, Richard Pryor (Warner Bros.)
Livin' inside Your Love, George Benson (Warner Bros.)
Live at Budokan, Cheap Trick (Epic)
Destiny, Jacksons (Epic)
Desolation Angels, Bad Company (Swan Song)
I Love You So, Natalie Cole (Capitol)
Van Halen II, Van Halen (Warner Bros.)
Go West, Village People (Casablanca)
Breakfast in America, Supertramp (A&M)
Parallel Lines, Blondie (Chrysalis)
We Are Family, Sister Sledge (Cotillion)
Evolution, Journey (Columbia)
Legend, Poco (MCA)
Music Box Dancer, Frank Mills (Polydor)
Instant Funk, Instant Funk (Salsoul)
Music Box, Evelyn "Champagne" King (RCA)
Inspiration, Maze featuring Frankie Beverly (Capitol)
Disco Nights, G.Q. (Arista)
George Harrison, George Harrison (Dark Horse)
Flag, James Taylor (Columbia)
Hair—motion picture soundtrack (RCA)
Greatest Hits, Waylon Jennings (RCA)
Take Me Home, Cher (Cassablanca)
Rickie Lee Jones, Rickie Lee Jones (Warner Bros.)
The Message Is Love, Barry White (Unlimited Gold Records)
Sooner or Later, Rex Smith (Columbia)
Night Owl, Gerry Rafferty (United Artists)
Dynasty, Kiss (Casablanca)
Teddy, Teddy Pendergrass (Phila. Intl.)
Underdog, Atlanta Rhythm Section (Polydor)
Monolith, Kansas (CBS-Kirshner)
Back to the Egg, Wings (Columbia)
Annie—original cast album (Columbia)
The Kids Are Alright, Starring The Who —motion picture soundtrack (MCA)
Communique, Dire Straits (Warner Bros.)
Best of Nat King Cole, Nat King Cole (Capitol)
Million Mile Reflections, Charlie Daniels (Epic)
Molly Hatchet, Molly Hatchet (Epic)
Classics, Kenny Rogers and Dottie West (United Artists)
Where I Should Be, Peter Frampton (A&M)
Get the Knack, Knack (Capitol)
The Music Band, War (MCA)
Waiting for Columbus, Little Feat (Warner Bros.)
Hot Property, Heatwave (Epic)
Candy-O, Cars (Elektra)
Queen Live Killers, Queen (Elektra)
Reality...What a Concept, Robin Williams (Casablanca)
One for the Road, Willie Nelson and Leon Russell (Columbia)
Decade, Neil Young (Warner-Reprise)
Bustin' Loose, Chuck Brown & the Soul Searchers (Source)
Rock On, Raydio (Arista)
In Color, Cheap Trick (Epic)
McFadden & Whitehead, McFadden and Whitehead (Phila. Intl.)
Street Life, Crusaders (MCA)
What 'Cha Gonna Do with My Lovin', Stephanie Mills (20th Century Fox)
A Night at Studio 54—various artists (Casablanca)
Candy, Con Funk Shun (Mercury)
Rust Never Sleeps, Neil Young (Warner-Reprise)

Morning Dance, Spyro Gyra (Infinity)
Under Wraps, Shaun Cassidy (Warner/Curb)
Look Sharp, Joe Jackson (A&M)
Dionne, Dionne Warwick (Arista)
Pleasure & Pain, Dr. Hook (Capitol)
The Main Event—motion picture soundtrack (CBS)
Bring It Back Alive, Outlaws (Arista)
Ronnie Milsap Live, Ronnie Milsap (RCA)
The Joy of Christmas, Mormon Tabernacle Choir (CBS)
Devotion, LTD (A&M)
Great Balls of Fire, Dolly Parton (RCA)
Voulez-Vouz, ABBA (Atlantic)
Adventures of Panama Red, New Riders of the Purple Sage (Columbia)
First under the Wire, Little River Band (Capitol)
Secret Omen, Cameo (Casablanca)
Nine Lives, REO Speedwagon (Epic)
The Muppet Movie—motion picture soundtrack (Atlantic)
Highway to Hell, AC/DC (Atlantic)
Chicago XIII, Chicago (Columbia)
Off the Wall, Michael Jackson (Epic)
Stay Free, Ashford & Simpson (Warner Bros.)
Give Me Your Love for Christmas, Johnny Mathis (Columbia)
Slow Train Coming, Bob Dylan (Columbia)
Home Free, Dan Fogelberg (Epic)
Identify Yourself, O'Jays (Phila. Intl.)
Volcano, Jimmy Buffett (MCA)

GOLD RECORD AWARDS—SINGLES
(1,000,000 units sold)

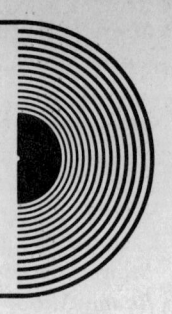

1958

"Catch a Falling Star," Perry Como (RCA Victor)
"He's Got the Whole World in His Hands," Laurie London (Capitol)
"Hard Headed Woman," Elvis Presley (RCA Victor)
"Patricia," Perez Prado (RCA Victor)

1959

"Tom Dooley," Kingston Trio (Capitol)

1960

None

1961

"Calcutta," Lawrence Welk (Dot)
"Big Bad John," Jimmy Dean (Columbia)

1962

"The Lion Sleeps," The Tokens (RCA Victor)
"Can't Help Falling in Love," Elvis Presley (RCA Victor)
"I Can't Stop Loving You," Ray Charles (ABC-Paramount)
"Roses Are Red," Bobby Vinton (Epic)
"Theme from a Summer Place," Percy Faith

1963

"Hey Paula," Paul and Paula (Philips)
"Sugar Shack," Jim Gilmer and the Fireballs (Dot)

1964

"I Want to Hold Your Hand," The Beatles (Capitol)
"Can't Buy Me Love," The Beatles (Capitol)
"Everybody Loves Somebody," Dean Martin (Reprise)
"Rag Doll," The 4 Seasons (Philips)
"A Hard Day's Night," The Beatles (Capitol)
"Oh, Pretty Woman," Roy Orbison (Monument)
"I Feel Fine," The Beatles (Capitol)

1965

"Downtown," Petula Clark (Warner Bros.)
"King of the Road," Roger Miller (Smash)

"Mrs. Brown You've Got a Lovely Daughter," Herman's Hermits (MGM)
"(I Can't Get No) Satisfaction," The Rolling Stones (London)
"Wooly Bully," Sam the Sham and the Pharoahs (MGM)
"I'm Henry VIII, I Am," Herman's Hermits (MGM)
"Help!" The Beatles (Capitol)
"Eight Days a Week," The Beatles (Capitol)
"I Got You Babe," Sonny and Cher (Atco)
"Yesterday," The Beatles (Capitol)
"A Lover's Concerto," The Toys (Dynovoice)

1966

"We Can Work It Out," The Beatles (Capitol)
"Ballad of the Green Berets," SSGT. Barry Sadler (RCA Victor)
"Sounds of Silence," Simon & Garfunkel (Columbia)
"These Boots Are Made for Walkin'," Nancy Sinatra (Reprise)
"Lightnin' Strikes," Lou Christie (MGM)
"No Where Man," The Beatles (Capitol)
"Soul and Inspiration," Righteous Brothers (Verve)
"California Dreamin'," Mamas and the Papas (Dunhill)
"Monday, Monday," Mamas and the Papas (Dunhill)
"Paperback Writer," The Beatles (Capitol)
"When a Man Loves a Woman," Percy Sledge (Atlantic)
"Lil' Red Riding Hood," Sam the Sham and the Pharoahs (MGM)
"Hanky Panky," Tommy James and the Shondells (Roulette)
"Yellow Submarine," The Beatles (Capitol)
"Summer in the City," Lovin' Spoonful (Kama Sutra)
"Sunny," Bob Hebb (Philips)
"Cherish," Association (Valiant)
"Last Train to Clarksville," The Monkees (Colgems)
"96 Tears,"? (Question mark) and the Mysterians (Cameo)
"I'm a Believer," The Monkees (Colgems)
"Winchester Cathedral," New Vaudeville Band (Fontana)
"Battle of New Orleans," Johnny Horton (Columbia)
"Good Vibrations," The Beach Boys (Capitol)

1967

"Snoopy vs. the Red Baron," The Guardsmen
"Mellow Yellow," Donovan (Epic)
"A Little Bit Me, a Little Bit You," The Monkees (Colgems)
"Penny Lane," The Beatles (Capitol)
"Sugartown," Nancy Sinatra (Reprise)
"There's a Kind of Hush (All over the Land)," Herman's Hermits (MGM)
"Somethin' Stupid," Frank and Nancy Sinatra (Reprise)
"This Diamond Ring," Gary Lewis (Liberty)
"Ruby Tuesday," The Rolling Stones (London)
"Happy Together," The Turtles (White Whale)
"Respect," Aretha Franklin (Atlantic)
"Green Onions," Booker T. & the MG's (Stax)
"Stranger on the Shore," Mr. Acker Bilk (Atco)
"I Never Loved a Man the Way I Love You," Aretha Franklin (Atlantic)
"Groovin'," The Young Rascals (Atlantic)
"Sweet Soul Music," Arthur Conley (Atco)
"Pleasant Valley Sunday," The Monkees (Colgems)

"Windy," Association (Warner Bros.)
"Little Bit O' Soul," Music Explosion (Laurie)
"Georgy Girl," The Seekers (Capitol)
"Baby I Love You," Aretha Franklin (Atlantic)
"Ode to Billie Joe," Bobby Gentry (Capitol)
"All You Need Is Love," The Beatles (Capitol)
"Light My Fire," The Doors (Elektra)
"Can't Take My Eyes Off You," Frankie Valli (Philips)
"The Letter," The Box Tops (Mala)
"Come Back When You Grow Up," Bobby Vee and the Strangers (Liberty)
"To Sir with Love," Lulu (Epic)
"Daydream Believer," The Monkees (Colgems)
"Soul Man," Sam and Dave (Stax)
"Never My Love," Association (Warner Bros.)
"Hello Goodbye," The Beatles (Capitol)
"Incense and Peppermints," Strawberry Alarm Clock (UNI)
"The Rain, the Park and Other Things," The Cowsills (MGM)

1968

"Chain of Fools," Aretha Franklin (Atlantic)
"Skinny Legs and All," Joe Tex (Dial)
"Judy in Disguise with Glasses," John Fred and the Playboys (Paula)
"Bend Me, Shape Me," American Breed (Acta)
"Woman, Woman," Union Gap (Columbia)
"Green Tambourine," The Lemon Pipers (Buddah)
"I Say a Little Prayer," Dionne Warwick (Scepter)
"Valleri," The Monkees (Colgems)
"Love Is Blue," Paul Mauriat (Philips)

"Simon Says," 1910 Fruitgum Co. (Buddah)
"(Sittin' on) the Dock of the Bay," Otis Redding (Volt)
"Since You've Been Gone," Aretha Franklin (Atlantic)
"Honey," Bobby Goldsboro (United Artists)
"Young Girl," Union Gap (Columbia)
"Lady Madonna," The Beatles (Capitol)
"Cry like a Baby," Box Tops (Mala)
"Cowboys to Girls," Intruders (Gamble)
"Tighten Up," Archie Bell and the Drells (Atlantic)
"Mrs. Robinson," Simon & Garfunkel (Columbia)
"Yummy, Yummy, Yummy," Ohio Express (Buddah)
"Beautiful Morning," The Rascals (Atlantic)
"Grazing in the Grass," Hugh Masekela (UNI)
"Lady Willpower," Gary Puckett and the Union Gap (Columbia)
"This Guy's in Love with You," Herb Alpert (A&M)
"Think," Aretha Franklin (Atlantic)
"The Horse," Cliff Nobles & Co. (Phil-L.A. Soul)
"People Got to Be Free," The Rascals (Atlantic)
"Harper Valley PTA," Jeannie C. Riley (Plantation)
"Hello, I Love You," The Doors (Elektra)
"Slip Away," Clarence Carter (Atlantic)
"Hey Jude," The Beatles (Capitol)
"Stoned Soul Picnic," 5th Dimension (Liberty)
"Born to Be Wild," Steppenwolf (Dunhill)
"1, 2, 3, Red Light," 1910 Fruitgum Co. (Buddah)
"Turn Around, Look at Me," The Vogues (Reprise)
"Sunshine of Your Love," Cream (Atco)
"I Say a Little Prayer," Aretha Franklin (Atlantic)

"Little Green Aapples," O. C. Smith (Columbia)
"Who's Making Love," Johnnie Taylor (Stax)
"Those Were the Days," Mary Hopkin (Apple)
"Girl Watcher," The O'Kaysions (ABC)
"Midnight Confession," Grassroots (Dunhill)
"Fire," Crazy World of Arthur Brown (Atlantic)
"I Love How You Love Me," Bobby Vinton (Epic)
"Over You," Union Gap (Columbia)

1969

"Chewy, Chewy," Ohio Express (Buddah)
"Abraham, Martin & John," Dion (Laurie)
"See Saw," Aretha Franklin (Atlantic)
"Soulful Strut," Young Holt Limited (Brunswick)
"Wichita Lineman," Glen Campbell (Capitol)
"Touch Me," The Doors (Elektra)
'Everyday People," Sly & the Family Stone (Epic)
"The Worst That Can Happen," Brooklyn Bridge (Buddah)
"Can I Change My Mind," Tyronne Davis (Dakar)
"Hooked on a Feeling," B. J. Thomas (Scepter)
"Too Weak to Fight," Clarence Carter (Atlantic)
"Stormy," Classics IV (Imperial)
"Build Me Up Buttercup," The Foundations (UNI)
"Dizzy," Tommy Roe (ABC)
"Magic Carpet Ride," Steppenwolf (Dunhill)
"Sheila," Tommy Roe (ABC)
"Sweet Pea," Tommy Roe (ABC)
"Indian Giver," 1910 Fruitgum Co. (Buddah)

"It's Your Thing," Isley Brothers (T-Neck)
"Time of the Season," Zombies (Date)
"Hair," The Cowsills (MGM)
"Only the Strong Survive," Jerry Butler (Mercury)
"Aquarius/Let the Sunshine In," 5th Dimension (Soul City)
"This Magic Moment," Jay and the Americans (United Artists)
"Get Back," The Beatles with Billy Preston (Apple)
"Oh Happy Day," Edwin Hawkins' Singers (Pavilion)
"You Make Me So Very Happy," Blood, Sweat and Tears (Columbia)
"The Chokin' Kind," Joe Simon (Sound Stage 7)
"Gitarzan," Roy Stevens (Monument)
"Grazin' in the Grass," Friends of Distinction (RCA)
"In the Ghetto," Elvis Presley (RCA)
"Love Theme from Romeo & Juliet," Henry Mancini (RCA)
"These Eyes," The Guess Who (RCA)
"In the Year 2525," Zager & Evans (RCA)
"Love Can Make You Happy," Mercy (Sundi)
"Ballad of John & Yoko," The Beatles (Capitol)
"Spinning Wheel," Blood, Sweat and Tears (Columbia)
"One," Three Dog Night (Dunhill)
"Color Him Father," Winstons (Metromedia)
"A Boy Named Sue," Johnny Cash (Columbia)
"Sweet Caroline," Neil Diamond (UMI)
"Honky Tonk Women," The Rolling Stones (London)
"Sugar, Sugar," Archies (Calendar)
"Put a Little Love in Your Heart," Jackie DeShannon (Imperial)
"I'll Never Fall in Love Again," Tom Jones (Parrot)
"Little Woman," Bobby Sherman (Metromedia)

"Get Together," Youngbloods (RCA)
"Jean," Oliver (CGC)
"Galveston," Glen Campbell (Capitol)
"Baby, I Love You," Andy Kim (Steed)
"Something," The Beatles (Apple)
"Laughing," The Guess Who (RCA)
"Suspicious Minds," Elvis Presley (RCA)
"Rudolph, the Red Nosed Reindeer," Gene Autry (Columbia)
"Wedding Bell Blues," 5th Dimension (Soul City)
"Na Na Hey Hey Kiss Him Goodbye," Steam (Fontana)
"Take a Letter Maria," R. B. Greaves (Atco)
"Going in Circles," Friends of Distinction (RCA)
"Simle a Little Smile for Me," Flying Machine (Congress)
"Raindrops Keep Falling on My Head," B. J. Thomas (Scepter)
"Back Field in Motion," Mel & Tim (Bamboo)
"Jet Plane," Peter, Paul & Mary (Warner Bros.)
"That'll Be the Day," Buddy Holly and the Crickets (Coral)
"Holly Holy," Neil Diamond (UNI)

1970

"And When I Die," Blood, Sweat and Tears (Columbia)
"Jam Up and Jelly Tight," Tommy Roe (ABC)
"La La La (If I Had You)," Bobby Sherman (Metromedia)
"Don't Cry Daddy," Elvis Presley (RCA)
"Venus," The Shocking Blue (Colossus)
"Jingle Jangle," Archies (Kirshner)
"Thank You (Falettinme Be Mice Elf Agin)," Sly & the Family Stone (Epic)
"Without Love,' Tom Jones (Parrot)
"Bridge over Troubled Water," Simon & Garfunkel (Columbia)
"Hey There Lonely Girl," Eddie Holman (ABC)
"Let It Be," The Beatles (Apple)
"Didn't I (Blow Your Mind This Time)," The Delfonics (Philly Groove)
"Rainy Night in Georgia," Brook Benton (Cotillion)
"The Rapper," Jaggerz (Kama Sutra)
"Easy Come, Easy Go," Bobby Sherman (Metromedia)
"Whole Lotta Love," Led Zeppelin (Atlantic)
"Arizona," Mark Lindsay (Columbia)
"Love Grows (Where My Rosemary Goes)," Edison Lighthouse (Bell)
"Spirit in the Sky," Norman Greenbaum (Reprise)
"House of the Rising Son," Frijid Pink (Parrot)
"Turn Back the Hands of Time," Tyrone Davis (Dakar)
"Give Me Just a Little More Time," Chairmen of the Board (Invictus)
"American Woman," The Guess Who (RCA)
"Love on a Two-way Street," Moments (Stang)
"Cecilia," Simon & Garfunkel (Columbia)
"Which Way You Goin' Billy," Poppy Family (London)
"Everything Is Beautiful," Ray Stevens (Barnaby)
"Hitchin' a Ride," Vanity Fair (Page One)
"Mama Told Me (Not to Come)," Three Dog Night (Dunhill)
"Band of Gold," Freda Payne (Invictus)
"Ride Captain Ride," Blues Image (Atco)
"Make It with You," Bread (Elektra)
"O-O-H Child," Stairsteps (Buddah)
"(They Long to Be) Close to You," Carpenters (A&M)
"The Wonder of You," Elvis Presley (RCA)
"In the Summertime," Mungo Jerry (Janus)
"Julie, Do Ya Love Me," Bobby Sherman (Metromedia)
"Patches," Clarence Carter (Atlantic)

"Spill the Wine," Eric Burdon and War (MGM)
"Candida," Dawn (Bell)
"Don't Play That Song," Aretha Franklin (Atlantic)
"Cracklin' Rosie," Neil Diamond (UNI)
"I Think I Love You," The Partridge Family (Bell)
"Groovy Situation," Gene Chandler (Mercury)
"We've Only Just Begun," The Carpenters (A&M)
"Snowbird," Anne Murray (Capitol)
"Somebody Has Been Sleeping in My Bed," 100 Proof (Hot Wax)
"One Less Bell to Answer," Fifth Dimension (Bell)
"Instant Karma," John Ono Lennon (Apple)
"My Sweet Lord," George Harrison (Apple)
"Down on the Corner," Creedence Clearwater Revival (Fantasy)
"Travelin' Band," Creedence Clearwater Revival (Fantasy)
"Bad Moon Rising," Creedence Clearwater Revival (Fantasy)
"Up around the Bend," Creedence Clearwater Revival (Fantasy)
"Lookin' Out My Back Door," Creedence Clearwater Revival (Fantasy)
"Knock Three Times," Dawn (Bell)

1971

"Groove Me," King Floyd (Chimneyville)
"Gypsy Woman," Brian Hyland (UNI)
"Rose Garden," Lynn Anderson (Columbia)
"One Bad Apple," The Osmonds (MGM)
"Precious, Precious," Jackie Moore (Atlantic)
"Doesn't Somebody Want to Be Wanted," The Partridge Family (Bell)
"Have You Ever Seen the Rain," Creedence Clearwater Revival (Fantasy)

"Don't Let the Green Grass Fool You," Wilson Pickett (Atlantic)
"She's a Lady," Tom Jones (Parrot)
"Amos Moses," Jerry Reed (RCA)
"Lonely Days," The Bee Gets (Atco)
"Joy to the World," Three Dog Night (ABC-Dunhill)
"For All We Know," The Carpenters (A&M)
"The Battle Hymn of Lt. Calley," Terry Nelson (Plantation)
"Help Me Make It through the Night," Sammi Smith (Mega)
"Put Your Hand in the Hand," Ocean (Kama Sutra)
"Proud Mary," Ike and Tina Turner (Liberty)
"Bridge over Troubled Water," Aretha Franklin (Atlantic)
"Want Ads," Honey Cone (Hot Wax)
"Stay Awhile," The Bells (Polydor)
"Don't Knock My Love," Wilson Pickett (Atlantic)
"Indian Reservation," Raiders (Columbia)
"Rainy Days & Mondays," The Carpenters (A&M)
"It's Too Late," Carole King (Ode)
"Treat Her like a Lady," Cornelius Brothers and Sister Rose (United Artists)
"It Don't Come Easy," Ringo Starr (Apple)
"Don't Pull Your Love," Hamilton, Joe Frank and Reynolds (ABC-Dunhill)
"Take Me Home, Country Roads," John Denver (RCA)
"How Can You Mend a Broken Heart," The Bee Gees (Atco)
"Spanish Harlem," Aretha Franklin (Atlantic)
"Bring the Boys Home," Freda Payne (Invictus)
"Sweet and Innocent," Donny Osmond (MGM)
"Signs," Five Man Electrical Band (Lionel)
"You've Got a Friend," James Taylor (Warner Bros.)

"She's Not Just Another Woman," 8th Day (Invictus)
"Uncle Albert/Admiral Halsey," Paul & Linda McCartney (Apple)
"Ain't No Sunshine," Bill Withers (Sussex)
"Stick-Up," Honey Cone (Hot Wax)
"Maggie May," Rod Stewart (Mercury)
"Go Away Little Girl," Donny Osmond (MGM)
"Superstar," The Carpenters (A&M)
"The Night They Drove Old Dixie Down," Joan Baez (Vanguard)
"Tired of Being Alone," Al Green (Hi)
"Thin Line Between Love and Hate," Persuaders (Atco)
"Yo-Yo," The Osmonds (MGM)
"Gypsys, Tramps & Thieves," Cher (Kapp)
"Easy Loving," Freddie Hart (Capitol)
"Family Affair," Sly & the Family Stone (Epic)
"Trapped by a Thing Called Love," Denise LaSalle (Westbound)
"Scorpio," Dennis Coffey and the Detroit Guitar Band (Sussex)
"Rock Steady," Aretha Franklin (Atlantic)
"Cherish," David Cassidy (Bell)
"Brand New Key," Melanie (Neighborhood)
"An Old Fashioned Love Song," Three Dog Night (ABC-Dunhill)
"Clean Up Woman," Betty Wright (Alston)

1972

"You Are Everything," Stylistics (Avco)
"American Pie," Don McLean (United Artists)
"Drowning in the Sea of Love," Joe Simon (Spring)
"Let's Stay Together," Al Green (Hi)
"Baby I'm a Want You," Bread (Elektra)
"Sunshine," Jonathan Edwards (Capricorn)
"I'd Like to Teach the World to Sing," New Seekers (Elektra)
"Precious and Few," Climax (Carousel)
"Hurting Each Other," The Carpenters (A&M)
"Without You," Nilsson (RCA)
"Day after Day," Badfinger (Apple)
"Kiss an Angel Good Mornin'," Charley Pride (RCA)
"The Lion Sleeps Tonight," Robert John (Atlantic)
"I Gotcha," Joe Tex (Dial)
"Jungle Fever," Chakachas (Polydor)
"Puppy Love," Donny Osmond (MGM)
"A Horse with No Name," America (Warner Bros.)
"Down by the Lazy River," The Osmonds (MGM)
"Ain't Understanding Mellow," Jerry Butler and Brenda Lee Eager (Mercury)
"Betcha by Golly, Wow," Stylistics (Avco)
"The First Time Ever I Saw Your Face," Roberta Flack (Atlantic)
"Day Dreaming," Aretha Franklin (Atlantic)
"Heart of Gold," Neil Young (Warner Bros.)
"Look What You've Done for Me," Al Green (Hi)
"Lean on Me," Bill Withers (Sussex)
"Nice to Be with You," Gallery (Sussex)
"Outa-Space," Billy Preston (A&M)
"Slippin' into Darkness," War (United Artists)
"Troglodyte," Jimmy Castor Bunch (RCA)
"Last Night I Didn't Get to Sleep at All," Fifth Dimension (Bell)
"Daddy Don't You Walk So Fast," Wayne Newton (Chelsea)
"Walking in the Rain with the One I Love," Love Unlimited (UNI)
"Song Sung Blue," Neil Diamond (UNI)
"Hey Girl," Donny Osmond (MGM)
"Sylvia's Mother," Dr. Hook and the Medicine Show (Columbia)

"The Way I Want to Touch You," Captain & Tennille (A&M)
"Convoy," C. W. McCall (MGM)

1976

"Love Rollercoaster," Ohio Players (Mercury)
"I Write the Songs," Barry Manilow (Arista)
"I Love Music," The O'Jays (Phila. Intl.)
"You Sexy Thing," Hot Chocolate (Big Tree)
"Proud Mary," Creedence Clearwater Revival (Fantasy)
"Theme from S.W.A.T.," Rhythm Heritage (ABC)
"Love to Love You Baby," Donna Summer (Oasis)
"Fox on the Run," Sweet (Capitol)
"Singasong," Earth, Wind & Fire (Columbia)
"Sweet Thing," Rufus featuring Chaka Khan (ABC)
"Disco Lady," Johnnie Taylor (Columbia)
"50 Ways to Leave Your Lover," Paul Simon (Columbia)
"December, 1963 (Oh, What a Night)," Four Seasons (Warner Bros.)
"Lonely Night (Angel Face)," Captain & Tennille (A&M)
"Love Hurts," Nazareth (A&M)
"Boogie Fever," Sylvers (Capitol)
"Dream Weaver," Gary Wright (Warner Bros.)
"All By Myself," Eric Carmen (Arista)
"Right Back Where We Started From," Maxine Nightingale (United Artists)
"Only Sixteen," Dr. Hook (Capitol)
"Welcome Back," John Sebastian (Warner-Reprise)
"I.O.U.," Jimmy Dean (GRT-Casino)
"Bohemian Rhapsody," Queen (Elektra)
"Get Up and Boogie," Silver Convention (Midland International-RCA)
"Silly Love Songs," Wings (Capitol)
"Kiss and Say Goodbye," The Manhattans (Columbia)
"Shannon," Henry Gross (Lifesong)
"Fooled Around and Fell in Love," Elvin Bishop (Capricorn)
"Sara Smile," Daryl Hall & John Oates (RCA)
"Afternoon Delight," Starland Vocal Band (Windsong)
"Shop Around," Captain & Tennille (A&M)
"Don't Go Breaking My Heart," Elton John and Kiki Dee (MCA-Rocket)
"You'll Never Find Another Love Like Mine," Lou Rawls (Phila. Intl.)
"Play That Funky Music," Wild Cherry (Epic-Sweet City)
"A Fifth of Beethoven," Walter Murphy and the Big Apple Band (Private Stock)
"Summer," War (United Artists)
"You Should Be Dancing," The Bee Gees (RSO)
"Heaven Must Be Missing an Angel," Tavares (Capitol)
"More, More, More," Andrea True Connection (Buddah)
"Disco Duck," Rick Dees and His Cast of Idiots (RSO)
"I'd Really Love to See You Tonight," England Dan & John Ford Coley (Big Tree)
"Tear the Roof Off the Sucker," Parliament (Casablanca)
"Devil Woman," Cliff Richard (MCA-Rocket)
"Let 'Em In," Wings (Capitol)
'If You Leave Me Now," Chicago (Columbia)
"Getaway," Earth, Wind & Fire (Columbia)
"Lowdown," Boz Scaggs (Columbia)
"Teddy Bear," Red Sovine (Gusto-Starday)
"You Don't Have to Be a Star (To Be in My Show)," Marilyn McCoo & Billy Davis, Jr. (ABC)
"Tonight's the Night (Gonna Be Alright)," Rod Stewart (Warner Bros.)

"The Rubberband Man," Spinners (Atlantic)
"Muskrat Love," Captain & Tennille (A&M)
"Car Wash," Rose Royce (MCA)
"You Make Me Feel Like Dancing," Leo Sayer (Warner Bros.)

1977

"Hot Line," Sylvers (Capitol)
"Beth," Kiss (Casablanca)
"I'll Be Good to You," Brothers Johnson (A&M)
"Nadia's Theme ('The Young & the Restless')," Barry DeVorzon and Perry Borkin, Jr. (A&M)
"Stand Tall," Burton Cummings (Portrait)
"Sorry Seems to Be the Hardest Word," Elton John (MCA)
"Enjoy Yourself," Jacksons (Epic)
"Torn between Two Lovers," Mary MacGregor (Capitol-Ariola America)
"After the Lovin'," Engelbert Humperdinck (Epic)
"Blinded by the Light," Manfred Mann's Earth Band (Warner Bros.)
"I Like Dreamin'," Kenny Nolan (20th Century Fox)
"New Kid in Town," Eagles (Asylum)
"Dancing Queen," ABBA (Atlantic)
"Evergreen (Theme from 'A Star Is Born')," Barbra Streisand (Columbia)
"Rich Girl," Daryl Hall & John Oates (RCA)
"I Never Cry," Alice Cooper (Warner Bros.)
"Don't Give Up on Us," David Soul (Private Stock)
"I've Got Love on My Mind," Natalie Cole (Capitol)
"The Things We Do for Love," 10CC (Phonogram-Mercury)
"Fly like an Eagle," Steve Miller Band (Capitol)
"Southern Nights," Glen Campbell (Capitol)
"Tryin' to Love Two," William Bell (Phonogram-Mercury)
"When I Need You," Leon Sayer (Warner Bros.)
"Hotel California," Eagles (Asylum)
"Ain't Gonna Bump No More," Joe Tex (Epic)
"Lucille," Kenny Rogers (United Artists)
"Undercover Angel," Alan O'Day (Atlantic)
"Gonna Fly Now (Theme from 'Rocky')," Bill Conti (United Artists)
"Angel in Your Arms," Hot (Atlantic-Big Tree)
"Da Doo Ron Ron," Shaun Cassidy (Warner Bros.)
"Best of My Love," Emotions (Columbia)
"I Just Want to Be Your Everything," Andy Gibb (RSO)
"Travelin' Man," Rick Nelson (United Artists-Imperial)
"Do You Wanna Make Love," Peter McCann (20th Century Fox)
"Float On," Floaters (ABC)
"(Your Love Has Lifted Me) Higher and Higher," Rita Coolidge (A&M)
"Looks Like We Made It," Barry Manilow (Arista)
"The King Is Gone," Ronnie McDowell (GRT)
"Way Down," Elvis Presley (RCA)
"Dreams," Fleetwood Mac (Warner Bros.)
"Telephone Line," Electric Light Orchestra (United Artists-Jet)
"Star Wars Theme/Cantina Band," Meco (Millennium)
"That's Rock 'n' Roll," Shaun Cassidy (Warner Bros.)
"Boogie Nights," Heatwave (Epic)
"It's Ecstasy When You Lay Down Next to Me," Barry White (20th Century Fox)
"Strawberry Letter 23," Brothers Johnson (A&M)
"You Light Up My Life," Debby Boone (Warner Bros.)
"Telephone Man," Meri Wilson (GRT)

"Nobody Does It Better," Carly Simon (Elektra)
"I Feel Love," Donna Summer (Casablanca)
"Don't It Make My Brown Eyes Blue," Crystal Gayle (United Artists)
"Swayin' to the Music," Johnny Rivers (Atlantic-Big Tree)
"Heaven on the 7th Floor," Paul Nicholas (RSO)
"How Deep Is Your Love," The Bee Gees (RSO)
"(Every Time I Turn Around) Back in Love Again," L.T.D. (A&M)

1978

"Baby Come Back," Player (RSO)
"My Way," Elvis Presley (RSA)
"Hey Deanie," Shaun Cassidy (Warner Bros.)
"Blue Bayou," Linda Ronstadt (Asylum)
"Short People," Randy Newman (Warner Bros.)
"We Are the Champions," Queen (Elektra)
"Stayin' Alive," Bee Gees (RSO)
"Here You Come Again," Dolly Parton (RCA)
"We're All Alone," Rita Coolidge (A&M)
"You're in My Heart," Rod Stewart (Warner Bros.)
"Emotion," Samantha Sang (Private Stock)
"Dance, Dance, Dance," Chic (Atlantic) lantic)
"Love Is Thicker than Water," Andy Gibb (RSO)
"Night Fever," Bee Gees (RSO)
"Sometimes When We Touch," Dan Hill (20th Century Fox)
"Just the Way You Are," Billy Joel (Columbia)
"Always and Forever," Heatwave (Epic)
"Our Love," Natalie Cole (Capitol)
"Can't Smile without You," Barry Manilow (Arista)

"You're the One That I Want," John Travolta and Olivia Newton-John RSO)
"Lay Down Sally," Eric Clapton (RSO)
"Flash Light," Parliament (Casablanca)
"Jack and Jill," Raydio (Arista)
"The Closer I Get to You," Roberta Flack and Donny Hathaway (Atlantic)
"If I Can't Have You," Yvonne Elliman (RSO)
"Too Much, Too Little, Too Late," Johnny Mathis and Deniece Williams (Columbia)
"Shadow Dancing," Andy Gibb (RSO)
"Use ta Be My Girl," O'Jays (Phila. Intl.)
"It's a Heartache," Bonnie Tyler (RCA)
"Dust in the Wind," Kansas (CBS-Kirshner)
"The Groove Line," Heatwave (Epic)
"Baker Street," Gerry Rafferty (United Artists)
"Last Dance," Donna Summer (Casablanca)
"Two out of Three Ain't Bad," Meat Loaf (Cleveland Intl.)
"Miss You," Rolling Stones (Rolling Stones)
"Grease," Frankie Valli (RSO)
"Take a Chance on Me," ABBA (Atlantic)
"Boogie Oogie Oogie," Taste of Honey (Capitol)
"Shame," Evelyn "Champagne" King (RCA)
"An Everlasting Love," Andy Gibb (RSO)
"King Tut," Steve Marting (Warner Bros.)
"Summer Nights," John Travolta, Olivia Newton-John and cast from Grease (RSO)
"Hopelessly Devoted to You," Olivia Newton-John (RSO)
"Copacabana," Barry Manilow (Arista)
"Hot Blooded," Foreigner (Atlantic)
"Got to Get You into My Life," Earth Wind & Fire (Columbia-ARC)

"Hot Child in the City," Nick Gilder (Chrysalis)
"Kiss You All Over," Exile (Warner-Curb)
"Close the Door," Teddy Pendergrass (Phila. Intl.)
"You Needed Me," Anne Murray (Capitol)
"MacArthur Park," Donna Summer (Casablanca)
"Macho Man," Village People (Casablanca)
"Magnet and Steel," Walter Egan (Columbia)
"Double Vision," Foreigner (Atlantic)
"Le Freak," Chic (Atlantic)
"You Don't Bring Me Flowers," Barbra Streisand and Neil Diamond (Columbia)
"One Nation under a Groove," Funkadelic (Warner Bros.)
"Too Much Heaven," Bee Gees (RSO)
"I Love the Night Life," Alicia Bridges (Polydor)
"YMCA," Village People (Casablanca)

1979

"Sharing the Night Together," Dr. Hook (Capitol)
"(Our Love) Don't Throw It All Away," Andy Gibb (RSO)
"Got to Be Real," Cheryl Lynn (Columbia)
"My Life," Billy Joel (Columbia)
"Instant Replay," Dan Hartman (CBS-Blue Sky)
"September," Earth, Wind & Fire (Columbia-ARC)
"Da Ya Think I'm Sexy," Rod Stewart (Warner Bros.)
"Every 1's a Winner," Hot Chocolate (Infinity)
"Tragedy," Bee Gees (RSO)
"Fire," Pointer Sisters (Planet-EA)
"I Will Survive," Gloria Gaynor (Polydor)
"A Little More Love," Olivia Newton-John (MCA)
"Hold the Line," Toto (Columbia)
"Shake Your Groove Thing," Peaches & Herb (Polydor)
"I Don't Know if It's Right," Evelyn "Champagne" King (RCA)
"I Want Your Love," Chic (Atlantic)
"Heaven Knows," Donna Summer with Brooklyn Dreams (Casablanca)
"Bustin' Loose," Chuck Brown & the Soul Searchers (Casablanca-Source)
"In the Navy," Village People (Casablanca)
"Knock on Wood," Amii Stewart (Ariola America)
"Music Box Dancer," Frank Mills (Polydor)
"I Got My Mind Made Up (You Can Get It Girl)," Instant Funk (RCA-Salsoul)
"What a Fool Believes," Doobie Brothers (Warner Bros.)
"Reunited," Peaches & Herb (Polydor)
"Heart of Glass," Blondie (Chrysalis)
"Livin' It Up," Bell & James (A&M)
"Love You Inside Out," Bee Gees (RSO)
"Shake Your Body," Jacksons (Epic)
"Hot Stuff," Donna Summer (Casablanca)
"Disco Nights (Rock-Freak)," G.Q. (Arista)
"Take Me Home," Cher (Casablanca)
"Ain't No Stopping Us Now," McFadden & Whitehead (Phila. Intl.)
"Good Night Tonight," Wings (Columbia)
"Boogie Wonderland," Earth, Wind & Fire with the Emotions (ARC)
"Stumblin' In," Suzi Quatro with Chris Norman (RSO)
"We Are Family," Sister Sledge
"Bad Girls," Donna Summer (Casablanca)
"Good Times," Chic (Atlantic)
"You Take My Breath Away," Rex Smith (Columbia)

"Makin' It," David Naughton (RSO)
"Just When I Needed You Most," Randy Vanwarmer (Bearsville)
"She Believes in Me," Kenny Rogers (United Artists)
"I Want You to Want Me," Cheap Trick (Epic)
"My Sharona," Knack (Capitol)
"I Was Made for Lovin' You," Kiss (Casablanca)
"Mama Can't Buy You Love," Elton John (MCA)
"The Devil Went Down to Georgia," Charlie Daniels Band (Epic)
"When You're in Love with a Beautiful Woman," Dr. Hook (Capitol)
"Main Event," Barbra Streisand (Columbia)
"You Gonna Make Me Love Somebody Else," Jones Girls (Phila. Intl.)
"Sad Eyes," Robert John (EMI)
"Rise," Herb Alpert (A&M)
"Lead Me On," Maxine Nightingale (Windsong)
"Knock On Wood," Amii Stewart (Ariola)
"Don't Stop 'till You Get Enough," Michael Jackson (Epic)
"Don't Bring Me Down," Electric Light Orchestra (Jet)
"I'll Never Love This Way Again," Dionne Warwick (Arista)
"Born to Be Alive," Patrick Hernandez (Columbia)
"After the Love Has Gone," Earth, Wind & Fire (Columbia-ARC)
"Pop Muzik," M (Warner Bros.)
"Ladies' Night," Kool & the Gang (Delite)
"Dim All the Lights," Donna Summer (Casablanca)

PLATINUM RECORD AWARDS—ALBUMS
(1,000,000 units sold)

1976

Eagles—Their Greatest Hits, Eagles (Asylum)
Desire, Bob Dylan (Columbia)
Frampton Comes Alive!, Peter Frampton (A&M)
Presence, Led Zeppelin (Swan Song)
Wings at the Speed of Sound, Wings (Capitol)
Rock 'n' Roll Music, The Beatles (Capitol)
Black and Blue, The Rolling Stones (Rolling Stone)
Rocks, Aerosmith (Columbia)
Breezin', George Benson (Warner Bros.)
Look Out for #1, Brothers Johnson (A&M)
Chicago X, Chicago (Columbia)
Membership Connection, Parliament (Casablanca)
Beautiful Noise, Neil Diamond (Columbia)
Silk Degrees, Boz Scaggs (Columbia)
Song of Joy, Captain & Tennille (A&M)
Fly Like an Eagle, Steve Miller Band (Capitol)
Spitfire, Jefferson Starship (Grunt)
Spirit, John Denver (RCA)
Spirit, Earth, Wind & Fire (Columbia)
Hasten Down the Wind, Linda Ronstadt (Asylum)
Dreamboat Annie, Heart (Mushroom)
Destroyer, Kiss (Casablanca)
The Song Remains the Same, Led Zeppelin (Swan Song)
Boston, Boston (Epic)
A Night on the Town, Rod Stewart (Warner Bros.)
The Outlaws, Waylon Jennings, Willie Nelson, Jessi Colter, Tompall Glaser (RCA)
Run with the Pack, Bad Company (Swan Song)
A New World Record, Electric Light Orchestra (United Artists)
Blue Moves, Elton John (MCA-Rocket)
Brass Construction, Brass Construction (United Artists)
Hotel California, Eagles (Asylum)
Wild Cherry, Wild Cherry (Epic-Sweet City)
Wings over America, Wings (Capitol)
Best of the Doobies, Doobie Brothers (Warner Bros.)
Children of the World, The Bee Gees (RSO)
One More for From the Road, Lynyrd Skynyrd (MCA)
Soul Searching, Average White Band

1977

Rock and Roll Over, Kiss (Casablanca)
Greatest Hits, War (United Artists)
This One's for You, Barry Manilow (Arista)
Greatest Hits, Linda Ronstadt (Asylum)
A Star Is Born, Barbra Streisand and Kris Kristofferson
All Things in Time, Lou Rawls (Phila. Intl.)
Rumours, Fleetwood Mac (Warner Bros.)

PLATINUM RECORD AWARDS—ALBUMS

Animals, Pink Floyd (Columbia)
Leftoverture, Kansas (Columbia-Kirshner)
Year of the Cat, Al Stewart (GRT-Janus)
Night Moves, Bob Seger and the Silver Bullet Band (Capitol)
The Pretender, Jackson Browne (Asylum)
Ask Rufus, Rufus featuring Chaka Khan (ABC)
After the Lovin', Engelbert Humperdinck (Epic)
Go for Your Guns, Isley Brothers (T-Neck)
Book of Dreams, Steve Miller Band (Capitol)
I'm in You, Peter Frampton (A&M)
Barry Manilow Live, Barry Manilow (Arista)
Rocky—motion picture soundtrack (United Artists)
Love Gun, Kiss (Casablanca)
Love at the Greek, Neil Diamond (Columbia)
Little Queen, Heart (Portrait)
Right on Time, Brothers Johnson (A&M)
Superman, Barbra Streisand (Columbia)
Foreigner, Foreigner (Atlantic)
Unpredictable, Natalie Cole (Capitol)
The Beatles at the Hollywood Bowl, The Beatles (Capitol)
Star Wars—motion picture soundtrack (20th Century Fox)
CSN, Crosby, Stills & Nash (Atlantic)
Rejoice, Emotions (Columbia)
J.T., James Taylor (Columbia)
Moody Blue, Elvis Presley (RCA)
Endless Flight, Leo Sayer (Warner Bros.)
Shaun Cassidy, Shaun Cassidy (Warner Bros.)
Cat Scratch Fever, Ted Nugent (Epic)
Free for All, Ted Nugent (Epic)
In Flight, George Benson (Warner Bros.)
The Floaters, The Floaters (ABC)
Ol' Waylon, Waylon Jennings (RCA)
Chicago XI, Chicago (Columbia)
Simple Dreams, Linda Ronstadt (Asylum)
In Concert, Elvis Presley (RCA)
Anytime . . . Anywhere, Rita Coolidge (A&M)
Elton John's Greatest Hits, Vol. II, Elton John (MCA)
Out of the Blue, Electric Light Orchestra (United Artists-Jet)
Barry White Sings for Someone You Love, Barry White (20th Century Fox)
James Taylor's Greatest Hits, James Taylor (Warner Bros.)
Here at Last . . . Bee Gees . . . Live, The Bee Gees (RSO)
Kiss Alive II, Kiss (Casablanca)
Point of Know Return, Kansas (Columbia-Kirshner)
Elvis Sings the Wonderful World of Christmas, Elvis Presley (RCA)
In Full Bloom, Rose Royce (Warner Bros.-Whitfield)
Down Two Then Left, Boz Scaggs (Columbia)
All 'n' All, Earth, Wind & Fire (Columbia)
Street Survivors, Lynyrd Skynyrd (MCA)
I'm Glad You're Here with Me Tonight, Neil Diamond (Columbia)
Draw the Line, Aerosmith (Columbia)
You Light Up My Life, Debby Boone (Warner Bros.)
Born Late, Shaun Cassidy (Warner Bros.)
Changes in Latitudes, Changes in Attitudes, Jimmy Buffett (ABC)
Greatest Hits, Olivia Newton-John (MCA)
'Live' Bullet, Bob Seger and the Silver Bullet Band (Capitol)
Foghat Live, Foghat (Bearsville)
Foot Loose & Fancy Free, Rod Stewart (Warner Bros.)
Too Hot to Handle, Heatwave (Epic)
The Grand Illusion, Styx (A&M)
Aja, Steely Dan (ABC)
News of the World, Queen (Elektra)

1978

Saturday Night Fever, Bee Gees (RSO)
The Stranger, Billy Joel (Columbia)
Greatest Hits, Etc., Paul Simon (Columbia)
We Must Believe in Magic, Crystal Gayle (United Artists)
Even Now, Barry Manilow (Arista)
Slowhand, Eric Clapton (RSO)
London Town, Paul McCartney & Wings (Capitol)
Waylon & Willie, Waylon Jennings and Willie Nelson (RCA)
Here You Come Again, Dolly Parton (RCA)
French Kiss, Bob Welch (Capitol)
Weekend in L.A., George Benson (Warner Bros.)
Showdown, Isley Brothers (T-Neck)
M.U.—The Best of Jethro Tull, Jethro Tull (Chrysalis)
Earth, Jefferson Starship (Grunt)
Funkentelechy vs. the Placebo Syndrome, Parliament (Casablanca)
Grease—motion picture soundtrack (RSO)
Let's Get Small, Steve Martin (Warner Bros.)
Son of a Son of a Sailor, Jimmy Buffett (ABC)
FM—motion picture soundtrack (MCA)
I Want to Live, John Denver (RCA)
Double Platinum, Kiss (Casablanca)
Feels So Good, Chuck Mangione (A&M)
Carolina Dreams, Marshall Tucker Band (Capricorn)
Stranger in Town, Bob Seger and the Silver Bullet Band (Capitol)
So Full of Love, O'Jays (Phila. Intl.)
Magazine, Heart (Mushroom)
Star Wars and Other Galactic Funk, Meco (Millenium)
Thank God It's Friday—motion picture soundtrack (Casablanca)
Shadow Dancing, Andy Gibb (RSO)
City to City, Gerry Rafferty (United Artists)
Central Heating, Heatwave (Epic)
Thankful, Natalie Cole (Capitol)
Teddy Pendergrass, Teddy Pendergrass (Phila. Intl.)
Double Vision, Foreigner (Atlantic)
Some Girls, Rolling Stones (Rolling Stones)
Darkness on the Edge of Town, Bruce Springsteen (Columbia)
You Light Up My Life, Johnny Mathis (Columbia)
Agents of Fortune, Blue Oyster Cult (Columbia)
Sgt. Pepper's Lonely Hearts Club Band—motion picture soundtrack (RSO)
Greatest Hits, ABBA (Atlantic)
Ten Years of Gold, Kenny Rogers (United Artists)
Double Live Gonzo, Ted Nugent (Epic)
Takin' It to the Streets, Doobie Brothers (Warner Bros.)
Flowing Rivers, Andy Gibb (RSO)
But Seriously, Folks, Joe Walsh (Asylum)
Boys in the Trees, Carly Simon (Elektra)
The Album, ABBA (Atlantic)
Don't Look Back, Boston (Epic)
Running on Empty, Jackson Browne (Asylum)
Natural High, Commodores (Motown)
Bat Out of Hell, Meat Loaf (Cleveland Intl.)
Life Is a Song Worth Singing, Teddy Pendergrass (Phila. Intl.)
Songbird, Barbra Streisand (Columbia)
Worlds Away, Pablo Cruise (A&M)
Togetherness, L.T.D. (A&M)
Blam, Brothers Johnson (A&M)
Who Are You, The Who (MCA)
Living in the U.S.A., Linda Ronstadt (Asylum)
Champagne Jam, Atlanta Rhythm Section (Polydor)
Kiss—Ace Frehley, Ace Frehley (Casablanca)
Kiss—Peter Criss, Peter Criss (Casablanca)
Kiss—Paul Stanley, Paul Stanley (Casablanca)

PLATINUM RECORD AWARDS—ALBUMS

Kiss—Gene Simmons, Gene Simmons (Casablanca)
A Taste of Honey, Taste of Honey (Capitol)
Pieces of Eight, Styx (A&M)
Van Halen, Van Halen (Warner Bros.)
Under Wraps, Shaun Cassidy (Warner-Curb)
Infinity, Journey (Columbia)
Nightwatch, Kenny Loggins (Columbia)
Live and More, Donna Summer (Casablanca)
52nd Street, Billy Joel (Columbia)
I Robot, Alan Parsons Project (Arista)
Dog and Butterfly, Heart (Portrait)
Hot Streets, Chicago (Columbia)
Tormato, Yes (Atlantic)
Sounds . . . and Stuff Like That, Quincy Jones (A&M)
Skynyrd's First and . . . Last, Lynyrd Skynyrd (MCA)
Backless, Eric Clapton (RSO)
A Single Man, Elton John (MCA)
Weekend Warriors, Ted Nugent (Epic)
Barbra Streisand's Greatest Hits, Volume II, Barbra Streisand (Columbia)
A Wild and Crazy Guy, Steve Martin (Warner Bros.)
Greatest Hits, Barry Manilow (Arista)
The Steve Miller Band's Greatest Hits 1974-78, Steve Miller Band (Capitol)
Jazz, Queen (Elektra)
Totally Hot, Olivia Newton-John (MCA)
Wings Greatest, Wings (Capitol)
You Don't Bring Me Flowers, Neil Diamond (Columbia)
The Best of Earth, Wind & Fire, Volume I, Earth, Wind & Fire (ARC)
Steely Dan's Greatest Hits, Steely Dan (ABC)
Twin Sons of Different Mothers, Dan Fogelberg and Tim Weisberg (Full Moon)
Cruisin', Village People (Casablanca)
You Get What You Play For, REO Speedwagon (Epic)
One Nation Under a Groove, Funkadelic (Warner Bros.)
Let's Keep It That Way, Anne Murray (Capitol)
Barry White, the Man, Barry White (20th Century Fox)
Live Bootleg, Aerosmith (Columbia)
Stardust, Willie Nelson (Columbia)
Macho Man, Village People (Casablanca)
The Cars, Cars (Elektra)
C'est Chic, Chic (Atlantic)
Blondes Have More Fun, Rod Stewart (Warner Bros.)

1979

Briefcase Full of Blues, Blues Brothers (Atlantic)
Elan, Firefall (Atlantic)
Brother to Brother, Gino Vannelli (A&M)
Toto, Toto (Columbia)
Octave, Moody Blues (London)
Spirits Having Flown, Bee Gees (RSO)
The Gambler, Kenny Rogers (United Artists)
Minute by Minute, Doobie Brothers (Warner Brothers)
Two for the Show, Kansas (Kirshner)
Time Passages, Al Stewart (Arista)
Love Tracks, Gloria Gaynor (Polydor)
Dire Straits, Dire Straits (Warner Bros.)
2 Hot! Peaches & Herb (Polydor)
Go West, Village People (Casablanca)
Desolation Angels, Bad Company (Swan Song)
Bad Girls, Donna Summer (Casablanca)
Destiny, Jacksons (Epic)
Van Halen II, Van Halen (Warner Bros.)
Breakfast in America, Supertramp (A&M)
Sleeper Catcher, Little River Band (Harvest)
Live at Budokan, Cheap Trick (Epic)
We Are Family, Sister Sledge (Atlantic)
Parallel Lines, Blondie (Chrysalis)
I Am, Earth, Wind & Fire (ARC)
Back to the Egg, Wings (Columbia)
Discovery, Electric Light Orchestra (Jet)
Dynasty, Kiss (Casablanca)

Teddy, Teddy Pendergrass (Phila. Intl.)
Get the Knack, Knack (Capitol)
Candy-O, Cars (Elektra)
Rickie Lee Jones, Rickie Lee Jones (Warner Bros.)
Million Mile Reflections, Charlie Daniels Band (Epic)
Greatest Hits, Waylon Jennings (RCA)
Midnight Magic, Commodores (Motown)
Evolution, Journey (Columbia)
The Kids Are Alright—motion picture soundtrack, The Who (MCA)
Disco Nights, G.Q. (Arista)
Evolution, Journey (CBS)
Eddie Money, Eddie Money (CBS)
First under the Wire, Little River Band (Capitol)
Risque, Chic (Atlantic)
Off the Wall, Michael Jackson (CBS)
Identify Yourself, O'Jays (Phila. Intl.)
Nether Lands, Dan Fogelberg (Epic)
Knock on Wood, Amii Stewart (Ariola)
Highway To Hell, AC-DC (Atlantic)
Evolution, Journey (Columbia)

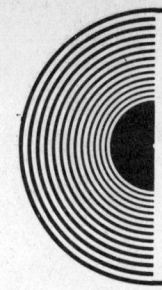

PLATINUM RECORD AWARDS—SINGLES
(2,000,000 units sold)

1976

"Disco Lady," Johnnie Taylor (Columbia)
"Kiss and Say Goodbye," The Manhattans (Columbia)
"Play That Funky Music," Wild Cherry (Epic-Sweet City)
"Disco Duck," Rick Dees and His Cast of Idiots (RSO)

1977

"Car Wash," Rose Royce (MCA)
"You Light Up My Life," Debby Boone (Warner Bros.)
"Boogie Nights," Heatwave (Epic)

1978

"Stayin' Alive," Bee Gees (RSO)
"Emotion," Samantha Sang (Private Stock)
"We Are the Champions," Queen (Elektra)
"Night Fever," Bee Gees (RSO)
"Star Wars Theme/Cantina Band," Meco (Millenium)
"Shadow Dancing," Andy Gibb (RSO)
"You're the One That I Want," (RSO)
"Boogie Oogie Oogie," Taste of Honey (Capitol)
"Grease," Frankie Valli (RSO)
"Le Freak," Chic (Atlantic)

1979

"Hot Child in the City," Nick Gilder (Chrysalis)
"YMCA," Village People (Casablanca)
"Too Much Heaven," Bee Gees (RSO)
"Da Ya Think I'm Sexy," Rod Stewart (Warner Bros.)
"I Will Survive," Gloria Gaynor (Polydor)
"Reunited," Peaches & Herb (Polydor)
"Tragedy," Bee Gees (RSO)
"Shake Your Body," Jacksons (Epic)
"Ain't No Stoppin' Us Now," McFadden & Whitehead (Phila. Intl.)
"Hot Stuff," Donna Summer (Casablanca)
"Knock on Wood," Amii Stewart (Ariola America)
"Bad Girls," Donna Summer (Casablanca)

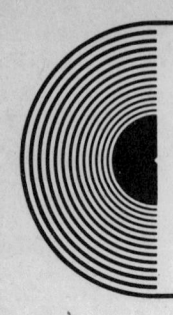

MILLION PERFORMANCE SONGS

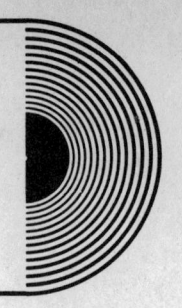

BMI-licensed compositions logging 1,000,000 radio-TV performances as of December 31, 1978. Foreign affiliates (PRS, SACM, etc.) are indicated in parentheses.

"*Abraham, Martin and John,*" Dick Holler (Regent Music Corp.)

"*Adios,*" Enric Madriguera, E. Woods (Peer International Corp.)

"*After the Lovin',*" Richard Ziegler, Alan Bernstein (Oceans Blue Music)

"*Again,*" Dorcas Cochran, Lionel Newman (Robbins Music)

"*All I Have to Do is Dream,*" Boudleaux Bryant (House of Bryant Publications)

"*All Shook Up,*" Otis Blackwell, Elvis Presley (Unart Music Corp., Elvis Presley Music, Inc.)

"*Almost Persuaded,*" Billy Sherrill, Glenn Sutton (Al Gallico Music Corp.)

"*Alone Again (Naturally),*" Gilbert O'Sullivan (PRS) (Management Agency and Music Publishing, Inc.)

"*Am I That Easy to Forget,*" Carl Belew, W. S. Stevenson, Shelby Singleton (Four Star Music Co., Inc.)

"*Amapola,*" Joseph M. LaSalle, Albert Gamse (E. B. Marks Music Corp.)

"*American Pie,*" Don McLean (Mayday Music, Inc.)

"*Amor,*" Gabriel Ruiz (SACM), Sunny Skylar, Ricardo Lopez Mendez (SACM) (Peer International Corp.)

"*And I Love Her,*" John Lennon (PRS), Paul McCartney (PRS) (Unart Music Corp., Maclen Music, Inc.)

"*And I Love You So,*" Don McLean (Mayday Music, Inc.)

"*Angel of the Morning,*" Chip Taylor, (Blackwood Music, Inc.)

"*Anna,*" R. Vatro (SIAE), R. Giordano (SIAE), William Engvick (Hollis Music, Inc.)

"*(Hey Won't You Play) Another Somebody Done Somebody Wrong Song,*" Chips Moman, Larry Butler (Screen Gems-EMI Music, Inc., Tree Publishing Co., Inc.)

"*Anytime,*" Herbert Happy Lawson (Unichappell Music, Inc.)

"*As Long As He Needs Me,*" Lionel Bart (PRS) (Hollis Music, Inc.)

"*Baby Don't Get Hooked on Me,*" Mac Davis (Screen Gems-EMI Music, Inc.)

"*Baby I'm Yours,*" Van McCoy, Blackwood Music, Inc.)

"*Baia,*" Ray Gilbert, Ary Barroso (SBACEM) (Peer International Corp.)

"*Ballin' The Jack,*" Chris Smith, James Burris (E. B. Marks Music Corp.)

"*Battle of New Orleans, The,*" Jimmie Driftwood (Warden Music Co., Inc.)

"*Behind Closed Doors,*" Kenny O'Dell (House of Gold Music, Inc.)

"*Besame Mucho,*" Chelo Velazquez (SACM), Sunny Skylar (Peer International Corp.)

"*Blue Bayou,*" Roy Orbison and Joe Melson (Acuff-Rose Publications, Inc.)

"Blue Suede Shoes," Carl L. Perkins (Hi-Lo Music, Inc., Unichappell Music, Inc.)

"Blue Velvet," Bernie Wayne, Lee Morris (Vogue Music, Inc.)

"Bluesette," Jean Thielemans, Norman Gimbel (Duchess Music Corp.)

"Bonaparte's Retreat," Pee Wee King, Redd Stewart (Acuff-Rose Publications, Inc.)

"Born Free," John Barry (PRS), Don Black (PRS) (Screen Gems-EMI Music, Inc.)

"Both Sides Now," Joni Mitchell (Siquomb Publishing Corp.)

"Brazil," Ary Barroso (SBACEM), S. K. Russell (Peer International Corp.)

"Breaking Up Is Hard To Do," Neil Sedaka, Howard Greenfield (Screen Gems-EMI Music, Inc.)

"Breeze and I, The," Ernesto Lecuona (SGAE), Al Stillman (E. B. Marks Music Corp.)

"Bridge Over Troubled Water," Paul Simon (Paul Simon Music)

"By The Time I Get To Phoenix," Jim Webb (The EMP Company)

"Bye Bye Love," Felice Bryant, Boudleaux Bryant (House of Bryant Publications)

"Cabaret," John Kander, Fred Ebb (Times Square Music Publications)

"Call Me," Tony Hatch (PRS) (Duchess Music Corp.)

"Canadian Sunset," Eddie Heywood, Norman Gimbel (Vogue Music, Inc.)

"Candida," Toni Wine, Irwin Levine (Big Apple Music Co.)

"Candy Kisses," George Morgan (Unichappell Music, Inc.)

"Candy Man, The," Leslie Bricusse, Anthony Newley (Taradam Music, Inc.)

"Can't Get Used to Losing You," Doc Pomus, Mort Shuman (Unichappell Music, Inc.)

"Can't Take My Eyes Off Of You," Bob Crewe, Bob Gaudio (Saturday Music, Inc., Seasons Four Music Corp.)

"Cast Your Fate to the Wind," Vince Guaraldi (Unichappell Music, Inc.)

"Cherish," Terry Kirkman (Beechwood Music Corp.)

"Chim Chim Cher-ee," Robert Sherman, Richard Sherman (Wonderland Music Co., Inc.)

"Classical Gas," Mason Williams (Irving Music, Inc.)

"Cold, Cold Heart," Hank Williams (Fred Rose Music, Inc., Hiriam Music)

"Come Closer To Me," Osvaldo Farres (SACEM), Al Stewart (Peer International Corp.)

"Come Softly To Me," Barbara Ellis, Gary R. Troxel, Gretchen Christopher (Cornerstone Publishing Co.)

"Cool Water," Bob Nolan (Unichappell Music, Inc., Elvis Presley Music, Inc.)

"Crying In The Chapel," Artie Glenn (Unichappell Music, Inc.)

"Daniel," Elton John (PRS), Bernie Taupin (PRS) (Dick James Music, Inc.)

"Danke Schoen," Bert Kaempfert (GEMA), Milt Gabler, Kurt Schwabach (GEMA) (Screen Gems-EMI Music, Inc.)

"Daydream," John Sebastian (The Hudson Bal Music Co.)

"Deep in the Heart of Texas," June Hershey, Don Swander (Melody Lane Publications, Inc.)

"Desafinado," Antonio Carlos Jobim, Newton Mendonca (SBAT) (Hollis Music, Inc.)

"Detour," Paul Westmoreland (Unichappell Music, Inc.)

"Diamond Girl," Jimmy Seals, Darrell Crofts (Dawnbreaker Music)

"Do You Want To Dance?," Bobby Freeman (Clockus Music, Inc.)

"(Sittin On) The Dock of the Bay," Otis Redding, Steve Cropper (East/Memphis Music Corp., Time Music Co., Inc.)

"Don't Be Cruel," Otis Blackwell, Elvis Presley (Unart Music Corp., Elvis Presley Music, Inc.)

"Don't Let the Stars Get in Your Eyes," Slim Willet (Four Star Music Co., Inc.)
"Don't Pull Your Love," Dennis Lambert, Brian Potter (Duchess Music Corp.)
"Don't Sleep in the Subway," Tony Hatch (PRS), Jackie Trent (PRS) (Duchess Music Corp.)
"Dream Baby," Cindy Walker (Combine Music Corp.)
"Dreams of the Everyday Housewife," Chris Gantry (Combine Music Corp.)
"Early in the Morning," Mike Leander (PRS), Eddie Seago (PRS) (Duchess Music Corp.)
"Earth Angel," Jesse Belvin (Dootsie Williams, Inc.)
"Easy Loving," Freddie Hart (Blue Book Music)
"El Condor Pasa, Paul Simon, Jorge Milchberg (SACEM), Daniel Robles (Paul Simon Music)
"El Paso," Marty Robbins (Elvis Presley Music, Inc., Paul Simon Music)
"Eleanor Rigby," John Lennon (PRS), Paul McCartney (PRS) (Maclen Music, Inc.)
"Elusive Butterfly," Bob Lind (Metric Music Co.)
"Endlessly," Clyde Otis, Brook Benton (Vogue Music, Inc.)
"Everybody's Talkin'," Fred Neil (Third Story Music, Inc.)
"Everything is Beautiful," Ray Stevens (Ahab Music Co., Inc.)
"Feel Like Makin' Love," Gene McDaniels (Skyforest Music Co., Inc.)
"Fever," John Davenport, Eddie Cooley (Fort Knox Music Co.)
"Fifty Ninth Street Bridge Song, The (Feelin' Groovy)," Paul Simon (Paul Simon Music)
"Fifty Ways to Leave Your Lover," Paul Simon (Paul Simon Music)
"Fire and Rain," James Taylor (Blackwood Music, Inc., Country Road Music, Inc.)
"First Time Ever I Saw Your Face," Ewan MacColl (PRS) (Stormking Music, Inc.)
"Flowers on the Wall," Lewis DeWitt (House of Cash, Inc., Unichappell Music, Inc.)
"Flying Home," Benny Goodman, Lionel Hampton (Regent Music Corp.)
"Folsom Prison," Johnny Cash (Hi-Lo Music, Inc.)
"For All We Know," Fred Karlin, Robb Royer, James Griffin (Duchess Music Corp., Al Gallico Music Corp.)
"For the Good Times," Kris Kristofferson (Buckhorn Music Publishing, Inc.)
"Four Walls," George Campbell, Marvin Moore (Unart Music Corp.)
"Frenesi," Alberto Dominguez (SACM), S. K. Russell (Peer International Corp.)
"Games People Play," Joe South (Lowery Music Co., Inc.)
"Gentle on My Mind," John Hartford (Ensign Music Corp.)
"Georgia on My Mind," Hoagy Carmichael, Stuart Gorrell (Peer International Corp.)
"Get Together," Chet Powers (Irving Music, Inc.)
"Girl From Ipanema, The," Antonio Carlos Jobim, Norman Gimbel, Vinicius de Moraes (SACEM) (Duchess Music Corp.)
"Glow Worm," Paul Lincke (GEMA), Lilla Robinson, Johnny Mercer (E. B. Marks Music Corp.)
"Go Away Little Girl," Gerry Goffin, Carole King (Screen Gems-EMI Music, Inc.)
"Goin' Out of My Head," Teddy Randazzo, Bobby Weinstein (Vogue Music, Inc.)
"Gone," Smokey Rogers (Elvis Presley Music, Inc., Dallas Music Co.)
"Good Vibrations," Brian Wilson, Mike Love (Irving Music, Inc.)
"Got to Get You Into My Life," John Lennon (PRS), Paul McCartney (PRS) (Maclen Music, Inc.)
"Gotta Travel On," Paul Clayton, Lee Hays, Fred Hellerman, Ronnie Gilbert, David Lazar, Pete Seeger, Larry

Ehrlich (Sanga Music, Inc.)
"*Granada,*" Agustin Lara (SACM) (Peer International Corp.)
"*Grazing in the Grass,*" Philemon Hou, Harry Elston (Cherio Corp.)
"*Green Door,*" Marvin Moore, Bob Davie (The Hudson Bay Music Co.)
"*Green Eyes,*" Nilo Menendez (SACM), Adolfo Utrera (SACM), E. Rivera, E. Woods (Peer International Corp.)
"*Green Fields,*" Frank Miller, Terry Gilkyson, Richard Dehr (Blackwood Music, Inc.)
"*Green Green Grass of Home,*" Curly Putman (Tree Publishing Co., Inc.)
"*Guantanamera,*" Pete Seeger, Hector Angulo, Jose Marti (Fall River Music, Inc.)
"*Gypsys, Tramps and Thieves,*" Robert Stone (Peso Music)
"*Half As Much,*" Curley Williams (Fred Rose Music, Inc.)
"*Handy Man,*" Jimmy Jones, Charles Merenstein, Otis Blackwell (Unart Music Corp., Bess Music Co.)
"*Happiest Girl in the USA, The,*" Donna Fargo (Algee Music Corp., Prima Donna Music Co.)
"*Happy Together,*" Alan Lee Gordon, Garry Bonner (The Hudson Bay Music Co.)
"*Hard Day's Night, A,*" John Lennon (PRS), Paul McCartney (PRS) (Unart Music Corp., Maclen Music, Inc.)
"*Harper Valley PTA,*" Tom T. Hall (Unichappell Music, Inc.)
"*Have You Never Been Mellow,*" John Farrar (Irving Music, Inc.)
"*(You're) Having My Baby,*" Paul Anka (Spanka Music Corp.)
"*He Don't Love You Like I Do,*" Jerry Butler, Curtis Mayfield, Calvin Carter (Conrad Music, Inc.)
"*Heartaches By The Number,*" Harlan Howard (Tree Publishing Co., Inc.)
"*Hearts of Stone,*" Rudy Jackson, Eddie Ray (Unart Music Corp., Regent Music Corp.)

"*He'll Have To Go,*" Joe Allison, Audrey Allison (Central Songs)
"*Hello It's Me,*" Todd Rundgren (Screen Gems-EMI Music, Inc.)
"*Help Me Make It Through The Night,*" Kris Kristofferson (Combine Music Corp.)
"*Here Comes The Sun,*" George Harrison (PRS), (Loaves and Fishes Music Co., Inc.)
"*Here There And Everywhere,*" John Lennon (PRS), Paul McCartney (PRS) (Maclen Music, Inc.)
"*Here You Come Again,*" Barry Mann, Cynthia Weil (Screen Gems-EMI Music, Inc., Summerhill Songs, Inc.)
"*Hey Jude,*" John Lennon (PRS), Paul McCartney (PRS) (Maclen Music, Inc.)
"*(Your Love Has Lifted Me) Higher and Higher,*" Carl Smith, Gary Jackson, Raynard Miner (BRC Music Corp., Chevis Publishing Corp., Warner-Tamerlane Publishing Corp.)
"*Homeward Bound,*" Paul Simon (Paul Simon Music)
"*Hooked on a Feeling,*" Mark James (Screen Gems-EMI Music, Inc.)
"*House of the Rising Sun, The,*" Alan Price (PRS) (Al Gallico Music Corp.)
"*How Can You Mend A Broken Heart,*" Robin Gibb (PRS), Barry Gibb (Front Wheel Music, Inc., Casserole Music, Inc.)
"*How Deep Is Your Love,*" Barry Gibb, Maurice Gibb, Robin Gibb (PRS) (Stigwood Music, Inc.)
"*How Sweet It Is To Be Loved By You,*" Eddie Holland, Brian Holland, Lamont Dozier (Stone Agate Music Corp.)
"*Hurt So Bad,*" Teddy Randazzo, Bobby Hart, Bobby Weinstein (Vogue Music, Inc.)
"*Hustle,*" Van McCoy (Warner-Tamerlane Publishing Corp., Van McCoy Music, Inc.)
"*I Almost Lost My Mind,*" Ivory Joe Hunter (Unichappell Music, Inc.)
"*I Am Woman,*" Helen Reddy, Ray

Burton (Irving Music, Inc., Buggerlugs Music)
"I Believe in Music," Mac Davis (Screen Gems-EMI Music, Inc.)
"I Can Help," Billy Swan (Combine Music Corp.)
"I Can't Help It," Hank Williams (Fred Rose Music, Inc., Hiriam Music)
"I Can't Stop Loving You," Don Gibson (Acuff-Rose Publications, Inc.)
"I Hear You Knocking," Pearl King, David Bartholomew (Unart Music Corp.)
"I Honesty Love You," Jeff Barry, Peter Allen (Irving Music, Inc., Broadside Music, Inc., Woolnough Music, Inc.)
"I Just Can't Help Believin'," Barry Mann, Cynthia Weil (Screen Gems-EMI Music, Inc.)
"I Just Want to be Your Everything," Barry Gibb (Stigwood Music, Inc.)
"I Love How You Love Me," Barry Mann, Larry Kolber (Screen Gems-EMI Music, Inc.)
"I Love You Because," Leon Payne (Fred Rose Music, Inc.)
"I Love You for Sentimental Reasons," Deke Watson, William Best (Duchess Music Corp.)
"I Love You So Much it Hurts," Floyd Tillman (Melody Lane Publications, Inc.)
"I Started Loving You Again," Bonnie Owens, Merle Haggard (Blue Book Music)
"I Walk the Line," Johnny Cash (Hi-Lo Music, Inc.)
"I Will Wait for You," Michel Legrand (SACEM), Jacques Demy (SACEM), Norman Gimbel (Vogue Music, Inc.)
"I Wonder Who's Kissing Her Now," William Hough, Frank Adams, Joe Howard (E. B. Marks Music Corp.)
"I'd Really Love to See You Tonight," Parker McGee (Dawnbreaker Music)
"If I Had a Hammer," Lee Hays, Pete Seeger (Ludlow Music, Inc.)
"If I Were A Carpenter," Tim Hardin (The Hudson Bay Music Co.)
"If You Go Away," Jacques Brel (SABAM), Rod McKuen (E. B. Marks Music Corp.)
"If You Love Me (Let Me Know)," John Rostill (PRS) (Al Gallico Music Corp.)
"I'll Be Around," Alec Wilder (Ludlow Music, Inc.)
"I'll Hold You in My Heart," Tommy Dilbeck, Eddy Arnold (Adams-Vee and Abbott, Inc.)
"I'm Leaving It All Up to You," Don Harris, Dewey Terry (Venice Music, Inc.)
"I'm So Lonesome I Could Cry," Hank Williams (Fred Rose Music, Inc., Hiriam Music)
"I'm Walkin'," Antoine Domino, Dave Bartholomew (Unart Music Corp.)
"Imagine," John Lennon (PRS) (Maclen Music, Inc.)
"It Is No Secret," Stuart Hamblen (Duchess Music Corp.)
"It's Just a Matter of Time," Belford Hendricks, Clyde Otis, Brook Benton (The Times Square Music Publications Co., Eden Music, Inc.)
"It's No Sin," George Hoven, Chester Shull (Robert Mellin Music)
"It's Not Unusual," Gordon Mills (PRS), Les Reed (PRS) (Duchess Music Corp.)
"It's Only Make Believe," Jack Nance, Conway Twitty (Twitty Bird Music Co.)
"Jambalaya," Hank Williams (Fred Rose Music, Inc.)
"Java," Freddy Friday, Allen Toussaint, Alvin Tyler, Marilyn Schack (Tideland Music Publishing Corp.)
"Jealous Heart," Jenny Lou Carson (Acuff-Rose Publications, Inc.)
"Joy to the World," Hoyt Axton (Lady Jane Music)
"Killing Me Softly with His Song," Charles Fox, Norman Gimbel (Fox-Gimbel Productions, Inc.)
"King of the Road," Roger Miller (Tree Publishing Co., Inc.)

MILLION PERFORMANCE SONGS 903

"Kiss of Fire," Robert Hill, Lester Allen (Duchess Music Corp.)
"Kisses Sweeter Than Wine," Paul Campbell, Pete Seeger, Fred Hellerman, Joel Newman, Ronnie Gilbert, Lee Hays (Folkways Music Publishers, Inc.)
"Knock Three Times," Irwin Levine, L. Russell Brown (Big Apple Music Co.)
"Last Date," Floyd Cramer (Acuff-Rose Publications, Inc.)
"Laughter in the Rain," Neil Sedaka, Philip Cody (Kiddio Music Co.)
"Lazy River," Hoagy Carmichael, Sid Arodin (Peer International Corp.)
"Let It Be," John Lennon (PRS), Paul McCartney (PRS) (Maclen Music, Inc.)
"Let Me Be There," John Rostill (PRS) (Al Gallico Music Corp.)
"Let Your Love Flow," Lawrence Williams (Loaves and Fishes Music Co., Inc.)
"Let's Dance," F. M. Baldridge, G. Stone, Josef Bonime (E. B. Marks Music Corp.)
"Letter, The," Wayne Thompson (Earl Barton Music, Inc.)
"Lion Sleeps Tonight, The," Paul Campbell, Hugo Peretti, George Weiss, Albert Stanton, Luigi Creatore, Solomon Linda (Folkways Music Publishers, Inc.)
"Live for Life," Francis Lai (SACEM), Norman Gimbel (Unart Music Corp.)
"Lonely Street," W. S. Stevenson, Carl R. Belew, Kenny Sowder (Four Star Music Co., Inc.)
"Long and Winding Road, The," John Lennon (PRS), Paul McCartney (PRS) (Maclen Music, Inc.)
"Love is Strange," Sylvia Robinson, Mickey Baker (SACEM), Ellas McDaniels (Ben-Ghazi Enterprises, Inc.)
"Love Me Tender," Elvis Presley, Vera Matson (Elvis Presley Music, Inc.)
"Love Me Tonight," Daniele Pace (SIAE), Mario Panzeri (SIAE), Barry Mason (PRS), Lorenzo Pilat (SIAE) (Duchess Music Corp.)
"Love Me With All Your Heart," Carlos Rigual (SACM), Mario Rigual (SACM), Carlos A. Martinoli (SADAIC), Sunny Skylar (Peer International Corp.)
"Love Will Keep Us Together," Neil Sedaka, Howard Greenfield (Kiddio Music Co.)
"Lover's Concerto, A," Denny Randall, Sandy Linzer (Screen Gems-EMI Music, Inc.)
"Lover's Question, A," Jimmy Williams, Brook Benton (The Times Square Music Publications Co., Unichappell Music, Inc., Eden Music, Inc.)
"Loves Me Like a Rock," Paul Simon (Paul Simon Music)
"Love's Theme," Barry White (Sa-Vette Music, Six Continents Music Publishing, Inc.)
"Lullaby of Birdland," George Shearing, George Weiss (Big Seven Music)
"Make the World Go Away," Hank Cochran (Tree Publishing Co., Inc.)
"Malaguena," Ernesto Lecuona (SGAE) (E. B. Marks Music Corp.)
"Mandy," Richard Kerr, Scott English (Screen Gems-EMI Music, Inc., Morris Music, Inc.)
"Manhattan," Richard Rodgers, Lorenz Hart (E. B. Marks Music Corp.)
"Margaritaville," Jimmy Buffett (Coral Reefer Music, Outer Banks Music)
"Maria Elena," Lorenzo Barcelata (SACM), S. K. Russell (Peer International Corp.)
"Marianne," Terry Gilkyson, Frank Miller, Richard Dehr (Blackwood Music, Inc.)
"Me and Bobby McGee," Kris Kristofferson, Fred L. Foster (Combine Music Corp.)
"Meditation,' Antonio Carlos Jobim, Newton Mendonca (SBACEM), Norman Gimbel (Duchess Music Corp.)
"Memories Are Made of This," Terry

Gilkyson, Richard Dehr, Frank Miller (Blackwood Music, Inc.)

"Michelle," John Lennon (PRS), Paul McCartney (PRS) (Maclen Music, Inc.)

"Misirlou," N. Roubanis (Misirlou Music, Inc.)

"Misty Blue," Bob Montgomery (Talmont Music, Inc.)

"More," Riz Ortolani (SIAE), Nino Oliviero (SIAE), Norman Newell (PRS), M. Ciorciolini (SIAE) (E. B. Marks Music Corp.)

"Morning After, The," Joel Hirschhorn, Al Kasha (Fox Fanfare Music, Inc.)

"Morning Has Broken," Cat Stevens (PRS), Eleanor Farjeon (PRS) (Island Music)

"Most Beautiful Girl, The," Norro Wilson, Billy Sherrill, Rory Bourke (Al Gallico Music Corp., Algee Music Corp.)

"Mr. Bojangles," Jerry Jeff Walker (Cotillion Music, Inc.)

"Mrs. Robinson," Paul Simon (Paul Simon Music)

"My Cherie Amour," Henry Cosby, Sylvia Moy, Stevie Wonder (Stone Agate Music Div.)

"My Elusive Dreams," Curly Putman, Billy Sherrill (Tree Publishing Co., Inc.)

"My Eyes Adored You," Bob Crewe, Kenny Nolan (Tannyboy Music Co., Stone Diamond Music Corp.)

"My Love," Tony Hatch (PRS) (Duchess Music Corp.)

"My Special Angel," Jimmy Duncan (Warner-Tamerlane Publishing Corp.)

"My Sweet Lord," George Harrison (PRS) (Loaves and Fishes Music Co., Inc.)

"My Way," Paul Anka, Jacques Revaux (SACEM), Claude Francois (SACEM) (Spanka Music Corp.)

"Never Can Say Goodbye," Clifton Davis (Portable Music Co., Inc.)

"Never My Love," Donald J. Addrisi, Richard P. Addrisi (Warner-Tamerlane Publishing Corp.)

"Never on Sunday," Manos Hadjidakis (SACEM), Billy Towne (Unart Music Corp., Llee Corp.)

"Night Train," Jimmy Forrest, Oscar Washington, Lewis C. Simpkins (Frederick Music Co.)

"Non Dimenticar," Shelley Dobbins, Michelle Galdieri (SIAE), P. G. Redi (SIAE) (Hollis Music, Inc.)

"Nothing From Nothing," Billy Preston, Bruce Fisher (Irving Music, Inc.)

"Ob La Di Ob La Da," John Lennon (PRS), Paul McCartney (PRS) (Maclen Music, Inc.)

"Oh, Lonesome Me," Don Gibson (Acuff-Rose Publications, Inc.)

"On Broadway," Cynthia Weil, Barry Mann, Jerry Leiber, Mike Stoller (Screen Gems-EMI Music, Inc.)

"One Tin Soldier," Dennis Lambert, Brian Potter (Duchess Music Corp.)

"Only You," Buck Ram, Ande Rand (Hollis Music, Inc.)

"Opus One," Sy Oliver, Sid Garris (Embassy Music Corp.)

"Paper Doll," Johnny Black (E. B. Marks Music Corp.)

"Parade of the Wooden Soldier," Leon Jessel (GEMA) (E. B. Marks Music Corp.)

"Peanut Vendor, The," Moises Simons, (SACEM), Marion Sunshine, L. Wolfe Gilbert (E. B. Marks Music Corp.)

"Penny Lane," John Lennon (PRS), Paul McCartney (PRS) (Maclen Music, Inc.)

"Perfidia," Alberto Dominguez (SACM), Milton Leeds (Peer International Corp.)

"Personality," Lloyd Price, Harold Logan (Lloyd and Logan Inc.)

"Petite Fleur," Sidney Bechet (Unichappell Music, Inc.)

"Please Mr. Postman," Robert Bateman, Brian Holland, Freddie Gorman (Stone Agate Music Corp.)

"Pledging My Love," Don Robey, Ferdi-

nand Washington (Duchess Music Corp., Wemar Music Corp.)
"Portrait of My Love," Cyril Ornadel (PRS), Norman Newell (PRS) (Piccadilly Music Corp.)
"Proud Mary," John C. Fogerty (Jondora Music)
"Put a Little Love in Your Heart," Jimmy Holiday, Randy Myers, Jackie DeShannon (Unart Music Corp.)
"Put Your Hand in the Hand," Gene MacLellan (PRO Canada) (Beechwood Music Corp.)
"Put Your Head on My Shoulder," Paul Anka (Spanka Music Corp.)
"Quiet Village," Les Baxter (Granson Music Co., Atlantic Music Corp.)
"Rainy Night in Georgia," Tony Joe White (Combine Music Corp.)
"Ramblin' Rose," Joe Sherman, Noel Sherman (ATV Music Corp.)
"Raunchy," William E. Justis Jr., Sidney Manker (Hi-Lo Music, Inc.)
"Release Me," Eddie Miller, W. S. Stevenson (Four Star Music Co., Inc.)
"Rhythm of the Rain," John Gummoe (Warner-Tamerlane Publishing Corp.)
"Rock the Boat," Waldo Holmes (Warner-Tamerlane Publishing Corp., Jimi Lane Music)
"Rockin' Robin," Jimmie Thomas (Recordo Music Publishers)
"Room Full of Roses," Tim Spencer (Unichappell Music, Inc.)
"(I Never Promised You A) Rose Garden, Joe South (Lowery Music Co., Inc.)
"Ruby Don't Take Your Love to Town," Mel Tillis (Cedarwood Publishing Co., Inc.)
"Say Has Anybody Seen My Sweet Gypsy Rose," Irwin Levine, L. Russell Brown (Levine and Brown Music, Inc.)
"Scarborough Fair/Canticle," Paul Simon, Arthur Garfunkel (Paul Simon Music)
"Seasons in the Sun," Jacques Brel (SABAM), Rod McKuen (E. B. Marks Music Corp.)

"Send Me the Pillow You Dream On," Hank Locklin (Four Star Music Co., Inc.)
"(Theme From) Shaft," Isaac Hayes (East/Memphis Music Corp.)
"Sincerely," Alan Freed, Harvey Fuqua (Arc Music Corp.)
"Singing the Blues," Melvin Endsley (Acuff-Rose Publications, Inc.)
"Sixteen Tons," Merle Travis (Unichappell Music, Inc., Elvis Presley Music, Inc.)
"Slow Poke," Redd Stewart, Pee Wee King, Chilton Price (Ridgeway Music)
"Smile A Little Smile," Geoffrey Stephens (PRS), Tony Macaulay (PRS) (Six Continents Music Publishing, Inc.)
"Snowbird," Gene MacLellan (PRO Canada) (Beechwood Music Corp.)
"Someday We'll Be Together," Harvey Fuqua, Jackey Beavers, Johnny Bristol (Stone Agate Music Corp.)
"Someday (You'll Want Me to Want You), Jimmie Hodges (Duchess Music Corp.)
"Somethin' Stupid," C. Carson Parks (Greenwood Music Co)
"Something," George Harrison (PRS) (Loaves and Fishes Music Co., Inc.)
"Song from Moulin Rouge, The," Georges Auric (SACEM), William Engvick (Screen Gems-EMI Music, Inc.)
"Song of the Islands," Charles E. King (E. B. Marks Music Corp.)
"Soulful Strut," William Sanders, Eugene Record (Warner-Tamerlane Publishing Corp., BRC Music Corp.)
"Sound of Philadelphia," Kenneth Gamble, Leon Huff (Mighty Three Music, Hip Trip Music Co.)
"Sound of Silence," Paul Simon (Paul Simon Music)
"Southern Nights," Allen Toussaint (Marsaint Music, Inc., Warner-Tamerlane Publishing Corp.)
"Spanish Eyes," Bert Kaempfert (GEMA), Charles Singleton, Eddie

Snyder (Screen Gems-EMI Music, Inc.)
"Spanish Harlem," Jerry Leiber, Phil Spector (Trio Music Co., Inc., Unichappell Music, Inc.)
"Spinning Wheel," David Clayton-Thomas (Blackwood Music, Inc.)
"Stand By Your Man," Tammy Wynette, Billy Sherrill (Al Gallico Music Corp.)
"Straight Life, The," Sonny Curtis (Warner-Tamerlane Publishing Corp.)
"Stranger on the Shore,' Acker Bilk (PRS), Robert Mellin (Robert Mellin Music)
"Strangers in the Night," Bert Kaempfert (GEMA), Charles Singleton, Eddie Snyder (Champion Music Corp., Screen Gems-EMI Music, Inc.)
"Sugar Sugar," Jeff Barry, Andy Kim (Don Kirshner Music, Inc.)
"Sukiyaki," Rokusuke Ei (JASRAC) Hachidai Nakamura (Beechwood Music Corp.)
"Summer Breeze," Jimmy Seals, Dash Crofts (Dawnbreaker Music, Inc., Duchess Music Corp.)
"Summer Samba," Norman Gimbel, Marcos Valle, Sergio Paulo Valle (Butterfield Music Corp., Duchess Music Corp.)
"Sunny," Bobby Hebb (Portable Music Co., Inc., MRC Music Corp.)
"Sunrise, Sunset," Jerry Bock, Sheldon Harnick (The Times Square Music Publications Co.)
"Superstar," Bonnie Bramlett, Leon Russell, (Delbon Publishing Co., Teddy Jack Music)
"Suspicious Minds," Mark James (Screen Gems-EMI Music, Inc.)
"Take a Letter Maria," R. B. Greaves (Vogue Music, Inc.)
"Tell Me Why," Marty Gold, Al Alberts (Spanka Music Corp., Rydal Music Co., Inc., Alstel Television Productions, Inc.)
"Tennessee Waltz," Pee Wee King, Redd Stewart (Acuff-Rose Publications, Inc.)

"Tequila," Chuck Rio (Jat Music, Inc., Modern Music Publishing Co.)
"That's All," Bob Haymes, Alan Brandt (Unart Music Corp.)
"Then You Can Tell Me Goodbye," John Loudermilk (Acuff-Rose Publications, Inc.)
"There Goes My Everything," Dallas Frazier (Husky Music Co., Inc., Acuff-Rose Publications, Inc.)
"There'll Be Some Changes Made," W. B. Overstreet, Billy Higgins (E. B. Marks Music Corp.)
"This Love of Mine," Sol Parker, Frank Sinatra, Hank Sanicola (Embassy Music Corp.)
"Tico-Tico," Zequinha Abreu (SBAT) Aloysio Oliveira (SBAT), Ervin Drake (Peer International Corp.)
"Tie a Yellow Ribbon Round the Ole Oak Tree," Irwin Levine, L. Russell Brown (Levine and Brown Music, Inc.)
"Til I Kissed You," Don Everly (Acuff-Rose Publications, Inc.)
"To Know Him is to Love Him," Phil Spector (Vogue Music, Inc.)
"To Sir, With Love," Don Black (PRS), Mark London (Screen Gems-EMI Music, Inc.)
"Torn Between Two Lovers," Peter Yarrow, Phil Jarrell (Muscle Shoals Sound Publishing Co., Inc.)
"Traces," Buddy Buie, James B. Cobb Jr., Emory Lee Gordy Jr. (Low-Sal Music Co.)
"Try a Little Kindness," Bobby Austin, Thomas Sapaugh (Allanwood Music, Airefield Music)
"Turn Around, Look at Me," Jerry Capehart (Warner-Tamerlane Publishing Corp., Elvis Presley Music, Inc., Unichappell Music, Inc.)
"Twilight Time," Buck Ram, Morty Nevins, Al Nevins (Devon Music, Inc.)
"Up, Up and Away," Jim Webb (The EMP Company)
"Walk in the Black Forest, A," Horst

Jankowski (GEMA) (MRC Music Corp.)
"Walk Right In," Gus Cannon, Hosea Woods, Erik Darling, Willard Svanoe (Peer International Corp., Silkie Music Publishers)
"Watch What Happens," Jacques Demy (SACEM), Michel Legrand (SACEM), Norman Gimbel (Vogue Music, Inc.)
"Watchin' Scotty Grow," Mac Davis (Screen Gems-EMI Music, Inc.)
"Wave," Antonio Carlos Jobim (Corcovado Music Corp.)
"Wedding Bell Blues," Laura Nyro (Tuna Fish Music, Inc.)
"We've Only Just Begun," Paul Williams, Roger Nichols (Irving Music, Inc.)
"What a Difference a Day Made," Maria Grever, Stanley Adams (E. B. Marks Music Corp.)
"What Kind of Fool Am I?," Leslie Bricusse, Anthony Newley (PRS) (Ludlow Music, Inc.)
"When Will I Be Loved," Phil Everly (Acuff-Rose Publications, Inc.)
"When Will I See You Again?" Kenneth Gamble, Leon Huff (Mighty Three Music)
"While We're Young," Alec Wilder, William Engvick, Morty Palitz (Ludlow Music, Inc.)
"White Silver Sands," Charles Matthews, Gladys Reinhardt (Sharina Music Co.)
"Who Can I Turn To?," Leslie Bricusse, Anthony Newley (PRS) (Musical Comedy Productions, Inc.)
"Wildfire," Michael Murphey, Larry Cansler (Warner-Tamerlane Publishing Corp.)
"Will You Love Me Tomorrow?," Gerry Goffin, Carole King (Screen Gems-EMI Music, Inc.)
"Windy," Ruthann Friedman (Irving Music, Inc.)
"With Pen in Hand," Bobby Goldsboro (Unart Music Corp., Detail Music, Inc.)

"Wonderful World," Sam Cooke, Lou Adler, Herb Alpert (Kags Music Corp.)
"Wonderland By Night," Klauss-Gunter Neuman (GEMA), Lincoln Chase (Screen Gems-EMI Music, Inc.)
"Yes Indeed," Sy Oliver (Embassy Music Corp.)
"Yesterday," John Lennon (PRS), Paul McCartney (PRS) (Maclen Music, Inc.)
"You Are My Sunshine," Jimmie Davis (Peer International Corp.)
"You Are So Beautiful," Billy Preston, Bruce Fisher (Irving Music, Inc.)
"You Belong to Me," Pee Wee King, Redd Stewart, Chilton Price (Studio Music Co., Ridgeway Music, Inc.)
"You Belong To My Heart (Solamente Una Vez),' Agustin Lara (SACM), Ray Gilbert (Peer International Corp.)
"You Send Me," Sam Cooke (Kags Music Corp.)
"You, You, You," Robert Mellin and Lotar Olias (GEMA) (Robert Mellin Music Publishing Corp.)
"Young At Heart," Johnny Richards, Carolyn Leigh (Cherio Corp.)
"Young Love," Ric Cartey, Carole Joyner (Lowery Music Co., Inc.)
"Your Cheatin' Heart," Hank Williams (Fred Rose Music, Inc.)
"Your Song," Elton John, Bernie Taupin (Dick James Music, Inc.)
"You're Sixteen," Richard Sherman, Robert Sherman (Warner-Tamerlane Publishing Corp.)
"Yours (Quiereme Mucho)," Gonzalo Roig, Albert Gamse (E. B. Marks Music Corp.)
"You've Lost That Lovin' Feelin'," Barry Mann, Cynthia Weil, Phil Spector (Screen Gems EMI Music, Inc.)
"You've Made Me So Very Happy," Frank Wilson, Brenda Holloway, Patrice Holloway, Berry Gordy Jr. (Stone Agate Music Corp.)

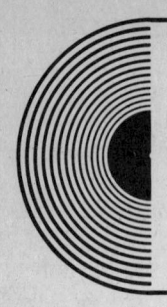

ACADEMY AWARD WINNERS

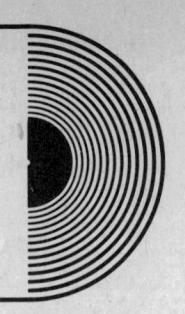

BEST SONG

1934 "The Continental," from *The Gay Divorcee* (RKO Radio). Con Conrad, music; Herb Magidson, lyrics.

1935 "Lullaby of Broadway," from *Gold Diggers of 1935* (Warner Bros.) Harry Warren, music; Al Dubin, lyrics.

1936 "The Way You Look Tonight," from *Swing Time* (RKO Radio) Jerome Kern, music; Dorothy Fields, lyrics.

1937 "Sweet Leilani," from *Waikiki Wedding* (Paramount). Harry Owens, music and lyrics.

1938 "Thanks for the Memory," from *Big Broadcast of 1938* (Paramount.) Ralph Rainger, music; Leo Robin, lyrics.

1939 "Over the Rainbow," from *The Wizard of Oz* (Metro-Goldwyn-Mayer). Harold Arlen, music; E. Y. Harburg, lyrics.

1940 "When You Wish upon a Star," from *Pinocchio* (Disney-RKO Radio). Leigh Harline, music; Ned Washington, lyrics.

1941 "The Last Time I Saw Paris," from *Lady Be Good* (Metro-Goldwyn-Mayer). Jerome Kern, music; Oscar Hammerstein II, lyrics.

1942 "White Christmas," from *Holiday Inn* (Paramount). Irving Berlin, music and lyrics.

1943 "You'll Never Know," from *Hello, Frisco, Hello* (20th Century Fox). Harry Warren, music; Mack Gordon, lyrics.

1944 "Swinging on a Star," from *Going My Way* (Paramount). James Van Heusen, music; Johnny Burke, lyrics.

1945 "It Might as Well Be Spring," from *State Fair* (20th Century Fox). Richard Rodgers, music; Oscar Hammerstein II, lyrics.

1946 "On the Atchison, Topeka and Santa Fe," from *The Harvey Girls* (Metro-Goldwyn-Mayer). Harry Warren, music; Johnny Mercer, lyrics.

1947 "Zip-a-Dee-Doo-Dah," from *Song of the South* (Disney-RKO Radio). Allie Wrubel, music; Ray Gilbert, lyrics.

1948 "Buttons and Bows," from *The Paleface* (Paramount). Jay Livingston, music; Ray Evans, lyrics.

1949 "Baby, It's Cold Outside," from *Neptune's Daughter* (Metro-Goldwyn-Mayer). Frank Loesser, music and lyrics.

*Given by the Academy of Motion Picture Arts and Sciences (the "Oscars").

ACADEMY AWARD WINNERS FOR BEST SONG

1950 "Mona Lisa," from *Captain Carey, USA* (Paramount). Ray Evans and Jay Livingston, music and lyrics.

1951 "In the Cool, Cool, Cool of the Evening," from *Here Comes the Groom* (Paramount). Hoagy Carmichael, music; Johnny Mercer, lyrics.

1952 "High Noon (Do Not Forsake Me, Oh My Darlin')," from *High Noon* (Kramer-United Artists). Dimitri Tiomkin, music; Ned Washington, lyrics.

1953 "Secret Love" from *Calamity Jane* (Warner Bros.). Sammy Fain, music; Paul Francis Webster, lyrics.

1954 "Three Coins in the Fountain," from *Three Coins in the Fountain* (20th Century Fox). Jule Styne, music; Sammy Cahn, lyrics.

1955 "Love Is a Many-Splendored Thing," from *Love Is a Many-Splendored Thing* (20th Century Fox). Sammy Fain, music; Paul Francis Webster, lyrics.

1956 "Whatever Will Be, Will Be (Que Sera, Sera)," from *The Man Who Knew Too Much* (Filwite Prods., Inc.-Paramount). Jay Livingston and Ray Evans, music and lyrics.

1957 "All the Way," from *The Joker Is Wild* (A.M.B.L. Prod.-Paramount). James Van Heusen, music; Sammy Cahn, lyrics.

1958 "Gigi," from *Gigi* (Arthur Freed Prods., Inc.-MGM). Frederick Loewe, music; Alan Jay Lerner, lyrics.

1959 "High Hopes," from *A Hole in the Head* (Sincap Prods.-United Artists). James Van Heusen, music; Sammy Cahn, lyrics.

1960 "Never on Sunday," from *Never on Sunday* (Melinafilm Prod.-Lopert Pictures Corp.). Manos Hadjidakis, music and lyrics.

1961 "Moon River," from *Breakfast at Tiffany's* (Jurow-Shepherd Prod.-Paramount). Henry Mancini, music; Johnny Mercer, lyrics.

1962 "Days of Wine and Roses," from *Days of Wine and Roses* (Martin Manulis-Jalem Prod.-Warner Bros.). Henry Mancini, music; Johnny Mercer, lyrics.

1963 "Call Me Irresponsible," from *Papa's Delicate Condition* (Amro Prod.-Paramount). James Van Heusen, music; Sammy Cahn, lyrics.

1964 "Chim Chim Cher-ee," from *Mary Poppins* (Walt Disney Prod.). Richard M. Sherman and Robert B. Sherman, music and lyrics.

1965 "The Shadow of Your Smile," from *The Sandpiper* (Filmways-Venice Prod.-MGM). Johnny Mandel, music; Paul Francis Webster, lyrics.

1966 "Born Free," from *Born Free* (Open Road Films, Ltd.-Atlas Films, Ltd. Prod.-Columbia). John Barry, music; Don Black, lyrics.

1967 "Talk to the Animals," from *Doctor Dolittle* (Apjac Prod.-20th Century Fox). Leslie Bricusse, music and lyrics.

1968 "The Windmills of Your Mind," from *The Thomas Crown Affair* (Mirisch-Simkoe-Solar Prod.-United Artists). Michel Legrand, music; Alan and Marilyn Bergman, lyrics.

1969 "Raindrops Keep Fallin' on My Head," from *Butch Cassidy and the Sundance Kid* (George Roy Hill-Paul Monash Prod.-20th Century Fox). Burt Bacharach, music; Hal David, lyrics.

1970 "For All We Know," from *Lovers and Other Strangers* (ABC Pictures Prod.-Cinerama). Fred Karlin, music; Robb Royer and James Griffin aka Robb Wilson and Arthur James, lyrics.

1971 "Theme from Shaft," from *Shaft*

(Shaft Prod. Ltd.-MGM). Isaac Hayes, music and lyrics.

1972 "The Morning After," from *The Poseidon Adventure* (Irwin Allen Prod.-20th Century Fox). Al Kasha and Joel Hirschhorn, music and lyrics.

1973 "The Way We Were," from *The Way We Were* (Rastar Prod.-Columbia). Marvin Hamlisch, music; Alan and Marilyn Bergman, lyrics.

1974 "We May Never Love Like This Again," from *The Towering Inferno* (Irwin Allen Prod.-20th Century Fox/Warner Bros.). Al Kasha and Joel Hirschhorn, music and lyrics.

1975 "I'm Easy," from *Nashville* (ABC Entertainment-Jerry Weintraub-Robert Altman Prod.-Paramount). Keith Carradine, music and lyrics.

1976 "Evergreen (Love Theme from A Star Is Born)," from *A Star Is Born,* (Barwood/Jon Peters Prod.-First Artists Presentation-Warner Bros.). Barbra Streisand, music; Paul Williams, lyrics.

1977 "You Light Up My Life," from *You Light Up My Life* (Session Company Prod.-Columbia). Joseph Brooks, music and lyrics.

1978 "Last Dance," from *Thank God It's Friday* (Casablanca-Motown Prod.-Columbia). Paul Jabara, music and lyrics.

BEST MUSICAL SCORING

1934 Victor Schertzinger and Gus Kahn, for *One Night of Love* (Columbia). Award presented to Columbia Studio Music Dept., Louis Silvers, Head.

1935 Max Steiner, for *The Informer* (RKO Radio). Award presented to RKO Radio Studio Music Dept., Max Steiner, Head.

1936 Erich Wolfgang Korngold, for *Anthony Adverse* (Warner Bros.). Award presented to Warner Bros. Studio Music Dept., Leo Forbstein, Head.

1937 Universal Studio Music Dept., Charles Previn, Head, for *One Hundred Men and a Girl* (Universal)

1938 Alfred Newman, for *Alexander's Ragtime Band* (20th Century Fox) Erich Wolfgang Korngold, for *The Adventures of Robin Hood* (Warner Bros.)

1939 Richard Hageman, Frank Harling, John Leipold and Leo Shuken, for *Stagecoach* (Walter Wanger-United Artists) Herbert Stothart, for *The Wizard of Oz* (Metro-Goldwyn-Mayer)

1940 Alfred Newman, for *Tin Pan Alley* (20th Century Fox) Leigh Harline, Paul J. Smith and Ned Washington, for *Pinocchio* (Disney-RKO Radio)

1941 Bernard Herrmann, for *All That Money Can Buy* (RKO Radio) Frank Churchill and Oliver Wallace, for *Dumbo* (Disney-RKO Radio)

1942 Max Steiner, for *Now, Voyager* (Warner Bros.) Ray Heindorf and Heinz Roemheld, for *Yankee Doodle Dandy* (Warner Bros.)

1943 Alfred Newman, for *The Song of Bernadette* (20th Century Fox)

ACADEMY AWARD WINNERS FOR BEST SONG

Ray Heindorf, for *This Is the Army* (Warner Bros.)
1944 Max Steiner, for *Since You Went Away* (Selznick-United Artists)
Carmen Dragon and Morris Stoloff, for *Cover Girl* (Columbia)
1945 Miklos Rozsa, for *Spellbound* (Selznick-United Artists)
Georgie Stoll, for *Anchors Aweigh* (Metro-Goldwyn-Mayer)
1946 Hugo Friedhofer, for *The Best Years of Our Lives* (Goldwyn-RKO Radio)
Morris Stoloff, for *The Jolson Story* (Columbia)
1947 Miklos Rozsa, for *A Double Life* (Kanin-U-I)
Alfred Newman, for *Mother Wore Tights* (20th Century Fox)
1948 Brian Easdale, for *The Red Shoes* (Rank-Archers-Eagle-Lion)
Johnny Green and Roger Edens, for *Easter Parade* (Metro-Goldwyn-Mayer)
1949 Aaron Copland, for *The Heiress* (Paramount)
Roger Edens and Lenni Hayton, for *On the Town* (Metro-Goldwyn-Mayer)
1950 Franz Waxman, for *Sunset Boulevard* (Paramount)
Adolph Deutsch and Roger Edens, for *Annie Get Your Gun* (Metro-Goldwyn-Mayer)
1951 Franz Waxman, for *A Place in the Sun* (Paramount)
Johnny Green and Saul Chaplin, for *An American in Paris* (Metro-Goldwyn-Mayer)
1952 Dimitri Tiomkin, for *High Noon* (Kramer-United Artists)
Alfred Newman, for *With a Song in My Heart* (20th Century Fox)
1953 Bronislau Kaper, for *Lili* (Metro-Goldwyn-Mayer)
Alfred Newman, for *Call Me Madam* (20th Century Fox)
1954 Dimitri Tiomkin, for *The High and the Mighty* (Wayne-Fellows Prod.-Warner Bros.)
Adolph Deutsch and Saul Chaplin, for *Seven Brides for Seven Brothers* (Metro-Goldwyn-Mayer)
1955 Alfred Newman, for *Love Is a Many-Splendored Thing* (20th Century Fox)
Robert Russell Bennett, Jay Blackton and Adolph Deutsch, for *Oklahoma!* (Rodgers & Hammerstein Pictures, Inc.-Magna Theatre Corp.)
1956 Victor Young, for *Around the World in 80 Days* (Michael Todd Co.-United Artists)
Alfred Newman and Ken Darby, for *The King and I* (20th Century Fox)
1957 Malcolm Arnold, for *The Bridge on the River Kwai* (Horizon Pictures-Columbia)
1958 Dimitri Tiomkin, for *The Old Man and the Sea* (Leland Hayward-Warner Bros.)
Andre Previn, for *Gigi* (Arthur Freed Prod.-MGM)
1959 Miklos Rozsa, for *Ben-Hur* (Metro-Goldwyn-Mayer)
Andre Previn and Ken Darby, for *Porgy and Bess* (Samuel Goldwyn Prod.)
1960 Ernest Gold, for *Exodus* (Carlyle-Alpina S.A. Prod.-United Artists)
Morris Stoloff and Harry Sukman, for *Song without End (The Story of Franz Liszt)* (Goetz-Vidor Pictures Prod.-Columbia)
1961 Henry Mancini, for *Breakfast at Tiffany's* (Jurow-Shepherd Prod.-Paramount)
Saul Chaplin, Johnny Green, Sid Ramin and Irwin Kostal, for *West Side Story* (Mirisch Pictures, Inc. and B and P Enterprises, Inc.-United Artists)
1962 Maurice Jarre, for *Lawrence of Arabia* (Horizon Pictures Ltd.-Sam Spiegel/David Lean Prod.-Columbia)
Ray Heindorf, for *The Music Man* (Warner Bros.)

ACADEMY AWARD WINNERS FOR BEST SONG

1963 John Addison, for *Tom Jones* (Woodfall Prod.-United Artists-Lopert Pictures)
Andre Previn, for *Irma La Douce* (Mirisch-Phalanx Prod.-United Artists)

1964 Richard M. Sherman and Robert B. Sherman, for *Mary Poppins* (Walt Disney Prod.)
Andre Previn, for *My Fair Lady* (Warner Bros.)

1965 Maurice Jarre, for *Doctor Zhivago* (Sostar S.A.-Metro-Goldwyn-Mayer British Studios, Ltd. Prod.-MGM)
Irwin Kostal, for *The Sound of Music* (Argyle Enterprises Prod.-20th Century Fox)

1966 John Barry, for *Born Free* (Open Road Films, Ltd-Atlas Films, Ltd. Prod.-Columbia)
Ken Thorne, for *A Funny Thing Happened on the Way to the Forum* (Melvin Frank Prod.-United Artists)

1967 Elmer Bernstein, for *Thoroughly Modern Millie* (Ross Hunter-Universal) Alfred Newman and Ken Darby, for *Camelot* (Warner Bros-7 Arts)

1968 John Barry, for *The Lion in Winter* (Haworth Prod.-Avco Embassy)
John Green, for *Oliver!* (Romulus Films-Columbia)

1969 Burt Bacharach, for *Butch Cassidy and the Sundance Kid* (George Roy Hill-Paul Monash Prod.-20th Century Fox)
Lennie Hayton and Lionel Newman, for *Hello, Dolly!* (Chenault Prod.-20th Century Fox)

1970 Francis Lai, for *Love Story* (The Love Story Company Prod.-Paramount) Beatles, for *Let It Be* (Beatles-Apple Prod.-United Artists)

1971 Michel Legrand, for *Summer of '42* (Robert Mulligan-Richard Alan Roth Prod.-Warner Bros.)
John Williams, for *Fiddler on the Roof* (Mirisch-Cartier Prod.-United Artists)

1972 Charles Chaplin, Raymond Rasch and Larry Russell, for *Limelight* (Charles Chaplin Prod.-Columbia)
Ralph Burns, for *Cabaret* (ABC Pictures Prod.-Allied Artists)

1973 Marvin Hamlisch, for *The Way We Were* (Rastar Prod.-Columbia)
Marvin Hamlisch, for *The Sting* (Universal-Bill/Phillips-George Roy Hill Film Prod., Zanuck/Brown Presentation-Universal)

1974 Nino Rota and Carmine Coppola, for *The Godfather Part II* (Coppola Company Prod.-Paramount)
Nelson Riddle, for *The Great Gatsby* (David Merrick Prod.-Paramount)

1975 John Williams, for *Jaws* (Universal-Zanuck/Brown Production-Universal) Leonard Rosenman, for *Barry Lyndon* (Hawk Films, Ltd. Prod.-Warner Bros.)

1976 Jerry Goldsmith, for *The Omen* (20th Century Fox)
Leonard Rosenman, for *Bound for Glory* (Bound for Glory Company Prod.-United Artists)

1977 John Williams, for *Star Wars* (Lucasfilm, Ltd. Prod.-20th Century Fox)
Jonathan Tunick, for *A Little Night Music* (Sascha-Wien Film Prod. in association with Elliott Kastner-New World Pictures)

1978 Giorgio Moroder, for *Midnight Express* (Casablanca Filmworks Prod.-Columbia)
Joe Renzetti, for *The Buddy Holly Story* (Innovisions-ECA Prod.-Columbia)

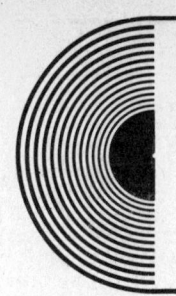

TONY AWARDS

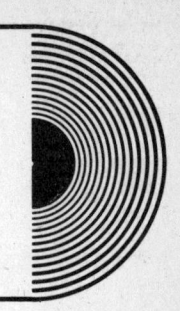

MUSICAL

1949 *Kiss Me Kate*
1950 *South Pacific*
1951 *Guys and Dolls*
1952 *The King & I*
1953 *Wonderful Town*
1954 *Kismet*
1955 *The Pajama Game*
1956 *Damn Yankees*
1957 *My Fair Lady*
1958 *The Music Man*
1959 *Redhead*
1960 *Fiorello!*
1961 *Bye, Bye Birdie*
1962 *How to Succeed in Business without Really Trying*
1963 *A Funny Thing Happened on the Way to the Forum*
1964 *Hello, Dolly!*
1965 *Fiddler on the Roof*
1966 *Man of La Mancha*
1967 *Cabaret*
1968 *Hallelujah, Baby!*
1969 *1776*
1970 *Applause*
1971 *Company*
1972 *Two Gentlemen of Verona*
1973 *A Little Night Music*
1974 *Raisin*
1975 *The Wiz*
1976 *A Chorus Line*
1977 *Annie*
1978 *Ain't Misbehavin'*
1979 *Sweeney Todd*

Given by the American Theatre Wing.

AUTHOR (Musical)

1949 Bella and Samuel Spewack, *Kiss Me Kate*
1950 Oscar Hammerstein II and Joshua Logan, *South Pacific*
1951 Jo Swerling and Abe Burrows, *Guys and Dolls*
1952 —
1953 Joseph Fields and Jerome Chodorov, *Wonderful Town*
1954 Charles Lederer and Luther Davis, *Kismet*
1955 George Abbott and Richard Bissell, *The Pajama Game*
1956 George Abbott and Douglass Wallop, *Damn Yankees*
1957 Alan Jay Lerner, *My Fair Lady*
1958 Meredith Willson and Franklin Lacey, *The Music Man*
1959 Herbert and Dorothy Fields, Sidney Sheldon and David Shaw, *Redhead*
1960 Jerome Weidman and George Abbott, *Fiorello!* Howard Lindsay and Russell Crouse, *The Sound of Music*
1961 Michael Stewart, *Bye, Bye Birdie*
1962 Abe Burrows, Jack Weinstock and Willie Gilbert, *How to Succeed in Business without Really Trying*
1963 Burt Shrevelove and Larry Gelbart, *A Funny Thing Happened on the Way to the Forum*
1964 Michael Stewart, *Hello, Dolly!*
1965 Joseph Stein, *Fiddler on the Roof*

PRODUCER (Musical)

1949 Saint-Subber and Lemuel Ayers, *Kiss Me Kate*
1950 Richard Rodgers, Oscar Hammerstein II and Joshua Logan, *South Pacific*
1951 Cy Feuer and Ernest Martin, *Guys and Dolls*
1952 —
1953 Robert Fryer, *Wonderful Town*
1954 Charles Lederer, *Kismet*
1955 Frederick Brisson, Robert Griffith and Harold S. Prince, *The Pajama Game*
1956 Frederick Brisson, Robert Griffith and Harold S. Prince in association with Albert B. Taylor, *Damn Yankees*
1957 Herman Levin, *My Fair Lady*
1958 Kermit Bloomgarden, Herbert Greene, Frank Productions, *The Music Man*
1959 Robert Fryer and Lawrence Carr, *Redhead*
1960 Leland Hayward and Richard Halliday, *The Sound of Music*
Robert Griffith and Harold Prince, *Fiorello!*
1961 Edward Padula, *Bye, Bye Birdie*
1962 Cy Feuer and Ernest Martin, *How to Succeed in Business without Really Trying*
1963 Harold Prince, *A Funny Thing Happened on the Way to the Forum*
1964 David Merrick, *Hello, Dolly!*
1965 Harold Prince, *Fiddler on the Roof*
1966 —
1967 —
1968 Albert Selden, Hal James, Jane C. Nussbaum and Harry Rigby, *Hallelujah, Baby!*
1969 —
1970 —
1971 Harold Prince, *Company*

DIRECTOR (Musical)

1960 George Abbott, *Fiorello!*
1961 Gower Champion, *Bye, Bye Birdie*
1962 Abe Burrows, *How to Succeed in Business without Really Trying*
1963 George Abbott, *A Funny Thing Happened on the Way to the Forum*
1964 Gower Champion, *Hello, Dolly!*
1965 Jerome Robbins, *Fiddler on the Roof*
1966 Albert Marre, *Man of La Mancha*
1967 Harold Prince, *Cabaret*
1968 Gower Champion, *The Happy Time*
1969 Peter Hunt, *1776*
1970 Ron Field, *Applause*
1971 Harold Prince, *Company*
1972 Harold Prince and Michael Bennett, *Follies*
1973 Bob Fosse, *Pippin*
1974 Harold Prince, *Candide*
1975 Geoffrey Holder, *The Wiz*
1976 Michael Bennett, *A Chorus Line*
1977 Gene Saks, *I Love My Wife*
1978 Richard Maltby, Jr., *Ain't Misbehavin'*
1979 Harold Prince, *Sweeney Todd*

COMPOSER AND LYRICIST

1949 Cole Porter, *Kiss Me Kate* (music and lyrics)
1950 Richard Rodgers, *South Pacific* (no lyricist category in 1950)
1951 Frank Loesser, *Guys and Dolls* (music and lyrics)
1952 —
1953 Leonard Bernstein, *Wonderful Town* (no lyricist category in 1953)
1954 Alexander Borodin, *Kismet* (no lyricist category in 1954)
1955 Richard Adler and Jerry Ross, *The Pajama Game* (music and lyrics)

1956 Richard Adler and Jerry Ross, *Damn Yankees* (music and lyrics)
1957 Frederick Loewe, *My Fair Lady* (no lyricist category in 1957)
1958 Meredith Willson, *The Music Man* (music and lyrics)
1959 Albert Hague, *Redhead* (no lyricist category in 1959)
1960 Jerry Bock, *Fiorello!* (no lyricist category in 1960)
Richard Rodgers, *The Sound of Music* (no lyricist category in 1960)
1961 —
1962 Richard Rodgers, *No Strings* (music and lyrics)
1963 Lionel Bart, *Oliver!* (music and lyrics)
1964 Jerry Herman, *Hello, Dolly!* (music and lyrics)
1965 Jerry Bock and Sheldon Harnick, *Fiddler on the Roof* (music and lyrics)
1966 Mitch Leigh and Joe Darion, *Man of La Mancha* (music and lyrics)
1967 John Kander and Fred Ebb, *Cabaret* (music and lyrics)
1968 Jule Styne, Betty Comden and Adolph Green, *Hallelujah, Baby!* (music and lyrics)
1969 —
1970 —
1971 Stephen Sondheim, *Company* (music and lyrics)
1972 Stephen Sondheim, *Follies* (music and lyrics)
1973 Stephen Sondheim, *A Little Night Music* (music and lyrics)
1974 Frederick Loewe (music) and Alan Jay Lerner (lyrics), *Gigi*
1975 Charlie Smalls, *The Wiz* (music and lyrics)
1976 Marvin Hamlisch (music) and Ed Kleban (lyrics), *A Chorus Line*
1977 Charles Strouse and Martin Charnin, *Annie* (music and lyrics)
1978 *Ain't Misbehavin'*
1979 Stephen Sondheim, *Sweeney Todd* (music and lyrics)

ACTRESS (Musical)

1948 Grace Hartman, *Angel with Wings*
1949 Nanette Fabray, *Love Life*
1950 Mary Martin, *South Pacific*
1951 Ethel Merman, *Call Me Madam*
1952 Gertrude Lawrence, *The King & I*
1953 Rosalind Russell, *Wonderful Town*
1954 Dolores Gray, *Carnival in Flanders*
1955 Mary Martin, *Peter Pan*
1956 Gwen Verdon, *Damn Yankees*
1957 Judy Holliday, *Bells Are Ringing*
1958 Thelma Ritter, *New Girl in Town*
Gwen Verdon, *New Girl in Town*
1959 Gwen Verdon, *Redhead*
1960 Mary Martin, *The Sound of Music*
1961 Elizabeth Seal, *Irma la Douce*
1962 Anna Maria Alberghetti, *Carnival*
Diahann Carroll, *No Strings*
1963 Vivien Leigh, *Tovarich*
1964 Carol Channing, *Hello, Dolly!*
1965 Liza Minnelli, *Flora, the Red Menace*
1966 Angela Lansbury, *Mame*
1967 Barbara Harris, *The Apple Tree*
1968 Patricia Routledge, *Darling of the Day*
Leslie Uggams, *Hallelujah, Baby!*
1969 Angela Lansbury, *Dear World*
1970 Lauren Bacall, *Applause*
1971 Helen Gallagher, *No, No, Nanette*
1972 Alexis Smith, *Follies*
1973 Glynis Johns, *A Little Night Music*
1974 Virginia Capers, *Raisin*
1975 Angela Lansbury, *Gypsy*
1976 Donna McKechnie, *A Chorus Line*
1977 Dorothy Loudon, *Annie*
1978 Liza Minnelli, *The Act*
1979 Angela Lansbury, *Sweeney Todd*

ACTOR (Musical)

1948 Paul Hartman, *Angel in the Wings*
1949 Ray Bolger, *Where's Charley?*
1950 Ezio Pinza, *South Pacific*
1951 Robert Alda, *Guys and Dolls*
1952 Phil Silvers, *Top Banana*
1953 Thomas Mitchell, *Hazel Flagg*

1954 Alfred Drake, *Kismet*
1955 Walter Slezak, *Fanny*
1956 Ray Walston, *Damn Yankees*
1957 Rex Harrison, *My Fair Lady*
1958 Robert Preston, *The Music Man*
1959 Richard Kiley, *Redhead*
1960 Jackie Gleason, *Take Me Along*
1961 Richard Burton, *Camelot*
1962 Robert Morse, *How to Succeed in Business without Really Trying*
1963 Zero Mostel, *A Funny Thing Happened on the Way to the Forum*
1964 Bert Lahr, *Foxy*
1965 Zero Mostel, *Fiddler on the Roof*
1966 Richard Kiley, *Man of La Mancha*
1967 Robert Preston, *I Do! I Do!*
1968 Robert Goulet, *The Happy Time*
1969 Jerry Orbach, *Promises, Promises*
1970 Cleavon Little, *Purlie*
1971 Hal Linden, *The Rothschilds*
1972 Phil Silvers, *A Funny Thing Happened on the Way to the Forum*
1973 Ben Vereen, *Pippin*
1974 Christopher Plummer, *Cyrano*
1975 John Cullum, *Shenandoah*
1976 George Rose, *My Fair Lady*
1977 Barry Bostwick, *The Robber Bridegroom*
1978 John Cullum, *On the Twentieth Century*
1979 Len Cariou, *Sweeney Todd*

1960 Patricia Neway, *The Sound of Music*
1961 Tammy Grimes, *The Unsinkable Molly Brown*
1962 Phyllis Newman, *Subways Are for Sleeping*
1963 Anna Quayle, *Stop the World—I Want to Get Off*
1964 Tessie O'Shea, *The Girl Who Came to Supper*
1965 Maria Karnilova, *Fiddler on the Roof*
1966 Beatrice Arthur, *Mame*
1967 Peg Murray, *Cabaret*
1968 Lillian Hayman, *Hallelujah, Baby!*
1969 Marian Mercer, *Promises, Promises*
1970 Melba Moore, *Purlie*
1971 Patsy Kelly, *No, No Nanette*
1972 Linda Hopkins, *Inner City*
1973 Patricia Elliot, *A Little Night Music*
1974 Janie Sell, *Over Here!*
1975 Dee Dee Bridgewater, *The Wiz*
1976 Carole Bishop, *A Chorus Line*
1977 Dolores Hall, *Your Arm's Too Short to Box with God*
1978 Nell Carter, *Ain't Misbehavin'*
1979 Carlin Glynn, *The Best Little Whorehouse in Texas*

ACTRESS, SUPPORTING OR FEATURED (Musical)

1950 Juanita Hall, *South Pacific*
1951 Isabel Bigley, *Guys and Dolls*
1952 Helen Gallagher, *Pal Joey*
1953 Sheila Bond, *Wish You Were Here*
1954 Gwen Verdon, *Can-Can*
1955 Carol Haney, *The Pajama Game*
1956 Lotte Lenya, *The Three Penny Opera*
1957 Edith Adams, *Li'l Abner*
1958 Barbara Cook, *The Music Man*
1959 Pat Stanley, *Goldilocks*
Cast, *La Plume de Ma Tante*

ACTOR, SUPPORTING OR FEATURED (Musical)

1947 David Wayne, *Finian's Rainbow*
1948 —
1949 —
1950 Myron McCormick, *South Pacific*
1951 Russell Nype, *Call Me Madam*
1952 Yul Brynner, *The King & I*
1953 Hiram Sherman, *Two's Company*
1954 Harry Belafonte, *John Murray Anderson's Almanac*
1955 Cyril Ritchard, *Peter Pan*
1956 Russ Brown, *Damn Yankees*
1957 Sydney Chaplin, *Bells Are Ringing*
1958 David Burns, *The Music Man*

1959 Russell Nype, *Goldilocks*
Cast, *La Plume de Ma Tante*
1960 Tom Bosley, *Fiorello!*
1961 Dick Van Dyke, *Bye, Bye Birdie*
1962 Charles Nelson Reilly, *How to Succeed in Business without Really Trying*
1963 David Burns, *A Funny Thing Happened on the Way to the Forum*
1964 Jack Cassidy, *She Loves Me*
1965 Victor Spinetti, *Oh, What a Lovely War*
1966 Frankie Michaels, *Mame*
1967 Joel Grey, *Cabaret*
1968 Hiram Sherman, *How Now, Dow Jones*
1969 Ronald Holgate, *1776*
1970 Rene Auberjonois, *Coco*
1971 Keene Curtis, *The Rothschilds*
1972 Larry Blyden, *A Funny Thing Happened on the Way to the Forum*
1973 George S. Irving, *Irene*
1974 Tommy Tune, *Seesaw*
1975 Ted Rose, *The Wiz*
1976 Sammy Williams, *A Chorus Line*
1977 Lenny Baker, *I Love My Wife*
1978 Kevin Kline, *On the Twentieth Century*
1979 Henderson Forsythe, *The Best Little Whorehouse in Texas*

PLAYBOY
MUSIC HALL OF FAME MEMBERS
in alphabetical order

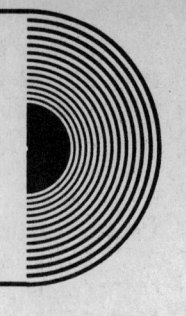

Duane Allman	Jimi Hendrix
Herb Alpert	Mick Jagger
Louise Armstrong	Elton John
Count Basie	Janis Joplin
Dave Brubeck	John Lennon
Ray Charles	Paul McCartney
Eric Clapton	Wes Montgomery
John Coltrane	Keith Moon
Miles Davis	Jim Morrison
Bob Dylan	Elvis Presley
Duke Ellington	Linda Ronstadt
Ella Fitzgerald	Frank Sinatra
Benny Goodman	Ringo Starr
George Harrison	Stevie Wonder

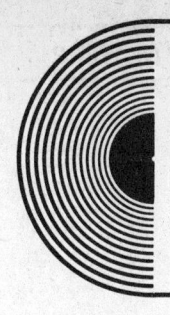

COUNTRY MUSIC ASSOCIATION AWARDS

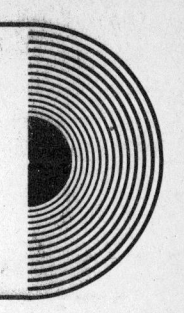

ENTERTAINER OF THE YEAR

1967 *Eddy Arnold*
1968 *Glen Campbell*
1969 *Johnny Cash*
1970 *Merle Haggard*
1971 *Charley Pride*
1972 *Loretta Lynn*
1973 *Roy Clark*
1974 *Charlie Rich*
1975 *John Denver*
1976 *Mell Tillis*
1977 *Ronnie Milsap*
1978 *Dolly Parton*
1979 *Willie Nelson*

ALBUM OF THE YEAR

1967 *There Goes My Everything,* Jack Greene (Decca)
1968 *Johnny Cash at Folsom Prison,* Johnny Cash (Columbia)
1969 *Johnny Cash at San Quentin Prison,* Johnny Cash (Columbia)
1970 *Okie from Muskogee,* Merle Haggard (Capitol)
1971 *I Won't Mention It Again,* Ray Price (Columbia)
1972 *Let Me Tell You about a Song,* Merle Haggard (Capitol)
1973 *Behind Closed Doors,* Charlie Rich (Epic)
1974 *A Very Special Love Song,* Charlie Rich (Epic)
1975 *A Legend in My Time,* Ronnie Milsap (RCA)
1976 *Wanted—The Outlaws,* Waylon Jennings, Jessie Colter, Tompall Glaser, Willie Nelson (RCA)
1977 *Ronnie Milsap Live,* Ronnie Milsap (RCA)
1978 *It Was Almost Like a Song,* Ronnie Milsap (RCA)
1979 *The Gambler,* Kenny Rogers (United Artists)

SINGLE OF THE YEAR

1967 "There Goes My Everything," Jack Greene (Decca)
1968 "Harper Valley PTA," Jeannie C. Riley (Plantation)
1969 "A Boy Named Sue," Johnny Cash (Columbia)
1970 "Okie from Muskogee," Merle Haggard (Capitol)
1971 "Help Me Make It Through the Night," Sammi Smith (Mega)
1972 "Happiest Girl in the Whole U.S.A.," Donna Fargo (Dot)
1973 "Behind Closed Doors," Charlie Rich (Epic)
1974 "Country Bumpkin," Cal Smith (MCA)
1975 "Before the Next Teardrop Falls," Freddy Fender (ABC-Dot)
1976 "Good Hearted Woman," Waylon Jennings and Willie Nelson (RCA)

Given by the Country Music Association.

1977 "Lucille," Kenny Rogers (United Artists)
1978 "Heaven's Just a Sin Away," Kendalls (Ovation)
1979 "The Devil Went Down To Georgia," Charlie Daniels Band (Epic)

SONG OF THE YEAR
(award to songwriter)

1967 "There Goes My Everything," Dallas Frazier
1968 "Honey," Bobby Russell
1969 "Caroll County Accident," Bob Ferguson
1970 "Sunday Morning Coming Down," Kris Kristofferson
1971 "Easy Loving," Freddie Hart
1972 "Easy Loving," Freddie Hart
1973 "Behind Closed Doors," Kenny O'Dell
1974 "Country Bumpkin," Don Wayne
1975 "Back Home Again," John Denver
1976 "Rhinestone Cowboy," Larry Weiss
1977 "Lucille," Roger Bowling, Hal Bynum
1978 "Don't It Make My Brown Eyes Blue," Richard Leigh
1979 "The Gambler," Don Schlitz

FEMALE VOCALIST OF THE YEAR

1967 Loretta Lynn
1968 Tammy Wynette
1969 Tammy Wynette
1970 Tammy Wynette
1971 Lynn Anderson
1972 Loretta Lynn
1973 Loretta Lynn
1974 Olivia Newton-John
1975 Dolly Parton
1976 Dolly Parton
1977 Crystal Gayle
1978 Crystal Gayle
1979 Barbara Mandrell

MALE VOCALIST OF THE YEAR

1967 Jack Greene
1968 Glen Campbell
1969 Johnny Cash
1970 Ronnie Milsap
1971 Charley Pride
1972 Charley Pride
1973 Charley Pride
1974 Ronnie Milsap
1975 Waylon Jennings
1976 Ronnie Milsap
1977 Ronnie Milsap
1978 Don Williams
1979 Kenny Rogers

VOCAL GROUP OF THE YEAR

1967 Stoneman Family
1968 Porter Wagoner and Dolly Parton
1969 Johnny Cash and June Carter
1970 Glaser Brothers
1971 Osborne Brothers
1972 Statler Brothers
1973 Statler Brothers
1974 Statler Brothers
1975 Statler Brothers
1976 Statler Brothers
1977 Statler Brothers
1978 Oak Ridge Boys
1979 Statler Brothers

VOCAL DUO OF THE YEAR

1970 Porter Wagoner and Dolly Parton
1971 Porter Wagoner and Dolly Parton
1972 Conway Twitty and Loretta Lynn
1973 Conway Twitty and Loretta Lynn
1974 Conway Twitty and Loretta Lynn
1975 Conway Twitty and Loretta Lynn
1976 Waylon Jennings and Willie Nelson
1977 Jim Ed Brown and Helen Cornelius
1978 Kenny Rogers and Dottie West
1979 Kenny Rogers and Dottie West

INSTRUMENTAL GROUP OR BAND OF THE YEAR

1967 Buckaroos
1968 Buckaroos
1969 Danny Davis and the Nashville Brass
1970 Danny Davis and the Nashville Brass
1971 Danny Davis and the Nashville Brass
1972 Danny Davis and the Nashville Brass
1973 Danny Davis and the Nashville Brass
1974 Danny Davis and the Nashville Brass
1975 Roy Clark and Buck Trent
1976 Roy Clark and Buck Trent
1977 Original Texas Playboys
1978 Oak Ridge Boys Band
1979 Charlie Daniels Band

INSTRUMENTALIST OF THE YEAR

1967 Chet Atkins
1968 Chet Atkins
1969 Chet Atkins
1970 Jerry Reed
1971 Jerry Reed
1972 Charlie McCoy
1973 Charlie McCoy
1974 Don Rich
1975 Johnny Gimble
1976 Hargus "Pig" Robbins
1978 Roy Clark
1979 Charlie Daniels

PUZZLES AND QUIZZES

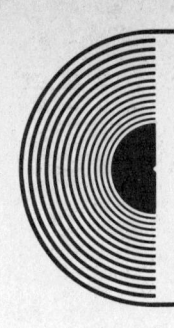

WORD CHOICE PUZZLES

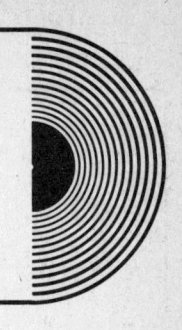

FEMALE ROCK STARS

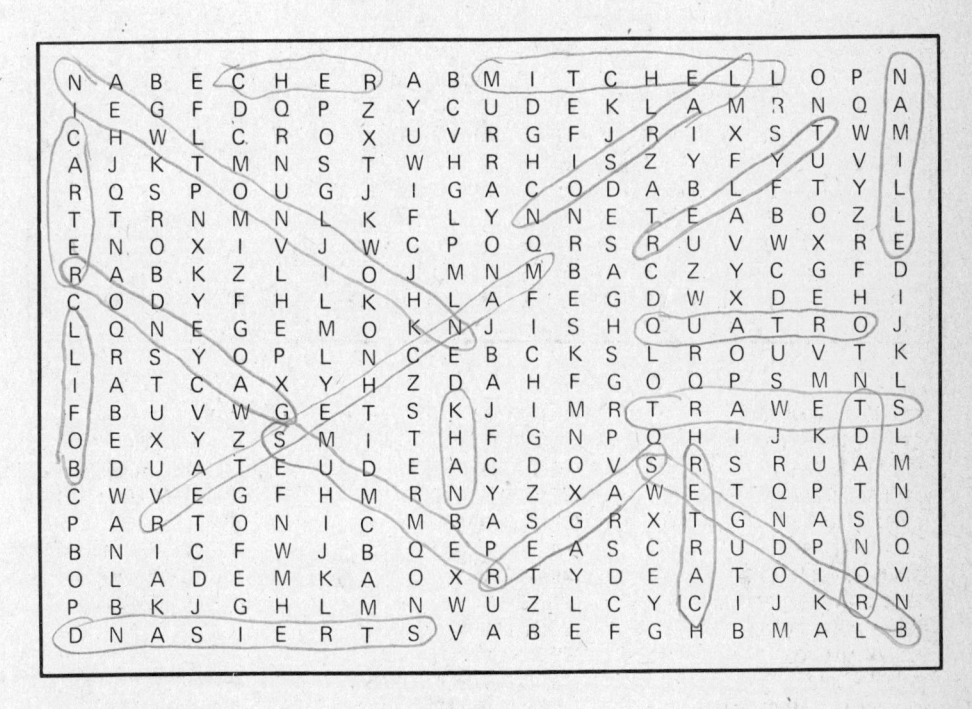

```
N A B E C H E R A B M I T C H E L L O P N
I E G F D Q P Z Y C U D E K L A M R N Q A
C H W L C R O X U V R G F J R I X S T W M
A R J K T M N S T W H R H I S Z Y F Y U I
R T Q S P O U G J I G A C O D A B L F T L
T E R N M N L K F L Y N N E T E A B O Z E
E R N O X I V J W C P O R S R U V W X R D
R C A B K Z L I O J M N M B A C Z Y C G F I
  L O D Y F H L K H L A F E G D W X D E H J
  L Q N E G E M O K N J I S H Q U A T R O J K
  I R S Y O P L N E B C K S L R O U V T K
  F A T C A X Y H Z D A H F G O O P S M N L
  O B U V W G E T S K J I M R T R A W E T S
  B E X Y Z S M I T H A C D O V S H I J K D L
  C D U A T E U D E N C Y Z X A W E R U A T M
  P W V E G F H M R N B A S G R X T Q P T N O
  B A R T O N I C M B A S G R X T G N A S Q
  O N I C F W J B Q E P E A S C R U D P N O V
  P L A D E M K A O X R T Y D E A T O I Q N
    B K J G H L M N W U Z L C Y C I J K R B
  D N A S I E R T S V A B E F G H B M A L B
```

(ANGELA) BOFILL
(ALICIA) BRIDGES
(CARLENE) CARTER
(VALERIE) CARTER
CHER
(LINDA) CLIFFORD
(NATALIE) COLE
(JUDY) COLLINS
(YVONNE) ELLIMAN
(CRYSTAL) GAYLE

(GLORIA) GAYNOR
(CHAKA) KHAN
(EVELYN "CHAMPAGNE") KING
(NICOLETTE) LARSON
(CHERYL) LYNN
(MELISSA) MANCHESTER
(JONI) MITCHELL
(ANNE) MURRAY
(OLIVIA) NEWTON—JOHN
(DOLLY) PARTON

(SUZI) QUATRO
(LINDA) RONSTADT
(DIANA) ROSS
(CAROLE BAYER) SAGER
(SAMANTHA) SANG
(PATTI) SMITH
(AMII) STEWART
(BARBRA) STREISAND
(DONNA) SUMMER
(BONNIE) TYLER

SM

The solution with 30 circled stars is on page 939.

MALE ROCK STARS

```
S H J K C O S T E L L O G H I J V A L L I
M T B A B D E F M E A T L O A F K M P N Q
K L E I J H G D C B Z Y X V U T L E O J R
N O N V S T E W A R T A R Z Y B C V A D S
M P S Q E H R S T U V E W X E F E G U T E
C A O R P N O N L K Y J I G H Z G O V R G
C Y N S Z A S P M A B L C M N E P Q Z W E
A X W I B K R I S T O F F E R S O N Y X R
R U V T L E L M D K J H I W X K U Q V I J
T S U O S O K C H E I F A Z Y G R S U T H
N R Q L P N W J G F D G B C E C H A F C L
E T E V Z Y H I U T I R A N T A E R L E M
Y Y J W B X B A S B S Q T R U R S E J D N
T A Y L O R Z N B S P Y W V R M W O Q P O
R L K B O W I E N O A X M N L E H S R T N
E D M W P G O L M H C R N K O N T P Y U O
F R N Q G S K R G S D O G J I S Z T X V M
F E J O I G J R E F T V W R H G I W Y A I
A S L Q M G I P E L U E X Y E V X R Z B S
R T Z E Y A G K M D L T W Z U D T S R C R
U Y W R H C I O N S N I B A F I N F D A P
V X C A S S I D Y E N O M G R H J E M N H
S P R I N G S T E E N C W D E T K L P O Q
```

(GEORGE) BENSON	(BILLY) JOEL	(CHRIS) REA
(STEPHEN) BISHOP	(ELTON) JOHN	(LEO) SAYER
(DAVID) BOWIE	(KRIS) KRISTOFFERSON	(BOZ) SCAGGS
(JACKSON) BROWNE	(KENNY) LOGGINS	(BOB) SEGER
(ERIC) CARMEN	(BARRY) MANILOW	(PAUL) SIMON
(SHAUN) CASSIDY	(PAUL) McCARTNEY	(BRUCE) SPRINGSTEEN
(ELVIS) COSTELLO	MEATLOAF	(AL) STEWART
(NEIL) DIAMOND	(STEVE) MILLER	(ROD) STEWART
(LEIF) GARRETT	(EDDIE) MONEY	(CAT) STEVENS
(MARVIN) GAYE	(TED) NUGENT	(JAMES) TAYLOR
(ANDY) GIBB	(TEDDY) PENDERGRASS	(FRANKIE) VALLI
(GEORGE) HARRISON	(ELVIS) PRESLEY	(BOB) WELCH
(MICK) JAGGER	(GERRY) RAFFERTY	(STEVIE) WONDER
		(WARREN) ZEVON

SM

The solution with 40 circled stars is on page 939.

ROCK GROUPS

```
K A B D C E Y N A P M O C D A B F G H I J
B C E Z Y L X W U V T S R Q P E N O M L K
E F I N M K L B R E H D N A S E H C A E P
A G H R I J M A N O P R Q T U G V X W L Y
C B A J T K L K F I C A R S A E B D A C Z
H D E I E P J L O E H J Q E T E S Y Z S Y
B F G H A F A N P M R G F U R S E R A X L
O E D Z E G F E V U O I K I V R L W B E D
Y C A F X Y H E H M N L F A J I G H D F C
S B G T Q W I M R C O D E U T V A Z W V H
C R F N L P J L N S N R A R S O E U X Y A
B D E A Y E K F C A O B Q X W P M T B Z L
S A H D Z T S E D S K N Z Y P N A D S T L
N M I Y X H G N M I H L S E A H B C P S A
O J V L W E I I J O D Q L T J S D A R E N
S L U E X W T H R S S I K I A U E P B F D
K T K E H H J L K O N M N H G R F Q M B O
C S V T W O E G P L T N K E P I S O A N A
A N R S R A F A B Y R M L O E J L H R B T
J A U Q N Z D E C S E Q K N H U D G I C E
E O P S Y S T I A R T S E R I D Q F E P S
```

ABBA
AEROSMITH
BAD COMPANY
BEACH BOYS
BEATLES
BEE GEES
CARS
CHEAP TRICK

DIRE STRAITS
EAGLES
EARTH, WIND AND FIRE
FIREFALL
HALL AND OATES
JACKSONS
JEFFERSON STARSHIP
KISS

LED ZEPPELIN
ORLEANS
PEACHES AND HERB
PLAYER
QUEEN
RUSH
STEELY DAN
THE WHO
YES

The solution with 25 circled groups is on page 940.

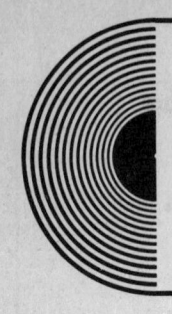

CROSSWORD PUZZLES

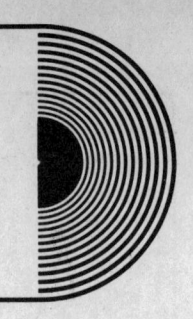

ROCK STARS

ACROSS

1 Canadian TV network
4 ——— up the engine
7 Family member
10 Hat
13 Above: (poet.)
14 Amin
15 Baseball great Mel
16 Pay TV org.
17 "Make Me Smile" group
19 Three men from Man
21 ——— Sutra
22 ——— carte
24 Sergio
25 Always
26 "Amos Moses" singer
28 ———-tse
29 Replace turf
31 Journey
33 "Magical Mystery ———"
36 Cut off
38 Leave out
40 19 Across's label
41 "Million Dollar Disco" group
46 "Long ——— Tomorrow"
47 Stalk
48 ——— Lanka
49 Repair
51 Carmen
53 Certain curves
57 Abba '75 hit
59 To be: (French)
61 Fork prong
62 Sing
65 David
66 Humorist Bombeck
67 "Stones" singer
69 McGovern
71 Beginning of the ———
72 Egg: comb. form
73 T.D.s: (abbr.)
74 Fed. defense group: (abbr.)
75 Drunkard
76 Color
77 "——— Cruise"
78 Tommy James '69 hit

DOWN

1 Joe from Sheffield
2 Mind
3 Felonies
4 Creek
5 Winter
6 Ultra ———
7 Type of story
8 Detail
9 Kind of band
10 "Strange Days" group
11 Busy as ———
12 Playwright Hart
18 "Tapestry" weaver
20 Little pest
23 "Dream On" group
27 Type of record
30 "Mad ——— and Englishmen"
32 Teases
34 "——— ta Be My Girl"
35 Acuff
37 Seeger
39 Lebanese sea port
41 McCartney album
42 Ice ———
43 Brown's friend
44 A ——— bag of shells
45 ——— Sledge
50 Ruin
52 Divers' ailments
54 Sea nymphs
55 Entangle
56 Medium's meeting
58 Headband
60 Gladden
62 ——— of March
63 ——— Rota
64 Covet
68 "Live and Let ———"
70 Made In ———

The answers are on page 941. JMS

HIT SONGS

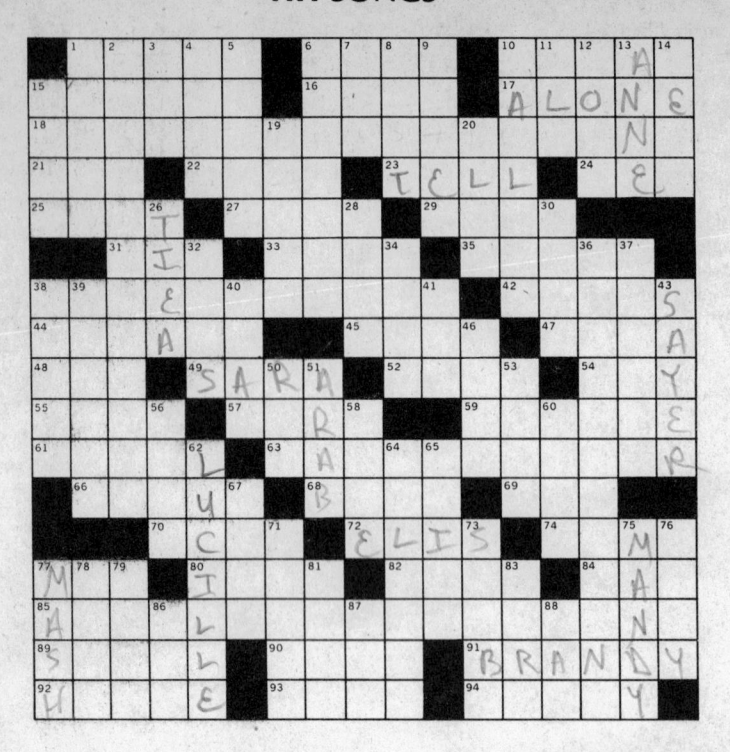

ACROSS

1. Audition discs
6. Gymnast Korbut
10. Springsteen gives a ——— performance!
15. Donovan '68 hit
16. Type of cloth
17. "——— Again (Naturally)"
18. Nilsson '69 hit
21. By way of
22. Superman's vision
23. "Show & ———": (Al Wilson)
24. McCann or Dudek
25. "——— Life Strange?": (Moody Blues)
27. Greek god of war
29. Homophone of scene
31. Petroleum
33. Apiece
35. "I Got A Name" name
38. James Taylor '70 hit
42. "The Great" & "The Terrible"
44. Infuriate
45. Phonogram recording artist McEntire
47. ——— boy!
48. Liberian native
49. "——— Smile": (Hall & Oates)
52. Pied Piper followers
54. "——— Baby": (Joplin)
55. Ham's partner
57. ——— Earth
59. Titter
61. Defiant one
63. Neil Diamond '72 hit
66. Vermont product
68. Radar spot
69. ——— degree
70. Business course: (abbr.)
72. "——— Coming": (Three Dog Night)
74. Freight trailer
77. Me, in Marseille
80. Pelvic bones
82. Moon goddess
84. Waddle
85. Merilee Rush '68 hit
89. Type of pigeon
90. "——— Drop City": (Monkees)
91. Looking Glass '72 hit
92. Lena
93. Yearns
94. The Hollies '75 hit

PUZZLES AND QUIZZES 931

DOWN

1 Mac
2 Beatles '66 hit
3 "La ———": (Debussy)
4 Cameo stone
5 Native-born Israeli
6 "Ring out the ———! Ring in the New!: (Jan. 1st toast)
7 Actress Myrna
8 Essence
9 Feeds the kitty
10 Monkees '68 hit
11 Sort; kind
12 Labor
13 Murray
14 Stretch one's ———
15 Stubbs of The Four Tops
19 Rowed
20 Actor Guinness
26 "——— Yellow Ribbon": (Orlando & Dawn)

28 ID mark
30 "Blame It On the Bossa ———": (Gorme)
32 Falls behind
34 "Yesterday," in Paris
36 Donovan '65 hit
37 Menu item
38 Rita Coolidge '72 hit
39 "I haven't seen you ———!"
40 "——— You": (Boz Scaggs)
41 Knicks' or Lakers' affil.
43 "When I Need You" singer
46 Attention: (abbr.)
50 Uncooked
51 "Ahab the ———": (Ray Stevens)
53 Stitched
56 Dried up
58 She, to Saint-Saëns
60 Food

62 Kenny Rogers '77 hit
64 Murderers
65 Type of den
67 Type of shirt
71 Stylish
73 Highbrows
75 Barry Manilow '74 hit
76 Pop of The Stooges
77 "The Monster ———": (1962)
78 Upon
79 Stravinsky
81 Done to———: (perfect)
83 Irish interjection
86 Eternity
87 Chinese dynasty
88 Fabray, to her friends

JMS

The answers are on page 941.

ROCK HISTORY

ACROSS

1. Parade exhibits
7. Air traffic controllers: (abbr.)
11. College in Blacksburg, Va.
14. Urge; spur
19. "——— Knowledge": (Ann-Margret movie)
20. "Never Never Gonna Give Ya Up" singer
22. June '66 Beatles single
23. First rock opera
24. ———'s Rubber Band
25. Type of holiday
26. Ye Olde ———
27. Gape
28. Particular
30. Stanley of Kiss
31. Saltpeter
33. Sit ———!: (Fonzie's line)
34. 1971 benefit at Madison Square Garden
40. "The ——— of Aquarius": (Fifth Dimension)
41. Himself, in Paris
42. Entire: Comb. form
43. Awards
47. Former Procol Harum member Robin
51. Imply
55. They headlined 98 Across
58. Friends of Sergio Mendes
60. Weisberg and Tiny
61. Of the age: (abbr.)
62. 180° from SSW
63. Nebraska city
65. Blockhead
67. Indicates: an earlier time
68. Org. founded by Victor Herbert in 1914
70. Split
73. 1967 event which introduced Joplin and Hendrix
77. Live
79. They record for Infinity
80. Galena and hematite, e.g.
81. Guided
85. "Mr. Lonely" singer
87. DJ who coined the term "rock 'n roll"
91. "In Cold Blood" author
92. Failed to keep a date
94. 55 Across is a good ———!
95. Dah's partner

97 "The ——— Birds": (McCullough novel)
98 Happening which 207,000 attended March 18, 1978
103 Summer drinks
104 Famous pig
107 Linear: (abbr.)
108 Give the eye to
109 Number in The Electric Light Orchestra
111 International Phonetic Alphabet: (abbr.)
112 So, in Glasgow
113 Weeder
115 Lives in

119 Ex-Beatle Stu
123 ——— Fetchit
125 Public address
126 Assault
127 Tub
129 Don Ho's food
131 Friar's title
132 August 23, 1966 New York spectacle
141 Indian prince
144 Puppeteer Lewis
145 Rich Little is one
146 Comedienne Himes
147 Worship
149 Angered

150 Slatted box
152 He also headlined 98 Across
156 Like some windows
157 Trick
158 Long-legged wading bird
159 Sci-Fi writer Isaac
160 Rex or O.C.
161 Detail: (abbr.)
162 Writer St. Vincent Millay
163 Hearing, touch, etc.

DOWN

1 Farm Credit Board: (abbr.)
2 ———-tse: (Chinese phil.)
3 Indicates: mountain
4 Prank
5 ——— of Honey
6 Foxier
7 Leather punch
8 Nilsson '71 tv special
9 Panatela
10 Rusty of baseball
11 ——— Fudge
12 Santa Maria's sister ship
13 "When ——— You": (Sayer)
14 Latin "ands"
15 "Let Me ———": (Warwick)
16 FBI agent
17 Biblical king of Israel
18 No, to Nureyev
21 Fitzgerald
22 He replaced Peter Best
29 Rockies, e.g.: (abbr.)
32 Transplant
34 "The ——— In The Cradle": (Chapin)
35 Fabled monster
36 "——— Rainbow": (Box Tops)
37 Enemy
38 Bruins or Flames affil.
39 What jrs. becomes
44 Metal in brass or bronze
45 Mount ———: (Eur. volcano)
46 ——— and The Limelites
48 1969 festival on Max Yasgur's farm

49 Ermine: (abbr.)
50 500 sheets of paper
52 "Ebb ———": (Damone)
53 Love, in Madrid
54 Scene of Dylan's '69 epic performance
56 Wyatt of the Old West
57 Shoals
59 "I ——— The Sheriff": (Clapton)
64 "My Way" composer
66 Son of Odin
67 ——— question: (asked)
68 Have ———: (sit down)
69 Recording artist Mills of RCA
70 ——— up: (accelerates)
71 Leave
72 ——— Tempo & April Stevens
74 Snitched
75 O follower
76 And so forth: (Abbr.)
78 "———'s the Day": (America)
82 Crucifix
83 To be, in Tours
84 Lairs
86 Not any: (law)
88 Arrangement: (abbr.)
89 Indicates: one-billionth of
90 Dulls
93 Rice dish
96 Row
99 Feudal estate
100 Medicinal plant
101 AMC product
102 Burl the folk singer

104 Leaning tower site
105 Musical work
106 The Good ———
110 What Kreskin has
112 "——— Marner": (Eliot novel)
114 Memorable Minnie
116 Defy: (French)
117 Pale brown
118 Sam The ———
120 1972 Liza Minnelli film
121 Shade the truth
122 Highest peak in the world
123 Station: (abbr.)
124 Opposite of taboo
128 Digression
130 Doctrine
133 Before degree or World
134 D.C. or Lash
135 Dashboard instrument, for short
136 Drinking bout
137 "I ——— It Through The Grapevine: (CCR)
138 Charles and Turner
139 Entertain
140 Entrench
141 Talks
142 Madam, I'm ———: (palindrome)
143 "Big Yellow Taxi" singer
148 Anglo-Saxon letter
151 Last Queen of Spain
153 German spa
154 Not otherwise enumerated: (abbr.)
155 RCA products

JMS

The answers are on page 942.

TRIVIA QUIZZES

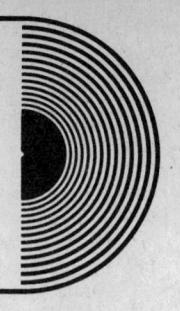

POP TRIVIA QUIZ
79 QUESTIONS TO TEST YOUR POP IQ

1. This British rock group may hold the record for best-educated band; three members hold degrees in either astronomy, biology, or electronics, and a fourth studied graphic design. Name the band.

2. Ace Frehley, Gene Simmons, Peter Criss, and Paul Stanley all have released successful solo albums. But they're still better known collectively as members of what group?

3. Which artist, or group, holds the record for having the most No. 1 singles on the United States' best-selling record charts in this decade?

4. Name the singer-composer who shocked some by posing in the buff with his wife for the cover of their "Wedding Album."

What's in a name? The next five names listed below are the ones the artist started out with. Give us the names under which they now perform.

5. Declan Patrick McManus

6. Perry Miller

7. Marvin Lee Aday

8. Roberta Joan Anderson

9. James Jewel Osterburg

10. The Rolling Stones recorded a song called "2120 S. Michigan Avenue." The title referred to the address of a Chicago-based company. Name it.

11. Robert Gordon, a former punk-rocker-turned-rockabilly-revivalist, recorded "Twenty Flight Rock" on a recent album. What noted rockabilly artist sang the same song in the 1950s film "The Girl Can't Help It"?

12. What rock band claims a pair of lips and a tongue as its corporate logo?

13. In the '60s, this onetime commercial aritst formed a band called David Jones and the Lower Third. Since then, he has been through a lot of changes. Name him.

14. Who owned the upstate New York farm where the Woodstock Music and Arts Fair, better known simply as Woodstock, was held in 1969?

15. Name the band whose music was featured in the sound tracks of the films "More," "Zabriskie Point," and "La Vallee."

16. Record producer Jaques Morali, who put together this act, named them for an area of New York City. Name the group.

17. Before becoming teen idols in the late '50s, Frankie Avalon and Bobby Rydell both were members of what Philadelphia band?

18. A well-known soul-rock-jazz band, whose music was featured in the 1970s film "That's the Way of the World," was founded by a musician whose past jobs included a stint as staff drummer for Chess Records and tours with Ramsey Lewis. Name him.

19. What singer starred in the reggae cult film "The Harder They Come"?

20. The St. Louis area was the birthplace of a white Ikette. Her name?

21. What song by Arlo Guthrie was also the title of a film starring the singer?

22. Born Jan. 8, 1935, in Mississippi, this performer won a state fair talent contest in the 1940s singing "Old Shep." Later, he went on to sell millions of records. His name?

23. In 1958, Gretchen, Gary, and Barbara met while attending Olympia High School in Washington. They began performing as Two Girls and a

Guy. The following year, they had two smash hit singles on Dolton Records after changing the group's name to what?

24. The 1959 plane crash that killed Ritchie Valens and the Big Bopper also took the life of a young singer and songwriter whose death figured heavily in Don McLean's song, "American Pie." Name him.

25. The singing daughter of a performer once famous for his white buck shoes, her recording of "You Light Up My Life" was a huge hit in 1977. Name her.

26. Before forming the Eagles, Don Henley and Glenn Frey both were backing musicians for a singer who had sung previously with the Stone Poneys. Name the singer.

27. What was the last Top-40 hit Diana Ross and the Supremes had before Ross left the group?

28. In the late '50s he and a bunch of clowns spread boogie woogie flu, sinus blues, and rockin' pneumonia. Name this carrier.

29. Of Little Richard, Little Eva, Little Walter, Little Anthony, and Big Tiny Little, who was noted for playing the harmonica?

30. In the fall of 1932, he and his band played the music for Sophie Tucker's shows at New York's Hotel Paramount Grill. In 1960 he played guitar on Ricky Nelson's recording of "Hello Mary Lou." Who was he?

31. According to a 1979 hit song, Guitar George played in what band?

32. Paul McCartney, George Harrison, and Ringo Starr recently performed on the same stage for the first time in years. The occasion was a party celebrating a rock performer's wedding. Name the rock artist.

33. The new wife of the rock performer in question No. 32 formerly was married to another celebrity. Name him.

34. RCA has the canine Little Nipper as its symbol. Which record company at one time depicted two halves of a dachshund on its label?

35. Its sarcastic "God Save the Queen" and "Anarchy in the U.K." did little to endear this now-defunct band to the British royal family. Name the group.

36. Name the Tokyo venue where both Bob Dylan and Cheap Trick recorded live albums.

37. This band, which began its career playing Chicago bars and clubs, took its original name from an advice column in a mechanics magazine. Later, they shortened their name to what?

38. Which member of Crosby, Stills, Nash, and Young once auditioned unsuccessfully for the Monkees?

39. Marty Balin, Signe Anderson, and Skip Spence were part of the lineup of this band in 1965. Name it.

40. Donald Fagen and Walter Becker took the name for their group from a steam-driven device mentioned in a novel. Name the novel.

41. What best-selling disco artist was a member of the Munich, Germany, production of the rock musical "Hair" in the 1960s?

42. What country-pop performer began her career as Porter Wagoner's singing partner?

43. Roger McGuinn, Gene Clark, and Chris Hillman, who currently perform as a trio, also performed together in what mid-'60s band?

44. Neil Young's album, "Tonight's the Night," was prompted, at least in part, by the drug-related deaths of two of his friends. Both are mentioned on the album, either in the songs or on the album jacket or inner sleeve. Name them.

45. Who saw Aunt Mary coming and ducked back in the alley in a popular '50s song?

46. Apollo C. Vermouth produced the 1968 British Top 10 hit "I'm the Urban Spaceman." Vermouth was, in reality, a pseudonym for one of the Beatles. Which one?

47. This singer and songwriter once cut a single, "The Ballad of the Yellow Beret," under an assumed name on the Are You Kidding Me label. His biggest successes, however, have been on Capitol Records, where he records under his real name. What is it?

48. Of Ronnie Hawkins, Edwin Hawkins, Screamin' Jay Hawkins, and Dale Hawkins, which one often used a coffin as a performing prop?

49. Who according to a song from the '60s "waits at the window, wearing the face that she keeps in a jar by the door"?

50. What song contains the following profound pieces of advice: "Walk on your tiptoes, don't try 'No Doz,' better stay away from those that carry around a fire hose ... don't wear sandals, try to aviod the scandals"?

PUZZLES AND QUIZZES

51. Before making his recording debut with "Greetings from Asbury Park, N.J.," this singer played in bands called Steel Mill, and Dr. Zoom and the Sonic Boom. Name him.

52. Most albums come with an inner sleeve. What artist once had his record packaged in panties?

53. They originally called their band Earth. But they found commercial, if not critical, success in the early '70s with droning slabs-of-sound music, a vaguely occult cachet, and a new name for the group. What was the new name?

54. The Pretty Things and the Rolling Stones paid tribute to this bluesman by recording two of his songs—"Rainin' in My Heart" and "I'm a King Bee," respectively. The bluesman's real name was James Moore, but he performed under another name. What was it?

Pop's bad boys (and girl): Match the five performers listed below with the crimes with which they have been charged at one time or another. Here are the crimes to choose from: assault and battery, possession of cocaine and heroin, indecent exposure, income tax evasion, and blocking the entrance to an induction center.

55. Jim Morrison

56. Chuck Berry

57. Joan Baez

58. Jerry Lee Lewis

59. Keith Richard

60. Today this band's albums regularly go platinum, but things haven't always shone so brightly. The group has survived several sessions of bad luck—at one point, one of the members disappeared and was later found to be hooked up with a religious cult; and in the early '70s, when the band was on the verge of breaking up, its manager put together a completely new band (using its name) and tried to tour with it. Name the group.

61. Name the record producers who ply their trade under the pseudonym "the Glimmer Twins."

62. What performer attended Beverly Hills (Cal.) High School, was a member of a quartet called Longfellow, and enjoyed his greatest success after turning television detective?

63. "Speedoo" (sometimes spelled Speedo) was his nickname; what was his real name?

64. Glen Campbell, James Guercio, and Daryl Dragon (also known as the Captain in the pop duo the Captain and Tennille) all have performed at various times as part of the lineup of what band?

65. Name the singer whose commercial ventures have included writing or rendering jingles for State Farm Insurance, Stridex, and Dr. Pepper.

66. Who wrote the lyrics to "I Think I'm Going to Kill Myself," "Roy Rogers," and "Social Disease"?

67. What performer named one of his children Moon Unit?

68. Whom did Charlie Watts replace as drummer when he joined the Rolling Stones?

69. Whom did Marky Ramone replace as drummer in the Ramones?

70. These two singer-songwriters have been performing together for more than 20 years, playing together in groups that included the Champs and the Dawnbreakers before trying their luck as a duo. Who are they?

71. Born in the Netherlands, these two brothers originally studied classical piano, but wound up making rock and roll in the U.S. Their first names are Alex and Edward. What's their last name?

72. Is-there-anybody-I-haven't-offended department: What country-rock performer's credits include writing and recording "Get Your Biscuits in the Oven and Your Buns in the Bed," "Top Ten Commandments," and "The Ballad of Charles Whitman"?

73. This singer's '60s credits include fronting a band that toured at one time as part of an Andy Warhol project called the Exploding Plastic Inevitable. Later, after going solo, he had a 1970s Top-40 hit single dealing with a fairly offbeat theme. Name this performer.

74. Lol Creme and Kevin Godley left 10cc to record with a device they developed that mechanically bowed the strings of a guitar. What did they call their invention?

75. Singer and actor Tim Curry toured last year to promote his pop album, but he remains better known for his role in "The Rocky Horror Picture Show." Name the kinky character Curry portrayed in the film.

76. What performer often has played club dates under the name Teddy Jack Eddy?

77. Which well-known rock band lost two of its members in motorcycle crashes in Macon, Ga.?

78. In 1977, only three singles were certified platinum (indicating sales of more than 2 million records) in the U.S. Of those three singles, only one of the songs was written by a member of the group that recorded it. Which song was it?

Answers are on page 943.

79. In the mid-'60s, this chap was part of a well-known British duo that launched their career with a Lennon-McCartney tune. These days, he manages some of the top rock talents. Name this musician-turned-manager.

LYM & TP

THE SPANISH INQUISITION

1. Name three of the "Roxy Girls".

2. On which label was Patti Smith's "Piss Factory" originally released?

3. These artists later became famous under what names? a) Ulysses Adrian Wood; b) Mary O'Brien; c) Paul Gadd; d) Roberta Joan Anderson; e) Eunice Waymon.

4. Which member of the Clash was originally in Johnny & The Vultures?

5. SEXIST SLOP is an anagram of which group?

6. What are the real names behind these nicknames or pseudonyms? a) Scratch; b) Big Youth; c) Stiggy; d) The Singing Brakemen; e) The Jersey Devil.

7. What was the great recording industry achievment of Joseph and Emil Berliner in 1897?

8. Which famous British playwright asked for the Beatles' "A Day in the Life" to be played at his funeral?

9. Name three TV pop series produced by Jack Good.

10. What's the link between "Wild Thing", the Sixties hit recorded by the Troggs, and film actor Jon Voight?

11. Complete the names of the following groups: a) Mike Sheridan and; b) Lothar and; c) Kingsize Taylor and; d) Mitch Ryder and; e) Spanky and.

12. Who said, "The dream is over"?

13. Which rock performer, later to become hugely successful in the Seventies, was called "the face of '68"?

14. Who was Dwight Frye, immortalised in Alice Cooper's "Ballad of Dwight Frye" (sic)?

15. From which Bob Dylan songs are these lines taken? a) "Brighton girls are like the moon"; b) "Jewels and binoculars hang from the head of the mule"; c) "In this age of fibreglass"; d) "The bridge at midnight trembles, the country doctor rambles"; e) "Someone's got it in for me, they're planting stories in the press".

16. Who was "El Toro Negro" on Minnie Ripperton's "Perfect Angel" album?

17. Which folksinger, one-half of a duo once very popular in America, recently played Sexton Blake in the kids' TV series?

18. Who wrote the story on which the film Saturday Night Fever was based?

19. Name four members of the Osmonds.

20. Of which regal New York band was Wayne County a member in the early Seventies?

21. Who formed the following record companies? a) Chiswick; b) Stiff; c) Sire; d) Reprise; e) Philadelphia International.

22. What was the original title of the Sex Pistols' film, and which notable American director was to have directed it?

23. What is a "snuff queen"?

24. Who, reportedly, said to whom, "Limp, you bugger, limp!"

25. Which song associated with Sesame Street and The Muppets did Van Morrison record?

26. Which name is given on the birth certificates of the following new-wave figures? a) Jake Riviera; b) Poly Styrene; c) Mark P; d) Tom Verlaine; e) Rat Scabies.

PUZZLES AND QUIZZES

27. Simon Dupree & The Big Sound later became which current British group?

28. Who was Python Lee Jackson?

29. Which country star played opposite Kirk Douglas in The Gunfight?

30. Who co-managed the Rolling Stones with Andrew Oldham in the group's early days? (And the answer's not Giorgio Gomelski).

31. Which two French words link Soft Machine to Matching Mole?

32. Salvador Dali was commissioned to do a hologram of which rock star?

33. When was the first electronic synthesizer built? a) 1948; b) 1955; c) 1961; d) 1966.

34. What are the titles of John Lennon's two books?

35. From which old blues artist did Ralph May get his new surname?

36. On which Ornette Coleman album does Jackson Pollock's White Light appear?

37. Which musicians wrote these books? a) Fry The Little Fishies; b) Really The Blues; c) Beneath The Underdog; d) Warlock of Love; e) The Trouble With Cinderella: An Outline of Identity.

38. Who was "born of Shawnee Indian stock in North Carolina in 1930, recorded for Cadence in the late Fifties, and enjoyed a huge hit that he could not follow"?

39. What was the Stax Records' house band in the mid-Sixties?

40. Who composed the sountracks for these films? a) You're A Big Boy Now; b) Barry Lyndon; c) Superfly; d) Sorcerer; e) What's Up Tiger Lily?

41. Quoting Shelley, who said of whom and in what place, "Peace, peace! He is not dead, he doth not sleep"?

42. With which better-known composers have these songwriters collaborated? a) Larry Beckett; b) Michael Moorcock; c) Jacques Levy; d) Jacob Brackman; e) Brian Jackson.

43. Jessi Colter is to Waylon Jennings what Charlotte Rampling is to whom?

44. Who sang the title song on the soundtrack of the movie High Noon?

45. Who was "The First Tycoon of Teen"?

46. Whom did Tiny Tim marry on television?

47. Who produced the following records? a) "Young Hearts Run Free"; b) "Ghosts Of Princes In Towers"; c) "Mythical Kings & Iguanas"; d) "Parallel Lines"; e) "Gonna Take A Miracle".

48. Whose life is said to have inspired Dorothy Baker's Jazz Age novel, Young Man With A Horn?

49. Identify three well-known bands who have taken their names from the works of William Burroughs.

50. Name two famous solo rock artists who have drawn self-portraits on the front covers of their albums.

51. What religions or cult practices are followed by the following aritsts; a) Ronnie Lane; b) Mike Love; c) Seals & Crofts; d) John Travolta; e) Carlos Santana.

Answers are on page 944.

ANSWERS

FEMALE ROCK STARS

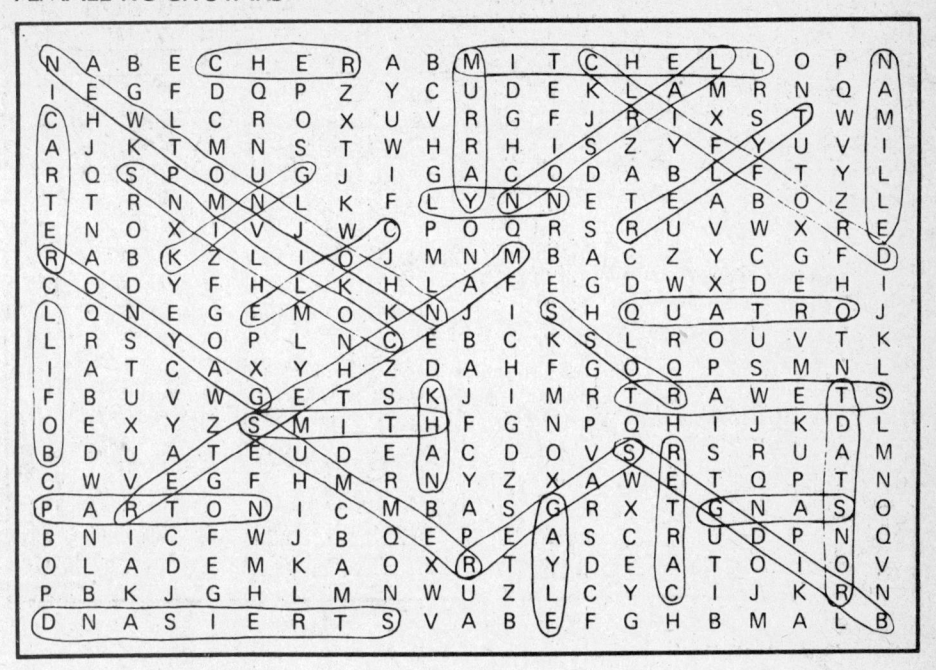

MALE ROCK STARS

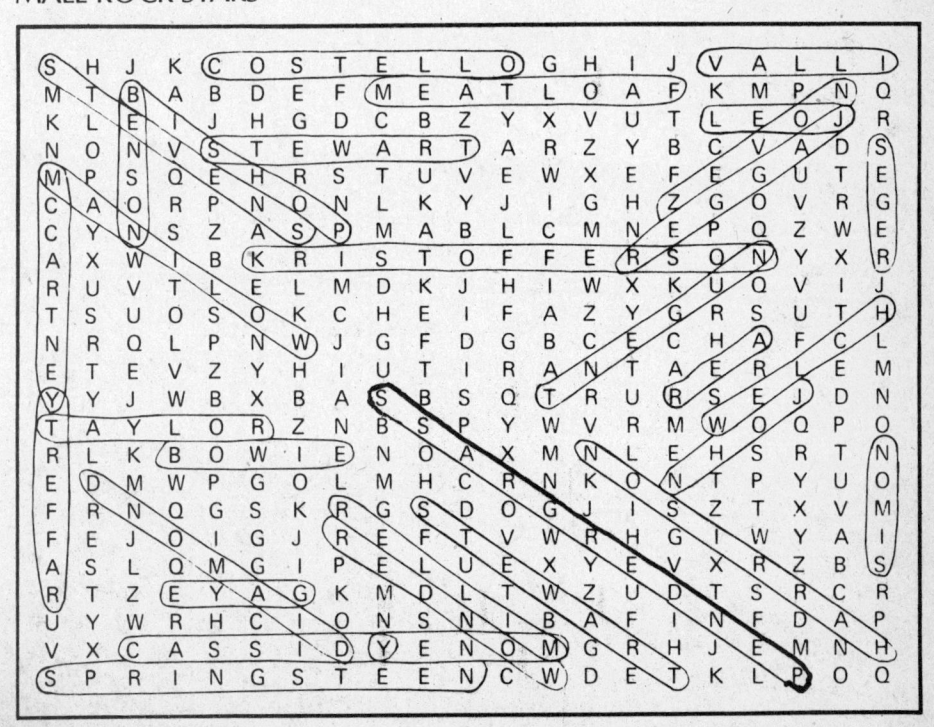

ROCK GROUPS

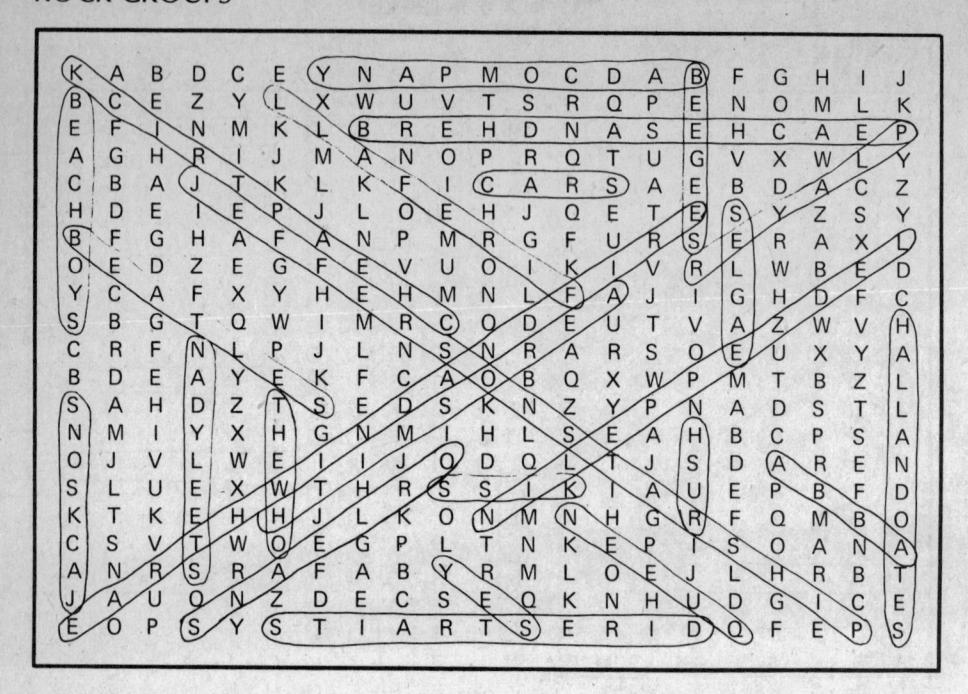

K	A	B	C	E	Y	N	A	P	M	O	C	D	A	B	F	G	H	I	J
B	C	E	Z	Y	L	X	W	U	V	T	S	R	Q	P	E	N	O	M	L	K
E	F	I	N	M	K	L	B	R	E	H	D	N	A	S	E	H	C	A	E	P
A	G	H	R	I	J	M	A	N	O	P	R	Q	T	U	G	V	X	W	L	Y
C	B	A	E	J	T	K	L	K	F	I	C	A	R	S	A	E	B	D	A	C	Z
H	D	E	I	E	P	J	L	O	E	H	J	Q	E	T	E	S	Y	Z	S	Y
B	F	G	H	A	F	A	N	P	M	R	G	F	U	R	S	E	R	A	X	L
O	E	D	Z	E	G	F	E	V	U	O	I	K	I	V	R	L	W	B	E	D
Y	C	A	F	X	Y	H	E	H	M	N	L	F	A	J	I	G	A	H	D	F	C
S	B	G	T	Q	W	I	M	R	C	O	D	E	U	T	V	A	Z	W	V	Y	H
C	R	F	N	L	P	J	L	N	S	N	R	A	R	S	O	E	U	X	Y	Z	A
B	D	E	A	Y	E	K	F	C	A	O	B	Q	X	W	P	M	T	B	Z	T	L
S	A	H	D	Z	T	S	E	D	S	K	N	Z	Y	P	N	A	B	D	S	T	L
N	M	I	Y	X	H	G	N	M	I	H	L	S	E	A	H	B	C	P	S	E	A
O	J	V	L	W	E	I	I	J	O	D	Q	L	T	J	S	D	A	R	E	F	N
S	L	T	U	E	W	X	T	H	R	S	S	I	K	I	U	E	P	B	F	D
K	T	K	V	E	H	H	J	L	K	O	N	M	N	H	G	R	F	Q	M	B	O
C	S	N	V	T	W	O	E	G	P	L	T	N	K	E	P	I	S	O	A	N	A
A	N	A	R	S	R	A	F	A	B	Y	R	M	L	O	E	J	L	H	R	B	T
J	A	U	O	N	Z	D	E	C	S	E	Q	K	N	H	U	D	G	I	C	P	E
E	O	P	S	Y	S	T	I	A	R	T	S	E	R	I	D	O	Q	F	E	P	S

ROCK STARS

C	B	C	■	R	E	V	■	S	I	S	■	T	A	M
O	E	R	■	I	D	I	■	O	T	T	■	H	B	O
C	H	I	C	A	G	O	■	B	E	E	G	E	E	S
K	A	M	A	■	A	L	A	■	M	E	N	D	E	S
E	V	E	R	■	R	E	E	D	■	L	A	O	■	■
R	E	S	O	D	■	T	R	E	K	■	T	O	U	R
■	■	■	L	O	P	■	O	M	I	T	■	R	S	O
R	A	R	E	G	E	M	S	O	D	Y	S	S	E	Y
A	G	O	■	S	T	E	M	■	S	R	I	■	■	■
M	E	N	D	■	E	R	I	C	■	E	S	S	E	S
■	■	S	O	S	■	E	T	R	E	■	T	I	N	E
I	N	T	O	N	E	■	H	A	L	■	E	R	M	A
D	I	A	M	O	N	D	■	M	A	U	R	E	E	N
E	N	D	■	O	V	I	■	P	T	S	■	N	S	C
S	O	T	■	D	Y	E	■	S	E	A	■	S	H	E

HIT SONGS

■	D	E	M	O	S	■	O	L	G	A	■	V	I	T	A	L
L	A	L	E	N	A	■	L	O	I	N	■	A	L	O	N	E
E	V	E	R	Y	B	O	D	Y	S	T	A	L	K	I	N	G
V	I	A	■	X	R	A	Y	■	T	E	L	L	■	L	E	S
I	S	N	T	■	A	R	E	S	■	S	E	E	N	■	■	■
■	■	O	I	L	■	E	A	C	H	■	C	R	O	C	E	■
F	I	R	E	A	N	D	R	A	I	N	■	I	V	A	N	S
E	N	R	A	G	E	■	R	E	B	A	■	A	T	T	A	■
V	A	I	■	S	A	R	A	■	R	A	T	S	■	C	R	Y
E	G	G	S	■	R	A	R	E	■	T	E	E	H	E	E	■
R	E	B	E	L	■	W	A	L	K	O	N	W	A	T	E	R
■	S	Y	R	U	P	■	B	L	I	P	■	N	T	H	■	■
■	■	E	C	O	N	■	E	L	I	S	■	S	E	M	I	■
M	O	I	■	I	L	I	A	■	L	U	N	A	■	W	A	G
A	N	G	E	L	O	F	T	H	E	M	O	R	N	I	N	G
S	T	O	O	L	■	T	E	A	R	■	B	R	A	N	D	Y
H	O	R	N	E	■	Y	E	N	S	■	S	A	N	D	Y	■

ROCK HISTORY

F	L	O	A	T	S	■	A	T	C	S	■	■	U	P	I	■	E	G	G	O	N
C	A	R	N	A	L	■	W	H	I	T	E	■	R	A	I	N	■	T	O	M	M	Y
B	O	O	T	S	Y	■	L	E	G	A	L	■	I	N	N	E	■	S	T	A	R	E
■	■	■	I	T	E	M	■	P	A	U	L	■	■	N	I	T	E	R	■	O	N	I	T
C	O	N	C	E	R	T	F	O	R	B	A	N	G	L	A	D	E	S	H	■	■
A	G	E	■	■	■	S	O	I	■	■	■	H	O	L	■	P	R	I	Z	E	S
T	R	O	W	E	R	■	E	N	T	A	I	L	■	A	E	R	O	S	M	I	T	H
S	E	N	O	R	E	S	■	T	I	M	S	■	■	A	E	T	■	■	N	N	E
■	■	O	M	A	H	A	■	D	O	L	T	■	P	R	E	■	A	S	C	A	P
R	E	N	D	■	M	O	N	T	E	R	E	Y	P	O	P	F	E	S	T	■
E	X	I	S	T	■	T	K	O	■	■	O	R	E	S	■	S	T	E	E	R	E	D
V	I	N	T	O	N	■	A	L	A	N	F	R	E	E	D	■	C	A	P	O	T	E
S	T	O	O	D	U	P	■	D	R	A	W	■	■	D	I	T	■	T	H	O	R	N
■	■	C	A	L	I	F	O	R	N	I	A	J	A	M	I	I	■	A	D	E	S
P	O	R	K	Y	■	L	I	N	■	O	G	L	E	■	S	E	V	E	N	■
I	P	A	■	■	S	A	E	■	■	H	O	E	R	■	R	E	S	I	D	E	S
S	U	T	C	L	I	F	F	E	■	S	T	E	P	I	N	■	S	P	E	E	C	H
A	S	S	A	I	L	■	■	V	A	T	■	■	P	O	I	■	■	F	R	A
■	B	E	A	T	L	E	S	A	T	S	H	E	A	S	T	A	D	I	U	M
R	A	J	A	■	S	H	A	R	I	■	A	P	E	R	■	M	I	M	I	■
A	D	O	R	E	■	I	R	E	D	■	C	R	A	T	E	■	N	U	G	E	N	T
P	A	N	E	D	■	R	U	S	E	■	H	E	R	O	N	■	A	S	I	M	O	V
S	M	I	T	H	■	D	E	T	■	■	E	D	N	A	■	S	E	N	S	E	S

POP TRIVIA QUIZ

1. Queen
2. Kiss
3. The Bee Gees
4. Question disqualified.
5. Elvis Costello
6. Jesse Colin Young
7. Meatloaf
8. Joni Mitchell
9. Iggy Pop
10. Chess Records (also acceptable: Checker Records or Chess Producing Corp.)
11. Eddie Cochran
12. Rolling Stones
13. David Bowie
14. Max Yasgur
15. Pink Floyd
16. Village People
17. Rocco and the Saints
18. Maurice White
19. Jimmy Cliff
20. Bonnie Bramlett
21. "Alice's Restaurant"
22. Elvis Presley
23. Fleetwoods
24. Buddy Holly
25. Debby Boone
26. Linda Ronstadt
27. "Someday We'll Be Together"
28. Huey Smith (also acceptable: Huey "Piano" Smith)
29. Little Walter
30. Ozzie Nelson
31. Sultans of Swing
32. Eric Clapton
33. George Harrison
34. End (or End Records)
35. Sex Pistols
36. Budokan (also acceptable: Nippon Budokan)
37. Rufus
38. Stills (or Stephen Stills)
39. Jefferson Airplane
40. "Naked Lunch"
41. Donna Summer
42. Dolly Parton
43. Byrds
44. Bruce Berry, Danny Whitten
45. Uncle John
46. Paul McCartney
47. Bob Seger
48. Screamin' Jay Hawkins
49. Eleanor Rigby
50. "Subterranean Homesick Blues"
51. Bruce Springsteen
52. Alice Cooper
53. Black Sabbath
54. Slim Harpo
55. Indecent exposure
56. Evasion of income tax
57. Blocking the entrance to an induction center
58. Assault and battery
59. Possession of cocaine and heroin
60. Fleetwood Mac
61. Mick Jagger, Keith Richard
62. Shaun Cassidy
63. Mr. Earl
64. Beach Boys
65. Barry Manilow
66. Bernie Taupin
67. Frank Zappa
68. Tony Chapman
69. Tommy Ramone (his real name, Tommy Erdelyi, is also acceptable)
70. Seals and Crofts (or Jim Seals and Dash Crofts)
71. Van Halen
72. Kinky Friedman
73. Lou Reed
74. The gizmo
75. Dr. Frank N. Furter
76. Gary Busey
77. Allman Brothers Band (Allman Brothers is also acceptable)
78. "Boogie Nights"
79. Peter Asher

THE SPANISH INQUISITION

1. Amanda Lear, Marilyn Cole, Kari-Ann, Jerry Hall.
2. Mer.
3. a) Roy Wood; b) Dusty Springfield; c) Gary Glitter; d) Joni Mitchell; e) Nina Simone.
4. Joe Strummer.
5. Sex Pistols.
6. a) Lee Perry; b) Augustus Manley Buchanan; c) Robert Stigwood; d) Jimmie Rodgers; e) Bruce Springsteen.
7. They invented the flat disc.
8. Joe Orton.
9. 6.5 Special, Oh Boy! Wham! and Boy Meets Girl (in Britain), Shindig (America).
10. Chip Taylor, who wrote "Wild Thing" is the brother of Jon Voight.
11. a) Mike Sheridan and the Nightriders; b) Lothar and the Hand People; c) Kingsize Taylor and the Dominoes; d) Mitch Ryder and the Detroit Wheels; e) Spanky and Our Gang.
12. John Lennon.
13. Peter Frampton.
14. A horror film actor.
15. a) "Sign On The Window"; b) "Visions Of Johanna"; c) "Dirge"; d) "Love Minus Zero/No Limit"; e) "Idiot Wind".
16. Stevie Wonder.
17. Jeremy Clyde.
18. Nik Cohn.
19. Osmonds—Alan, Wayne Merrill, Jay, Donny, Marie and Jimmy.
20. Queen Elizabeth.
21. a) Ted Carroll; b) Jake Riviera and Dave Robinson; c) Seymour Stein and Richard Gottehrer; d) Frank Sinatra and e) Kenny Gamble and Leon Huff.
22. Who Killed Bambi?—Russ Meyer.
23. The Country musician's term for a groupie.
24. Jack Good/Gene Vincent.
25. "Green".
26. a) Andrew Jakeman; b) Marion Elliot; c) Mark Perry; d) Tom Miller; e) Chris Miller.
27. Gentle Giant.
28. Rod Stewart.
29. Johnny Cash.
30. Eric Easton.
31. "Machine Mollie".
32. Alice Cooper.
33. 1955.
34. A Spaniard In The Works and In His Own Write.
35. Blind Willie McTell.
36. "Free Jazz".
37. a) Matt McGinn; b) Mezz Mezzrow; c) Charles Mingus; d) Marc Bolan and e) Artie Shaw.
38. Link Wray.
39. Booker T. and The MGs with the Mar-Keys horn section.
40. a) John Sebastian; b) The Chieftains; c) Curtis Mayfield; d) Tangerine Dream and e) John Sebastian.
41. Mick Jagger of Brian Jones at the Hyde Park Festival.
42. a) Tim Buckley; b) Hawkwind and Robert Calvert; c) Bob Dylan and Roger McGuinn; d) Carly Simon and e) Gil Scott-Heron.
43. Jean-Michel Jarre.
44. Tex Ritter.
45. Phil Spector.
46. Miss Vicki.
47. a) Dave Crawford; b) Mick Ronson; c) Nik Vennet; d) Mike Chapman and e) Gamble & Huff.
48. Bix Beiderbecke.
49. Soft Machine, Dead Fingers Talk, Heavy Metal Kids, Steely Dan, Nova.
50. Joni Mitchell, Bob Dylan, John Lennon.
51. a) Meher Baba; b) Transcendental Meditation; c) Ba'hai; d) Scientology and e) Sri Chinmoy.

Acknowledgments

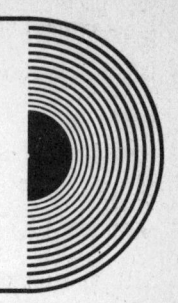

Based on an original concept by David Krebs and Steven Leber of Contemporary Communications Corp.

RESEARCH COORDINATOR: Linda Bullied
RESEARCH ASSISTANT: Sandra Sawotka
GENERAL ASSISTANT: Laura Gordon
PHOTOGRAPH EDITOR: Victoria North

Contributors

DF David Fricke. *Who's Who*.

DL Dennis Lambert. "How To Become a Record Producer" from *Producing Hit Records*, New York, Schirmer Books, 1980.

DM David Marsh. *Rock 'n' Roll Films. The 10 Best/10 Worst Rock 'n' Roll Films*.

ED Eric Doctorow. *So You Want to Be a Record Executive*.

FMIW Father Michael Ignatius Watts. "The Spanish Inquisition," Copyright 1979 *Melody Maker*. Used by permission.

HS Howard Stein. "Getting Talent for Rock Concerts" from *Promoting Rock Concerts*, New York, Schirmer Books, 1979.

IAR Ira A. Robbins. *New Wave Music*.

IBS Ira B. Stechel. *How to Organize Your Business*.

JK James Karnbach. *Rock 'n' Roll Film Directory*.

JM John Morthland. *Who's Who*.

JMS J. M. Samson. *Crossword Puzzles*.

JP Jeffrey Peisch. *Rock Events 1979*.

J.S. John Swenson. *Who's Who*.

KAM Kendall A. Minter. *Introductions* to *Music Business Contracts*.

LF Leonard Feldman. *New Technology.*

LK Laura Kaufmann. *Choosing the Right Publicist.*

LVM & TP Lynn Van Matre and Tom Popson. "Pop Music Trivia Quiz" From the *Chicago Tribune.* Copyright © 1979 Chicago Tribune. All Rights Reserved. Used by permission.

MM Mark Mehler. *Who's Who.*

MP Martin Porter. *Best American Recording Studios 1979. Greatest Events in Rock 'n' Roll History.*

RA Robert Angus. *Important Music Inventions.*

RB Richard Blackburn. "Rock 'n' Roll Disc Jockeys," originally titled "Alan Freed May Have Invented Rock 'n' Roll Radio But He Had Help," from *Waxpaper.* Reprinted by permission Warner Bros. Records, Inc. © 1979.

RCH Randal C. Hill. *Rock's Most Collectible Discs.*

RED Robert Edward Donnelly. *Choosing the Right Attorney.*

RH Richard Hogan. *Twenty-five Years of Rock 'n' Roll.*

RMN Ralph M. Newman. "The Motown Sound Revisited—Come and Get These Memories," from *New York Rocker*, January, 1979. Reprinted by Permission *New York Rocker*, © 1979.

RSD R. Serge Denisoff. *Contemporary Music Bibliography.*

RZ Ronald Zalkind. "How To Raise Money," from *Getting Ahead In the Music Business*, New York, Schirmer Books, 1979.

SM Scott Morrison. *Word Choice Puzzles*: "Male Rock Stars," "Female Rock Stars," and "Rock Groups," from *Rock Love*, 1979. Used by permission.

WMB William M. Borchard. *Trademarks In the Music Business.*

WW Walter Wager, public relations advisor to the National Music Publishers' Association, and former Director of Public Relations for ASCAP. *How To Get Your Song Published.* Copyright Walter Wager, used by permission.

We wish to acknowledge the efforts of Gail Katz, Bobby Sands, Rob Bidney, Laurie Steinberg, Bob Merlis, Lenny Kalikow, Neil McIntyre, Ira Mayer, Gene Sculatti, Travis Milner, Rosa, J.R. Smalling, Paul G. Gallo, Joe Cohen, Henry Brief, Arma Andon, Russell Sanjek, Howard Colson, Michael Kerker, Andrew Schwartz, Richard Williams, Paul Trolio, Eugene Fischer, Elaine Bailly, Robin Budin, Howie Cohen, Patrick Culley, Katie Fares, Karol Kamin, Louis Levin, Kevin McShane, Peter Mensch, Vicki Maistowski, Bruce Palley, Julie Rader, Noel Love, Viera Rysula, Evan Trievitz, David Wilkes, Helene Elenko, Stanley Garrett, Martha Zalkind and Ira Herzog for their excellent help in the preparation of this work.

Reader Questionnaire

Please help us make the *Contemporary Music Almanac* even better next year.

What is your age? _____

Are you male or female? _____

What is your occupation? _____

What is your favorite kind of music?
_____ contemporary rock   _____ country
_____ rock from the 60s   _____ rock from the 50s
_____ rhythm and blues   _____ disco
_____ other

Who is your favorite group? _____

Who is your favorite artist? _____

What is your favorite part(s) of this almanac?

What subject(s) would you like to see covered in the next edition?

Is there any topic or section you'd like covered more completely?

Thank you in advance for your cooperation.

Please send the completed questionnaire to Schirmer Books, 866 Third Avenue, New York, N. Y. 10022.